Dictionary of
American Literary
Characters

Dictionary of American Literary Characters

Edited by
Benjamin Franklin V
Associate Editors
Gary Geer and Judith Haig

A Bruccoli Clark Layman Book

New York • Oxford • Sydney

Dictionary of American Literary Characters

Library of Congress Cataloging-in-Publication Data

Dictionary of American literary characters/edited by Benjamin Franklin V; associate editors, Gary Geer and Judith Haig.
    p. cm.
  "A Bruccoli Clark Layman book."
  ISBN 0-8160-1917-7
  1. American fiction—Dictionaries. 2. Characters and characteristics in literature—Dictionaries. I. Franklin, Benjamin, 1939- . II. Geer, Gary. III. Haig, Judith Giblin.
PS374.C43D5 1990
813.009'2303—dc20   89-25820
                            CIP
British CIP information available on request

Designed by Quentin Fiore

Printed in the United States of America

10 9 8 7 6 5 4 3 2 1

To my lunch companions, James Dickey and Don Greiner, who don't need this book.

Preface

This book describes the major characters in significant American novels—in addition to those in some uncelebrated novels and in a sampling of best sellers—from William Hill Brown's *The Power of Sympathy* (1789) through 1979. By "novels" I mean long works of fiction, or what is presented as fiction, although a few of the books are often referred to as novellas, and some as "non-fiction novels." Because a novelist is included does not mean that characters from all of his or her novels are described. I stopped with the year 1979 in order to permit critical consensus to evolve. Space limitations have dictated omitting some novels that otherwise would have been included. The entries are factual: they contain little interpretation. Users of this book who cannot recall the name of a character in a novel, and therefore cannot turn directly to the desired character's entry, should consult the index, where characters are listed alphabetically by novel. Although some characters, such as Babe Ruth and George Washington, are historical figures, they are treated in precisely the same manner as obviously fictional characters. Unnamed characters are not included.

Dictionary of
American Literary
Characters

A

A. Daughter of Nimni and Ohiro-Moldona-Fivona in Herman Melville's *Mardi*.

Captain (Aarfy) Aardvaark. Fraternity man and navigator in Yossarian's squadron; rapes an Italian chambermaid and throws her out a window to her death to avoid a blot on his reputation in Joseph Heller's *Catch-22*.

Aaron. Hebrew son of Amram, brother of Miriam (and perhaps of Moses), and first high priest of the Israelites; killed and entombed by Moses on Mount Hor in Zora Neale Hurston's *Moses, Man of the Mountain*.

Jimmy Aaron. Young black man who is murdered when he returns to the plantation to organize and lead his people during the civil rights movement in Ernest J. Gaines's *The Autobiography of Miss Jane Pittman*.

Mother Abagail. See Abagail Freemantle.

Horace Abbeville. Bigamist and debtor; commits suicide after settling accounts with Lee Chong the grocer by exchanging a fish-meal storage building for his debt in John Steinbeck's *Cannery Row*.

Elizabeth (Liz, Gillespie Emerson) Abbott. Woodcarver and clock winder who reconstitutes the Emerson family and salvages their neglected Baltimore home; as Gillespie, becomes the wife of Matthew Emerson and the mother of two children in Anne Tyler's *The Clock Winder*.

Horace Abbott. Gentle husband of Sally Page Abbott; dies of a heart attack as a result of a Halloween prank in John Gardner's *October Light*.

John Abbott. Pastor of Faith Baptist Church in Ellington, North Carolina, and father of Elizabeth Abbott in Anne Tyler's *The Clock Winder*.

Julia Abbott. Wife of John Abbott and mother of Elizabeth Abbott in Anne Tyler's *The Clock Winder*.

Sally Page Abbott. Eighty-year-old liberal who in self-defense plans the injury or death of her brother, James Page, until she nearly kills her niece, Ginny Hicks; widow of Horace Abbott in John Gardner's *October Light*.

Abby. See Abagail Freemantle.

Aunt Abby (Nab). Maiden sister and ward of John Bellmont; tries to protect Frado from Mrs. Bellmont in Harriet E. Wilson's *Our Nig*.

Abe. Elderly government lawyer running away from corrupt politics and grief over the death of his wife and son; befriended by Anne and Phil Sorenson before plunging off a cliff to his death in Frederick Busch's *Manual Labor*.

Abe. Son of Lucy; slave who is sent to sea, where he dies trying to assist distressed sailors in John Pendleton Kennedy's *Swallow Barn*.

Uncle Abednego. Elderly black from the almshouse who is the Birdsongs' gardener in Ellen Glasgow's *The Sheltered Life*.

Abel (Abelito). American Indian and World War II veteran who is imprisoned for murder in N. Scott Momaday's *House Made of Dawn*.

James Abel. Poor Farm inmate and witch digger in Jessamyn West's *The Witch Diggers*.

Mary Abel. Poor Farm inmate and witch digger; sets the fire that kills Christian Fraser in Jessamyn West's *The Witch Diggers*.

Carol Abernathy. Wife of Hunt Abernathy and mistress of Ron Grant; head of Hunt Hills Little Theatre and occultist in James Jones's *Go to the Widow-Maker*.

Hunt Abernathy. Husband of Carol Abernathy and friend of Ron Grant; general manager of a brickmaking and lumberyard establishment in Indianapolis in James Jones's *Go to the Widow-Maker*.

Abilene. Pool shark, oil-well driller, and richest man (in cash) in Thalia, Texas, in Larry McMurtry's *The Last Picture Show*.

Mike Abrams. Lawyer; early romantic interest and later good friend of Salley Gardens in Susan Cheever's *Looking for Work*.

Dr. Abe Abramson. Physician; older cousin and surrogate father of Zeke Gurevich; patron of freethinkers in Greenwich Village in William Herrick's *The Itinerant*.

Abrazza. Bachelor king of Bonovona in Herman Melville's *Mardi*.

Abyssinia (Sister 'ssinia). Dressmaker who travels with Arista Prolo as a costume designer; confides the story of Arista's life and death to Black Will in Carlene Hatcher Polite's *Sister X and the Victims of Foul Play*.

Josh Ace. Son of a team of Hollywood screenwriters from the 1930s and lover of Isadora Wing in Erica Jong's *How to Save Your Own Life*.

Achille. See Lafitte.

Achilles. Greek hero and lover of Helen; joins her in Egypt in H. D.'s *Helen in Egypt.*

Charlie Achorn. Cracker-barrel philosopher, temporary farmhand, and resident of Pretty Pass in Peter De Vries's *I Hear America Swinging.*

Noah Ackerman. Lonely Jewish social worker whose marriage to Hope Plowman deeply enriches his life; drafted into the army during World War II, where he is subjected to anti-Semitic taunts and distinguishes himself as a hero, in Irwin Shaw's *The Young Lions.*

Robert Ackley. Ill-groomed student who lives next to Holden Caulfield at Pencey Prep in J. D. Salinger's *The Catcher in the Rye.*

Acoraci. Guard at the exit from NESTER in Scott Spencer's *Last Night at the Brain Thieves Ball.*

Elizabeth (Lizzie) Acton. Guileless sister of Robert Acton; marries Clifford Wentworth in Henry James's *The Europeans.*

Mrs. Acton. Invalid mother of Robert and Lizzie Acton in Henry James's *The Europeans.*

Robert Acton. Sophisticated, well-traveled cousin of William Wentworth; courts Eugenia Münster in Henry James's *The Europeans.*

Ace Adair. Husband of Jewel Adair; killed by a train in William Goyen's *Come, The Restorer.*

Addis Adair. Adopted son of Ace and Jewel Adair; searches for his biological father and becomes a saintlike figure in the wilderness in William Goyen's *Come, The Restorer.*

Jewel Adair. Wife of Ace Adair; seeks to fulfill her lustful desires in William Goyen's *Come, The Restorer.*

Walter (Wat, Watty) Adair. North Carolina Tory sympathizer who betrays Arthur Butler; captured following the battle of King's Mountain; dies of a bite from a rabid wolf in John Pendleton Kennedy's *Horse-Shoe Robinson.*

Adam. Texas soldier who has an affair with Miranda; dies from influenza in Katherine Anne Porter's *Pale Horse, Pale Rider.*

Captain Jacob R. Adam. Owner of the S.S. *Thespian,* home of *Adam's Original and Unparalleled Floating Opera,* and master of ceremonies of the minstrel show in John Barth's *The Floating Opera.*

Alice (Lady Alicia, Alys Tuttle) Adams. Daughter of Virgil Adams; has a summer-long romance with Arthur Russell, but gives up her dreams of a life in high society and enrolls in a business college in Booth Tarkington's *Alice Adams.*

Amos Adams. Philosophic and idealistic editor of the Harvey *Tribune*; husband of Mary Adams, father of Grant Adams, and grandfather of Kenyon Adams in William Allen White's *In the Heart of a Fool.*

Carter Adams. American acquaintance who introduces Charlie Stark to the beauty of the Hawaiian Islands in Peter Matthiessen's *Raditzer.*

Mrs. Charles Fine Adams. Elderly woman who brings to the narrator's library a book on growing flowers in hotel rooms by candlelight in Richard Brautigan's *The Abortion.*

Grandfather Adams. Grandfather of Pookie Adams; supplies Pookie with "Casey Ruggles" comic strips in John Nichols's *The Sterile Cuckoo.*

Grandfather Adams. Grandfather of Stephen Grendon; takes Grendon's side in arguments and teaches him that "all love is just a fight against time" in August Derleth's *Evening in Spring*; also appears in *The Shield of the Valiant.*

Grant Adams. Father of Kenyon Adams; carpenter, reformer, and labor organizer in love with Laura Nesbit Van Dorn and killed by an anti-union mob in William Allen White's *In the Heart of a Fool.*

Jake Adams. Streetwise eighteen year old who makes his living in the drug underworld of St. Louis; main character in Herbert Simmons's *Corner Boy.*

John Adams. See Alexander Smith.

John R. Adams. Major, veteran of the Philippine campaign, and commander of the 1st Marine battalion in France during World War I in Thomas Boyd's *Through the Wheat.*

Kay Adams. College girlfriend and later the second wife of Michael Corleone in Mario Puzo's *The Godfather.*

Kenyon Adams. Illegitimate son of Grant Adams and Margaret Müller; reared as the son of Amos and Mary Adams; musician and artist who marries Lila Van Dorn in William Allen White's *In the Heart of a Fool.*

Marian and Bob Adams. Aunt and uncle of Pookie Adams; their Los Angeles home is a haven for Pookie in John Nichols's *The Sterile Cuckoo.*

Mary Sands Adams. Wife of Amos Adams and mother of Grant Adams; with the help of James Nesbit, claims her grandson Kenyon Adams as her own son in William Allen White's *In the Heart of a Fool*.

Mildred Adams. See Mildred Adams Gale.

Mrs. Adams. Wife of Virgil Adams and mother of Alice and Walter Adams; nags her husband to start his own factory so she and their daughter can join high society in Booth Tarkington's *Alice Adams*.

Old Man Adams. Father of Jake Adams; factory worker close to retirement in Herbert Simmons's *Corner Boy*.

Phil Adams. Boyhood friend of Tom Bailey; teaches Bailey self-defense; becomes the consul at Shanghai in Thomas Bailey Aldrich's *The Story of a Bad Boy*.

Pookie (Pooks) Adams. Girlfriend of Jerry Payne; whimsical storyteller who falls in and out of love and finally commits suicide in John Nichols's *The Sterile Cuckoo*.

Virgil (Virg) Adams. Father of Alice and Walter Adams; longtime loyal employee of J. A. Lamb; starts his own glue factory, but is eventually bought out by Lamb, in Booth Tarkington's *Alice Adams*.

Walter (Wallie) Adams. Son of Virgil Adams; despises the high society his mother and sister Alice aspire to; takes up with disreputable companions and becomes an embezzler in Booth Tarkington's *Alice Adams*.

Captain Willie Adams. Boat owner who warns Harry Morgan that Morgan's bootlegging has been discovered in Ernest Hemingway's *To Have and Have Not*.

Gerard (Gerry) Adamson. Chairman of the English department at Quirn College, philosopher-poet, and husband of Louise Adamson, who leaves him for Vadim Vadimovich, in Vladimir Nabokov's *Look at the Harlequins!*

Louise Adamson. Young wife of Gerry Adamson, whom she leaves for a less than felicitous marriage to Vadim Vadimovich, whose third wife she becomes, in Vladimir Nabokov's *Look at the Harlequins!*

Frances (F. Jasmine, Frankie) Addams. Twelve-year-old protagonist infatuated with her brother and his bride; disrupts their wedding in an attempt to accompany them on their honeymoon in Carson McCullers's *The Member of the Wedding*.

Jarvis Addams. Older brother of Frankie Addams; bridegroom in Carson McCullers's *The Member of the Wedding*.

Royal Quincy Addams. Jewelry store owner, father of Frankie and Jarvis Addams, and employer of Berenice Sadie Brown in Carson McCullers's *The Member of the Wedding*.

Judah Addison. Investor in Frank Cowperwood's natural gas project in Theodore Dreiser's *The Titan*.

Adele. Daughter of Lillian in Anaïs Nin's *Ladders to Fire* and *Seduction of the Minotaur*.

Adelina. Mexican wife of Harrison; asphyxiated in Nicholas Delbanco's *News*.

Adeppi. Young orphaned street singer in the Italian village of Castiglione; befriends Nino and lives with Arsella and Pipistrello in John Hawkes's *The Goose on the Grave*.

Adler. Member of Ward Bennett's crew seeking and failing to reach the North Pole; loyally remains with Bennett afterwards, encouraging him to make another voyage to the Arctic, in Frank Norris's *A Man's Woman*.

Dr. Adler. Vain physician and professor of internal medicine who lives in comfortable retirement in New York's Hotel Gloriana; uncaring father of Tommy Wilhelm in Saul Bellow's *The Victim*.

Liza Adler. Marxist who corresponds with Paul Hobbes in John Clellon Holmes's *Go*.

Myron (Mike) Adler. Successful and even-tempered businessman who, out of friendship and concern, reveals Joseph's decline into bad temper in Saul Bellow's *Dangling Man*.

Adraste. Maid of Helen; becomes pregnant by Damastor in John Erskine's *The Private Life of Helen of Troy*.

Boris (B., King B.) Adrian. Critically respected film director who directs a pornographic movie in Terry Southern's *Blue Movie*.

Anthony (Toni) Adverse. Illegitimate son of Maria Bonnyfeather and heir of John Bonnyfeather; has many adventures in his travels as he makes his fortune in Hervey Allen's *Anthony Adverse*.

Aegisthus. Lover of Clytemnestra; conspires with her to murder Clytemnestra's husband, Agamemnon; killed by Orestes in John Erskine's *The Private Life of Helen of Troy*.

Aeore (Child-Star, Riri'an). Niaruna Indian warrior who becomes a jaguar-shaman and chief rival of Lewis Moon in Peter Matthiessen's *At Play in the Fields of the Lord*.

African Flower. See Abeba Williams Lavoisier Torch.

After Birth Tycoon. See Salvador Hassan O'Leary.

Agamemnon. Brother of Menelaos and husband of Clytemnestra; killed by Clytemnestra and her lover Aegisthus in John Erskine's *The Private Life of Helen of Troy*.

Robert Agar. Specialist in keys and safecracking and an accomplice of Edward Pierce, whom Agar turns in to the police, in Michael Crichton's *The Great Train Robbery*.

Agatha. Beauty parlor assistant and girlfriend of Raymond; at Raymond's request, she visits the ailing Jake Brown in Claude McKay's *Home to Harlem*.

Bill Agatson. Former Harvard University student who drinks heavily and craves excess; killed in the New York subway in John Clellon Holmes's *Go*.

Aglone. Former slave who lives with the Pinseau family after the Civil War as their cook and housekeeper in Grace King's *The Pleasant Ways of St. Médard*.

Roland (Rollie) Agni. Talented rookie outfielder forced to play on the worst team in the Patriot League and bat eighth all year; reminds Angela Whittling Trust of her only true love, Luke Gofannon, in Philip Roth's *The Great American Novel*.

Agocho (Agocho Koh Tli-chu, Fig Tree John, John, Red Fire Bird). Apache Indian who seeks revenge on all whites for his wife's murder in Edwin Corle's *Fig Tree John*.

Mme. Agoropoulos. Woman kept from the social gatherings of the Cabala; honored when Alix d'Espoli accepts her invitation in Thornton Wilder's *The Cabala*.

Agravaine. Brother of Gawaine in Thomas Berger's *Arthur Rex*.

Ahab. Captain of the *Pequod* whose pursuit of Moby Dick leads to the death of everyone aboard the ship except Ishmael in Herman Melville's *Moby-Dick*.

Gil Ahab. Night-shift worker whose truck is used to transport workers to the Past Bay Manufacturing Company factory during the strike; religious fanatic in Robert Cantwell's *The Land of Plenty*.

Mickey Ahearn. Unmarried mother of a child she calls Willy and sends via railroad freight to Will Brady in Wright Morris's *The Works of Love*.

Ah Fong. Chinese baker on Manukura who dies in the hurricane before he can return to China in Charles Nordhoff and James Norman Hall's *The Hurricane*.

K. Y. Ahmed. See Salvador Hassan O'Leary.

Forney Aiken. Alcoholic photographer who darkens his skin while researching his latest book on black life in the South in Walker Percy's *The Last Gentleman*.

Aimata. See Pomaree Vahinee I.

Mollie Ainslie. Massachusetts teacher who becomes a major landowner in Kansas; marries Hesden Le Moyne in Albion W. Tourgee's *Bricks without Straw*.

Oscar Ainslie. Brother of Mollie Ainslie; makes Mollie promise, as he is dying of consumption, that she will remain in a healthful Southern climate in Albion W. Tourgee's *Bricks without Straw*.

Noel (Saul Ehrmann) Airman. Songwriter with a crooked arm who is the social director and head of the entertainment staff at South Wind, an adult camp; love of Marjorie Morningstar in Herman Wouk's *Marjorie Morningstar*.

Robert Aitken. Philadelphia printer who hires Thomas Paine to start the *Pennsylvania Magazine*, only to fire him when Paine starts writing too plainly about American independence, in Howard Fast's *Citizen Tom Paine*.

A. J. (Merchant of Sex). Financier of Islam Inc.; international playboy and practical joker in William S. Burroughs's *Naked Lunch*; sponsor of Homer Mandrill for president in *Exterminator!*; also appears in *The Soft Machine* and *The Wild Boys*.

Ajax. See Albert Jacks.

Alamo. Lead steer of the Del Sol trail herd that travels from Texas to Abilene in Emerson Hough's *North of 36*.

Alan. Husband of Sabina in Anaïs Nin's *A Spy in the House of Love*.

Alanno. Chief of Hio-Hio who criticizes King Bello in Herman Melville's *Mardi*.

Arthur Alarcon. Los Angeles Superior Court judge who replaces Alfred Peracca in the second trial of Gregory Powell and Jimmy Smith in Joseph Wambaugh's *The Onion Field*.

Bert Albany. Former miner who works in Zar's saloon; courts and marries a prostitute, with whom he leaves Hard Times when Clay Turner returns to raze the town, in E. L. Doctorow's *Welcome to Hard Times*.

Albert. Friend of Cecil Braithwaite in John Edgar Wideman's *Hurry Home*.

Alberta. Maid with mixed blood who is the object of Gamaliel Bland Honeywell's early desires in Ellen Glasgow's *The Romantic Comedians*.

Salathiel (Little Turtle) Albine. Child captured and reared by Indians; eventually works his way from life in the forest to one of civilization in Philadelphia in Hervey Allen's *The Forest and the Fort, Bedford Village*, and *Toward the Morning*.

Helen Albury. Sister of Robert Albury determined to prove her brother's innocence in Dashiell Hammett's *Red Harvest*.

Robert Albury. Assistant cashier of the First National Bank in Personville who is desperately in love with Dinah Brand, embezzles money to court her, and is charged with the murder of Donald Willsson in Dashiell Hammett's *Red Harvest*.

Maria Katerina Lorca Guerrera (Kat) Alcazar. American lesbian of Cuban descent; hired by Angel Stone as companion, secretary, bodyguard, and detective; narrator of M. F. Beal's *Angel Dance*.

Harriet Bumstead Alden. Mother of Oliver Alden in George Santayana's *The Last Puritan*.

Nathaniel Alden. Boston landlord and half brother of Peter Alden in George Santayana's *The Last Puritan*.

Oliver Alden. Idealistic student of philosophy; the "last Puritan" in George Santayana's *The Last Puritan*.

Peter Alden. Father of Oliver Alden in George Santayana's *The Last Puritan*.

Roberta (Mrs. Clifford Golden, Mrs. Carl Graham, Ruth Howard) Alden. Lover of Clyde Griffiths and pregnant by him; falls from a boat and drowns as Griffiths fails to attempt her rescue in Theodore Dreiser's *An American Tragedy*.

Thomas (Tom, Tommy) Alden. Davenport author who sponsors Felix Fay at literary activities, even though Fay is a socialist, in Floyd Dell's *Moon-Calf*.

Sir John Alderston. An owner of South Eastern Railway in Michael Crichton's *The Great Train Robbery*.

Karen Susan Aldrich. Former mental patient who finally succeeds in committing suicide in Judith Guest's *Ordinary People*.

Aline Aldridge. See Aline Aldridge Grey.

Rodney Aldwick. Friend of Neil Kingsblood; turns against his friend when Kingsblood's black ancestry is discovered in Sinclair Lewis's *Kingsblood Royal*.

Aleck Sander. Black friend of Chick Mallison in William Faulkner's *Intruder in the Dust* and *The Town*.

Aleema. Priest from Amma who is killed by Taji in Herman Melville's *Mardi*.

Fred Aleman. Sober businessman to whom Joan Mitchell is engaged in Shirley Ann Grau's *The House on Coliseum Street*.

Alex (Uncle Alex). Alabama farmer, husband of Caroline, and employer and benefactor of Ollie in George Wylie Henderson's *Ollie Miss* and *Jule*.

Dr. Alexander. Assistant lecturer in Biodynamics and government agent; brings Adam Krug to a university meeting the night Krug's wife, Olga, dies; later exterminated for bungling in Vladimir Nabokov's *Bend Sinister*.

Roland Alexander. Four-year-old boy who dies after accidentally swallowing rat poison left in his bedroom; as a result of this tragedy, his father almost beats his mother to death before being locked up by police in Alexis Deveaux's *Spirits in the Street*.

Suicide Alexander. Manager of the California baseball team that signs Henry Wiggen when Wiggen is released from the New York Mammoths in Mark Harris's *It Looked Like For Ever*.

Aunt Alexandra. Sister of Atticus Finch and aunt of Scout and Jem Finch; moves into the Finch home to help turn Scout into a southern lady in Harper Lee's *To Kill a Mockingbird*.

Leonid Andreich Alexandrov. Self-effacing Russian professor of engineering blinded by Peter Greene in John Barth's *Giles Goat-Boy*.

Alexis. Budding playwright and narrator who records the thwarted lives of young people living in her Harlem neighborhood in Alexis Deveaux's *Spirits in the Street*.

Alexis. See James Potts.

Alex Alexson. Second husband of Sophia Grieve Ryder in Djuna Barnes's *Ryder*.

Alfonso. Male canary Birdy buys from Mr. Lincoln to mate with Birdie in William Wharton's *Birdy*.

Alfonso (Fonso). Wife beater and cousin of Eva Medina Canada in Gayl Jones's *Eva's Man*.

Alfrado (Frado, Nig). Spirited mulatto girl indentured to the Bellmont family; tells the story of her mistreatment and growth to adulthood in Harriet E. Wilson's *Our Nig*.

Alfred (Alfy). Bouncer, protector, and watchman of the Bear Flag restaurant, a bar and brothel, in John Steinbeck's *Cannery Row*.

Algernon. White mouse used for experiments involving increased intelligence who is treated by Charlie Gordon, another experimental subject, as Gordon's only peer in Daniel Keyes's *Flowers for Algernon*.

Ali (Eli). Divorced Jewish father; first man Theresa Dunn allows to pick her up in a bar in Judith Rossner's *Looking for Mr. Goodbar*.

Alice. Wife of an unnamed sailor stationed in Newport; wants a baby so badly that she urges Theophilus North to impregnate her in Thornton Wilder's *Theophilus North*.

Alisande de la Carteloise. See Sandy.

Alix. Soon-to-be second wife of Ted in Reynolds Price's *Love and Work*.

John F. Alkahest. Bizarre paraplegic in violent pursuit of drug dealers in *The Smugglers of Lost Souls' Rock*, the interior novel within John Gardner's *October Light*.

Allan. Wealthy white radical, now a recluse in Vermont, in Nicholas Delbanco's *News*.

Kirby Allbee. Anti-Semite and weak-willed drunk who blames Asa Leventhal for his own moral degeneration, persecuting and finally attempting to murder him in retaliation, in Saul Bellow's *The Victim*.

Betsy Allbright. Romantic, much-married, and retired actress in Ludwig Bemelmans's *Dirty Eddie*.

Bobbie Allen. Waitress and prostitute who is Joe Christmas's first love in William Faulkner's *Light in August*.

Ethan (Ticonderoga) Allen. Enormous prisoner of war in Pendennis Castle, Falmouth, England, whom Israel Potter observes, in Herman Melville's *Israel Potter*.

Jim Allen. Fellow employee of Falton Harron at Watkins & Company, manufacturer of microscopes, in Susan Sontag's *Death Kit*.

Liddy Allen. Maid of Rachel Innes; believes murder and break-ins are the work of ghosts in Mary Roberts Rinehart's *The Circular Staircase*.

Madge Allen (Kramer). Puma trainer who goes on a short trip to Mexico with Frank Chambers in James M. Cain's *The Postman Always Rings Twice*.

Miss Allen. Nurse at St. Vincent's Hospital; befriends and loves Jason Wheeler in Albert Halper's *Union Square*.

Reverend Allen. Hypocritical minister in Winston Churchill's *Richard Carvel*.

Risa Allen. Woman with whom Edwin Locke becomes romantically obsessed in Joyce Carol Oates's *Cybele*.

Abigail Allerton. Friend of Hamm Rufe; forced to resign her university history assistantship because of her frankness in writing the political history of the town of Franklin in Mari Sandoz's *Capital City*.

Landon Allgood. Uncle of Mildred Sutton; sleeps in a church pew waiting for his niece's funeral in Reynolds Price's *A Long and Happy Life*.

Svetlana Alliluyeva. Daughter of Joseph Stalin; neighbor of George Levanter in Princeton in Jerzy Kosinski's *Blind Date*.

Anna Allston. Cousin and friend of Cornelia Wilton; becomes ill and dies following the disappearance of her husband, Lewis Barnwell, shortly after their wedding in Caroline Gilman's *Recollections of a Southern Matron*.

Joseph (Joe) Allston. Retired literary agent who befriends the Catlins; narrator of Wallace Stegner's *All the Little Live Things*; goes to Denmark to learn about his mother; narrator of *The Spectator Bird*.

Ruth Allston. Wife of Joe Allston in Wallace Stegner's *All the Little Live Things* and *The Spectator Bird*.

Almanni. Warrior who rules Odo during Media's absence in Herman Melville's *Mardi*.

The Greek Almas. Partner in the Regents Sportsmen's Club, Inc., and loan shark to whom Jerry Doherty owes $18,000; kills Croce Torre in a gun battle in George V. Higgins's *The Digger's Game*.

Elizabeth Almond. Aunt of Catherine Sloper; hosts a party at which Catherine meets Morris Townsend in Henry James's *Washington Square*.

Marian Almond. Pretty cousin of Catherine Sloper; marries Arthur Townsend and introduces Catherine to Arthur's cousin, Morris Townsend, in Henry James's *Washington Square*.

Almsbury. See John Randolph, Earl of Almsbury.

Lady Emily Almsbury. Meek and faithful wife of John Randolph, Earl of Almsbury, in Kathleen Winsor's *Forever Amber*.

Frank Alpine. Gentile drifter who becomes assistant storekeeper in Bernard Malamud's *The Assistant*.

Gerald (Jerry) Alsop. Self-styled moral advisor with deep respect for conventions and clean living whose close friendship with George Webber breaks down at Harvard when Webber begins to question Alsop's values in Thomas Wolfe's *The Web and the Rock*.

Isaac Alston. Elderly town patriarch disabled by a stroke in Reynolds Price's *A Long and Happy Life*.

Marina (Miss Marina) Alston. Elderly and eccentric sister of Isaac Alston in Reynolds Price's *A Long and Happy Life*.

Alva. Son of an American mulatto mother and Filipino father; employed as a presser in a costume house; has an affair with Emma Lou Morgan and fathers an illegitimate child by Geraldine in Wallace Thurman's *The Blacker the Berry*.

Captain Alvarado. Friend of Madre María del Pilar; urges Esteban to go to sea with him as an escape from the loss of Thornton Wilder's *The Bridge of San Luis Rey*.

Madame (Manueleta [Manuelata] Hernandez) Alvarez. Ambitious, aristocratic, Spanish-born wife of President Alvarez of Olancho in Richard Harding Davis's *Soldiers of Fortune*.

Manuel (Manny) Alvarez. Friend of Ruben Fontanez and Marty; dances in the subway for money in Jay Neugeboren's *Listen Ruben Fontanez*.

Maria Alvarez. Child patient at Sacred Heart Hospital, where she is a victim of attempted rape; dies of pneumonia in Edward Lewis Wallant's *The Children at the Gate*.

Pepe Alvarez. Prizefighter once managed by Ed Sansom; former lover of Randolph Lee Skully and the focus of his life in Truman Capote's *Other Voices, Other Rooms*.

President Alvarez. President of Olancho who aspires to establish a dictatorship but is overthrown and executed in Richard Harding Davis's *Soldiers of Fortune*.

Barone Alvarito. Duck-hunting companion of Col. Richard Cantwell in Ernest Hemingway's *Across the River and into the Trees*.

Elizabeth Thornwell (Betty) Alvin. Granddaughter of Cornelia Thornwell; leaves her parents' comfortable home to live modestly with her grandmother; becomes an antiestablishment activist; marries a socialist journalist and fights to save Sacco and Vanzetti from execution in Upton Sinclair's *Boston*.

Blessed (Bles) Alwyn. Favorite pupil of Mary Taylor; lover and later husband of Zora; fails as a Washington politician and returns to Alabama to help blacks free themselves from the sharecropping system in W. E. B. Du Bois's *The Quest of the Silver Fleece*.

Lady Amalthea. Unicorn who leaves the forest to discover if she is the last of her kind; turned into Lady Amalthea by Schmendrick in order to save her from Red Bull in Peter S. Beagle's *The Last Unicorn*.

John (Johnny, Squirrel) Amato. Compulsive gambler who plans the robbery of a mob-run card game with Frankie and Russell; killed by Jackie Cogan in George V. Higgins's *Cogan's Trade*.

Amber. Female healer who befriends Teray in Octavia E. Butler's *Patternmaster*.

Amber. See Amber St. Clare.

George Amberson. Brother of Isabel Amberson Minafer and uncle of George Amberson Minafer; former congressman and a business failure in Booth Tarkington's *The Magnificent Ambersons*.

Isabel Amberson. See Isabel Amberson Minafer.

Major Amberson. Head of a prominent family whose fortunes dwindle so much that he leaves no estate in Booth Tarkington's *The Magnificent Ambersons*.

Ambrosius. Young Franciscan monk who, in 1680, murders Benedicta, the hangman's daughter, to save her from a romance with Rochus in Ambrose Bierce's adaptation of *The Monk and the Hangman's Daughter*.

Amelia. Black maid and youthful friend of the narrator of Aline Bernstein's *The Journey Down*.

Prince Amerigo. Italian nobleman who marries Maggie Verver and who had a previous attachment to Charlotte Stant in Henry James's *The Golden Bowl*.

Bob Ames. Cousin of Mrs. Vance; encourages Carrie Meeber to become an actress in Theodore Dreiser's *Sister Carrie*.

Cathy Ames. See Cathy Ames Trask.

Charlotte Ames. See Charlotte Ames Emory.

Charlotte Ames. Wife of Harry Ames and, on one occasion, sexual partner of Max Reddick in John A. Williams's *The Man Who Cried I Am*.

Dalton Ames. Lover of Caddy Compson and the father of Quentin Compson II in William Faulkner's *The Sound and the Fury*.

Harry Ames. Leading Afro-American novelist of his time; murdered by the CIA in order to suppress publication of a contingency plan, code named King Alfred, for removing the minority population of the United States into concentration camps in John A. Williams's *The Man Who Cried I Am*.

Lacey Debney Ames. Obese mother of Charlotte Emory and wife of Murray Ames in Anne Tyler's *Earthly Possessions*.

Mat Ames. Youth who leads a group of boys in the snowball fight against the boys led by Jack Harris in Thomas Bailey Aldrich's *The Story of a Bad Boy*.

Murray Ames. Dour photographer father of Charlotte Emory and husband of Lacey Debney Ames in Anne Tyler's *Earthly Possessions*.

Catherine Amesbury. See Cathy Ames Trask.

Amigo. Mexican cowhand for Major Willard Tetley; convinces the lynch mob to seek the rustlers on a trail different from that pursued by Sheriff Risley in Walter Van Tilburg Clark's *The Ox-Bow Incident*.

Jasper Ammen. Egoist who, as a "study," plots the murder of a stranger in Conrad Aiken's *King Coffin*.

Amos. Minister who attempted to burn down his own church; golf partner of Thomas Marshfield at the retreat in John Updike's *A Month of Sundays*.

Amos. Prosperous member of the Chicago Stock Exchange who disapproves of his impractical and nonmaterialistic brother, Joseph, in Saul Bellow's *Dangling Man*.

Amos. Television character who turns in moochers Kingfish Stevens and Andy Brown to the police for robbing his place in Ishmael Reed's *The Last Days of Louisiana Red*.

Mr. Amos. Valet of Congressman Doolittle; keeps Sara Andrews informed of his employer's failing health in W. E. B. Du Bois's *Dark Princess*.

Amram. Hebrew father of Aaron and Miriam, and perhaps of Moses as well; slave in Goshen in Zora Neale Hurston's *Moses, Man of the Mountain*.

Harriet Shippen Amron. Philadelphia blue blood married to Saul Amron in Paule Marshall's *The Chosen Place, the Timeless People*.

Saul Amron. American anthropologist who goes to the Caribbean as the leader of a research project designed to improve life for the poor people of Bourne Island; husband of Harriet Shippen Amron in Paule Marshall's *The Chosen Place, the Timeless People*.

Mrs. Amsden. American expatriate and friend of Evalina Bowen; concerned with the affairs of others in William Dean Howells's *Indian Summer*.

Jack Amsterdam. Corrupt construction contractor for the Catholic church and business and golf partner of Desmond Spellacy; arrested for the murder of Lois Fazenda in John Gregory Dunne's *True Confessions*.

Jules Amthor. "Psychic consultant" in Raymond Chandler's *Farewell, My Lovely*.

Amula. Young woman jealous of the attention Rochus gives Benedicta; comforts Ambrosius before his execution in Ambrose Bierce's adaptation of *The Monk and the Hangman's Daughter*.

Amy. Aunt of Miranda; romanticized by her family as a model of Southern beauty; marries Gabriel Breaux, her longtime suitor, and dies shortly thereafter of tuberculosis in Katherine Anne Porter's *Old Mortality*.

Amyas le Poulet. See Clarence.

Anacleto. Eccentric Filipino manservant excessively devoted to Alison Langdon; disappears shortly after her death in Carson McCullers's *Reflections in a Golden Eye*.

Jack Analysis. Journalist of Greek parentage and former lover of Molly Calico in Peter De Vries's *The Mackerel Plaza*.

Dame Anaïtis (Lady of the Lake). Ruler of the enchanted island Cocaigne; becomes Jurgen's first wife when he begins a yearlong dalliance in the dream realm in pursuit of his wife Dame Lisa in James Branch Cabell's *Jurgen*.

Albert Ancke. Times Square night person and drug addict in John Clellan Holmes's *Go.*

Francisco Domingo Carlos Andres Sebastián (Frisco) d'Anconia. Successful industrialist who destroys his international copper empire when he joins the strike in Ayn Rand's *Atlas Shrugged.*

Frau Anders. Mistress of Hippolyte; sells her into slavery in Susan Sontag's *The Benefactor.*

John Anders. Police captain who investigates the murder of Angela Black in Michael Crichton's *The Terminal Man.*

Alfred (Al) Anderson. Proprietor of Al's Lunch Wagon; sympathetic to the Communist labor organizers; helps feed the strikers in John Steinbeck's *In Dubious Battle.*

Andy Anderson. Chief bugler of G Company; feels his position threatened by Robert E. Lee Prewitt; coauthors *The Re-Enlistment Blues* with Prewitt and Sal Clark in James Jones's *From Here to Eternity.*

Argustus (Mr. Andy) Anderson. Father of Mac Douglas; musician and supporter of his grandson, Raymond Douglas, in Herbert Simmons's *Man Walking on Eggshells.*

Bess (Bessie) Anderson. Daughter of Tillie and Ern Anderson and sister of Nonnie and Ed Anderson; college-educated maid in Lillian Smith's *Strange Fruit.*

Betty Anderson. Daughter of mill workers; becomes pregnant by Rodney Harrington and is bought off by his father, Leslie Harrington, in Grace Metalious's *Peyton Place.*

Brigham M. (Brig) Anderson. Senior senator from Utah and chairman of the Senate Foreign Relations Subcommittee on the nomination of Robert Leffingwell in Allen Drury's *Advise and Consent.*

Charley Anderson. World War I Ace who has a mercurial career as an airplane parts manufacturer after the war; his obsession with the stock market and his lack of moral principles lead to his ruin in John Dos Passos's *U.S.A.* trilogy.

Dolly Anderson. Self-loathing teenaged daughter of Viola Anderson; given to flights of fantasy which are a pretext for her murder in Hal Bennett's *The Black Wine.*

Ed (Eddie) Anderson. Son of Tillie and Ern Anderson, brother of Nonnie and Bessie Anderson, and killer of Tracy Deen in Lillian Smith's *Strange Fruit.*

Ern Anderson. Husband of Tillie Anderson and father of Nonnie, Bessie, and Ed Anderson in Lillian Smith's *Strange Fruit.*

Homer Anderson. Sociologist and factory personnel administrator and neighbor of Gertie and Clovis Nevels in Harriette Arnow's *The Dollmaker.*

Jan Anderson. Strong-willed young protagonist who shoots Uncle Hake Nolan to protect his sister, Timmie Anderson, in Fred Chappell's *The Inkling.*

Jaw Buster Anderson. Neighbor of Nunn Ballew, fox hunter, and owner of a logging truck often used to transport neighbors to town from their isolated community in Harriette Arnow's *Hunter's Horn.*

Jenny Nolan Anderson. Widowed mother of Jan and Timmie Anderson and sister of Hezekiah Nolan; gradually loses control of her household and eventually dies of cancer in Fred Chappell's *The Inkling.*

Leon Anderson. Communications expert at NESTER in Scott Spencer's *Last Night at the Brain Thieves Ball.*

Mrs. Anderson. Neighbor of Gertie and Clovis Nevels and wife of Homer Anderson; brings Gertie the message that the wife of a factory executive wants dolls to be carved for a Christmas bazaar in Harriette Arnow's *The Dollmaker.*

Nonnie (Non) Anderson. Daughter of Tillie and Ern Anderson and sister of Bessie and Ed Anderson; black lover of Tracy Deen and mother of their unborn child in Lillian Smith's *Strange Fruit.*

Dr. Robert Anderson. Principal of a southern black school; moves to New York, where he meets and marries Anne Grey, in Nella Larsen's *Quicksand.*

Tillie Anderson. Mother of Nonnie, Bessie, and Ed Anderson and wife of Ern Anderson; works in white households as a cook in Lillian Smith's *Strange Fruit.*

Timmie Anderson. Violently insane sister of Jan Anderson; tries to deflect Jan's penetrating gaze by persuading him to wear glasses and hopes to give him insight by cutting eyelike gashes in his hands and feet in Fred Chappell's *The Inkling.*

Viola Anderson. Friend of Eloise McLindon, cynical political activist, whorehouse madam, and mother of Dolly Anderson in Hal Bennett's *The Black Wine* and *Seventh Heaven.*

Wilbur Anderson. Son of Argustus Anderson and uncle of Raymond Douglas; trumpet player who buys Douglas his first trumpet and helps to influence his musical style in Herbert Simmons's *Man Walking on Eggshells*.

Andreas. Franciscan Superior of the Monastery of Berchtesgaden in Ambrose Bierce's adaptation of *The Monk and the Hangman's Daughter*.

Andrés. Member of Pablo's partisan group in Ernest Hemingway's *For Whom the Bell Tolls*.

Andrew. Suitor and spiritual advisor of Mary Pinesett, husband of Doll, elder at Heaven's Gate Church, blacksmith, and carpenter at Blue Brook Plantation in Julia Peterkin's *Scarlet Sister Mary*.

Captain Donald Andrews. Math expert and friend of Captain Nathaniel Hicks; Acting Chief of the Statistical Section in James Gould Cozzens's *Guard of Honor*.

Elizabeth (Polly) Andrews. Medical technician and first employer of Libby MacAusland; member of the Group in Mary McCarthy's *The Group*.

Gerald Andrews. Neighbor of Adah Logan and friend of the Mitchells; soldier killed during World War II in Susan Glaspell's *Judd Rankin's Daughter*.

Sara Andrews. See Sara Andrews Towns.

Thomas T. (Dad) Andrews. Father of Todd Andrews; commits suicide on February 2, 1930, after the collapse of his personal finances in the stock market crash of 1929; cofounder of the law firm Andrews and Bishop in John Barth's *The Floating Opera*.

Todd Andrews. Fifty-four-year-old lawyer who attempts suicide; narrator and central figure in John Barth's *The Floating Opera*.

Walter Andrews. Man who, seventy years earlier, owned the property and mansion which is the poorhouse in John Updike's *The Poorhouse Fair*.

Andrei Androfski. Brother of Deborah Bronski, friend of Alexander Brandel and Christopher de Monti, and lover of Gabriela Rak; leads the Warsaw Ghetto Revolt in Leon Uris's *Mila 18*.

Nick Andros. Deaf-mute chosen to lead The Stand, but who is killed unexpectedly, in Stephen King's *The Stand*.

Andy. Freedman who tells Comfort Servosse about the local chapter of the Union League; caretaker at Warrington Place who tends to the dying Servosse in Albion W. Tourgee's *A Fool's Errand*.

Miss Ange. Drag queen in New Orleans who dresses as Scarlett O'Hara, Desdemona, and Drusilla Duncan in John Rechy's *City of Night*.

Stella Bast Angel (Engels). Cousin of Edward Bast; schemes to gain control of her family's General Roll Corporation in William Gaddis's *JR*.

Sister Angelica. Nun who is Father Trask's apprentice; helps lead the wake for Chalmers Egstrom in William Goyen's *In a Farther Country*.

Angélique. Discarded mistress of Count Armand de Sacy; courtesan living in forced exile at Bréda in Arna Wendell Bontemps's *Drums at Dusk*.

Dr. Angelo. Handsome middle-aged Italian physician at the Diamond County Home for the Aged; treats George Lucas's chronic ear infection in John Updike's *The Poorhouse Fair*.

Max Angelo. Sculptor; sometime lover of Salley Gardens in Susan Cheever's *Looking for Work*.

Angel of Death. See John Sallow.

Angie (Ange). Married woman who claims she is pregnant by her lover Billy Phelan in order to test Phelan's love for her in William Kennedy's *Billy Phelan's Greatest Game*.

Earl Angstrom. Husband of Mary Angstrom and father of Rabbit and Miriam Angstrom; works as a printer in John Updike's *Rabbit, Run* and *Rabbit Redux*.

Harry (Rabbit) Angstrom. Husband of Janice Springer Angstrom and father of Nelson Angstrom; talented former basketball player entangled in adult responsibilities in John Updike's *Rabbit, Run* and *Rabbit Redux*.

Janice Springer (Jan) Angstrom. Wife of Rabbit Angstrom and mother of Nelson Angstrom; accidentally drowns her infant daughter in John Updike's *Rabbit, Run*; has an affair with Charlie Stavros in *Rabbit Redux*.

Mary Angstrom. Wife of Earl Angstrom and mother of Rabbit and Miriam Angstrom in John Updike's *Rabbit, Run*; suffers from Parkinson's disease in *Rabbit Redux*.

Miriam (Mim) Angstrom. Younger sister of Rabbit Angstrom in John Updike's *Rabbit, Run* and *Rabbit Redux*.

Nelson Frederick Angstrom. Son of Janice and Rabbit Angstrom in John Updike's *Rabbit, Run* and *Rabbit Redux*.

Rebecca June Angstrom. Infant daughter of Janice and Rabbit Angstrom; drowns in a bathtub in John Updike's *Rabbit, Run*.

Arch Anker. See The County Clerk.

Ann. Traveling companion and supporter of Francis Starwick in Thomas Wolfe's *Of Time and the River*.

Miss Ann (Our Lady of the Limitless Bladder). Client of C. Card and an accomplished beer drinker; kills the prostitute whose body she hires Card to steal from the morgue in Richard Brautigan's *Dreaming of Babylon*.

Anna. Traumatized victim of sexual assault who may be the saving love of Lancelot Lamar's new world in Walker Percy's *Lancelot*.

Annatoo. Wife of Samoa; lost at sea in Herman Melville's *Mardi*.

Anne-Marie. Student who serves on the Cinema Committee with Hill Gallagher during the student rebellion in James Jones's *The Merry Month of May*.

Anna Annesley. Genteel sister-in-law of John Osborne; cares for Mildred and Helen Osborne following their mother's death in Paul Laurence Dunbar's *The Love of Landry*.

Annette. Discarded mistress of Count Armand de Sacy; courtesan living in forced exile at Bréda in Arna Wendell Bontemps's *Drums at Dusk*.

Annette. See Anna Ivanovna Blagovo.

Annixter. Wheat rancher in the San Joaquin Valley who attempts to influence the state's railroad commission and fails; shot by a railroad agent in Frank Norris's *The Octopus*.

Anselm (Arthur, Saint Anselm). Religious poet and bitter friend of Stanley in William Gaddis's *The Recognitions*.

Anselmo. Old man who is Robert Jordan's guide in Ernest Hemingway's *For Whom the Bell Tolls*.

Karen Anson. Assistant to Mark Hall in Project Wildfire in Michael Crichton's *The Andromeda Strain*.

Anterrabae. Forceful god in Yr, the mental world of Deborah Blau, in Hannah Green's *I Never Promised You a Rose Garden*.

Antheil. "Regulatory agent" who forces John Converse to locate Marge Converse, who he believes has the smuggled heroin, in Robert Stone's *Dog Soldiers*.

Anthony. Hospital orderly whom Willie Hall tries to indoctrinate politically in John Edgar Wideman's *The Lynchers*.

Mr. Antolini. Former English teacher of Holden Caulfield at Elkton Hills and a refuge for Holden in New York City; gives Holden a pat on the head, a drunkenly intimate gesture that frightens Holden away, in J. D. Salinger's *The Catcher in the Rye*.

Anton (the Quail). Son of Makar and lover of his sister, Ewka, in Jerzy Kosinski's *The Painted Bird*.

Spiros Antonapoulos. Moronic deaf-mute idealized by John Singer; dies of nephritis in an insane asylum in Carson McCullers's *The Heart Is a Lonely Hunter*.

Antone. Middle-aged Portuguese sailor flogged for fighting aboard the *Neversink* in Herman Melville's *White-Jacket*.

Brother (Father) Antonio. Capuchin monk with a mysterious past; model for Miriam's artwork; killed by Donatello in Nathaniel Hawthorne's *The Marble Faun*.

Marc Antony. Nephew of Julius Caesar; caught attempting to seduce Cleopatra and leaving Rome soon after, in Thornton Wilder's *The Ides of March*.

Anulka. Local witch who cures the narrator of a kick in the stomach by applying a dead mole to his abdomen in Jerzy Kosinski's *The Painted Bird*.

Aonetti (Deer Eyes). Indian maiden enamored of Koningsmarke in James Kirke Paulding's *Koningsmarke*.

Apeyahola (Indian Jory). American sailor imprisoned by Tripoli pirates; Creek Indian, trader, pioneer, and cofounder of a town in Oklahoma in H. L. Davis's *Harp of a Thousand Strings*.

Catharine Bosworth Apley. Boston aristocrat chosen by George Apley's family to be his wife in John P. Marquand's *The Late George Apley*.

Eleanor (El) Apley. Daughter of George and Catharine Apley; rebels against her social class and marries an outsider in John P. Marquand's *The Late George Apley*.

George William Apley. Boston aristocrat and lawyer; son of Thomas Apley, husband of Catharine Apley, and father of John and Eleanor Apley; upholds the family tradition and social convention in John P. Marquand's *The Late George Apley*.

John Apley. Son of George and Catharine Apley; rebels against family tradition but returns to assume his role as head of the family and as a proper Bostonian in John P. Marquand's *The Late George Apley*.

Thomas Apley. Boston aristocrat and textile merchant; molds his son George Apley into a proper

Bostonian while maintaining an illegitimate family in New York in John P. Marquand's *The Late George Apley.*

William Apley. Manager of the Apley family textile mills; considers his nephew George incompetent to enter the business in John P. Marquand's *The Late George Apley.*

Appleby. Fellow squadron member who reports Yossarian for refusing to take atabrine tablets in Joseph Heller's *Catch-22.*

Frank Appleby. Bank trust officer married to Janet Appleby in John Updike's *Couples.*

Janet Appleby. Seductive wife of Frank Appleby; they couple swap with Marcia and Harold Smith in John Updike's *Couples.*

Alf Applegate. Elderly bachelor neighbor of the Birdwells in Jessamyn West's *The Friendly Persuasion.*

Mr. Applegate. Vicar of Christ Church in St. Botolph's; alcoholic whose weakness is responsible for his colorful sermons in John Cheever's *The Wapshot Scandal.*

Corinna Appleton. Mother of Skippy Appleton, possibly by Louis Zimmerman rather than by Harry Appleton, the husband she abandons, in John Updike's *The Centaur.*

Harry (Doc) Appleton. Physician who treats the Caldwell family; belongs to no church and subscribes to no belief system; twin brother of Hester Appleton; abandoned by his wife, Corinna Appleton; his son, Skippy Appleton, is possibly not his but Louis Zimmerman's in John Updike's *The Centaur.*

Hester Appleton. Spinster sister of Doc Appleton; teacher of Latin and French; harbors longtime fantasies about her colleague George Caldwell in John Updike's *The Centaur.*

Skippy Appleton. Son of Corinna Appleton and possibly of Louis Zimmerman in John Updike's *The Centaur.*

Stella Appleton. First girlfriend of Eugene Witla in Theodore Dreiser's *The "Genius."*

Apraxine. One of the many ill or handicapped people cared for by Chrysis in Thornton Wilder's *The Woman of Andros.*

Rachel (Little Mother) Apt. Leader of a group of Jewish resistance fighters battling the Nazis from well-concealed bunkers and in the sewers of occupied Warsaw in John Hersey's *The Wall.*

Julia (Donna Julia) d'Aquilanera. Daughter of Leda Matilda Colonna d'Aquilanera and half sister of Marcantonio d'Aquilanera in Thornton Wilder's *The Cabala.*

Leda Matilda Colonna, La Duchessa d'Aquilanera. Mother of Marcantonio and Julia d'Aquilanera; enlists Samuele's help in curbing Marcantonio's sensual life-style in Thornton Wilder's *The Cabala.*

Marcantonio d'Aquilanera. Son of Leda Matilda Colonna d'Aquilanera; adopts a life of dissipation and commits suicide in Thornton Wilder's *The Cabala.*

Arabella. Lesbian movie star who acts in Boris Adrian's pornographic movie in Terry Southern's *Blue Movie.*

Arai. Younger daughter of Fakahau and Mata, sister of Marama, and servant to Madame de Laage; survives the hurricane in Charles Nordhoff and James Norman Hall's *The Hurricane.*

Julius Arcenaux. Owner of a grocery store, the central gathering place on the Isle aux Chiens, in Shirley Ann Grau's *The Hard Blue Sky.*

Cora (Mamma) Archbald. Widowed daughter-in-law of General Archbald; reared on *Little Women,* she tries to rear her daughter, Jenny Blair Archbald, in the same manner in Ellen Glasgow's *The Sheltered Life.*

General David (Grandfather) Archbald. Patriarch who idealizes Eva Birdsong in Ellen Glasgow's *The Sheltered Life.*

Etta (Aunt Etta) Archbald. Daughter of General Archbald; invalid, hysterical, and unmarried aunt of Jenny Blair Archbald in Ellen Glasgow's *The Sheltered Life.*

Isabella (Aunt Isabella) Archbald. Bold and beautiful aunt of Jenny Blair Archbald; marries Joseph Crocker in Ellen Glasgow's *The Sheltered Life.*

Jenny Blair Archbald. Woman who, at age nine, begins keeping a secret with George Birdsong and, at age eighteen, thinks she is in love with him in Ellen Glasgow's *The Sheltered Life.*

Archbishop of Chicago. Religious leader who invites Roger Ashley to dinner at the height of Roger's journalistic fame and tells him the parable of the walls in Thornton Wilder's *The Eighth Day.*

Alan Archdale. White counsel for Peter in DuBose Heyward's *Porgy.*

Adeline Archer. Widowed mother of Newland Archer in Edith Wharton's *The Age of Innocence.*

Alice Archer. Sensitive friend of Sally Manchester and Cecilia Vaughan; dies of a broken heart when Cecilia, her best friend, marries Arthur Kavanagh, Alice's secret love, in Henry Wadsworth Longfellow's *Kavanagh.*

Dallas Archer. Son of Newland and May Archer in Edith Wharton's *The Age of Innocence.*

Isabel Archer. Charming, intellectual, strong-willed heroine who seeks to expand her life experiences in Europe; marries Gilbert Osmond in Henry James's *The Portrait of a Lady.*

Iva Archer. Miles Archer's wife, with whom Sam Spade is attempting to end an affair in Dashiell Hammett's *The Maltese Falcon.*

John Archer. Doctor who assists Perry Dart in solving a murder case in Rudolph Fisher's *The Conjure-Man Dies.*

Lew Archer. California private detective; the hero in eighteen of Ross Macdonald's novels starting with *The Moving Target.*

May Archer. See May Welland.

Miles Archer. Sam Spade's partner, who is murdered while shadowing Brigid O'Shaughnessy and Floyd Thursby at the beginning of Dashiell Hammett's *The Maltese Falcon.*

Newland Archer. Fiancé of May Welland; falls in love with his cousin, Ellen Olenska, in Edith Wharton's *The Age of Innocence.*

Doctor Howard Archie. Small-town doctor who recognizes the musical intelligence of Thea Kronborg; helps her move to Chicago to study music and underwrites her studies in Germany in Willa Cather's *The Song of the Lark.*

Arfretee. Wife of Deacon Eeremear Po-Po in Herman Melville's *Omoo.*

Harry Argent. Generous, energetic lover of Eliza Quarles; movie producer in Alice Adams's *Listening to Billie.*

Argo. Sister of Pamphilus in Thornton Wilder's *The Woman of Andros.*

Jacques d'Argus. See Jakob Gradus.

Arheetoo. Tahitian casuist who asks Typee to forge documents in Herman Melville's *Omoo.*

Ariane. Young woman of twenty six who is the shipboard lover of both Allert Vanderveenan and Olaf; disappears mysteriously from the cruise ship in John Hawkes's *Death, Sleep & the Traveler.*

Robert Ariyoshi. Japanese fisherman who takes Charlie Stark fishing in Peter Matthiessen's *Raditzer.*

Arkie. See James Parker McClellan.

Margotte Arkin. Widowed niece of Artur Sammler's dead wife; earnest and goodhearted but clumsy and verbose woman in whose apartment Sammler is provided a room in Saul Bellow's *Mr. Sammler's Planet.*

Madge Arlen. Friend of India Bridge and member of the Women's Auxiliary in Evan Connell's *Mrs. Bridge* and *Mr. Bridge.*

Armand. Oldest living vampire who introduces Louis and Claudia to the Théâtre des Vampires in Anne Rice's *Interview with the Vampire.*

Richie Armbriste. Young pornography magnate in search of a movie erroneously thought to include footage of Hitler at an orgy in Don DeLillo's *Running Dog.*

Lewis (Lew, Lo) Armistead. Seasoned Confederate general in charge of one of George Pickett's brigades in Michael Shaara's *The Killer Angels.*

William (Bill) Armiston. Activist who betrays the group, brings a bomb into their home, and murders three of the men; murdered by Kam Wright in M. F. Beal's *Amazon One.*

Henry Armstid. Poor farmer in William Faulkner's *As I Lay Dying, Light in August, The Hamlet, The Town,* and *The Mansion.*

Martha (Lula) Armstid. Wife of Henry Armstid in William Faulkner's *As I Lay Dying, Light in August,* and *The Hamlet.*

Arnold (Aubrey Wallace) Armstrong. Son of Paul Armstrong; as Aubrey Wallace he marries and abandons Lucy Haswell; murdered in Mary Roberts Rinehart's *The Circular Staircase.*

Fanny B. (F. B. A.) Armstrong. Wife of Paul Armstrong; insists that Rachel Innes give up her lease to Sunnyside in Mary Roberts Rinehart's *The Circular Staircase.*

Louise Armstrong. Daughter of Paul Armstrong; secretly returns to Sunnyside when she discovers her father's plot in Mary Roberts Rinehart's *The Circular Staircase.*

Paul Armstrong. President of the Traders' Bank who embezzles money and frames John Bailey for the crime in Mary Roberts Rinehart's *The Circular Staircase.*

Clifford Armytage. See Merton Gill.

Armenta Arnez. Middle-class high school girl to whom Jake Adams is attracted in Herbert Simmons's *Corner Boy.*

Edna Arnez. Wife of Henry Arnez and mother of Armenta Arnez in Herbert Simmons's *Corner Boy.*

Henry Arnez. Husband of Edna Arnez and father of Armenta Arnez in Herbert Simmons's *Corner Boy.*

Arnold. Heavy-set young man who lives with his parents; eventually goes to live in the house of Christina Goering with his father and Lucie Gamelon in Jane Bowles's *Two Serious Ladies.*

Benedict Arnold. American Revolutionary War colonel who leads an overland attack on Quebec in Kenneth Roberts's *Arundel.*

Julie Hempel Arnold. Schoolgirl friend of Selina Peake DeJong; the friendship is renewed later in life in Edna Ferber's *So Big.*

Alcée Arobin. Seducer who has an affair with Edna Pontellier in Kate Chopin's *The Awakening.*

Carmen Arrellano. Girlfriend of Gerardo Strasser-Mendana and later of Antonio Strasser-Mendana in Joan Didion's *A Book of Common Prayer.*

Lady Susannah Arrow. Wealthy anarchist and bisexual lover in Paul Theroux's *The Family Arsenal.*

Arrowhead. Untrustworthy Tuscarora Indian who informs the French of the position of the relief party in James Fenimore Cooper's *The Pathfinder.*

Joyce Lanyon Arrowsmith. See Joyce Lanyon.

Leora Tozer Arrowsmith. See Leora Tozer.

Martin Arrowsmith. Medical doctor and researcher frustrated by the commercial and confining aspects of his work in Sinclair Lewis's *Arrowsmith.*

Arsella. Servant of a contessa; wife of Pipistrello; Adeppi stays with her family in John Hawkes's *The Goose on the Grave.*

Art. Friend of a friend of the narrator; lives in Hotel Trout Fishing in America with a prostitute and a cat in Richard Brautigan's *Trout Fishing in America.*

Arthur. Headmaster of a boys' boarding school and companion of Mrs. Montague; patrols Hill House by night with a revolver in Shirley Jackson's *The Haunting of Hill House.*

Arthur. Lifelong naif compromised by his vulnerability but sustained by his idealism; eponymous character in Thomas Berger's *Arthur Rex.*

Arthur (Jones). King of England who, while posing as a peasant with Hank Morgan, is captured and sold into slavery; rescued by Clarence in Samuel Langhorne Clemens's *A Connecticut Yankee in King Arthur's Court.*

Curt Arvey. Head of Arvey Film Studio; lends Vito Orsini money to produce a film and then attempts to wrest control of it from Orsini in the middle of production in Judith Krantz's *Scruples.*

Stephan Asche. See Wyatt Gwyon.

Jacob (Jake) Ascher. Lawyer and friend of the Isaacsons, whom he defends during their espionage trial; his defense is partially responsible for the Isaacsons being convicted and executed in E. L. Doctorow's *The Book of Daniel.*

Susan Ash. Maid of Beale Farange in Henry James's *What Maisie Knew.*

Edward Ashe. Illegitimate son of Elias McCutcheon and Ellen Poe Ashe; falls in love with Betsy, fathers a child by her, and flees with them to Canada in Jesse Hill Ford's *The Raider.*

Ellen Poe Ashe. Woman abandoned by her husband; falls in love with Elias McCutcheon and bears their son, Edward Ashe; later marries Colonel Ennis Dalton in Jesse Hill Ford's *The Raider.*

Brewster (Brew) Ashenden. Millionaire playboy and eligible bachelor who copulates with a bear to save his life; narrator of *The Making of Ashenden,* a novella in Stanley Elkin's *Searches and Seizures.*

Colonel Argall Ashendyne. Father of Medway Ashendyne; leads the family's attempt to force traditional womanhood on his granddaughter, Hagar Ashendyne, in Mary Johnston's *Hagar.*

Hagar Ashendyne. Independent girl who grows to overcome her family and culture; becomes a famous author and an advocate for women's rights in Mary Johnston's *Hagar.*

Medway Ashendyne. Father of Hagar Ashendyne; travels to Europe during her childhood; when he is injured, Hagar assumes responsibility for him in Mary Johnston's *Hagar.*

Luann Asher. Half-white, pill-addicted orphan adopted by Simon Asher; rejected by persons of both races in Hal Bennett's *A Wilderness of Vines.*

Reed Ashford. Lover of Daria Worthington and Eliza Quarles and love object of Evan Quarles; morose about his affair with Daria, takes an overdose of pills and dies in Alice Adams's *Listening to Billie*.

Benish (Rabbi Benish) Ashkenazi. Revered leader in the Jewish community of Goray, Poland, and father of Levi Ashkenazi; temporarily exiled from Goray after the Chmielnicki massacre of 1648; later returns and remains studiously faithful to the Torah and Jewish tradition, rejecting the Sabbatai Zevi sect as blasphemous, in Isaac Bashevis Singer's *Satan in Goray*.

Levi Ashkenazi. Youngest son of Rabbi Benish Ashkenazi; disdains his father's orthodoxy and leads the followers of Sabbatai Zevi in Isaac Bashevis Singer's *Satan in Goray*.

Baron Ashkenazy. See Tateh.

Beata Kellerman Ashley. See Beata Kellerman-Ashley.

Lady Brett Ashley. English fiancée of Michael Campbell and former lover of Robert Cohn; has an affair with Pedro Romero in Ernest Hemingway's *The Sun Also Rises*.

Constance (Constance Ashley-Nishimura) Ashley. Youngest of the Ashley children; develops sympathy for the downtrodden and becomes internationlly acclaimed as a social activist in Thornton Wilder's *The Eighth Day*.

Senator Godfrey Ashley. A leading citizen of and chronicler of important social activities in Far Edgerley; junior warden of St. John's Episcopal Church in Constance Fenimore Woolson's *For the Major*.

John Barrington Ashley. Wrongly convicted murderer of Breckenridge Lansing; stolen from a train by unknown men; flees to Chile and later drowns at sea in Thornton Wilder's *The Eighth Day*.

Lily Scolastica Ashley. Oldest of the Ashley children; leaves Coaltown to become a world-famous concert singer in Thornton Wilder's *The Eighth Day*.

Marie-Louise Scolastique Dubois Ashley. Grandmother of John Ashley; she is the only member of his early family whose influence he consciously feels; he remembers her prayer to be used in the unfolding of God's plan in Thornton Wilder's *The Eighth Day*.

Roger Berwyn (Trent Frazier) Ashley. Only son of John and Beata Ashley and the first Ashley child to flee Coaltown; becomes a famous journalist in Chicago under the name of Trent Frazier and later as Berwyn Ashley; marries Félicité Lansing in Thornton Wilder's *The Eighth Day*.

Sophia Ashley. Daughter of John and Beata Ashley; after her father's disappearance, she takes control of the family's fortune in such enterprises as selling lemonade and books to travelers; insists on turning the family home into a boardinghouse; her hard work leads to a mental breakdown from which she never recovers in Thornton Wilder's *The Eighth Day*.

Constance Ashley-Nishimura. See Constance Ashley.

Jefferson Ashton. Inexperienced and opportunistic attorney retained to defend six blacks accused of raping a white woman in T. S. Stribling's *Unfinished Cathedral*.

Julia Ashton. American poet in London during World War I and wife of Rafe Ashton in H. D.'s *Bid Me to Live*.

Rafe Ashton. Poet and soldier married to Julia Ashton but having an affair with Bella Carter in H. D.'s *Bid Me to Live*.

Joe Askew. Army officer who sets up an airplane parts business in partnership with Charley Anderson after the war; when the business is successful, Anderson, who had been living with the Askew family, sells his partner out in a stock exchange deal in John Dos Passos's *U.S.A.* trilogy.

Askwani. White youth reared by the Cherokee of Crow Town; devoted protégé of Ewen Warne; husband of Ruhama Warne in H. L. Davis's *Beulah Land*.

Lucas (Luke) Asphalter. Zoologist at the University of Chicago who tells Moses Herzog, his dearest friend, that Madeleine Herzog has cuckolded him with Val Gersbach; stands by Herzog in his time of emotional turmoil in Saul Bellow's *Herzog*.

Brian Aspinwall. Young teacher at Justin Martyr School and confidant of headmaster Francis Prescott; principal narrator who keeps a journal of various accounts of Prescott's life in Louis Auchincloss's *The Rector of Justin*.

Fanny Assingham. American-born wife of the retired British army officer Robert Assingham; becomes a confidante of Maggie Verver and breaks the golden bowl in Henry James's *The Golden Bowl*.

Col. Robert (Bob) Assingham. Retired British army officer and husband of Fanny Assingham; listens to his wife's schemes with detachment in Henry James's *The Golden Bowl*.

Theodore (Teddy) Ast. Women's garment salesman and manufacturer; gets out of his partnership with Harry Bogen in Apex Modes before it goes bankrupt in Jerome Weidman's *I Can Get It for You Wholesale*; starts his own garment firm and steals Martha Mills from Bogen in *What's in It for Me?*

Asta. Schnauzer of Nick and Nora Charles in Dashiell Hammett's *The Thin Man*.

China Aster. Candlemaker from Marietta, Ohio, whose attempts to repay loans drive him into poverty in Herman Melville's *The Confidence-Man*.

Lieutenant Aster. Nineteen-year-old female psychiatrist who attempts a "therapeutic reprise" on Georgie Cornell in Thomas Berger's *Regiment of Women*.

Mack Aston. Dance-marathon contestant in Horace McCoy's *They Shoot Horses, Don't They?*

Astrid. Twenty-six-year-old estranged wife of the nameless narrator of Nicholas Delbanco's *Grasse 3/23/66*.

Atherton. Boston attorney and friend of Bartley Hubbard in William Dean Howells's *A Modern Instance*.

Miss Atkins. Orphanage dietician whom Joe Christmas sees having sex with an intern in William Faulkner's *Light in August*.

George P. Atkinson. Manufacturer of cotton seed products and employer of Mamba in DuBose Heyward's *Mamba's Daughters*.

Lissa Atkinson. Mulatto daughter of Hagar and granddaughter of Mamba; talented singer who appears in a black folk opera at the Metropolitan Opera House in DuBose Heyward's *Mamba's Daughters*.

Miss Maudie Atkinson. Neighbor who defends Atticus Finch to his children; her house is burned down in Harper Lee's *To Kill a Mockingbird*.

Gordon Atterbury. Rejected suitor of Alison Parr in Winston Churchill's *The Inside of the Cup*.

Atti. Lioness kept by King Dahfu in the lower reaches of his castle; aids the transformation of Eugene Henderson from pig man to leonine kingly spirit in Saul Bellow's *Henderson the Rain King*.

Louise Attwater. See Louise Attwater Eborn.

Atwater. Architect of expensive homes in Henry Blake Fuller's *The Cliff-Dwellers*.

Mr. Aubineau. Henpecked host in James Kirke Paulding's *The Dutchman's Fireside*.

Mrs. Aubineau. Shrewish hostess in James Kirke Paulding's *The Dutchman's Fireside*.

Audrey. Name assumed at majority by the narrator's wife, Aurora, in Peter De Vries's *The Tunnel of Love*.

Augie (Little Augie, Little Poison). Tiny black jockey born with a caul; succeeds despite a series of setbacks; protagonist of Arna Wendell Bontemps's *God Sends Sunday*.

Julia Cornelia Augusta. Wealthy young Roman who befriends the destitute Hipparchia in H. D.'s *Palimpsest*.

Augustín. Member of Pablo's partisan group in Ernest Hemingway's *For Whom the Bell Tolls*.

Augustine. Sober French maid of Eugenia Münster in Henry James's *The Europeans*.

Julian Augustus. Roman emperor who struggles unsuccessfully to discredit Christianity and restore worship of the Greek gods; assassinated by Callistus in Gore Vidal's *Julian*.

Aurora. See Audrey.

Benny Austin. Best friend and business partner of Harry Wyeth in Joan Didion's *Play It As It Lays*.

Henry (Hank) Austin. Father of four children who is fired from his job as truckman by Old Running Water in Albert Halper's *Union Square*.

Ava (Delilah Lee). Aspiring dancer and lover of Isolde; names herself after Ava Gardner in Marilyn French's *The Women's Room*.

Buchanan Malt (Malty) Avis. West Indian friend of Banjo in Claude McKay's *Banjo*.

Captain Andrew Avers. Father of Raib Avers and Desmond Eden; dies aboard the *Lillias Eden* in Peter Matthiessen's *Far Tortuga*.

Jim Eden (Buddy) Avers. Quiet and frightened seventeen-year-old son of Raib Avers; determined to be a turtler even though he gets seasick and lacks ability; dies following the wreck of the *Lillias Eden* in Peter Matthiessen's *Far Tortuga*.

Captain Raib Avers. Skilled turtler and captain of the *Lillias Eden*; embittered by changes he has witnessed in the fishery business; attempts to take his crew over Misteriosa Reef at night, but wrecks his boat and loses his life and the lives of all but one of his crew, in Peter Matthiessen's *Far Tortuga*.

Avery. Original owner of the Silver Sun Saloon; tries to persuade Molly Riordan to kill Clay Turner; dies when Turner burns the Silver Sun in E. L. Doctorow's *Welcome to Hard Times*.

Avey. Independent northern black woman; the narrator mistakes her indifference toward him as indolence in Jean Toomer's *Cane*.

Arthur Axelrod. Father of David Axelrod and a lawyer in Scott Spencer's *Endless Love*.

David (Dave) Axelrod. Obsessive lover of Jade Butterfield; narrator of Scott Spencer's *Endless Love*.

Dr. Marcus J. Axelrod. Boyhood friend of Herman Gold and prosperous Lower East Side physician in Michael Gold's *Jews without Money*.

Rose Axelrod. Wife of Arthur Axelrod and mother of David Axelrod in Scott Spencer's *Endless Love*.

Willie Duke Aycock. Sexual rival of Rosacoke Mustian for the affections of Wesley Beavers in Reynolds Price's *A Long and Happy Life*.

Bartolomeo Aymo. Ambulance driver in the command of Frederic Henry; shot and killed by fellow Italian soldiers in the confusion of a retreat in Ernest Hemingway's *A Farewell to Arms*.

Ayres. British army major who attends the yacht party in William Faulkner's *Mosquitoes*.

Azarian. Rock musician who becomes leader of a band when singer Bucky Wunderlick drops out; ultimately murdered in Don DeLillo's *Great Jones Street*.

Azarina. Black servant of Eugenia Münster in Henry James's *The Europeans*.

Fernande (Nande) Azeredo. Exotic Frenchwoman who has an affair with Sam Dodsworth in Sinclair Lewis's *Dodsworth*.

President Azureus. Head of the university who calls a meeting to require the faculty to sign papers of allegiance to the new regime; Adam Krug, whose wife dies only hours before the meeting, alone refuses to sign the declaration in Vladimir Nabokov's *Bend Sinister*.

Azusa. Common-law wife to whom Wolfie yearns to return in Peter Matthiessen's *At Play in the Fields of the Lord*.

B

Eleazar (Reb Eleazar) Babad. Wealthiest man in Goray before the 1648 invasion and massacre; afterward, a widower, wanderer, and father who abandons Rechele Babad to relatives in Isaac Bashevis Singer's *Satan in Goray*.

Rechele Babad. Epileptic daughter of Reb Eleazar Babad, wife of Reb Itche Mates in an unconsummated marriage, and mistress and later wife of Reb Gedaliya; called a prophetess by the people of Goray, she is tormented and impregnated by Satan in Isaac Bashevis Singer's *Satan in Goray*.

Babbalanja. Philosopher from Odo and Taji's companion in Herman Melville's *Mardi*.

Eunice Littlefield Babbitt. See Eunice Littlefield.

George F. (Georgie) Babbitt. Realtor and faithful Zenith civic booster who fails to find happiness upholding community values in Sinclair Lewis's *Babbitt*; also appears in *Elmer Gantry*.

Katherine (Tinka) Babbitt. Daughter of George and Myra Babbitt; adored by her father in Sinclair Lewis's *Babbitt*.

Myra Thompson Babbitt. Patient wife of George Babbitt; mother of Katherine, Theodore, and Verona Babbitt in Sinclair Lewis's *Babbitt*.

Theodore Roosevelt (Ted) Babbitt. Son of George and Myra Babbitt; would-be automobile mechanic who elopes with Eunice Littlefield in Sinclair Lewis's *Babbitt*.

Verona (Rone) Babbitt. Daughter of George and Myra Babbitt; Bryn Mawr graduate who marries Kenneth Escott in Sinclair Lewis's *Babbitt*.

Dwight Babcock. Stodgy member of the Knickerbocker Trust Company who is Patrick Dennis's trustee and Mame Dennis's nemesis in Patrick Dennis's *Auntie Mame* and *Around the World with Auntie Mame*

Babe. See Beatrice Greene.

Meyer Babushkin. Partner of Harry Bogen in Apex Modes, a women's garments manufacturing company; goes to jail because of Bogen's stealing from the firm in Jerome Weidman's *I Can Get It for You Wholesale*.

Baby Igor. See Metzger.

Baby Thor. Son of Amanda Ziller conceived during an electrical storm in Tom Robbins's *Another Roadside Attraction.*

Jesus de Baca. Old, poor priest of Isleta whose sole worldly possession is a wooden parrot in Willa Cather's *Death Comes for the Archbishop*.

Bach. Crippled ex-Nazi married to a woman who is half-Jewish in Thomas Berger's *Crazy in Berlin*.

Richard Bache. Son-in-law of Benjamin Franklin; gets Thomas Paine a job as a tutor when Paine first arrives in America in Howard Fast's *Citizen Tom Paine*.

Octave Bacheron. White pharmacist who supports the civil rights efforts of the Reverend Phillip Martin in Ernest J. Gaines's *In My Father's House*.

Linda (Lin) Bachofen. Beautiful blonde government enforcer and sister of Mariette Bachofen; comes with her fiancé to arrest Mr. Ember and later appears with another fiancé, Doctor Alexander, to arrest Adam and David Krug; executed for her mistakes in Vladimir Nabokov's *Bend Sinister*.

Mariette (Mariechen) Bachofen. Young sister of Linda Bachofen who becomes David Krug's nurse; probably informs on Adam Krug; dies after being raped by forty soldiers in Vladimir Nabokov's *Bend Sinister*.

Abra Bacon. Young woman engaged to marry Aron Trask but who feels unworthy of his extreme virtue and trapped by his narrow view of life and love; realizes that Caleb Trask is the one she truly loves in John Steinbeck's *East of Eden*.

Sir Francis Bacon. Writer and courtier in George Garrett's *Death of the Fox*.

Lillian Bacon. Dance-marathon partner of Pedro Ortega; violently attacked by Ortega when he learns that Rocky Gravo attempted to seduce her in Horace McCoy's *They Shoot Horses, Don't They?*

The Bad Priest. See V.

Miriam Bader. Wife of Shmuel Bader; helps David Lurie with his German studies in Chaim Potok's *In the Beginning*.

Shmuel Bader. Torah teacher of David Lurie and European field director of an organization that brings Polish Jews to the United States in Chaim Potok's *In the Beginning*.

Ray Badger. Ne'er-do-well first husband of Melissa Scaddon Wapshot; jewel thief and rival to Moses Wapshot in John Cheever's *The Wapshot Chronicle*.

Proctor (Proc) Baggart. Bigoted and disreputable magistrate charged with keeping blacks subservient and with maintaining law and order in the district outside Charleston where Charles Raymond's Phosphate Mining Company is located in DuBose Heyward's *Mamba's Daughters*.

Dr. Bagley. President of Polycarp College in Peter De Vries's *Let Me Count the Ways*.

Father Battista Baglione. Catholic priest and member of the Common Sense Committee in Robert Coover's *The Origin of the Brunists*.

John (Alex, Alexander Graham, Jack) Bailey. Bank cashier accused of murdering Arnold Armstrong and of causing the Traders' Bank to fail; disguises himself as a gardener in order to clear his name in Mary Roberts Rinehart's *The Circular Staircase*.

Thomas (Tom) Bailey. Youth who has numerous adventures in Rivermouth; narrator of Thomas Bailey Aldrich's *The Story of a Bad Boy*.

Raymond Baillet. Obliging Parisian taxi driver; may have inspired Jean-Louis Lebris de Kérouac's *satori*, or "sudden illumination," in Jack Kerouac's *Satori in Paris*.

Bump Baily. Outfielder for the Knights, practical joker, and lover of Memo Paris; dies going after a fly ball in Bernard Malamud's *The Natural*.

Eva Baily. Sister of Minna Baily; lives with Minna and their nephew in a 70th Street apartment building managed by Norman Moonbloom in Edward Lewis Wallant's *The Tenants of Moonbloom*.

Joe Baily. Rival of Augie; a "bad nigger" who contends with Tom Wright for the affection of Florence Dessau in Arna Wendell Bontemps's *God Sends Sunday*.

Minna Baily. Sister of Eva Baily; lives with Eva and their nephew in a 70th Street apartment building managed by Norman Moonbloom in Edward Lewis Wallant's *The Tenants of Moonbloom*.

Guitar Bains. Best friend of Milkman and member of a racial revenge group called the Seven Days in Toni Morrison's *Song of Solomon*.

Lulu Bains. Daughter of a church deacon; Elmer Gantry narrowly escapes having to marry her, although he later has an affair with her, in Sinclair Lewis's *Elmer Gantry*.

Jeff Baird. Director of comedy films who gives Merton Gill his first starring role in Harry Leon Wilson's *Merton of the Movies*.

Baker. Friend who visits Anne and Phil Sorenson to recover from a divorce and clumsily seduces Anne

in Frederick Busch's *Manual Labor*.

April Baker. Spaced-out teenaged sister of Nicole Baker Barrett; innocent companion of Gary Gilmore during his first murderous spree in Norman Mailer's *Executioner's Song*.

Colonel Baker. Orthopedic surgeon at Kilrainey Army Hospital who wants to amputate the right leg of Bobby Prell in James Jones's *Whistle*.

Helen Baker. Friend of Larry Donovan; works at a hot dog stand in Jack Conroy's *The Disinherited*.

Jordan Baker. Dishonest friend of Daisy Buchanan; romantically involved with Nick Carraway in F. Scott Fitzgerald's *The Great Gatsby*.

Lou Garbo (Left Bank, Montana Lou) Baker. Bohemian and writer; mistress of Jesse Proctor in Wright Morris's *The Huge Season*.

Miss Baker. Elderly woman who falls in love with Old Grannis in Frank Norris's *McTeague*.

Mr. Baker. President of the First National Bank in New Baytown who tries to use Ethan Allen Hawley to gain additional wealth and power for himself in John Steinbeck's *The Winter of Our Discontent*.

Mrs. Samuel Baker. Widow of a Washington lobbyist and client of John Carrington, to whom she reveals the improper dealings of Senator Ratcliffe, in Henry Adams's *Democracy*.

Nancy May Baker. Lover of Marshall Pearl; ornithologist studying eagles in New Mexico for the University of Chicago in Mark Helprin's *Refiner's Fire*.

Nicole Baker. See Nicole Kathryne Baker Barrett.

Rena Baker. Dying sanitorium patient beloved and mourned by Don Wanderhope in Peter De Vries's *The Blood of the Lamb*.

Steve Baker. Actor on the *Cotton Blossom* who leaves the showboat with his wife Julie Dozier in Edna Ferber's *Show Boat*.

Gus Bakewell. Thug and associate of Donald Washburn in Thomas Berger's *Who Is Teddy Villanova?*

Annabel Balch. Fiancée of Lucius Harney and rival of Charity Royall in Edith Wharton's *Summer*.

George Baldwin. Unscrupulous attorney who rises to the top of his profession and becomes the third husband of Ellen Thatcher in John Dos Passos's *Manhattan Transfer*.

Baldy. Scotch sailor aboard the *Neversink* whose life is saved by Cadwallader Cuticle in Herman Melville's *White-Jacket*.

Simon Bale. Religious fanatic whose wife dies in their burning house; accidentally killed by Henry Soames in John Gardner's *Nickel Mountain*.

Balfour. Merchant who rescues Constantia Dudley from a group of ruffians; Constantia rejects him after a subsequent courtship in Charles Brockden Brown's *Ormond*.

Lord Balham. Englishman and commissioner for refugees of the Society of Nations; Mary Douglas solicits his aid in blocking the expulsion order for German and Austrian refugees in Martha Gellhorn's *A Stricken Field*.

Professor Ball. Headmaster of an academy for boys and a leader of the Free Farmers' Brotherhood of Protection and Control, a vigilante organization designed to control tobacco prices by any means necessary, in Robert Penn Warren's *Night Rider*.

Gregory (Greg) Ballard. Black fisherman from Cape Cod who fights for the loyalists in the Spanish civil war and against the racial hatred of Hitler; friend of Jake Starr in William Herrick's *Hermanos!*

John (Old John, Uncle John) Ballew. Second cousin of Nunn Ballew; prosperous, highly respected farmer in Harriette Arnow's *Hunter's Horn*; sells land to Gertie Nevels in *The Dollmaker*.

Lee Roy Ballew. Eldest son of Nunn and Milly Ballew; assumes responsibilities as "man of the house" while his father fox hunts in Harriette Arnow's *Hunter's Horn*.

Lucy Ballew. Youngest daughter of Nunn and Milly Ballew in Harriette Arnow's *Hunter's Horn*.

Milly Ballew. Long-suffering, hardworking wife of Nunn Ballew and mother of five living children and two others who died young in Harriette Arnow's *Hunter's Horn*.

Nunnely Danforth (Nunn) Ballew. Kentucky fox hunter obsessed with chasing the fox called King Devil; husband of Milly Ballew in Harriette Arnow's *Hunter's Horn*.

Suse Ballew. Intelligent, sensitive adolescent daughter of Nunn and Milly Ballew; longs to escape her family's poverty in Little Smokey Creek, Kentucky, in Harriette Arnow's *Hunter's Horn*.

William Danforth (Bill Dan) Ballew. Baby son of Nunn and Milly Ballew in Harriette Arnow's *Hunter's Horn*.

Drew Ballinger. Sales supervisor for a large soft-drink company; spokesman for the laws of civilization who is killed during the three-day canoe trip on the Cahulawassee River in James Dickey's *Deliverance*.

Old Bull (Old Bull Lewis, Smiley Bull Balloon) Balloon (Baloon). Alcoholic gambler who sells flyswatters door-to-door with Cody Pomeray, Sr., in Jack Kerouac's *Visions of Cody*; plays pool with Doctor Sax in *Doctor Sax*; appears as W. C. Fields in *Book of Dreams*; and drinks with Emil Duluoz in *Visions of Gerard*.

Baltimore. Black cook aboard the *Julia* who delivers the round robin to the English consul on Tahiti in Herman Melville's *Omoo*.

Lord Baltimore. See Charles Calvert, Lord Baltimore.

Rocco (Bullets) Bambarella. Macho gambler and police detective in Joseph Wambaugh's *The Black Marble*.

Hugo Bamman. World War I ambulance driver, freelance journalist and documentary novelist, communist, and former schoolmate of the narrator in Edmund Wilson's *I Thought of Daisy*.

Catherine Banahan. Fiancée of Studs Lonigan; conceives their child, although he dies before they can wed, in James T. Farrell's *Judgment Day*.

Joseppi Banascalco. Captain of the Europe-bound *Castel Felice*, on which most of the action occurs in Calvin Hernton's *Scarecrow*.

George R. (Brass Band, Tall George) Band. First lieutenant in C-for-Charlie Company who replaces James Stein as company commander; his lust for heroism earns him the hatred of his men, and he is eventually relieved of command for failing to communicate with headquarters in James Jones's *The Thin Red Line*.

Cesare (Rico) Bandello. Ambitious and ruthless gang leader who takes over Sam Vettori's gang; enjoys seven years of success and fame before he is forced to flee Chicago and is killed in Toledo, Ohio, in William Riley Burnett's *Little Caesar*.

Isabel (Bell) Banford. Apparently the illegitimate daughter of Pierre Glendinning II; she and Pierre Glendinning III pretend to be married in Herman Melville's *Pierre*.

Thomas Buckminster (Tommy) Bangs. Sociable, mischievous boy in Louisa May Alcott's *Little Men*.

Joe Banion. Black hired hand on Mat Feltner's Kentucky tobacco farm; husband of Nettie Banion in Wendell Berry's *A Place on Earth* and *The Memory of Old Jack*.

Nettie Banion. Black housekeeper and cook on Mat Feltner's Kentucky tobacco farm; wife of Joe Banion in Wendell Berry's *A Place on Earth* and *The Memory of Old Jack*.

William Hays (Will) Banion. Kentuckian who leads the Liberty covered wagon train in Emerson Hough's *The Covered Wagon*.

Alonzo (Lonnie) Banks. Younger brother of the black councilman Randolph Banks; dedicated Communist expelled from the party for opposing its stand on domestic issues in Julian Mayfield's *The Grand Parade*.

Banjo. See Lincoln Agrippa Daily.

Billy Banks. School friend of Terry Wilson, whom he tries to help get off drugs, in Donald Goines's *Dopefiend*.

Freddie Banks. Twelve-year-old "boyfriend" of Jane Baxter in Booth Tarkington's *Seventeen*.

Joseph Banks. President of the Royal Society who secures Roger Byam a midshipman's berth on HMS *Bounty* so Byam can compile a dictionary of the Tahitian language; provides for Byam's defense after he is returned to England as a mutineer in Charles Nordhoff and James Norman Hall's *Mutiny on the Bounty*.

Randolph (Randy) Banks. Black city councilman and Harvard Law School graduate; brother of Lonnie Banks and lover of Patty Speed in Julian Mayfield's *The Grand Parade*.

Si Banks. Leftist writer and friend of the narrator in Edmund Wilson's *Memoirs of Hecate County*.

Wallace Banks. Obsequious friend of William Baxter; usually gets the unenviable jobs of master of ceremonies and money taker for the jaunts of the young townspeople in Booth Tarkington's *Seventeen*.

Judge Goodwill Banner. Owner of the New York Knights baseball team in Bernard Malamud's *The Natural*.

Ethel Banning. Instructor of Spanish and French and one of Jacob Horner's interviewers at Wicomico State Teachers College in John Barth's *The End of the Road*.

Thomas Bannister. Barrister who represents Abe Cady in Leon Uris's *QB VII*.

Homer Lisle (Granddad) Bannon. Second husband of Jewel Bannon and grandfather of Lonnie Bannon; ranch owner with a diseased cattle herd; killed by his stepson Hud in Larry McMurtry's *Horseman, Pass By*.

Jewel Bannon. Second wife of Homer Bannon, mother of Hud, and stepgrandmother of Lonnie Bannon in Larry McMurtry's *Horseman, Pass By*.

Lonnie Bannon. Stepnephew of Hud; leaves the ranch after the death of his grandfather, Homer Bannon; narrator of Larry McMurtry's *Horseman, Pass By*.

Roger Bannon. Ambitious building contractor who attracts Grace Caldwell Tate in John O'Hara's *A Rage to Live*.

Scott (Hud, Huddie) Bannon. See Hud.

Henry (Hank) Banta. Mean boy, "a compound of deceit and resentment," who causes Ralph Hartsook trouble in Edward Eggleston's *The Hoosier Schoolmaster*.

Jean (The Homesteader, St. John the Baptist) Baptiste. Black homesteader; would-be lover of Agnes Stewart and husband of Orlean McCarthy in Oscar Micheaux's *The Homesteader*.

Antonina Barabo. Elder daughter of Signor Barabo; fascinated by the power of Il Gufo, she declares her love and offers herself to him in John Hawkes's *The Owl*.

Ginevra Barabo. Younger sister of Antonina Barabo; attacked by Il Gufo's pet owl in John Hawkes's *The Owl*.

Signor Barabo. Father of Antonina and Ginevra Barabo; tries to obtain the release of a prisoner to marry Antonina in John Hawkes's *The Owl*.

Tommy Barban. Soldier of fortune who becomes Nicole Warren Diver's second husband in F. Scott Fitzgerald's *Tender Is the Night*.

Barbara. Attorney and agent of Henry Wiggen in Mark Harris's *It Looked Like For Ever*.

Barbara. Sexual conquest of Carol Severin Swanson in Jim Harrison's *Wolf*.

Captain Barbatov. Russian military martinet outsmarted by George Levanter in Jerzy Kosinski's *Blind Date*.

Arthur Barber. Student council president who tries to convince Dr. Charles Osman to change his mind about failing Raymond Blent in Howard Nemerov's *The Homecoming Game*.

Helen Van Vleck Barber. First love of Nelson Dewey; marries Joel Barber and dies in childbirth in August Derleth's *The Shadow in the Glass*.

Joel Barber. Law partner of Nelson Dewey; successfully competes with Dewey for Helen Van Vleck in August Derleth's *The Shadow in the Glass*.

Márgara Bárcenas. Beautiful daughter of a fugitive of the Revolution and lover of Domingo Vázquez de Anda in Josefina Niggli's *Step Down, Elder Brother*.

Edith Barclay. Secretary to Frank Hirsh; later becomes his second mistress but leaves for Chicago after Agnes Hirsh discovers their affair in James Jones's *Some Came Running*.

Jane Mason Barclay. Wife of John Barclay and mother of Jeanette Barclay; her death from typhoid fever is indirectly caused by her husband's greed in William Allen White's *A Certain Rich Man*.

Jeanette Barclay. Daughter of John and Jane Barclay; marries Neal Dow Ward after her father is rid of his fortune in William Allen White's *A Certain Rich Man*.

John (Johnnie) Barclay. Capitalist who founds the Golden Belt Wheat Company monopoly; husband of Jane Barclay and father of Jeanette Barclay; after his wife's death, he dismantles his fortune and returns to Sycamore Ridge in William Allen White's *A Certain Rich Man*.

Amanda (Miss Manda) Barcroft. Jilted lover of Harley Drew in Shelby Foote's *Love in a Dry Season*.

Florence (Miss Flaunts) Barcroft. Invalid sister of Amanda Barcroft in Shelby Foote's *Love in a Dry Season*.

Major Malcolm Barcroft. Cotton factor in Bristol, Mississippi, and father of Amanda and Florence Barcroft in Shelby Foote's *Love in a Dry Season*.

Bardianni. Sage who influences Babbalanja in Herman Melville's *Mardi*.

Carbon Bareau. Mountaineer who identifies Arnaud du Tilh as his nephew in Janet Lewis's *The Wife of Martin Guerre*.

Juanita Collins Harmeyer (Mother Goddam) Barefoot. Madam and friend of Perry in James Leo Herlihy's *Midnight Cowboy*.

Tombaby (Princess) Barefoot. Son of Juanita Barefoot in James Leo Herlihy's *Midnight Cowboy*.

Mr. Barham. English visitor to Kentucky in James Kirke Paulding's *Westward Ho!*.

Damon Barker. Lost father of Agnes Deming and loyal father-surrogate to Jo Erring and Ned Westlock in E. W. Howe's *The Story of a Country Town*.

Ned Barker. Bullying, blundering boy in Louisa May Alcott's *Little Men*.

Penny Barker. Former girlfriend of Clyde Stout, whose grammar she corrects, in Jack Matthews's *Hanger Stout, Awake!*

Catherine Barkley. English volunteer hospital worker in Italy at the beginning of World War I; falls in love with Frederic Henry and dies of hemorrhaging after the Caesarean delivery of their stillborn son in Ernest Hemingway's *A Farewell to Arms*.

King Barlo. Charismatic black preacher and field laborer famous for his cane-cutting and his attractiveness to women in Jean Toomer's *Cane*.

Barlow. Mugger turned cabdriver who works for Edward Pierce in Michael Crichton's *The Great Train Robbery*.

Barlow. Vampire and owner, with his partner Richard Straker, of Marsten House in Stephen King's *'Salem's Lot*.

Frank X. Barlow. See Dr. Robert Fender.

Joel Barlow. American expatriate in France who helps arrange for the publication of Thomas Paine's *The Age of Reason* in Howard Fast's *Citizen Tom Paine*.

Augustus Barnard. Spirited friend of Arthur Gordon Pym; arranges Pym's stowaway on the *Grampus*; wounded in the retaking of the ship from mutineers; dies from exposure and malnutrition in Edgar Allan Poe's *The Narrative of Arthur Gordon Pym*.

Mr. Barnard. Father of Augustus Barnard and captain of the *Grampus*; set adrift when the ship's crew mutinies in Edgar Allan Poe's *The Narrative of Arthur Gordon Pym*.

Benecia Wallin Barnes. Wife of Solon Barnes and mother of five children, including Etta and Stewart Barnes, in Theodore Dreiser's *The Bulwark*.

Etta Barnes. Daughter of Solon and Benecia Barnes; disregards her parents' wishes and attends the University of Wisconsin; mistress of Willard Kane; returns home following the suicide of her brother Stewart Barnes in Theodore Dreiser's *The Bulwark*.

Hannah and Rufus Barnes. Quaker parents of Solon Barnes in Theodore Dreiser's *The Bulwark*.

Jacob (Jake) Barnes. American newspaperman in Paris rendered impotent by a war wound; narrator of Ernest Hemingway's *The Sun Also Rises*.

Lett Barnes. Poet and friend of Julia Ashton in H. D.'s *Bid Me to Live*.

Mattie Barnes. Original dance-marathon partner of Kid Kamm; collapses and is eliminated from the competition in Horace McCoy's *They Shoot Horses, Don't They?*

Osella Barnes. Childhood nurse of Gavin Hexam and later maid for Gavin and N. Hexam; quits her job as maid because she believes N. Hexam is a witch in Diane Johnson's *The Shadow Knows*.

Solon Barnes. Quaker farmer and businessman who attempts to be both successful and a good Quaker in Theodore Dreiser's *The Bulwark*.

Stewart (Stew) Barnes. Son of Solon and Benecia Barnes; commits suicide following his involvement in the death of Psyche Tanzer in Theodore Dreiser's *The Bulwark*.

Edith Dewar Barnstorff. Grandmother of Jane Clifford in Gail Godwin's *The Odd Woman*.

Anna Allston Barnwell. See Anna Allston.

Bill Barnwell. Slave beaten by his master Lewis Barnwell in Caroline Gilman's *Recollections of a Southern Matron*.

Lewis Barnwell. Girlhood boyfriend of Cornelia Wilton; disappears shortly after his marriage to Anna Allston in Caroline Gilman's *Recollections of a Southern Matron*.

Arthur (Art) Baron. Company division head responsible for replacing Andy Kagle with Bob Slocum in Joseph Heller's *Something Happened*.

Amadeus Baroque. Mill worker who finds and reads the only extant manuscript of Doctor Sax, written under the pen name Adolphus Asher Ghoulens, in Jack Kerouac's *Doctor Sax*.

Augustus M. Barr. Unscrupulous ex-minister; steals Peter Kaden's beloved in Oscar Micheaux's *The Homesteader*.

Lilli Barr. See Ellen Tolliver.

Celestine Barre. Wife of Raoul Barre in Allen Drury's *Advise and Consent*.

Raoul Barre. French ambassador to the United States; with his wife, Celestine Barre, and the British ambassador, expresses the NATO countries' viewpoint in Allen Drury's *Advise and Consent*.

Ed Barrett. Father of Will Barrett; his suicide haunts Will in Walker Percy's *The Last Gentleman*.

Jennifer Cavilleri (Jenny) Barrett. Daughter of Philip Cavilleri; working-class Radcliffe graduate who marries Oliver Barrett IV against his family's wishes; dies of leukemia in Erich Segal's *Love Story*.

Nicole Kathryne Baker (Nicole Kathryne Gilmore, Nucoa Butterball) Barrett. Girlfriend of Gary Gilmore in Norman Mailer's *The Executioner's Song*.

Sylvia (Syl) Barrett. First-year teacher who learns the intricacies of life at Calvin Coolidge High School; finds herself buried in meaningless paperwork with little time or support to teach in Bel Kaufman's *Up the Down Staircase*.

Willston Bibb (Billy, Will) Barrett. Humidification engineer who crosses America trying to live as the epitome of Southern honor in Walker Percy's *The Last Gentleman*.

Oliver (Old Stonyface) Barrett III. Olympic rower, textile mill owner, and father of Oliver Barrett IV; disapproves of his son's wife in Erich Segal's *Love Story*; brings his son into the family firm in *Oliver's Story*.

Oliver (Ollie) Barrett IV. Wealthy Harvard graduate who marries Jennifer Cavilleri, a working-class woman, against his family's wishes in Erich Segal's *Love Story*; falls in love with Marcie Binnendale Nash, but finds that she is shallow and unethical, in *Oliver's Story*.

Paul Barringer. Glamour boy of the Calvin Coolidge High School English faculty; unpublished writer who composes a poem for every occasion; pursues Sylvia Barrett; responds to a love letter from a student by correcting it grammatically in Bel Kaufman's *Up the Down Staircase*.

Delia Barron. Unrelenting flirt whose interest in George Birdsong causes one of Eva Birdsong's early attacks of neuralgia in Ellen Glasgow's *The Sheltered Life*.

Grace Barron. Wife of Virgil Barron and friend of the Bridges; commits suicide in Evan Connell's *Mrs. Bridge* and *Mr. Bridge*.

Virgil Barron. Bank executive, husband of Grace Barron, and friend of the Bridges in Evan Connell's *Mrs. Bridge* and *Mr. Bridge*.

Wilkie Barron. Acquaintance of Jeremiah Beaumont in law school and successful politician; preserves Beaumont's manuscript and shoots himself "tidily through the heart" in Robert Penn Warren's *World Enough and Time*.

Barrow. Friend of Berkeley (Howard Tracy) in Samuel Langhorne Clemens's *The American Claimant*.

G. H. Barrow. Randy labor lobbyist whom J. Ward Morehouse uses to forge a cooperative spirit between management and labor; lover of Mary French in John Dos Passos's *U.S.A.* trilogy.

Fred T. Barry. Wealthy businessman and arts patron in Kurt Vonnegut's *Breakfast of Champions*.

Bart. Hangman who executes Ben Harper in Davis Grubb's *The Night of the Hunter*.

Bart. Son of Utch Thalhammer and the unnamed narrator, brother of Jack, and playmate and friend of Fiordiligi and Dorabella Winter; favored by Severin Winter, who thinks that Bart will be an excellent one-hundred seventy-seven-pound wrestler in John Irving's *The 158-Pound Marriage*.

Lily Bart. Well-bred but poor New York socialite whose futile attempts to arrange a suitable marriage for herself initiate the central plot of Edith Wharton's *The House of Mirth*.

Bartlett. Rancher who sways the mob to the idea of lynching the rustlers in Walter Van Tilburg Clark's *The Ox-Bow Incident*.

Arlene Bartlett. Mother of Laney Bartlett; poor but vital widow who takes several lovers and is frequently pregnant in Joyce Carol Oates's *Childwold*.

Dickie Bartlett. Teenaged helper of Clem Streeter; held prisoner and then released by Legs Diamond in William Kennedy's *Legs*.

Edith Bartlett. Nineteenth-century fiancée of Julian West in Edward Bellamy's *Looking Backward*.

Evangeline Ann (Laney) Bartlett. Teenager from an impoverished rural area who becomes the focus of the eccentric Fitz John Kasch's obsession; daughter of Arlene Bartlett in Joyce Carol Oates's *Childwold*.

Vale Bartlett. Embittered Vietnam veteran and son of Arlene Bartlett in Joyce Carol Oates's *Childwold*.

Birchie Bartley. Insane twelve-year-old daughter of Lizzie Bartley and Blessed Belshazzar; her trial for murder is used by the state of Virginia to punish blacks for the crime of pretending to be white in Hal Bennett's *A Wilderness of Vines*.

Calvin LeRoy Bartley. Youngest son of Lizzie Bartley; rejected by Darlene Mosby, he commits suicide by covering himself with pitchlime in Hal Bennett's *A Wilderness of Vines*.

Lizzie Bartley. Matriarch of the Bartley clan noted for dark skins, good looks, and virility; also mother by Blessed Belshazzar of Birchie Bartley in Hal Bennett's *A Wilderness of Vines* and *The Black Wine*.

Robert Bartley. Father of thirteen children and lover of Neva Stapleton and Eloise McLindon; responsible for the death of Otha Manning during World War I in Hal Bennett's *A Wilderness of Vines* and *The Black Wine*.

Count Bartolomé. Attractive, courtly man who allows the difficult child Robin Empson to ride on his palomino mare in Gail Godwin's *The Perfectionists*.

Barton. Twenty-first century minister who preaches to thousands via telephone in Edward Bellamy's *Looking Backward*.

Miss Lavinia Barton. Mother of Odessa Barton Market and disapproving mother-in-law of Joe Market in Hal Bennett's *Lord of Dark Places*.

Odessa Barton. See Odessa Barton Market.

Mistress Bartram. Teacher who bears a child by Portius Wheeler; the child is named Rosa Tench after Bartram marries Jake Tench in Conrad Richter's *The Fields*; becomes a recluse in *The Town*.

Brush Bascom. Political manipulator and dispenser of bribes in Winston Churchill's *Mr. Crewe's Career*.

Chaplain Bascom. Baptist chaplain and friend of Father Donovan; rushes to save Donovan but is crushed by the same lorry that kills his friend in John Horne Burns's *The Gallery*.

Lena Bascombe. Actress playing the mother in the film version of Osgood Wallop's *The Duchess of Obloquy* in Peter De Vries's *Mrs. Wallop*.

Basellecci. Elderly teacher of Italian; afflicted with cancer of the bowel; lives in the Mott Street building managed by Norman Moonbloom in Edward Lewis Wallant's *The Tenants of Moonbloom*.

Bashele. Wife of Zelig, mother of Shosha, and mother-in-law of Aaron Greidinger in Isaac Bashevis Singer's *Shosha*.

Bashti. Island chief who leads the destruction of the *Arangi* and is Jerry's keeper in Jack London's *Jerry of the Islands*.

Herman Baskerville. Homosexual mentor of Bill Kelsey and student of racial mythology and revolution in Hal Bennett's *Seventh Heaven*.

George Baso. Japanese Zen master suffering from tuberculosis; friend visited by Jack Duluoz and Dave Wain in Jack Kerouac's *Big Sur*.

Jethro Bass. Devious political boss who is personally a kind and genuinely concerned leader; loves Cynthia Ware; guardian of Cynthia Wetherell in Winston Churchill's *Coniston*.

Jonathan Staunch Bass. Son of Pourty F. Bloodworth; half brother of Amos-Otis Thigpen, LaDonna Scales, Regal Pettibone, and Noah Grandberry; minister who counsels Thigpen and Abraham Dolphin in Leon Forrest's *The Bloodworth Orphans*.

Lucy Nelson Bassart. Granddaughter of Willard Carroll and daughter of Myra and Duane Nelson; her dreams of independence are thwarted by premarital pregnancy; marriage to Roy Bassart and motherhood bring her no happiness in Philip Roth's *When She Was Good*.

Roy Bassart. Dreamy World War II veteran who becomes a photographer and marries his pregnant girlfriend, Lucy Nelson, in Philip Roth's *When She Was Good*.

Claude Bassett. Educated orphan and drifter; "seasonal" husband of Maggie Moore who returns every winter and leaves every spring until his death in Betty Smith's *Maggie-Now*.

Ethel Bassett. First wife of Will Brady; spends their wedding night rolled in a sheet and later abandons him in Wright Morris's *The Works of Love*.

Georgie (The Little Gentleman) Bassett. Boy whose excellent behavior and refined ways irritate Penrod Schofield in Booth Tarkington's *Penrod, Penrod and Sam*, and *Penrod Jashber*.

Edward Bast. Young composer who reluctantly becomes JR's business representative in William Gaddis's *JR*.

Bastock. Driver for Huguenine's circus who trains Caroline Trid to be Carolina, lady high rider, in Walter D. Edmonds's *Chad Hanna*.

Bat. Motion picture mechanic who lives at Queenie's Boarding House; part of the group that sings with George Brush in Thornton Wilder's *Heaven's My Destination*.

Obed (Dr. Battius) Bat. Naturalist full of book knowledge but deficient in common sense; accompanies Ishmael Bush and clan onto the prairie; serves as a comic foil to Natty Bumppo in James Fenimore Cooper's *The Prairie*.

Carole (C. B.) Batelle. Single mother of Dawn Batelle; activist and only member of the group to be captured; serving an indeterminate prison sentence at the end of M. F. Beal's *Amazon One*.

Dawn Melody (Dawn Melody Topp) Batelle. Illegitimate daughter of Carole Batelle; reareed to age seven by Topper; after her mother's arrest, sent to live with foster parents in M. F. Beal's *Amazon One*.

Glen Bateman. Sociology professor and fourth lead in The Stand in Stephen King's *The Stand*.

Digby Bates. Deputy chief of the Los Angeles Police Department; publicity hound in JosephWambaugh's *The Black Marble*.

Henry Bates. Mulatto lover of Teresa Cary; forced away on the day of their elopement by Teresa's mother, Olivia Cary, in Jessie Redmon Fauset's *Comedy, American Style*.

James Bates. Dance-marathon contestant who, with his wife, Ruby, is Robert Syverten's and Gloria Beatty's best friend in the marathon in Horace McCoy's *They Shoot Horses, Don't They?*

Joseph Bates. New England tutor of Cornelia Wilton and her brothers in Caroline Gilman's *Recollections of a Southern Matron*.

Ruby Bates. Dance partner and wife of James Bates; her participation in a marathon while pregnant is protested by the Mothers' League for Good Morals in Horace McCoy's *They Shoot Horses, Don't They?*

Sue Lathrop Bates. Head of Chicago society in Henry Blake Fuller's *With the Procession*; also appears in *The Cliff-Dwellers*.

Hymie Bateshaw. Mad pseudoscientist who studies boredom and thus claims to have discovered how to generate life; survives the shipwreck of the *Sam MacManus* with Augie March, whom he attacks viciously, in Saul Bellow's *The Adventures of Augie March*.

Billy Batson. Leader of the warrior faction of the Indians; committed to fighting government troops head-on and dying rather than dispersing peacefully throughout the United States in Marge Piercy's *Dance the Eagle to Sleep*.

Miss Priscilla Batte. Majestic teacher at Dinwiddie Academy for Young Ladies, guardian of the old order, and matchmaker in Ellen Glasgow's *Virginia*.

Camille Turner Batterson. Retired teacher of writing and symbol of civilized behavior in Randall Jarrell's *Pictures from an Institution*.

Cynthia Battiloro. Former love of William Demarest, whom she meets unexpectedly aboard ship in Conrad Aiken's *Blue Voyage*.

Max Battisfore. Sheriff of Iron Cliffs County in Robert Traver's *Anatomy of a Murder*.

Baucis. Male slave on the Sawyer plantation; accompanies the Laceys to Beulah and returns with them to the Tidewater in Mary Lee Settle's *O Beulah Land*.

Eva (Greek) Baum. Femme fatale of Earl Horter in Wright Morris's *Love among the Cannibals*.

Karl Baumgartner. Alcoholic lawyer from Mexico City traveling with his abused wife and fearful son in Katherine Anne Porter's *Ship of Fools*.

Baxter. Puritan preacher whose attempts to eliminate heresy and "anarchic distemper" in Cromwell's army force the soldiers to begin meeting secretly in order to obtain privacy in Mary Lee Settle's *Prisons*.

Baxter. See Hagar.

Abner Baxter. Violent coal miner who succeeds Ely Collins as the pastor of the Nazarene church in Robert Coover's *The Origin of the Brunists*.

Charlie Ryan Baxter. Writer of experimental novels in Alison Lurie's *Real People*.

Ezra Ezekial (Pa, Penny) Baxter. Honest and hardworking man who affectionately oversees the boyhood of his son Jody Baxter in Marjorie Kinnan Rawlings's *The Yearling*.

Frances (Black Piggy, Franny) Baxter. Daughter of Abner and Sarah Baxter in Robert Coover's *The Origin of the Brunists*.

Jane (Little Jane) Baxter. Ten-year-old sister of William Baxter; pesters her brother while he is suffering the pangs of adolescent love in Booth Tarkington's *Seventeen*.

Jody Baxter. Adolescent who adopts an orphaned fawn; matures when his mother shoots the fawn to save the family food supply in Marjorie Kinnan Rawlings's *The Yearling*.

Mrs. Baxter. Patient, sympathetic, and long-suffering mother of William Baxter; tries to cope with her son's infatuation with Miss Lola Pratt during his seventeenth summer in Booth Tarkington's *Seventeen*.

Nathan (Black Hand, Nat) Baxter. Son of Abner and Sarah Baxter in Robert Coover's *The Origin of the Brunists*.

Ory (Ma) Baxter. Hardworking mother of Jody Baxter in Marjorie Kinnan Rawlings's *The Yearling*.

Paul (Black Peter, Paulie) Baxter. Son of Abner and Sarah Baxter in Robert Coover's *The Origin of the Brunists*.

Sarah Baxter. Devoted friend of Constantia Dudley; reveals to Constantia a connection between Ursula Monrose and Ormond; loses her husband and their two daughters to yellow fever in Charles Brockden Brown's *Ormond*.

Sarah Baxter. Intimidated wife of Abner Baxter in Robert Coover's *The Origin of the Brunists*.

William Sylvanus (Silly Bill) Baxter. Seventeen-year-old who makes a fool of himself when he falls "in love" with Miss Lola Pratt in Booth Tarkington's *Seventeen*.

Arthur Bayson. Ineffectual husband of Betty Starr Bayson in Thomas Berger's *Killing Time*.

Betty Starr Bayson. Venal woman whose mother and sister were murdered by Joseph Detweiler in Thomas Berger's *Killing Time*.

Bea. Operator and mistress of ceremonies in the Hippodrome; mother of Iris; dies of a heart attack in Cyrus Colter's *The Hippodrome*.

Alice (Alie) Beach. Younger sister of Lucy Beach; at forty-three, senses that her life lacks meaning but ignores her sister's encouragement to leave their mother in William Maxwell's *Time Will Darken It*.

Lucy Beach. Older sister of Alice Beach; given musical training but denied a career by her mother; expresses her frustration near the end of William Maxwell's *Time Will Darken It*.

Major General Ira N. (Bus) Beal. Commander at Ocanara Army Air Base whose leadership is tested when black officers attempt to use the officers' club in James Gould Cozzens's *Guard of Honor*.

Miss Beale. Temperance and religious activist who teaches Patience Sparhawk about people's obsessive roles in Gertrude Atherton's *Patience Sparhawk and Her Times*.

Mrs. Beale. See Mrs. Beale Farange.

Elizabeth (Lizzie) Bean. Honey-blonde psychological counselor at a college in upstate New York; pregnant by Horace L'Ordinet, she gives birth to the baby boy later adopted by Annie and Phil

Sorenson; lover of Eli Silver in Frederick Busch's *Rounds*.

Titus Bean. Journalist and friend of Mabry Jenkins; writes scripts for pornographic movies in addition to writing stories about a chemical company's illicit activities in Peter Gent's *Texas Celebrity Turkey Trot*.

John Bear. Deaf-mute Pawnee Indian who helps Molly Riordan when she is burned; flees town when Clay Turner appears for a second time in E. L. Doctorow's *Welcome to Hard Times*.

Dr. Shakespeare Agamemnon Beard. Black founder of the National Social Equality League in George S. Schuyler's *Black No More*.

Angus Beaton. Arrogant art director of the magazine *Every Other Week* in William Dean Howells's *A Hazard of New Fortunes*.

Mr. Beaton. Secretary and general counsel for Typon International whose admiration for Amy Joubert leads him to plot for her control of the company in William Gaddis's *JR*.

Beatty. Captain of the firemen who burn books in Ray Bradbury's *Fahrenheit 451*.

Gloria Beatty. Cynical aspiring actress who convinces Robert Syverten to enter the dance marathon with her; killed by Syverten at her request in Horace McCoy's *They Shoot Horses, Don't They?*

Bobo Beauchamp. Groom in William Faulkner's *The Reivers*.

Emily Crayton Beauchamp. Daughter of Colonel Crayton and only true friend of Charlotte Temple among the gentility in the United States; writes to Charlotte's parents in England to explain the plight of their daughter in Susanna Rowson's *Charlotte*.

Henry Beauchamp. Son of Lucas and Mollie Beauchamp in William Faulkner's *Go Down, Moses*.

Hubert Beauchamp. Plantation owner and uncle of Ike McCaslin in William Faulkner's *Go Down, Moses*.

James Thucydides (Tennie's Jim, Thucydus) Beauchamp. Son of Tomey's Turl and Tennie Beauchamp in William Faulkner's *Go Down Moses*; grandfather of Bobo Beauchamp in *The Reivers*.

Lucas Quintus Carothers McCaslin Beauchamp. Son of Tomey's Turl and Tennie Beauchamp; accused of murdering Vinson Gowrie; appears in William Faulkner's *Go Down, Moses*; *Intruder in the Dust*; and *The Reivers*.

Molly (Mollie) Beauchamp. Wife of Lucas Beauchamp in William Faulkner's *Go Down, Moses* and *Intruder in the Dust*.

Philip Manigault Beauchamp. Soldier who helps execute General Gragnon in William Faulkner's *A Fable*.

Samuel Worsham Beauchamp. Grandson of Lucas and Molly Beauchamp; executed for killing a Chicago policeman in William Faulkner's *Go Down, Moses*.

Sophonsiba Beauchamp. See Sophonsiba Beauchamp McCaslin.

Tennie Beauchamp. Wife of Tomey's Turl and mother of James Thucydides (Tennie's Jim), Lucas, and Sophonsiba Beauchamp in William Faulkner's *Go Down, Moses*; great-grandmother of Bobo Beauchamp in *The Reivers*.

Tomey's Turl Beauchamp. Husband of Tennie Beauchamp and father of James Thucydides (Tennie's Jim), Lucas, and Sophonsiba Beauchamp in William Faulkner's *Go Down, Moses*; a character of the same name appears in *The Town*.

Bob Beaudreau. Football fanatic and financier who loses his girlfriend to Phil Elliott in Peter Gent's *North Dallas Forty*.

Julius Beaufort. Husband of Regina Beaufort; wealthy banker of mysterious origins and dissipated habits in Edith Wharton's *The Age of Innocence*.

Maria McInnis Beaufort. Banker's daughter who marries a university professor-psychiatrist after an affair with Jed Tewksbury in Robert Penn Warren's *A Place to Come To*.

Regina Dallas Beaufort. Wife of Julius Beaufort and ostentatious hostess for old New York society in Edith Wharton's *The Age of Innocence*.

Jeremiah (Jerry, William K. Grierson) Beaumont. Altruist and author of the manuscript that provides the plot of the novel; kills Colonel Cassius Fort, escapes from jail, but is caught and decapitated in Robert Penn Warren's *World Enough and Time*.

Ned Beaumont. Gambler who investigates murder charges against his friend, political boss Paul Madvig, in Dashiell Hammett's *The Glass Key*.

Rachel Jordan Beaumont. Wife of Jeremiah Beaumont and former lover of Colonel Cassius Fort, father of her first child, in Robert Penn Warren's *World Enough and Time*.

Pussy (Mrs. Beau) Beauseigneur. Example of encroaching commuters in Woodsmoke, Connecticut; employs Frank Spofford as a handyman in Peter De Vries's *Reuben, Reuben*.

Beauty (Chips). Ugly carpenter aboard the *Julia* in Herman Melville's *Omoo*.

Martinette de Beauvais (Ursula Monrose). Purchaser of the lute Constantia Dudley sells to alleviate her family's financial distress; revealed to be the sister of Ormond, from whom she was separated during adolescence, in Charles Brockden Brown's *Ormond*.

Ollie Totem Head Water Beaver. Guide on the Alaskan hunting expedition in Norman Mailer's *Why Are We in Vietnam?*

Tug Beavers. Poor-white teamster on a railroad construction gang who is murdered by Peck Bradley in T. S. Stribling's *Teeftallow*.

Wesley Beavers. Sexually magnetic protagonist in Reynolds Price's *A Long and Happy Life*.

Hannah Bech. Mother of Henry Bech; dies in a Riverdale nursing home in John Updike's *Bech: A Book*.

Henry Bech. Middle-aged Jewish writer from New York; experiences writer's block after publishing two novels, *Travel Light* and *The Chosen*, the novella *Brother Pig*, and two collections, *When the Saints* and *The Best of Bech*; his travels take him to Russia, Rumania, Bulgaria, London, Martha's Vineyard, and Virginia in John Updike's *Bech: A Book*.

Craig Beckerman. Electrode implantation volunteer at Neuropsychiatric Research Unit in Michael Crichton's *The Terminal Man*.

Becky. White southerner who bears two black sons; dies alone, rejected by both black and white religious communities, in Jean Toomer's *Cane*.

Duncan Bedford. Son of Malcolm and Sarah Bedford; after serving in the Confederate army, he returns to Portobello plantation and marries Julia Valette Somerville in Stark Young's *So Red the Rose*.

Lieutenant Bedford. Platoon leader in France during World War I who is killed at the battle of Soissons in Thomas Boyd's *Through the Wheat*.

Malcolm (Mac) Bedford. Husband of Sarah Tate Bedford, father of Duncan Bedford, and owner of Portobello plantation in Natchez; joins the Confederate army and dies of typhus in Stark Young's *So Red the Rose*.

Sarah Tate (Sallie, Tait) Bedford. Wife of Malcolm Bedford and mother of Duncan Bedford; widowed during the Civil War, she manages Portobello plantation until Duncan returns from the army in Stark Young's *So Red the Rose*.

Record Head (Bednarski) Bednar. Veteran Chicago police captain who bears the guilt of the criminals with whom he has dealt in Nelson Algren's *The Man with the Golden Arm*.

Mrs. Beech. President of the Women's City Club interested in political reform in Chicago; in an attempt to join forces with others who share her reform interests, she is one of the white guests at Sara Andrews Towns's dinner party in W. E. B. Du Bois's *Dark Princess*.

Beulah Beecham. See Beulah Beecham Renfro.

Clara Beechum. See Clara Beechum Pettit.

Jack (Old Jack) Beechum. Subsistence farmer and representative patriarch of Port William, Kentucky; overextending his farm to please his wife, Ruth Lightwood, he becomes estranged from her and has an affair with Rose McInnis; central presence whose thoughts organize Wendell Berry's *The Memory of Old Jack*; also appears in *Nathan Coulter* and *A Place on Earth*.

Nancy Beechum. See Nancy Beechum Feltner.

Ruth Beechum. See Ruth Lightwood.

Cyrus U. (Beeky) Beekman. Cunning and devious opportunist and Union army officer who exploits southern whites and blacks; carpetbag candidate for governor of Alabama who advocates a New South commercial ethic in T. S. Stribling's *The Forge* and *The Store*.

Sir Francis (Piggie) Beekman. Wealthy man attracted to Lorelei Lee; she is affectionate to him long enough to gain a diamond tiara that his wife desires for herself in Anita Loos's *"Gentlemen Prefer Blondes."*

Gracie Beekman. See Gracie Vaiden.

Old Man Beeler. Retired pharmacist living with his daughter, Sheryl Beeler, in a Mott Street apartment managed by Norman Moonbloom in Edward Lewis Wallant's *The Tenants of Moonbloom*.

Sheryl Beeler. Daughter of Old Man Beeler; exchanges sexual favors with Norman Moonbloom for rent cuts in Edward Lewis Wallant's *The Tenants of Moonbloom*.

Hiram Beers. Horse trainer and menial-for-hire for Norwood; serves as an ambulance driver during the Civil War and becomes Reuben Wentworth's stable hand in Henry Ward Beecher's *Norwood*.

Shep Beery. Accomplice of Gerry Kells in Paul Cain's *Fast One*.

Edmond (Sordino) Behr-Bleibtreau. Psychologist and hypnotist who disrupts a radio talk show hosted by Dick Gibson in Stanley Elkin's *The Dick Gibson Show*.

S. Behrman. Railroad agent in the San Joaquin Valley who manipulates the law to the disadvantage of the wheat growers in Frank Norris's *The Octopus*.

Thami Beidaoui. Family outcast; Moroccan friend and victim of Nelson Dyar in Paul Bowles's *Let It Come Down*.

Dr. Beineke. Fantasy leader of an expedition with which Margaret Reynolds travels to the interior of the Amazon to study the primitive Itwo tribe in Anne Richardson Roiphe's *Up the Sandbox!*

Bel. See Isabel.

Carl Belcher. Incompetent night foreman at the Past Bay Manufacturing Company factory who precipitates the strike in Robert Cantwell's *The Land of Plenty*.

Belcour. Unscrupulous friend of Jack Montraville; convinces Montraville to desert Charlotte Temple on the claim that she is faithless; dies at the hands of Montraville when Montraville learns of the deception in Susanna Rowson's *Charlotte*.

Amy Belden. Widow who helps Mary Leavenworth and Henry Clavering elope, and who hides the maid Hannah Chester after the murder of Horatio Leavenworth, in Anna Katharine Green's *The Leavenworth Case*.

Gilbert Belden. Partner with David Marshall in a wholesale grocery in Henry Blake Fuller's *With the Procession*.

Judy Belden. See Jennie Denton.

Belfast X. "Black Irish London junkie" who sells a virgin-wool sports jacket to Black Will during one of Black Will's junkets in Carlene Hatcher Polite's *Sister X and the Victims of Foul Play*.

Belinda (Marie O'Neill). Movie star at Olympia Studios; married to Maurice Cassard in Ludwig Bemelmans's *Dirty Eddie*.

Bell. Proprietor of a sugar plantation in Taloo; married to a beautiful woman from Sydney in Herman Melville's *Omoo*.

Clinton Harkavy Bell. Advertising executive and father of David Bell; figures prominently in his son's extended flashback in Don DeLillo's *Americana*.

David Bell. New York television producer who travels west with friends to make a documentary about the Navaho but becomes obsessed with a zany film of his own creation; narrator of Don DeLillo's *Americana*.

Diana Bell. Older daughter of a prominent Newport family who is about to elope with Hilary Jones, a married man, until Theophilus North manages to halt them in Thornton Wilder's *Theophilus North*.

Irene Bell. Actress who leaves Willie Spearmint for Harry Lesser in Bernard Malamud's *The Tenants*.

Joe Bell. Lexington Avenue bartender who takes messages for Holly Golightly in Truman Capote's *Breakfast at Tiffany's*.

John Bell. Private, then sergeant, stationed in the Pacific; haunted by memories of his wife; receives news of his promotion to lieutenant the same day he learns of his wife's intention to leave him for another man in James Jones's *The Thin Red Line*.

Bella. Dark-haired lesbian prostitute who enthusiastically tattoos and tortures Peter Leland in Fred Chappell's *Dagon*.

Belladonna. Female piglet in Ludwig Bemelmans's *Dirty Eddie*.

Alice Bellantoni. Daughter of Polina Bellantoni in Rita Mae Brown's *Rubyfruit Jungle*.

Polina Bellantoni. Columbia University professor, mother of Alice Bellantoni, and lover of Paul Digita and Molly Bolt in Rita Mae Brown's *Rubyfruit Jungle*.

Blondy Belle. Former moll and girlfriend of Little Arnie Worch; takes up with Rico Bandello and alerts him to Arnie's cheating on Rico in William Riley Burnett's *Little Caesar*.

Claire de Bellegarde. See Claire de Bellegarde de Cintré.

Emmeline de Bellegarde. Murderer of her husband and mother of Claire de Cintré; opposes the marriage of Claire and Christopher Newman in Henry James's *The American*.

Henri-Urban de Bellegarde. Husband of Emmeline de Bellegarde and father of Claire, Urban, and Valentin de Bellegarde; murdered by his wife and Urban because he opposed Claire's first marriage in Henry James's *The American*.

Madame Urbain de Bellegarde. Unhappily married wife of Urbain de Bellegarde; encourages Christopher Newman's suit of Claire de Cintré in Henry James's *The American*.

Urbain de Bellegarde. Eldest son of Emmeline de Bellegarde, with whom he plots to kill his father; despises Christopher Newman in Henry James's *The American*.

Valentin de Bellegarde. Younger brother of Urbain de Bellegarde and friend of Christopher Newman; killed by Stanislas Kapp in a duel over Noémie Nioche in Henry James's *The American*.

Bellerophon. King of Lycia and slayer of the chimera; must leave his city and assume an artificial identity in the *Bellerophoniad*, a novella in John Barth's *Chimera*.

Amy (Anne Frank) Bellette. Librarian and former student of E. I. Lonoff; wants Lonoff to leave his wife and live with her in Italy; imagined by Nathan Zuckerman to be Anne Frank in Philip Roth's *The Ghost Writer*.

Clare Bellew. See Clare Kendry.

John Bellew. White husband of Clare Kendry; businessman and former South American adventurer; after discovering Clare is black, he confronts her in a Harlem apartment, where she falls to her death, in Nella Larsen's *Passing*.

Margery Bellew. Daughter of John Bellew and Clare Kendry; attends boarding school in Switzerland in Nella Larsen's *Passing*.

Bellingham. Governor of Massachusetts Bay who wants to take Pearl from her mother, Hester Prynne, in Nathaniel Hawthorne's *The Scarlet Letter*.

Louis (Schemer) Bellini. Family man who leads a double life; dies from a gunshot wound suffered in a robbery in William Riley Burnett's *The Asphalt Jungle*.

John R. (Boss) Bellmann. Politician elected on a reform platform and later murdered in Paul Cain's *Fast One*.

James Bellmont. Abolitionist sympathizer who befriends Frado; business associate of his brother, Lewis Bellmont, and husband of Susan Bellmont; dies after a lingering illness in Harriet E. Wilson's *Our Nig*.

Jane Bellmont. Invalid daughter of John and Mrs. Bellmont; marries George Means against her mother's will in Harriet E. Wilson's *Our Nig*.

Jenny Bellmont. Young woman from a poor family in the West; marries Jack Bellmont and suffers the hatred and lies of her mother-in-law, Mrs. Bellmont, in Harriet E. Wilson's *Our Nig*.

John Bellmont. Kind patriarch of the Bellmont family who tries to protect Frado from the cruelty of Mrs. Bellmont in Harriet E. Wilson's *Our Nig*.

John (Jack) Bellmont. Youngest son of John and Mrs. Bellmont; befriends Frado and defies his mother and sister on her behalf, claiming her as "his coloured protegé"; husband of Jenny Bellmont in Harriet E. Wilson's *Our Nig*.

Lewis Bellmont. Son of John and Mrs. Bellmont; lives in Baltimore, where he is associated in business first with his brother James and later with his brother Jack in Harriet E. Wilson's *Our Nig*.

Mary Bellmont. Younger daughter of John and Mrs. Bellmont; follows her mother's example in tormenting Frado, whom Mary attempts to kill by hurling a knife at her, in Harriet E. Wilson's *Our Nig*.

Mrs. Bellmont. Tyrannical and sadistic persecutor of Frado; professed Christian and wife of John Bellmont in Harriet E. Wilson's *Our Nig*.

Susan Bellmont. Descendant of a wealthy Baltimore family; wife of James Bellmont in Harriet E. Wilson's *Our Nig*.

Bello. Humpbacked ruler of Dominora in Herman Melville's *Mardi*.

Mildred Belloussovsky-Dommergues. Often-married writer seated next to Henry Bech at his induction ceremony in John Updike's *Bech: A Book*.

Esther Leonie Beloff. Sensual daughter of the Reverend Marian Miles Beloff and the object of religious leader Nathan Vickery's tormented sexual attraction in Joyce Carol Oates's *Son of the Morning*.

Reverend Marian Miles Beloff. Exploitative, materialistic religious leader who employs the young Nathan Vickery in his ministry; father of Leonie Beloff in Joyce Carol Oates's *Son of the Morning*.

Blessed Belshazzar. Escaped rapist, leader of the sect of the Blessed Belshazzar, and father of Birchie Bartley in Hal Bennett's *A Wilderness of Vines*.

A. M. Belshue. Atheistic and freethinking jeweler and husband of Nessie Sutton; commits suicide in

T. S. Stribling's *Teeftallow*.

Belt (Alonzo Fiber). Master of the dojo at the Sun N Fun motel in Florida in Harry Crews's *Karate Is a Thing of the Spirit*.

Bembo (Mowree). New Zealand harpooner who, as temporary captain of the *Julia*, tries to wreck the ship near Tahiti in Herman Melville's *Omoo*.

Elijah Westlake (Lige) Bemis. County attorney, federal judge, and protector of John Barclay's monopoly in William Allen White's *A Certain Rich Man*.

Luther (Lute) Bemis. Former partner of Jud Clasby; convicted and hanged for his part in the Indian massacre in Jessamyn West's *The Massacre at Fall Creek*.

Ora (Ory) Bemis. Wife of Luther Bemis in Jessamyn West's *The Massacre at Fall Creek*.

Ben. Drug supplier and friend of Arthur Ketcham in John Clellon Holmes's *Go*.

Ben. Large and menacing gangster whom Christina Goering meets in a bar; he deserts her in Jane Bowles's *Two Serious Ladies*.

Ben. Name used for two slaves, designated big Ben and little Ben, who are opossum hunters in John Pendleton Kennedy's *Swallow Barn*.

Ben (Old Ben). Slave and house servant of Moseley Sheppard in Arna Wendell Bontemps's *Black Thunder*.

David Ben Ami. Israeli member of the Palmach; uses biblical passages as military strategies in Leon Uris's *Exodus*.

Akiva Ben Canaan. Brother of Barak Ben Canaan and uncle of Ari and Jordana Ben Canaan; heads illegal terrorist activities against the British forces in Palestine in Leon Uris's *Exodus*.

Ari Ben Canaan. Lover of Kitty Fremont; soldier in the Israeli War of Independence and smuggler of Jews into Palestine, his home, in Leon Uris's *Exodus*.

Barak Ben Canaan. Father of Ari and Jordana Ben Canaan and brother of Akiva Ben Canaan; political head of Palestine in Leon Uris's *Exodus*.

Jordana Ben Canaan. Sister of Ari Ben Canaan and lover of David Ben Ami; Israeli sabra and fighter in Leon Uris's *Exodus*.

Ben Benally. Friend and roommate of Abel in N. Scott Momaday's *House Made of Dawn*.

Belle Mitchell Benbow. Mother of Titania Mitchell, divorced from Harry Mitchell, and married to Horace Benbow; appears in William Faulkner's *Sartoris (Flags in the Dust)* and *Sanctuary*.

Horace Benbow. Attorney in William Faulkner's *Sartoris (Flags in the Dust)* and *Sanctuary*.

Narcissa Benbow. See Narcissa Benbow Sartoris.

George James Bender. Excellent wrestler who injures his knee as a sophomore at Iowa State and fails to win the Big Eight championship; beaten by Willard Buzzard because Edith Winter tries to seduce and humble Bender in John Irving's *The 158-Pound Marriage*.

Albert F. Bendix. Brother of H. W. and R. N. Bendix; famous for giving large tips in Henry Miller's *Black Spring*.

H. W. Bendix. Brother of Albert F. and R. N. Bendix; wealthy merchant who complains about the quality of merchandise and services in Henry Miller's *Black Spring*.

R. N. Bendix. Brother of Albert F. and H. W. Bendix; unable to visit the tailor shop because he has had his legs amputated in Henry Miller's *Black Spring*.

Alan Benedict. Doctor in Piedmont, Arizona, who opens the Scoop VII satellite and unleashes the Andromeda Strain in Michael Crichton's *The Andromeda Strain*.

Baldwin (Bawley) Benedict. Unmarried uncle of Bick Benedict; runs a small cattle operation in Edna Ferber's *Giant*.

Juana Benedict. Wife of Jordy Benedict in Edna Ferber's *Giant*.

Leslie Lynnton (Les) Benedict. Wife of Bick Benedict and mother of Jordy Benedict and Luz Benedict II; forsakes her pleasant Virginia homestead for the rigors of rural Texas and the husband she loves in Edna Ferber's *Giant*.

Luz Benedict (I). Sister of Bick Benedict; manages the Reata household and helps oversee the ranch in Edna Ferber's *Giant*.

Luz Benedict (II). Daughter of Bick and Leslie Benedict in Edna Ferber's *Giant*.

Jordan (Bick) Benedict the Third. Husband of Leslie Lynnton Benedict and father of Jordy Benedict and Luz Benedict II; manages Reata, the huge family cattle estate, in Edna Ferber's *Giant*.

Jordan (Jordy) Benedict the Fourth. Son of Jordan and Leslie Benedict and husband of Juana Benedict; becomes a physician in Edna Ferber's *Giant*.

Benedicta. Apparently the illegitimate daughter of a hangman but actually the daughter of the Saltmaster and the hangman's wife; secretly loves Ambrosius, a monk, who murders her in Ambrose Bierce's adaptation of *The Monk and the Hangman's Daughter*.

Maria Beñes. Daughter of the designer of a black housing development and married lover of Bill Kelsey; dispatching black rivals, she proves the strength of white juju in Hal Bennett's *Seventh Heaven*.

Cleo Benham. Wife of Elmer Gantry and mother of their two children in Sinclair Lewis's *Elmer Gantry*.

Benjamin. See Benjamin Eliezer.

Casimir (Casey) Benkowski. Washed-up Polish boxer, minor hood, and Bruno Lefty Bicek's boxing manager in Nelson Algren's *Never Come Morning*.

Issachar Bennet. Shaker missioner who helps Jerry Fowler rescue Norah Sharon in Walter D. Edmonds's *Erie Water*.

Cuthbert (Couth) Bennett. Friend of Fred Trumper; catches a venereal disease from Elsbeth Malkas; caretaker at the Pillsbury Estate who eventually marries Sue Kunft Trumper and cares for Colm Trumper in John Irving's *The Water-Method Man*.

George Bennett. Former army buddy of Jack Sellars; persuades Jack and Bebe Sellars to manage his property at Pickerel Beach in Doris Betts's *The River to Pickle Beach*.

Sue Kunft Trumper (Biggie) Bennett. Mother, by her husband Fred Trumper, of Colm Trumper; divorces Trumper and marries Cuthbert Bennett in John Irving's *The Water-Method Man*.

Ward Bennett. Arctic explorer who courts Lloyd Searight, contributing to the death of Richard Ferriss as he does so, in Frank Norris's *A Man's Woman*.

Lov Bensey. Railroad coal chute worker whose child-wife, Pearl Lester Bensey, abandons him in Erskine Caldwell's *Tobacco Road*.

Pearl Lester Bensey. Daughter of Ada Lester; abandons her husband, Lov Bensey, in Erskine Caldwell's *Tobacco Road*.

Bob Benson. Friend of Jule Jackson in New York; helps Jule become a printer's apprentice in George Wylie Henderson's *Jule*.

George Benson. Murderer of Folded Leaf; convicted and hanged in Jessamyn West's *The Massacre at Fall Creek*.

Harold Franklin (Harry) Benson. Computer scientist upon whom the stage-three operation is performed in Michael Crichton's *The Terminal Man*.

Steven (Chuckie, Dandy, Steve, Stevie) Benson. Narrator and central character in Ed Bullins's *The Reluctant Rapist*.

Walter Arlis Benson. See Walter Boyle.

Elspeth (Aunt Jetty) Bent. Granddaughter of Jess and Eliza Birdwell and daughter of Mattie Birdwell and Gardiner Bent in Jessamyn West's *The Friendly Persuasion* and *Except for Me and Thee*.

Gardiner (Gard) Bent. Fiancé and then husband of Mattie Birdwell in Jessamyn West's *The Friendly Persuasion* and *Except for Me and Thee*.

Mattie Bent. See Martha Truth Birdwell.

Horace Bentley. Generous friend of the poor after being ruined by Eldon Parr in Winston Churchill's *The Inside of the Cup*.

Jesse Bentley. Son of Tom Bentley; assumes responsibility for the Bentley farm after his father's retirement; injured by his grandson David Hardy in Sherwood Anderson's *Winesburg, Ohio*.

Katherine Bentley. Wife of Jesse Bentley; dies giving birth to Louise Bentley in Sherwood Anderson's *Winesburg, Ohio*.

Louise Bentley. See Louise Bentley Hardy.

Nat Benton. Stockbroker who advises Charley Anderson, allowing him to garner enough of stock in Askew-Merritt to sell out his senior partner, Joe Askew; Benton supplies Anderson with tips throughout the market boom in John Dos Passos's *U.S.A.* trilogy.

Sheila Benton. Health and beauty editor for *Vogue* magazine who is obsessed by her passion for Ambrose Clay in Gail Godwin's *Violet Clay*.

Billy Bentson. Small-time Dallas gambler and friend of Mabry Jenkins; reaches the big time by taking Junior Everett for several hundred thousand dollars in Peter Gent's *Texas Celebrity Turkey Trot*.

Dr. (Doc) Benway. Mad scientist and surgeon; "manipulator and coordinator of symbol systems and expert in all phases of interrogation, brainwashing, and control"; director of the Reconditioning Center in William S. Burroughs's *Naked Lunch*; also appears in *Nova Express*, *The Soft Machine*, and *Exterminator!*

Natalie Benziger. See Natalie Benziger Eaton.

Zeydel (Reb Zeydel) Ber. Ritual slaughterer, widower, uncle of Rechele Babad, and son-in-law of Granny; provides food, clothing, and shelter for Rechele until his death in Isaac Bashevis Singer's *Satan in Goray*.

Montgomery (Monty) Beragon (Bergoni). Polo-playing lover and later husband of Mildred Pierce; wastes Mildred's money and betrays her by sleeping with her daughter, Veda Pierce, in James M. Cain's *Mildred Pierce*.

Berbelang. Leader of the group of Third World art-nappers who return art from Western museums to its true owners; killed by Biff Musclewhite because Berbelang trusted the idealistic Thor Wintergreen too much in Ishmael Reed's *Mumbo Jumbo*.

Marquis René-Victor de Bercy. French nobleman engaged to Thérèse de Fontenay in H. L. Davis's *Harp of a Thousand Strings*.

Marija Berczynskas. Cousin of Ona Rudkus; lends money to Jurgis Rudkus to buy a house; becomes a prostitute to support the family in Upton Sinclair's *The Jungle*.

Mack Berg. Volunteer in an American battalion in the Spanish civil war; killed and mutilated in the loyalists' efforts to raise the siege of Madrid in William Herrick's *Hermanos!*

Miriam Berg. See Miriam Berg Stone.

Theodore (Teddy) Berg. Famous American composer in Alison Lurie's *Real People*.

P. O. Bergdahl. Mysterious character; possibly the father of O. P. Dahlberg or possibly Dahlberg himself in Wright Morris's *The Fork River Space Project*.

Minna Bergen. Spoiled neighbor of Ada Fincastle and Ralph McBride; pursues Ralph in Ellen Glasgow's *Vein of Iron*.

Helga Bergenstrohm. Wife of Swede Bergenstrohm; washerwoman and cook for the miners; fights with Molly Riordan over feeding Jimmy Fee in E. L. Doctorow's *Welcome to Hard Times*.

Swede Bergenstrohm. Hardworking husband of Helga Bergenstrohm; killed by Clay Turner in E. L. Doctorow's *Welcome to Hard Times*.

Tyrone C. Berger. Psychiatrist who counsels Conrad Jarrett after his suicide attempt in Judith Guest's *Ordinary People*.

Hogo (Roy) de Bergerac. Loathsome troublemaker and anti-prince in Donald Barthelme's *Snow White*.

Vinny Bergerac. Madcap boyhood friend of Jack Duluoz; known for cursing in Jack Kerouac's *Doctor Sax*, *Maggie Cassidy*, and *Book of Dreams*.

Alexandra Bergson. Smart, ambitious, but lonely farmer who becomes successful because she plans for the future in Willa Cather's *O Pioneers!*

Emil Bergson. Restless, college-educated brother of Alexandra Bergson; loves Marie Shabata and is killed by her husband, Frank Shabata, in Willa Cather's *O Pioneers!*

John Bergson. Swedish immigrant; hardworking but unsuccessful farmer who leaves his farm to his daughter, Alexandra Bergson, in Willa Cather's *O Pioneers!*

Lou Bergson. Greedy and bigoted brother of Alexandra Bergson; becomes a populist agitator in Willa Cather's *O Pioneers!*

Mrs. Bergson. Wife of John Bergson; longs for Sweden in Willa Cather's *O Pioneers!*

Oscar Bergson. Greedy and bigoted son of Mr. and Mrs. John Bergson; resents his brother Emil Bergson's intellectual tendencies and his sister Alexandra Bergson's farming success in Willa Cather's *O Pioneers!*

Kirkcudbright Llanover Marjoribanks Sellers (Howard Tracy), Viscount Berkeley. Son of the Earl of Rossmore; wishes to renounce his title and live in America; falls in love and marries Sally Sellers in Samuel Langhorne Clemens's *The American Claimant*.

Lightening Berlew. Hired hand of Mat Feltner and husband of Sylvania Berlew; alienated from the land Wendell Berry's *The Memory of Old Jack*.

Sylvania (Smoothbore) Berlew. Wife of Lightening Berlew in Wendell Berry's *The Memory of Old Jack*.

Paul Berlin. Army infantry specialist stationed in Vietnam; compelled to imagine the diverse realities of the war in Tim O'Brien's *Going after Cacciato*.

Benjamin Samson (Ben) Berman. Jewish father of Samuel Paul Berman; retired cabdriver and former radio actor in Jay Neugeboren's *Sam's Legacy*.

Morrie Berman. Former pimp, gambler, and backer of Billy Phelan's bowling and pool games; involved in Charlie Boy McCall's kidnapping in William Kennedy's *Billy Phelan's Greatest Game*.

O. J. Berman. Hollywood agent who helps change Holly Golightly from a hillbilly to a potential starlet in Truman Capote's *Breakfast at Tiffany's*.

Samuel Paul (Sam) Berman. Son of Benjamin Samson Berman, professional gambler, and lover of Stella; moves to California to escape paying gambling debts in Jay Neugeboren's *Sam's Legacy*.

Bernard. Student who serves on the Cinema Committee with Hill Gallagher during the student rebellion in James Jones's *The Merry Month of May*.

Jefferson (Jeff) Bernard. Aged recluse whose explanation of Mildred Latham's past to Sidney Wyeth causes Wyeth to return to her in Oscar Micheaux's *The Forged Note*.

Jesse (Jess) Bernarr. Active telepath who joins the Pattern, a "vast network of mental links," in Octavia E. Butler's *Mind of My Mind*.

Bernice. See Bernice Stockton.

Madame Anna Bernstein. Member of the Cabala and "the power behind the German banking house" in Thornton Wilder's *The Cabala*.

Lieutenant Paco Berrendo. Member of Captain Mora's fascist group in Ernest Hemingway's *For Whom the Bell Tolls*.

Blues Berry. Prisoner in the stockade; beaten to death by guards led by Fatso Judson in James Jones's *From Here to Eternity*.

Dolek Berson. Member of the Nazi-dominated *Judenrat* forced to coordinate the so-called "resettlement" of Polish Jews; becomes the strategic leader of the final battle against total Nazi destruction of the Warsaw ghetto in John Hersey's *The Wall*.

Bertha. See Chatelaine of La Trinité.

Bertha Mae. Teenaged lover of Jule Jackson; eventually moves with him from Alabama to New York in George Wylie Henderson's *Jule*.

Louis Berthold. French journalist with everchanging politics; colleague of Mary Douglas in Martha Gellhorn's *A Stricken Field*.

Bertie. Victim of Harry Cresswell's sexual abuse and mother by him of a mulatto child, Emma, in W. E. B. Du Bois's *The Quest of the Silver Fleece*.

Bertilia (Bert). Daughter of Suzanne Winograd who behaves more maturely than her mother in Mark

Harris's *It Looked Like For Ever*.

Alexander (Alex) BeShears. Store owner and neighbor of the Vaidens; father of Ponny BeShears and victim of the Leatherwood gang's violence in T. S. Stribling's *The Forge* and *The Store*.

Ponny BeShears. Daughter of Alex BeShears, lover of Polycarp Vaiden, and first wife of Miltiades Vaiden; dies during childbirth; appears in T. S. Stribling's *The Forge* and *The Store*.

Bess. Mistress of Crown, who deserts her; taken in by Porgy, from whom she runs away, in DuBose Heyward's *Porgy*.

Aunt Bess (Bessie). Wife of Uncle Clyde; boards Dandy Benson at her Maryland farm during summers in his boyhood in Ed Bullins's *The Reluctant Rapist*.

Travis (Blix) Bessemer. Friend of Condé Rivers; helps Rivers become a writer and falls in love with him in the process in Frank Norris's *Blix*.

Bessie. Girlfriend of Van Norden; obsessed with "technique" in Henry Miller's *Tropic of Cancer*.

Bessy Mae. Sister of Teddy, who steals Bessy Mae's ADC check to support his heroin addiction, in Donald Goines's *Dopefiend*.

Samuel Bester. Chairman of the language arts department at Calvin Coolidge High School; observes teachers and leaves extensive memos; believes all students should read Charles Dickens and Shakespeare in Bel Kaufman's *Up the Down Staircase*.

Wilfrid (Wilf) Bestudik. Dimwitted priest, rector of St. Clement's Hill Retreat House, and superior of Father Urban in J. F. Powers's *Morte D'Urban*.

Brother Bethune. Baptist minister at the Beecham family reunion in Eudora Welty's *Losing Battles*.

Betsy. Slave owned by Ellen Ashe and sold after Edward Ashe falls in love with her; Edward finds Betsy and their child and moves with them to Canada in Jesse Hill Ford's *The Raider*.

Betsy. Wholesome friend of Esther Greenwood and her fellow guest editor at a New York fashion magazine; she and Esther suffer ptomaine poisoning at a *Ladies' Day* magazine banquet in Sylvia Plath's *The Bell Jar*.

Lulu Bett. Spinster sister of Ina Bett Deacon; released from domestic drudgery when she marries, inadvertently, Ninian Deacon, a man already married; marries Neil Cornish in Zona Gale's *Miss Lulu*

Bett.

Mrs. Bett. Mother of Ina and Lulu Bett and mother-in-law of Dwight Deacon, in whose house she lives, in Zona Gale's *Miss Lulu Bett.*

Thomas (Tommy) Bettersworth. Small-town businessman who is killed in a fight over his wife's reputation in Mary Austin's *A Woman of Genius.*

Betty. Fiancée of Miss Lonelyhearts in Nathanael West's *Miss Lonelyhearts.*

Betty. Window designer for Saks who does layouts for Renate's planned magazine in Anaïs Nin's *Collages.*

Lillian Beye. Woman always fighting inner turmoil and seeking self-fulfillment; pianist in Anaïs Nin's *Ladders to Fire, Children of the Albatross,* and *Seduction of the Minotaur.*

Friedrich (Fritz) Bhaer. Kindly, eccentric German tutor who marries Jo March in Louisa May Alcott's *Little Women;* also appears in *Little Men.*

Jo March Bhaer. See Jo March.

Robin (Rob, Robby) Bhaer. Enthusiastic chatterbox at Plumfield; son of Jo and Friedrich Bhaer in Louisa May Alcott's *Little Men.*

Bella Biaggi. See Bella Biaggi Dehn.

Bianca. Former lover of Bill Agatson and former fiancée of Arthur Ketcham in John Clellon Holmes's *Go.*

Billy Biasse. Friend of Jake Brown and host to the longshoremen's gaming rendezvous in Claude McKay's *Home to Harlem.*

William (Billy, Club) Bibbit. Stuttering, mother-dominated mental patient who slits his throat in response to the domination of Big Nurse in Ken Kesey's *One Flew Over the Cuckoo's Nest.*

Lila Chand Bibi. Name assumed by Arista Prolo on tour in Tokyo in Carlene Hatcher Polite's *Sister X and the Victims of Foul Play.*

B. A. Bibokov. Investigating magistrate for Cases of Extraordinary Importance; tries to help clear Yakov Bok of murder charges in Bernard Malamud's *The Fixer.*

Bruno (Lefty) Bicek. Polish hood and boxer who betrays his girlfriend Steffi Rostenkowski into prostitution and who commits a senseless murder in Nelson Algren's *Never Come Morning.*

Fanny Bick. Young woman who has an intense affair with the much older William Dubin in Bernard Malamud's *Dubin's Lives.*

Alexander Biddenhurst. English visitor to Virginia by way of Philadelphia; proponent of liberty and agitator of the revolt against planter-aristocrats in Henrico County, Virginia, in Arna Wendell Bontemps's *Black Thunder.*

Wing (Adolph Myers) Biddlebaum. Former teacher who works on farms in Winesburg, Ohio; morbidly obsessed with his hands because of a scandal that nearly resulted in his lynching in Sherwood Anderson's *Winesburg, Ohio.*

Bidet. French commander in William Faulkner's *A Fable.*

Dr. Zbigniew (Papa) Bieganśka. Polish professor, author of an anti-Semitic pamphlet, and father of Sophie Zawistowska; executed by the Nazis in William Styron's *Sophie's Choice.*

Paul (Polly) Biegler. Lawyer from the Michigan Upper Peninsula who defends Frederic Manion; narrator of Robert Traver's *Anatomy of a Murder.*

Big Bertha. Black cook on the wandering island in John Hawkes's *Second Skin.*

Big Bertha of Heaven. See Blackman.

Ruby Big Elk. Daughter of the former chief of the Osage nation, wife of Cimarron Cravat, and mother of two children in Edna Ferber's *Cimarron.*

Big Ellis. Kentucky farmer and drinking partner of Burley Coulter in Wendell Berry's *Nathan Coulter* and *A Place on Earth.*

Reverend Doctor James Bigelow. Traveling evangelist who shocks George Brush in Thornton Wilder's *Heaven's My Destination.*

Roxie Biggers. Sister of Perry Northcutt; pietistic busybody and gossip who is opposed to Sunday baseball in T. S. Stribling's *Teeftallow.*

Chester Biggs. Trainer and handler of Victoria Regina, a miniature schnauzer stolen in Joseph Wambaugh's *The Black Marble.*

Lytle (Little) Biggs. Cynical, swaggering swindler in E. W. Howe's *The Story of a Country Town.*

Big Hing. See Kheng Fatt, Chop Hing.

Big Laura. Leader of a group of ex-slaves heading north after the Civil War; killed while defending them from vengeful whites in Ernest J. Gaines's *The Autobiography of Miss Jane Pittman.*

Luther Biglin. Jailer in William Faulkner's *The Mansion.*

Big Lot. Young man who spends the night with Charlie and causes the break up in the relationship between Charlie and the male narrator of Tennessee Williams's *Moise and the World of Reason*.

Big Nurse. See Nurse Ratched.

Theresa (Theresa Haug) Bigoness. Coworker of Martha Reganhart; becomes pregnant by a man other than her husband, passes herself off as single, bears a daughter, gives the child up for adoption, and returns to her harsh marriage in Philip Roth's *Letting Go*.

Big Sally. Black woman who drives a Mercedes and talks of her oppression in Ishmael Reed's *The Last Days of Louisiana Red*.

Big-Tooth. Mid-Pleistocene ancestor of the narrator; member of a race about to make evolutionary gains in Jack London's *Before Adam*.

Big Tub. Leader of the Rastas in Mark Helprin's *Refiner's Fire*.

Big Turtle. Shawnee Indian who captures Salathiel Albine and gives him the name of Little Turtle in Hervey Allen's *The Forest and the Fort*.

Bildad. An owner of the *Pequod* in Herman Melville's *Moby-Dick*.

John Little Bilham. Aspiring artist who is a friend of Chad Newsome and a confidant of Lambert Strether; becomes engaged to Mamie Pocock in Henry James's *The Ambassadors*.

Bill. Leader of the seven impotent capitalists who live with Snow White, wash windows, and make Chinese baby food; hanged for throwing two six-packs of beer through a windshield in Donald Barthelme's *Snow White*.

Bill. Reporter for *Field and Stream* and lover of Lisa in Anaïs Nin's *Collages*.

Bill. Editor of Miranda in Katherine Anne Porter's *Pale Horse, Pale Rider*.

M. A. (Medium Asshole) Bill. Personnel director for Pure Pores Filters Company; goes on the Alaskan hunting expedition in Norman Mailer's *Why Are We in Vietnam?*

Miss Billie. Friend of Marie Canada and mother of Charlotte; gives a wooden bracelet to Eva Medina Canada in Gayl Jones's *Eva's Man*.

George Billings. Former astronaut who serves as Jace Everett's troubleshooter; hires Mabry Jenkins to work for Everett's radio station but fires him when the ratings slip in Peter Gent's *Texas Celebrity Turkey Trot*.

Roe Billins. College roommate of Jerry Payne; spring house-party date of Nancy Putnam in John Nichols's *The Sterile Cuckoo*.

Billy. Retarded and abandoned sweeper of a pool hall who is employed and protected by Sam the Lion; butt of practical jokes; killed by a truck while sweeping the streets in Larry McMurtry's *The Last Picture Show*.

Billy. Vietnam veteran who is impatient with passive Civil Rights era methods of the Reverend Phillip Martin in Ernest J. Gaines's *In My Father's House*.

Uncle Billy. Belly-bumping champion whom Skipper defeats and from whom Skipper receives the crucifix he later gives to Catalina Kate in John Hawkes's *Second Skin*.

Lucius Binford. Common-law husband of Reba Rivers in William Faulkner's *Sanctuary*, *The Mansion*, and *The Reivers*.

Doc Bingham. Disreputable book peddler who hires Mac in Chicago and, after being caught in bed with a farmer's wife, flees, leaving Mac stranded in rural Michigan in John Dos Passos's *U.S.A.* trilogy.

Jo-Lea Bingham. Pregnant daughter of Timothy Bingham in Robert Penn Warren's *The Cave*.

Thomas (Tom) Bingham. Architect who encourages his friend David Marshall to endow a college building in Henry Blake Fuller's *With the Procession*.

Timothy Bingham. Father of Jo-Lea Bingham and "chief stockholder, president, and cashier" of the People's Security Bank of Johntown, Tennessee; arranges for Jo-Lea to have an abortion in Robert Penn Warren's *The Cave*.

Marcie Binnendale. See Marcie Binnendale Nash.

Beansy Binz. Young left-handed pitcher who replaces Henry Wiggen on the New York Mammoths in Mark Harris's *It Looked Like For Ever*.

Jimmy Biondo. Gangster who threatens to kill Legs Diamond in William Kennedy's *Legs*.

Harvey Birch. Mysterious peddler thought to be a spy for the British army but who is, in fact, George Washington's most trusted agent; his actions are marked by a selfless devotion to his country in James Fenimore Cooper's *The Spy*.

Master Lazarus Birchem. Schoolmaster in James Kirke Paulding's *Koningsmarke*.

Marilyn Birchfield. Kindhearted social worker who tries to befriend Sol Nazerman in Edward Lewis Wallant's *The Pawnbroker*.

Harriet Bird. Beautiful woman who shoots athletes with silver bullets in Bernard Malamud's *The Natural*.

Henry Bird. Employee of the *Free Press* who fights with Bartley Hubbard over Hannah Morrison in William Dean Howells's *A Modern Instance*.

Miss Iris (Aunt Iris) Bird. Crippled spinster biology teacher who chaperones a beach house party for Cress Delahanty and friends in Jessamyn West's *Cress Delahanty*.

Pete Bird. Unemployed, debt-plagued amateur poet and friend of Daisy Meissner in Edmund Wilson's *I Thought of Daisy*.

Senator and Mrs. Bird. Ohio couple who aid Eliza and Harry Harris as they flee the Shelby estate in Harriet Beecher Stowe's *Uncle Tom's Cabin*.

Birdie. Female canary and the mother of Birdy's flock in William Wharton's *Birdy*.

Miss Birdseye. Elderly philanthropist and leader of New England reform movements who dies at Marmion, the summer cottage of Olive Chancellor, in Henry James's *The Bostonians*.

Dabney Birdsong. Brilliant engineer and architect who becomes the lover of Annabel Upchurch, his childhood friend, after she marries Judge Honeywell in Ellen Glasgow's *The Romantic Comedians*.

Eva Howard Birdsong. Famous Queensborough beauty of the 1890s who gives up a career in opera for the great passion of loving the unfaithful George Birdsong in Ellen Glasgow's *The Sheltered Life*.

George Birdsong. Charming but struggling attorney who marries Eva Howard; lover of Memoria and other women, including Jenny Blair, in Ellen Glasgow's *The Sheltered Life*.

Eliza Cope Birdwell. Recorded Quaker minister and wife of Jess Birdwell in Jessamyn West's *The Friendly Persuasion* and *Except for Me and Thee*.

Jane Birdwell. Younger daughter of Jess and Eliza Birdwell in Jessamyn West's *The Friendly Persuasion*.

Little Jess Birdwell. Youngest child of Jess and Eliza Birdwell in Jessamyn West's *The Friendly Persuasion* and *Except for Me and Thee*.

Jesse Griffith (Jess) Birdwell. Quaker nurseryman and husband of Eliza Birdwell in Jessamyn West's *The Friendly Persuasion* and *Except for Me and Thee*.

Joshua (Josh) Birdwell. Son of Jess and Eliza Birdwell in Jessamyn West's *The Friendly Persuasion* and *Except for Me and Thee*.

Laban (Labe) Birdwell. Son of Jess and Eliza Birdwell in Jessamyn West's *The Friendly Persuasion* and *Except for Me and Thee*.

Martha Truth (Mattie) Birdwell. Daughter of Jess and Eliza Birdwell; marries Gardiner Bent; appears in Jessamyn West's *The Friendly Persuasion* and *Except for Me and Thee*.

Sarah Birdwell. Daughter of Jess and Eliza Birdwell who dies young; appears in Jessamyn West's *The Friendly Persuasion* and *Except for Me and Thee*.

Stephen (Steve) Birdwell. Youngest son of Jess and Eliza Birdwell; marries Lidy Cinnamond in Jessamyn West's *The Friendly Persuasion*.

Birdy. Patient in an army psychiatric hospital who is obsessed with birds and who has an elaborate fantasy in which he is a bird; a narrator of William Wharton's *Birdy*.

Kareen Birkman. Young girlfriend and lover left behind by Joe Bonham in Dalton Trumbo's *Johnny Got His Gun*.

Mike Birkman. Father of Kareen Birkman in Dalton Trumbo's *Johnny Got His Gun*.

B. D. Bisbee. Friend of Chad Hanna, advance man for Huguenine's circus, and eventually part-owner of the circus in Walter D. Edmonds's *Chad Hanna*.

Bisch. Prison cellmate of Leo Feldman; tailor who creates Feldman's fool suit in Stanley Elkin's *A Bad Man*.

Bernice Bishop. Welfare worker who with Mr. Rayber attempts to get Francis Marion Tarwater away from his great-uncle; failing, she marries Rayber but deserts him after bearing their idiot son, Bishop Rayber, in Flannery O'Connor's *The Violent Bear It Away*.

Clare Bishop. Former mistress and secretary of Sebastian Knight during the six years in which he wrote his first two novels; eventually marries someone else and dies without ever speaking to V. in Vladimir Nabokov's *The Real Life of Sebastian Knight*.

Ephraim (Eef) Bishop. Sheriff in William Faulkner's *The Mansion*.

Jesse Bishop. Congressional Medal of Honor winner and member of the 918th Bomb Group; dies in battle in Beirne Lay, Jr., and Sy Bartlett's *Twelve O'Clock High!*

Meg Bishop. Judgmental journalist who accuses Mrs. Karen Stone of escapism as a way to forget her husband in Tennessee Williams's *The Roman Spring of Mrs. Stone.*

Leota B. Bisland. Sixth-grade classmate and first lover of Molly Bolt in Rita Mae Brown's *Rubyfruit Jungle.*

Agate Bissell. Strong-willed servant-for-hire who does her Christian duty for all the citizens of Norwood; serves as a hospital administrator and member of the Sanitary Commission during the Civil War and marries Parson Buell after his first wife dies in Henry Ward Beecher's *Norwood.*

Joe (Iddiboy, Iddyboy) Bissonnette. Muscular boyhood friend of Jack Duluoz in Jack Kerouac's *Doctor Sax* and *Maggie Cassidy.*

Roderick Magsworth (Roddy) Bitts, Junior. Scion of a snobbish, well-to-do family; his infrequent encounters with Penrod Schofield usually come to disastrous conclusions in Booth Tarkington's *Penrod, Penrod and Sam,* and *Penrod Jashber.*

Jimmy Bivens. White grocer beaten by Sonny Boy Mosby; his death convinces the town of Somerton that blacks have set out to kill all the white people in Jesse Hill Ford's *The Liberation of Lord Byron Jones.*

Luella Bixby. Aunt of Serena Lindley; member of numerous church societies and organizations for social improvement in Mary Austin's *Santa Lucia.*

B. J.. Character addressed by William Lee in William S. Burroughs's *The Ticket That Exploded*; consultant to the CIA on the fate of the British monarchy in *Exterminator!*

Bea Sorenson Bjornstam. See Bea Sorenson.

Angela (Doris Blankfurt) Black. Stripper killed by Harold Benson in Michael Crichton's *The Terminal Man.*

Capitola Black. See Capitola Le Noir.

Captain Black. Squadron intelligence officer who spearheads the Glorious Loyalty Oath Campaign in Joseph Heller's *Catch-22.*

Harry Black. Machinist, union shop steward, and strike leader who resents the sexual demands of his wife and who, despite his apparent total masculinity, becomes intrigued by, then infatuated with,

and later scorned by a series of male homosexuals and transvestites; ultimately sexually molests a ten-year-old boy and is beaten by a mob in Hubert Selby, Jr.'s *Last Exit to Brooklyn.*

Iris Black. Beautiful sister of Ivor Black and first wife of Vadim Vadimovich; killed by a crazed lover in front of her brother and husband, who claims that Iris and his unnamed fourth wife were the only women he truly loved, in Vladimir Nabokov's *Look at the Harlequins!*

Ivor Black. Brother of Iris Black and Cambridge friend of Vadim Vadimovich, whom he offhandedly invites to his Riviera villa, where Vadim meets Iris, in Vladimir Nabokov's *Look at the Harlequins!*

James (J.B.) Black. Community storyteller who takes pride in his African roots in George Cain's *Blueschild Baby.*

Josina Kugler Black. Owner of the Black Motor company in Mari Sandoz's *Capital City.*

Mr. Black. Ironside minister; usually humane man and a saint of misery until World War I unleashes his sermons on God's righteous wrath in Ellen Glasgow's *Vein of Iron.*

Willis B. Black. See Black Will.

Black Antler. Seneca Indian and follower of a Seneca prophet in Jessamyn West's *The Massacre at Fall Creek.*

Black Cat. Guitar player who plays while Ideal, as a little girl, is "implored to dance a big brass bed" in Carlene Hatcher Polite's *The Flagellants.*

Black Christopher. See Christopher Hall.

Black Donald. Wily chief of a bandit gang and supposed henchman of the villain Gabriel Le Noir; befriended by Capitola Le Noir in E.D.E.N. Southworth's *The Hidden Hand.*

Black Guinea (Ebony, Guinea). Crippled black who catches coins in his mouth in Herman Melville's *The Confidence-Man.*

Black Herman. Noted occultist in Ishmael Reed's *Mumbo Jumbo.*

Black Hetty. Devoted servant to Colonel James B. Brewton's family; assigned to care for the children in Conrad Richter's *The Sea of Grass.*

Black One. Six-year-old narrator who, beginning in 1939, wanders throughout eastern Europe and experiences the cruelty and barbarity of those who shun him in Jerzy Kosinski's *The Painted Bird.*

Black Warrior. Primitive Indian philosopher in James Kirke Paulding's *Westward Ho!*

Black Will (Willis B. Black). Well-traveled Afro-American and confidant of Abyssinia in Carlene Hatcher Polite's *Sister X and the Victims of Foul Play.*

Black Wolf. College-educated Sioux Indian who is a friend of Aaron Gadd; murdered and scalped by the Ojibway Indians in Sinclair Lewis's *The God-Seeker.*

Mrs. Blackett. Aged but cheerful and self-reliant widowed mother of Mrs. Almira Blackett Todd and William Blackett in Sarah Orne Jewett's *The Country of the Pointed Firs.*

William Blackett. Neat, handsome, and shy farmer-fisherman who is the brother of Mrs. Almira Todd; marries Esther Hight, whom he has secretly courted for forty years, in Sarah Orne Jewett's *The Country of the Pointed Firs.*

Jerry Blackford. Tenant farmer, husband of Judith Pippinger, and father of three children in Edith Summers Kelley's *Weeds.*

Judith Pippinger (Judy) Blackford. Daughter of Bill and Annie Pippinger, wife of Jerry Blackford, and mother of three children in Edith Summers Kelley's *Weeds.*

Wyeth Blackford. Feckless best friend of Anson Page and curator of a hunt club in Hamilton Basso's *The View from Pompey's Head.*

Captain Abraham Blackman. Black career soldier cut down by snipers in Vietnam; participates through delirium in outstanding moments of black military history from the Battle of Bunker Hill in the American Revolution to the Abraham Lincoln Brigade in the Spanish Civil War in John A. Williams's *Captain Blackman.*

Blackman (Big Bertha of Heaven). Itinerant fundamentalist preacher who conducts a revival in Irontown, Tennessee, in T. S. Stribling's *Teeftallow.*

Charles Blackwood. Brother of Julian Blackwood and cousin of Constance and Mary Katherine Blackwood; enters the Blackwood home to secure the family fortune for himself and brings about the destruction of house and family in Shirley Jackson's *We Have Always Lived in the Castle.*

Constance Blackwood. Older sister of Mary Katherine Blackwood and nominal head of the household; accused but acquitted of the Blackwood family poisoning; never leaves the house and grounds because she is feared and hated in the village in Shirley Jackson's *We Have Always Lived in the Castle.*

Julian Blackwood. Elderly invalid uncle of Constance and Mary Katherine Blackwood; sole survivor of the Blackwood family poisoning, about which he is writing a book, in Shirley Jackson's *We Have Always Lived in the Castle.*

Mary Katherine (Merricat) Blackwood. Reclusive, psychotic eighteen year old who lives in the family manse with her older sister, Constance Blackwood, and her uncle, Julian Blackwood; as a child, poisoned most of her family in Shirley Jackson's *We Have Always Lived in the Castle.*

Harlow Blade, Jr.. Teenaged author of a book on masturbation, which he delivers to the narrator's library, in Richard Brautigan's *The Abortion.*

Anna Ivanovna (Annette) Blagovo. Typist for Vadim Vadimovich; becomes his second wife and the mother of their daughter, Isabel; leaves Vadim under the influence of Ninel Langley, with whom she drowns in floods resulting from a hurricane, in Vladimir Nabokov's *Look at the Harlequins!*

Amory Blaine. "Romantic egotist" in and hero of F. Scott Fitzgerald's *This Side of Paradise.*

Beatrice O'Hara Blaine. Extravagant and alcoholic mother of Amory Blaine in F. Scott Fitzgerald's *This Side of Paradise.*

Edith Lawrence Blair. Childhood friend of Ruth Holland; stops seeing her after Ruth runs away with Stuart Williams, a married man, in Susan Glaspell's *Fidelity.*

Hugh Blair. Editor in chief of *The Townsman* in Peter De Vries's *The Tunnel of Love.*

James Blair. Friend of Samuele; graduate of Harvard University in classical studies who travels to Europe as an archaeological adviser to a film company in Thornton Wilder's *The Cabala.*

Jenny Blair. See Jenny Blair Archbald.

Alice Blake. Student at Calvin Coolidge High School who throws herself out of a window because of her unreturned love for English teacher Paul Barringer, whose response to her love letter was to correct it grammatically, in Bel Kaufman's *Up the Down Staircase.*

Ben Blake. Aspiring law student and first serious boyfriend of Francie Nolan in Betty Smith's *A Tree Grows in Brooklyn.*

Betty Blake. Daughter of Rachel Colbert Blake; dies in an outbreak of diphtheria in Willa Cather's *Sapphira and the Slave Girl*.

Blacky Blake. Forest ranger who supervises and befriends Glacier District lookouts Jarry Wagner and Jack Duluoz in Jack Kerouac's *Desolation Angels*.

Hagar Weylin Blake. Great-grandmother of Dana Franklin in Octavia E. Butler's *Kindred*.

Harry Blake. Boyhood friend of Tom Bailey; inveterate carver of his initials in Thomas Bailey Aldrich's *The Story of a Bad Boy*.

Mabel Blake. Widowed mother of Tony Blake; stabbed to death by Erskine Fowler in Richard Wright's *Savage Holiday*.

Macijah Blake. Citizen of New Economy; informs Preacher of Pearl and John Harper's presence in the town in Davis Grubb's *The Night of the Hunter*.

Mary (Molly) Blake. Daughter of Rachel Colbert Blake; survives a diphtheria epidemic in Willa Cather's *Sapphira and the Slave Girl*.

Michael Blake. United States congressman from Virginia; husband of Rachel Colbert Blake; dies of yellow fever during an epidemic in Willa Cather's *Sapphira and the Slave Girl*.

Mrs. Blake. Employment agency worker; advises Emma Lou Morgan to return to school and helps her find temporary work in Wallace Thurman's *The Blacker The Berry*.

Nathaniel (Nat) Blake. Orphaned street musician who is sent to Plumfield in Louisa May Alcott's *Little Men*.

Rachel Colbert Blake. Daughter of Sapphira and Henry Colbert; widow of Michael Blake; helps her mother's slave Nancy escape to Canada in Willa Cather's *Sapphira and the Slave Girl*.

Ron Blake. Teenaged beatnik and singer; admirer of Evelyn Pomeray and companion of Jack Duluoz during a retreat to a remote cabin in Jack Kerouac's *Big Sur*.

Tony Blake. Young son of Mabel Blake; accidentally falls from the balcony of his apartment after being frightened by the sudden appearance of Erskine Fowler in Richard Wright's *Savage Holiday*.

William Blake. English poet and illustrator who helps Thomas Paine flee from England after Paine's *The Rights of Man* creates a furor in Howard Fast's *Citizen Tom Paine*.

Captain Blakely. Presiding officer at the court-martial of Lieutenant Steve Maryk for mutiny in Herman Wouk's *The Caine Mutiny*.

Roger Blakesley. Rival of Charles Gray; loses the bank vice-presidency to Gray in John P. Marquand's *Point of No Return*.

Clinton W. Blalock. Friend who tries to get Lee Youngdahl a teaching position at Harvard in Mark Harris's *Wake Up, Stupid*.

Estel Blanc. Abyssinian mortician and an eccentric; first person Malcolm visits on his journey through life in James Purdy's *Malcolm*.

Augusta Blanchard. Young American painter who belongs to the artistic fraternity of Rome; fiancée of Mr. Leavenworth in Henry James's *Roderick Hudson*.

Rita Blanchard. Paramour of Walter Knight and one-time owner of a ranch coveted by Joe Templeton in Joan Didion's *Run River*.

Blanche. Prostitute with Jake Jackson when he is robbed by a pickpocket in Richard Wright's *Lawd Today*.

Bland. Master-at-arms who runs an alcohol-smuggling ring aboard the *Neversink* in Herman Melville's *White-Jacket*.

Gerald Bland. Harvard classmate of Quentin Compson I in William Faulkner's *The Sound and the Fury*.

Madame Sisseretta (Mrs. Sari Blandine) Blandish. Owner of a Harlem hair-straightening parlor; when the Black-No-More process makes all blacks white, she develops a process to stain white skin light brown in George S. Schuyler's *Black No More*.

Alexander Blaney. Homosexual killed accidentally by Los Angeles policeman Sam Niles in Joseph Wambaugh's *The Choirboys*.

Ethel Blaney. Teacher and sister of Elizabeth Blaney Morison in William Maxwell's *They Came Like Swallows*.

Jim Blankenship. Chief minister of the Pine Street Methodist Church; initiator of extravagant fund-raising schemes for building a large nonsectarian cathedral in T. S. Stribling's *Unfinished Cathedral*.

Doris Blankfurt. See Angela Black.

Deborah (Deb) Blau. Mentally ill teenaged Jewish heroine committed to a mental hospital in Hannah Green's *I Never Promised You a Rose Garden*.

Esther Blau. Distraught, yet strong mother of Deborah Blau; has to fight herself and her family to help her daughter by committing her to a mental hospital in Hannah Green's *I Never Promised You a Rose Garden*.

Jacob Blau. Accountant whose family emigrated from Poland; father of Deborah Blau; feels the pressures of guilt, failure, and love in Hannah Green's *I Never Promised You a Rose Garden*.

Susan (Suzy) Blau. Younger sister of Deborah Blau; has to live in the shadow of a sister who is not present in Hannah Green's *I Never Promised You a Rose Garden*.

A. Hebert Bledsoe. President of a southern black college who expels the narrator and sends him to New York in Ralph Ellison's *Invisible Man*.

Chris Bledsoe. Nephew of Lee Buck Cal; attracted to Louisa Sheridan, who feels herself falling in love with him; killed in a feud in Harriette Simpson Arnow's *Mountain Path*.

Bleecker. Host of the party at which George Kelcey gets drunk in Stephen Crane's *George's Mother*.

Queen Blenda. Mother of Charles Xavier, the last king of Zembla; erects a tasteless monument on the site of her husband's death in Vladimir Nabokov's *Pale Fire*.

Raymond (Ray) Blent. Star football player who purposely fails two courses to cover up his accepting a bribe to lose a game; boyfriend of Lily Sayre in Howard Nemerov's *The Homecoming Game*.

Shenandoah Blessing. Army lieutenant and friend of Sean O'Sullivan; heads police services in Rombaden in post-World War II Germany in Leon Uris's *Armageddon*.

Colonel Bletheram. Rakish octogenarian in Ellen Glasgow's *The Romantic Comedians*; also appears in *They Stooped to Folly*.

Deni Bleu. Seaman and friend of Jack Duluoz in New York in Jack Kerouac's *Visions of Cody*; also appears in *Book of Dreams* and *Desolation Angels*.

Captain Dominus Blicero. See Lieutenant Weissmann.

William Bligh. Captain of the HMS *Bounty* whose harsh treatment of his men leads them to rebel in Charles Nordhoff and James Norman Hall's *Mutiny on the Bounty*; set adrift with eighteen men in a small boat and brings all but one of them to safety in *Men against the Sea*.

Mr. Blimin. Member of the Communist party's Central Committee in New York; questions Lionel Lane about his true identity and political beliefs and about the murders of Langley Herndon, Gilbert Blount, and Jack Hilton in Richard Wright's *The Outsider*.

Blind Pig (Piggy-O). Blind, filthy drug deliverer and later drug dealer in Nelson Algren's *The Man with the Golden Arm*.

Mr. Blint. Member of the Ververs' social circle who is the object of Lady Castledean's romantic interest in Henry James's *The Golden Bowl*.

Betty Bliss. Plump, earnest graduate student of Russian; writes a paper on Dostoyevski for Professor Pnin in Vladimir Nabokov's *Pnin*.

Mattie Bliss. See Nina Carrington.

Mabel Blitch. See Mabel Blitch Lipscomb.

Blix. See Travis Bessemer.

Shifrah Puah Bloch. Polish concentration camp survivor and mother of Masha Tortshiner in Isaac Bashevis Singer's *Enemies, A Love Story*.

Doremus (Reme) Blodgett. Hosiery salesman who is the first of many people to be shocked by George Brush's unusual theories in Thornton Wilder's *Heaven's My Destination*.

Joseph Bloeckman (Black). Movie producer in F. Scott Fitzgerald's *The Beautiful and Damned*.

Hafen Blok. Hessian deserter and Indian fighter; heavy drinking, storytelling vagrant in John Pendleton Kennedy's *Swallow Barn*.

Dr. Jules Blomburg. First of John Wilder's psychiatrists; Wilder calls him a "dead-silent bullshit artist" in Richard Yates's *Disturbing the Peace*.

Moll (Mother Blonay) Blonay. Poor, elderly, potion-selling woman living in a hovel near Dorchester, South Carolina; assists her son Ned Blonay in betraying Major Singleton's partisan band to the British in William Gilmore Simms's *The Partisan*.

Ned (Goggle) Blonay. Son of Moll Blonay; betrays Major Singleton's partisan band to the British in William Gilmore Simms's *The Partisan*.

Lydia (Lily, Lurella, Lyddy) Blood. Niece of Maria Latham and the Erwins and granddaughter of Deacon Latham; becomes, on her trip to Venice, the "Lady of the Aroostook"; marries James Staniford in William Dean Howells's *The Lady of the Aroostook*.

Arlington Bloodworth, Sr.. Plantation and slave owner who adopts and rears Pourty Bloodworth in Leon Forrest's *The Bloodworth Orphans*.

Arlington Bloodworth III. Father, by Rachel Rebecca Carpenter Flowers, of Industrious Bowman and Carl-Rae Bowman in Leon Forrest's *The Bloodworth Orphans*.

Pourty Ford Worthy Bloodworth y Bloodworth. Foundling reared by Arlington Bloodworth, Sr.; father of LaDonna Scales, Regal Pettibone, Amos-Otis Thigpen, Noah Grandberry, and Jonathan Bass; kills his foster father in Leon Forrest's *The Bloodworth Orphans*.

Isaac Nathan Bloom. Army private who boxes for the regimental team; commits suicide after being implicated in a military investigation of homosexual activity in James Jones's *From Here to Eternity*.

Anatole Bloomberg. Tackle for the Logos College football team and philosophizing roommate of Gary Harkness in Don DeLillo's *End Zone*.

Harold Bloomguard. Los Angeles policeman and organizer of off-duty "meetings" in MacArthur Park; one of ten protagonists in Joseph Wambaugh's *The Choirboys*.

Angus Blount. Young scamp who jilts Annabel Upchurch in Ellen Glasgow's *The Romantic Comedians*.

Eva Blount. Artist married to Gilbert Blount; becomes involved in an affair with Lionel Lane after Blount's death; commits suicide by jumping from a window of an apartment building in Richard Wright's *The Outsider*.

Gilbert (Gil) Blount. Communist party official married to Eva Blount; attempts to recruit Lionel Lane; murdered by Lane in Langley Herndon's apartment in Richard Wright's *The Outsider*.

Jake Blount. Itinerant labor organizer who confides his dreams to the deaf-mute John Singer in Carson McCullers's *The Heart Is a Lonely Hunter*.

Blue. Self-appointed mayor and chronicler of Hard Times; marries Molly Riordan and cares for Jimmy Fee; ambushes and mortally wounds Clay Turner; narrator of E. L. Doctorow's *Welcome to Hard Times*.

Billy Blue. Gangster who attempts to assassinate Legs Diamond and is eventually killed by Diamond in William Kennedy's *Legs*.

Walden Blue. Tenor saxophonist in John Clellon Holmes's *The Horn*.

Blue Back. Old Oneida Indian and friend of Gil Martin in Walter D. Edmonds's *Drums along the Mohawk*.

Blue Billie. Childhood foe and later ally of Jimmie Johnson in Stephen Crane's *Maggie: A Girl of the Streets*; hoodlum whose impending fight with George Kelcey is interrupted by news of Kelcey's mother's illness in *George's Mother*.

Blue Fairy Godmother. See Frank Wirtanen.

Blue Juice. Pimp who assaults Jake Jackson after Jackson accuses the prostitute Blanche of picking his pocket in Richard Wright's *Lawd Today*.

Julian Blumberg. Weak, struggling novelist and screenwriter who unwittingly becomes a ghostwriter for Sammy Glick in Budd Schulberg's *What Makes Sammy Run?*

Monroe Blumenfeld. First child to have his Bar Mitzvah in the temple David Dehn builds; announces at his Bar Mitzvah that as an adult he will live in Israel in Jerome Weidman's *The Temple*.

Jack Blunt. Irish cockney sailor aboard the *Highlander* who uses hair darkener and tries to interpret his dreams in Herman Melville's *Redburn*.

Gilly (Prince) Bluton. Sensuous, hedonistic, aggressive mulatto who attempts to seduce Lissa Atkinson; employee of and informer for Proctor Baggart; murdered by Hagar in DuBose Heyward's *Mamba's Daughters*.

Terrence (Terry) Bluvard. Writer and wealthy white lesbian lover of Renay Davis in Ann Allen Shockley's *Loving Her*.

Cornelia Bly. Abstract artist and mistress of Augie Poole; bears a child by Poole that Poole unwittingly adopts in Peter De Vries's *The Tunnel of Love*.

Major Boam. Frequent visitor to the Wandrous home; his pedophiliac behavior traumatizes Gloria Wandrous in John O'Hara's *Butterfield 8*.

Milly Boardman. Teenaged daughter of Quincy Boardman and student at a Massachusetts boarding school in Albert Halper's *Union Square*.

Quincy (Boardie) Boardman. Widower father of Milly Boardman; executive who lives, with his mistress Margie, in the Glen Cove Apartments in Albert Halper's *Union Square*.

Boaz. Martian army sergeant in Kurt Vonnegut's *The Sirens of Titan*.

Moses Lincoln Boatwright. Black, Harvard-educated philosopher who murdered and cannibalized his victim; interviewed in prison by Max Reddick in John A. Williams's *The Man Who Cried I Am.*

Bob. Husband of Constance Marlow, obsessive reader of the *Greek Anthology*, and "minor-league" sadist; the Logan brothers mistake Bob and Constance for bowling trophy thieves and shoot both in Richard Brautigan's *Willard and His Bowling Trophies.*

Captain Bob. Tahitian jailer and linguist in Herman Melville's *Omoo.*

Bobbie. Homosexual friend of Alva in Wallace Thurman's *The Blacker the Berry.*

Helen Bober. Twenty-three-year-old daughter of Morris and Ida Bober; pursued by Frank Alpine in Bernard Malamud's *The Assistant.*

Ida Bober. Wife of Morris Bober in Bernard Malamud's *The Assistant.*

Morris Bober. Jewish storekeeper in Bernard Malamud's *The Assistant.*

Bobochka. Soviet Writers' Union official in charge of Henry Bech's itinerary in Russia in John Updike's *Bech: A Book.*

Billy Bocksfuss. See George Giles.

Junior (Speedy, Speedy-Boy) Bodden. Tough and determined crew member of the *Lillias Eden* and only survivor of its wrecking in Peter Matthiessen's *Far Tortuga.*

Gabriella Bodeen. Glamorous actress with whom Lee Youngdahl believes himself in love in Mark Harris's *Wake Up, Stupid.*

Bodger. Dean of students at Steering School and friend of Jennie Fields and Garp in John Irving's *The World According to Garp.*

Bodien. Disbarred plumber employed by Norman Moonbloom in Edward Lewis Wallant's *The Tenants of Moonbloom.*

Pig Bodine. Former shipmate of Benny Profane; involved with the Whole Sick Crew in Thomas Pynchon's *V.*; possibly Seaman Bodine in *Gravity's Rainbow.*

Seaman Bodine. AWOL seaman who befriends Tyrone Slothrop and Roger Mexico in Thomas Pynchon's *Gravity's Rainbow*; possibly Pig Bodine in *V.*

William Yancey Bodine. Organizer of a secret association to advance Americanism and to persecute Jews, blacks, and Catholics in T. S. Stribling's *Unfinished Cathedral.*

William S. (Willie) Body (Bloodworth). Lover of Lavinia Masterson and father, by his half sister Carrie Trout, of Abraham Dolphin in Leon Forrest's *The Bloodworth Orphans.*

Léry Bogard. Scholar who accompanies Samuele to the Villa Horace for a weekend visit as the guest of Marie-Astrée-Luce de Morfontaine in Thornton Wilder's *The Cabala.*

Jack (Jackie, Jacques) Bogardes. Wealthy but neurotic journalist who lives with his mother on Park Avenue; friend of Eric Eisner and lover of Marie Curtin in Phillip Lopate's *Confessions of Summer.*

Peter Bogardus. Orderly in a Chicago hospital where Roger Ashley works briefly; the first to expose Ashley to the concept of reincarnation in Thornton Wilder's *The Eighth Day.*

Dr. Dominie Bogart. Clergyman and longtime friend of Aaron Burr; officiates at Burr's marriage to Eliza Bowen Jumel in Gore Vidal's *Burr.*

Marin Bogart. Daughter of Charlotte Douglas and Warren Bogart; runs off with leftist revolutionaries in Joan Didion's *A Book of Common Prayer.*

Mrs. Bogart. Strict Baptist and neighbor of the Kennicotts in Sinclair Lewis's *Main Street.*

Warren Bogart. Wandering ne'er-do-well; first husband of Charlotte Douglas and later her lover; father of Marin Bogart in Joan Didion's *A Book of Common Prayer.*

Harry (Heshalle, Heshie) Bogen. Women's garment manufacturer who steals from his own firm, Apex Modes, and makes his partner, Meyer Babushkin, take the blame and go to jail; narrator of Jerome Weidman's *I Can Get It for You Wholesale*; enters into partnership with and steals from Hrant Yazdabian; has his own money stolen by Martha Mills, his girlfriend; narrator of *What's in It for Me?*

Mrs. Bogen. Mother of Harry Bogen in Jerome Weidman's *I Can Get It for You Wholesale*; becomes ill and dies while Harry is trying to escape to Europe in *What's in It for Me?*

George Bogger. Epileptic who lives with his parents and works as a roadman with the highway department; dies during a seizure while hunting frogs in Mark Steadman's *A Lion's Share.*

Elizaveta Innokentievna Bogolepov. See Dr. Elizaveta Innokentievna Bogolepov Pnin Wind.

Bohack. Leader of Happy Valley Commune in Don DeLillo's *Great Jones Street.*

Lotte Böhm. Lover of Igor Karlovy in Leon Uris's *Armageddon*.

Harry Bohn. Friend of Luke Lampson; born of his dead mother's body; helps to bury Hattie Lampson in John Hawkes's *The Beetle Leg*.

Boise (Boy). Cat that is Thomas Hudson's companion in Ernest Hemingway's *Islands in the Stream*.

Yakov Shepsovitch (Yakov Ivanovitch Dologushev) Bok. Jewish handyman arrested for the murder of a young boy and sent to prison in Bernard Malamud's *The Fixer*.

Miss Boke. Fat and friendly newcomer whose monopolization of William Baxter at Miss Lola Pratt's going-away party almost induces him to commit mayhem in Booth Tarkington's *Seventeen*.

Bokonon. See Lionel Boyd Johnson.

Paul (Kid Faro, Scot, Scotch, Scotcho, Scotty) Boldieu. Baseball pitcher and boyhood friend of Jack Duluoz in Jack Kerouac's *Doctor Sax*, *Maggie Cassidy*, and *Book of Dreams*.

Joe Boleo. Skilled woodsman and courier for the American forces in the Mohawk Valley; instrumental in saving Gil Martin's family from destruction in Walter D. Edmonds's *Drums along the Mohawk*.

Lester Bolin. Scientist who assists Robert Softly in developing a cosmic language based on mathematical principles in Don DeLillo's *Ratner's Star*.

Dr. Bolling. Romantic and restless father of Binx Bolling; joins the R.C.A.F. and dies during World War II in Walker Percy's *The Moviegoer*.

Emily Bolling. See Emily Bolling Cutrer.

John Bickerson (Binx, Jack) Bolling. New Orleans stockbroker and film buff who pursues money, women, and God; narrator of Walker Percy's *The Moviegoer*.

Kate Cutrer Bolling. See Kate Cutrer.

Brother Bolo. Priest who smuggles religious artifacts out of Castiglione; friend of Dolce, with whom he made a hair shirt out of rat skins for Arsella's mother, in John Hawkes's *The Goose on the Grave*.

Cameron Bolt. Husband of Francesca Fox Bolt; district attorney seeking election as Attorney General of California in Gail Godwin's *Glass People*.

Carl Bolt. Adoptive father of Molly Bolt in Rita Mae Brown's *Rubyfruit Jungle*.

Carrie Bolt. Adoptive mother of Molly Bolt in Rita Mae Brown's *Rubyfruit Jungle*.

Francesca Fox Bolt. Wife of Cameron Bolt and, briefly, seeker of her own identity in Gail Godwin's *Glass People*.

Molly (Moll) Bolt. Illegitimate child, adopted daughter of Carl and Carrie Bolt, lesbian heroine, and narrator of Rita Mae Brown's *Rubyfruit Jungle*.

Rachel Bolt. Confidante and New York guide of Hagar Ashendyne; recovers from her husband's abuse in Mary Johnston's *Hagar*.

Chick Bolton. Black racketeer obsessed with hatred for all whites; counterpart of Hank Dean in Julian Mayfield's *The Grand Parade*.

Harry (Bury) Bolton. Mysterious friend of Redburn; crushed to death between a whale and a ship in Herman Melville's *Redburn*.

Oliver Bolton. Farmer and caretaker of the Kilburn estate in William Dean Howells's *Annie Kilburn*.

Pauliny Bolton. Wife of Oliver Bolton and proud housekeeper of the Kilburns in William Dean Howells's *Annie Kilburn*.

Ruth Bolton. Philadelphia Quaker; medical student and girlfriend of Philip Sterling in Samuel Langhorne Clemens and Charles Dudley Warner's *The Gilded Age*.

Bella-Lenore Boltwood. Associate of Nathaniel Turner Witherspoon and lover of fairy tales in Leon Forrest's *The Bloodworth Orphans*.

Bombie of the Frizzled Head (Snow Ball). Witch-like black servant of Heer Peter Piper in James Kirke Paulding's *Koningsmarke*.

Charles Bon. Probably the son of Thomas Sutpen and his first wife, Eulalia Bon; engaged to his probable half sister Judith Sutpen in William Faulkner's *Absalom, Absalom!*

Charles Etienne Saint-Valery Bon. Son of Charles Bon and his octoroon mistress; father of Jim Bond in William Faulkner's *Absalom, Absalom!*

Eulalia Bon. See Eulalia Bon Sutpen.

Angela (Angie) Bonali. Daughter of Vince Bonali; necks in a car during a high school basketball game while the mine accident occurs in Robert Coover's *The Origin of the Brunists*.

Charlie Bonali. Disaffected wastrel son of Vince Bonali; goes AWOL from the marines in Robert Coover's *The Origin of the Brunists*.

Etta Bonali. Fat, long-suffering wife of Vince Bonali in Robert Coover's *The Origin of the Brunists*.

Vince Bonali. Supervisor at the Deepwater Mine who becomes involved in efforts to stop the Brunist cult in Robert Coover's *The Origin of the Brunists*.

Napoleon Bonaparte. French dictator who seeks Thomas Paine's support to add legitimacy to his regime in Howard Fast's *Citizen Tom Paine*.

Napoleon Bonaparte. French ruler and lover of Angela Guessippi in Hervey Allen's *Anthony Adverse*.

Sidney Bonbon. Cajun plantation overseer who kills Marcus Payne in Ernest J. Gaines's *Of Love and Dust*.

Louise Bonbon. Childish wife of Sidney Bonbon; ignored by her husband, she becomes romantically involved with Marcus Payne in Ernest J. Gaines's *Of Love and Dust*.

Remi Boncoeur. Prep school friend of Sal Paradise; works as a barracks guard in Jack Kerouac's *On the Road*.

Hamish (Old Man Bond, 'Sieur 'Amsh, Alec Hinks, Captain Strike-down-then-make-the-Palaver) Bond. Slave runner turned New Orleans plantation owner who buys the mulatto Amantha Starr and takes her as a mistress; hangs himself while a captive of Rau-Ru and black rioters in 1866 in Robert Penn Warren's *Band of Angels*.

Jim Bond. Idiot son of Charles Etienne Saint-Valery Bon and a black woman in William Faulkner's *Absalom, Absalom!*

Aldo Bonello. Italian ambulance driver in the command of Frederic Henry during the retreat from Caporetto; wanders off with the hope of being taken prisoner by the Germans in Ernest Hemingway's *A Farewell to Arms*.

Blanche Lebanon Timberlane Boneyard. First wife of Cass Timberlane in Sinclair Lewis's *Cass Timberlane*.

Ann Chapin Bongiorno. See Ann Chapin.

Charley Bongiorno. Jazz saxophonist and Ann Chapin's first husband in John O'Hara's *Ten North Frederick*.

Al Bonham. Expert skin diver and small businessman in Ganado Bay, Jamaica; teaches Ron Grant to skin-dive in James Jones's *Go to the Widow-Maker*.

Joe Bonham. American soldier who suffers nearly complete physical incapacitation as the result of wounds received in World War I; his dreams and reminiscences comprise Dalton Trumbo's *Johnny Got His Gun*.

Letta Bonham. Jamaican schoolteacher and wife of Al Bonham; divorces Bonham and moves to Kingston in James Jones's *Go to the Widow-Maker*.

Bonkers (Bonkie). Newfoundland retriever who bites off part of Garp's left ear; Garp bites off one of Bonkers's ears in John Irving's *The World According to Garp*.

Benny Bonner. Psychology student and older maternal cousin who practices analysis on Joe Sandwich in Peter De Vries's *The Vale of Laughter*.

Dolly Bonner. Mistress of Milton Loftis in William Styron's *Lie Down in Darkness*.

Nicholas de Bonneville. French newspaper editor who helps shelter Thomas Paine in Paris and who later sends his family to Paine in America during the Napoleonic regime in Howard Fast's *Citizen Tom Paine*.

John Bonnyfeather. Prominent Leghorn merchant; maternal grandfather of Anthony Adverse, whom he gives a surname and educates, in Hervey Allen's *Anthony Adverse*.

Maria (Marquise da Vincitata) Bonnyfeather. Mother, by Denis Moore, of Anthony Adverse in Hervey Allen's *Anthony Adverse*.

Booker. Middle-aged pool hall owner who allows his customers—mostly corner boys—to play dice in the back room in Herbert Simmons's *Corner Boy*.

Knobby Booker. Informer for Bumper Morgan against Timothy Landry in Joseph Wambaugh's *The Blue Knight*.

Calvin (Uncle Cal) Bookwright. Bootlegger in William Faulkner's *The Town*, *The Mansion*, and *The Reivers*.

Odum Bookwright. Wealthy farmer and one of the buyers of Old Frenchman's Place; appears in William Faulkner's *The Hamlet* and *The Mansion*.

Father Boomer. Nondescript priest who baptizes the dying Jamie Vaught in Walker Percy's *The Last Gentleman*.

Daniel Boone. Frontiersman who marries Diony Hall Jarvis and Evan Muir in Elizabeth Madox Roberts's *The Great Meadow*.

Borabolla. Fat king of Mondoldo in Herman Melville's *Mardi*.

Dolly von Borg. Granddaughter of Russian friends of Vadim Vadimovich, the object of a childhood crush and later her lover, in Vladimir Nabokov's *Look at the Harlequins!*

Paul R. Borg. Self-satisfied lawyer and friend of John and Janice Wilder in Richard Yates's *Disturbing the Peace.*

Isabelle Borgé. First love of Amory Blaine while he is at Princeton in F. Scott Fitzgerald's *This Side of Paradise.*

Katje (Domina Nocturna) Borgesius. Agent of Dutch descent with no fixed allegiance; involved in various sexual liaisons with Lieutenant Weissmann, Tyrone Slothrop, Gottfried, Pirate Prentice, and Brigadier Ernest Pudding in Thomas Pynchon's *Gravity's Rainbow.*

Boris. "Weather prophet" living with Henry Miller at the Villa Borghese in Henry Miller's *Tropic of Cancer.*

Thaddeus (Ned) Bork. Effeminate assistant minister to Thomas Marshfield; sleeps with Alicia Crick; professes liberal political and social ideas in John Updike's *A Month of Sundays.*

Boronai. Leader of the tribe of Niaruna Indians into which Lewis Moon comes as a spirit leader in Peter Matthiessen's *At Play in the Fields of the Lord.*

Borowski. Accordion-playing friend of Henry Miller; gives Miller lunch on Wednesdays in Henry Miller's *Tropic of Cancer.*

Sergeant Leonard Borth. Fearless M.P. in charge of security during the allied occupation of Adano in John Hersey's *A Bell for Adano.*

Emory Bortz. Professor of English and editor of the Lectern Press edition of Richard Wharfinger's *The Courier's Tragedy* in Thomas Pynchon's *The Crying of Lot 49.*

Dr. Bosco. Boston surgeon who becomes so fascinated with the hints that Theophilus North effects cures with his hands that he urges North to become associated with Bosco's medical practice in Thornton Wilder's *Theophilus North.*

James Boswell. Professional strongman and collector of great men; yearns for immortality and authors a diary in Stanley Elkin's *Boswell.*

Margaret Boswell. See Principessa Margaret dei Medici.

Catharine Bosworth. See Catharine Bosworth Apley.

Dr. James McHenry Bosworth. Former diplomat and author of several books on American architecture; elderly resident of Newport who is a virtual captive in his home because of incontinence, a problem Theophilus North helps alleviate, in Thornton Wilder's *Theophilus North.*

Sarah Bosworth. Daughter of Dr. James Bosworth; because she dislikes Theophilus North, she seeks to hinder his efforts to aid her father in Thornton Wilder's *Theophilus North.*

Jacob (Jake) Botcher. Behind-the-scenes political manipulator and dispenser of bribes in Winston Churchill's *Mr. Crewe's Career.*

Doctor Botot. Wealthy widower and physician who cares for the residents of St. Médard parish in Grace King's *The Pleasant Ways of St. Médard.*

Loretta Botsford. See Loretta Botsford Wendall.

Happy Bottom. Buxom nurse, letter writer extraordinaire, and bedmate of Justin Miller in Robert Coover's *The Origin of the Brunists.*

Pierre Bouc. See Piotr.

Sulie Boudrault. Longtime servant in the Peck household; widow of a ragtime pianist in Anne Tyler's *Searching for Caleb.*

Hal Boudreau. Hired hand and tenant on the Sherbrooke estate; drunkard and possible lover of Maggie Sherbrooke in Nicholas Delbanco's *Sherbrookes.*

Angelina (Nanane) Bouie. Aged godmother of the Reverend Phillip Martin in Ernest J. Gaines's *In My Father's House.*

Michelle Bouilloux. Longtime secret lover of Harry Ames entrusted to deliver his message from beyond the grave to Max Reddick in John A. Williams's *The Man Who Cried I Am.*

Boukman. Ugly, menacing black leader of a group of rebel slaves in Arna Wendell Bontemps's *Drums at Dusk.*

Raoul de Bourggraff. Masterful art department head at Olympia Studios in Ludwig Bemelmans's *Dirty Eddie.*

Garan Bourke. New York lawyer who rescues his lover Patience Sparhawk from execution for murder in Gertrude Atherton's *Patience Sparhawk and Her Times.*

Dolly Boutts. Flirt interested in John Gwynne; rival of Isabel Otis in Gertrude Atherton's *Ancestors.*

Matt Bowden. Opportunist who pursues Major Grumby in William Faulkner's *The Unvanquished*.

Charles Bowen. Elderly friend of Laura Fairford; philosophizes about the male passion for money-making that relegates women to the periphery of men's lives in Edith Wharton's *The Custom of the Country*.

Effie Bowen. Daughter of Evalina Bowen and admirer of Theodore Colville in William Dean Howells's *Indian Summer*.

Evalina Ridgely (Lina) Bowen. Widow who marries her friend Theodore Colville; mother of Effie Bowen and temporary guardian of Imogene Graham in William Dean Howells's *Indian Summer*.

Jack Bowen. Brother of Marie Ann Bowen and friend of Steve Benson from summers in Maryland in Ed Bullins's *The Reluctant Rapist*.

Lora Bowen. See Lora Bowen Nolan.

Marie Ann Bowen. Sister of Jack Bowen and girlfriend of Dandy Benson in Ed Bullins's *The Reluctant Rapist*.

Frederika Bowers. Chief mistress of Prince Cabano; helps her rival Estella Washington escape from Cabano in Ignatius Donnelly's *Caesar's Column*.

James (Jim) Bowers. Employee at a funeral home owned by Tyree Tucker; proposes marriage to Emma Tucker after Tyree Tucker's death in Richard Wright's *The Long Dream*.

Madison Bowers. Fashionable but excellent Chicago voice teacher with whom Thea Kronborg studies in Willa Cather's *The Song of the Lark*.

Florence Cochran (Mrs. Ralph) Bowlsby. Divorcée and friend of Garp; teaches English at a university where she has affairs with senior faculty members in John Irving's *The World According to Garp*.

Carl-Rae Bowman. Son of Arlington Bloodworth III and Rachel Rebecca Carpenter Flowers; brother of Industrious Bowman in Leon Forrest's *The Bloodworth Orphans*.

Industrious Bowman. Son of Arlington Bloodworth III and Rachel Rebecca Carpenter Flowers; brother of Carl-Rae Bowman; associate of Nathaniel Turner Witherspoon in Leon Forrest's *The Bloodworth Orphans*.

Deighton Boyce. Free-spirited father of Selina Boyce; commits suicide within sight of the coast of Barbados after trying to find himself in New York in Paule Marshall's *Brown Girl, Brownstones*.

Ina Boyce. Sister of Selina Boyce; quiet, soft-spoken young woman who is devoted to her church; settles into an uneventful life and a dull marriage in Paule Marshall's *Brown Girl, Brownstones*.

Selina (Deighton Selina) Boyce. Daughter of Silla and Deighton Boyce and sister of Ina Boyce; unsettled heroine who returns to the Caribbean after becoming disillusioned with America in Paule Marshall's *Brown Girl, Brownstones*.

Silla (Silla-gal) Boyce. Wife of Deighton Boyce and mother of Selina and Ina Boyce; driven woman determined to control the lives of those in her family in Paule Marshall's *Brown Girl, Brownstones*.

Beverly (Bev) Boyd. Homosexual college instructor rejected by Peter Gale in Louis Adamic's *Grandsons*.

Gordon Boyd. "Wild" boyhood friend of Walter McKee; writer and self-proclaimed failure in Wright Morris's *The Field of Vision* and *Ceremony in Lone Tree*.

Mrs. Boyd. See Daughter.

J. Boyer. Accomplished clergyman attracted to Eliza Wharton in Hannah Webster Foster's *The Coquette*.

Miss Tee (Auntee) Boykin. Loving presence and mother of Scooter in Albert Murray's *Train Whistle Guitar*.

Orren Boyle. Failing industrialist who seeks government protection against free market competition in Ayn Rand's *Atlas Shrugged*.

Walter (Walter Arlis Benson) Boyle. Salesman, sometimes sanctimonious, sometimes involved in petty crimes; lives separate lives under different names in John Gardner's *The Sunlight Dialogues*.

Jim Boynton. Friend who encourages Clyde Stout to stop letting people take advantage of him; owns a 1963 Corvette in Jack Matthews's *Hanger Stout, Awake!*

Eloisa Brace. Resident at the fourth address to which Mr. Cox sends Malcolm; painter who often invites musicians to her house in James Purdy's *Malcolm*.

Jerome Brace. Ex-convict and husband of Eloisa Brace; because he sees Malcolm as "the spirit of life," begs Malcolm for his friendship in James Purdy's *Malcolm*.

Sarah Bracknell. See Sarah Bracknell Hazlett.

Nelson Goodfellow (Big Nellie) Bradbury. American journalist who first reports the Berlin airlift in Leon Uris's *Armageddon*.

Henry Bradford. Saloon owner who nearly beats Adolph Myers to death because Myers supposedly molested Bradford's son in Sherwood Anderson's *Winesburg, Ohio*.

Bradish. New York artist friend and studio mate of Richard Dale in Sarah Orne Jewett's *A Marsh Island*.

Ardis Bradley. Wife of Tuck Bradley in Joan Didion's *A Book of Common Prayer*.

Austin Bradley. Owner of Happy's Café, following Tadpole McCormick's ownership of it, in Gayl Jones's *Corregidora*.

Jessie Bradley. First wife of George Ogden; her spending ruins Ogden financially in Henry Blake Fuller's *The Cliff-Dwellers*.

Peck Bradley. Poor-white hill man who is lynched for murdering Tug Beavers in T. S. Stribling's *Teeftallow*.

Thorne Bradley. Friend of Forrest Mayfield; refuses to continue their friendship after Forrest elopes in Reynolds Price's *The Surface of Earth*.

Tuck Bradley. American ambassador to Boca Grande in Joan Didion's *A Book of Common Prayer*.

Colonel Bradly. Member of the expedition against the wild boys; later joins them and shoots a movie of them in William S. Burroughs's *The Wild Boys*.

Brady. Irish schoolmaster who cares for Morton Goodwin and Kike Lumsden; marries Lumsden's mother in Edward Eggleston's *The Circuit Rider*.

Cecilia Brady. Daughter of Pat Brady; her love for Monroe Stahr is unrequited; narrator of F. Scott Fitzgerald's *The Last Tycoon*.

Pat Brady. Father of Cecilia Brady and treacherous partner of Monroe Stahr in F. Scott Fitzgerald's *The Last Tycoon*.

Will Jennings Brady. Unsuccessful entrepreneur, hotel lobby dweller; dies while dressed for the role of Santa Claus in Wright Morris's *The Works of Love*.

Willy Brady, Jr.. Son of Mickey Ahearn "adopted" by Will Brady in Wright Morris's *The Works of Love*.

Clinton Bragg. Early suitor and second husband of Mateel Shepherd, whose first husband, Jo Erring, kills him in E. W. Howe's *The Story of a Country Town*.

Braid-Beard. See Mohi.

Abbie Brainard. Daughter of Abigail and Erastus Brainard; second wife of George Ogden in Henry Blake Fuller's *The Cliff-Dwellers*.

Abigail Brainard. Wife of Erastus Brainard and mother of Abbie, Burton, and Marcus Brainard in Henry Blake Fuller's *The Cliff-Dwellers*.

Burton Tillinghast (Burt) Brainard. Son of Abigail and Erastus Brainard and vice president of his father's bank; his financial schemes drive the family into poverty in Henry Blake Fuller's *The Cliff-Dwellers*.

Cornelia McNabb Tillinghast (Nealie) Brainard. Waitress and then stenographer in the Clifton; wife of Burt Brainard in Henry Blake Fuller's *The Cliff-Dwellers*.

Erastus M. Brainard. Husband of Abigail Brainard and father of Abbie, Burton, and Marcus Brainard; president of the Underground National Bank; killed by his son Marcus in Henry Blake Fuller's *The Cliff-Dwellers*.

Marcus Brainard. Son of Abigail and Erastus Brainard; frustrated artist who kills his father, strangles his brother, Burt, and commits suicide in Henry Blake Fuller's *The Cliff-Dwellers*.

Marigold Shoemaker Brainerd. Philadelphian living in Paris; rival of Aileen Cowperwood for the affections of Bruce Tollifer in Theodore Dreiser's *The Stoic*.

Cecil Otis Braithwaite. Black lawyer, janitor, and hairdresser who travels to Europe and Africa before returning to his wife in John Edgar Wideman's *Hurry Home*.

Esther Brown Braithwaite. Wife of Cecil Braithwaite, whom she supports through law school, only to have him desert her, in John Edgar Wideman's *Hurry Home*.

Simon Braithwaite. Stillborn son of Esther Brown and Cecil Braithwaite in John Edgar Wideman's *Hurry Home*.

Della Brame. Young black woman whose several sexual encounters with Buck Russell may have produced her son in Reynolds Price's *A Generous Man*.

Kate Helen Branch. Mother of Burley Coulter's bastard son in Wendell Berry's *Nathan Coulter*.

Battle John Brand. Hellfire and brimstone revival preacher in Harriette Arnow's *Hunter's Horn* and *The Dollmaker*.

Bobby Brand. Vietnam veteran and former junkie who accompanies David Bell and friends on a trip west to make a documentary film in Don DeLillo's

Americana.

Charlotte Wentworth Brand. See Charlotte Wentworth.

Dinah Brand. Golddigger who provides information and companionship to the Op in Dashiell Hammett's *Red Harvest.*

Mr. Brand. Unitarian minister who courts Gertrude Wentworth but who ultimately marries Charlotte Wentworth in Henry James's *The Europeans.*

Alexander (Alex) Brandel. Father of Wolf Brandel and friend of Andrei Androfski; historian of the Warsaw ghetto and leader of the Bathyran Zionist Executive Council; scholar and pacifist turned activist; diarist/journalist in Leon Uris's *Mila 18.*

Wolf Brandel. Son of Alexander Brandel and lover of Rachel Bronski; leads survivors from the Warsaw ghetto in Leon Uris's *Mila 18.*

George Sylvester Brander. Ohio senator who dies before he can marry his lover Jennie Gerhardt in Theodore Dreiser's *Jennie Gerhardt.*

Mark Brandler. California Superior Court judge who presides at the first trial of Gregory Powell and Jimmy Smith in Joseph Wambaugh's *The Onion Field.*

Cousin Annie Brandon. See Annie Brandon O'Neill.

Backwater Brandon. Tidewater gentleman living in Fluvanna County; never adapts to frontier ways and so is always at odds with his neighbors in Mary Lee Settle's *O Beulah Land.*

Constancia Brown (Constance, Lady Macbeth, Mrs. Shakespeare) Brandon. Garrulous, pretentious hostess of a salon in Harlem's Striver's Row; satirized, along with an outrageous assortment of her guests, in Countee Cullen's *One Way to Heaven.*

Dr. George Brandon. Husband of Constancia Brandon in Countee Cullen's *One Way to Heaven.*

Gregory Brandon. Sir Walter Ralegh's executioner in George Garrett's *Death of the Fox.*

Oliver Brandon. Black companion and employee of William Howland; helps Abigail Tolliver fight a mob and save the Howland home in Shirley Ann Grau's *The Keepers of the House.*

Stuart Brandon. Wastrel brother of Mamie Brandon Catlett and father of Annie Brandon O'Neill in Mary Lee Settle's *Know Nothing.*

Percy Brandreth. Petitioner for Mrs. Munger; male lead in *Romeo and Juliet* in William Dean Howells's *Annie Kilburn.*

Mrs. Homer Branney. See Mabel Blitch Lipscomb.

Bob Brannom. Corrupt district attorney who is killed by Dix Handley in William Riley Burnett's *The Asphalt Jungle.*

Alice Brannon. Little-mourned wife of Biff Brannon; dies following surgery in Carson McCullers's *The Heart Is a Lonely Hunter.*

Bartholomew (Biff) Brannon. Methodical and observant café owner who is fond of freaks; husband of Alice Brannon in Carson McCullers's *The Heart Is a Lonely Hunter.*

Bras-Coupé. Former African prince; tortured and dies following an attempted escape from slavery in George Washington Cable's *The Grandissimes.*

Etta Brashear. Cincinnati working woman who befriends Susan Lenox; marries a rich brewer in order to avoid a life of poverty and prostitution in David Graham Phillips's *Susan Lenox.*

Luca Brasi. Close friend of Don Corleone; killed by rival gangsters in Mario Puzo's *The Godfather.*

Shah of Bratpuhr. Religious leader of the Kalhouri sect who visits the United States in Kurt Vonnegut's *Player Piano.*

Carlton Braun. See Carl Brown.

Inez Braverman. Widow of Leslie Braverman in Wallace Markfield's *To an Early Grave.*

Leslie Braverman. Deceased writer who is the subject of recollections by several of his friends in Wallace Markfield's *To an Early Grave.*

Richard Braxley. Lawyer for Major Roland Forrester; tries to cheat Edith Forrester of her inheritance in Robert Montgomery Bird's *Nick of the Woods.*

Braxton. Unemployed gambler and hustler; shares an apartment with Alva in Wallace Thurman's *The Blacker The Berry.*

Harold (Harry) Bray. Protean figure; the false Grand Tutor whom George Giles drives out of the college in John Barth's *Giles Goat-Boy.*

Catherine Bread. Servant of the de Bellegardes; reveals to Christopher Newman that Emmeline and Urbain de Bellegarde killed Urbain's father in Henry James's *The American.*

Gabriel (Gabe) Breaux. Drinker and gambler who courts and marries Amy in Katherine Anne Porter's *Old Mortality.*

Gavin Breckbridge. Fiancé of Drusilla Hawk; killed at Shiloh in William Faulkner's *The Unvanquished*.

Myra (Myron) Breckinridge. Female transsexual, born Myron Breckinridge, seeking to destroy traditional sex roles; anally rapes Rusty Godowsky and tries to seduce Mary-Ann Pringle; reverts to her original sex and marries Pringle in Gore Vidal's *Myra Breckinridge*.

Edmonia Honeywell Bredalbane. Liberated, promiscuous, oft-married twin sister of Judge Gamaliel Bland Honeywell in Ellen Glasgow's *The Romantic Comedians*.

Ralph Bredalbane. Young and poor fourth husband of Edmonia Bredalbane, on whose money he lives, in Ellen Glasgow's *The Romantic Comedians*.

Nathan Brederhagan. Profligate rake who stabs Christina Jansen during an attempted rape in Ignatius Donnelly's *Caesar's Column*.

Baroness Bredow (née Tolstoy). Extraordinary aunt of Vadim Vadimovich who exhorted him as a child to quit moping and use his imagination to invent reality by looking at the harlequins in Vladimir Nabokov's *Look at the Harlequins!*

Cholly Breedlove. Alcoholic husband of Pauline Breedlove; rapes his eleven-year-old daughter Pecola in Toni Morrison's *The Bluest Eye*.

Hallie Breedlove. Mulatto prostitute with a fierce sense of independence in Nelson Algren's *A Walk on the Wild Side*.

Monica Breedlove. Neighbor and friend of Christine Penmark; senses fear and worry in Christine, but is oblivious to the evil in Rhoda Penmark, in William March's *The Bad Seed*.

Pauline Williams (Polly) Breedlove. Wife of Cholly Breedlove and mother of Pecola and Sammy Breedlove; works as a maid in Toni Morrison's *The Bluest Eye*.

Pecola Breedlove. Daughter of Pauline and Cholly Breedlove who is raped and impregnated by her father; desires blue eyes in Toni Morrison's *The Bluest Eye*.

Sammy Breedlove. Son of Cholly and Pauline Breedlove and brother of Pecola Breedlove in Toni Morrison's *The Bluest Eye*.

Yancey Breedlove. Young deputy who is second-in-command of the hunt for Rato Mustian, the dog, and the snake in Reynolds Price's *A Generous Man*.

Charlie Breene. Wealthy suitor of Dorothy Shaw; their marriage is cruelly opposed by his parents; when he is penniless and her husband is dead, they marry in Anita Loos's *"But Gentlemen Marry Brunettes."*

Captain Elijah (Lige) Brent. Riverboat captain and devoted friend of Colonel Carvel, and therefore of the South, in Winston Churchill's *The Crisis*.

Ellen Brent. Pregnant wife of Henry Brent; scared into her grave by her husband's mad delusions in Andrew Lytle's *A Name for Evil*.

Frederick (Fred, Freddie) Brent. Ward of Hester Prime; Baptist pastor in Dexter, Ohio, who leaves his post in disgrace and migrates to Cincinnati, where he meets his father, a born-again Christian, in Paul Laurence Dunbar's *The Uncalled*.

Henry Brent. Haunted man who undertakes the restoration of his ancestor's farm; narrator of Andrew Lytle's *A Name for Evil*.

Major Brent. Former owner of The Grove and felt to be its ghostly inhabiter by his descendant Henry Brent in Andrew Lytle's *A Name for Evil*.

Margaret (Mag, Margar't) Brent. Wife of Tom Brent and mother of Frederick Brent; dies from alcoholism in Paul Laurence Dunbar's *The Uncalled*.

Robert Brent. New York playwright who helps Susan Lenox become an actress and dies through the plotting of her jealous lover, Freddie Palmer, in David Graham Phillips's *Susan Lenox*.

Tom Brent. Drunkard who abuses and later abandons his wife, Margaret Brent, and son, Frederick Brent; becomes a born-again Christian and is reunited with his son in Paul Laurence Dunbar's *The Uncalled*.

Tony Brenzo. Liberal white policeman, friend of Joe Market, and eloquent foe of narcissism and nihilism in Hal Bennett's *Lord of Dark Places*.

Nina Brett. Chic young woman who interviews Francesca Bolt at an employment agency in Gail Godwin's *Glass People*.

Maud Brewster. Shipwrecked woman rescued by the *Ghost*; assists Hump Van Weyden in navigating the ship to the United States in Jack London's *The Sea-Wolf*.

Rev. Evan Brewster. Minister of the Ebenezer Baptist Church in Sinclair Lewis's *Kingsblood Royal* and *Cass Timberlane*.

Brock (Brock Chamberlain) Brewton. Son of Lutie Brewton and Brice Chamberlain, although Colonel James B. Brewton refuses to accept this fact; becomes a gambler and then an outlaw; killed by a posse in Conrad Richter's *The Sea of Grass.*

Harry (Hal) Brewton. Nephew of Colonel James Brewton; becomes a medical doctor; narrator of Conrad Richter's *The Sea of Grass.*

Colonel James B. (Jim) Brewton. Powerful cattle baron and rancher who battles against nester settlements until government laws restrain his actions; welcomes the return of his errant wife Lutie in Conrad Richter's *The Sea of Grass.*

Lutie Cameron Brewton. Wife of Colonel James B. Brewton; has an affair with Brice Chamberlain and has a son by him; deserts her family because of boredom with pioneer life, but returns home fifteen years later, in Conrad Richter's *The Sea of Grass.*

Margaret Brice. Mother of Stephen Brice in Winston Churchill's *The Crisis.*

Stephen Atterbury (Steve) Brice. Antislavery lawyer who marries Virginia Carvel in Winston Churchill's *The Crisis.*

Virginia Carvel Brice. See Virginia Carvel.

Bridesman. Flight commander in William Faulkner's *A Fable.*

Bridewell. First lieutenant aboard the *Neversink* in Herman Melville's *White-Jacket.*

Hannah Bridewell. See Hannah Bridewell Cadett.

Carolyn (Corky) Bridge. Daughter of Walter and India Bridge; marries and moves to Parallel, Kansas, in Evan Connell's *Mrs. Bridge* and *Mr. Bridge.*

Douglas Bridge. Son of Walter and India Bridge; frequently in trouble as a child; later joins the army in Evan Connell's *Mrs. Bridge* and *Mr. Bridge.*

India Bridge. Wife of Walter Bridge and mother of Ruth, Carolyn, and Douglas Bridge in Evan Connell's *Mrs. Bridge* and *Mr. Bridge.*

Ma'am Bridge. Washerwoman for Clarissa Packard's mother in Caroline Gilman's *Recollections of a Housekeeper.*

Ruth Bridge. Daughter of Walter and India Bridge; moves to New York City and takes a job with a women's magazine in Evan Connell's *Mrs. Bridge* and *Mr. Bridge.*

Walter Bridge. Husband of India Bridge and father of Ruth, Carolyn, and Douglas Bridge; dies in his Kansas City law office in Evan Connell's *Mrs. Bridge* and *Mr. Bridge.*

Jim Bridger. Mountaineer who aids the wagon train and Molly Wingate in Emerson Hough's *The Covered Wagon.*

Cicily Carver Bridges. See Cicily Carver Bridges Lancaster.

James (John) Bridges. One of three Englishmen, sympathetic to the American cause, who send Israel Potter as courier to Benjamin Franklin in Herman Melville's *Israel Potter.*

Charley Bridwell. Reclusive father of Jed Bridwell in Vardis Fisher's *In Tragic Life.*

Jed Bridwell. Untamed boy who lives across the Snake River from Vridar Hunter in Vardis Fisher's *In Tragic Life*; also appears in *Orphans in Gethsemane.*

Lela Bridwell. Mother of Jed Bridwell and friend of Prudence Hunter; leaves her husband, Charley Bridwell, after years of suffering with him in Vardis Fisher's *In Tragic Life.*

Henry (Harry) Brierly. College friend of Philip Sterling, with whom Brierly goes West to make money in railroads; business partner of Beriah Sellers; loves but is rejected by Laura Hawkins in Samuel Langhorne Clemens and Charles Dudley Warner's *The Gilded Age.*

Hortense Briggs. Shop employee admired by Clyde Griffiths in Theodore Dreiser's *An American Tragedy.*

Mona Brigstock. Owen Gereth's vulgar and domineering fiancée and, finally, wife in Henry James's *The Spoils of Poynton.*

Mrs. Brigstock. Mother of Mona Brigstock and mistress of the Waterbath estate in Henry James's *The Spoils of Poynton.*

Bella (Belle) Brill. Daughter of Clothilde Wright and cousin of Jim Calder; makes opportunistic marriages with Joe Stowe and Allen Southby in John P. Marquand's *Wickford Point.*

Clothilde Brill. See Clothilde Brill Wright.

Harry Brill. Parasitical son of Clothilde Wright and cousin of Jim Calder; preoccupied with maintaining his social position in John P. Marquand's *Wickford Point.*

Brimmer. Communist labor organizer in F. Scott Fitzgerald's *The Last Tycoon*.

Dr. Myron T. Brink. Second psychiatrist of John Wilder; prescribes large quantities of drugs to treat Wilder's emotional breakdowns in Richard Yates's *Disturbing the Peace*.

Grace Brissenden. Gossip married to Guy Brissenden, a man nearly half her age, in Henry James's *The Sacred Fount*.

Guy (Briss) Brissenden. Young man married to Grace Brissenden, a woman nearly twice his age; acts as a front for the affair between Gilbert Long and Lady John in Henry James's *The Sacred Fount*.

Russ Brissenden. Socialist poet who encourages and inspires Martin Eden; commits suicide in Jack London's *Martin Eden*.

Judge Bristline. Comical judge who loses his coat and shoes during the Confederate raid on Chambersburg in Hervey Allen's *Action at Aquila*.

Wellington (Don Velantón Bristó) Bristow. American businessman who keeps a "rat list" of wanted men in Thornton Wilder's *The Eighth Day*.

Cora Brittain. Surreptitious racial avenger emulated by her grandson Kevin Brittain in Hal Bennett's *Wait Until the Evening*.

Dolores Brittain. Adopted daughter of Grandpa Brittain and wife of Henry Robinson, who murders her as she gives birth to her lover's child, in Hal Bennett's *Wait Until the Evening*.

Kevin Brittain. Admitted mediocrity given insight into the confluence of racism, duplicity, and death; son of Minnie and Percy Brittain; narrator of Hal Bennett's *Wait Until the Evening*.

Minnie Brittain. Wife of Percy Brittain and mother of eight; frees her family from the despotism of her father-in-law in Hal Bennett's *Wait Until the Evening*.

Paul Brittain. Son of Minnie and Percy Brittain; tricked into hanging himself by his brother Kevin Brittain in Hal Bennett's *Wait Until the Evening*.

Percy Brittain. Philandering husband of Minnie Brittain and father of eight; marked for death by his son Kevin Brittain in Hal Bennett's *Wait Until the Evening*.

Shadrach (Grandpa, Mr. Brittain) Brittain. Former slave and tyrannical owner of the farm on which his family work as sharecroppers; husband of Cora Brittain in Hal Bennett's *Wait Until the Evening*.

Mr. Britten. Employee of Henry Dalton; questions Bigger Thomas about the disappearance of Mary Dalton in Richard Wright's *Native Son*.

Nan Britton. Faithful maid and confidante of Amber St. Clare in Kathleen Winsor's *Forever Amber*.

Donald R. Broadbent. Inept counsel for the State Senate Standing Committee on Education, Welfare, and Public Morality investigating the propriety of an attempt to purchase a brilliant child in John Hersey's *The Child Buyer*.

Thomas Broaden. Prosperous, college-educated mulatto banker who promotes high culture in the upper echelon of the black community in DuBose Heyward's *Mamba's Daughters*.

Dorothy (Dotty) Brock. American Red Cross worker in Luxembourg and lover of Lieutenant Colonel John Dawson Smithers in Martha Gellhorn's *Wine of Astonishment*.

Lucius Brockway. Supervisor at Liberty Paints in Ralph Ellison's *Invisible Man*.

Herman Broder. Member of a well-to-do Polish family who survived World War II by being hidden in a hayloft after a witness reported that the Nazis had killed his wife and children; later marries the servant who hid him and immigrates to America, where he poses as a traveling book salesman in order to have time to spend with his mistress and serve as a ghostwriter for a successful rabbi, in Isaac Bashevis Singer's *Enemies, A Love Story*.

Tamara Luria Broder. Polish upper-class activist and first wife of Herman Broder; shot and left to die by Nazis but survives her wounds and, subsequently, Russian work camps; learns after the war that her husband is alive and follows him to New York in Isaac Bashevis Singer's *Enemies, A Love Story*.

Yadwiga Pracz Broder. Polish Catholic; former servant and later wife of Herman Broder; immigrates with him to America, where she gives birth to a daughter named after his mistress, in Isaac Bashevis Singer's *Enemies, A Love Story*.

Mrs. Brodhag. Devoted housekeeper of Don and Carol Wanderhope in Peter De Vries's *The Blood of the Lamb*.

Brodie. Tattooed bomber and anorexic teenaged girl in Paul Theroux's *The Family Arsenal*.

Ellen Brody. Wife of Martin Brody; unsympathetic toward her husband's concerns about the Great White Shark; becomes so bored that she has an affair with Matt Hooper in Peter Benchley's *Jaws*.

Martin Brody. Chief of police in Amity determined to protect people from the Great White Shark; sole survivor of the attempt to hunt the shark in Peter Benchley's *Jaws*.

Sally Broke. Snobbish, young society woman in Winston Churchill's *Coniston*.

Austin (Irwin Swenson) Bromberg. Erudite essayist and owner of an impressive private library; host of Leo Percepied in Jack Kerouac's *The Subterraneans*; mentioned in *Book of Dreams*.

Chief Broom (Big Chief) Bromden. Large, half-native American inmate of a mental hospital who hallucinates and pretends to be deaf and mute before Randle McMurphy restores his self-confidence; narrator of Ken Kesey's *One Flew Over the Cuckoo's Nest*.

Charlie Bronski. Young Los Angeles vice detective in the Red Scalotta case in Joseph Wambaugh's *The Blue Knight*.

Deborah Androfski Bronski. Sister of Andrei Androfski, wife of Paul Bronski, and lover of Christopher de Monti; becomes active in the Warsaw ghetto resistance in Leon Uris's *Mila 18*.

Paul Bronski. Husband of Deborah Bronski; heads the Jewish Civil Authority for Warsaw after the Nazi occupation; commits suicide in Leon Uris's *Mila 18*.

Rachael Bronski. Daughter of Paul and Deborah Bronski and lover of Wolf Brandel; resistance fighter in the Warsaw ghetto in Leon Uris's *Mila 18*.

George H. Bronson. Newly elected prosecuting attorney who sees the trial of Ralph Hartsook as an opportunity to distinguish himself in Edward Eggleston's *The Hoosier School-Master*.

Mackey Brood. Friend and lover of Jack Curran; gives birth to a son nine months after her last night with Curran before his death in Mark Steadman's *A Lion's Share*.

Daisy (Posy, Mrs. Shakespeare Smith) Brooke. Twin sister of Demijohn Brooke in Louisa May Alcott's *Little Women*; also appears in *Little Men*.

John Brooke. Sensible tutor of Theodore Laurence; marries Meg March in Louisa May Alcott's *Little Women*; also appears in *Little Men*.

John (Demi, Demijohn) Brooke. Twin brother of Daisy Brooke and son of Meg and John Brooke in Louisa May Alcott's *Little Women*; also appears in *Little Men*.

Margaret March Brooke. See Margaret March.

Mrs. Edward (Mrs. Brook) Brookenham. Daughter of Lady Julia and leader of a social group; ambitious mother of Nanda Brookenham in Henry James's *The Awkward Age*.

Fernanda (Nanda) Brookenham. Daughter of Mrs. Brookenham; loves Van Vanderbank; lives in London with her godfather, Mr. Longdon, in Henry James's *The Awkward Age*.

Pierce R. (P. R.) Brooks. Los Angeles homicide detective sergeant; investigating officer in the death of Ian Campbell in Joseph Wambaugh's *The Onion Field*.

J. Jerome (Jerry) Brophy. District attorney who offers to dismiss a rape charge against Ralph Detweiler if Arthur Winner will support his quest for a judgeship in James Gould Cozzens's *By Love Possessed*.

Bo Browder. Childhood acquaintance of Thomas Eborn; policeman who investigates the break-in at the house of Louise Eborn in Reynolds Price's *Love and Work*.

Brower. Insurance adjuster and roommate of George Ogden in Henry Blake Fuller's *The Cliff-Dwellers*.

Theodore Brower. Settlement house resident who courts Jane Marshall in Henry Blake Fuller's *With the Procession*.

Andy Brown. Radio character jailed for robbing Amos's place; freed from jail by Minnie Yellings in Ishmael Reed's *The Last Days of Louisiana Red*.

Annie McGairy Brown. Eighteen-year-old bride of Carl Brown; budding writer and heroine of Betty Smith's *Joy in the Morning*.

Benson Brown. Light-skinned black man attracted to Emma Lou Morgan; eventually marries Gwendolyn Johnson in Wallace Thurman's *The Blacker The Berry*.

Berenice Sadie Brown. Black cook and confidante of Frankie Addams in Carson McCullers's *The Member of the Wedding*.

Betty Brown. See Eliza Mellon Swain.

Biglow (Papa Biglow) Brown. Magnificent ginger-colored giant and rival of Augie for the affection of Della Green in Arna Wendell Bontemps's *God Sends Sunday*.

Bo-jo Brown. Harvard football hero and classmate of Harry Pulham; organizes their twenty-fifth class reunion in John P. Marquand's *H. M. Pulham, Esquire*.

Bobby Brown. See Wilbur Rockefeller Daffodil-11 Swain.

Bubber Brown. Comical friend of Jinx Jenkins in Rudolph Fisher's *The Walls of Jericho* and *The Conjure-Man Dies*.

Buddy Brown. Rival of Tom More; doctor who defends the use of euthanasia with the elderly in Walker Percy's *Love in the Ruins*.

Bunny Brown. Harlem friend of Max Disher; becomes white through the Black-No-More process and helps Disher run the Knights of Nordia in George S. Schuyler's *Black No More*.

Carl (Carlton Braun) Brown. Struggling law student at a midwestern university in 1927; husband of Annie McGairy Brown in Betty Smith's *Joy in the Morning*.

Charles Brown. Beloved of Mary Conant banished from New England because he is an Episcopalian; returns to wed Conant and adopt her half-Indian son in Lydia Maria Child's *Hobomok*.

Corporal Brown. Union soldier who befriends the black child Ticey and renames her Jane in Ernest J. Gaines's *The Autobiography of Miss Jane Pittman*.

Cyril Brown. Marine killed on Saipan in Leon Uris's *Battle Cry*.

Dick Brown. Second-rate commercial artist; married man and first lover of Dorothy Renfrew in Mary McCarthy's *The Group*.

Dick Brown. Humpbacked, cheerful boy in Louisa May Alcott's *Little Men*.

Esther Brown. See Esther Brown Braithwaite.

Fats Brown. Bartender at the Grove in Richard Wright's *The Long Dream*.

Fran Brown. College friend of Renay Davis and babysitter for Denise Davis in Ann Allen Shockley's *Loving Her*.

Frederick (Steely) Brown. Ten-year-old son of Paul and Mae Brown; reader sees ghetto life from his viewpoint in Julian Mayfield's *The Long Night*.

Hattie Brown. Wife of Heck Brown, daughter of Ma Sigafoos, and client of Billy Bumpers in Peter De Vries's *I Hear America Swinging*.

Helen Brown. See Angela Sterling.

Herkimer (Heck) Brown. Renegade farmer, husband of Hattie Brown, son-in-law of Ma Sigafoos, and client of Billy Bumpers in Peter De Vries's *I Hear America Swinging*.

Herman (Wimpy) Brown. Heroin addict and informer for Bumper Morgan in Joseph Wambaugh's *The Blue Knight*.

Honey Camden Brown. Foster brother of Berenice Sadie Brown; imprisoned for breaking into a drugstore in Carson McCullers's *The Member of the Wedding*.

Jackie Brown. Hard-bitten gun dealer who acts as middleman for those who sell guns and those who want them for illegal reasons in George V. Higgins's *The Friends of Eddie Coyle*.

Jake Brown. Longshoreman who returns to Harlem longing to embrace friends and familiar places; meets the girl of his dreams, Felice, his first night home, loses her the next day, therefore spending the rest of the novel trying to find his "little brown" in Claude McKay's *Home to Harlem*; expatriate returning to the United States from Marseilles in *Banjo*.

Jane Brown. See Miss Jane Pittman.

Jayhu (Jehu) Brown. Union man whose cough keeps him from being drafted into the Confederate army; assists Union prisoners of war who escape from Salisbury prison in Albion W. Tourgee's *A Fool's Errand*.

Jenny (Jane, Jenny Angel, Johanna Engel) Brown. American painter traveling with David Scott, with whom she has a tumultuous relationship, in Katherine Anne Porter's *Ship of Fools*.

Joe Brown. See Lucas Burch.

Johnny Brown. Sales executive under Andy Kagle in Joseph Heller's *Something Happened*.

Mae Brown. Long-suffering wife of Paul Brown, by whom she is temporarily deserted, and mother of Steely Brown in Julian Mayfield's *The Long Night*.

Mike Brown. Revolutionary War veteran; drunken farmer and blacksmith whose family deserts him in John Pendleton Kennedy's *Swallow Barn*.

Ned Brown. See Edward Stephen Douglass.

Paul Brown. Father of Steely Brown and husband of Mae Brown; defeated by ghetto life in Julian Mayfield's *The Long Night*.

Recktall Brown. Corrupt businessman who talks Wyatt Gwyon into forging paintings in William Gaddis's *The Recognitions*.

Sheldon Brown. Los Angeles deputy district attorney; co-prosecutor in the second murder trial of Gregory Powell and Jimmy Smith in Joseph Wambaugh's *The Onion Field*.

Sergeant William (Willie) Brown. Misogynistic soldier in Norman Mailer's *The Naked and the Dead*.

Elizabeth Browne. See Elizabeth Browne Rogers.

Katherine Morley (Kitty) Brownell. American visitor to Schloss Riva and friend to Warren Howe; possibly (and briefly) Etienne Dulac's mistress in Wright Morris's *Cause for Wonder*.

Adrian Pericles Brownwell. Owner and editor of the Sycamore Ridge *Banner* whose modest wealth saves John Barclay's bank early in Barclay's career and who, with Barclay's help, marries Molly Culpepper in William Allen White's *A Certain Rich Man*.

Molly Culpepper Brownwell. Daughter of Martin Culpepper and wife of Adrian Brownwell; loves Bob Hendricks in William Allen White's *A Certain Rich Man*.

Bruce. Pan-like bisexual friend and lover of Renate who travels with her through Mexico and periodically lives with her in Anaïs Nin's *Collages*.

Rev. Calvin Bruce. Chicago minister in Charles M. Sheldon's *In His Steps*.

Colonel Bruce. Commander of the station outpost in Robert Montgomery Bird's *Nick of the Woods*.

Dr. Bruce (Doc). Black physician and business partner of Tyree Tucker in Richard Wright's *The Long Dream*.

Walter Bruch. Sixty-year-old musicologist and baritone who likes to enact his own funeral and is a compulsive masturbator when excited by women's arms, a weakness he confesses regularly to Artur Sammler, in Saul Bellow's *Mr. Sammler's Planet*.

Victor Bruge. Friend of Stewart Barnes; gives Psyche Tanzer a fatal dose of a drug he believes is an aphrodisiac in Theodore Dreiser's *The Bulwark*.

Joe Brundige. Author of a story in the *Evening News* reporting how he undergoes a scientific body transfer with a Mayan so he can destroy the Mayan control machine in William S. Burroughs's *The Soft Machine*.

Eddie Brunner. Platonic friend of Gloria Wandrous; struggles to find work as a commercial artist while working as a night man in a brothel in John O'Hara's *Butterfield 8*.

Antonio Bruno. Father of Giovanni and Marcella Bruno; dies in front of a television set in Robert Coover's *The Origin of the Brunists*.

Emilia Bruno. Mother of Giovanni and Marcella Bruno in Robert Coover's *The Origin of the Brunists*.

Giovanni Bruno. Catholic coal miner who, during a mine disaster, claims to have been visited by the Virgin Mary, thereby inaugurating the chiliastic cult of the Brunists in Robert Coover's *The Origin of the Brunists*.

Marcella Bruno. Innocent sister of Giovanni Bruno and Justin Miller's object of infatuation; hit and killed by a car in Robert Coover's *The Origin of the Brunists*.

Elizabeth Martin Brush. See Elizabeth Martin.

George Marvin (George Busch, James Bush, Jim) Brush. Innocent, religiously and socially conservative representative of a textbook company in Thornton Wilder's *Heaven's My Destination*.

James Bruton. English fiancé, for a brief period, of Jane Clifford in Gail Godwin's *The Odd Woman*.

Marcus Junius Brutus. Former enemy of Caesar; recalled from Gaul by Caesar to become Praetor; one of Caesar's assassins in Thornton Wilder's *The Ides of March*.

Bobby Bryant. Alcoholic friend of Bill Kelsey; committed to winning government money by becoming the first male to bear a child in Hal Bennett's *Seventh Heaven*.

Clarke Bryant. Charismatic white supremacist and political leader against school integration in Julian Mayfield's *The Grand Parade*.

Malcolm (Malc) Bryant. Anthropologist-sociologist who analyzes the class structure of the town of Clyde in John P. Marquand's *Point of No Return*.

William Cullen Bryant. Poet and editor of the *Evening Post* in Gore Vidal's *Burr*.

Bubbles. See Richard Wiggins.

Lacy Gore Buchan. Fifteen-year-old son of Major Lewis Buchan; friend of George Posey and in love with Jane Posey; tries to understand both the Buchan and Posey families; joins the Confederate army after the death of his father; narrator of Allen Tate's *The Fathers*.

Major Lewis Buchan. Father of Semmes, Susan, and Lacy Buchan; member of an old Virginia family; remains loyal to the Union but is killed by the Union army in Allen Tate's *The Fathers*.

Semmes (Brother Semmes) Buchan. Son disowned by Major Lewis Buchan; Virginia native who joins the Confederate army against his father's wishes; loves and plans to marry Jane Posey; killed by George Posey in Allen Tate's *The Fathers*.

Susan Buchan. See Susan Buchan Posey.

Daisy Fay Buchanan. Wife of Tom Buchanan and treacherous lost love of Jay Gatsby in F. Scott Fitzgerald's *The Great Gatsby*.

Doctor Buchanan. Golf partner and doctor of Judge Honeywell in Ellen Glasgow's *The Romantic Comedians*.

Rosemarie (Rosie) Buchanan. Friend of Ray Smith and mistress of Cody Pomeray; leaps off an apartment building to her death during an attack of paranoia in Jack Kerouac's *The Dharma Bums*; also appears in *Book of Dreams* and *Big Sur*.

Tom Buchanan. Unfaithful millionaire husband of Daisy Buchanan in F. Scott Fitzgerald's *The Great Gatsby*.

Buchwald. Army private who helps execute General Gragnon in William Faulkner's *A Fable*.

Buck. Dog who leads a dog team and twice saves the life of John Thornton, whose death Buck mourns, in Jack London's *The Call of the Wild*.

Joe (Cowboy, Tex) Buck. Would-be hustler and grandson of Sally Buck; travels from Albuquerque to Houston and New York, where he befriends Ratso Rizzo, in James Leo Herlihy's *Midnight Cowboy*.

Sally Buck. Grandmother of Joe Buck; dies while Joe is in the army in James Leo Herlihy's *Midnight Cowboy*.

Uncle Buck. See Theophilus McCaslin.

Buckingham. See George Villiers.

Helen Buckle. Outspoken wife of Slim Buckle in Jack Kerouac's *Visions of Cody*.

Slim (Ed Buckle) Buckle. Cross-country traveling companion of Cody Pomeray and Jack Duluoz; husband of Helen Buckle in Jack Kerouac's *Visions of Cody*; also appears in *Book of Dreams*.

David A. Buckley. State's attorney who prosecutes Bigger Thomas for the murder of Mary Dalton in Richard Wright's *Native Son*.

Asher Buckner. Maternal uncle of Paul Herz; lives an unattached life as a painter in Philip Roth's *Letting Go*.

Eleanor Apley Budd. See Eleanor Apley.

Irma Barnes Budd. Wealthy American heiress and wife of Lanny Budd in Upton Sinclair's *Dragon's Teeth*.

Lanning Prescott (Lanny) Budd. Wealthy American son of an arms manufacturer; helps secure the release of Johannes and Freddi Robin from the Nazis in Upton Sinclair's *Dragon's Teeth*.

William (Baby, Beauty, Billy) Budd. Handsome sailor aboard the *Rights-of-Man* impressed into service on the *Indomitable*; when falsely accused of planning a mutiny, he accidentally kills his accuser John Claggart in Herman Melville's *Billy Budd*.

Budda Ben. Crippled son of Maum Hannah and advice-giver to Mary Pinesett; banished from Heaven's Gate Church for cursing, but later reinstated, in Julia Peterkin's *Scarlet Sister Mary*.

Uncle Buddy. See Amodeus McCaslin.

Buell. Intelligent, unemotional minister of Norwood whose sermons are filled with carefully crafted scholarship and who marries Agate Bissell after the death of his first wife in Henry Ward Beecher's *Norwood*.

Elgin Buell. Spy and personal cinematographer in Lancelot Lamar's quest to see sin in Walker Percy's *Lancelot*.

Buffalo Wallow Woman. Wife of Old Lodge Skins in Thomas Berger's *Little Big Man*.

John Buford. Adept cavalry officer who is the first Northern general to arrive at Gettysburg in Michael Shaara's *The Killer Angels*.

Dr. Samuel Buggerie. White statistician who discovers that over half the Anglo-Saxon population of the United States has black ancestors; eventually lynched in George S. Schuyler's *Black No More*.

Herr Ottokar Bukuwky. Employee of the von Studenitz family and husband of Frau Natalie Schuschnigg; instrumental in arranging restoration of Rudolf Stanka to family position in Louis Adamic's *Cradle of Life*.

Professor Bulgaraux. Leader of the Autogenists in Susan Sontag's *The Benefactor*.

Bulkington. Popular crewman from the *Grampus* who signs aboard the *Pequod* in Herman Melville's *Moby-Dick*.

Joe Bullitt. Friend of William Baxter; one of Baxter's rivals for the affections of Miss Lola Pratt in Booth Tarkington's *Seventeen*.

Major Rupert Bullock. Close friend of Judge Clinton McKelva; informs Fay McKelva's family that the judge has died in Eudora Welty's *The Optimist's Daughter*.

Tennyson Bullock. Close friend of Becky McKelva; wife of Major Bullock and mother of Tish Bullock in Eudora Welty's *The Optimist's Daughter*.

Tish Bullock. Bridesmaid and close friend of Laurel McKelva Hand; daughter of Major and Tennyson Bullock in Eudora Welty's *The Optimist's Daughter*.

Absalom Bulrush. Poor white whose farm is mortgaged to Frank Meriwether in John Pendleton Kennedy's *Swallow Barn*.

Emil (Saüre) Bummer. German dope dealer and former cat burglar in Thomas Pynchon's *Gravity's Rainbow*.

Stanley Bumpas. Policeman who thirteen years before beat Sonny Boy Mosby; an accomplice of Willie Joe Worth in the murder of Lord Byron Jones in Jesse Hill Ford's *The Liberation of Lord Byron Jones*.

William (Billy) Bumpers. Marriage counselor who earned a doctorate by submitting a rejected sociology dissertation to the English department as an experimental novel; narrator of Peter De Vries's *I Hear America Swinging*.

Nathaniel (Deerslayer, Hawkeye, Leather-stocking, la Longue Carabine, Natty, Pathfinder) Bumppo. White woodsman and guide with knowledge of Indian ways; helps Chingachgook rescue Wah-ta!-Wah and protects the Hutter family in James Fenimore Cooper's *The Deerslayer*; guide and escort to Major Heyward and the Munro sisters in *The Last of the Mohicans*; experiences love for Mabel Dunham in *The Pathfinder*; comes into conflict with the settlers of Templeton in *The Pioneers*; dies on the prairie in *The Prairie*.

Dr. Bumstead. Father of Harriet Bumstead Alden; briefly cares for Peter Alden in George Santayana's *The Last Puritan*.

Harriet Bumstead. See Harriet Bumstead Alden.

Byron Bunch. Mill worker who befriends Lena Grove in William Faulkner's *Light in August*.

Pauline (Polly) Buncombe. Wife of Willis Buncombe; helps her husband in their grocery store at Pickerel Beach and hides Bible verses among the vegetables in Doris Betts's *The River to Pickle Beach*.

Willis Buncombe. Husband of Pauline Buncombe; proprietor of a small grocery store at Pickerel Beach in Doris Betts's *The River to Pickle Beach*.

Nat Bundle. Press agent for Harry Mercury in Peter De Vries's *Through the Fields of Clover*.

Addie Bundren. First wife of Anse Bundren and mother of five children, one of whom, Jewel, is fathered by the minister Whitfield; following Addie's death, the family carries her body to Jefferson in William Faulkner's *As I Lay Dying*.

Anse Bundren. Husband of Addie Bundren and father of four children; honors his wife's request to be buried in Jefferson, Mississippi; remarries soon after Addie's funeral in William Faulkner's *As I Lay Dying*.

Cash Bundren. Son of Anse and Addie Bundren; carpenter who builds his mother's coffin in William Faulkner's *As I Lay Dying*.

Darl Bundren. Son of Anse and Addie Bundren; committed to an asylum in William Faulkner's *As I Lay Dying*.

Dewey Dell Bundren. Daughter of Anse and Addie Bundren; impregnated by Lafe in William Faulkner's *As I Lay Dying*.

Jewel Bundren. Son of Addie Bundren and her lover Whitfield in William Faulkner's *As I Lay Dying*.

Vardaman Bundren. Son of Anse and Addie Bundren in William Faulkner's *As I Lay Dying*.

Bundy (Old Bundy). Aging, bald, and extremely thin slave with a predilection for alcohol; dies as a result of a whipping administered by Thomas Prosser in Arna Wendell Bontemps's *Black Thunder*.

Bungs. Cooper aboard the *Julia* in Herman Melville's *Omoo*.

Gloria Bunshaft. Featherbrained wife of Wally Hines and paramour of Joe Sandwich in Peter De Vries's *The Vale of Laughter*.

Amanita Buntline. Wealthy lesbian friend of Caroline Rosewater in Kurt Vonnegut's *God Bless You, Mr. Rosewater*.

Doctor Burch. Young New York doctor who loves Dorinda Oakley and guides her emotional recovery and intellectual development in Ellen Glasgow's *Barren Ground*.

Lucas Burch (Joe Brown). Braggart mill worker and bootlegger who fathers Lena Grove's child in William Faulkner's *Light in August.*

Ellis (Scholarly Attorney) Burden. Lawyer who marries Jack Burden's mother and moves her from Arkansas to Burden's Landing; leaves her when Jack is about six years old in Robert Penn Warren's *All the King's Men.*

Jack (Jackie, Jackie-Bird, Jackie-Boy) Burden. Student of history, friend of Anne and Adam Stanton, son of Judge Irwin, and cynical righthand man for Willie Stark; narrator of Robert Penn Warren's *All the King's Men.*

Jim Burden. Lawyer for a railroad company who recalls his friendship with Ántonia Shimerda; narrator of Willa Cather's *My Ántonia.*

Joanna Burden. Daughter of Nathaniel Burden and his second wife; lover of Joe Christmas, who murders her, in William Faulkner's *Light in August*; also appears in *The Mansion.*

Juana Burden. First wife of Nathaniel Burden and mother of Calvin Burden II in William Faulkner's *Light in August.*

Martha Burden. White New York artist friend of Angela Murray in Jessie Redmon Fauset's *Plum Bun.*

Milly Burden. Defiant and unsettling secretary of Virginius Littlepage; seduced, impregnated, and abandoned by Martin Welding in Ellen Glasgow's *They Stooped to Folly.*

Nathaniel Burden. Father of Calvin Burden II (by Juana Burden) and Joanna Burden (by his second wife) in William Faulkner's *Light in August.*

Calvin Burden (I). Father of Nathaniel Burden; John Sartoris kills Burden and Calvin Burden II in William Faulkner's *Light in August.*

Calvin Burden (II). Son of Nathaniel and Juana Burden; John Sartoris kills Burden and Calvin Burden I in William Faulkner's *Light in August.*

Alberta Ross Burdick. See Alberta Ross.

Clark Burdon. Gunman and homesteader who befriends Clay Clavert in H. L. Davis's *Honey in the Horn.*

Wally Burgan. Shady lawyer and former business partner of Herbert Pierce; lover of Mildred Pierce in James M. Cain's *Mildred Pierce.*

Milton Burgess. Owner of a general store and rival merchant of Jasper Lathrop in Wendell Berry's *A Place on Earth* and *The Memory of Old Jack.*

Richard Burgess. Guard for the South Eastern Railway who is bribed into helping Edward Pierce in Michael Crichton's *The Great Train Robbery.*

Matthew (Matt) Burke. Teacher who befriends Ben Mears; assists in destroying the evil that surrounds the Marsten House in Stephen King's *'Salem's Lot.*

Nancy Burke. Assistant costume designer and friend of Delia Poole in Janet Flanner's *The Cubical City.*

Sadie Burke. Private secretary to and mistress of Willie Stark; her jealousy leads to Stark's assassination in Robert Penn Warren's *All the King's Men.*

Studsy Burke. Ex-con, owner of the speakeasy The Pigiron Club in Dashiell Hammett's *The Thin Man.*

Teddy Burke. Pickpocket who pretends to pick Edgar Trent's pocket, thus permitting Edward Pierce to gain information on safe keys, in Michael Crichton's *The Great Train Robbery.*

Toonker Burkette. Dentist who tells of Eleanor Fite's murder and Thomas McCutcheon's suicide in Jesse Hill Ford's *Mountains of Gilead*; mentioned in *The Liberation of Lord Byron Jones.*

Johnnie Price Burkhalter. Hardware dealer in Somerton and tennis partner of Steve Mundine in Jesse Hill Ford's *The Liberation of Lord Byron Jones.*

George Burkin. Fellow inmate of George Brush in an Ozarksville, Missouri, jail in Thornton Wilder's *Heaven's My Destination.*

Burleigh. Lawyer who gains acquittal for Royal Earle Thompson in Katherine Anne Porter's *Noon Wine.*

John Burleson. Friend of Melville Gurney and chief of the county Ku Klux Klan; speaks out against murdering Comfort Servosse and tends to the dying Servosse; ultimately denounces the Klan in Albion W. Tourgee's *A Fool's Errand.*

Jean Burling. Lover of Nicholas Delbanco in Nicholas Delbanco's *In the Middle Distance.*

Henry Burlingame III. Gifted tutor who gives Ebenezer Cooke an unusually comprehensive education in John Barth's *The Sot-Weed Factor.*

Robert Burlingham. Showboat owner and Susan Lenox's protector in David Graham Phillips's *Susan Lenox.*

Johnny Burnecker. Well-meaning Iowa farm youth who joins the army and is inspired by the example of Noah Ackerman in Irwin Shaw's *The Young Lions.*

Frank Burnham. Stunt pilot killed in an airplane crash in William Faulkner's *Pylon*.

Mr. Burns. Employment manager at the Cosmodemonic Telegraph Company of North America in Henry Miller's *Tropic of Capricorn*.

Beauregard Jackson Pickett (Beau) Burnside. Southern millionaire who marries Mame Dennis after she sells him twenty pairs of roller skates; dies thirteen months after their wedding in Patrick Dennis's *Auntie Mame*.

Elmore Jefferson Davis Burnside. Obnoxious southerner, ladies' underwear salesman, and cousin of Mame Dennis's dead husband; tries to court Mame until her nephew arranges to have him arrested by Fascists in Patrick Dennis's *Around the World with Auntie Mame*.

Mame Dennis Burnside. See Mame Dennis.

Aaron Burr. Conspirator to conquer and rule in Mexico; opponent of Thomas Jefferson; acquitted at a trial for treason in Mary Johnston's *Lewis Rand*.

Col. Aaron Burr. Third vice-president of the United States; accused of killing Alexander Hamilton in a duel and arrested for treason in Gore Vidal's *Burr*.

Theodosia Burr. Daughter of Aaron Burr and wife of Joseph Alston; believed to have drowned in Gore Vidal's *Burr*.

Henry Burrage. Son of Mrs. Burrage; Harvard student who proposes marriage to Verena Tarrant in Henry James's *The Bostonians*.

Mrs. Burrage. Society hostess who entertains Verena Tarrant in New York in Henry James's *The Bostonians*.

Nathaniel Burrington. Father of Calvin Burden I in William Faulkner's *Light in August*.

Anthony (Tony) Burton. President of the Stuyvesant Bank who awards the vice-presidency of the bank to Charles Gray in John P. Marquand's *Point of No Return*.

Bertrand Burton. Manservant of Ebenezer Cooke; temporarily becomes a king in John Barth's *The Sot-Weed Factor*.

Charles (Barton) Burton. Baylor University pathologist and member of the scientist group at Project Wildfire in Michael Crichton's *The Andromeda Strain*.

Doc Burton. Physician who treats the migrant workers and supports their strike in John Steinbeck's *In Dubious Battle*.

Ralph Burton. English officer friendly to Johnny Lacey; brings Lacey news of Braddock's death after the defeat outside Fort Duquesne in Mary Lee Settle's *O Beulah Land*.

Thomas Burton. One of the soldiers who tries to make a deal with Richard Mast for the pistol Mast possesses in James Jones's *The Pistol*.

Tom (Big Boy) Burwell. Southern black laborer who resents white Bob Stone's advances toward his girlfriend Louisa; in self-defense he cuts Stone's throat and is lynched by a white mob in Jean Toomer's *Cane*.

Asa Bush. Firstborn son of Ishmael and Esther Bush; shot in the back by his uncle, Abiram White, who tries to blame Natty Bumppo for Asa's murder, in James Fenimore Cooper's *The Prairie*.

Esther (Eester) Bush. Powerful and fearless wife of Ishmael Bush; concurs with Ishmael in imposing a death sentence on her brother, Abiram White, in James Fenimore Cooper's *The Prairie*.

Ike (Al Kennedy) Bush. Fighter dissuaded from taking a dive by the Op in Dashiell Hammett's *Red Harvest*.

Esther (Eester) Bush. Powerful and fearless wife of Ishmael Bush; concurs with Ishmael in imposing a death sentence on her brother, Abiram White, in James Fenimore Cooper's *The Prairie*.

Ike (Al Kennedy) Bush. Fighter dissuaded from taking a dive by the Op in Dashiell Hammett's *Red Harvest*.

Ishmael (the Great Buffalo) Bush. Squatter, patriarch, and law unto himself; husband of Esther Bush and brother-in-law of Abiram White; with White, kidnapper of Inez de Certavallos in James Fenimore Cooper's *The Prairie*.

Ambrose Bushfield. Frontiersman in James Kirke Paulding's *Westward Ho!*

Otto Bussen. Mathematics student at the University of Berlin; roomer in Rosa Reichl's boardinghouse in Katherine Anne Porter's *The Leaning Tower*.

Buster (Bus). Friend and playmate of Sandy Rodgers; passes for white in Langston Hughes's *Not Without Laughter*.

Seth Buswell. Owner and editor of the *Peyton Place Times* who gives Allison MacKenzie her first job in Grace Metalious's *Peyton Place*.

Buteo. Native of South America and king-to-be when the revolution is won; fights alongside Ramón

Cordes and feels brotherhood with him in William Herrick's *The Last to Die*.

Butler. Mysterious stranger who abducts Ellen Langton; falls from a cliff and dies while fighting Fanshawe in Nathaniel Hawthorne's *Fanshawe*.

Aileen (Ai) Butler. See Aileen Butler Cowperwood.

Arthur Butler. Patriot hero captured by the Tories; rescued by Horse Shoe Robinson in time to fight at King's Mountain; husband of Mildred Lindsay in John Pendleton Kennedy's *Horse-Shoe Robinson*.

Edward Malia (Eddie) Butler. Father of Aileen Butler; uses his political influence to ruin Frank Cowperwood in Theodore Dreiser's *The Financier*.

Eugenie Victoria Butler. Daughter of Scarlett O'Hara and Rhett Butler; killed in a horse-riding accident in Margaret Mitchell's *Gone with the Wind*.

Michael X. (Butty) Butler. First husband of Rozelle Hardcastle; dies in a yachting accident in Robert Penn Warren's *A Place to Come To*.

Rhett K. Butler. Successful blockade runner during the Civil War; third husband of Scarlett O'Hara, whom he leaves, in Margaret Mitchell's *Gone with the Wind*.

Widow Butler. Invalid mother of Butler; lives with her sister in Nathaniel Hawthorne's *Fanshawe*.

Ann Butterfield. Wife of Hugh Butterfield and mother of Jade, Sam, and Keith Butterfield in Scott Spencer's *Endless Love*.

Hugh Butterfield. Doctor and father of Jade, Sam, and Hugh Butterfield; killed by a taxi while pursuing David Axelrod in Scott Spencer's *Endless Love*.

Jade Butterfield. Subject of David Axelrod's obsessive love in Scott Spencer's *Endless Love*.

Keith Butterfield. Son of Hugh and Ann Butterfield in Scott Spencer's *Endless Love*.

Sam (Sammy) Butterfield. Son of Hugh and Ann Butterfield in Scott Spencer's *Endless Love*.

Clara Butterworth. Daughter of Tom Butterworth and student at Ohio State University; thoughtful young woman who marries Hugh McVey in Sherwood Anderson's *Poor White*.

Tom Butterworth. Ohio farmer and father of Clara Butterworth; invests in the factory that produces Hugh McVey's inventions in Sherwood Anderson's *Poor White*.

Willard Buzzard. Iowa State wrestler who beats his former teammate George Bender in the champi-

onship for the one-hundred fifty-eight-pound division in John Irving's *The 158-Pound Marriage*.

Roger Byam. Midshipman on the HMS *Bounty* who narrates the events of the voyage to Tahiti, his efforts to compile a dictionary of the Tahitian language, the mutiny, his return to England in chains, and his narrow escape from being hanged as a mutineer in Charles Nordhoff and James Norman Hall's *Mutiny on the Bounty*.

Peter Bye. Doctor of mixed racial heritage; husband of Joanna Marshall in Jessie Redmon Fauset's *There Is Confusion*.

Mr. Byfield. Track coach of Homer Macauley at Ithaca High School; prejudiced against students from immigrant families in William Saroyan's *The Human Comedy*.

Anthony Byrd. Florist, aspiring writer, and friend of Annie Brown in Betty Smith's *Joy in the Morning*.

Crowell Byrd. Father of Susan Byrd and son of Heddy Byrd in Toni Morrison's *Song of Solomon*.

Heddy Byrd. Indian woman who finds and rears Jake (Macon Dead I) when he is dropped by his father, the flying African; mother of Sing and Crowell Byrd and grandmother of Susan Byrd in Toni Morrison's *Song of Solomon*.

Sing Byrd. Wife of Macon Dead I, daughter of Heddy Byrd, and mother of Pilate Dead and Macon Dead II; dies in childbirth in Toni Morrison's *Song of Solomon*.

Susan Byrd. Granddaughter of Heddy Byrd and cousin of Milkman; tells Milkman during his visit to Shalimar, Virginia, of the flying powers of his great-grandfather in Toni Morrison's *Song of Solomon*.

Raymond Byrne. Los Angeles deputy district attorney; co-prosecutor in the second murder trial of Gregory Powell and Jimmy Smith in Joseph Wambaugh's *The Onion Field*.

Mrs. Bywaters. Frederick County postmistress who helps Nancy escape to Canada in Willa Cather's *Sapphira and the Slave Girl*.

BZ. Homosexual film producer and husband of Helene; commits suicide in Joan Didion's *Play It As It Lays*.

Jan Bzik. Sickly Polish peasant, father of Wanda Bzik, and owner of the slave Jacob Eliezer in Isaac Bashevis Singer's *The Slave*.

C

Prince Cabano (Jacob Isaacs). Jewish banker and a leader in the Oligarchy who attempts to deflower Estella Washington; killed during an apocalyptic revolution in Ignatius Donnelly's *Caesar's Column*.

Lionel Cabot. Best friend of Ulysses Macauley in William Saroyan's *The Human Comedy*.

Cacciato. American infantryman in Vietnam who is pursued by his own squad; deserter who leaves the war for Paris in Tim O'Brien's *Going after Cacciato*.

Rheinhold Cacoethes. San Francisco literary critic in Jack Kerouac's *The Dharma Bums*.

Matteo Cacopardo. Sulphur processor who advises Major Joppolo to secure a bell for the town in John Hersey's *A Bell for Adano*.

Mr. Cadwalader. Leader of the Progressive group and official head of the Farmer-Labor Party in Chicago with whom Mrs. Beech seeks an alliance in W. E. B. Du Bois's *Dark Princess*.

Abraham (Abe) Cady. American Jewish author of *The Holocaust*, a book that charges Adam Kelno with sterilizing healthy Jewish patients without the use of an anaesthetic in the Jadwiga concentration camp; defendant in a libel suit; lover of Sarah Wydman in Leon Uris's *QB VII*.

Alex Cady. Bigoted and violent poor-white tenant farmer who persecutes blacks; destroys a wagon belonging to Miltiades Vaiden and leads a mob that lynches Toussaint Vaiden in T. S. Stribling's *The Store*.

Ben Cady. Son of Abe Cady; Israeli pilot killed during the Arab-Israeli conflict in Leon Uris's *QB VII*.

Dr. Benjamin Cady. Nobel Prize winner, one of Jesse Vogel's medical heroes, and father of Helene Cady Vogel in Joyce Carol Oates's *Wonderland*.

Eph Cady. Son of Alex Cady; assassinates Miltiades Vaiden in T. S. Stribling's *Unfinished Cathedral*.

Helene Cady. See Helene Cady Vogel.

Augustus (Gus) Caesar. Former slave of Richard Cameron; rapes Marion Lenoir and is lynched by the Ku Klux Klan in Thomas Dixon's *The Clansman*.

Caius Julius Caesar. Dictator of Rome whose death occurs on the ides of March in Thornton Wilder's *The Ides of March*.

Brian (Art) Caffrey. Grandson of Katherine Brownell and heir apparent to Etienne Dulac's audacity in Wright Morris's *Cause for Wonder*.

Rollo Cage. Loyal white friend of Jule Jackson and son of a store owner in George Wylie Henderson's *Jule*.

Matthew (Matt) Cahn. Handsome Arab; second husband of Rachel Farrell in William Herrick's *The Itinerant*.

Eddie Cahow. Ubiquitous barber with genealogical genius in Wright Morris's *The Man Who Was There* and *The Home Place*.

Anna Oliver Caillet. Beautiful and artistic older daughter of Thomas Oliver; marries Oliver's adopted son, Robert Caillet, and bears a son to carry on the family name in Shirley Ann Grau's *The Condor Passes*.

Anthony Caillet. Son of Anna and Robert Caillet destined to carry on the family name; commits suicide, driving his parents to despair, in Shirley Ann Grau's *The Condor Passes*.

Aurelie Caillet. Mother of Joan Mitchell and four other daughters from five successive marriages in Shirley Ann Grau's *The House on Coliseum Street*.

Robert Caillet. "Adopted" son Thomas Oliver picked up off the streets; unfaithful husband of Anna Oliver Caillet and father of Anthony Caillet in Shirley Ann Grau's *The Condor Passes*.

Amanda (Mandy) Cain. Adulteress whose infidelity, discovered by Ellen Chesser, causes the suicide of Cassie Beal MacMurtrie in Elizabeth Madox Roberts's *The Time of Man*.

George (Georgie, Daddy George, Junior) Cain. Harlem basketball star and community hero unable to handle the pressure in a private school, which he attends as a token black; becomes a drug addict and ex-convict; narrator of George Cain's *Blueschild Baby*.

Keith (Raschid) Cain. Brother of George Cain; involved in urban street violence; becomes a Muslim in George Cain's *Blueschild Baby*.

Mom Cain. Deeply religious mother of George Cain in George Cain's *Blueschild Baby*.

Pop (Grandad) Cain. Ambitious government worker and father of George Cain in George Cain's *Blueschild Baby*.

Joel Cairo. Homosexual pursuer of the jewel-encrusted statuette who forms a temporary alliance with Brigid O'Shaughnessy in Dashiell Hammett's *The Maltese Falcon*.

Cal. Favorite student of Thomas Eborn; Eborn dreams Cal has died on the evening Eborn's mother actually dies in Reynolds Price's *Love and Work*.

Corie Cal. See Corie Calhoun.

Haze Cal. See Haze Calhoun.

Rie Cal. See Rie Calhoun.

Calamity Jane (Martha Jane Canary). Childhood friend of Morissa Kirk; drunkenly taunts Morissa about being illegitimate in Mari Sandoz's *Miss Morissa*.

Joseph P. (Gentleman Joe) Calash. Highwayman who helps Daniel Harrow escape a beating and who is later helped to escape by Harrow and Molly Larkins, only to be shot by a posse, in Walter D. Edmonds's *Rome Haul*.

Jim Calder. Successful writer of magazine fiction and cousin of the Brills; alternately drawn to and repelled by Wickford Point; narrator of John P. Marquand's *Wickford Point*.

Brock Caldwell. Idle, sarcastic older brother of Grace Caldwell Tate; gradually matures and becomes head of the Caldwell family in John O'Hara's *A Rage to Live*.

Catherine Kramer (Cassie, Chariclo) Caldwell. Wife of George Caldwell, mother of Peter Caldwell, and daughter of Pop Kramer in John Updike's *The Centaur*.

Duck Caldwell. Hired worker for the Crooms; represents "a high manifestation of ordinary life" in Lionel Trilling's *The Middle of the Journey*.

Dr. Edward (Ned) Caldwell. Father of William Caldwell; beloved country doctor injured in a buggy accident in Mary Austin's *Santa Lucia*.

Elias (Old Man) Caldwell. Neighbor of the Holbrooks who, dying, tries to tell Mazie Holbrook what he has learned about life and wills her books which her father sells for fifty cents in Tillie Olsen's *Yonnondio*.

Emily Caldwell. Wife of Duck Caldwell and lover of John Laskell; her "unreality" distances the Crooms in Lionel Trilling's *The Middle of the Journey*.

George W. (Chiron, Sticks) Caldwell. Husband of Cassie Caldwell and father of Peter Caldwell; high school general science teacher and swimming coach preoccupied with death and mythic delu-

sions that he is the perpetually wounded Chiron, noblest of all centaurs; narrates part of John Updike's *The Centaur*.

Grace Brock Caldwell. See Grace Brock Caldwell Tate.

Maude Caldwell. West Indian neighbor of the Coffin family and twelve-year-old best friend of Francie Coffin in Louise Meriwether's *Daddy Was a Number Runner*.

Peter Caldwell. Son of George and Cassie Caldwell; cares deeply about his father but is often embarrassed by him; longs to be an artist; narrates part of John Updike's *The Centaur*.

Professor Caldwell. Professor of English who helps Martin Eden expand his interests in Jack London's *Martin Eden*.

Rebecca (Becky) Caldwell. Sixteen-year-old sister of Maude Caldwell and neighbor and friend of Francie Coffin in Louise Meriwether's *Daddy Was a Number Runner*.

Sam Caldwell. Railroad man in William Faulkner's *The Reivers*.

Susan Caldwell. Daughter of Duck and Emily Caldwell; John Laskell becomes friendly with her in Lionel Trilling's *The Middle of the Journey*.

Vallejo (Vallie) Caldwell. Neighbor of Francie Coffin; arrested and sentenced to die for the robbery and murder of a white shoe salesman in Louise Meriwether's *Daddy Was a Number Runner*.

William (Billy) Caldwell. Ebullient daughter of Doctor Caldwell; loved by Edward Jasper and successfully courted by George Rhewold in Mary Austin's *Santa Lucia*.

Bud Calhoun. Lazy genius inventor who joins revolutionaries in Kurt Vonnegut's *Player Piano*.

Corie (Corie Cal) Calhoun. Wife of Lee Buck Calhoun and mother of Rie Calhoun and five other children in Harriette Simpson Arnow's *Mountain Path*.

Gerald (Bull's-eye, Jerry) Calhoun. Former college quarterback ashamed of his father; in love with Sue Murdock, daughter of his employer, Bogan Murdock, in Robert Penn Warren's *At Heaven's Gate*.

Haze (Haze Cal) Calhoun. Brother, neighbor, and moonshining partner of Lee Buck Calhoun in Harriette Simpson Arnow's *Mountain Path*.

Lee Buck Calhoun. Calhoun family patriarch, farmer, school trustee, moonshiner, fiddler, and landlord of Louisa Sheridan in Harriette Simpson Arnow's *Mountain Path.*

Mabel Calhoun. Daughter of Haze Calhoun; cousin and schoolmate of Rie Calhoun in Harriette Simpson Arnow's *Mountain Path.*

Rie (Rie Cal) Calhoun. Oldest daughter of Lee Buck and Corie Calhoun; student of Louisa Sheridan in Harriette Simpson Arnow's *Mountain Path.*

Professor Seth Calhoun. Bigot and author of *The Menace of the Negro to Our American Civilization;* invited by Constancia Brandon to speak at a soiree in her salon in Countee Cullen's *One Way to Heaven.*

Molly Calico. Clerk of the zoning board and later parish secretary; clandestinely courted and affianced by Andrew Mackerel during the period of mourning for his late wife; finally marries Mike Todarescu in Peter De Vries's *The Mackerel Plaza.*

Pippa Calico. Mother of Molly Calico and temporary housekeeper for Andrew Mackerel in Peter De Vries's *The Mackerel Plaza.*

Donald Callahan. Pastor of Jerusalem's Lot who seeks to help Matt Burke destroy vampires in Stephen King's *'Salem's Lot.*

Maria Callas. Singer and subjunctive girlfriend of Trout Fishing in America in Richard Brautigan's *Trout Fishing in America.*

Mindy Callender. Young and pregnant girlfriend of Jake Simms in Anne Tyler's *Earthly Possessions.*

Dante Callicchio. Former boxer and wrestler and father of three children; severely beats the federal men in New York so Fred Trumper can flee them in John Irving's *The Water-Method Man.*

Dutt Callister. Neighbor who accompanies Elias McCutcheon on the raid of the Horse Pens and later to the Civil War in Jesse Hill Ford's *The Raider.*

Fancy Callister. Wife of Dutt Callister; bears several children and constantly complains in Jesse Hill Ford's *The Raider.*

Callistus. Servant and bodyguard assigned to Julian Augustus by a cabal of Christian military officers; assassinates Julian at the height of a military skirmish with the Persians in Gore Vidal's *Julian.*

Caroline Calloway. Intellectual mother of Louisa Calloway; suffers from periods of depression in Alice Adams's *Families and Survivors.*

Jack Calloway. Tobacco-rich father of Louisa Calloway; vocal in his prejudice against FDR, unions, blacks, Jews, and spending life in and out of sanitoriums in Alice Adams's *Families and Survivors.*

Louisa (Lou, Louisa Jeffreys, Louisa Wasserman) Calloway. Modern southern belle rebelling against family wealth and tradition; protagonist of Alice Adams's *Families and Survivors.*

Zeb Calloway. See Boone Caudill.

Calpurnia. Housekeeper for the Finch family and mother substitute for Scout and Jem Finch in Harper Lee's *To Kill a Mockingbird.*

Calpurnia. Last wife of Caesar; they are married weeks before his death in Thornton Wilder's *The Ides of March.*

Charles Calvert, Lord Baltimore. Lord Proprietary of the Province of Maryland in John Barth's *The Sot-Weed Factor.*

Clay Calvert. Orphan adopted by Uncle Preston Shiveley in H. L. Davis's *Honey in the Horn.*

Calvin. Black homosexual who befriends Molly Bolt on her arrival in New York City in Rita Mae Brown's *Rubyfruit Jungle.*

Calyxa. Mythical figure who is also a student writing a thesis on Perseus in the *Perseid,* a novella in John Barth's *Chimera.*

Camara (Princess). Six-year-old daughter of Truman Held and Lynne Rabinowitz; dies as the result of a violent, unspecified crime in Alice Walker's *Meridian.*

Thomas Cambridge. Maternal uncle of Clara and Theodore Wieland; reveals to Clara that Theodore killed his own wife and children at Carwin's instigation in Charles Brockden Brown's *Wieland.*

Cameron. Professional killer, companion of Greer, habitual counter, and destroyer of the Hawkline Monster; plans to but does not marry Susan Hawkline in Richard Brautigan's *The Hawkline Monster.*

Ben Cameron. Confederate colonel who organizes the Ku Klux Klan to overthrow the black-dominated government of Reconstruction in Thomas Dixon's *The Clansman.*

Henry Cameron. Pioneer in modern architecture; defies mediocrity but finally is crushed by it in Ayn Rand's *The Fountainhead.*

Kenneth Cameron. New York producer who marries Kim Ravenal in Edna Ferber's *Show Boat.*

Kim Ravenal Cameron. Daughter of Magnolia and Gaylord Ravenal; New York actress who marries Kenneth Cameron in Edna Ferber's *Show Boat*.

Dr. Lemuel (Bracciani) Cameron. Site director of Talifer Missile Base known for his ruthlessness and brilliance; discredited in a congressional hearing in John Cheever's *The Wapshot Scandal*.

Margaret Cameron. Sister of Ben Cameron; loves Phil Stoneman in Thomas Dixon's *The Clansman*.

Richard Cameron. Father of Ben and Margaret Cameron; physician who identifies Augustus Caesar as Marion Lenoir's assailant in Thomas Dixon's *The Clansman*.

Camille. Second wife of Dean Moriarty; following a third marriage, he returns to her in Jack Kerouac's *On the Road*.

Flora Camp. Youngest daughter of Tom Camp; abducted and killed, apparently by Dick, in Thomas Dixon's *The Leopard's Spots*.

Reuben (Reub) Camp. Unsuccessful farmer who agrees with many of Homos's criticisms of America in William Dean Howells's *A Traveler from Altruria*.

Tom Camp. Poor, crippled Confederate veteran who becomes insane after his daughters are killed by blacks in Thomas Dixon's *The Leopard's Spots*.

Adah Campbell. Former Las Vegas showgirl; wife of Ian Campbell in Joseph Wambaugh's *The Onion Field*.

Chrissie Campbell. Mother of Ian Campbell in Joseph Wambaugh's *The Onion Field*.

Howard W. Campbell, Jr.. American playwright turned Nazi propagandist and U.S. spy; narrator of Kurt Vonnegut's *Mother Night* and the "American Quisling" in *Slaughterhouse-Five*.

Ian James Campbell. Los Angeles policeman killed by Gregory Powell and Jimmy Smith in Joseph Wambaugh's *The Onion Field*.

Kay (Kay-Kay, The Pumpkin) Campbell. English literature major from Iowa and lover of Alex Portnoy; her refusal to convert to Judaism prompts Portnoy to end their relationship in Philip Roth's *Portnoy's Complaint*.

Michael (Mike) Campbell. Heavy-drinking British fiancé of Lady Brett Ashley in Ernest Hemingway's *The Sun Also Rises*.

Milly Campbell. Wife of Shep Campbell and mother of their four sons; contented with her suburban life in Richard Yates's *Revolutionary Road*.

Nicholas Campbell. First love of Phebe Grant and the husband of one of her friends in Jessie Redmon Fauset's *Comedy, American Style*.

Sheppard Sears (Shep) Campbell. Well-educated and affluent engineer who adopts a self-created mask of boorish masculinity; secretly in love with April Wheeler in Richard Yates's *Revolutionary Road*.

Terrence (Terry) Campbell. Ward of Adam Kelno and friend of Stephan Kelno; medical doctor in Leon Uris's *QB VII*.

Tunis G. Campbell. Antislavery activist, author of a memoir, and subject of Sam's research in Nicholas Delbanco's *News*; mentioned in *In the Middle Distance*.

Virgil Campbell. Wily country storekeeper and school board member who gives David Christopher the job as principal of Cornhill Grammar School in Fred Chappell's *It Is Time, Lord*.

Camper. Traveler who helped to build the dam originally and who witnessed the mud slide that killed Mulge Lampson; helps to bury Hattie Lampson in John Hawkes's *The Beetle Leg*.

Dan T. Campion. Corrupt contractor and important member of the Catholic church in John Gregory Dunne's *True Confessions*.

Luis Campion. Homosexual expatriate in F. Scott Fitzgerald's *Tender Is the Night*.

Eva Medina (Eve, Sweet) Canada. Narrator who, as a young woman, is sentenced to a reformatory for having stabbed Moses Tripp in the hand; married for two years to James Hunn; murders her lover Davis Carter and is imprisoned in a psychiatric prison in Gayl Jones's *Eva's Man*.

John Canada. Husband of Marie Canada and father of Eva Medina Canada in Gayl Jones's *Eva's Man*.

Marie Canada. Wife of John Canada, mother of Eva Medina Canada, and lover of Tyrone in Gayl Jones's *Eva's Man*.

Martha Jane Canary. See Calamity Jane.

Canby. Eponymous owner of the only saloon in the town of Bridger's Wells in Walter Van Tilburg Clark's *The Ox-Bow Incident*.

Candy. Aging ranch hand who dreams of making a new start with George Milton and Lennie Small in John Steinbeck's *Of Mice and Men*.

Candy. See Candy Christian.

Mrs. Candy. Housekeeper and cook for Doremus Jessup; quiet supporter of the New Underground in Sinclair Lewis's *It Can't Happen Here.*

Lash Canino. Killer in Raymond Chandler's *The Big Sleep.*

Audrey Cannon. Assistant professor of dance and theater arts who limps because of an accident with a lawn mower; has an affair with Severin Winter in John Irving's *The 158-Pound Marriage.*

Rinaldo (Ronald) Cantabile. Flashy criminal and would-be mafia operator who smashes Charlie Citrine's Mercedes over a welched bet and tries to exploit Citrine's writings for personal profit in Saul Bellow's *Humboldt's Gift.*

Gerald (Chief) Cantley. White chief of police who receives kickbacks from Tyree Tucker's illegal businesses; murders Tyree Tucker and arrests Fish Tucker for attempted rape in Richard Wright's *The Long Dream.*

John (Johnny) Cantloe. Puritan soldier and follower of Johnny Church and Thankful Perkins; condemned to death for mutiny but spared in Cromwell's blanket pardon in Mary Lee Settle's *Prisons.*

Davey Cantor. Fellow student and friend of Reuven Malter in Chaim Potok's *The Chosen.*

Richard (Dick, Ricardo) Cantwell. American army officer who, fatally ill, returns to Venice to visit a lover and hunt for ducks in Ernest Hemingway's *Across the River and into the Trees.*

John Canty. Cruel father of Tom Canty; introduces Edward Tudor, disguised as Tom Canty, to thieves and beggars in Samuel Langhorne Clemens's *The Prince and the Pauper.*

Tom Canty. Boy from the London slums who looks exactly like Edward Tudor; exchanges identity with Edward and learns the burdensome duties of royal life in Samuel Langhorne Clemens's *The Prince and the Pauper.*

Charles Cap. Sea captain who is uneasy on land and inland waters in James Fenimore Cooper's *The Pathfinder.*

Benjamin (Ben) Cape. Son of Caleb and Lizzie Cape; witnesses the murder of his friend Folded Leaf in Jessamyn West's *The Massacre at Fall Creek.*

Caleb (Cale) Cape. Husband of Lizzie Cape and unordained preacher to the settlement in Jessamyn West's *The Massacre at Fall Creek.*

Hannah (Hannay) Cape. Daughter of Caleb and Lizzie Cape; courted by Charles Fort and Oscar Dilk in Jessamyn West's *The Massacre at Fall Creek.*

Lizzie Cape. Wife of Caleb Cape in Jessamyn West's *The Massacre at Fall Creek.*

Luigi and Angelo Capello. Italian twins blamed for the murder of York Driscoll in Samuel Langhorne Clemens's *Pudd'nhead Wilson.*

Mrs. Capon. Woman with whom Frado leaves her son until she can regain strength and find a livelihood in Harriet E. Wilson's *Our Nig.*

Barry Caprio. Brother of Steve Caprio and former navy boxer; hired by Jackie Cogan to beat a confession out of Mark Trattman in George V. Higgins's *Cogan's Trade.*

Steve Caprio. Mafia thug and brother of Barry Caprio; hired by Jackie Cogan to beat a confession out of Mark Trattman in George V. Higgins's *Cogan's Trade.*

Captain. Lover of Ida Farange while she is married to Sir Claude in Henry James's *What Maisie Knew.*

la Longue Carabine. See Nathaniel Bumppo.

Caraher. Anarchist saloon keeper in the San Joaquin Valley who influences Presley to bomb S. Behrman's home in Frank Norris's *The Octopus.*

Richard (Dick) Caramel. Successful novelist and friend of Anthony Patch in F. Scott Fitzgerald's *The Beautiful and Damned.*

Judge Darwin Carberry. Judge who ultimately frees George Brush from an Ozarksville, Missouri, jail in Thornton Wilder's *Heaven's My Destination.*

C. (Eye, Stew Meat) Card. Spanish Civil War veteran and down-and-out private detective given to daydreaming about Babylon; hired to steal a corpse in Richard Brautigan's *Dreaming of Babylon.*

Carey. Slave of Frank Meriwether; coachman and butler in John Pendleton Kennedy's *Swallow Barn.*

Colonel Cargill. Former marketing executive famed for failure; now troubleshooter for General Peckem in Joseph Heller's *Catch-22.*

Carl. Farm boy who is the first love of Rose Dutcher in Hamlin Garland's *Rose of Dutcher's Coolly.*

Carl. Former lover from whom the narrator receives a bottle of brandy she later gives to her new suitor, a talented and passionate young writer, in Aline Bernstein's *The Journey Down.*

Carl. Husband of Vera; kills her lover, E. L. Fletcher, in Jerry Bumpus's *Anaconda*.

Carl. Navy combat veteran whose plan to murder Raditzer is thwarted in Peter Matthiessen's *Raditzer*.

Carl (Joe). Writer who has written no book; hates Paris in Henry Miller's *Tropic of Cancer*.

Carla. Mental patient who becomes Deborah Blau's friend in Hannah Green's *I Never Promised You a Rose Garden*.

Darlene Mosby Carlisle. Best friend of Neva Manning and former lover of Calvin Bartley in Hal Bennett's *A Wilderness of Vines*.

Ida (Cordelia) Carlisle. Powerful preserver of a social system based on differences in skin color among blacks in Burnside, Virginia; convicted of pretending to be white; dies in a home for the criminally insane; appears in Hal Bennett's *A Wilderness of Vines*, *The Black Wine*, and *Wait Until the Evening*.

Carlo. Handsome, teenaged hand-organ player aboard the *Highlander* in Herman Melville's *Redburn*.

Carlos. Proprietor of a wine cellar in John Edgar Wideman's *Hurry Home*.

Carlos. Neighbor of Harry Meyers; often beats his wife Nydia, and threatens Meyers in Jay Neugeboren's *Listen Ruben Fontanez*.

Carlotta. Mother of BZ; gives BZ and Helene money to stay married in Joan Didion's *Play It As It Lays*.

Christina Carlson. See Christina Jansen.

Claudia Carlstadt. Woman hired by Frank Cowperwood to seduce the mayor of Chicago so Cowperwood can blackmail him in Theodore Dreiser's *The Titan*.

Lady (Corinna) Carlton. Beautiful wife of Bruce Carlton; her faithfulness eventually persuades him to give up his relationship with Amber St. Clare in Kathleen Winsor's *Forever Amber*.

Lord (Bruce) Carlton. Dashing cavalier, privateer, only real love of Amber St. Clare, and father of two of her children; begins a King's grant plantation in Virginia with his wife, Corinna, in Kathleen Winsor's *Forever Amber*.

Carma. Muscular black southerner whose denial of adultery results in her husband's being sentenced to a chain gang in Jean Toomer's *Cane*.

Carmelo. Hired hand of Sparicio; works the tiller and sings a Mediterranean ballad in Lafcadio Hearn's *Chita*.

Frank Carmichael. Chief of police in Peter De Vries's *Comfort Me with Apples*.

John Carmichael. Hard-drinking executive of a meat packing firm in Robert Herrick's *The Memoirs of an American Citizen*.

Margaret Carmichael. See Margaret Carmichael Howland.

Robert Carmichael. See Robert Carmichael Howland.

Frank Carmody. Writer and drug addict; companion of Adam Moorad and Leo Percepied in Jack Kerouac's *The Subterraneans*.

Jersey Carmody. Single mother, writer, and helper of the other activists in M. F. Beal's *Amazon One*.

Lucette Carmody. Crippled child evangelist whose preaching fascinates both Mr. Rayber and young Francis Marion Tarwater in Flannery O'Connor's *The Violent Bear It Away*.

Carnashan. Alcoholic messenger hired by Henry Miller in Henry. Miller's *Tropic of Capricorn*.

Cassius P. (Cash) Carney. Boyhood friend of John Wickliff Shawnessy; financier in Ross Lockridge, Jr.'s *Raintree County*.

Caroline. Wife of Uncle Alex; nurses Ollie from wounds received in a knife fight in George Wylie Henderson's *Ollie Miss*; appears also in *Jule*.

Aunt Caroline. Relative with whom Henry Miller spends a summer; notable for her kindness to him and her pockmarked face in Henry Miller's *Tropic of Capricorn*.

Joe Carp. Bakery worker with Charlie Gordon in Daniel Keyes's *Flowers for Algernon*.

Belle Carpenter. Employee in a millinery shop who allows herself to be courted by George Willard because of her distrust of Ed Handby in Sherwood Anderson's *Winesburg, Ohio*.

David (Davey) Carpenter. Infant son of Patsy and Jim Carpenter in Larry McMurtry's *Moving On*.

James (Jim) Carpenter. Husband of Patsy White Carpenter and father of Davey Carpenter; leaves Patsy for fellow Rice University graduate student Clara Clark in Larry McMurtry's *Moving On*.

Patsy White Carpenter. Wife of Jim Carpenter and mother of Davey Carpenter; takes Hank Malory as a lover and loses her husband to Clara Clark in Larry McMurtry's *Moving On*.

Carey Carr. Minister who presides at the funeral of Peyton Loftis; confidant of Helen Loftis in William Styron's *Lie Down in Darkness*.

Nick Carraway. Neighbor and befriender of Jay Gatsby; narrator of F. Scott Fitzgerald's *The Great Gatsby*.

Sir Robert Carre. Military leader for Governor Lovelace in James Kirke Paulding's *Koningsmarke*.

Lieutenant Colonel Benny Carricker. Young fighter pilot and war hero whose punching of a black pilot is partly responsible for triggering unrest among black officers in James Gould Cozzens's *Guard of Honor*.

Carrie. Mute slave who befriends Dana Franklin and marries Nigel in Octavia E. Butler's *Kindred*.

Sister Carrie. See Caroline Meeber.

James Lawford Carrington. Nashville sculptor and second husband of Rozelle Hardcastle; dies of a heroin overdose in Robert Penn Warren's *A Place to Come To*.

John Carrington. Washington lawyer whom Senator Ratcliffe sends to Mexico in order to get him away from Madeleine Lee in Henry Adams's *Democracy*.

Nina (Mattie Bliss) Carrington. Chambermaid at the hotel where Paul Armstrong fakes his death; tries to blackmail Frank Walker in Mary Roberts Rinehart's *The Circular Staircase*.

Rebecca Carrington. See Rebecca Carrington Jones-Talbot.

Rozelle Hardcastle Butler (Beauty Queen of Dugton High, Miss Pritty-Pants, Rose) Carrington. Wife successively of Michael X. Butler, J. Lawford Carrington, and a black man posing as a swami; lover of Jed Tewksbury in Robert Penn Warren's *A Place to Come To*.

Madam Marion More Morris Carroll. Second wife of Major Carroll, stepmother of Sara Carroll, and mistress of the Carroll Farms; forced by her husband's mental decline to protect him and the community from each other in Constance Fenimore Woolson's *For the Major*.

Sara Carroll. Daughter of Major Carroll and beloved of Frederick Owen; responds diplomatically to the needs of both her father and stepmother, Marion More Carroll, in Constance Fenimore Woolson's *For the Major*.

Scar Carroll. Son of Major Carroll and Marion More Carroll and stepbrother of Sara Carroll in Constance Fenimore Woolson's *For the Major*.

Major Scarborough Carroll. Owner of the Carroll Farms, first citizen of Far Edgerley, and senior warden of St. John's Episcopal Church; subject of protective attention from his wife Marion More Carroll and daughter, Sara Carroll, as senility and blindness threaten his position in the community in Constance Fenimore Woolson's *For the Major*.

Willard Carroll. Paterfamilias and grandfather of Lucy Nelson Bassart in Philip Roth's *When She Was Good*.

Amy Carruthers. Wealthy North Carolina socialite who becomes Harley Drew's lover in Shelby Foote's *Love in a Dry Season*.

Jeff Carruthers. Husband and cousin of Amy Carruthers in Shelby Foote's *Love in a Dry Season*.

Christopher (Kit) Carson. Mountaineer and scout who brings news of the discovery of gold in California in Emerson Hough's *The Covered Wagon*.

Edward (Ed, Kit, Pimples) Carson. Acne-ridden seventeen-year-old apprentice mechanic to Juan Chicoy; interested in the electrifying Camille Oaks in John Steinbeck's *The Wayward Bus*.

Frederic Augustus Carson. Suitor of Nina Gordon, whom he loses to Edward Clayton, in Harriet Beecher Stowe's *Dred*.

Jonah Dean (J. D.) Carson. Powerful political ally of Angus Cleveland under indictment for theft of political funds; manipulator of anti-school integration demonstrations in Julian Mayfield's *The Grand Parade*.

Kit (Christóbal) Carson. Explorer, trapper, and Indian hunter; friend of Bishop Latour in Willa Cather's *Death Comes for the Archbishop*.

Audrey Carsons. American child who becomes a wild boy in William S. Burroughs's *The Wild Boys*; creates his lover Jerry in his story, "The Autobiography of a Wolf," and participates in the attempt to blow up the nerve-gas train in *Exterminator!*

Ardis Carter. See Ardis Ross.

Bella Carter. Mistress of Rafe Ashton in H. D.'s *Bid Me to Live*.

Cyrus Carter. President of a railroad, employer of Oliver Tappan, and uncle of Madeline Carter in Hjalmar Hjorth Boyesen's *The Golden Calf*.

Davis (Davy) Carter. Kentuckian who is murdered by his lover, Eva Medina Canada, in Gayl Jones's *Eva's Man.*

Faron Carter. Fishing guide who works out of Key West in Thomas McGuane's *Ninety-Two in the Shade.*

Gil Carter. Rowdy best friend of Art Croft in Walter Van Tilburg Clark's *The Ox-Bow Incident.*

Dr. Harry Carter. Teacher of psychology and one of Jacob Horner's interviewers at Wicomico State Teachers College in John Barth's *The End of the Road.*

Hattie (Hattie Starr) Carter. Proprietor of a Louisville brothel; mother of Berenice Fleming in Theodore Dreiser's *The Stoic* and *The Titan.*

John T. Carter. Southern gentleman serving in the Union army during the Civil War who marries Lillie Ravenel despite the objections of her father; dies in battle shortly after the discovery of his affair with Lillie's aunt, Mrs. Larue, in John William DeForest's *Miss Ravenel's Conversion from Secession to Loyalty.*

Lillie Ravenel Carter. Louisiana belle who, through a series of adventures and marriages, becomes firmly attached to the Union cause in the Civil War in John William DeForest's *Miss Ravenel's Conversion from Secession to Loyalty.*

Madam Fannie Rosalie de Carter. Neighbor of Aunt Hager Williams; fights for women's suffrage and prohibition in Langston Hughes's *Not Without Laughter.*

Madeline Carter. Aristocratic New Yorker and niece of Cyrus Carter; marries Oliver Tappan and inspires his corruption in Hjalmar Hjorth Boyesen's *The Golden Calf.*

Ravenel (Ravvie) Carter. Son of John and Lillie Ravenel Carter; his presence and need for attention occupies Lillie after her husband's infidelity is discovered in John William DeForest's *Miss Ravenel's Conversion from Secession to Loyalty.*

Ted Carter. Young man who, to the chagrin of his social-climbing family, loves the socially unacceptable Selena Cross in Grace Metalious's *Peyton Place.*

William Carter. See Jackson Yeager.

Charles Carteret. Friend of Nick Dormer; urges Dormer to enter politics in Henry James's *The Tragic Muse.*

Major Philip Carteret. Aristocratic white newspaper owner and adversary of Dr. William Miller in Charles W. Chesnutt's *The Marrow of Tradition.*

Elijah J. (Hookworm) Cartwright. Sex-driven Tennessee mountain boy who is a member of Big Red Smalley's traveling gospel show in George Garrett's *Do, Lord, Remember Me.*

Lettie Cartwright. Midwife of Tangierneck in Sarah E. Wright's *This Child's Gonna Live.*

Colonel Comyn Carvel. Grandson of Dorothy Manners and Richard Carvel; father of Virginia Carvel; proslavery aristocrat in Civil War St. Louis in Winston Churchill's *The Crisis.*

Dorothy Manners Carvel. See Dorothy Manners.

Grafton Carvel. Deceitful, unprincipled uncle of Richard Carvel in Winston Churchill's *Richard Carvel.*

Lionel Carvel. Kindly man who rears the orphaned Richard Carvel in Winston Churchill's *Richard Carvel.*

Philip Carvel. Ne'er-do-well son of Grafton Carvel in Winston Churchill's *Richard Carvel.*

Richard (Dick) Carvel. Manly Marylander who suffers greatly as an American supporter during the Revolutionary War; husband of Dorothy Manners; narrator of Winston Churchill's *Richard Carvel.*

Virginia (Jinny) Carvel. Descendant of Richard Carvel; spirited and high-minded supporter of her Maryland ancestors and of slavery; marries Stephen Brice in Winston Churchill's *The Crisis.*

Alden Carver, Junior. Bachelor brother of Stephen Carver; succeeds his father as a bank president; appears in Margaret Ayer Barnes's *Years of Grace* and *Wisdom's Gate.*

Cicily Carver. See Cicily Carver Bridges Lancaster.

Cicily (Silly) Carver. Unmarried sister of Stephen Carver in Margaret Ayer Barnes's *Years of Grace.*

Jane Ward (Mumsy) Carver. Daughter of John and Lizzie Ward, wife of Stephen Carver, and mother of three children, including Cicily Carver; despite her education and opportunities, she accepts a conventional life in Margaret Ayer Barnes's *Years of Grace* and *Wisdom's Gate.*

Captain Jonathan Carver. Officer in Rogers' Rangers who later betrays Major Robert Rogers in Kenneth Roberts's *Northwest Passage.*

Lawyer Carver. Attorney who reads Peregrine Lacey Catlett's will to the Catlett family in Mary Lee Settle's *Know Nothing.*

Maury Carver. Loudmouth member of Johnny Catlett's militia unit in Mary Lee Settle's *Know Nothing*.

Mother Carver. Wise old frontier woman who settles with her family at Beulah; tries to help Sally Lacey adapt to frontier life but is scorned in Mary Lee Settle's *O Beulah Land*.

Preston Carver. Eighteen-year-old dandy and subordinate officer in Johnny Catlett's Confederate army unit in Mary Lee Settle's *Know Nothing*.

Stephen Carver. Boston banker married to Jane Ward Carver; father of three children, including Cicily Carver, in Margaret Ayer Barnes's *Years of Grace* and *Wisdom's Gate*.

Francis Carwin. Biloquist who wreaks havoc on the lives of Clara Wieland, her family, and her friends in Charles Brockden Brown's *Wieland*.

Christopher Fidele Cary. Husband of Olivia Cary; a doctor who refuses to "pass for white" in Jessie Redmon Fauset's *Comedy, American Style*.

Edward Cary. Son of Warwick Cary, brother of Judith Cary, nephew of Fauquier Cary, and husband of Désirée Gaillard; fights with the Confederate navy in Virginia and Mississippi in Mary Johnston's *The Long Roll* and *Cease Firing*.

Fairfax Cary. Brother of Ludwell Cary; postpones engagement to Unity Dandridge to pursue his brother's murderer in Mary Johnston's *Lewis Rand*.

Fauquier Cary. Uncle of Judith and Edward Cary and cousin of Richard Cleave; Whig veteran of the Mexican War who wants to preserve the Union, until the battle at Fort Sumter; promoted to the rank of general and loses an arm at Sharpsburg; appears in Mary Johnston's *The Long Roll* and *Cease Firing*.

Judith Jacqueline Cary. Daughter of Warwick Cary, sister of Edward Cary, and niece of Fauquier Cary; attends wounded Confederate troops in Richmond, and marries Richard Cleave; appears in Mary Johnston's *The Long Roll* and *Cease Firing*.

Lucy Cary. Aunt of Judith and Edward Cary and sister of Fauquier Cary; makes shirts, from family curtains, for Confederate troops in Mary Johnston's *The Long Roll*.

Ludwell Cary. Brother of Fairfax Cary; rival in politics and romance of Lewis Rand, by whom he is murdered, in Mary Johnston's *Lewis Rand*.

Oliver Cary. Dark-skinned son of Olivia Cary; driven to suicide by his mother's treatment of him in Jessie Redmon Fauset's *Comedy, American Style*.

Olivia Blanchard Cary. Upper-class, light-skinned woman who eventually destroys two of her children by her obsession with skin color in Jessie Redmon Fauset's *Comedy, American Style*.

Teresa (Tess, Treesa) Cary. Light-skinned mulatto daughter of Olivia Cary; forced by her mother to give up her dark-skinned lover to marry the white Aristide Pailleron in Jessie Redmon Fauset's *Comedy, American Style*.

Christopher Blanchard (Chris) Cary, Jr.. Son of Olivia Cary; saved from her influence by his father and his wife's claiming of their black heritage in Jessie Redmon Fauset's *Comedy, American Style*.

Prince Casamassima. Young and exceedingly wealthy Italian prince married to Christina Light in Henry James's *Roderick Hudson*; pursues his runaway wife in an attempt to convince her to return home in *The Princess Casamassima*.

Princess Casamassima. See Christina Light.

Jock Casey. Imaginary pitcher who kills Damon Rutherford with a bean ball in Robert Coover's *The Universal Baseball Association, Inc., J. Henry Waugh, Prop*.

Margaret Casey. Manipulative Irish Catholic housekeeper to whom Isabel Moore makes a final conscience payment in Mary Gordon's *Final Payments*.

Leni Cass. Unemployed actress living with her son in a Second Avenue apartment managed by Norman Moonbloom in Edward Lewis Wallant's *The Tenants of Moonbloom*.

Cassandra (Candy). Daughter of Skipper and Gertrude, mother of Pixie, and wife of Fernandez; commits suicide by jumping from the top of a lighthouse in John Hawkes's *Second Skin*.

Maurice (Joe) Cassard. French screenwriter who marries Belinda in Ludwig Bemelmans's *Dirty Eddie*.

Casse-tête. Thief executed with Stefan in William Faulkner's *A Fable*.

Maggie (M. C.) Cassidy. First love of Jack Duluoz; ultimately rejects him in Jack Kerouac's *Maggie Cassidy*; mentioned in *Book of Dreams* and *Desolation Angels*.

Cassie. Fiancée of Bumper Morgan and teacher of French at Los Angeles City College in Joseph Wambaugh's *The Blue Knight*.

Cassy (Miss Cassy). Mysterious, unwilling slave mistress to Simon Legree; manages the escape of herself and Emmeline, her daughter, with the help of Uncle Tom and is reunited by chance with Eliza Harris in Harriet Beecher Stowe's *Uncle Tom's Cabin.*

Minnie Castevet. Wife of Roman Castevet; prepares the mysterious daily drinks for Rosemary Woodhouse during Rosemary's pregnancy with Satan's son in Ira Levin's *Rosemary's Baby.*

Roman Castevet. Warlock who poses as a kindly old neighbor of Rosemary and Guy Woodhouse; orchestrates Satan's seduction of Rosemary Woodhouse in Ira Levin's *Rosemary's Baby.* See also Steven Marcato.

Joe Castiglione. Miner who initiates a new recruit by sodomizing him with an air hose in Robert Coover's *The Origin of the Brunists.*

Alejandro Castillo. Younger son of the valley's richest man and lover of the beautiful María de las Garzas; friend of Bob Webster; married to a woman he does not love; dies tragically in Josefina Niggli's *Mexican Village.*

Joaquín Castillo. Older son of the valley's richest man; leaves Hidalgo to fight in the Revolution of 1910; returns incognito as an actor with a wandering troupe and reclaims his position in the village, eventually becoming a close friend of Bob Webster, in Josefina Niggli's *Mexican Village.*

James Castle. Elkton Hills student who commits suicide rather than retract his statement accusing another student of conceit in J. D. Salinger's *The Catcher in the Rye.*

Julian Castle. Operator of a jungle hospital; Albert Schweitzer-figure in Kurt Vonnegut's *Cat's Cradle.*

Philip Castle. Son of Julian Castle; hotelkeeper and author of a book on San Lorenzo in Kurt Vonnegut's *Cat's Cradle.*

Lady Castledean. Member of the Ververs' social circle who is romantically interested in Mr. Blint in Henry James's *The Golden Bowl.*

Castlemaine. See Barbara Palmer, Lady Castlemaine.

Fidel Castro. Cuban dictator who, in Margaret Reynolds's fantasy, is really a woman disguised as a man in Anne Richardson Roiphe's *Up the Sandbox!*

Jim Casy. Former preacher who baptized the infant Tom Joad (II); inspires Tom to correct some social wrongs in John Steinbeck's *The Grapes of Wrath.*

Catalina Kate. See Kate.

Governor John (Black Jack) Cates. Head of Typhon International; great-uncle of Amy Joubert in William Gaddis's *JR.*

Abiah Cathcart. Stolid New Englander who rises from poverty to become a leading citizen of Norwood, owning the best set of matched horses in town and fathering an enormous family, in Henry Ward Beecher's *Norwood.*

Alice Cathcart. Friend of Rose Wentworth; joins Wentworth and Agate Bissell in Northern hospital duty during the Civil War, only to see her true love, Thomas Heywood, die fighting for the South at Gettysburg, in Henry Ward Beecher's *Norwood.*

Barton Cathcart. Son of Abiah and Rachel Cathcart; practical yet mystical graduate of Amherst who becomes the Norwood schoolmaster; rises to a Union generalship in the Civil War despite being wounded and captured several times; marries Rose Wentworth in Henry Ward Beecher's *Norwood.*

Colonel Cathcart. Air force officer whose desire for personal glory causes him to keep raising the number of bombing missions Yossarian's squadron must fly in Joseph Heller's *Catch-22.*

Rachel Liscomb Cathcart. Sensitive wife of Abiah Cathcart; passes on some of her mystical spirit to her son Barton Cathcart in Henry Ward Beecher's *Norwood.*

Andrew (Andy) Cather. Husband of Bertha Cather; at age twelve he found the body of his drowned mother; narrates part of Conrad Aiken's *Great Circle.*

Bertha (Berty) Cather. Wife of Andrew Cather; has an affair with Tom Crapo in Conrad Aiken's *Great Circle.*

David Cather. Uncle of Andrew Cather and brother of John Cather; drowns with his lover Doris Cather in Conrad Aiken's *Great Circle.*

Doris Cather. Mother of Andrew Cather; drowns with her lover David Cather in Conrad Aiken's *Great Circle.*

John Cather. Father of Andrew Cather in Conrad Aiken's *Great Circle.*

Catherine. Wife of Hugh, lover of Cyril, and mother of Meredith, Dolores, and Eveline; once forced by Hugh to wear a chastity belt in an attempt to stop her affair with Cyril; collapses at Hugh's funeral and spends time in a village sanctuary in John Hawkes's *The Blood Oranges.*

Queen Catherine (Infanta Catherine of Portugal). Barren queen of Restoration England's Charles II; tolerates his many mistresses out of love for him and the hope that she will eventually give him a legitimate heir to the English throne in Kathleen Winsor's *Forever Amber*.

George Catherwood. Brother of Tom Catherwood; Confederate soldier in a divided family in Winston Churchill's *The Crisis*.

Tom Catherwood. Brother of George Catherwood; Union soldier in a divided family in Winston Churchill's *The Crisis*.

Doc Cathey. Physician and small-town philosopher; long-term companion and comforter to Henry Soames in John Gardner's *Nickel Mountain*.

Andy Catlett. Oldest son of Bess and Wheeler Catlett in Wendell Berry's *A Place on Earth* and *The Memory of Old Jack*.

Bess Feltner Catlett. Daughter of Mat and Margaret Feltner; wife of Wheeler Catlett and mother of Andy and Henry Catlett in Wendell Berry's *A Place on Earth* and *The Memory of Old Jack*.

Ezekiel (Zeke) Catlett. Eldest son of Jeremiah and Hannah Catlett; marries Sara Lacey and becomes Johnny Lacey's heir; kills Witcikti, using the English tomahawk once stolen from Witcikti himself, in Mary Lee Settle's *O Beulah Land*.

Hannah Bridewell Catlett. London pickpocket transported to Virginia; as a captive of Shawnee Indians, she is the first white settler to see Beulah land; killed by Witcikti in the last Indian raid at Beulah; wife of Jeremiah and mother of Ezekiel and Rebecca Catlett in Mary Lee Settle's *O Beulah Land*.

Henry Catlett. Youngest son of Bess and Wheeler Catlett in Wendell Berry's *A Place on Earth* and *The Memory of Old Jack*.

Jeremiah Catlett. Illiterate farmer and "New Light" preacher led to escape his indentures, travel west, rescue Hannah Bridewell Catlett, his future wife, in the wilderness, and move to Beulah, where he is killed in the last Indian raid; father of Ezekiel and Rebecca Catlett in Mary Lee Settle's *O Beulah Land*.

Johnny Catlett. Younger son of Leah and Peregrine Lacey Catlett; leaves Beulah to avoid commitment to Melinda Lacey; goes to Missouri and Kansas, but returns to take over Beulah from his father; eventually enlists in the Confederate army but without believing in the southern position or the possibility of success in Mary Lee Settle's *Know Nothing*.

Leah Cutwright Catlett. Descendant of Doggo Cutwright; Ohio-born wife of Peregrine Lacey Catlett and mother of Lewis, Johnny, and Lydia Catlett; an outsider who is initially an abolitionist, she becomes willing to sell slaves and more approving of slavery than is her husband in Mary Lee Settle's *Know Nothing*.

Lewis Catlett. Elder son of Leah and Peregrine Lacey Catlett; inherits his mother's antislavery attitudes, religious piety, and sense of being an outsider; becomes a preacher and an abolitionist; leaves Beulah and eventually enlists in the Union army in Mary Lee Settle's *Know Nothing*.

Lydia Catlett. See Lydia Catlett Neill.

Mamie Brandon Catlett. Descendant of Backwater Brandon and the Kreggs; daughter-in-law of Ezekiel Catlett and mother of Peregrine Lacey Catlett in Mary Lee Settle's *Know Nothing*.

Peregrine Lacey Catlett. Grandson of Ezekiel Catlett, proprietor of Beulah, husband of Leah Cutwright Catlett, and father of Lewis, Johnny, and Lydia Catlett and of the slave Toey; deplores the responsibilities of being a slaveowner and supports the Union in Mary Lee Settle's *Know Nothing*.

Rebecca (Becky) Catlett. Daughter of Jeremiah and Hannah Catlett and sister of Ezekiel Catlett in Mary Lee Settle's *O Beulah Land*.

Sara Lacey (Mrs. Ezekiel Catlett) Catlett. Daughter of Johnny and Sally Lacey, sister of Peregrine and Montague Lacey, and wife of Ezekiel Catlett; only child of Johnny Lacey to share his love for Beulah land and his egalitarian ideas, she eventually inherits Beulah in Mary Lee Settle's *O Beulah Land*.

Sara Lacey (Mrs. Lewis Catlett) Catlett. Daughter of Brandon and Sally Lacey; beautiful child who, as an adult, becomes gawky, religious, and conscious of being a poor relation; marries Lewis Catlett and adopts his attitudes in Mary Lee Settle's *Know Nothing*.

Wheeler Catlett. Lawyer in Port William, Kentucky, and son-in-law of Mat Feltner; husband of Bess Catlett and father of Andy and Henry Catlett in Wendell Berry's *A Place on Earth* and *The Memory of Old Jack*.

Debby Catlin. Daughter of John and Marian Catlin in Wallace Stegner's *All the Little Live Things*.

Henry (Hank) Catlin. Depression-era newcomer to California from the Midwest; defeats Walter Knight for a seat in the state legislature in Joan Didion's *Run River*.

Jeremiah Catlin. Union soldier from Lane County, Tennessee, who is imprisoned by the Confederates; husband of Marcia Vaiden in T. S. Stribling's *The Store.*

Jerry Catlin the Second. Son of Jerry and Marcia Catlin; seduces Pammy Lee Sparkman; Methodist minister infatuated with Sydna Crowninshield Vaiden but who marries Aurelia Swartout; appears in T. S. Stribling's *The Store* and *Unfinished Cathedral.*

John Catlin. Husband of Marian Catlin in Wallace Stegner's *All the Little Live Things.*

Marcia Vaiden Catlin. See Marcia Vaiden.

Marian Catlin. Neighbor of the Allstons; dies of cancer while pregnant in Wallace Stegner's *All the Little Live Things.*

Katherine Cattleman. Wife of Paul Cattleman; becomes the lover of Iz Einsam, a psychiatrist for whom she works as a research assistant at UCLA, in Alison Lurie's *The Nowhere City.*

Paul Cattleman. History researcher, husband of Katherine Cattleman, and lover of Ceci O'Connor in Alison Lurie's *The Nowhere City.*

Gaius Valerius Catullus. Young poet with great potential; first an enemy of Caesar and then a friend; loves Clodia Pulcher, who rejects him, in Thornton Wilder's *The Ides of March.*

Boone (Zeb Calloway) Caudill. Fledgling mountain man who leaves his Kentucky home to trap furs in the Rocky Mountains in A. B. Guthrie's *The Big Sky.*

Charlotte Ann Caulder. Former girlfriend of Bob Beaudreau, who shoots her after she becomes Phil Elliott's lover, in Peter Gent's *North Dallas Forty.*

Allie Caulfield. Sensitive younger brother of Holden Caulfield; dies of leukemia in J. D. Salinger's *The Catcher in the Rye.*

D. B. Caulfield. Older brother of Holden Caulfield; writer of sensitive short stories who now writes movie scripts in Hollywood in J. D. Salinger's *The Catcher in the Rye.*

Holden Caulfield. Seventeen-year-old prep school dropout who recounts the events leading to his confinement in a sanitorium; narrator of J. D. Salinger's *The Catcher in the Rye.*

Phoebe Josephine Caulfield. Ten-year-old sister of Holden Caulfield; writes short stories about "Hazle" Weatherfield in J. D. Salinger's *The Catcher in the Rye.*

Rita Cavanagh. Actress turned lyric poet and Greenwich Village celebrity in Edmund Wilson's *I Thought of Daisy.*

Melissa Cavanaugh. Lover of Tommy Douglas in Scott Spencer's *Preservation Hall.*

Theodore (Ted) Cavanaugh. President of West Condon's First National Bank who is behind the efforts of the Common Sense Committee to disband the Brunists in Robert Coover's *The Origin of the Brunists.*

Tommy (Kit, Kitten) Cavanaugh. Son of Ted Cavanaugh; follows in the footsteps of Justin Miller as a high school basketball star in Robert Coover's *The Origin of the Brunists.*

Jennifer (Jenny) Cavilleri. See Jennifer Cavilleri Barrett.

Philip (Phil) Cavilleri. Rhode Island pastry chef and father of Jennifer Cavilleri Barrett; approves of his daughter's marriage to Oliver Barrett IV in Erich Segal's *Love Story;*. consoles Barrett after Jenny's death in *Oliver's Story.*

Dorinda (D'rindy) Cayce. Attractive daughter of John Cayce; scorns the suit of Rick Tyler and believes that Hiram Kelsey is similar to an Old Testament prophet in Mary Noailles Murfree's *The Prophet of the Great Smoky Mountains.*

John Cayce. Moonshiner and father of Dorinda Cayce in Mary Noailles Murfree's *The Prophet of the Great Smoky Mountains.*

Ceci. See Cecile O'Connor.

Mr. Cedarquist. Wealthy manufacturer and shipbuilder who sees a great future in grain exports to the Far East in Frank Norris's *The Octopus.*

Mrs. Cedarquist. Wife of Mr. Cedarquist and supporter of the arts, including artists of dubious merit, in Frank Norris's *The Octopus.*

Cederberge. Chief inspector in the international marine police; investigates the disappearance of Hellos in Calvin Hernton's *Scarecrow.*

Cinquo (Sinker) Centavos. Young Mexican horse wrangler with the Del Sol trail herd in Emerson Hough's *North of 36.*

Inez de Certavallos. Sixteen-year-old daughter of a wealthy Spanish nobleman in Louisiana and bride of Duncan Uncas Middleton; kidnapped on her wedding night by Abiram White and Ishmael Bush; later rescued by Middleton, with the help of

Natty Bumppo, in James Fenimore Cooper's *The Prairie*.

Dr. Chadwick. Black general practitioner who comforts John Wilder during Wilder's last emotional breakdown in Richard Yates's *Disturbing the Peace*.

Freddy Chaikin. Agent for Maria Wyeth in Joan Didion's *Play It As It Lays*.

Jud Chain. Professional gambler and business associate of Bo Mason in Wallace Stegner's *The Big Rock Candy Mountain*.

Chairman Mao's Robot. Chinese woman delegate to a youth festival in Moscow; kidnapped and sexually exploited by George Levanter and Romarkin in Jerzy Kosinski's *Blind Date*.

Conrad Chakravorti. Indian who rents the Adirondack cabin inhabited by Ambrose Clay; mishap prevents his discovery of Clay's suicide in Gail Godwin's *Violet Clay*.

Lieutenant Commander Jack Challee. Navy judge advocate who prosecutes Lieutenant Steve Maryk for mutiny in Herman Wouk's *The Caine Mutiny*.

Beryl Challenor. Childhood friend and playmate of Selina Boyce; values prestige and material gain in Paule Marshall's *Brown Girl, Brownstones*.

Percy Challenor. Father of Beryl Challenor and a leader of the Association of Barbadian Homeowners and Businessmen in Paule Marshall's *Brown Girl, Brownstones*.

Madame Charles (Anastasia Petrovna Potapov) Chamar. Russian mother of Armande Chamar Person; product of a noble family ruined by the revolution in Vladimir Nabokov's *Transparent Things*.

Brice Chamberlain. Prominent lawyer who supports the nesters; paramour of Lucie Brewton and father of Brock Brewton; becomes judge of the district court in Conrad Richter's *The Sea of Grass*.

Joshua Lawrence Chamberlain. Brilliant Union colonel who defends a rocky hill called Little Round Top against a rebel onslaught at Gettysburg in Michael Shaara's *The Killer Angels*.

Frank Chambers. Drifter who works for Nick Papadakis and is the lover of Cora Papadakis; with Cora, he murders Nick, but is acquitted; later convicted of murdering Cora, who dies accidentally, in James M. Cain's *The Postman Always Rings Twice*.

Edith de Chambrolet. Wealthy expatriate American who takes in McKenna Gallagher after Louisa

Gallagher's suicide attempt in James Jones's *The Merry Month of May*.

Chance (Chauncey Gardiner). Gardener, idiot, and hero who is propelled to fame in Jerzy Kosinski's *Being There*.

George (Fat) Chance. Portly inspector and chief of detectives in Peter De Vries's *The Mackerel Plaza*.

Vic Chance. Airplane builder in William Faulkner's *Pylon*.

Kate Chanceller. Feminist, socialist, and student at Ohio State University; becomes a good friend of Clara Butterworth in Sherwood Anderson's *Poor White*.

Olive Chancellor. Radical Boston spinster who opposes the marriage of her protégée Verena Tarrant in Henry James's *The Bostonians*.

Cathie Chandler. See Cathie Chandler Finer.

Tom Chaney. Hired hand and outlaw who kills two men and who is pursued by Mattie Ross, Rooster Cogburn, and LaBoeuf in Charles Portis's *True Grit*.

Luke Channell. Disgusting rogue and secret first husband of Amber St. Clare in Kathleen Winsor's *Forever Amber*.

Mrs. Luke Channell. See Amber St. Clare.

Christina Channing. Singer with a symphony orchestra and mistress of Eugene Witla in Theodore Dreiser's *The "Genius."*

Nancy Dupree (Bugsy) Channing. Bay Area socialite who marries and divorces Ryder Channing in Joan Didion's *Run River*.

Ryder Channing. Entrepreneur and real estate developer; seducer of Martha McClellan and Lily Knight McClellan; murdered by Everett McClellan in Joan Didion's *Run River*.

Chantal. Daughter of Papa and Honorine, older sister of Pascal, and lover of Henri for five years; with Henri, an unwilling passenger in the car in John Hawkes's *Travesty*.

Madame de Chantelle. Mother-in-law of Anna Leath; represents aristocratic French propriety in spite of her American origins in Edith Wharton's *The Reef*.

Mateo Chapa. Mestizo chauffeur whose entrepreneurial ambitions and intelligence accelerate his rise in the Monterrey business world; marries Sofía Vázquez de Anda in Josefina Niggli's *Step Down, Elder Brother*.

Ann Chapin. Daughter of Edith and Joe Chapin I in John O'Hara's *Ten North Frederick*.

Benjamin Chapin. Father of Joe Chapin I in John O'Hara's *Ten North Frederick*.

Charlotte Hofman Chapin. Wife of Benjamin Chapin and mother of Joe Chapin I in John O'Hara's *Ten North Frederick*.

Edith Stokes Chapin. Wife and widow of Joe Chapin I in John O'Hara's *Ten North Frederick*.

Joseph (Joe) Benjamin Chapin. Gibbsville, Pennsylvania, lawyer who aspires to be president of the United States in John O'Hara's *Ten North Frederick*.

Joseph Benjamin (Joby, Joe) Chapin, Jr.. Son of Edith and Joe Chapin I; jazz pianist unappreciated by his parents; works for the OSS in John O'Hara's *Ten North Frederick*.

Celia Chapman. Eighteen-year-old cleaning woman who loves Leon Fisher in Albert Halper's *Union Square*.

Ali Juan (God of Street Boys) Chapultepec. Street boy in William S. Burroughs's *The Soft Machine*; as Clinch Smith's houseboy, he runs amok and is killed in *Exterminator!*; appears also in *Nova Express*, *The Ticket That Exploded*, and *The Wild Boys*.

Anna-Maria Charaiambos. Sister of Orsetta Procopirios in Nicholas Delbanco's *The Martlet's Tale*.

John F. (Jack) Charisma. Martyred United States president and rival of Trick E. Dixon in Philip Roth's *Our Gang*.

Charitas. Conventional neighbor of Helen; shocked by Helen's views of love and morality; forces her son Damastor to leave home after he impregnates Helen's maid Adraste in John Erskine's *The Private Life of Helen of Troy*.

Charity. Wife of Lazarus and nurse to Johnny Church, his mother, and his aunt, Nell Lacy, in Mary Lee Settle's *Prisons*.

Charlemont. St. Louis merchant who bankrupts himself to help a needy friend in Herman Melville's *The Confidence-Man*.

Charles. Young street hustler and drug addict; sent to a school for delinquent boys at age fourteen for stealing; homeless after his release because his mother is hospitalized and his father has disappeared in Alexis Deveaux's *Spirits in the Street*.

Anatole Charles. Art dealer who sponsors a show of Eugene Witla's work in Theodore Dreiser's *The "Genius."*

Nick Charles. Out-of-retirement private detective in Dashiell Hammett's *The Thin Man*.

Nora Charles. Wealthy wife of Nick Charles in Dashiell Hammett's *The Thin Man*.

Vera Charles. Famed actress and best friend of Mame Dennis in Patrick Dennis's *Auntie Mame* and *Around the World with Auntie Mame*.

Charles II. See Charles Stuart.

Charles II. See Charles Xavier Vseslav.

Inez Dresden Charlesbois. Piano and accordion teacher idealized by Cress Delahanty until Cress learns of her affair with Don Rivers in Jessamyn West's *Cress Delahanty*.

Luther Charlesbois. Husband of Inez Charlesbois in Jessamyn West's *Cress Delahanty*.

Lester Charley. Bookstore owner and later a canaller who rents a room to Jerry and Mary Fowler in Walter D. Edmonds's *Erie Water*.

Charlie. Large, kind, black male nurse on the Men's Violent Ward of Bellevue Mental Hospital, where John Wilder is a patient, in Richard Yates's *Disturbing the Peace*.

Charlie. Painter from Texas whose affair with Big Lot inspires the male narrator, Charlie's lover, to write Tennessee Williams's *Moise and the World of Reason*.

Charlotte. Daughter of Miss Billie in Gayl Jones's *Eva's Man*.

Charlotte. French trainee PaPa LaBas hires to replace Berbelang; becomes an assistant in a stage show and, because she helps Berbelang return art stolen by Western museums to the original owners, is killed by Biff Musclewhite in Ishmael Reed's *Mumbo Jumbo*.

Charlotte. Viennese prostitute questioned about lust by Jenny Fields; has sex with Garp, becomes a close friend of his, and dies of uterine cancer in John Irving's *The World According to Garp*.

Ed Charney. Gibbsville bootlegger and keeper of Helene Holman in John O'Hara's *Appointment in Samarra*.

Duke of Chartersea. Degenerate, immoral suitor of Dorothy Marmaduke and rival of Richard Carvel in Winston Churchill's *Richard Carvel*.

Jack Chase. Respected British captain of the main-top aboard the *Neversink*; deserts ship to fight for Peru; secures liberty for the crew in Rio in Herman Melville's *White-Jacket*.

Jasper Chase. Local society novelist in love with but rejected by Rachel Winslow in Charles M. Sheldon's *In His Steps*.

Joseph Raymond (Joe, Joey) Chase. Brother of Orpha Chase; Quaker minister and faith healer charged with manslaughter in the death of Marie Griswold in Jessamyn West's *The Life I Really Lived*.

Mary Eliza Chase. Niece of Eliza Bowen Jumel; marries Nelson Chase in Gore Vidal's *Burr*.

Nelson Chase. Nephew by marriage of Eliza Bowen Jumel and husband of Mary Eliza Chase in Gore Vidal's *Burr*.

Orpha (Mrs. Dudley, Mrs. Hesse, Tumbleweed) Chase. Novelist; sister of Joseph Chase; wife of Alonzo Dudley, Jacob Hesse, and Ralph Navarro; lover of Tom O'Hara and Gregory McGovern; adoptive mother of Wanda; narrator of Jessamyn West's *The Life I Really Lived*.

Chatelaine of La Trinité (Bertha). Chatelaine of a community in the High Alps; travels through Europe with Aurelia West, dilettantes, and minor nobles in Henry Blake Fuller's *The Chatelaine of La Trinité*.

Denise Chatillion. Early settler of Fort Hill and wife of Pettecasockee in Jesse Hill Ford's *The Raider*.

Chaucer. Chief writer for comedian Harry Mercury in Peter De Vries's *Through the Fields of Clover*.

Ellen Chauncey. Pleasant young woman Ellen Montgomery meets at the Marshmans' Christmas dinner; they become bosom friends in Susan Warner's *The Wide, Wide World*.

Mary Cheap. Elderly Jewish store owner who insists Joe Market end her life as he did his son's in Hal Bennett's *Lord of Dark Places*.

Comte Raymond de Chelles. Third husband of Undine Spragg; enraged when Undine attempts to sell his family's Louis Quinze tapestries hanging in his chateau de Saint Désert in Edith Wharton's *The Custom of the Country*.

Countess Raymond de Chelles. See Undine Spragg.

Albert Chenal. White merchant in protest of whom the Reverend Phillip Martin is organizing the black community in Ernest J. Gaines's *In My Father's House*.

Celia Chentshiner. Intellectual wife of Haiml Chentshiner and lover of Morris Feitelzohn and Aaron Greidinger in Isaac Bashevis Singer's *Shosha*.

Haiml Chentshiner. Well-to-do husband of Celia Chentshiner and friend and benefactor of Aaron Greidinger in Isaac Bashevis Singer's *Shosha*.

Coralie Chépé. Governess for the Talbot family before the Civil War; strips their abandoned house of its remaining valuables and refuses to help them when they return to New Orleans destitute after the war in Grace King's *The Pleasant Ways of St. Médard*.

Cherry. See Cherry Melanie.

Mary Cherry. Opinionated spinster who moves from family to family in the Natchez plantation society; during the Civil War, sneaks messages and medicines through the picket lines in Stark Young's *So Red the Rose*.

Pete (The Smoothie) Cheshire. Ex-convict and attempted blackmailer in Peter De Vries's *Comfort Me with Apples*.

Stella Chesney. Beautiful actress, fugitive from a jealous lover in Mexico, and finally wife of Augie March and starlet in the French movie *Les Orphelines* in Saul Bellow's *The Adventures of Augie March*.

Ellen (Ellie) Chesser. Daughter of an itinerant farmer; engaged to Jonas Prather but marries Jasper Kent and has many children in Elizabeth Madox Roberts's *The Time of Man*.

Henry Chesser. Itinerant farmer who is the husband of Nellie Chesser and the father of Ellen Chesser in Elizabeth Madox Roberts's *The Time of Man*.

Nellie Chesser. Wife of Henry Chesser and mother of Ellen Chesser in Elizabeth Madox Roberts's *The Time of Man*.

Hannah Chester. Maid to Eleanore and Mary Leavenworth; discovered to be missing following the murder of Horatio Leavenworth in Anna Katharine Green's *The Leavenworth Case*.

Charles (Cheswickle) Cheswick. Blustering but insecure mental patient who apparently drowns himself in Ken Kesey's *One Flew Over the Cuckoo's Nest*.

Chiang (Elder Gull, The Elder). Leader of the flock of seagulls who are perfecting their flying skills; helps Jonathan Livingston Seagull become a better flyer in Richard Bach's *Jonathan Livingston Seagull*.

Bebe (Francois Parmentier) Chicago. West Indian homosexual with political connections to the *guerrilleros* and to Gerardo Strasser-Mendana in

Joan Didion's *A Book of Common Prayer*.

Chicken Little. Young boy who, during a child's game, slips from Sula's hands and drowns in Toni Morrison's *Sula*.

Chicken Number Two. Lifetime convict who, in his dying days, evokes a transforming sympathy in Zeke Farragut that results in Farragut's escape in John Cheever's *Falconer*.

Crystal Chickering. Fiancée, then wife of Chick Swallow in Peter De Vries's *Comfort Me with Apples*.

Clayton (Bloody) Chiclitz. American industrialist and president of Yoyodyne, Inc., in Thomas Pynchon's *V.* and *The Crying of Lot 49*; toy manufacturer involved in black-marketeering with Major Duane Marvy in *Gravity's Rainbow*.

Alice Chicoy. Querulous, bored, and alcoholic wife of Juan Chicoy; helps at her husband's diner and fears that Juan will leave her in John Steinbeck's *The Wayward Bus*.

Juan Chicoy. Irish-Mexican mechanic, bus driver, and owner of a gas station/diner; considers abandoning his mud-stuck bus and his troublesome passengers to start a carefree life away from his gas station and his alcoholic wife in John Steinbeck's *The Wayward Bus*.

Chief Broom. See Chief Broom Bromden.

Roger Chillingworth. Name assumed by the husband of Hester Prynne; conceals his identity, with Hester's help, in order to seek revenge on Arthur Dimmesdale, his wife's lover, in Nathaniel Hawthorne's *The Scarlet Letter*.

Doctor Reverend Wesley Augustus Chillingworth. Professor of ethics at the divinity school Thomas Marshfield attended; father of Jane Chillingworth Marshfield in John Updike's *A Month of Sundays*.

China Mary. Longtime housekeeper for the McClellan family in Joan Didion's *Run River*.

Chinatown. See Chinatown Moss.

Ching. Honest and industrious farmer and overseer of Wang Lung's land in Pearl Buck's *The Good Earth*.

Chingachgook (Great Serpent, Indian John, John Mohegan). Noble Indian who is the last of his tribe, the father of Uncas, and the companion of Natty Bumppo; enlists Bumppo's help in rescuing Wahta!-Wah in James Fenimore Cooper's *The Deerslayer*; helps Bumppo fight Magua in *The Last of the Mohicans*; helps Bumppo guide Mabel Dunham to

her father in *The Pathfinder*; converted to Christianity, he lives in a cabin near Templeton, where he dies in a fire, in *The Pioneers*.

Chink. Keeper of the clockworks, shaman of Siwash Ridge, and impregnator of Sissy Hankshaw Gitche in Tom Robbins's *Even Cowgirls Get the Blues*.

Elly Chipley (Lenore La Verne). Actress on the *Cotton Blossom* in Edna Ferber's *Show Boat*.

Chippo. See Erin Simon.

Edith Chipps. English radio and television writer; wife, then widow of Gowan McGland and paramour of Alvin Mopworth in Peter De Vries's *Reuben, Reuben*.

Chips. See Beauty.

Deputy Warden Chisholm. Unsympathetic supervisor at Falconer prison whose denial of drugs to Zeke Farragut gives the convict periods of extreme agony in John Cheever's *Falconer*.

Aunt Chloe. Black nurse of Tom Bailey in New Orleans in Thomas Bailey Aldrich's *The Story of a Bad Boy*.

Aunt Chloe. Wife of Uncle Tom and mother of three children; suffers greatly when Tom is sold and attempts to earn the money to buy Tom back by cooking on other plantations in Harriet Beecher Stowe's *Uncle Tom's Cabin*.

Chloris. Denizen of the enchanted forest Leuke; becomes Jurgen's second wife after his apotheosis as a solar legend and subsequent exile from Cocaigne following the vernal equinox in James Branch Cabell's *Jurgen*.

Chief Choate. Full-blooded Indian corporal who boxes on the regimental team in James Jones's *From Here to Eternity*.

Choh. Artisan and Tehkohn wife of Gehnahteh; fosters Tien in Octavia E. Butler's *Survivor*.

Bill Chokee. Pawnbroker from whom Edward Pierce buys guns and bullets in Michael Crichton's *The Great Train Robbery*.

Luzana (Old Luze) Cholly. Legendary bluesman idolized by Scooter in Albert Murray's *Train Whistle Guitar*.

Lee Chong. Chinese grocer who owns and operates the largest and most eclectically stocked general store in the Cannery Row section of Monterey, California, in John Steinbeck's *Cannery Row*.

Chorus. Ancient chorus upset with Antigone for taking away its lines; shoots Minnie Yellings aboard an airplane she is hijacking; the airplane captain, mistaking Chorus for a hijacker, shoots it to death in Ishmael Reed's *The Last Days of Louisiana Red*.

Choucoune. Tiny mulatto modiste who sometimes sews at Bréda in Arna Wendell Bontemps's *Drums at Dusk*.

Emilia Chrabotzky. Catholic widow of a professor and mother of Halina Chrabotzky; beloved friend of Yasha Mazur in Isaac Bashevis Singer's *The Magician of Lublin*.

Halina Chrabotzky. Sickly daughter of Emilia Chrabotzky; her youth, beauty, and precocity sexually attract Yasha Mazur, unbeknown to Emilia, and to Yasha's admitted shame, in Isaac Bashevis Singer's *The Magician of Lublin*.

Chremes. Father of Philumena; does not understand why Simo does not insist that Pamphilus marry Philumena in Thornton Wilder's *The Woman of Andros*.

Jesus Christ. See The Corpse.

Bill Christian. Member of the board of directors of the Association of Growers of Dark Fired Tobacco, an organization designed to influence tobacco prices; supporter of the night riders in Robert Penn Warren's *Night Rider*.

Candy Christian. Innocent who, in her search for love, has a number of bizarre sexual encounters in Terry Southern and Mason Hoffenberg's *Candy*.

Fletcher Christian. Master's mate on HMS *Bounty* who marries Maimiti and who leads the rebellion against Captain Bligh in Charles Nordhoff and James Norman Hall's *Mutiny on the Bounty*; leads a group of mutineers and Tahitians to an isolated island where he attempts to establish a democracy, only to see it fail when the tension between the Tahitians and the whites erupts into violence, to which he falls victim, in *Pitcairn's Island*.

Jack Christian. Identical twin of Sidney Christian, husband of Livia Christian, and uncle of Candy Christian, whom he seduces on the floor of her father's hospital room, in Terry Southern and Mason Hoffenberg's *Candy*.

Livia Christian. Vulgar, sex-starved wife of Jack Christian and aunt of Candy Christian in Terry Southern and Mason Hoffenberg's *Candy*.

Lucille (Sukie) Christian. Daughter of Bill Christian and lover of Percy Munn in Robert Penn Warren's *Night Rider*.

Sidney Christian. Father of Candy Christian; suffers a partial lobotomy at the hands of his gardener but reappears as a dung-covered holy man in Terry Southern and Mason Hoffenberg's *Candy*.

Uncle Willy Christian. Drugstore operator in William Faulkner's *The Town*, *The Mansion*, and *The Reivers*.

Christine. Blonde wife of Max; impregnated by Gene Pasternak in John Clellon Holmes's *Go*.

Christine. Worker in a laundry across from Sebastian Dangerfield's house; becomes one of Sebastian's girlfriends in J. P. Donleavy's *The Ginger Man*.

Joe Christmas. Possibly a half-black who is the lover and murderer of Joanna Burden; castrated by Percy Grimm in William Faulkner's *Light in August*.

Cory Christopher. Wife of David Christopher, mother of James and Julia Christopher, and daughter of the owners of the farm where the Christophers live in Fred Chappell's *It Is Time, Lord*.

David (Davy) Christopher. Husband of Cory Christopher and father critical of his son, James, but indulgent toward his daughter, Julia; teacher fired for his teaching of science but too proud to ask for reinstatement in Fred Chappell's *It Is Time, Lord*.

James (Jimmy) Christopher. Son of Cory and David Christopher and husband of Sylvia Christopher; quits his job as production manager of Winton College Press to come to terms with his past and his own identity; eventually starts over by reapplying for his job and returning to his family; narrator of Fred Chappell's *It Is Time, Lord*.

Julia Christopher. Younger sister of James Christopher; model child and responsible adult who claims she always has protected James from the consequences of his actions in Fred Chappell's *It Is Time, Lord*.

Sylvia Christopher. Understanding wife of James Christopher in Fred Chappell's *It Is Time, Lord*.

Chrono. Son of Malachi Constant and Beatrice Rumfoord in Kurt Vonnegut's *The Sirens of Titan*.

Chrysanthi (Chrýsomou). Lover of Sotiris Procopirios in Athens in Nicholas Delbanco's *The Martlet's Tale*.

Chrysis. The woman of Andros who comes to Brynos, to the dismay of the Greek citizens there whose sons frequent her dinners and discussions, in Thornton Wilder's *The Woman of Andros.*

Chub. Irish immigrant and Presbyterian minister; friend of Frank Meriwether, collector of the classical library, and tutor in John Pendleton Kennedy's *Swallow Barn.*

Eustace Chubb. Poet known for his Cold War verse in John Updike's *Bech: A Book.*

Laurence Chubb, Jr.. Head of Chubb's safe-making company who shows the South Eastern Railway safes to Miss Miriam in Michael Crichton's *The Great Train Robbery.*

Corporal Jonathan (Johnny) Church. Young rebel who is disowned by his father and enlists in Cromwell's army at age sixteen; opposes Cromwell's Irish campaign but is offered a pardon if he will recant his democratic views; chooses to be executed by a firing squad; fathers a child by Nell Lacy; narrator of Mary Lee Settle's *Prisons.*

Roy Church. Agent for the Kansas Bureau of Investigation; works with Harold Nye in breaking the false story of Richard Hickock in Truman Capote's *In Cold Blood.*

Soaphead Church. See Elihue Micah Whitcomb.

Horace (Woody) Church-Woodbine. Irresponsible banjo player from a family of wealthy horse fanciers; employer of Bad-foot Dixon and Augie in Arna Wendell Bontemps's *God Sends Sunday.*

Alfred Churchill. Rambunctious son of the Churchills who grows to manhood in Henry Wadsworth Longfellow's *Kavanagh.*

Edward Churchill. Uncle of Jacqueline Churchill, whose marriage to Lewis Rand he opposes; Federalist and veteran of Yorktown in Mary Johnston's *Lewis Rand.*

Jacqueline Churchill. Niece of Edward Churchill; refuses Ludwell Cary's marriage proposal and offends her family by marrying Lewis Rand in Mary Johnston's *Lewis Rand.*

Mary Churchill. Wife of Churchill; encourages her husband to write and scolds him when he does not do so in Henry Wadsworth Longfellow's *Kavanagh.*

Mr. Churchill. Schoolmaster who tries unsuccessfully to write a romance in Henry Wadsworth Longfellow's *Kavanagh.*

Cicero. Roman senator who becomes one of the conspirators against Caesar in Thornton Wilder's *The Ides of March.*

Cinder. Rival of Mary Pinesett; lover of July, whom she wins by means of a love charm, in Julia Peterkin's *Scarlet Sister Mary.*

Lidy Cinnamond. Wife of Stephen Birdwell and lover of Mel Venters in Jessamyn West's *The Friendly Persuasion.*

Claire de Bellegarde de Cintré. Young widow whose family hopes she will marry a rich man; becomes a nun because her family will not let her marry Christopher Newman in Henry James's *The American.*

Cipher X. Designer of hoopla hoops in Ishmael Reed's *The Free-Lance Pallbearers.*

Circe. Midwife and housekeeper on the Butler plantation in Danville, Pennsylvania; secretly cared for Pilate Dead and Macon Dead II after their father was killed in Toni Morrison's *Song of Solomon.*

Charles (Charlie) Citrine. Author of the Broadway play *Von Trenck,* which wins a Pulitzer Prize and becomes a successful film; friend of Von Humboldt Fleisher, jilted lover of Renata Koffritz, and seeker after a quiet life through anthroposophy; narrator of Saul Bellow's *Humboldt's Gift.*

John (Jemmy Legs) Claggart. Master-at-arms aboard the *Indomitable* who, upon falsely accusing Billy Budd of planning a mutiny, is killed by Budd in Herman Melville's *Billy Budd.*

Claire. Deceased wife of Konrad Vost and mother of Mirabelle in John Hawkes's *The Passion Artist.*

Claire. Discarded mistress of Count Armand de Sacy; courtesan living in forced exile at Bréda in Arna Wendell Bontemps's *Drums at Dusk.*

Claire. Syphilitic store owner and wife of Jimmy in Jerry Bumpus's *Anaconda.*

Clem (Cousin Clem) Clammidge. Farmhand turned "primitive" art critic; writes for the *Daily Bugle* in Peter De Vries's *I Hear America Swinging.*

Harry Clammidge. Publisher of the *Picayune Blade* and employer of Chick Swallow in Peter De Vries's *Comfort Me with Apples.*

DeYancey Clanahan. Grandson of Tip Clanahan; defense attorney for Daniel Ponder in Eudora Welty's *The Ponder Heart.*

Tip Clanahan. Friend of Sam Ponder; judge who helps commit Daniel Ponder to an asylum in Jackson, Mississippi, in Eudora Welty's *The Ponder Heart.*

William de la Touche Clancey. "Tory sodomite" and editor of the anti-American magazine *America* in Gore Vidal's *Burr*.

Clancy. Displaced archetypal 1890s police officer in William S. Burroughs's *Exterminator!*

Mr. Clancy. General manager of the Cosmodemonic Telegraph Company; hires Henry Miller to spy on and to fire employees in Henry Miller's *Tropic of Capricorn*.

Judge Fox Clane. Prejudiced judge and retired statesman whose idea to convince the government to redeem Confederate money leads to Sherman Pew's rebellion and death in Carson McCullers's *Clock without Hands*.

John Jester Clane. Grandson of Judge Fox Clane and son of Johnny Clane; determined to discover the reason for his father's suicide; loves Sherman Pew in Carson McCullers's *Clock without Hands*.

Johnny Clane. Son of Judge Fox Clane and father of John Jester Clane; commits suicide after he learns the woman he loves, Joy Little, detests him and loves Nigra Jones in Carson McCullers's *Clock without Hands*.

Captain Daniel Clapsaddle. Bluff American patriot in Winston Churchill's *Richard Carvel*.

Hugh Clapton. Royalist clergyman and teacher of Johnny Fraser in James Boyd's *Drums*.

Clara. Middle child of the three orphans in the care of Rachel Cooper in Davis Grubb's *The Night of the Hunter*.

Doña Clara. See Doña Clara de Montemayor.

Clarence (Amyas le Poulet). Sixth-century associate of Hank Morgan; with Morgan's help, publishes a newspaper in Samuel Langhorne Clemens's *A Connecticut Yankee in King Arthur's Court*.

Clarendon. See Edward Hyde, Earl of Clarendon.

Claret. Captain of the *Neversink* in Herman Melville's *White-Jacket*.

Clarice. Illegitimate daughter of Arthur Wiatte, niece of Euphemia Lorimer, and fiancée of Clithero Edny in Charles Brockden Brown's *Edgar Huntly*.

Stormy Claridge. Girlfriend of Ezra Lyttle; uses sex to further her career in Peter Gent's *Texas Celebrity Turkey Trot*.

Clarie. See Clarence Henderson.

Clarissa. Mira's friend in graduate school; abandons her traditional marriage for a lesbian relationship in Marilyn French's *The Women's Room*.

Sister Clarisse. Widow to whom Hubert Cooley is attracted in Julian Mayfield's *The Hit*.

Clara Clark. Rice University graduate student and lover of Jim Carpenter in Larry McMurtry's *Moving On*.

Paul Clark. Suave rival of Homer Zigler for the affections of Frances Harbach in Clyde Brion Davis's *"The Great American Novel–."*

Robert (Bob, David Hawke) Clark. Writer and teacher whom Vridar Hunter meets in New York in Vardis Fisher's *No Villain Need Be*; also appears as David Hawke in *Orphans in Gethsemene*.

Salvatore (Friday, Sal) Clark. Bugler for G Company; shares Andy Anderson's and Robert E. Lee Prewitt's love of the blues in James Jones's *From Here to Eternity*.

Sam Clark. Owner of a hardware store and friend of Will Kennicott in Sinclair Lewis's *Main Street*.

Seward Trewlove Clark. Unitarian minister from California who predicts a murder aboard ship in Conrad Aiken's *Blue Voyage*.

Clarke. Overseer in Kirby & John's mill in Rebecca Harding Davis's *Life in the Iron Mills*.

Helen Clarke. Only "friend" of Mary Katherine, Constance, and Julian Blackwood and only regular visitor to the family home in Shirley Jackson's *We Have Always Lived in the Castle*.

Henry Clarke. Capable certified public accountant with Glymmer, Read who is relatively unaffected by the firm's bankruptcy in Nathan Asch's *The Office*.

Jim Clarke. Husband of Helen Clarke in Shirley Jackson's *We Have Always Lived in the Castle*.

Maxwell E. Clarke. Principal of Calvin Coolidge High School; manages to stay in his office all day, except for a rare public appearance to give a speech on lofty ideals, in Bel Kaufman's *Up the Down Staircase*.

Jud Clasby. Hunter, trapper, and instigator of the Indian massacre in Jessamyn West's *The Massacre at Fall Creek*.

Mlle. Claude. Prostitute with whom Henry Miller briefly thinks he is in love in Henry Miller's *Tropic of Cancer*.

Sir Claude. Dashing young man with an eye for the ladies who marries Ida Farange and becomes involved with Mrs. Beale Farange; loving stepfather of Maisie Farange in Henry James's *What Maisie Knew.*

Claudia. Child vampire whom Louis treats as a daughter; destroyed by Lestat in Anne Rice's *Interview with the Vampire.*

Clausen. Sexually frustrated murderer and suicide in Henry Miller's *Tropic of Capricorn.*

Anna Clausen. Sister-in-law of Orin Clausen and neighbor of Chris Van Eenanam and Ellen Strohe in Larry Woiwode's *What I'm Going to Do, I Think.*

Orin Clausen. Brother-in-law of Anna Clausen and Michigan-woods neighbor of Chris Van Eenanam and Ellen Strohe in Larry Woiwode's *What I'm Going to Do, I Think.*

Henry Ritchie (Le Roy Robbins) Clavering. Englishman who secretly marries Mary Leavenworth in Anna Katharine Green's *The Leavenworth Case.*

Lee (Clavey) Clavering. New York journalist and playwright who offers his lover Countess Marie Zattiany a return to youthful passion in Gertrude Atherton's *Black Oxen.*

Clif Clawson. Medical school roommate of Martin Arrowsmith; drops out of school and becomes an automobile salesman in Sinclair Lewis's *Arrowsmith.*

Ambrose Valentine Clay. Uncle of Violet Clay; dabbles at writing, is briefly married to Carol Gruber, and shoots himself in Gail Godwin's *Violet Clay.*

Catherine Clay. South Carolinian and former lover of Chester Hunnicutt Pomeroy; produces a Panamanian marriage certificate showing her marriage to Pomeroy in Thomas McGuane's *Panama.*

Collis Clay. Unsuccessful suitor of Rosemary Hoyt in F. Scott Fitzgerald's *Tender Is the Night.*

Robert Clay. Adventurer and self-taught engineer in charge of an iron-mining operation in Olancho; enamored of socialite Alice Langham in Richard Harding Davis's *Soldiers of Fortune.*

Violet Isabel Clay. Aspiring artist who leaves her unsatisfactory work in New York as an illustrator of Gothic novels to work seriously on her painting in an isolated cabin; narrator of Gail Godwin's *Violet Clay.*

Anne Clayton. Owner, with her brother Edward Clayton, of Magnolia Grove plantation; institutes educational and disciplinary reforms on the plantation, which arouse the ire of her neighbors, in Harriet Beecher Stowe's *Dred.*

Edward Clayton. Son of Judge Clayton and fiancé of Nina Gordon; sides increasingly with the abolitionists until he is forced to give up the plantation system and move to Canada with his emancipated slaves in Harriet Beecher Stowe's *Dred.*

Judge Clayton. Father of Edward and Anne Clayton; as a North Carolina superior court judge, he is forced to overturn a ruling that Edward won ensuring humane treatment of slaves in Harriet Beecher Stowe's *Dred.*

Sean Cleary. Unprincipled, self-serving director of guidance for the public schools of Pequot; aids Wissey Jones's attempt to purchase a child-genius for experimental research in John Hersey's *The Child Buyer.*

Richard (Dick, Philip Deaderick) Cleave. Captain of the 65th Virginia Infantry under General Jackson; temporarily disgraced and forced to fight under an assumed name, but restored to command; marries Judith Cary after heroic action and revelation of a rival's plotting; appears in Mary Johnston's *The Long Roll* and *Cease Firing.*

Harry C. Clegg. Newspaper reporter in Thomas Berger's *Killing Time.*

Hattie Clegg. Old-maid neighbor of the Ganchions who moves to Houston in William Goyen's *The House of Breath.*

Hiram Clegg. Brunist and eventually bishop of Randolph Junction in Robert Coover's *The Origin of the Brunists.*

Donald Clellon. First fiancé of Sarah Grimes Wilson; lies about his age and background, causing the engagement to be broken, in Richard Yates's *Easter Parade.*

Clem. One of the "seven dwarfs" who wash windows, make Chinese baby food, and live with Snow White in Donald Barthelme's *Snow White.*

Clematis (Clem). Mongrel dog of Genesis; his antics embarrass William Baxter in Booth Tarkington's *Seventeen.*

Clemence. Black street woman who assists Palmyre la Philosophe in seeking revenge on Agricola Fusilier in George Washington Cable's *The Grandissimes.*

Sam Clemence. Boyfriend of Mary Kettlesmith in Bernard Malamud's *The Tenants.*

Karen Hansen Clement. Surrogate daughter of Kitty Fremont, lover of Dov Landau, and Jewish refugee in Cyprus; killed during the Israeli War of Independence in Leon Uris's *Exodus*.

Mrs. Clement. Prostitute whom Bert Albany trades for another prostitute in E. L. Doctorow's *Welcome to Hard Times*.

Laurence G. Clements. Scholar at Waindell College; his wife rents a room to Timofey Pnin until their daughter returns and forces Pnin to move out in Vladimir Nabokov's *Pnin*.

Peter Clemenza. Gangster who remains loyal to the Corleone family in Mario Puzo's *The Godfather*.

Clemmie. Ambitious prostitute who tells Arkie McClellan a lie about her new pimp and so causes him to shoot Zebulon Johns Mackie in Fred Chappell's *The Gaudy Place*.

Cleo. Divorced, consumptive, pot-smoking member of the Hippodrome's cast in Cyrus Colter's *The Hippodrome*.

Cleo. Piano player with Walden Blue in John Clellon Holmes's *The Horn*.

Cleopatra. Queen of Egypt and lover of Caesar, by whom she has borne a son; visits Rome on a state visit in Thornton Wilder's *The Ides of March*.

Gaston Cleric. Classical scholar and teacher who inspires Jim Burden in Willa Cather's *My Ántonia*.

Angus Cleveland. Powerful, corrupt seventy-year-old political leader, former mayor of Gainesboro, and benefactor of Douglas Taylor, his successor, in Julian Mayfield's *The Grand Parade*.

Mr. Cleveland. Chauffeur of Miss Ann and her accomplice in crime in Richard Brautigan's *Dreaming of Babylon*.

Clevenger. Car test-track owner who takes the hitchhiking David Bell to Texas at the end of Don DeLillo's *Americana*.

Helena (Hellen) Cleves. Friend and employer of Constantia Dudley; her reputation is ruined by Ormond's refusal to marry her; dies of yellow fever in Charles Brockden Brown's *Ormond*.

Clevinger. Friend and fellow squadron member of Yossarian; Harvard undergraduate with "lots of intelligence and no brains"; hounded as a troublemaker by Lieutenant Scheisskopf in Joseph Heller's *Catch-22*.

Leland Clewes. Former state department friend whom Walter F. Starbuck "betrays"; husband of Sarah Wyatt in Kurt Vonnegut's *Jailbird*.

Jane Clifford. Teacher of English at a midwestern university and lover of Gabriel Weeks in Gail Godwin's *The Odd Woman*.

Brother Tod Clifton. Member of the Brotherhood who is killed by the police and becomes a Brotherhood martyr in Ralph Ellison's *Invisible Man*.

Schuyler Clinton. New York senator and chairman of the Foreign Relations Committee; admirer of Madeleine Lee in Henry Adams's *Democracy*.

Percy Clocklan. Dublin friend of Sebastian Dangerfield; fakes suicide in the Irish sea and later re-emerges in London as a mysteriously wealthy man in J. P. Donleavy's *The Ginger Man*.

Cletus James (C. J.) Clovis. Entrepreneur who builds bat towers for insect control in Thomas McGuane's *The Bushwhacked Piano*.

Esther Clumly. Blind wife of Fred Clumly; helps temper his zeal for obedience to laws in John Gardner's *The Sunlight Dialogues*.

Fred Clumly. Police chief of Batavia, New York, who finally understands what makes "The Sunlight Man" behave like a criminal; husband of Esther Clumly in John Gardner's *The Sunlight Dialogues*.

Bonnie Fox Clutter. Wife of Herbert Clutter and mother of their four children; ill with emotional and physical ailments, she is the last member of the family murdered in Truman Capote's *In Cold Blood*.

Herbert William Clutter. Prominent and wealthy owner of River Valley Farm in Holcomb, Kansas; victim of the first and most brutal murder by Perry Smith in Truman Capote's *In Cold Blood*.

Kenyon Clutter. Youngest child and only son of Bonnie and Herbert Clutter; shot to death in Truman Capote's *In Cold Blood*.

Nancy Clutter. Talented and much admired sixteen-year-old daughter of Bonnie and Herbert Clutter; third murder victim in Truman Capote's *In Cold Blood*.

Albert Cluveau. Cajun who is the occasional fishing companion of Miss Jane Pittman and the hired killer of Ned Douglass in Ernest J. Gaines's *The Autobiography of Miss Jane Pittman*.

Uncle Clyde. Husband of Aunt Bessie; Dandy Benson boards at their Maryland farm during summers in his boyhood in Ed Bullins's *The Reluctant Rapist*.

Frances Clyne. Lover of Robert Cohn in Ernest Hemingway's *The Sun Also Rises*.

Clytemnestra. Sister of Helen and wife of Agamemnon; conspires with her lover Aegisthus to murder Agamemnon; killed in turn by her son Orestes in John Erskine's *The Private Life of Helen of Troy*.

Charles (Cobby) Cobb. Greedy and crafty bookie who helps finance a jewelry robbery in William Riley Burnett's *The Asphalt Jungle*.

Georgiana Cobb. Fiancée of her neighbor Adam Moss in James Lane Allen's *A Kentucky Cardinal*; dies after giving birth to their son, Adam Cobb Moss, in *Aftermath*.

Jeremiah Cobb. Judge who sentences Nat Turner and Hark to be hanged; Job-figure and lonely widower in William Styron's *The Confessions of Nat Turner*.

Joe R. Cobb. Air exec with the 918th Bomb Group in Beirne Lay, Jr., and Sy Bartlett's *Twelve O'Clock High!*

Joseph Cobb. Brother of Georgiana Cobb; West Point cadet in James Lane Allen's *A Kentucky Cardinal*; also appears in *Aftermath*.

Margaret Cobb. Mother of Georgiana Cobb in James Lane Allen's *A Kentucky Cardinal* and *Aftermath*.

Maybelline (Mae) Cobb. Defiant, bedridden wife of Winston Cobb; killed in a fire set by her husband; appears in Hal Bennett's *A Wilderness of Vines*, *The Black Wine*, *Wait Until the Evening*, and *Seventh Heaven*.

Sylvia Cobb. Sister of Georgiana and Joseph Cobb; flirts with Adam Moss in James Lane Allen's *A Kentucky Cardinal*; also appears in *Aftermath*.

Reverend Winston Cobb. Preacher in Burnside, Virginia; sex-show performer, blackmailer, and perfume salesman; father of David Hunter, mentor of Kevin Brittain, alter ego of Bill Kelsey, and slayer of his wife, Mae Cobb; apprehended in New Jersey for murdering Dolly Anderson and visited in prison by Joe Market; appears in Hal Bennett's *A Wilderness of Vines*, *The Black Wine*, *Lord of Dark Places*, *Wait Until the Evening*, and *Seventh Heaven*.

Ensign Peregrine Cockburn. English cousin of Johnny Lacey; sent to Virginia as part of Braddock's force against Fort Duquesne; killed by Indians and stripped of his possessions by Squire Raglan in Mary Lee Settle's *O Beulah Land*.

Jack Cockerell. Head of the English department at Waindell College; does near-perfect but mean impersonations of Timofey Pnin in Vladimir Nabokov's *Pnin*.

Cockney. See Shorty.

Wayne Codd. Cowboy and ranch foreman who hits Nicholas Payne, possibly causing Payne brain damage, in Thomas McGuane's *The Bushwhacked Piano*.

Dan Cody. Millionaire miner who employs the young James Gatz for five years; leaves money to Gatz, which he does not receive, in F. Scott Fitzgerald's *The Great Gatsby*.

James M. (Jimmy) Cody. Doctor who concludes that Danny Glick was killed by vampires in Stephen King's *'Salem's Lot*.

Edward R. (Instant) Coffee. Impulsive presiding judge; character in Osgood Wallop's *The Duchess of Obloquy* in Peter De Vries's *Mrs. Wallop*.

Mr. Coffee. Ragman and vagrant in Carlene Hatcher Polite's *The Flagellants*.

China Doll Coffin. Older sister of Sukie Maceo and neighborhood prostitute in 1930s Harlem; stabs and kills her pimp in Louise Meriwether's *Daddy Was a Number Runner*.

Francie Coffin. Twelve-year-old only girl and youngest child of Henrietta and Adam Coffin; comes of age in mid-1930s Harlem; narrator of Louise Meriwether's *Daddy Was a Number Runner*.

Henrietta Coffin. Wife of Adam Coffin and mother of James Junior, Sterling, and Francie Coffin; becomes the primary support of the family after her husband abandons them in a Harlem tenement in Louise Meriwether's *Daddy Was a Number Runner*.

James Adam Coffin. Husband of Henrietta Coffin and father of James Junior, Sterling, and Francie Coffin; becomes a number runner and eventually abandons his family after legal fees for Junior absorb his income in Louise Meriwether's *Daddy Was a Number Runner*.

James Adam (James Junior, Junior) Coffin, Jr. Fifteen-year-old brother of Sterling and Francie Coffin; arrested for the robbery and murder of a white shoe salesman, but released in Louise Meriwether's *Daddy Was a Number Runner*.

Sterling Coffin. Fourteen-year-old brother of Francie and James Junior Coffin; quits high school to take a job because he sees no future as a black person with a diploma in Louise Meriwether's *Daddy Was a Number Runner*.

Jack (Jackie) Cogan. Mafia enforcer who restores order to mob-run enterprises; kills Frankie, Mark

Trattman, and Squirrel Amato in George V. Higgins's *Cogan's Trade*.

Reuben (Rooster) Cogburn. United States marshall and bounty hunter who is hired by Mattie Ross to capture Tom Chaney in Charles Portis's *True Grit*.

Anna Cohen. Worker burned to death in a fire at Mme. Soubrine's, a fashionable millinery shop in John Dos Passos's *Manhattan Transfer*.

Archie Cohen. Young American volunteer in the Spanish civil war; eventually denounces the Communist party in William Herrick's *Hermanos!*

Gabriel (Dutch) Cohen. Friend of Samuel Paul Berman since grade school in Jay Neugeboren's *Sam's Legacy*.

Genghis Cohen. Eminent philatelist hired to appraise Pierce Inverarity's stamp collection in Thomas Pynchon's *The Crying of Lot 49*.

Joey Cohen. Russian-born childhood friend of Michael Gold in Michael Gold's *Jews without Money*.

Morris (Mike Palgrave) Cohen. Architect who designs a temple for David Dehn; adopts Dehn's daughter, Rachel Dehn, in Jerome Weidman's *The Temple*.

Rachel Cohen. Daughter of David Dehn and Bella Biaggi Dehn, and adopted daughter of Morris Cohen; friend of the reporter who discovers the source of David Dehn's wealth in Jerome Weidman's *The Temple*.

Robert Cohn. Jewish American novelist in Paris; in love with and violently jealous of Lady Brett Ashley in Ernest Hemingway's *The Sun Also Rises*.

Henry Colbert. Miller and husband of Sapphira Dodderidge Colbert; gives their daughter, Rachel Colbert, money to smuggle Nancy to Canada in Willa Cather's *Sapphira and the Slave Girl*.

Martin Colbert. Rakish nephew of Henry Colbert; his repeated advances toward Nancy cause her to escape to Canada in Willa Cather's *Sapphira and the Slave Girl*.

Rachel Colbert. See Rachel Colbert Blake.

Sapphira Dodderidge (Sapphy, The Mistress) Colbert. Wealthy Virginia slave owner, wife of Henry Colbert, and mother of Rachel Colbert in Willa Cather's *Sapphira and the Slave Girl*.

Colbrook. Marine corporal aboard the *Neversink* who saves White-Jacket from a flogging in Herman Melville's *White-Jacket*.

Edward (Cap) Colburne. New England lawyer who relinquishes Lillie Ravenel to John Carter and serves as a captain under Carter in the Civil War; marries Lillie after Carter's death in John William DeForest's *Miss Ravenel's Conversion from Secession to Loyalty*.

Lillie Ravenel Carter Colburne. See Lillie Ravenel Carter.

Cold Cuts. Alcoholic nightclub singer who works in a morgue and speaks sixteen languages; friend of Jay in Anaïs Nin's *A Spy in the House of Love*.

Ellen Coldfield. See Ellen Coldfield Sutpen.

Goodhue Coldfield. Father of Ellen and Rosa Coldfield in William Faulkner's *Absalom, Absalom!*

Rosa Coldfield. Daughter of Goodhue Coldfield in and one of the narrators of William Faulkner's *Absalom, Absalom!*

George (Stuffy) Cole. Big boy with an overindulgent mother in Louisa May Alcott's *Little Men*.

King Cole. Marine whose guitar playing entertains his platoon mates; wounded in France during World War I in Thomas Boyd's *Through the Wheat*.

Miranda Cole. High school teacher and girlfriend of Thomas Skelton in Thomas McGuane's *Ninety-Two in the Shade*.

Pauline (M. C. Number Two, Moe) Cole. High school cheerleader and girlfriend abandoned by Jack Duluoz in favor of Maggie Cassidy in Jack Kerouac's *Maggie Cassidy*; mentioned in *Book of Dreams* and *Desolation Angels*.

Raymond Cole. Fighter and heavy drinker; combat veteran who freezes to death in a cornfield in James Jones's *Some Came Running*.

William Cole. Boatswain on HMS *Bounty* whose loyalty to Captain Bligh and his regard for Admiralty law cause him to be set adrift with Bligh after the mutiny in Charles Nordhoff and James Norman Hall's *Mutiny on the Bounty*; his faith in God and Bligh, as well as his great strength, help him survive being cast adrift at sea in *Men against the Sea*.

Alice E. Coleman. Wife of a northerner who, after being ambushed, dies in her arms in Albion W. Tourgee's *A Fool's Errand*.

Claris Coleman. Daughter of Colonel Coleman and first lover of Clay-Boy Spencer in Earl Hamner, Jr.'s *Spencer's Mountain*.

Colonel Coleman. General manager of the New Dominion Stone Company; buys Clay Spencer's mountain property so Spencer can send his oldest son to college in Earl Hamner, Jr.'s *Spencer's Mountain*.

Daisy Meissner Coleman. Broadway chorus girl and wife of Ray Coleman in Edmund Wilson's *I Thought of Daisy*.

Ray Coleman. Husband of Daisy Meissner Coleman; reporter for the *Telegram-Dispatch* and then for the tabloid *Daily Sketch* in Edmund Wilson's *I Thought of Daisy*.

Vance R. (Professor, Slim) Coleman. Book salesman and would-be entrepreneur; friend of Sidney Wyeth in Oscar Micheaux's *The Forged Note*.

Anne-Marion Coles. College roommate and later correspondent of Meridian Hill in Alice Walker's *Meridian*.

Clarence Colfax. Hotheaded but noble Confederate soldier; suitor of Virginia Carvel in Winston Churchill's *The Crisis*.

Andrew Collier. Journalist and half brother of Daniel Compton Wills; discovers his supposed benefactor, Daniel Cable Wills, is his father and a former member of the OSS and CIA in George V. Higgins's *Dreamland*.

John Collier. Bearer of a marriage proposal from James Hopkins to Sally Oldham; she encourages Collier to advance his own suit and becomes his wife in Lydia Maria Child's *Hobomok*.

Sally Oldham Collier. Friend of Mary Conant; rejects the written marriage proposal of James Hopkins in favor of its bearer, John Collier, in Lydia Maria Child's *Hobomok*.

Collins. American sailor who often pays for drinks and entertainment for Henry Miller, Kruger, and Fillmore in Henry. Miller's *Tropic of Cancer*.

Clara Collins. Widow of Ely Collins and leader of the Circle in Robert Coover's *The Origin of the Brunists*.

Elaine Collins. Repressed daughter of Ely Collins; falls in love with Carl Dean Palmers in Robert Coover's *The Origin of the Brunists*.

Ely Collins. Preacher and coal miner; deceased husband of Clara Collins in Robert Coover's *The Origin of the Brunists*.

Hannah Ann Collins. Old and blind Alabama poetess in John Updike's *Bech: A Book*.

Henry Collins. Rich, cranky Englishman who marries Marian Forrester and makes her final years secure in Willa Cather's *A Lost Lady*.

Jasper Collins. Companion of Larry Donovan and Nat Moore in the search for jobs and a meaningful life in Jack Conroy's *The Disinherited*.

Kitty (Mrs. Benjamin Watson, Mrs. Catherine) Collins. Maid at the Hutter house; married to Benjamin Watson, who returns to her after an absence of ten years, in Thomas Bailey Aldrich's *The Story of a Bad Boy*.

Lieutenant Collins. Leader of an expedition with Dick Gibson in search of the last living dodo bird on the island of Mauritius during World War II in Stanley Elkin's *The Dick Gibson Show*.

Rupe (Rupie) Collins. Bully who encourages Penrod Schofield's antics to take a more aggressive form in Booth Tarkington's *Penrod*.

William David Collins. Name given to the baby Leslie Collins adopts in Harriette Simpson Arnow's *The Kentucky Trace*.

William David Leslie Collins II. Son of Virginia gentry and patriot covertly involved in the American Revolution; shoots his own brother at the battle of Camden; cares for and ultimately adopts a child in Harriette Simpson Arnow's *The Kentucky Trace*.

Collyer. British adjutant in William Faulkner's *A Fable*.

Joe Colper. Sales manager of Harris Towers, a condominium complex, in *The Condominium*, a novella in Stanley Elkin's *Searches and Seizures*.

Ann Colt. Wife of Timothy Colt; shy, awkward former English major who remains devoted to her husband despite his affair with Eileen Shallcross; returns to him after his trial in Louis Auchincloss's *The Great World and Timothy Colt*.

Timothy (Timmy) Colt. Idealistic but angry young lawyer who becomes a partner in a large Manhattan law firm and almost destroys his career and marriage through unethical conduct; husband of Ann Colt in Louis Auchincloss's *The Great World and Timothy Colt*.

Colton. Unknown outsider who becomes the first elected sheriff of Tooms County, Alabama, and vows to destroy blacks any way possible to prevent them from advancing in W. E. B. Du Bois's *The Quest of the Silver Fleece*.

Anabel Colton. Friend of Isabel Otis, wife of Tom Colton, and a mother submerged in domesticity in Gertrude Atherton's *Ancestors*.

Thomas (Tom) Colton. Practical California businessman, husband of Anabel Colton, politician eager to become a United States senator, and rival of John Gwynne in Gertrude Atherton's *Ancestors*.

Ralph Coltsworth. Suitor preferred by Hagar Ashendyne's family; opposes Hagar's beliefs, but is determined to marry her until she resists his physical advances in Mary Johnston's *Hagar*.

Alfonso (Al) Columbato. Longtime friend of Birdy; patient in an army hospital who gets Birdy to stop acting like a bird; a narrator of William Wharton's *Birdy*.

Bess Columbine. Mistress and partner in crime of Black Jack Mallard; jealous of Mallard's friendship with Amber St. Clare in Kathleen Winsor's *Forever Amber*.

Theodore Colville. Newspaper editor living in Florence; briefly engaged to Imogene Graham, but marries the more suitable Evalina Bowen in William Dean Howells's *Indian Summer*.

Aycock Comfort. Friend of Jack Renfro sentenced with him to Parchman State Penitentiary; maintains the balance of Maud Eva Moody's car while it hangs on the edge of Banner Top in Eudora Welty's *Losing Battles*.

Dan Comisky. Gambler who promotes free-hanging as a sport and urges Clyde Stout to compete in it in Jack Matthews's *Hanger Stout, Awake!*

Benjamin (Benjy, Maury) Compson. Idiot son of Caroline Bascomb and Jason Lycurgus Compson III; brother of Caddy Compson, Quentin Compson I, and Jason Compson IV; castrated and committed to an asylum; appears in William Faulkner's *The Sound and the Fury* and *The Mansion*.

Candace (Caddy) Compson. Daughter of Caroline Bascomb and Jason Lycurgus Compson III; sister of Benjy Compson, Quentin Compson I, and Jason Compson IV; mother of Quentin Compson II; appears in William Faulkner's *The Sound and the Fury* and *The Mansion*.

Caroline Bascomb Compson. Wife of Jason Lycurgus Compson III; mother of Benjy and Caddy Compson, Quentin Compson I, and Jason Compson IV in William Faulkner's *The Sound and the Fury*.

Jason Lycurgus Compson (I). Indian agent who trades a racing mare to Ikkemotubbe for a square mile of land that becomes the center of Jefferson, Mississippi; appears in William Faulkner's *The Sound and the Fury* and *Requiem for a Nun*.

Jason Lycurgus Compson (II). Hunter and Civil War general; only real friend of Thomas Sutpen; appears in William Faulkner's *The Sound and the Fury*; *Absalom, Absalom!*; *The Unvanquished*; *Go Down, Moses*; *Intruder in the Dust*; *Requiem for a Nun*; *The Town*; and *The Reivers*.

Jason Lycurgus Compson (III). Husband of Caroline Bascomb; father of Benjy and Caddy Compson, Quentin Compson I, and Jason Compson IV; appears in William Faulkner's *The Sound and the Fury* and *Absalom, Absalom!*

Jason Lycurgus Compson (IV). Son of Caroline Bascomb and Jason Lycurgus Compson III; brother of Benjy and Caddy Compson and Quentin Compson I; appears in William Faulkner's *The Sound and the Fury*, *The Town*, and *The Mansion*.

Quentin Compson (I). Son of Caroline Bascomb and Jason Lycurgus Compson III; brother of Benjy and Caddy Compson and Jason Compson IV; following a year at Harvard, he commits suicide; appears in William Faulkner's *The Sound and the Fury*; *Absalom, Absalom!* (in which he is one of the narrators); and *The Mansion*.

Quentin Compson (II). Illegitimate daughter of Caddy Compson and Dalton Ames; appears in William Faulkner's *The Sound and the Fury* and *The Mansion*.

Ben Compton. Radical intellectual devoted to proletarian issues who is jailed for subversive activities in John Dos Passos's *U.S.A.* trilogy.

Gladys Compton. Secretary whom J. Ward Morehouse asks to watch over Janey Williams and whose family, as a result, boards her temporarily; sister of Ben Compton in John Dos Passos's *U.S.A.* trilogy.

Edgar Comroe. Night officer at Vandenberg Air Force Base in Michael Crichton's *The Andromeda Strain*.

Charlie Comstock. Reformed alcoholic, pious parishioner of Andrew Mackerel, and copublisher of the *Globe* in Peter De Vries's *The Mackerel Plaza*.

Lord (Jack) Comyn. Generous nobleman secretly sympathetic to the American cause; friend of Richard Carvel in Winston Churchill's *Richard Carvel*.

Charles Hobomok Conant. Son of Mary Conant and Hobomok in Lydia Maria Child's *Hobomok*.

Jerry Conant. Designer and animator of television commercials; husband of Ruth Conant and lover of Sally Mathias in John Updike's *Marry Me*.

Mary Conant. Bride of Hobomok and later of Charles Brown; mother of Charles Hobomok Conant and heroine of Lydia Maria Child's *Hobomok.*

Mrs. Mary Conant. Daughter of an English earl, wife of Roger Conant, and mother of Mary Conant; dies in the Puritan settlement at Salem in Lydia Maria Child's *Hobomok.*

Roger Conant. Stern Puritan father of Mary Conant and husband of Mrs. Mary Conant; forbids his daughter to marry the Episcopalian Charles Brown in Lydia Maria Child's *Hobomok.*

Ruth Conant. Wife of Jerry Conant and lover of Richard Mathias in John Updike's *Marry Me.*

Catherine M. (Cate) Conboy. Daughter of Lincoln and Elizabeth Conboy; loves Christian Fraser but marries Ferris Thompson in Jessamyn West's *The Witch Diggers.*

Elizabeth (Lib) Conboy. Wife of Lincoln Conboy and mother of Catherine, James, and Emma Conboy in Jessamyn West's *The Witch Diggers.*

Emma Jane (Em) Conboy. Younger daughter of Lincoln and Elizabeth Conboy in Jessamyn West's *The Witch Diggers.*

James (Dandie, Jim) Conboy. Son of Lincoln and Elizabeth Conboy; marries Poor Farm inmate Norah Tate in Jessamyn West's *The Witch Diggers.*

Lincoln (Link) Conboy. Superintendent of Poor Farm, husband of Elizabeth Conboy, and father of Catherine, James, and Emma Conboy in Jessamyn West's *The Witch Diggers.*

Sophie Concord. Negro nurse and friend of Neil Kingsblood in Sinclair Lewis's *Kingsblood Royal.*

La Condesa. Insane, drug-addicted Spanish noblewoman deported from Cuba for her political activities; loved by the ship's doctor, Schumann, in Katherine Anne Porter's *Ship of Fools.*

Signor (Cee-Pee) Condotti-Pignata. Painter who imagines Cynthia Pomeroy as Primavera in Wright Morris's *What a Way to Go.*

Count Condu. Hungarian vampire imagined by Jack Duluoz in Jack Kerouac's *Doctor Sax.*

Mame and Max Confrey. Restaurateurs in William Faulkner's *Light in August.*

Congo. Sailor without attachments or responsibilities; he is an "intellectual anarchist" against whom free-spirited but otherwise encumbered characters are measured in John Dos Passos's *Manhattan Transfer.*

Jim Conklin. Tall soldier fatally wounded in battle; Henry Fleming witnesses his grotesque death throes in Stephen Crane's *The Red Badge of Courage.*

Will (Willie) Conklin. Chief of the Emerald Isle Engine Company; he and his men destroy the Model T of Coalhouse Walker, Jr., and cause the death of many innocent people in E. L. Doctorow's *Ragtime.*

Conmal (Duke of Aros). Renowned translator of Shakespeare into Zemblan; uncle who influences Charles Xavier, the last king of Zembla, to be passionately addicted to literature in Vladimir Nabokov's *Pale Fire.*

Alec Connage. Princeton classmate of Amory Blaine and brother of Rosalind Connage in F. Scott Fitzgerald's *This Side of Paradise.*

Rosalind Connage. Great love of Amory Blaine; marries a rich man in F. Scott Fitzgerald's *This Side of Paradise.*

Stephen Conner. Current superintendent of the Diamond County Home for the Aged; holds certain ideals about serving humanity and the need for impartiality in dealing with the residents; stoned by some of the old people in John Updike's *The Poorhouse Fair.*

Betsy Jekyll Connolly. See Betsy Jekyll.

Hector Connolly. Irish-Catholic newspaperman and author; marries Betsy Jekyll in Nancy Hale's *The Prodigal Women.*

Lizzie Connolly. Occasional girlfriend of Martin Eden in Jack London's *Martin Eden.*

Professor Connolly. Fawning head of the drama department at Webster, an Ivy League school, whom Victor Milgrim courts in hopes of obtaining an honorary degree in Budd Schulberg's *The Disenchanted.*

Phil Connor. Boss of Ona Rudkus; coerces her into having sex with him in Upton Sinclair's *The Jungle.*

Walt Connor. Night-shift worker at the Past Bay Manufacturing Company factory who is promoted by Carl Belcher and sides with management during the strike; briefly kidnaps Marie Turner and has a relationship with Rose MacMahon in Robert Cantwell's *The Land of Plenty.*

Mary Connynge. Deceitful mistress of John Law and, later, of Philippe of Orleans in Emerson Hough's *The Mississippi Bubble.*

Andrea Biddle Conover. Washington mistress of Bruce Gold and daughter of Pugh Biddle Conover in Joseph Heller's *Good as Gold*.

Pugh Biddle Conover. Member of well-connected Virginia gentry and father of Andrea Biddle Conover in Joseph Heller's *Good as Gold*.

Sarah (Sally) Conover. Lover of Ian Sherbrooke in Nicholas Delbanco's *Sherbrookes*.

Gabriel (John Doe, Johnny Dumbledee, Gabe) Conroy. Gentle giant of a man; good but somewhat clumsy protagonist of Bret Harte's *Gabriel Conroy*.

Grace Conroy. See DonXa Dolores Salvatierra.

Olympia (Olly) Conroy. Dutiful wife of Gabriel Conroy in Bret Harte's *Gabriel Conroy*.

Malachi (Space Wanderer, Unk) Constant. Millionaire, messiah, and space traveler in Kurt Vonnegut's *The Sirens of Titan*.

Constantin. United Nations simultaneous interpreter and blind date of Esther Greenwood in Sylvia Plath's *The Bell Jar*.

Carol Constantine. Painter and wife of Eddie Constantine; they are involved in couple swapping, with homosexual overtones, with Irene and Ben Saltz in John Updike's *Couples*.

Eddie Constantine. Airline pilot married to Carol Constantine in John Updike's *Couples*.

Constantius Augustus (Constans). Roman emperor who methodically exterminates all other surviving male members of his family with the exception of his cousins Gallus and Julian in Gore Vidal's *Julian*.

Contessa. Elderly woman who arranges meetings between handsome Italian gigolos she calls "marchettas" and rich men and women; introduces Mrs. Karen Stone to Paolo in Tennessee Williams's *The Roman Spring of Mrs. Stone*.

The Continental Op. Nameless detective for the Continental Detective Agency who heads the investigation into corruption in Personville in Dashiell Hammett's *Red Harvest*.

John Converse. American journalist in Vietnam who tries to get rich by smuggling heroin into the United States but is captured by Antheil and forced to locate his wife, Marge Converse, who has the heroin, in Robert Stone's *Dog Soldiers*.

Marge Bender Converse. Wife of John Converse; pursued by Antheil's men in Robert Stone's *Dog Soldiers*.

Bill Conway. Boyhood foe of Tom Bailey, until Tom beats him in a fight; tells Ezra Wingate that Tom and others stole Ezra's stagecoach; becomes a grocer with Seth Rodgers in Thomas Bailey Aldrich's *The Story of a Bad Boy*.

Dodo Conway. Often-pregnant Catholic housewife and neighbor of Esther Greenwood in Sylvia Plath's *The Bell Jar*.

Durfee (Duff) Conway. Jazz cornet player executed for murder in Shelby Foote's *Jordan County*.

Nora Conway. Mother of Duff Conway in Shelby Foote's *Jordan County*.

Widow Conway. Dressmaker and mother of Bill Conway in Thomas Bailey Aldrich's *The Story of a Bad Boy*.

John Coode. Antithesis of Lord Baltimore; possible hero, possible villain, or possible figment of the imagination in John Barth's *The Sot-Weed Factor*.

Signora Coogan. Rich woman who pays for the companionship of Paolo and takes him to Capri; ridiculed by Paolo and the Contessa in Tennessee Williams's *The Roman Spring of Mrs. Stone*.

Al Cook. See Alexandr Petrovich Kukolnikov.

Mrs. Beatrice Latchett (Bea) Cook. Mistress of Henry Bech following her sister, Norma Latchett; bland and gentle thirty-four-year-old mother of three in the process of divorcing her husband in John Updike's *Bech: A Book*.

Lois Cook. Unkempt author of *The Gallant Gallstone* who exalts decadence in order to spite beauty in Ayn Rand's *The Fountainhead*.

Thomas (Tommy) Cook. Law clerk who takes over Mr. Talbot's practice during the Civil War but relinquishes it to Talbot when he returns to New Orleans after the war in Grace King's *The Pleasant Ways of St. Médard*.

Wilmer Cook. Boyish thug who works for Casper Gutman and whom Sam Spade calls a gunsel in Dashiell Hammett's *The Maltese Falcon*.

Anna Cooke. Twin sister of Ebenezer Cooke who, Henry Burlingame suggests, might be in reality the woman Cooke really loves in John Barth's *The Sot-Weed Factor*.

Ebenezer (Eben) Cooke. American-born Londoner forced to cross the Atlantic to claim his father's Maryland estates in John Barth's *The Sot-Weed Factor*.

Judge Charlie Cool. Defender and protector of Dolly Talbo; proposes to her shortly before her death in Truman Capote's *The Grass Harp*.

Joe Cool. Prison inmate who entrusts Erwin Riemenschneider with Cool's big robbery plan, provided that Riemenschneider will try to get Cool paroled, in William Riley Burnett's *The Asphalt Jungle*.

Gertrude Cooley. Long-suffering wife of Hubert Cooley and mother of James Lee Cooley in Julian Mayfield's *The Hit*.

Hubert Cooley. Fifty-year-old husband of Gertrude Cooley and father of James Lee Cooley in Julian Mayfield's *The Hit*.

James Lee Cooley. Twenty-six-year-old son of Hubert and Gertrude Cooley, lover of Essie Turner in Julian Mayfield's *The Hit*.

Seabright B. (Seab) Cooley. Senior senator from South Carolina and President Pro Tempore of the Senate who helps defeat two of his enemies, the President and the President's nominee for Secretary of State, in Allen Drury's *Advise and Consent*.

Jasper Coon. Free Soiler who questions why he fights for the Confederacy in Jesse Hill Ford's *The Raider*.

Coonskins. See Pitch.

Rachel Cooper. Elderly woman who takes in Pearl and John Harper after their flight down the river; protects the children from Preacher in Davis Grubb's *The Night of the Hunter*.

Reverend Cooper. Minister in Danville, Pennsylvania, who helps Milkman find his family farm in Toni Morrison's *Song of Solomon*.

Coot. See Asa Bruce Harcoot.

Carmen Sylva (Sylvy) Cope. Cousin and fiancée of Christian Fraser; loses him first to Catherine Conboy and then to death in Jessamyn West's *The Witch Diggers*.

Benedict Mady Copeland. Ascetic black physician committed to racial progress; his children ignore his teachings in Carson McCullers's *The Heart Is a Lonely Hunter*.

Brownfield (Brown) Copeland. Crazed son of Margaret and Grange Copeland; kills his wife, Mem Copeland, and is later murdered by his father in Alice Walker's *The Third Life of Grange Copeland*.

Daphne (Daffy) Copeland. Eldest daughter of Mem and Brownfield Copeland; committed to an insane asylum in Alice Walker's *The Third Life of Grange Copeland*.

Grandpapa Copeland. Elderly preacher; father and final refuge of Benedict Mady Copeland in Carson McCullers's *The Heart Is a Lonely Hunter*.

Grange Copeland. Georgia black redeemed by love for his granddaughter, Ruth Copeland; his life is chronicled from prohibition to the civil rights movement in Alice Walker's *The Third Life of Grange Copeland*.

Josie Copeland. One-time prostitute and owner of the Dew Drop Inn; vacillates in her allegiance to Grange Copeland, whom she marries, and his son Brownfield Copeland in Alice Walker's *The Third Life of Grange Copeland*.

Margaret Copeland. First wife of Grange Copeland; commits suicide after poisoning her illegitimate son Star in Alice Walker's *The Third Life of Grange Copeland*.

Mem R. Copeland. Teacher demoralized by her husband, Brownfield Copeland, who shoots her to death in front of their children, in Alice Walker's *The Third Life of Grange Copeland*.

Ornette Copeland. Middle daughter of Mem and Brownfield Copeland; becomes a prostitute in Alice Walker's *The Third Life of Grange Copeland*.

Ruth Copeland. Youngest daughter of Mem and Brownfield Copeland; reared by her grandfather, Grange, who is slain by police after attempting to save her from her father's custody, in Alice Walker's *The Third Life of Grange Copeland*.

Ted (Teddy) Copeland. First fiancé of Aline Grey; dies of the flu during World War I in Sherwood Anderson's *Dark Laughter*.

William (Willie) Copeland. Son of Benedict Mady Copeland and brother of Portia; negligent prison guards cause the amputation of his feet from frostbite in Carson McCullers's *The Heart Is a Lonely Hunter*.

Beverly Copfee. Prostitute employed by Maurice Cassard in Ludwig Bemelmans's *Dirty Eddie*.

Frieda Copperfield. Wife of J. C. Copperfield, friend of Christina Goering, and intimate companion of Pacifica in Jane Bowles's *Two Serious Ladies*.

J. C. Copperfield. Husband of Frieda Copperfield; enthusiastic man who loves to travel; Frieda finally leaves him in Jane Bowles's *Two Serious Ladies*.

Cora. Young, impoverished black student of Eric Eisner's literacy program; suffers from depression and suicidal tendencies in Phillip Lopate's *Confessions of Summer*.

Aunt Cora Lou. Sister of Bertha Ann Upshur, mother of Lil Bits and Mamie, and friend to Mariah Upshur; outcast of Tangierneck in Sarah E. Wright's *This Child's Gonna Live*.

Coransee. Brother of Teray and son of Rayal and Jansee; challenges his brother for the Pattern, a "vast network of mental links," in Octavia E. Butler's *Patternmaster*.

Myna Corbett. Overweight health food advocate and occasional companion of Gary Harkness at Logos College in Don DeLillo's *End Zone*.

Corbitant. Enemy of Hobomok and the Puritan settlers in Lydia Maria Child's *Hobomok*.

Fidsey Corcoran. Young hoodlum whom George Kelcey helps win a fistfight in Stephen Crane's *George's Mother*.

Jesus Maria Corcoran. Alcoholic, dissipated acquaintance of Pilon, who invites Corcoran to live with him because Corcoran has three dollars, in John Steinbeck's *Tortilla Flat*.

Rina Marlowe Cord. See Rina Marlowe.

Jonas Cord, Jr.. Magnate who takes control of Cord Explosives upon the death of his father and develops an aircraft company, an electronics firm, and a movie company; sacrifices personal happiness for power in Harold Robbins's *The Carpetbaggers*.

Jonas Cord, Sr.. Father of Jonas Cord, Jr., and founder of Cord Explosives and the Cord fortune; dies of an encephalic embolism in Harold Robbins's *The Carpetbaggers*.

Ramón (Cortés) Cordes. Itinerant professional revolutionary with a fatal attraction to lost causes; leader of a band of revolutionaries who is taken prisoner and awaits execution in William Herrick's *The Last to Die*.

Cordelia Swain Cordiner. Psychologist who separates the Swain twins, Wilbur and Eliza, in Kurt Vonnegut's *Slapstick*.

Corey. Leader of the Indians, a youth movement revolting against an authoritarian United States; his followers disperse and survive in ragtag groups in Marge Piercy's *Dance the Eagle to Sleep*.

Anna Bellingham Corey. Wife of Bromfield Corey; opposes the attachment of her son, Tom Corey, to Penelope Lapham in William Dean Howells's *The Rise of Silas Lapham*.

Bromfield Corey. Boston aristocrat who tries to accept the relationship of his son, Tom Corey, with the Laphams in William Dean Howells's *The Rise of Silas Lapham*.

Judge Leonidas Corey. Member of the educational committee in Morganville, Oklahoma; tries to interest George Brush in Corey's daughter in Thornton Wilder's *Heaven's My Destination*.

Mississippi Corey. Daughter of Judge Leonidas Corey; dines with George Brush and shocks him with her references to drinking and smoking in Thornton Wilder's *Heaven's My Destination*.

Mister Corey. Minister imported by Sally Lacey for Sara Lacey's marriage to Ezekiel Catlett in Mary Lee Settle's *O Beulah Land*.

Tom Corey. Son of Bromfield and Anna Corey; employee in Silas Lapham's paint factory who marries Penelope Lapham in William Dean Howells's *The Rise of Silas Lapham*.

Constanzia (Connie) Corleone. Daughter of Vito Corleone and wife of the abusive Carlo Rizzi in Mario Puzo's *The Godfather*.

Kay Corleone. See Kay Adams.

Michael Corleone. Youngest son of Don Corleone; originally determined to stay out of the family business, he takes the place of his father after the old man's death and proceeds to murder all of his family's enemies in Mario Puzo's *The Godfather*.

Santino (Sonny) Corleone. Acting head of the family during the convalescence of his father, Don Corleone, until he himself is killed by rival gangsters in Mario Puzo's *The Godfather*.

Vito (Don Corleone, The Godfather) Corleone. Head of a powerful family of Sicilian gangsters in Mario Puzo's *The Godfather*.

Aunt Cornelia (Cornie). Aunt of Honey Winthrop; takes over Winthrop's upbringing, allows her to go to Paris for a year, and enrolls her in the Katie Gibbs Secretarial School in New York in Judith Krantz's *Scruples*.

Frank (Frankie, Mark) Cornelius. Dying tubercular who is the object of Cress Delahanty's infatuation in Jessamyn West's *Cress Delahanty*.

Joyce Cornelius. School bus driver and wife of Frank Cornelius in Jessamyn West's *Cress Delahanty*.

Georgie Cornell. Twenty-first-century man living in a society dominated by women; escapes enslavement by females in a fantasy of role reversals; protagonist of Thomas Berger's *Regiment of Women*.

Neil Cornish. Piano teacher and would-be law student who marries Lulu Bett in Zona Gale's *Miss Lulu Bett*.

Cornwallis. Head of the British forces in the South; graciously receives Mildred and Henry Lindsay in John Pendleton Kennedy's *Horse-Shoe Robinson*.

Corporal. See Stefan.

The Corpse. Mummified and later plastered body of Jesus Christ stolen from the Vatican by Plucky Purcell; incinerated along with John Paul Ziller and Mon Cul on the Icarus XC solar balloon in Tom Robbins's *Another Roadside Attraction*.

Corregidora. Portuguese sea captain who, in Brazil, is a "slave breeder and whoremonger"; in fathering two females by his own daughters, he ultimately influences the life of Ursa Corregidora in Gayl Jones's *Corregidora*.

Correy (Mama) Corregidora. Daughter of Gram Corregidora and Corregidora; mother, by Martin, of Ursa Corregidora in Gayl Jones's *Corregidora*.

Dorita (Great Gram) Corregidora. Slave of Corregidora, by whom she has Gram Corregidora; great-grandmother of Ursa Corregidora, in Gayl Jones's *Corregidora*.

Gram (Grandmama) Corregidora. Daughter of Dorita and Corregidora; mother, by Corregidora, of Correy Corregidora; grandmother of Ursa Corregidora, in Gayl Jones's *Corregidora*.

Ursa (U. C., Ursa Corre, Urs, Ursie) Corregidora. Blues singer descended from the whoremonger Corregidora and instructed by her female forebears to "make generations"; because her husband, Mutt Thomas, throws her, pregnant, down a flight of stairs, she undergoes a hysterectomy; narrator of Gayl Jones's *Corregidora*.

Alfredo Corregio. Portuguese fisherman who lives for a time with his family in the Meserve's servant house before returning to the shrimping business to handle Jim Meserve's boats in Zora Neale Hurston's *Seraph on the Suwanee*.

Miss Corrie. See Everbe Corinthia Hogganbeck.

Corruthers. Political crony of Sammy Scott; known for his underground dirty work in W. E. B. Du Bois's *Dark Princess*.

Corson. Veteran army lieutenant who yearns for the "old" army in Tim O'Brien's *Going after Cacciato*.

Sheldon Corthell. Esthete who courts Laura Dearborn and then attempts to win her once more after her marriage to Curtis Jadwin in Frank Norris's *The Pit*.

Edith Cortright. American-born widow of a British diplomat; lover and traveling companion of Sam Dodsworth in Sinclair Lewis's *Dodsworth*.

Billy Cosgrove. Wealthy acquaintance of Father Urban and patron of the Order of St. Clement; offended by Father Urban's attempt to correct his behavior, he abandons both priest and Order in J. F. Powers's *Morte D'Urban*.

Michael Cosman. General practitioner; best friend and "almost lover" of Isadora Wing; tells Isadora of her husband's affair in Erica Jong's *How to Save Your Own Life*.

Bill Costello. Sponsor of John Wilder in Alcoholics Anonymous; well-intentioned but platitudinous in Richard Yates's *Disturbing the Peace*.

Ivan Costello. First boyfriend of Maria Wyeth in New York in Joan Didion's *Play It As It Lays*.

Mrs. Costello. Aunt of Frederick Winterbourne; thinks that the Millers are common, dreadful, and vulgar in Henry James's *Daisy Miller*.

Euphrasia (Phrasie) Cotton. Spinster housekeeper of Hilary Vane; friend of Austen Vane in Winston Churchill's *Mr. Crewe's Career*.

Ralph (Ralphie) Cotton. Rich and snobbish black student—one of only two—at a private academy; his family discourages his association with George Cain in George Cain's *Blueschild Baby*.

Burley (Uncle Burley) Coulter. Wayward bachelor brother of Jarrat Coulter; his wild antics provide down-home Kentucky humor in Wendell Berry's *Nathan Coulter*, *A Place on Earth*, and *The Memory of Old Jack*.

David (Dave) Coulter. Father of Jarrat and Burley Coulter and "Grandpa" to Nathan Coulter in Wendell Berry's *Nathan Coulter*; also appears in *The Memory of Old Jack*.

Hannah Coulter. Wife of Nathan Coulter and mother of Mattie Coulter; widow of Virgil Feltner and mother by him of Little Margaret Feltner in Wendell Berry's *A Place on Earth* and *The Memory of Old Jack*.

Jarrat Coulter. Widowed subsistence tobacco farmer in Port William, Kentucky; father of Tom Coulter and "Daddy" to Nathan Coulter in Wendell Berry's *Nathan Coulter*, *A Place on Earth*, and *The Memory of*

Old Jack.

Mathew Burley (Mattie) Coulter. Son of Nathan and Hannah Coulter in Wendell Berry's *The Memory of Old Jack.*

Nathan Coulter. Kentucky tobacco farmer and second husband of widowed Hannah Feltner; narrator of Wendell Berry's *Nathan Coulter*; also appears in *A Place on Earth* and *The Memory of Old Jack.*

Tom Coulter. Oldest son of Jarrat Coulter; leaves home after a fight with his father; killed during World War II in Wendell Berry's *A Place on Earth*; also appears in *Nathan Coulter.*

Count of Monte Beni. See Donatello.

Countess. Physically ugly but wealthy American lover of Beale Farange while he is married in Henry James's *What Maisie Knew.*

Countess. Epicene tycoon of feminine hygiene products and owner of the Rubber Rose Ranch; makes Sissy Hankshaw his star model as the Yoni Yum/ Dew Girl in Tom Robbins's *Even Cowgirls Get the Blues.*

The County Clerk (Arch Anker). Obscene civil servant working out of the Old Court House in Pigeon Hole; person to whom civil cases are referred so they will not be resolved in William S. Burroughs's *Naked Lunch* and *The Soft Machine.*

Olive de Courcy. Red Cross volunteer in France who passes out stocks of American supplies to the villagers in Willa Cather's *One of Ours.*

Landry Court. Boyish suitor of Laura Dearborn and worshipful colleague of Curtis Jadwin at the Chicago Board of Trade; marries Laura's sister Page Dearborn and remains determined to become like Jadwin, despite Jadwin's failure as a speculator, in Frank Norris's *The Pit.*

Mont Court. Parole officer of Gary Gilmore in Norman Mailer's *The Executioner's Song.*

Adele Courtland. Neighbor of the McKelvas and sister of Nate Courtland in Eudora Welty's *The Optimist's Daughter.*

Nate Courtland. New Orleans eye specialist and family friend of the McKelvas; treats both Clinton and Becky McKelva's vision problems in Eudora Welty's *The Optimist's Daughter.*

Jim Courtney. Police captain killed by Rico Bandello in the New Year's Eve holdup of the Casa Alvarado nightclub in William Riley Burnett's *Little Caesar.*

Tom Courtney. *New York Times* reporter who conducts the first interview with Chance in Jerzy Kosinski's *Being There.*

Miles Coverdale. Narrator who observes the people and events at Blithedale and who claims to have loved Priscilla in Nathaniel Hawthorne's *The Blithedale Romance.*

Major — de Coverley. Magisterially photogenic officer responsible for renting apartments for the use of officers and enlisted men on rest leave in Europe in Joseph Heller's *Catch-22.*

Daisy Patricia Cowan. Sister of Jim Cowan and fiancée of Phillip Laurie in Nathan Asch's *Pay Day.*

Eugene Cowan. Brother of Jim and Daisy Cowan; killed at Verdun in Nathan Asch's *Pay Day.*

James (Jim) Cowan. Dissatisfied bookkeeper who wants to be a traveling salesman and who wanders around New York the night of the Sacco-Vanzetti executions in Nathan Asch's *Pay Day.*

Martha Cowan. Mother of Jim and Daisy Cowan; tries to keep the family together in Nathan Asch's *Pay Day.*

Ebenezer Cowley. Owner of Cowley & Son's store whose reputation as "queer" torments his son Elmer Cowley in Sherwood Anderson's *Winesburg, Ohio.*

Elmer Cowley. Junior partner of Cowley & Son's store; beats George Willard and leaves Winesburg in a frustrated attempt to deal with his family's reputation as "queer" in Sherwood Anderson's *Winesburg, Ohio.*

Aileen Butler (Ai, Mrs. Montague) Cowperwood. Mistress of Frank Cowperwood in Theodore Dreiser's *The Financier*; unhappily married wife of Cowperwood in *The Stoic* and *The Titan.*

Frank Algernon (Dickson, Montague) Cowperwood. Stockbroker and friend of Philadelphia politicians; husband of Lillian Semple Cowperwood and lover of Aileen Butler; convicted and jailed for unscrupulous business deals in Theodore Dreiser's *The Financier*; released from jail, he is active in the natural gas business; marries Aileen Butler in *The Titan*; attempts to monopolize the London streetcar and subway system; dies in *The Stoic.*

Henry Worthington Cowperwood. Father of Frank Cowperwood; resigns his bank presidency following Frank's involvement in a scandal in Theodore Dreiser's *The Financier.*

Lillian Semple (Anna Wheeler) Cowperwood. Widow of Alfred Semple and first wife of Frank Cowperwood in Theodore Dreiser's *The Financier*; also appears in *The Stoic*, where she is called Anna Wheeler, and *The Titan*.

George Cox. Friend of Nelson Dewey; involves Dewey in mining investments that lead to the wealth of both men in August Derleth's *The Shadow in the Glass*.

Hillary Cox. Innocent disfigured by an anarchist's bomb in Robert Herrick's *The Memoirs of an American Citizen*.

Mr. Cox. Astrologer who meets Malcolm on a hotel bench and helps introduce him to life by sending him to the homes of acquaintances in James Purdy's *Malcolm*.

Eddie (Eddie Fingers, Paulie) Coyle. Convicted small-time criminal who sells out other criminals in order to make a deal with federal authorities in George V. Higgins's *The Friends of Eddie Coyle*.

Coyotito. Infant son of Kino and Juana; refused medical treatment after being stung by a scorpion because his parents are poor; shot to death by a thief in John Steinbeck's *The Pearl*.

Crab. Teacher at Swallow Barn; preceptor of Ned Hazard in John Pendleton Kennedy's *Swallow Barn*.

Caroline (Calamity Jane) Crabb. Sister of Jack Crabb in Thomas Berger's *Little Big Man*.

Jack (Little Big Man) Crabb. One-hundred-eleven-year-old survivor of the Battle of Little Bighorn; picaresque hero and narrator of Thomas Berger's *Little Big Man*.

Olga Crabb. Wife of Jack Crabb and mother of their son in Thomas Berger's *Little Big Man*.

Mr. Craft. Partner in Aaron Burr's law firm in Gore Vidal's *Burr*.

Thomas Craig. Employee of Stephen Dudley; his embezzlement causes Dudley's financial ruin; kills Dudley, at Ormond's bidding, and is himself killed by Ormond in Charles Brockden Brown's *Ormond*.

Crainpool. Dickensian-like secretary to Alexander Main; forced to flee for his life for jumping bail in *The Bailbondsman*, a novella in Stanley Elkin's *Searches and Seizures*.

Keg Head Cramer. Neighbor of Nunn Ballew; crass, self-righteous father-in-law of Lureenie Cramer in Harriette Arnow's *Hunter's Horn*.

Lureenie Cramer. Mother of three at age twenty; dreamer deserted by her husband, Rans Cramer; nearly starves to death with her family; dies in childbirth in Harriette Arnow's *Hunter's Horn*.

Mark Cramer. Son of Keg Head Cramer; works in Detroit and fathers a child by Suse Ballew out of wedlock in Harriette Arnow's *Hunter's Horn*.

Nurse Cramer. Freckled army nurse and friend of Sue Ann Duckett in Joseph Heller's *Catch-22*.

Rans Cramer. Husband who deserts Lureenie Cramer; flees the community to avoid arrest and returns after he "gets religion" in Harriette Arnow's *Hunter's Horn*.

Agatha Cramp. Wealthy white woman dedicated to social service to blacks but opposed to an integrated neighborhood in Rudolph Fisher's *The Walls of Jericho*.

Esther Crane. Daughter of a prosperous black grocer; fascinated by King Barlo in Jean Toomer's *Cane*.

Helga Crane. Daughter of a Danish immigrant mother and black American father; resigns as a teacher and travels to Harlem and Denmark; becomes the sickly and overburdened wife of the Reverend Mr. Pleasant Green in Nella Larsen's *Quicksand*.

Jasper Crane. Black Virginian who claims to live with his brother in Harlem; meets Emma Lou Morgan in a movie theater, borrows five dollars from her, and vanishes in Wallace Thurman's *The Blacker the Berry*.

Kelcey Crane. Young trumpeter in John Clellon Holmes's *The Horn*.

Lewis Crane. Army electronics technician who looks for the downed Scoop VII satellite in Michael Crichton's *The Andromeda Strain*.

Nebraska (Bras) Crane. Part-Cherokee Indian boyhood friend of George Webber in Thomas Wolfe's *You Can't Go Home Again* and *The Web and the Rock*.

Emile Cranmer. Grocery delivery boy with whom Melissa Wapshot has an affair in John Cheever's *The Wapshot Scandal*.

Mrs. Amelia Cranston. Operator of a boardinghouse for Newport servants in Thornton Wilder's *Theophilus North*.

Thomas (Tom) Lowell Crapo. Friend of Andrew Cather and lover of Cather's wife Bertha Cather in Conrad Aiken's *Great Circle*.

Crash. Naval officer convicted of having an illicit affair with a fourteen-year-old Polynesian female in Herman Melville's *Omoo*.

Cimarron (Cim) Cravat. Son of Sabra and Yancey Cravat and husband of Ruby Big Elk; field geologist in Edna Ferber's *Cimarron*.

Donna Cravat. Daughter of Sabra and Yancey Cravat and wife of the multimillionaire Tracy Wyatt in Edna Ferber's *Cimarron*.

Sabra Venable Cravat. Daughter of Felice and Lewis Venable, wife of Yancey Cravat, and mother of Cimarron and Donna Cravat; strong pioneer who becomes an important newspaper editor and an Oklahoma congresswoman in Edna Ferber's *Cimarron*.

Yancey (Cimarron) Cravat. Husband of Sabra Venable Cravat and father of Cimarron and Donna Cravat; lawyer and newspaperman who becomes governor of the Oklahoma Territory and then joins Teddy Roosevelt's Rough Riders in Edna Ferber's *Cimarron*.

Marcella L. (Queenie) Craven. Owner of Queenie's Boarding House in Kansas City, where George Brush stays; devout Catholic in Thornton Wilder's *Heaven's My Destination*.

Wanda Cravens. Dimwitted widow who is readily seduced by both Justin Miller and Vince Bonali in Robert Coover's *The Origin of the Brunists*.

Andrew Crawford. Husband for one summer of Emily Grimes; impotent, he hates Emily's sexuality in Richard Yates's *Easter Parade*.

Brandon Crawford. Brother-in-law of Sally Lacey; helps Johnny Lacey with his land claims and is elected with him to the House of Burgesses in Mary Lee Settle's *O Beulah Land*.

Elise Crawford. Sister of Maija von Einzeedle, wife of Reuben Crawford, and lover of Anthony Hope-Harding in Nicholas Delbanco's *Small Rain*.

Frank Crawford. Father of Sonny Crawford, former high school principal, and proprietor of a domino parlor in Larry McMurtry's *The Last Picture Show*.

Haim Crawford. Cousin of Bannie Upshire Dudley; member of the Paddy Rollers of Mantipico County in Sarah E. Wright's *This Child's Gonna Live*.

Janie Mae Crawford. Heroine who becomes the wife of Logan Killicks, Jody Starks, and Vergible Woods before becoming completely herself in Zora Neale Hurston's *Their Eyes Were Watching God*.

Melancthon Crawford. American sailor imprisoned by Tripoli pirates; Indian trader and pioneer who is a cofounder of a town in Oklahoma in H. L. Davis's *Harp of a Thousand Strings*.

Reuben Crawford. Husband of Elise Crawford in Nicholas Delbanco's *Small Rain*.

Sonny Crawford. Athlete at Thalia High School, roommate of Duane Moore, and lover of Ruth Popper; initiated into adulthood in Larry McMurtry's *The Last Picture Show*.

Miss Stephanie Crawford. Gossipy neighbor of Atticus Finch and one of the family who constantly spread rumors about Boo Radley in Harper Lee's *To Kill a Mockingbird*.

Colonel Crayton. Father of Mrs. Beauchamp and husband of Mademoiselle La Rue in Susanna Rowson's *Charlotte*.

Mrs. Crayton. See Mademoiselle La Rue.

Crazy Carl. Retarded adult in the town of Maxwell, Georgia, on whose word Henry McIntosh is mistakenly identified as the murderer of Tracy Deen in Lillian Smith's *Strange Fruit*.

William Cream. Barber who offers no trust to his customers in Herman Melville's *The Confidence-Man*.

Lady Creamhair. See Virginia R. Hector.

Louis Credenza. Senior member of a large property-owning family in northwest Iowa that controls the radio station that employs Dick Gibson in Stanley Elkin's *The Dick Gibson Show*.

Captain Joe Cree. First husband of Julia Cropleigh Cree and pillar of the community; his suicide sets in motion the events of Andrew Lytle's *The Velvet Horn*.

Julia Cropleigh Cree. Youngest of the orphaned Cropleigh children and mother of Lucius Cree; object of the long-suffering love of Pete Legrand, the crazed passion of her brother, Duncan Cropleigh, and the formal devotion of her husband, Joe Cree, in Andrew Lytle's *The Velvet Horn*.

Lucius Cree. Son of Joe and Julia Cropleigh Cree; forced to face the mystery of his family's past when his father commits suicide in Andrew Lytle's *The Velvet Horn*.

Emmett Creed. Head football coach in his first year at Logos College; has a no-nonsense attitude and reputation for winning in Don DeLillo's *End Zone*.

Catherine Creek. Black woman who insists she is an Indian; from childhood on, lives with the Talbo sisters, adoring Dolly and despising Verena, in Truman Capote's *The Grass Harp*.

Carrie Cressler. Confidante of Laura Dearborn; encourages Laura to marry Curtis Jadwin in Frank Norris's *The Pit*.

Charles (Charlie) Cressler. Dealer in grain at the Chicago Board of Trade who is ruined by speculation and commits suicide in Frank Norris's *The Pit*.

Harry Cresswell. Congressman who opposes the education of his black tenants; son of Colonel St. John Cresswell, husband of Mary Taylor, and father of Bertie's mulatto child Emma in W. E. B. Du Bois's *The Quest of the Silver Fleece*.

Helen Cresswell. Self-centered daughter of Colonel St. John Cresswell and wife of John Taylor in W. E. B. Du Bois's *The Quest of the Silver Fleece*.

Mary Taylor Cresswell. See Mary Taylor.

Colonel St. John Cresswell. Southern aristocrat who owns almost everything in Tooms County, Alabama; father of Helen and Harry Cresswell in W. E. B. Du Bois's *The Quest of the Silver Fleece*.

Creuzot. Tall, fair-skinned Frenchman who operates his own print shop; afflicted with a lung disease in Arna Wendell Bontemps's *Black Thunder*.

Alice Pomfret Crewe. See Alice Pomfret.

Humphrey Crewe. Unskilled amateur politician who becomes increasingly shrewd and reforming; unsuccessful suitor of Victoria Flint and husband of Alice Pomfret in Winston Churchill's *Mr. Crewe's Career*.

Tony Crews. Black poet; Emma Lou Morgan meets him at a rent party in Wallace Thurman's *The Blacker the Berry*.

Cribbens (Crib). Prospector with whom McTeague discovers gold in the Panamint Range in Frank Norris's *McTeague*.

Cribiche. Young orphan reared by Père Philéas in Grace King's *The Pleasant Ways of St. Médard*.

Alicia Crick. Lover of the Reverend Thomas Marshfield in the first of his many adulterous affairs; later lover of Ned Bork; church organist and divorced mother of three in John Updike's *A Month of Sundays*.

Avis Criley. See Avis Criley Elderman.

Bradd Criley. Grand Republic attorney, friend of Cass Timberlane, and lover of Jinny Timberlane in Sinclair Lewis's *Cass Timberlane*.

Crimson Rambler. See Clarence Rambo.

John Cripps. Illiterate and cruel husband of Sue Seymour Cripps; following her death, turns their children's home into a low tavern in Harriet Beecher Stowe's *Dred*.

Sue Seymour (Suse) Cripps. Daughter of formerly aristocratic Virginian parents and wife of the illiterate John Cripps; owner of Tiff Peyton; dies in poverty after the birth of her third child in Harriet Beecher Stowe's *Dred*.

Amy Crittenden. Mother of John Buddy Pearson and wife of Ned Crittenden in Zora Neale Hurston's *Jonah's Gourd Vine*.

Ned Crittenden. Stepfather of John Buddy Pearson and husband of Amy Crittenden in Zora Neale Hurston's *Jonah's Gourd Vine*.

Elizabeth Crittendon. Southern lady who has an affair with Nathaniel Franklin after he burns her house in Hervey Allen's *Action at Aquila*.

Margaret Crittendon. Daughter of Elizabeth Crittendon; has an affair with a doomed Confederate soldier in Hervey Allen's *Action at Aquila*.

Croaker. Savage, uneducated sexual brute who rapes Anastasia Stoker in John Barth's *Giles Goat-Boy*.

Joseph Crocker. Handsome carpenter whom Isabella Archbald elects to marry in Ellen Glasgow's *The Sheltered Life*.

Hartshorn Priss Crockett. Introverted New York socialite and member of the Group in Mary McCarthy's *The Group*.

Art Croft. Narrator of Walter Van Tilburg Clark's *The Ox-Bow Incident*.

Staff Sergeant Samuel (Sam) Croft. Fascistic commander of a reconnaissance unit who arranges the death of Robert Hearn in Norman Mailer's *The Naked and the Dead*.

Professor Crofts. Condescending Emersonian scholar and Shep Stearns's former teacher in Budd Schulberg's *The Disenchanted*.

Mrs. Crofut. Woman who George Brush believes has many daughters, when in fact she operates a house of prostitution, in Thornton Wilder's *Heaven's My Destination*.

Miss Croly. Grade-school teacher of Felix Fay; encourages Fay to use his imagination in Floyd Dell's *Moon-Calf*.

Hugh and Sarah Hutchins (Widow Hutchins) Crombie. Operators of the Hand and Bottle Inn in Nathaniel Hawthorne's *Fanshawe*.

Clarence (Sinbad) Cromwell. Veteran black Los Angeles police detective; friend of A. M. Valnikov in Joseph Wambaugh's *The Black Marble*.

Oliver (Ironsides) Cromwell. Commander of the Parliamentary army; originally appears to consider his soldiers equals but is corrupted by power and property, betraying his promises to the soldiers opposed to his Irish campaign, in Mary Lee Settle's *Prisons*.

Jabberwhorl (Jab) Cronstadt. Friend of Henry Miller; provides one free meal per week for Miller in Henry Miller's *Tropic of Cancer*; poet, musician, weatherman, herbologist, and linguist in *Black Spring*.

Katya Cronstadt. Daughter of Jabberwhorl Cronstadt in Henry Miller's *Black Spring*.

Eugene (Gene) Crook. Crooked banker who swindles Jean Baptiste in Oscar Micheaux's *The Homesteader*.

Dr. Junius (Doc) Crookman. Black biologist and physician who develops the Black-No-More process to make blacks white in George S. Schuyler's *Black No More*.

Crooks. Black ranch hand who hesitatingly befriends Lennie Small in John Steinbeck's *Of Mice and Men*.

Arthur Croom. Friend of John Laskell; arranges for Laskell's care during his illness in Lionel Trilling's *The Middle of the Journey*.

Nancy (Nan) Croom. Wife of Arthur Croom; refuses to accept the reality of death in Lionel Trilling's *The Middle of the Journey*.

George Crooper. Cousin of Johnnie Watson; his prodigious appetite causes him trouble, to the delight of William Baxter, Johnnie Watson, and Joe Bullitt, in Booth Tarkington's *Seventeen*.

Annie Crop. Young daughter of Gideon and Ida Crop; swept off a country bridge to her death during a flood in Wendell Berry's *A Place on Earth*.

Gideon Crop. Tenant farmer of Roger Merchant, husband of Ida Crop, and father of Annie Crop in Wendell Berry's *A Place on Earth*.

Ida Crop. Wife of Gideon Crop, mother of Annie Crop, and object of Ernest Finley's unrequited love in Wendell Berry's *A Place on Earth*.

Beverly Cropleigh. Woodsman and eldest of the Cropleigh siblings; retreats to Parcher's Cove after his parents are killed in a steamboat disaster in Andrew Lytle's *The Velvet Horn*.

Dickie Cropleigh. Physician and brother of Julia Cropleigh Cree in Andrew Lytle's *The Velvet Horn*.

Duncan Cropleigh. Jealous brother of Julia Cropleigh Cree and probable biological father of her son, Lucius Cree; blown up with his brother Beverly in a dynamite explosion during the Civil War in Andrew Lytle's *The Velvet Horn*.

Jack (Uncle Jack) Cropleigh. Brother of Julia Cropleigh Cree and garrulous uncle of Lucius Cree; tries to instruct and protect his nephew, in the end lunging in front of the bullet intended for Lucius; principal narrator of Andrew Lytle's *The Velvet Horn*.

Julia Cropleigh. See Julia Cropleigh Cree.

H. Lowe Crosby. Midwestern entrepreneur and patriot; husband of Hazel Crosby in Kurt Vonnegut's *Cat's Cradle*.

Hazel (Mom) Crosby. Hoosier wife of H. Lowe Crosby; sews the U.S. flag in Kurt Vonnegut's *Cat's Cradle*.

Anthony (Anthony Cruz) Cross. Poor, light-skinned love and eventual mate of Angela Murray in Jessie Redmon Fauset's *Plum Bun*.

Lucas Cross. Drunken shack-dweller whose abuse of his stepdaughter, Selena Cross, drives her to murder him and causes the suicide of his wife, Nellie Cross, in Grace Metalious's *Peyton Place*.

Nadine Cross. Woman chosen to bear Randall Flagg's child in Stephen King's *The Stand*.

Nellie Cross. Wife of Lucas Cross and mother of Selena Cross; hangs herself in the MacKenzie home as a result of her husband's raping and impregnating her daughter in Grace Metalious's *Peyton Place*.

Selena Cross. Daughter of Nellie Cross, stepdaughter of Lucas Cross, and best friend of Allison MacKenzie; kills her abusive stepfather during an attempted rape and is acquitted of the murder but henceforth shunned by the respectable townspeople in Grace Metalious's *Peyton Place*.

Crotti. Cocaine merchant involved in a struggle for control of Los Angeles in Paul Cain's *Fast One*.

Frank Crotty. Los Angeles policeman and partner of Thomas Spellacy in John Gregory Dunne's *True Confessions*.

Martha Crouch. Wife of Samuel Crouch; landlady and secret lover of N'Gana Frimbo in Rudolph Fisher's *The Conjure-Man Dies*.

Samuel (Easley Jones) Crouch. Harlem mortician, husband of Martha Crouch, and landlord of N'Gana Frimbo, whom Crouch kills, in Rudolph Fisher's *The Conjure-Man Dies*.

Jonah (J., Jayber, Jaybird) Crow. Barber of Port William, Kentucky, and self-taught philosopher in Wendell Berry's *A Place on Earth* and *The Memory of Old Jack*.

Ben Crowder. Tough-minded manager of the Washington baseball team in Mark Harris's *It Looked Like For Ever*.

Crown. Catfish Row cotton stevedore and lover of Bess; murders Robbins and is fatally stabbed by Porgy in DuBose Heyward's *Porgy*.

Alberta Sydna Crowninshield. See Alberta Sydna Crowninshield Vaiden.

Drusilla Lacefield (Dru) Crowninshield. Daughter of Caruthers Lacefield; elopes with Emory Crowninshield the day before she is to marry Miltiades Vaiden; mother of Sydna Crowninshield; appears in T. S. Stribling's *The Forge*, *The Store*, and *Unfinished Cathedral*.

Emory Crowninshield. Southern genteel aristocrat and husband of Drusilla Lacefield; Confederate major and ardent defender of chattel slavery; appears in T. S. Stribling's *The Forge*.

Kate Croy. Secret fiancée of Merton Densher and friend of the dying Mildred Theale; plots to have Densher marry Theale and inherit her money in Henry James's *The Wings of the Dove*.

Sarah Croyden. Actress, confidante of Olivia Lattimore, and abandoned lover and later the wife of Leon Lawrence in Mary Austin's *A Woman of Genius*.

Cruz. Indian woman, addict, and companion of Tristessa in Jack Kerouac's *Tristessa*.

Anthony Cruz. See Anthony Cross.

Cuckold. Wife murderer and convict who runs a private commissary and tells of a homosexual relationship which parallels that of Zeke Farragut in John Cheever's *Falconer*.

Cuckoo. Mistress of Old Lord in the House of Hwang; procuress who moves to Wang Lung's home as Lotus's meddling servant in Pearl Buck's *The Good Earth*.

Cudjoe. Deformed slave fiercely faithful to Lafitte in Joseph Holt Ingraham's *Lafitte*.

Daddy Cudjoe. Conjure doctor at Blue Brook Plantation; dispenser of a successful love charm to Cinder and of an unsuccessful antidote to Mary Pinesett in Julia Peterkin's *Scarlet Sister Mary*.

Moll Cudlip. Cutpurse sentenced for life to Australia; escapes and lives with her aborigine lover in Charles Nordhoff and James Norman Hall's *Botany Bay*.

Cuffee. Slave and miller at Beulah; sold as punishment for trying to run away in Mary Lee Settle's *Know Nothing*.

Cuffee Ned. Hero of the poor blacks on Bourne Island; led the largest and most successful slave revolt in the island's history in Paule Marshall's *The Chosen Place, the Timeless People*.

Tom Cullen. Slightly retarded man who, under the influence of Nick Andros's spirit, saves Stuart Redman's life in Stephen King's *The Stand*.

Norah (Norry) Culligan. Landlady and lover of Charles Fort in Jessamyn West's *The Massacre at Fall Creek*.

Captain Cully. Would-be minstrel and leader of a band of ineffective outlaws in Peter S. Beagle's *The Last Unicorn*.

Lieutenant Culpepper. Third-generation army officer; serves as defense counsel for Robert E. Lee Prewitt's trial in James Jones's *From Here to Eternity*.

Martin (Mart) Culpepper. Town developer and partner of John Barclay; saved from disgrace and financial ruin when his daughter, Molly Culpepper, marries Adrian Brownwell in William Allen White's *A Certain Rich Man*.

Molly Culpepper. See Molly Culpepper Brownwell.

Lieutenant Jack Culver. Lawyer on Marine reserve duty and closest friend of Captain Mannix; one of the men ordered on a useless thirty-six-mile hike in William Styron's *The Long March*.

Thwaite Cumberly. Philadelphian hired by MacDougal to work with Marietta McGee-Chavéz to populate her Spain in William Goyen's *In a Farther Country*.

Major General Edward Cummings. Commander of troops on the island of Anopopei; predicts a totalitarian future for America in Norman Mailer's *The Naked and the Dead.*

Candace (Candy, The One Who Is Always Wrapped, The Muffled One) Cunningham. Blonde American second wife of Colonel Ellelloû; fellow student with him at McCarthy College in Wisconsin; wears full purdah to survive the coup Ellelloû leads against foreigners; leaves him after his own government falls in John Updike's *The Coup.*

John Cunningham. Father of Avis Cunningham Everhard; physics professor who is fired for publishing a prolabor book; disappears during the rise of the Iron Heel in Jack London's *The Iron Heel.*

Miz Cunningham. Woman who looks after John and Pearl Harper while Willa Harper is at work; attempts to coerce John into revealing the whereabouts of hidden money in Davis Grubb's *The Night of the Hunter.*

Mr. Cunningham. Old man cared for until his death by Elizabeth Abbott in Anne Tyler's *The Clock Winder.*

Billy Cupcake. Television evangelist who delivers a eulogy for Trick E. Dixon in Philip Roth's *Our Gang.*

Cupid. Arrogant, perverted policeman in Wright Morris's *My Uncle Dudley.*

Miss Lavinia Curdy. Friend of Gin-head Susy; searches successfully for a lover in Claude McKay's *Home to Harlem.*

Curley. Friend admired by Henry Miller because he has no morals or sense of shame; has affairs with three women at the same time in Henry Miller's *Tropic of Capricorn.*

Curley. Part-owner of a ranch who vows to kill Lennie Small for having raped Curley's wife in John Steinbeck's *Of Mice and Men.*

Jack Curran. Son of Kathleen and Johnny Curran; football star of Boniface College, beer truck driver, and wrestler; falls in love with and marries Mary Odell, who later leaves him; dies fighting a fire in Mark Steadman's *A Lion's Share.*

Johnny (Old Johnny) Curran. Father of Jack Curran and ex-husband of Kathleen Reilley in Mark Steadman's *A Lion's Share.*

Kathleen Curran. See Kathleen Lynch Reilley.

Mary Cheney Odell Curran. First real love of Jack Curran; marries Curran against her parents' wishes and later divorces him in Mark Steadman's *A Lion's Share.*

Ned Currie. Reporter for the *Winesburg Eagle* who leaves his lover Alice Hindman for greater opportunities in Chicago in Sherwood Anderson's *Winesburg, Ohio.*

Honey Curry. Small-time Irish hoodlum who is involved in Charlie Boy McCall's kidnapping; killed in Newark in a gun battle with the police in William Kennedy's *Billy Phelan's Greatest Game.*

James (Peppercorn) Curry. British dragoon who bribes Wat Adair to betray Arthur Butler; killed at King's Mountain in John Pendleton Kennedy's *Horse-Shoe Robinson.*

Marie Curtin. Asthmatic young socialite and part-time model and writer; lover of Jack Bogardes, Teddy Forster, and Eric Eisner in Phillip Lopate's *Confessions of Summer.*

Curtin (Curtis, Curty). American drifter who meets Dobbs in a Mexican oil camp and joins him on a search for gold in B. Traven's *The Treasure of the Sierra Madre.*

George Armstrong Custer. Army general defeated at Little Bighorn in Thomas Berger's *Little Big Man.*

Cadwallader Cuticle. Surgeon aboard the *Neversink* who is interested in morbid anatomy; saves the life of Baldy, and kills another sailor by operating on him unnecessarily, in Herman Melville's *White-Jacket.*

Rav Yosef Cutler. Mashpia of Asher Lev; treats Lev compassionately until Lev exhibits his masterpieces in Chaim Potok's *My Name Is Asher Lev.*

Emily Bolling Cutrer. Stoical and aristocratic great aunt and patron of Binx Bolling in Walker Percy's *The Moviegoer.*

Jules Cutrer. Worldly and wealthy husband of Emily Bolling Cutrer and father of Kate Cutrer in Walker Percy's *The Moviegoer.*

Kate Cutrer. Despairing daughter of Jules Cutrer and stepdaughter of Emily Bolling Cutrer; marries Binx Bolling in Walker Percy's *The Moviegoer.*

Wycliffe (Wick) Cutter. Merciless moneylender who tries to seduce Ántonia Shimerda; murders his wife and commits suicide in Willa Cather's *My Ántonia.*

Doggo Cutwright. Braggart, provincial soldier, and lazy settler at Beulah; moves west beyond Beulah because he hates all symbols of refinement, but leaves his children behind so they can be educated; eventually sides with Johnny Lacey's political opponents in Mary Lee Settle's *O Beulah Land*.

Jacob Cutwright. Drunkard and brother of Doggo Cutwright; tears up and fouls Jarcey Pentacost's books before leaving Beulah with a band of white outlaws who raid the settlement during Johnny Lacey's absence in Mary Lee Settle's *O Beulah Land*.

Leah Cutwright. See Leah Cutwright Catlett.

Maggie Cutwright. Half-Indian wife of Doggo Cutwright; insulted by the women of Beulah, she steals Sally Lacey's china cup before leaving the settlement in Mary Lee Settle's *O Beulah Land*.

Anton Cuzak. Husband of Ántonia Shimerda at the conclusion of Willa Cather's *My Ántonia*.

Cynthia. Girlfriend, briefly, of Jesse; leaves him just before he joins Lee Mellon at Big Sur in Richard Brautigan's *A Confederate General from Big Sur*.

Lily Shane de Cyon. See Lily Shane.

René de Cyon. French diplomat who marries Lily Shane in Louis Bromfield's *The Green Bay Tree*.

Cyril. Husband of Fiona, lover of Catherine, and employer of Rosella; narrator of John Hawkes's *The Blood Oranges*.

Cytheris. Famous actress who instructs Pompeia for a part in the Mysteries; visits Turrinus in his self-imposed exile in Thornton Wilder's *The Ides of March*.

Sybil Czap. Mother who sells the story of her son's death to Waldo in Paul Theroux's *Waldo*.

Casimir (Polack) Czienwicz. Polish-American soldier who believes he can beat the system in Norman Mailer's *The Naked and the Dead*.

D

D. Passenger on the *Here They Come* who plans to buy the English language in Gregory Corso's *The American Express*.

Anthony X. (Tony) D'Alessandro. Lover of Bella Biaggi before and after her marriage to David Dehn; dies with Biaggi in an automobile accident in Jerome Weidman's *The Temple*.

Annie D'Alfonso. See Annie Landry.

Ignatius (Inky) D'Alfonso. Marooned skipper of the *Pixie* who becomes the lover and then husband of Annie Landry in Shirley Ann Grau's *The Hard Blue Sky*.

Stephanie D'Alfonso. See Stephanie Maria D'Alfonso Oliver.

Thomas Parke D'Invilliers. Literary Princeton classmate of Amory Blaine in F. Scott Fitzgerald's *This Side of Paradise*.

Lou Da Silva. Chairman of the student honor committee and forceful advocate of Raymond Blent's eligibility to play football in Howard Nemerov's *The Homecoming Game*.

Elliott Dabney. Four-year-old son of Billie Dabney; rival of Jack Duluoz for Billie's attention in Jack Kerouac's *Big Sur*.

Willamine (Billie) Dabney. Blonde model whose beauty reminds Jack Duluoz of Julien Love; mother of Elliott Dabney, mistress of Cody Pomeray, and lover of Jack Duluoz in Jack Kerouac's *Big Sur*.

Daisy Dacey. Traveling companion of Pauline Faubion in Conrad Aiken's *Blue Voyage*.

Daddy. Talented and exuberant actor; father of the narrator of Aline Bernstein's *The Journey Down*.

Daddy Big. Cousin of Bindy McCall; former gambler and pool hustler jailed for two years for a crime he did not commit; assisted by Billy Phelan in William Kennedy's *Billy Phelan's Greatest Game*.

Daddy Faith. Preacher who conducts a riverside baptismal service in William Styron's *Lie Down in Darkness*.

Elaine Dade. Jamaican lover of Allan and mother of their child in Nicholas Delbanco's *News*.

Herbert Hamilton Dade. Young entrepreneur whose courtship of Margaret Schofield is undermined by her brother, Penrod Schofield, in Booth Tarkington's *Penrod Jashber*.

Private Luther Dade. Confederate rifleman from Mississippi; narrates part of Shelby Foote's *Shiloh*.

Anne Dadier. Pregnant wife of Richard Dadier in Evan Hunter's *The Blackboard Jungle*.

Richard (Richie, Rick) Dadier. First-year teacher at a New York vocational school who wins the respect of the problem student Gregory Miller in Evan Hunter's *The Blackboard Jungle*.

Steven (Steve) Dagg. Drunken, malingering, and scavenging backwoodsman who serves as a foot soldier under General Jackson; delivers a false message, which leads to the destruction of Richard Cleave's Stonewall Brigade; deserts the military to live with a widow in the mountains; appears in Mary Johnston's *The Long Roll* and *Cease Firing*.

Daggett. Lawyer for the Ross family in Charles Portis's *True Grit*.

Daggoo. Black harpooner for Flask in Herman Melville's *Moby-Dick*.

Dagon. Phoenician fertility god, half-man and half-fish; subject of Peter Leland's investigations and the deity to whom he is finally sacrificed in Fred Chappell's *Dagon*.

Urban Dagonet. Grandfather of Ralph Marvell and head of the prestigious old New York family whose locus is a house on Washington Square in Edith Wharton's *The Custom of the Country*.

Dahfu. King of the Wariri tribe of African lion worshippers; former medical student and later philosophical mentor and friend of Eugene Henderson in Saul Bellow's *Henderson the Rain King*.

Gjermund Dahl. Norwegian political leader in O. E. Rölvaag's *Peder Victorious* and *Their Father's God*.

Katrina Nilssen Dahl. Maternal aunt of Helga Crane and wife of Poul Dahl; encourages Helga to marry an artist in Copenhagen and remain in Denmark in Nella Larsen's *Quicksand*.

Mona Dahl. Best friend of Dolores Haze at Beardsley School; knows about Haze's involvement with Clare Quilty and helps her keep secrets from Humbert Humbert in Vladimir Nabokov's *Lolita*.

Poul Dahl. Uncle by marriage of Helga Crane and husband of Katrina Dahl; encourages Helga to become an expatriate and remain in Denmark in Nella Larsen's *Quicksand*.

O. P. Dahlberg. Handyman and writer who runs off with Alice Kelcey in Wright Morris's *The Fork River*

Space Project. See also P. O. Bergdahl.

Claude Daigle. Schoolmate of Rhoda Penmark; murdered by Rhoda because he received a penmanship medal that Rhoda thought she should have won in William March's *The Bad Seed.*

Lincoln Agrippa (Banjo) Daily. Black American expatriate living in Marseilles; hangs out with a group of black expatriates from Africa and the Caribbean in Claude McKay's *Banjo.*

Hube Dakens. River flatboatman in H. L. Davis's *Beulah Land.*

Richard (Dick) Dale. Wealthy young New York painter who becomes more serious about both his life and his art after spending a month on a New England farm in Sarah Orne Jewett's *A Marsh Island.*

Sheridan Dale. Shady lawyer who heads the trusts and estates department and becomes managing partner of Sheffield, Knox after the death of Henry Knox; under his influence Timothy Colt commits a breach of trust in Louis Auchincloss's *The Great World and Timothy Colt.*

Suzanne Dale. Daughter of Eugene Witla's landlady; attracts Witla, whom she distracts from his work, in Theodore Dreiser's *The "Genius."*

Cal Dalhart. Cowboy who falls in love with Taisie Lockhart and murders his rival, Del Williams, in Emerson Hough's *North of 36.*

Brother Dallas. See L. Westminster Purcell III.

Major Dalleson. Officer who accidentally wins the Battle of Anopopei in Norman Mailer's *The Naked and the Dead.*

Julia Sherringham Dallow. Widow engaged to Nick Dormer until he chooses art over politics in Henry James's *The Tragic Muse.*

Amy Paget Dalrymple. Attractive, opulent neighbor of Virginius Littlepage; seeks Littlepage's legal advice in Ellen Glasgow's *They Stooped to Folly.*

Col. Ennis Dalton. Yankee officer and later husband of Ellen Poe Ashe in Jesse Hill Ford's *The Raider.*

Dalton (Diddy) Harron. Public relations man determined to discover whether he has actually committed a murder; his dying fantasies upon his suicide constitute the events of Susan Sontag's *Death Kit.*

Henry G. Dalton. Father of Mary Dalton; wealthy philanthropist who hires Bigger Thomas as a chauffeur in Richard Wright's *Native Son.*

Mary Dalton. Daughter of the wealthy Dalton family and girlfriend of Jan Erlone sympathetic to Communist ideology; suffocated with a pillow by Bigger Thomas in Richard Wright's *Native Son.*

Mrs. Dalton. Blind wife of Henry G. Dalton and mother of Mary Dalton in Richard Wright's *Native Son.*

Mr. Dalzell. Hospital roommate of Judge Clinton McKelva; convinces himself that the judge is his long-lost son in Eudora Welty's *The Optimist's Daughter.*

Damastor. Cowardly son of Charitas; forced to leave home after impregnating Adraste in John Erskine's *The Private Life of Helen of Troy.*

Stuart Dameron. Chief of the Campbell County Ku Klux Klan in Thomas Dixon's *The Leopard's Spots.*

Vern Damico. Uncle who gives Gary Gilmore a job when Gilmore first gets out of prison in Norman Mailer's *The Executioner's Song.*

Cross (Lionel Lane) Damon. Postal worker believed by his family and friends in Chicago to have been killed in a train accident; escapes to New York, where he assumes another identity, commits three murders, and is himself murdered by members of the Communist party, in Richard Wright's *The Outsider.*

Damuddy. Grandmother of Benjy and Caddy Compson, Jason Compson IV, and Quentin Compson I in William Faulkner's *The Sound and the Fury.*

Dan. New leader of Snow White's "seven dwarfs" after Bill's execution in Donald Barthelme's *Snow White.*

Dan. Rough, rebellious orphan in Louisa May Alcott's *Little Men.*

Dan Cupid. Mischievous grandson of Bombie of the Frizzled Head in James Kirke Paulding's *Koningsmarke.*

Dan'l. Black servant of Mulberry Sellers in Samuel Langhorne Clemens's *The American Claimant.*

Seth Dana. Active telepath who joins the "vast network of mental links" known as the Pattern in Octavia E. Butler's *Mind of My Mind.*

Troy Dana. Hollow actor who plays the mysterious savior in the Southern melodrama being filmed in Walker Percy's *Lancelot.*

Hugh Danaher. Catholic cardinal and superior of Desmond Spellacy in John Gregory Dunne's *True Confessions.*

Danby. Dissolute American husband of Handsome Mary in Herman Melville's *Redburn.*

Molly Dance. Whore and mother of ten; lover of Wendell Ryder and Dr. Matthew O'Connor in Djuna Barnes's *Ryder.*

Nichol Dance. Key West fishing guide whose feud with Thomas Skelton leads to the burning of Dance's boat and the deaths of both Skelton and Dance in Thomas McGuane's *Ninety-Two in the Shade.*

Claude Dancer. Lawyer who takes over Mitch Lodwick's prosecution of Frederic Manion in Robert Traver's *Anatomy of a Murder.*

Unity Dandridge. Niece of Edward Churchill and cousin of Jacqueline Churchill; engaged to Fairfax Cary in Mary Johnston's *Lewis Rand.*

Doc Daneeka. Brooding medical officer who introduces Yossarian to Catch-22; because his name falsely appears on the manifest of a crashed plane, he is declared officially dead, despite his obvious continued existence, in Joseph Heller's *Catch-22.*

Danforth. See Gerald Stanhope.

Lady Danforth. See Amber St. Clare.

Cornelia Dangerfield. Wife of Cuthbert Dangerfield in James Kirke Paulding's *Westward Ho!*

Colonel Cuthbert Dangerfield. Displaced Virginian and founder of a Kentucky frontier village in James Kirke Paulding's *Westward Ho!*

Leonard Dangerfield. Son of Cornelia and Cuthbert Dangerfield; politician in James Kirke Paulding's *Westward Ho!*

Marion Dangerfield. English wife of Sebastian Dangerfield; in exasperation, she leaves him, taking their daughter with her, in J. P. Donleavy's *The Ginger Man.*

Mrs. Samuel Dangerfield. See Amber St. Clare.

Samuel Dangerfield. Extremely wealthy elderly commoner and second husband of Amber St. Clare; gives her second child by Bruce Carlton his name and then dies, leaving her a rich widow, in Kathleen Winsor's *Forever Amber.*

Sebastian Dangerfield. American law student at Trinity College, Dublin, which he flees in order to escape creditors; narrator of J. P. Donleavy's *The Ginger Man.*

Virginia Dangerfield. Daughter of Cornelia and Cuthbert Dangerfield; high-spirited heroine of James Kirke Paulding's *Westward Ho!*

Daniel. Friend of Fonny Hunt; recently released from prison in James Baldwin's *If Beale Street Could Talk.*

Daniel. Student who serves on the Cinema Committee with Hill Gallagher during the student rebellion in James Jones's *The Merry Month of May.*

The Dankster (Board-Her-in-the-Smoke). Mainmastman aboard the *Indomitable* who tells Billy Budd that John Claggart dislikes Budd in Herman Melville's *Billy Budd.*

Ragnar Danneskjold. Aristotelian philosopher who turns pirate in order to exact justice in Ayn Rand's *Atlas Shrugged.*

Danny. Happily vagrant and alcoholic young man who inherits two small houses and quickly finds himself beset by friends who come to live in his houses; becomes so depressed from the restrictive life-style of owning property that he dies from a fall, his houses burn, and all his friends disperse after his burial in John Steinbeck's *Tortilla Flat.*

Danton. Leader of the French Jacobites who, opposed to Thomas Paine and the Girondists, unleashes The Terror on France, only to be a victim of it himself, in Howard Fast's *Citizen Tom Paine.*

Daphne. Passenger on the *Here They Come* who designs a replacement ship, *There They Go,* in Gregory Corso's *The American Express.*

Lady Darah. Patternist who leads a faction against Teray and Amber in Octavia E. Butler's *Patternmaster.*

Monsignor Thayer Darcy. Worldly Roman Catholic priest who becomes a father-substitute for Amory Blaine in F. Scott Fitzgerald's *This Side of Paradise.*

Victoria Dare. Frequenter of Washington parties; keeps Madeleine Lee and Sybil Ross informed of the latest gossip; engaged to Lord Dunberg in Henry Adams's *Democracy.*

Darlene. Performer in the Hippodrome; rescued from a tavern by Bea; attempts to save Jackson Yeager in Cyrus Colter's *The Hippodrome.*

Mrs. Edward Darley. See Flora Deland.

Emil Lazarus (Laz) Darlovsky. Handsome, "mystic," fifteen-and-a-half-year-old brother of Simon Darlovsky in Jack Kerouac's *Desolation Angels.*

Simon (The Mad Russian) Darlovsky. Poet, companion and lover of Irwin Garden, and older brother of Lazarus Darlovsky in Jack Kerouac's *Desolation Angels.*

Austin Darnley. Father of James and Rose Darnley; English vicar and philosophical adviser to Oliver Alden in George Santayana's *The Last Puritan.*

James (Jim, Lord Jim) Darnley. Captain of the yacht owned by Peter Alden and friend of Oliver Alden in George Santayana's *The Last Puritan.*

Rose Darnley. Sister of James Darnley; rejects the marriage proposal of Oliver Alden in George Santayana's *The Last Puritan.*

George Darrow. Middle-aged diplomat and former suitor of Anna Leath; when they renew their relationship, he lies about his connection with Sophy Viner, with whom he has had an affair, in Edith Wharton's *The Reef.*

Dart. See D'Artagnan Foxx.

Perry Dart. Police detective in Rudolph Fisher's *The Conjure-Man Dies.*

James W. (Jim) Darwent. Kindly dean of the law school and friend to Carl and Annie Brown in Betty Smith's *Joy in the Morning.*

Beagle Hamlet Darwin. Character in a novel Balso Snell reads; impregnates Janey Davenport but will not marry her in Nathanael West's *The Dream Life of Balso Snell.*

Basil Dashwood. Actor who marries Miriam Rooth in Henry James's *The Tragic Muse.*

Miriam Rooth Dashwood. See Miriam Rooth.

Dates. Servitor to the Glendinnings in Herman Melville's *Pierre.*

Edward Daugherty. Husband of Katrina Daugherty, father of Martin Daugherty, and lover of Melissa Spencer; author of two plays in William Kennedy's *Billy Phelan's Greatest Game.*

Katrina Daugherty. Wife of Edward Daugherty and mother of Martin Daugherty; burned in the Delavan Hotel fire and dies from smoke inhalation in the Brothers' School fire in William Kennedy's *Billy Phelan's Greatest Game.*

Martin Daugherty. Husband of Mary Daugherty, father of Peter Daugherty, and lover of Melissa Spencer; go-between in Charlie Boy McCall's kidnapping; chastises the McCalls for their treatment of his friend Billy Phelan in William Kennedy's *Billy Phelan's Greatest Game.*

Mary Daugherty. Wife of Martin Daugherty and mother of Peter Daugherty in William Kennedy's *Billy Phelan's Greatest Game.*

Peter Daugherty. Son of Mary and Martin Daugherty; joins the Catholic priesthood, to his mother's delight and his father's chagrin, in William Kennedy's *Billy Phelan's Greatest Game.*

Daughter (Mrs. Boyd). Companion of Gordon Boyd; poses as his wife in Wright Morris's *Ceremony in Lone Tree.*

Kitty Daumler. Earthy and uncomplicated mistress of Joseph for a brief time in Saul Bellow's *Dangling Man.*

Dauphin (Edmund Kean, Elexander Blodgett, Looy the Seventeen, Harvey Wilks). Confidence man and accomplice of the Duke of Bridgewater in Samuel Langhorne Clemens's *Adventures of Huckleberry Finn.*

Janey Davenport. Character in a novel Balso Snell reads; wants Snell to kill Beagle Darwin in Nathanael West's *The Dream Life of Balso Snell.*

Keith Davenport. Commanding officer of the 918th Bomb Group who overidentifies with his men; replaced by Frank Savage in Beirne Lay, Jr., and Sy Bartlett's *Twelve O'Clock High!*

David. American youth living in Paris and trying to come to terms with his sexual identity; breaks his engagement to Hella when he falls in love with Giovanni; narrator of James Baldwin's *Giovanni's Room.*

Dave Davidoff. Public relations director first for Typhon International, then for JR's company in William Gaddis's *JR.*

Helena Davidson. Highly educated daughter of a wealthy Ohio family; roommate of Kay Leiland Strong and member of the Group in Mary McCarthy's *The Group.*

Rachel Davidson. Healer who joins the "vast network of mental links" known as the Pattern in Octavia E. Butler's *Mind of My Mind.*

Scott Davidson. Lover of Hildegaard Falkenstein; pilot killed during the Berlin airlift in Leon Uris's *Armageddon.*

Arthur Davies. General-store owner who opposes the lynch mob but rides with it in hopes of averting the hanging in Walter Van Tilburg Clark's *The Ox-Bow Incident.*

Davis. See Davis Carter.

Avis Davis. House-party participant, identical twin of Mavis Davis, and schoolmate of Cress Delahanty in Jessamyn West's *Cress Delahanty*.

Barney Davis. Supervisor of the Deepwater Mine in Robert Coover's *The Origin of the Brunists*.

Becky Davis. Schoolgirl who appears slutty to her teacher, George Caldwell, in John Updike's *The Centaur*.

Charles (Chappie) Davis. Coach and spiritual father of the alumni of a black high school athletic team and neighborhood gang, the Junior Bachelor Society, which holds a reunion to celebrate his seventieth birthday in John A. Williams's *The Junior Bachelor Society*.

Denise Davis. Daughter of Renay and Jerome Lee Davis; killed in an automobile accident in Ann Allen Shockley's *Loving Her*.

Exum Davis. Confederate veteran who, because he sells land and stock to his black hands, is threatened by the Regulators in Albion W. Tourgee's *A Fool's Errand*.

Jack Davis. Convict husband of Judy Davis; beats Preacher Smathers and causes his death in Fred Chappell's *It Is Time, Lord*.

Jerome Lee Davis. Ex-athlete, philanderer, alcoholic, abusive husband of Renay Davis, and father of Denise Davis in Ann Allen Shockley's *Loving Her*.

John (Jack) Davis. Young Goose Creek native recruited for Major Singleton's partisan band; his love for Bella Humphries embroils him in a dispute with Sergeant Hastings in William Gilmore Simms's *The Partisan*.

Judy Davis. Millworker and prostitute involved first with Preacher Smathers and then also with James Christopher; wife of Jack Davis in Fred Chappell's *It Is Time, Lord*.

Lancy Davis. White-hating black youth killed in a race riot in Carson McCullers's *The Heart Is a Lonely Hunter*.

Louise (Lou) Davis. College-educated girlfriend of Jule Jackson in New York; has an affair with Jeff Gordon in George Wylie Henderson's *Jule*.

Matthew L. (Matt) Davis. Newspaper editor, historian, and official biographer of Aaron Burr; conspiratorial political activist in Gore Vidal's *Burr*.

Mavis Davis. House party participant, identical twin of Avis Davis, and schoolmate of Cress Delahanty in Jessamyn West's *Cress Delahanty*.

Mississippi Davis. Driver of rigs for hire in New Orleans in Arna Wendell Bontemps's *God Sends Sunday*.

Peggy Davis. Attractive widow returning to Wales; "The Welsh Rarebit" in Conrad Aiken's *Blue Voyage*.

Renay Davis. Musician, mother of Denise Davis, wife of Jerome Lee Davis, and black lover of Terry Bluvard in Ann Allen Shockley's *Loving Her*.

Roger Davis. American novelist and friend of Thomas Hudson in Ernest Hemingway's *Islands in the Stream*.

Seneca Davis. Uncle of Frank Cowperwood and owner of a Cuban sugar plantation in Theodore Dreiser's *The Financier*.

Hope Davison. Friend of Sally Forbes; secretly in love with Lymie Peters in William Maxwell's *The Folded Leaf*.

Phoebe Davison. Granddaughter of Garrett Pendergass and true love of Salathiel Albine in Hervey Allen's *Bedford Village*.

Meredith (Mered) Dawe. Young counterculture artist, mystic, and prophet who is imprisoned and later defended by lawyer Jack Morrissey in Joyce Carol Oates's *Do with Me What You Will*.

Charles Proctor Dawn. Attorney engaged by Helen Albury to defend her brother and whom the Op is accused of murdering in Dashiell Hammett's *Red Harvest*.

Dave Dawson. Albino conjure man; kidnapped to locate a lode of gold on Ty Ty Walden's farm in Erskine Caldwell's *God's Little Acre*.

Francis (Frank) Dawson. Schoolmaster in colonial North Carolina who avoids punishment for his rebellion by fleeing to Tennessee in Caroline Gordon's *Green Centuries*.

Joanna Dawson. Teenaged traveling companion and first wife of Cody Pomeray in Jack Kerouac's *Visions of Cody*.

Jocasta Dawson. See Jocasta Dawson Outlaw.

Joe Dawson. Laundry room supervisor of Martin Eden in Jack London's *Martin Eden*.

Mr. and Mrs. Luke Dawson. Wealthiest couple in Gopher Prairie in Sinclair Lewis's *Main Street*.

George Daxter. Obese, half-white mortician; tries to seduce Meridian Hill in Alice Walker's *Meridian*.

Clara Day. Daughter of Traverse Rocke's benefactor and later fiancée of Rocke in E.D.E.N. Southworth's *The Hidden Hand*.

Diana Day. Intellectual daughter of Burden Day and wife of Billy Thorne; hopelessly in love with Peter Sanford in Gore Vidal's *Washington, D.C.*

James Burden Day. Flawed, idealistic senator whose fall from power drives him to suicide in Gore Vidal's *Washington, D.C.*

Kitty Day. Eccentric wife of Burden Day; known for blurting out embarrassing truths in Gore Vidal's *Washington, D.C.*

Norma Day. Girlfriend of Eddie Brunner; lends clothes to Gloria Wandrous in John O'Hara's *Butterfield 8*.

Diana (Di) Deacon. Daughter of Dwight Deacon; talked out of eloping with Bobby Larkin by Lulu Bett in Zona Gale's *Miss Lulu Bett*.

Dwight Herbert (Bertie) Deacon. Husband of Ina Deacon and brother-in-law of Lulu Bett; dentist and justice of the peace who inadvertently marries his brother Ninian Deacon to Lulu Bett in Zona Gale's *Miss Lulu Bett*.

Ina Bett (Inie) Deacon. Sister of Lulu Bett, wife of Dwight Deacon, and stepmother of Diana Deacon in Zona Gale's *Miss Lulu Bett*.

Ninian Deacon. Globe-trotting brother of Dwight Deacon; husband of Lulu Bett until his long-lost wife is discovered to be alive in Zona Gale's *Miss Lulu Bett*.

First Corinthians Dead. Daughter of Macon Dead II and Ruth Foster Dead; sister of Mary Magdalene Dead and Milkman; falls in love with Henry Porter in Toni Morrison's *Song of Solomon*.

Hagar Dead. Daughter of Reba Dead and granddaughter of Pilate Dead; obsessed with her love for her cousin Milkman in Toni Morrison's *Song of Solomon*.

Macon (Jake) Dead I. Ex-slave whose name was changed erroneously by a drunken Civil War soldier; youngest son of Solomon, the flying African; because of his wealth and independence, he is killed by resentful white landowners in Toni Morrison's *Song of Solomon*.

Macon Dead II. Son of Macon Dead I and Sing Byrd; brother of Pilate Dead, husband of Ruth Foster Dead, and father of Milkman, First Corinthians, and Mary Magdalene Dead in Toni Morrison's *Song of Solomon*.

Macon (Milk, Milkman) Dead III. Son of Macon Dead II and Ruth Foster Dead; hero who discovers in a journey to Shalimar, Virginia, the history and mythical powers of his African great-grandfather in Toni Morrison's *Song of Solomon*.

Mary Magdalene (Lena) Dead. Daughter of Macon Dead II and Ruth Foster Dead; sister of First Corinthians and Milkman Dead in Toni Morrison's *Song of Solomon*.

Pilate Dead. Sister of Macon Dead II, daughter of Sing Byrd and Macon Dead I, mother of Hagar and Reba Dead; known for her independence, use of conjure, and absence of a navel in Toni Morrison's *Song of Solomon*.

Rebecca (Reba) Dead. Daughter of Pilate Dead and sister of Hagar Dead in Toni Morrison's *Song of Solomon*.

Ruth Foster (Miss Rufie) Dead. Daughter of the town's only black doctor; wife of Macon Dead II and mother of Mary Magdalene, First Corinthians, and Milkman Dead in Toni Morrison's *Song of Solomon*.

The Dead Father. Abstract hero who slowly loses limbs on the journey to his grave in Donald Barthelme's *The Dead Father*.

Mr. Deak. Bracktown store owner in Gayl Jones's *Corregidora*.

Jim Deakins. Young sidekick of Boone Caudill; killed by Caudill, who suspects Deakins of making love to Teal Eye, in A. B. Guthrie's *The Big Sky*.

Fred Dealey. Realistic judge who believes that "Whatever happens, happens because a lot of other things have happened already" in James Gould Cozzens's *By Love Possessed*.

Eliza Dean. First fiancée of Francis Prescott; broke the engagement after he announced his intention to become a clergyman and educator in Louis Auchincloss's *The Rector of Justin*.

Hank Dean. White supremacist follower of Clarke Bryant; assassin of integrationist mayor Douglas Taylor in Julian Mayfield's *The Grand Parade*.

Jean (Jane Provost) Dean. Former secretary of John Shade; arranges a disastrous blind date between Hazel Shade and her cousin Pete Dean; supposedly, Charles Kinbote's source of information about Hazel in Vladimir Nabokov's *Pale Fire*.

Laura Dearborn. See Laura Dearborn Jadwin.

Page Dearborn. Younger sister of Laura Dearborn; ingénue who loves her sister's former suitor Landry Court in Frank Norris's *The Pit*.

Deborah (Deb). Cousin of Hugh Wolfe; her theft of a pocketbook results in his imprisonment in Rebecca Harding Davis's *Life in the Iron Mills*.

Miss Debry. Day-nurse of John Laskell in Lionel Trilling's *The Middle of the Journey*.

Daniel (Danny) Deck. Husband of Sally Bynum Deck, father of Lorena Deck, and lover of Jill Peel; aspiring novelist who travels from Texas to California and back to Texas; disappears into the Rio Grande River; narrator of Larry McMurtry's *All My Friends Are Going to Be Strangers*; lover of Emma Horton in *Terms of Endearment*.

Lorena Deck. Daughter of Daniel and Sally Deck in Larry McMurtry's *All My Friends Are Going to Be Strangers*.

Sally Bynum Deck. Wife of Daniel Deck and mother of Lorena Deck; after her marriage fails, she refuses to permit Daniel to see Lorena in Larry McMurtry's *All My Friends Are Going to Be Strangers*.

Johnny Dedman. Delinquent held back in school in John Updike's *The Centaur*.

Leonard Dedman. Friend and victim of Leo Feldman in Stanley Elkin's *A Bad Man*.

Alma Mathews Deen. Mother of Tracy and Laura Deen and wife of Dr. Tutwiler Deen; driving force to get Tracy married and in the church in Lillian Smith's *Strange Fruit*.

Laura Deen. Sister of Tracy Deen and daughter of Alma and Dr. Tutwiler Deen; northern-educated young southern woman in Lillian Smith's *Strange Fruit*.

Tracy Deen. Son of Alma and Dr. Tutwiler Deen and brother of Laura Deen; white lover of a black woman, Nonnie Anderson; murdered by Ed Anderson in Lillian Smith's *Strange Fruit*.

Dr. Tutwiler (Tut) Deen. Husband of Alma Deen and father of Tracy and Laura Deen; physician to White Town of Maxwell, Georgia, in Lillian Smith's *Strange Fruit*.

Lord Deepmore. English aristocrat who becomes friendly with Noémie Nioche in Henry James's *The American*.

Deerslayer. See Nathaniel Bumppo.

Flora Dees. Foster mother of Tisha Dees and wife of Squire Dees in Arthenia J. Bates's *The Deity Nodded*.

Heflin (Hef) Dees. Foster brother of Tisha Dees and legal son of Flora and Squire Dees in Arthenia J. Bates's *The Deity Nodded*.

Katie Mae (Plump) Dees. Foster sister of Tisha Dees, legal daughter of Flora and Squire Dees, and wife of Obidiah Funches in Arthenia J. Bates's *The Deity Nodded*.

Ludd Dees. Foster brother of Tisha Dees and legal son of Flora and Squire Dees in Arthenia J. Bates's *The Deity Nodded*.

Lyman Portland (Pa) Dees. Father of Squire Dees and foster grandfather of Tisha Dees in Arthenia J. Bates's *The Deity Nodded*.

Squire Dees. Foster father of Tisha Dees and husband of Flora Dees in Arthenia J. Bates's *The Deity Nodded*.

Tisha (Chip, Tish) Dees. Foster daughter of Flora and Squire Dees, teenaged bride of Kovel Henry, and Black Muslim convert in Arthenia J. Bates's *The Deity Nodded*.

Duffy Deeter. Visitor to the Rattlesnake Roundup from Gainesville, Florida, in Harry Crews's *A Feast of Snakes*.

Bernadine (Nedra) Deevers. Friend and schoolmate of Cress Delahanty in Jessamyn West's *Cress Delahanty*.

Dad Deform. Hunchbacked passenger on the *Here They Come* who makes bombs for Hinderov and religious statues for Simon in Gregory Corso's *The American Express*.

Jack Degree. See Jakob Gradus.

Mr. Degré. See Jakob Gradus.

Bella Biaggi Dehn. First wife of David Dehn and lover of Anthony X. D'Alessandro; owner of the land on which Dehn builds a temple in Jerome Weidman's *The Temple*.

David (Dave) Dehn. Builder of a temple and founder and leader of the Beechwood, New York, Jewish community in Jerome Weidman's *The Temple*.

Alfred Dehner. Antique dealer who rents out upstairs rooms to male university students; landlord of Spud Latham and Lymie Peters in William Maxwell's *The Folded Leaf*.

Ray (Deify) Deifendorf. Ace swimmer and student of George Caldwell who accidentally breaks the grille on Caldwell's car in John Updike's *The Centaur*.

Dirk (So Big, Sobig) DeJong. Son of Selina and Pervus DeJong; studies architecture and becomes a bond salesman in Edna Ferber's *So Big*.

Pervus DeJong. Truck farmer and widower who marries Selina Peake in Edna Ferber's *So Big*.

Selina Peake DeJong. Daughter of Simeon Peake; teacher in a country school near Chicago who marries Pervus DeJong and becomes a successful truck farmer following his death; mother of Dirk DeJong in Edna Ferber's *So Big*.

Delores del Ruby. Lesbian forewoman of the Rubber Rose Ranch in Tom Robbins's *Even Cowgirls Get the Blues*.

Crescent (Cress, Cressy) Delahanty. Daughter of John and Gertrude Delahanty who grows from twelve to sixteen in Jessamyn West's *Cress Delahanty*.

Gertrude Delahanty. Wife of John Delahanty and mother of Cress Delahanty in Jessamyn West's *Cress Delahanty*.

John Delahanty. Rancher, school board clerk, husband of Gertrude Delahanty, and father of Cress Delahanty in Jessamyn West's *Cress Delahanty*.

Flora (Mrs. Edward Darley) Deland. Newspaper gossip writer in Thornton Wilder's *Theophilus North*.

Delaney. Foreman of the Quien Sabe ranch discharged because of Annixter's jealousy; joins the railroad agents who oppose the wheat ranchers in the San Joaquin Valley; dies during a gunfight with the ranchers in Frank Norris's *The Octopus*.

Grace Delaney. Managing editor of *Running Dog* and lover of Lomax in Don DeLillo's *Running Dog*.

Patrick (Packy) Delaney. Owner of the Parody Club and bartender at the Kenmore Hotel in William Kennedy's *Legs*.

Edward Delatte. Lawyer hired by Abigail Tolliver to help her keep the Howland fortune intact in Shirley Ann Grau's *The Keepers of the House*.

Andrea Delbanco. Sister of Nicholas Delbanco in Nicholas Delbanco's *In the Middle Distance*.

Barbara Delbanco. Wife of Nicholas Delbanco in Nicholas Delbanco's *In the Middle Distance*.

Evelyn (Eve) Delbanco. Daughter of Nicholas and Barbara Delbanco in Nicholas Delbanco's *In the Middle Distance*.

Michael Delbanco. Son of Nicholas and Barbara Delbanco; accidentally killed at age thirteen in Nicholas Delbanco's *In the Middle Distance*.

Nicholas (Nicky) Delbanco. Architect and would-be novelist; narrator of Nicholas Delbanco's *In the Middle Distance*.

Delbert (Delly). Owner of the rum shop and leader in the village of Spiretown, center of the poorest section of Bourne Island, in Paule Marshall's *The Chosen Place, the Timeless People*.

Delgado. Former Cuban pickpocket and brothel exhibitionist; member of Ramón Cordes's band of revolutionaries in William Herrick's *The Last to Die*.

Della. Schofield family cook who manages to keep Penrod Schofield out of trouble in her domain in Booth Tarkington's *Penrod, Penrod and Sam*, and *Penrod Jashber*.

Pauline Delos. Bisexual mistress of Earl Janoth and sometime lover of George Stroud; killed by Janoth in Kenneth Fearing's *The Big Clock*.

Del Rio. Boxer and aspiring actor; lives in the Thirteenth Street building managed by Norman Moonbloom in Edward Lewis Wallant's *The Tenants of Moonbloom*.

Ida (Ida Bitch) Delson. Worker in a textile union office in New Jersey; first wife of Zeke Gurevich; transvestite in William Herrick's *The Itinerant*.

Angelo DeMarco. Nineteen-year-old pharmacist's assistant; beneficiary of Sammy Kahan's insurance policy in Edward Lewis Wallant's *The Children at the Gate*.

Esther DeMarco. Widowed mother of Angelo and Theresa DeMarco in Edward Lewis Wallant's *The Children at the Gate*.

Frank DeMarco. Cousin of Angelo and Theresa DeMarco; owner of a pharmacy and employer of Angelo in Edward Lewis Wallant's *The Children at the Gate*.

Theresa DeMarco. Mentally retarded sister of Angelo DeMarco and daughter of Esther DeMarco; dies of a congenital heart ailment in Edward Lewis Wallant's *The Children at the Gate*.

William Demarest. Author traveling by ship from New York to London in Conrad Aiken's *Blue Voyage*.

Alice (Legs) Dembosky. Baton twirler and fiancée of Heshie Portnoy in Philip Roth's *Portnoy's Complaint*.

Alonzo I. R. Demby. Former linebacker and current teacher of Afro-American studies at a college in upstate New York; office mate of Phil Sorenson and Turner's eventual roommate; dismissed from the college faculty on grounds of moral turpitude in Frederick Busch's *Rounds*.

Demetrius. Poet who invites Hedylus to a school in Alexandria in H. D.'s *Hedylus*.

Agnes Deming. Daughter of Damon Barker; school-teacher and later the wife of Ned Westlock in E. W. Howe's *The Story of a Country Town*.

Carol Deming. Aspiring actress who plays a role in David Bell's documentary film in Don DeLillo's *Americana*.

Demion. Former lover of Hedyle who befriends her son Hedylus in H. D.'s *Hedylus*.

Marthe (Magda) Demont. Sister of Marya and Stefan in William Faulkner's *A Fable*.

Salvatore (Sal) De Muccio. Son of Italian immigrants, owner of Superior Shoeshine Parlor, and husband of Reenie O'Farron in Betty Smith's *Tomorrow Will Be Better*.

Jim Denby. Boyfriend of Gertrude Donovan in Nathan Asch's *The Office*.

Homer Denham. Orphan befriended by Jess Birdwell in Jessamyn West's *The Friendly Persuasion*.

Norma Denitz. Daughter of a psychiatrist; jealously claims that Callie Wells's pregnancy was entrapment in John Gardner's *Nickel Mountain*.

Reva Denk. Beautiful blonde woman with whom Jesse Vogel falls obsessively in love in Joyce Carol Oates's *Wonderland*.

Stephen Denleigh. Doctor who successfully courts Laurentine Strange in Jessie Redmon Fauset's *The Chinaberry Tree*.

Ep Denman. Husband of Jennifer Denman, father of Leroy and Ted Denman, and uncle of Molly Bolt in Rita Mae Brown's *Rubyfruit Jungle*.

Jennifer (Jenna) Denman. Wife of Ep Denman, mother of Leroy and Ted Denman, aunt of Molly Bolt; dies of cancer in Rita Mae Brown's *Rubyfruit Jungle*.

Leroy Denman. Cousin of Molly Bolt in Rita Mae Brown's *Rubyfruit Jungle*.

Ted Denman. Cousin of Molly Bolt in Rita Mae Brown's *Rubyfruit Jungle*.

Cornet Henry (Harry) Denne. Chaplain in Cromwell's army and one of two officers to remain with the dissenting soldiers; confesses and implicates Johnny Church and Thankful Perkins; sentenced to death but recants and is pardoned in Mary Lee Settle's *Prisons*.

Weede Denney. Television executive and David Bell's boss in Don DeLillo's *Americana*.

Burke Dennings. British film director and friend of Chris MacNeil; murdered by Captain Howdy, the demon, in William Peter Blatty's *The Exorcist*.

Mame (Auntie Mame) Dennis. Flamboyant heiress whose unorthodox ideas and lifestyle are the basis of Patrick Dennis's *Auntie Mame* and *Around the World with Auntie Mame*.

Michael Dennis. Son of Patrick Dennis and Pegeen Ryan in Patrick Dennis's *Around the World with Auntie Mame*.

Patrick Dennis. Young boy who comes of age under the influence of his flamboyant aunt; narrator of Patrick Dennis's *Auntie Mame* and *Around the World with Auntie Mame*.

Pegeen Dennis. See Pegeen Ryan.

Wallace French (Wally) Dennis. Writer and winner of the Parkman College Creative Writing Fellowship; lover of Dawn Hirsh; killed in the Korean War in James Jones's *Some Came Running*.

Will Dennison. Friend of David Stofsky in John Clellon Holmes's *Go*.

Garrett Denniston. Land speculator who hopes to make Cassville Wisconsin's state capital in August Derleth's *The Shadow in the Glass*.

William (Wilhelm) Denny. Chemical engineer from Texas in Katherine Anne Porter's *Ship of Fools*.

Merton Densher. Journalist secretly engaged to Kate Croy; plots with Croy to marry the dying Mildred Theale and inherit her money; cannot go through with the plot, and refuses Theale's fortune when he inherits it in Henry James's *The Wings of the Dove*.

Bobby Denton. Revivalist preacher in Kurt Vonnegut's *The Sirens of Titan*.

George (Crazy George) Denton. Insane friend of Henry Miller in Henry Miller's *Black Spring*.

Jennie (Judy Belden, Sister M. Thomas) Denton. Young woman, raped as a teenager, who escapes her neighborhood through a nursing school scholarship; turns from nursing to prostitution; becomes a movie star and the lover and fiancée of Jonas Cord, Jr., but breaks the engagement after telling him of her past; becomes a nun in Harold Robbins's *The Carpetbaggers*.

Thomas Denton. Union man who is the intended victim of a Ku Klux Klan ambush in Albion W. Tourgee's *A Fool's Errand*.

Virginia Depre. See Virginia Du Pre.

Edgar Derby. Former teacher and leader of American prisoners of war in Kurt Vonnegut's *Slaughterhouse-Five*.

Annie Derrick. Wife of Magnus Derrick, with whom she lives on a wheat ranch; refined woman fearful of nature in Frank Norris's *The Octopus*.

Harran Derrick. Loyal son of Magnus and Annie Derrick and one of the ranchers slain by the railroad agents at the irrigation-ditch gunfight in Frank Norris's *The Octopus*.

Lyman Derrick. San Francisco attorney with gubernatorial ambitions; betrays his father, Magnus Derrick, and other San Joaquin Valley wheat ranchers in order to obtain the railroad's support in Frank Norris's *The Octopus*.

Magnus Derrick. Proprietor of the Los Muertos wheat ranch in the San Joaquin Valley; resorts to bribery to effect a change of grain-hauling rates and loses his reputation and sanity in the process as the railroad finally defeats him in Frank Norris's *The Octopus*.

Der Springer. See Gerhardt von Göll.

Diron Desautels. Handsome young nephew of Philippe Desautels and member of *Les Amis des Noirs*, an antislavery faction; with Toussaint, co-protagonist of Arna Wendell Bontemps's *Drums at Dusk*.

Philippe Desautels. Elderly aristocrat recently fired as naval commissioner of Colonial Haiti in Arna Wendell Bontemps's *Drums at Dusk*.

Miriam Desebour. See Miriam Desebour Kranz.

Miss Desjardin. Sympathetic gym teacher of Carrie White in Stephen King's *Carrie*.

Lorency Desmit. See Lorency.

Nimbus Desmit. See Nimbus.

Colonel Potem (Potestatem Dedimus Smith) Desmit. Son of Peter Smith; owner of numerous North Carolina plantations, where he breeds slaves scientifically; owner of Nimbus, whom Desmit cheats in the sale of the Red Wing plantation, in Albion W. Tourgee's *Bricks without Straw*.

Bernie Despain. Bookie who holds IOUs from Taylor Henry and who owes Ned Beaumont money in Dashiell Hammett's *The Glass Key*.

Raoul-Ernest-Louis Desrivières. Husband of Aimée Peyronnette and father of Mayotte; shot to death in Lafcadio Hearn's *Youma*.

Florence Dessau. Church-going New Orleans woman who captures Augie's attention and at whose heels Joe Baily and Tom Wright follow; involved in a secret affair with Horace Church-Woodbine in Arna Wendell Bontemps's *God Sends Sunday*.

Dessie. Girlfriend of Henry McIntosh and maid in Tom Harris's household in Lillian Smith's *Strange Fruit*.

Miss Destiny. Flamboyant drag queen who dreams of a grand Hollywood-style wedding for herself in John Rechy's *City of Night*.

Anne Dettrey. Clever magazine editor who is a friend and supporter of Phil Green, unaware he is not really Jewish, in Laura Z. Hobson's *Gentleman's Agreement*.

Helen Detweiler. Secretary of Arthur Winner and sister of Ralph Detweiler; commits suicide because of troubles brought by her brother in James Gould Cozzens's *By Love Possessed*.

Joseph (Joe) Detweiler. Deranged murderer in Thomas Berger's *Killing Time*.

Ralph Detweiler. Brother of Helen Detweiler; charged with rape; his subsequent flight contributes to his sister's suicide in James Gould Cozzens's *By Love Possessed*.

Brockhurst (Broc, Broccoli) Detwiler. Childhood friend of Molly Bolt who exposes himself in a scheme for the two children to make money in Rita Mae Brown's *Rubyfruit Jungle*.

Samantha (Sam) De Vere. Self-sufficient carpenter in Gail Godwin's *Violet Clay*.

Jack Devlin. Childhood friend and later fiancé of Derrick Thornton; although a socialist and a pacifist, he fights in World War I and is killed in action in Helen Hooven Santmyer's *Herbs and Apples*.

DeVoss. Manager of the Bronze Peacock nightclub in William Riley Burnett's *Little Caesar*.

Josiah Devotion. See Squire Raglan.

Colonel Devries. War hero and congressman in William Faulkner's *The Mansion*.

Cleva Dewar. Sister of Edith Barnstorff who figures in Jane Clifford's family lore; left the South for New York with a traveling actor in 1905 and died in childbirth, unwed and deserted, in Gail Godwin's *The Odd Woman*.

Dewey. Name given to three indigent children who live in the home of Eva Peace in Toni Morrison's *Sula*.

Alvin Adams (Al) Dewey. Member of the Kansas Bureau of Investigation; appointed chief investigator in the Clutter murder case; breaks the case with the assistance of three other agents in Truman Capote's *In Cold Blood*.

Charles (Charlie) Dewey. Elder son of Nelson and Katherine Dewey; his death in childhood causes difficulties between his parents in August Derleth's *The Shadow in the Glass*.

Katherine Dunn (Kate, Katie) Dewey. Wife of Nelson Dewey; after being the first lady of Wisconsin, she cannot live easily in a lesser role in August Derleth's *The Shadow in the Glass*.

Katie Dewey. Daughter of Nelson and Katherine Dewey; becomes the agency by which her mother is able to separate herself from Nelson Dewey in August Derleth's *The Shadow in the Glass*.

Nelson (Nels) Dewey. Lawyer, land speculator, mining and railroad investor, and politician who becomes the first governor of Wisconsin; his determination to live as a country squire leads to his disappointment and despair in August Derleth's *The Shadow in the Glass*.

Nelson (Nettie) Dewey. Younger son of Nelson and Katherine Dewey; leaves college to seek a fortune in the West, but disappears and is not heard from again in August Derleth's *The Shadow in the Glass*.

Josiah Dexter. Newport mechanic who buys Theophilus North's car, rents North a bicycle, and sells him a car in Thornton Wilder's *Theophilus North*.

Paul Dexter. Regular customer at the tailor shop; moves to New York from Indiana in Henry Miller's *Black Spring*.

Alice Diamond. Wife of Legs Diamond; tends to her husband following the various assassination attempts against him and tolerates his affair with Kiki Roberts in William Kennedy's *Legs*.

Eddie Diamond. Brother of Legs Diamond; suffers from tuberculosis and moves to Denver, where he escapes an assassination attempt, in William Kennedy's *Legs*.

John Thomas (Jack, Legs) Diamond. Husband of Alice Diamond and lover of Kiki Roberts; gangster who survives five assassination attempts before being killed in William Kennedy's *Legs*; also appears in *Billy Phelan's Greatest Game*.

Diana. Flamboyant collector of textiles, paintings, and jewelry; resident of Golconda and friend of Lillian Beye and Fred in Anaïs Nin's *Seduction of the Minotaur*.

Mammy Diana. Slave who prophesies marriage between the Hazard and Tracy families as the only way of settling the lawsuit over worthless land in John Pendleton Kennedy's *Swallow Barn*.

Diane. Third wife of Cody Pomeray in Jack Kerouac's *Visions of Cody*.

Dib. Contact of Johnny with the wild boys in William S. Burroughs's *The Wild Boys*; also appears in *Exterminator!*

Dicey. Common-law wife of Bill Kelsey and mother of seven; slain by white magic in Hal Bennett's *Seventh Heaven*.

Dick. Cartoon editor for *The Townsman*; friend and neighbor of Augie Poole; narrator of Peter De Vries's *The Tunnel of Love*.

Dick. Communist organizer and ladies' man known as a "bedroom radical" in John Steinbeck's *In Dubious Battle*.

Dick. Dishonest black who is lynched for apparently having murdered Flora Camp in Thomas Dixon's *The Leopard's Spots*.

Dick. Son of Wolfie and Azusa; preys constantly on his father's mind in Peter Matthiessen's *At Play in the Fields of the Lord*.

Nathaniel G. Dick. Union colonel in William Faulkner's *The Unvanquished*.

Pamela Dickensen. Actress who performs a lesbian scene with Arabella in Boris Adrian's pornographic movie in Terry Southern's *Blue Movie*.

Danny Dickerson. Pathetic, has-been performer who approaches Miranda about an unfavorable review she gave him in Katherine Anne Porter's *Pale Horse, Pale Rider*.

Foley Dickinson. Refugee from an Ivy League college who lives for several months at Pickerel Beach; Bebe Sellars tries to reunite him with his parents in Maryland in Doris Betts's *The River to Pickle Beach*.

Geordie Dickson. Jazz singer discovered by Edgar Pool in John Clellon Holmes's *The Horn*.

Bud Diefendorf. Former physicist turned philosopher, Buddhist, and janitor; friend of Ray Smith in Jack Kerouac's *The Dharma Bums.*

Mr. Diefendorf. Newport chief of police who is frequently consulted as Theophilus North becomes involved in local conflicts in Thornton Wilder's *Theophilus North.*

Cathleen Diehl. Married woman involved in an adulterous love affair with Edwin Locke in Joyce Carol Oates's *Cybele.*

Christian Diestl. Ex-communist German officer who joins the Nazi party and gradually becomes a fanatical fascist, losing moral principles in a series of brutal acts; killed by Michael Whitacre at the end of World War II in Irwin Shaw's *The Young Lions.*

Dieter. Drug guru who lives in the desert and provides a hiding place for Marge Converse in Robert Stone's *Dog Soldiers.*

Bob (Bobby) Dietz. Son of the Reata ranch boss; becomes a self-employed agronomist after refusing to operate the ranch in Edna Ferber's *Giant.*

Digby. Owner of the Past Bay Manufacturing Company in Robert Cantwell's *The Land of Plenty.*

Paul Digita. New York University professor of English and lover of Polina Bellantoni and Molly Bolt in Rita Mae Brown's *Rubyfruit Jungle.*

Oscar Achilles (O.A., Ossie) Dilk. Assistant prosecutor who courts Hannah Cape in Jessamyn West's *The Massacre at Fall Creek.*

Gracie Dill. See Gracie Vaiden.

William Howard Taft ('Bama) Dillert. Flamboyant gambler and drinker; protector of Dave Hirsh in James Jones's *Some Came Running.*

John (Johnny) Dillinger. Head of a gang of robbers in William Riley Burnett's *High Sierra.*

Dillon. Full-time bartender and part-time hit man who works for the mob but also snitches to the police when it suits him in George V. Higgins's *The Friends of Eddie Coyle.*

Dilsey. See Dilsey Gibson.

Abner Dilworthy. United States senator investigated for bribery in Samuel Langhorne Clemens and Charles Dudley Warner's *The Gilded Age.*

Mr. Dimick. Insurance man from Albany, New York, and a courier of messages for the New Underground in Sinclair Lewis's *It Can't Happen Here.*

Arthur Dimmesdale. Minister, lover of Hester Prynne, and father of Pearl; dies after acknowledging his paternity of Pearl in Nathaniel Hawthorne's *The Scarlet Letter.*

Nancy Dimock. Mistress of the Blue Ball Inn and friend of the Lindsays, Arthur Butler, and Horse Shoe Robinson in John Pendleton Kennedy's *Horse-Shoe Robinson.*

Dinadan. Camelot humorist who tells old jokes in Samuel Langhorne Clemens's *A Connecticut Yankee in King Arthur's Court.*

Dinah. First wife of Hart Kennedy in John Clellon Holmes's *Go.*

Myrtle Dinardo. Parasol-wielding accomplice of Mother Ormsby in upstaging the navy during ceremonies dedicating the USS *Ormsby* in Wright Morris's *Man and Boy.*

Mabel Budd Detaze (Beauty) Dingle. Oft-married mother of Lanny Budd in Upton Sinclair's *Dragon's Teeth.*

Parsifal Dingle. Latest husband of Mabel Dingle; spiritualist and devotee of New Thought literature in Upton Sinclair's *Dragon's Teeth.*

Willie Dinsmore. Playwright from whom Michael Lovett gets a boardinghouse room in Norman Mailer's *Barbary Shore.*

Dirty Eddie. Black piglet from a San Fernando Valley farm who achieves stardom in a musical film in Ludwig Bemelmans's *Dirty Eddie.*

Disa, Duchess of Payn (Queen Disa). Cherished wife of Charles II; once copied into her album a quatrain from a poem by John Shade in Vladimir Nabokov's *Pale Fire.*

Max (Matthew [Matt] Fisher, William Small) Disher. Harlem man about town and first recipient of the Black-No-More treatment; after becoming white, marries the daughter of the Imperial Grand Wizard of the Knights of Nordica in George S. Schuyler's *Black No More.*

Benny Diskin. Delicatessen counterboy who serves J. Henry Waugh his meals in Robert Coover's *The Universal Baseball Association, Inc., J. Henry Waugh, Prop.*

Ditcher. Barrel-chested black overseer on the Bowler plantation; champion fist fighter until conquered by Gabriel Prosser; the two become friends and co-generals in the slave uprising in Arna Wendell Bontemps's *Black Thunder.*

Ditmas. Cynical and freethinking engineer on a railroad construction gang who is the chief proponent of Sunday baseball in T. S. Stribling's *Teeftallow.*

Diut. Tehkohn tribal leader who marries Alanna Verrick and fathers Tien; narrates part of Octavia E. Butler's *Survivor.*

Nicole Warren Diver. Wealthy young woman who suffers a mental collapse as a result of an incestuous relationship with her father; wife of Dick Diver in F. Scott Fitzgerald's *Tender Is the Night.*

Richard (Dick) Diver. Brilliant young psychiatrist who undergoes a process of decline after marrying mental patient Nicole Warren in F. Scott Fitzgerald's *Tender Is the Night.*

Alonzo Divich. Frequently married carnival owner in Anne Tyler's *Searching for Caleb.*

Jerry Divine. Sportscaster with whom Henry Wiggen does some announcing in Mark Harris's *It Looked Like For Ever.*

Bad-foot (Mistah Bad-foot Man) Dixon. Club-footed stableman who gives Augie a home and a chance to become a jockey in Arna Wendell Bontemps's *God Sends Sunday.*

Trick E. (Tricky, Tricky D) Dixon. Double-talking United States president who champions the unborn and directs the invasion of Denmark; dies when stuffed naked, in a fetal position, into a water-filled baggie in Philip Roth's *Our Gang.*

D. J. (Jellicoe Jethroe, Ranald Jethroe). Eighteen year old who remembers an Alaskan hunting expedition on the night before going to Vietnam; narrator of Norman Mailer's *Why Are We in Vietnam?*

Djuna. Dancer, friend and possibly lover of Lillian, and lover of Rango; appears in Anaïs Nin's *Ladders to Fire, Children of the Albatross, The Four-Chambered Heart, A Spy in the House of Love,* and *Seduction of the Minotaur.*

Dill Doak. Black burlesque entertainer who tries to convert Cass McKay to communism in Nelson Algren's *Somebody in Boots.*

Ben Doaks. Cattle herder and farmer who loves Lethe Sayles in Mary Noailles Murfree's *In the Clouds.*

Dobbs. Copilot who wrestles the controls from Huple on a fateful bombing mission over Avignon; urges the assassination of Colonel Cathcart in Joseph Heller's *Catch-22.*

Dobbs (Dobby). American drifter in Mexico; works in an oil camp and lives as a panhandler before searching for gold in B. Traven's *The Treasure of the Sierra Madre.*

Doc. Easygoing physician aboard the *Reluctant*; friend and confidant of Mr. Roberts in Thomas Heggen's *Mister Roberts.*

Doc. Owner of the Western Biological Laboratory, a marine-specimen supply company, in John Steinbeck's *Cannery Row.*

Uncle Doc. Friend of Jake Brown; owns a saloon that the longshoremen frequent in Claude McKay's *Home to Harlem.*

Mrs. Dockey. Receptionist and nurse at the Remobilization Farm in John Barth's *The End of the Road.*

Doctor. Director of the Remobilization Farm and Jacob Horner's personal psychotherapist in John Barth's *The End of the Road.*

Frank Dodd. Psychotic rapist and murderer whose true identity Johnny Smith's psychic ability helps reveal in Stephen King's *The Dead Zone.*

Henry Dodge. Territorial governor of Wisconsin and United States senator in August Derleth's *The Shadow in the Glass.*

Pardon Dodge. Frontier settler who kills Richard Braxley while Braxley is abducting Edith Forrester in Robert Montgomery Bird's *Nick of the Woods.*

Brent Dodsworth. Son of Fran and Sam Dodsworth and a student at Yale University in Sinclair Lewis's *Dodsworth.*

Emily Dodsworth. See Emily Dodsworth McKee.

Frances Voelker (Fran) Dodsworth. Europhile wife of Sam Dodsworth; runs off with her lover Count Kurt von Obersdorf in Sinclair Lewis's *Dodsworth.*

Samuel (Sam, Sammy) Dodsworth. President of Revelation Motor Company in Zenith; travels with his wife, Fran, to Europe, where their marriage breaks up, in Sinclair Lewis's *Dodsworth.*

Abel Doe. Renegade white man who has become a Piankeshaw Indian warrior in Robert Montgomery Bird's *Nick of the Woods.*

Telie Doe. Daughter of Abel Doe and guide to Captain Roland and Edith Forrester in Robert Montgomery Bird's *Nick of the Woods.*

William (Little Will) Dogood. Fifteen-year-old Puritan soldier and follower of Johnny Church; beaten for refusing to sign Cromwell's petition asking pardon and sentenced to death for mutiny; saved by Cromwell's blanket pardon in Mary Lee Settle's *Prisons*.

Charles (Charley) Doheny. Irish farmer who is the brother of Susie Doheny and the friend of Peder Holm in O. E. Rölvaag's *Peder Victorious* and *Their Father's God*.

Susie Doheny. Devout Irish Catholic neighbor of the Norwegian Holms in O. E. Rölvaag's *Peder Victorious*; marries the Lutheran Peder Holm, and religion becomes the basis for conflict between them in *Their Father's God*.

Jerry (Digger) Doherty. Boston criminal and owner of the bar, The Bright Red; owes the mob $18,000; resorts to theft and other crimes in George V. Higgins's *The Digger's Game*.

Paul Doherty. Catholic priest and brother of Jerry Doherty; attempts to keep his brother out of trouble with the mob and the police in George V. Higgins's *The Digger's Game*.

Professor (Dr.) Dohmler. Swiss psychiatrist and mentor of Dick Diver in F. Scott Fitzgerald's *Tender Is the Night*.

Dolce. Priest who stays at the Caffé Gatto; as a novice, he and Brother Bolo made a hair shirt of rat skins for Arsella's mother in John Hawkes's *The Goose on the Grave*.

Della Dole. Former lover of Jule and rival of Ollie; dies before the conclusion of George Wylie Henderson's *Ollie Miss*.

Doll. Unpleasant wife of Andrew and rival of Mary Pinesett in Julia Peterkin's *Scarlet Sister Mary*.

Don Doll. Naive Virginian private in C-for-Charlie Company who is distressed that his cowardice is mistaken for bravery in James Jones's *The Thin Red Line*.

Engelbert Dollfuss. Chancellor of Austria killed by his brother in John Irving's *Setting Free the Bears*.

Yakov Ivanovitch Dologushev. See Yakov Shepsovitch Bok.

Dolores. Daughter of Hugh and Catherine, younger sister of Meredith, twin sister of Eveline in John Hawkes's *The Blood Oranges*.

Abraham Ulysses (Abe) Dolphin. Son of William Body and Carrie Trout; grandson of Arlington Bloodworth, Sr., in Leon Forrest's *The Bloodworth Orphans*.

Domiron. Spirit contact of Eleanor Norton in Robert Coover's *The Origin of the Brunists*.

Donald. Flamboyant, effeminate man who becomes one of Sabina's lovers but treats her as a mother-figure in Anaïs Nin's *A Spy in the House of Love*.

Donald. Homosexual member of the Hippodrome's cast; solicits Jackson Yeager in Cyrus Colter's *The Hippodrome*.

Donald. Lover of Michael in Anaïs Nin's *Children of the Albatross*.

Geoffrey (Fife of Fain) Donald. Established San Francisco poet and benefactor of Jack Duluoz in Jack Kerouac's *Desolation Angels*.

Vincent (Socks) Donald. Promoter of the dance marathon; loses his struggle against the Mothers' League for Good Morals after a shooting in the bar adjoining the dance hall in Horace McCoy's *They Shoot Horses, Don't They?*

Donatello. (Count of Monte Beni). Faunlike Italian who loves Miriam Schaefer and kills Brother Antonio in Nathaniel Hawthorne's *The Marble Faun*.

Eddie Donato. Sicilian grocery store owner who hides Dix Handley and Erwin Riemenschneider in William Riley Burnett's *The Asphalt Jungle*.

Nick Donato. Unconventional painter who is the lover of Janet Belle Smith in Alison Lurie's *Real People*.

Jim Donell. Chief of the village fire department; most vocal and only identified individual in an otherwise anonymous crowd of cruel villagers in Shirley Jackson's *We Have Always Lived in the Castle*.

Donjalolo (Fonoo). Effeminate ruler of Juam in Herman Melville's *Mardi*.

Sean Xavier (Mike) Donnigan. Master construction worker and friend of Howard Roark in Ayn Rand's *The Fountainhead*.

Father Donovan. Catholic chaplain and friend of Chaplain Bascom; run over by an English lorry while trying to save a young girl in John Horne Burns's *The Gallery*.

Gertrude (Gert, Gerty) Donovan. Stenographer-typist for Glymmer, Read; consents to marry Jim Denby when she discovers that she is unable to marry one of the firm's junior partners in Nathan Asch's *The Office*.

Larry Donovan. Rakish railroad conductor who plans to marry Ántonia Shimerda, but abandons her after impregnating her in Willa Cather's *My Ántonia*.

Larry Donovan. Young workingman who travels through the American Midwest in the years leading up to the Great Depression in search of jobs and a meaningful life; narrator of Jack Conroy's *The Disinherited*.

Tom Donovan. Ex-Catholic priest, coal miner, labor organizer, and father of Larry Donovan in Jack Conroy's *The Disinherited*.

Ramona Donsell. Lexington Avenue florist, beautiful divorcée, and graduate student in art history enrolled in Moses Herzog's evening course; resilient survivor and Herzog's mistress and priestess of love in Saul Bellow's *Herzog*.

Neloa (Nell) Doole. Wife of Vridar Hunter; in order to punish him for her frustrating life with him, she commits suicide; appears in Vardis Fisher's *In Tragic Life*, *Passions Spin the Plot*, *We Are Betrayed*, and *Orphans in Gethsemene*.

Gene Doolie. Heroin customer of William Lee; possibly a police informer in William S. Burroughs's *Junkie*.

Congressman Doolittle. White legislator whose vacant seat Sammy Scott and Matthew Towns attempt to win in W. E. B. Du Bois's *Dark Princess*.

Hiram Doolittle. Templeton architect who has Natty Bumppo imprisoned for hunting out of season in James Fenimore Cooper's *The Pioneers*.

Doom. See Ikkemotubbe.

Bukka (Make-um-shit) Doopeyduk. Narrator and resident of HARRY SAM who wants to become the first black bacteriological warfare expert; flunks out of college, loses his job as a hospital orderly, marries Fannie Mae, has the hoodoo put on him by her grandmother, has it removed by U2 Polyglot, is divorced from his wife, and meets HARRY SAM in Ishmael Reed's *The Free-Lance Pallbearers*.

Doreen. Cynical fellow guest editor with Esther Greenwood on a New York fashion magazine and Esther's companion during a sexual escapade in Sylvia Plath's *The Bell Jar*.

Dorfû. Astute spy for Michaelis Ezana; becomes the new president of Kush and exiles the fallen Colonel Ellelloû in John Updike's *The Coup*.

Earl of Dorincourt. See John Arthur Molyneux Errol.

Dorine. Commune-mate of Beth Walker; acquires self-esteem in Marge Piercy's *Small Changes*.

Doris. Flirtatious sister of Joan Mitchell and daughter of Aurelie Caillet; dates Michael Kern in Shirley Ann Grau's *The House on Coliseum Street*.

Lady Agnes Dormer. Mother of Biddy, Grace, Nick, and Percy Dormer in Henry James's *The Tragic Muse*.

Bridget (Biddy) Dormer. Younger sister of Nick Dormer; loves Peter Sherringham in Henry James's *The Tragic Muse*.

Grace Dormer. Older sister of Nick Dormer in Henry James's *The Tragic Muse*.

Nicholas (Nick) Dormer. Man who chooses art over politics, which leads Julia Sherringham Dallow to break their engagement in Henry James's *The Tragic Muse*.

Percival (Percy) Dormer. Older brother of Nick Dormer in Henry James's *The Tragic Muse*.

Doro. Nubian male who can change bodies and live indefinitely in Octavia E. Butler's *Mind of My Mind*.

Dorothy la Désirée (Heart's Desire, Madame Dorothy). First true love of Jurgen; appears to him as the perfect woman and epitome of lost love throughout his yearlong journey in James Branch Cabell's *Jurgen*.

Dorris. Artistic dancer barred by class differences from a romance with the brother of her employer in Jean Toomer's *Cane*.

Bertha Dorset. Wealthy New York socialite who tries to conceal her own infidelity by insinuating that her husband, George Dorset, is involved with Lily Bart in Edith Wharton's *The House of Mirth*.

George Dorset. Unhappily married, wealthy businessman who falls in love with Lily Bart but is rejected by her in Edith Wharton's *The House of Mirth*.

Fidelia (Delia) Dosson. Sister of Francie Dosson in Henry James's *The Reverberator*.

Francina (Francie) Dosson. Daughter of Whitney Dosson; gives an interview to her friend George Flack which, when published, scandalizes her family in Henry James's *The Reverberator*.

Whitney Dosson. Wealthy American who takes his daughters, Delia and Francie Dosson, to Europe in Henry James's *The Reverberator*.

Dot. See Dorothy Powers.

Lob (Jumping Sturgeon) Dotterel. Busybody constable adopted by the Indians in James Kirke Paulding's *Koningsmarke*.

Olga Sergeievna Doubkov. Russian dressmaker living in Coaltown; befriends the Ashley and Lansing families; influences George Lansing by teaching him Russian and encouraging his interest in acting in Thornton Wilder's *The Eighth Day*.

Douceline. Mother of Youma; dies when her son is young in Lafcadio Hearn's *Youma*.

Thomas Dougherty. Butler in the Leavenworth house who discovers the body of Horatio Leavenworth in Anna Katharine Green's *The Leavenworth Case*.

Douglas. Man who reads the governess's manuscript about Miles, Flora, and the ghosts in Henry James's *The Turn of the Screw*.

Banny Douglas. Religious grandmother of Hosea Douglas; storyteller of the lives of black heroes in Herbert Simmons's *Man Walking on Eggshells*.

Charlotte Amelia (Char) Douglas. Wife of Leonard Douglas and formerly of Warren Bogart; mother of Marin Bogart; killed in a coup d'état in Boca Grande in Joan Didion's *A Book of Common Prayer*.

Helen Douglas. Sister of Raymond Douglas in Herbert Simmons's *Man Walking on Eggshells*.

Hosea Douglas. Husband of Mae Douglas and father of Raymond Douglas; aspiring football player who, in 1927, is unable to play professionally because he is black in Herbert Simmons's *Man Walking on Eggshells*.

Leonard Douglas. San Francisco attorney, second husband of Charlotte Douglas, and father of their hydrocephalic baby; possible power broker in Boca Grande in Joan Didion's *A Book of Common Prayer*.

Lillian Belsito Douglas. See Lillian Belsito Douglas Morgan.

Mae Douglas. Wife of Hosea Douglas and mother of Raymond Douglas; becomes insane as a result of her hatred of whites and her son's preference for music over any other career in Herbert Simmons's *Man Walking on Eggshells*.

Mary Douglas. American journalist and anti-Fascist in Czechoslovakia between the time of the Munich Pact and the Anschluss in Martha Gellhorn's *A Stricken Field*.

Old Douglas. Racist who initially denies Jule Jackson a membership card in Typographical Union No. 6 in George Wylie Henderson's *Jule*.

Raymond Charles Douglas. Son of Mae and Hosea Douglas; grows up in St. Louis's black belt during the Depression and becomes a jazz musician in Herbert Simmons's *Man Walking on Eggshells*.

Thomas (Tom, Tommy) Douglas. Prisoners' rights activist who is accidentally killed by his stepbrother Virgil Morgan in Scott Spencer's *Preservation Hall*.

Widow Douglas. Sister of Miss Watson and guardian of Huck Finn in Samuel Langhorne Clemens's *The Adventures of Tom Sawyer* and *Adventures of Huckleberry Finn*.

Chet Douglass. Student at Devon School and rival of Gene Forrester for class academic honors in John Knowles's *A Separate Peace*.

Edward Stephen (Ned, Ned Brown) Douglass. Son of Big Laura reared by Miss Jane Pittman; murdered for his efforts to improve the condition of his people in Ernest J. Gaines's *The Autobiography of Miss Jane Pittman*.

Monsieur Douperie. French dancing master driven to distraction by his student Teague Oregan in Hugh Henry Brackenridge's *Modern Chivalry*.

Douris. Ruler of Samos in Hellenistic times, lover of Hedyle, and patron of Hedyle's son, Hedylus, in H. D.'s *Hedylus*.

Hercules Dousman. Entrepreneur in the early development of Wisconsin; helps Nelson Dewey with railroad investments in August Derleth's *The Shadow in the Glass*.

The Dove. See Hilda.

Hettie Dowler. Zenith church secretary who attempts to blackmail her lover, the Methodist minister Elmer Gantry, in Sinclair Lewis's *Elmer Gantry*.

Oscar Dowler. Husband of Hettie Dowler; helps his wife attempt to blackmail Elmer Gantry in Sinclair Lewis's *Elmer Gantry*.

Margo Dowling. Chorus girl who marries unhappily and is unable to rid herself permanently of her leeching Cuban husband; mistress of Charley Anderson in John Dos Passos's *U.S.A.* trilogy.

Frances Lonigan Dowson. See Frances Lonigan.

Fay Doyle. Wife of Peter Doyle; writes to Miss Lonelyhearts and seduces him in Nathanael West's *Miss Lonelyhearts*.

Peter Doyle. Crippled husband of Fay Doyle; shoots Miss Lonelyhearts in Nathanael West's *Miss Lonelyhearts*.

Count Alphonse (Henri) D'Oyley. Twin brother and nemesis of Lafitte in Joseph Holt Ingraham's *Lafitte*.

Beckwith Dozer. Proud black man who becomes the central figure in racially tense Winfield County, Mississippi, in Elizabeth Spencer's *The Voice at the Back Door*.

Julie Dozier. Actress who is forced to leave the *Cotton Blossom* when people learn that her mother is a black in Edna Ferber's *Show Boat*.

Hella (Helen Drake) Drachenfels. Nazi at Buchenwald and a prostitute following World War II; second wife of David Dehn, the source of whose money she reveals; murdered by Fanny Mintz in Jerome Weidman's *The Temple*.

Jonathan Bailey (Johnny B.) Draeger. Union official who comes from California to Oregon to supervise the suppression of the Stamper family's non-union logging operation in Ken Kesey's *Sometimes a Great Notion*.

Ada Dragan. Active telepath who founds a school for Patternists in Octavia E. Butler's *Mind of My Mind*.

Dragon. Guardian of a personal treasure hoard who cynically denies any freedom of will in a world of chance in John Gardner's *Grendel*.

Augusta Drake. Friend of Susan Ward and wife of Thomas Hudson; artist living in the East in Wallace Stegner's *Angle of Repose*.

Hubert Drake. Brother of Temple Drake in William Faulkner's *Sanctuary*.

Judge Drake. Father of Hubert and Temple Drake in William Faulkner's *Sanctuary*.

Susanna Drake. Lovely, scarred, and mad Southern belle who marries John Wickliff Shawnessy; dies during the Civil War in Ross Lockridge, Jr.'s *Raintree County*.

Temple Drake. See Temple Drake Stevens.

Alice Draper. Troubled wife of Jack Draper; has an affair with Jean-Paul La Prade in Richard Yates's *A Good School*.

Jack Draper. Polio-crippled, alcoholic, cynical chemistry master at Dorset Academy; characteristically botches an attempt to hang himself in his lab with a Brooks Brothers belt in Richard Yates's *A Good School*.

Dred. See Dred Vesey.

General Dreedle. Rival of General P. P. Peckem; prevented from pinning a medal on Yossarian when Yossarian appears at the ceremony naked in Joseph Heller's *Catch-22*.

Samuel Dreff. Retired Jewish accountant who spends one night in a shelter on an Appalachian mountain trail with Mac Miller in Frederick Busch's *Domestic Particulars*.

Sam Dreiman. American builder and investor who leaves his estranged wife and children to live and travel with Betty Slonim; finances Aaron Greidinger's first play, *The Ludmir Maiden*, in Isaac Bashevis Singer's *Shosha*.

Inez Dresden. See Inez Dresden Charlesbois.

Harley Drew. Ambitious cotton merchant and banker engaged to Amanda Barcroft; lover of Amy Carruthers in Shelby Foote's *Love in a Dry Season*.

Harley Drew. Owner of the largest ranch in Bridger's Wells; sells Donald Martin the cattle Martin is accused of rustling in Walter Van Tilburg Clark's *The Ox-Bow Incident*.

Rev. John Jennison Drew. Pastor of the Chatham Road Presbyterian Church, of which George Babbitt is a member, in Sinclair Lewis's *Babbitt*.

Ruby Drew. Black cleaning woman who tries to save her fair sister, Savata; narrator of William Goyen's *The Fair Sister*.

Margaret Jane (Polly) Drewry. Caretaker, sometime daughter substitute, and sometime mistress of Robinson Mayfield in Reynolds Price's *The Surface of Earth*.

Dr. Felix Dreyfus. Plastic surgeon who operates on one of Sissy Hankshaw Gitche's thumbs; later creates the first Cubist nose in Tom Robbins's *Even Cowgirls Get the Blues*.

Randolph Driblette. Actor and director who stages a performance of Richard Wharfinger's *The Courier's Tragedy* in which he delivers a variant line that mentions the Tristero; commits suicide by walking into the ocean in Thomas Pynchon's *The Crying of Lot 49*.

Percy Northumberland Driscoll. Father of Thomas à Becket Driscoll and brother of York Driscoll; rears Valet de Chambre in Samuel Langhorne Clemens's *Pudd'nhead Wilson*.

Robert (Bob, Pop) Driscoll. Assistant English master popular with his students and his colleagues; loves Dorset Academy and tries to believe it is "a good school" in Richard Yates's *A Good School*.

Thomas à Becket (Chambers, Valet de Chambre) Driscoll. Son of Percy Driscoll; switched at birth with Valet de Chambre and reared as a slave named Chambers in Samuel Langhorne Clemens's *Pudd'nhead Wilson*.

York Leicester Driscoll. Judge and leading citizen of Dawson's Landing; murdered by Valet de Chambre in Samuel Langhorne Clemens's *Pudd'nhead Wilson*.

Stanley Drobeck. Captain of the Wilshire Police Station, base of the ten Los Angeles policemen-protagonists of Joseph Wambaugh's *The Choirboys*.

George Drobes. Bronx suitor of Marjorie Morningstar in Herman Wouk's *Marjorie Morningstar*.

Natasha and Otto (Vanya) Drollinger. Married couple who are non-Communist Russophiles and residents of the Glen Cove Apartments in Albert Halper's *Union Square*.

Charles H. (Charlie) Drouet. Traveling salesman and first lover of Carrie Meeber in Theodore Dreiser's *Sister Carrie*.

Henry Iverson Dround. Old-fashioned and philanthropic meat packer in Robert Herrick's *The Memoirs of an American Citizen*.

Jane Dround. Forceful and brilliant wife of Henry Dround and adviser of Edward Van Harrington in Robert Herrick's *The Memoirs of an American Citizen*.

Dr. Roy Drover. President of the Federal Club, from which Neil and Robert Kingsblood resign, in Sinclair Lewis's *Kingsblood Royal*; friend of Cass Timberlane in *Cass Timberlane*.

Drucilla. Black cook for Moseley Sheppard in Arna Wendell Bontemps's *Black Thunder*.

Kate Drummond. New York roommate of Ann Chapin; lover of Joe Chapin I in John O'Hara's *Ten North Frederick*.

Christine (Chris) and Mela (Mely) Dryfoos. Daughters of Jacob Dryfoos who are eager to find their place in New York society in William Dean Howells's *A Hazard of New Fortunes*.

Conrad Dryfoos. Son of Jacob Dryfoos and publisher of *Every Other Week*; killed while helping the people involved in a streetcar strike in William Dean How-

ells's *A Hazard of New Fortunes*.

Jacob Dryfoos. Millionaire from oil found on his farm; backer of the magazine *Every Other Week* who has difficulty fitting into high society in William Dean Howells's *A Hazard of New Fortunes*.

Jack Duane. Jail inmate with Jurgis Rudkus; introduces Jurgis to a life of crime and Chicago politics in Upton Sinclair's *The Jungle*.

Larry Duane. Young lawyer married to a daughter of Henry Knox; defends Timothy Colt in his trial for breach of trust in Louis Auchincloss's *The Great World and Timothy Colt*.

Gerald Dubin. See Gerald Willis.

Kitty Willis Dubin. Widow who marries William Dubin; mother of Gerald Willis and Maud Dubin in Bernard Malamud's *Dubin's Lives*.

Maud Dubin. Daughter of William and Kitty Dubin; as a college student, becomes pregnant by a much older professor who is both married and of a different race in Bernard Malamud's *Dubin's Lives*.

William B. Dubin. Biographer; husband of Kitty Dubin, father of Maud Dubin, and adoptive father of Gerald Willis; has a passionate extramarital affair with the much younger Fanny Bick in Bernard Malamud's *Dubin's Lives*.

Chloe Duboise. Mistress of both Hans and Alexander Mueller and mother by one of them of Robert Mueller in Nicholas Delbanco's *Fathering*.

Captain Clarence Duchemin. Enthusiastic voluptuary of the Reports Section at Ocanara Army Air Base whose influence secures an apartment for himself, Captain Nathaniel Hicks, and Captain Donald Andrews in James Gould Cozzens's *Guard of Honor*.

Dr. Pete Duchesne. Physician and hero of Bret Harte's *Gabriel Conroy*.

Sue Ann Duckett. Army nurse and occasionally lover of Yossarian in Joseph Heller's *Catch-22*.

Bernard Ducrot. Aide to the retired Archbishop Latour in Willa Cather's *Death Comes for the Archbishop*.

Dudley. Caretaker at Hill House and husband of Mrs. Dudley in Shirley Jackson's *The Haunting of Hill House*.

Alonzo T. (Lon, Lonnie) Dudley. First husband of Orpha Chase; murders Crit Matthews and then kills himself to prevent Orpha's learning of his homosexuality in Jessamyn West's *The Life I Really*

Lived.

Bannie Upshire Dudley. White second cousin of Margaret Upshur, lover of Percy Upshur, and mother of Dr. Albert Grene; holds the deed to the Upshur land in Sarah E. Wright's *This Child's Gonna Live.*

Bruce (John Stockton) Dudley. Dissatisfied newspaper reporter who flees from his job and his wife in Chicago and returns to his boyhood home of Old Harbor, Indiana, under an assumed name; runs away with the wife of the richest man in town in Sherwood Anderson's *Dark Laughter.*

Constantia (Constance) Dudley. Young woman whose efforts to support her father and herself lead her into a battle of wills with the sinister Ormond in Charles Brockden Brown's *Ormond.*

Mrs. Dudley. Officious housekeeper and cook who refuses to stay at Hill House after dark in Shirley Jackson's *The Haunting of Hill House.*

Mrs. Dudley. See Orpha Chase.

Stephen Dudley. Father of Constantia Dudley; supported by Constantia after he loses his business to Thomas Craig's embezzlement; murdered by Craig in Charles Brockden Brown's *Ormond.*

Angus Duer. Medical school classmate of Martin Arrowsmith; Arrowsmith's rival for the affections of Leora Tozer in Sinclair Lewis's *Arrowsmith.*

Margaret (Margy) Duff. First lover of Eugene Witla in Theodore Dreiser's *The "Genius."*

J. D. Duffey. Well-known moonshiner in Harriette Arnow's *Hunter's Horn.*

Leo Duffy. Composition instructor at Cascadia College; his high standards, radical thinking, and liaison with Pauline Gilley cause his demise at that institution and his eventual suicide in Bernard Malamud's *A New Life.*

Tiny Duffy. Lieutenant governor under Willie Stark and Stark's reminder to himself of political corruption; sets in motion the events leading to Stark's assassination in Robert Penn Warren's *All the King's Men.*

Maribeth Dufour. Schoolmate of Cress Delahanty, house party participant, and niece of Miss Iris Bird in Jessamyn West's *Cress Delahanty.*

Yuro Dug. Husband of Dora Dugova and father of Zorka Dugova; imprisoned for robbery; murderer of several foster children in Louis Adamic's *Cradle of Life.*

Sheik Dugan. Bullying thug who terrorizes Sammy Glick in elementary school and later becomes his factotum in Budd Schulberg's *What Makes Sammy Run?*

Charlene Duggs. Girlfriend of Sonny Crawford, who outgrows her, in Larry McMurtry's *The Last Picture Show.*

Dora (Doramamo) Dugova. Croatian peasant who is the wife of Yuro Dug, mother of Zorka Dugova, and foster mother of Rudolf Stanka; murderer of several foster children in Louis Adamic's *Cradle of Life.*

Zorka Dugova. Peasant daughter of Dora Dugova and Yuro Dug; marries Rudolf Stanka in Louis Adamic's *Cradle of Life.*

Leo Dugovka. Gentile friend of David Schearl in Henry Roth's *Call It Sleep.*

Duke. Patient, long-suffering dog of Penrod Schofield; his loyalty to his master results in his being subjected to numerous experiments in Booth Tarkington's *Penrod, Penrod and Sam,* and *Penrod Jashber.*

Duke of Bridgewater (Bilgewater, David Garrick, William Wilks). Confidence man and accomplice of the Dauphin in Samuel Langhorne Clemens's *Adventures of Huckleberry Finn.*

The Duke (Herr Duke). German cannibal who carves up and devours a child in John Hawkes's *The Cannibal.*

Nathaniel (Nat, Sir Nat) Dukinfield. Dissipated, sports-loving baronet who attracts Johnny Fraser at Edenton in James Boyd's *Drums.*

Etienne Dulac. Owner of the Austrian castle Schloss Riva and weaver of fantasies; his alleged death brings the characters together in Wright Morris's *Cause for Wonder.*

Ange (Angie, Angy, Ma, Memère) Duluoz. Wife of Emil Duluoz and mother of Gerard, Catherine, and Jean Duluoz in Jack Kerouac's *Doctor Sax, Maggie Cassidy, Book of Dreams, Big Sur, Visions of Gerard,* and *Desolation Angels.*

Catherine (Nin, Ti Nin) Duluoz. Older sister of Jean Duluoz in Jack Kerouac's *Doctor Sax, Maggie Cassidy, Book of Dreams, Visions of Gerard, Desolation Angels,* and *Visions of Cody.*

Emil Alcide (Emilio, Emil Kerouac, Emil Pop, Leo, Pa) Duluoz. Husband of Ange Duluoz and father of Gerard, Catherine, and Jean Duluoz in Jack

Kerouac's *Doctor Sax, Maggie Cassidy, Book of Dreams, Big Sur, Visions of Gerard,* and *Desolation Angels.*

Gerard (Gerardo, Ti Gerard) Duluoz. Saintly older brother of Jean Duluoz; dies at age nine of a rheumatic heart in Jack Kerouac's *Visions of Gerard;* appears briefly in *Doctor Sax, Maggie Cassidy, Book of Dreams, Big Sur, Desolation Angels,* and *Visions of Cody.*

Jean Louis (Jack, Jackie, Jacky, J. D., John, Ti Jean, Ti Loup, Ti Pousse [Little Thumb], Zagg, Zaggo, Zagguth) Duluoz. Autobiographical French Canadian hero and narrator of Jack Kerouac's *Doctor Sax, Maggie Cassidy, Visions of Gerard, Desolation Angels,* and *Visions of Cody.*

Du Mesne. French-Canadian guide and boatman for John Law in Emerson Hough's *The Mississippi Bubble.*

Jack Dumbrowski. Neighbor and antagonist of Alvin Mopworth; popular novelist whose narrative style is satirically demonstrated in Peter De Vries's *Reuben, Reuben.*

Royal Dumphry. Homosexual expatriate in F. Scott Fitzgerald's *Tender Is the Night.*

Peter Dumphy. Conniving villain; specialist in California land fraud schemes in Bret Harte's *Gabriel Conroy.*

Kenneth (Snake) Dumpson. Housing commissioner and former member of the black high school athletic team and neighborhood gang gathering for a birthday testimonial honoring Chappie Davis in John A. Williams's *The Junior Bachelor Society.*

René Dumur. Suitor of Annette Slogum; castrated by Butch Haber in Mari Sandoz's *Slogum House.*

Dunbar. Air force lieutenant and friend of Yossarian; malingerer who believes he will live longer if he makes time pass slowly in Joseph Heller's *Catch-22.*

Lord Dunbeg. Irishman visiting Washington to study Americans; fascinated by Victoria Dareto, to whom he becomes engaged, in Henry Adams's *Democracy.*

Anthony Duncan. Popular author who attempts to fake his disappearance in East Germany; after Tarden exposes him, Duncan is found dead in his car in Denmark, near the German border, in Jerzy Kosinski's *Cockpit.*

Charles Duncan. New England tutor of Cornelia Wilton and her brothers in Caroline Gilman's *Recollections of a Southern Matron.*

Mary Beth Duncan. Secretary of James Quinn in Thomas McGuane's *The Sporting Club.*

Whitey Duncan. Veteran Los Angeles policeman and alcoholic partner of Roy Fehler; dies of cirrhosis of the liver in Joseph Wambaugh's *The New Centurions.*

Duncan of Lundie. Commander of Fort Oswego in James Fenimore Cooper's *The Pathfinder.*

Lieutenant Dundy. Police detective antagonistic toward Sam Spade who is investigating the murders of Miles Archer and Floyd Thursby in Dashiell Hammett's *The Maltese Falcon.*

Charley Dunham. Friend of James Staniford; marries Miss Hibbard in William Dean Howells's *The Lady of the Aroostook.*

Mabel (Magnet) Dunham. Daughter of Serjeant Dunham and the only woman Natty Bumppo ever loves; loves and marries Jasper Western in James Fenimore Cooper's *The Pathfinder.*

Mrs. Dunham. See Miss Hibbard.

Serjeant Dunham. Father of Mabel Dunham, whom he wishes to marry Natty Bumppo; killed in an ambush in James Fenimore Cooper's *The Pathfinder.*

Brace Dunlap. Suitor of Benny Phelps; conspires with Jubiter Dunlap to kill their brother, Jake Dunlap, and frame Silas Phelps in Samuel Langhorne Clemens's *Tom Sawyer, Detective.*

Ed Dunkel. Complacent friend of Dean Moriarty in Jack Kerouac's *On the Road.*

Doctor J. Dunlap. Hospital director who fondles the unconscious Candy Christian in Terry Southern and Mason Hoffenberg's *Candy.*

Jake Dunlap. Jewel thief murdered by his brothers Brace and Jubiter Dunlap in Samuel Langhorne Clemens's *Tom Sawyer, Detective.*

Jubiter Dunlap. Twin brother of Jake Dunlap; conspires with his brother Brace Dunlap to kill Jake and frame Silas Phelps in Samuel Langhorne Clemens's *Tom Sawyer, Detective.*

Rosie Dunlup. Wife of Royce Dunlup and housekeeper for Aurora Greenway in Larry McMurtry's *Terms of Endearment.*

Royce Dunlup. Husband of Rosie Dunlup; has an affair and is stabbed to death in Larry McMurtry's *Terms of Endearment.*

Brigid Dunn. See Brigid Dunn Kelly.

Charles Dunn. Judge who examines Nelson Dewey for the bar and who becomes Dewey's father-in-law in August Derleth's *The Shadow in the Glass*.

Katherine Dunn. See Katherine Dunn Dewey.

Katherine (Kitty) Dunn. Older and more liberal sister of Theresa Dunn; introduces Theresa to drugs in Judith Rossner's *Looking for Mr. Goodbar*.

Theresa (Terry, Tessie, Theresita) Dunn. Young Catholic teacher who frequents bars to meet men; murdered by one of her pickups, Gary Cooper White, in Judith Rossner's *Looking for Mr. Goodbar*.

Thomas Dunn. Older brother of Theresa Dunn; dies in Vietnam when Theresa is very young in Judith Rossner's *Looking for Mr. Goodbar*.

Howard Dunninger. Lawyer and final lover of Emily Grimes; leaves her to return to his young second wife in Richard Yates's *Easter Parade*.

Clarence Duntz. Agent for the Kansas Bureau of Investigation; works with Alvin Dewey to break down the lies of murderer Perry Smith in Truman Capote's *In Cold Blood*.

Brother Dunwoodie. Leader of the August evangelist tent revival; at Alma Deen's request, he counsels Tracy Deen into church and marriage in Lillian Smith's *Strange Fruit*.

Peyton Dunwoodie. Major of the Virginia dragoons who is torn between his friendship with Henry Wharton and the patriot cause; marries Frances Wharton and later becomes a general in James Fenimore Cooper's *The Spy*.

Dunyazade (Doony). Younger sister of Scheherazade in the *Dunyazadiad*, a novella in John Barth's *Chimera*.

Louis Eugene (Julian Morris) Dupont. Visitor to Carroll Farms who is revealed to be Marion More Carroll's lost son in Constance Fenimore Woolson's *For the Major*.

Virginia (Miss Jenny) Du Pre (Depre). Sister of John Sartoris in William Faulkner's *Sartoris (Flags in the Dust)*, *Sanctuary*, *The Unvanquished*, *Requiem for a Nun*, *The Town*, and *The Mansion*.

Sergio (Serge) Duran. Mexican-American Los Angeles policeman who grows to accept his heritage in Joseph Wambaugh's *The New Centurions*.

Borsfa Durd. Slovenian peasant killed by Ustashi terrorists in John Irving's *Setting Free the Bears*.

Julian Durgo. Detective sergeant who investigates the rape of Laura Manion and the shooting of Barney

Quill in Robert Traver's *Anatomy of a Murder*.

Mrs. John Durham. Aristocratic former slave owner who rears Allan McLeod in Thomas Dixon's *The Leopard's Spots*.

Rev. John Durham. North Carolina preacher who turns down a lucrative job offer from a Boston church in Thomas Dixon's *The Leopard's Spots*.

André Duroy. Sculptor and first boyfriend of Jane Ward in Margaret Ayer Barnes's *Years of Grace*.

Reverend Paul Durrell. Civil rights leader resembling Martin Luther King, Jr., in John A. Williams's *The Man Who Cried I Am*.

Dr. Walter Dürrfeld. Director of a German industrial conglomerate for which the Auschwitz concentration camp furnishes labor in William Styron's *Sophie's Choice*.

John Dutcher. Farmer and father of Rose Dutcher; reluctantly supports Rose's university education and life in the city in Hamlin Garland's *Rose of Dutcher's Coolly*.

Rose (Rosie) Dutcher. Farm girl reared by her father, John Dutcher; college graduate whose independence and natural grace gain her access to Chicago society; marries Warren Mason in Hamlin Garland's *Rose of Dutcher's Coolly*.

Dori Duz. Shameless sexual exploiter of men; loved by Yossarian in Joseph Heller's *Catch-22*.

Gora Dwight. Novelist aware of the recklessness of Lee Clavering and Mary Ogden's passion in Gertrude Atherton's *Black Oxen*.

Nelson Dyar. New York bank teller who travels to Tangier; protagonist of Paul Bowles's *Let It Come Down*.

Inspector Dyce. Detective who investigates N. Hexam's claim that Evalin McCabe Wilson was murdered in Diane Johnson's *The Shadow Knows*.

Billie Dyer. Son of Malcolm Dyer and friend of Paul Hardin; recipient of a dog cart made by J. Hardin; drowned in a swimming accident in Brand Whitlock's *J. Hardin & Son*.

Dave Dyer. Gopher Prairie druggist in Sinclair Lewis's *Main Street*.

Malcolm Dyer. Father of Billie and Winona Dyer; wealthy landowner and idol of Paul Hardin; dies of pneumonia after rescuing Evelyn Walling from an icy creek in Brand Whitlock's *J. Hardin & Son*.

Winona (Winifred, Winnie) Dyer. Daughter of Malcolm Dyer and wife of Paul Hardin; temporarily separated from her husband when his affair with Evelyn Walling is exposed in Brand Whitlock's *J. Hardin & Son*.

Dyke. Wrongfully discharged railroad employee who turns to hop-growing, only to be ruined by the railroad's shipping rates; becomes a train robber in Frank Norris's *The Octopus*.

E

Earl of Hertford. Uncle of Edward Tudor; advisor to Tom Canty (disguised as Edward) in Samuel Langhorne Clemens's *The Prince and the Pauper*.

Earl of Rossmore. Father of Berkeley; annoyed by Mulberry Sellers's claim of the Rossmore title in Samuel Langhorne Clemens's *The American Claimant*.

Roy Earle. See Johnston Wade.

Roy (Mad Dog) Earle. Pardoned convict who is sent to California to rob a resort hotel; hunted down and killed after he becomes America's New Public Enemy No. 1 in William Riley Burnett's *High Sierra*.

Edward Easterly. Partner of the late Mr. Job Grey and executor of the Grey fortune; chairman of the Republican State Committee of New Jersey in W. E. B. Du Bois's *The Quest of the Silver Fleece*.

Elinor (Lakey) Eastlake. Taciturn brunette beauty who studies art in Paris after graduating from Vassar; believed by other members of the Group to be homosexual in Mary McCarthy's *The Group*.

William Washington Eathorne. President of the First State Bank of Zenith; works with George Babbitt to increase Sunday School enrollment in Sinclair Lewis's *Babbitt*.

Brother Eaton. Second Avenue evangelist in Henry Miller's *Black Spring*.

Martha Johnson Eaton. Wife of Samuel Eaton and mother of Alfred Eaton; falls in love with two other men and becomes an invalid alcoholic in John O'Hara's *From the Terrace*.

Mary St. John Eaton. Woman who breaks off her engagement to another man to marry Alfred Eaton in John O'Hara's *From the Terrace*.

Natalie Benziger Eaton. Young Mountain City woman with whom Alfred Eaton falls in love at first sight; becomes Eaton's mistress and later his wife in John O'Hara's *From the Terrace*.

Raymond Alfred Eaton. Second son of Samuel and Martha Eaton; after World War I he becomes a private banker in New York; an assistant secretary to the navy in World War II in John O'Hara's *From the Terrace*.

Rowland Eaton. First son of Alfred and Mary Eaton; World War II navy pilot who dies on a training mission in John O'Hara's *From the Terrace*.

Samuel Eaton. Father of Alfred Eaton and autocratic owner of Eaton Iron & Steel in John O'Hara's *From the Terrace*.

Athens Ebanks. Incompetent and insubordinate crew member of the *Lillias Eden*, said to be a thief; jumps ship to join Desmond Eden's crew in Peter Matthiessen's *Far Tortuga*.

Janet Eberly. Crippled woman loved by Sam McPherson in Sherwood Anderson's *Windy McPherson's Son*.

Ebony. See Black Guinea.

Jane Eborn. Wife of Thomas Eborn in Reynolds Price's *Love and Work*.

Jim Eborn. Father of Todd Eborn and grandfather of Thomas Eborn in Reynolds Price's *Love and Work*.

Louise Attwater (Lou) Eborn. Mother of Thomas Eborn; her death sets off her son's questioning of his own life in Reynolds Price's *Love and Work*.

Thomas (Tom) Eborn. Professor of English whose elderly mother's death sets in motion the events of Reynolds Price's *Love and Work*.

Todd Eborn. Deceased father of Thomas Eborn and husband of Louise Eborn in Reynolds Price's *Love and Work*.

Jack Eccles. Episcopalian minister who counsels Rabbit Angstrom in John Updike's *Rabbit, Run*.

Lucy Eccles. Wife of Jack Eccles; physically attracted to Rabbit Angstrom in John Updike's *Rabbit, Run*.

Echegaray. Gentle wood-carver of animals who drowns after saving a dog thrown overboard by Ric and Rac in Katherine Anne Porter's *Ship of Fools*.

Char Ecktin. Young dramatist in John Updike's *Bech: A Book*.

Ecrest. Psychiatrist who treats David Axelrod in Scott Spencer's *Endless Love*.

Simeon Ecuyer. Swiss soldier-of-fortune in charge of Fort Pitt; appears in Hervey Allen's *The Forest and the Fort* and *Bedford Village*.

Eddie. Part-time bartender who supplies the Palace Flophouse and Grill with stolen liquor in John Steinbeck's *Cannery Row*.

Eddie. Teenaged husband of Meridian Hill and father of Eddie, Jr; divorces Meridian in Alice Walker's *Meridian*.

Eddie. Store clerk who brings the resurrected road runner to Marietta McGee-Chavéz in William Goyen's *In a Farther Country*.

Eddie Jr. (Rundi). Son of Meridian Hill and Eddie; she gives him away so she can resume her education in Alice Walker's *Meridian*.

Eddy. Bimini fisherman admired by the Hudsons in Ernest Hemingway's *Islands in the Stream*.

Captain Desmond Eden. "Outside child" of Captain Andrew Avers and half brother of Raib Avers, who hates him; reputed to be a pirate and smuggler; competes with Raib Avers for turtles in Peter Matthiessen's *Far Tortuga*.

Martin (Bill) Eden. Sailor who becomes a successful author; commits suicide when he is unable to find happiness in Jack London's *Martin Eden*.

Michael (Mike) Eden. Former psychology professor who works to rescue Jews from Nazi Germany; meets Marjorie Morningstar on a ship sailing to France in Herman Wouk's *Marjorie Morningstar*.

Homer Edge. Promoter of Herman Mack's attempt to eat a Ford Maverick at the Hotel Sherman in Harry Crews's *Car*.

Carothers (Roth) Edmonds. Son of Zack Edmonds and father of McCaslin Edmonds in William Faulkner's *Go Down, Moses*; *Intruder in the Dust*; *The Town*; and *The Reivers*.

Carothers McCaslin (Old Cass) Edmonds. Woodsman and father of Zack Edmonds in William Faulkner's *Go Down, Moses*; *The Town*; and *The Reivers*.

Zachary Taylor (Zack) Edmonds. Son of McCaslin Edmonds; almost murdered by Lucas Beauchamp; appears in William Faulkner's *Go Down, Moses* and *The Reivers*.

Edmund. Drunken, fat, illegitimate son of The Dead Father in Donald Barthelme's *The Dead Father*.

Clithero Edny.. Deranged Irishman who murders Arthur Wiatte; attempts further murder because of insane delusions; ultimately commits suicide in Charles Brockden Brown's *Edgar Huntly*.

Edouard. Friend of Nino; attacked by his former partner, Jacopo, in John Hawkes's *The Goose on the Grave*.

First Lieutenant James A. Edsell. Champion of justice and equality whose pleasure in making trouble renders his liberal principles suspect in James Gould Cozzens's *Guard of Honor*.

King Edumu IV, Lord of Wanjiji. Aged king of Noire deposed by his adopted son, Colonel Hakim Félix Ellelloû; beheaded by Ellelloû to restore rain to the land; his severed head is used by the Soviets and Ellelloû's enemies as a fake oracle to stir up dissent in John Updike's *The Coup*.

Edward. Ex-violinist who lives in a trailer on the beach in Golconda with his many children in Anaïs Nin's *Seduction of the Minotaur*.

Edward. One of the "seven dwarfs" who wash windows, make Chinese baby food, and live with Snow White in Donald Barthelme's *Snow White*.

Agnes and Esther Edwards. Elderly aunts of Guy Grand in Terry Southern's *The Magic Christian*.

Alfonse Edwards. Black CIA agent involved in undercover counterintelligence activities, including assassination, while posing as a writer in John A. Williams's *The Man Who Cried I Am*.

Edward Edwards. Captain of HMS *Pandora* who, sent to capture mutineers, captures and returns to England both the guilty and innocent, and treats them all inhumanely, in Charles Nordhoff and James Norman Hall's *Mutiny on the Bounty*.

Foxhall (Fox) Edwards. Editor, mentor, and best friend of George Webber in Thomas Wolfe's *You Can't Go Home Again*.

Henry Edwards. Elderly friend of Julien La Brierre; dies at Viosca's Point before La Brierre can reach him in Lafcadio Hearn's *Chita*.

Josh Edwards. Teacher whose students destroy his prized record collection in Evan Hunter's *The Blackboard Jungle*.

Oliver Edwards. See Oliver Effingham.

Ralph Edwards. Pharmacy student who seduces Barbara Mintner at a drive-in theater in Terry Southern's *Flash and Filigree*.

Wesley Edwards. Presbyterian minister in Robert Coover's *The Origin of the Brunists*.

Edwin. Querulous and conventional father of Waldo in Paul Theroux's *Waldo*.

Mehmet Effendi. Turkish friend of Alexis Saranditis and lover of Saranditis's daughter in Nicholas Delbanco's *The Martlet's Tale*.

Oliver (Oliver Edwards) Effingham. Young hunter who returns to Templeton to claim land once owned by his father but now owned by Judge Marmaduke Temple; marries Elizabeth Temple in

James Fenimore Cooper's *The Pioneers*.

Mrs. Efrim. Operator of a small store where George Brush assists a thief in taking her money in order to prove his theory of *ahimsa* in Thornton Wilder's *Heaven's My Destination*.

Frances Egan. School nurse at Calvin Coolidge High School who sends memos pronouncing, "Poor nutrition is frequently the cause of poor marks," in Bel Kaufman's *Up the Down Staircase*.

Norah Egan. Chicago prostitute and Cass McKay's only love in Nelson Algren's *Somebody in Boots*.

Egbert. Disciple of Mark Winsome; tells the story of China Aster in Herman Melville's *The Confidence-Man*.

Chalmers Egstrom. Fat, laughing man who brings a mandolin with strings made of a woman's hair into Marietta McGee-Chavéz's Spain; dies and is resurrected in William Goyen's *In a Farther Country*.

Harriet Ehrlich. Fiancée, then wife of Ron Patimkin in Philip Roth's *Goodbye, Columbus*.

Billy Ehrmann. Son of a Supreme Court justice, brother of Saul Ehrmann (Noel Airman), student at Columbia University, and suitor of Marjorie Morningstar in Herman Wouk's *Marjorie Morningstar*.

Saul Ehrmann. See Noel Airman.

Frederick Eichner. Renowned dermatologist who causes a fatal automobile accident and inexplicably attacks and later kills his patient Felix Treevly in Terry Southern's *Flash and Filigree*.

Eblis Eierkopf. Physically deficient and impotent scientist in John Barth's *Giles Goat-Boy*.

Thomas Eigen. Author of an important novel, reduced to doing public relations work for Typhon International in William Gaddis's *JR*.

Dudley Eigenvalue, D.D.S.. Practitioner of psychodontia; Herbert Stencil's consultant in Thomas Pynchon's *V.*

William Einhorn. Full-time employer and part-time mentor of Augie March during March's high school years; paralytic schemer, bluffer, survivor, womanizer, and philosopher of high aspirations in Saul Bellow's *The Adventures of Augie March*.

Dr. Isidore (Iz) Einsam. Psychiatrist, husband of Glory Green, and lover of Katherine Cattleman in Alison Lurie's *The Nowhere City*.

Harald von Einzeedle. Husband of Maija von Einzeedle in Nicholas Delbanco's *Small Rain*.

James von Einzeedle. Son of Maija and Harald von Einzeedle in Nicholas Delbanco's *Small Rain*.

Maija von Einzeedle. Former wife of Harald von Einzeedle and lover of Anthony Hope-Harding in Nicholas Delbanco's *Small Rain*.

Thomas von Einzeedle. Son of Harald and Maija von Einzeedle in Nicholas Delbanco's *Small Rain*.

Eisen. Ex-husband of Shula Sammler; toeless, handsome, mentally unstable artist manqué who gleefully smashes the head of a black pickpocket with his art objects in Saul Bellow's *Mr. Sammler's Planet*.

Norman Eisenberg. White lover of Eloise McLindon, unsuspecting father of Clair Hunter, and self-appointed moral guide of David Hunter in Hal Bennett's *The Black Wine*.

Ruth Eisenbraun. English instructor and Lanier Club adviser at a Virginia women's college; arranges for Henry Bech's visit and offers to sleep with him in John Updike's *Bech: A Book*.

Dwight David Eisenhower. President of the United States and most recent incarnation of Uncle Sam Slick in Robert Coover's *The Public Burning*.

Gus Eisman. "Button King" who is "interested in educating" his mistress, Lorelei Lee; she remains attentive to him throughout her adventures and does not drop him until she marries Henry Spoffard in Anita Loos's *"Gentlemen Prefer Blondes."*

Eric Eisner. Columbia University graduate, former journalist, and current teacher in the New York City literacy program; friend of Jack Borgardes and lover of Marie Curtin; narrator of Phillip Lopate's *Confessions of Summer*.

Charles Francis (Charley) Eitel. Movie director who eventually testifies before an antisubversive congressional committee in Norman Mailer's *The Deer Park*.

Pepe El Culito. See Salvador Hassan O'Leary.

El Hombre Invisible. See William Lee.

Eladio. Member of Pablo's partisan group in Ernest Hemingway's *For Whom the Bell Tolls*.

Elaine. Lover of Jesse; they meet in a Monterey bar in Richard Brautigan's *A Confederate General from Big Sur*.

Elan. "Soul at the seventh aspect" of Eleanor Norton in Robert Coover's *The Origin of the Brunists*.

Donald Merwin (Trashcan Man) Elbert. Pyromaniac and devoted servant to Randall Flagg; inadvertently destroys Flagg's forces, thus saving The Free Zone, in Stephen King's *The Stand*.

Elder. See Nung En.

Avis Criley Elderman. Sister of Bradd Criley; cares for Jimmy Timberlane in Sinclair Lewis's *Cass Timberlane*.

Mr. Eldridge. Maternal grandfather of Charlotte Temple; despite his grief at the loss of Charlotte, he manages to enjoy her child for several years in Susanna Rowson's *Charlotte*.

Eleanor. Friend of Gerda Mulvaney in Chicago; tells Jane Clifford the story of her marriage and her husband's new fiancée in Gail Godwin's *The Odd Woman*.

Benjamin Eliezer. Son of Jacob Eliezer and Wanda Bzik; grows up in Jerusalem and becomes a teacher in the yeshiva and the father of three children in Isaac Bashevis Singer's *The Slave*.

Jacob (Reb Jacob) Eliezer. Jewish slave of Polish peasants after the Chmielnicki massacres, in which his wife and children were murdered; falls in love with Wanda Bzik and lives in Pilitz with her as husband and wife until she dies in childbirth; dies and is buried next to her two decades later in Isaac Bashevis Singer's *The Slave*.

Elijah. Mysterious figure who warns Ishmael and Queequeg about Ahab in Herman Melville's *Moby-Dick*.

Elinor. Married woman who leaves her family to join Francis Starwick in France; supports Starwick financially and is erroneously thought to be his mistress in Thomas Wolfe's *Of Time and the River*.

Elizabeth. Part-time prostitute and Lee Mellon's part-time lover; visits Mellon and Jesse at Big Sur in Richard Brautigan's *A Confederate General from Big Sur*.

Elizabeth I. Queen of England in George Garrett's *Death of the Fox*.

Colonel Hakim Félix (Bini, Happy) Ellelloû. Ill-fated, American-trained creator and dictator-president of the imaginary African nation of Kush; struggles with the meaning of freedom and identity in John Updike's *The Coup*.

Maggie (Mag) Ellersley. Friend of the Marshall family; wife of Henderson Neal and then of Peter Marshall; successful businesswoman after Peter's death in Jessie Redmon Fauset's *There Is Confusion*.

Tex Ellery. See Dick Gibson.

Bob Ellgood. Robust brother of Geneva Ellgood; farms scientifically and takes an interest in Dorinda Oakley in Ellen Glasgow's *Barren Ground*.

Geneva Ellgood. Wealthy, ugly blonde whose family pressures Jason Greylock to marry her after she claims they were engaged in New York; drowns on Dorinda Oakley's wedding day in Ellen Glasgow's *Barren Ground*.

James (Jim) Ellgood. Father of Geneva and Bob Ellgood; experimental and successful stock farmer who forces Jason Greylock to marry Geneva in Ellen Glasgow's *Barren Ground*.

Francis Bosworth (Frank) Ellinger. Handsome bachelor of ambiguous morals, lover of Marian Forrester during her husband's illness, and husband of Constance Ogden in Willa Cather's *A Lost Lady*.

Ed Elliott. Boyhood friend of Niel Herbert, whom Elliott tells, much later, about the final years and death of Marian Forrester, in Willa Cather's *A Lost Lady*.

Jim Elliott. Secretary of the West Condon Chamber of Commerce in Robert Coover's *The Origin of the Brunists*.

Peter (Spider) Elliott. New York fashion photographer who, after being fired from various jobs, moves to California with his partner, Valentine O'Neill, to run Scruples, Billy Ikehorn Orsini's boutique, in Judith Krantz's *Scruples*.

Phillip J. (Bertrand, Phil) Elliott. Dallas Cowboy wide receiver and loner who is released from the team for "behavior detrimental to professional football" in Peter Gent's *North Dallas Forty*.

Edward Elton (Ed, Eddie) Ellis. Worker at Red Cloud Agency and friend of gamblers and horse thieves; husband of Morissa Kirk in Mari Sandoz's *Miss Morissa*.

John Ellis. Neurosurgeon who performs the stage-three operation on Harold Benson in Michael Crichton's *The Terminal Man*.

Morissa Kirk Ellis. See Morissa Kirk.

Puss Ellis. Town's "loose woman" in Reynolds Price's *A Generous Man*.

Steve Ellis. Television producer and "sugar daddy" to Ida Scott in James Baldwin's *Another Country*.

Alice Ellish. Roommate of Natalie Novotny in Thomas Berger's *Who Is Teddy Villanova?*

Kitty Ellison. Cousin of Richard Ellison; befriends Isabel March in William Dean Howells's *Their Wedding Journey.*

Lucy Ellison. Classmate of Mollie Ainslie; teacher at Red Wing school, until her marriage to an army officer, in Albion W. Tourgee's *Bricks without Straw.*

Richard and Fanny Ellison. Married couple traveling across New York and Canada in William Dean Howells's *Their Wedding Journey.*

Ted Elmer. See Dick Gibson.

William Elphinstone. Master-at-arm's mate on HMS *Bounty* who is set adrift with Captain Bligh in Charles Nordhoff and James Norman Hall's *Mutiny on the Bounty*; the ordeal at sea causes his mind to snap in *Men against the Sea.*

Elsa. Young German woman living with Henry Miller and Boris in Henry Miller's *Tropic of Cancer.*

Ted Elson. See Dick Gibson.

Elspeth. Haglike mother of Zora; allows Harry Cresswell and his cronies to carouse with the young girls in her cabin in W. E. B. Du Bois's *The Quest of the Silver Fleece.*

Elvira. See Elvira Moody.

Elvira Jane. Great granddaughter of Veenie Goodwin and, through an affair with Robinson Mayfield, mother of Rover Walters in Reynolds Price's *The Surface of Earth.*

Elzbieta (Teta Elzbieta). Stepmother of Ona Rudkus in Upton Sinclair's *The Jungle.*

Mr. Ember. Obscure scholar, translator of Shakespeare, and friend of Adam Krug, with whom he carries on a lengthy conversation about *Hamlet*; later arrested for his association with Krug in Vladimir Nabokov's *Bend Sinister.*

Andrew Emerson. Son of Pamela Emerson; one of seven Emerson siblings and twin of the ill-fated Timothy Emerson; brother-in-law of Elizabeth Abbott in Anne Tyler's *The Clock Winder.*

Fortune Emerson. Half sister of Captain Morgan Montgomery and strict guardian of Ellen Montgomery when Ellen's parents go abroad in Susan Warner's *The Wide, Wide World.*

Gillespie Emerson. See Elizabeth Abbott.

Margaret Emerson. Daughter of Pamela Emerson; one of seven Emerson siblings and sister-in-law of Elizabeth Abbott in Anne Tyler's *The Clock Winder.*

Matthew Emerson. Newspaperman; son of Pamela Emerson and, eventually, husband of Elizabeth Abbott and father of their two children in Anne Tyler's *The Clock Winder.*

Pamela Emerson. Baltimore matron and mother of four sons and three daughters; saved from neglect by Elizabeth Abbott, who becomes her daughter-in-law, in Anne Tyler's *The Clock Winder.*

Peter Emerson. Vietnam veteran; youngest child of Pamela Emerson and brother-in-law of Elizabeth Abbott in Anne Tyler's *The Clock Winder.*

Timothy Emerson. Medical student who shoots himself; son of Pamela Emerson and twin of Andrew Emerson in Anne Tyler's *The Clock Winder.*

Enoch Emery. Young man with "wise blood" who steals a mummy from the zoo museum to be the "new Jesus" for Hazel Motes's Church Without Christ; later disappears wearing a gorilla suit in Flannery O'Connor's *Wise Blood.*

Stan Emery. Would-be architect who feels imprisoned within the artlessness of the buildings and the intellectual stagnation of New York; burns the building in which he lives in a suicidal gesture in John Dos Passos's *Manhattan Transfer.*

Emil. Quick-tempered, restless boy in Louisa May Alcott's *Little Men.*

Emile. Taxi driver, friend of the French consul, and painter from Marseilles in Anaïs Nin's *Collages.*

George Emlen. Obnoxious businessman whom Timothy Colt represents in several corporate transactions; as trustee of Emlen family holdings, Colt helps George by concealing the true value of stock in a textile firm, thus breaking his trust to other family members, in Louis Auchincloss's *The Great World and Timothy Colt.*

Emma. Buxom daughter of The Dead Father in Donald Barthelme's *The Dead Father.*

Emma. Mean-spirited, one-eyed mother of Waldo in Paul Theroux's *Waldo.*

Emma. Mulatto daughter of Harry Cresswell and Bertie; grows into a fine young woman with Zora's guidance in W. E. B. Du Bois's *The Quest of the Silver Fleece.*

Emma (Em). Ibo woman who can heal herself and shift her shape and thus live indefinitely in Octavia E. Butler's *Mind of My Mind.*

Emmanuel. Mexican gardener who, upon being caught having sex with Candy Christian, attacks her father with a trowel in Terry Southern and Mason Hoffenberg's *Candy*.

Emmeline. Beautiful young slave bought by Simon Legree to be his mistress; escapes with Cassy to Canada and then to Europe in Harriet Beecher Stowe's *Uncle Tom's Cabin*.

Alonzo D. (Lon) Emmerich. Corrupt criminal lawyer who commits suicide rather than face exposure and prison in William Riley Burnett's *The Asphalt Jungle*.

Emmy. Housekeeper for the Mahons; loves Donald Mahon before and after his injuries in William Faulkner's *Soldiers' Pay*.

Alberta Emory. Gypsy-like mother of Amos, Saul, Linus, and Julian Emory in Anne Tyler's *Earthly Possessions*.

Amos Emory. Musician brother of Saul Emory and would-be lover of Saul's wife, Charlotte Emory, in Anne Tyler's *Earthly Possessions*.

Catherine (Selinda) Emory. Daughter of Charlotte and Saul Emory who adopts the name and identity of an imaginary playmate in Anne Tyler's *Earthly Possessions*.

Charlotte Ames Emory. Wife of Saul Emory, mother of Selinda Emory, and foster mother of Jiggs Emory; photographer whose longing to travel is fulfilled only when she is kidnapped by Jake Simms in Anne Tyler's *Earthly Possessions*.

Jiggs Emory. Foster son of Charlotte and Saul Emory in Anne Tyler's *Earthly Possessions*.

Julian Emory. Shiftless but mechanically talented brother of Saul Emory and brother-in-law of Charlotte Emory in Anne Tyler's *Earthly Possessions*.

Linus Emory. Carver of dollhouse furniture; brother of Saul Emory and brother-in-law of Charlotte Emory in Anne Tyler's *Earthly Possessions*.

Saul Emory. Bible-toting pastor of Holy Basis Church in Clarion, Maryland; oldest and gravest of Alberta Emory's sons; husband of Charlotte Emory, father of Selinda Emory, and foster father of Jiggs Emory in Anne Tyler's *Earthly Possessions*.

Empire State. Townsman who never speaks; member of a racial revenge group called the Seven Days in Toni Morrison's *Song of Solomon*.

Dane Tarrant Empson. Former magazine writer, wife of John Empson, and stepmother of Robin Empson in Gail Godwin's *The Perfectionists*.

John Dominick Empson. Unconventional psychotherapist, husband of Dane Empson, and father, by an earlier liaison, of Robin Empson in Gail Godwin's *The Perfectionists*.

Robin (Robin Redbreast) Empson. Three-year-old illegitimate son of John Empson; silent child who engages in a battle of wills with his new stepmother, Dane Empson, in Gail Godwin's *The Perfectionists*.

Governor Endicott. Chief magistrate of the Puritan settlement at Salem; banishes Charles Brown in Lydia Maria Child's *Hobomok*.

Henrik Endor. Mathematician for Field Experiment Number One who becomes disillusioned and retreats to a hole in the ground for the rest of his life in Don DeLillo's *Ratner's Star*.

Endymion. Slave of Mildred Lindsay in John Pendleton Kennedy's *Horse-Shoe Robinson*.

Lou Engel. Lover of classical music and steak; attempts to save J. Henry Waugh's job in Robert Coover's *The Universal Baseball Association, Inc., J. Henry Waugh, Prop.*

Martin Engle. English professor who becomes Theresa Dunn's first lover in Judith Rossner's *Looking for Mr. Goodbar*.

Caroline Walker English. Wife of Julian English in John O'Hara's *Appointment in Samarra*.

Julian McHenry English. Unhappy Gibbsville Cadillac dealer; protagonist in John O'Hara's *Appointment in Samarra*; also appears in *A Rage to Live*.

William Dilworth English. Prominent Gibbsville doctor and father of Julian English in John O'Hara's *Appointment in Samarra*; appears in *Ten North Frederick*.

Enid. Blonde lesbian prostitute who anticipates becoming Mina Morgan's next victim when the disintegration of Peter Leland is completed in Fred Chappell's *Dagon*.

Donny Ennis. Mentally handicapped boy befriended by Tim Neumiller in Larry Woiwode's *Beyond the Bedroom Wall*.

Enos Enoch. First Grand Tutor of New Tammany College whose influence has weakened in John Barth's *Giles Goat-Boy*.

Bartholomew Enright. Broadway producer to whom Lee Youngdahl takes his play in Mark Harris's *Wake Up, Stupid*.

Father Enright. Confessor of the young Joe Sandwich in Peter De Vries's *The Vale of Laughter*.

Reverend Wilbur Entwistle. See Stingo.

Envelove. Head of the legal department at Olympia Studios in Ludwig Bemelmans's *Dirty Eddie*.

Oberst Enzian. Leader of the Herero group known as the Schwarzkommando, who attempt to build a rocket in occupied Germany; half brother of Vaslav Tchitcherine and former lover of Lieutenant Weissmann in Thomas Pynchon's *Gravity's Rainbow*.

Jaja Enzkwu. African diplomat assassinated for uncovering a CIA contingency plan for removing the minority population of the United States into concentration camps in John A. Williams's *The Man Who Cried I Am*.

Ephum. Loyal slave in Winston Churchill's *The Crisis*.

Horst von Epp. Head of the Department of Propaganda and Press in Warsaw after Nazi occupation; friend of Christopher de Monti in Leon Uris's *Mila 18*.

Reverend Alexander Eppes. Backwoods preacher who buys Nat Turner from Samuel Turner and hires him out to his congregation; eventually sells him back into slavery in William Styron's *The Confessions of Nat Turner*.

Nathan Epstein. Philosophy professor at Marlowe College; campus favorite whose students refer to him as "God" in Richard Yates's *Disturbing the Peace*.

Margherita (Greta, Gretel) Erdmann. German actress and star of Gerhardt von Göll's semi-pornographic horror films; sometime lover of Tyrone Slothrop in Thomas Pynchon's *Gravity's Rainbow*.

Clem Ergot. Brother of Jody Ergot; oldtime vaudeville hoofer who works as a Russian agent to represent the United States in an unfavorable light in William S. Burroughs's *Naked Lunch*.

Jody Ergot. Brother of Clem Ergot; with him, works as a Russian agent to discredit the United States in William S. Burroughs's *Naked Lunch*.

Lord Eric. Lover of Ida Farange during her marriage to Sir Claude in Henry James's *What Maisie Knew*.

Lars Ericson. Handsome merchant marine who leaves Emily Grimes for a male lover in Richard Yates's *Easter Parade*.

Augusta Erlich. Mother of a college friend of Claude Wheeler; befriends Wheeler with adoration and introduces him to a social and cultural arena in Willa Cather's *One of Ours*.

Jan Erlone. Communist party member and boyfriend of Mary Dalton; secures an attorney to defend Bigger Thomas after Thomas is charged with Mary's murder in Richard Wright's *Native Son*.

Jo Erring. Uncle and closest friend of Ned Westlock; divorces Mateel Shepherd and kills her second husband, Clinton Bragg; commits suicide in E. W. Howe's *The Story of a Country Town*.

Cedric (Ceddie, Lord Fauntleroy) Errol. American-born grandson of the Earl of Dorincourt; returns to England as his grandfather's heir in Frances Hodgson Burnett's *Little Lord Fauntleroy*.

Captain Cedric Errol. Third son of the Earl of Dorincourt; marries an American, fathers Cedric Errol, and dies young in Frances Hodgson Burnett's *Little Lord Fauntleroy*.

Mrs. Cedric (Dearest) Errol. American widow of Captain Cedric Errol and mother of Cedric Errol in Frances Hodgson Burnett's *Little Lord Fauntleroy*.

John Arthur Molyneux (Earl of Dorincourt) Errol. British nobleman who disinherits his son yet brings his grandson, Cedric Errol, to England as his heir in Frances Hodgson Burnett's *Little Lord Fauntleroy*.

Henshaw Erwin. Second husband of Josephine Erwin; eccentric Englishman fascinated by the United States in William Dean Howells's *The Lady of the Aroostook*.

Josephine Erwin. Aunt of Lydia Blood; invites Lydia to visit her in Italy in William Dean Howells's *The Lady of the Aroostook*.

Joaquín Escalona. Mayor of a Mexican village; captures Miguel and Miguel's bandits in B. Traven's *The Treasure of the Sierra Madre*.

Baron Carola von Eschenbach. Practical joker who once worked in Hollywood; claims to have been wealthy, but is now broke and has a venereal disease in Henry Miller's *Black Spring*.

Kenneth Escott. Newspaper reporter with liberal political views; marries Verona Babbitt in Sinclair Lewis's *Babbitt*.

Verona Babbitt Escott. See Verona Babbitt.

Frank Esel. Painter summering in Norwood who, rejected by Rose Wentworth, becomes a superior artist before becoming a Union colonel in Barton Cathcart's regiment during the Civil War in Henry Ward Beecher's *Norwood*.

Esme. Schizophrenic model for Wyatt Gwyon in William Gaddis's *The Recognitions*.

Jean Espagnol. Soldier of fortune who identifies Arnaud du Tilh in Janet Lewis's *The Wife of Martin Guerre*.

Princess Alix d'Espoli. Member of the Cabala; brilliant conversationalist who, although married, falls in love with many younger men, including James Blair, in Thornton Wilder's *The Cabala*.

Elena Esposito. Mistress of Charles Eitel and later of Marion Faye in Norman Mailer's *The Deer Park*.

Constance (Connie) Estabrook. Aunt of Margery Estabrook; stops interfering with Stephen Grendon's love for Margery when he points out some of Connie's son's clandestine activities in August Derleth's *Evening in Spring*.

Margery Estabrook. Protestant girlfriend of Stephen Grendon in August Derleth's *Evening in Spring*.

Esteban. Identical twin of Mañuel; goes to sea with Captain Alvarado to cope with his grief over Mañuel's death; dies in the fall of the bridge in Thornton Wilder's *The Bridge of San Luis Rey*.

Estelle. Secretary at a New York export firm with whom Paul Hobbes is unable to consummate an affair in John Clellon Holmes's *Go*.

Estelle. Sister of Mildred Sutton in Reynolds Price's *A Long and Happy Life*.

Esther. Lover of Gabriel Grimes and mother of Royal; dies in childbirth in James Baldwin's *Go Tell It on the Mountain*.

Princess Lili Estradina. Eminent figure in Paris's Faubourg Saint Germain society; lively companion of Undine Spragg and cousin of Raymond de Chelles in Edith Wharton's *The Custom of the Country*.

Eteoneus. Gatekeeper who believes that men should be brutelike and that women should submit to men in John Erskine's *The Private Life of Helen of Troy*.

Etta. Spoiled but attractive fifteen-year-old niece of Joseph; her taunts lead Joseph to family violence in Saul Bellow's *Dangling Man*.

Eugenio. Courier traveling with the Millers in Henry James's *Daisy Miller*.

Eunice. Mother of Tomasina and wife of Thucydides in William Faulkner's *Go Down, Moses*.

Eusabio. Navajo friend of Bishop Latour; appeals to Latour to help the Navajos, who are being driven from their land, in Willa Cather's *Death Comes for the Archbishop*.

Eusebia. Roman empress who intercedes with her husband, Constantius, on behalf of Julian in Gore Vidal's *Julian*.

Kate Eustis. Wife of Luther Eustis; narrates part of Shelby Foote's *Follow Me Down*.

Luther Dade (Luke Gowan) Eustis. Religious fundamentalist, murderer of Beulah Ross, and central narrator of Shelby Foote's *Follow Me Down*.

Eva. See Eva Medina Canada.

Brownie Evans. Son of Lije and Rebecca Evans, husband of Mercy McBee, and capable sidekick of Dick Summers in A. B. Guthrie's *The Way West*.

Harold Evans. First husband of Lucy Henley; archaeologist working in Kenya; dies young in Shirley Ann Grau's *Evidence of Love*.

Janice Evans. Bride of Jarvis Addams; Frankie Addams disrupts their wedding in CarsonMcCullers's *The Member of the Wedding*.

June Evans. See June.

Lije Evans. Missouri farmer who travels to Oregon with a wagon train; husband of Rebecca Evans and father of Brownie Evans in A. B. Guthrie's *The Way West*.

Lucy Evans. See Lucy Roundtree Evans Henley.

M (Em, Thelma Postgate) Evans. Eccentric bald woman who has rejected her former name; hires Francesca Bolt as an amanuensis in Gail Godwin's *Glass People*.

Rebecca (Becky) Evans. Wife of Lije Evans and mother of Brownie Evans in A. B. Guthrie's *The Way West*.

Ricardo S. (Rick) Evans. Black nationalist figure in Ed Bullins's *The Reluctant Rapist*.

Mrs. Eveleigh. Wealthy plantation widow whom Captain Porgy contemplates marrying in William Gilmore Simms's *Woodcraft*.

Eveline. Daughter of Hugh and Catherine, younger sister of Meredith, twin sister of Dolores in John Hawkes's *The Blood Oranges*.

Floyd Evenwrite. Bumbling local union leader in conflict with the Stamper family in Ken Kesey's *Sometimes a Great Notion*.

Elwood Everett. Crass businessman and father of Richard Everett in Joyce Carol Oates's *Expensive*

People.

Farah Everett. Wife of Junior Everett; leaves him for Mabry Jenkins in Peter Gent's *Texas Celebrity Turkey Trot.*

Jace Everett. Wealthy Texan whose business empire includes the radio station where Mabry Jenkins works, the chemical company that Titus Bean is trying to expose, and the celebrity tournaments that George Billings oversees in Peter Gent's *Texas Celebrity Turkey Trot.*

Natashya Romanov (Nada, Tashya) Everett. Mother of Richard Everett; self-centered, destructive woman and object of her son's murderous fantasies in Joyce Carol Oates's *Expensive People.*

Richard (Dickie) Everett. Son of Nada and Elwood Everett; teenaged memoirist who recounts his childhood experiences in the affluent suburbs of Detroit in Joyce Carol Oates's *Expensive People.*

Jace (Junior) Everett, Jr.. Son of Jace Everett; leaves his wife and son for Stephano Valentine, who helps him perpetuate a massive swindle, in Peter Gent's *Texas Celebrity Turkey Trot.*

Jason (Trey) Everett III. Son of Junior and Farah Everett; watches television no matter what is happening around him in Peter Gent's *Texas Celebrity Turkey Trot.*

Avis Cunningham (Felice Van Verdighan) Everhard. Daughter of John Cunningham and wife of Ernest Everhard; author and narrator of a book, published in the distant future, that chronicles the rise of the Iron Heel in Jack London's *The Iron Heel.*

Ernest Everhard. Martyr of the anti-Oligarchy revolution who foresees the rise of the Iron Heel; husband of Avis Cunningham Everhard in Jack London's *The Iron Heel.*

Eli Everjohn. Private detective from Caro Mill, Maryland; hired to locate Daniel Peck's missing half brother, Caleb, in Anne Tyler's *Searching for Caleb.*

Cudjo Evers. Prosperous blue-collar worker and former member of the black high school athletic team and neighborhood gang gathering for a birthday testimonial honoring Chappie Davis in John A.

Williams's *The Junior Bachelor Society.*

Vemon Dilbert (Blue Nose) Evers. Experienced sailor aboard the *Lillias Eden* and sometime drunkard; left by Captain Raib Avers in Nicaragua when Evers leaves the boat overnight in Peter Matthiessen's *Far Tortuga.*

Mark Eversley. Great tragic actor and mentor of Olivia Lattimore in Mary Austin's *A Woman of Genius.*

Samantha-Marie (Sam) Everton. Expatriate American who has affairs with Dave Weintraub, Hill Gallagher, and Harry Gallagher in James Jones's *The Merry Month of May.*

Mayella Violet Ewell. Abused daughter of Bob Ewell; accuses Tom Robinson of rape in Harper Lee's *To Kill a Mockingbird.*

Richard (Dick, Baldy) Ewell. Southern general whose recent loss of a leg affects his self-confidence in Michael Shaara's *The Killer Angels.*

Robert E. Lee (Bob) Ewell. Father of Mayella Ewell, accuser of Tom Robinson, and attempted murderer of Scout and Jem Finch in Harper Lee's *To Kill a Mockingbird.*

Walter Ewell. Hunter in William Faulkner's *Go Down, Moses*; *The Mansion*; and *The Reivers.*

Miss Ewing. Longtime legal secretary who becomes mentally unstable in William Maxwell's *Time Will Darken It.*

Ewka. Daughter of Makar and first sexual partner of the narrator; also has sex with goats and her brother, Anton, in Jerzy Kosinski's *The Painted Bird.*

Mr. Eyebright. Prominent Union man to whom Ralph Kirkwood confesses the details of Jerry Hunt's murder; opposes the Ku Klux Klan; helps tend to the dying Comfort Servosse in Albion W. Tourgee's *A Fool's Errand.*

Michaelis Ezana. Fastidious minister of the interior under Colonel Ellelloû; specializes in statistics and regulations and loves forbidden luxuries from the West; imprisoned by Ellelloû, he escapes to help overthrow the government; becomes the lover of Angelica Gibbs in John Updike's *The Coup.*

F

Gregario Fabbisogno. One of two carabinieri who attack and then release Jacopo; later beats Adeppi in John Hawkes's *The Goose on the Grave.*

Faber. Former professor of English who teaches Guy Montag about books and helps him escape arrest in Ray Bradbury's *Fahrenheit 451.*

Fabio. Troubled friend of Paolo; swindled by a corrupt Vatican-connected priest; Paolo wants Mrs. Karen Stone to help Fabio financially in Tennessee Williams's *The Roman Spring of Mrs. Stone.*

Moses Fable. President of Olympia Studios who suffers with Dirty Eddie's owners until the piglet becomes a box-office sensation in Ludwig Bemelmans's *Dirty Eddie.*

Ben Fagan. Poet, Buddhist, and drinking companion of Jack Duluoz in Jack Kerouac's *Big Sur.*

Battle (Fire-eater) Fairchild. Father of the bride, Dabney Fairchild, husband of Ellen Fairchild, and owner of the Delta plantation Shellmound in Eudora Welty's *Delta Wedding.*

Dabney (Miss Dab) Fairchild. Daughter of Battle and Ellen Fairchild; seventeen-year-old bride in Eudora Welty's *Delta Wedding.*

David Fairchild. Fashionable interior decorator known for his acerbic wit; confidant of Eileen Shallcross in Louis Auchincloss's *The Great World and Timothy Colt.*

Dawson Fairchild. Novelist who attends the yacht party in William Faulkner's *Mosquitoes.*

Denis Fairchild. Brother of Battle Fairchild and father of Maureen Fairchild; killed in France during World War I in Eudora Welty's *Delta Wedding.*

Ellen Dabney Fairchild. Pregnant wife of Battle Fairchild and Virginia-born mother of eight, including the bride, in Eudora Welty's *Delta Wedding.*

George Fairchild. Memphis lawyer, youngest brother of Battle Fairchild, and best man in the wedding of his niece Dabney Fairchild; risks his life to free his niece Maureen Fairchild's foot from the path of an oncoming train, in Eudora Welty's *Delta Wedding.*

India Primrose Fairchild. Nine-year-old daughter of Battle and Ellen Fairchild and first cousin of Laura McRaven in Eudora Welty's *Delta Wedding.*

Jim Allen Fairchild. Unmarried deaf sister of Battle Fairchild; lives at the Grove plantation in Eudora Welty's *Delta Wedding.*

Maureen Fairchild. Nine-year-old daughter of Denis Fairchild living with the Battle Fairchild family; suffers from brain damage and impaired speech after her mother drops her on her head in infancy in Eudora Welty's *Delta Wedding.*

Primrose Fairchild. Unmarried sister of Battle Fairchild; lives at the Grove plantation in Eudora Welty's *Delta Wedding.*

Roberta Reid (Robbie) Fairchild. Wife of George Fairchild; leaves her husband but returns to him at Shellmound before the wedding in Eudora Welty's *Delta Wedding.*

Roy Fairchild. Eight-year-old son of Battle and Ellen Fairchild; pushes his cousin Laura McRaven into the Yazoo River in Eudora Welty's *Delta Wedding.*

Shelley Fairchild. Eighteen-year-old oldest child of Battle and Ellen Fairchild; plans to go to Europe with an aunt after her sister Dabney's wedding in Eudora Welty's *Delta Wedding.*

Sir Thomas (Black Tom) Fairfax. Second-in-command to Oliver Cromwell at the Battle of Naseby and one of those present when Johnny Church and Thankful Perkins are condemned to death and executed in Mary Lee Settle's *Prisons.*

Grace Fairfield. Writer for *Chatelaine West* who wants to interview Francesca Bolt in Gail Godwin's *Glass People.*

Laura Fairford. Sister of Ralph Marvell and member of one of the old families of New York's Washington Square in Edith Wharton's *The Custom of the Country.*

Father Fairing. Jesuit priest who attempts to convert the rats in the New York sewers of the 1930s; keeps a journal which mentions a specific rat, Veronica, whom he refers to as V.; also involved with Sydney Stencil and Veronica Manganese in the politics of Valetta, Malta, in 1919, in Thomas Pynchon's *V.*

Ulysses S. (Mistah Baseball) Fairsmith. Devout Christian manager of the Ruppert Mundys and baseball missionary to Africa; dies in the dugout after a stupid play by one of his players in Philip Roth's *The Great American Novel.*

Helen Fairwood. American tourist in Egypt; main character in H. D.'s *Palimpsest.*

Fakahau. Father of Marama, husband of Mata, and chief of the island of Manukura; shelters his fugitive son-in-law Terangi; dies during the hurricane in Charles Nordhoff and James Norman Hall's *The Hurricane.*

Julian Falck. Amherst College student and boyfriend of Sissy Jessup; sent to a concentration camp for having infiltrated the Minute Men as a member of the New Underground in Sinclair Lewis's *It Can't Happen Here.*

Reverend Falck. Episcopal minister and grandfather of Julian Falck; beaten to death in a concentration camp in Sinclair Lewis's *It Can't Happen Here.*

Sharon Falconer. Evangelist and faith healer whose assistant is Elmer Gantry; killed in a fire during a revival in Sinclair Lewis's *Elmer Gantry.*

Harley Falk. Itinerant cobbler with a blind horse; informs Mary Fowler of Jerry Fowler's affair with Norah Sharon in Walter D. Edmonds's *Erie Water.*

Ernestine (Erna) Falkenstein. Niece and caretaker of Ulrich Falkenstein, sister of Hildegaard Falkenstein, and lover of Sean O'Sullivan; bears the brunt of Nazi guilt and commits suicide in Leon Uris's *Armageddon.*

Hildegaard (Hilde Diehl) Falkenstein. Niece of Ulrich Falkenstein, sister of Ernestine Falkenstein, and lover of Scott Davidson; reformed prostitute from post-World War II Berlin in Leon Uris's *Armageddon.*

Ulrich Falkenstein. Uncle of Ernestine and Hildegaard Falkenstein; survivor of Schwabenwald; pre-Nazi head of the Social Democrats; post-World War II head of the new Democratic party in Berlin in Leon Uris's *Armageddon.*

Mike Fallopian. Member of the Peter Pinguid Society, involved with an alternate mail system, in Thomas Pynchon's *The Crying of Lot 49.*

Falsgrave. Clergyman and frustrated suitor of Mary Glendinning in Herman Melville's *Pierre.*

Grace Fanhall. Socialite pursued and won by Billie Hawker; gives him three violets in Stephen Crane's *The Third Violet.*

Fannie Mae. Wife of Bukka Doopeyduk; divorces him in Ishmael Reed's *The Free-Lance Pallbearers.*

Lieutenant Tod Fanning. Shipmate of Claude Wheeler aboard the *Anchises*; contracts pneumonia, but survives because of Wheeler's care, in Willa Cather's *One of Ours.*

Shirley Fanon. Attorney for the condominium where Marshall Preminger lives after his father's death in *The Condominium*, a novella in Stanley Elkin's *Searches and Seizures.*

Fanshawe. Serious Harley College student; loves Ellen Langton and rescues her from Butler, but does not marry her, in Nathaniel Hawthorne's *Fanshawe.*

Doctor Faraday. Large and genial New York surgeon who rescues Dorinda Oakley after she steps in front of a horse-drawn vehicle; gives Dorinda work and teaches her to think biologically in Ellen Glasgow's *Barren Ground.*

Beale Farange. Father of Maisie Farange; materialistic, showy man with lecherous tendencies; husband of both Ida Farange and Mrs. Beale Farange in Henry James's *What Maisie Knew.*

Mrs. Beale (Miss Overmore) Farange. Governess of Maisie Farange; involved with Sir Claude in Henry James's *What Maisie Knew.*

Ida Farange. Mother of Maisie Farange; similar to her husband Beale Farange in being materialistic and lascivious, but she is also moody and charming; wife of both Farange and Sir Claude in Henry James's *What Maisie Knew.*

Maisie Farange. Child who "saw too much" while in her innocence, acting as a cover for many adulterous affairs in Henry James's *What Maisie Knew.*

Farani. Husband of Hitia and son-in-law of Tavi and Marunga; survives the hurricane in Charles Nordhoff and James Norman Hall's *The Hurricane.*

Lou Farbstein. Cynical and fast-talking police beat reporter for the *World* newspaper in William Riley Burnett's *The Asphalt Jungle.*

Gertrude (Gerty) Farish. Destitute cousin of Lawrence Selden; remains a loyal friend to Lily Bart throughout Edith Wharton's *The House of Mirth.*

Farley. Computer specialist at Autotronics who allows Robert Morris to examine Harold Benson's desk in Michael Crichton's *The Terminal Man.*

Jean Farlow. First cousin and wife of John Farlow and closest friend in Ramsdale of Charlotte Haze; with her husband, attends the Haze-Humbert wedding in Vladimir Nabokov's *Lolita.*

John Farlow. Husband of Jean Farlow; manages the Haze property after Charlotte Haze dies until the death of his own wife in Vladimir Nabokov's *Lolita.*

Gladys Farmer. Poor but extravagant high school teacher who is pursued by Bayliss Wheeler in Willa Cather's *One of Ours.*

Nate Farmer. Tough, young black Los Angeles police detective in Joseph Wambaugh's *The Black Marble*.

Jeff Farnley. Best friend of alleged murder victim Larry Kinkaid, employee of Harley Drew, and focal point of the lynch mob in Walter Van Tilburg Clark's *The Ox-Bow Incident*.

Hubert H. (Skeeter) Farnsworth. Black radical Vietnam veteran arrested for drug pushing; escapes and hides at Rabbit Angstrom's house in John Updike's *Rabbit Redux*.

Virgie Farnum. Friend of Silla Boyce; unlike most Barbadian women, has pale skin and gray eyes in Paule Marshall's *Brown Girl, Brownstones*.

Cecily Saunders Farr. Wife of George Farr, after having been engaged to Donald Mahon, in William Faulkner's *Soldiers' Pay*.

George Farr. Georgian who marries Cecily Saunders in William Faulkner's *Soldiers' Pay*.

M. J. Farr. District Attorney under whom Ned Beaumont ostensibly operates as a special investigator in Dashiell Hammett's *The Glass Key*.

Captain John Farrago. Bachelor, often disappointed in love, who travels between Pittsburgh and Philadelphia with his servant Teague Oregan, to whom Farrago administers lessons in servile behavior, in Hugh Henry Brackenridge's *Modern Chivalry*.

Eben Farragut. Selfish brother who hates Zeke Farragut from childhood and who even in death is the agent of Zeke's betrayal in John Cheever's *Falconer*.

Ezekiel (Zeke) Farragut. University professor and drug addict who accidentally kills his insufferable brother, Eben Farragut; achieves a new vision of life based on his association with other convicts in Falconer prison in John Cheever's *Falconer*.

Marcia Farragut. Narcissistic wife of Zeke Farragut whose contempt for him is one of the destructive forces in his life in John Cheever's *Falconer*.

Farrell. Northern Irish Protestant and mercenary soldier in Jamaica, where he masterminds the raid on the Rasta camp; rival of Marshall Pearl in Mark Helprin's *Refiner's Fire*.

Rachel Mary Conyngham Farrell. Young Irish girl, twice married, and enduring love of Zeke Gurevich in William Herrick's *The Itinerant*.

Simon Xavier Farrell. Sickly photographer, painter, and sculptor; first husband of Rachel Farrell in William Herrick's *The Itinerant*.

Mrs. Farrinder. Campaigner for the emancipation of women who is skeptical of inspirational views in Henry James's *The Bostonians*.

Ensign Farrington. Replacement officer aboard the USS *Caine* who assists Willie Keith in saving the ship after a kamikaze attack in Herman Wouk's *The Caine Mutiny*.

Farris. Judge who spies against Randall Flagg in Stephen King's *The Stand*.

Gene Farrow. Husband of Lois Farrow and father of Jacy Farrow; rich from oil leases, but hard-pressed to remain rich, in Larry McMurtry's *The Last Picture Show*.

Jacy Farrow. Daughter of Gene and Lois Farrow; spoiled and naive girlfriend of Duane Moore; elopes with Sonny Crawford, although the marriage is annulled, in Larry McMurtry's *The Last Picture Show*.

Lois Farrow. Wife of Gene Farrow, mother of Jacy Farrow, and lover of Sam the Lion; cynical drunk who is practical in matters of sex in Larry McMurtry's *The Last Picture Show*.

Father. Father of Henry Miller; becomes ill when he stops drinking, remains a semi-invalid for a year, and spends his free time sitting on a bench in the cemetery in Henry Miller's *Tropic of Capricorn*.

Father. Husband of Mother and father of Little Boy; owner of a company that makes flags, buntings, and fireworks; accompanies Admiral Peary's expedition to the North Pole; intermediary during Coalhouse Walker, Jr.'s siege at the Morgan Library; dies on the *Lusitania* in E. L. Doctorow's *Ragtime*.

Sam Fathers. Son of Ikkemotubbe; teaches Ike McCaslin about the woods and hunting in William Faulkner's *Go Down, Moses*; also appears in *Intruder in the Dust* and *The Reivers*.

Pauline Faubion. Flirtatious American "fleshpot" in Conrad Aiken's *Blue Voyage*.

Fauntleroy. See Moodie.

Lord Fauntleroy. See Cedric Errol.

Faustin the Zombie. Witness to and commentator on, but not participant in, life in Anaïs Nin's *Children of the Albatross*.

Harriot (Rosebud) Fawcet. Companion to Mrs. Francis; dies after learning that her beloved, Tommy Harrington, is her halfbrother in William Hill Brown's *The Power of Sympathy*.

Maria Fawcet. Mother, by J. Harrington, of Harriot Fawcet in William Hill Brown's *The Power of Sympathy*.

Felix Fay. Socialist reformer in Davenport, Iowa, in Floyd Dell's *Moon-Calf*.

John Fay. Bridge-building engineer who receives Hagar Ashendyne's declaration of love and promise of marriage as they drift off the coast of Brittany after a shipwreck in Mary Johnston's *Hagar*.

Fayaway. Female friend of Tommo in Herman Melville's *Typee*.

Marion (Marion O'Faye) Faye. Bisexual, pimp, drug dealer, and beat-nihilist; son of Dorothea O'Faye in Norman Mailer's *The Deer Park*.

Lois Fazenda. Prostitute and murder victim in John Gregory Dunne's *True Confessions*.

Walter Feather. Saxophone player and rival of Willie Keith for the affections of May Wynn in Herman Wouk's *The Caine Mutiny*.

Feather Mae. Great-grandmother of Meridian Hill; fought to preserve sacred Indian burial mounds in Alice Walker's *Meridian*.

Fedallah. Mysterious Parsee whom Ahab smuggles aboard the *Pequod* in Herman Melville's *Moby-Dick*.

Beatrice (Bea, Bee) Fedder. Wife of Niles Fedder in Thomas Berger's *Reinhart in Love*.

Niles Fedder. Neighbor of Carl Reinhart in Vetsville in Thomas Berger's *Reinhart in Love*.

Samson-Aaron (The Uncle) Feder. Brother of Rose Morgenstern in Herman Wouk's *Marjorie Morningstar*.

Fee. Town carpenter and father of Jimmy Fee; killed by Clay Turner in E. L. Doctorow's *Welcome to Hard Times*.

Jimmy Fee. Orphan cared for by Blue and Molly Riordan, whom he accidentally kills, in E. L. Doctorow's *Welcome to Hard Times*.

Cheops Feeley. Scientist who wants to implant an electrode in Billy Twillig's head to boost the power of his left brain in Don DeLillo's *Ratner's Star*.

Lionel Feffer. Former reader for poor-sighted Artur Sammler; academic operator who arranges Sammler's Bloomsbury talk at Columbia University; causes a violent street scene by photographing the black pickpocket who menaces Sammler in Saul Bellow's *Mr. Sammler's Planet*.

Roy Fehler. Recovered alcoholic and Los Angeles policeman; killed at the end of Joseph Wambaugh's *The New Centurions*.

Hannah Portnoy Feibish. Sister of Alex Portnoy in Philip Roth's *Portnoy's Complaint*.

Mendel (The Ox) Feinstein. Weightlifter and Legs Diamond's henchman; dies from a heart attack in William Kennedy's *Legs*.

Morris Feitelzohn. Agnostic philosopher and lecturer, woman-chaser, and zloty-borrowing friend of Aaron Greidinger in Isaac Bashevis Singer's *Shosha*.

Billy Feldman. Son of Leo Feldman in Stanley Elkin's *A Bad Man*.

Isidore Feldman. Jewish peddler and father of Leo Feldman; teaches Leo the fundamentals and ethics of selling in Stanley Elkin's *A Bad Man*.

Leo Feldman. Department store owner and purveyor of The Basement, where he does favors; sentenced to a year in prison for the crime of being himself in Stanley Elkin's *A Bad Man*.

Lilly Feldman. Wife of Leo Feldman in Stanley Elkin's *A Bad Man*.

Felice. "Little brown" whom Jake Brown believes is the love of his life and for whom he searches Harlem; they leave Harlem together for Chicago in Claude McKay's *Home to Harlem*.

Luke (Paragon) Fellinka. Head guide on Rusty Jethroe's hunting expedition into the Brooks Range in Norman Mailer's *Why Are We in Vietnam?*

Ben Feltner. Father of Mat Feltner and husband of Nancy Beechum Feltner in Wendell Berry's *The Memory of Old Jack*.

Bess Feltner. See Bess Feltner Catlett.

Hannah Feltner. See Hannah Coulter.

Margaret (Little Margaret) Feltner. Daughter of Virgil and Hannah Feltner; born after the death of her father in Wendell Berry's *A Place on Earth*; also appears in *The Memory of Old Jack*.

Margaret Finley Feltner. Wife of Mat Feltner and mother of Virgil Feltner and Bess Feltner Catlett; brings her daughter-in-law, Hannah Feltner, to live with her family following the death of Virgil in Wendell Berry's *A Place on Earth*; also appears in *Nathan Coulter* and *The Memory of Old Jack*.

Mat Feltner. Subsistence tobacco farmer in Port William, Kentucky; son of Ben and Nancy Feltner and husband of Margaret Feltner; centered consciousness of Wendell Berry's *A Place on Earth*; also appears in *Nathan Coulter* and *The Memory of Old Jack*.

Nancy Beechum Feltner. Wife of Ben Feltner, mother of Mat Feltner, and sister of Old Jack Beechum in Wendell Berry's *The Memory of Old Jack*.

Virgil Feltner. Son of Mat and Margaret Feltner, first husband of Hannah Coulter, and father of Little Margaret Feltner; dies in World War II in Wendell Berry's *A Place on Earth*.

Thea Fenchel. Heiress to a million-dollar mineral water business; brash and spoiled seeker after goddesslike perfection; her affair with Augie March lasts only as long as her abortive attempt in Mexico to hunt iguanas with eagles in Saul Bellow's *The Adventures of Augie March*.

Dr. Robert (Frank X. Barlow, Kilgore Trout) Fender. Prisoner with Walter F. Starbuck; writes science fiction pseudonymously in Kurt Vonnegut's *Jailbird*.

Edward B. (Ed, Eddie) Fenig. Writer who lives upstairs from Bucky Wunderlick in Don DeLillo's *Great Jones Street*.

Henry Fenn. Drunken lawyer and first husband of Margaret Müller; reformed railroad shopkeeper in William Allen White's *In the Heart of a Fool*.

Julian Fenn. Colleague of Holman Turner in the English department at Convers College in Alison Lurie's *Love and Friendship*.

Miranda Fenn. Wife of Julian Fenn in Alison Lurie's *Love and Friendship*.

Lee Fenner. Silent partner of the *Coast Guardian*, which publishes information damaging to John Bellmann, in Paul Cain's *Fast One*.

Captain Jack Fenwick. Half-mad mountaineer whose parents were killed by Indians; becomes a killer of Indians in Hervey Allen's *Bedford Village*.

Charles Fenwick. Proud and arrogant youth with stunted social development; aided by Theophilus North in Thornton Wilder's *Theophilus North*.

Collin Talbo Fenwick. Southern boy who lives with his cousins, the Talbo sisters, during his adolescent years; narrator of Truman Capote's *The Grass Harp*.

Eloise Fenwick. Sister of Charles Fenwick; introduces her brother to Theophilus North, who has been her tennis instructor, in Thornton Wilder's *Theophilus North*.

Feral. Senegalese actor who performs in a sex scene with Angela Sterling in Boris Adrian's pornographic movie in Terry Southern's *Blue Movie*.

Ferguson. Tory partisan leader killed at King's Mountain in John Pendleton Kennedy's *Horse-Shoe Robinson*.

Ferguson (Fergy). Worker at the Cane Vale sugar factory in Bournehills, the poorest section of Bourne Island, in Paule Marshall's *The Chosen Place, the Timeless People*.

Duncan Ferguson. Educated, moral, and philosophical servant who becomes Captain John Farrago's bog-trotter, after Teague Oregan is appointed as exciseman, in Hugh Henry Brackenridge's *Modern Chivalry*.

Helen (Fergy) Ferguson. Scottish nurse in Italy at the beginning of World War I; friend and confidante of Catherine Barkley in Ernest Hemingway's *A Farewell to Arms*.

Jeb Ferguson. Boorish farmer whom Susan Lenox is forced to marry and from whom she flees in David Graham Phillips's *Susan Lenox*.

Swoop Ferguson. Corrupt policeman never allowed to join his contemporaries in the Junior Bachelor Society; tries to humiliate them by arresting Moon Porter at the testimonial for Coach Chappie Davis in John A. Williams's *The Junior Bachelor Society*.

Burgess, Claudia, and Octavia Fern. Sisters who own the Fern Grammar School, where Rhoda Penmark is enrolled, in William March's *The Bad Seed*.

Fernandez. Husband of Cassandra and son-in-law of Skipper; leaves Cassandra for Harry and is found dead by Skipper, strangled by a guitar string, in John Hawkes's *Second Skin*.

Fernando (Fernandito). Member of Pablo's partisan group in Ernest Hemingway's *For Whom the Bell Tolls*.

Joseph (Joe) Ferone. Problem student at Calvin Coolidge High School whom Sylvia Barrett works desperately to help; very bright teenager who is a product of the streets in Bel Kaufman's *Up the Down Staircase*.

Luther Ferrari. High school boyfriend of Brenda Patimkin; teammate of Ron Patimkin and best man at his wedding in Philip Roth's *Goodbye, Columbus*.

Floyd Ferris. Major coordinator of the State Science Institute who is responsible for Project X and Project F in Ayn Rand's *Atlas Shrugged*.

Richard (Dick) Ferriss. Best friend of Ward Bennett; dies of typhoid fever when his nurse, Lloyd Searight, is prevented by Bennett from doing her duty in Frank Norris's *A Man's Woman*.

Earl Fetner. Husband of Tweet Fetner, brother of Bebe Sellars, and owner of a used car lot in Doris Betts's *The River to Pickle Beach*.

Grace Fetner. Mother of Bebe Sellars; disapproves of her daughter's marriage, fearing that Jack Sellars has inherited mental problems, in Doris Betts's *The River to Pickle Beach*.

Mary Ruth Packard Fetner. Wife of Troy Fetner and mother of Randy Fetner in Doris Betts's *The River to Pickle Beach*.

Randy Fetner. Young son of Troy and Mary Ruth Fetner; nearly drowns in a pond during a family outing in Doris Betts's *The River to Pickle Beach*.

Treva (Tweet) Fetner. Wife of Earl Fetner; her home exhibits multiple decorating clichés in Doris Betts's *The River to Pickle Beach*.

Troy Fetner. Brother of Bebe Sellars and Earl Fetner; family jester who writes ads for Earl's used car business in Doris Betts's *The River to Pickle Beach*.

William Fetters. White cotton mill owner who exploits his employees and traffics in convict labor in Charles W. Chesnutt's *The Colonel's Dream*.

Jesus Fever. Ancient little black man who drives a mule and wagon; his death changes the life of his granddaughter, Missouri Fever, in Truman Capote's *Other Voices, Other Rooms*.

Missouri (Zoo) Fever. Granddaughter of Jesus Fever; her husband cut her throat when she was a teen-aged bride; becomes a religious fanatic after being gang-raped in Truman Capote's *Other Voices, Other Rooms*.

Fiammetta. French prostitute who, regardless of the amount of money, refuses Tarden in Jerzy Kosinski's *Cockpit*.

Fibby. See Phoebe.

Alonzo Fiber. See Belt.

Fidelia. Young woman whose abduction before her marriage leads to Henry's suicide in William Hill Brown's *The Power of Sympathy*.

Achsa Fielding. Supposedly widowed English Jewess who promises to marry Arthur Mervyn in Charles Brockden Brown's *Arthur Mervyn*.

Charles (Charlie) Fielding. Musician, conductor, and composer; begins writing symphonies but never finishes them; first lover of Isadora Wing after her first marriage in Erica Jong's *Fear of Flying*.

Roger Fielding. Rich white lover of Angela Murray in Jessie Redmon Fauset's *Plum Bun*.

Jennifer (Jenny) Fields. Mother of T. S. Garp; seduces Garp's dying father because she wants a child without the problems of marriage; writes an autobiography, *A Sexual Suspect*; sympathizes with the Ellen Jamesians and is assassinated at a political rally by Kenny Truckenmiller in John Irving's *The World According to Garp*.

Corporal Fife. Clerk in C-for-Charlie Company and close friend of Private Witt; his combat experiences cause a series of recurring nightmares in James Jones's *The Thin Red Line*.

Fig Tree John. See Agocho.

Angela Figueroa. Oldest child in the Figueroa family; physically abused by her father; escapes from a girls' shelter to which she has been sent and hides out with her sixteen-year-old boyfriend, Buddy Rivers, in June Jordan's *His Own Where*.

Mr. Filer. Agent of Olive Chancellor; tries to convince Verena Tarrant to go on stage in Henry James's *The Bostonians*.

Charlie Filetti. Friend of Legs Diamond; involved in the Hotsy Totsy Club shootout in William Kennedy's *Legs*.

Fillmore. Friend of Henry Miller; employed in the diplomatic service; assaulted by a prostitute, hospitalized, and forced to leave Paris in order to escape from Ginette in Henry Miller's *Tropic of Cancer*.

Filthy Herman. Double amputee and sexual pervert in Joseph Wambaugh's *The Choirboys*.

Fin-de-Siècle. Parisian count, writer, and traveling companion of Aurelia West and the Chatelaine in Henry Blake Fuller's *The Chatelaine of La Trinité*.

Ada Fincastle. Heroine who challenges Janet Rowan for the love of Ralph McBride, loses him, bears their child, marries him, but has difficulty keeping him in Ellen Glasgow's *Vein of Iron*.

Grandmother Fincastle. Mother of John Fincastle and grandmother of Ada Fincastle; of unquestioning religion, thinks her son a heretic in Ellen Glasgow's *Vein of Iron*.

John (Father) Fincastle. Presbyterian minister and philosopher of idealism who loses his church because of a book he publishes; spends his life as a poor schoolmaster; father of Ada Fincastle in Ellen Glasgow's *Vein of Iron.*

Maggie (Aunt Maggie) Fincastle. Sister of John Fincastle and aunt of Ada Fincastle; does not accept her brother's religious doubts in Ellen Glasgow's *Vein of Iron.*

Mary Evelyn (Mrs. John, Mother) Fincastle. Poor, orphaned Tidewater belle who marries John Fincastle, but who becomes uneasy in their life of poverty in Ellen Glasgow's *Vein of Iron.*

Atticus Finch. Father of Scout and Jem Finch and lawyer who defends Tom Robinson; right-minded citizen and parent who says it is a "sin to kill a mockingbird" in Harper Lee's *To Kill a Mockingbird.*

Jean Louise (Scout) Finch. Curious and defiant youngster who begins to accept her role as a female; daughter of Atticus Finch and narrator of Harper Lee's *To Kill a Mockingbird.*

Jeremy Atticus (Jem) Finch. Proud older brother of Scout Finch; comes to appreciate and understand his father, Atticus Finch, in Harper Lee's *To Kill a Mockingbird.*

Katharine Finch. Secretary to Paul Proteus in Kurt Vonnegut's *Player Piano.*

Miriam Finch. Sculptress and lover of Eugene Witla in Theodore Dreiser's *The "Genius."*

Sadie Finch. Chief clerk at Calvin Coolidge High School who sends out memos such as "Please ignore the bells"; signs in for Paul Barringer so he can slip in late undetected in Bel Kaufman's *Up the Down Staircase.*

Sondra Finchley. Wealthy girlfriend of Clyde Griffiths, who sees in her a chance to improve his social standing, in Theodore Dreiser's *An American Tragedy.*

Sidney Fineman. Influential and pioneering Hollywood producer whose position as production chief is usurped by Sammy Glick in Budd Schulberg's *What Makes Sammy Run?*

Cathie Chandler Finer. Wife of Sam Finer; a lover, briefly, of Ron Grant; caught in adultery with Al Bonham in a motel in James Jones's *Go to the Widow-Maker.*

Sam Finer. Wisconsin businessman who loans Al Bonham money to buy the schooner *Naiad*; marries Cathie Chandler in James Jones's *Go to the Widow-Maker.*

Eddie Fingers. See Eddie Coyle.

Mike Fink. Mississippi River flatboatman and mail rider in Eudora Welty's *The Robber Bridegroom.*

Morris Fink. Handyman and resident of the apartment house also occupied by Stingo, Nathan Landau, and Sophie Zawistowska in William Styron's *Sophie's Choice.*

Dauphine Finkel. Second wife of Jed Tewksbury; introduces Tewksbury "to all the ideas that were going to redeem the world" in the early 1940s in Robert Penn Warren's *A Place to Come To.*

Judith Finkel. Grandmother of Jerry Kaplan and one of only two whites living in the black Cousinville, New Jersey, ghetto in Hal Bennett's *The Black Wine.*

Sanford (Sandy, Zed) Finkelstein. Owner of Krishna Bookshop and lover of Erica Tate in Alison Lurie's *The War Between the Tates.*

Angela Finlay. Beautiful woman who provides an alibi for Alonzo D. Emmerich in William Riley Burnett's *The Asphalt Jungle.*

Ernest (Shamble) Finley. Crippled brother of Margaret Feltner; commits suicide because of unrequited love for Ida Crop in Wendell Berry's *A Place on Earth.*

Huckleberry (George Jackson, George Peters, Huck, Sarah Mary Williams, Tom Sawyer) Finn. Son of Pap Finn; witnesses Injun Joe's murder of Dr. Robinson and rescues Widow Douglas in Samuel Langhorne Clemens's *The Adventures of Tom Sawyer*; runs away with Jim and narrates *Adventures of Huckleberry Finn*; accompanies Tom Sawyer on a balloon trip across North Africa and narrates *Tom Sawyer Abroad*; helps Tom Sawyer solve a murder and narrates Clemens's *Tom Sawyer, Detective.*

Pap Finn. Town drunk and father of Huckleberry Finn in Samuel Langhorne Clemens's *The Adventures of Tom Sawyer* and *Adventures of Huckleberry Finn.*

Edward Francis (Ed) Finnerty. Best friend of Paul Proteus; joins the Ghost Shirt revolution in Kurt Vonnegut's *Player Piano.*

Oliver Finnerty. Panderer, pimp, and peepshow proprietor in Nelson Algren's *A Walk on the Wild Side.*

Samson Finney. Lawyer and old friend of Judah Sherbrooke in Nicholas Delbanco's *Possession* and *Sherbrookes.*

Thomas (Colonel, Curn, Curny) Finnley. Iconoclastic and successful trumpeter in John Clellon

Holmes's *The Horn*.

Finny. See Phineas.

Alvin Finque. Los Angeles police lieutenant in the Wilshire Station in Joseph Wambaugh's *The Choirboys*.

Julius Finsberg. Old business partner of Ben Flesh's father in the costume industry; father of the eighteen Finsberg children; grants to Ben the gift of the "prime interest rate" in Stanley Elkin's *The Franchiser*.

Patty Finsberg. One of eighteen children of Julius Finsberg and favorite god-cousin of Ben Flesh; cannot hear loud noises in Stanley Elkin's *The Franchiser*.

Finsberg children. Eighteen children of Julius Finsberg, four sets of triplets and three sets of twins, all named for musical stage personalities Patty, LaVerne, Maxene, Oscar, Ethel, Lorenz, Jerome, Irving, Noël, Gertrude, Kitty, Helen, Sigmund-Rudolf, Mary, Moss, Gus-Ira, Lotte, and Cole; all suffer from strange, mortal diseases in Stanley Elkin's *The Franchiser*.

Fiona. Sensual wife of Cyril and lover of Hugh; departs with Meredith, Dolores, and Eveline after Hugh's death and Catherine's collapse in John Hawkes's *The Blood Oranges*.

Jack Fiori. See Jack Flowers.

Carol Ann Firebaugh. College student who spends a summer as a Red Cross Grey Lady in Kilrainey Army Hospital during World War II; becomes involved with Marion Landers and later, more seriously, with Martin Winch in James Jones's *Whistle*.

Firebird. Wild horse of Leonora Penderton; throws Captain Penderton and brings about his chance meeting with the naked Private Ellgee Williams in Carson McCullers's *Reflections in a Golden Eye*.

Gary Fish. Friend and business associate of Tracy Morgan in Scott Spencer's *Preservation Hall*.

Sweeney Fishberg. Grand Republic attorney and friend of Jinny Timberlane in Sinclair Lewis's *Cass Timberlane*.

Bruno Fisher. Classmate of Eric Eisner at Columbia University and New York social worker; finds Eric a job with the literacy program for the disadvantaged in Phillip Lopate's *Confessions of Summer*.

Carry Fisher. Twice-divorced New York socialite who tries to help Lily Bart find a husband and, later, a job in Edith Wharton's *The House of Mirth*.

Helen Givens Fisher. Daughter of the Imperial Grand Wizard of the Knights of Nordica; marries whitened black man Matthew Fisher and gives birth to a mulatto son in George S. Schuyler's *Black No More*.

Leon Fisher. Idealistic Communist artist and friend of Jason Wheeler; unhappily in love with Helen Jackson, but loved by Celia Chapman, in Albert Halper's *Union Square*.

Matthew (Matt) Fisher. See Max Disher.

Pop Fisher. Manager of the Knights and uncle of Memo Paris in Bernard Malamud's *The Natural*.

Wally Fisher. Owner of a West Condon hotel; rents the ground on which the Brunists believe they will ascend to heaven to the operators of a fair in Robert Coover's *The Origin of the Brunists*.

Warden Fisher. Warden of a surreal prison; terrorizes Leo Feldman in Stanley Elkin's *A Bad Man*.

Eddy Fiske. Police officer who investigates Frederick Eichner's automobile accident in Terry Southern's *Flash and Filigree*.

Eddie Fislinger. College classmate of Elmer Gantry, president of the local YMCA, and Baptist minister in Sinclair Lewis's *Elmer Gantry*.

Johann Fist. Captain of a motley crew of smugglers and a Satanic/Faustian figure in *The Smugglers of Lost Souls' Rock*, the interior novel within John Gardner's *October Light*.

Eleanor Fite. Memphis socialite engaged to Gratt Shafer; murdered at her wedding by Thomas McCutcheon in Jesse Hill Ford's *Mountains of Gilead*.

Ann Fitzgerald. Photographer who travels with her lover Nicholas Payne, but marries another; her photographs of Payne receive critical acclaim in Thomas McGuane's *The Bushwhacked Piano*.

Duke and Edna (La) Fitzgerald. Parents of Ann Fitzgerald; dislike Nicholas Payne in Thomas McGuane's *The Bushwhacked Piano*.

Captain Basil Fitz-Hugh. Handsome, genteel British nobleman who romances Mame Dennis and marries Vera Charles in Patrick Dennis's *Around the World with Auntie Mame*.

Atty Fitzpatrick. Lover of Conor Larkin and member of the Irish Republican Brotherhood in Leon Uris's *Trinity*.

Mrs. Fitzpatrick. Heavy drinker who becomes blasphemous and makes a fool of herself when drunk in Carlene Hatcher Polite's *The Flagellants*.

George P. (or M.) Flack. American reporter for *The Reverberator* who publishes a story about his friend Francie Dosson and her family in Henry James's *The Reverberator*.

Flag. Orphaned fawn Jody Baxter takes as a pet and companion in Marjorie Kinnan Rawlings's *The Yearling*.

Celia Flagg. Ex-wife of Mason Flagg; also loved by Peter Leverett in William Styron's *Set This House on Fire*.

Charles Evans (Charlie) Flagg. Communist party organizer, civil rights activist, and coworker of Zeke Gurevich in William Herrick's *The Itinerant*; battalion commander of loyalist forces in the Spanish civil war in *Hermanos!*

Mason Flagg. American playboy living in Rome whose sadistic behavior and decadent life-style destroy many lives and culminate in the rape and murder of Francesca Ricci and his own subsequent death in William Styron's *Set This House on Fire*.

Randall Flagg. Former faceless entity materialized into human form; leads the forces of evil in Stephen King's *The Stand*.

Jim Flaherty. Veteran Irish police detective who is Rico Bandello's antagonist and close observer in William Riley Burnett's *Little Caesar*.

Guy Flamm. Shady theatrical producer in Herman Wouk's *Marjorie Morningstar*.

Elizabeth (Betty) Flanagan. Washerwoman, cook, and "petticoat doctor" to the American troops in James Fenimore Cooper's *The Spy*.

Jack Flanders. Young man with a scarred face who wants to be an actor; enters Marietta McGee-Chavéz's Spain in William Goyen's *In a Farther Country*.

John (Jack) Flanders. Divorced poet who takes Emily Grimes with him when he accepts a teaching post at the University of Iowa Writers' Workshop; she rejects his marriage proposal and returns to New York without him in Richard Yates's *Easter Parade*.

Flask (King-Post). Third mate aboard the *Pequod* in Herman Melville's *Moby-Dick*.

Troy Flavin. Thirty-four-year-old Fairchild overseer from the Tishomingo Hills of Mississippi; marries Dabney Fairchild in Eudora Welty's *Delta Wedding*.

Kathleen (Kathleen Tigler) Fleisher. Wife of Von Humboldt Fleisher and friend of Charlie Citrine,

with whom she shares the money collected from the lawsuit against literary pirates who stole the *Caldofredo* script, in Saul Bellow's *Humboldt's Gift*.

Von Humboldt Fleisher. Friend and literary father of Charlie Citrine, author of *Harlequin Ballads*, and collaborator with Citrine on the film script for *Caldofredo*, later pirated and the subject of a lawsuit; "poet, thinker, problem drinker, pill-taker, man of genius, manic depressive, intricate schemer," and compulsive talker whose body Citrine arranges to have moved from an obscure pauper's grave in New Jersey to Valhalla Cemetery and whose wisdom–"Remember: we are not natural beings but supernatural beings"–Citrine receives as a gift in Saul Bellow's *Humboldt's Gift*.

Berenice (Bevy, Kathryn Trent) Fleming. Daughter of Hattie Carter and lover of Frank Cowperwood in Theodore Dreiser's *The Titan*; moves to London with Cowperwood and plans to build a hospital after his death in *The Stoic*.

Henry (Flem) Fleming. Youthful Union soldier who deserts his regiment; a spurious wound emboldens him to return and fight fearlessly in Stephen Crane's *The Red Badge of Courage*.

Joe Fleming. Boxer who will not give up his sport despite the pleas of his girlfriend, Genevieve; killed in a prizefight in Jack London's *The Game*.

Robert Fleming. Solicitor who encourages Hugh Tallant to seek redress in England after the American Revolution and who later gets Tallant pardoned when Tallant returns to England after escaping from the Australian penal colony in Charles Nordhoff and James Norman Hall's *Botany Bay*.

Benjamin (Ben) Flesh. Franchiser who travels to his businesses throughout America; god-cousin to the eighteen Finsberg children and sufferer from multiple sclerosis in Stanley Elkin's *The Franchiser*.

Adaline Fletcher. Disturbed, eccentric wife of E. L. Fletcher in Jerry Bumpus's *Anaconda*.

Alice (Quiet Alice) Fletcher. Wife of Harrison Fletcher; has an affair with T. S. Garp; unable to finish her second novel; dies in an airplane crash in John Irving's *The World According to Garp*.

E. L. Fletcher. Oil-field roughneck, husband of Adaline Fletcher, and lover of Vera; killed by Vera's husband, Carl, in Jerry Bumpus's *Anaconda*.

Everell Fletcher. Son of William Fletcher and betrothed of Hope Leslie; captured by Indians and saved from execution by Magawisca in Catharine Maria Sedgwick's *Hope Leslie*.

Gid Fletcher. Avaricious blacksmith who captures Rick Tyler in Mary Noailles Murfree's *The Prophet of the Great Smoky Mountains*.

Harrison (Harry) Fletcher. Husband of Alice Fletcher and professor who has affairs with his students; dies in an airplane crash in John Irving's *The World According to Garp*.

William Fletcher. Puritan settler, father of Everell Fletcher, and guardian of Faith and Hope Leslie in Catharine Maria Sedgwick's *Hope Leslie*.

Mr. Flick. Musician and shipboard gigolo with whom the narrator dances en route from Europe to America in Aline Bernstein's *The Journey Down*.

Wilbur Flick. Alcoholic scion of a wealthy family who, following the stock market crash, becomes a communist and a profesional magician in Edmund Wilson's *Memoirs of Hecate County*.

Kate (Kate Harrington) Flickinger. Red-haired childhood friend of Louisa Calloway; happily married in Alice Adams's *Families and Survivors*.

Private Otto Flickner. Union cannoneer from Minnesota; narrates part of Shelby Foote's *Shiloh*.

Lucius Fliegend. Jewish owner of Fliegend Fancy Box and Pasteboard Toy Manufacturing Company, which employs Jinny Timberlane, in Sinclair Lewis's *Cass Timberlane*.

Luther Leroy (Lute) Fliegler. Employee of Julian English, to whom Fliegler gives good advice, in John O'Hara's *Appointment in Samarra*.

Augustus P. (Gus) Flint. Tyrannical railroad executive who controls state politics; father of Victoria Flint in Winston Churchill's *Mr. Crewe's Career*.

Jere Flint. Dance-marathon contestant who is unfairly eliminated from a derby race through the machinations of the marathon officials in Horace McCoy's *They Shoot Horses, Don't They?*

Victoria Flint. Privileged daughter of Augustus P. Flint; matures and becomes the wife of Austen Vane in Winston Churchill's *Mr. Crewe's Career*.

Flip. Coworker who warns Will Harris that if southern blacks do not accept subservience, they will suffer the consequences in Junius Edwards's *If We Must Die*.

Evy Rommely Flittman. Older sister of Katie Nolan and "refined" aunt of Francie Nolan in Betty Smith's *A Tree Grows in Brooklyn*.

Flo. Manager of a charity rummage shop in Jay Neugeboren's *Sam's Legacy*.

Renata Flonzaley. See Renata Koffritz.

Captain Flood. Operator of a riverboat and friend of Johnny Fraser in James Boyd's *Drums*.

Charles Curtis (Curt) Flood. Baseball player who leaves the Washington Senators; charged by Trick E. Dixon with attempting to destroy baseball and corrupt the youth of America in Philip Roth's *Our Gang*.

Dora Flood. Madam and proprietor of the Bear Flag Restaurant, a popular brothel, in John Steinbeck's *Cannery Row*.

Mrs. Flood. Landlady of Hazel Motes who, though at first attracted only by his money, becomes fascinated by his eyes after he blinds himself and takes him in before his death in Flannery O'Connor's *Wise Blood*.

Nora Flood. American socialite and lover of Robin Vote; after losing Robin to Jenny Petherbridge, she observes Robin's confrontation with the dog and Robin's bestial nature in Djuna Barnes's *Nightwood*.

Flopit. Spoiled lapdog of Miss Lola Pratt in Booth Tarkington's *Seventeen*.

Flora. Angelic girl under the care of the governess; sister of Miles; becomes frightened of and hateful toward the governess when the governess confronts her about the ghosts in Henry James's *The Turn of the Screw*.

Florence. Student who serves on the Cinema Committee with Hill Gallagher during the student rebellion in James Jones's *The Merry Month of May*.

Florimel. Vampire who becomes Jurgen's third wife during his sojourn in the Hell of his father following Jurgen's departure from Leuke in James Branch Cabell's *Jurgen*.

Flossie. Goodnatured prostitute who appears to radiate health but afflicts both Dolly Haight and Vandover with a venereal disease in Frank Norris's *Vandover and the Brute*.

Flossie (Floss, Queen of Stars). Beautiful prostitute and friend of Legs Diamond and Marcus Gorman in William Kennedy's *Legs*.

Effie (Mrs. Effie, Mrs. Senator James Knox Floud) Floud. Cousin of Egbert G. Floud and leader of the Red Gap social set; wants Marmaduke Ruggles to teach Egbert how to dress and behave as a gentleman in Harry Leon Wilson's *Ruggles of Red Gap*.

Egbert G. Floud. Cousin of Effie Floud; wins the valet Marmaduke Ruggles from George Augustus Vane-

Basingwell in a poker game and takes Ruggles to the United States in Harry Leon Wilson's *Ruggles of Red Gap.*

Jack Flowers (Fiori). American pimp, philosopher, and romantic visionary in Singapore in Paul Theroux's *Saint Jack.*

Rachel Rebecca Carpenter (Sister Rache) Flowers. Blind priestess and mother of Industrious and Carl-Rae Bowman in Leon Forrest's *The Bloodworth Orphans.*

Mr. Floyd. Bracktown resident who attempts to court Correy Corregidora in Gayl Jones's *Corregidora.*

Mrs. Floyd. Boardinghouse operator in Charles Portis's *True Grit.*

Captain Flume. Squadron public relations officer frightened of his tentmate, Chief White Halfoat, in Joseph Heller's *Catch-22.*

Terry Flynn. Handsome, swaggering, athletic student who is two years behind his classmates in reading skills; characterized by his ringing "Bubba-hah! Bubba-hah-hah!" laugh in Richard Yates's *A Good School.*

Joe (Speed) Fogarty. Principal sidekick of Legs Diamond in William Kennedy's *Legs.*

Eliezer Fogel. Anti-Zionist Jewish professor whose ideas Daniel Ginsberg admires but disagrees with in Jay Neugeboren's *An Orphan's Tale.*

Penny Fogleman. Girlfriend of Peter Caldwell in John Updike's *The Centaur.*

Folded Leaf. Seneca Indian boy taught by Black Antler and murdered by George Benson in Jessamyn West's *The Massacre at Fall Creek.*

Dave (Foles) Foley. Pragmatic federal agent who listens to the snitching of Eddie Coyle and the other punks in George V. Higgins's *The Friends of Eddie Coyle.*

Dick Foley. Continental Detective Agency operative who answers the Continental Op's call for assistance and quits the job because of his scrupulous attitude in Dashiell Hammett's *Red Harvest.*

Edward (Eddie) Foley. Junior partner with Glymmer, Read who, when the firm becomes bankrupt, turns to alcohol in Nathan Asch's *The Office.*

Peter Nielson Foley. Ineffectual pacifist and author of an unfinished manuscript, "The Strange Captivity," about the charismatic influence of Charles Lawrence in Wright Morris's *The Huge Season.*

Alwin Folger. Aristocratic neighbor of the Crooms; host of John Laskell as Laskell recuperates from scarlet fever in Lionel Trilling's *The Middle of the Journey.*

Eunice (Eunie) Folger. Nursemaid for the son of Nancy and Arthur Croom in Lionel Trilling's *The Middle of the Journey.*

Mrs. Folger. Wife of Alwin Folger; her interest in John Laskell's intellectual life facilitates his recovery from scarlet fever in Lionel Trilling's *The Middle of the Journey.*

Willard Follansbee. Deputy who hopes to become sheriff of Winfield County, Mississippi; pawn of corrupt forces in Elizabeth Spencer's *The Voice at the Back Door.*

Catherine Follet. Daughter of Jay and Mary Follet and younger sister of Rufus Follet in James Agee's *A Death in the Family.*

Jay Follet. Father of Rufus Follet and husband of Mary Follet; dies in an automobile accident while driving home to Knoxville, Tennessee, after an emergency visit to his father, who was wrongly believed to be dying, in James Agee's *A Death in the Family.*

Mary Follet. Pious, prudish wife of Jay Follet and mother of Rufus Follet; widowed when her husband dies in an automobile accident in James Agee's *A Death in the Family.*

Ralph Follet. Younger brother of Jay Follet and uncle of Rufus Follet; undertaker and an alcoholic; phones Jay with the mistaken news that their father is dying and sets Jay upon the journey that ends with his death in an automobile accident in James Agee's *A Death in the Family.*

Rufus Follet. Six-year-old son of Jay and Mary Follet; protagonist of James Agee's *A Death in the Family.*

Louie (Nifty) Fomorowski. Drug dealer in Chicago's Polish neighborhoods in Nelson Algren's *The Man with the Golden Arm.*

Fondriere. Corporal who refuses to use his authority to order Grace to return the pistol stolen from Richard Mast in James Jones's *The Pistol.*

Fonoo. See Donjalolo.

Johnny Fontane. Popular singer whose career is promoted by Don Corleone in Mario Puzo's *The Godfather.*

Ruben Fontanez. Troublesome Puerto Rican student of Harry Meyers; becomes Meyers's friend in Jay

Neugeboren's *Listen Ruben Fontanez*.

Jeanne-Marie Ignace Thérèse Cabarrus de Fontenay. French noblewoman and former wife of Jean-Lambert Tallien in H. L. Davis's *Harp of a Thousand Strings*.

Clinton Foote. Universally hated general manager and director of player personnel of the Dallas Cowboys in Peter Gent's *North Dallas Forty*.

Foppl. Plantation owner in Germany's Protectorate in South-West Africa in 1922; holds a "Siege Party" which includes Kurt Mondaugen, Lieutenant Weissmann, and Vera Meroving and fondly recalls the extermination of the native Herero population in Thomas Pynchon's *V*.

Eva Grumbauer Forbes. Plain, conventional older sister of Alice Prentice; both praises and chides Alice's "independence of spirit" in Richard Yates's *A Special Providence*.

Father Vincent Forbes. Freethinking Catholic priest who introduces Theron Ware to higher criticism; Ware later wrongly suspects Forbes of an affair with Celia Madden in Harold Frederic's *The Damnation of Theron Ware*.

John Kingsgrant Forbes. New England novelist of manners who receives the Medal for Modern Fiction in John Updike's *Bech: A Book*.

Owen Forbes. Lumbering, drunken husband of Eva Grumbauer Forbes; claims to be writing a history of World War I in Richard Yates's *A Special Providence*.

Sally Forbes. Daughter of a university professor and friend of Lymie Peters and Hope Davison; loves Spud Latham in William Maxwell's *The Folded Leaf*.

Jack Ford. Sly, tight-fisted boy in Louisa May Alcott's *Little Men*.

W. W. W. (C. C. C., W. A. D., W. F.) Ford. Spiritualist and master of disguises in Leon Forrest's *The Bloodworth Orphans*.

Buck Forrester. Neighbor who helps the Baxters when Penny Baxter becomes ill in Marjorie Kinnan Rawlings's *The Yearling*.

Captain Daniel Forrester. Pioneer and railroad builder who loses his fortune rather than sacrifice his honor; marries Marian Ormsby after saving her life in Willa Cather's *A Lost Lady*.

Daniel (Danny) Forrester. Marine radio operator wounded at Saipan in Leon Uris's *Battle Cry*.

Edith Forrester. Niece of Major Roland Forrester, cousin of Captain Roland Forrester, and heir to her uncle's wealth in Robert Montgomery Bird's *Nick of the Woods*.

Fodder-wing Forrester. Crippled boy who raises wild animals and who is Jody Baxter's best friend in Marjorie Kinnan Rawlings's *The Yearling*.

Gene Forrester. Best friend of Finny and probably the cause of the accident that cripples him; narrator of John Knowles's *A Separate Peace*.

Kyla Forrester. Mira's friend in graduate school; leaves her husband for a lesbian lover in Marilyn French's *The Women's Room*.

Lem Forrester. Drunken, mean neighbor of the Baxters; becomes Oliver Hutto's enemy in Marjorie Kinnan Rawlings's *The Yearling*.

Marian Ormsby (Maidy) Forrester. Wife of Daniel Forrester, who is twenty-five years her senior, and first lady of Sweet Water; turns to alcohol and other men because of her husband's illness; as a widow marries Henry Collins, a rich Englishman, in Willa Cather's *A Lost Lady*.

Captain Roland Forrester. Cousin of Edith Forrester and nephew of Major Roland Forrester; written out of his uncle's will when he fights on the American side in the Revolutionary War in Robert Montgomery Bird's *Nick of the Woods*.

Major Roland (Roly) Forrester. Former Tory and wealthy uncle of Captain Roland Forrester and Edith Forrester; wishes to keep his wealth from his nephew in Robert Montgomery Bird's *Nick of the Woods*.

Teddy Forster. Canadian living in London; talent agent, drug dealer, and former lover of Marie Curtin; introduces Eric Eisner to the "beautiful people" of London in Phillip Lopate's *Confessions of Summer*.

Dr. Abdul Forsythe. Villain who changes people into shadows in C. Card's latest daydream of Babylon in Richard Brautigan's *Dreaming of Babylon*.

Fort. See Luther.

Colonel Cassius (Old Cass) Fort. Lawyer and prominent politician who becomes Jeremiah Beaumont's mentor; Beaumont kills him for seducing Rachel Jordan in Robert Penn Warren's *World Enough and Time*.

Charles (Charlie) Fort. Defense lawyer who successfully courts Hannah Cape in Jessamyn West's *The Massacre at Fall Creek*.

Malory Forten. Conventional young man discovered to be the half brother of Melissa Paul just before his marriage to her in Jessie Redmon Fauset's *The Chinaberry Tree.*

Fortescue. Centennial Club member who collects military miniatures and heads up a group to track down and punish Earl Olive in Thomas McGuane's *The Sporting Club.*

Hugh Fortescue. British seaman and New World colonist whose settlement disappears without a trace, giving rise to the legend of the Lost Colony, in Thomas Wolfe's *The Hills Beyond.*

Don Fortgang. Member of the Beechwood community before David Dehn builds a temple; opposes Dehn's plans and commits suicide after losing an election to Dehn in Jerome Weidman's *The Temple.*

Brother Fortinbride. Methodist preacher who once fought with John Sartoris's regiment in William Faulkner's *The Unvanquished.*

Mommy Fortuna. Witch who captures the unicorn (Lady Amalthea) for her Midnight Carnival in Peter S. Beagle's *The Last Unicorn.*

Susan Fosdick. Elderly widow famous for her skill at "visiting"; although called "a strange sail" for her tendency to arrive without warning, her entertaining stories make her a welcome guest in Sarah Orne Jewett's *The Country of the Pointed Firs.*

Billy Fosnacht. Son of Peggy Fosnacht and friend of Nelson Angstrom in John Updike's *Rabbit Redux.*

Peggy Fosnacht. Mother of Billy Fosnacht and lover for one night of Rabbit Angstrom in John Updike's *Rabbit Redux.*

Foster. Library employee, cave worker, and friend of Vida Kramar and the narrator in Richard Brautigan's *The Abortion.*

Dr. Foster. Minister of India and Walter Bridge in Evan Connell's *Mrs. Bridge.*

Kenneth Foster. University art teacher and friend of Janet Belle Smith in Alison Lurie's *Real People.*

Roger Foster. Impersonator of Colonel Sanders; teaches Ben Flesh lessons in salesmanship in Stanley Elkin's *The Franchiser.*

Roger Foster. Librarian and intermittent suitor of Fanny Bick in Bernard Malamud's *Dubin's Lives.*

Silas Foster. Farmer and overseer of Blithedale in Nathaniel Hawthorne's *The Blithedale Romance.*

Stephen (Steve) Foster. Patriot frontiersman who teaches woodcraft and the art of war to the young Henry Lindsay in John Pendleton Kennedy's *Horse-Shoe Robinson.*

Tom Foster. Young man who comes to Winesburg from Cincinnati; in a drunken state he fabricates a sexual encounter between himself and Helen White in Sherwood Anderson's *Winesburg, Ohio.*

Fouché. French minister of police in H. L. Davis's *Harp of a Thousand Strings.*

Captain Walter Fountain. Ohio native who dies in the first Confederate advance; narrates part of Shelby Foote's *Shiloh.*

Erskine Fowler. Retired insurance company employee partly responsible for the accidental death of Tony Blake; murderer of Mabel Blake in Richard Wright's *Savage Holiday.*

Henry Fowler. General manager of the banking firm of Huddleston & Bradford who unwittingly gives information to Edward Pierce in Michael Crichton's *The Great Train Robbery.*

Jeremiah (Jerry) Fowler. Young man bound for the Holland Patent to buy farmland; instead buys the papers of Mary Goodhill, whom he later marries; carpenter who builds locks on the Erie Canal in Walter D. Edmonds's *Erie Water.*

Mary Goodhill Fowler. Indentured servant redeemed by Jerry Fowler; Fowler's long-suffering wife in Walter D. Edmonds's *Erie Water.*

Georgie (Syph) Fox. Small-time hoodlum who bungles a robbery and is ostracized by the McCalls; commits suicide by leaping from a viaduct in William Kennedy's *Billy Phelan's Greatest Game.*

Madeline Fox. Graduate student in English who is engaged to Martin Arrowsmith until he meets Leora Tozer in Sinclair Lewis's *Arrowsmith.*

Mardou (Irene May) Fox. Independent black woman, former mental patient, and lover of Leo Percepied in Jack Kerouac's *The Subterraneans*; also appears in *Book of Dreams.*

D'Artagnan (Dart) Foxx. Concert singer and former member of the black high school athletic team and neighborhood gang gathering for a birthday testimonial honoring Chappie Davis in John A. Williams's *The Junior Bachelor Society.*

Foxy Lady. Transsexual scion of an influential Moslem family; lover of George Levanter in Jerzy Kosinski's *Blind Date.*

Frado. See Alfrado.

Juan Reyes Fragua. Albino killed by Abel in N. Scott Momaday's *House Made of Dawn*.

Eunice Fraley. Elderly, timid New England spinster tyrannized by her mother in Sarah Orne Jewett's *A Country Doctor*.

Frampton. Goose Creek native who, demented, avenges his wife's death in William Gilmore Simms's *The Partisan*.

Lancelot (Lance) Frampton. Youth who, following his mother's murder, joins Major Singleton's group of partisans and becomes Singleton's protégé in William Gilmore Simms's *The Partisan*; partisan lieutenant of Captain Porgy in *Woodcraft*.

Dolph Franc. Chief of a corrupt police force in William Riley Burnett's *The Asphalt Jungle*.

Francie. Friend who visits the narrator and her young writer-lover at Ambleside and takes the pair on a tour of the English countryside in Aline Bernstein's *The Journey Down*.

Francie. Girlfriend of Henry Miller; enjoys describing her sexual experiences with other men; attempts to seduce her brother in Henry Miller's *Tropic of Capricorn*.

Dr. Francis. Famous humanitarian of the Babylon of C. Card's daydreams in Richard Brautigan's *Dreaming of Babylon*.

Mrs. Francis. Companion to Harriot Fawcet in William Hill Brown's *The Power of Sympathy*.

Francisco. Illegitimate son of Fray Nicolás; Abel's grandfather in N. Scott Momaday's *House Made of Dawn*.

Albert B. Francoeur. Second of seven Francoeur brothers; marine officer who provides money to his parents and for his brothers' education; strives to keep the family together in David Plante's *The Family*.

André J. Francoeur. Fifth of seven Francoeur brothers; aspiring singer and amateur painter who tries a business career before joining the navy in David Plante's *The Family*.

Aricie Melanie Atalie Lajoie (Reena) Francoeur. Wife of Arsace Francoeur and mother of seven sons; devotes herself to her family and her house; becomes emotionally ill after her husband disowns their son Philip Francoeur in David Plante's *The Family*.

Arsace Louis Pylade (Jim) Francoeur. Husband of Aricie Francoeur and father of seven sons; loses his foreman's job because of union pressure and becomes a day laborer; fails to be elected as a state representative in David Plante's *The Family*.

Daniel R. Francoeur. Sixth of seven Francoeur brothers; struggles to understand his father's failures, his mother's emotional illness, and the conflicts between his sexuality and Catholicism in David Plante's *The Family*.

Edmond R. Francoeur. Third of seven Francoeur brothers; because he thinks that the family takes him for granted, he tries, unsuccessfully, to break from the family in David Plante's *The Family*.

Julien E. Francoeur. Youngest of seven Francoeur brothers; quiet and unassertive in a family that is often emotional and talkative in David Plante's *The Family*.

Philip P. Francoeur. Fourth of seven Francoeur brothers; after graduating from MIT, he joins the air force; breaks with his father after marrying and failing to honor a promise to help buy a house for his parents in David Plante's *The Family*.

Richard A. Francoeur. Eldest of seven Francoeur brothers; fails in his business ambitions in David Plante's *The Family*.

Dominique Francon. Independent misanthrope and Howard Roark's mistress in Ayn Rand's *The Fountainhead*.

Andre Franconi. Syphilitic barber, reputed Lothario, and resident of the Glen Cove Apartments in Albert Halper's *Union Square*.

Frank. Car thief who uses a revolver with dum-dum bullets; boyfriend of Rosie in Jim Harrison's *A Good Day to Die*.

Anne Frank. See Amy Bellette.

Rose Frank. Hostess of a party in Paris which the Walkers and Aline Aldridge attend and where Aline meets Fred Grey, her future husband, in Sherwood Anderson's *Dark Laughter*.

Frankie. Friend of Harry Morgan; introduces Morgan to Mr. Sing in Ernest Hemingway's *To Have and Have Not*.

Frankie. Mildly retarded boy befriended by Doc; institutionalized following his theft of an expensive clock to give as a birthday gift to Doc in John Steinbeck's *Cannery Row*.

Frankie. Partner of Squirrel Amato and Russell in robbing a mob-run card game; killed by Jackie Cogan in George V. Higgins's *Cogan's Trade*.

Amy Forrester Franklin. Recent bride of Dr. Deane Franklin; leaves him because of his friendship with Ruth Holland in Susan Glaspell's *Fidelity*.

Benjamin Franklin. American ambassador to France to whom Israel Potter delivers a message in Herman Melville's *Israel Potter*.

Benjamin Franklin. American statesman and philosopher who provides the means for Thomas Paine to immigrate to America in Howard Fast's *Citizen Tom Paine*.

Dr. Deane Franklin. Unconventional small-town physician who helps and defends Ruth Holland in Susan Glaspell's *Fidelity*.

Edana (Dana) Franklin. Contemporary black woman pulled into the past by the needs of her white ancestor; narrator of Octavia E. Butler's *Kindred*.

Julia Franklin. Replacement for Charlotte Temple in the affections of Jack Montraville and eventually his wife in Susanna Rowson's *Charlotte*.

Kevin Franklin. White husband of Dana Franklin in Octavia E. Butler's *Kindred*.

Nathaniel T. (Nat) Franklin. Union army colonel who dies on his front porch while watching young soldiers march off to war with Spain in Hervey Allen's *Action at Aquila*.

Thomas Franklin. Young lawyer who evicts Chance and subsequently comes closest to guessing the identity of Chauncey Gardiner in Jerzy Kosinski's *Being There*.

Tommy Franklin. Resident of the Diamond County Home for the Aged; files peachstones into the shapes of small animals and baskets to sell at the annual fair; befriends Elizabeth Heinemann and escorts her to meals in John Updike's *The Poorhouse Fair*.

Don Franyo. Priest-tutor of Rudolf Stanka; uncovers Stanka's gift of communion with birds in Louis Adamic's *Cradle of Life*.

Franz. Tall Germanic domestic boy in Louisa May Alcott's *Little Men*.

Christian J. (Christie) Fraser. Insurance salesman who loves both Catherine Conboy and Sylva Cope in Jessamyn West's *The Witch Diggers*.

John (Dadder) Fraser. Scotch Presbyterian loyalist, well-to-do farmer, and father of Johnny Fraser in James Boyd's *Drums*.

John (Johnny) Fraser, Jr.. Loyalist turned patriot who is wounded aboard the *Bonhomme Richard* in James Boyd's *Drums*.

Simon Frasier. Black attorney who represents blacks in the police and magistrate courts of Charleston in DuBose Heyward's *Porgy*.

Cora Frawley. Mother of Ralph Frawley; gossip-mongering acquaintance of Emma Wallop in Peter De Vries's *Mrs. Wallop*.

Stephen Frazer. Friend of Felix Fay, whom Frazer introduces to atheist thought, in Floyd Dell's *Moon-Calf*.

Fred. Name Holly Golightly gives to the otherwise unnamed young writer and narrator of Truman Capote's *Breakfast at Tiffany's*.

Fred. Student from the University of Chicago who works at the hotel in Golconda translating letters from prospective guests; friend of Lillian Beye and Diana in Anaïs Nin's *Seduction of the Minotaur*.

Fred. Stuttering minister who plays poker with Thomas Marshfield at the retreat in John Updike's *A Month of Sundays*.

Freddie. Janitor of a local department store and neighborhood handyman and messenger in Toni Morrison's *Song of Solomon*.

Freddy. Dance-marathon contestant who is eliminated when his partner is revealed to be a minor who ran away from home in Horace McCoy's *They Shoot Horses, Don't They?*

Doris Frederic. English teacher and lover of 'Bama Dillert in James Jones's *Some Came Running*.

Frederick (Frederico, Rico). Controversial poet and novelist; friend of Julia Ashton in H. D.'s *Bid Me to Live*.

Elsa Frederick. Wife of Frederick in H. D.'s *Bid Me to Live*.

Mr. Freed. Manager at the St. Mark's Hotel who gives Sam Spade information from the hotel registry about Brigid O'Shaughnessy in Dashiell Hammett's *The Maltese Falcon*.

Dr. Freedman. Physician who provides illegal drugs and abortions to Leo Feldman in Stanley Elkin's *A Bad Man*.

Dave Freeland. Husband of Felise Freeland and Harlem socialite in whose apartment the confrontation between John Bellew and Clare Kendry, which ends in Clare's death, occurs in Nella Larsen's *Passing*.

Felise Freeland. Member of Harlem's black bourgeoisie, wife of Dave Freeland, and friend of Irene Redfield; hosts a party at which Clare Kendry falls to her death from a sixth floor window in Nella Larsen's *Passing*.

Freeman. Drifter who commits himself to helping people along the way, making them his substitute family, in John Gardner's *The Sunlight Dialogues*.

Jerry Freeman. Young newspaper feature writer who is assigned to interview Cameron Bolt and later goes to work for him in Gail Godwin's *Glass People*.

Lucy Freeman. See Lucy Freeman Sumner.

Ludie Freeman. First and favorite husband of Berenice Sadie Brown in Carson McCullers's *The Member of the Wedding*.

Abagail (Abby, Mother Abagail) Freemantle. Prophetess chosen by God to establish forces in the Free Zone against Randall Flagg in Stephen King's *The Stand*.

Arthur Lyon Fremantle. Englishman who sympathizes with the Confederate cause and offers advice and good cheer to the rebel leaders in Michael Shaara's *The Killer Angels*.

Katherine (Kitty) Fremont. Friend of Mark Parker, lover of Ari Ben Canaan, and surrogate mother of Karen Clement; American Christian nurse in post-World War II refugee centers and in Israel in Leon Uris's *Exodus*.

Ezra French. Bidwell, Ohio, farmer who influences Hugh McVey's ideas for a mechanical cabbage patch in Sherwood Anderson's *Poor White*.

Gabe French, Sr.. Wheelchair-bound invalid who isolates himself in one room of his house with a black servant to wait on him in Jesse Hill Ford's *Mountains of Gilead*.

Gabriel (Gabe) French. Land speculator in Jesse Hill Ford's *The Raider*; ancestor of Gabe French, Sr., in *Mountains of Gilead*.

Guinevere (Gwen) French. English teacher at Parkman College and thwarted lover of Dave Hirsh; edits his comic combat novel after his death in James Jones's *Some Came Running*.

Col. Henry French. Civil War veteran who offends his southern neighbors by his color-blind attitudes in business in Charles W. Chesnutt's *The Colonel's Dream*.

Mary French. Devoted radical who works as secretary to G. H. Barrow and provides a home for Ben Compton when he gets out of jail in John Dos Passos's *U.S.A.* trilogy.

Mattie French. Unmarried daughter of Gabe French and best friend of Patsy Jo McCutcheon; works in a jewelry store in Jesse Hill Ford's *Mountains of Gilead*.

Robert Ball French. Poet and retired English teacher; father of Gwen French; amateur philosopher and drinker in James Jones's *Some Came Running*.

Babette Freniere. Louisianian whom Louis loves after he becomes a vampire; she thinks that he is an evil monster in Anne Rice's *Interview with the Vampire*.

Willard Freund. Father of a son, Jimmy, by Callie Wells; abandons both mother and child to free himself for college and a career in John Gardner's *Nickel Mountain*.

Wilhelm Freytag. Aryan oilman who is refused seating at the captain's table because he admits to having a Jewish wife in Katherine Anne Porter's *Ship of Fools*.

Frick and Frack. Team of Los Angeles homicide investigators in Joseph Wambaugh's *The Black Marble*.

Doctor Fried. German psychiatrist who treats Deborah Blau at the mental hospital in Hannah Green's *I Never Promised You a Rose Garden*.

Ella Friedenberg. Guidance counselor at Calvin Coolidge High School who keeps extensive records on students and insists that teachers acquaint themselves with the PPP of each student's PRC and believes that everything will be OK if teachers write a CC for student records; also uses many Freudian terms in Bel Kaufman's *Up the Down Staircase*.

Fortune Friendly. Gambler and preacher who drives for Daniel Harrow; buys the *Ella-Romeyn* when Harrow returns to farming in Walter D. Edmonds's *Rome Haul*.

N'Gana Frimbo. Harvard-educated Harlem conjure-man and secret lover of his landlady Martha Crouch; killed by Samuel Crouch in Rudolph Fisher's *The Conjure-Man Dies*.

Colonel Nathan (One-Eye) Frisbie. Abolitionist, house burner, and commander of the Union gunboat *Starlight* in Shelby Foote's *Jordan County*.

Frisco. See Francisco d'Anconia.

Frog. Youth who learned the art of tightrope walking from a European circus performer in Carlene Hatcher Polite's *The Flagellants*.

Desmond Frogget. Drinking buddy of Jack Flowers at the Bandung in Singapore in Paul Theroux's *Saint Jack*.

Ethan (Ethe) Frome. New England farmer whose life is ruined by poverty and his sickly, malicious wife, Zenobia Frome, in Edith Wharton's *Ethan Frome*.

Zenobia Pierce (Zeena) Frome. Shrewish, hypochondriacal wife and cousin of Ethan Frome in Edith Wharton's *Ethan Frome*.

Frony. See Frony Gibson.

Lilly Frost. Tweed-wearing spinster and botanist who rooms with the Dangerfields in Dublin; later Sebastian Dangerfield's reluctant lover in J. P. Donleavy's *The Ginger Man*.

Mark Frost. Poet who attends the yacht party in William Faulkner's *Mosquitoes*.

Martin Frost. Private detective hired by Frederick Eichner to investigate Felix Treevly in Terry Southern's *Flash and Filigree*.

Captain Frounier. Cursing, toothless, ninety-one-year-old owner of a fleet of sailing vessels in Haiti in Arna Wendell Bontemps's *Drums at Dusk*.

Joseph Frowenfeld. Young American pharmacist who marries Clotilde Nancanou and whose liberal views are opposed by the old Louisiana society in George Washington Cable's *The Grandissimes*.

Horatio (Sgarlotto) Frump. Detective who seeks to uncover the plans of the passengers on the *Here They Come* in Gregory Corso's *The American Express*.

Indiana Frusk. See Indiana Frusk Rolliver.

Adam Fry. Father of Gideon Fry; leaves the ranch to his son and commits suicide in Larry McMurtry's *Leaving Cheyenne*.

Gideon (Gid) Fry. Son of Adam Fry, husband of Mabel Peters Fry, father of Jimmy, lover of Molly Taylor White, and friend of Johnny McCloud; owner of a large Texas ranch; dies after falling from a windmill; narrates part of Larry McMurtry's *Leaving Cheyenne*.

Mabel Peters Fry. Wife of Gideon Fry in Larry McMurtry's *Leaving Cheyenne*.

Thomas (Happy Tom) Fry. Cripple aboard the *Fidèle* in Herman Melville's *The Confidence-Man*.

John Fryer. Master of HMS *Bounty* who treats the crew decently, but who is forced to join Captain Bligh in being set adrift after the rebellion in Charles Nordhoff and James Norman Hall's *Mutiny on the Bounty*; because of his strength and navigational skills, he is of great assistance while adrift at sea in *Men against the Sea*.

Lois Fuchs. Large, earthy woman from Louisiana who tells of her passionate affair with a boy in William Goyen's *In a Farther Country*.

Otto Fuchs. Hired man of the Burdens; admired by Jim Burden in Willa Cather's *My Ántonia*.

Alistair Fuchs-Forbes. Spiritual con man whose pop transcendentalism seduces Doris More in Walker Percy's *Love in the Ruins*.

Dolores de la Fuente (y Someruelos). Second wife of Anthony Adverse in Hervey Allen's *Anthony Adverse*.

Padre Fuentes. Roman Catholic missionary murdered by the Niaruna Indians he comes to serve in Peter Matthiessen's *At Play in the Fields of the Lord*.

Elizabeth (E. F.) Fuess. Deceased girlfriend of John Laskell in Lionel Trilling's *The Middle of the Journey*.

Dino Fulgoni. Los Angeles prosecutor in the second murder trial of Jimmy Smith in JosephWambaugh's *The Onion Field*.

Fulkerson. Magazine sponsor who convinces Basil March to edit *Every Other Week* in William Dean Howells's *A Hazard of New Fortunes*.

Governor Alvin Tufts (Allie) Fuller. Former trick bicycle rider and racer who rises to great wealth and prominence; in his dislike of "Reds," he refuses to grant Sacco and Vanzetti a new trial, despite evidence that Webster Thayer, who presided at the earlier trial, had engaged in numerous improprieties in Upton Sinclair's *Boston*.

Professor George Orson Fuller. Doctor of phrenology who patents a cap to mould the shape of the head, thereby influencing mental capabilities, in Gore Vidal's *Burr*.

Dr. Joel Fuller. Veterinarian who threatens to put Rato Mustian's dog to sleep in Reynolds Price's *A Generous Man*.

Obidiah Funches. Husband of Katie Mae Dees in Arthenia J. Bates's *The Deity Nodded*.

Fuqua. Police captain who tries to use the Fazenda murder to further his career in John Gregory Dunne's *True Confessions*.

Reverend Jethro (Furb) Furber. Preacher haunted by sexual passion and obsessed by the seemingly impenetrable ease of Brackett Omensetter; Furber's roiling stream of consciousness dominates part of William Gass's *Omensetter's Luck*.

Loretta Furlong. See Loretta Botsford Wendall.

Patrick (Pat) Furlong. Brutish man who marries Loretta Wendall and badly beats his stepdaughter, Maureen Wendall, in Joyce Carol Oates's *them*.

Furman. Southern jail inmate and model of audacity to Dudley Osborn in Wright Morris's *My Uncle Dudley*.

Flora Furness. Daughter of Lily Furness, cousin of Stephen Carver, and schoolmate of Jane Ward in Margaret Ayer Barnes's *Years of Grace* and *Wisdom's Gate*.

Lily Furness. Mother of Flora Furness; commits suicide when Albert Lancaster, the man she loves, marries Muriel Lester in Margaret Ayer Barnes's *Years of Grace*.

Frank Fusco. Art critic who prepares a retrospective exhibit of the photography of Maude Coffin Pratt in Paul Theroux's *Picture Palace*.

Agricola (Agricole) Fusilier. Creole uncle of Honoré Grandissime in George Washington Cable's *The Grandissimes*.

Allen Fuso. American anthropologist who is second in command on the research project designed to help poor blacks on Bourne Island in Paule Marshall's *The Chosen Place, the Timeless People*.

Nick Fuso. Young mechanic and upstairs tenant of Morris Bober in Bernard Malamud's *The Assistant*.

G

Gabriel. See Gabriel Breaux.

Gabriel (Gabou). Servant of Louis Desrivières and lover of Youma, whom he fails to rescue from a burning house, in Lafcadio Hearn's *Youma*.

Reverend Gabrielsen. Preacher who advocates English services in the Norwegian Lutheran Church; presses Peder Holm to join the ministry in O. E. Rölvaag's *Peder Victorious*.

Aaron Gadd. New England carpenter, missionary to the Sioux Indians in the Minnesota territory, and later a builder in St. Paul; husband of Selene Lanark in Sinclair Lewis's *The God-Seeker*.

Elijah Gadd. Brother of Aaron Gadd and labor organizer in the Minnesota territory in Sinclair Lewis's *The God-Seeker*.

Selene Lanark Gadd. See Selene Lanark.

Uriel Gadd. New England farmer, Calvinist deacon, and father of Aaron and Elijah Gadd; helps slaves escape to Canada in Sinclair Lewis's *The God-Seeker*.

Errante Gaetano. Sleeping cart driver whose failure to leave the road leads to General Marvin's order forbidding carts to enter Adano in John Hersey's *A Bell for Adano*.

Gaffett. Old seafarer who tells Captain Littlepage about a city of ghosts near the North Pole in Sarah Orne Jewett's *The Country of the Pointed Firs*.

Gagnon. Bird lover; friend and killer of Konrad Vost in John Hawkes's *The Passion Artist*.

Wendy (Wendee) Gahaghan. Graduate student and lover of Brian Tate in Alison Lurie's *The War Between the Tates*.

Jean Gail. White lesbian ex-lover of Terry Bluvard; jealous of the relationship between Bluvard and Renay Davis in Ann Allen Shockley's *Loving Her*.

Désirée Gaillard. Wife of Edward Cary; attacked and killed by Sherman's drunken marauders in Mary Johnston's *Cease Firing*.

Bull (Old Bull, Señor Gahr-va) Gaines. Cincinnati-born, sixty-year-old morphine addict living in Mexico City in Jack Kerouac's *Tristessa* and *Desolation Angels*.

Lawrence Mason (Larry) Gaines. Handsome, intelligent, popular Student Council President at Dorset Academy; joins the Merchant Marine, has a tender sexual initiation with Edith Stone, and dies when his ship explodes ten miles out of New York harbor in Richard Yates's *A Good School*.

Bill Gains. Friend and heroin connection of William Lee in New York; later comes to Mexico City in William S. Burroughs's *Junkie*; also appears in *Naked Lunch* and *The Soft Machine*.

Neil Gaither. Woman John Wickliff Shawnessy should marry but does not in Ross Lockridge, Jr.'s *Raintree County*.

Paul Lloyd Galambos. Psychologist kidnapped to work at NESTER; narrator of Scott Spencer's *Last Night at the Brain Thieves Ball*.

Andrew (Andy, George Andrews, Miles-Away-Andrews) Gale, Jr.. Grandson of Slovenian immigrant Anton Galé and contributor to liberal causes; killed gangland style in Louis Adamic's *Grandsons*.

Andrew (Andy) Gale, Sr.. Son of Anton Galé and father of Andy, Margaret, and Peter Gale; worker who becomes a middle-class salesman in Louis Adamic's *Grandsons*.

Anthony Adams (Tony) Gale. Son of Mildred Adams Gale and Jack Gale in Louis Adamic's *Grandsons*.

Anton Galé. Slovenian immigrant who is killed in the Haymarket Riot; father of Andrew Gale, Sr., and Tony Gale; grandfather of Andy, Margaret, Peter, and Jack Gale in Louis Adamic's *Grandsons*.

Jack Gale. Grandson of Anton Galé and son of Tony Gale; murdered because of his I. W. W. organizing activities in Louis Adamic's *Grandsons*.

Margaret Gale. See Margaret Gale Stedman.

Mildred Adams Gale. Wife of Jack Gale and mother of Anthony Adams Gale; supporter of liberal causes in Louis Adamic's *Grandsons*.

Peter (Jack McLeish) Gale. Rootless grandson of Anton Galé; assumes the identity of Jack McLeish, a character in his proposed novel "Grandsons," in Louis Adamic's *Grandsons*.

Tony Gale. Steelworker son of Anton Galé and father of Jack Gale in Louis Adamic's *Grandsons*.

Harry Gallagher. Expatriate American screenwriter; married to Louisa Gallagher; has an affair with Samantha Everton and follows her from Paris to Rome and then to Tel Aviv in James Jones's *The Merry Month of May*.

Hill Gallagher. Son of Harry Gallagher; becomes involved in student riots in Paris, has an affair with Samantha Everton, and moves to Spain to live in a cave in James Jones's *The Merry Month of May*.

Honor Gallagher. Best friend in childhood of Cress Delahanty in Jessamyn West's *Cress Delahanty.*

Jane Gallagher. Former neighbor and friend of Holden Caulfield; always kept her kings in the back row when playing checkers; Holden worries about her date with Ward Stradlater in J. D. Salinger's *The Catcher in the Rye.*

Louisa Dunn Hill Gallagher. Wife of Harry Gallagher; suffers brain damage after a suicide attempt in James Jones's *The Merry Month of May.*

Matt Gallagher. Partner of Piet Hanema and husband of Terry Gallagher in John Updike's *Couples.*

McKenna Hartley Gallagher. Young daughter of Harry and Louisa Gallagher; godchild of Jack Hartley in James Jones's *The Merry Month of May.*

Roy Gallagher. Boston-Irish soldier who suffers a nervous breakdown when he hears of his wife's death in Norman Mailer's *The Naked and the Dead.*

Terry Gallagher. Potter and musician; wife of Matt Gallagher in John Updike's *Couples.*

Gallegos. Corrupt priest who is suspended by Bishop Latour in Willa Cather's *Death Comes for the Archbishop.*

Gallen (Gallen von St. Leonhard). Lover of Hannes Graff; helps Graff free the animals in John Irving's *Setting Free the Bears.*

Sedaya (Sede) Gallet. Cherokee Indian who betrays a rebellious tribesman in return for Crow Town's exemption from removal; later the wife of Ewen Warne in H. L. Davis's *Beulah Land.*

Gallus. Ambitious, violent-tempered brother of Julian; elevated to the position of Caesar by Constantius but ultimately executed by him in Gore Vidal's *Julian.*

Ike Galovitch. Hardheaded Yugoslavian-American platoon guide who dislikes Robert E. Lee Prewitt in James Jones's *From Here to Eternity.*

John Galt. Brilliant research engineer for Twentieth Century Motor Company; organizes a strike against self-immolation in Ayn Rand's *Atlas Shrugged.*

Lucie Gamelon. Cousin of Christina Goering's governess and later companion of Christina; eventually lives with Arnold in Jane Bowles's *Two Serious Ladies.*

Gilbert (Gil) Gamesh. Egocentric but unbeatable pitcher who kills umpire Mike Masterson with a pitch; banished from baseball but later returns to expose Communist influence in the Patriot League in Philip Roth's *The Great American Novel.*

General Aubrey T. Gammage. Friend and confidant of Daniel Cable Wills and principal agent in a program of industrial sabotage and trade sanctions against the Nazis during World War II in George V. Higgins's *Dreamland.*

Gamow. Psychoanalyst whom Will Barrett entertains by playing the ideal patient in Walker Percy's *The Last Gentleman.*

David Gamut. Psalm singer accompanying Duncan Heyward and the Munroe sisters in James Fenimore Cooper's *The Last of the Mohicans.*

Berryben Ganchion. See Berryben Starnes.

Boy Ganchion. A main voice/narrator of William Goyen's *The House of Breath.*

Christy Ganchion. Son of Granny Ganchion; fails to save his wife from drowning in William Goyen's *The House of Breath.*

Folner (Follie) Ganchion. Son of Granny Ganchion; runs away with a circus and later commits suicide in William Goyen's *The House of Breath.*

Hannah (Granny) Ganchion. Mother of Christy and Folner Ganchion; grandmother of Boy Ganchion and Berryben Starnes in William Goyen's *The House of Breath.*

Benjamin (Ben) Harrison Gant. Beloved older brother of Eugene Gant in Thomas Wolfe's *Look Homeward, Angel*; dies of pneumonia caused by years of neglect by his parsimonious parents in *Of Time and the River.*

Eliza E. Pentland Gant. Wife of Oliver Gant and mother of Eugene Gant; her fear of poverty and fervent belief in the work ethic ultimately destroy her family in Thomas Wolfe's *Look Homeward, Angel* and *Of Time and the River.*

Eugene Gant. Shy, studious boy from a large, parsimonious North Carolina family; his youth and young manhood are chronicled in Thomas Wolfe's *Look Homeward, Angel* and *Of Time and the River.*

Oliver Gant. Unfaithful husband of Eliza Gant and father of Eugene Gant; drunken womanizer who dies of cancer in Thomas Wolfe's *Look Homeward, Angel.*

Elmer Gantry. Midwesterner who, after working as a revivalist, becomes a powerful, less-than-ethical Methodist minister in Sinclair Lewis's *Elmer Gantry*; radio minister with ties to various charitable organizations that employ Gideon Planish in *Gideon Planish*.

Mrs. Elmer Gantry. See Cleo Benham.

Mrs. Logan Gantry. Dress shop owner with great hopes for her son, Elmer Gantry, in Sinclair Lewis's *Elmer Gantry*.

Eddie (Uncle Ganooch) Ganucci. Organized crime leader who is caught in a five-car pileup when Stephen Rojack throws Deborah Rojack's body from a window in Norman Mailer's *An American Dream*.

Louis Garafolo. Old boxing manager of Lee Youngdahl in Mark Harris's *Wake Up, Stupid*.

Garbos. Farmer who hangs the narrator from the ceiling and tortures him with a dog in Jerzy Kosinski's *The Painted Bird*.

Doctor Garcia. Tijuana abortionist who performs an abortion on Vida Kramar in Richard Brautigan's *The Abortion*.

Irwin Garden. Homosexual poet and friend of Jack Duluoz in Jack Kerouac's *Visions of Cody*; also appears in *Book of Dreams*, *Big Sur*, and (as the author of the poem "Howling") in *Desolation Angels*.

Jason Gardens. Magazine editor and husband of Salley Gardens; their marriage presents the central problem in Susan Cheever's *Looking for Work*.

Salley Gardens. Protagonist and dissatisfied wife who finds marriage a trap from which serious employment is conceived of as an escape in Susan Cheever's *Looking for Work*.

Chauncey Gardiner. See Chance.

Sir Philip Gardiner. Villain who is unsuccessful in his attempt to abduct Hope Leslie in Catharine Maria Sedgwick's *Hope Leslie*.

Jeff Gardner. Bowlegged thug employed by Shad O'Rory; enjoys beating Ned Beaumont in Dashiell Hammett's *The Glass Key*.

Adela Gareth. Mother of Owen Gareth and mistress of Poynton; attempts to enlist Fleda Vetch's assistance in maintaining control of the Poynton furnishings in Henry James's *The Spoils of Poynton*.

Owen Gareth. Weak-willed son of Adela Gareth; attracted to Fleda Vetch but marries Mona Brigstock in Henry James's *The Spoils of Poynton*.

Critchwood Laverne (Chick, Chicken, Chicky) Garfield. Football coach of Jack Curran at Boniface College in Mark Steadman's *A Lion's Share*.

Tony Garido. Cuban husband of Margo Dowling who drives her away with his abuse and yet periodically seeks her help in John Dos Passos's *U.S.A.* trilogy.

Vin Garl. Day-shift worker at the Past Bay Manufacturing Company factory; Finnish immigrant and former Wobbly who proposes the strike in Robert Cantwell's *The Land of Plenty*.

Mary Garland. Cousin of Sarah Hudson and fiancée of Roderick Hudson; loved by Rowland Mallet, Hudson's patron, in Henry James's *Roderick Hudson*.

Joe (José) Garms. Street fighter, army deserter, and volunteer in an American battalion in the Spanish civil war; friend of Jake Starr in William Herrick's *Hermanos!*

George D. Garnett (Garnet). Southern planter opposed to slavery; buys slaves and lets them work for their freedom; expelled from the Mayfield Baptist Church for supporting Comfort Servosse's sabbath school for freedom at Warrington; attacked unsuccessfully by the Ku Klux Klan in Albion W. Tourgee's *A Fool's Errand*.

Louisa Garnett (Garnet). Daughter of George Garnett; her hair turns from brown to white as a result of the Ku Klux Klan attack on her home in Albion W. Tourgee's *A Fool's Errand*.

Richard Brooke (Dick) Garnett. Southern general accused of cowardice for withdrawing from an encounter with Union troops; placed in charge of the second of George Pickett's brigades in Michael Shaara's *The Killer Angels*.

Pete Garolian. Serbian proprietor of the Crystal Lunchroom in Albert Halper's *Union Square*.

Duncan Garp. First child of T. S. Garp and Helen Holm; loses an eye in an automobile crash and an arm in a motorcycle accident; marries one of Roberta Muldoon's transsexual friends; dies by choking to death on an olive while laughing too hard at one of his own jokes in John Irving's *The World According to Garp*.

Helen Holm Garp. See Helen Holm.

Jenny Garp. Third child of T. S. Garp and Helen Holm; twice-married doctor and cancer researcher who dies of cancer in John Irving's *The World According to Garp*.

T. S. Garp. Son of Technical Sergeant Garp and Jenny Fields, husband of Helen Holm, and father of Duncan, Walt, and Jenny Garp; wrestler who becomes a wrestling coach; devoted friend of Ellen

James; killed by Pooh Percy in John Irving's *The World According to Garp*.

Technical Sergeant Garp. Father of T. S. Garp; dies from a flak wound in John Irving's *The World According to Garp*.

Walt Garp. Second child of T. S. Garp and Helen Holm; dies in an automobile accident in John Irving's *The World According to Garp*.

Helmeth Garrett. Engineer and self-made man; Olivia Lattimore's first romance and later her lover; alienated from Lattimore when she refuses to halt her stage career should they marry in Mary Austin's *A Woman of Genius*.

Moon Garrett. Member of Ned Pepper's outlaw gang that holds captive Mattie Ross, Rooster Cogburn, and LaBoeuf in Charles Portis's *True Grit*.

Joe Garrity. High school track coach of Jack Duluoz in Jack Kerouac's *Maggie Cassidy*.

Marie Garson. Dime-a-dance woman on whom Roy Earle becomes emotionally dependent in William Riley Burnett's *High Sierra*.

Nat Garth. Feebleminded adopted son of Nellie Garth Goodwin; becomes a thief so he can join Nellie in Australia, only to die en route, in Charles Nordhoff and James Norman Hall's *Botany Bay*.

Nellie Garth. See Nellie Garth Goodwin.

Georgia Garveli. Daughter of Pop Garveli and friend of Jake Adams, whose car crashes with Georgia in it, in Herbert Simmons's *Corner Boy*.

Pop Garveli. Father of Georgia Garveli and friend of Jake Adams; white grocery store owner who operates a store in St. Louis's black belt in Herbert Simmons's *Corner Boy*.

Richard Garvin. Investor in Consolidated Tractions; driven to financial ruin and suicide by Eldon Parr in Winston Churchill's *The Inside of the Cup*.

Maria de las Garzas. Loveliest woman in Hidalgo, but an outcast; loves Alejandro Castillo and is murdered by his wife in Josefina Niggli's *Mexican Village*.

Amos G. Gashwiler. Storekeeper in Simsbury, Illinois, who promises to hold Merton Gill's job in case Merton does not succeed in Hollywood in Harry Leon Wilson's *Merton of the Movies*.

Captain Amos Gaskens. Former plantation owner who leads a band of Tories in William Gilmore Simms's *The Partisan*.

Charles (Charlie) Gaston. Son of a Confederate hero and husband of Sallie Worth; organizes the Red Shirts in opposition to the Reconstruction government and is elected governor of North Carolina in Thomas Dixon's *The Leopard's Spots*.

Nelson (Nelse) Gaston. Faithful slave of the Gastons; refuses to join the Union League in Thomas Dixon's *The Leopard's Spots*.

Ben Gately. Graduate of the United States Military Academy and commander of the Leper Colony in the 918th Bomb Group in Beirne Lay, Jr., and Sy Bartlett's *Twelve O'Clock High!*

Dr. Gates. Former Confederate doctor who also practiced among the Northerners and thought secession was folly; cares for Comfort Servosse during Servosse's final illness in Albion W. Tourgee's *A Fool's Errand*.

General Horatio Gates. Commander of the American forces at the Battle of Camden in William Gilmore Simms's *The Partisan*.

Jo Gates. Formerly married girlfriend of the narrator in Edmund Wilson's *Memoirs of Hecate County*.

Jay (James Gatz) Gatsby. Man of a mysterious background who hosts lavish parties on Long Island in the 1920s; seeks to recover Daisy Buchanan's love in F. Scott Fitzgerald's *The Great Gatsby*.

Henry C. Gatz. Father of James Gatz in F. Scott Fitzgerald's *The Great Gatsby*.

James Gatz. See Jay Gatsby.

Seymour Gatz. Salvage expert and patron of Warren Howe in Wright Morris's *Cause for Wonder*.

Adam Gaudylock. Backwoodsman, friend of Lewis Rand, and innocent participant in a plan to settle the West in Mary Johnston's *Lewis Rand*.

Norman Gaul. Drunken college halfback who spits into the punchbowl at the party Jane and Thomas Eborn chaperone in Reynolds Price's *Love and Work*.

Gavrila. Political officer who befriends and indoctrinates the narrator and gives him Gorky's *Childhood* in Jerzy Kosinski's *The Painted Bird*.

Gawaine. Nephew of Arthur, faithful husband of Ragnell, dutiful father, proven warrior, and the "finest man" in Thomas Berger's *Arthur Rex*.

Ralph C. (Rafie) Gawber. Middle-aged accountant who fears and witnesses apocalyptic turmoil in Paul Theroux's *The Family Arsenal*.

Denny Gayde. Escaped convict aided by the child Hagar Ashendyne; becomes a Socialist speaker in Mary Johnston's *Hagar.*

Squire Gaylord. Publisher of the *Free Press* and father of Marcia Gaylord Hubbard in William Dean Howells's *A Modern Instance.*

Thomas (Tom) Gaylord. Friend of Hilary and Austen Vane; lumber executive and political worker in Winston Churchill's *Mr. Crewe's Career.*

William (Bill) Gaylord. American infantry lieutenant killed in action in World War II in Martha Gellhorn's *Wine of Astonishment.*

Major Gazaway. Politician and soldier in John Carter's regiment; his connections keep him ahead of Edward Colburne despite Gazaway's obvious cowardice and ineptness at command in John William DeForest's *Miss Ravenel's Conversion from Secession to Loyalty.*

Charlie Geary. Self-serving, manipulative Darwinian who strips Vandover of his inheritance in Frank Norris's *Vandover and the Brute.*

Orlando Geary. Early settler and deputy sheriff in Shoestring Valley, Oregon, in H. L. Davis's *Honey in the Horn.*

Reb Gedaliya. Ritual slaughterer, cabalist, and follower of Sabbatai Zevi; Satan figure who leads the townspeople of Goray into evil; seduces and then marries Rechele Babad; finally leaves Goray and turns apostate in Isaac Bashevis Singer's *Satan in Goray.*

Abigail (Aunt Abigail) Geddy. Member of the only "colored family" in Ironside; independent woman proud of her Indian blood and pragmatic about killing chickens in Ellen Glasgow's *Vein of Iron.*

Bernard Geffen. Shady Detroit businessman who hires Jules Wendall as his driver; through Geffen, Wendall meets Geffen's niece, Nadine Greene, in Joyce Carol Oates's *them.*

Gehl. Garkohn huntress who befriends Alanna Verrick in Octavia E. Butler's *Survivor.*

Gehnahteh. Artisan and Tehkohn husband of Choh; fosters Tien in Octavia E. Butler's *Survivor.*

Hans von Gehring. Facially scarred roomer at Rosa Reichl's boardinghouse; student on leave from Heidelberg University in Katherine Anne Porter's *The Leaning Tower.*

Arthur Gwynn Geiger. Pornography dealer and blackmailer who is murdered in Raymond Chandler's *The Big Sleep.*

Phil Gelvin. Mundane shoe salesman whose unimaginative lovemaking drives Bab Masters to fantasy and prolonged complaint about the unconscientiousness of lovers and readers alike in William Gass's *Willie Masters' Lonesome Wife.*

Susan Gender. Girlfriend of Duffy Deeter; student at the University of Florida in Harry Crews's *A Feast of Snakes.*

Genesis. Black handyman of the Baxters; unintentionally but effectively deflates William Baxter's ego in Booth Tarkington's *Seventeen.*

Mr. Genesis. Father of Genesis; whittles toys for Jane Baxter in Booth Tarkington's *Seventeen.*

Genevieve. Girlfriend of Joe Fleming, with whom she pleads to give up boxing, in Jack London's *The Game.*

Genial. See Terrence Weld.

Genie. Fantastic character who must devise a new approach to the writing of fiction in the *Dunyazadiad,* a novella in John Barth's *Chimera.*

Genslinger. Newspaper editor loyal to railroad interests who reveals Magnus Derrick's resort to bribery as a means of reducing the rates for shipping wheat in Frank Norris's *The Octopus.*

Sarah Gentles. Wife of Van Harrington in Robert Herrick's *The Memoirs of an American Citizen.*

Ed Gentry. Graphic artist who achieves complete renewal by identifying himself with nature; narrator-protagonist of James Dickey's *Deliverance.*

George. Black employee of Joe Lon Mackey; brother of Lummy in Harry Crews's *A Feast of Snakes.*

George. Female impersonator and dancer at the Iron Horse in Harry Crews's *Karate Is a Thing of the Spirit.*

George III. King of England who hires Israel Potter as a gardener in Herman Melville's *Israel Potter.*

Tobey George. Army friend of Marcus Macauley; visits the Macauley family following Marcus's death in William Saroyan's *The Human Comedy.*

Georgia. Cousin of Daniel Verger, with whom she has an affair, in John Clellon Holmes's *Go.*

Georgiana. Girlfriend of Henry Miller known for having changed her name and for creating her own identity in Henry Miller's *Tropic of Capricorn.*

Letty Pace Gerald. Childhood sweetheart and later wife of Lester Kane, who cannot love her as he loved Jennie Gerhardt, in Theodore Dreiser's *Jennie Gerhardt*.

Geraldine. Girlfriend of Alva; becomes pregnant and gives birth to their illegitimate, deformed child in Wallace Thurman's *The Blacker The Berry*.

Gerard. Early lover of Lillian; frightened by her power in Anaïs Nin's *Ladders to Fire*.

Sophie Geratis. Greek chambermaid in a luxury hotel with whom Augie March has a brief affair during his period as a labor organizer for the CIO in Saul Bellow's *The Adventures of Augie March*.

Gerhard. Computer specialist at the Neuropsychiatric Research Unit who designs the computer that is implanted in Harold Benson in Michael Crichton's *The Terminal Man*.

Lieutenant David Gerhardt. Handsome officer from New York and friend of Claude Wheeler; respected by fellow soldiers because he could have been in the military band but chose to serve in the infantry in Willa Cather's *One of Ours*.

Genevieve (Jennie, Mrs. J. G. Stover) Gerhardt. Lover of George Brander, by whom she has a child; nurse and lover of Lester Kane; unwed mother who tries to improve her life but suffers many setbacks in Theodore Dreiser's *Jennie Gerhardt*.

Joe (Joey) Gerhardt. Childhood friend of Henry Miller; considered a "gentleman" for having beaten up another youth in Henry Miller's *Tropic of Capricorn*.

William Gerhardt. Father of Jennie Gerhardt, with whom he lives after his wife dies, in Theodore Dreiser's *Jennie Gerhardt*.

Germaine. Prostitute with gold teeth who becomes a friend of Henry Miller in Henry Miller's *Tropic of Cancer*.

Emmeline Gerrish. Childhood friend of Annie Kilburn and proud wife of William Gerrish in William Dean Howells's *Annie Kilburn*.

William B. (Bill) Gerrish. Successful businessman who leads the revolt against Julius W. Peck in William Dean Howells's *Annie Kilburn*.

George Gerry. Handsome New England lawyer; after being angered by Miss Nan Prince's rejection of his marriage proposal, he admires the dedication that leads her to choose a career in medicine; becomes more serious as a result of his relationship with

Nan in Sarah Orne Jewett's *A Country Doctor*.

Valentine (Val) Gersbach. Radio personality with flaming copper hair, boisterous surface emotions, flawed Yiddish, and a wooden leg; false friend to Moses Herzog and adulterous lover of Madeleine Herzog in Saul Bellow's *Herzog*.

Rav Gershenson. Orthodox Talmudic scholar who teaches both Danny Saunders and Reuven Malter in Chaim Potok's *The Chosen*; persuades Rav Jacob Kalman to ordain Saunders as a rabbi in *The Promise*.

Gershon. Arrogant, ignorant, and nepotistic tax collector, town bully, foe of Jacob Eliezer, and warden of the burial society who forbids the performance of sacred rituals on the body of Jacob's wife, Wanda Bzik, in Isaac Bashevis Singer's *The Slave*.

Will Gerstenslager. Widowed lawyer; friend, financial adviser, and suitor of Emma Wallop in Peter De Vries's *Mrs. Wallop*.

Gerta. Girlfriend of Jasper Ammen in Conrad Aiken's *King Coffin*.

Gertrude. Wife of Skipper and mother of Cassandra; commits suicide sixteen months after the birth of her granddaughter Pixie in John Hawkes's *Second Skin*.

Lucy Gessler. Neighbor of Mildred Pierce and bartender in Mildred's restaurant in James M. Cain's *Mildred Pierce*.

Sister Geter. Pentecostal Fire Baptized Believer who tries to evangelize Ray, Banjo, and the other expatriates in Claude McKay's *Banjo*.

Millie Muldoon Gharoujian. Owner of a miniature schnauzer used by Philo Skinner in his dognapping scheme in Joseph Wambaugh's *The Black Marble*.

Adolphus Asher Ghoulens. See Doctor Sax.

Cavaliere Giuseppino Giacosa. Former secret lover of Mrs. Light and father, by her, of Christina Light; escorts Christina and Mrs. Light to the watering-places of Europe in Henry James's *Roderick Hudson*.

Mr. Giardineri. Owner of the Aaron Burr, a local college restaurant; pretends to have contacts with organized crime concerning the bribe money Raymond Blent took to lose a football game in Howard Nemerov's *The Homecoming Game*.

Lester (Les) Gibbons. Cowardly and envious neighbor of the Stamper family in Ken Kesey's *Sometimes*

a Great Notion.

Angelica Gibbs. Blond American widow of Donald Gibbs; comes to Kush to avenge her husband's death and instead stays to adopt an African life style as Michaelis Ezana's lover in John Updike's *The Coup.*

Donald "X." Gibbs. Immolated USAID officer whose pyre is mounds of cereal and junk food meant as relief food for famine victims of Kush but rejected by Colonel Ellellou; after Ellellou is ousted, the new government memorializes Gibbs by naming a shopping center after him in John Updike's *The Coup.*

Miss Dorothy Gibbs. Operator of the Female Institute in Thomas Bailey Aldrich's *The Story of a Bad Boy.*

Jack Gibbs. Failed writer and polymath; once worked for the General Roll Corporation, but now teaches science and plays the horses in William Gaddis's *JR.*

Stanley Gibbs. Gravedigger for Port William, Kentucky, in Wendell Berry's *A Place on Earth.*

Gibby. American heiress and lover of Woytek; slain with him and others in a Charles Manson-style massacre in Jerzy Kosinski's *Blind Date.*

Dick (Tex Ellery, Ted Elmer, Ted Elson, Ellery Loyola, Marshall Maine, etc.) Gibson. Itinerant radio announcer on a lifelong apprenticeship in search of the meaning of America; adopts numerous aliases in Stanley Elkin's *The Dick Gibson Show*; also appears in *The Franchiser.*

Dilsey Gibson. Cook for the Compsons; married to Roskus Gibson and the mother of Frony, T. P., and Versh Gibson in William Faulkner's *The Sound and the Fury.*

Drag Gibson. Western capitalist who French kisses a green horse; orders brides through the mail and kills them by feeding them to his swine; dying from having been poisoned by Mustache Sal until he recovers miraculously upon learning that the Pope is visiting the West in Ishmael Reed's *Yellow Back Radio Broke-Down.*

Fannie Gibson. See Fannie Hamilton.

Frony Gibson. Daughter of Dilsey and Roskus Gibson; sister of T. P. and Versh Gibson in William Faulkner's *The Sound and the Fury.*

Jim Gibson. Journeyman harnessmaker who helps his employer Joseph Wainsworth improve his business; murdered by Wainsworth when he publicly humiliates Wainsworth for his old-fashioned business ways in Sherwood Anderson's *Poor White.*

Roskus Gibson. Husband of Dilsey; father of Frony, T. P., and Versh Gibson in William Faulkner's *The Sound and the Fury.*

T. P. Gibson. Son of Dilsey and Roskus Gibson; brother of Frony and Versh Gibson in William Faulkner's *The Sound and the Fury.*

Versh Gibson. Son of Dilsey and Roskus Gibson; brother of Frony and T. P. Gibson in William Faulkner's *The Sound and the Fury.*

Gifford (Gip). White leader of a group of militant black revolutionaries; commits suicide in Nicholas Delbanco's *News.*

Gignoux. Spy and traitor in Winston Churchill's *The Crossing.*

Gil. Proprietor of and bartender at Gil's Tavern who is able to place George Stroud with Pauline Delos on the day of her murder in Kenneth Fearing's *The Big Clock.*

Gloria Gilbert. See Gloria Gilbert Patch.

Ted Gilbert. Americanized Norwegian teacher who shocks Beret Holm by producing a play in O. E. Rölvaag's *Peder Victorious.*

George (Billy Bocksfuss, Georgie, Goat-Boy) Giles. Hero, raised as a goat, who becomes the Grand Tutor; narrator of John Barth's *Giles Goat-Boy.*

Grace Giles. Black student at the University of Southern California; friendly toward Emma Lou Morgan but not popular with the other students in Wallace Thurman's *The Blacker the Berry.*

Jimmie Giles. Cheerful young porter who befriends Matthew Towns and is lynched after being accused of attacking a white woman in W. E. B. Du Bois's *Dark Princess.*

Stoker (Giles Stoker) Giles. Supposed son of George Giles, "whereabouts unknown, existence questionable"; claims to be the editor of the text of John Barth's *Giles Goat-Boy.*

Colonel Barry Fitzgerald Macartney Gilfillan. British officer in James Kirke Paulding's *The Dutchman's Fireside.*

Father (Gilly) Gilhooley. Priest of the Lonigans in James T. Farrell's *Young Lonigan*; builds a new church as blacks move into the South Chicago neighborhood in *The Young Manhood of Studs Lonigan* and *Judgment Day.*

Kenny Gill. Thief and partner of Russell in a dog-stealing racket; betrays Russell to Jackie Cogan in George V. Higgins's *Cogan's Trade*.

Merton (Clifford Armytage) Gill. Small-town store clerk who becomes a Hollywood film actor under the name of Clifford Armytage in Harry Leon Wilson's *Merton of the Movies*.

Miss Gillespie. Cold, defiant school principal who snubs Matthew Towns because he is a Pullman porter in W. E. B. Du Bois's *Dark Princess*.

Dr. Gerald Gilley. Director of composition and later chair of the English department at Cascadia College; husband of Pauline Gilley in Bernard Malamud's *A New Life*.

Pauline Gilley. Wife of Gerald Gilley; has affairs with Leo Duffy and Seymour Levin in Bernard Malamud's *A New Life*.

Dr. Gillies. Best physician in Coaltown whose wisdom is often sought; introduces at a turn-of-the-century party the idea that men of the new century were children of the eighth day in Thornton Wilder's *The Eighth Day*.

Joe (Yaphank) Gilligan. Army private who helps care for Donald Mahon in William Faulkner's *Soldiers' Pay*.

Joan Gilling. Fellow inmate with Esther Greenwood at a private mental hospital; hangs herself in Sylvia Plath's *The Bell Jar*.

Hayden Gillis. Representative of the governor of the Dakota Territory; consults with Blue about Hard Times in E. L. Doctorow's *Welcome to Hard Times*.

Bessie Gilmore. Mother of Gary Gilmore in Norman Mailer's *The Executioner's Song*.

Gary Mark Gilmore. First American to be executed after a ten-year moratorium; protagonist of Norman Mailer's *The Executioner's Song*.

Mikal Gilmore. Brother of Gary Gilmore in Norman Mailer's *The Executioner's Song*.

Anthony Gilray. English judge who presides over the libel suit between Adam Kelno and Abe Cady in Leon Uris's *QB VII*.

John Gilson. Schoolboy who, in order to impress his teacher, pretends to be Fyodor Dostoyevski's character Raskolnikov in Nathanael West's *The Dream Life of Balso Snell*.

Ginette. Prostitute involved with Fillmore; becomes pregnant and has a venereal disease in Henry Miller's *Tropic of Cancer*.

Gin-head Susy (Susy). Woman with a "yellow complex" who searches for a lover; dispenses free gin at socials she gives in Brooklyn; Zeddy Plummer later becomes her live-in lover in Claude McKay's *Home to Harlem*.

Ginny. Lover of Shawn; develops a skill for raising vegetables and has the first Indian baby after the dispersement of the Indians in Marge Piercy's *Dance the Eagle to Sleep*.

Ginny. Roommate of Louella and volunteer Red Cross worker in John Horne Burns's *The Gallery*.

Joe Ginotta. Brother of Pete Ginotta; bootlegger and restaurant manager in William Faulkner's *Mosquitoes* and *Pylon*.

Pete Ginotta. Brother of Joe Ginotta; boyfriend of Jenny Steinbauer, with whom he attends the yacht party, in William Faulkner's *Mosquitoes*; also appears in *Pylon*.

Daniel (Charles Fogelstein, Danny) Ginsberg. Orphan at the Maimonides Home for Jewish Boys who wants Charlie Sapistein to adopt him; author of a diary in Jay Neugeboren's *An Orphan's Tale*.

Jack Gioncarlo. Sailor befriended by Charlie Stark; helps thwart the murder of Raditzer in Peter Matthiessen's *Raditzer*.

Terry Gionoffrio. Young runaway chosen to be the mother of Satan's son; killed when she refuses to consent to the plan in Ira Levin's *Rosemary's Baby*.

Giovanelli. Handsome Italian who declares the innocence of his companion Daisy Miller following her death in Henry James's *Daisy Miller*.

Giovanni. Italian lover of David and rival of Hella in James Baldwin's *Giovanni's Room*.

Zito Giovanni. Former fascist informer who retains his position as town usher and becomes an assistant to Major Joppolo in John Hersey's *A Bell for Adano*.

Girard Girard. Billionaire notorious for being unfaithful to his wife; becomes enamored of Malcolm and wants to become his substitute father in James Purdy's *Malcolm*.

Madame (Doddy) Girard. Wife of Girard Girard; somewhat mad, she becomes obsessively infatuated with Malcolm and nurses him on his deathbed in James Purdy's *Malcolm*.

Christopher Gist. Indian agent who fails to understand why the Catawba warriors leave Braddock's camp in Mary Lee Settle's *O Beulah Land*.

Julian Gitche. Full-blooded Mohawk Indian pianist and New York/Yale wimp who marries Sissy Hankshaw; she leaves him and he turns to drink in Tom Robbins's *Even Cowgirls Get the Blues.*

Sissy Hankshaw Gitche. Big-thumbed model and hitchhiker extraordinaire who marries Julian Gitche; lover of Bonanza Jellybean, the Chink, and Delores del Ruby; jumpsuited heroine of Tom Robbins's *Even Cowgirls Get the Blues.*

Giulia. Young Italian woman who falls in love with an American captain and agrees to sleep with him on the night he must leave for the front in John Horne Burns's *The Gallery.*

Uncle Dan Givens. Notorious teller of tall tales about his past in Cudge Windsor's pool hall in Langston Hughes's *Not Without Laughter.*

Helen Givens. See Helen Givens Fisher.

Reverend Henry Givens. Former Ku Klux Klansman, now Imperial Grand Wizard of the Knights of Nordica; discovered to have black ancestors in George S. Schuyler's *Black No More.*

Mrs. Helen Givings. Garrulous real estate agent; neighbor who befriends the Wheelers in a vain effort to find companions for her schizophrenic son in Richard Yates's *Revolutionary Road.*

Howard Givings. Husband of Helen Givings; reads newspapers and turns off his hearing aid whenever he tires of listening to her in Richard Yates's *Revolutionary Road.*

John Givings. Paranoid schizophrenic son of Helen and Howard Givings; perceiving and commenting on the falsehoods in other people's lives and plans, he ends friendless in a mental institution in Richard Yates's *Revolutionary Road.*

James Callowhill Gladwin. Spokesman for Masonry on the frontier in Hervey Allen's *Bedford Village.*

Gladys. Estranged wife of Cross Damon; refuses to grant him a divorce; demands that he borrow $800 and give her the title to the house and car in Richard Wright's *The Outsider.*

Gladys. Girlfriend of Fish Tucker; dies in a fire at the Grove in Richard Wright's *The Long Dream.*

Gladys. Prostitute in Jack Flowers's stable in Singapore in Paul Theroux's *Saint Jack.*

Aunt Gladys. Newark relative with whom Neil Klugman lives in Philip Roth's *Goodbye, Columbus.*

Diana Moon Glampers. "Patient" of Eliot Rosewater in Kurt Vonnegut's *God Bless You, Mr. Rosewater.*

Zahn Glanz. High school lover of Hilke Marter; Vienna taxi driver who disappears after apparently driving into Hungary in John Irving's *Setting Free the Bears.*

Vera Glavanakova. Bulgarian poet of warmth and intelligence; Henry Bech falls in love with her in John Updike's *Bech: A Book.*

E. M. Glavis. Husband of Ethel McCarthy Glavis in Oscar Micheaux's *The Homesteader.*

Ethel McCarthy Glavis. Sister of Orlean McCarthy; sides with their father, Newton Justine McCarthy, against Jean Baptiste in Oscar Micheaux's *The Homesteader.*

Josh Glazer. Aging playwright, lyricist, and Broadway wit in John Updike's *Bech: A Book.*

Glenda (Gilded Girl). Stripper and informer for Bumper Morgan in Joseph Wambaugh's *The Blue Knight.*

Dorothea Glendinning. Sister of Pierre Glendinning II; gives a portrait of him as a young man to Pierre Glendinning III in Herman Melville's *Pierre.*

Mary Glendinning. Wife of Pierre Glendinning II and mother of Pierre Glendinning III; disowns her son and makes Glendinning Stanly the beneficiary of her estate in Herman Melville's *Pierre.*

Pierre Glendinning (I). Father of Pierre Glendinning II and horse-loving general in Herman Melville's *Pierre.*

Pierre Glendinning (II). Father of Pierre Glendinning III and apparently the father of Isabel Banford in Herman Melville's *Pierre.*

Pierre Glendinning (III). Son of Mary and Pierre Glendinning II; by pretending to be the husband of Isabel Banford, apparently his half sister, he causes the death of himself and others in Herman Melville's *Pierre.*

Nelly Glentworth. Nineteen-year-old engaged woman loved by the adolescent Tom Bailey in Thomas Bailey Aldrich's *The Story of a Bad Boy.*

Daniel Francis (Danny) Glick. Brother of Ralphie Glick; becomes a vampire after being bitten by his brother in Stephen King's *'Salem's Lot.*

Ralphie Glick. Brother of Danny Glick; killed by the vampire, Barlow, in Stephen King's *'Salem's Lot.*

Sammy (Sammele Glickstein) Glick. Ruthlessly ambitious copyboy who rises to the position of production chief of a major Hollywood studio in Budd Schulberg's *What Makes Sammy Run?*

Israel Glickstein. Brother of Sammy Glick; unlike his sibling, Israel observes the traditions of the Jewish faith in Budd Schulberg's *What Makes Sammy Run?*

Yuri Gligoric. Brash young poet and sexual rival of Leo Percepied in Jack Kerouac's *The Subterraneans.*

Johnny Glimmergarden. Second husband of Evelyn Marvel in Peter De Vries's *Through the Fields of Clover.*

Globke. Manager of Bucky Wunderlick and employee of Transparanoia organization in Don DeLillo's *Great Jones Street.*

Karl Glocken. Hunchbacked tobacco salesman from Mexico City who is returning to Germany in Katherine Anne Porter's *Ship of Fools.*

Gloriani. American sculptor of European extraction; member of the artistic fraternity in Rome and commentator on Roderick Hudson's sculptures in Henry James's *Roderick Hudson.*

Glover. Harley College student and friend of Edward Walcott in Nathaniel Hawthorne's *Fanshawe.*

Glycerium. Fifteen-year-old sister of Chrysis; falls in love with Pamphilus; before the question of their marriage is resolved, she dies in childbirth in Thornton Wilder's *The Woman of Andros.*

John T. Glymmer. Forceful senior partner of Glymmer, Read and former Secretary of the Treasury of the United States in Nathan Asch's *The Office.*

Glynda, Girl of the Glen. See Arista Prolo.

Glyp. Ancient Egyptian tomb robber in a dream had by Alexander Main in *The Bailbondsman,* a novella in Stanley Elkin's *Searches and Seizures.*

Goat. Young man with whom Salome Musgrove conspires to kill her stepdaughter Rosamond in Eudora Welty's *The Robber Bridegroom.*

Goat-Boy. See George Giles.

Goat Lady (Mother). Cryptic figure who takes her cart to the road in search of her son and is accidentally killed by George Loomis in John Gardner's *Nickel Mountain.*

God. The burning bush, Voice, Lord, pillar of cloud, and pillar of fire that guides Moses in Zora Neale Hurston's *Moses, Man of the Mountain.*

God of Street Boys. See Ali Juan Chapultepec.

Louisa Goddard. Wealthy and frugal intellectual loved by Marmaduke Littlepage, whose brother, Virginius Littlepage, she has loved for over thirty years, in Ellen Glasgow's *They Stooped to Folly.*

Michael Godfrey. Student debtor who tutors Amber St. Clare in upper-class speech and helps her escape from the criminal environment of Black Jack Mallard and Mother Red Cap in Kathleen Winsor's *Forever Amber.*

Gaston Godin. Bachelor professor of French at Beardsley College, friend of Humbert Humbert, and fancier of young boys; finds a home for Humbert and Dolores Haze near Beardsley School in Vladimir Nabokov's *Lolita.*

Reverend Marcus Augustus Godley. Bethel Church minister whose horse loses an unofficial race with Jess Birdwell's horse in Jessamyn West's *The Friendly Persuasion.*

Evan Godolphin. Son of Hugh Godolphin; aids his father and encounters Victoria Wren and Sydney Stencil in Florence in 1899; after extensive plastic surgery, becomes Veronica Manganese's caretaker on Malta in 1919 in Thomas Pynchon's *V.*

Hugh Godolphin. Explorer of the Antarctic and father of Evan Godolphin; may have discovered the mythical land of Vheissu in 1884; encounters V. as Victoria Wren in Florence in 1899 and as Vera Meroving in South-West Africa in 1922 in Thomas Pynchon's *V.*

Ma Godolphin. Rural tycoon and land baroness; reigning celebrity and competitor of Ma Sigafoos; client and briefly paramour of Billy Bumpers in Peter De Vries's *I Hear America Swinging.*

Rusty (Ace Mann) Godowsky. Macho boyfriend of Mary-Ann Pringle; anally raped by Myra Breckinridge; later a successful movie star and lover of Letitia Van Allen in Gore Vidal's *Myra Breckinridge.*

Christina Goering. Friend of Frieda Copperfield and, for a while, lover of Andrew McClane in Jane Bowles's *Two Serious Ladies.*

Luke (Luke the Loner) Gofannon. Legendary Patriot League centerfielder and the only man Angela Whittling Trust ever loved in Philip Roth's *The Great American Novel.*

Allan Gold. Schoolmaster and scout for General Jackson; wounded in the battle at Gaines's Mill; transformed into a fierce warrior by action at Sharpsburg; appears in Mary Johnston's *The Long Roll* and *Cease Firing.*

Belle Gold. Patient wife of the social climbing Bruce Gold in Joseph Heller's *Good as Gold.*

Bruce Gold. Dissatisfied college professor and aspiring cabinet officer; at work on a book on the Jewish-American experience in Joseph Heller's *Good as Gold.*

Esther Gold. Sister of Michael Gold; killed by a truck in New York's Lower East Side in Michael Gold's *Jews without Money.*

Gussie Gold. Slightly crazed stepmother of Bruce Gold; descended from Richmond and Charleston Jewish aristocracy in Joseph Heller's *Good as Gold.*

Herman Gold. Rumanian-born father of Michael Gold; owns a suspender shop, but is reduced to painting houses and finally to peddling bananas in New York's Lower East Side in Michael Gold's *Jews without Money.*

Jackson (Crazy Jack) Gold. Sixteen-year-old playmate of Abeba Torch during her childhood in rural North Carolina in Ellease Southerland's *Let the Lion Eat Straw.*

Julius Gold. Irascible father of Bruce Gold in Joseph Heller's *Good as Gold.*

Katie Gold. Hungarian-born mother of Michael Gold in Michael Gold's *Jews without Money.*

Michael (Mikey) Gold. Jewish narrator who tells of his family's life in New York's Lower East Side in Michael Gold's *Jews without Money.*

Sid Gold. Older brother and irritant of Bruce Gold in Joseph Heller's *Good as Gold.*

Rosalie Goldbaum. Naive young woman to whom Sammy Glick proposes in New York and then abandons when he moves to Hollywood in Budd Schulberg's *What Makes Sammy Run?*

Alvah Goldbook. Poet and friend of Ray Smith; author of the poem "Wail" in Jack Kerouac's *The Dharma Bums.* See also Irwin Garden.

Laura (Daphne Fountain, Vivi Lamar, Diana Lord) Golden. Successful actress who threatens John Wickliff Shawnessy's idealism in Ross Lockridge, Jr.'s *Raintree County.*

Rabbi Goldfarb. Rabbi of the synagogue the young David Dehn attends; murdered on the day of Dehn's Bar Mitzvah in Jerome Weidman's *The Temple.*

Dave Goldman. Jewish childhood friend of Phil Green, recently discharged from the army; becomes the sounding board for Green's experiences and frustrations in Laura Z. Hobson's *Gentleman's Agreement.*

Emma (Red Emma) Goldman. Anarchist who gives Evelyn Nesbit a massage and influences the political ideas of Mother's Younger Brother in E. L. Doctorow's *Ragtime.*

Sidney Jerome (Sid) Goldman. Hard-hitting Jewish first baseman for the New York Mammoths in Mark Harris's *The Southpaw, Bang the Drum Slowly, A Ticket for a Seamstitch,* and *It Looked Like For Ever.*

Jòrgen Josiah (Goldy) Goldschmidt. English publisher of Henry Bech in John Updike's *Bech: A Book.*

Frances (Frannie) Goldsmith. Pregnant woman concerned that her child will develop the disease that has destroyed most of humanity in Stephen King's *The Stand.*

Goldstein. Broadway producer of lavish spectacles; loves Delia Poole in Janet Flanner's *The Cubical City.*

Britt Goldstein. Film producer who wants to obtain the screen rights to Isadora Wing's novel *Candida Confesses* in Erica Jong's *How to Save Your Own Life.*

Joey Goldstein. Jewish-American soldier in Norman Mailer's *The Naked and the Dead.*

Maxine Goldstein. Former girlfriend of Jake Adams; seeks fame as a dancer in Herbert Simmons's *Corner Boy.*

Sandy Goldstone. Son of the owner of Lamm's department store and suitor of Marjorie Morningstar in Herman Wouk's *Marjorie Morningstar.*

Judge Hugh Warren Goldsworth. Distinguished authority on Roman law and intended target of a madman's bullet which kills John Shade by mistake; rents his house to Charles Kinbote, thus making Kinbote a neighbor of John Shade in Vladimir Nabokov's *Pale Fire.*

Doc Golightly. Horse doctor from Tulip, Texas; took in Lulamae Barnes and her brother, Fred, as children and married the fourteen-year-old girl in Truman Capote's *Breakfast at Tiffany's.*

Holiday (Holly, Lulamae Barnes) Golightly. Nineteen-year-old girl about town living in New York in the 1940s; married to Doc Golightly in Tulip, Texas, when she was fourteen in Truman Capote's *Breakfast at Tiffany's.*

Gerhardt (Der Springer) von Göll. German filmmaker and black-marketeer; symbolized by a knight chess piece in Thomas Pynchon's *Gravity's Rainbow.*

Marfa Vladimirovna Golov. Mother of Zhenia Golov in Bernard Malamud's *The Fixer.*

Zhenia (Zhenechka) Golov. Twelve-year-old boy murdered in Bernard Malamud's *The Fixer.*

Comrade General Golz (Hotze). Officer who orders Robert Jordan to blow up a bridge in Ernest Hemingway's *For Whom the Bell Tolls.*

John Golz. Clean-cut young writer; downstairs neighbor and friend of Mardou Fox in Jack Kerouac's *The Subterraneans.*

Joseph (Joe, Spanish) Gomez. Marine troublemaker who dies heroically at Saipan in Leon Uris's *Battle Cry.*

Captain Rogelio Gomez. Republican army officer who escorts Andrés through the Republican lines in Ernest Hemingway's *For Whom the Bell Tolls.*

Goneril. Vain and apparently deranged woman whose husband, John Ringman, leaves her in Herman Melville's *The Confidence-Man.*

Pepe Gonzales. Clever jokester and friend of Bob Webster; one of his pranks settles a longstanding feud with a neighboring village in Josefina Niggli's *Mexican Village.*

Agnes Gooch. Prim secretary who, under the influence of Mame Dennis, becomes pregnant; marries one of Patrick Dennis's schoolmasters moments before her baby is born in Patrick Dennis's *Auntie Mame.*

Eunice Goode. Alcoholic expatriate and Nelson Dyar's sexual rival in Paul Bowles's *Let It Come Down.*

Mary Goodhill. See Mary Goodhill Fowler.

Jim Goodhue. Dispossessed Ohio farmer who befriends Roy Earle in William Riley Burnett's *High Sierra.*

Velma Goodhue. Clubfooted woman in William Riley Burnett's *High Sierra.*

Adrian Goodlove. English psychoanalyst and lover of Isadora Wing in Erica Jong's *Fear of Flying.*

Goodman. Son-in-law of Zuckor and minor employee of Glymmer, Read in Nathan Asch's *The Office.*

Francis (Frank) Goodman. Cosmopolitan who encounters Mark Winsome, Egbert, and William Cream, among others, in Herman Melville's *The Confidence-Man.*

Lyra Goodman. See Lyra Goodman Wilmington.

Mr. Goodman. Unscrupulous secretary of Sebastian Knight; writes a biography of his former employer after Knight's death in Vladimir Nabokov's *The Real Life of Sebastian Knight.*

Clyde Goodson. Baptist minister who teaches Latin to Clay-Boy Spencer to help him qualify for admission to the University of Richmond in Earl Hamner, Jr.'s *Spencer's Mountain.*

Washington Goodspeed. Northern congressman with whom Hesden Le Moyne discusses the need for federal aid to local schools and other educational projects in Albion W. Tourgee's *Bricks without Straw.*

Goodwell. Friend of Wellingborough Redburn; tries to care for Harry Bolton in New York in Herman Melville's *Redburn.*

Bella Goodwin. First wife of Dan Goodwin; though a free person, accompanies her convict husband to Australia; dies as they escape the penal colony in Charles Nordhoff and James Norman Hall's *Botany Bay.*

Dan Goodwin. English smuggler imprisoned in Australia; after his first wife dies and after he returns to England, he marries Nellie Garth, whereupon they immigrate to America, in Charles Nordhoff and James Norman Hall's *Botany Bay.*

Felicia Goodwin. Wife of Les Goodwin in Joan Didion's *Play It As It Lays.*

Lee Goodwin. Bootlegger who is lynched in William Faulkner's *Sanctuary.*

Les Goodwin. Husband of Felicia Goodwin; lover of Maria Wyeth and father of her aborted baby in Joan Didion's *Play It As It Lays.*

Lewis (Marcus Burchard, Lew, Pinkey) Goodwin. Older brother of Morton Goodwin; outlaw believed to be dead but actually living as Burchard, a local sheriff, and Pinkey, a notorious desperado, in Edward Eggleston's *The Circuit Rider.*

Morton (Mort) Goodwin. Rough southern Ohio youth who, following his conversion to Methodism and subsequent rejection as a suitor by Patty Lumsden, becomes a circuit rider in Edward Eggleston's *The Circuit Rider.*

Nellie Garth Goodwin. Widowed owner of a small English farm who is sent to Australia for having harbored highwayman Tom Oakley; after escaping from the penal colony, she marries Dan Goodwin, with whom she immigrates to America, in Charles Nordhoff and James Norman Hall's *Botany Bay.*

Veenie Goodwin. Elderly black woman who has worked for the Mayfield family in the past; great grandmother of Walter Grainger and grandmother of Rover Walters in Reynolds Price's *The Surface of Earth*.

Caspar Goodwood. Resolute American suitor of Isabel Archer in Henry James's *The Portrait of a Lady*.

Brother Joe C. Goodyhay. Minister in William Faulkner's *The Mansion*.

Lorenz T. Goodykuntz. Proprietor of the Universal College of Metaphysical Knowledge, a mail order degree mill, in Thomas Berger's *Reinhart in Love*.

Goosey. Flute player who plays jazz with Banjo in Claude McKay's *Banjo*.

Gopi. Cripple from birth whom Jack Flowers helps in Singapore in Paul Theroux's *Saint Jack*.

Gordon. Sculptor who attends the yacht party in William Faulkner's *Mosquitoes*.

Abraham Gordon. Excommunicated Jewish scholar whose books questioning the literal truth of the Bible cause his son, Michael Gordon, to become catatonic in Chaim Potok's *The Promise*.

Charles (Charlie) Gordon. Author of progress reports; retarded man whose intelligence quotient is raised to over 200, although he loses the new intelligence, in Daniel Keyes's *Flowers for Algernon*.

Cora Gordon. See Cora Gordon Stewart.

Doctor Gordon. Male psychiatrist who administers shock treatments to Esther Greenwood before her suicide attempt in Sylvia Plath's *The Bell Jar*.

Harry Gordon. Half brother of Nina and Tom Gordon and husband of Lisette Gordon; quadroon manager of Canema plantation who, inspired by Dred Vesey, flees the plantation for the Dismal Swamp and joins Edward Clayton as a free man in Canada in Harriet Beecher Stowe's *Dred*.

Helen Gordon. Unhappy wife of Richard Gordon in Ernest Hemingway's *To Have and Have Not*.

Jeff Gordon. Wealthy businessman and friend and lover of Louise Davis in George Wylie Henderson's *Jule*.

John Gordon. Uncle of Nina Gordon and owner of the plantation neighboring Canema; aids an indigent white family who are squatters on his land in Harriet Beecher Stowe's *Dred*.

Joseph Gordon. Father of Rachel Gordon and brother of Abraham Gordon in Chaim Potok's *The Promise*.

Aunt Katy Gordon. See Aunt Katy.

Lisette Gordon. Wife of Harry Gordon; bought by Nina Gordon to protect Lisette from Tom Gordon's lecherous pursuit in Harriet Beecher Stowe's *Dred*.

Michael Gordon. Disturbed son of Abraham Gordon; his catatonia is treated by Danny Saunders in Chaim Potok's *The Promise*.

Nina Gordon. Vivacious owner of Canema plantation and fiancée of Edward Clayton; undergoes conversion to Christianity and abolitionism in Harriet Beecher Stowe's *Dred*.

Rachel Gordon. Wife of Danny Saunders in Chaim Potok's *The Promise*.

Richard (Dick) Gordon. Writer in Ernest Hemingway's *To Have and Have Not*.

Sarah Gordon. Wife of Joseph Gordon and mother of Rachel Gordon in Chaim Potok's *The Promise*.

Thomas (Tom) Gordon. Dissolute brother of Nina Gordon; inherits Canema plantation and begins leading lynch mobs which attack Edward Clayton and kill Dred Vesey in Harriet Beecher Stowe's *Dred*.

Hermann Wilhelm Göring. Nazi Reichminister who forces Johannes Robin to give his wealth to the Nazis; makes a deal with Lanny Budd for the release of Freddi Robin from Dachau in Upton Sinclair's *Dragon's Teeth*.

Dennis P. (Dinny) Gorman. Supporter of the Democratic party in James T. Farrell's *Young Lonigan*; influential judge and member of the Order of Christopher in *The Young Manhood of Studs Lonigan* and *Judgment Day*.

Marcus Gorman. Criminal lawyer and friend of Legs Diamond; narrator of William Kennedy's *Legs*; also appears in *Billy Phelan's Greatest Game*.

Levi Gorringe. Lawyer and Methodist church trustee who befriends Alice Ware in Harold Frederic's *The Damnation of Theron Ware*.

Bill Gorton. Friend of Jake Barnes; accompanies Barnes on a trip to Spain in Ernest Hemingway's *The Sun Also Rises*.

Heine Gortz. Leader of Gottlob Wut's German Motorcycle Unit Balkan 4 when Wallner is relieved of command; helps kill Wut in an outhouse in John Irving's *Setting Free the Bears*.

Restore Gosling. Witness against Koningsmarke in James Kirke Paulding's *Koningsmarke.*

Maria Gostrey. Friend and confidante of Lambert Strether, with whom she ultimately falls in love; friend of Madame de Vionnet in Henry James's *The Ambassadors.*

Gottfried. Pawn in Lieutenant Weissmann's sexual intrigues; launched by Weissmann in rocket 00000, known as the Schwarzgerät, in Thomas Pynchon's *Gravity's Rainbow.*

August (Auggie) Gottlieb. Newspaperboy and leader of the neighborhood gang in William Saroyan's *The Human Comedy.*

Max Gottlieb. Behaviorist psychiatrist and best friend of Tom More in Walker Percy's *Love in the Ruins.*

Professor Max Gottlieb. Medical school bacteriology professor who is dismissed for his eccentric ideas but who later becomes director of the McGurk Institute of Biology in Sinclair Lewis's *Arrowsmith.*

Governor. Governor of an unnamed state who impregnates Lily Shane but will not marry her in Louis Bromfield's *The Green Bay Tree.*

Governor. Amateur naturalist and antiquarian; French and German cosmopolite who is the godfather and traveling companion of the Chatelaine in Henry Blake Fuller's *The Chatelaine of La Trinité.*

Harmon Gow. Former stage driver who tells the narrator part of Ethan Frome's story in Edith Wharton's *Ethan Frome.*

Judge James Bartholomew Gowan. Judge who serves as an authority figure for the young Ellen Chesser in Elizabeth Madox Roberts's *The Time of Man.*

Luke Gowan. See Luther Dade Eustis.

Reginald Gower. Printer and bookstore owner who wants to print a pamphlet for Charles Schuyler in Gore Vidal's *Burr.*

Bilbo Gowrie. Son of Nub Gowrie and twin of Vardaman Gowrie in William Faulkner's *Intruder in the Dust.*

Bryan Gowrie. Son of Nub Gowrie in William Faulkner's *Intruder in the Dust.*

Crawford Gowrie. Son of Nub Gowrie; military deserter who murders his brother Vinson Gowrie and Jake Montgomery in William Faulkner's *Intruder in the Dust.*

N. B. Forrest Gowrie. Son of Nub Gowrie in William Faulkner's *Intruder in the Dust.*

Nub Gowrie. Father of six sons and bootlegger in William Faulkner's *Intruder in the Dust, The Town,* and *The Mansion.*

Vardaman Gowrie. Son of Nub Gowrie and twin of Bilbo Gowrie in William Faulkner's *Intruder in the Dust.*

Vinson Gowrie. Youngest son of Nub Gowrie; murdered by his brother Crawford Gowrie in William Faulkner's *Intruder in the Dust.*

Dr. Frederika Gozar. Principal of Lincoln Elementary School and mentor of child-genius Barry Rudd; resists the bribes and seductive reasoning of Wissey Jones in an attempt to make Barry one of his "specimens" in John Hersey's *The Child Buyer.*

Comte Edouard de la Cote de Grace. Poor French count who refuses to marry Billy Winthrop when he discovers that she has no money in Judith Krantz's *Scruples.*

Doc Graaf. Mennonite physician who examines Mary Robinson after her "attack" in John Updike's *Of the Farm.*

Grace. Beautiful young nurse for Dr. Angelo; comes to the fair to meet her boyfriend and another couple; all four sneak up to the sick ward to deliver candies to the patients in John Updike's *The Poorhouse Fair.*

Grace. Soldier who fights for the pistol that Richard Mast possesses in James Jones's *The Pistol.*

Mr. Gracie. Harvard undergraduate and friend of Henry Burrage in Henry James's *The Bostonians.*

Jakob (Jacques d'Argus, James de Gray, Mr. Degré, Jack Degree, Jacques de Grey, G, Jack Grey, Ravenstone, Ravus, Vinogradus) Gradus. Assassin who stalks Charles II, the exiled King of Zembla, and mistakenly kills John Shade, according to Charles Kinbote; may be a figment of Kinbote's imagination in Vladimir Nabokov's *Pale Fire.*

Grady. Newspaper reporter in William Faulkner's *Pylon.*

Delbert Grady. Former winter caretaker of the Overlook Hotel who kills his wife and daughters; appears as a ghost to John Torrance in Stephen King's *The Shining.*

Harold Graebner. Army friend of Binx Bolling; saves Bolling's life during the Korean War in Walker Percy's *The Moviegoer.*

Dr. Graf. Attending physician of John Laskell in Lionel Trilling's *The Middle of the Journey*.

Wilibald Graf. Dying religious fanatic who perceives himself as a faith healer in Katherine Anne Porter's *Ship of Fools*.

Hannes Graff. Friend of Siggy Javotnik and lover of Gallen; frees the animals; narrator of John Irving's *Setting Free the Bears*.

Stanley Graff. Realtor with George Babbitt's agency; fired for dishonesty in Sinclair Lewis's *Babbitt*.

Grafton. Former lover of Delia Poole in Janet Flanner's *The Cubical City*.

Charles Gragnon. General against whom Stefan and others mutiny in William Faulkner's *A Fable*.

Alexander Graham. See John Bailey.

Eustace Graham. District attorney in William Faulkner's *Sartoris (Flags in the Dust)* and *Sanctuary*.

Imogene Graham. Protégée of Evalina Bowen and fiancée of Theodore Colville in William Dean Howells's *Indian Summer*.

Mr. Graham. Chairman of the Republican County Central Committee and one of the white guests at Sara Andrews Towns's dinner party in W. E. B. Du Bois's *Dark Princess*.

Mrs. Graham. Elderly New England widow whose wisdom and kindness make her a favorite confidante of both Dr. John Leslie and Nan Prince in Sarah Orne Jewett's *A Country Doctor*.

Mrs. Graham. Mother of Imogene Graham; requests that Imogene be released from her engagement to Theodore Colville in William Dean Howells's *Indian Summer*.

Walter S. Grainger. Son of Rover Walters; becomes a combination servant and friend of Forrest and Rob Mayfield in Reynolds Price's *The Surface of Earth*.

Grammy. Grandmother of Waldo; ate dandelions during the Depression in Paul Theroux's *Waldo*.

Gran Boz (La Grand' Bosse, Louis Caddo, Louis Cadeau, Ole Big Hump). Humpbacked river pirate and trader who shelters Jeremiah and Rachel Beaumont after they escape from jail in Robert Penn Warren's *World Enough and Time*.

Gran Maestro (Grand Master). Italian friend of Richard Cantwell; Maitre d'Hotel at the Gritti Palace in Ernest Hemingway's *Across the River and into the Trees*.

George Francis Granberry. Husband of Myra Granberry; his wealth keeps him from finding an outlet for his energies; his claims for being an inventor are shown to be false; seeks help from Theophilus North for Myra in Thornton Wilder's *Theophilus North*.

Myra Granberry. Wife of George Granberry; confined to home because she is pregnant following two miscarriages; Theophilus North reads to her and helps improve her education in Thornton Wilder's *Theophilus North*.

Julia Granby. Society friend of Eliza Wharton in Hannah Webster Foster's *The Coquette*.

Guy Grand. Eccentric billionaire who amuses himself by paying large sums of money for people to degrade themselves in Terry Southern's *The Magic Christian*.

Noah Ridgerook Grandberry. Son of Pourty Bloodworth and half brother of Amos-Otis Thigpen, LaDonna Scales, Regal Pettibone, and Jonathan Bass; associate of Nathaniel Turner Witherspoon in Leon Forrest's *The Bloodworth Orphans*.

Achille Grandissime. Cousin of Honoré Grandissime in George Washington Cable's *The Grandissimes*.

Honoré Grandissime. Member of the Creole aristocracy and head of the Grandissimes; marries Aurora Nancanou in George Washington Cable's *The Grandissimes*.

Honoré Grandissime f.m.c. Quadroon half brother of Honoré Grandissime; landlord who commits suicide because Palmyre la Philosophe refuses to marry him in George Washington Cable's *The Grandissimes*.

Sylvestre Grandissime. Nephew of Agricola Fusilier, from whom Grandissime is saved from dueling, in George Washington Cable's *The Grandissimes*.

Madame Grandoni. Friend and neighbor of Augusta Blanchard, friend of Mrs. Light and Christina Light, and confidante of Rowland Mallet in Henry James's *Roderick Hudson*.

Granger. Leader of a group of underground intellectuals who have memorized great works of literature in order to preserve them in a bookless society in Ray Bradbury's *Fahrenheit 451*.

Emmeline Grangerford. Deceased daughter of Colonel Grangerford; author of "Ode to Stephen Dowling Bots, Dec'd" in Samuel Langhorne Clemens's *Adventures of Huckleberry Finn*.

Colonel Saul Grangerford. Head of the Grangerford family that is feuding with the Shepherdsons; is killed in a battle with them in Samuel Langhorne Clemens's *Adventures of Huckleberry Finn.*

Sophia Grangerford. Daughter of Colonel Grangerford; elopes with Harney Shepherdson, thus precipitating a deadly battle between the Grangerfords and Shepherdsons, in Samuel Langhorne Clemens's *Adventures of Huckleberry Finn.*

Old Grannis. Elderly man who falls in love with Miss Baker in Frank Norris's *McTeague.*

Granny. Deceased grandmother who had a profound influence on Lutie Johnson in Ann Petry's *The Street.*

Granny. Mother-in-law of Reb Zeydel Ber and grandmother figure to Rechele Babad; superstitious old woman whose stories of witches, goblins, and demons and whose death on the eve of Yom Kippur negatively influence the impressionable and epileptic Rechele in Isaac Bashevis Singer's *Satan in Goray.*

S. Granquist. Accomplice of Gerry Kells; accused of murdering John Bellmann, whom she had tried to blackmail, in Paul Cain's *Fast One.*

Louisa Grant. Friend of Elizabeth Temple in James Fenimore Cooper's *The Pioneers.*

Lucia Angelina Elena Videndi (Lucky) Grant. Lover and wife of Ron Grant and daughter of a New York bootlegger; holds a master's degree in political philosophy in James Jones's *Go to the Widow-Maker.*

Phebe Grant. Light-skinned mulatto who refuses to "pass for white"; becomes the loyal wife of Christopher Cary, Jr., in Jessie Fauset's *Comedy, American Style.*

Ron Grant. Famous playwright and naval veteran; marries Lucky Videndi and suspects her of adultery with Jim Grointon; protagonist of James Jones's *Go to the Widow-Maker.*

Bud Grantham. Father of Bella Grantham Tallant and friend and partner of Jimmy Tallant; like Jimmy, he undergoes a favorable character transformation in Elizabeth Spencer's *The Voice at the Back Door.*

Gerald (Gerry) Grass. Young antiestablishment poet in Alison Lurie's *Real People.*

Christabel Grau. Young landlady in love with Cass Timberlane in Sinclair Lewis's *Cass Timberlane.*

Hermione Gravell-Pitt. Con artist with prominent teeth; promises to have Mame Dennis presented at court but instead bilks her out of a great deal of money in Patrick Dennis's *Around the World with Auntie Mame.*

George Graves. Friend of Eugene Gant in Thomas Wolfe's *Look Homeward, Angel.*

Muley Graves. Oklahoma farmer and neighbor of the Joad family; tells Tom Joad II about how their families were forced to abandon their farms and journey to California to find work in John Steinbeck's *The Grapes of Wrath.*

Rocky Gravo. Master of ceremonies for the dance marathon; known for his indiscretions with female contestants in Horace McCoy's *They Shoot Horses, Don't They?*

Belfreda Gray. Black maid of the Kingsbloods in Sinclair Lewis's *Kingsblood Royal.*

Charles (Charley) Gray. Lower-upper-class native of Clyde who becomes vice-president of Stuyvesant Bank in John P. Marquand's *Point of No Return.*

James de Gray. See Jakob Gradus.

John Gray. Father of Charles Gray; makes and loses several fortunes in John P. Marquand's *Point of No Return.*

Mortimer (Mort, Speedy, Tex) Gray. Marine who survives campaigns at Tarawa and Saipan in Leon Uris's *Battle Cry.*

Nancy (Nance) Gray. Wife of Charles Gray; helps her husband achieve business success in John P. Marquand's *Point of No Return.*

Thomas R. Gray. Defense attorney who reads Nat Turner's confession to the court in William Styron's *The Confessions of Nat Turner.*

Gray Beaver. Cruel Indian master of White Fang; sells White Fang to Beauty Smith for a bottle of whiskey in Jack London's *White Fang.*

Lewin Lockridge Grayle. Devoted millionaire husband of the former Velma Valento in Raymond Chandler's *Farewell, My Lovely.*

Rev. Thomas Grayson. Educated mulatto minister from New York City who tries unsuccessfully to establish a new church for the black workers of the Phosphate Mining Company; assumes pastorate of a Harlem Episcopal church and helps Lissa Atkinson become a successful singer in DuBose Heyward's *Mamba's Daughters.*

Great White Shark. Enormous shark that terrorizes the town of Amity in Peter Benchley's *Jaws*.

Great World Snake (Palalakonuh, Serpent of Eternity, Snake of Evil, World Sun Snake). Monstrous embodiment of evil defeated by the forces of good in an apocalyptic Judgment Day at the end of Jack Kerouac's *Doctor Sax*.

Montague Greaves. English engineer who interests Frank Cowperwood in the London subway system in Theodore Dreiser's *The Stoic*.

Wodie Greaves. One-eyed believer in magic; joins the crew of the *Lillias Eden* to escape someone who seeks his death but dies when the boat wrecks on Misteriosa Reef in Peter Matthiessen's *Far Tortuga*.

Al (Ed Charney, Anthony Joseph Murascho) Grecco. Driver and helper for Ed Charney in John O'Hara's *Appointment in Samarra*.

Mrs. Greco. Lonely white neighbor of Bill Kelsey; after the death of her only friend, allows cockroaches to overrun her apartment in Hal Bennett's *Seventh Heaven*.

Maxwell Greech. Satanic-looking manager of South Wind camp for adults where Marjorie Morningstar meets Noel Airman in Herman Wouk's *Marjorie Morningstar*.

Della Green. Mulatto former prostitute who becomes Augie's mistress after his success as a jockey in Arna Wendell Bontemps's *God Sends Sunday*.

Elijah Green. Follower who calls the Reverend Phillip Martin "our Martin Luther King" in Ernest J. Gaines's *In My Father's House*.

Glory Green. Actress and wife of Iz Einsam in Alison Lurie's *The Nowhere City*.

Harvey Green. Professional gambler who corrupts the youth of Cedarville and murders Willy Hammond in T. S. Arthur's *Ten Nights in a Bar-Room*.

Jack Green. Head of market research, rival of Andy Kagle, and boss and principal antagonist of Bob Slocum in Joseph Heller's *Something Happened*.

Aunt Mehitable Green. Former slave and present conjure woman who informs Dorinda Oakley that Dorinda is pregnant in Ellen Glasgow's *Barren Ground*.

Micajah ('Cajah) Green. Sheriff of Shaftsville who identifies the location of the Cayce still and who loses his job because of his inability to capture Rick Tyler in Mary Noailles Murfree's *The Prophet of the Great Smoky Mountains*.

Mr. Green. Grand Dragon of the Ku Klux Klan convinced by Sara Andrews to support Matthew Towns's release from prison as a good political move in W. E. B. Du Bois's *Dark Princess*.

Ned Green. Mississippi-born expatriate black poet in Copenhagen in Cecil Brown's *The Life and Loves of Mr. Jiveass Nigger*.

Pauly Green. World War II veteran and owner of a café in Bristol, Mississippi; fires his pistol at customers in Shelby Foote's *Jordan County*.

Philip (Phil, Schuyler) Green. Widowed thirty-five-year-old writer on his first magazine assignment; pretending he is Jewish, devises a new slant for articles on anti-Semitism in Laura Z. Hobson's *Gentleman's Agreement*.

Reverend Mr. Pleasant Green. Southern black preacher who meets Helga Crane in a Harlem storefront church, marries her, and returns with her to rural Alabama in Nella Larsen's *Quicksand*.

Schuyler Green. See Philip Green.

Tom (Tommy) Green. Bright and loving eight-year-old son of Phil Green; experiences ridicule from his peers because he pretends to be Jewish in Laura Z. Hobson's *Gentleman's Agreement*.

Tony Green. Member of the Nova Mob in William S. Burroughs's *Nova Express* and *The Soft Machine*; appears also in *The Wild Boys*.

Greene. Young man who reports the alleged murder by rustlers of Larry Kinkaid in Walter Van Tilburg Clark's *The Ox-Bow Incident*.

Beatrice (Babe) Greene. Black singer at Jimbo's bar; befriends Jill Pendleton and sends her to live with Harry Angstrom in John Updike's *Rabbit Redux*.

Nadine Greene. Mentally unstable young woman from the affluent Detroit suburb Grosse Pointe; shoots her lover, Jules Wendall, in Joyce Carol Oates's *them*.

General Nathanael Greene. American Revolutionary War general who tries to persuade Thomas Paine to join his command and who relies upon Paine to explain to the soldiers what they are fighting for, thereby keeping their allegiance, in Howard Fast's *Citizen Tom Paine*.

Pete Greene. Free black man; friend and coworker of Jim in Harriet E. Wilson's *Our Nig*.

Peter (Pete) Greene. Optimistic, innocent, but self-reliant and selfish American in John Barth's *Giles Goat-Boy*.

Phillip (Phil) Greene. Famous editor and friend of Garvin Wales in Hamilton Basso's *The View from Pompey's Head*.

Faye Greener. Aspiring actress who cares only about advancing her career; romantically involved with Tod Hackett and Earle Shoop in Nathanael West's *The Day of the Locust*.

Harry Greener. Former vaudevillian clown who is the father of Faye Greener and a friend of Tod Hackett in Nathanael West's *The Day of the Locust*.

General Lewis (Colonel) Greenfield. Citizen of Saint Louis who leads the expedition against the wild boys in William S. Burroughs's *The Wild Boys*.

Dr. Fowler Greenhill. Medical doctor and husband of Mary Jessup Greenhill; executed by firing squad for refusing to become a medical officer in the Minute Men in Sinclair Lewis's *It Can't Happen Here*.

Mary Jessup Greenhill. Older daughter of Doremus Jessup and wife of Dr. Fowler Greenhill; joins the Corpo Women's Flying Corps and deliberately crashes her plane into Effingham Swan's in order to kill Swan in Sinclair Lewis's *It Can't Happen Here*.

Drexel Greenshaw. Black headwaiter in the Fiesole Room at the Pineland Hotel in Sinclair Lewis's *Kingsblood Royal*.

Lionel (Bulldog) Greenspan. Jewish FBI agent who tails Bruce Gold in Joseph Heller's *Good as Gold*.

Lieutenant Barney Greenwald. Attorney for accused mutineer Lieutenant Steve Maryk in Herman Wouk's *The Caine Mutiny*.

Aurora Starrett Greenway. Widowed mother of Emma Horton, mother-in-law of Thomas Horton, grandmother of Melanie, Teddy, and Tommy Horton, and lover of General Hector Scott in Larry McMurtry's *Terms of Endearment*.

Alice Greenwood. See Alice Greenwood Weylin.

Esther (Elly Higginbottom) Greenwood. Brilliant college student and aspiring writer who attempts suicide after a 1953 summer stint as a college guest editor of a New York fashion magazine; narrator of Sylvia Plath's *The Bell Jar*.

Mrs. Greenwood. Mother of Esther Greenwood; finds her daughter in the crawl space under the house after Esther attempts suicide with an overdose of sleeping pills in Sylvia Plath's *The Bell Jar*.

Greer. Professional killer, companion of Cameron, and lover and briefly husband of Jane Hawkline;

hired by the Hawkline sisters to destroy the monster created by their father in Richard Brautigan's *The Hawkline Monster*.

Mrs. Greer. Disseminator of village gossip, especially about the Carroll Farms, in Constance Fenimore Woolson's *For the Major*.

Colonel Walter Greer. Holder of a life-grant for Red Wing plantation, which Potem Desmit buys and sells fraudulently to Nimbus, in Albion W. Tourgee's *Bricks without Straw*.

Count Greffi. Ninety-four-year-old former diplomat who drinks champagne and plays billiards with Frederic Henry in Ernest Hemingway's *A Farewell to Arms*.

Billy Gregg. Seventy-year-old resident of the Diamond County Home for the Aged; former Newark electrician; small, angry man who, emboldened by George Lucas's bottle of rye, throws the first stones at Stephen Conner in John Updike's *The Poorhouse Fair*.

Franz Gregorovious. Swiss psychiatrist and disloyal partner of Dick Diver in a mental clinic in F. Scott Fitzgerald's *Tender Is the Night*.

Kaethe Gregorovious. Wife of Franz Gregorovious; resents Dick and Nicole Diver in F. Scott Fitzgerald's *Tender Is the Night*.

Aaron (Arele, Tsutsik) Greidinger. Playwright and novelist in Warsaw prior to and during Hitler's regime; forms sexual liaisons with Dora Stolnitz, Betty Slonim, Celia Chentshiner, and Tekla, but marries his childhood love, Shosha; narrator of Isaac Bashevis Singer's *Shosha*.

Grendel (Cowface). Enlightened "monster" who seeks brotherhood with the Scyldings, who assign him the role of ravager; narrator of John Gardner's *Grendel*.

Mrs. Harry (Tishy) Grendon. Hostess of Nanda Brookenham in Henry James's *The Awkward Age*.

Stephen (Steve) Grendon. Successful author, member of the school board, and Sac Prairie celebrity in August Derleth's *The Shield of the Valiant*; Roman Catholic whose love for the Protestant Margery Estabrook is opposed by his family, except for Grandfather Adams; narrator of *Evening in Spring*.

Will and Rose Grendon. Parents of Stephen Grendon in August Derleth's *Evening in Spring*.

Dr. Albert Grene. Black physician of Calvertown; son of Bannie Upshire Dudley and Percy Upshur and father of Mariah Upshur's daughter, Bardetta

Tometta Upshur, in Sarah E. Wright's *This Child's Gonna Live*.

Louis Grenier. A founder of Jefferson and original owner of Old Frenchman's Place in William Faulkner's *Intruder in the Dust, Requiem for a Nun, The Town,* and *The Reivers*.

Catherine (Katty) Grenville. Young woman who becomes romantically involved with Roger Bannon in John O'Hara's *A Rage to Live*.

Samuel (Sam) Gretry. Broker at the Chicago Board of Trade who handles Curtis Jadwin's attempt to corner the American wheat market in Frank Norris's *The Pit*.

Nancy Grewell. Black midwife who saves the infant Capitola Le Noir from being murdered at birth by her villainous uncle in E.D.E.N. Southworth's *The Hidden Hand*.

Aline Aldridge Grey. Wife of Fred Grey; fantasizes about one of her husband's workers, Bruce Dudley; pregnant by Dudley, she runs away with him in Sherwood Anderson's *Dark Laughter*.

Anne Grey. Widowed niece of Jeanette Hayes-Rore and member of Harlem's young black socialites; takes Helga Crane into her home as a guest; meets Robert Anderson through Helga and later marries him in Nella Larsen's *Quicksand*.

Fred Grey. Owner of a wheel factory in Old Harbor, Indiana, and husband of Aline Aldridge Grey; leads an unhapy life and eventually loses his wife to Bruce Dudley, one of his former workers, in Sherwood Anderson's *Dark Laughter*.

Jack Grey. See Jakob Gradus.

Jacques de Grey. See Jakob Gradus.

Mr. Job Grey. Deceased husband of Mrs. Grey in W. E. B. Du Bois's *The Quest of the Silver Fleece*.

Mrs. Grey. Wealthy New York widow of Job Grey; shows concern for blacks and promises financial support for Miss Sarah Smith's school in W. E. B. Du Bois's *The Quest of the Silver Fleece*.

Doctor Greylock. Cruel, drink-crazed father of Jason Greylock; lives amid his mixed-race offspring and backs Jason's marriage to Geneva Ellgood in Ellen Glasgow's *Barren Ground*.

Jason Greylock. Personable but weak-willed doctor who sacrifices himself for his father; seduces Dorinda Oakley, marries Geneva Ellgood, and succumbs to alcohol in Ellen Glasgow's *Barren Ground*.

Herbert Greyson. Young protector of Capitola Le Noir and later her husband in E.D.E.N. Southworth's *The Hidden Hand*.

Amelia de Grier. Wife of Wendell Ryder and mother of five in Djuna Barnes's *Ryder*.

Elizabeth Grier. Member of the Cabala who lives at the Palazzo Barberini; hosts numerous dinners in Thornton Wilder's *The Cabala*.

Jenny (Ma) Grier. Only female member of the lynch mob; uses her femininity to shame doubtful members of the mob into certainty concerning the need for a hanging in Walter Van Tilburg Clark's *The Ox-Bow Incident*.

William K. Grierson. See Jeremiah Beaumont.

Irma Griese. See Zofia Maria Biegańska Zawistowska.

'Gustus Thomas (Gus, Tom) Griff. Uncle of Tad; owner of a mill that is, presumably, destroyed by Mink Lorey in Mary Noailles Murfree's *In the Clouds*.

Julius Griffin. Los Angeles psychiatrist; treats Karl Hettinger after the murder of Hettinger's partner in Joseph Wambaugh's *The Onion Field*.

Leon Griffin. See Leon Lawrence.

Mrs. Griffin. Widow to whom Captain Porgy is attracted in William Gilmore Simms's *Woodcraft*.

Walter (Wat) Griffin. Whig farmer captured by the Tory Amos Gaskens; saved from hanging by Major Singleton in William Gilmore Simms's *The Partisan*.

Asa Griffiths. Traveling evangelist, husband of Elvira Griffiths, and father of Clyde Griffiths in Theodore Dreiser's *An American Tragedy*.

Clyde (Baker, Clifford Golden, Carl Graham, Harry Tenet) Griffiths. Son of Asa and Elvira Griffiths; lover of Roberta Alden, whom he plots to kill when he has the opportunity to raise his social standing by marrying Sondra Finchley; executed for having murdered Alden in Theodore Dreiser's *An American Tragedy*.

Elvira Griffiths. Traveling evangelist, wife of Asa Griffiths, and mother of Clyde Griffiths in Theodore Dreiser's *An American Tragedy*.

Harold Griffiths. Melodramatic poet and newspaper columnist in Gore Vidal's *Washington, D.C.*

Samuel Griffiths. Uncle of Clyde Griffiths; gives his nephew an important job and introduces him to upper-class life in Theodore Dreiser's *An American Tragedy*.

L. J. Griggs. See Big Red Smalley.

Carrol Grilhiggen. Passenger on the *Here They Come* who plans to return Lucifer to heaven in Gregory Corso's *The American Express*.

The Grim Reaper. See John Sallow.

Deborah Grimes. First wife of Gabriel Grimes; made sterile when raped by white men at the age of sixteen in James Baldwin's *Go Tell It on the Mountain*.

Elizabeth Grimes. Common law wife of Richard and mother by him of John Grimes; marries Gabriel Grimes after Richard's suicide in James Baldwin's *Go Tell It on the Mountain*.

Emily (Emmy) Grimes. Younger sister of Sarah Grimes Wilson; pursues a series of love affairs, but late in life is friendless and alone, relying on a nephew as a guardian, in Richard Yates's *Easter Parade*.

Esther (Pookie) Grimes. Mother of Sarah Grimes Wilson and Emily Grimes; childish yet ambitious for social status; falls while drunk and dies in a state hospital in Richard Yates's *Easter Parade*.

Florence Grimes. Oppressed black woman who desperately surrenders to Christianity; sister of Gabriel Grimes in James Baldwin's *Go Tell It on the Mountain*.

Gabriel Grimes. Deacon at the Temple of the Fire Baptized, a black evangelical church in Harlem; frustrated by years of white oppression, he is driven to violence and hypocrisy; stepfather of John Grimes and husband of Deborah Grimes and later Elizabeth Grimes in James Baldwin's *Go Tell It on the Mountain*.

John Grimes. Harlem adolescent who eventually commits himself to Christianity after a torturous search for his black identity in a white world; brother of Roy Grimes, stepson of Gabriel Grimes, and son of Elizabeth Grimes in James Baldwin's *Go Tell It on the Mountain*.

Roy Grimes. Rebellious black youth and brother of John Grimes in James Baldwin's *Go Tell It on the Mountain*.

Walter Grimes. Estranged husband of Esther Grimes; writes headlines for the *New York Sun* and dotes on his daughters, Sarah Grimes Wilson and Emily Grimes, in Richard Yates's *Easter Parade*.

Percy Grimm. National guardsman who castrates Joe Christmas in William Faulkner's *Light in August*.

Mr. Grimshaw. Teacher at the Temple Grammar School in Thomas Bailey Aldrich's *The Story of a Bad Boy*.

Grindle. Mystic leader of a utopian community who seduces Candy Christian in Terry Southern and Mason Hoffenberg's *Candy*.

Grippenwald. Veterinarian to Hollywood animals, including Dirty Eddie, in Ludwig Bemelmans's *Dirty Eddie*.

David (Davey) Griscam. Wall Street lawyer and early graduate of Justin Martyr School whose efforts as trustee and fundraiser lead to institutional growth but loss of the original vision of the school; author of notes compiled by Brian Aspinwall in Louis Auchincloss's *The Rector of Justin*.

Jules Griscam. Son of David Griscam and graduate of Justin Martyr School; bitter young man who dies in an automobile crash and is Francis Prescott's greatest failure as headmaster in Louis Auchincloss's *The Rector of Justin*.

Griswold. Messenger hired by Henry Miller; former army sergeant who goes crazy and destroys the office; eventually promoted to a clerkship in Henry Miller's *Tropic of Capricorn*.

Burt Griswold. Husband of Marie Griswold; testifies against Joseph Chase in Jessamyn West's *The Life I Really Lived*.

Colonel Sandy Griswold. Cavalry officer who aids the Del Sol cowboys during their troubles with Indians and rustlers in Emerson Hough's *North of 36*.

Marie Shields Griswold. Wife of Burt Griswold; her death from cancer prompts the manslaughter charges against Joseph Chase in Jessamyn West's *The Life I Really Lived*.

Griza. Computer operator at Talifer Missile Base who helps Coverly Wapshot do a computer analysis of Keats's poetry in John Cheever's *The Wapshot Scandal*.

William (Willie) Grogan. Night wire-chief and confidant of Homer Macauley; dies of a heart attack while receiving a telegraph message about Marcus Macauley's death in William Saroyan's *The Human Comedy*.

Jim Grointon. American skindiver out of Kingston, Jamaica; takes Lucky and Ron Grant diving and asks Lucky to leave Ron and marry him in James Jones's *Go to the Widow-Maker*.

Gregor Gronfein. Wealthy prisoner who offers to smuggle letters out of prison for Yakov Bok and later turns in Bok to the warden in Bernard Malamud's *The Fixer*.

LD Groover. Roommate of Mabry Jenkins; member of the Dallas Cowboys who writes in his spare time and is cut from the team at the end of the season in Peter Gent's *Texas Celebrity Turkey Trot*.

H. M. Grosbeake. Professor of philosophy and the narrator's spiritual mentor in Edmund Wilson's *I Thought of Daisy*.

Mrs. Grose. Housekeeper and motherly friend to the governess; gradually reveals the history of Bly in Henry James's *The Turn of the Screw*.

Mrs. Hugo Gross. See Felix Treevly.

Rhino (O-Daddy) Gross. Disqualified gynecologist, one-time abortionist, and maker of "O-Daddy, The Condom of Tomorrow" in Nelson Algren's *A Walk on the Wild Side*.

Velma Gross. Ex-convict and maker, with her husband, Rhino, of O-Daddy condoms in Nelson Algren's *A Walk on the Wild Side*.

Dora Grossbart. Fantasy friend of Margaret Reynolds and fellow worker in Another Mother for Peace; travels with Reynolds to Vietnam to spread the word about the peace movement in Anne Richardson Roiphe's *Up the Sandbox!*

Lena Grove. Poverty-stricken woman who travels to Jefferson in search of Lucas Burch, the father of her unborn child, in William Faulkner's *Light in August*.

William (Bill) Grove. Shy, awkward student who develops a measure of self-confidence by becoming chief writer and editor of the Dorset Academy *Chronicle* in Richard Yates's *A Good School*.

Sally Grover. Associate of Horace Bentley and friend of the poor in Winston Churchill's *The Inside of the Cup*.

Grown Boy. Retarded nephew of Verily; accidentally killed by mill hands and a policeman when Jester Clane chases him in Carson McCullers's *Clock without Hands*.

Maureen Grube. Small-town girl living in New York City; easy sexual conquest for Frank Wheeler in Richard Yates's *Revolutionary Road*.

Carol M. Gruber. Successful owner of several factories; married briefly to Ambrose Clay in Gail Godwin's *Violet Clay*.

Vladislav Grigorievitch Grubeshov. Prosecuting attorney and procurator of the Kiev Superior Court; tries to convict Yakov Bok of murder in Bernard Malamud's *The Fixer*.

Joe Grubner. Great high-school athlete on whom Pookie Adams has a crush; dies in an automobile accident while on a date with Pookie in John Nichols's *The Sterile Cuckoo*.

Molly Grue. Cook for Captain Cully's outlaws; leaves Cully to join the unicorn in Peter S. Beagle's *The Last Unicorn*.

Major Grumby. Leader of Grumby's Independents who murders Rosa Millard and who in turn is murdered by her grandson, Bayard Sartoris II; appears in William Faulkner's *The Unvanquished* and *The Hamlet*.

Mose Grundy. Bracktown barber in Gayl Jones's *Corregidora*.

Angela Gruner. Niece of Artur Sammler and estranged daughter of Arnold Gruner; confesses to Sammler her sexual exploits and her indifference to her father's disapproval in Saul Bellow's *Mr. Sammler's Planet*.

Dr. Arnold (Elya) Gruner. Physician and benevolent Jewish patriarch who disapproves of his son's schemes and his daughter's sexual liberation; provides care and security for Artur and Shula Sammler and, apparently, abortions for the Mafia; dies of a brain aneurysm in Saul Bellow's *Mr. Sammler's Planet*.

Ebenezer Gryce. New York police detective who investigates the murder of Horatio Leavenworth in Anna Katharine Green's *The Leavenworth Case*.

Percy Gryce. Dull but wealthy collector of Americana; one of several men Lily Bart attempts to marry in Edith Wharton's *The House of Mirth*.

Guenever. Queen; wife of Arthur in Samuel Langhorne Clemens's *A Connecticut Yankee in King Arthur's Court*.

Princess Guenevere (Phyllida). Woman whom Jurgen rescues; through her, he becomes acquainted with Dame Anaïtis in James Branch Cabell's *Jurgen*.

Bea Guerin. Wife of Roger Guerin and lover of Piet Hanema in John Updike's *Couples*.

Pauline Guerin. Black woman who gains small material and emotional amenities as the mistress of Sidney Bonbon in Ernest J. Gaines's *Of Love and Dust*.

Roger Guerin. Independently wealthy husband of Bea Guerin in John Updike's *Couples*.

Guerlac. See Henri Guerlac de Sabrevois.

Martin Guerre. Husband of Bertrande de Rols; many years after deserting his wife, he returns to find her living with Arnaud du Tilh, who resembles Guerre and who has pretended to be him, in Janet Lewis's *The Wife of Martin Guerre.*

Madame Martin Guerre. See Bertrande de Rols.

Monsieur Guerre. Demanding father of Martin Guerre; thrown from a horse and killed in Janet Lewis's *The Wife of Martin Guerre.*

Pierre Guerre. Brother of Monsieur Guerre; becomes head of the Guerre family following his brother's death in Janet Lewis's *The Wife of Martin Guerre.*

Sanxi Guerre. Son of Bertrande de Rols and Martin Guerre in Janet Lewis's *The Wife of Martin Guerre.*

Angela (Angela Maea) Guessippi. Lover of Anthony Adverse and later of Napoleon Bonaparte in Hervey Allen's *Anthony Adverse.*

Il Gufo (Padrone). Hangman and only marriageable man in the village of Sasso Fetore (Tomb Stench); known as "the owl"; narrator of John Hawkes's *The Owl.*

Caporale Guiglielmo. One of two carabinieri who attack and then release Jacopo in John Hawkes's *The Goose on the Grave.*

John Guild. Police lieutenant investigating the murder of Julia Wolf and the disappearance of Clyde Wynant in Dashiell Hammett's *The Thin Man.*

Guillaume. Homosexual who humiliates Giovanni and is murdered by him in James Baldwin's *Giovanni's Room.*

Guinea. See Black Guinea.

Philomena Guinea. Wealthy patroness of scholarship student Esther Greenwood; finances Esther's psychiatric recovery from suicidal depression in a private sanitarium in Sylvia Plath's *The Bell Jar.*

Guinevere. Wife of King Arthur and mistress of Launcelot in Thomas Berger's *Arthur Rex.*

Beverly Guinevere. See Beverly Guinevere McLeod.

Monina Guinevere. See Monina.

Bernard (Bernar', Bernie) Guizot. Young hustler and, briefly, lover of Leslie McGivers; tries unsuccessfully to come between McGivers and her friend Honor Rogers in Marge Piercy's *The High Cost of Living.*

Luther Gulliday. Victim of Stuart McKay's murderous anger and resentment when Gulliday takes McKay's job in Nelson Algren's *Somebody in Boots.*

Gun-Deck. Man-of-war's man aboard the *Highlander* in Herman Melville's *Redburn.*

Vergil Gunch. President of the Boosters' Club of which George Babbitt is a member; pressures Babbitt to join the Good Citizens' League in Sinclair Lewis's *Babbitt.*

Ma Gundel. Motherly waitress to and confidante of Moses Fable in Ludwig Bemelmans's *Dirty Eddie.*

Gunstone. Client for whom Jack Flowers provides women in Paul Theroux's *Saint Jack.*

Betty June Gunter. Adolescent friend of Todd Andrews and his first sexual partner; later, as a prostitute, attacks Andrews in a Baltimore brothel in John Barth's *The Floating Opera.*

Theda Gunther. Secretary and mistress of Adrian Lynch in Joseph Wambaugh's *The Choirboys.*

Arnold Gupton. Oldest Gupton brother; bachelor with no palate in his mouth; cheats at cards in Reynolds Price's *A Long and Happy Life.*

Frederick Gupton. Infant son of Marise and Macey Gupton; plays Baby Jesus to Rosacoke Mustian's Virgin Mary in Reynolds Price's *A Long and Happy Life.*

Macey Gupton. Childhood friend of Milo Mustian in Reynolds Price's *A Long and Happy Life*; joins Milo in sexual experimentation with an unnamed black girl in *A Generous Man.*

Marise Gupton. Sister of Willie Duke Aycock; married to Macey Gupton in Reynolds Price's *A Long and Happy Life* and *A Generous Man.*

Pacifici Bartola Ahmed Gurevich. Second wife of Zeke Gurevich and mother of his children in William Herrick's *The Itinerant.*

Samuel Ezekiel (Jakie, Red, Zeke) Gurevich. Son of a poor Jewish family in New York City; civil rights activist; itinerant soldier in the Spanish civil war and World War II; lover and rebel in William Herrick's *The Itinerant.*

Lucy Gurget. Cook for Solomon Tinkle and motherly friend of Daniel Harrow and Molly Larkins in Walter D. Edmonds's *Rome Haul.*

Forbes Gurney. Poet and lover of Stephanie Platow in Theodore Dreiser's *The Titan.*

General Marion Gurney. Confederate veteran and prominent politician who opposes Reconstruction; sends an anonymous warning that enables Lily Servosse to save her father and Thomas Denton from the Ku Klux Klan ambush; opposes his son's marriage to Lily in Albion W. Tourgee's *A Fool's Errand*.

Melville Gurney. Son of General Marion Gurney; sentinel during the Ku Klux Klan's abortive ambush of Thomas Denton; vows to marry Lily Servosse in Albion W. Tourgee's *A Fool's Errand*.

Mr. Gurney. Minister in Lionel Trilling's *The Middle of the Journey*.

Gus. Black youth assaulted by Bigger Thomas in Richard Wright's *Native Son*.

Gus (Brownie). Friend of Melba; picks up Malcolm at the horticultural gardens and prepares him for marriage to Melba in James Purdy's *Malcolm*.

Eleanor Guthrie. Wealthy Texas heiress and lover of Sonny Shanks in Larry McMurtry's *Moving On*.

Ephraim (Eph) Guthrie. Low-keyed brother of Fee Guthrie in Mary Noailles Murfree's *In the "Stranger People's" Country*.

Felix (Fee) Guthrie. Owner of the "stranger people's" burial ground; loves Litt Pettingill intensely, and beats Leonard Rhodes savagely; dies because of a sheriff's mistake in Mary Noailles Murfree's *In the "Stranger People's" Country*.

Casper Gutman. Criminal mastermind whose research has identified the jewel-encrusted statuette given as a tribute to Charles V by the Hospitalers of St. John in the sixteenth century and whose ruthless persistence has led him to San Francisco in search of it in Dashiell Hammett's *The Maltese Falcon*.

Rhea Gutman. Daughter of Casper Gutman; drugged in Dashiell Hammett's *The Maltese Falcon*.

Father Gutstadt. Catholic villain who follows the trail of The Corpse to the zoo in Tom Robbins's *Another Roadside Attraction*.

Captain Guy. Part owner and captain of the schooner *Jane Guy* who rescues Arthur Gordon Pym and Dirk Peters after the wreck of the *Grampus*; murdered with his crew on the island of Tsalal in Edgar Allan Poe's *The Narrative of Arthur Gordon Pym*.

Guy (Cabin Boy, Paper Jack). Captain of the *Julia* in Herman Melville's *Omoo*.

El Comandante Rufino Guzmán. Prefect of Oriente State bent on forcibly bringing the Niaruna Indians under his control over the objections of the missionaries in Peter Matthiessen's *At Play in the Fields of the Lord*.

Fausto Guzmán. Son of Comandante Guzmán in Peter Matthiessen's *At Play in the Fields of the Lord*.

Señora Dolores Estella Carmen Maria Cruz y Peralta Guzmán. Wife of Comandante Guzmán in Peter Matthiessen's *At Play in the Fields of the Lord*.

James (Jeemes, Jim) Gwinnan. Judge at Mink Lorey's trial who is, Lorey thinks, in love with Lethe Sayles; disliked by Lorey's attorney Bob Harshaw in Mary Noailles Murfree's *In the Clouds*.

John Elton Cecil (Jack) Gwynne. American-born English aristocrat and lover of Isabel Otis; willing to give up his inherited seat in the British government for a political career in the United States in Gertrude Atherton's *Ancestors*.

Nell (Nelly) Gwynne. Famous actress and one of the many mistresses of Charles II in Kathleen Winsor's *Forever Amber*.

Lady Victoria Gwynne. Beautiful widowed mother of John Gwynne; forced to choose between the ennui of expected social class behavior and the expression of her intellectual, sensuous nature in Gertrude Atherton's *Ancestors*.

Camilla Gwyon. Wife of Reverend Gwyon; dies when their son, Wyatt Gwyon, is three and haunts him throughout William Gaddis's *The Recognitions*.

Esther Gwyon. Aspiring writer and wife of Wyatt Gwyon in William Gaddis's *The Recognitions*.

Reverend Gwyon. Protestant minister who turns to pagan religion after the death of his wife in William Gaddis's *The Recognitions*.

Wyatt (Stephan Asche, Stephen) Gwyon. Painter who turns to forgery; later an expatriate in Spain; protagonist of William Gaddis's *The Recognitions*.

Gypsy (Zuleika). Pony of Tom Bailey; becomes a trick pony in a circus in Thomas Bailey Aldrich's *The Story of a Bad Boy*.

H

Mamma Habblesham. Midwife who rears Abeba Torch before the six-year-old child's mother takes her to New York in Ellease Southerland's *Let the Lion Eat Straw.*

Butch (Butch Braley) Haber. Convict brother of Gulla Slogum; castrates René Dumur, Annette Slogum's suitor, on her mother's orders in Mari Sandoz's *Slogum House.*

Regula (Gulla) Haber. See Regula Haber Slogum.

Eunice Habersham. Spinster granddaughter of Doctor Habersham in William Faulkner's *Intruder in the Dust* and *The Town.*

Doctor Samuel Habersham. Early settler of Jefferson in William Faulkner's *Intruder in the Dust, Requiem for a Nun,* and *The Town.*

Hugh Habershaw. North Carolina Tory partisan who captures Arthur Butler; killed by Horse-Shoe Robinson in John Pendleton Kennedy's *Horse-Shoe Robinson.*

Dr. Habicht. Father of Ferdinand and Minna; scholarly, idealistic German who educates the young Oliver Tappan in Hjalmar Hjorth Boyesen's *The Golden Calf.*

Ferdinand Habicht. Ne'er-do-well brother of Minna Habicht; studies in a German university; upon returning to the United States, he borrows money from Oliver Tappan in Hjalmar Hjorth Boyesen's *The Golden Calf.*

Minna Habicht. Simple, pretty, and uncorrupt daughter of Dr. Habicht; once engaged to Oliver Tappan in Hjalmar Hjorth Boyesen's *The Golden Calf.*

Jerome (Jerry) Hack. Mediocre but reliable screenwriter at Olympia Studios in Ludwig Bemelmans's *Dirty Eddie.*

Philip (Phil) Hackett. Respectable yet ultimately disloyal friend of Laurentine Strange in Jessie Redmon Fauset's *The Chinaberry Tree.*

Tod Hackett. Lover of Faye Greener and painter for a movie studio who observes Hollywood decadence, which inspires his painting, *The Burning of Los Angeles,* in Nathanael West's *The Day of the Locust.*

Elmo C. Hacketts, Jr.. Army private in Kurt Vonnegut's *Player Piano.*

Harriet N. Q. (Hattie) Haddock. Wife of William P. Haddock and mother of Mildred Haddock in Donald Ogden Stewart's *Mr and Mrs Haddock Abroad.*

Mildred Haddock. Ten-year-old daughter of Harriet and William Haddock in Donald Ogden Stewart's *Mr and Mrs Haddock Abroad.*

William P. (Will) Haddock. Husband of Harriet Haddock and father of Mildred Haddock; takes his wife and daughter on a voyage to Europe, on which they have strange experiences, in Donald Ogden Stewart's *Mr and Mrs Haddock Abroad.*

Hadija. Child prostitute pursued by Nelson Dyar and Eunice Goode in Paul Bowles's *Let It Come Down.*

Brinker Hadley. Class leader and politican who later joins the Coast Guard to avoid combat during World War II in John Knowles's *A Separate Peace.*

Ellen Shipp Hadley. Wife of Daniel Compton Wills, daughter of a well-to-do Boston family, and graduate of Wellesley; discovers her husband has seduced the wife of Andrew Collier in George V. Higgins's *Dreamland.*

Mr. Hadley. Father of Brinker Hadley and exponent of traditional values concerning patriotism and duty in John Knowles's *A Separate Peace.*

Reba (Dickless Tracy, No-Balls) Hadley. Intelligent, articulate, and courageous Los Angeles policewoman in Joseph Wambaugh's *The Choirboys.*

Mr. Hadwin. Quaker benefactor of Arthur Mervyn; dies in the yellow-fever epidemic of 1793 in Charles Brockden Brown's *Arthur Mervyn.*

Mr. Haecker. Retired high school principal and resident of the Dorset Hotel in John Barth's *The Floating Opera.*

Alonso Hagan. Frustrated fisherman who never caught a trout; his fishing diary is found in his sister's attic by the narrator of Richard Brautigan's *Trout Fishing in America.*

Hagar (Baxter). Daughter of Mamba and mother of Lissa Atkinson; banned from Charleston because of her drunkenness and violent and disorderly conduct; murdered by Gilly Bluton in DuBose Heyward's *Mamba's Daughters.*

Hagen. Father of Johnny Hagen; longtime night-crew electrician at the Past Bay Manufacturing Company factory who is feared and distrusted by Carl Belcher; shot by police during the strike in Robert Cantwell's *The Land of Plenty.*

Herman Hagen. Head of the German department at Waindell College and Timofey Pnin's protector in Vladimir Nabokov's *Pnin*.

John (Johnny) Hagen. Son of Hagen; recently hired night-crew worker at the Past Bay Manufacturing Company factory who falls in love with Ellen Turner in Robert Cantwell's *The Land of Plenty*.

Steve Hagen. Second in command to Earl Janoth at Janoth Enterprises; conceives a plan to locate the unidentified witness who can link Janoth to the murder of Pauline Delos; a narrator of Kenneth Fearing's *The Big Clock*.

Thomas (Tom) Hagen. Lawyer and counselor to the Corleone family; taken in and reared by the Corleones after being orphaned in Mario Puzo's *The Godfather*.

King Haggard. Ruler of Hagsgate in Peter S. Beagle's *The Last Unicorn*.

Paul (Paulie) Haggerty. Friend of Studs Lonigan in James T. Farrell's *Young Lonigan*; pressured into marrying; dies of a venereal disease in *The Young Manhood of Studs Lonigan*.

Mister Haggin. Plantation owner and Jerry's original master in Jack London's *Jerry of the Islands*.

Hagood. Newspaper editor in William Faulkner's *Pylon*.

Edgar Rice Burroughs Hagstrohm. "Average man" and inhabitant of the dystopian Homestead in Kurt Vonnegut's *Player Piano*.

Augustus M. Haguenin. Editor of a Chicago newspaper who endorses Frank Cowperwood's streetcar plans in exchange for a streetcar line past his office in Theodore Dreiser's *The Titan*.

Cecily Haguenin. Daughter of Augustus Haguenin and lover of Frank Cowperwood in Theodore Dreiser's *The Titan*.

Dolliver (Dolly) Haight. Virtuous man who contracts a venereal disease from the prostitute Flossie "via a kiss upon his cut lip" in Frank Norris's *Vandover and the Brute*.

Lonzo Hait. Husband of Mannie Hait in William Faulkner's *The Town*; mule and horse trader in *The Mansion*.

Mannie Hait. Wife of Lonzo Hait in William Faulkner's *The Town*.

Vashti (Vash) Hake. See Vashti Hake Snyth.

Hal. Soldier who wants to help the sorrowing world, but lands in a hospital with paranoia and delusions of persecution in John Horne Burns's *The Gallery*.

Lisa Halder. Jamaican wife of René Halder; engineers the wedding of Lucky Videndi and Ron Grant in James Jones's *Go to the Widow-Maker*.

René Halder. Owner of Grand Hotel Crount, Kingston; old friend of Lucky Videndi in James Jones's *Go to the Widow-Maker*.

Arnold Haldmarne. Husband of Willa Haldmarne and father of Kerrin, Marget, and Merle Haldmarne; farmer who battles drought and depression in Josephine Johnson's *Now in November*.

Kerrin Haldmarne. Eldest daughter of Arnold and Willa Haldmarne; emotionally unstable; commits suicide in Josephine Johnson's *Now in November*.

Marget Haldmarne. Middle daughter of Arnold and Willa Haldmarne; narrator of Josephine Johnson's *Now in November*.

Merle Haldmarne. Youngest daughter of Arnold and Willa Haldmarne in Josephine Johnson's *Now in November*.

Willa Haldmarne. Wife of Arnold Haldmarne and mother of Kerrin, Marget, and Merle Haldmarne; dies of burns while trying to save the family farm from fire in Josephine Johnson's *Now in November*.

Bona Hale. White southerner attracted to Paul Johnson, a fellow student she suspects might be black, in Jean Toomer's *Cane*.

Mrs. Hale. Invalid wife of a clergyman; employs Frado after she leaves Mrs. Moore in Harriet E. Wilson's *Our Nig*.

Ruth Varnum (Mrs. Ned Hale) Hale. Widow and old acquaintance of Ethan Frome; declines to enlighten the narrator about Frome's story in Edith Wharton's *Ethan Frome*.

Dan Haley. Slave dealer who buys Harry Harris and Uncle Tom from the Shelbys in Harriet Beecher Stowe's *Uncle Tom's Cabin*.

James J. (Jim) Halford. Lover of Julia Maybury Stairs; leaves the United States believing that Julia will not accompany him in Mary Austin's *Santa Lucia*.

Colonel (Sir Peter) Halkett. Scottish regimental commander of the British army; possesses second sight and so knows the day he will die in Mary Lee Settle's *O Beulah Land*.

Betty Hall. Feminine sister of Diony Hall in Elizabeth Madox Roberts's *The Great Meadow.*

Christopher (Black Christopher) Hall. Harlem radical; lover and valet of Leo Proudhammer in James Baldwin's *Tell Me How Long the Train's Been Gone.*

Cubsy Hall. Seven-year-old preacher whom Ruby Drew tries to take from Orondo McCabe in William Goyen's *The Fair Sister.*

Diony Hall. See Diony Hall Jarvis.

George (Ike) Hall. Itinerant socialist who befriends Mac in John Dos Passos's *U.S.A.* trilogy.

James Hall. Cigar-smoking judge and source of Charlie Noble's story about John Moredock in Herman Melville's *The Confidence-Man.*

Mark William Hall. Surgeon who is the "odd man" member of the scientist group at Project Wildfire in Michael Crichton's *The Andromeda Strain.*

Polly Brook Hall. Mother of Diony Hall in Elizabeth Madox Roberts's *The Great Meadow.*

Thomas Hall. Father of Diony Hall and philosopher of the spread of civilization in Elizabeth Madox Roberts's *The Great Meadow.*

Willie (Littleman) Hall. Angry, crippled young black who plots to lynch a white policeman in John Edgar Wideman's *The Lynchers.*

Betsey (Ma) Halleck. Matriarch of the family that transports Jerry and Mary Fowler to Utica; owner of a large farm at which Mary takes refuge when separating from Jerry in Walter D. Edmonds's *Erie Water.*

Ezra Ben Halleck. Wealthy Bostonian who remains loyal to Marcia Gaylord Hubbard during her divorce proceedings in William Dean Howells's *A Modern Instance.*

Douglas Halliday. Spoiled, angry son of Manley and Jere Halliday in Budd Schulberg's *The Disenchanted.*

Jere Halliday. See Jere Wilder-Halliday.

Manley Halliday. Brilliant, accomplished American novelist in decline, famous for his chronicling of the 1920s; an alcoholic in debt and poor health, he agrees to collaborate with a young junior writer on a screenplay for a low-budget college musical; a drinking spree culminates in his death in Budd Schulberg's *The Disenchanted.*

Rachel Halliday. Center of the Quaker household where Eliza Harris and her husband are reunited before being aided by the Quaker community on their flight north in Harriet Beecher Stowe's *Uncle Tom's Cabin.*

Hallie. See Hallie Breedlove.

Dick Hallorann. Black chef at the Overlook Hotel who uses his ability to communicate psychically with Daniel Torrance to rescue Torrance and Torrance's mother from John Torrance in Stephen King's *The Shining.*

Colonel Halloway. White lover of Sal Strange and father of Laurentine Strange in Jessie Redmon Fauset's *The Chinaberry Tree.*

Halmea. Black housekeeper at Homer Bannon's ranch, which she leaves after being raped by Hud, in Larry McMurtry's *Horseman, Pass By.*

Bob Halpin. Businessman who employs Virgil Morgan in Scott Spencer's *Preservation Hall.*

Phil Halpin. Los Angeles deputy district attorney; second prosecutor of Gregory Powell and Jimmy Smith in Joseph Wambaugh's *The Onion Field.*

Catherine (Katie) Halsey. Orphaned niece of Ellsworth Toohey vitiated by her uncle's counsel and Peter Keating's betrayal in Ayn Rand's *The Fountainhead.*

Fred Halsey. Black owner of a wagon shop who befriends Ralph Kabnis in Jean Toomer's *Cane.*

Lanning Halsey. Cousin of Delia Ralston; courts Clementina Lovell and plans to marry her after she is adopted by her wealthy aunt Delia in Edith Wharton's *The Old Maid.*

Doctor Ewing J. Halyard. State Department guide for the Shah of Bratpuhr in Kurt Vonnegut's *Player Piano.*

Carl Halzer. Farmer, labor organizer, and legislator in Mari Sandoz's *Capital City.*

Brother Hambro. Chief theoretician of the Brotherhood who teaches the narrator the Brotherhood's doctrine in Ralph Ellison's *Invisible Man.*

Abdul Hamid. Black Muslim leader who believes that in the United States something is successful in direct proportion to how it is put over; murdered in Ishmael Reed's *Mumbo Jumbo.*

Hamilton. Surgeon aboard the HMS *Pandora* who tries to alleviate the inhumane treatment of the *Bounty* prisoners and who assists Roger Byam at Byam's trial in Charles Nordhoff and James Norman Hall's *Mutiny on the Bounty.*

Alexander Hamilton. Leader who persuades the Federalist party to vote for Thomas Jefferson over Aaron Burr for president after an election tie in 1800; killed by Burr in a duel in Gore Vidal's *Burr*.

Anise Hamilton. Girlfriend who provides Braxton with spending money until she discovers he is spending it on other women in Wallace Thurman's *The Blacker the Berry*.

Berry (Be'y) Hamilton. Hard-working, loyal butler falsely accused of stealing money from Francis Oakley and sentenced to ten years at hard labor; husband of Fannie Hamilton and father of Joe and Kitty Hamilton in Paul Laurence Dunbar's *The Sport of the Gods*.

Charles (Charlie) Hamilton. First husband of Scarlett O'Hara; dies from pneumonia and measles during the early stages of the Civil War in Margaret Mitchell's *Gone with the Wind*.

Fannie (Fannie Gibson) Hamilton. Housekeeper on the estate of Maurice Oakley, wife of Berry Hamilton, and mother of Joe and Kitty Hamilton; migrates to New York City, where she is tricked into marriage by a man who beats her and reduces her to poverty, in Paul Laurence Dunbar's *The Sport of the Gods*.

Joe Hamilton. Son of Berry and Fannie Hamilton; migrates to New York City, where he becomes a dandy, an alcoholic, and the murderer of his sweetheart, in Paul Laurence Dunbar's *The Sport of the Gods*.

Kitty (Kit) Hamilton. Daughter of Berry and Fannie Hamilton; becomes a vaudeville dancer and singer in Paul Laurence Dunbar's *The Sport of the Gods*.

Melanie Hamilton. See Melanie Hamilton Wilkes.

Milo (Arabella Stone) Hamilton. Close friend of Violet Clay and writer of Gothic novels in Gail Godwin's *Violet Clay*.

Roy Hamilton. Californian who has come east to discover the identity of his father; admired by Henry Miller in Henry Miller's *Tropic of Capricorn*.

Samuel (Sam) Hamilton. Salinas Valley farmer who befriends the settler Adam Trask and, just before he dies, convinces Trask to name Trask's sons and reveals that Trask's wife, Cathy Ames Trask, is operating a successful brothel in Salinas in John Steinbeck's *East of Eden*.

Sarah Jane Hamilton. Spinster aunt of Charles and Melanie Hamilton; receives the mourning Scarlett O'Hara in Atlanta following the death of Charles Hamilton, Scarlett's first husband, in Margaret Mitchell's *Gone with the Wind*.

Uncle Hamilton. Wealthy maternal uncle and frequent houseguest of Joe Sandwich; becomes infatuated with and later marries Laura Pribble in Peter De Vries's *The Vale of Laughter*.

Will Hamilton. Son of Samuel Hamilton and business partner of Caleb Trask in the bean venture which makes them both wealthy during the wartime food shortages in John Steinbeck's *East of Eden*.

Jack Hamlin. Gambler with a heart of gold in Bret Harte's *Gabriel Conroy*.

John Hamlin. Lover of Audrey Carsons in William S. Burroughs's *The Wild Boys*.

Laila Hammad. Belly dancer and prostitute who asks Bumper Morgan for help when she is pregnant in Joseph Wambaugh's *The Blue Knight*.

Ambrose Hammer. Retired postal worker researching and writing a book on black history; boarder of Clotilda Pilgrim; adopts Lester Parker after Pilgrim's death in Cyrus Colter's *The Rivers of Eros*.

Bert Hammer. American soldier; pal and bunkmate of Jacob Levy in Martha Gellhorn's *Wine of Astonishment*.

Marietta Drum Hammer. Wife of Paul Hammer; tender toward him only when there is a public disaster in John Cheever's *Bullet Park*.

Paul Hammer. Warped idealist who seeks to wake up the world by the attempted sacrifice of a model citizen (later substituting the citizen's son) in John Cheever's *Bullet Park*.

Caleb Hammil. Utica contractor who hires Jerry Fowler to build first canal locks in Walter D. Edmonds's *Erie Water*.

Hallie Rufer Hammond. Daughter of George Rufer, widow of Michael Hammond, and mother of Rufer Hammond; political radical in her youth and early in her marriage; owner of Hammonds, Franklin's largest department store, in Mari Sandoz's *Capital City*.

Lois Hammond. Teacher whom Richard Dadier saves from rape and who tries to seduce Dadier in Evan Hunter's *The Blackboard Jungle*.

Miss Hammond. Nurse who cares for Elsa Mason as she is dying from cancer in Wallace Stegner's *The Big Rock Candy Mountain*.

Reverend Hammond. Pastor of the church attended by Bigger Thomas's mother; visits Thomas in jail and attempts to convert him to Christianity in Richard Wright's *Native Son*.

Rufer Hammond. See Hamm Rufe.

Willy Hammond. Young man from Cedarville who becomes a gambler and is murdered by Harvey Green in T. S. Arthur's *Ten Nights in a Bar-Room*.

Richard (Dicky) Hampshire. Boyhood friend who draws cartoons with Jack Duluoz in Jack Kerouac's *Doctor Sax*.

Opel Hampson. Drug-using rock groupie who dies suddenly in bed; her New York apartment is a refuge for Bucky Wunderlick in Don DeLillo's *Great Jones Street*.

Hope (Hub) Hampton (I). Sheriff of Yoknapatawpha County in William Faulkner's *The Hamlet, Intruder in the Dust, The Town, The Mansion,* and *The Reivers*.

Hope (Little Hub) Hampton (II). Son of Hub Hampton and sheriff of Yoknapatawpha County in William Faulkner's *The Mansion* and *The Reivers*.

Judge Horace Hanby. Former carpetbag governor of a southern state; keeps the citizens of Bidwell, Ohio, informed about his prophetic and philosophical ideas of the future of industry in the midwest in Sherwood Anderson's *Poor White*.

Samuel Hanby. Puritanical principal of a black training school who demands the resignation of Ralph Kabnis in Jean Toomer's *Cane*.

Winfield Scott Hancock. Former hero in the Mexican War and friend of Lewis Armistead; Northern general who takes possession of Cemetery Hill during the Battle of Gettysburg in Michael Shaara's *The Killer Angels*.

Caroline Hand. Wife of Hosmer Hand; lover of Frank Cowperwood in Theodore Dreiser's *The Titan*.

Hosmer Hand. Investor who seeks revenge on Frank Cowperwood, who has been sleeping with Hand's wife, in Theodore Dreiser's *The Titan*.

Laurel McKelva (Polly) Hand. Chicago fabric designer; daughter of Clinton and Becky McKelva and widow of Philip Hand in Eudora Welty's *The Optimist's Daughter*.

Philip Hand. Husband of Laurel McKelva Hand; killed during World War II in Eudora Welty's *The Optimist's Daughter*.

John Handback. Owner of a plantation store who cheats black as well as white sharecroppers; financially ruined because of Miltiades Vaiden's vengeance; appears in T. S. Stribling's *The Forge* and *The Store*.

Lucius Handback. Son of John Handback; marries Sydna Crowninshield Vaiden; appears in T. S. Stribling's *The Store* and *Unfinished Cathedral*.

Ed Handby. Bartender who courts Belle Carpenter and takes her from George Willard in Sherwood Anderson's *Winesburg, Ohio*.

Dix (Dixie, William Tuttle Jamieson) Handley. Once-famous criminal who dies in his native South, ironically fulfilling his dream of returning, in William Riley Burnett's *The Asphalt Jungle*.

Handsome Mary. English wife of Danby and proprietor of the Baltimore Clipper boardinghouse in Liverpool in Herman Melville's *Redburn*.

Martin Handson. Uncle and manager of Putsy Handson in Calvin Hernton's *Scarecrow*.

Orville Handson. Racist, sadistic, and murderous army sergeant; killed in Korea by Scarecrow in Calvin Hernton's *Scarecrow*.

Putsy Handson. Successful model, daughter of Orville Handson, and lover of Wantman Krane in Calvin Hernton's *Scarecrow*.

Angela Hanema. Wife of Piet Hanema and mother of Ruth and Nancy Hanema in John Updike's *Couples*.

Foxy Hanema. See Elizabeth Fox Whitman.

Nancy Hanema. Younger daughter of Piet and Angela Hanema in John Updike's *Couples*.

Piet Hanema. Philandering husband of Angela Hanema and later of Foxy Whitman; father of Ruth and Nancy Hanema in John Updike's *Couples*.

Ruth Hanema. Older daughter of Piet and Angela Hanema in John Updike's *Couples*.

Hanes. Assistant to Globke in Transparanoia organization; steals a mysterious drug in Don DeLillo's *Great Jones Street*.

Hania. Redheaded prison companion of Eva Laubenstein and seducer of Laubenstein's son, Konrad Vost, in John Hawkes's *The Passion Artist*.

Hank. Airport announcer in William Faulkner's *Pylon*.

Hank. Friend of Joe Gilligan in William Faulkner's *Soldiers' Pay*.

Sissy Hankshaw. See Sissy Hankshaw Gitche.

Ray Hanley. Law partner and friend of Calvin Jarrett in Judith Guest's *Ordinary People*.

Caroline Trid Hanna. See Caroline Trid.

Chad Hanna. Orphan hotel hostler who joins Huguenine's Great and Only International Circus, marries Caroline Trid, and becomes ringmaster in Walter D. Edmonds's *Chad Hanna*.

Maum Hannah. Mother of Budda Ben and guardian of and midwife for Mary Pinesett; matriarch of Blue Brook Plantation and important member of Heaven's Gate Church in Julia Peterkin's *Scarlet Sister Mary*.

Hans. German socialist, veteran of World War I, labor agitator, and Larry Donovan's political mentor in Jack Conroy's *The Disinherited*.

Beret Holm Hansa. Wife of Per Hansa and mother of Peder Victorious Holm in O. E. Rölvaag's *Giants in the Earth*; widowed, she often succumbs to madness, but still establishes a successful farm as her children become Americanized, in *Peder Victorious* and *Their Father's God*.

Per (Peder) Hansa (Holm). Innovative pioneer farmer married to Beret Holm; leader of the Norwegian settlement in the Dakota territory; successfully battles nature, but dies in a winter storm, in O. E. Rölvaag's *Giants in the Earth*.

Andrew Jackson (Chip) Hansen. Army general, superior to Sean O'Sullivan, and first military governor of post-World War II Germany in Leon Uris's *Armageddon*.

Arne Hansen. Volatile Swede in Katherine Anne Porter's *Ship of Fools*.

Mr. Hansen. Tall, blond Austrian who owns the Black Pearl nightclub in Golconda where Lillian Beye plays piano in Anaïs Nin's *Seduction of the Minotaur*.

Margo Hansmon. Friendly landlady; baker of Annie and Carl Brown's wedding cake in Betty Smith's *Joy in the Morning*.

George (Georgette) Hanson. Transvestite and homosexual who professes to be pleased with his sexual orientation; almost aggressively defensive about his sexuality, he nonetheless becomes a creature for pity because of rejection by his beloved Vinnie in Hubert Selby, Jr.'s *Last Exit to Brooklyn*.

Minnie Meeber Hanson. Sister of Carrie Meeber; Carrie lives with her in Theodore Dreiser's *Sister Carrie*.

Countess Berthe von Happel. Viennese divorcée who marries into Boston society; only hostess who invites Sonia Marburg to her salon in Jean Stafford's *Boston Adventure*.

Count Rudolf von Hapsburg. Lover of Zdenka von Studenitz, father of Rudolf Stanka, and murderer of a mistress; commits suicide in Louis Adamic's *Cradle of Life*.

Frances Harbach. True love of Homer Zigler in Clyde Brion Davis's *"The Great American Novel—."*

Asa Bruce (Coot) Harcoot. Former bank president who lives as a philosophical bum in Herb's Addition; built the first brick kilns in Franklin in Mari Sandoz's *Capital City*.

Gregory W. Harcourt. Psychiatrist whose testimony for the prosecution is discredited by Paul Biegler in Robert Traver's *Anatomy of a Murder*.

Billie Harcum. Stereotyped Memphis belle of Irwin K. Macgregor and later his wife in Wright Morris's *Love among the Cannibals*.

Tandy Hard. Winesburg citizen whose childhood encounter with a drunken stranger changes her life in Sherwood Anderson's *Winesburg, Ohio*.

Tom Hard. Religious fanatic who, with his daughter Tandy, befriends a drunken stranger in Sherwood Anderson's *Winesburg, Ohio*.

Hard Heart. Noble Pawnee chieftain and ally of Natty Bumppo; kills enemy chief Mahtoree in fierce combat and claims his scalp in James Fenimore Cooper's *The Prairie*.

Rozelle Hardcastle. See Rozelle Hardcastle Butler Carrington.

Hardee-Hardee. See Lem Hardy.

Gretchen Hardenburg. Unfaithful wife of Lieutenant Hardenburg; undermines the character of Christian Diestl by initiating an affair with him in Irwin Shaw's *The Young Lions*.

Lieutenant Hardenburg. Callous Nazi officer whose heinous crimes against humanity serve as an example for Christian Diestl in Irwin Shaw's *The Young Lions*.

J. (Joshua) Hardin. Father of Paul Hardin; carriage maker and crusading prohibitionist who protests alone against the mob that lynched Smoke in Brand Whitlock's *J. Hardin & Son*.

John Wesley Hardin. Racist hired by Drag Gibson to defeat the Loop Garoo Kid, but unable to do so in Ishmael Reed's *Yellow Back Radio Broke-Down*.

Paul Hardin. Rebellious son of J. Hardin and husband of Winona Dyer; bank vice president who is a successful oil speculator and landowner in Brand Whitlock's *J. Hardin & Son*.

Winona Dyer Hardin. See Winona Dyer.

Annie Harding. High-spirited girl who comes to live at Plumfield in Louisa May Alcott's *Little Men*.

Dale Harding. Most intelligent and articulate of the intimidated mental patients who respond to Randle McMurphy's example in resisting Big Nurse in Ken Kesey's *One Flew Over the Cuckoo's Nest*.

Reverend Hardman. Episcopal minister and Christian Socialist in Robert Herrick's *The Memoirs of an American Citizen*.

Alva Hardwick. Demented man employed by Donald Martin; accuses Juan Martinez of murdering Larry Kinkaid; lynched by the mob in Walter Van Tilburg Clark's *The Ox-Bow Incident*.

Albert Hardy. Father of John and Mary Hardy; allows Louise Bentley to board at his family's home while she attends school in Sherwood Anderson's *Winesburg, Ohio*.

Coach Hardy. Football coach for "the College" and plea bargainer for Raymond Blent's football career in Howard Nemerov's *The Homecoming Game*.

David Hardy. Son of Louise and John Hardy; leaves home after an incident in which he fears he has accidentally killed his grandfather, Jesse Bentley, in Sherwood Anderson's *Winesburg, Ohio*.

Harriet Hardy. Daughter of Albert Hardy; shuns Louise Bentley when the elder Hardy prefers Louise to her and her sister Mary Hardy in Sherwood Anderson's *Winesburg, Ohio*.

John Hardy. Winesburg banker and husband of Louise Hardy; works with Jesse Bentley to have David Hardy moved to Bentley's farm in Sherwood Anderson's *Winesburg, Ohio*.

Lem (Hardee-Hardee) Hardy. English military leader of Hannamanoo whom the natives tattoo in Herman Melville's *Omoo*.

Louise Bentley Hardy. Daughter of Jesse Bentley and mother of David Hardy; her cynicism isolates her from the rest of the townspeople in Sherwood Anderson's *Winesburg, Ohio*.

Mary Hardy. Daughter of Albert Hardy; her tryst with a young man strengthens Louise Bentley's resolve to have a suitor in Sherwood Anderson's *Winesburg, Ohio*.

Theo J. Hardy. New, honest, and hardworking police chief who is determined to reform the department in William Riley Burnett's *The Asphalt Jungle*.

Rev. Balthazar Harge. Superintendent of the Bois des Morts Mission in the Minnesota territory; convinces Aaron Gadd to become a missionary to the Indians in Sinclair Lewis's *The God-Seeker*.

Mercie Harge. Wife of Balthazar Harge; dies of consumption in Sinclair Lewis's *The God-Seeker*.

Christine (Chris) Hargensen. Classmate who torments Carrie White in Stephen King's *Carrie*.

Manson Hargrove. Man who shot Estelle in the chest without killing her in Reynolds Price's *A Long and Happy Life*.

Hark (Hercules). Slave and closest friend of Nat Turner; Hark's wife and son are sold to another plantation in William Styron's *The Confessions of Nat Turner*.

Daniel Harkavy. Trade-journal editor and friend of Asa Leventhal; warns Leventhal, as a fellow Jew, not to be hypersensitive or defensive about his Jewishness, in Saul Bellow's *The Victim*.

Gary Harkness. Football halfback for Logos College who is preoccupied by nuclear cataclysm; narrator of Don DeLillo's *End Zone*.

Joe Harland. Bum who has fallen from a position of prominence in the business world in John Dos Passos's *Manhattan Transfer*.

Frances (Frankie) Harlow. Member of Thomas Marshfield's congregation who complains of too much music in the services and not enough excitement in her marriage; Marshfield is unable to make love to her in John Updike's *A Month of Sundays*.

Gerald (Gerry) Harlow. Husband of Frankie Harlow; banker and a deacon of Thomas Marshfield's church in John Updike's *A Month of Sundays*.

Whizzer Harlow. Old beatnik friend of Lee Youngdahl in Mark Harris's *Wake Up, Stupid*.

Effie (Mamma Effie) Harmon. Wife of Pop Harmon and mother of Mariah Upshur in Sarah E. Wright's *This Child's Gonna Live*.

Pop Harmon. Husband of Effie Harmon and father of Mariah Upshur in Sarah E. Wright's *This Child's Gonna Live*.

Rocco (Little Rock, Little Rock Harmony, Rock) Harmonia. Boyfriend of Winnie in John Clellon Holmes's *Go*.

Lucius Harney. Young architect who, on a visit to his cousin in North Dormer, becomes Charity Royall's lover and impregnates her in Edith Wharton's *Summer*.

Harold. Father of a child by the young May Alice in Gayl Jones's *Corregidora*.

A. J. Harper. Abusive lover of Evalin McCabe Wilson in Diane Johnson's *The Shadow Knows*.

Al Harper. Quick, conniving Hollywood agent in Budd Schulberg's *The Disenchanted*.

Andrew T. Harper. Father of Linn Harper and husband of Katherine Harper; assistant professor of history at William Watson College and reluctant collaborator in Zebulon Johns Mackie's history of Bunker County in Fred Chappell's *The Gaudy Place*.

Ben Harper. Father of Pearl and John Harper; executed for robbery and murder in Davis Grubb's *The Night of the Hunter*.

Duncan (Happy) Harper. Racial moderate and candidate for sheriff in Winfield County, Mississippi; dies in a car wreck with a black man in his protection in Elizabeth Spencer's *The Voice at the Back Door*.

Henry Harper. Nine-year-old orphan who calls a late-night radio talk show in Stanley Elkin's *The Dick Gibson Show*.

John Harper. Son of Ben and Willa Harper; flees with his sister Pearl rather than reveal to Preacher the whereabouts of stolen money he has sworn to his father to protect in Davis Grubb's *The Night of the Hunter*.

Joseph (Joe) Harper. Pal of Tom Sawyer in Samuel Langhorne Clemens's *The Adventures of Tom Sawyer*.

Katherine (Katy) Harper. Mother of Linn Harper, wife of Andrew Harper, and niece of Zebulon Johns Mackie; insists on calling Mackie to get Linn out of jail in Fred Chappell's *The Gaudy Place*.

Linn Harper. Seventeen-year-old son of Andrew and Katherine Harper; inspired by the works of Albert Camus to commit the "gratuitous act" of breaking into the Spartan Stock Feed Products Mill to steal chicken feed in Fred Chappell's *The Gaudy Place*.

Col. Looseleaf Harper. Pilot who dropped the atomic bomb on Nagasaki; Eliot Rosewater's pilot in Kurt Vonnegut's *Breakfast of Champions*.

Louise Taylor (Tinker) Harper. Wife and eventual widow of Duncan Harper and object of Jimmy Tallant's romantic affection in Elizabeth Spencer's *The Voice at the Back Door*.

Pearl Harper. Younger sister of John Harper and daughter of Ben and Willa Harper; flees with her brother to avoid giving Preacher the stolen money hidden in her rag doll in Davis Grubb's *The Night of the Hunter*.

Willa Harper. Mother of Pearl and John Harper and widow of Ben Harper; marries and is murdered by Preacher in Davis Grubb's *The Night of the Hunter*.

Edward Harranby. Scotland Yard man who captures Edward Pierce in Michael Crichton's *The Great Train Robbery*.

Celia Hornby (Baby, Ceeley, Doll-Baby, Honey-Baby) Harrick. Wife of Jack Harrick and teacher in Robert Penn Warren's *The Cave*.

Jasper (Big Bubba) Harrick. Older son of John T. and Celia Hornby Harrick and a hero in the Korean War; dies trapped in a cave near Johntown, Tennessee, in Robert Penn Warren's *The Cave*.

John T. (Jack, Jumping Jack, Ole Jack) Harrick. Dying husband of Celia Hornby Harrick; soldier in World War II and blacksmith by trade; known as a hell-raiser in his younger days in Robert Penn Warren's *The Cave*.

Harriet (Harry the Rapist). Lover of Georgie Cornell in Thomas Berger's *Regiment of Women*.

Harriett. Maid and cook for India and Walter Bridge in Evan Connell's *Mrs. Bridge* and *Mr. Bridge*.

Kerfoot (Carl) Harriman. Marine sergeant in France during World War I who, upon learning of his girlfriend's interest in another man, shoots himself in the foot in Thomas Boyd's *Through the Wheat*.

Harrington. Customer at Jerry Doherty's bar; becomes an accomplice with Doherty in a fur theft and turns him in to the FBI when he feels cheated with his share of the take in George V. Higgins's *The Digger's Game*.

Harrington. Father of Laurette Harrington; chairman of the board of World-Wide Studios responsible for the ousting of Sidney Fineman as production chief and the promotion of Sammy Glick to take his place in Budd Schulberg's *What Makes Sammy Run?*

Amelia Harrington. Wife of J. Harrington and mother of Tommy Harrington in William Hill Brown's *The Power of Sympathy.*

Edward Harrington. See Edward Van Harrington.

J. Harrington. Father, by his wife Amelia Harrington, of Tommy Harrington and, by Maria Fawcet, of Harriot Fawcet in William Hill Brown's *The Power of Sympathy.*

Kate Harrington. See Kate Flickinger.

Laurette Harrington. Beautiful, arrogant daughter of the chairman of the board of World Wide Studios; marries Sammy Glick in Budd Schulberg's *What Makes Sammy Run?*

Leslie Harrington. Wealthy mill owner who uses his money and power to control people in Grace Metalious's *Peyton Place.*

May Rudge Harrington. Wife of Will Harrington in Robert Herrick's *The Memoirs of an American Citizen.*

Myra Harrington. Sister of Tommy Harrington; loves Jack Worthy in William Hill Brown's *The Power of Sympathy.*

Rodney Harrington. Spoiled son of Leslie Harrington; selfish womanizer who impregnates Betty Anderson and is later killed in an automobile accident in Grace Metalious's *Peyton Place.*

Sarah Gentles Harrington. See Sarah Gentles.

Tommy Harrington. "Moralist and amoroso" and brother of Myra Harrington; commits suicide after discovering that his beloved, Harriot Fawcet, is his halfsister in William Hill Brown's *The Power of Sympathy.*

Will Harrington. Principled and poor brother of Edward Van Harrington and husband of May Rudge Harrington in Robert Herrick's *The Memoirs of an American Citizen.*

Harris. New Orleans steamboat captain and market contractor; searches island and coastal areas for survivors following the storm that destroys Last Island in Lafcadio Hearn's *Chita.*

Charles Baker (Dill) Harris. Nephew of Miss Rachel Haverford and excitable summer neighbor of Scout and Jem Finch in Harper Lee's *To Kill a Mockingbird.*

Eliza Harris. Slave to the Shelbys, who have treated her almost as a daughter; wife of George Harris and mother of Harry Harris; flees across the partially frozen Ohio River to the North and then to Canada when she learns that Harry has been sold in Harriet Beecher Stowe's *Uncle Tom's Cabin.*

George Harris. Harvard-educated black who, unable to find work, turns to crime in Thomas Dixon's *The Leopard's Spots.*

George Harris. Husband of Eliza Harris and father of Harry Harris; skilled machinist who flees to Canada when his owner becomes threatened by Harris's superior talents in Harriet Beecher Stowe's *Uncle Tom's Cabin.*

Harry .Harris. Son of the slaves Eliza and George Harris; taken north by his mother after she learns that he has been sold in Harriet Beecher Stowe's *Uncle Tom's Cabin.*

Jack Harris. Boyhood friend of Tom Bailey; leads boys in the snowball fight; dies in the battle of the Seven Pines in Thomas Bailey Aldrich's *The Story of a Bad Boy.*

Podjo (Podj) Harris. White kidnapper, ex-convict, and gambler in Shelby Foote's *September September.*

Sid Harris. Condominium president who duns Marshall Preminger for back rent in *The Condominium,* a novella in Stanley Elkin's *Searches and Seizures.*

Stink Harris. Army infantryman in Vietnam noted for his toughness, pettiness, and distrust in Tim O'Brien's *Going after Cacciato.*

Tom Harris. Leading citizen of Maxwell, Georgia; owner of its sawmills and turpentine stills in Lillian Smith's *Strange Fruit.*

Will Harris. Veteran who returns from Korea to the South to live and become an active citizen; prevented from registering to vote because he is black in Junius Edwards's *If We Must Die.*

Harrison (Hal, Harry). White organizer of the Irredentist movement in Mexico; murdered by Mexican police in Nicholas Delbanco's *News.*

C. D. Harrison. Necrophiliac father of Les Harrison; essentially owns Metropolitan Pictures in Terry Southern's *Blue Movie.*

Charlie Harrison. Friend and co-worker of Georgie Cornell in Thomas Berger's *Regiment of Women.*

Fido Harrison. Head broker at MacNaughton and Blair; friend and supervisor of Joe Sandwich in Peter De Vries's *The Vale of Laughter.*

Frederick Harrison. Man who charters the *South Florida* and turns in Harry Morgan to the authorities in Ernest Hemingway's *To Have and Have Not.*

John Harrison. Suicide for whose death Inspector Lee blames Terrence Weld in William S. Burroughs's *The Ticket That Exploded.*

Les (Rat Prick) Harrison. Son of C. D. Harrison and vice president of Metropolitan Pictures; kept under sedation to prevent his learning about explicit sex scenes in Boris Adrian's pornographic movie in Terry Southern's *Blue Movie.*

Mrs. Phelps (Dolly) Harrison. Wealthy Washington society leader and widow involved with Bob Munin Allen Drury's *Advise and Consent.*

William (Willie) Harrison. Mill owner whose proposal of marriage Lily Shane rejects in Louis Bromfield's *The Green Bay Tree.*

Dalton (Diddy) Harron. Public relations man determined to discover whether he has actually committed a murder; his dying fantasies upon his suicide constitute the events of Susan Sontag's *Death Kit.*

Joan Harron. Ex-wife of Dalton Harron in Susan Sontag's *Death Kit.*

Paul Harron. Younger brother of Dalton Harron in Susan Sontag's *Death Kit.*

Daniel (Dan, Dan'l) Harrow. Farmer who works as a driver, inherits a canal boat, becomes lover of Molly Larkins, and returns to farming in Walter D. Edmonds's *Rome Haul*; appears as a dairyman in *The Big Barn.*

Harry. Chronically cold passenger on the *Here They Come* who plans to make the world warmer in Gregory Corso's *The American Express.*

Harry. Clerk in a record store with extensive knowledge of jazz; contributor to Renate's planned magazine in Anaïs Nin's *Collages.*

Harry. Elderly resident of the Golden Years Community; pays a janitress to permit him to shave her pubic hair with his electric shaver in Jerzy Kosinski's *Cockpit.*

Harry. English groom in William Faulkner's *A Fable.*

Harry. Gunner's mate for whom Fernandez leaves Cassandra; dies in a hotel room trying to save Fernandez in John Hawkes's *Second Skin.*

Harry. Brother of Amy and father of Miranda and Maria; shoots a man suspected of having kissed Amy in Katherine Anne Porter's *Old Mortality.*

Judge Harry. Corrupt white judge who awards wife-slayer Brownfield Copeland custody of his daughter Ruth Copeland in Alice Walker's *The Third Life of Grange Copeland.*

Harry the Rapist. See Harriet.

Andor Harsanyi. Chicago pianist and teacher who encourages Thea Kronborg to study voice in Willa Cather's *The Song of the Lark.*

Bob Harshaw. Attorney who defends Mink Lorey and who becomes the enemy of James Gwinnan in Mary Noailles Murfree's *In the Clouds.*

Henrietta Hart. Maternal elderly widow who befriends Dane Empson in Majorca in Gail Godwin's *The Perfectionists.*

Jesse (Jesse Pedersen, Jesse Vogel) Harte. Boy who escapes his father's murderous rampage and as an adult becomes a brain surgeon; having legally changed his name, he pursues the American dream and the mystery of his own identity; husband of Helene Cady Vogel in Joyce Carol Oates's *Wonderland.*

Nelson Hartis. Presbyterian minister who marries Ellen Strohe and Chris Van Eenanam in Larry Woiwode's *What I'm Going to Do, I Think.*

Eleanor Hartley. Ex-wife of Jack Hartley in James Jones's *The Merry Month of May.*

Jonathan James (Jack) Hartley III. Editor of *The Two Islands Review* and friend of the Gallagher family; narrator of James Jones's *The Merry Month of May.*

Miss Hartley. Nurse from Mobile, Alabama, called to care for Helga Crane after the birth of Helga's fourth child in Nella Larsen's *Quicksand.*

Reverend Curtis Hartman. Presbyterian minister who is driven to distraction by his voyeuristic obsession with Kate Swift in Sherwood Anderson's *Winesburg, Ohio.*

George Hartshorn. Jealous white man who loves Slim Girl in Oliver La Farge's *Laughing Boy.*

Ralph Hartsook. Young schoolmaster whose first assignment is in the 1850s in Flat Creek, Indiana, where he matches wits with recalcitrant pupils and corrupt locals, but where he also finds love, in Edward Eggleston's *The Hoosier School-Master.*

Caroline Harvey. Society matron and wife of Willis Harvey; accepts and coaches Rose Dutcher in Chicago society in Hamlin Garland's *Rose of Dutcher's Coolly.*

Elbert Harvey. Son of Caroline and Willis Harvey; offers wealth and good character in his courtship of Rose Dutcher in Hamlin Garland's *Rose of Dutcher's Coolly.*

Willis Harvey. Wealthy, enlightened Chicago businessman and husband of Caroline Harvey in Hamlin Garland's *Rose of Dutcher's Coolly*.

Bess Harvill. Close friend of N. Hexam in Diane Johnson's *The Shadow Knows*.

Esther Harvitz. Roommate of Rachel Owlglass; has an affair with the plastic surgeon who performs her nose job in Thomas Pynchon's *V.*

James Trueman Harwell. Murderer of Horatio Leavenworth, whom he had served as secretary, in Anna Katharine Green's *The Leavenworth Case*.

Nat Haskell. Freedman who tells Comfort Servosse about overhearing Marcus Thompson relate how John Walters was murdered by a group of ten men, including Thompson himself, in Albion W. Tourgee's *A Fool's Errand*.

Bonny Fern Haskin. Childhood and adult companion of Larry Donovan and female counterpart of the itinerant male worker during hard times in the American Midwest in Jack Conroy's *The Disinherited*.

Hassan. See Salvador Hassan O'Leary.

Eva Hassel. Classmate and early love interest of Henry Bech in John Updike's *Bech: A Book*.

Martha Hastings. See Martha Hastings King.

Sergeant Hastings. British sergeant serving in Dorchester, South Carolina; bully whose lust for Bella Humphries leads to his death in William Gilmore Simms's *The Partisan*.

Jake Hasty. Dog-show handler at the fair in Reynolds Price's *A Generous Man*.

Lucy Haswell. Wife of Arnold Armstrong, whom she knows as Aubrey Wallace; dies giving birth to their son, Lucien Wallace, in Mary Roberts Rinehart's *The Circular Staircase*.

Homer T. Hatch. Bounty hunter killed by Royal Earle Thompson in Katherine Anne Porter's *Noon Wine*.

Miss Hatchard. Cousin of Lucius Harney and supervisor of the North Dormer library in which Charity Royall works for a short time in Edith Wharton's *Summer*.

Hatcher. American engineer who comes to Mexico to forget his past, but cannot in Anaïs Nin's *Seduction of the Minotaur*.

James Graves Hatcher. Professor of dramatics at Harvard who teaches Eugene Gant in Thomas Wolfe's *Of Time and the River*.

Tilda Hatter. Former landlady of Jinny Timberlane; plaintiff in a court case before Cass Timberlane in Sinclair Lewis's *Cass Timberlane*.

Angeline Hatton. See Angeline Meserve.

Theresa Haug. See Theresa Bigoness.

Hausenfield. Undertaker in the first Hard Times; placed alive in his own hearse by Clay Turner and sent to the flats, where he dies, in E. L. Doctorow's *Welcome to Hard Times*.

Bobby Hauser. Son of Sherman and Carol Hauser; dies accidentally in Edward Lewis Wallant's *The Tenants of Moonbloom*.

Carol Hauser. Wife of Sherman Hauser and mother of Bobby Hauser; lives in the 70th Street building managed by Norman Moonbloom in Edward Lewis Wallant's *The Tenants of Moonbloom*.

Herman Hauser. Owner of the Little Rialto burlesque house in Chicago in Nelson Algren's *Somebody in Boots*.

Horse Hauser. Foul-mouthed and hilarious ne'er-do-well friend of Ralph Sandifer in Thomas Berger's *Sneaky People*.

Sherman Hauser. Husband of Carol Hauser and father of Bobby Hauser; tenant in the 70th Street building managed by Norman Moonbloom in Edward Lewis Wallant's *The Tenants of Moonbloom*.

Hautia. Queen of Flozella a Nina who apparently captures Yillah in Herman Melville's *Mardi*.

Ernest Havel. Bohemian immigrant and Claude Wheeler's best boyhood friend in Willa Cather's *One of Ours*.

Miss Rachel Haverford. Neighbor of Atticus Finch and aunt of Dill Harris in Harper Lee's *To Kill a Mockingbird*.

Captain Havermeyer. Sharpshooter and lead bombardier in Yossarian's squadron; refuses to take evasive action in battle in Joseph Heller's *Catch-22*.

T. Havisham. Attorney for the Earl of Dorincourt; brings Cedric Errol to England in Frances Hodgson Burnett's *Little Lord Fauntleroy*.

Horace Havistock. Wealthy American expatriate and esthete living in Paris; schoolmate and boyhood friend of Francis Prescott and author of "The Art of Friendship" about their relationship in Louis Auchincloss's *The Rector of Justin*.

Ally Hawes. Poorest girl in North Dormer and friend of Charity Royall; sews for Annabel Balch in Edith Wharton's *Summer*.

Julia Hawes. North Dormer "bad girl" and sister of Ally Hawes; seen by Charity Royall carousing with Lawyer Royall in a nearby town in Edith Wharton's *Summer*.

Hawk. Talented military subordinate of Wang the Tiger; eventually establishes himself as leader of a rival bandit group and is then captured and killed by his former leader in Pearl Buck's *Sons*.

Dr. Archibald Hawk. Byronically romantic man who presents himself so as to be attractive to women; engaged to Gertrude Larkin, until she discovers that he desires her money, in Hjalmar Hjorth Boyesen's *The Mammon of Unrighteousness*.

Drusilla Hawk. See Drusilla Hawk Sartoris.

Louisa (Louise) Hawk. Mother of Drusilla Hawk in William Faulkner's *The Unvanquished*.

David Hawke. See Robert Clark.

Harrison (Woolf) Hawke. Fraudulent psychiatrist in Vardis Fisher's *No Villain Need Be*; also appears as Harrison Woolf in *Orphans in Gethsemene*.

William (Billie, Will) Hawker. Struggling artist in love with a woman of superior wealth and social status in Stephen Crane's *The Third Violet*.

Hawkeye. See Nathaniel Bumppo.

George Washington Hawkins. Brother of Laura and Henry Clay Hawkins; with Laura, plans to sell their land in Tennessee and build Knobs Industrial University for blacks in Samuel Langhorne Clemens and Charles Dudley Warner's *The Gilded Age*; congressional delegate from the Cherokee Strip and friend of Mulberry Sellers in Clemens's *The American Claimant*.

Henry Clay Hawkins. Brother of Laura and George Washington Hawkins; inept Confederate soldier who later, from his Australian business ventures, supports the Hawkins family in Samuel Langhorne Clemens and Charles Dudley Warner's *The Gilded Age*.

Hiram Adolphus Hawkins. Poet who dies of a broken heart when Cecilia Vaughan rejects him and marries Arthur Kavanagh in Henry Wadsworth Longfellow's *Kavanagh*.

Laura Van Brunt Hawkins. Daughter of the Van Brunts who is adopted by the Hawkinses after the Van Brunts are thought to be killed in a steamboat crash; becomes an influential Washington lobbyist; murders George Selby, but is acquitted; dies believing she is a failure in Samuel Langhorne Clemens and Charles Dudley Warner's *The Gilded Age*.

Martha Hawkins. Kindly niece of Squire Hawkins; wins the affection of Bud Means in Edward Eggleston's *The Hoosier School-Master*.

Martha Amelia Hawkins. Sister of Adolphus Hawkins; helps him in his unsuccessful pursuit of Cecilia Vaughan in Henry WadsworthLongfellow's *Kavanagh*.

Sadie Hawkins. Daughter of a taverner; tricks Leslie Collins into marrying her and gives birth to another man's son six months later in Harriette Simpson Arnow's *The Kentucky Trace*.

Squire Hawkins. Former poor Yankee schoolmaster who becomes one of the influential men of Flat Creek, Indiana, in Edward Eggleston's *The Hoosier School-Master*.

Wibird Hawkins. Rivermouth minister in Thomas Bailey Aldrich's *The Story of a Bad Boy*.

Jane Hawkline. Twin sister of Susan Hawkline and daughter of Professor Hawkline; hires Cameron and Greer to destroy the Hawkline Monster in Richard Brautigan's *The Hawkline Monster*.

Professor Hawkline. Father of Susan and Jane Hawkline; Harvard chemistry professor whose experiments create the Hawkline Monster, which turns him into an elephant-foot umbrella stand, from which transformation he is rescued by Greer and Cameron, in Richard Brautigan's *The Hawkline Monster*.

Susan Hawkline. Twin sister of Jane Hawkline and daughter of Professor Hawkline; hires Cameron and Greer to destroy the Hawkline Monster; plans to but does not marry Cameron in Richard Brautigan's *The Hawkline Monster*.

Hawkline Monster. Sentient, malevolent creature of light, accompanied by a beneficent if inept shadow; created in Professor Hawkline's chemistry experiments and destroyed by Cameron in Richard Brautigan's *The Hawkline Monster*.

Captain Andy Hawks. Owner of the *Creole Belle* and later of the showboat *Cotton Blossom* in Edna Ferber's *Show Boat*.

Asa Hawks. Bogus street preacher who pretends to be blind but actually lost his nerve in the attempt to blind himself; father of Sabbath Lily Hawks in Flannery O'Connor's *Wise Blood*.

Magnolia Hawks. See Magnolia Hawks Ravenal.

Parthenia Ann (Parthy) Hawks. Former teacher from Massachusetts, wife of Andy Hawks, and mother of Magnolia Hawks Ravenal in Edna Ferber's *Show Boat*.

Sabbath Lily Hawks. Illegitimate daughter of Asa Hawks; pursues Hazel Motes and tries to live with him when her father leaves town in Flannery O'Connor's *Wise Blood*.

Ethan Allen (Eth) Hawley. Grocery clerk at Marullo's Fruit and Fancy Groceries who regains ownership of the store by having Alfio Marullo deported; son of a formerly prominent family who takes possession of the most valuable land in New Baytown by manipulating his childhood friend Danny Taylor, thus restoring money and respect to the Hawley family, in John Steinbeck's *The Winter of Our Discontent*.

Mary Hawley. Dance-marathon contestant who agrees to marry her partner Vee Lovell in a publicity-oriented wedding arranged by the managers of the contest in Horace McCoy's *They Shoot Horses, Don't They?*

Mary Hawley. Devoted wife of Ethan Allen Hawley; encourages her husband to rise above the level of grocery clerk so their family will have the financial status to be respected among the people of New Baytown in John Steinbeck's *The Winter of Our Discontent*.

Jack Haxby. Jealous husband of Lucille Haxby; celebrity dentist who maliciously pulls the wrong tooth from Gowan McGland, precipitating McGland's suicide, in Peter De Vries's *Reuben, Reuben*.

Lucille Haxby. Wife of Jack Haxby and paramour of Gowan McGland in Peter De Vries's *Reuben, Reuben*.

August Hay. Former ice-cream vendor, now derelict resident of the Diamond County Home for the Aged; laughs at everything and shares George Lucas's bottle of rye at the fair in John Updike's *The Poorhouse Fair*.

Clarence Hay-Lawrence. Pretentious, monocled chess opponent of William Demarest in Conrad Aiken's *Blue Voyage*.

Dr. Kenneth Hale Hayden. Jewish physician who diagnoses and treats J. T. Malone for leukemia; exposes Malone's prejudice in Carson McCullers's *Clock without Hands*.

Harry and Juanita Haydock. Owners of the Bon Ton Store in Sinclair Lewis's *Main Street*.

Sally Hayes. Friend Holden Caulfield takes to the theater; he invites her to run away with him in J. D. Salinger's *The Catcher in the Rye*.

Val Hayes. Mentor of Cody Pomeray and friend at Columbia University of Jack Duluoz; introduces Duluoz to Pomeray in Jack Kerouac's *Visions of Cody*.

Jeanette Hayes-Rore. Widow of a black Chicago politician; a "race" woman, active in Negro Women's Clubs; becomes the employer, benefactor, and friend of Helga Crane in Nella Larsen's *Quicksand*.

Charles Hayman. Pioneer who in 1876 settled beside a creek that now bears his name in Richard Brautigan's *Trout Fishing in America*.

Andrew Haynes. Schoolmaster in Harriette Arnow's *Hunter's Horn*.

Flagler Haynes. Book publisher, then editor of the *Booklover*, and finally publisher's reader and reviewer in Edmund Wilson's *Memoirs of Hecate County*.

Miss Haynsworth. Winner of the poetry contest Henry Bech judges at a Virginia women's college in John Updike's *Bech: A Book*.

Arnold Hayward. White lawyer of Fonny Hunt in James Baldwin's *If Beale Street Could Talk*.

Thomas Hayward. Cowardly midshipman who reveals his cruelty by testifying against both the mutineers and those who are forced to stay aboard the HMS *Bounty* after the mutiny in Charles Nordhoff and James Norman Hall's *Mutiny on the Bounty*; set adrift with Captain Bligh in *Men against the Sea*.

Bill Haywood. IWW leader portrayed in John Dos Passos's *U.S.A.* trilogy.

Arthur (Art) Hazard. Black musician who teaches Rick Martin how to play the trumpet; member of Jeff Williams's band in Dorothy Baker's *Young Man with a Horn*.

Edward Hazard. Father of Walter Hazard and grandfather of Ned Hazard; ambitious politician whose misdirected schemes at agricultural improvement help encumber his estate and instigate the eventual lawsuit between Frank Meriwether and Isaac Tracy over worthless land separating their plantations in John Pendleton Kennedy's *Swallow Barn*.

Lucretia Hazard. See Lucretia Hazard Meriwether.

Ned Hazard. Son and heir of Walter Hazard and brother of Lucretia Hazard Meriwether; irresponsible but good-natured gentleman and sportsman who is expelled from Princeton; assists in operating Frank Meriwether's plantation in John Pendleton Kennedy's *Swallow Barn*.

Walter Hazard. Father of Ned Hazard and Lucretia Hazard Meriwether in John Pendleton Kennedy's *Swallow Barn*.

Charlotte Haze. See Charlotte Becker Haze Humbert.

Dolores (Dolly, Lo, Lolita) Haze. Precocious nymphet, daughter of Charlotte Haze, stepdaughter and mistress of Humbert Humbert, and wife of Richard Schiller in Vladimir Nabokov's *Lolita*.

Sarah Bracknell Hazlett. Girlfriend of Johnny Smith; marries another man while Smith is in a coma following an automobile accident in Stephen King's *The Dead Zone*.

Neal Hazzard. Commandant for the American sector of Berlin in Leon Uris's *Armageddon*.

Sidney Herbert Head. Banker married to and quickly divorced from Caddy Compson in William Faulkner's *The Sound and the Fury*.

Gerald Healey. Minister who marries Earl Morgan and Lillian Douglas in Scott Spencer's *Preservation Hall*.

Vince Healy. Famous newspaper reporter in William Riley Burnett's *High Sierra*.

Ruth Heaper. Lover of Jack Duluoz in New York in Jack Kerouac's *Desolation Angels*.

Lieutenant Robert (Bobby) Hearn. Harvard-educated assistant to General Cummings; resists Cummings's authority and is made head of a reconnaissance patrol; dies by Japanese sniper fire after Sergeant Croft withholds information in Norman Mailer's *The Naked and the Dead*.

Arthur Heathcote. Englishman who unsuccessfully woos Mildred Osborne in Paul Laurence Dunbar's *The Love of Landry*.

The Heavy Metal Kid. See Uranian Willy.

Marshall Hebert. White plantation owner whose past criminal activities are known by Sidney Bonbon and Aunt Julie Rand in Ernest J. Gaines's *Of Love and Dust*.

Hector. Faithful hound of Natty Bumppo in James Fenimore Cooper's *The Prairie* and *The Pioneers*.

Virginia R. (Lady Creamhair, Creamie) Hector. Virgin mother of George Giles, whom he almost rapes; daughter of the former Chancellor of New Tammany College in John Barth's *Giles Goat-Boy*.

Sybil Hedden. Date of Todd Eborn on the day he meets Louise Attwater in Reynolds Price's *Love and Work*.

Oman Hedgepath. Most prominent lawyer in Somerton and nephew and law partner of Steve Mundine; hired by Lord Byron Jones to win a divorce from Emma Jones; narrates part of Jesse Hill Ford's *The Liberation of Lord Byron Jones*.

Virgil (Virge) Hedgepath. Marine colonel and friend of the Meecham family; godfather of Ben Meecham in Pat Conroy's *The Great Santini*.

Mrs. Hedges. Mysterious woman who operates a whorehouse in the apartment building where Lutie Johnson lives; close friend and informal partner of Mr. Junto in Ann Petry's *The Street*.

Robert Thomas Hedrick IV. School friend of Susie Schnitzer; their "dates" are a pretense which allows her to visit her maternal grandmother in Harriette Simpson Arnow's *The Weedkiller's Daughter*.

Professor Hedron. Mathematician and childhood friend of Adam Krug; arrested and later commits suicide in prison in Vladimir Nabokov's *Bend Sinister*.

Hedyle. Athenian courtesan, consort of Douris of Samos, and mother of Hedylus in H. D.'s *Hedylus*.

Hedylus. Adolescent poet of the Hellenistic Age who rebels against his mother, Hedyle; invited by Demion to leave Samos for India in H. D.'s *Hedylus*.

Mrs. Heeny. Society manicurist and masseuse who provides Undine Spragg with social gossip in Edith Wharton's *The Custom of the Country*.

Mrs. Heimowitz. Mother of Murray Heimowitz and upstairs neighbor of Mrs. Bogen in Jerome Weidman's *I Can Get It for You Wholesale*; cares for the dying Mrs. Bogen in *What's in It for Me?*

Murray Heimowitz. Lawyer engaged to Ruthie Rivkin in Jerome Weidman's *What's in It for Me?*

Elizabeth Heinemann. Blind resident of the Diamond County Home for the Aged; speaks of her hopes for an afterlife in John Updike's *The Poorhouse Fair*.

Heinie. See Vahine.

Heinrich. Twelve-year prisoner of Dachau and Jacob Levy's guide to the concentration camp in Martha

Gellhorn's *Wine of Astonishment*.

Truman (True) Held. Artist and civil rights activist; husband of Lynne Rabinowitz, father of Camara, and friend and occasional lover of Meridian Hill in Alice Walker's *Meridian*.

Ana Helein. Viennese social worker raped and murdered by a Russian checkpoint guard in John Irving's *Setting Free the Bears*.

Helen. Girlfriend of Jim Cowan; she is with Eddie Mitchell the night of the Sacco-Vanzetti executions in Nathan Asch's *Pay Day*.

Helen. Wife of Menelaos and sister of Clytemnestra; her liberal views of love, morality, and life upset others in John Erskine's *The Private Life of Helen of Troy*.

Helen (Helena, Helen of Troy). Greek heroine mysteriously transported to Egypt for the duration of the Trojan War in H. D.'s *Helen in Egypt*.

Helena. Wife of Julian and sister of Constantius; after learning that her infant children have been secretly murdered by Eusebia, Helena encourages Julian to overthrow Constantius in Gore Vidal's *Julian*.

Helene. Wife of BZ; has an affair with Carter Lang in Joan Didion's *Play It As It Lays*.

Hella. Young American woman courted and later jilted by David in James Baldwin's *Giovanni's Room*.

Heller. Old Dutch janitor at Olinger High School in John Updike's *The Centaur*.

Heimie Hellman. Bootlegging associate of Harry (Bo) Mason in Wallace Stegner's *The Big Rock Candy Mountain*.

Hello. Joint king, with Piko, of Diranda; they control the population size by holding deadly games in Herman Melville's *Mardi*.

Hellos. Voluptuous woman of supernatural powers; murdered by Scarecrow in Calvin Hernton's *Scarecrow*.

Adam Helmer. Giant, womanizing woodsman who outruns a party of Mohawks to warn of an impending attack on German Flats in Walter D. Edmonds's *Drums along the Mohawk*.

Olaf Eric Helton. Escapee from an insane asylum; makes Royal Earle Thompson's farm profitable in Katherine Anne Porter's *Noon Wine*.

August (Aug) Hempel. Father of Julie Hempel Arnold; butcher who later owns the Hempel Packing

Company in Edna Ferber's *So Big*.

Brooks Hendell. Divorced Jewish lawyer who marries and divorces Katherine Dunn in Judith Rossner's *Looking for Mr. Goodbar*.

Katherine Dunn Hendell. See Katherine Dunn.

Clarence (Clarie) Henderson. Professor of English at the University of California and former member of the black high school athletic team and neighborhood gang gathering for a birthday testimonial honoring Chappie Davis in John A. Williams's *The Junior Bachelor Society*.

Ed Henderson. Brigadier general and bomber commander in Beirne Lay, Jr., and Sy Bartlett's *Twelve O'Clock High!*

Eugene H. (Captain Henderson, Gene, Henderson-Sungo, Leo E., Rain King, Sungo) Henderson. Twice-married American millionaire with a master's degree, a face like an "unfinished church," and a voice within crying "I want, I want" that drives him in an earnest search for higher reality in Africa; discovers his answer in service to others as a joyful affirmer and an aspiring physician in Saul Bellow's *Henderson the Rain King*.

Riley Henderson. Independent and admired friend of Collin Fenwick; helps fight the battlers of the tree house in Truman Capote's *The Grass Harp*.

Rose Henderson. First love of Felix Fay and lover, with him, of French literature in Floyd Dell's *Moon-Calf*.

Sam Henderson. Fat horse trader who is actually an undercover police agent pursuing Gentleman Joe Calash in Walter D. Edmonds's *Rome Haul*.

Will Henderson. Editor of the *Winesburg Eagle* in Sherwood Anderson's *Winesburg, Ohio*.

Miles Hendon. Former soldier who is the guardian and protector of Edward Tudor (disguised as Tom Canty); made an earl when Edward becomes king in Samuel Langhorne Clemens's *The Prince and the Pauper*.

Mrs. (Suzy) Hendrick. Owner of the small-town Kentucky hotel in which Old Jack Beechum lives out his final days in Wendell Berry's *A Place on Earth* and *The Memory of Old Jack*.

Pamela (Pam) Hendricks. Sexually aggressive young mistress of John Wilder; encourages him to make a movie about his mental hospital experiences in Richard Yates's *Disturbing the Peace*.

Robert (Bob) Hendricks. Fund-raiser for John Barclay; loses Molly Culpepper to Adrian Brownwell, who murders Hendricks, although the death is ruled a suicide, in William Allen White's *A Certain Rich Man.*

Abigail Morton Henley. First wife of Edward Henley; divorces him after he pays a sixteen-year-old Irishwoman $10,000 to bear his child in Shirley Ann Grau's *Evidence of Love.*

Edward Milton Henley. Veteran of several marriages and numerous love affairs; focal character who narrates part of Shirley Ann Grau's *Evidence of Love.*

Eleanor Halsey Henley. Second wife of Edward Henley in Shirley Ann Grau's *Evidence of Love.*

Lucy Roundtree Evans Henley. First wife of Stephen Henley; narrates part of Shirley Ann Grau's *Evidence of Love.*

Stephen Henley. Son of Edward Henley and a young Irishwoman; becomes a Unitarian minister; narrates part of Shirley Ann Grau's *Evidence of Love.*

Thomas Henley. Son of Lucy and Stephen Henley; takes after his promiscuous grandfather, Edward Henley; lives in Chicago and collects art in Shirley Ann Grau's *Evidence of Love.*

Millicent (Milly) Henning. Childhood friend of Hyacinth Robinson; becomes acquainted with a group of revolutionaries in Henry James's *The Princess Casamassima.*

Lloyd Henreid. Aide to Randall Flagg in Stephen King's *The Stand.*

Henri. Chef for the Paradise Inn who is dazzled by the past; contributes recipes to Renate's planned magazine in Anaïs Nin's *Collages.*

Henri. Lover of Chantal and Honorine; poet, former mental patient, and closest friend of Papa; with Chantal, an unwilling passenger in the car in John Hawkes's *Travesty.*

Henri. See Count Alphonse D'Oyley.

Henry. Crew member on Thomas Hudson's anti-submarine patrol boat in Ernest Hemingway's *Islands in the Stream.*

Henry. Crusty but benevolent grocer; friend of Annie Brown and inspiration for her first paid piece of writing in Betty Smith's *Joy in the Morning.*

Henry. Lover of Fidelia, whose abduction leads to his suicide, in William Hill Brown's *The Power of Sympathy.*

Henry. One of the "seven dwarfs" who wash windows, make Chinese baby food, and live with Snow White in Donald Barthelme's *Snow White.*

Billy James Henry. Juilliard-trained bassist in John Clellon Holmes's *The Horn.*

Frederic Henry. American serving as a lieutenant in the Italian army at the beginning of World War I; deserts with his lover Catherine Barkley to neutral Switzerland, where she dies in childbirth; narrator of Ernest Hemingway's *A Farewell to Arms.*

Janet Henry. Daughter of Senator Henry; romantically pursued by Paul Madvig, whom she despises; falls in love with Ned Beaumont in Dashiell Hammett's *The Glass Key.*

Judge Henry. Employer of the Virginian in Owen Wister's *The Virginian.*

Kovel (Shot) Henry. Husband of Tisha Dees in Arthenia J. Bates's *The Deity Nodded.*

Senator Ralph Bancroft Henry. U.S. senator whose son is murdered in Dashiell Hammett's *The Glass Key.*

Susan Henry. Lover of Jade Butterfield before Jade's reunion with David Axelrod in Scott Spencer's *Endless Love.*

Taylor Henry. Son of Senator Henry; the last person to see his murdered father in Dashiell Hammett's *The Glass Key.*

Tisha Dees Henry. See Tisha Dees.

John Everett Henshaw. Rancher and first husband of Tasmania Orcino in Jessamyn West's *A Matter of Time.*

Philip Henshaw. English engineer who interests Frank Cowperwood in the London subway system in Theodore Dreiser's *The Stoic.*

Arvay (Arvie) Henson. Poor backwoods heroine who marries Jim Meserve; sister of Larraine Henson Middleton and mother of Earl, Angeline, and Kenny Meserve in Zora Neale Hurston's *Seraph on the Suwanee.*

Larraine Henson. See Larraine Henson Middleton.

Matthew (Matt) Henson. Neighbor of Angela and Virginia Murray; eventual love of Virginia in Jessie Redmon Fauset's *Plum Bun.*

Andrew (Jake) Hepburn III. Close friend of Robert Mueller; killed in a mugging in Nicholas Delbanco's *Fathering.*

Mr. Herald. Apartment building manager who tells Terry Bluvard to get rid of her black friend or leave in Ann Allen Shockley's *Loving Her*.

Niel Herbert. Friend of Daniel and Marian Forrester; goes east to study architecture in Willa Cather's *A Lost Lady*.

Jimmy Herf. Newspaperman who aspires to authorship; married, for a time, to Ellen Thatcher; the central observer of the action in John Dos Passos's *Manhattan Transfer*.

Grandmother Herkimer. Elderly woman influenced by Agee Ward; her funeral is detailed in Wright Morris's *The Man Who Was There*.

Nicholas Herkimer. Stolid, courageous commander of the American militia at the battle of Oriskany; dies after amputation of a leg fails to halt gangrene in Walter D. Edmonds's *Drums along the Mohawk*.

Leon Herlitz. Ironic psychologist who counsels James Boswell to become a strongman; the result is a fate in direct opposition to Boswell's character in Stanley Elkin's *Boswell*.

Herman. Cardshark who poses as a diamond trader to cover up his illicit trading in women; eventually runs away with Zeftel and operates a brothel with her in Buenos Aires in Isaac Bashevis Singer's *The Magician of Lublin*.

Herman. Drug addict who moves in with William Lee and sells marijuana with him in William S. Burroughs's *Junkie*.

Herman. Black neighbor of Penrod Schofield; with his brother, Verman, Herman provides the manpower for Penrod's grand schemes in Booth Tarkington's *Penrod*, *Penrod and Sam*, and *Penrod Jashber*.

Annie Morris Herman. Spirited, supportive high school classmate of Ruth Holland in Susan Glaspell's *Fidelity*.

Hermione. Daughter of Helen and Menelaos; rejects her mother's views of love and morality and runs off with Orestes in John Erskine's *The Private Life of Helen of Troy*.

Doctor Hernandez. Mexican physician of Golconda who becomes a friend of Lillian Beye and is murdered for opposing drug trafficking in his community in Anaïs Nin's *Seduction of the Minotaur*.

Langley Herndon. Owner of the apartment building where Gilbert and Eva Blount live; argues with Gilbert about Gilbert's allowing Lionel Lane to live there despite rules excluding blacks; Lane murders

both men in Richard Wright's *The Outsider*.

Isabel Herrick. Physician who supports women's equality with men in career and marriage; marries Dr. Sanborn in Hamlin Garland's *Rose of Dutcher's Coolly*.

Josie (Jo) Herrick. High-society woman whom Ross Wilbur rejects in favor of Moran Sternersen in Frank Norris's *Moran of the Lady Letty*.

George Herrold. Black man who hears George Giles crying in the computer and pulls him out; later rendered insane in John Barth's *Giles Goat-Boy*.

Sam Herschberger. War comrade who loans C. Card five dollars in Richard Brautigan's *Dreaming of Babylon*.

David Herschmidt. See David L. Hirsh.

Vic (Old Man) Herschmidt. Father of Frank and David Hirsh; leaves his wife to elope with the doctor's wife; town drunk in James Jones's *Some Came Running*.

Elizabeth DeWitt (Libby) Herz. Unhealthy and unhappy young woman married to Paul Herz; finds some measure of contentment in her role as an adoptive mother in Philip Roth's *Letting Go*.

Karen Herz. Young farm woman involved in an obsessive love affair in Joyce Carol Oates's *With Shuddering Fall*.

Mr. Herz. Stern farmer and father of Karen Herz in Joyce Carol Oates's *With Shuddering Fall*.

Paul Herz. Aspiring novelist and professor of English whose marriage to Libby DeWitt alienates his parents and creates many responsibilities and difficulties for him in Philip Roth's *Letting Go*.

Hermann Herzenbrecher. Pharmacist and employer of Konrad Vost in John Hawkes's *The Passion Artist*.

June (Junie) Herzog. Precocious small daughter of Moses Herzog who loves his "most of every type" stories and whose ostensible vulnerability to emotional pain almost leads Herzog to murder Val Gersbach in Saul Bellow's *Herzog*.

Madeleine Pontritter (Mady) Herzog. Unfaithful second wife of Moses Herzog, mother of June Herzog, and lover of Val Gersbach; intelligent, beautiful, haughty, histrionic, unpredictable, and vindictive in Saul Bellow's *Herzog*.

Mim Herzog. School board member accidentally discovered by George Caldwell to be having an affair with Louis Zimmerman in John Updike's *The Centaur*.

Moses Elkanah (Butterfingers, Fishbones, Fucky-knuckles, Ikey-Fishbones, Ikey-Moe, Mose, Moshe) Herzog. Unemployed history professor with a Ph.D., wealthy siblings, displaced children, an adulterous second wife, an important scholarly book (*Romanticism and Christianity*), a faithful friend, a devoted mistress, a disorderly career, and assorted problems that intensify the central conflict between his intellect and his sensibilities; tormented protagonist and "suffering joker" of Saul Bellow's *Herzog*.

Harvey Hess. Pool player who thinks he can beat Billy Phelan; wears expensive suits and atrocious ties and socks in William Kennedy's *Billy Phelan's Greatest Game*.

Jacob (Jake) Hesse. Owner of a chain of shoe stores and second husband of Orpha Chase in Jessamyn West's *The Life I Really Lived*.

Mrs. Hesse. See Orpha Chase.

Lorena (Rena) Hessenwinkle. Secretary at the Friendly Hearth Wood Yard; former lover of Fen Redcliff, by whom she has a son, and later wife of Fen's brother, Tat Redcliff, in Josephine Pinckney's *Three O'Clock Dinner*.

Hester. Would-be love of Tom More in the counterculture, which has rejected technology to live in the swamps, in Walker Percy's *Love in the Ruins*.

Helen (Moms) Hettinger. Wife of Karl Hettinger in Joseph Wambaugh's *The Onion Field*.

Karl Hettinger. Los Angeles policeman and partner of Ian Campbell; kidnapped and nearly killed by Gregory Powell and Jimmy Smith in Joseph Wambaugh's *The Onion Field*.

Hevaneva. Idol maker and canoe builder on Maramma in Herman Melville's *Mardi*.

Gavin Hexam. Lawyer and former husband of N. Hexam in Diane Johnson's *The Shadow Knows*.

N. Hexam. Paranoid narrator who believes someone is plotting to kill her; lover of Andrew Mason and former wife of Gavin Hexam in Diane Johnson's *The Shadow Knows*.

Karl Heykoop. Dutch husband of Polly Heykoop and philanderer who has an affair with Penelope MacMahon in Gail Godwin's *The Perfectionists*.

Polly Heykoop. American wife of Karl Heykoop and mother of twin girls; keeps a secret photograph album of her husband's sexual conquests in Gail Godwin's *The Perfectionists*.

Duncan Heyward. British major charged with taking Cora and Alice Munro to Fort William Henry; led astray by Magua, Heyward enlists the help of Natty Bumppo, Chingachgook, and Uncas to protect the Munro sisters in James Fenimore Cooper's *The Last of the Mohicans*.

Marvin Heywood. Owner of the Pink Dragon Bar, watering hole for petty criminals on patrolman Bumper Morgan's beat, in Joseph Wambaugh's *The Blue Knight*.

Thomas J. Heywood. Virginia gentleman summering in Norwood who, feeling caught between two cultures and rejected by Rose Wentworth, becomes swept up in the war fever; fights for the South at Gettysburg in Henry Ward Beecher's *Norwood*.

Li Van Hgoc. Major in the Fourth Vietcong Battalion who is in charge of the tunnel system; a condemned deserter who believes that the land is America's enemy in Vietnam in Tim O'Brien's *Going after Cacciato*.

Angeline (Angie) Hibbard. Mother-in-law and ideological opposite of Caddy Hibbard; triumphs by outliving Caddy in Wright Morris's *The World in the Attic*.

Bud Hibbard. Conventional rural boyhood friend whom Clyde Muncy revisits in Wright Morris's *The World in the Attic*.

Caddy Hibbard. Childless daughter-in-law of Angie Hibbard; her death and funeral are the key events in Wright Morris's *The World in the Attic*.

Clark Hibbard. Editor and publisher of the *Parkman Oregonian*; helps Frank Hirsh develop Parkman Village at the bypass in James Jones's *Some Came Running*.

Clinton Hibbard. Deceased husband of Caddy Hibbard and son of Angie Hibbard; the basis of conflict between the two women in Wright Morris's *The World in the Attic*.

Miss Hibbard. Wealthy, unattractive fiancée of Charley Dunham; marries Dunham in William Dean Howells's *The Lady of the Aroostook*.

Nellie Hibbard. Wife considered by Bud Hibbard "the finest creature on God's earth" in Wright Morris's *The World in the Attic*.

Preston Hibbard. Former prep-school classmate of Bing Lockwood; marries Tina Lockwood in John O'Hara's *The Lockwood Concern*.

Mistress Hibbins. Sister of Governor Bellingham; hanged as a witch in Nathaniel Hawthorne's *The*

Scarlet Letter.

Richard Eugene (Dick) Hickock. Mastermind of the crime against the Clutter family; persuades Perry Smith to become his partner in robbery and murder in Truman Capote's *In Cold Blood.*

James Butler (Duck Bill, Wild Bill) Hickok. Nervous gunslinger of the American West and friend of Jack Crabb in Thomas Berger's *Little Big Man.*

Wild Bill Hickok. Marshall of Hays City, Kansas, in Emerson Hough's *North of 36.*

Dickey Hicks. Son adopted by Lewis and Ginny Hicks in an attempt to assuage the loss by suicide of her brother, Richard Page, in John Gardner's *October Light.*

Lewis Hicks. Swamp Yankee and part-Indian handyman whose closeness to the rhythms of nature helps restore a sense of balance in the conflict between James Page and Sally Page Abbott in John Gardner's *October Light.*

Miss Hicks. High school history teacher of Homer Macauley; tries to promote goodwill among students of different ethnic backgrounds in William Saroyan's *The Human Comedy.*

Mr. Hicks. Prodigal son whose trip aboard the *Aroostook* fails to cure him of his alcoholism in William Dean Howells's *The Lady of the Aroostook.*

Captain Nathaniel Hicks. Former magazine editor who represents the viewpoint of the intelligent, reasonable civilian drafted to be a soldier in James Gould Cozzens's *Guard of Honor.*

Raymond (Cap, Ray) Hicks. American sailor who smuggles heroin into the United States for John Converse; chased into hiding by Antheil in Robert Stone's *Dog Soldiers.*

Virginia Page (Ginny) Hicks. Sensible daughter of James Page; her unintentional near-death at the hands of Sally Page Abbott quiets the violence within the family in John Gardner's *October Light.*

William Hicks. Marine automatic rifleman in France during World War I who is transformed into a hardened veteran in Thomas Boyd's *Through the Wheat.*

Mrs. Higbee. Housekeeper for Cass Timberlane in Sinclair Lewis's *Cass Timberlane.*

Mrs. J. Franklin Higby. President of the Mothers' League for Good Morals in Horace McCoy's *They Shoot Horses, Don't They?*

Bernard Higginbotham. Brother-in-law of Martin Eden; believes that Eden is a worthless drunk in Jack London's *Martin Eden.*

Elly Higginbottom. See Esther Greenwood.

Dinah Blackford Higgins. Sister of Wyeth Blackford and childhood sweetheart of Anson Page; marries Mico Higgins in order to restore her family's faded fortunes in Hamilton Basso's *The View from Pompey's Head.*

Doc Higgins. Proprietor of Doc Higgins' Tonsorial Palace; bribes his friend, a postmaster, to prevent Jack Jackson's being fired in Richard Wright's *Lawd Today.*

Hondo Higgins. Television star and pornographic movie mogul who helps Stormy Claridge further her career in return for sexual favors in Peter Gent's *Texas Celebrity Turkey Trot.*

Hop Higgins. Night watchman of Winesburg in Sherwood Anderson's *Winesburg, Ohio.*

Mico (Mickey) Higgins. Outsider who becomes a successful entrepreneur and a social climber in Hamilton Basso's *The View from Pompey's Head.*

Ned Higgins. Boy who visits Hepzibah Pyncheon's cent-shop in Nathaniel Hawthorne's *The House of the Seven Gables.*

Frances Higginson. College roommate of and later resident of the same New York apartment with Derrick Thornton in Helen Hooven Santmyer's *Herbs and Apples.*

Highboy. Husband of Portia and companion of her brother Willie Copeland in Carson McCullers's *The Heart Is a Lonely Hunter.*

Frances Highsmith. Aggressive woman who dominates Johnny Strange and causes his belated sexual awakening in James Jones's *Whistle.*

Robert Highsmith. Lawyer for Adam Kelno, member of the House of Commons, and head of the British office of Sanctuary International in Leon Uris's *QB VII.*

Esther (Dunnet Shepherdess) Hight. Spinster shepherdess whose hard outdoor life supporting herself and her aged, difficult mother is rewarded when, at her mother's death, she marries William Blackett, who has courted her for forty years, in Sarah Orne Jewett's *The Country of the Pointed Firs.*

Gail Hightower. Presbyterian minister forced to resign from his church following his wife's suicide in William Faulkner's *Light in August.*

Mrs. Gail Hightower. Disturbed wife of Gail Hightower; commits suicide by jumping from a hotel window in Memphis in William Faulkner's *Light in August.*

Dr. Hilarius. Psychotherapist of Oedipa Maas; conducts experiments with LSD; formerly worked at Buchenwald in Thomas Pynchon's *The Crying of Lot 49.*

Hilda. Fellow guest editor with Esther Greenwood for a New York fashion magazine; pleased that the Rosenbergs will be executed in Sylvia Plath's *The Bell Jar.*

Hilda (The Dove). Copier of famous paintings in Rome who lives in a tower surrounded by doves and who witnesses the murder of Brother Antonio; marries Kenyon in Nathaniel Hawthorne's *The Marble Faun.*

Hildesheim. Physician who restores Miranda's health in Katherine Anne Porter's *Pale Horse, Pale Rider.*

Ambrose Powell Hill. Irritable Southern general in Michael Shaara's *The Killer Angels.*

Dr. Hill. Well-meaning young obstetrician who unknowingly turns Rosemary Woodhouse over to devil worshippers when she comes to him for help in Ira Levin's *Rosemary's Baby.*

Eliab Hill. Crippled black shoemaker, preacher, and teacher who is freed by Casaubon Le Moyne and who is taught to read and write by Hester Le Moyne; rescued from the Ku Klux Klan by Nimbus; receives a college education in the North in Albion W. Tourgee's *Bricks without Straw.*

Fiorio (Fifi) Hill. Brilliant film director who wins an Oscar as best director for his work on Vito Orsini's *Mirrors* in Judith Krantz's *Scruples.*

Gertrude Hill. Former teacher, mother of Meridian Hill, and earliest source of her daughter's feelings of guilt in Alice Walker's *Meridian.*

Meridian Hill. Compassionate civil rights activist who suffers from psychosomatic paralysis in Alice Walker's *Meridian.*

Hillentafel. Father of Kuno; furniture maker in Texas in Katherine Anne Porter's *The Leaning Tower.*

Kuno Hillentafel. Dead friend of Charles Upton; inspires Upton's visit to Berlin in Katherine Anne Porter's *The Leaning Tower.*

Boyd (B. H.) Hiller. Estranged husband of Irene Blaney Hiller in William Maxwell's *They Came Like Swallows.*

Irene Blaney Hiller. Sister of Elizabeth Morison; estranged from Boyd Hiller, she considers his request for a reconciliation but chooses instead to help rear Elizabeth's children in William Maxwell's *They Came Like Swallows.*

Joshua Isaiah (Josh) Hillman. Lawyer for Billy Orsini; handles all of her business affairs and falls in love with Valentine O'Neill in Judith Krantz's *Scruples.*

John (Jack) Hilton. Communist party member and member of the editorial board for the *Daily Worker*; murdered by Lionel Lane in Richard Wright's *The Outsider.*

Ralph Himebaugh. Sexually repressed attorney whose numerological model of the end of the world is merged with Eleanor Norton's mystic model in Robert Coover's *The Origin of the Brunists.*

Sandor Himmelstein. Chicago lawyer of Madeleine Herzog; provides temporary lodging and fierce advice to the displaced Moses Herzog in Saul Bellow's *Herzog.*

Hinderov. Passenger on the *Here They Come* who plans to use an American Express office as a distribution center for bombs in Gregory Corso's *The American Express.*

Alice Hindman. Clerk in Winney's Dry Goods Store; spinster because of her devotion to her departed lover, Ned Currie, in Sherwood Anderson's *Winesburg, Ohio.*

Eupheus (Doc) and Mrs. Hines. Parents of Milly Hines and grandparents of Joe Christmas in William Faulkner's *Light in August.*

Milly Hines. Daughter of Eupheus and Mrs. Hines; dies giving birth to Joe Christmas in William Faulkner's *Light in August.*

Mother Hines. Possessive mother of Wally Hines in Peter De Vries's *The Vale of Laughter.*

Wally Hines. Psychology instructor at Wilton College, theorist of comedy and laughter, and former teacher of Joe Sandwich; Sandwich cuckolds him and later marries his widow; narrates part of Peter De Vries's *The Vale of Laughter.*

Alec Hinks. See Hamish Bond.

Horace Hinton. Black director of the social services office where Bruno Fisher and Eric Eisner work; carries a gun in order to intimidate students in Phillip Lopate's *Confessions of Summer.*

Hipparchia. Greek poet-courtesan; lives with Marius and later Verrus in H. D.'s *Palimpsest*.

Hippolyte. Narrator who recounts his dream and real life in Susan Sontag's *The Benefactor*.

Buck Hipps. Texan who auctions the spotted horses in William Faulkner's *The Hamlet*.

Heinrich Hirsch. Secretary of education, culture, and information in post-World War II Berlin who defects to the American sector in Leon Uris's *Armageddon*.

Mr. Hirsch. Uncle of Aaron Lublin; moves into the Lublin family's 70th Street apartment in Edward Lewis Wallant's *The Tenants of Moonbloom*.

Agnes Marie Towns Hirsh. Wife of Frank Hirsh and mother of Dawn and Walter Hirsh; hypochondriac who resents her husband's mistresses in James Jones's *Some Came Running*.

David L. (Dave, David Herschmidt) Hirsh. Talented writer and World War II veteran; loves Gwen French but marries Ginnie Moorehead, whose ex-husband kills him, in James Jones's *Some Came Running*.

Dawn (Dawnie) Hirsh. Daughter of Frank and Agnes Hirsh and aspiring actress; lover of Wally Dennis but marries another man in order to forget him in James Jones's *Some Came Running*.

Frank Hirsh. Leading citizen of Parkman, Illinois, and brother of Dave Hirsh; becomes a wealthy peeping tom in James Jones's *Some Came Running*.

Mrs. Elvira Hirsh. Wife of Vic Hershmidt and member of the Church of Christ Saved in James Jones's *Some Came Running*.

Walter Hirsh. Seven-year-old adopted son of Frank and Agnes Hirsh; loves engineering and heavy equipment in James Jones's *Some Came Running*.

Hist-oh!-Hist. See Wah-ta!-Wah.

Mrs. Wally Bee Hitchcock. Woman encountered by Hazel Motes on his train ride to Taulkinham in Flannery O'Connor's *Wise Blood*.

Hitia. Daughter of Marunga and Tavi and wife of Farani; survives the hurricane, during which she gives birth to a son, in Charles Nordhoff and James Norman Hall's *The Hurricane*.

Hitihiti. Tahitian subchieftain with whom Roger Byam resides and who helps Byam compile a dictionary of the Tahitian language in Charles Nordhoff and James Norman Hall's *Mutiny on the Bounty*.

Adolph (the Führer, Adi Schicklgruber) Hitler. Leader of the National Socialist revolution in Germany; discusses politics and art with Lanny Budd in Upton Sinclair's *Dragon's Teeth*.

Hivohitee. Pontiff of Maramma in Herman Melville's *Mardi*.

Mr. and Mrs. Hoaglund. Managers of N. Hexam's apartment in Diane Johnson's *The Shadow Knows*.

Hoak. Sailor who helps Charlie Stark save Raditzer from murder in Peter Matthiessen's *Raditzer*.

Miss Hobbe. Landlady of Miranda; threatens to evict the ill Miranda in Katherine Anne Porter's *Pale Horse, Pale Rider*.

Kathryn (Cousin Angie) Hobbes. Cynical and aggressive wife of Paul Hobbes; has an affair with Gene Pasternak in John Clellan Holmes's *Go*.

Paul (H.) Hobbes. Twenty-five-year-old novelist and poet married for six years to Kathryn Hobbes; unable to consummate a relationship with Estelle in John Clellon Holmes's *Go*.

Corporal Hobbs. Joker from Oklahoma and radioman in William Styron's *The Long March*.

Roy Hobbs. Star outfielder for the New York Knights; a rookie in his late thirties who succumbs to a gambling scheme involving his team's owner in Bernard Malamud's *The Natural*.

Silas Hobbs. New York grocer and friend of Cedric Errol in Frances Hodgson Burnett's *Little Lord Fauntleroy*.

Hobomok. Noble Indian chieftain who weds Mary Conant but relinquishes her and their son on the return of Mary's first love, Charles Brown, in Lydia Maria Child's *Hobomok*.

Alison Parr Hodder. See Alison Parr.

John Hodder. Clergyman who reevaluates his religious beliefs in light of modern social problems; marries Alison Parr in Winston Churchill's *The Inside of the Cup*.

Baron (Putzi) von Hodenlohern. Nazi who nearly tricks Mame Dennis in Patrick Dennis's *Around the World with Auntie Mame*.

Arthur Taggert (Old Man) Hodge, Sr. Patriarch known for his tolerance of each of his children's search for selfhood—the equivalent of his view, as a congressman, of democracy—in John Gardner's *The Sunlight Dialogues*.

Benjamin (Ben) Hodge, Sr. Foster father of Indian brothers after the death of his own son in Korea in John Gardner's *The Sunlight Dialogues*.

Kathleen Paxton Hodge. Wife of Taggert Hodge; driven into a catatonic state by her father, Clive Paxton, in John Gardner's *The Sunlight Dialogues*.

Luke Hodge. Son of Millie and William Hodge, Sr.; sacrifices his life to reunite his parents; his death persuades his uncle, Taggert Hodge, to surrender to the law in John Gardner's *The Sunlight Dialogues*.

Mildred Jewel (Millie) Hodge. Divorced wife of William Hodge, Sr., and mother of Luke Hodge; almost committed as insane by William, because she understands the complexities of love which seem clear and simple to him, in John Gardner's *The Sunlight Dialogues*.

Taggert Faeley (The Sunlight Man, Tag) Hodge. Husband of Kathleen Paxton Hodge; returns to Batavia, New York, to avenge her brutalization by Clive Paxton in John Gardner's *The Sunlight Dialogues*.

William B. (Will) Hodge, Sr. Lawyer enraged that he is only the second choice of his wife, Millie Hodge; love for their son, Luke, redeems him in John Gardner's *The Sunlight Dialogues*.

Eliphalet (Brother Hodges, 'Liph, 'Liphalet) Hodges. Husband of Hester Prime; adoptive father of Frederick Brent in Paul Laurence Dunbar's *The Uncalled*.

Marion (Sister Mary) Hodgkiss. Intellectual Marine radio operator and friend of Danny Forrester; killed at Saipan in Leon Uris's *Armageddon*.

Captain Hodgson. Captain of the lifeboat station in San Francisco Bay who discovers Moran Sternersen's corpse and reports her murder to Ross Wilbur in Frank Norris's *Moran of the Lady Letty*.

James Vaiden Hodige. Mulatto great-grandson of Miltiades Vaiden; one of six blacks standing trial for raping a white woman; escapes to safety in T. S. Stribling's *Unfinished Cathedral*.

Dr. Luther Hodler. Swiss physician who imagines Cynthia Pomeroy as Nausicaä in Wright Morris's *What a Way to Go*.

Angela (Mrs. Harrison C. Conners) Hoenikker. Saxophonist and sister of Newton and Frank Hoenikker in Kurt Vonnegut's *Cat's Cradle*.

Dr. Felix Hoenikker. Father of the atom bomb, Ice-9, and Frank, Angela, and Newton Hoenikker in

Kurt Vonnegut's *Cat's Cradle*.

Franklin (Frank) Hoenikker. Older brother of Newton and Angela Hoenikker and adviser to President Papa Monzano in Kurt Vonnegut's *Cat's Cradle*.

Newton (Little Newt) Hoenikker. Midget brother of Frank and Angela Hoenikker; painter in Kurt Vonnegut's *Cat's Cradle*.

Fred Hoff. IWW instigator who recruits Mac to work for a Wobbly newspaper in John Dos Passos's *U.S.A.* trilogy.

Ferenc Hofmann-Beck. Employee of a French publishing company and friend of the Gallaghers; appears for many of the gatherings of expatriate Americans at the Gallagher home in James Jones's *The Merry Month of May*.

Major Hogan. Antagonistic and disapproving doctor at Kilrainey Army Hospital whose responsibility it is to return wounded men to duty as soon as possible in James Jones's *Whistle*.

Violet Mauling Hogan. Secretary to Thomas Van Dorn; becomes a prostitute after being widowed, but reforms with the help of Henry Fenn in William Allen White's *In the Heart of a Fool*.

Boon Hogganbeck. Hunter or stable hand in William Faulkner's *Go Down, Moses* (where he kills Old Ben), *Intruder in the Dust*, *The Town*, and *The Reivers*.

Everbe Corinthia (Miss Corrie) Hogganbeck. Prostitute who marries Boon Hogganbeck in William Faulkner's *The Reivers*.

Lucius Priest Hogganbeck. Son of Boon and Corrie Hogganbeck in William Faulkner's *The Town*, *The Mansion*, and *The Reivers*.

Mrs. Hoggs. Woman who boards sick people who are wards of the state; betrays Frado, claiming she is not an invalid and is capable of work, in Harriet E. Wilson's *Our Nig*.

Prince Moritz Franz Ernst Felix von Hohenauer. Austrian diplomat who convinces Marie Zattiany to gain political power by marrying him rather than to marry Lee Clavering for love in Gertrude Atherton's *Black Oxen*.

Prince Arbogast (Arbo) von Hohengraetz. Liberal nobleman who directs Rudolf Stanka's maturation and reveals Stanka's true identity in Louis Adamic's *Cradle of Life*.

Dr. Rippleton Holabird. Head of the physiology department and later director of the McGurk Institute of Biology in Sinclair Lewis's *Arrowsmith*.

Anna Holbrook. Wife of Jim Holbrook and mother of Mazie and other Holbrook children; inspires her poor family with her poetic yearnings in Tillie Olsen's *Yonnondio*.

Jim Holbrook. Bitter husband and father of a 1920s family brutalized by poverty; searches from mining town to farm to industrial city for a better way of life in Tillie Olsen's *Yonnondio*.

Mazie (Big-eyes) Holbrook. Oldest Holbrook child who, though often terrified by life, still wonders and dreams about the world in Tillie Olsen's *Yonnondio*, much of which is told from Mazie's point of view.

Holgrave. Daguerreotypist, descendant of Matthew Maule, and resident of the Pyncheon house; marries Phoebe Pyncheon in Nathaniel Hawthorne's *The House of the Seven Gables*.

Billie Holiday. Singer whose life and music are invoked in Alice Adams's *Listening to Billie*.

Burne Holiday. Princeton friend of Amory Blaine; social reformer in F. Scott Fitzgerald's *This Side of Paradise*.

Cyrus (Cy) Holland. Unforgiving brother of Ruth Holland in Susan Glaspell's *Fidelity*.

Ruth Holland. Independent-minded, small-town young woman who scandalizes local society by running away with Stuart Williams, a married man, in Susan Glaspell's *Fidelity*.

Ted Holland. Supportive younger brother of Ruth Holland in Susan Glaspell's *Fidelity*.

Hollingsworth. Selfish reformer who uses Zenobia and who loves Priscilla in Nathaniel Hawthorne's *The Blithedale Romance*.

Ed Leroy Hollingsworth. Government agent who pursues and interrogates William McLeod; lover of Beverly Guinevere McLeod in Norman Mailer's *Barbary Shore*.

Blix Murphy Hollister. Younger sister of Tasmania Orcino; enlists Tasmania's help in dying when her cancer becomes unbearable in Jessamyn West's *A Matter of Time*.

John (Jack) Hollister. Columnist and managing editor of the Fort Penn *Sentinel* whose casual friendship with Grace Caldwell Tate, his employer, leads to an affair with her in John O'Hara's *A Rage to Live*.

Milt Hollister. Young widower who becomes Blix Hollister's husband in Jessamyn West's *A Matter of Time*.

Charles Hollopeter. Pasadena attorney who defends Jimmy Smith in Smith's second murder trial in Joseph Wambaugh's *The Onion Field*.

Jebb Holloway. Rival of Jasper Harrick and former basketball star; goes into the cave with Isaac Sumpter but lies about reaching the trapped Harrick in Robert Penn Warren's *The Cave*.

Holly. Lover and coworker of Molly Bolt in New York City in Rita Mae Brown's *Rubyfruit Jungle*.

Holly. See Holly Webster Wiggen.

Anna Marie (And-Ongen) Holm (Hansa). Daughter of Beret Holm and Per Hansa and sister of Peder Holm (Hansa) in O. E. Rölvaag's *Giants in the Earth*, *Peder Victorious*, and *Their Father's God*.

Beret Holm. See Beret Holm Hansa.

Ernie Holm. Divorced father of Helen Holm; Steering School wrestling coach who dies while reading a pornographic magazine in John Irving's *The World According to Garp*.

Helen Holm. Wife of T. S. Garp and mother of Duncan, Walt, and Jenny Garp; respected college English teacher who has an affair with Michael Milton; cremated in John Irving's *The World According to Garp*.

Henry Percival Holm. Son of Store-Hans Holm in O. E. Rölvaag's *Peder Victorious*.

Ole Haldor (Olamand) Holm (Hansa). Son of Per Hansa and Beret Holm in O. E. Rölvaag's *Giants in the Earth*; marries and moves farther west in *Peder Victorious*.

Peder Emmanuel (Lisj-Per, Patrick St. Olaf, Petie) Holm. Son of Peder Holm and Susie Doheny Holm; his parents' religious conflict leads to his being christened secretly by both his grandmother and his mother in O. E. Rölvaag's *Their Father's God*.

Peder Victorious (Permand) Holm. Son of Per Hansa and Beret Holm; focus of his mother's sanity and madness in O. E. Rölvaag's *Giants in the Earth*; marries Susie Doheny, an Irish Catholic, in *Peder Victorious*; abandons the ministry for politics in *Their Father's God*.

Per Holm. See Per Hansa.

Susie Doheny Holm. See Susie Doheny.

Store-Hans (Hans Kristian) Holm (Hansa). Son of Per Hansa and Beret Holm in O. E. Rölvaag's *Giants in the Earth*; marries and buys a farm in *Peder Victorious*; opposes his brother Peder Hansa's marriage and politics in *Their Father's God*.

Helene Holman. Torch singer and Ed Charney's girlfriend in John O'Hara's *Appointment in Samarra*.

Ben Holmes. Black friend of Susie Schnitzer in Harriette Simpson Arnow's *The Weedkiller's Daughter*.

Bradley Holmes. Editor of Allison MacKenzie; becomes her lover without telling her he is married in Grace Metalious's *Peyton Place*.

Captain Dana E. (Dynamite) Holmes. Company commander and coach of the regimental boxing team; orders the Treatment for Robert E. Lee Prewitt after Prewitt refuses to box in James Jones's *From Here to Eternity*.

Jack Holmes. Parachute jumper and possibly the father of Jack Shumann in William Faulkner's *Pylon*.

Karen Holmes. Wife of Dana Holmes; has an affair with Milton Warden; leaves Oahu for the mainland after Holmes and Warden receive their orders to go overseas in James Jones's *From Here to Eternity*.

Mrs. Eliza Holmes. Bookish, meditative, and sentimental resident of Belleview; reveals that Tommy Harrington and Harriot Fawcet have the same father in William Hill Brown's *The Power of Sympathy*.

Alexander Holston. A founder of Jefferson in William Faulkner's *Absalom, Absalom!*, *Intruder in the Dust*, *Requiem for a Nun*, *The Town*, and *The Mansion*.

Tina Marie (Teeny Marie) Holt. Bald, breastless, one-legged, one-eyed actress in Terry Southern's *Blue Movie*.

Andrew Holte. Minister who advocates abandoning the Norwegian for the evangelical in the Lutheran church in O. E. Rölvaag's *Peder Victorious*; also appears in *Their Father's God*.

Onnie Jay Holy. See Hoover Shoats.

Konrad Holzapfel. German tourist baited by Jewish Adrien Perkheimer in Wright Morris's *What a Way to Go*.

Morris Homestead. Aristocratic fraternity brother of Abraham Lockwood; later Lockwood's banker and investment partner in John O'Hara's *The Lockwood Concern*.

Homos (Altrurian). Visitor to America from the European utopia of Altruria; critic of American life in William Dean Howells's *A Traveler from Altruria*.

Honest Lil (Lillian). Cuban prostitute and friend of Thomas Hudson in Ernest Hemingway's *Islands in the Stream*.

Little Homer Honey. Son of Sister Ida Honey and star of the Honey family; preaches, rope twirls, and helps with collections in Truman Capote's *The Grass Harp*.

Sister Ida Honey. Impoverished traveling revivalist; mother of fifteen children, most of them illegitimate, in Truman Capote's *The Grass Harp*.

Miss Honey. Second wife of Gabriel Breaux in Katherine Anne Porter's *Old Mortality*.

Jason Honeygale. Tennessee writer in John Updike's *Bech: A Book*.

Annabel Upchurch Honeywell. See Annabel Upchurch.

Clarence Honeywell. Black mechanic employed by Buddy Sandifer in Thomas Berger's *Sneaky People*.

Judge Gamaliel Bland Honeywell. Wealthy, decorous, and recently widowed man who marries Annabel Upchurch, a woman over forty years his junior, in Ellen Glasgow's *The Romantic Comedians*.

Honorine. Mother of Pascal and Chantal, wife of Papa, and lover of Henri; has a tattoo of pale purple grapes with yellow stems below her navel; sleeps at home, unaware of her husband's grisly plan, in John Hawkes's *Travesty*.

Wayne Hoobler. Prison parolee drawn to Dwayne Hoover in Kurt Vonnegut's *Breakfast of Champions*.

Valentine (Val) Hood. Fugitive American consul in Vietnam; involved with gunrunners and would-be terrorists in London in Paul Theroux's *The Family Arsenal*.

Ezekiel Hook. See John Treeworgy.

John F. (Hookie) Hook. Ninety-four-year-old resident of the Diamond County Home for the Aged; respected former schoolteacher who sees his friend Billy Gregg as his "final pupil" in John Updike's *The Poorhouse Fair*.

Andrew (Andy) Hookans. Marine radio operator who loses a leg at Saipan in Leon Uris's *Battle Cry*.

Charlie Hooker. Lover of Neva Manning and farm worker intent on founding a religion based on honesty, self-acceptance, and racial reconciliation in Hal Bennett's *A Wilderness of Vines*.

Skipper (Cap, Hipless) Hooker. Fanatical deep-sea fisherman and Los Angeles police captain of Hollywood Station's detective division in Joseph Wambaugh's *The Black Marble*.

Bentley T. Hooks. Disillusioned son of a revival preacher; offers Brooke Kincaid her one chance to live authentically in Lee Smith's *Something in the Wind*.

Hookworm. See Elijah J. Cartwright.

Matthew (Matt) Hooper. Oceanographer who helps identify and hunt the Great White Shark in Peter Benchley's *Jaws*.

Hank Hoos. "Kansas primitive" sanitorium roommate of Don Wanderhope in Peter De Vries's *The Blood of the Lamb*.

Minna Hooven. Daughter of Mrs. Hooven; driven by want—because the railroad forced her out of her home—to prostitution in Frank Norris's *The Octopus*.

Mrs. Hooven. Mother of Minna Hooven; victim of the railroad's chicanery who, having lost her home, starves to death in Frank Norris's *The Octopus*.

Celia Hoover. Wife of Dwayne Hoover and mother of Bunny Hoover; commits suicide in Kurt Vonnegut's *Breakfast of Champions*.

Dwayne Hoover. Husband of Celia Hoover, father of Bunny Hoover, and Pontiac dealer who goes insane in Kurt Vonnegut's *Breakfast of Champions*.

George (Bunny) Hoover. Homosexual pianist and son of Dwayne and Celia Hoover in Kurt Vonnegut's *Breakfast of Champions*.

Anthony (Jeeves) Hope-Harding. Frame-maker and lover of two sisters, Maija von Einzeedle and Elise Crawford; dies of cancer in Nicholas Delbanco's *Small Rain*.

Janet Hope-Harding. Mother of Anthony Hope-Harding in Nicholas Delbanco's *Small Rain*.

James Hopkins. Rejected suitor of Sally Oldham in Lydia Maria Child's *Hobomok*.

Eliphalet Hopper. Sycophantic and unscrupulous war profiteer; suitor of Virginia Carvel in Winston Churchill's *The Crisis*.

Sally Thwaites Hopwood. Fallen-away Catholic and daughter of Mrs. Andrew Thwaites; alone on an island in a small lake with Father Urban, she proposes a swim in the nude and disrobes in front of him; insulted by his refusal of the seduction, she maroons him in J. F. Powers's *Morte D'Urban*.

Sim Hornby. Half-breed and one of Jane Nail's attackers; killed in the raid on the Horse Pens in Jesse Hill Ford's *The Raider*.

Jacob (Jake) Horner. Teacher of prescriptive grammar at Wicomico State Teachers College and lover of Rennie Morgan; narrator of John Barth's *The End of the Road*.

Charles Ames Horney. Educator and author; fearfully eschews the past in Wright Morris's *Cause for Wonder*.

Mrs. Horowitz. Superstitious neighbor of the Luries who leaves David Lurie a collection of books on higher Biblical criticism in Chaim Potok's *In the Beginning*.

Earl Horter. Writer of popular song lyrics who is attracted to Eva Baum; narrator of Wright Morris's *Love among the Cannibals*.

Emma Greenway Horton. Daughter of Aurora Greenway, wife of Thomas Horton, and mother of Melanie, Teddy, and Tommy Horton; following the collapse of her marriage, she dies of cancer in Larry McMurtry's *Terms of Endearment*; appears in *Moving On* and *All My Friends Are Going to Be Strangers*.

Ernest Horton. Traveling novelty salesman from the Little Wonder Company who impresses the passengers on Juan Chicoy's bus with his ingenious merchandise, including the "Little Wonder Artificial Sore Foot," in John Steinbeck's *The Wayward Bus*.

Ginger Horton. Writer and friend of Guy Grand in Terry Southern's *The Magic Christian*.

Melanie, Teddy, and Tommy Horton. Children of Emma and Thomas Horton and grandchildren of Aurora Greenway in Larry McMurtry's *Terms of Endearment*; Teddy and Tommy also appear in *Moving On*; Tommy also appears in *All My Friends Are Going to Be Strangers*.

Thomas (Flap) Horton. Husband of Emma Greenway Horton, father of Melanie, Teddy, and Tommy Horton, and son-in-law of Aurora Greenway; second-rate graduate student and professor of English; appears in Larry McMurtry's *Terms of Endearment*, *Moving On*, and *All My Friends Are Going to Be Strangers*.

Hospital Tommy. Co-owner of a local barbershop and member of the racial revenge group known as the Seven Days in Toni Morrison's *Song of Solomon*.

Rudolph Franz Höss. Commandant of Auschwitz concentration camp and employer of Sophie

Zawistowska for a brief period; sentenced and executed during the Nuremberg trials in William Styron's *Sophie's Choice*.

Harry (Erich Weiss) Houdini. Magician and escape artist who stops at Father's house and who tries to contact his dead mother through seances in E. L. Doctorow's *Ragtime*.

Ely Houston. New York district attorney who investigates the murders of Gilbert Blount, Langley Herndon, and Jack Hilton in Richard Wright's *The Outsider*.

Jack (Zack) Houston. Farmer murdered by Mink Snopes; appears in William Faulkner's *The Hamlet*, *The Town*, and *The Mansion*.

Paul (Mr. Bug Gatherer) Hover. Kentucky-born bee hunter who follows his beloved Ellen Wade onto the prairie; joins Natty Bumppo and Duncan Uncas Middleton in rescuing Inez de Certavallos in James Fenimore Cooper's *The Prairie*.

Howard. Only black member of the board of review for the post office in Richard Wright's *Lawd Today*.

Howard (Howy). Experienced prospector who helps Dobbs and Curtin search for gold in B. Traven's *The Treasure of the Sierra Madre*.

Pembroke Howard. Courtroom opponent of Pudd'nhead Wilson; prosecutes Luigi and Angelo Capello for the murder of York Driscoll in Samuel Langhorne Clemens's *Pudd'nhead Wilson*.

Rosanna Howard. Wealthy student of Isadora Wing and her lover in Erica Jong's *How to Save Your Own Life*.

Captain (Nowonmai, Satan) Howdy. Overpowering demonic possessor of Regan MacNeil's mind and body in William Peter Blatty's *The Exorcist*.

Elena Ross (Elena Kármán) Howe. Beautiful young blonde married to the domineering lawyer Marvin Howe; seeks to define herself through an adulterous affair with Jack Morrissey in Joyce Carol Oates's *Do with Me What You Will*.

Marvin Howe. Brilliant but ruthless attorney who marries Elena Ross in Joyce Carol Oates's *Do with Me What You Will*.

Marybeth Howe (Lynn Lord). Student radical and fugitive who boards with Anton and Theo Wait under the assumed name of Lynn Lord in Diane Johnson's *Lying Low*.

Warren P. Howe. Author and television writer; narrator of events taking place at Schloss Riva in Wright Morris's *Cause for Wonder*.

Pappy Howell. Horse-race gambler found shot to death and robbed of his winnings, for which Wade Shiveley is unjustly blamed, in H. L. Davis's *Honey in the Horn*.

Abigail Howland. See Abigail Howland Mason.

Hatton Howland. Yankee husband of Angeline Meserve and entrepreneur land-developer in Zora Neale Hurston's *Seraph on the Suwanee*.

Margaret Carmichael Howland. Black housekeeper, mistress, and later wife of William Howland; mother of Robert Carmichael in Shirley Ann Grau's *The Keepers of the House*.

Robert Carmichael Howland. Mulatto son of William Howland and Margaret Carmichael; reveals his parents' secret marriage to the press and thereby ruins the political career of John Tolliver in Shirley Ann Grau's *The Keepers of the House*.

William Howland. Patriarch of the Howland family secretly married to his black housekeeper; narrates part of Shirley Ann Grau's *The Keepers of the House*.

Rosemary Hoyt. Beautiful young movie actress who falls in love with Dick Diver in F. Scott Fitzgerald's *Tender Is the Night*.

Hrothgar. King of the Scyldings who, having conquered all adjacent lands, seeks the meaning of life in his old-age ruminations in John Gardner's *Grendel*.

Hrothulf. Orphaned nephew of Hrothgar; becomes a pretender to Hrothgar's throne in John Gardner's *Grendel*.

Bartley Hubbard. Newspaperman married to Marcia Gaylord Hubbard; given to affairs and plagiarism; murdered by an outraged citizen in William Dean Howells's *A Modern Instance*; interviews Silas Lapham in *The Rise of Silas Lapham*.

Bull (Big Bull) Hubbard. Novelist and drug addict; accidentally shoots and kills his wife, June, in Jack Kerouac's *Visions of Cody*; also appears in *Doctor Sax*, *Book of Dreams*, and (as the author of *Nude Supper*) in *Desolation Angels*.

Marcia Gaylord (Marsh) Hubbard. Wife of Bartley Hubbard; after he deserts her, she divorces him in William Dean Howells's *A Modern Instance*; also appears in *The Rise of Silas Lapham*.

Caroline Weed Hubble. Daughter of Frederick

Weed, wife of Roger Hubble, mother of Jeremy Hubble, and friend of Conor Larkin in Leon Uris's *Trinity*.

Jeremy Hubble. Son of Caroline and Roger Hubble; friend, protégé, and fellow athlete of Conor Larkin; lover of a Catholic woman in Leon Uris's *Trinity*.

Roger Hubble. Owner of Hubble Manor who heads and supports the Ulster Protestants against Irish Catholics; husband of Caroline Weed Hubble and father of Jeremy Hubble in Leon Uris's *Trinity*.

Hubby. Exhibitionist who periodically disrobes before his front window during his wife's pregnancy in Carlene Hatcher Polite's *Sister X and the Victims of Foul Play*.

Andy Huben. American missionary and wife of Leslie Huben; gradually disillusioned by her husband's childish radical Christianity in Peter Matthiessen's *At Play in the Fields of the Lord*.

Leslie (Les) Huben. American missionary, husband of Andy Huben, and bitter foe of Roman Catholicism; mistakenly believes he can convert the Niaruna Indians of South America to his brand of Protestant Christianity in Peter Matthiessen's *At Play in the Fields of the Lord*.

Hubert. Maternal grandfather of Cress Delahanty in Jessamyn West's *Cress Delahanty*.

Hubert. One of the "seven dwarfs" who wash windows, make Chinese baby food, and live with Snow White in Donald Barthelme's *Snow White*.

Huck (Old Huck). Friend from New York of Bull Hubbard and Irwin Garden; develops boils while visiting Hubbard in Jack Kerouac's *Visions of Cody*; also appears in *Book of Dreams* and *Desolation Angels*.

Hud (Huddie). Son of Jewel Bannon and stepuncle of Lonnie Bannon; rapes Halmea and kills his stepfather, Homer Bannon, in Larry McMurtry's *Horseman, Pass By*.

Zachary (Zack) Huddlestone. New Yorker and friend of Mark Littleton in John Pendleton Kennedy's *Swallow Barn*.

Andrew Hudson. Son of Thomas Hudson; killed in an automobile accident in Ernest Hemingway's *Islands in the Stream*.

David (Dave, Davy, Mr. David) Hudson. Son of Thomas Hudson; almost catches a huge fish off

Bimini; killed in an automobile accident in Ernest Hemingway's *Islands in the Stream*.

Harley M. Hudson. Vice-President of the United States; appears weak until thrust into the Presidency by the President's death in Allen Drury's *Advise and Consent*.

Roderick Hudson. Young American sculptor studying art in Europe and patronized by Rowland Mallet; fiancé of Mary Garland, but in love with Christina Light; dies tragically in Henry James's *Roderick Hudson*.

Sarah Hudson. Widowed mother of Roderick Hudson and cousin of Mary Garland; visits her son in Europe in Henry James's *Roderick Hudson*.

Thomas Hudson. Husband of Augusta Drake; Susan Ward's editor in Wallace Stegner's *Angle of Repose*.

Thomas (Mr. Tom, Tomás) Hudson. American painter who helps track down German U-boat sailors in the Caribbean in Ernest Hemingway's *Islands in the Stream*.

Tom (Schatz) Hudson. Eldest son of Thomas Hudson; visits his father in Bimini and is later killed in World War II in Ernest Hemingway's *Islands in the Stream*.

Mrs. Hudspeth. Widow who trades horses with Jess Birdwell in Jessamyn West's *The Friendly Persuasion*.

Saved from Captivity (Cap) Huff. Friend of Steven Nason; marches to Quebec with Benedict Arnold in Kenneth Roberts's *Arundel*.

Isaac Huffacre. Man who teaches Leslie Collins woods skills for survival in Harriette Simpson Arnow's *The Kentucky Trace*.

Clifford Huffley. Ordinary but effective successor of the Reverend Jethro Furber after Furber's breakdown in William Gass's *Omensetter's Luck*.

Samuel (Sam) Hugg. River barge captain and teller of tall tales in James Kirke Paulding's *Westward Ho!*

Hugh. One-armed husband of Catherine, father of Meredith, Dolores, and Eveline, and lover of Fiona; photographer and collector of pornography; forces Catherine to wear a chastity belt in an attempt to stop her affair with Cyril; accidentally hangs himself in his photography studio in John Hawkes's *The Blood Oranges*.

Charles Windham Hughes. Friend who Brooke Kincaid says "made her mind"; his death precipitates the action of Lee Smith's *Something in the Wind*.

Elbert Hughes. Youth with remarkable skill at duplicating the handwriting of others; trapped in a scheme to forge famous letters and documents in Thornton Wilder's *Theophilus North*.

Ronny (Root) Hughes. Youngster responsible for the unjust punishment of Jan Anderson; later imprisoned by Anderson in a box supposedly filled with poisonous spiders but actually filled with mice in Fred Chappell's *The Inkling*.

Alonzo Dent (A. D.) Huguenine. Farmer who becomes a circus owner and struggles to recoup his investment in Huguenine's Great and Only International Circus in Walter D. Edmonds's *Chad Hanna*.

Bettina (Bettina Billings) Huguenine. Wife of A. D. Huguenine; as Bettina Billings, she is the fat lady in Huguenine's circus; matronly protector of the circus workers in Walter D. Edmonds's *Chad Hanna*.

Alain Hugues. Husband of Chantal Hugues and guardian of the young Robert Mueller in Nicholas Delbanco's *Fathering*.

Chantal Hugues. Wife of Alain Hugues and guardian of Robert Mueller as a child in Nicholas Delbanco's *Fathering*.

Andy Hull. Son of a preacher; eighth-grade classmate of Suse Ballew in Harriette Arnow's *Hunter's Horn*; serves in Europe in World War II in *The Dollmaker*.

Charlotte Becker Haze Humbert. Mother of Dolores Haze and second wife of Humbert Humbert; struck and killed by a car as she runs out of her house in a fit of anger against Humbert in Vladimir Nabokov's *Lolita*.

Humbert (Edgar H. Humbert, Hummy) Humbert. European author who tells of his obsession with the nymphet Dolores Haze; narrator of Vladimir Nabokov's *Lolita*.

Claude Humbold. Real estate huckster and employer of Carl Reinhart in Thomas Berger's *Reinhart in Love*.

George Humbolt. See Uncle Peepee Marshmallow.

Al Hummel. Owner of Hummel's Garage and school board member responsible for George Caldwell's appointment as a teacher; husband of Vera Hummel and nephew of Pop Kramer in John Updike's *The Centaur*.

Vera Hummel. Girls' physical education teacher at Olinger High School, widely rumored to have had numerous affairs; wife of Al Hummel in John Updike's *The Centaur*.

Hump. Cheyenne war chief in Thomas Berger's *Little Big Man*.

Alice Humphreys. Young woman who befriends and teaches Ellen Montgomery while Ellen lives with her aunt near Thirlwall; dies at age twenty-four in Susan Warner's *The Wide, Wide World*.

John Humphreys. Ministerial student and brother of Alice Humphreys; becomes Ellen Montgomery's beloved teacher and finally her husband in Susan Warner's *The Wide, Wide World*.

Mr. Humphreys. Country minister and father of Alice and John Humphreys; Ellen Montgomery moves to his home and cares for him after Alice's untimely death in Susan Warner's *The Wide, Wide World*.

Bella (Bell) Humphries. Daughter of Richard Humphries; her suitors include the British sergeant Hastings and the partisan John Davis in William Gilmore Simms's *The Partisan*.

Richard (Old Dick) Humphries. Taverner and father of Bella and William Humphries in William Gilmore Simms's *The Partisan*.

William (Bill) Humphries. Son of Richard Humphries and brother of Bella Humphries; trusted lieutenant of Major Singleton in William Gilmore Simms's *The Partisan*.

Hungry Joe. Hero who holds an air force record for flying the most combat tours of duty; has nightmares when grounded in Joseph Heller's *Catch-22*.

James (Hawk) Hunn. Husband of Eva Medina Canada; kills a man in a dispute over a woman in Gayl Jones's *Eva's Man*.

Adam B. Hunt. Ambitious party man but unsuccessful candidate for the gubernatorial nomination in Winston Churchill's *Mr. Crewe's Career*.

Adrienne Hunt. Older of Fonny Hunt's "uppity" sisters in James Baldwin's *If Beale Street Could Talk*.

Alonzo (Fonny) Hunt. Aspiring sculptor and lover of Tish Rivers; sent to prison for rape in James Baldwin's *If Beale Street Could Talk*.

Frank Hunt. Father of Fonny Hunt in James Baldwin's *If Beale Street Could Talk*.

Jason Hunt. Husband of Nan Hunt and father of Cissy Hunt and Marcia Mae Hunt O'Donnell; wealthy, socially prominent, and politically influential figure in Elizabeth Spencer's *The Voice at the Back Door*.

Jerry (Uncle Jerry) Hunt. Crippled freedman and charismatic preacher whose warning saves Comfort Servosse from an ambush; hanged by the Ku Klux Klan following a vision in which he reveals the details of John Walter's murder in Albion W. Tourgee's *A Fool's Errand*.

Laura Hunt. Black fiancée of Roy Fehler; helps him recover from divorce and alcoholism in Joseph Wambaugh's *The New Centurions*.

Marjorie Angeline (Cissy) Hunt. Younger daughter of Nan and Jason Hunt and fiancée of Kerney Woolbright in Elizabeth Spencer's *The Voice at the Back Door*.

Mrs. Hunt. Pious wife of Frank Hunt and mother of Fonny Hunt in James Baldwin's *If Beale Street Could Talk*.

Nan Hunt. Patrician wife of Jason Hunt and mother of Marcia Mae Hunt O'Donnell and Cissy Hunt in Elizabeth Spencer's *The Voice at the Back Door*.

Sheila Hunt. Younger of Fonny Hunt's "uppity" sisters in James Baldwin's *If Beale Street Could Talk*.

Angele Lorelei Lee Hunter. First lover, then mistress, and third wife of Vridar Hunter in Vardis Fisher's *Orphans in Gethsemene*.

Clair Hunter. Daughter of Eloise McLindon and Norman Eisenberg and half sister of David Hunter; seized and killed by an eagle in Hal Bennett's *The Black Wine*.

Conrad R. Hunter. Wealthy owner of the Dallas Cowboys in Peter Gent's *North Dallas Forty*.

David Hunter. Troubled son of Eloise McLindon and Winston Cobb; his initiation into adulthood is the central focus of Hal Bennett's *The Black Wine*.

Diana Hunter. Sister of Vridar Hunter and the only Hunter child who does not forsake the parents' Mormon strictures in Vardis Fisher's *In Tragic Life, Passions Spin the Plot, We Are Betrayed,* and *Orphans in Gethsemene*.

Dock Hunter. Good-humored brother of Joe Hunter in Vardis Fisher's *In Tragic Life* and *Orphans in Gethsemene*.

Eloise Hunter. See Eloise McLindon.

Emmett John Hunter. Fiancé of Joanne Remington; business failure who is made president of the Dallas Cowboys by his brother, Conrad Hunter, in Peter Gent's *North Dallas Forty*.

Henry Hunter. Common-law husband of Eloise McLindon and Korean War veteran dispirited by the segregated North; leaves an ambiguous legacy for his putative son, David Hunter, in Hal Bennett's *The Black Wine*.

Joseph Charles (Joe) Hunter. Cold father of Vridar Hunter in Vardis Fisher's *In Tragic Life, Passions Spin the Plot, We Are Betrayed, No Villain Need Be,* and *Orphans in Gethsemene*.

Mertyl (Mert) Hunter. Cross-eyed and persecuted brother of Vridar Hunter in Vardis Fisher's *In Tragic Life, Passions Spin the Plot, We Are Betrayed, No Villain Need Be,* and *Orphans in Gethsemene*.

Neloa Doole Hunter. See Neloa Doole.

Prudence Branton Hunter. Stern mother of Vridar Hunter in Vardis Fisher's *In Tragic Life, Passions Spin the Plot, We Are Betrayed, No Villain Need Be,* and *Orphans in Gethsemene*.

Robert (Bob) Hunter. Black railway worker fired from his job; briefly involved with the Communist party, whose members turn him in to the immigration authorities for deportation to Jamaica, in Richard Wright's *The Outsider*.

Sarah Hunter. Wife of Bob Hunter in Richard Wright's *The Outsider*.

Steve Hunter. Business school graduate who builds a factory to produce Hugh McVey's mechanical inventions and persuades local citizens to invest in it; shot and wounded by Joseph Wainsworth for contributing to the industrialization of the community, therefore changing it, in Sherwood Anderson's *Poor White*.

Vridar Baroledt (Vreed) Hunter. Child of a religious Utah family; grows up to be an intellectual and writes an autobiographical novel; appear in Vardis Fisher's *In Tragic Life, Passions Spin the Plot, We Are Betrayed, No Villain Need Be,* and *Orphans in Gethsemene*.

Edgar Huntly. Narrator who relates the tale of how his insane compulsions, although with good motives, misled him, bringing about disastrous consequences, in Charles Brockden Brown's *Edgar Huntly*.

Huple. Fifteen-year-old pilot who lied about his age

to join the air force; lives with his cat in a tent with Hungry Joe in Joseph Heller's *Catch-22*.

Iris Hurley. God-fearing friend of Silla Boyce in Paule Marshall's *Brown Girl, Brownstones*.

Will Hurley. Drugstore clerk who unsuccessfully courts Alice Hindman in Sherwood Anderson's *Winesburg, Ohio*.

George W. (George Wheeler) Hurstwood. Married saloon manager who steals money from the saloon and flees to New York with his lover, Carrie Meeber; dies in a flophouse fire in Theodore Dreiser's *Sister Carrie*.

Julia Hurstwood. Estranged wife of George Hurstwood in Theodore Dreiser's *Sister Carrie*.

Anatole Husac. "Father of Neo-Figurism" in John Updike's *Bech: A Book*.

Edward (Hutch) Hutchins. English-born New York novelist who befriends Rosemary Woodhouse and is killed trying to protect her from devil worshippers in Ira Levin's *Rosemary's Baby*.

Eveline Hutchins. Friend and partner of Eleanor Stoddard who develops her interest in art and high culture into a social skill; her flirtatious manner attracts an array of well-heeled suitors despite her marriage in John Dos Passos's *U.S.A.* trilogy.

Rachel Hutchins. Beautiful, seriously disturbed woman who marries Rob Mayfield and dies in childbirth in Reynolds Price's *The Surface of Earth*.

Raven Hutchins. Father of Rachel Hutchins in Reynolds Price's *The Surface of Earth*.

Sarah (Widow Hutchins) Hutchins. See Sarah Hutchins Crombie.

Lyle Hutson. Most successful lawyer on Bourne Island and a senator in the legislature in Paule Marshall's *The Chosen Place, the Timeless People*.

Hutten. Professor married to Käthe Hutten in Katherine Anne Porter's *Ship of Fools*.

Käthe Hutten. Childless wife of Professor Hutten; speaks publicly against her husband in Katherine Anne Porter's *Ship of Fools*.

Hetty Hutter. Simpleminded sister of Judith Hutter; loves Henry March; accidentally killed in an Indian attack in James Fenimore Cooper's *The Deerslayer*.

Judith Hutter. Beautiful stepdaughter of Thomas Hutter; tries unsuccessfully to inspire love in Natty Bumppo in James Fenimore Cooper's *The Deerslayer*.

Thomas (Thomas Hovey) Hutter. Stepfather of Judith and Hetty Hutter; lives on the ark that he built on Lake Glimmerglass; scalped by the Indians and laid to rest at the bottom of Glimmerglass in James Fenimore Cooper's *The Deerslayer*.

Grandma Hutto. Friend of Penny Baxter; once shared her home with the Baxter family in Marjorie Kinnan Rawlings's *The Yearling*.

Oliver Hutto. Seafaring son of Grandma Hutto; his love for Twink Weatherby causes his mother to move away in Marjorie Kinnan Rawlings's *The Yearling*.

Rufus (Rufe) Hutton. White kidnapper and ex-convict killed in Shelby Foote's *September September*.

Samuel (Sam) Huxley. Marine captain killed at Saipan in Leon Uris's *Battle Cry*.

Lord (Old Lord) Hwang. Patriarch of the House of Hwang in Pearl Buck's *The Good Earth*.

Liff Hyatt. Mountain child who occasionally works for farmers in Edith Wharton's *Summer*.

Mary Hyatt. Destitute mother of Charity Royall whom Charity does not know until she attends Mary's primitive burial on the Mountain in Edith Wharton's *Summer*.

Anne Hyde. Rather homely daughter of the Earl of Clarendon and wife of the Duke of York in Kathleen Winsor's *Forever Amber*.

Edward Hyde, Earl of Clarendon. Highly influential, envied, and disliked Chancellor of Restoration England who aids Charles II but finally falls out of favor and is ousted from power in Kathleen Winsor's *Forever Amber*.

Gottfried (Son of Gutsy, Texas) Hyde, Jr. Best friend of D. J.; goes on the Alaskan hunting expedition in Norman Mailer's *Why Are We in Vietnam?*

Gottfried (Gotsie, Gutsy) Hyde, Sr. Undertaker and father of Tex Hyde in Norman Mailer's *Why Are We in Vietnam?*

Hygmod. Lord of the Helmings; overcome in battle, he surrenders his sister Wealtheow to the victorious Hrothgar in John Gardner's *Grendel*.

Jesse Hyman. Son of Squire Nathaniel Hyman; because he favors Reconstruction, he is beaten by the Ku Klux Klan; sent to Kansas, where he is befriended by a preacher who was beaten at Flat Rock twelve years earlier, in Albion W. Tourgee's *A Fool's Errand*.

Squire Nathaniel Hyman. Neighbor of Comfort Servosse and a community spokesman in warning the Servosses against associating with Northern teachers from the freedmen's school at Verdenton; presides at the trial of three Negro men accused of murdering Tom Savage in Albion W. Tourgee's *A Fool's Errand*.

Mr. Hyslop. Secretary of A. J. in William S. Burroughs's *Naked Lunch*.

I

I. Daughter of Nimni and Ohiro-Moldona-Fivona in Herman Melville's *Mardi*.

I&I. See The Intolerable Kid.

Ideal. Young woman who explores the mental and physical dimensions of love with her lover Jimson; together they constitute the title characters in Carlene Hatcher Polite's *The Flagellants*.

The Idiot. Retarded white lover of Dolores Brittain; slain by black women of Burnside, Virginia, during an Easter pageant in Hal Bennett's *Wait Until the Evening*.

Idomeneus. Unconventional suitor of Helen and the first soldier to return from the Trojan War in John Erskine's *The Private Life of Helen of Troy*.

Finger Idzikowski. Friend and boxing trainer of Bruno Lefty Bicek; hexes Bicek's opponents in Nelson Algren's *Never Come Morning*.

Ike (Old Ike). Friend and heroin connection of William Lee in Mexico City in William S. Burroughs's *Junkie* and *Naked Lunch*.

Billy Ikehorn. See Wilhelmina Hunnenwell Winthrop Ikehorn Orsini.

Ellis Ikehorn. Wealthy businessman who marries his secretary, Billy Winthrop, and who leaves her his fortune in Judith Krantz's *Scruples*.

Ikkemotubbe (Doom). Chickasaw chief in William Faulkner's *Absalom, Absalom!*; *Go Down, Moses*; *Requiem for a Nun*; *The Town*; and *The Reivers*.

Art Immelmann. Mephistophelean funding officer who tempts Tom More to pursue a life of abstraction and eroticism in Walker Percy's *Love in the Ruins*.

Angelo (Joe) Incardona. Railroad trackman killed by Dalton Harron in Susan Sontag's *Death Kit*.

Myra Incardona. Widow of the murdered Angelo Incardona in Susan Sontag's *Death Kit*.

Ned Inching. London pickpocket imprisoned in Australia; escapes from the penal colony and returns to London in Charles Nordhoff and James Norman Hall's *Botany Bay*.

Indian Jenny. Solitary old woman who drinks, dabbles in the occult, and carries a grudge against the Stamper family in Ken Kesey's *Sometimes a Great Notion*.

El Indio. Morphine addict and friend of Tristessa in Jack Kerouac's *Tristessa*.

Inez. Notorious character in Ideal's neighborhood; dies a "bloody, unsolved death" while her neighbors sleep in Carlene Hatcher Polite's *The Flagellants*.

Inez. Third wife of Dean Moriarty in Jack Kerouac's *On the Road*.

Tory Ingersoll. Homosexual anthologist of "new" 1960s poetry in John Updike's *Bech: A Book*.

Arthur J. Ingles. Husband of Cecilia Ingles; owner of the Clifton, a Chicago skyscraper, in Henry Blake Fuller's *The Cliff-Dwellers*.

Cecilia Ingles. Wife of Arthur J. Ingles; rules Chicago society in Henry Blake Fuller's *The Cliff-Dwellers*.

Allen Ingram. Teacher of creative writing on the faculty at Convers College in Alison Lurie's *Love and Friendship*.

Andrew Ingram. Friend and teacher of Conor Larkin and Seamus O'Neill in Leon Uris's *Trinity*.

Zell Ingram. Commercial artist; friend of Jule Jackson and fellow resident at the YMCA in New York City in George Wylie Henderson's *Jule*.

Injun Joe. Half-breed who murders Dr. Robinson and frames Muff Potter; dies when he is accidentally sealed in a cave in Samuel Langhorne Clemens's *The Adventures of Tom Sawyer*.

Raoul Innerarity. Creole who helps Joseph Frowenfeld in Frowenfeld's drug store in George Washington Cable's *The Grandissimes*.

Gertrude Innes. Niece of Rachel Innes and fiancée of John Bailey in Mary Roberts Rinehart's *The Circular Staircase*.

Halsey B. Innes. Nephew of Rachel Innes; kidnapped when he discovers that Paul Armstrong is alive in Mary Roberts Rinehart's *The Circular Staircase*.

Rachel (Aunt Ray) Innes. Middle-aged spinster who rents Sunnyside and who helps solve the murder of Arnold Armstrong; narrator of Mary Roberts Rinehart's *The Circular Staircase*.

Innis. Tory partisan leader in Charleston, South Carolina, who imprisons Arthur Butler in John Pendleton Kennedy's *Horse-Shoe Robinson*.

Innocent (Pope). Pope who appears in the West to fight the Loop Garoo Kid, which he does successfully; rejects Drag Gibson's request to kill Loop in Ishmael Reed's *Yellow Back Radio Broke-Down*.

The Intolerable Kid (I&I). Member of the Nova Mob who spreads havoc through slander in William S. Burroughs's *Nova Express*.

Pierce Inverarity. California real estate mogul who names Oedipa Maas as executrix of his estate, which contains a stamp collection that leads Oedipa into her search for the meaning of Tristero, in Thomas Pynchon's *The Crying of Lot 49*.

Invicta. Black-cloaked, melodramatic actress who informs Tony Smith of Moise's financial needs and searches for Big Lot, her missing lover, in Tennessee Williams's *Moise and the World of Reason*.

Iray. Young wife of Teray in Octavia E. Butler's *Patternmaster*.

Hettie Irden. Frowsy B-girl whom J. Henry Waugh entertains in Robert Coover's *The Universal Baseball Association, Inc., J. Henry Waugh, Prop.*

Latham Ireland. Lawyer who rivals Martin Arrowsmith for the affections of Joyce Lanyon in Sinclair Lewis's *Arrowsmith*.

Irene. Adolescent friend of Hedylus who considers leaving Samos with him in H. D.'s *Hedylus*.

Iris. Daughter of Bea; hawker of cigarettes, old beyond her years, in Cyrus Colter's *The Hippodrome*.

Daniel Webster (Dan) Irving. College professor blacklisted for his outspoken opposition to United States involvement with Russia during World War I; journalist who exposes the oil scandal in the Harding administration in Upton Sinclair's *Oil!*

Washington Irving. Pseudonym used by Yossarian and Major Major Major Major in Joseph Heller's *Catch-22*.

Irwin. Professor from Cambridge, Massachusetts, whom Esther Greenwood seduces and to whom she loses her virginity on an overnight release from a mental hospital in Sylvia Plath's *The Bell Jar*.

Alexander Irwin. Young heavyweight boxer in whom Lee Youngdahl has an investment in Mark Harris's *Wake Up, Stupid*.

Judge Montague M. (Monty) Irwin. Respected citizen of Burden's Landing and father of the illegitimate Jack Burden; backs the political opposition to Willie Stark in Robert Penn Warren's *All the King's Men*.

Isaac. Elderly slave at Dove Cote; accompanies the Lindsays and Horse Shoe Robinson on their visit

to Cornwallis to assure Arthur Butler's fair treatment in John Pendleton Kennedy's *Horse-Shoe Robinson*.

Jacob Isaacs. See Prince Cabano.

Daniel Isaacson. See Daniel Isaacson Lewin.

Paul (Pauly) Isaacson. Husband of Rochelle Isaacson and father of Daniel Isaacson Lewin and Susan Isaacson Lewin; radio shop operator who becomes a member of the Communist party; convicted as a spy and electrocuted in E. L. Doctorow's *The Book of Daniel*.

Rochelle Isaacson. Wife of Paul Isaacson and mother of Daniel Isaacson Lewin and Susan Isaacson Lewin; becomes a member of the Communist party and is convicted as a spy and electrocuted in E. L. Doctorow's *The Book of Daniel*.

Susan Isaacson. See Susan Isaacson Lewin.

Isabel (Bel). Daughter of Annette Blagovo and Vadim Vadimovich; marries a self-proclaimed revolutionary and flees to Russia, where she becomes ill and poverty stricken; Vadim rushes in vain to help the daughter he neglected most of her life in Vladimir Nabokov's *Look at the Harlequins!*

Isaiah. Ex-slave and servant of Felice and Lewis Venable; runs away to Oklahoma with Sabra Venable and her new husband, Yancey Cravat, in Edna Ferber's *Cimarron*.

Ishmael. Narrator; sole survivor of the *Pequod*'s pursuit of Moby Dick in Herman Melville's *Moby-Dick*.

Doug Ismaileh. Playwright from Hunt Hills Theatre Group and imitator of Ron Grant; invited by Carol Abernathy to skindive in Jamaica with the group in James Jones's *Go to the Widow-Maker*.

Isold of the White Hands. Look-alike of La Belle Isold; Tristram marries her but is not happy with only the image of his true love, La Belle Isold, in Thomas Berger's *Arthur Rex*.

Isolde (Iso). Lesbian prominent among Mira's friends in graduate school in Marilyn French's *The Women's Room*.

Issetibbeha. Chickasaw chief in William Faulkner's *Go Down, Moses*; *Requiem for a Nun*; *The Town*; and *The Reivers*.

Itelo. Prince of the Arnewi tribe of African cow worshippers; welcomes Eugene Henderson to the drought-stricken village with a ritual wrestling match that Henderson wins, making Itelo a bosom friend, in Saul Bellow's *Henderson the Rain King*.

Ito. Giggling Japanese houseboy noted for his terrible driving in Patrick Dennis's *Auntie Mame* and *Around the World with Auntie Mame*.

Iva (née Almstadt). Librarian and long-suffering wife of Joseph in Saul Bellow's *Dangling Man*.

Walter Ivans. Disgruntled associate of Paul Madvig's who feels that Madvig should arrange the release of his brother, Tim Ivans, in Dashiell Hammett's *The Glass Key*.

Crazy Ivar. Eccentric Norwegian hermit who works with animals on Alexandra Bergson's farm in Willa Cather's *O Pioneers!*

Ives. Silent, elderly linguist whom Tom More saves from enforced euthanasia in Walker Percy's *Love in the Ruins*.

Izzy the Push. Member of the Nova Mob in William S. Burroughs's *Nova Express* and *The Ticket that Exploded*.

J

Jacataqua. Abenaki Indian blood sister of Steven Nason; accompanies Benedict Arnold's army to Quebec in Kenneth Roberts's *Arundel*.

Jacinto. Indian guide who shows Bishop Latour a sacred Indian cave in Willa Cather's *Death Comes for the Archbishop*.

Jack. Writer and would-be painter adventuring in the drug underworld of Mexico City; narrator of Jack Kerouac's *Tristessa*.

Jack. Son of Utch Thalhammer and the unnamed narrator, brother of Bart, and playmate and friend of Dorabella and Fiordiligi Winter in John Irving's *The 158-Pound Marriage*.

Brother Jack. Leader of the Brotherhood who recruits the narrator into his organization in Ralph Ellison's *Invisible Man*.

Captain Jack. Keeper of a lifesaving station in San Francisco Bay who provides plots and details to the would-be author Condé Rivers in Frank Norris's *Blix*.

Esther Jack. Stage-set designer, wife of Frederick Jack, and lover of George Webber in Thomas Wolfe's *You Can't Go Home Again* and *The Web and the Rock*.

Frederick (Fritz) Jack. Wealthy New York businessman and husband of Esther Jack in Thomas Wolfe's *You Can't Go Home Again*; also appears in *The Web and the Rock*.

Albert (Ajax) Jacks. Town dandy and lover of Sula in Toni Morrison's *Sula*.

Jackson. Illiterate atheist who bullies the *Highlander*'s sailors in Herman Melville's *Redburn*.

Jackson. Murderer of Gil Santini; captured by Harry Meyers in Jay Neugeboren's *Listen Ruben Fontanez*.

Jackson. Worker who loses his arm in an industrial accident and is denied compensation by his employer in Jack London's *The Iron Heel*.

Alice Jackson. See Alice Greenwood Weylin.

Art Jackson. Parachute jumper in William Faulkner's *Pylon*.

Beth Jackson. Senior nurse at the Hauptman Clinic in Terry Southern's *Flash and Filigree*.

Bill Jackson. Mountaineer who helps Will Banion protect the wagon train; kills Sam Woodhull in Emerson Hough's *The Covered Wagon*.

Chester (Ches) Jackson. Porter; brother-in-law of Clotilda Pilgrim and father of their daughter, Ruby Parker; deceased in Cyrus Colter's *The Rivers of Eros*.

Douglas MacArthur Jackson. Lover of Miriam Berg; intellectual who is occasionally emotionally abusive in Marge Piercy's *Small Changes*.

Ezzard (Chops, Ezz) Jackson. Assistant editorial director of Lawrence Publications and former member of the black high school athletic team and neighborhood gang gathering for a birthday testimonial honoring Chappie Davis in John A. Williams's *The Junior Bachelor Society*.

Father Jackson. Priest who comforts Mary Follet after the death of her husband in James Agee's *A Death in the Family*.

Harry Jackson. Butler and chauffeur for Edith and Joe Chapin I; confidant of Ann Chapin in John O'Hara's *Ten North Frederick*.

Helen Jackson. New Orleans Communist and resident of Twenty-Door City; mistress of José Morales and loved by Leon Fisher in Albert Halper's *Union Square*.

Jake Jackson. Postal worker who is deeply in debt; wife beater, card player, and heavy drinker in Richard Wright's *Lawd Today*.

Jordan Jackson. Poor white who rises to the rank of lieutenant in the Confederate army; saves the life of Hesden Le Moyne in battle, and makes money in trade following the war; whipped by the Ku Klux Klan for running on the same political ticket as a black and for advocating a political alliance of blacks and poor whites in Albion W. Tourgee's *Bricks without Straw*.

Jule (Mr. Man, Schoolboy) Jackson. Illegitimate son of Ollie and Big Jule, lover of Bertha Mae, and protagonist of George Wylie Henderson's *Jule*.

Lil Jackson. Wife of Jake Jackson and frequent victim of his physical abuse; needs an operation in Richard Wright's *Lawd Today*.

Martha Jackson. Friend who encourages Mira to return to college in Marilyn French's *The Women's Room*.

Pearl (Pearlie) Jackson. Wife of Chester Jackson and sister of Clotilda Pilgrim in Cyrus Colter's *The Rivers of Eros*.

Peter Jackson. Sixty-nine-year-old man who survives the Andromeda Strain attack in Michael Crichton's *The Andromeda Strain*.

T5 Ronald Jackson. Driver for Richard Cantwell in Ernest Hemingway's *Across the River and into the Trees*.

Sillerton Jackson. Bachelor and social gossip in Edith Wharton's *The Age of Innocence*; mentioned in *The Old Maid*.

Stuart Jackson. Wealthy midwestern suitor who is rejected by Adah Logan in Susan Glaspell's *Judd Rankin's Daughter*.

General Thomas Jonathan (Stonewall) Jackson. Professor of natural philosophy and military tactics at Virginia Military Institute; earns a reputation as an eccentric but brilliant tactician; apotheosized when accidentally killed by Confederate troops in Mary Johnston's *The Long Roll*.

Jacob. See Jacob Eliezer.

Baron Jacobi. Bulgarian minister who lectures on the corruptness of Americans and who whacks Senator Ratcliffe with a cane; friend of Madeleine Lee in Henry Adams's *Democracy*.

Capt. Jacobi. Ship's captain of *La Paloma* who delivers a falcon statuette to Sam Spade in Dashiell Hammett's *Maltese Falcon*.

Bob (Satan) Jacobs. Black American hairdresser in Copenhagen; married to a rich Swedish woman in Cecil Brown's *The Life and Loves of Mr. Jiveass Nigger*.

Constance Jacobs. Sister of Wilson Jacobs; befriends Mildred Latham in Oscar Micheaux's *The Forged Note*.

Samuel (Sammy) Jacobs. Elderly Jewish store owner who is disappointed when his son loses his job with Glymmer, Read in Nathan Asch's *The Office*.

Wilson Jacobs. Minister, fund-raiser for the YMCA, and brother of Constance Jacobs; falls in love with Mildred Latham in Oscar Micheaux's *The Forged Note*.

Lena Jacobson. Old woman saved by Marshall Preminger from drowning in *The Condominium*, a novella in Stanley Elkin's *Searches and Seizures*.

Arnold Jacoby. Tenant of the 70th Street building managed by Norman Moonbloom; lives with his common-law wife, Betty Jacoby, in Edward Lewis Wallant's *The Tenants of Moonbloom*.

Betty Jacoby. Common-law wife of Arnold Jacoby and tenant of the 70th Street building managed by Norman Moonbloom in Edward Lewis Wallant's *The Tenants of Moonbloom*.

Janos Jacoby. Lover of Margot Lamar and co-director of the film being shot at Belle Isle in Walker Percy's *Lancelot*.

Jacopo. Accordion player in the Caffé Gatto; attacks his former partner, Edouard, in John Hawkes's *The Goose on the Grave*.

Ernestine (Winnie) Jacques. Long-lost sister whom Mildred Latham meets by coincidence; wife of the physician who treats Sidney Wyeth for typhoid in Oscar Micheaux's *The Forged Note*.

Father Jacques. Frontier priest in James Kirke Paulding's *Westward Ho!*

Curtis (J.) Jadwin. Real estate baron, romantic lover, and then the "Great Bull" of the Chicago Board of Trade; attempts to corner the American wheat market, losing his fortune and almost losing his wife, in Frank Norris's *The Pit*.

Laura Dearborn Jadwin. Wife of Curtis Jadwin; nearly driven insane by Jadwin's neglect in Frank Norris's *The Pit*.

Sid Jaffe. Respectable and responsible lawyer whose pursuit of Martha Reganhart involves him in doing free legal work for Paul and Libby Herz in Philip Roth's *Letting Go*.

Jaggers. Reconnaissance-photography interpreter who examines the film taken by Samuel Wilson in Michael Crichton's *The Andromeda Strain*.

Don Jaime. See Don Jaime de Ribera.

Jake. Faithful former slave of Richard Cameron; helps get Cameron released from jail in Thomas Dixon's *The Clansman*.

Jake. See Macon Dead I.

Jake. See Pete.

Jake. Black fisherman and resident of Catfish Row; killed in a Charleston hurricane in DuBose Heyward's *Porgy*.

James I (James VI of Scotland). King of England who was King James VI of Scotland in George Garrett's *Death of the Fox*.

Earl James. White playmate and friend of Sandy Rodgers; does not understand why Sandy is not admitted to "Children's Day" at the amusement park in Langston Hughes's *Not Without Laughter*.

Ellen James. Rape victim whose attackers cut off her tongue; martyr for the Ellen Jamesians, whom she does not admire; drowns at Dog's Head Harbor in John Irving's *The World According to Garp.*

Jefferson James. Physician and friend of Frank Cowperwood in Theodore Dreiser's *The Stoic.*

Jesse James. Gunfighter and legendary outlaw whose death Chester Pomeroy denies; appears to Pomeroy at the end of Thomas McGuane's *Panama.*

Laura James. First love of Eugene Gant; leaves Gant to marry her hometown boyfriend in Thomas Wolfe's *Look Homeward, Angel.*

Miss James. Telephone operator with Glymmer, Read who is relatively unconcerned when the firm declares bankruptcy in Nathan Asche's *The Office.*

Nathan James. Young missionary doctor in Octavia E. Butler's *Survivor.*

Clive Jameson. Famous Civil War general and son of Isaac Jameson in Shelby Foote's *Jordan County.*

Dorothy Jameson. Painter who attends the yacht party in William Faulkner's *Mosquitoes.*

Isaac Jameson. First white settler and plantation developer on Lake Jordan in Shelby Foote's *Jordan County.*

Professor Doctor Laszlo Jamf. German scientist who developed Imipolex G and conducted Pavlovian experiments which presumably conditioned Tyrone Slothrop's responses to the V-2 rocket in Thomas Pynchon's *Gravity's Rainbow.*

Jamie Ray. Homosexual minister and golf player at the retreat in John Updike's *A Month of Sundays.*

Jamieson. Detective who investigates Arnold Armstrong's murder in Mary Roberts Rinehart's *The Circular Staircase.*

Mary (Bessie) Jamiesson. Resident of the Diamond County Home for the Aged; homely, heavy woman with a gift for flirting, affection, and patience; bears the emotional scars of having had a beautiful, unloving mother in John Updike's *The Poorhouse Fair.*

Oliver (O. J.) Jamison. Reform-school buddy of Jake Simms in Anne Tyler's *Earthly Possessions.*

Tom Jamison. Hometown friend for whom a delirious soldier mistakes Henry Fleming in Stephen Crane's *The Red Badge of Courage.*

Jane. Pretentious older woman; sometime companion and lover of Vivaldo Moore in James Baldwin's *Another Country.*

Jane. Promiscuous pilot who becomes involved with drug dealers in *The Smugglers of Lost Souls' Rock,* the interior novel within John Gardner's *October Light.*

Jane. See Jane Villiers de l'Isle-Adam.

Duchess Jane. Friend of Mrs. Brookenham in Henry James's *The Awkward Age.*

Janey. Child protected by Hugh Wolfe and his relatives in Rebecca Harding Davis's *Life in the Iron Mills.*

Janey. Lover of Vernor Stanton in Thomas McGuane's *The Sporting Club.*

Mrs. Janney. Mother of Rena Janney; killed in an automobile crash in August Derleth's *The Shield of the Valiant.*

Rena (Miss Lolly C., Mouse, Renchen) Janney. Girlfriend of Kivden Sewall and a victim of Sac Prairie gossip; moves to Madison to live with her mother and becomes a jazz singer in August Derleth's *The Shield of the Valiant.*

Earl Janoth. Publisher and head of Janoth Enterprises; lover and murderer of Pauline Delos; a narrator of Kenneth Fearing's *The Big Clock.*

Pauline Janowski. Adolescent who asks Henry Miller for a job as a messenger; he seduces her and leaves her on the highway in the middle of the night to hitch a ride to Cleveland in Henry Miller's *Tropic of Capricorn.*

Jansee. Lead wife and sister of Patternmaster Rayal in Octavia E. Butler's *Patternmaster.*

Christina Jansen (Christina Carlson). Wife of Maximilian Petion; poor music hall singer whom Nathan Brederhagan stabs during an attempted rape in Ignatius Donnelly's *Caesar's Column.*

Samuel Japson. Quaker trader who befriends Salathiel Albine; appears in Hervey Allen's *The Forest and the Fort* and *Bedford Village.*

Willard Jarkins. Broker for Frank Cowperwood; handles Cowperwood's interest in the London subway system in Theodore Dreiser's *The Stoic.*

Jarl (Skyeman, Viking). Companion of Taji; killed by Aleema's sons in Herman Melville's *Mardi.*

Father Jarnatt. Village priest who befriends Jean-Lambert Tallien in H. L. Davis's *Harp of a Thousand Strings.*

Beth Jarrett. Wife of Calvin Jarrett and mother of Jordan and Conrad Jarrett in Judith Guest's *Ordinary People*.

Calvin (Cal) Jarrett. Successful tax attorney, husband of Beth Jarrett, and father of Jordan and Conrad Jarrett in Judith Guest's *Ordinary People*.

Conrad Keith (Con) Jarrett. Younger son of Calvin and Beth Jarrett; returns home a year after his suicide attempt in Judith Guest's *Ordinary People*.

Jordan (Buck, Bucky) Jarrett. Older son of Calvin and Beth Jarrett; dies in a boat accident in Judith Guest's *Ordinary People*.

Berk Jarvis. Pioneer who marries Diony Hall; captured by Indians, but escapes and reclaims Diony, who has married Evan Muir, in Elizabeth Madox Roberts's *The Great Meadow*.

Diony Hall (Diny) Jarvis. Imaginative daughter of a planter family; marries Berk Jarvis, who is later captured by the Indians and presumed dead; marries Evan Muir, but chooses Jarvis over Muir when Jarvis returns, in Elizabeth Madox Roberts's *The Great Meadow*.

Elvira Jarvis. Mother of Berk Jarvis in Elizabeth Madox Roberts's *The Great Meadow*.

Major Gordon Jarvis. Defense counsel for Jacob Levy in Martha Gellhorn's *Wine of Astonishment*.

Paul Jarvis. Fiancé of Delia Poole; taken into his uncle's business and subsequently ordered to the Philippines in Janet Flanner's *The Cubical City*.

Edward K. (Jap) Jasper. Former medical student disabled by mental collapse; finally able to complete his studies after having served as Doctor Caldwell's faithful assistant; silently in love with William Caldwell in Mary Austin's *Santa Lucia*.

Madame de Jaume. Witty friend of Adela Gareth in Henry James's *The Spoils of Poynton*.

Siegfried (Siggy) Javotnik. Friend of Hannes Graff; persuades Graff to help free the animals; stung to death by bees in John Irving's *Setting Free the Bears*.

Vratno Javotnik. Husband of Hilke Marter-Javotnik and father of Siggy Javotnik; linguist and friend of Gottlub Wut; murdered by Todor Slivinca in John Irving's *Setting Free the Bears*.

Jay. Pianist in a movie house, drunkard, and artist whose paintings decorate Mambo's nightclub; friend of Sabina and Djuna and husband of Lillian in Anaïs Nin's *Ladders to Fire, Children of the Albatross, The Four-Chambered Heart, A Spy in the House of Love*, and *Seduction of the Minotaur*.

Charlie Jay. Devil-may-care boyhood friend of Brock Caldwell; has sex with Grace Brock Caldwell when they both are teenagers; becomes mayor of Fort Penn in John O'Hara's *A Rage to Live*.

Jay Cee. Brainy literary editor of a New York fashion magazine and supervisor who tries to nurture Esther Greenwood's literary aspirations in Sylvia Plath's *The Bell Jar*.

Leon Jazinski. Employee of Piet Hanema's construction firm in John Updike's *Couples*.

J. B. See James Black. f lJealous. Miller who removes his ploughboy's eyes with a spoon in Jerzy Kosinski's *The Painted Bird*.

Jean. Masochistic wife of Alfonso in Gayl Jones's *Eva's Man*.

Jean. Soldier in William Faulkner's *A Fable*.

Jean-baby. Friend of Martin Frost; puts hashish in Frederick Eichner's drink in Terry Southern's *Flash and Filigree*.

Jean-Jacques. Struggling writer, part-time prostitute and petty thief, and best friend of Hippolyte in Susan Sontag's *The Benefactor*.

Jeff. Attacker who attempts to castrate Will Harris in Junius Edwards's *If We Must Die*.

Roscoe Jeffcoat. Jailer in Shelby Foote's *Follow Me Down*.

Jefferson (Jeff). Impotent husband of Till and slave of Sapphira Dodderidge Colbert in Willa Cather's *Sapphira and the Slave Girl*.

Frannie Jefferson. Teacher, community leader, and wife of Ol Jefferson in Sarah E. Wright's *This Child's Gonna Live*.

Ol Jefferson. Husband of Frannie Jefferson; eccentric peddler and spreader of community history in Sarah E. Wright's *This Child's Gonna Live*.

Thomas Jefferson. Principal author of the Declaration of Independence and third president of the United States; orders Aaron Burr arrested for treason in Gore Vidal's *Burr*.

Thomas Jefferson. President of the United States who helps Lewis Rand become an attorney; withholds a letter which would reveal Rand's part in the Burr conspiracy in Mary Johnston's *Lewis Rand*.

Thomas (Tom) Jefferson. Virginia gentleman who helps Thomas Paine formulate revolutionary ideas and who incorporates many of them in The Declaration of Independence in Howard Fast's *Citizen Tom Paine*.

Woodrow Wilson Jefferson. Black Marxist who believes that Marx and Engels are alive and wants to meet them; makes the Negro Viewpoint in Hinckle Von Vampton's novel-within-the-novel *The Benign Monster*, but is saved by his preacher father, in Ishmael Reed's *Mumbo Jumbo*.

John Jeffreys. Older, silver-haired second husband of Louisa Calloway in Alice Adams's *Families and Survivors*.

Louisa Jeffreys. See Louisa Calloway.

Jeffy (Jeff). Young teenaged girl who makes sexual advances toward Ursa Corregidora in Gayl Jones's *Corregidora*.

Betsy Jekyll. Younger sister of Maizie Jekyll; fashion model and a free-spirited woman until she marries Hector Connolly in Nancy Hale's *The Prodigal Women*.

Minnie May Jekyll. Wife of Thomas Jekyll and mother of Maizie and Betsy Jekyll; urges her husband to move the family from Virginia to Massachusetts in Nancy Hale's *The Prodigal Women*.

Minnie May (Maizie) Jekyll. Virginia beauty who marries Lambert Rudd and has a nervous breakdown shortly after their daughter is born in Nancy Hale's *The Prodigal Women*.

Thomas (Tom) Jekyll. Lawyer from Virginia who never adjusts to life in the North after moving to Massachusetts with his family in Nancy Hale's *The Prodigal Women*.

Bonanza (Sally Elizabeth Jones) Jellybean. Cutest and best cowgirl and the first cowgirl to die; leads the revolt on the Rubber Rose Ranch; lover of Sissy Hankshaw Gitche in Tom Robbins's *Even Cowgirls Get the Blues*.

Jinx Jenkins. Furniture mover and comical friend of Bubber Brown in Rudolph Fisher's *The Walls of Jericho*; *The Conjure-Man Dies*.

Mabry Jenkins. Dallas Cowboy defensive back whose life falls apart when he is cut from the team in Peter Gent's *Texas Celebrity Turkey Trot*.

Leo (Dead-Eye) Jenks. Stupid sharpshooter who becomes sheriff of the second Hard Times; killed by Clay Turner in E. L. Doctorow's *Welcome to Hard Times*.

Captain Jenness. Captain of the *Aroostook* and guardian of Lydia Blood while she is aboard in William Dean Howells's *The Lady of the Aroostook*.

Jabe Jenney. Farmer and friend of Austen Vane in Winston Churchill's *Mr. Crewe's Career*.

Betsey Jennings. Liverpool woman who starves to death with her three children in Herman Melville's *Redburn*.

W. B. Jennings. Newspaper reporter and writer of boys' adventure books; outside observer of events at Tom Scanlon's ninetieth birthday in Wright Morris's *Ceremony in Lone Tree*.

Myrtle Jennison. Tim Noonan's lover who inspires Whisper Thaler's jealousy in Dashiell Hammett's *Red Harvest*.

Jenny. Boyhood sweetheart of Israel Potter; marries Sergeant Singles in Herman Melville's *Israel Potter*.

Jenny. Prostitute working in the Chicago hotel where Cross Damon stays before leaving for New York; tries to convince Damon to take her with him in Richard Wright's *The Outsider*.

Jenny. See Virginia Du Pre and Genevieve Steinbauer.

John Jermin. Chief mate of the *Julia* and nemesis of Captain Guy in Herman Melville's *Omoo*.

Jero. African in Copenhagen who injures George Washington in a fight in Cecil Brown's *The Life and Loves of Mr. Jiveass Nigger*.

Melvin (Doc) Jerrell. Philosophical black homosexual physician in Copenhagen in Cecil Brown's *The Life and Loves of Mr. Jiveass Nigger*.

Jerry. Carpenter and former slave of the Talbot family in Grace King's *The Pleasant Ways of St. Médard*.

Jerry. Easygoing Italian-American and, for a short time, lover of Barbara King in James Baldwin's *Tell Me How Long the Train's Been Gone*.

Jerry. Irish terrier pup "born to hate niggers" who travels with Van Horn to the British Solomons; must search for a white master after Van Horn is killed in Jack London's *Jerry of the Islands*.

Jerry (the Lemon Kid). Wolf mate of Audrey Carsons in Audrey's story, "The Autobiography of a Wolf," in William S. Burroughs's *Exterminator!*

Jesse. Lover of Elaine, friend of Lee Mellon, and narrator of Richard Brautigan's *A Confederate General from Big Sur*.

Miss Jessel. Ghost of a governess and apparently a lover of Peter Quint in Henry James's *The Turn of the Screw*.

Cecilia (Sissy) Jessup. Younger daughter of Doremus Jessup; active in the New Underground in Sinclair Lewis's *It Can't Happen Here*.

Doremus Jessup. Editor of the Fort Beulah *Daily Informer* and later publisher of anti-government leaflets for the New Underground; after being beaten in a concentration camp, he escapes to Canada in Sinclair Lewis's *It Can't Happen Here*.

Emma Jessup. Solid, kindly wife of Doremus Jessup in Sinclair Lewis's *It Can't Happen Here*.

Leroy Jessup. Janitor at the Penmarks' apartment complex; murdered by Rhoda Penmark when she learns that he knows of her evil deeds in William March's *The Bad Seed*.

Mary Jessup. See Mary Jessup Greenhill.

Philip Jessup. Son of Doremus Jessup; attorney and later a Corporatist judge in Sinclair Lewis's *It Can't Happen Here*.

Jesting Squaw's Son. Devoted friend of Laughing Boy in Oliver La Farge's *Laughing Boy*.

Jesus Christ. See The Corpse.

Jethro. Black slave and childhood companion of Leslie Collins; later given to Leslie in Harriette Simpson Arnow's *The Kentucky Trace*.

Jethro (Ruel). Mentor and father-in-law of Moses and father of Zipporah; Kenites priest with whom Moses lives for twenty years before accepting Jethro's challenge to deliver the Israelites from Egypt in Zora Neale Hurston's *Moses, Man of the Mountain*.

Alice Hallie Lee (Death-row Jethroe) Jethroe. Mother of D. J. in Norman Mailer's *Why Are We in Vietnam?*

Ranald Jethroe. See D. J.

Rusty (David Rutherford Jethroe Jellicoe Jethroe, Sir Jet-Throne) Jethroe. Husband of Alice Jethroe and father of D. J.; organizes the Alaskan hunting expedition in Norman Mailer's *Why Are We in Vietnam?*

Helen Jewett. Mistress of Charles Schuyler; murdered at the brothel of Rosanna Townsend in Gore Vidal's *Burr*.

Jezebel. Ninety-five-year-old slave of Sapphira Dodderidge Colbert and the last of the African-born Colbert slaves in Willa Cather's *Sapphira and the Slave Girl*.

Jibbenainosay. See Nathan Slaughter.

Jiggs. Mechanic in William Faulkner's *Pylon*.

Jim. Free black man, husband of Mag Smith, and father of Frado in Harriet E. Wilson's *Our Nig*.

Jim. Personal slave of Peregrine Lacey Catlett and husband of Minna in Mary Lee Settle's *Know Nothing*.

Jim. Tahiti harbor pilot in Herman Melville's *Omoo*.

Jim. Runaway slave of Miss Watson in Samuel Langhorne Clemens's *Adventures of Huckleberry Finn*; accompanies Huck Finn and Tom Sawyer on a balloon trip across North Africa in *Tom Sawyer Abroad*.

Jesus Jiminez. I.W.W. organizer killed with Jack Gale in Louis Adamic's *Grandsons*.

Jimmy. Illegitimate son of Callie Wells and Willard Freund; reared by Henry Soames in John Gardner's *Nickel Mountain*.

Jimmy. Illegitimate son of Molly Taylor White and Gideon Fry and halfbrother of Joe; killed in World War I in Larry McMurtry's *Leaving Cheyenne*.

Jimmy. Mercenary rover who escorts Toby to a whaling ship in Herman Melville's *Typee*.

Jimmy. Store owner and husband of Claire in Jerry Bumpus's *Anaconda*.

Jimmy (Jim). Cousin of Mutt Thomas in Gayl Jones's *Corregidora*.

William Hezekiah Jimson. Fundamentalist minister in Shelby Foote's *Follow Me Down*.

Jimson (Jim). Lover of Ideal; together they constitute the title characters in Carlene Hatcher Polite's *The Flagellants*.

Joachim. Housemaster to whom Teray is apprenticed in Octavia E. Butler's *Patternmaster*.

Madame Joachim. Creole neighbor of the Talbots in Grace King's *The Pleasant Ways of St. Médard*.

Al Joad. Brother of Tom Joad II; moves west with the family in John Steinbeck's *The Grapes of Wrath*.

John (Uncle John) Joad. Brother of Tom Joad I and uncle of Tom Joad II; helps the Joad family move west in John Steinbeck's *The Grapes of Wrath*.

Ma Joad. Mother of Tom II, Noah, Rose of Sharon, and Al Joad, among others; rejoices at Tom's release from prison, but worries about his involvement in rebellious activities at the California work farm in John Steinbeck's *The Grapes of Wrath*.

Noah Joad. Brother of Tom Joad II; moves west with the family in John Steinbeck's *The Grapes of Wrath*.

Rose of Sharon Joad. See Rose of Sharon Joad Rivers.

Tom (Pa) Joad (I). Father of Tom Joad II; leads his family west to look for work and a new start in life in John Steinbeck's *The Grapes of Wrath*.

Tom (Tommy) Joad (II). Young man who questions the injustices of Depression-era America while journeying west with his family in John Steinbeck's *The Grapes of Wrath*.

Jo-Ann. Daughter of Monica Winthrop and, it is later revealed, Jonas Cord, Jr., in Harold Robbins's *The Carpetbaggers*.

Joanna. Member of the Indians and lover of Corey; captured and brainwashed to embrace Freudian femininity in Marge Piercy's *Dance the Eagle to Sleep*.

Joaquín. Member of El Sordo's partisan group in Ernest Hemingway's *For Whom the Bell Tolls*.

Joby. Sartoris slave and father of Loosh in William Faulkner's *Sartoris (Flags in the Dust)* and *The Unvanquished*.

Dame Jocelyn. Aged storyteller with whom George Washington possibly once flirted in Thomas Bailey Aldrich's *The Story of a Bad Boy*.

Jochebed. Wife of Amram and Hebrew mother of Aaron, Miriam, and a third child who may be Moses in Zora Neale Hurston's *Moses, Man of the Mountain*.

Jody. Con man and homosexual lover of Zeke Farragut; makes a dramatic escape from Falconer prison in John Cheever's *Falconer*.

Joe. Highway patrolman and boyfriend of Junell Mack in Harry Crews's *Car*.

Joe. Illegitimate son of Molly Taylor White and Johnny McCloud and halfbrother of Jimmy; killed in World War I in Larry McMurtry's *Leaving Cheyenne*.

Joe. Killer of Kai-a in Edwin Corle's *Fig Tree John*.

Sergeant Joe (Jo-Jo). American soldier who contracts syphilis in Naples in John Horne Burns's *The Gallery*.

Uncle Joe. See Uncle Joe Morgan.

Johann. Nurse who despises his dying uncle, Wilibald Graf, in Katherine Anne Porter's *Ship of Fools*.

Johansen. Cruel mate on the *Ghost* in Jack London's *The Sea-Wolf*.

Nikoline Johansen. Intellectual Norwegian friend of Peder Holm (Hansa); abandons America for Norway in O. E. Rölvaag's *Their Father's God*.

John. Clairvoyant film critic and contributor to Renate's planned magazine in Anaïs Nin's *Collages*.

John. Dark-skinned black man who helps Emma Lou Morgan find a place to live and pay her rent; she refuses to continue their relationship because she feels his skin is too dark in Wallace Thurman's *The Blacker the Berry*.

John. Fantasy lover of Margaret Reynolds; leader of PROWL, a secret subversive organization whose plan is to blow up the George Washington Bridge to isolate Manhattan for black solidarity, in Anne Richardson Roiphe's *Up the Sandbox!*

John. Grounded British aviator in World War I who restlessly rides a bicycle around New York City; one of Sabina's lovers in Anaïs Nin's *A Spy in the House of Love*.

John. Lover of Patricia and finder of the Logan brothers' bowling trophies, which he keeps in the apartment he shares with Patricia beneath the apartment of Constance Marlow and Bob, in Richard Brautigan's *Willard and His Bowling Trophies*.

John. Sailor aboard the *Neversink* who precipitates the fighting that leads to the fighters' flogging in Herman Melville's *White-Jacket*.

John (Harry, Harry Hotspur, Northumberland, Parsifal, Percival, Prince Hal, Pussy). Priest-physician whose virtual silence enables his long-time friend Lancelot Lamar to confess; narrator of Walker Percy's *Lancelot*.

John (Jonah). Fiancé of Mona Aamons Monzano and narrator of Kurt Vonnegut's *Cat's Cradle*.

Lady John. Noblewoman who is having an affair with Gilbert Long in Henry James's *The Sacred Fount*.

Johnny. Narrator who goes to find the wild boys in William S. Burroughs's *The Wild Boys*; also appears in *Exterminator!*

Johnny. Young man sodomized in William S. Burroughs's *Naked Lunch*, *Nova Express*, *The Soft Machine*, and *The Ticket That Exploded*.

Howard Johns. Gynecologist who "examines" Candy Christian in the men's room of a bar in Terry Southern and Mason Hoffenberg's *Candy*.

Johnson. British doctor on Tahiti in Herman Melville's *Omoo*.

Johnson. Brutal, abusive father of Maggie and Jimmie Johnson in Stephen Crane's *Maggie*.

Johnson. Servile black man who betrays other blacks as they attempt to become independent of the Cresswells; lynched by a mob led by Sheriff Colton in W. E. B. Du Bois's *The Quest of the Silver Fleece*.

Johnson (Yonson). Crewman on the *Ghost* who drowns while attempting to escape the brutality on ship in Jack London's *The Sea-Wolf*.

Agnes Johnson. See Agnes Johnson Trent.

Albert (Al) Johnson. Overweight friend of Jake Jackson and fellow postal worker in Richard Wright's *Lawd Today*.

Amos (Brick) Johnson. Star pitcher with the Brooklyn Royal Dodgers and teammate of Mason Tidewater, of whom Johnson is jealous, in Jay Neugeboren's *Sam's Legacy*.

Barmy Johnson. Cellmate of Roy Earle; dies after having taught Earle how to deal with the loneliness of prison life in William Riley Burnett's *High Sierra*.

Bub Johnson. Eight-year-old son of Lutie Johnson in Ann Petry's *The Street*.

Canaan Johnson. Teacher at and business manager of the Light of the World Holiness Church; deserts Savata in William Goyen's *The Fair Sister*.

Clara Johnson. Twenty-six-year-old daughter of Margaret Johnson and her mother's traveling companion on a lengthy holiday in Italy, where Fabrizio Naccarelli falls hopelessly in love with her; has the mental acumen of a ten year old because of a childhood accident in Elizabeth Spencer's *The Light in the Piazza*.

Earl Johnson. Poolroom companion of Cody Pomeray in Denver in Jack Kerouac's *Visions of Cody*.

Gertrude (Mrs. Sidney Bacon) Johnson. Southern novelist and would-be satirist; teaches writing for a semester at Benton College in Randall Jarrell's *Pictures from an Institution*.

Gwendolyn Johnson. Young friend of Emma Lou Morgan; marries Benson Brown in Wallace Thurman's *The Blacker the Berry*.

Helen Johnson. Wyoming native; wife of Earl Johnson in Jack Kerouac's *Visions of Cody*.

Jeremy Johnson, Sr. Owner of fighting dogs who sells a dog to Edward Pierce in Michael Crichton's *The Great Train Robbery*.

Jim Johnson. Estranged husband of Lutie Johnson in Ann Petry's *The Street*.

Jimmie Johnson. Brother of Maggie Johnson; a tough youth who is similar to his brutal father in Stephen Crane's *Maggie*.

Lionel Boyd (Bokonon) Johnson. Guru, philosopher, priest, and author in Kurt Vonnegut's *Cat's Cradle*.

Lutie Johnson. Determined young woman who hopes that hard work and sacrifice will enable her to leave Harlem and improve life for her young son, Bub Johnson; heroine of Ann Petry's *The Street*.

Lyin' B. Johnson. United States president before Trick E. Dixon in Philip Roth's *Our Gang*.

Maggie (Mag) Johnson. New Yorker who "blossomed in a mud-puddle"; works in a sweatshop, and is seduced and deserted by Pete; becomes a prostitute and commits suicide in Stephen Crane's *Maggie*; appears in *George's Mother*.

Margaret Johnson. Middle-aged American traveling abroad with her retarded daughter, with whom a young Italian falls in love, in Elizabeth Spencer's *The Light in the Piazza*.

Mary Johnson. Angry, violent mother of Maggie and Jimmie Johnson; rejects her daughter when Maggie tries to return home in Stephen Crane's *Maggie*.

Mary (Duchess of Uganda) Johnson. Satirical character and follower of Marcus Garvey in Countee Cullen's *One Way to Heaven*.

Mattie Johnson. Deeply religious maid of Constancia Brandon and innocent heroine duped into trusting and marrying Sam Lucas in Countee Cullen's *One Way to Heaven*.

Mr. Johnson. Man who charters Harry Morgan's boat for fishing, but does not pay for it, in Ernest Hemingway's *To Have and Have Not*.

Mrs. Johnson. Resident of the Diamond County Home for the Aged; tends the candy stand at the annual fair in John Updike's *The Poorhouse Fair*.

Noel Johnson. Cigarette industry executive who remains helplessly in the United States when his wife informs him from Italy that their retarded adult daughter is in love with a young Italian, and he with her, in Elizabeth Spencer's *The Light in the Piazza*.

Norman Johnson. Income tax official who pursues Honora Wapshot from St. Botolph's to Rome in John Cheever's *The Wapshot Scandal*.

Oscar Johnson. Black army sergeant in Vietnam who plans most of the military operations in Tim O'Brien's *Going after Cacciato*.

Paul Johnson. Southern mulatto whose attraction to a white fellow student, Bona Hale, emphasizes his ambivalence about racial identity in Jean Toomer's *Cane*.

Sister Sarah Johnson. Friend of Aunt Hager Williams; claims white oppression made her leave home in Langston Hughes's *Not Without Laughter*.

Wade Johnson. Teacher who lives in a Second Avenue apartment managed by Norman Moonbloom in Edward Lewis Wallant's *The Tenants of Moonbloom*.

Walter Johnson. Cousin of Ralph Hartsook; studies medicine with Dr. Henry Small, but becomes a member of Small's band of robbers, in Edward Eggleston's *The Hoosier School-Master*.

Sir William Johnson. British administrator in North America and enemy of Major Robert Rogers in Kenneth Roberts's *Northwest Passage*.

Sir William Johnson. British commander in James Kirke Paulding's *The Dutchman's Fireside*.

Willie-Mae Johnson. Granddaughter of Sarah Johnson and playmate of Sandy Rodgers in Langston Hughes's *Not Without Laughter*.

Malcolm Johnsprang. Realtor, suitor of Lee Mercury, chauvinistic New Englander from the Deep South, and "an interesting bore, an intelligent ass" in Peter De Vries's *Through the Fields of Clover*.

Joseph Eggleston Johnston. Commander of the Confederate troops in the West when Vicksburg is lost; quarrels with and reprimanded by Jefferson Davis; asked to halt Sherman's march in Mary Johnston's *Cease Firing*; mentioned in *The Long Roll*.

Jo-Jo. Actor, first husband of Ellen Thatcher in John Dos Passos's *Manhattan Transfer*.

Jolene. Small-town beauty who entangles George Levanter in her divorce proceedings in Jerzy Kosinski's *Blind Date*.

Jonah. See John.

Jonathan. Second husband of Kate and stepfather of Francesca Fox Bolt in Gail Godwin's *Glass People*.

Jones. Envious preacher who attempts to undermine Zora's efforts to help his congregation free themselves from their sharecropping status in W. E. B. Du Bois's *The Quest of the Silver Fleece*.

Jones. New Yorker who befriends Redburn in Herman Melville's *Redburn*.

Adelaide (Addy) Jones. Daughter of Railroad Jones and lover of Abner Teeftallow; leaves Lane County, Tennessee, to join her missionary lover in India in T. S. Stribling's *Teeftallow*.

Alice Jones. Gardener's daughter who plays often with Carolyn Bridge; because of her race, she is snubbed by the Bridge family in Evan Connell's *Mrs. Bridge* and *Mr. Bridge*.

Alpha Jones. See Alpha Jones Neumiller.

Anna Jones. Widowed mulatto and mother of Garvin Jones in Hamilton Basso's *The View from Pompey's Head*.

Barney Jones. Lazy, loud-mouthed young black man from the Piney Woods of Texas; famous for his lies in Arna Wendell Bontemps's *God Sends Sunday*.

Charley (Charlie) Jones. Jovial drinker who guides George Kelcey's descent into alcohol in Stephen Crane's *George's Mother*.

Conrad Jones. Son of Ed and Electra Jones; killed in a car-train accident in Larry Woiwode's *Beyond the Bedroom Wall*.

David (Railroad) Jones. Crafty and unscrupulous entrepreneur who promotes the construction of a railroad through Lane County, Tennessee; murdered by James Sandage in T. S. Stribling's *Teeftallow*.

Easley Jones. See Samuel Crouch.

Edward (Ed) Jones. Crusty, baseball-obsessed husband of Electra Jones and father of Alpha Jones Neumiller and four sons in Larry Woiwode's *Beyond the Bedroom Wall*.

Electra Jones. Wife of Ed Jones and mother of Alpha Jones Neumiller and four sons in Larry Woiwode's *Beyond the Bedroom Wall*.

Elling Jones. Son of Ed and Electra Jones; killed in a car-train accident in Larry Woiwode's *Beyond the Bedroom Wall*.

Emma Lee Lessenbery Jones. Wife of Lord Byron Jones and lover of the white police officer Willie Joe Worth, by whom she bears a son, in Jesse Hill Ford's *The Liberation of Lord Byron Jones*.

Eric Jones. Disenfranchised "rich kid" from Alabama who becomes an international actor; lover and patron of Yves and lover of Cass Silenski in James Baldwin's *Another Country*.

Garwood B. Jones. Former schoolmate of John Wickliff Shawnessy; opportunistic United States senator in Ross Lockridge, Jr.'s *Raintree County*.

George Gordon Lord Byron (L. B.) Jones. Black undertaker in Somerton who seeks a divorce from Emma Jones; brutally murdered and his body mutilated by Willie Joe Worth in Jesse Hill Ford's *The Liberation of Lord Byron Jones*; also appears in *Mountains of Gilead*.

Hilary Jones. Married man with a daughter; almost runs away with Diana Bell before Theophilus North intervenes in Thornton Wilder's *Theophilus North*.

Januarius Jones. Obese sensualist in William Faulkner's *Soldiers' Pay*.

Jefferson Jones. Ohio State University wrestler who defeats Severin Winter for sixth place in the national championship; becomes the wrestling coach at a Cleveland high school in John Irving's *The 158-Pound Marriage*.

Jerome Jones. Son of Ed and Electra Jones; victim of a childhood drowning accident in Larry Woiwode's *Beyond the Bedroom Wall*.

Brother John Jones. Self-centered president of the Universal Mutual Insurance Company, at whose home Matthew Towns learns the identity of the woman who snubs him, in W. E. B. Du Bois's *Dark Princess*.

John Paul Jones. Captain of the *Ranger*, *Bon Homme Richard*, and *Ariel*; who befriends Israel Potter in Herman Melville's *Israel Potter*.

John Paul Jones. Captain of the *Bonhomme Richard*, during whose victory over the *Serapis* Johnny Fraser is wounded, in James Boyd's *Drums*.

Joshua (Shine) Jones. Ambitious moving van driver who falls in love with Linda Young in Rudolph Fisher's *The Walls of Jericho*.

Karl N. Jones. Intended murder victim of Jasper Ammen in Conrad Aiken's *King Coffin*.

Lamont Cranston Jones. Black homosexual and writer driven to suicide by Joe Market in Hal Bennett's *Lord of Dark Places*.

Lamont Quincy (L. Q.) Jones. Marine radio operator killed at Saipan in Leon Uris's *Battle Cry*.

Lionell Jones. Son of Ed and Electra Jones in Larry Woiwode's *Beyond the Bedroom Wall*.

Lou Jones. Cynical assistant and boy-of-all-work to Justin Miller; loses his job when he photographs Miller's failed attempt to seduce Marcella Bruno in Robert Coover's *The Origin of the Brunists*.

Love Jones. Provocative black woman over whom Willie Copeland fights Junebug in Carson McCullers's *The Heart Is a Lonely Hunter*.

Marjorie Jones. Object of Penrod Schofield's affections in Booth Tarkington's *Penrod*, *Penrod and Sam*, and *Penrod Jashber*.

Marvin Cora Jones. Barbed-wire drummer who shares a stagecoach with Greer, Cameron, and Magic Child in Richard Brautigan's *The Hawkline Monster*.

Milly Jones. Mother, by Thomas Sutpen, of a daughter; her grandfather, Wash Jones, kills her, Sutpen, and the baby in William Faulkner's *Absalom, Absalom!*

Mitchell (Mitchy-Mitch) Jones. Brother of Marjorie Jones; frequently interrupts Penrod Schofield's attempts to gain Marjorie's attention in Booth Tarkington's *Penrod*.

Nevada Jones. Showgirl, ex-prostitute, who marries Congo in John Dos Passos's *Manhattan Transfer*.

Nigra Jones. Black man accused of murdering Ossie Little and defended by Johnny Clane; lover of Joy Little and father of Sherman Pew in Carson McCullers's *Clock Without Hands*.

Olin Jones. Harelipped northern drifter and consummate panhandler who passes on his skill to Cass McKay in Nelson Algren's *Somebody in Boots*.

Lieutenant Oliver Cromwell Jones. See Rau-Ru.

Captain Osborn Jones. Retired oyster dredger and a resident of the Dorset Hotel in John Barth's *The Floating Opera*.

Peter (Pete) Jones. Corrupt county commissioner and father of seven schoolchildren in Edward Eggleston's *The Hoosier School-Master*.

Richard (Dickon) Jones. Templeton architect and sheriff who imprisons Natty Bumppo for hunting out of season in James Fenimore Cooper's *The Pioneers*.

Sally Elizabeth Jones. See Bonanza Jellybean.

Sherman Jones. See Sherman Pew.

Simolean (Sim) Jones. Friend of Steven Grendon in August Derleth's *The Shield of the Valiant*; also appears in *Evening in Spring*.

Theophilus Jones. Abolitionist preacher beaten by a mob during a meeting at Flat Rock; blames Nathaniel Hyman for directing the mob to the meeting, but provides protection and patronage for Jesse Hyman, in Albion W. Tourgee's *A Fool's Errand*.

Wash Jones. Grandfather of Milly Jones; kills her, her baby, and the baby's father, Thomas Sutpen, in William Faulkner's *Absalom, Absalom!*

William (Super) Jones. Mentally unbalanced superintendent of the apartment building where Lutie Johnson lives; gets Bub Johnson in trouble with the law after Lutie rejects Jones's advances in Ann Petry's *The Street*.

Wissey Jones. Executive of the United Lymphomilloid Company and "Child Buyer" who comes to the town of Pequot to "purchase a specimen" for his company's experimental research in John Hersey's *The Child Buyer*.

Rebecca Carrington (Dee-Dee, Mrs. David McInnis) Jones-Talbot. Aunt of J. Lawford Carrington; leaves her English husband for an Italian lover and eventually returns to Nashville society in Robert Penn Warren's *A Place to Come To*.

Major Victor Joppolo. Allied Occupation officer in Adano who seeks advice from townspeople, shows them respect, and secures the town a bell in John Hersey's *A Bell for Adano*.

Jordan. English printer who encourages Thomas Paine and who is jailed for publishing Paine's *The Rights of Man* in Howard Fast's *Citizen Tom Paine*.

Amos Jordan. See Amos Winthrop.

Daniel (Dan, Smoke) Jordan. Black drummer who meets Rick Martin in a bowling alley; member of Jeff Williams's band in Dorothy Baker's *Young Man with a Horn*.

Rachel Jordan. See Rachel Jordan Beaumont.

Robert (Inglés, Roberto) Jordan. American volunteer with the Spanish Republican Army whose mission is to blow up a bridge in Ernest Hemingway's *For Whom the Bell Tolls*.

Zeke (Zeki-O) Jordan. Friend of Fish Tucker; enlists in the army and is sent to France in Richard Wright's *The Long Dream*.

Christian Jorgensen (Sidney Kelterman). Conniving second husband of Mimi Jorgensen in Dashiell Hammett's *The Thin Man*.

Mimi Jorgensen. Money-hungry former wife of Clyde Wynant in Dashiell Hammett's *The Thin Man*.

Jose. Friend of George Cain; disillusioned when Cain does not become a successful role model for youngsters in the community in George Cain's *Blueschild Baby*.

Jose. Mexican worker who befriends Johnny Mack and sells him a Ford car in Edwin Corle's *Fig Tree John*.

Joseph. Volatile, interpretive intellectual and fumbler with his own freedom; dangler and diarist-narrator of Saul Bellow's *Dangling Man*.

Chief Joseph. Brilliant military strategist and leader of the Nez Perce Indians in Jim Harrison's *A Good Day to Die*.

Moredecai (Reb Mordecai) Joseph. Cabalist and one-time foe of Rabbi Benish Ashkenazi; beguiled but ultimately disillusioned by the messianic claims of Sabbatai Zevi; exorcises the demon from Rechele Babad's body in Isaac Bashevis Singer's *Satan in Goray*.

Joshua. Confidant and "adopted son" of Moses and leader of the Israelite army in Zora Neale Hurston's *Moses, Man of the Mountain*.

Sister Josie. Young black nun with gold teeth; attends Catalina Kate on the wandering island in John Hawkes's *Second Skin*.

Amy Moncrieff Joubert. Wealthy heiress and JR's teacher; has a brief affair with Jack Gibbs in William Gaddis's *JR*.

Mme. Joubert. Kindly but sad Frenchwoman in whose home Claude Wheeler and David Gerhardt stay when they are not fighting on the front in Willa Cather's *One of Ours*.

Jourdonnais. French sidekick of Boone Caudill and Dick Summers; killed in an Indian raid in A. B. Guthrie's *The Big Sky*.

Joy. Elderly lame labor organizer who is killed during the strike in John Steinbeck's *In Dubious Battle*.

Joy. Hippie; girlfriend of Stanley and traveling companion of Floyd Warner and Kermit Oelsligle in Wright Morris's *Fire Sermon*.

Mary Joy. See Naomi Sandifer.

Edward Joyner. Only son of Robert Joyner in Thomas Wolfe's *The Hills Beyond*.

Emily Drumgoole Joyner. Wife of Theodore Joyner and mother of Gustavus Adolphus Joyner in Thomas Wolfe's *The Hills Beyond*.

Gustavus Adolphus (Dolph, Silk) Joyner. Younger son of Theodore and Emily Joyner; becomes a lawyer and goes West in Thomas Wolfe's *The Hills Beyond*.

Mag Joyner. Hypochondriac who exploits and dominates her husband, Mark Joyner, and is disliked by her nephew George Webber in Thomas Wolfe's *You Can't Go Home Again* and *The Web and the Rock*.

Mark Joyner. Maternal uncle of George Webber in Thomas Wolfe's *You Can't Go Home Again* and *The Web and the Rock*.

Maw Joyner. Spinster aunt who rears George Webber after the death of his long-suffering mother in Thomas Wolfe's *You Can't Go Home Again* and *The Web and the Rock*.

Robert Joyner. Brother of Zachariah Joyner; lawyer with a reputation for honesty in Thomas Wolfe's *The Hills Beyond*.

Theodore Joyner. Youngest son of William Joyner; founds the first school of higher learning in Libya Hill and later becomes a Confederate colonel in the Civil War in Thomas Wolfe's *The Hills Beyond*.

William (Bear) Joyner. Founder of the Joyner clan, father of Zachariah Joyner, and ancestor of George Webber in Thomas Wolfe's *The Hills Beyond*.

Zachariah (Zack) Joyner. Son of William Joyner; governor of the state of Catawba and later a United States senator in Thomas Wolfe's *The Hills Beyond*.

JP. Eastern European fencing champion imprisoned and tortured for refusing to become a spy; avenged by his friend George Levanter in Jerzy Kosinski's *Blind Date*.

Juan Tomás. Brother of Kino; hides his brother and Kino's family after their home is burned and after Kino kills a thief in John Steinbeck's *The Pearl*.

Juana. Slave of Lafitte; tends to Constanza Velasquez in Joseph Holt Ingraham's *Lafitte*.

Juana. Wife of Kino; attempts to persuade her husband to return the pearl to the sea, once she sees that the pearl will bring them grief and danger, in John Steinbeck's *The Pearl*.

Juanita. First girlfriend of Scarecrow; moves from Chattanooga, Tennessee, to New York, where she becomes a heroin addict and dies of an overdose, in Calvin Hernton's *Scarecrow*.

Juba. Teenaged paramour and confidante of Gabriel Prosser in Arna Wendell Bontemps's *Black Thunder*.

Jude. Husband of Nel Wright in Toni Morrison's *Sula*.

Tanis Judique. Attractive widow who rents an apartment from George Babbitt and becomes his mistress in Sinclair Lewis's *Babbitt*.

Judith. Depraved young woman who joins Big Red Smalley's traveling gospel show in George Garrett's *Do, Lord, Remember Me*.

Judith. Maid of Clara Wieland; Carwin uses her to familiarize himself with Clara's habits in Charles Brockden Brown's *Wieland*.

Fred (Old Man) Judkins. Old-timer, folk philosopher, and diner habitué in John Gardner's *Nickel Mountain*.

James (Fatso) Judson. Sadistic chief guard at the Schofield Barracks Post Stockade who persecutes Angelo Maggio and oversees the fatal beating of Blues Berry; killed by Robert E. Lee Prewitt to avenge Berry's death in James Jones's *From Here to Eternity*.

Mrs. Judson. Housekeeper who helps Marmaduke Ruggles with his new restaurant and eventually marries him in Harry Leon Wilson's *Ruggles of Red Gap*.

Jug. Newspaper photographer in William Faulkner's *Pylon*.

Jule (Big Jule). Renegade lover of Ollie and father out of wedlock of their son, Jule Jackson, in George Wylie Henderson's *Ollie Miss* and *Jule*.

Julia. Pregnant psychology professor, partner of Angel Stone, and lover of Kat Alcazar; helps Kat unravel the secret of Angel in M. F. Beal's *Angel Dance*.

Julia. Secretary of Walter Bridge in Evan Connell's *Mrs. Bridge* and *Mr. Bridge*.

Cousin Julia. Sophisticated British writer and relative of the narrator of Aline Bernstein's *The Journey Down*.

Lady Julia. Deceased mother of Mrs. Brookenham and friend of Mr. Longdon in Henry James's *The Awkward Age*.

Julie. Motherless daughter of The Dead Father in Donald Barthelme's *The Dead Father*.

Eliza Bowen Jumel. Second wife of Aaron Burr; divorces him in Gore Vidal's *Burr*.

June (June Evans). Benzedrine addict accidentally shot and killed by her husband, Bull Hubbard, in Jack Kerouac's *Visions of Cody*; also appears in *Book of Dreams* and *Desolation Angels*.

Junebug. Rival wounded by Willie Copeland in a knife fight over Love Jones in Carson McCullers's *The Heart Is a Lonely Hunter*.

Heinrich Jung. Nazi friend of Lanny Budd in Upton Sinclair's *Dragon's Teeth*.

Brother Juniper. Red-haired Franciscan monk who witnesses the fall of the bridge and decides to document the lives of those who died; as a result of his research, he and his book are burned in Thornton Wilder's *The Bridge of San Luis Rey*.

Mr. (Old Man Junto) Junto. White owner of bars, whorehouses, and dance halls in Harlem; lusts after Lutie Johnson and inadvertently helps destroy her life in Ann Petry's *The Street*.

Jurgen. Middle-aged pawnbroker and failed poet who through flattery regains his youth for one year in James Branch Cabell's *Jurgen*.

Jutta. Younger sister of Stella Snow and mistress of Zizendorf; mother of the child cannibalized in John Hawkes's *The Cannibal*.

Céleste Juvet. Pretty fifteen-year-old daughter of Hugo Juvet and granddaughter of Mme. Jacques Juvet; eventually wins the heart of Diron Desautels in Arna Wendell Bontemps's *Drums at Dusk*.

Hugo Juvet. Drunken, nomadic son of Mme. Juvet and natural father of Céleste Juvet in Arna Wendell Bontemps's *Drums at Dusk*.

Mme. Jacques Juvet. Ugly former house servant at Bréda; matron in her fifties thought by the plantation's slaves to be a witch in Arna Wendell Bontemps's *Drums at Dusk*.

K

Ralph Kabnis. Northern black professor and poet who goes south to educate underprivileged blacks; his fear of racial violence renders him ineffective as an educator in Jean Toomer's *Cane*.

Peter Kaden. German immigrant and farmer; driven to suicide by Augustus M. Barr in Oscar Micheaux's *The Homesteader*.

Nathan Kadish. Childhood friend of Sonia Marburg, later loved by Marburg for the deformity caused by a large birthmark on his face; leaves Boston to study in Paris in Jean Stafford's *Boston Adventure*.

Kadongolimi. Obese first wife of Colonel Ellelloû; marries him when he is an unproven boy and tries to preserve the African ways of their youth in John Updike's *The Coup*.

Edwin L. Kaffrath. Director of the Chicago natural gas company in Theodore Dreiser's *The Titan*.

Harry Kagan. Self-styled political leader of students at Calvin Coolidge High School; accomplished "apple polisher" in Bel Kaufman's *Up the Down Staircase*.

Andy Kagle. Head of the sales department, rival of Jack Green, and friend and colleague of Bob Slocum until Slocum supplants him and has him pensioned off in Joseph Heller's *Something Happened*.

Samuel Abel (Sammy) Kahan. Jewish orderly at Sacred Heart Hospital who sells drugs to patients; dies in a freak accident on the hospital steps in Edward Lewis Wallant's *The Children at the Gate*.

Kitty Kahl. Marine corporal and former lightweight boxer; killed in France during World War I in Thomas Boyd's *Through the Wheat*.

Paul (Paula) Kahler. Transsexual and psychotic killer; understood by Dr. Leopold Lehmann as a symbol of the possibilities of transformation in Wright Morris's *The Field of Vision*.

Jacob Kahn. Nonreligious Jewish sculptor who becomes Asher Lev's art teacher and mentor in Chaim Potok's *My Name Is Asher Lev*.

Tanya Kahn. Russian wife of Jacob Kahn; encourages her husband's artistic endeavors in Chaim Potok's *My Name Is Asher Lev*.

Kai-a (Bi-Tli-Kai, Nalin, White Deer's Daughter). Apache Indian wife of Agocho and mother of Johnny Mack; murdered, raped, and burned by Joe in Edwin Corle's *Fig Tree John*.

John Kaimon. Drifter who joins Belt's dojo; leaves with Gaye Nell Odell at the end of Harry Crews's *Karate Is a Thing of the Spirit*.

Kaisa. Garrulous aspiring actress; roommate of Hellos aboard the *Castel Felice* in Calvin Hernton's *Scarecrow*.

Don (Doc) Kaiser. Psychiatrist and flight surgeon for the 918th Bomb Group in Beirne Lay, Jr., and Sy Bartlett's *Twelve O'Clock High!*

Albert Kalandyk. See Alberto Mogadiscio.

General Johann De Kalb. German commander of the Continental Regulars under Horatio Gates at the Battle of Camden in William Gilmore Simms's *The Partisan*.

Rav Jacob Kalman. Holocaust survivor and Talmudic scholar who almost refuses to ordain Reuven Malter in Chaim Potok's *The Promise*.

Kamikazee. See Heritage Wright.

Kid Kamm. Contestant in the dance marathon; partnered with Jackie Miller after his original partner Mattie Barnes collapses in Horace McCoy's *They Shoot Horses, Don't They?*

Irving Kanarek. Los Angeles defense attorney; second defender of Jimmy Smith in Joseph Wambaugh's *The Onion Field*.

Archibald Kane. Wealthy manufacturer and father of Lester Kane; stipulates in his will that Lester must either marry or leave Jennie Gerhardt in order to receive his inheritance in Theodore Dreiser's *Jennie Gerhardt*.

Lester Kane. Son of Archibald Kane; loves Jennie Gerhardt, but leaves her in order to inherit his father's money; marries Letty Pace Gerald, but cannot love her as he loves Gerhardt in Theodore Dreiser's *Jennie Gerhardt*.

Letty Pace Gerald Kane. See Letty Pace Gerald.

Robert Kane. Older brother of Lester Kane, whose relationship with Jennie Gerhardt Robert opposes in Theodore Dreiser's *Jennie Gerhardt*.

Willard Kane. New York painter and lover of Etta Barnes in Theodore Dreiser's *The Bulwark*.

Sulo Kangas. Jailer in Robert Traver's *Anatomy of a Murder*.

Morton L. (Morty) Kanovitz. Production manager of Boris Adrian's pornographic movie in Terry Southern's *Blue Movie*.

Sol (Uncle Sol) Kantor. Friend of Charlie Sapistein; travels the country visiting friends he knew at the Maimonides Home for Jewish Boys in Jay Neugeboren's *An Orphan's Tale*.

Dominie Kanttwell. Village clergyman in James Kirke Paulding's *Koningsmarke*.

Jerry Kaplan. Grandson of Judith Finkel; spends a summer exploring race, sexuality, and friendship with David Hunter in Hal Bennett's *The Black Wine*.

Stanislas Kapp. Heir to a brewery; quarrels with Valentin de Bellegarde about Noémie Nioche in Henry James's *The American*.

Rabo Karabekian. Minimalist painter in Kurt Vonnegut's *Breakfast of Champions*.

Karakoee. Former shipmate of Tommo; helps Tommo escape from the Typees in Herman Melville's *Typee*.

Karen. Wealthy ex-wife of Gifford in Nicholas Delbanco's *News*.

Karintha. Beautiful black woman warped by a premature sexual experience in Jean Toomer's *Cane*.

Karkov. Russian journalist who is a friend of Robert Jordan in Ernest Hemingway's *For Whom the Bell Tolls*.

Karky. Typean tattoo artist in Herman Melville's *Typee*.

Karloff. Huge one-hundred-four-year-old Russian immigrant who dies in a Thirteenth Street apartment managed by Norman Moonbloom in Edward Lewis Wallant's *The Tenants of Moonbloom*.

Igor Karlovy. Russian colonel and chief of engineers in post–World War II Berlin; friend of Sean O'Sullivan and lover of Lotte Böhm in Leon Uris's *Armageddon*.

Karmin. "Soul at the seventh aspect" of Carl Dean Palmers in Robert Coover's *The Origin of the Brunists*.

Julius Karp. Proprietor of a wine and liquor store near Morris Bober's grocery store in Bernard Malamud's *The Assistant*.

Louis Karp. Son of Julius Karp and would-be suitor of Helen Bober in Bernard Malamud's *The Assistant*.

Damien Karras. Jesuit priest, psychiatrist, and counselor who is forced to confront his faith in God in the presence of the demonic possession of Regan MacNeil in William Peter Blatty's *The Exorcist*.

Marina (Rina) Karsh. Activist on the run after an explosion; escapes the country with the aid of her father in M. F. Beal's *Amazon One*.

Max Kasavubu. Professor and agent for the Louisiana Red Corporation who believes that Richard Wright's Bigger Thomas was not executed but was smuggled out of prison; dreams that he is Mary, about to be raped by Thomas, and then sees himself as Thomas and kills Nanny Lisa, his Louisiana Red co-conspirator, in Ishmael Reed's *The Last Days of Louisiana Red*.

Fitz John Kasch. Reclusive writer and academic who becomes obsessed with an impoverished rural family, the Bartletts, especially teenaged Laney Bartlett, in Joyce Carol Oates's *Childwold*.

Kate (Catalina Kate). Young black woman who gives birth to a child by Skipper on the Night of All Saints in John Hawkes's *Second Skin*.

Kate (Katie). Mother of Francesca Fox Bolt; lives in the mountains with Ware Smith and bears their child in Gail Godwin's *Glass People*.

Kate-Careless. Lover of Wendell Ryder and mother of three in Djuna Barnes's *Ryder*.

Katherine. Lover of Harry Miller; breaks off their relationship after her ex-husband beats him up in Frederick Busch's *Domestic Particulars*.

Katie. High-class prostitute who wants to marry Bruce Pearson for his insurance money in Mark Harris's *Bang the Drum Slowly*.

Katje. See Katje Borgesius.

Aunt Katy. Slave housekeeper of Canema plantation; owned by Nina Gordon in Harriet Beecher Stowe's *Dred*.

Katya. See Katya Cronstadt.

Katz. Crooked lawyer who defends Frank Chambers; cheats Chambers and gets the insurance money and Nick Papadakis's restaurant in James M. Cain's *The Postman Always Rings Twice*.

Stanley Katz. Trumpet player who lives with Jer Sidone in the Seventieth Street building managed by Norman Moonbloom; attempts suicide in Edward Lewis Wallant's *The Tenants of Moonbloom*.

Julius Kauffman. Brother of Eva Wiseman; attends the yacht party in William Faulkner's *Mosquitoes*.

Kauka. Manukuran who survives the hurricane in Charles Nordhoff and James Norman Hall's *The*

Hurricane.

Beulah Land.

Princess Kautilya (Dark Princess, Maharanee of Bwodpur). Young princess concerned for the uniting of the colored races of the world against racism; marries Matthew Towns and bears their child, the future Maharajah of Bwodpur, in W. E. B. Du Bois's *Dark Princess.*

Arthur Kavanagh. Minister who marries Cecilia Vaughan in Henry Wadsworth Longfellow's *Kavanagh.*

Kay-Kay. See Kay Campbell.

Julia Kaye. Strong-willed Englishwoman seeking power through marriage to an influential man, such as John Gwynne, in Gertrude Atherton's *Ancestors.*

Kaysinata. Shawnee Indian who serves as Salathiel Albine's adoptive father in Hervey Allen's *The Forest and the Fort.*

Kazak. Time-traveling dog of Winston Niles Rumfoord in Kurt Vonnegut's *The Sirens of Titan*; Doberman guard dog in *Breakfast of Champions.*

Johnny Kazarakis. Talented athlete and track teammate of Jack Duluoz in Jack Kerouac's *Maggie Cassidy.*

Ardis Kármán. See Ardis Ross.

Elena Kármán. See Elena Ross Howe.

Doctor Kearsley. Physician who nurses Thomas Paine back to health when Paine first arrives in America in Howard Fast's *Citizen Tom Paine.*

Peter (Petey) Keating. Ambitious architect; compromises self-esteem and happiness for shallow accolades in Ayn Rand's *The Fountainhead.*

Tracy Keating. See Tracy Keating Morgan.

Mrs. Doris Keefe. Landlady of Theophilus North in Thornton Wilder's *Theophilus North.*

Roland Keefer. Son of a politician, military school graduate, and friend of Willie Keith in Herman Wouk's *The Caine Mutiny.*

Thomas (Tom) Keefer. Half brother of Roland Keefer; communications officer on the USS *Caine* who plants seeds of mutiny and becomes captain of the *Caine* in Herman Wouk's *The Caine Mutiny.*

Keekee. See Zeke.

Azariah Keel. Frontiersman who calls Johnny Lacey a Tuckahoe and a turncoat, nearly starting a fight with Solomon McKarkle, in Mary Lee Settle's *O*

Doctor Charlie Keene. Physician friend of Joseph Frowenfeld; loves Aurora Nancanou in George Washington Cable's *The Grandissimes.*

Rolfe Keepsake. Fascist son ignored by Rolfe Ruskin; killed in the Spanish civil war in William Herrick's *Hermanos!*

Kegerise. Brightest student of George Caldwell in John Updike's *The Centaur.*

Fred Kegerise. Former burgess of Andrews; brings his eight-year-old grandson to the fair in John Updike's *The Poorhouse Fair.*

Edwin (Ed, Eddy, Keggsy) Keggs. Former high-school algebra teacher who joins the navy and is assigned to a minesweeper-destroyer; friend of Willie Keith in Herman Wouk's *The Caine Mutiny.*

Compton J. Keith. Wealthy coal mine owner infatuated with Delia Poole; eventually marries Mercy Wellington in Janet Flanner's *The Cubical City.*

Ensign James L. (Jim) Keith. Green officer who tries to follow navy regulations until he gets drunk with some enlisted men; provides comic relief in Thomas Heggen's *Mister Roberts.*

Mrs. Keith. Mother of Willie Keith in Herman Wouk's *The Caine Mutiny.*

Willis Seward (Keither, Willie) Keith. Princeton graduate and former nightclub pianist who supports the mutiny and serves as the last captain of the USS *Caine* in Herman Wouk's *The Caine Mutiny.*

Kelcey (Serenus Vogel). Magazine writer who investigates the Fork River project; narrator of Wright Morris's *The Fork River Space Project.*

Alice Kelcey. Wife of Kelcey; runs off with O. P. Dahlberg to parts unknown in Wright Morris's *The Fork River Space Project.*

George (Georgie, Kel') Kelcey. Young slum resident who learns to drink, fight, and swear in front of his long-suffering mother in Stephen Crane's *George's Mother.*

John (Jack) Kelleher. Priest of the Order of St. Clement; exiled along with Father Urban to Duesterhaus, Minnesota, to help convert a sanitarium into a retreat house in J. F. Powers's *Morte D'Urban.*

Beata Kellerman-Ashley. Wife of John Ashley, by whom she has four children; moves to California long after her husband's death in Thornton Wilder's *The Eighth Day.*

Gerry Kells. Los Angeles gangster who tries to benefit financially from being caught in a power struggle in Paul Cain's *Fast One*.

Barney Oswald Kelly. Father of Deborah Kelly Rojack; multimillionaire who wishes to appear with Stephen Rojack at his daughter's funeral in Norman Mailer's *An American Dream*.

Bill Kelly. Oldest brother of Mick Kelly in Carson McCullers's *The Heart Is a Lonely Hunter*.

Brigid Dunn Kelly. Younger sister of Theresa Dunn; happily married and mother of three children in Judith Rossner's *Looking for Mr. Goodbar*.

Deborah Caughlin Mangaravidi Kelly. See Deborah Kelly Rojack.

Etta Kelly. Older sister of Mick Kelly; Etta's illness forces Mick to quit school and go to work in Carson McCullers's *The Heart Is a Lonely Hunter*.

Frank James (Jim, Geam) Kelly. Survival-wise black man who vainly counsels Marcus Payne; narrator of Ernest J. Gaines's *Of Love and Dust*.

George (Baby-Killer, Bubber) Kelly. Younger brother of Mick Kelly; accidentally shoots and wounds four-year-old Baby Wilson in Carson McCullers's *The Heart Is a Lonely Hunter*.

Hazel Kelly. Oldest sister of Mick Kelly in Carson McCullers's *The Heart Is a Lonely Hunter*.

Knute Kelly. Sharecropper who works on a fifty-fifty basis with Uncle Alex in George Wylie Henderson's *Ollie Miss*.

Mick Kelly. Adolescent girl trapped by her family's poverty; abandons her dreams of musical fame to drop out of school and take a job at Woolworth's in Carson McCullers's *The Heart Is a Lonely Hunter*.

Mike Kelly. Unemployed, unambitious lower class urban male, supported by his wife, in Hubert Selby, Jr.'s *Last Exit to Brooklyn*.

Ralph Kelly. Baby brother of Mick Kelly in Carson McCullers's *The Heart Is a Lonely Hunter*.

Wilbur Kelly. Disabled father of Mick Kelly and Mick's five brothers and sisters; tries to work as a watch repairman in Carson McCullers's *The Heart Is a Lonely Hunter*.

Adam Kelno. Former doctor at Jadwiga concentration camp, where he performed sterilization experiments on Jewish prisoners; knighted doctor in London; plaintiff in a libel suit against author Abe Cady in Leon Uris's *QB VII*.

Angela Brown Kelno. British nurse and wife of Adam Kelno in Leon Uris's *QB VII*.

Stephan Kelno. Architect son of Adam and Angela Kelno in Leon Uris's *QB VII*.

Bill Kelsey. Self-satisfied middle-aged hustler and dreamer fought over and controlled by female conjurers; submits to the will of Maria Beñes in Hal Bennett's *Seventh Heaven*.

Dessie Kelsey. Black midwife, laundress, and helpmate to the Meserves; wife of Joe Kelsey in Zora Neale Hurston's *Seraph on the Suwanee*.

Hiram (Hi) Kelsey. Young, handsome, and intense preacher whose faith is severely tried by the mountaineers he serves; dies under ironic circumstances in Mary Noailles Murfree's *The Prophet of the Great Smoky Mountains*.

Joe Kelsey. Black friend, confidant, and hired hand of Jim Meserve and blues-picking musician who teaches Kenny Meserve to play the guitar; husband of Dessie Kelsey in Zora Neale Hurston's *Seraph on the Suwanee*.

Rob't Kelsey. Kentucky wagon driver who drowns crossing the Snake River in Emerson Hough's *The Covered Wagon*.

Serena Kelsey. Mother of Bill Kelsey and practitioner of juju; defeated by the superior magic of Aunt Keziah in Hal Bennett's *Seventh Heaven*.

Zachary Kelsey. Schizophrenic father of Bill Kelsey in Hal Bennett's *Seventh Heaven*.

Georgia Kelterman. Wife of Christian Jorgensen (Sidney Kelterman), whom he failed to divorce before marrying Mimi Wynant Jorgensen, in Dashiell Hammett's *The Thin Man*.

Detroit (Pumpkin Kitty) Kemp. Friend of Tisha Dees in Arthenia J. Bates's *The Deity Nodded*.

Ken. Opium addict and early lover of Bruce in Anaïs Nin's *Collages*.

Bedford Kendal. Father of Eva Kendal in Reynolds Price's *The Surface of Earth*.

Charlotte Watson Kendal. Mother of Eva Kendal; commits suicide by drinking a glass of lye on hearing that Eva has had a child; leaves a letter blaming Eva for the suicide in Reynolds Price's *The Surface of Earth*.

Eva Kendal. Protagonist whose elopement with her Latin teacher sets events in motion in Reynolds Price's *The Surface of Earth*.

Kennerly Kendal. Brother of Eva Kendal, whom he blames for the suicide of their mother, in Reynolds Price's *The Surface of Earth*.

Rena Kendal. Sister of Eva Kendal; first Eva's ally and then her enemy in Reynolds Price's *The Surface of Earth*.

Ellen Kendall. Aunt of Joel Harrison Knox; takes care of him after his mother's death but is deceived into sending him to stay at Skully's Landing in Truman Capote's *Other Voices, Other Rooms*.

Gretchen Kendall. Feminist lawyer and close friend of Isadora Wing in Erica Jong's *How to Save Your Own Life*.

Major Kendall. Companion of William Demarest; pursues Peggy Davis in Conrad Aiken's *Blue Voyage*.

Henley Kendrick. Brother of Gertie Nevels; killed in World War II in Harriette Arnow's *The Dollmaker*.

Mrs. Kendrick. Mother of Gertie Nevels; persuades John Ballew not to sell the Tipton Place to Gertie so Gertie will join her husband in Detroit in Harriette Arnow's *The Dollmaker*.

Bob Kendry. Alcoholic father of Clare Kendry and impoverished college-educated janitor of a Chicago apartment building; killed in a saloon fight in Nella Larsen's *Passing*.

Clare Kendry. Daughter of Bob Kendry; passes for white and marries John Bellew, who doesn't know she is black; dies in a fall from a Harlem apartment after a confrontation with Bellew in Nella Larsen's *Passing*.

Harley (Husband-Man) and Villa (Wife-Woman) Kennan. White tourists on a cruise ship to which Jerry swims to escape Bashti in Jack London's *Jerry of the Islands*.

Frank Kennedy. Second husband of Scarlett O'Hara; killed by Union soldiers while involved in a Ku Klux Klan raid in Margaret Mitchell's *Gone with the Wind*.

Hart Kennedy. Denver jazz fan and philanderer in John Clellon Holmes's *Go*.

Ray H. Kennedy. Freethinking railroad conductor; admires Thea Kronborg and leaves money for her musical studies in Willa Cather's *The Song of the Lark*.

Watt Kennedy. Sheriff in William Faulkner's *Light in August*.

Kate Kenner. Leader of the Red Gap Bohemian set; marries Nevil Vane-Basingwell in Harry Leon Wil-son's *Ruggles of Red Gap*.

Carol Milford (Carrie) Kennicott. Librarian from St. Paul who marries Will Kennicott and moves to his home in Gopher Prairie, Minnesota, in Sinclair Lewis's *Main Street*.

Dr. Will Kennicott. Doctor who marries Carol Milford; cannot understand why his wife is unhappy living in Gopher Prairie in Sinclair Lewis's *Main Street*.

Ruby (Rube) Kenny. Model and lover of Eugene Witla in Theodore Dreiser's *The "Genius."*

Caroline Kent. Proprietor of Illyria in Alison Lurie's *Real People*.

Chick Kent. Infant son of Ellen Chesser and Jasper Kent in Elizabeth Madox Roberts's *The Time of Man*.

Ellen Chesser Kent. See Ellen Chesser.

Jasper Kent. Tenant farmer and husband of Ellen Chesser; has an affair and is accused of barn burning in Elizabeth Madox Roberts's *The Time of Man*.

Vance Kenton. Wealthy white artist, owner of Sherwood Forest Inn, and lesbian in Ann Allen Shockley's *Loving Her*.

Kenyon. American sculptor and friend of Miriam Schaefer; suspicious of her relationship with Brother Antonio; marries Hilda in Nathaniel Hawthorne's *The Marble Faun*.

David Alan (Dave) Kepesh. Professor of comparative literature who is transformed into a six-foot-long breast; narrator of Philip Roth's *The Breast*.

Kepi. Friend of Nanantatee; carries an address book listing the Paris brothels in Henry Miller's *Tropic of Cancer*.

Michael Kern. Young college professor who has an affair with Joan Mitchell; she destroys his career by revealing that he is having an affair with an undergraduate in Shirley Ann Grau's *The House on Coliseum Street*.

Emil Kerouac. See Emil Duluoz.

Jean-Louis Lebris (Jack, John Louis Kerouac) de Kérouac. American writer visiting France in search of his family origins; narrator of Jack Kerouac's *Satori in Paris*.

John (Jack) Kerouac. Dreamer and narrator of Jack Kerouac's *Book of Dreams*.

Patrick (Emerald Pat) Kerrigan. Saloon owner and second ward boss in Theodore Dreiser's *The Titan*.

Kersaint. Medical officer for the Tuamotu Group; tells his colleague Vernier about the hurricane in Charles Nordhoff and James Norman Hall's *The Hurricane*.

de Kersaint (I). Host of thirty relatives on the eve of the black emancipation in the West Indies; dies bravely in the fire at his house in Lafcadio Hearn's *Youma*.

de Kersaint (II). Son of de Kersaint I; incites the black rioters by shooting their leader Sylvain in Lafcadio Hearn's *Youma*.

Alexis Kessler. Musician and music professor at Woodslee University; becomes involved in a turbulent love affair with fellow academic Brigit Stott in Joyce Carol Oates's *Unholy Loves*.

Charles Kessler. Millionaire father of the murdered Paulie Kessler in Meyer Levin's *Compulsion*.

Jonas Kessler. Brother of Charles Kessler; discovers that Paulie Kessler has been killed in Meyer Levin's *Compulsion*.

Martha Kessler. Wife of Charles Kessler and mother of the murdered Paulie Kessler in Meyer Levin's *Compulsion*.

Paulie Kessler. Son of Charles and Martha Kessler; kidnapped and murdered by Artie Straus and Judd Steiner in Meyer Levin's *Compulsion*.

Arthur Ketcham. Drinking friend of Paul Hobbes in John Clellan Holmes's *Go*.

Mr. Kettledrum. Postman in Ellen Glasgow's *Barren Ground*.

Kevin. One of the "seven dwarfs" who wash windows, make Chinese baby food, and live with Snow White in Donald Barthelme's *Snow White*.

Boykin Keye. Lecherous white farmer who employs Jule Jackson as a farmhand and fights with him over Jackson's sixteen-year-old girlfriend, Bertha Mae, in George Wylie Henderson's *Jule*.

Evelyn Keyes. Fiancée of Spider in Herbert Simmons's *Corner Boy*.

Keziah. Obese great-aunt of Miranda in Katherine Anne Porter's *Old Mortality*.

Aunt Keziah. Powerful Burnside, Virginia, conjurer; surrogate mother and sexual enslaver of Bill Kelsey in Hal Bennett's *Seventh Heaven*.

Krishna (K. K.) Khaleel. Indian ambassador to the United States and voice of the Third World with his constant concern for placating the USSR in Allen Drury's *Advise and Consent*.

Chop Hing Kheng Fatt (Big Hing). Ship chandler and Chinese boss of Jack Flowers in Paul Theroux's *Saint Jack*.

Mrs. Edwin Kibbler. Mother of Edwin Kibbler, Jr.; believes Cress Delahanty has purposely injured her son in Jessamyn West's *Cress Delahanty*.

Edwin Kibbler, Jr. Schoolmate who becomes a close friend of Cress Delahanty in Jessamyn West's *Cress Delahanty*.

Kiche. Wolf; mate of One Eye and mother of White Fang in Jack London's *White Fang*.

Kid. Nephew and companion of Dudley Osborn; narrator of Wright Morris's *My Uncle Dudley*.

The Kid. Thug bodyguard of Bernie Despain in Dashiell Hammett's *The Glass Key*.

Susan Kidwell. Closest friend and confidante of Nancy Clutter; discovers Nancy's body the morning after the crime in Truman Capote's *In Cold Blood*.

Kiki. Homosexual street boy in William S. Burroughs's *The Soft Machine*; possessed by Ali in *The Ticket That Exploded*; serves as a "deep trance medium" to the Mayan Death God in *The Wild Boys*; also appears in *Nova Express*.

Annie Kilburn. Only child of Judge Rufus Kilburn; wealthy spinster who tries to do good but discovers that charity alone is inadequate in William Dean Howells's *Annie Kilburn*.

Judge Rufus Kilburn. Father of Annie Kilburn; dies in Italy in William Dean Howells's *Annie Kilburn*.

Logan Killicks. Middle-aged farmer who becomes sixteen-year-old Janie Crawford's first husband in Zora Neale Hurston's *Their Eyes Were Watching God*.

Andy Kilvinsky. Veteran Los Angeles policeman, partner of Gus Plebesly, "philosopher," and eventual suicide in Joseph Wambaugh's *The New Centurions*.

Lucius (Dr. Mootry) Kimbell. Sharecropper who works for Uncle Alex in George Wylie Henderson's *Jule*.

Merle Kinbona. Emotionally unstable but strong-minded Bourne Island woman who dreams of a better life for the poor blacks of Bournehills in Paule Marshall's *The Chosen Place, the Timeless People*.

Dr. Charles (K.) Kinbote. Mad editor of John Shade's poem *Pale Fire*; his commentaries interpret the work as the story of his own life as an exiled monarch, Charles Xavier Vseslav, last king of Zembla, in Vladimir Nabokov's *Pale Fire*.

Brooke Kincaid. College student who divides herself into Brooke, her real self, and Brooke Proper, her social persona; desperately seeks a language of the heart and then throws away her one chance for it in Bentley T. Hooks; narrator of Lee Smith's *Something in the Wind*.

Carolyn Kincaid. Ephemeral and emotionally unavailable mother of Brooke Kincaid in Lee Smith's *Something in the Wind*.

Carter Kincaid. Cynical brother of Brooke Kincaid in Lee Smith's *Something in the Wind*.

Sharon Kincaid. Girlfriend of Binx Bolling in Walker Percy's *The Moviegoer*.

T. Royce Kincaid. Lawyer father of Brooke Kincaid; shields himself from his children by clichés in Lee Smith's *Something in the Wind*.

Andrew Kincannon. Lover of Maggie Sherbrooke in Nicholas Delbanco's *Sherbrookes*.

William F. Kinderman. Persevering and insatiably curious homicide detective whose investigation of a bizarre murder leads him to the MacNeil family in William Peter Blatty's *The Exorcist*.

Lydia Kindle. University of Iowa student with whom Fred Trumper is unable to make love in John Irving's *The Water-Method Man*.

King. Black bisexual lover of Louisa Calloway; outspoken about the rich South in Alice Adams's *Families and Survivors*.

Abbey (Ab) King. Four-year-old daughter of Austin and Martha King; eavesdrops on adult conversations, spends time in the kitchen with Rachel, and begins to adjust to the idea of a baby sister in William Maxwell's *Time Will Darken It*.

Austin King. Lawyer whose perseverance wins the hand of Martha Hastings; pays off debts of foster relatives, though not legally obligated to do so; his kindness to his foster cousin, Nora Potter, causes gossip in William Maxwell's *Time Will Darken It*.

Barbara King. White actress from a well-to-do Kentucky family; becomes the friend, lover, and eventually lifelong companion of Leo Proudhammer in James Baldwin's *Tell Me How Long the Train's Been Gone*.

Belle King. Nouveau riche sister of Phil Green; angered because her socialite friends think she is Jewish and will exclude her from their circle and their clubs in Laura Z. Hobson's *Gentleman's Agreement*.

Bill King. Advertising agent and friend and classmate of Harry Pulham; becomes the lover of Kay Motsford Pulham in John P. Marquand's *H. M. Pulham, Esquire*.

Chad King. Friend of Sal Paradise; works in a Denver library in Jack Kerouac's *On the Road*.

Ed King. Middle-aged homosexual who has a brief paid sexual encounter with the unnamed protagonist of John Rechy's *City of Night*.

Edward King. Father of Sarah King; feared by the people of Winesburg but befriended by Joe Welling in Sherwood Anderson's *Winesburg, Ohio*.

Martha Hastings King. Wife of Austin King; defends her husband against rumors that he is unfaithful, though she is frustrated by the differences between them, in William Maxwell's *Time Will Darken It*.

Reginald (Reggie) King. Wealthy yachtsman, travel writer, and friend of Alice Langham in Richard Harding Davis's *Soldiers of Fortune*.

Sarah King. Daughter of Edward King; courted by Joe Welling in Sherwood Anderson's *Winesburg, Ohio*.

Tom King. Son of Edward King; befriended by Joe Welling in Sherwood Anderson's *Winesburg, Ohio*.

King Devil. Elusive fox that often leads Nunn Ballew to neglect his family in Harriette Arnow's *Hunter's Horn*.

Elizabeth (Biddy) Kingsblood. Daughter of Neil and Vestal Kingsblood in Sinclair Lewis's *Kingsblood Royal*.

Faith Kingsblood. Mother of Neil Kingsblood; learns that she is one-sixteenth black in Sinclair Lewis's *Kingsblood Royal*.

Dr. Kenneth M. Kingsblood. Dentist and father of Neil Kingsblood; dies when he learns that his wife Faith is part black in Sinclair Lewis's *Kingsblood Royal*.

Neil Kingsblood. Junior bank officer and family man who loses his standing in the community upon the discovery that he is one-thirty-second black in Sinclair Lewis's *Kingsblood Royal*.

Robert Kingsblood. Brother of Neil Kingsblood in Sinclair Lewis's *Kingsblood Royal*.

Vestal Kingsblood. Supportive wife of Neil Kingsblood; member of the Junior League in Sinclair Lewis's *Kingsblood Royal*.

Laurence Liam (Larry) Kinkaid. Alleged murder victim of rustlers in Walter Van Tilburg Clark's *The Ox-Bow Incident*.

J. Kinnear. Government agent who has infiltrated a terrorist group plotting a bombing of the New York Stock Exchange in Don DeLillo's *Players*.

Kinney. Storyteller whose work Bartley Hubbard sells without permission in William Dean Howells's *A Modern Instance*.

Alice Kinnian. Teacher who selects Charlie Gordon for an experiment involving increased intelligence in Daniel Keyes's *Flowers for Algernon*.

Kino. Impoverished Indian fisherman who finds a giant pearl and dreams of becoming rich; becomes disillusioned when pearl dealers attempt to cheat him and when others attempt to deprive him of his pearl in John Steinbeck's *The Pearl*.

Kinosling. New pastor of the Schofields' church; his brief flirtation with Margaret Schofield ends when her brother Penrod fills Kinosling's hat with tar in Booth Tarkington's *Penrod*.

Eben Kinship. Black husband of Martha Kinship and father of Teddy and Lucinda Kinship in Shelby Foote's *September September*.

Julia Kinship. Girlfriend of Duff Conway in Shelby Foote's *Jordan County*.

Lucinda (Sister Baby) Kinship. Six-year-old younger sister of Teddy Kinship in Shelby Foote's *September September*.

Martha Wiggins Kinship. Black wife of Eben Kinship, daughter of Theo Wiggins, and mother of Teddy and Lucinda Kinship in Shelby Foote's *September September*.

Theo (Ted, Teddy) Kinship. Eight-year-old son of Martha and Eben Kinship; kidnapped in Shelby Foote's *September September*.

Cass Kinsolving. Alcoholic American painter on his way down; manipulated by Mason Flagg in William Styron's *Set This House on Fire*.

Poppy Kinsolving. Wife of Cass Kinsolving in William Styron's *Set This House on Fire*.

Mrs. Gert Kipfer. Owner of the brothel at which Alma Schmidt works in James Jones's *From Here to Eternity*.

Temperance Kipp. Maid-servant at the New England Owen farm who has money of her own; stays on with the Owens more as an equal than as a servant because she has always been with the family in Sarah Orne Jewett's *A Marsh Island*.

Kirby. Callous scion of a mill owner in Rebecca Harding Davis's *Life in the Iron Mills*.

Morissa (Issy) Kirk. Stepdaughter of Robin Thomas; flees the charge of being an illegitimate child by going west; doctor unable to save her husband, Eddie Ellis, from disgrace and death in Mari Sandoz's *Miss Morissa*.

Christian Kirke. Yale University anthropologist whose appendicitis attack prevents him from joining the group of scientists at Project Wildfire in Michael Crichton's *The Andromeda Strain*.

Mary-Jane (Madeleine) Saxon Kirkland. Widow of a wealthy industrialist; dies of cancer after her marriage to George Levanter in Jerzy Kosinski's *Blind Date*.

Ralph Kirkwood. Ku Klux Klan member who guides the raiding party to Jerry Hunt's house; in confessing to Comfort Servosse and Thomas Denton, Kirkwood reveals the names of many Klan leaders in Albion W. Tourgee's *A Fool's Errand*.

Leo Kirsch. Repressed momma's boy and used car salesman in Thomas Berger's *Sneaky People*.

Mary Randolph (Rannie) Kirsted. New neighbor of the Baxters; a ten-year-old who incites Jane Baxter to help Jane's brother, William, make a fool of himself at Miss Lola Pratt's departure in Booth Tarkington's *Seventeen*.

Flossie Kiskadden. Daughter of a minister; has a romantic but somber love for a Confederate soldier in Hervey Allen's *Action at Aquila*.

Kisu-Mu. See Meriwether Lewis Moon.

Captain Alvinza Kitchell. Piratical captain of the *Bertha Millner* who shanghaies the dandified Ross Wilbur in San Francisco in Frank Norris's *Moran of the Lady Letty*.

Campbell Kitchen. Retired white author who promotes interest in black cultural and social life in Harlem; employs Emma Lou Morgan as a personal maid for his wife in Wallace Thurman's *The Blacker the Berry*.

Opal Kitchener. Sculptress and sometime member of a ménage à trois with Heck and Hattie Brown in Peter De Vries's *I Hear America Swinging*.

K.K. See Krishna Khaleel.

Abner Klang. Unlettered literary agent of Lee Youngdahl in Mark Harris's *Wake Up, Stupid*.

Don Klausmeyer. Employee of Janoth Enterprises who brings Louise Patterson to the *Crimeways* office to identify the missing witness in Kenneth Fearing's *The Big Clock*.

Solly Klein. Cynical teacher at North Manual Trades High School in Evan Hunter's *The Blackboard Jungle*.

R.V. Kleppmann. Confidence man and gangster in John Gardner's *The Sunlight Dialogues*.

Dr. Klinger. Psychoanalyst of David Kepesh in Philip Roth's *The Breast*.

Menasha Klinger. Companion of Waldemar and ancient tenor who sings arias over Von Humboldt Fleisher's last resting place in Saul Bellow's *Humboldt's Gift*.

Klinker. See William Lee.

Ewing Klipspringer. Frequent guest at Jay Gatsby's house in F. Scott Fitzgerald's *The Great Gatsby*.

Mr. Klipspringer. United States government contact of Michaelis Ezana; responsible for new international investments in Kush; becomes adviser to the new government when Colonel Ellelloû is overthrown in John Updike's *The Coup*.

Jotham Klore. Lover of Molly Larkins and bully of the canal; eventually beaten in a fight by Daniel Harrow in Walter D. Edmonds's *Rome Haul*.

Neil Klugman. Librarian and lover of Brenda Patimkin; narrator of Philip Roth's *Goodbye, Columbus*.

Zivan Knezevich. Olympic wrestler and Chetnik freedom fighter who flees Tito's Yugoslavia to live in Vienna; teaches his nephew Severin Winter to wrestle in John Irving's *The 158-Pound Marriage*.

Edith Knight. Wife of Walter Knight and mother of Lily Knight McClellan in Joan Didion's *Run River*.

Gaylord Knight. Superintendent for the four Moonbloom Realty buildings managed by Norman Moonbloom in Edward Lewis Wallant's *The Tenants of Moonbloom*.

Sebastian Knight. Russian-born English writer whose elusive past becomes the obsession of his half brother and biographer, V., in Vladimir Nabokov's *The Real Life of Sebastian Knight*.

Virginia Knight. English mother of Sebastian Knight, who adopts her maiden name; abandons her family for another man in Vladimir Nabokov's *The Real Life of Sebastian Knight*.

Walter Knight. Rancher and father of Lily Knight McClellan; once hoped to become governor of California in Joan Didion's *Run River*.

K9. Agent for the Nova Police in William S. Burroughs's *Nova Express*, *The Soft Machine*, and *The Ticket That Exploded*.

W. Alcott (Old Bottle-ass) Knoedler. Headmaster of Dorset Academy; spends most of his time trying to recruit students and secure funding for the ill-fated school in Richard Yates's *A Good School*.

Lady Catharine (Lady Kitty) Knollys. Love interest of John Law in Emerson Hough's *The Mississippi Bubble*.

Carl Knox. Police detective in Thomas Berger's *Who Is Teddy Villanova?*

Henry Knox. Senior partner in Sheffield, Knox law firm; mentor and father-figure to Timothy Colt in Louis Auchincloss's *The Great World and Timothy Colt*.

Joel Harrison Knox. Thirteen-year-old boy who goes to live with his paralyzed father, his stepmother, and her cousin at Skully's Landing, where he learns about homosexuality, in Truman Capote's *Other Voices, Other Rooms*.

Orrin Knox. Senior senator from Illinois, two-time loser of his party's presidential nomination, and best friend of Senator Brigham Anderson; leads the fight against the nomination of Robert Leffingwell for Secretary of State after the suicide of Brigham Anderson in Allen Drury's *Advise and Consent*.

Fireball Kodadek. Henchman of Bonifacy Konstantine and adversary of Bruno Lefty Bicek; rapes Bicek's girlfriend Steffi Rostenkowski in Nelson Algren's *Never Come Morning*.

Franz Koenig. Nazi supporter and colleague of Paul Bronski in Leon Uris's *Mila 18*.

Dr. Schlichter von Koenigswald. Reformed Nazi and physician in Julian Castle's hospital in Kurt Vonnegut's *Cat's Cradle*.

Renata (Fat-Tits, Renata Flonzaley, Miss Universe) Koffritz. Earthy and beautiful hedonist and interior decorator who serves as Charlie Citrine's mistress until she dumps her son on him and marries a wealthy undertaker named Flonzaley in Saul Bellow's *Humboldt's Gift*.

Barton Kohl. Husband of Linda Snopes in William Faulkner's *The Mansion*.

Linda Snopes Kohl. Illegitimate daughter of Eula Varner Snopes and Hoake McCarron in William Faulkner's *The Town*; wife of Barton Kohl in *The Mansion*.

Else von Kohler. German woman with whom George Webber becomes involved in Thomas Wolfe's *You Can't Go Home Again*.

Kojak. Dog of Glen Bateman; helps save Stuart Redman in Stephen King's *The Stand*.

Stephani Kolhoff. Estranged wife of Hamm Rufe; labor activist in Mari Sandoz's *Capital City*.

Ko-li. "Soul at the seventh aspect" of Colin Meredith in Robert Coover's *The Origin of the Brunists*.

Mathilde Kollwitz. School teacher and companion to Winifred Throop in Wright Morris's *What a Way to Go*.

Kolory. Lord primate of Typee in Herman Melville's *Typee*.

Koningsmarke (Long Finne). Young hero in James Kirke Paulding's *Koningsmarke*.

Bonifacy (The Barber) Konstantine. Polish barber, brothel owner, and leader of a group of neighborhood Polish hoods in Nelson Algren's *Never Come Morning*.

Kooloo. Tahitian who befriends and then deserts Typee in Herman Melville's *Omoo*.

Cardinal von Kopf. Official of the Liechtenstein Catholic Church who confiscates Boris Adrian's pornographic movie in Terry Southern's *Blue Movie*.

Odis Korby. Undertaker in Jessamyn West's *The Witch Diggers*.

Kori. Leader of an outcast band of Niaruna Indians who live on the generosity of the missionaries in Peter Matthiessen's *At Play in the Fields of the Lord*.

Lieutenant Colonel Korn. Scheming assistant to Colonel Cathcart in Joseph Heller's *Catch-22*.

Bud Korpenning. Drifter who murders his father in a fit of anger and is so haunted by guilt that he jumps off the Brooklyn Bridge in John Dos Passos's *Manhattan Transfer*.

Kory-Kory. Servitor to Tommo in Herman Melville's *Typee*.

Koshchei the Deathless. Changeling god and creator of things as they are; sets Jurgen on the road that leads him through a year of regained youth in James Branch Cabell's *Jurgen*.

Violet Koskozka. Lusty woman whose boyfriend lives with her and her husband in Nelson Algren's *The Man with the Golden Arm*.

Anna Kossowski. Drunken childhood guardian of Konrad Vost in John Hawkes's *The Passion Artist*.

Stanley Koteks. Engineer at Yoyodyne, Inc.; tells Oedipa Maas about the Nefastis machine in Thomas Pynchon's *The Crying of Lot 49*.

Dr. Bernard M. (Bernie) Kotelchuk. Veterinarian who becomes Danielle Zimmern's lover in Alison Lurie's *The War Between the Tates*.

Nat Kott. Childhood friend and schoolmate of Nicholas Delbanco in Nicholas Delbanco's *In the Middle Distance*.

Grant Koven. Hired hand of Arnold Haldmarne; experiences unrequited love for Merle Haldmarne in Josephine Johnson's *Now in November*.

Yozhé Kozak. Slovenian artist employed to develop Rudolf Stanka's artistic talents in Louis Adamic's *Cradle of Life*.

George Kraft. Soviet spy and friend of Howard Campbell in Kurt Vonnegut's *Mother Night*.

Peter Krajiek. Bohemian immigrant who sells the Shimerdas a house at an unfair price; feels guilt at Shimerda's suicide in Willa Cather's *My Ántonia*.

Kram. Hunchbacked artist who lives in a Mott Street apartment managed by Norman Moonbloom in Edward Lewis Wallant's *The Tenants of Moonbloom*.

Vida Kramar. Nineteen-year-old beauty and lover of Mr. Librarian; has an abortion in Tijuana in Richard Brautigan's *The Abortion*.

Pop Kramer. Elderly father of Cassie Caldwell, grandfather of Peter Caldwell, and father-in-law of George Caldwell in John Updike's *The Centaur*.

Wantman Krane. Beat poet, lover of Hellos and later of Putsy Handson, and friend of Scarecrow in Calvin Hernton's *Scarecrow*.

Doctor Irving Krankeit. See Irving Semite.

Kranmer. Corrupt vice squad lieutenant who is killed by Roy Earle in William Riley Burnett's *High Sierra*.

Marc Krantz. Junior partner at Glymmer, Read who decides to become a writer in Paris when the firm goes bankrupt in Nathan Asch's *The Office*.

Miriam Desebour Kranz. Hospital nurse in Morristown, New Jersey, who teaches Dick Gibson the secret of the "dead room" in Stanley Elkin's *The Dick Gibson Show*.

Sidney H. (Sid) Krassman. Film producer who arranges the financing for Boris Adrian's pornographic movie and acts in one of its sex scenes in Terry Southern's *Blue Movie*.

Jozef Muck-Horch von Kretschmann. Half brother of Wanda Muck-Horch von Kretschmann and lover of Sophie Zawistowska; assassin for the Polish resistance forces in Warsaw; murdered by Ukranian guards in William Styron's *Sophie's Choice*.

Wanda Muck-Horch von Kretschmann. Half sister of Jozef Muck-Horch von Kretschmann; Polish resistance leader captured by Nazis and confined in Birkenau in William Styron's *Sophie's Choice*.

Brandon Kregg. Wealthy proprietor of Albion, devout Presbyterian, and husband of Sally Crawford Lacey's oldest sister; refuses a loan to Brandon and Sally Lacey in Mary Lee Settle's *Know Nothing*.

Crawford (Fish) Kregg. Son of Brandon Kregg, roommate of Johnny Catlett at the University of Virginia, and one of the wealthiest young men in Virginia; marries Melinda Lacey, compromises his principles for a political career, hates Johnny Catlett because he knows Melinda always loved Johnny and bore his child, and finally joins the Confederate army hoping to be killed in Mary Lee Settle's *Know Nothing*.

Dr. Noah Kregg. Cousin of Crawford Kregg and physician who attends Melinda Lacey Kregg in her final illness in Mary Lee Settle's *Know Nothing*.

Lacey Kregg. Daughter of Melinda Kregg and, supposedly, Crawford Kregg; her natural father is Johnny Catlett in Mary Lee Settle's *Know Nothing*.

Melinda Lacey Kregg. Granddaughter of Peregrine Lacey and ward of Peregrine Lacey Catlett; loved by Lewis and Johnny Catlett but marries Crawford Kregg for security; bears two children by Crawford and one child by Johnny before she dies of a broken spirit in Mary Lee Settle's *Know Nothing*.

Moses Kregg. Bachelor lawyer, storekeeper, justice of the peace in Fluvanna County, and friend of Johnny Lacey in Mary Lee Settle's *O Beulah Land*.

Sanhedron Kregg. Keeper of the land office of Fluvanna County and friend of Johnny Lacey; with his three brothers, controls the settlement at Kreggs' Crossing in Mary Lee Settle's *O Beulah Land*.

Minor Kretz. Owner of Minor's Luncheonette; fearful of communism in John Updike's *The Centaur*.

Reb Yudel Krinsky. Russian-born Jew who is rescued from Siberia by Aryeh Lev and who encourages Asher Lev's interest in art in Chaim Potok's *My Name Is Asher Lev*.

Kristel. Assistant to Anna Kossowski and would-be seducer of Konrad Vost in John Hawkes's *The Passion Artist*.

Charles (Charlie) Kroegel. Friend and classmate of Eric Eisner at Columbia University and presently a graduate student at Columbia; lends Eric his New York apartment in Phillip Lopate's *Confessions of Summer*.

Mr. and Mrs. Peter Kronborg. Parents of Thea Kronborg; he is a small-town Methodist minister in Willa Cather's *The Song of the Lark*.

Thea Kronborg. Daughter of a small-town minister; studies voice in Chicago and New York and becomes a leading opera singer in Willa Cather's *The Song of the Lark*.

Professor Adam (Adamka, Adam the Ninth, Mugakrad, Gumakrad) Krug. Influential philosopher, husband of Olga Krug, and father of David Krug; the government unsuccessfully tries to persuade him to accept the new regime by arresting his friends and relatives and even torturing and murdering his son; goes mad before he is killed in Vladimir Nabokov's *Bend Sinister*.

David Krug. Eight-year-old son of Adam and Olga Krug kidnapped by the government to force his father to accept the new regime; through apparent bungling on the part of government thugs, he dies after being tortured in Vladimir Nabokov's *Bend Sinister*.

Olga Krug. Beloved wife of Adam Krug and mother of David Krug; dies following a kidney operation; persecution of her husband begins the day after her death in Vladimir Nabokov's *Bend Sinister*.

Kruger. Artist and sculptor who lends money to Henry Miller and permits Miller to live in his studio in Henry Miller's *Tropic of Cancer*.

Marie Krull. Wife of Charles Neumiller (I) and cousin of Father Krull in Larry Woiwode's *Beyond the Bedroom Wall*.

Selmer Krull. Catholic priest and spiritual adviser to Martin Neumiller in Courtenay, North Dakota;

performs the marriage ceremony of Neumiller and Alpha Jones in Larry Woiwode's *Beyond the Bedroom Wall*.

Fritz Kruppenbach. Lutheran minister who refuses to intervene in Rabbit Angstrom's marital problems in John Updike's *Rabbit, Run*.

Stepan Krylenko. Russian friend of the Shanes who becomes an international Communist leader in Louis Bromfield's *The Green Bay Tree*.

Kudashvili. Russian captain who discovers Utch Thalhammer inside a dead cow's carcass and becomes Utch's guardian; killed in Budapest in John Irving's *The 158-Pound Marriage*; also appears in *Setting Free the Bears*.

Alexandr Petrovich (Al Cook) Kukolnikov. Americanized Russian émigré and husband of Susan Kukolnikov; during alternate summers opens his New England country home to other Russian émigré friends in Vladimir Nabokov's *Pnin*.

Susan Marshall (Susanna Karlovna) Kukolnikov. American wife of Alexandr Petrovich Kukolnikov and gracious hostess to Russian and American friends at The Pines, a country home inherited from her father, in Vladimir Nabokov's *Pnin*.

Eddie Kulanski. Catholic neighbor of the Luries; his virulent anti-Semitism takes the form of endlessly tormenting David Lurie in Chaim Potok's *In the Beginning*.

Larry Kulik. Gangster lawyer in Joan Didion's *Play It As It Lays*.

Sue (Biggie) Kunft. See Sue Kunft Trumper Bennett.

Kuno. See Kuno Hillentafel.

Abe Kusich. Dwarf who befriends Tod Hackett in Nathanael West's *The Day of the Locust*.

Cousin Kvorka. Neighborhood police sergeant who warns Frankie Machine of his imminent arrest in Nelson Algren's *The Man with the Golden Arm*.

L

L. Slovenian immigrant worker-writer and eventual author of Peter Gale's proposed novel "Grandsons"; narrator of Louis Adamic's *Grandsons*.

Eugene de Laage. French colonial administrator of the Tuamotu Group who attempts unsuccessfully to capture Terangi in Charles Nordhoff and James Norman Hall's *The Hurricane*.

Germaine Anne Marie de Laage. Wife of Eugene de Laage; rescued by Terangi during the hurricane; later helps him escape in Charles Nordhoff and James Norman Hall's *The Hurricane*.

PaPa (Papa) LaBas. God of the crossroads in the New World and an astro-detective in Ishmael Reed's *Mumbo Jumbo* and *The Last Days of Louisiana Red*.

La Belle Isold. Lover of Tristram; dies when his body is found in Thomas Berger's *Arthur Rex*.

Labina. Halfhearted prostitute who finds the narrator frozen in the woods and takes him home in Jerzy Kosinski's *The Painted Bird*.

LaBoeuf. Texas Ranger who hunts the murderer Tom Chaney in Charles Portis's *True Grit*.

General Labonne. Frenchman whom Mary Douglas convinces to accompany Lord Balham in his attempt to help the German and Austrian refugees in Martha Gellhorn's *A Stricken Field*.

Labove. Teacher who attempts to seduce Eula Varner in William Faulkner's *The Hamlet*.

Julien Raymond (Papa Zulien) La Brierre. New Orleans doctor brought, by chance, to Viosca's Point eleven years after the supposed drowning of his daughter Chita Viosca in Lafcadio Hearn's *Chita*.

Zozo Labrique. Charter member of the American Hoo-Doo Church in Ishmael Reed's *Yellow Back Radio Broke-Down*.

Robert W. Lacaud. Persistent prospector who follows Curtin to the gold mine and causes dissent among the other miners in B. Traven's *The Treasure of the Sierra Madre*.

Nate Lace. Exotic-foods restaurateur whose establishment is intended as the gathering place for The Club in Stanley Elkin's *Boswell*.

A. Gray Lacefield. Son of Caruthers Lacefield, brother of Drusilla Lacefield, and betrothed of Marcia Vaiden; plantation aristocrat who becomes editor of a newspaper in Florence, Alabama; appears in T. S. Stribling's *The Forge* and *The Store*.

Caruthers Lacefield. Landed aristocrat and slave owner; patriarch of Lacefield Manor and father of A. Gray and Drusilla Lacefield in T. S. Stribling's *The Forge*.

Drusilla Lacefield. See Drusilla Lacefield Crowninshield.

Lucy Lacefield. See Lucy Lacefield Vaiden.

Brandon Lacey. Great-grandson of Montague Lacey, proprietor of Crawford's Landing plantation, and husband of Sally Crawford Lacey; bankrupted by the Panic of 1837 in Mary Lee Settle's *Know Nothing*.

Jonathan (Johnny) Lacey. Provincial captain and survivor of Braddock's army, frontier landholder, and member of the Virginia House of Burgesses; descendant of Johnny Church and husband of Sally Sawyer Lacey in Mary Lee Settle's *O Beulah Land*.

Katherine (Kathy) Lacey. Divorced teacher who falls in love with Phil Green and finds she is more concerned about appearances than about individuals in Laura Z. Hobson's *Gentleman's Agreement*.

Melinda Lacey. See Melinda Lacey Kregg.

Montague Crawford Bacchus Lacey. Eldest son of Johnny and Sally Lacey; marries Brandon Crawford's daughter and becomes his heir in Mary Lee Settle's *O Beulah Land*.

Peregrine Lacey. Son of Johnny and Sally Lacey; shares his mother's disdain for frontier settlers, hates his father for bringing him to the frontier, and is disinherited for his part in the massacre of Shawnee Indians in Mary Lee Settle's *O Beulah Land*; returns to Beulah to die in *Know Nothing*.

Sally Crawford (Sal) Lacey. Frivolous wife of Brandon Lacey, niece of Mamie Brandon Catlett, and mother-in-law of Lewis Catlett in Mary Lee Settle's *Know Nothing*.

Sally Sawyer (Sal) Lacey. Shallow, blonde wife of Johnny Lacey; considers the frontier settlers her inferiors and so is never satisfied or accepted at Beulah; eventually has her hair forcibly cut off because of her aristocratic pretensions and goes mad as a result in Mary Lee Settle's *O Beulah Land*.

Sara Lacey. See Sara Lacey (Mrs. Ezekiel) Catlett and Sara Lacey (Mrs. Lewis) Catlett.

Lactamaeon. Tormentor of Deborah Blau in Yr, the mental world of Deborah's creation, in Hannah

Green's *I Never Promised You a Rose Garden*.

Nell Lacy. Younger sister of Johnny Church's mother, wife of Sir Valentine Lacy, mother of Peregrine Lacy and of a child by Johnny Church in Mary Lee Settle's *Prisons*.

Peregrine Lacy. Son of Nell and Sir Valentine Lacy; cousin and childhood playmate of Johnny Church; dies fighting with the king's army at the siege of Bristol in Mary Lee Settle's *Prisons*.

Sir Valentine Lacy. Husband of Nell Lacy and father of Peregrine Lacy; befriends Johnny Church despite political and religious differences; expresses a dying wish for another child and so causes the sexual encounter between Nell and Johnny in Mary Lee Settle's *Prisons*.

Lady of the Lake. Benevolent mythic character in Thomas Berger's *Arthur Rex*.

Lafayette. French nobleman who fights in the American Revolution and later supports Thomas Paine's efforts in the French Revolution in Howard Fast's *Citizen Tom Paine*.

Lafe. Father of Dewey Dell Bundren's unborn child in William Faulkner's *As I Lay Dying*.

Zoot Lafferty. Street bookie for Red Scalotta and informer for Bumper Morgan in Joseph Wambaugh's *The Blue Knight*.

Lafitte (Achille). Twin brother of Count Alphonse D'Oyley, impulsive pirate, and patriotic hero-villain in Joseph Holt Ingraham's *Lafitte*.

Lafon. French nobleman and father of the twins Lafitte and Count Alphonse D'Oyley in Joseph Holt Ingraham's *Lafitte*.

Rosemarie de Laframboise. Long Island socialite living in Rome as the mistress of Mason Flagg in William Styron's *Set This House on Fire*.

Timothy (Snail) Laird. Free black man who works for both sides in the Civil War by selling stolen goods, helping runaway slaves, and running guns in Jesse Hill Ford's *The Raider*.

Julia Lake. Fifty-year-old secretary to Todd Andrews in John Barth's *The Floating Opera*.

Roger Burns Lakeside. Mortician presiding over the funeral of Grandmother Herkimer in Wright Morris's *The Man Who Was There*.

Dr. V. Govinda Lal. Space scientist, author of the book *Future of the Moon*, and advocate of inhabitation of the moon; Shula Sammler steals his lecture notes and Artur Sammler subsequently holds philosophical discussions with him in Saul Bellow's *Mr. Sammler's Planet*.

Lallemont. General and corps commander in William Faulkner's *A Fable*.

Lamai. Island boy who finds Jerry in the sea after the *Arangi* is destroyed in Jack London's *Jerry of the Islands*.

Lancelot Andrewes (Lance) Lamar. Crazed lawyer who tells how he wreaked apocalyptic vengeance for his wife's adultery; narrator of Walker Percy's *Lancelot*.

Lily Lamar. Mother of Lancelot Lamar; Lancelot suspects her of having committed adultery with her distant cousin in Walker Percy's *Lancelot*.

Lucy Lamar. Daughter of Lancelot and Lucy Cobb Lamar; plans to join the ménage of Raine Robinette and Troy Dana in Walker Percy's *Lancelot*.

Lucy Cobb Lamar. Dead and highly romanticized first wife of Lancelot Lamar in Walker Percy's *Lancelot*.

Mary Margaret Reilly (Margot) Lamar. Second wife of Lancelot Lamar; stars in a movie co-directed by Robert Merlin, her former lover, and Janos Jacoby, her latest lover, in Walker Percy's *Lancelot*.

Maury Lamar. Feckless and politically corrupt father of Lancelot Lamar in Walker Percy's *Lancelot*.

Ruby Lamar. Common-law wife of Lee Goodwin in William Faulkner's *Sanctuary*.

J. A. Lamb. Head of a wholesale drug firm; employer of Virgil Adams until Adams takes a formula for glue and starts his own factory; eventually buys out Adams's company in Booth Tarkington's *Alice Adams*.

Letitia (Letty) Lamb. Close friend of Harriet Alden in George Santayana's *The Last Puritan*.

Mary Lambert. Wife of Thomas Paine; dies of a fever in England, leaving Paine alone and emotionally drained before he immigrates to America, in Howard Fast's *Citizen Tom Paine*.

Tom Lambert. American journalist and colleague of Mary Douglas in Martha Gellhorn's *A Stricken Field*.

Maurice Lamotta. Unscrupulous business manager for Thomas Oliver; arranges Oliver's marriage to Stephanie D'Alfonso in Shirley Ann Grau's *The Condor Passes*.

Rabbi Milton Lampert. Noted scholar whose publications and lectures are written for him by Herman Broder; grows wealthy from ventures in real estate, gambling, and the stock market in Isaac Bashevis Singer's *Enemies, A Love Story*.

Rose Lampkin. Suspected mistress of Gilbert Blount in Richard Wright's *The Outsider*.

Hattie Lampson. Dead mother of Luke and Mulge Lampson and mother-in-law of Ma Lampson; buried on the side of the dam overlooking the area where Mulge died in John Hawkes's *The Beetle Leg*.

Luke (Cowboy) Lampson. Younger son of Hattie Lampson and Cap Leecher; while fishing by the dam, he snares a human fetus, which he throws back; lives with Ma Lampson and Maverick in John Hawkes's *The Beetle Leg*.

Ma Lampson. Widow of Mulge Lampson, sister-in-law of Luke Lampson, and daughter-in-law of Hattie Lampson; lives with Luke Lampson and Maverick and searches for Mulge's grave with a divining rod in John Hawkes's *The Beetle Leg*.

Gerald Lamson. English novelist with whom Lorelei Lee takes up when Gus Eisman is out of town, using him to gain leverage with Gus, in Anita Loos's *"Gentlemen Prefer Blondes."*

Caesar Lanark. Minnesota landowner and fur trader; father of Selene Lanark in Sinclair Lewis's *The God-Seeker*.

Selene (Princess) Lanark. Half-Sioux daughter of Caesar Lanark; wife of Aaron Gadd in Sinclair Lewis's *The God-Seeker*.

Albert Lancaster. Chicago socialite and husband of Muriel Lester Lancaster in Margaret Ayer Barnes's *Years of Grace*.

Cicily Carver Bridges Lancaster. Daughter of Stephen and Jane Ward Carver in Margaret Ayer Barnes's *Years of Grace*; independent woman who defies convention and divorces Jack Bridges to marry Albert Lancaster, Jr.; comes to terms with Lancaster's infidelity in *Wisdom's Gate*.

Muriel Lester Lancaster. Schoolmate of Jane Ward, wife of Albert Lancaster, and mother of Albert Lancaster, Jr.; marries Ed Brown after Albert Lancaster's death in Margaret Ayer Barnes's *Years of Grace*; also appears in *Wisdom's Gate*.

Lance. Attractive black figure skater who dies of a drug overdose while skating; first lover of the male narrator of Tennessee Williams's *Moise and the World of Reason*.

Valerie (Val) Land. Niece of George Atkinson, daughter of an aspiring but unsuccessful painter, and lover and eventual wife of Saint Wentworth in DuBose Heyward's *Mamba's Daughters*.

Dov Landau. Survivor of the Warsaw Ghetto Revolt and Auschwitz; a runner and forger in the Warsaw ghetto; lover of Karen Clement in Leon Uris's *Exodus*.

Nathan Landau. Paranoid schizophrenic posing as a research biologist; befriends Stingo; commits double suicide with his lover, Sophie Zawistowska, in William Styron's *Sophie's Choice*.

Landers. Republican postmaster and proponent of justice and equality for blacks; opposed to mob violence but unable to prevent the lynching of Toussaint Vaiden in T. S. Stribling's *The Store*.

Marion Landers. Company clerk who returns from duty in the South Pacific with an injured ankle and, once in the United States, stays in trouble because of his chronic violent behavior and disrespect for the army; kills himself by stepping in front of a moving car in James Jones's *Whistle*.

Mavis Landour. London society woman and lover of Freddie Ransome in H. D.'s *Palimpsest*.

Adele Landry. Wife of Al Landry and stepmother of Annie Landry in Shirley Ann Grau's *The Hard Blue Sky*.

Alistair (Al) Landry. Widowed father of Annie Landry; makes his daughter jealous when he marries Adele Landry in Shirley Ann Grau's *The Hard Blue Sky*.

Annie Landry. Bored sixteen year old who falls in love with Inky D'Alfonso and marries him in Shirley Ann Grau's *The Hard Blue Sky*.

Timothy G. Landry. Armed robber against whom patrolman Bumper Morgan offers perjured testimony in Joseph Wambaugh's *The Blue Knight*.

Stewart Landsborough. Publisher of war books who is temporarily mistaken by Violet Clay for a publisher of pornography in Gail Godwin's *Violet Clay*.

Asshur Lane. Unconventional but faithful friend and eventual mate of Melissa Paul in Jessie Redmon Fauset's *The Chinaberry Tree*.

Jimmy (Jimmie) Lane. Friend and playmate of Sandy Rodgers; his mother dies and he quits school to become a bell-hop in Langston Hughes's *Not Without Laughter*.

Lionel Lane. See Cross Damon.

Silvia Lane. Dishonest secretary to Leo Feldman in Stanley Elkin's *A Bad Man.*

Carter Lang. Womanizing movie director and husband of Maria Wyeth in Joan Didion's *Play It As It Lays.*

Kate Lang. Institutionalized retarded daughter of Maria Wyeth and Carter Lang in Joan Didion's *Play It As It Lays.*

Mrs. Lang. Name Maria Wyeth never calls herself in Joan Didion's *Play It As It Lays.*

Susan Lang. Prostitute who gets information about gold shipments from her client Henry Fowler in Michael Crichton's *The Great Train Robbery.*

Alison Langdon. Frail wife of Major Morris Langdon and employer of Anacleto; loses her baby daughter and dies shortly after being institutionalized for mental problems in Carson McCullers's *Reflections in a Golden Eye.*

Fred Langdon. Boyhood friend of Tom Bailey; captured in the snowball fight; becomes a California vintner in Thomas Bailey Aldrich's *The Story of a Bad Boy.*

Major Morris (The Buffalo) Langdon. Unfaithful husband of Alison Langdon and lover of Leonora Penderton; feels guilt and remorse at the death of his wife in Carson McCullers's *Reflections in a Golden Eye.*

Wolfgang Langfanger. Potter and councilman in James Kirke Paulding's *Koningsmarke.*

Torquemada Langguth. California writer in John Updike's *Bech: A Book.*

Alice Langham. Elder daughter of Andrew Langham; socialite who fascinates Robert Clay in Richard Harding Davis's *Soldiers of Fortune.*

Andrew Langham. Eastern tycoon who finances the Olancho Mining Company in Richard Harding Davis's *Soldiers of Fortune.*

Hope Langham. Younger daughter of Andrew Langham; falls in love with Robert Clay in Richard Harding Davis's *Soldiers of Fortune.*

Theodore Langham. Son of Andrew Langham; college student sent to Olancho to oversee his father's mining interests in Richard Harding Davis's *Soldiers of Fortune.*

Ninel Ilinishna (Ninella, Nonna) Langley. Landlady of Annette Blagovo and Vadim Vadimovich; takes Annette and Bel to live with her in her cottage and perishes along with Annette in floods caused by a hurricane in Vladimir Nabokov's *Look at the Harlequins!*

Lady Aurora Langrish. Spinster philanthropist who ministers to the poor and admires the revolutionary Paul Muniment in Henry James's *The Princess Casamassima.*

Ellen Langton. Ward of the Melmoths; abducted by Butler and rescued by Fanshawe; marries Edward Walcott in Nathaniel Hawthorne's *Fanshawe.*

John Langton. Evil rival for power with George Posey; captain of a company of Confederate soldiers; killed by Posey in Allen Tate's *The Fathers.*

John Langton. Father of Ellen Langton; presumed lost at sea in Nathaniel Hawthorne's *Fanshawe.*

Gertrude Langueville. Frenchwoman who inspires love and murder in Joseph Holt Ingraham's *Lafitte.*

Lewis Lanier. Ex-husband of Violet Clay in Gail Godwin's *Violet Clay.*

Anne Lansing. Youngest Lansing child and her father's favorite; becomes deeply attached to her brother George Lansing in Thornton Wilder's *The Eighth Day.*

Breckenridge (Breck) Lansing. Loud and boisterous managing director of some of Coaltown's mines; murder victim in Thornton Wilder's *The Eighth Day.*

Eustacia Sims (Eustachie, Stacey) Lansing. Wife of Breckenridge Lansing; native of St. Kitts, where she operated a store; endures much from her husband but remains faithful to him even after his death in Thornton Wilder's *The Eighth Day.*

Félicité Marjolaine Dupuy Lansing. Second Lansing daughter; has ambitions of becoming a nun; uncovers the mystery of her father's death and marries Roger Ashley in Thornton Wilder's *The Eighth Day.*

Fisher Lansing. Iowa farmer who is the brother of Breckenridge Lansing; takes charge of much of Eustacia Lansing's business after his brother's murder; manages to sell some of the inventions of John Ashley as if they were Breck's work in Thornton Wilder's *The Eighth Day.*

George Sims Lansing. Troubled son of Breckenridge and Eustacia Lansing; becomes fascinated with the Russian language and the theater and runs away to pursue both interests; admits to having killed his father in Thornton Wilder's *The Eighth Day.*

Joyce Lanyon. Unhappily married second wife of Martin Arrowsmith in Sinclair Lewis's *Arrowsmith*.

Irene Lapham. Daughter of Silas and Persis Lapham; falls in love with Tom Corey in William Dean Howells's *The Rise of Silas Lapham*.

Penelope (Pen) Lapham. Daughter of Silas and Persis Lapham; marries Tom Corey in William Dean Howells's *The Rise of Silas Lapham*.

Persis (Pert) Lapham. Wife of Silas Lapham; former country schoolteacher who is uneasy in Boston society in William Dean Howells's *The Rise of Silas Lapham*.

Silas Lapham. Wealthy businessman without social background; loses his fortune when he refuses to enter into an unethical business deal in William Dean Howells's *The Rise of Silas Lapham*.

Lapin. Thief executed with Stefan in William Faulkner's *A Fable*.

Volida La Porte. Friend of Etta Barnes, whom La Porte encourages to attend the University of Wisconsin, in Theodore Dreiser's *The Bulwark*.

Jean-Paul (Frenchy) La Prade. Self-centered, "wonderfully Gallic" French master at Dorset Academy; has an affair with Alice Draper and then in a self-dramatizing gesture joins the Office of Strategic Services during World War II in Richard Yates's *A Good School*.

Mlle Ida (Mlle L., Guillaume de Monparnasse) Larivière. Governess of Ada and Lucette Veen who, using a pseudonym, becomes a famous author in Vladimir Nabokov's *Ada*.

Alexander (Aleck) Larkin. Nephew of Obed Larkin; lawyer in partnership with his brother Horace until Aleck discovers that Horace is using the firm to advance his political ambitions; idealist who quests for the meaning of life and marries Gertrude Larkin in Hjalmar Hjorth Boyesen's *The Mammon of Unrighteousness*.

Bobby Larkin. Friend of Diana Deacon, with whom he plans to elope until dissuaded by Lulu Bett, in Zona Gale's *Miss Lulu Bett*.

Brigid Larkin. Sister of Conor Larkin; runs the family farm in Leon Uris's *Trinity*.

Conor Larkin. Blacksmith, Gaelic football player, and revolutionary for the Irish Catholics; lover of Shelley MacLeod and Atty Fitzpatrick in Leon Uris's *Trinity*.

Dary Larkin. Catholic priest; helps his brother Conor Larkin escape from prison in Leon Uris's *Trinity*.

Gertrude (Gertie) Larkin. Adopted daughter of Obed Larkin; an aspiring sculptress; engaged to Dr. Archibald Hawk until she discovers that he wants her money; marries Aleck Larkin in Hjalmar Hjorth Boyesen's *The Mammon of Unrighteousness*.

Horace Larkin. Nephew of Obed Larkin; lawyer and politician who marries Kate Van Schaak and, because of her, establishes a career in diplomacy in Hjalmar Hjorth Boyesen's *The Mammon of Unrighteousness*.

Karl Larkin. Active telepath and husband of Mary Larkin in Octavia E. Butler's *Mind of My Mind*.

Liam Larkin. Brother of Conor Larkin; moves to Australia to farm his own land in Leon Uris's *Trinity*.

Mary Larkin. Wife of Karl Larkin, daughter of Doro, and granddaughter of Emma; establisher of the "vast network of mental links" known as the Pattern and narrator of parts of Octavia E. Butler's *Mind of My Mind*.

Maude Larkin. Affluent but impractical friend who encourages Alice Prentice to live beyond her means in Richard Yates's *A Special Providence*.

Obed Larkin. Uncle and adoptive father of Aleck and Horace Larkin and adoptive father of Gertrude Larkin; philanthropist and founder of Larkin University in Hjalmar Hjorth Boyesen's *The Mammon of Unrighteousness*.

Molly Larkins. Lover of Daniel Harrow in Walter D. Edmonds's *Rome Haul*.

Laroussel. Creole traveling with Captain Harris; interrogates Chita Viosca and discovers her Creole background in Lafcadio Hearn's *Chita*.

Larry. Anticivilization sailor aboard the *Highlander* in Herman Melville's *Redburn*.

Larry. Husband of Lillian in Anaïs Nin's *Ladders to Fire* and *Seduction of the Minotaur*.

Death Larsen. Brother of Wolf Larsen and captain of the *Macedonia* in Jack London's *The Sea-Wolf*.

Wolf Larsen. Brutal captain of the *Ghost* in Jack London's *The Sea-Wolf*.

Gummy Larson. Contractor to whom Willie Stark gives the hospital contract in exchange for political support in Robert Penn Warren's *All the King's Men*.

Mademoiselle La Rue (Mrs. Crayton). Teacher at Charlotte Temple's school who aids Jack Montraville in Charlotte's seduction; briefly she is the romantic interest of Belcour, only to abandon him for marriage to Colonel Crayton, whom she meets on her journey from England to the United States in Susanna Rowson's *Charlotte*.

Mrs. Larue. Sister-in-law of Dr. Ravenel; her rank opportunism and amoral behavior lead her to an affair with John Carter, despite his marriage to her niece, in John William DeForest's *Miss Ravenel's Conversion from Secession to Loyalty*.

Reverend James J. Lasher. Spiritual leader of the Ghost Shirt Society's revolt in Kurt Vonnegut's *Player Piano*.

John Laskell. Young liberal searching for the middle ground between conflicting absolutist ideologies in Lionel Trilling's *The Middle of the Journey*.

Richard Lasker. Publisher and editor of *Great Naval Battles*; Tarden exposes Lasker's involvement in a plot to boost book sales by faking the disappearance of one of his authors behind the Iron Curtain in Jerzy Kosinski's *Cockpit*.

Norma Latchett. Thirty-six-year-old mistress of Henry Bech for two and a half years; tense, critical woman with a sharp tongue; replaced as mistress by her sister, Bea Latchett Cook, in John Updike's *Bech: A Book*.

Charles (Spud) Latham. Son of Evans Latham and Mrs. Latham and best friend of Lymie Peters; loves Sally Forbes in William Maxwell's *The Folded Leaf*.

Deacon Latham. Father of Maria Latham and grandfather of Lydia Blood in William Dean Howells's *The Lady of the Aroostook*.

Evans Latham. Father of Helen and Spud Latham in William Maxwell's *The Folded Leaf*.

Helen Latham. Sister of Spud Latham in William Maxwell's *The Folded Leaf*.

Maria Latham. Aunt and guardian of Lydia Blood in William Dean Howells's *The Lady of the Aroostook*.

Mildred Latham. Woman with a mysterious past who loves Sidney Wyeth, sells his book, and eventually marries him in Oscar Micheaux's *The Forged Note*.

Mrs. Latham. Mother of Helen and Spud Latham in William Maxwell's *The Folded Leaf*.

Phil Latham. Wrestling coach at Devon School in John Knowles's *A Separate Peace*.

Frank Lathrop. Lifetime farming friend and neighbor of Mat Feltner; together they own the building used by Jasper Lathrop for his general store, the central meeting place for many of the conversations in Wendell Berry's *A Place on Earth* and *The Memory of Old Jack*.

Jasper Lathrop. Son of Frank Lathrop and owner of a general store in Port William, Kentucky, in Wendell Berry's *A Place on Earth* and *The Memory of Old Jack*.

Latnah. Woman who supports the black expatriates in Marseilles in Claude McKay's *Banjo*.

Clarence Latouche. Murderer of Asa Stryker in Edmund Wilson's *Memoirs of Hecate County*.

Jean Marie Latour. French missionary appointed vicar apostolic of New Mexico and later archbishop; oversees reforms in the New Mexico church and builds a cathedral in Santa Fe in Willa Cather's *Death Comes for the Archbishop*.

Ephemia (Effie) Lattimore. Homemaker sister of Olivia and Forester Lattimore in Mary Austin's *A Woman of Genius*.

Forester (Forrie) Lattimore. Brother of Olivia and Effie Lattimore and the favored child of the widowed Sally Lattimore; small-town shopkeeper in Mary Austin's *A Woman of Genius*.

Olivia May Lattimore. Sister of Effie and Forester Lattimore; widow of Tommy Bettersworth, lover of Helmeth Garrett, and longtime friend and probable future wife of Gerald McDermott; gifted and successful actress hampered by roles traditionally imposed on women; narrator of Mary Austin's *A Woman of Genius*.

Sally Lattimore. Widowed mother of Olivia, Forester, and Effie Lattimore in Mary Austin's *A Woman of Genius*.

Eva Laubenstein. Mother of Konrad Vost imprisoned for murdering Konrad Vost the Father; engineers her son's sexual liberation during a revolt of women prisoners in John Hawkes's *The Passion Artist*.

Hymie Laubscher. Assistant to Henry Miller at the telegraph company; frequently lends him money in Henry Miller's *Tropic of Capricorn*.

Harold Emery Lauder. Adolescent in love with Frances Goldsmith; joins forces with Randall Flagg in Stephen King's *The Stand*.

Laughing Boy (Blind Eyes, Horse Trader, My Slayer of Enemy Gods, Sings Before Spears, Turns His

Back, Went Away). Skilled horseman and artisan of silver jewelry who makes bowguards and is married to Slim Girl in Oliver La Farge's *Laughing Boy*.

Peter Laughlin. Speculator and member of the Chicago Board of Trade; business partner of Frank Cowperwood in Theodore Dreiser's *The Titan*.

Launcelot. Lover of Guinevere and antagonist of Arthur; describes himself as "not a leader, but . . . always led" in Thomas Berger's *Arthur Rex*.

Count Laundromat. Austrian who runs a laundromat near Renate's home in Anaïs Nin's *Collages*.

Amy March Laurence. See Amy Curtis March.

Bess Laurence. Daughter of Amy March and Theodore Laurence; stays briefly at Plumfield in Louisa May Alcott's *Little Men*.

James Laurence. Wealthy, elderly grandfather of Theodore Laurence in Louisa May Alcott's *Little Women*.

Theodore (Laurie, Teddy) Laurence. Wealthy grandson of James Laurence; proposes marriage to Jo March, but ultimately marries Amy March in Louisa May Alcott's *Little Women*; also appears in *Little Men*.

Laurent. Young helper in Creuzot's print shop; harassed by Virginians, who pejoratively label him a Jacobin, in Arna Wendell Bontemps's *Black Thunder*.

Laurie. Sexual conquest of Carol Severin Swanson in Jim Harrison's *Wolf*.

Phillip Laurie. Fiancée of Daisy Cowan; smug, eager businessman in Nathan Asch's *Pay Day*.

Grandma Lausch. Imperious ruler of the March household until she is consigned to an institution for the elderly, where she dies, in Saul Bellow's *The Adventures of Augie March*.

Albert (Kid Lousy, Louse, Kid Louso, Lousy) Lauzon. Boyhood friend and companion of Jack Duluoz in Jack Kerouac's *Doctor Sax*, *Maggie Cassidy*, and *Book of Dreams*.

Arial Lavalina. Handsome young novelist introduced to Frank Carmody by Leo Percepied in Jack Kerouac's *The Subterraneans*.

Lavender. Mulatto steward aboard the *Highlander* in Herman Melville's *Redburn*.

Jay Laverick. Playboy friend of Cass and Jinny Timberlane in Sinclair Lewis's *Cass Timberlane*.

Lenore La Verne. See Elly Chipley.

Eleanor Lavery. Lifelong friend who helps liberate Isabel Moore from bondage to the past in Mary Gordon's *Final Payments*.

Angela Williams Lavoisier. Fierce mother of Abeba Torch, her only child, in Ellease Southerland's *Let the Lion Eat Straw*.

Arthur Lavoisier. Loving stepfather of Abeba Torch in Ellease Southerland's *Let the Lion Eat Straw*.

Mama Lavorn. Operator of a black café and tourist home, a front for prostitution; dying of cancer, she narrates part of Jesse Hill Ford's *The Liberation of Lord Byron Jones*.

Catharine Law. Illegitimate daughter of John Law and Mary Connynge in Emerson Hough's *The Mississippi Bubble*.

John (Beau, Jack, Jean L'as, Jessamy) Law. Precocious, arrogant gambler and financial wizard in Emerson Hough's *The Mississippi Bubble*.

Will (Guillaume L'as) Law. Brother of John Law in Emerson Hough's *The Mississippi Bubble*.

Lawrence. Eccentric window dresser and friend who paints Djuna's apartment with phosphorescent paint in Anaïs Nin's *Children of the Albatross*.

Amy Lawrence. Girlfriend of Tom Sawyer until Becky Thatcher comes to town in Samuel Langhorne Clemens's *The Adventures of Tom Sawyer*.

Major Billy Lawrence. Second-in-command to Colonel Templeton on the thirty-six-mile hike in William Styron's *The Long March*.

Charles Gans Lawrence. Wealthy college tennis star with a magnetic personality and a "habit of perfection"; gored in an amateur bullfight and later kills himself in Wright Morris's *The Huge Season*.

Leon (Griffin) Lawrence. Actor who seduces and later marries Sarah Croyden; as Leon Griffin, he is the friend and would-be lover of Olivia Lattimore in Mary Austin's *A Woman of Genius*.

Jack Laws. Lover of Ethan Segal and friend of Pammy Wynant; commits suicide while the three are vacationing in Maine in Don DeLillo's *Players*.

Maureen Fairchild (Great-Aunt Mac) Laws. Widowed aunt of Battle Fairchild; lives at Shellmound plantation in Eudora Welty's *Delta Wedding*.

Berry Lawson. Former slave who moves to the Red Wing settlement; flees with Nimbus after the battle with the Ku Klux Klan, but reappears years later as a settler in Eupolia, Kansas, in Albion W. Tourgee's *Bricks without Straw*.

Catherine (Cat, Catty) Lawson. Hair straightener who tends to Ursa Corregidora following Ursa's operation in Gayl Jones's *Corregidora*.

Jack Lawson. Best friend of Henry Miller; remains ill for a year and dies; Miller claims to have forgotten him immediately after his death in Henry Miller's *Tropic of Capricorn*.

Sally Ann Lawson. Wife of Berry Lawson, with whom she moves to Red Wing and flees following the Ku Klux Klan attack; returns with their children to Red Wing, and is resettled, by Mollie Ainslie, in Kansas, in Albion W. Tourgee's *Bricks without Straw*.

Captain John (Jack) Lawton. Fearless captain of the Virginia dragoons who tries to track down Harvey Birch; fatally wounded toward the end of the Revolutionary War in James Fenimore Cooper's *The Spy*.

Mrs. Layden. Wealthy observer of the dance marathon who chooses Robert Syverten and Gloria Beatty as her favorite couple; accidentally killed in the shooting in the Palm Garden in Horace McCoy's *They Shoot Horses, Don't They?*

Edgar Laydon. Teacher of literature and first love of Hagar Ashendyne in Mary Johnston's *Hagar*.

Solace Layfield. False prophet hired by Hoover Shoats as Hazel Motes's double; Motes kills him by running over him with a rat-colored Essex in Flannery O'Connor's *Wise Blood*.

Lazarus. Ex-insurance salesman; bouncer at the Iron Horse and student at Belt's dojo in Harry Crews's *Karate Is a Thing of the Spirit*.

Lazarus. Servant of Johnny Church's family; sent to fight in Cromwell's army; captured by the king's army, who cut off his ears and his tongue, in Mary Lee Settle's *Prisons*.

Joe (Joey, Laze) Lazenby. High school friend of Conrad Jarrett in Judith Guest's *Ordinary People*.

Rose Wise (Mrs. Rose, Rosey) Lazuli. San Francisco socialite who directs poetry readings and entertains Jack Duluoz in Jack Kerouac's *Desolation Angels*.

Paul Lazzaro. Prisoner of war and murderer of Billy Pilgrim in Kurt Vonnegut's *Slaughterhouse-Five*.

George Leach. Former cabin boy who attempts to murder the captain and cook aboard the *Ghost* in Jack London's *The Sea-Wolf*.

Leah. Older sister of Augie; rears him after the death of their mother in Arna Wendell Bontemps's *God Sends Sunday*.

Zelda Leah. First wife of Jacob Eliezer, engaged to him at the age of ten, and mother of their three children; killed with her children in the Chmielnicki massacre in Isaac Bashevis Singer's *The Slave*.

Veronica Leary. Army nurse and romantic love interest of Carlo Reinhart in Thomas Berger's *Crazy in Berlin*.

Anna Leath. Wealthy American woman living in France after her marriage to Fraser Leath; widowed and pained by her reticence and inability to experience passion, she renews a relationship with George Darrow, a former suitor who has recently had an affair with Sophy Viner, governess to Anna's daughter, in Edith Wharton's *The Reef*.

Effie Leath. Daughter of Anna and Fraser Leath in Edith Wharton's *The Reef*.

Fraser Leath. Deceased husband of Anna Leath; cosmopolitan man who collected enamelled snuff boxes and painted in watercolors in Edith Wharton's *The Reef*.

Owen Leath. Stepson of Anna Leath; his wish to marry Sophy Viner eventually causes George Darrow, Anna's fiancé, to reveal his affair with Sophy in Edith Wharton's *The Reef*.

Leather-stocking. See Nathaniel Bumppo.

Woodrow (Woody) Leathers. World War II friend of Orlando Pratt; sleeps with Maude Coffin Pratt, who thinks Leathers is her brother Orlando, in Paul Theroux's *Picture Palace*.

Bill Leatherwood. Leader of a band of ruthless, fortune-seeking marauders in T. S. Stribling's *The Forge*.

Eleanore Leavenworth. Cousin of Mary Leavenworth; niece of Horatio Leavenworth, whom she is suspected of having murdered, in Anna Katharine Green's *The Leavenworth Case*.

Horatio Leavenworth. Wealthy man found murdered in his library in Anna Katharine Green's *The Leavenworth Case*.

Mary Leavenworth. Cousin of Eleanore Leavenworth; sole heir of her uncle Horatio Leavenworth, until he discovers her secret marriage to Henry Clavering, an Englishman, in Anna Katharine Green's *The Leavenworth Case*.

Mr. Leavenworth. Rich American widower traveling in Europe who becomes engaged to Augusta Blanchard; commissions Roderick Hudson to sculpt a representation of Intellectual Refinement in Henry James's *Roderick Hudson*.

Peter Leavitt. Clinical microbiologist and member of the scientist group at Project Wildfire in Michael Crichton's *The Andromeda Strain*.

Le Balafré. Venerable Sioux leader, father of Tachechana, and father-in-law of Mahtoree; offers to adopt and thereby save Mahtoree's captive, Hard Heart, in James Fenimore Cooper's *The Prairie*.

Nikolai Maximovitch Lebedev. Owner of a brickyard; hires Yakov Bok as foreman after Yakov saves his life in Bernard Malamud's *The Fixer*.

Zinaida Nikolaevna (Zina) Lebedev. Daughter of Nikolai Lebedev; tries to seduce Yakov Bok and later testifies against him in Bernard Malamud's *The Fixer*.

Dmitri Lebedov. Elderly Russian orderly at Sacred Heart Hospital; confesses to Angelo DeMarco that he attempted to rape Maria Alvarez in Edward Lewis Wallant's *The Children at the Gate*.

Ulysse Lebris. Restaurateur in Brittany and distant relative discovered by Jean-Louis Lebris de Kérouac in Jack Kerouac's *Satori in Paris*.

Madame Lebrun. Owner of an island resort where the Pontelliers, the Ratignolles, and Mademoiselle Reisz vacation; mother of Robert Lebrun in Kate Chopin's *The Awakening*.

Robert Lebrun. Young man with whom Edna Pontellier falls in love; son of Madame Lebrun in Kate Chopin's *The Awakening*.

Madame Lecerf. See Nina Toorovetz de Rechnoy.

Le Loup Cervier. Indian brave who gives Natty Bumppo the name Hawkeye; first man killed by Bumppo in James Fenimore Cooper's *The Deerslayer*.

Dr. Ledsmar. Scientist and student of Darwinian theory consulted by Theron Ware; Ledsmar derisively names a lizard after Ware in Harold Frederic's *The Damnation of Theron Ware*.

Oscar (Shad) Ledue. Surly peasant, hired man of Doremus Jessup, and captain of the local Minute Men; caught embezzling funds, he is sent to a concentration camp, where he is killed by people he

sent there, in Sinclair Lewis's *It Can't Happen Here*.

Thomas Ledward. Acting surgeon aboard HMS *Bounty* in Charles Nordhoff and James Norman Hall's *Mutiny on the Bounty*; set adrift with Captain Bligh; narrator of *Men against the Sea*.

Lee (Ching Chong). Wise Chinese servant in the Trask household; helps to rear the twins Caleb and Aron Trask and acts as friend and advisor to Adam Trask in John Steinbeck's *East of Eden*.

Buddy Lee. Sensitive twin whose brother died of cancer at age fifteen; works for Stephen Conner as secretary and confidant in John Updike's *The Poorhouse Fair*.

Dixie Lee. Pioneer who becomes a brothel madam and later an oil baron in Edna Ferber's *Cimarron*.

Inspector J. Lee. See William Lee.

Lorelei Lee. Blonde diarist and intercontinental adventuress who, accompanied by Dorothy Shaw, collects amours and diamonds; her diary constitutes Anita Loos's *"Gentlemen Prefer Blondes"*; chronicles further adventures and the life of Dorothy in *"But Gentlemen Marry Brunettes."*

Madeleine Ross (Mrs. Lightfoot Lee) Lee. Young widow who moves to Washington to observe democracy in action and starts a salon where various personalities meet for lively conversation; accepts the marriage proposal of Senator Ratcliffe, then rejects it after learning of his improper political dealings, in Henry Adams's *Democracy*.

Mavis (China Doll) Lee. Prostitute in Decatur, New Jersey; becomes involved with murder and drug dealing in Hal Bennett's *Lord of Dark Places*.

Robert Edward Lee. Confederate general commanding the Army of Northern Virginia; hopes to destroy Union forces through a second invasion of the North, but loses decisively at Gettysburg, in Michael Shaara's *The Killer Angels*.

William (Bill, Billy, Lee the Agent, El Hombre Invisible, Inspector J. Lee, Klinker, William Seward) Lee. Heroin addict and petty criminal in New York, New Orleans, Texas, and eventually Mexico City; narrator of William S. Burroughs's *Junkie*; appears also in *Naked Lunch, Nova Express, The Soft Machine, The Ticket That Exploded*, and *Exterminator!*

Lee the Agent. See William Lee.

Lee Buck Cal. See Lee Buck Calhoun.

Cap Leech. Father of Luke and Mulge Lampson; lives with the Indians and practices irregular and illegal medicine; delivers Harry Bohn from the body of the infant's dead mother in John Hawkes's *The Beetle Leg*.

George (Grig) Leeds. Abyssinian piano player with whom Malcolm shares a room in the house of Eloisa and Jerome Brace in James Purdy's *Malcolm*.

Leete. Twenty-first century doctor and father of Edith Leete; discusses the advances of society in the time Julian West has been asleep in Edward Bellamy's *Looking Backward*.

Edith Leete. Daughter of Doctor Leete and descendant of Edith Bartlett; loves Julian West in Edward Bellamy's *Looking Backward*.

Leevey. American military overseer of a partitioned Germany; pursued by Zizendorf in John Hawkes's *The Cannibal*.

Mary Agnes LeFabre. Creole black woman who rejects the advances of white Tee Bob Samson in Ernest J. Gaines's *The Autobiography of Miss Jane Pittman*.

Jim Lefferts. College roommate and close friend of Elmer Gantry; they drift apart when Gantry decides to enter the ministry in Sinclair Lewis's *Elmer Gantry*.

Lawrence Lefferts. Member of the old New York social set; known as the authority on correct form in Edith Wharton's *The Age of Innocence*.

Robert A. (Bob) Leffingwell. Highly controversial presidential nominee for Secretary of State in Allen Drury's *Advise and Consent*.

Will Legate. Hunter in William Faulkner's *Go Down, Moses* and protector of Lucas Beauchamp in *Intruder in the Dust*.

Dr. Leggett. Marine biologist on the *Sea Beast*; student of "the primeval ooze of life" in Wright Morris's *Love among the Cannibals*.

William Leggett. Consumptive editor of the *Evening Post*; invites Charles Schuyler to write Aaron Burr's story; convinced that Martin Van Buren is Burr's illegitimate son in Gore Vidal's *Burr*.

Peter Legrand. Mill owner and moneylender; spends half a lifetime longing for Julia Cropleigh Cree and the child he thinks is his own in Andrew Lytle's *The Velvet Horn*.

Julian Legree. Matinee idol and frequent drinker in Henry Miller's *Black Spring*.

Simon Legree. Cruel, opportunistic former slave owner who gains political power during Recon-

struction in Thomas Dixon's *The Leopard's Spots*.

Simon Legree. Final owner of Uncle Tom, whom he tortures to death in an effort to make Tom reveal the whereabouts of two escaped female slaves, in Harriet Beecher Stowe's *Uncle Tom's Cabin*.

Legs (Red). Gambler and bootlegger; shares a room with Sidney Wyeth in Oscar Micheaux's *The Forged Note*.

Dr. Leopold Lehmann. Pseudo-psychiatrist specializing in cases of human transformation; guardian of Paula Kahler in Wright Morris's *The Field of Vision*.

Annabel Leigh. First love of Humbert Humbert and source of his passion for Dolores Haze; dies of typhus four months after her Riviera summer with him in Vladimir Nabokov's *Lolita*.

William Leigh. Friend of Jack Flowers; dies suddenly in Paul Theroux's *Saint Jack*.

Alma Leighton. Artist romantically interested in Angus Beaton in William Dean Howells's *A Hazard of New Fortunes*.

Patricia (Pat) Leighton. New York advertising agent and lover of Jim Calder; attempts to free Calder from his attachment to the Brills and Wickford Point in John P. Marquand's *Wickford Point*.

Lekh. Birdcatcher and lover of Stupid Ludmila; paints the bird in the title of Jerzy Kosinski's *The Painted Bird*.

Annie Leland. Grandmother of Peter Leland; forces her grandson to look at his mannacled father and later wills him the house where his father was imprisoned in the attic in Fred Chappell's *Dagon*.

Peter Leland. Methodist minister, author of "Remnants of Pagan Forces in American Puritanism," and drunken subject of Mina Morgan's humiliations, mutilations, and human sacrifice; protagonist of Fred Chappell's *Dagon*.

Sheila Leland. Wife of Peter Leland; presumably murdered by him in Fred Chappell's *Dagon*.

Iris Lemon. Woman who brings Roy Hobbs out of his batting slump and to whom he goes after being sold out by Memo Paris in Bernard Malamud's *The Natural*.

Mr. Lemon. Caretaker of the trailer park where the Manions live; Frederic Manion turns himself in to Lemon, a deputy sheriff, after shooting Barney Quill in Robert Traver's *Anatomy of a Murder*.

Casaubon Le Moyne. Father of Hesden Le Moyne; Unionist who is the only Whig to have represented

Horsford County in the North Carolina legislature in Albion W. Tourgee's *Bricks without Straw*.

Hesden Le Moyne. Southern gentleman and Unionist whose code of honor leads him to enlist as a private in the Confederate army; befriends Eliab Hill and Nimbus; repudiates the racial prejudice of his Southern neighbors; marries Mollie Ainslie in Albion W. Tourgee's *Bricks without Straw*.

Hester Richards Le Moyne. Granddaughter of Black Jim Richards, from whom she inherits Mulberry Hill plantation, and mother of Hesden Le Moyne; treats Mollie Ainslie as her social inferior until Mollie shames her by demonstrating a rigorous code of personal honor in Albion W. Tourgee's *Bricks without Straw*.

Hildreth Le Moyne. Son of Hesden and Julia Lomax Le Moyne; dies of yellow fever, despite the nursing of Mollie Ainslie, whom he loves from the moment they meet, in Albion W. Tourgee's *Bricks without Straw*.

Julia Lomax Le Moyne. First wife of Hesden Le Moyne; dies while giving birth to Hildreth Le Moyne in Albion W. Tourgee's *Bricks without Straw*.

Lemsford. Poet friend of White-Jacket in Herman Melville's *White-Jacket*.

Lena. See Mary Magdalene Dead.

Lenard (Len). Lover of Lou Ellen and party host in Ed Bullins's *The Reluctant Rapist*.

Judith (Judy) Lengel. Stupid but determined student of George Caldwell in John Updike's *The Centaur*.

Anna Lenihan (Lenihanova). Impoverished dance-hall hostess and then a waitress who is one of the narrator's mistresses in Edmund Wilson's *Memoirs of Hecate County*.

Sylvia Lennox. Corrupt wife of Terry Lennox; murder victim in Raymond Chandler's *The Long Goodbye*.

Terry Lennox. War hero suspected of murdering his wife; befriended by Philip Marlowe in Raymond Chandler's *The Long Goodbye*.

Alexander (Uncle Aleck) Lenoir. Simpleminded former slave of Jeannie Campbell Lenoir; elected to the state legislature in Thomas Dixon's *The Clansman*.

Capitola (Cap Black) Le Noir. Fiesty heroine who first appears disguised as a newsboy and continues her adventures as a "damsel errant," fighting

duels, capturing bandits, and rescuing damsels in distress, in E.D.E.N. Southworth's *The Hidden Hand*.

Craven Le Noir. Bumbling son of Gabriel Le Noir; falls in love with Capitola Le Noir in E.D.E.N. Southworth's *The Hidden Hand*.

Gabriel Le Noir. Villainous uncle of Capitola Le Noir; conspires to obtain her fortune and that of Clara Day in E.D.E.N. Southworth's *The Hidden Hand*.

Jeannie Campbell Lenoir. Widow and mother of Marion Lenoir; commits suicide with her daughter after Marion is raped in Thomas Dixon's *The Clansman*.

Marion Lenoir. Sweetheart of Ben Cameron; commits suicide after being raped by Augustus Caesar in Thomas Dixon's *The Clansman*.

Lenore. Radical left-wing contact of Kat Alcazar; recommended Kat to Angel Stone in M. F. Beal's *Angel Dance*.

Susan (Lorna Sackville, Susie) Lenox. Mistress of Rod Spenser and of Freddie Palmer; factory worker and prostitute in Cincinnati and New York before becoming an acclaimed actress in David Graham Phillips's *Susan Lenox*.

Leola. Second cousin by marriage to Shokotee McNeilly; comes to live with Elias McCutcheon and Jane Nail at the birth of their first child and remains in Jesse Hill Ford's *The Raider*.

Leona (Anne). Poor white woman from Georgia whom Rufus Scott loves and abuses in James Baldwin's *Another Country*.

Foscoe Leonard. Homesteader and minister who is killed when a posse overtakes Wade Shiveley; his death helps cause Shiveley's hanging in H. L. Davis's *Honey in the Horn*.

Margaret Leonard. Consumptive woman who befriends Eugene Gant in Thomas Wolfe's *Look Homeward, Angel*.

Ruth Leonard. Lover of Rabbit Angstrom; becomes pregnant by him in John Updike's *Rabbit, Run*.

Leontine. Black singer at the Paradise Inn nightclub in Anaïs Nin's *Collages*.

Leopard. Greedy and fierce robber chief killed by Wang the Tiger in Pearl Buck's *Sons*.

J. T. Leopold. Retired painter and husband of Milly Leopold; occupies a Second Avenue apartment managed by Norman Moonbloom in Edward

Lewis Wallant's *The Tenants of Moonbloom.*

Milly Leopold. Wife of J. T. Leopold; lives in a Second Avenue apartment managed by Norman Moonbloom in Edward Lewis Wallant's *The Tenants of Moonbloom.*

Elwin (Leper) Lepellier. Clumsy schoolmate of Gene Forrester and Finny; suffers a mental breakdown after joining the Ski Patrol and receives a dishonorable discharge in John Knowles's *A Separate Peace.*

Harry LeSabre. Transvestite Pontiac salesman in Kurt Vonnegut's *Breakfast of Champions.*

Thomas Le Sage. Los Angeles Superior Court judge who replaces Arthur Alarcon in the second trial of Gregory Powell and Jimmy Smith in Joseph Wambaugh's *The Onion Field.*

Leslie. Republican judge who teaches democracy and American politics to John Gwynne in Gertrude Atherton's *Ancestors.*

Dr. John Leslie. Widowed New England country doctor who has avoided the cities and great hospitals to minister instead to country folk; guardian of Nan Prince in Sarah Orne Jewett's *A Country Doctor.*

Faith Leslie. Sister of Hope Leslie; captured by Indians and married to the Pequod Oneco in Catharine Maria Sedgwick's *Hope Leslie.*

Hope Leslie. Savior of the Indians Nelema and Magawisca; betrothed of Everell Fletcher in Catharine Maria Sedgwick's *Hope Leslie.*

Harry Lesser. Jewish novelist struggling to finish his third novel; criticizes the writing of Willie Spearmint and falls in love with Irene Bell in Bernard Malamud's *The Tenants.*

Lestat. Vampire who makes Louis a vampire; kills Claudia and Madeleine in Anne Rice's *Interview with the Vampire.*

Lester. Saxophonist whom Dorothy Shaw marries despite his ugliness and, as it turns out, homosexuality; bribed by Charlie Breene's parents to prevent a divorce, then murdered at their instigation in Anita Loos's *"But Gentlemen Marry Brunettes."*

Ada Lester. Mother of seventeen children, not all by her husband Jeeter Lester; longs to be buried in a new dress in Erskine Caldwell's *Tobacco Road.*

Dan Lester. Young New England farmer-blacksmith who almost loses his lifelong love, Doris Owen, to Dick Dale, but finally marries her, in Sarah Orne Jewett's *A Marsh Island.*

Dude Lester. Sixteen year old who marries Bessie Rice, an itinerant preacher, in Erskine Caldwell's *Tobacco Road.*

Ellie May Lester. Harelipped daughter of Jeeter and Ada Lester; leaves her parents to become the mate of Lov Bensey, a man her younger sister Pearl Lester deserted, in Erskine Caldwell's *Tobacco Road.*

Howard Lester. Judge who presides over Frederick Eichner's grand jury hearing in Terry Southern's *Flash and Filigree.*

Jeeter Lester. Georgia tenant farmer whose obsession with the soil causes him to reject the financial security of the cotton mills in Erskine Caldwell's *Tobacco Road.*

Mother Lester. Half-starved grandmother of the Lester children; run over by an automobile driven by her grandson Dude Lester and buried in a field before she is dead in Erskine Caldwell's *Tobacco Road.*

Muriel Lester. See Muriel Lester Lancaster.

Abe (Lynx) Letterman. Agent for Angela Sterling and for Dave and Debbie Roberts in Terry Southern's *Blue Movie.*

Madame Leuwen. Pseudonym under which one of Tarden's unidentified lovers checks into Hotel de la Mole in Jerzy Kosinski's *Cockpit.*

Lev (Arieh Ben Barak). Husband of Katrina Perlé and father of Marshall Pearl; Russian Jew who commands the Israeli Second Mountain Brigade in Mark Helprin's *Refiner's Fire.*

Aryeh Lev. Father of Asher Lev; breaks with his son over Asher's art; assists European Jews in Chaim Potok's *My Name Is Asher Lev.*

Asher Lev. Narrator whose art causes his rejection by the Jewish community in Chaim Potok's *My Name Is Asher Lev.*

Rivkeh Lev. Mother of Asher Lev; torn between her son's artistic talent and her husband's disdain of that talent in Chaim Potok's *My Name Is Asher Lev.*

Yitzchok Lev. Supportive uncle of Asher Lev in Chaim Potok's *My Name Is Asher Lev.*

George (Lev) Levanter. Russian émigré, international businessman, and adventurer; protagonist of Jerzy Kosinski's *Blind Date.*

Irving Levenspiel. Jewish landlord who wants Harry Lesser to move so he can tear down the building in Bernard Malamud's *The Tenants.*

Asa Leventhal. Middle-aged New York Jew and trade-journal editor who must cope with his fears of loneliness, anti-Semitism, displacement, and death in order to strike an informed balance between what he owes to others and what he owes to himself in Saul Bellow's *The Victim*.

Peter Charles Leverett. Young attorney from Virginia and childhood friend of Mason Flagg; narrator of William Styron's *Set This House on Fire*.

Jake Levin. Jewish marine radio operator and friend of Mortimer Gray; killed on Tarawa in Leon Uris's *Battle Cry*.

Seymour (Sam, Sy) Levin. Thirty-year-old composition instructor at Cascadia College who has an affair with Pauline Gilley that eventually leads to his resignation from the college; central character in Bernard Malamud's *A New Life*.

Gerald David Levine. R.A.F. pilot who commits suicide in William Faulkner's *A Fable*.

Holly Levine. Literary critic and friend of Leslie Braverman in Wallace Markfield's *To an Early Grave*.

Noach Levinson. Recordkeeper for the *Judenrat* (a Nazi-controlled governing body) and principal narrator of an account of the Nazi occupation of Poland and the Jewish resistance movement in a Warsaw ghetto in John Hersey's *The Wall*.

Matt Levitt. Mechanic enamored of Linda Snopes in William Faulkner's *The Town*.

Jacob (Jake, Jawn) Levy. Jewish jeep driver for Lieutenant Colonel John Dawson Smithers; lover and fiancé of Kathe Limpert; deliberately runs over three Germans after visiting Dachau in Martha Gellhorn's *Wine of Astonishment*.

Lydia Levy. American Jew who is the sister of Paul Levy and the wife of Marshall Pearl; understands her husband's "visions" and supports his search for his family in Mark Helprin's *Refiner's Fire*.

Maurice Levy. Rival of Penrod Schofield for the attention of Marjorie Jones; alternates between being Penrod's bitter foe and one of his regular playmates in Booth Tarkington's *Penrod, Penrod and Sam*, and *Penrod Jashber*.

Paul Levy. American Jew who is the brother of Lydia Levy and the protector of Marshall Pearl; Navy officer who, as captain of the *Lindos Transit*, tries unsuccessfully to help transport European Jews to Palestine in Mark Helprin's *Refiner's Fire*.

Sol Levy. Osage, Oklahoma, Jew who rises from street peddler to prosperous and respected businessman in Edna Ferber's *Cimarron*.

Daniel Isaacson (Danny) Lewin. Son of Paul and Rochelle Isaacson reared by Robert and Lise Lewin following his parents' execution; Ph.D. candidate at Columbia University who physically abuses his wife and is a radical protester; narrator of parts of E. L. Doctorow's *The Book of Daniel*.

Lise Lewin. Wife of Robert Lewin and foster-mother of Daniel Isaacson Lewin and Susan Isaacson Lewin in E. L. Doctorow's *The Book of Daniel*.

Robert Lewin. Husband of Lise Lewin and foster-father of Daniel Isaacson Lewin and Susan Isaacson Lewin; Boston College law professor who knows that the Isaacsons' trial was a travesty in E. L. Doctorow's *The Book of Daniel*.

Susan Isaacson (Susy, Susyanna) Lewin. Daughter of Paul and Rochelle Isaacson reared by Robert and Lise Lewin following her parents' execution; institutionalized after attempting suicide; retreats into her madness and dies in E. L. Doctorow's *The Book of Daniel*.

John Lewis. Numbers runner who fails to pay off Hubert Cooley's $7.00 bet on 417 in Julian Mayfield's *The Hit*.

Shepherd (Shep) Lewis. Black school teacher and friend of Elijah Green; takes a special, but not necessarily benevolent, interest in Robert X in Ernest J. Gaines's *In My Father's House*.

Spotteswood Lewis. Tuckahoe gentleman and Provincial officer in charge of Fort Young; snubbed by Sally Lacey because he lives with an Indian squaw in Mary Lee Settle's *O Beulah Land*.

Stanley Lewis. Elihu Willsson's secretary in Dashiell Hammett's *Red Harvest*.

Tony Lewis. Good-looking homosexual in his thirties; lover of Sebastian Michael and friend of Johnny Rio in John Rechy's *Numbers*.

Lieutenant Leznicki. New York detective who first accuses Stephen Rojack of murdering Deborah Rojack in Norman Mailer's *An American Dream*.

Mélanie (La Jarretière) L'Heuremaudit. Young French ballet star; has an affair with V. in Paris in 1913; dies during a performance as the result of an accident or suicide in Thomas Pynchon's *V.*

Libanius. Hellenist scholar and philosopher whose teachings are much admired by Julian; narrates part of Gore Vidal's *Julian*.

Lu Libble. Football coach of Jack Duluoz at Columbia University in Jack Kerouac's *Maggie Cassidy*; appears as Lou Little in *Visions of Cody*.

Bayou de Libertas. Overseer of the plantation at Bréda known for his kind treatment of slaves; friend of Captain Frounier in Arna Wendell Bontemps's *Drums at Dusk*.

Mr. Librarian (Candyman). Caretaker of an unusual San Francisco library and lover of Vida Kramar; narrator of Richard Brautigan's *The Abortion*.

Ernest Lieberman. Psychiatrist at Gan Dafna kibbutz who works with concentration camp survivors in Leon Uris's *Exodus*.

Maxwell (Skip) Lieberman. Coney Island schoolmate of Bruce Gold and now manager of a small intellectual magazine that publishes Gold's articles in Joseph Heller's *Good as Gold*.

The Lie Detector. Man who assumes that Sabina is guilty and follows her and other artists, extracting confessions from them, in Anaïs Nin's *A Spy in the House of Love* and *Seduction of the Minotaur*.

Lietta. Oldest daughter of Edward in Anaïs Nin's *Seduction of the Minotaur*.

Emily Liggett. Wife of Weston Liggett; does not suspect her husband's infidelity in John O'Hara's *Butterfield 8*.

Weston Liggett. Wealthy, Yale-educated husband of Emily Liggett and lover of Gloria Wandrous; his double life finally is exposed when he returns home beaten up and drunk in John O'Hara's *Butterfield 8*.

Christina (Princess Casamassima) Light. Beautiful, illegitimate daughter of Mrs. Light and the Cavaliere Giacosa; loved by Roderick Hudson, but marries Prince Casamassima, in Henry James's *Roderick Hudson*; leaves her husband to pursue revolutionary activity in *The Princess Casamassima*.

Gracie Light. See Gracie Vaiden.

Mrs. Light. Widowed mother, by the Cavaliere Giacosa, of Christina Light; obsessed with making a great fortune by marriage for her daughter in Henry James's *Roderick Hudson*.

Lightborne. Owner of a Soho gallery and erotic art dealer in Don DeLillo's *Running Dog*.

Amanda Lightfoot. Feminine ideal of the young Gamaliel Bland Honeywell; remains faithful to him in their brief engagement to him in Ellen Glasgow's *The Romantic Comedians*.

Charlie Lightfoot. Veteran Los Angeles police detective and former partner of A.M. Valnikov; a suicide in Joseph Wambaugh's *The Black Marble*.

Maria Lightfoot. Mulatto grandmother of Emma Lou Morgan in Wallace Thurman's *The Blacker the Berry*.

Samuel Lightfoot. Mulatto grandfather of Emma Lou Morgan in Wallace Thurman's *The Blacker the Berry*.

Shining Lighttower. Marine radio operator wounded at Saipan in Leon Uris's *Battle Cry*.

Ruth Lightwood. Bitter wife of Jack Beechum; refuses to sleep with her husband after the birth of their daughter, Clara Beechum, in Wendell Berry's *The Memory of Old Jack*.

Lil Bits. Daughter of Aunt Cora Lou and sister of Mamie in Sarah E. Wright's *This Child's Gonna Live*.

Lillian. See Honest Lil.

Lillian. See Lillian Beye.

Lily. Mira's friend; driven insane by the cruelty of her father, husband, and son in Marilyn French's *The Women's Room*.

Kathe Limpert. Catholic waitress in Luxembourg; lover and intended wife of Jacob Levy in Martha Gellhorn's *Wine of Astonishment*.

Abraham Lincoln. President of the United States who pardons Ben Cameron and whose assassination leads to the radical Republican policies of Reconstruction in Thomas Dixon's *The Clansman*.

Mr. Lincoln. Black Philadelphian who raises canaries and teaches Birdy about breeding them in William Wharton's *Birdy*.

Berthold Lindau. German-born American socialist who is the editor of *Every Other Week* and is fired by Jacob Dryfoos; killed by the police during a streetcar workers' strike in William Dean Howells's *A Hazard of New Fortunes*.

Evan Lindley. Progress-minded attorney; learns prudence from his wife Serena Lindley after suffering financial reverses in Mary Austin's *Santa Lucia*.

Serena Haven Lindley. Wife of Evan Lindley; frustrated from exclusion from her husband's business affairs until financial reverses force an end to his protectiveness in Mary Austin's *Santa Lucia*.

Mrs. Lindow. Plump and pleasant grandmotherly housekeeper who prepares meals for the narrator and her young writer-lover during their stay at

Ambleside in Aline Bernstein's *The Journey Down.*

Henry Lindsay. Son of Philip Lindsay, brother of Mildred Lindsay, and friend of Stephen Foster; visits Cornwallis to assure Arthur Butler's fair treatment in John Pendleton Kennedy's *Horse-Shoe Robinson.*

Mildred Lindsay. Daughter of Philip Lindsay, sister of Henry Lindsay, and wife of Arthur Butler; visits Cornwallis to assure her husband's fair treatment; reunited with Butler at King's Mountain in John Pendleton Kennedy's *Horse-Shoe Robinson.*

Mr. Lindsay. Scottish uncle of Ellen Montgomery; supervises her training and education while she lives in Scotland in Susan Warner's *The Wide, Wide World.*

Mrs. Lindsay. Scottish grandmother of Ellen Montgomery; disowned Ellen's mother after she married an American, but rears Ellen as a teenager in Susan Warner's *The Wide, Wide World.*

Philip Lindsay. Father of Henry and Mildred Lindsay; master of Dove Cote; dies in a misdirected effort to pursue his daughter and join the British and Tory forces at King's Mountain in John Pendleton Kennedy's *Horse-Shoe Robinson.*

Mickey Linehan. Continental Detective Agency operative who answers the Continental Op's call for assistance in Dashiell Hammett's *Red Harvest.*

Lena Lingard. Jim Burden's girlfriend while he is in college in Willa Cather's *My Ántonia.*

Byron Linkhorn. Brother of Dove Linkhorn; his death causes the passion to go out of his father's sermons in Nelson Algren's *A Walk on the Wild Side.*

Dove Linkhorn. Innocent involved in numerous shady schemes in Nelson Algren's *A Walk on the Wild Side.*

Fitz Linkhorn. Father of Byron and Dove Linkhorn; drunken fire-and-brimstone preacher in Nelson Algren's *A Walk on the Wild Side.*

Mr. Linnehan. High school principal of Henry Bech in John Updike's *Bech: A Book.*

Colonel Linscomb. Horse owner in William Faulkner's *The Reivers.*

Carl Linstrum. Childhood friend of Alexandra Bergson, whom he marries, in Willa Cather's *O Pioneers!*

Lion. Dog in William Faulkner's *Go Down, Moses* (where he helps capture Old Ben) and *The Town.*

Lip-lip. Dog of Gray Beaver; killed by White Fang in Jack London's *White Fang.*

Private Lipido. Defender of Mother Ormsby; companion to Warren K. Ormsby in ceremonies dedicating the USS *Ormsby* in Wright Morris's *Man and Boy.*

Mabel Blitch Lipscomb. Childhood friend of Undine Spragg; divorces and remarries to enhance her social status in Edith Wharton's *The Custom of the Country.*

Jane Löes Lipton. World traveler and philanthropist, sufferer from lupus erythematosus, and friend of Brewster Ashenden in *The Making of Ashenden*, a novella in Stanley Elkin's *Searches and Seizures.*

Prince Lír. Adopted son of King Haggard; falls in love with Lady Amalthea and performs heroic deeds to win her favor in Peter S. Beagle's *The Last Unicorn.*

Lisa. Exotic woman in Acapulco who looks like a combination of a Toulouse-Lautrec painting and the jungle; moves back to New York with her lover Bill; friend of Renate in Anaïs Nin's *Collages.*

Dame Lisa (Adelais). Shrewish wife of Jurgen in James Branch Cabell's *Jurgen.*

Lissus. Opponent wounded with a machete during a fight with Augie in Arna Wendell Bontemps's *God Sends Sunday.*

Binky Lister. Secretary of David Bell at a New York television network; while on the road, Bell calls her regularly for home office news in Don DeLillo's *Americana.*

Barry Little. Black American student at McCarthy College in Wisconsin who befriends the young Hakim Ellelloû in John Updike's *The Coup.*

Joy (Mrs. Ossie Little) Little. Wife of Ossie Little, lover of Nigra Jones, and mother by Jones of the mulatto Sherman Pew; Johnny Clane falls in love with her and commits suicide after she gives birth to her son in Carson McCullers's *Clock Without Hands.*

Lou Little. See Lu Libble.

Ossie Little. Preacher whom Nigra Jones is accused of murdering; husband of Joy Little in Carson McCullers's *Clock Without Hands.*

Little Big Man. See Jack Crabb.

Little Boy. Son of Father and Mother; becomes a star in Our Gang comedies in E. L. Doctorow's *Ragtime.*

Little Brother Leaping Fish. Lone young Indian whom Leslie Collins meets in the forest and names in Harriette Simpson Arnow's *The Kentucky Trace*.

Joe Little Fox. Indian boatbuilder for Backwater Brandon and lover of Lyddy; burned to death by the Kreggs when they hear that the land beyond the mountains is reserved for the Indians in Mary Lee Settle's *O Beulah Land*.

The Little Girl. Daughter of Mameh and Tateh; befriended by Evelyn Nesbit in E. L. Doctorow's *Ragtime*.

Little Harp. Bandit who discovers that Jamie Lockhart is both a robber and a gentleman in Eudora Welty's *The Robber Bridegroom*.

Little Horse. "Heemaneh" Indian in Thomas Berger's *Little Big Man*.

Little Luke. See Luther.

Henry van der Luyden. Husband of Louisa van der Luyden; one of the last remaining members of an aristocratic New York family and so considered a source of social wisdom in Edith Wharton's *The Age of Innocence*; mentioned in *The Old Maid*.

Louisa Dagonet van der Luyden. Wealthy New York aristocrat revered by other old New York families; wife of Henry van der Luyden in Edith Wharton's *The Age of Innocence*; mentioned in *The Old Maid*.

Little Rock. Night-crew hoist man at the Past Bay Manufacturing Company factory killed during the power outage in Robert Cantwell's *The Land of Plenty*.

Little Sunshine. Hermit figure who lives at the Cloud Hotel on Drownin Pond; maker of charms in Truman Capote's *Other Voices, Other Rooms*.

Eunice Littlefield. Daughter of Howard Littlefield and neighbor of the Babbitts; elopes with Theodore Babbitt in Sinclair Lewis's *Babbitt*.

Howard Littlefield. Father of Eunice Littlefield and neighbor of George Babbitt; employment manager of the Zenith Street Traction Company in Sinclair Lewis's *Babbitt*.

Norman (Norm) Littlefield. Head of the English department at Polycarp College; dies of stress from paying life insurance premiums in Peter De Vries's *Let Me Count the Ways*.

Mary Littlejohn. New friend of Frankie Addams; her arrival allows Frankie to ignore the death of John Henry West in Carson McCullers's *The Member of the Wedding*.

Mrs. Littlejohn. Boardinghouse owner in William Faulkner's *The Hamlet* and *The Town*.

Ulysses Littlejohn. Spendthrift companion of Cuthbert Dangerfield in James Kirke Paulding's *Westward Ho!*

Littleman. See Willie Hall.

Agatha (Aunt Agatha) Littlepage. Aunt of Virginius Littlepage; condemned to her third-story back bedroom because of an early indiscretion with Colonel Bletheram in Ellen Glasgow's *They Stooped to Folly*.

Captain Littlepage. Stately and refined retired sea captain and lover of the poets Shakespeare and Milton; haunted by a story about a city of ghosts near the North Pole in Sarah Orne Jewett's *The Country of the Pointed Firs*.

Curle Littlepage. Popular, vulgar, and naively optimistic son of Victoria and Virginius Littlepage in Ellen Glasgow's *They Stooped to Folly*.

Duncan Littlepage. Spoiled son of Victoria and Virginius Littlepage; demoralized by World War I in Ellen Glasgow's *They Stooped to Folly*.

Marmaduke Littlepage. Byronic older brother of Virginius Littlepage; modernist painter and opponent of "Victorian psychology" in Ellen Glasgow's *They Stooped to Folly*.

Mary Victoria Littlepage. See Mary Victoria Littlepage Welding.

Victoria Brooke Littlepage. Wealthy and orderly wife of Virginius Littlepage in Ellen Glasgow's *They Stooped to Folly*.

Virginius Curle Littlepage. Pillar of society who, as he is attracted to Amy Dalrymple, begins to find his happy marriage monotonous in Ellen Glasgow's *They Stooped to Folly*.

Mortimer Lonzo Littlepaugh. Counsel for the American Electric Power Company; commits suicide when replaced as counsel by Judge Irwin in Robert Penn Warren's *All the King's Men*.

Mark Littleton. New Yorker who visits his cousin and friend Ned Hazard in Virginia; narrator of John Pendleton Kennedy's *Swallow Barn*.

Henry Livaudais. Eighteen-year-old resident of Isle aux Chiens; runs away with a young woman from a neighboring island but is believed to be dead in Shirley Ann Grau's *The Hard Blue Sky*.

Pete Livaudais. Brother of Henry Livaudais; sets fire to several buildings on a rival island, Terre Haute, exacerbating a feud in Shirley Ann Grau's *The Hard Blue Sky*.

Lieutenant Crofts Livingston. Officer in charge of harbor facilities who aids Major Joppolo in securing a bell for the town in John Hersey's *A Bell for Adano*.

Livingston (Lischinsky). Harvard-educated Russian Jew reared in New York and Arizona; successful businessman who supports the attempts of his adopted son, Marshall Pearl, to locate Pearl's family in Mark Helprin's *Refiner's Fire*.

Richard Olney (Dickie) Livingston III. Language tutor and playboy; brings to an anniversary gathering the gun that killed Charles Lawrence in Wright Morris's *The Huge Season*.

Aunt Llanyllyn. Aunt of Lucy Tartan in Herman Melville's *Pierre*.

Loady. Personal slave of Mamie Brandon Catlett; mother of the slave sold to pay for the Catletts' trip to Egeria Springs in Mary Lee Settle's *Know Nothing*.

Lobo. See Carl Logan.

Cynthia Locke. Wife of adulterous Edwin Locke in Joyce Carol Oates's *Cybele*.

Edwin Locke. Husband of Cynthia Locke, involved in a tragi-comic midlife crisis; seeks salvation through a series of romantic obsessions and marital infidelities in Joyce Carol Oates's *Cybele*.

Townsend Pederson (Towny) Locke. Visiting conventioneer whom Joe Buck beats up and robs for money with which to take Ratso Rizzo to Florida in James Leo Herlihy's *Midnight Cowboy*.

Major Clyde Lockert. Cocoa grower from British Guiana; friend of Fran and Sam Dodsworth in Europe in Sinclair Lewis's *Dodsworth*.

Anastasie (Taisie) Lockhart. Owner of Texas cattle; accompanies the trail herd to Abilene in Emerson Hough's *North of 36*.

Gertrude (Dirty Gertie) Lockhart. Promiscuous housewife in Proxmire Manor repeatedly thwarted by modern appliances and plumbing; eventually commits suicide in John Cheever's *The Wapshot Scandal*.

Jamie Lockhart. Bandit who becomes the robber bridegroom and hides his identity from his bride, Rosamond Musgrove, in Eudora Welty's *The Robber Bridegroom*.

Rosamond Musgrove Lockhart. Daughter of Clement Musgrove; lover and wife of the robber bridegroom, Jamie Lockhart, in Eudora Welty's *The Robber Bridegroom*.

Abraham Lockwood. Son of Moses Lockwood and the first Lockwood to attend college; expands the family wealth by investing outside the town of Swedish Haven; conceives of his family as the "Concern" in John O'Hara's *The Lockwood Concern*.

Adelaide Hoffner Lockwood. Pennsylvania Dutch wife of Abraham Lockwood in John O'Hara's *The Lockwood Concern*.

Agnes Wynne Lockwood. Invalid first wife of George Lockwood; mother of Bing and Tina Lockwood in John O'Hara's *The Lockwood Concern*.

Ernestine (Tina) Lockwood. Daughter of Agnes and George Lockwood; returns from Europe in John O'Hara's *The Lockwood Concern*.

George Bingham Lockwood. Scion of a wealthy rural Pennsylvania family; consolidates the family fortunes and builds a large country estate outside Swedish Haven in John O'Hara's *The Lockwood Concern*.

George Bingham (Bing) Lockwood, Jr. Son of Agnes and George Lockwood; expelled from Princeton; makes his fortune in California oil in John O'Hara's *The Lockwood Concern*.

Geraldine Lockwood. Second wife of George Lockwood in John O'Hara's *The Lockwood Concern*.

Moses Lockwood. First Lockwood in Swedish Haven, Pennsylvania; suspicious and violent, he amasses a fortune in real estate, coal-dredging, bank stock, and a distillery; builds a large house surrounded by a high wall in John O'Hara's *The Lockwood Concern*.

Penrose Lockwood. Younger brother of George Lockwood and his partner in Lockwood & Co. in John O'Hara's *The Lockwood Concern*.

Wilma Lockwood. Wife of Penrose Lockwood in John O'Hara's *The Lockwood Concern*.

Mitch Lodwick. District attorney prosecuting Frederic Manion; longtime rival of Paul Biegler in Robert Traver's *Anatomy of a Murder*.

Ann (Annie) Loeb. Young film editor; Manley Halliday's companion, nurse, confidante, and lover in Budd Schulberg's *The Disenchanted*.

Helen Peyton Loftis. Mother of Peyton and Maudie Loftis and wife of Milton Loftis in William Styron's *Lie Down in Darkness*.

Maudie (Maudie-poo) Loftis. Second child of Helen and Milton Loftis and younger sister of Peyton Loftis; dies after a childhood accident in William Styron's *Lie Down in Darkness*.

Milton (Bunny, Cap'n Milton, Milt) Loftis. Father of Peyton and Maudie Loftis, husband of Helen Loftis, and lover of Dolly Bonner in William Styron's *Lie Down in Darkness*.

Peyton Loftis. Twenty-two-year-old daughter of Milton and Helen Loftis; a suicide whose funeral is being conducted in William Styron's *Lie Down in Darkness*.

Rosemary Loftus. Dance-marathon contestant who lures Robert Syverten into a sexual liaison under the bandstand in Horace McCoy's *They Shoot Horses, Don't They?*

Sonny Loftus. Army lieutenant whose attention to Mary Pilant makes Barney Quill jealous in Robert Traver's *Anatomy of a Murder*.

Adah Elwood (Cousin Adah) Logan. Vivacious midwestern socialite; wife of Joe Logan and second cousin of Judd Rankin in Susan Glaspell's *Judd Rankin's Daughter*.

Carl (Lobo) Logan. Gang leader and schoolmate of Raymond Douglas; murders a policeman out of revenge in Herbert Simmons's *Man Walking on Eggshells* and in *Corner Boy*.

Jesse Logan. Drifter/cowhand on Homer Bannon's ranch, which he is forced to leave following the slaughter of Homer's diseased cattle herd, in Larry McMurtry's *Horseman, Pass By*.

Joe Logan. Wealthy inventor and husband of Adah Elwood Logan in Susan Glaspell's *Judd Rankin's Daughter*.

Mr. Valentino (Val) Logan. Neighbor who saves the young Eva Medina Canada from sexual molesting, but who makes his own sexual advances toward her, in Gayl Jones's *Eva's Man*.

Logan brothers. Three brothers whose lifetime of bowling success is destroyed when their trophies are stolen; turn to crime in search of the trophies, eventually shooting Constance Marlow and Bob under the impression they are the trophy thieves, in Richard Brautigan's *Willard and His Bowling Trophies*.

Tom Loker. Slave catcher who pursues Eliza Harris and her family; gives up his trade after being wounded and then cared for by the Quakers in Harriet Beecher Stowe's *Uncle Tom's Cabin*.

Robbie Lokyar. Youthful Puritan soldier who turns the soldiers' secret meetings from religion to politics; admired by Johnny Church for his "impassioned hatred of all forms of neglect of man"; shot for mutiny, becoming a martyr and uniting opposition to Cromwell, in Mary Lee Settle's *Prisons*.

Lolita. See Dolores Haze.

Lomax. Employee of Earl Mudger in Radial Matrix, an intelligence organization fronting as a business, in Don DeLillo's *Running Dog*.

Hetty Lomax. Sister of Julia Lomax Le Moyne and cousin of Hester Le Moyne, who wills Hetty a half-interest in Mulberry Hill plantation, in Albion W. Tourgee's *Bricks without Straw*.

Michael Lomax. Twenty-nine-year-old American who owns a house in an ancient city four hours from Golconda to which he brings Lillian Beye; has buried all his emotions in Anaïs Nin's *Seduction of the Minotaur*.

Lombardo. Author of *Koztanza*, a masterpiece admired by Babbalanja, in Herman Melville's *Mardi*.

Caesar Lomellini. Commanding general of the Brotherhood of Destruction who leads a revolution against the Oligarchy; murdered by his own followers in Ignatius Donnelly's *Caesar's Column*.

Royal (Roy) Lommax. American army cook in Luxembourg; wounded in the stomach by a shell fragment from a tank cannon in Martha Gellhorn's *Wine of Astonishment*.

London. Leader of the migrant workers who strike during apple picking in John Steinbeck's *In Dubious Battle*.

Miss Lonelyhearts. Male advice columnist burdened by his inability to assist those who write for help in Nathanael West's *Miss Lonelyhearts*.

Buck (Ted Percey) Loner. Uncle of Myra/Myron Breckinridge and owner of an acting school; his tape recorded reports reveal that Myra and Myron are the same person in Gore Vidal's *Myra Breckinridge*.

Lonesome Blue. Friend of Banjo and Ray; deported from France in Claude McKay's *Banjo*.

Gertrude Long. Hotel cigar counter clerk, then second wife of Will Brady in Wright Morris's *The Works of Love*.

Gilbert Long. Young gentleman who is having an affair with Lady John in Henry James's *The Sacred Fount*.

Long Ghost (Long Doctor, Peter). Doctor aboard the *Julia* and Typee's companion in Herman Melville's *Omoo*.

Mr. Longdon. Wealthy friend of Lady Julia and Mrs.

Brookenham in Henry James's *The Awkward Age*.

Walter Longknife. Indian to whom Meridian Hill's father tries unsuccessfully to give farmland containing sacred Indian burial mounds in Alice Walker's *Meridian*.

James (Old Pete, The Dutchman) Longstreet. Southern general who is the right-hand man of Robert E. Lee; opposes Lee's plan to undertake the offensive against the Union army at Gettysburg in Michael Shaara's *The Killer Angels*.

Frances (Fran, Frances Dowson) Lonigan. Sister of Studs Lonigan in James T. Farrell's *Young Lonigan*; appears in *The Young Manhood of Studs Lonigan*; happily married, as Frances Dowson, in *Judgment Day*.

Loretta (Fritzie) Lonigan. Sister of Studs Lonigan in James T. Farrell's *Young Lonigan*; girlfriend of Phillip Rolfe in *The Young Manhood of Studs Lonigan*; happily married to Rolfe in *Judgment Day*.

Mary Lonigan. Mother of Studs Lonigan; envisions her son as a priest in James T. Farrell's *Young Lonigan*; also appears in *The Young Manhood of Studs Lonigan* and *Judgment Day*.

Patrick J. (Paddy, Pat) Lonigan. Father of Studs Lonigan in James T. Farrell's *Young Lonigan*; gets successful contracts by paying kickbacks in *The Young Manhood of Studs Lonigan*; loses most of his money in the Depression in *Judgment Day*.

William (Bill, Studs) Lonigan. South Chicago grammar school graduate who spends an aimless summer hanging out and daydreaming in James T. Farrell's *Young Lonigan*; works for his father and frequents pool rooms and brothels in *The Young Manhood of Studs Lonigan*; engaged to marry Catherine Banahan, but dies before he can wed her, in *Judgment Day*.

Emanuel Isidore (E. I., Manny) Lonoff. Jewish literary hero of Nathan Zuckerman; invites the younger writer to spend the night at his house; feels he has lived his life only in the fantasy of his works in Philip Roth's *The Ghost Writer*.

Hope (Hopie) Lonoff. Unhappy wife of E. I. Lonoff; offers to leave Lonoff and Amy Bellette to live together when she feels unloved by Lonoff in Philip Roth's *The Ghost Writer*.

Loo. Daughter of Arfretee and Deacon Ereemear Po-Po; fends off Long Ghost's advances in Herman Melville's *Omoo*.

George Loomis. One-armed, gimpy veteran of the Korean War who nevertheless manages his own farm; accidentally kills Goat Lady in John Gard-

ner's *Nickel Mountain*.

Howie Loomis. Local merchant who helps sponsor Big Red Smalley's traveling gospel show in George Garrett's *Do, Lord, Remember Me*.

Imogen Loomis. Crippled young married woman seduced by the narrator in Edmund Wilson's *Memoirs of Hecate County*.

Loop Garoo Kid. Black cowboy who fights with whips and Hoo-Doo and who is an antagonist of the Pope; believes that a novel can be anything it wants to be in Ishmael Reed's *Yellow Back Radio Broke-Down*.

Loosh. See Lucius.

Lop-Ear. Friend of Big-Tooth; after learning to paddle a log, he travels away from the tribe in Jack London's *Before Adam*.

Tony Lopanto. Parking garage employee who picks up Theresa Dunn in a bar and becomes her sexual partner in Judith Rossner's *Looking for Mr. Goodbar*.

Earl Scheib Lopez. Eleven-year-old Cuban bicycle thief in Joseph Wambaugh's *The Black Marble*.

Dr. Maria Lopez. Fantasy female chief of Havana Main Hospital who is interviewed by Margaret Reynolds the journalist; introduces Reynolds to Fidel Castro, who is really a woman disguised as a man, in Anne Richardson Roiphe's *Up the Sandbox!*

Aggie Lopin. Spinster and gossip; owns a dry goods store in Betty Smith's *Joy in the Morning*.

Goldie Lopin. Common-law wife of an Indian storekeeper; adviser on pregnancy and motherhood to Annie Brown in Betty Smith's *Joy in the Morning*.

Fran LoPresti. Sculptor and neighbor of Joe Allston in Wallace Stegner's *All the Little Live Things*.

Julie LoPresti. Daughter of Fran LoPresti; becomes pregnant at Jim Peck's commune in Wallace Stegner's *All the Little Live Things*.

LoQuadro. Mathematician who secretly sells excess time on the Space Brain computer in Don DeLillo's *Ratner's Star*.

Harry Lorbeer. Plumber; proprietor and mentor-priest of the space project in Wright Morris's *The Fork River Space Project*.

Bradley Lord. Sycophantic team secretary of the New York Mammoths in Mark Harris's *The Southpaw*.

Lynn Lord. See Marybeth Howe.

Horace L'Ordinet. Professor of English and father of Elizabeth Bean's baby; kidnaps the infant and, after his arrest, pleads temporary insanity; his black ancestry is discovered when the baby is found to have sickle-cell anemia in Frederick Busch's *Rounds*.

Lorency. Cook at Knapp-of-Reeds plantation and mother of Nimbus; traded South following Nimbus's marriage; dies in Louisiana during a journey back to North Carolina in Albion W. Tourgee's *Bricks without Straw*.

Reuben (Mink) Lorey. Troublesome woodsman who, if he is responsible for destroying Gus Griff's mill, is responsible for Tad's presumed death in Mary Noailles Murfree's *In the Clouds*.

Euphemia Wiatte Lorimer. Benefactress of Clithero Edny; aunt of Clarice Wiatte Lorimer, to whom Edny is engaged; sister of Arthur Wiatte, who drives away her lover, Sarsefield, whom she ultimately marries; victim of attempted murder by Clithero Edny in Charles Brockden Brown's *Edgar Huntly*.

Linda Loring. Sister of Sylvia Lennox; Philip Marlowe's lover in Raymond Chandler's *The Long Goodbye*.

Laverne Linda Hogan Lorraine. Mistress of Buddy Sandifer and lover of Ralph Sandifer in Thomas Berger's *Sneaky People*.

Lottie Mae. Maid of Big Joe Mackey and murderer of Buddy Matlow in Harry Crews's *A Feast of Snakes*.

Lotus (Lotus Flower). Teahouse prostitute bought as a concubine by Wang Lung, whose son she also attracts, in Pearl Buck's *The Good Earth*.

Louella. Volunteer Red Cross worker in Naples and comforter to all lost American soldiers in John Horne Burns's *The Gallery*.

Lou Ellen. Lover of Lenard and party hostess in Ed Bullins's *The Reluctant Rapist*.

Louie. Bus driver who becomes so attracted to Camille Oaks that he reserves a seat behind his in an attempt to make a date with her, despite the protests of an elderly passenger who desires to sit in the reserved seat, in John Steinbeck's *The Wayward Bus*.

Louie. Hospital chemist living at Queenie's boardinghouse in Thornton Wilder's *Heaven's My Destination*.

Louis. Louisiana plantation owner who, after being made a vampire by Lestat, seeks out other vampires; morally disturbed by his need to kill in order to survive; tells his story to an interviewer in Anne Rice's *Interview with the Vampire*.

Louis. Crew member on the *Ghost* who is kind to Hump Van Weyden in Jack London's *The Sea-Wolf*.

Louisa. Southern black woman desired by both Tom Burwell, a black laborer, and Bob Stone, son of her white employer, in Jean Toomer's *Cane*.

Louisa. Woolworth floorwalker in William Goyen's *In a Farther Country*.

Sister Louise. Administrator of Sacred Heart Hospital in Edward Lewis Wallant's *The Children at the Gate*.

Louvinia. Wife of Joby's; Ringo's grandmother in William Faulkner's *Sartoris (Flags in the Dust)* and *The Unvanquished*.

Louvinie. Slave and storyteller whose tongue is cut out by the plantation owner; her buried tongue nourishes a fabled magnolia tree in Alice Walker's *Meridian*.

Julien Love. Friend of Bull Hubbard and Jack Duluoz in Jack Kerouac's *Visions of Cody*; also appears in *Book of Dreams*, *Big Sur*, and *Desolation Angels*.

Colonel Richard Lovelace. English governor in James Kirke Paulding's *Koningsmarke*.

Sally Lovelace. Well-to-do third wife of John Buddy Pearson in Zora Neale Hurston's *Jonah's Gourd Vine*.

Charlotte (Chatty) Lovell. Poor cousin of Delia Ralston; mother of Clementina Ralston by Delia's former suitor, Clement Spender; the "old maid" of Edith Wharton's *The Old Maid*.

Clementina Lovell. See Clementina Lovell Ralston.

Eddie Lovell. Unreflecting investor and husband of Nell Lovell in Walker Percy's *The Moviegoer*.

Jessica (Jessie) Lovell. Member of the Clyde upper class; discouraged by her father from marrying her first love, Charles Gray; marries Jackie Mason in John P. Marquand's *Point of No Return*.

Laurence Lovell. Father of Jessica Lovell; opposes his daughter's marriage to Charles Gray in John P. Marquand's *Point of No Return*.

Nell Lovell. Glibly humanistic cousin of Binx Bolling and wife of Eddie Lovell in Walker Percy's *The Moviegoer*.

Vee Lovell. Dance partner of Mary Hawley; agrees to marry Mary during the marathon as a publicity ploy in Horace McCoy's *They Shoot Horses, Don't They?*

Lord Lovely. Elegant man in Liverpool whom Harry Bolton avoids in Herman Melville's *Redburn*.

Butch Lovemaiden. Deputy in William Faulkner's *The Reivers.*

Michael (Mike) Lovett. Amnesia victim, retainer of William McLeod's "black box," and narrator of Norman Mailer's *Barbary Shore.*

Jimmy Low. Friend of Cody Pomeray; participates in the taped conversations of Jack Kerouac's *Visions of Cody.*

Maud Lowder. Aunt of Kate Croy; opposes Croy's engagement to Merton Densher because he has no money in Henry James's *The Wings of the Dove.*

David Lowe. Professor Joseph Moore's prize student; Lowe's dalliance with Moore's daughter presumably causes Moore's stroke in Mary Gordon's *Final Payments.*

Geneve Lowe. First mistress of Frank Hirsh and ambitious buyer for the Mode Shop in James Jones's *Some Came Running.*

Julian Lowe. Flight cadet in William Faulkner's *Soldiers' Pay.*

Everett Lowell. Boston congressman who supports political equality for blacks but opposes social integration in Thomas Dixon's *The Leopard's Spots.*

Hope Lowell. Muse and fairy godmother to Isadora Wing in Erica Jong's *How to Save Your Own Life.*

Johnny Lowell. Job supervisor of Jimson in Carlene Hatcher Polite's *The Flagellants.*

Julius Lowenthal. Jewish manufacturer of Catholic religious objects and church furnishings who isolates himself from Gentiles, whom he distrusts and dislikes, in Katherine Anne Porter's *Ship of Fools.*

Edna Lown. Colleague and lover of Robert Softly; works on a project for developing a cosmic language based on mathematical principles in Don DeLillo's *Ratner's Star.*

Lowry. Lover of Clara Walpole and father of her son, Swan Revere, in Joyce Carol Oates's *A Garden of Earthly Delights.*

Ella Lowry. See Ella Lowry Sturgis.

Ellery Loyola. See Dick Gibson.

Aaron Lublin. Husband of Sarah Lublin and father of their two children; Jewish refugee who lives in one of the Seventieth Street apartments managed by Norman Moonbloom in Edward Lewis Wallant's *The Tenants of Moonbloom.*

Sarah Lublin. Wife of Aaron Lublin and mother of their two children; tenant in one of the apartments managed by Norman Moonbloom in Edward Lewis Wallant's *The Tenants of Moonbloom.*

George R. Lucas. Resident and pig-tender at the Diamond County Home for the Aged; husband of Martha Lucas; former truck farmer whose land was requisitioned by the Federal Department of Conservation; brings bottles of rye to the fair and participates in the stoning of Stephen Conner in John Updike's *The Poorhouse Fair.*

Martha (Marty) Lucas. Resident of the Diamond County Home for the Aged and wife of George Lucas; complaining woman with bad legs and a love for her pet parakeet in John Updike's *The Poorhouse Fair.*

Mattie Johnson Lucas. See Mattie Johnson.

Sam Lucas. Con man who marries and betrays Harlem innocent Mattie Johnson; redeems himself at the conclusion of Countee Cullen's *One Way to Heaven.*

Carl Luce. Columbia University student and former adviser of Holden Caulfield at the Whooton School; meets Holden at the Wicker Bar for a drink and a conversation about sex in J. D. Salinger's *The Catcher in the Rye.*

Marino Lucero. Poor priest of Arroyo Hondo who accumulates great wealth and fears that it will be stolen in Willa Cather's *Death Comes for the Archbishop.*

Luciana. Voluptuous and independent Italian woman whose back was scarred in an air raid; Yossarian falls in love with her in Joseph Heller's *Catch-22.*

Lucius (Loosh). Son of Joby; Sartoris slave in William Faulkner's *The Unvanquished.*

Achsa Luckett. Daughter of Worth and Jary Luckett; steals Louie Scurrah from her sister Genny Luckett and runs off with him to the western territory in Conrad Richter's *The Trees*; after Scurrah's death, she lives with another man in *The Fields.*

Genny (Ginny) Luckett. Beautiful sister of Sayward Luckett; after her husband Louie Scurrah deserts her, she is so frightened by a panther that for a time she becomes deranged; eventually hires out for work with a nearby family in Conrad Richter's *The Trees*; continues in this position until she marries a boatyard owner in *The Fields*; dies in *The Town.*

Jary Luckett. Wife of Worth Luckett; distressed to leave her Pennsylvania birthplace and settle in the Ohio territory; rears five children and dies of a fever in Conrad Richter's *The Trees.*

Sayward (Saird) Luckett. Oldest daughter of Worth and Jary Luckett; marries Portius Wheeler and becomes a heroic, energetic, capable homemaker; watches as the forest area grows toward civilization; has nine living children; performs herculean tasks under primitive conditions, but when the family becomes prosperous she acquiesces to having a large home built in Americus, Ohio, where she lives; principal character in Conrad Richter's *The Fields, The Town,* and *The Trees.*

Sulie Luckett. Youngest child of Worth and Jary Luckett; disappears in the woods in Conrad Richter's *The Trees;* marries an Indian and wants no contact with her white family in *The Town.*

T. P. Luckett. Chicken egg entrepreneur; model of success to Will Brady in Wright Morris's *The Works of Love.*

Worth Luckett. Head of a pioneer family that travels into the Ohio territory and builds a home there; after his wife's death, he eventually leaves his family in the charge of his eldest daughter, Sayward Luckett, and travels further into the midwestern wilderness in Conrad Richter's *The Trees;* returns to what is now a thriving town and lives primitively there until his death in *The Town.*

Wyitt Luckett. Son of Worth and Jary Luckett; in his eagerness to hunt and be a woodsman he takes after his father in Conrad Richter's *The Trees;* strikes out for the distant western territory in *The Fields;* the family wonders about his fate in *The Town.*

Lucrezia. Daughter of Frau Anders and later mistress of Hippolyte in Susan Sontag's *The Benefactor.*

Lucy. Maid of the Churchills; her unhappy relationship with a foreign bootmaker leads to her suicide in Henry Wadsworth Longfellow's *Kavanagh.*

Lucy. Widowed slave who goes mad awaiting the return of her drowned son Abe in John Pendleton Kennedy's *Swallow Barn.*

Ludus. Black livery stable worker in William Faulkner's *The Reivers.*

Luff. See Wymontoo-Hee.

Lugena. Wife of Nimbus; refuses to tell the Ku Klux Klan the whereabouts of Eliab Hill; resettles with her children in Kansas on land purchased for her by Mollie Ainslie in Albion W. Tourgee's *Bricks without Straw.*

Luke. Attacker who joins Jeff and Tom in an attempt to castrate Will Harris in Junius Edwards's *If We Must Die.*

Luluque. Soldier in William Faulkner's *A Fable.*

Corporal Lumbowski. Army corporal whom Columbato strikes in William Wharton's *Birdy.*

Lumen. Professor and advocate of social Darwinism in William Dean Howells's *A Traveler from Altruria.*

William Wigglesworth (Billy) Lumkin. Dean of Convers College in Alison Lurie's *Love and Friendship.*

Lummy. Black employee of Joe Lon Mackey; brother of George in Harry Crews's *A Feast of Snakes.*

Captain Enoch (Nuck) Lumsden. Large landholder whose manipulative, controlling, and acquisitive nature causes his estrangement from his daughter, Patty Lumsden, and from his nephew, Kike Lumsden, in Edward Eggleston's *The Circuit Rider.*

Hezekiah (Kike) Lumsden. Delicate youth who converts to Methodism and becomes a zealous circuit rider, endangering his already frail health, in Edward Eggleston's *The Circuit Rider.*

Patty Lumsden. Beautiful and aristocratic daughter of Enoch Lumsden; refuses to see Morton Goodwin following his conversion to Methodism, although she herself eventually converts, in Edward Eggleston's *The Circuit Rider.*

Adeline Luna. Worldly sister of Oliver Chancellor; takes an interest in Basil Ransom in Henry James's *The Bostonians.*

Isaac Lund. Son of a homesteader; shot by Clay Calvert while trying to rob Calvert's wagon in H. L. Davis's *Honey in the Horn.*

Captain Adam Lundy. Union officer who burns Isaac Jameson's home in Shelby Foote's *Jordan County.*

Claire (Misty) de Lune. Secretary to Artie Pringle; marries Billy Bumpers in Peter De Vries's *I Hear America Swinging.*

Lurene. Mother of Jeffy; works the night shift at a factory in Gayl Jones's *Corregidora.*

Alex Lurie. Brother of David Lurie; his love of English literature and his tendency to act rather than think draw him away from his Jewish faith in Chaim Potok's *In the Beginning.*

David (Davey) Lurie. Narrator who overcomes a series of childhood illnesses and misfortunes and goes on to apply his brilliant mind and thirst for knowledge to higher Biblical criticism despite his family's disapproval in Chaim Potok's *In the Beginning.*

Max Lurie. Father of David Lurie; after serving in the Polish army in World War I, he founds an organization to bring Polish Jews to the United States in Chaim Potok's *In the Beginning.*

Meyer Lurie. Brother of Max Lurie; follows Max to the United States and serves with him in an organization to bring Polish Jews to America in Chaim Potok's *In the Beginning*.

Ruth Lurie. Wife of Max Lurie and mother of David Lurie in Chaim Potok's *In the Beginning*.

Sarah Lurie. Wife of Meyer Lurie; helps comfort the Polish Jewish community during their struggles in the United States in Chaim Potok's *In the Beginning*.

Saul (Rav Shaul) Lurie. Son of Meyer Lurie; cares for his cousin David Lurie while they are in school together; becomes a rabbi in Chaim Potok's *In the Beginning*.

Luster. Servant or stable worker in William Faulkner's *The Sound and the Fury*; *Absalom, Absalom!*; and *The Reivers*.

Dotty and Kitty Lutch. American friends of Maggie Verver in Henry James's *The Golden Bowl*.

Luter. Foreman at a print shop who tries to seduce Genya Schearl in Henry Roth's *Call It Sleep*.

Luther (Fort). Transient from Fort Meyers, Florida, who likes chocolate ice in Nelson Algren's *A Walk on the Wild Side*.

Luther (Little Luke). Transient who leads Dove Linkhorn into fraudulent sales pitches in Nelson Algren's *A Walk on the Wild Side*.

Lutte. Beautiful German model who dances with Charles Upton at a Berlin cabaret in Katherine Anne Porter's *The Leaning Tower*.

Grandma Luttrell. Herb doctor and adventurer in H. L. Davis's *Beulah Land*.

Heinrich Lutz. Swiss hotelier who is traveling with his wife and their unattractive daughter in Katherine Anne Porter's *Ship of Fools*.

Louie Lutz. Son of Naomi Lutz; accompanies George Swiebel to Africa and gets into trouble trying to learn obscenities in Swahili in Saul Bellow's *Humboldt's Gift*.

Naomi Lutz. Childhood sweetheart of Charlie Citrine; persuades George Swiebel to take her son, Louie Lutz, with him to Africa in Saul Bellow's *Humboldt's Gift*.

Luz (Luce). Daughter of a horse trader; love of Clay Calvert and his guide to an understanding and acceptance of the necessary evil in human nature in H. L. Davis's *Honey in the Horn*.

Luzana Cholly (Old Luze). Legendary and idolized bluesman in Albert Murray's *Train Whistle Guitar*.

Lydia (Lyddy). Mulatto slave and daughter of Backwater Brandon and lover of Joe Little Fox; loves Johnny Lacey, who buys her after Brandon's death and brings her to Beulah, in Mary Lee Settle's *O Beulah Land*.

Lykin. Astronaut who crash-lands with Bradly and later turns into a Green Fish Boy in William S. Burroughs's *The Ticket That Exploded*.

Eric Lyle. Thief who travels with his mother in Paul Bowles's *The Sheltering Sky*.

Mrs. Lyle. Australian travel writer and mother of Eric Lyle in Paul Bowles's *The Sheltering Sky*.

Lyman. Judge and anti-temperance congressman who is beaten up by a mob angry over the death of Willy Hammond in T. S. Arthur's *Ten Nights in a Bar-Room*.

Adrian Lynch. Deputy chief of the Los Angeles Police Department; sloganeer and buffoon in Joseph Wambaugh's *The Choirboys*.

Andrew Lynch. Painter; brother of Mary Follet and uncle of Rufus Follet; sent to the scene of Jay Follet's automobile accident, he confirms Jay's death to his waiting family; describes Jay's funeral to Rufus in James Agee's *A Death in the Family*.

Catherine Lynch. Mother of Mary Follet and grandmother of Rufus Follet in James Agee's *A Death in the Family*.

Hannah Lynch. Aunt of Mary Follet and great aunt of Rufus Follet; comforts Mary, whose husband has died in an automobile accident, in James Agee's *A Death in the Family*.

Joel Lynch. Father of Mary Follet and grandfather of Rufus Follet in James Agee's *A Death in the Family*.

Silas Lynch. Black lieutenant governor of South Carolina in Thomas Dixon's *The Clansman*.

Lynda. High-spirited teenager who is suspended from school and sent to a detention home for girls for slapping a teacher; after her release, she hangs out on the street smoking cigarettes and drinking wine in Alexis Deveaux's *Spirits in the Street*.

Polk Lynde. Wealthy playboy and lover of Aileen Cowperwood in Theodore Dreiser's *The Titan*.

Buddy van der Lynn. Romantic leading man in Ludwig Bemelmans's *Dirty Eddie*.

Ezra Lyttle. Boyfriend of Stormy Claridge; Dallas Cowboy defensive back whose business ventures collapse after he is caught exposing himself in Peter Gent's *Texas Celebrity Turkey Trot*.

M

M/Neighbor. Neighbor of Bukka Doopeyduk; his mother lost his name in a lottery in Ishmael Reed's *The Free-Lance Pallbearers.*

Arthur Ma. Son of a prominent Chinatown family in San Francisco; friend and companion of Lorenz Monsanto and Jack Duluoz in Jack Kerouac's *Big Sur.*

Atlas Androgyne (Atlas Atlantis) Maartens. Usually-stoned security guard and friend of Kam Wright; aids the activists in M. F. Beal's *Amazon One.*

Oedipa (Oed) Maas. Wife of Wendell Maas; becomes executrix of Pierce Inverarity's will and searches for the meaning of the mysterious Tristero system; heroine of Thomas Pynchon's *The Crying of Lot 49.*

Wendell (Mucho) Maas. Husband of Oedipa Maas, disc-jockey on a California radio station who experiments with LSD in Thomas Pynchon's *The Crying of Lot 49.*

Mac. Marine sergeant in and narrator of Leon Uris's *Battle Cry.*

Mac. See Fenian McCreary.

Mrs. Macallister. Flirtatious acquaintance of Bartley Hubbard in William Dean Howells's *A Modern Instance.*

Maria Miranda Macapa. Psychologically peculiar cleaning woman who marries Zerkow; murdered by Zerkow in Frank Norris's *McTeague.*

Herbert Macaulay. Attorney who administers the affairs of Clyde Wynant in Dashiell Hammett's *The Thin Man.*

Homer Macauley. Fourteen-year-old night messenger for Western Union whose job brings him into contact with various aspects of life in Ithaca, California, in William Saroyan's *The Human Comedy.*

Marcus Macauley. Brother of Homer and Ulysses Macauley; killed in World War II in William Saroyan's *The Human Comedy.*

Ulysses Macauley. Four-year-old brother of Homer and Marcus Macauley; curious about everything around him in William Saroyan's *The Human Comedy.*

Elizabeth (Libby) MacAusland. Translator of Italian for a literary agent; eventually marries an actor; member of the Group in Mary McCarthy's *The Group.*

Doctor (Mac) MacDonald. Son-in-law of Professor Ball and leader of the Bardsville raid on tobacco buyers' warehouses in Robert Penn Warren's *Night Rider.*

General MacDonald. Editor of the *Chicago Inquirer* in Theodore Dreiser's *The Titan.*

Truman Leslie MacDonald. Son of General MacDonald; demands railway stock in exchange for supporting Frank Cowperwood's streetcar plans in Theodore Dreiser's *The Titan.*

MacDoon. Undergarment designer and London friend of Sebastian Dangerfield in J. P. Donleavy's *The Ginger Man.*

Thomas Harold MacDougal. Artisan in stone and plaster of Paris, and owner of Artifacts of Spain; husband of Marietta McGee-Chavéz in William Goyen's *In a Farther Country.*

Sukie Maceo. Sister of China Doll Maceo and friend of Francie Coffin in Louise Meriwether's *Daddy Was a Number Runner.*

Don Joaquin MacGillivray. American boatman and trader who kidnaps Commodore Robinette in H. L. Davis's *Harp of a Thousand Strings.*

Hector Macgoblin. Secretary of State under Lee Sarason; flees to Cuba after shooting Sarason in Sinclair Lewis's *It Can't Happen Here.*

MacGregor. Friend of Henry Miller; drinks in bars without having money to pay his tab; brings his girlfriends home to spend the night and asks his mother to serve them breakfast in bed in Henry Miller's *Tropic of Capricorn.*

Irwin K. (Mac) Macgregor. Writer of popular music and partner of Earl Horter; marries Billie Harcum in Wright Morris's *Love among the Cannibals.*

Maggie (Shirley Silverstein) MacGregor. Journalist and television personality who makes a living interviewing and reporting on celebrities, including Billy Ikehorn Orsini, Vito Orsini, and Spider Elliott, in Judith Krantz's *Scruples.*

Macha. Former Russian princess who moves in with Fillmore; spends her time in bed reading Russian newspapers and avoiding Fillmore's advances in Henry Miller's *Tropic of Cancer.*

James Duncan MacHardie. Wealthy and powerful New York financier who hires Alfred Eaton after Eaton rescues MacHardie's young grandson, who had fallen through the ice while skating, in John O'Hara's *From the Terrace.*

Frankie Machine. See Francis Majcinek.

Oliver Cromwell MacIvor. Minister who incites Protestants against Catholics in Leon Uris's *Trinity*.

Balliol (Jones, Mac, James Watson) MacJones. Successful chronicler of the beat generation and literary rival of Leo Percepied in Jack Kerouac's *The Subterraneans*; also appears in *Book of Dreams*.

Mack. Leader of the group of vagrant men who frequent Lee Chong's grocery; convices Chong to appoint him and the others guardians of the building Chong received from Horace Abbeville; names the building the Palace Flophouse and Grill in John Steinbeck's *Cannery Row*.

Easton (Easy) Mack. Father of Herman Mack and owner of Auto-Town and Salvage House; kills himself in a car crusher in Harry Crews's *Car*.

George Mack. Ranch owner who employs Johnny Mack (who takes George's surname) and Jose in Edwin Corle's *Fig Tree John*.

Herman Mack. Son of Easy Mack; tries to eat a Ford Maverick bumper to bumper in Harry Crews's *Car*.

Jane Paulsen Mack. Wife of Harrison Mack and mother of Jeannine Mack; occasional mistress of Todd Andrews between 1932 and 1937 in John Barth's *The Floating Opera*.

Jeannine Paulsen Mack. Daughter of Jane Mack by either Harrison Mack or Todd Andrews in John Barth's *The Floating Opera*.

Johnny (Fig Tree Junior, Great Spirits, Juanito Fig Tree, N'Chai Chidn) Mack. Apache son of Agocho and Kai-a; marries the Mexican Maria and gradually loses his Indian heritage in Edwin Corle's *Fig Tree John*.

Junell Mack. Daughter of Easy Mack and girlfriend of Joe; drives the tow truck for Auto-Town in Harry Crews's *Car*.

Mister Mack. Son of Easy Mack; replaces Herman Mack in trying to eat a Ford Maverick in Harry Crews's *Car*.

Harrison A. Mack, Jr. Manager of his father's canning empire and heir to his fortune; friend of Todd Andrews and husband of Jane Mack in John Barth's *The Floating Opera*.

Gideon MacKarkle. Highland Scot who introduces Johnny Church to the realities of war; remains loyal to democratic ideals and is sentenced to death for mutiny, but is saved by Cromwell's blanket pardon; tells others about Virginia but insists he will not move his nine sons and seven grandchildren in Mary Lee Settle's *Prisons*.

Barney MacKean. Playmate rejected by Frankie Addams after they commit "a secret and unknown sin" in Carson McCullers's *The Member of the Wedding*.

Allison MacKenzie. Daughter of Constance MacKenzie; aspiring writer who looks upon the scandal and social injustice of her hometown as material for a novel in Grace Metalious's *Peyton Place*.

Constance (Connie, Constance Standish) MacKenzie. Mother of Allison MacKenzie; assumes the name of her married lover after bearing their illegitimate daughter and moves to the small town where she opens a dress shop and passes herself off as a widow; later marries Tomas Makris in Grace Metalious's *Peyton Place*.

Shreve MacKenzie. Harvard roommate of Quentin Compson I in William Faulkner's *The Sound and the Fury*. Also see Shrevlin McCannon.

Reverend Andrew Mackerel. Widowed pastor of the People's Liberal Church in Avalon, Connecticut; narrator of Peter De Vries's *The Mackerel Plaza*.

Ida May Mackerel. Late wife of Andrew Mackerel; founder of a clinic ("She was crazy about mental health.") and memorial dedicatee of the Ida May Mackerel Plaza and shopping center in Peter De Vries's *The Mackerel Plaza*.

Beatriz Dargan (Beeder) Mackey. Sister of Joe Lon Mackey; driven crazy after finding her mother's body in Harry Crews's *A Feast of Snakes*.

Big Joe Mackey. Brutal father of Joe Lon Mackey in Harry Crews's *A Feast of Snakes*.

Joe Lon Mackey. Former Boss Rattler; murders Luther Peacock and Berenice Sweet in a shooting spree in Harry Crews's *A Feast of Snakes*.

Mabel Mackey. Harlem neighbor of the Coffin family; frequent number player who runs poker games; Adam Coffin moves in with her when he leaves his family in Louise Meriwether's *Daddy Was a Number Runner*.

Mary Lamar Mackey. Best friend of Dabney Fairchild; plays the piano at Dabney's wedding in Eudora Welty's *Delta Wedding*.

Zebulon Johns (Zeb) Mackie. City councilman, political boss, owner of construction and sewage companies awarded city contracts, purchaser of Gimlet Street property, and would-be historian of Bunker County in Fred Chappell's *The Gaudy Place*.

Mack MacLeod. Alcoholic owner of an Alabama plantation in George Wylie Henderson's *Ollie Miss*.

Shelley MacLeod. Protestant lover of Conor Larkin; killed by Protestant fanatics for loving a Catholic in Leon Uris's *Trinity*.

Bonnie MacMahon. Cocktail waitress who serves "Breakfast of Champions" in Kurt Vonnegut's *Breakfast of Champions*.

Charles (Mac) MacMahon. Father of Rose MacMahon and manager of the Past Bay Manufacturing Company factory in Robert Cantwell's *The Land of Plenty*.

Penelope MacMahon. Unhappy but hopeful young woman who vacations in Majorca with her psychotherapist and his wife, John and Dane Empson; has an affair there with Karl Heykoop in Gail Godwin's *The Perfectionists*.

Rose (Kitten, Kitty) MacMahon. Daughter of Charles MacMahon; while possibly pregnant by Roger Schwartz, she begins a relationship with Walt Connor in Robert Cantwell's *The Land of Plenty*.

Cassie Beal MacMurtrie. Wife of Scott MacMurtrie, whose infidelity leads Cassie to suicide in Elizabeth Madox Roberts's *The Time of Man*.

Scott MacMurtrie. Husband of Cassie Beal MacMurtrie and lover of Amanda Cain in Elizabeth Madox Roberts's *The Time of Man*.

MacNaughton. Partner in MacNaughton-Blair brokerage; father-in-law and employer of Joe Sandwich in Peter De Vries's *The Vale of Laughter*.

Betty (Naughty) MacNaughton. Plump, chaste fiancée, long-suffering wife, then widow of Joe Sandwich; ultimately marries Wally Hines in Peter De Vries's *The Vale of Laughter*.

Chris MacNeil. Celebrated actress and divorced, frantic mother of Regan MacNeil, who is possessed by a demon, in William Peter Blatty's *The Exorcist*.

Regan Teresa (Rags) MacNeil. Eleven-year-old daughter of Chris MacNeil; victim of demonic possession in William Peter Blatty's *The Exorcist*.

Adèle Macomb. Rich, popular bully who marries James March and is Leda March's nemesis in Nancy Hale's *The Prodigal Women*.

Bob MacSwain. One-time detective in the Personville Police Department fired by Chief Noonan for suspicion of covering up Tim Noonan's murder in Dashiell Hammett's *Red Harvest*.

Mr. Mactabb. Creditor of Cuthbert Dangerfield in James Kirke Paulding's *Westward Ho!*

Claudia MacTeer. Playmate of Pecola Breedlove; narrator of Toni Morrison's *The Bluest Eye*.

Frieda MacTeer. Sister of Claudia McTeer in Toni Morrison's *The Bluest Eye*.

John MacWalsey (McWalsey). Professor vacationing in the Florida Keys who becomes involved with Helen Gordon in Ernest Hemingway's *To Have and Have Not*.

MacWilliams. Civil engineer and Robert Clay's ablest assistant in Richard Harding Davis's *Soldiers of Fortune*.

Mad Jack. Brandy-drinking lieutenant who defies the captain to save the *Neversink* during a gale off Cape Horn and who puts down a mutiny aboard the same ship in Herman Melville's *White-Jacket*.

Maddalena. Cook of Evalina Bowen; sings to Effie Bowen in William Dean Howells's *Indian Summer*.

Celia Madden. Voluptuous church organist and freethinker; Theron Ware mistakes her avowal of women's independence for sexual license in Harold Frederic's *The Damnation of Theron Ware*.

Jeremiah (Jerry) Madden. Wealthy but unpretentious sawmill owner; father of Celia, Michael, and Theodore Madden in Harold Frederic's *The Damnation of Theron Ware*.

Michael Madden. Consumptive brother of Celia Madden; advises Theron Ware to stop meddling, but Ware ignores the advice in Harold Frederic's *The Damnation of Theron Ware*.

Terence (Theodore) Madden. Dissolute younger brother of Celia Madden; Celia's trip to New York to aid him is misinterpreted by Theron Ware in Harold Frederic's *The Damnation of Theron Ware*.

Madeleine. Parisian vampire, friend of Louis, and surrogate mother to Claudia; killed by Lestat in Anne Rice's *Interview with the Vampire*.

Lannie Madison. Disturbed young woman whose testimony erodes William McLeod's resistance in Norman Mailer's *Barbary Shore*.

Robert (Bob) Madison. Fellow postal worker and friend of Jake Jackson; suffers from venereal disease in Richard Wright's *Lawd Today*.

Mara Madoff. Daughter of a clothier; murdered by Hitler's Brownshirts; her body is found in the Vienna State Opera House in John Irving's *Setting Free the Bears*.

Opal Madvig. Daughter of Paul Madvig who is enamored of Taylor Henry, the man her father is accused of murdering, in Dashiell Hammett's *The Glass Key.*

Paul Madvig. Political boss who is accused of murdering the son of a U.S. Senator in Dashiell Hammett's *The Glass Key.*

Mae. Unidentified woman whose name Wesley Beavers calls out while making love to Rosacoke Mustian in Reynolds Price's *A Long and Happy Life.*

Maestro. Old and lecherous lover of Lucrezia in Susan Sontag's *The Benefactor.*

Emory Mafferson. Employee of Janoth Enterprises who covers the police investigation of the murder of Pauline Delos and reports privately to George Stroud; a narrator of Kenneth Fearing's *The Big Clock.*

Mag. Black servant in the Kendal household in Reynolds Price's *The Surface of Earth.*

Magawisca. Daughter of the Pequod chief Mononotto and sister of Oneco; risks her life to save Everell Fletcher from execution in Catharine Maria Sedgwick's *Hope Leslie.*

Magdalena (Ma). Fruit store operator who serves as Rico Bandello's fence in William Riley Burnett's *Little Caesar.*

Tia Magdalena. Housekeeper for Bob Webster; feared and respected by the townspeople because she is a witch in Josefina Niggli's *Mexican Village.*

Eric (Cop) Magee. White policeman determined to prove Kevin Brittain guilty of murder in Hal Bennett's *Wait Until the Evening.*

Janet Magee. Invalid sister of Cop Magee and unintended murder victim of Cora Brittain in Hal Bennett's *Wait Until the Evening.*

Teacake Magee. See Teacake Sistrunk Magee Ponder.

Maggie. See Margaret Stevens Mallison.

Angelo Maggio. Gambling, sarcastic private in G Company who befriends Robert E. Lee Prewitt; discharged with a Section 8 after being persecuted by Fatso Judson in the stockade in James Jones's *From Here to Eternity.*

Magic Child. Temporary identity of one of the Hawkline sisters (whether Susan or Jane is never revealed) while under the influence of the Hawkline Monster, whom she hires Greer and Cameron to destroy, in Richard Brautigan's *The Hawkline Monster.*

Mr. Magruder. Methodist circuit rider and elder who supervises and advises Morton Goodwin in Edward Eggleston's *The Circuit Rider.*

Magua (le Renard Subtil). Indian guide who, seeking revenge against Colonel Munro, leads Duncan Heyward into dangerous territory and later abducts Cora Munro to be Magua's wife in James Fenimore Cooper's *The Last of the Mohicans.*

Mahailey. Faithful servant to the Wheeler family in Willa Cather's *One of Ours.*

Clarabelle Mahon. Teacher who tries to make her immigrant students into homogeneous Americans, but suffers disenchantment and a breakdown, in O. E. Rölvaag's *Peder Victorious.*

Donald Mahon. Disfigured American R.A.F. pilot who returns to Georgia and marries Margaret Powers in William Faulkner's *Soldiers' Pay.*

Margaret Powers Mahon. Widow of Richard Powers and wife of Donald Mahon in William Faulkner's *Soldiers' Pay.*

The Reverend (Uncle Joe) Mahon. Episcopalian minister and father of Donald Mahon in William Faulkner's *Soldiers' Pay.*

Mahtoree. Treacherous Sioux chieftain; villainous but courageous opponent slain by the noble Hard Heart in single combat in James Fenimore Cooper's *The Prairie.*

Maida. Secretary to Paul Biegler in Robert Traver's *Anatomy of a Murder.*

Fausto Maijstral. Maltese poet and father of Paola Maijstral; recounts his encounter with the Bad Priest in his "confessions" in Thomas Pynchon's *V.*

Paola (Ruby) Maijstral. Daughter of Fausto Maijstral; keeps the ivory comb of the lady V.; gives Herbert Stencil the Confessions of Fausto and thereby convinces Stencil to go to Malta in Thomas Pynchon's *V.*

Maimiti. Strong-willed Tahitian who marries Fletcher Christian in Charles Nordhoff and James Norman Hall's *Mutiny on the Bounty*; joins Christian in attempting to establish a democracy on an isolated island, where she provides strong leadership for the women and children when violence erupts, in *Pitcairn's Island.*

Alexander (the Bailbondsman, Phoenician) Main. Cincinnati bailbondsman obsessed by life's mysteries; claims descent from the ancient Phoenicians; narrator of *The Bailbondsman*, a novella in Stanley Elkin's *Searches and Seizures.*

Marshall Maine. See Dick Gibson.

Raymond (Captain Bruno Storm) Mainwaring. Son of Splendor Mainwaring in Thomas Berger's *Vital Parts*.

Splendor Gallant Mainwaring. Black friend of Carlo Reinhart in Thomas Berger's *Reinhart in Love* and *Vital Parts*.

Honora Tremont Mairs. Adopted orphan cousin of Beverly Peele, whom Mairs murders out of jealousy, in Gertrude Atherton's *Patience Sparhawk and Her Times*.

Francis (Automatic, Frankie Machine) Majcinek. Card hustler and morphine addict who cannot break his habit in Nelson Algren's *The Man with the Golden Arm*.

Sophie (Zoschka, Zosh) Majcinek. Wheelchair-bound and shrewish wife of Frankie Machine in Nelson Algren's *The Man with the Golden Arm*.

Major Major Major Major. Painfully shy squadron commander named by a father fond of practical jokes and "promoted by an I.B.M. machine with a sense of humor" in Joseph Heller's *Catch-22*.

Makar. Farmer and rabbit expert at whose house the narrator is introduced to sex, incest, and bestiality in Jerzy Kosinski's *The Painted Bird*.

Mrs. Makely. Society woman who believes that Homos is an American posing as an Altrurian in William Dean Howells's *A Traveler from Altruria*.

Mako. Son of Tavi and Marunga and altar boy and servant to Father Paul; reveals Terangi's hiding place to Eugene de Laage shortly before the hurricane, which Mako fails to survive, in Charles Nordhoff and James Norman Hall's *The Hurricane*.

Constance Makris. See Constance MacKenzie.

Tomas (Tom, Michael Rossi) Makris. Greek from New York hired as a small-town school principal; lover and later husband of Constance MacKenzie in Grace Metalious's *Peyton Place*.

Tony Malarkey. Dublin friend of Sebastian Dangerfield; barricades himself in his flat to prevent eviction in J. P. Donleavy's *The Ginger Man*.

Malcolm. Fifteen year old in search of his father; through the auspices of Mr. Cox, begins an adventure through the stages of life in James Purdy's *Malcolm*.

Elsbeth Malkas. Supposed artist who gives a venereal disease to Fred Trumper and Cuthbert Bennett in John Irving's *The Water-Method Man*.

Black Jack Mallard. Highwayman who saves Amber St. Clare by taking her with him when he escapes from Newgate Prison; instructs her in survival by crime in Kathleen Winsor's *Forever Amber*.

Rowland Mallet. Wealthy American art lover traveling in Europe; patron of Roderick Hudson and in love with Hudson's fiancée, Mary Garland, in Henry James's *Roderick Hudson*.

Mary (Marie de Sabrevois) Mallinson. Childhood love of Steven Nason; abducted by Guerlac in Kenneth Roberts's *Arundel*.

Charles Mallison. Husband of Margaret Stevens and father of Chick Mallison in William Faulkner's *Intruder in the Dust*, *The Town*, and *The Mansion*.

Charles (Chick) Mallison. Son of Charles and Margaret Stevens Mallison in William Faulkner's *Intruder in the Dust*, *The Town*, and *The Mansion*.

Margaret Stevens (Maggie) Mallison. Sister of Gavin Stevens, wife of Charles Mallison, and mother of Chick Mallison in William Faulkner's *Intruder in the Dust*, *Requiem for a Nun*, *The Town*, and *The Mansion*.

Pamela (Pam) Mallory. Flight lieutenant and girlfriend of Frank Savage in Beirne Lay, Jr., and Sy Bartlett's *Twelve O'Clock High!*

Steven (Steve) Mallory. Sculptor whose work reflects the heroic in man in Ayn Rand's *The Fountainhead*.

Jimmy Malloy. Alcoholic newspaper reporter who meets Eddie Brunner at a jam session and later tries to find out about Gloria Wandrous from him in John O'Hara's *Butterfield 8*.

John J. (Jack) Malloy. Former IWW member and stockade prisoner who attempts to teach Robert E. Lee Prewitt the value of passive resistance; escapes from the stockade in James Jones's *From Here to Eternity*.

Moose Malloy. Ex-convict who hires Philip Marlowe to find his lost love, Velma Valento—who murders him—in Raymond Chandler's *Farewell, My Lovely*.

Frances Xavier (Frankie) Malone. Son of Nora and Patrick Malone, ambitious messenger boy for a Wall Street brokerage firm, and first boyfriend and later husband of Margy Shannon in Betty Smith's *Tomorrow Will Be Better*.

J. T. Malone. Pharmacist dying of leukemia who tries to deny the truth about his impending death; refuses to bomb the house of Sherman Pew in Carson McCullers's *Clock Without Hands*.

Margy Malone. See Margy Shannon.

Martha Malone. Wife of J. T. Malone who helps nurse her husband while he dies of leukemia; owns Coca-Cola stock in Carson McCullers's *Clock Without Hands*.

Nathan (Lips) Malone. Accountant and gopher for Sid Krassman; procures corpses for C. D. Harrison to have sex with in Terry Southern's *Blue Movie*.

Nora Malone. Wife of Patrick Malone and possessive mother of Frankie Malone in Betty Smith's *Tomorrow Will Be Better*.

Patrick (Patsy) Malone. Joker and Brooklyn police officer; correspondence student of embalming, a profession for his retirement; husband of Nora Malone and father of Frankie Malone in Betty Smith's *Tomorrow Will Be Better*.

Maloney the Areopagite. Catholic mystic and biographer of Saint Puce, a holy flea, in Nathanael West's *The Dream Life of Balso Snell*.

Hank Malory. Rice University graduate student and lover of Patsy Carpenter in Larry McMurtry's *Moving On*.

Hubert Maloy. Member of Legs Diamond's gang in William Kennedy's *Legs*; a kidnapper of Charlie Boy McCall in *Billy Phelan's Greatest Game*.

David Malter. Renowned Zionist and Talmudic scholar who teaches his son Reuven to find his own way between old beliefs and new scholarship in Chaim Potok's *The Chosen* and *The Promise*.

Reuven (Bobby) Malter. Son of David Malter; helps his friend Danny Saunders come to terms with his intelligence and his Jewish heritage in Chaim Potok's *The Chosen*, which he narrates; chooses to become a rabbi rather than a mathematician in *The Promise*.

Malty. See Buchanan Malt Avis.

Tootsie Maltz. Radical whom Harry Bogen uses to start a strike of shipping clerks in the women's garment industry; becomes Bogen's partner in a delivery service, and then becomes sole owner of the service, in Jerome Weidman's *I Can Get It for You Wholesale*.

Mama (Ma). Impoverished widow and mother of Thomas Henry Oliver in Shirley Ann Grau's *The Condor Passes*.

Mamba. Grandmother of Lissa Atkinson and mother of Hagar; domestic servant of the Wentworths and later of the Atkinsons in DuBose Heyward's *Mamba's Daughters*.

Mambo. Black Caribbean musician and nightclub singer; one of Sabina's lovers in Anaïs Nin's *A Spy in the House of Love*.

Mameh. Wife of Tateh and mother of The Little Girl; becomes a prostitute in E. L. Doctorow's *Ragtime*.

Mamie. Daughter of Aunt Cora Lou and sister of Lil Bits in Sarah E. Wright's *This Child's Gonna Live*.

Aunt Mamie. Boardinghouse proprietor who offers bountiful meals, chaos, and love to the narrator of Aline Bernstein's *The Journey Down*.

Mammy. Personal slave of Marie St. Clare and mother figure to Eva St. Clare in Harriet Beecher Stowe's *Uncle Tom's Cabin*.

Mammy. Slave who is Scarlett O'Hara's nanny in Margaret Mitchell's *Gone with the Wind*.

Arthur Manchek. Officer in charge at Vandenberg Air Force Base who declares a state of emergency in Michael Crichton's *The Andromeda Strain*.

Sally Manchester. Friend of Alice Archer; tends to Alice's mother and rejects men following a broken engagement in Henry Wadsworth Longfellow's *Kavanagh*.

Charlie Mandarin. Cousin of Honoré Grandissime; attempts to lynch Clemence in George Washington Cable's *The Grandissimes*.

Dr. Mandelet. Physician who perceives Edna Pontellier's awakening to individuality and sensuality in Kate Chopin's *The Awakening*.

Agnes Mandeville. Foster mother of Margo Dowling who takes the child after her father disappears in John Dos Passos's *U.S.A.* trilogy.

Frank Mandeville. Vaudevillian who introduces his foster daughter, Margo Dowling, to show business; she elopes after he rapes her in John Dos Passos's *U.S.A.* trilogy.

Homer (Purple Better One) Mandrill. Presidential candidate presented by A. J. to the Democratic National Convention in William S. Burroughs's *Exterminator!*

Mandy. Mixed-blood washerwoman fired by Belinda Treadwell a month before Mandy's white son is born of her union with Cyrus Treadwell in Ellen Glasgow's *Virginia*.

Aunt Mandy. Wise, matriarchal protector of Mattie Johnson in Countee Cullen's *One Way to Heaven*.

Veronica Manganese. See V.

Al Manheim. Drama critic turned screenwriter; narrator of Budd Schulberg's *What Makes Sammy Run?*

Frederic (Manny) Manion. Army lieutenant whose wife, Laura Manion, Barney Quill allegedly rapes; pleads temporary insanity to the charge of murdering Quill in Robert Traver's *Anatomy of a Murder.*

Laura Manion. Wife of Frederic Manion; allegedly raped by Barney Quill in Robert Traver's *Anatomy of a Murder.*

Doctor Mann. Israeli who tracks down female writers and is preparing an art exhibition in Israel in Anaïs Nin's *Collages.*

Justin G. Mannerly. Denver school teacher; benefactor of Cody Pomeray in Jack Kerouac's *Visions of Cody.*

Dorothy (Dolly) Manners. Frivolous, socially ambitious young woman who matures and becomes the worthy wife of Richard Carvel in Winston Churchill's *Richard Carvel.*

Margaret Manners. Wife of Marmaduke Manners and mother of Dorothy Manners in Winston Churchill's *Richard Carvel.*

Marmaduke Manners. Devious, social-climbing fop; husband of Margaret Manners and father of Dorothy Manners in Winston Churchill's *Richard Carvel.*

Nancy Mannigoe. Maid of Gowan and Temple Drake Stevens; hanged for murdering the Stevenses' baby daughter in William Faulkner's *Requiem for a Nun.*

Janus Manning. Black plantation owner, husband of Neva Stapleton, and leader in an effort to unseat the head of the color hierarchy in Burnside, Virginia, in Hal Bennett's *A Wilderness of Vines.*

Janus Eugene (Gene) Manning II. Slow-witted adolescent sexually attracted to his mother, Neva Stapleton Manning, in Hal Bennett's *A Wilderness of Vines.*

Neva Blanche Stapleton Manning. Widow of Janus Manning, mother of Gene Manning, and lover of Charlie Hooker; abandons the South and sexual repression at the close of Hal Bennett's *A Wilderness of Vines.*

Otha Manning. Son of Janus Manning; killed in France during World War I in Hal Bennett's *A Wilderness of Vines.*

Captain Al Mannix. Jewish Marine from Brooklyn and closest friend of Lieutenant Culver; scorns the Marine Corps and openly hates Colonel Templeton in William Styron's *The Long March.*

Mannock. British pilot in William Faulkner's *A Fable.*

Manolin. Young Cuban friend of Santiago in Ernest Hemingway's *The Old Man and the Sea.*

Manon. Retired psychiatrist who counsels against the stage-three operation on Harold Benson in Michael Crichton's *The Terminal Man.*

Senator Aaron Mansfield. Presiding member of the committee investigating the attempted "purchase" of Barry Rudd; tries unsuccessfully to make sense of circuitous and conflicting testimony in John Hersey's *The Child Buyer.*

Marchioness Medora Manson. Eccentric aunt who takes charge of Ellen Olenska after the death of Ellen's parents in Edith Wharton's *The Age of Innocence.*

Signor Rafael Mantissa. Italian intriguer; enlists the aid of the Gaucho in the aborted attempt to steal Botticelli's *Venus* in Florence in 1899 in Thomas Pynchon's *V.*

Manuel. Helper in Emil Duluoz's print shop in Jack Kerouac's *Visions of Gerard.*

Mañuel. Twin brother of Esteban; falls in love with Camila Perichole and dies from an accident in Thornton Wilder's *The Bridge of San Luis Rey.*

Manya. Russian housekeeper for David and Reuven Malter in Chaim Potok's *The Chosen* and *The Promise.*

Charles Maple. Los Angeles public defender of Gregory Powell during Powell's second trial for the murder of Ian Campbell in Joseph Wambaugh's *The Onion Field.*

Ezra Maple. Proprietor of the Hard Times general store, which Clay Turner burns; helps Blue bury the dead and then leaves town in E. L. Doctorow's *Welcome to Hard Times.*

Isaac Maple. Brother of Ezra Maple; rebuilds his brother's store and cares for Helga Bergenstrohm; financially ruined in E. L. Doctorow's *Welcome to Hard Times.*

Father Mapple. New Bedford preacher who delivers a sermon about Jonah in Herman Melville's *Moby-Dick.*

Marama. Daughter of Fakahau and Mata, sister of Arai, and wife of Terangi; faithfully waits for her husband while he is in jail, helps him rescue Madame de Laage during the hurricane, and escapes with him after the storm in Charles Nordhoff and James Norman Hall's *The Hurricane*.

Jerry Marble. Fat church deacon who, despite the scolding of his late wife, is inordinately fond of jokes and laughter in Henry Ward Beecher's *Norwood*.

Marbonna. Marquesan nurse of Queen Pomaree's children in Herman Melville's *Omoo*.

Hermann Marburg. German-born father of Sonia and Ivan Marburg and husband of Shura Korf Marburg; deserts his family before Ivan's birth in Jean Stafford's *Boston Adventure*.

Ivan Marburg. Brother of Sonia Marburg; dies in childhood and is given a pauper's burial in Jean Stafford's *Boston Adventure*.

Shura Korf Marburg. Mentally deranged Russian-born mother of Sonia and Ivan Marburg and wife abandoned by Hermann Marburg in Jean Stafford's *Boston Adventure*.

Sonia (Sonie) Marburg. Daughter of impoverished immigrant parents; realizes her childhood dream when she becomes secretary to Miss Pride; narrator of Jean Stafford's *Boston Adventure*.

Steven (Roman Castevet) Marcato. Son of an infamous devil worshipper in the 1890s; changes his name and carries on his father's practices in Ira Levin's *Rosemary's Baby*.

March. High-minded, impecunious father of Meg, Jo, Beth, and Amy March; his war service keeps him away from home in Louisa May Alcott's *Little Women*.

Amy Curtis (Mrs. Theodore Laurence) March. Artistic and sensitive but vain and self-centered youngest sister of Meg, Jo, and Beth March; and ultimately marries Theodore Laurence in Louisa May Alcott's *Little Women*; also appears in *Little Men*.

Augie (Bolingbroke) March. Picaresque hero and quester after a "worthwhile fate" through adventures in Chicago, Canada, Mexico, the African Sea, and Paris; marries Stella Chesney and plans to establish a home for orphans; narrator of Saul Bellow's *The Adventures of Augie March*.

Aunt March. Wealthy, prim aunt of Meg ,Jo, Beth, and Amy March; leaves her home to Jo March in Louisa May Alcott's *Little Women*.

Basil March. Husband of Isabel March; travels across New York and Canada on their honeymoon in William Dean Howells's *Their Wedding Journey*; leaves a dull insurance job in Boston to edit a literary magazine in New York in *A Hazard of New Fortunes*; narrator of *The Shadow of a Dream*.

Elizabeth (Beth) March. Quiet, gentle, domestic sister of Meg, Jo, and Amy March; dies after being weakened by scarlet fever in Louisa May Alcott's *Little Women*.

Georgie March. Mentally retarded but gentle younger brother of Augie March; institutionalized by Grandma Lausch and becomes a competent and content shoe repairman in Saul Bellow's *The Adventures of Augie March*.

Henry (Hurry Harry) March. Untrustworthy and careless woodsman who wants to marry Judith Hutter in James Fenimore Cooper's *The Deerslayer*.

Isabel March. Wife of Basil March; travels across New York and Canada on their honeymoon in William Dean Howells's *Their Wedding Journey*; makes an uneasy adjustment to New York City in *A Hazard of New Fortunes*; appears in *The Shadow of a Dream*.

James March. Doctor and first cousin of Leda March; marries Leda and then Adèle Macomb in Nancy Hale's *The Prodigal Women*.

Jo (Mrs. Friedrich Bhaer) March. Awkward, straightforward tomboy who aspires to be a writer and who ultimately marries Friedrich Bhaer in Louisa May Alcott's *Little Women*; also appears in *Little Men*.

Leda March. Awkward girl who grows into a great beauty, but remains insecure; wife of James March, mother of Treat March, and lover of Lambert Rudd in Nancy Hale's *The Prodigal Women*.

Mama March. Simple-minded mother of Simon, Augie, and Georgie March; placed in a nursing home when the boys grow up in Saul Bellow's *The Adventures of Augie March*.

Margaret (Meg, Mrs. John Brooke) March. Eldest sister of Jo, Beth, and Amy March; becomes a governess and ultimately marries John Brooke in Louisa May Alcott's *Little Women*; also appears in *Little Men*.

Miss March. Compassionate teacher who befriends Frado; lectures the class against prejudice in Harriet E. Wilson's *Our Nig*.

Mrs. (Marmee) March. Wise and understanding mother of Meg, Jo, Beth, and Amy March in Louisa May Alcott's *Little Women*.

Reverend March. Unmarried minister of the Reformed Church in Olinger; interested in Vera Hummel in John Updike's *The Centaur.*

Treat March. Son of Leda and James March and friend of Betsy Jekyll in Nancy Hale's *The Prodigal Women.*

Dr. Oliver Marchand. Physician who treats Caribbean victims of the plague in Sinclair Lewis's *Arrowsmith.*

Morton Marcher. Rich planter and maternal grandfather of Jeremiah Beaumont in Robert Penn Warren's *World Enough and Time.*

Julia Marcia. Aunt of Caesar; has great political insight and influence in Thornton Wilder's *The Ides of March.*

Marco. Peruvian, woman-hating escort of Esther Greenwood to a country club dance; she bloodies his nose to prevent his sexual advances in Sylvia Plath's *The Bell Jar.*

Marcus. Leader of a black ghetto youth gang who takes his group to the Catskills; distrusts the Indians but joins them after his group members are killed in Marge Piercy's *Dance the Eagle to Sleep.*

Kate Marcy. Lover of Preston Parr; driven to alcoholism and prostitution by Eldon Parr in Winston Churchill's *The Inside of the Cup.*

Charley Marden. Boyhood friend of Tom Bailey in Thomas Bailey Aldrich's *The Story of a Bad Boy.*

Katrina Marek. Viennese actress who takes the paintings of her husband Kurt Winter to London; mother of Severin Winter in John Irving's *The 158-Pound Marriage.*

Marengo (Ringo). Boyhood friend of Bayard Sartoris II in William Faulkner's *The Unvanquished.*

Margaret (Margo). Prostitute and girlfriend of Herman Mack in Harry Crews's *Car.*

Margawse. Mother of Agravaine, Gawaine, and Mordred; half sister of Arthur and sister of Morgan la Fey in Thomas Berger's *Arthur Rex.*

Margie. Unfaithful mistress of Quincy Boardman and resident of the Glen Cove Apartments in Albert Halper's *Union Square.*

Margo. Ticket seller at The Go Hole in John Clellan Holmes's *Go.*

Marguerite. Native of South America and a tough professional revolutionary; loved by Ramón Cordes but used by his superiors to seduce him

into submission in William Herrick's *The Last to Die.*

Marheyo. Father of Kory-Kory in Herman Melville's *Typee.*

Maria. Brilliant and talented twenty-five-year-old black woman who holds a law degree from Columbia University and has the image of a she-fox on her belly; masochistic lover of Scarecrow finally killed by him in Calvin Hernton's *Scarecrow.*

Maria. Member of Pablo's partisan group who is raped and becomes the lover of Robert Jordan in Ernest Hemingway's *For Whom the Bell Tolls.*

Maria. Mexican wife of Hatcher in Anaïs Nin's *Seduction of the Minotaur.*

Maria. Aged black proprietor of a Catfish Row cook shop; formidable foe of disruptive and debilitating influences, such as Sportin' Life, in DuBose Heyward's *Porgy.*

Maria. Mexican servant who marries Johnny Mack, raped by Agocho, her father-in-law, in Edwin Corle's *Fig Tree John.*

Maria. Older sister of Miranda in Katherine Anne Porter's *Old Mortality.*

Maria (Rachel). Slave who accompanies Sally and Brandon Lacey on their visit to Beulah; renamed by Sally after visiting France in Mary Lee Settle's *Know Nothing.*

Miss Marie (Maginot Line). Physically formidable prostitute in Toni Morrison's *The Bluest Eye.*

Arthur Marion. Planter, owner of Roseland and Bellevue plantations, and husband of Cornelia Wilton Marion; badly burned while rescuing slaves and other property from a fire in Caroline Gilman's *Recollections of a Southern Matron.*

Cornelia Wilton Marion. See Cornelia Wilton.

Francis (The Swamp Fox) Marion. Colonel of the partisan cavalry who offers his services to Horatio Gates for the Battle of Camden in William Gilmore Simms's *The Partisan.*

Lorna Maris. Dancer and mistress of Frank Cowperwood in Theodore Dreiser's *The Stoic.*

Maritze. White tenant of Silla Boyce; despises the fact that she must rent from a black person in Paule Marshall's *Brown Girl, Brownstones.*

Marius. Roman officer and lover of Hipparchia in H. D.'s *Palimpsest.*

Mark. Middle-aged sailor flogged for fighting aboard the *Neversink* in Herman Melville's *White-Jacket.*

Lord Mark. English gentleman who, after being rejected by Mildred Theale, tells her about Kate Croy and Merton Densher's plot in Henry James's *The Wings of the Dove.*

Harvey Marker. Author of *Naked and the Doomed* and husband of Jack Duluoz's "old flame" in Jack Kerouac's *Desolation Angels.*

Madame Eudora Market. Founder of The Church of Stephen Martyr and grandmother of Joe Market in Hal Bennett's *Lord of Dark Places.*

Joe Market. Son of Titus and Ramona Market; picaresque hero who appears as Naked Disciple, prostitute, student, husband, soldier, detective, Christ-figure, and condemned murderer in Hal Bennett's *Lord of Dark Places* and *Wait Until the Evening.*

Odessa Barton Market. Wife of Joe Market; believes she is responsible for their son's death in Hal Bennett's *Lord of Dark Places.*

Ramona Market. Self-sacrificing wife of Titus Market and mother of Joe Market in Hal Bennett's *Lord of Dark Places.*

Roosevelt Market. Nephew, husband, and disciple of Madame Eudora Market; his lynching and castration are witnessed by his son, Titus Market, in Hal Bennett's *Lord of Dark Places.*

Titus Market. Son of Madame Eudora and Roosevelt Market; prophet of black salvation through moral inversion and worship of his son, Joe Market, in Hal Bennett's *Lord of Dark Places* and *Wait Until the Evening.*

Bojack Markham. Longtime black housekeeper for the Shafer family; prays to live until Gratt and Patsy Jo Shafer's baby is born and dies one month after the birth of Adam Gideon Shafer in Jesse Hill Ford's *Mountains of Gilead.*

Frau Markheim. Swedish wife of a Jewish Czechoslovakian doctor; solicits the aid of Mary Douglas in escaping the Nazi occupation of Czechoslovakia in Martha Gellhorn's *A Stricken Field.*

Virginia (Virgin) Markowitz. Twenty-one-year-old receptionist in the insurance company where Bob Slocum had his first job; always imagined by Slocum as seated under a Western Union clock, she remains his lifelong image of feminine seductiveness in Joseph Heller's *Something Happened.*

Sonia Marks. Friend of Jane Clifford; teaches a Women in Literature course in Gail Godwin's *The Odd Woman.*

Lester Marlow. Native of Wichita Falls who uses his friend Jacy Farrow to enter the "fast" crowd in Thalia in Larry McMurtry's *The Last Picture Show.*

Marlowe. Alcoholic reviewer and translator who can articulate only one phrase, "You pay"; asks Henry Miller and Carl to review for him while he is in San Francisco in Henry Miller's *Tropic of Cancer.*

Geraldine Marlowe. Adoptive mother of Rina Marlowe in Harold Robbins's *The Carpetbaggers.*

Harrison (Harry) Marlowe. Adoptive father of Rina Marlowe; adopts her after her mother, his cook, dies in Harold Robbins's *The Carpetbaggers.*

Philip Marlowe. Los Angeles private detective; the hero in all of Raymond Chandler's novels: *The Big Sleep*; *Farewell, My Lovely*; *The High Window*; *The Lady in the Lake*; *The Little Sister*; *The Long Goodbye*; and *Playback.*

Rina (Katrina Osterlaag) Marlowe. Orphan adopted by Harrison and Geraldine Marlowe; marries Jonas Cord, Sr., whom she meets while dating his son; later, widowed, she marries Nevada Smith and becomes a movie star; confesses on her deathbed her longstanding love for Jonas Cord, Jr., in Harold Robbins's *The Carpetbaggers.*

Ronald (Laddie) Marlowe. Adoptive brother and first lover of Rina Marlowe in Harold Robbins's *The Carpetbaggers.*

Marquis de Marnessie. French emigrant who hosts Captain John Farrago and Duncan Ferguson in Hugh Henry Brackenridge's *Modern Chivalry.*

Marnoo. English-speaking native who helps Tommo escape from the Typees in Herman Melville's *Typee.*

Marquis of Tempo-Rubato. Freethinking Italian son of the Duke of Largo and friend of Count Fin-de-Siècle; gives a rare, perfect bloom from his conservatory in tribute to the Chatelaine in Henry Blake Fuller's *The Chatelaine of La Trinité.*

Lindsay Marriott. Blackmailer who is murdered in Raymond Chandler's *Farewell, My Lovely.*

Eddie Mars. Racketeer in Raymond Chandler's *The Big Sleep.*

Mona Mars. Wife of Eddie Mars; she helps Philip Marlowe escape from her husband in Raymond Chandler's *The Big Sleep.*

James T. (Jimmy) Marsala. Italian-American brother-in-arms to Carlo Reinhart in Thomas Berger's *Crazy in Berlin.*

President Donald Marsh. President of Lincoln College and critic of local politics in Charles M. Sheldon's *In His Steps.*

Hattie (Puss) Marsh. Daughter of Rachael Marsh; attracted to Berkeley, whom she knows as Howard Tracy, in Samuel Langhorne Clemens's *The American Claimant.*

Rachael Marsh. Landlady of Berkeley, whom she knows as Howard Tracy, in Samuel Langhorne Clemens's *The American Claimant.*

Verena Marsh. Deaf housekeeper hired to cook for Charity Royall and her guardian, Lawyer Royall, after he makes sexual advances toward Charity in the doorway of her bedroom in Edith Wharton's *Summer.*

David Marshall. Husband of Eliza Marshall and father of Jane, Rosamund, Roger, and Truesdale Marshall, wealthy Chicago wholesale grocer in Henry Blake Fuller's *With the Procession.*

Eddie (Eddy) Marshall. Alcoholic friend and boat's helper of Harry Morgan in Ernest Hemingway's *To Have and Have Not.*

Eliza Marshall. Wife of David Marshall and mother of Jane, Rosamund, Roger, and Truesdale Marshall in Henry Blake Fuller's *With the Procession.*

Jane Marshall. Daughter of Eliza and David Marshall; attempts to restore her family's lost social standing; establishes a club for working women; falls in love with Theodore Brower in Henry Blake Fuller's *With the Procession.*

Joanna (Janna) Marshall. Young dancer battling racial prejudice who eventually chooses marriage to Peter Bye over her career in Jessie Redmon Fauset's *There Is Confusion.*

Joel Marshall. Inspirational father of Joanna Marshall in Jessie Redmon Fauset's *There Is Confusion.*

Little Buddy Marshall. Friend of Scooter in a series of boyhood adventures in Albert Murray's *Train Whistle Guitar.*

Philip Marshall. Brother of Joanna Marshall working with interracial organizations; second husband of Maggie Ellersley in Jessie Redmon Fauset's *There Is Confusion.*

Richard Truesdale (Dick) Marshall. Son of Eliza and David Marshall; dilettante artist called home to Chicago from Europe in Henry Blake Fuller's *With the Procession.*

Roger Marshall. Son of Eliza and David Marshall; lawyer and real estate speculator who manages his father's interests in Henry Blake Fuller's *With the Procession.*

Rosamund (Rosy) Marshall. Daughter of Eliza and David Marshall; leaves Chicago for England, where she lives with her husband, in Henry Blake Fuller's *With the Procession.*

Susan Marshall. See Susan Marshall Kukolnikov.

Sylvia Marshall. Domestic sister of Joanna Marshall in Jessie Redmon Fauset's *There Is Confusion.*

Jane Chillingworth Marshfield. Wife of Thomas Marshfield and mother of Martin and Stephen Marshfield; takes a liberal, ethical approach to living and enjoys long, boozy discussions with Ned Bork in John Updike's *A Month of Sundays.*

Martin Marshfield. Sixteen-year-old son of Tom and Jane Marshfield; unhappy bully in John Updike's *A Month of Sundays.*

Reverend Thomas (Tom) Marshfield. Adulterous Episcopal minister who sleeps with a number of his parishioners; rationalizes all sex as creative and positive and defines himself as a "believing unbeliever"; husband of Jane Chillingworth Marshfield and father of Martin and Stephen Marshfield; narrator-diarist of John Updike's *A Month of Sundays.*

Stephen Marshfield. Fourteen-year-old son of Tom and Jane Marshfield; worldly, good-looking young man in John Updike's *A Month of Sundays.*

Virginia (Jinny) Marshland. See Virginia Marshland Timberlane.

Uncle Peepee (George Humbolt) Marshmallow. Eccentric and village exhibitionist in John Cheever's *The Wapshot Chronicle.*

George Marshman. Kindly gentleman who befriends Ellen Montgomery on her lonely trip to Thirlwall; later she learns he is of the Marshman family of Ventnor in Susan Warner's *The Wide, Wide World.*

Mr. Marshman. Country gentleman who befriends Ellen Montgomery at his Christmas party; proprietor of Ventnor in Susan Warner's *The Wide, Wide World.*

Marta. Old woman whom the narrator accidentally immolates at the beginning of Jerzy Kosinski's *The Painted Bird.*

Mrs. Martello. Private nurse for the hospitalized Judge Clinton McKelva in Eudora Welty's *The Opti-*

mist's Daughter.

Marter. Father of Hilke Marter; head librarian at the International Student House and later postmaster at Kaprun; commits suicide by riding his mail sled down the Kitzsteinhorn in John Irving's *Setting Free the Bears.*

Muttie Marter. Mother of Hilke Marter; accidentally killed by a Russian machine gunner as she shouts from a window about her grandson's birth in John Irving's *Setting Free the Bears.*

Hilke Marter-Javotnik. High school sweetheart of Zahn Glanz; wife of Vratno Javotnik and mother of Siggy Javotnik in John Irving's *Setting Free the Bears.*

Martha. Mad typist whom Bob Slocum finally has removed from his office in Joseph Heller's *Something Happened.*

Marthe (Magda). See Marthe Demont.

Martin. Father, by Correy Corregidora, of Ursa Corregidora in Gayl Jones's *Corregidora.*

Martin. See Mr. Bradly Mr. Martin.

Abby (Queen's Twin) Martin. Lonely widow who collects memorabilia about Queen Victoria, who was born on the same day as Abby, in Sarah Orne Jewett's *The Country of the Pointed Firs.*

Alma Martin. Second-year student at the University of Southern California in Wallace Thurman's *The Blacker the Berry.*

Alma Martin. Wife of the Reverend Phillip Martin in Ernest J. Gaines's *In My Father's House.*

Bob Martin. Thrifty and industrious freedman blacksmith who refuses to work for white men who owe him money; achieves no legal redress for his whipping or for his wife and daughter's abuse in Albion W. Tourgee's *A Fool's Errand.*

Donald Martin. Rancher hanged by the lynch mob because he cannot produce a bill of sale for the cattle he bought from Harley Drew and because Larry Kinkaid's pistol is found in the possession of Juan Martinez, Martin's employee, in Walter Van Tilburg Clark's *The Ox-Bow Incident.*

Edward Richard (Rick) Martin. Musician who rises to stardom as a jazz trumpeter, but dies at a young age because of alcohol and drug abuse, in Dorothy Baker's *Young Man with a Horn.*

Elizabeth Martin. Daughter of Herb Martin, who, before he dies, gives her to George Brush, in Thornton Wilder's *Heaven's My Destination.*

Gertrude Martin. Light-skinned black woman who can pass for white; grows up on the south side of Chicago with Clare Kendry; marries a white butcher who accepts her being black in Nella Larsen's *Passing.*

Gilbert (Gil) Martin. Young settler in Deerfield who fights as an American militiaman against the Indians and irregulars in Walter D. Edmonds's *Drums along the Mohawk.*

Herbert (Herb) Martin. Newspaperman living at Queenie's Boarding House; before dying, he gives his daughter, Elizabeth Martin, to George Brush in Thornton Wilder's *Heaven's My Destination.*

Laodocious Martin. Friend of Johnny Church at Oxford; arrested with him for writing "Astrologia non est scientia" on the door of Lauds College in Mary Lee Settle's *Prisons.*

Lucinda Martin. See Lucinda Martin Stone.

Magdelana Borst (Lana) Martin. Wife of Gilbert Martin; miscarries their first child but bears two other children in Walter D. Edmonds's *Drums along the Mohawk.*

Mr. Bradly Mr. Martin (Bradly, Martin, Mr. & Mrs. D, The Ugly Spirit). Leader of the Nova Mob; heavy-metal addict, inventor of the double cross, biggest operator in any universe, and a master of transfer in William S. Burroughs's *Nova Express, The Soft Machine,* and *The Ticket That Exploded.*

Mr. Martin. Seducer of Ophelia Shepherd, his wife's sister, in William Hill Brown's *The Power of Sympathy.*

Mrs. Martin. Rhode Island cousin of Mrs. Francis in William Hill Brown's *The Power of Sympathy.*

Reverend Phillip J. Martin. Black leader losing the influence he had during the civil rights movement who is surprised by the appearance of his philosophically antagonistic, illegitimate son, Robert X, whom Martin has not seen since infancy, in Ernest J. Gaines's *In My Father's House.*

Shago Martin. Black jazz singer in Norman Mailer's *An American Dream.*

Shep Martin. Boyfriend of Berenice Sweet; student at the University of Georgia in Harry Crews's *A Feast of Snakes.*

Sidney Martin. Graduate of West Point and army lieutenant in Vietnam, where he is fragged, in Tim O'Brien's *Going after Cacciato.*

Sponge Martin. Co-worker and friend of Bruce Dudley in Old Harbor, Indiana; free-spirited man who foresees the attraction between Aline Grey and Dudley in Sherwood Anderson's *Dark Laughter*.

Betty Martindale. Childhood friend and later the sympathetic and level-headed confidante of Grace Caldwell Tate in John O'Hara's *A Rage to Live*.

Martine. Mistress of a wealthy banker connected with the French government; passes along some of her inside information to her lover, Jack Hartley, in James Jones's *The Merry Month of May*.

Martinez. Los Angeles policeman who beats up Abel after attempting to rob him in N. Scott Momaday's *House Made of Dawn*.

Antonio José Martínez. Wealthy priest in Taos who ignores his celibacy vows in Willa Cather's *Death Comes for the Archbishop*.

Juan (Francisco Morez) Martinez. Mysterious Mexican employee of Donald Martin; his possession of Larry Kinkaid's pistol convinces the mob that he is one of Kinkaid's murderers; hanged with Alva Hardwick and Martin in Walter Van Tilburg Clark's *The Ox-Bow Incident*.

Sergeant Julio Martinez. Mexican-American soldier who helps Sergeant Croft arrange the death of Lieutenant Hearn in Norman Mailer's *The Naked and the Dead*.

Marty. Latino proud of his Indian heritage; cares for the ill Harry Meyers and takes him to a black magic ritual in Jay Neugeboren's *Listen Ruben Fontanez*.

André Marty. Commissar who detains Andrés and Captain Rogelio Gomez in Ernest Hemingway's *For Whom the Bell Tolls*.

Maruca. Quadroon former slave and wife of Perrault in H. L. Davis's *Beulah Land*.

Alfio Marullo. Italian Catholic immigrant and owner of Marullo's Fruit and Fancy Groceries who sells the store to his seemingly good and faithful clerk Ethan Allen Hawley; deported as the result of an anonymous phone call to immigration officials in John Steinbeck's *The Winter of Our Discontent*.

Marunga. Wife of Tavi and mother of Hitia and Mako; survives the hurricane in Charles Nordhoff and James Norman Hall's *The Hurricane*.

Alma (Moo Moo) Marvel. Wife of Ben Marvel and mother of Elsie, Evelyn, Bushrod, and Cotton Marvel; celebrates her fortieth wedding anniversary in Peter De Vries's *Through the Fields of Clover*.

Ben Marvel. Husband of Alma Marvel, with whom he is celebrating their fortieth wedding anniversary, and father of Elsie, Evelyn, Bushrod, and Cotton Marvel; author of the "Edgewise" column in the Hickory, Massachusetts, *Blade* in Peter De Vries's *Through the Fields of Clover*.

Bushrod Marvel. Son of Alma and Ben Marvel; stereotypical comic liberal and secretary of the Civil Liberties League in Peter De Vries's *Through the Fields of Clover*.

Clara Marvel. Wife of Bushrod Marvel; guiltridden for her "prejudice" after objecting to Bushrod's kissing "the colored maid" in Peter De Vries's *Through the Fields of Clover*.

Cotton Marvel. Twenty-six-year-old divorced youngest child of Ben and Alma Marvel; lives at home working on "The Seven Who Stank," a play, in Peter De Vries's *Through the Fields of Clover*.

Elsie Marvel. Daughter of Alma and Ben Marvel; former wife of Harry Mercury, and others, in Peter De Vries's *Through the Fields of Clover*.

Evelyn Shaw Glimmergarden Marvel. Daughter of Ben and Alma Marvel; her father's favorite, "a golden feminine flame," in Peter De Vries's *Through the Fields of Clover*.

Athene Marvell. Graduate student with Vridar Hunter in Vardis Fisher's *We Are Betrayed*; Hunter's second wife in *No Villain Need Be*; divorced from Hunter in *Orphans in Gethsemene*.

Mrs. Marvell. Widowed mother of Ralph Marvell and member of the prestigious New York Marvell and Dagonet families in Edith Wharton's *The Custom of the Country*.

Paul Marvell. Son of Ralph Marvell and Undine Spragg; after divorcing Ralph, Undine uses Paul to blackmail him in Edith Wharton's *The Custom of the Country*.

Ralph Marvell. Reserved husband of Undine Spragg; writes poetry and hopes to rescue her from the influence of unprincipled social flatterers; commits suicide after Undine tries to blackmail him in Edith Wharton's *The Custom of the Country*.

Undine Marvell. See Undine Spragg.

Marx Marvelous. Ex-think tanker, later just a thinker and manager of the zoo; suffers hemorrhoids, lust for Amanda Ziller, and doubt; brilliant but frivolous author in Tom Robbins's *Another Roadside Attraction*.

Marvin. Female impersonator and dancer at the Iron Horse in Harry Crews's *Karate Is a Thing of the Spirit*.

General Marvin. Officer regarded by his subordinates as callous and arbitrary; transfers Major Joppolo to Algiers for countermanding an order banning carts in Adano in John Hersey's *A Bell for Adano*.

Phoebe Marvin. Tomboy who sails a sloop and accompanies Benedict Arnold's army to Quebec; marries Steven Nason in Kenneth Roberts's *Arundel*.

Major Duane Marvy. Fat American officer stationed in the Zone; involved in black-marketeering with Bloody Chiclitz; nemesis of Tyrone Slothrop and Oberst Enzian; eventually castrated because of mistaken identity in Thomas Pynchon's *Gravity's Rainbow*.

Carlo Marx. Sorrowful, poetic con man; friend of Sal Paradise and Dean Moriarty in Jack Kerouac's *On the Road*.

Mary. Nurse to Paul and Dalton Harron as children in Susan Sontag's *Death Kit*.

Mary. One of Sebastian Dangerfield's girlfriends; leaves her sadistic father and follows Sebastian to London, where she has a promising start as an actress, in J. P. Donleavy's *The Ginger Man*.

Mary. Youngest of the orphaned girls in the care of Rachel Cooper in Davis Grubb's *The Night of the Hunter*.

Miss Mary. Dying senile tenant of Silla Boyce; mother of Maritze and friend of Selina Boyce in Paule Marshall's *Brown Girl, Brownstones*.

Marya. Sister of Marthe and half sister of Stefan in William Faulkner's *A Fable*.

Lieutenant Stephen (Steve) Maryk. Executive officer who seizes control of the USS *Caine* from Captain Queeg during a typhoon in Herman Wouk's *The Caine Mutiny*.

Marylou. First wife of Dean Moriarty in Jack Kerouac's *On the Road*.

Mrs. Mash. Caseworker for "Crib" adoption agency in Peter De Vries's *The Tunnel of Love*.

Abigail Howland Mason. Daughter of William Howland by his first wife and mother of Abigail Mason Tolliver in Shirley Ann Grau's *The Keepers of the House*.

Andrew Mason. Lawyer and lover of N. Hexam in Diane Johnson's *The Shadow Knows*.

Bruce Mason. Younger son of Elsa and Bo Mason; resents his intimidating father; interrupts law school to be with his dying mother; after his mother's death he is estranged from his father, whom he views as ineffectual, exploitative, and self-indulgent, in Wallace Stegner's *The Big Rock Candy Mountain*.

Chester (Chet) Mason. Eldest son of Elsa and Bo Mason; relinquishes a chance at a baseball career after a humiliating arrest due to his father's bootlegging activities; precipitously marries his high school sweetheart; dies of pneumonia as a young man who had already become discouraged about his future in Wallace Stegner's *The Big Rock Candy Mountain*.

Elsa Norgaard Mason. Devoted long-suffering wife of Bo Mason and daughter of Nels Norgaard; leaves her Minnesota home as a young woman after her father marries her friend Sarah; goes to live with her uncle in North Dakota, where she meets her future husband; dies of cancer, leaving her husband bereft, in Wallace Stegner's *The Big Rock Candy Mountain*.

Gloria Mason. Girlfriend of Tyree Tucker; possesses cancelled bribery checks written by Tyree Tucker to Gerald Cantley in Richard Wright's *The Long Dream*.

Gregory Edward Mason. Englishman who marries Abigail Howland; father of Abigail Mason Tolliver in Shirley Ann Grau's *The Keepers of the House*.

Harry G. (Bo) Mason. Peripatetic opportunist who moves his family from place to place in the West in search of elusive prosperity and lasting security; murders Elaine Nesbitt, with whom he had an extramarital affair, and commits suicide when his last years find him living in poverty and despair in Wallace Stegner's *The Big Rock Candy Mountain*.

Hazel Mason. Black student from Texas who flunks out of college; disliked by Emma Lou Morgan because of her "Negro mannerisms" in Wallace Thurman's *The Blacker the Berry*.

Jack (Jackie) Mason. Upper-middle-class boyhood friend of Charles Gray; becomes successful in Clyde and marries Jessica Lovell in John P. Marquand's *Point of No Return*.

Jessica Lovell Mason. See Jessica Lovell.

Laura Mason. High school sweetheart of Chet Mason; later marries him, a decision which meets with the disapproval of Chet's parents; becomes a young widow after Chet's untimely death from pneumonia in Wallace Stegner's *The Big Rock Candy Mountain*.

Mr. Mason. Second mate aboard the *Aroostook* in William Dean Howells's *The Lady of the Aroostook*.

Opal Mason. Prostitute who laughs at Will Brady's offer of marriage in Wright Morris's *The Works of Love*.

Rose Dutcher Mason. See Rose Dutcher.

Mrs. Stacy McAndrews Mason. Aunt of Sally Lacey; sees her first husband tortured and scalped by Indians but survives to remarry and raise a total of nine children in Mary Lee Settle's *O Beulah Land*.

Warren Mason. Newspaperman and aspiring novelist; proposes marriage apologetically to Rose Dutcher, who accepts his liberal conditions, in Hamlin Garland's *Rose of Dutcher's Coolly*.

Joe (Gentleman Joe) Massara. Handsome and debonair member of the Vettori gang who wishes to leave it in order to pursue a dancing career in William Riley Burnett's *Little Caesar*.

Richard Mast. Army private who struggles to maintain possession of a pistol he believes will someday save him from a Japanese major with a Samurai saber in James Jones's *The Pistol*.

Cass Mastern. Maternal uncle of Ellis Burden; his letters during the Civil War serve as a basis for Jack Burden's doctoral dissertation in Robert Penn Warren's *All the King's Men*.

Babs Masters. Lyrical babbler who gives instructions in patience and attentiveness in the loving of a woman and the reading of a book, which are revealed as equivalent activities, as she narrates William Gass's *Willie Masters' Lonesome Wife*.

Lavinia Masterson. Lover of William Body in Leon Forrest's *The Bloodworth Orphans*.

Michael (Mike, Mike the Mouth) Masterson. Respected and feared umpire whose arguments with Gil Gamesh lead to Masterson's death; killed by a pitched ball in Philip Roth's *The Great American Novel*.

Mat. See Mat Moss.

Mata. Wife of Fakahau and mother of Marama and Arai; dies during the hurricane in Charles Nordhoff and James Norman Hall's *The Hurricane*.

Matches. Black hobo arrested in El Paso with Cass McKay in Nelson Algren's *Somebody in Boots*.

Tio Mate. Mexican *pistolero* in William S. Burroughs's *The Wild Boys*; participates in the attempt to blow up the nerve-gas train in *Exterminator!*

Mateo. English-speaking employee of Feliu Viosca, for whom Mateo acts as an interpreter, in Lafcadio Hearn's *Chita*.

Benjamino (Benjy, Mino) Matera. Young man who loses his feet in an accident; Theophilus North helps him adjust to his handicap and meet young women in Thornton Wilder's *Theophilus North*.

Itche (Gelding, Reb Itche) Mates. Ascetic packman and follower of Sabbatai Zevi; weds Rechele Babad but never consummates the marriage; travels to foreign places with Reb Mordecai Joseph bearing the good news of the Messiah's advent in the person of Sabbatai Zevi, but returns to Goray disillusioned in Isaac Bashevis Singer's *Satan in Goray*.

Hopestill (Hope) Mather. Rebellious niece and ward of Miss Pride; marries Dr. Philip McAllister after being impregnated by Harry Morgan; dies in a riding accident in Jean Stafford's *Boston Adventure*.

Richard (Dick) Mathias. Liquor store owner, husband of Sally Mathias, and lover of Ruth Conant in John Updike's *Marry Me*.

Sally Mathias. Wife of Richard Mathias and lover of Jerry Conant in John Updike's *Marry Me*.

Matilda. Small crazy woman who sits on benches near the river for twenty years waiting for her lover to return in Anaïs Nin's *Children of the Albatross*.

Matilda (Mat). Worker at Hosea Ortman's farm and lover of Paul Hardin; causes the quarrel that leads to Smoke's lynching in Brand Whitlock's *J. Hardin & Son*.

Buddy Matlow. Lecherous sheriff and Public Safety Director of Lebeau County in Harry Crews's *A Feast of Snakes*.

Matt. Dog-musher who helps Weedon Scott tame White Fang in Jack London's *White Fang*.

Alice Matthews. Friend of Rachel Hutchins at whose father's sanitarium Rachel has recovered from her "nerves"; only person to advise Rachel strongly against marrying Rob Mayfield in Reynolds Price's *The Surface of Earth*.

Crit Matthews. Neighbor murdered by Alonzo Dudley in Jessamyn West's *The Life I Really Lived*.

Ebon Matthews. Homosexual lover of Alonzo Dudley in Jessamyn West's *The Life I Really Lived*.

Eloise Matthews. Wife of H. K. Matthews who makes a pass at Ned Beaumont on the evening of her husband's suicide in Dashiell Hammett's *The Glass Key*.

H. K. Matthews. Publisher of the *Observer* who attempts to use his influence to get Paul Madvig indicted for the murder of Senator Henry in Dashiell Hammett's *The Glass Key*.

Lord Claude Maudulayne. British ambassador to the United States; with French ambassador Raoul Barre, presents the view of the NATO countries in Allen Drury's *Advise and Consent*.

Lady Kitty Maudulayne. Wife of Lord Claude Maudulayne in Allen Drury's *Advise and Consent*.

Thomas Maule. Son of Matthew Maule I; architect and builder of the Pyncheon house; hides the Pyncheon land deed in Nathaniel Hawthorne's *The House of the Seven Gables*.

Matthew Maule (I). Father of Thomas Maule; hanged for witchcraft; curses the Pyncheon family in Nathaniel Hawthorne's *The House of the Seven Gables*.

Matthew Maule (II). Son of Thomas Maule; hypnotizes Alice Pyncheon in Nathaniel Hawthorne's *The House of the Seven Gables*.

Sarah Abbott (The Pilgrim) Maulsby. Massachusetts debutante and lover of Alex Portnoy in Philip Roth's *Portnoy's Complaint*.

Maum Netta (Mauma). Old mulatto servant of the Wentworths in DuBose Heyward's *Mamba's Daughters*.

Patricia Maurier. Wealthy widow who hosts the yacht party in William Faulkner's *Mosquitoes*.

Maverick. Mandan Indian woman who lives with Luke and Ma Lampson in John Hawkes's *The Beetle Leg*.

Mavis. Sister of Judy Davis and companion of James Christopher at the Apex Longleaf Club; tells Christopher about Jack Davis's beating of Preacher Smathers and accuses him of being ultimately responsible for Smathers's injuries in Fred Chappell's *It Is Time, Lord*.

Mawakis. Shawnee Indian who serves as Salathiel Albine's adoptive mother in Hervey Allen's *The Forest and the Fort*.

Max. Argentinian and second in command of the revolutionary forces in South America; strong, intelligent, and intuitive man who loves power in William Herrick's *The Last to Die*.

Max. Attorney secured by Jan Erlone to defend Bigger Thomas against the charge of murdering Mary Dalton in Richard Wright's *Native Son*.

Max. Machinist and cold husband of Christine in John Clellon Holmes's *Go*.

Max. Obese, megalomaniacal auto race manager in Joyce Carol Oates's *With Shuddering Fall*.

Max. Photographer and contributor to Renate's planned magazine in Anaïs Nin's *Collages*.

Max (Red Max). Hot-tempered sailor, with two wives, who befriends Redburn in Herman Melville's *Redburn*.

Captain Harris Maxey. First officer of B Company and Claude Wheeler's captain in Willa Cather's *One of Ours*.

Gifford (Giff) Maxim. Political revolutionary disowned by the Party in Lionel Trilling's *The Middle of the Journey*.

Maximov. Husband of Anna Petrovna Maximov; arrested with her while Adam Krug and Krug's son stay with them at their country home in Vladimir Nabokov's *Bend Sinister*.

Anna Petrovna Maximov. Kind old woman and wife of Maximov; arrested while caring for David Krug in Vladimir Nabokov's *Bend Sinister*.

Maximus. Magician, seer, and pseudo-philosopher who ingratiates himself with Julian, to the dismay of Julian's more scholarly friends, in Gore Vidal's *Julian*.

Henry Maxwell. Minister of the First Church of Raymond, Kansas, who asks his parishioners to ask themselves "What would Jesus do?" in Charles M. Sheldon's *In His Steps*.

John Maxwell. Advertising manager for Jonathan Beer, the company that, at Mrs. Layden's suggestion, sponsors Robert Syverten and Gloria Beatty in the dance marathon in Horace McCoy's *They Shoot Horses, Don't They?*

Seth Maxwell. Party-loving Dallas Cowboy starting quarterback and friend of Phil Elliott in Peter Gent's *North Dallas Forty*.

May. Neighbor of Daniel Verger; moves in with Bill Agatson, who throws her out three days before he is killed, in John Clellon Holmes's *Go*.

John May. Physician and would-be philanthropist in Rebecca Harding Davis's *Life in the Iron Mills*.

May (Aunt May). Daughter of Grandfather Adams and aunt of Stephen Grendon; meddler who opposes Grendon's dating of Margery Estabrook in August Derleth's *Evening in Spring*.

May Alice. Girlhood friend of Ursa Corregidora; sexually active at a young age, she has a baby by Harold in Gayl Jones's *Corregidora*.

Kate Maybone. Mother who charges Duncan Ferguson with bastardy in Hugh Henry Brackenridge's *Modern Chivalry*.

Julia Maybury. Socialite wife of Antrim Stairs; driven to suicide by his refusal to divorce her so she can marry Jim Halford in Mary Austin's *Santa Lucia*.

Anna Goodwin Mayfield. Dead mother of Forrest Mayfield in Reynolds Price's *The Surface of Earth*.

Eva Kendal Mayfield. See Eva Kendal.

Forrest Mayfield. Latin teacher who elopes with his sixteen-year-old pupil, Eva Kendal, in Reynolds Price's *The Surface of Earth*.

Hattie (Hatt Shorter) Mayfield. Sister of Forrest Mayfield and wife of the deceased James Shorter in Reynolds Price's *The Surface of Earth*.

Aunt Mannie Mayfield. Elderly aunt of Mildred Sutton in Reynolds Price's *A Long and Happy Life*.

Rachel Hutchins Mayfield. See Rachel Hutchins.

Raven Hutchins (Hutch) Mayfield. Child of Rachel Hutchins and Rob Mayfield in Reynolds Price's *The Surface of Earth*.

Robinson Mayfield. Estranged father of Forrest Mayfield in Reynolds Price's *The Surface of Earth*.

Robinson (Rob) Mayfield. Son of Eva Kendal and Forrest Mayfield in Reynolds Price's *The Surface of Earth*.

Mayhew. Florence, Alabama, peace officer who conspires with John Handback to find the money Miltiades Vaiden stole from Handback in T. S. Stribling's *The Store*.

Caroline Peck Mayhew. Hypochondriac mother of Justine Peck and wife of Sam Mayhew; commits suicide after her husband's death in Anne Tyler's *Searching for Caleb*.

Jessie Mayhew. College student working at Camp Morgan who attracts George Brush's interest until he learns that she believes in evolution in Thornton Wilder's *Heaven's My Destination*.

Sam Mayhew. Husband of Caroline Peck Mayhew in Anne Tyler's *Searching for Caleb*.

Mayo (May, Sandra). Lover of Valentine Hood and wife of Sweeney in Paul Theroux's *The Family Arsenal*.

The Mayor of the Twentieth Century. Murderer who once disguised himself as Trout Fishing in America in Richard Brautigan's *Trout Fishing in America*.

Mayotte. Daughter of Aimée Peyronnette and Louis Desrivières; nurtured by her beloved foster-mother Youma in Lafcadio Hearn's *Youma*.

Esther Mazur. Devoted wife of Yasha Mazur, despite his lechery; unable to bear children, she spends her days as a head seamstress, meticulously abiding by Jewish customs, in Isaac Bashevis Singer's *The Magician of Lublin*.

Rutka Mazur. Member of a Zionist youth movement; joins Jewish resistance fighters in Warsaw and, hiding in a bunker from Nazi soldiers walking overhead, endures a comrade's putting to death her incessantly crying baby in John Hersey's *The Wall*.

Yasha (Magician of Lublin, Reb Jacob the Penitent) Mazur. Adulterous husband of Esther Mazur and itinerant magician; lover of Magda Zbarski and Zeftel and would-be husband of Emilia Chrabotzky; after Magda's death, he repents, changes his name, lives hermetically, and becomes famous for his piety and healing powers in Isaac Bashevis Singer's *The Magician of Lublin*.

Dr. Philip (Perly) McAllister. Aristocratic Boston physician secretly loved by Sonia Marburg; marries Hopestill Mather in Jean Stafford's *Boston Adventure*.

Reverend Charles McAndrews. Virginia gentleman who becomes a fundamentalist preacher and abolitionist, and eventually dies in Kansas for his beliefs, in Mary Lee Settle's *Know Nothing*.

James McArdle. Fanatical evangelist; appears in Hervey Allen's *Bedford Village* and *The Forest and the Fort*.

Dirk McArthur. Self-centered playboy whom Eveline Hutchins meets aboard ship and with whom she has an affair that ends because of his drunkenness in John Dos Passos's *U.S.A.* trilogy.

Terry McBain. Aspiring woman writer involved in a flirtation with the narrator of Peter De Vries's *The Tunnel of Love*.

Mrs. McBales. See Mrs. McKeckeran.

Henry (Hank) McBee. Stingy, no-account plebeian for the captain of the wagon train in A. B. Guthrie's *The Way West*.

Mercy McBee. Sensual daughter of Hank McBee; lover of Curtis Mack, by whom she has a child; wife of Brownie Evans in A. B. Guthrie's *The Way West.*

Ada Fincastle McBride. See Ada Fincastle.

Mrs. McBride. Strict mother of Ralph McBride; product of curdled Calvinism, her values are based on hatred; consigns her son to a forced marriage to Janet Rowan and military service in Ellen Glasgow's *Vein of Iron.*

Ralph McBride. Brilliant and headstrong man trapped by the forces of morality and money into marrying Janet Rowan; later marries Ada Fincastle in Ellen Glasgow's *Vein of Iron.*

Ranny McBride. Handsome, intelligent, and illegitimate son of Ada Fincastle and Ralph McBride; insists on social change in Ellen Glasgow's *Vein of Iron.*

Dean McCabe. First husband of Peggy McCabe Robinson; assistant dean at Yale University in John Updike's *Of the Farm.*

Earl McCabe. Marine deserter who, as a partner of Lionel Boyd Johnson, becomes ruler of San Lorenzo in Kurt Vonnegut's *Cat's Cradle.*

Orondo McCabe. Owner of a Philadelphia nightclub and manager of Cubsy Hall in William Goyen's *The Fair Sister.*

Richard McCabe. Eleven-year-old stepson of Joey Robinson and son of Peggy McCabe Robinson and Dean McCabe; serious boy with a passion for reading and for knowledge of the natural world in John Updike's *Of the Farm.*

Alonzo (Lon) McCaferty. Ex-actor and alcoholic tramp; returns to his hometown to die in Jerry Bumpus's *Anaconda.*

Bindy McCall. Brother of Patsy and Matt McCall and father of Charlie Boy McCall; controls Albany's nighttime world, which he closes to Billy Phelan because Phelan refused to spy on Morrie Berman, in William Kennedy's *Billy Phelan's Greatest Game.*

Charlie Boy McCall. Son of Bindy McCall; kidnap victim in William Kennedy's *Billy Phelan's Greatest Game.*

Matt McCall. Brother of Patsy and Bindy McCall and uncle of Charlie Boy McCall; political strategist and spokesman in William Kennedy's *Billy Phelan's Greatest Game.*

Patsy McCall. Brother of Bindy and Matt McCall and uncle of Charlie Boy McCall; establishes the powerful Irish-Democratic McCall political machine in

William Kennedy's *Billy Phelan's Greatest Game.*

Anse McCallum. Son of Buddy McCallum; fights Matt Levitt in William Faulkner's *The Town.*

Buddy McCallum. Father of Anse McCallum in William Faulkner's *Intruder in the Dust* and *The Town.*

Lafe McCallum. See Lafe.

Bridget McCandliss. Girl whose parents are lost in an Indian raid and who is returning to relatives in Carlisle, Pennsylvania, in Hervey Allen's *Toward the Morning.*

Mickey McCane. Former Army buddy of Jack Sellars; makes passes at Bebe Sellars and finally goes berserk, murdering the idiot boy Pinhead and Miss Whitaker, his black nurse, in Doris Betts's *The River to Pickle Beach.*

Shrevlin (Shreve) McCannon. Harvard roommate of Quentin Compson I and one of the narrators of William Faulkner's *Absalom, Absalom!* See also Shreve MacKenzie.

Hoake McCarron. Tennesseean who fathers Eula Varner's daughter Linda Snopes; appears in William Faulkner's *The Hamlet, The Town,* and *The Mansion.*

Mike McCarthy. Irish idler admired by young Sam McPherson in Sherwood Anderson's *Windy McPherson's Son.*

Newton Justine (Brother McCarthy, Colonel, Judge, Mac, Newt, N. J., Papa, Prince of Evil) McCarthy. Unscrupulous minister; turns his daughter Orlean against Jean Baptiste and is murdered by her in Oscar Micheaux's *The Homesteader.*

Orlean E. McCarthy. Wife of Jean Baptiste and daughter of Newton Justine McCarthy; kills her father and herself in Oscar Micheaux's *The Homesteader.*

Parnell Emmett Joseph (Parn) McCarthy. Alcoholic lawyer who makes a comeback by assisting Paul Biegler in defending Frederic Manion in Robert Traver's *Anatomy of a Murder.*

Amodeus (Uncle Buddy) McCaslin. Son of Carothers McCaslin and twin of Theophilus (Uncle Buck) McCaslin; appears in William Faulkner's *The Unvanquished* and *Go Down, Moses.*

Carothers McCaslin. See Lucius Quintus Carothers McCaslin.

Isaac (Ike) McCaslin. Son of Theophilus (Buck) and Sophonsiba Beauchamp McCaslin; renounces his birthright; appears in William Faulkner's *The Ham-*

let; *Go Down, Moses*; *Intruder in the Dust*; *The Town*; *The Mansion*; and *The Reivers*.

Lucius Quintus Carothers (Old Carothers) McCaslin. Father of Amodeus (Buddy) McCaslin, Theophilus (Buck) McCaslin, a daughter, and, by the slave Tomasina, Tomey's Turl; appears in William Faulkner's *Go Down, Moses*; *Intruder in the Dust*; and *The Reivers*.

Ned McCaslin. Grandson of Carothers McCaslin in William Faulkner's *The Reivers*.

Sophonsiba Beauchamp McCaslin. Wife of Theophilus (Buck) McCaslin, and mother of Ike McCaslin in William Faulkner's *Go Down, Moses*.

Theophilus (Uncle Buck) McCaslin. Son of Carothers McCaslin, husband of Sophonsiba Beauchamp McCaslin, and the father of Ike McCaslin; appears in William Faulkner's *Absalom, Absalom!*; *The Unvanquished*; *The Hamlet*; *Go Down, Moses*; and *The Reivers*.

Polly Ann Ripley McChesney. See Polly Ann Ripley.

Thomas (Tom) McChesney. Strong and faithful Kentucky pioneer; husband of Polly Ann Ripley and friend of David Ritchie in Winston Churchill's *The Crossing*.

Reba McClain. Girlfriend of Red Scalotta and bet recorder in Joseph Wambaugh's *The Blue Knight*.

Clarisse McClellan. Young neighbor of Guy Montag; her unconventional ideas inspire Montag to rebel against the antiliterate society in Ray Bradbury's *Fahrenheit 451*.

Everett Currier McClellan. Hop farmer and husband of Lily Knight McClellan; murders Ryder Channing before shooting himself in Joan Didion's *Run River*.

James Parker (Arkie) McClellan. Fourteen-year-old Gimlet Street hustler who shoots Zebulon Johns Mackie in a misguided attempt to protect Clemmie in Fred Chappell's *The Gaudy Place*.

Julia Knight (Julie) McClellan. Daughter of Everett and Lily Knight McClellan in Joan Didion's *Run River*.

Knight McClellan. Son of Everett and Lily Knight McClellan in Joan Didion's *Run River*.

Lily Knight McClellan. Wife of Everett McClellan and daughter of Walter and Edith Knight; has several affairs, most importantly with Ryder Channing, in Joan Didion's *Run River*.

Martha Currier McClellan. Sister of Everett McClellan and lover of Ryder Channing; buried on the family farm by Everett after her possibly suicidal drowning in Joan Didion's *Run River*.

A. M. (Forenoon) McClintock. Hedonistic college roommate of Vridar Hunter in Vardis Fisher's *Passions Spin the Plot*.

Jonathan (Johnny) McCloud. Lover of Molly Taylor White, father of Joe White, and friend of Gideon Fry; cowboy on Fry's ranch; narrates part of Larry McMurtry's *Leaving Cheyenne*.

Mark McCluskey. Police captain in the pay of Virgil Sollozzo; killed by Michael Corleone in revenge for the shooting of Vito Corleone in Mario Puzo's *The Godfather*.

Codene McClusky. Girlfriend of Raymond Douglas in Herbert Simmons's *Man Walking on Eggshells*.

Father McConagha. Catholic priest at St. Dominick's church in Chicago in William Riley Burnett's *Little Caesar*.

Alexander Hamilton McCone. Stuttering son of Daniel McCone and patron of Walter F. Starbuck in Kurt Vonnegut's *Jailbird*.

Daniel McCone. Industrialist and father of Alexander McCone in Kurt Vonnegut's *Jailbird*.

McCord. Newspaperman in William Faulkner's *The Wild Palms*.

Pat McCormick. Oil camp contractor who employs Dobbs and Curtin; pays his employees only when threatened with death in B. Traven's *The Treasure of the Sierra Madre*.

Tadpole (Crawdad, Tad, Taddy) McCormick. Owner of Happy's Café, where Ursa Corregidora sings; tends to Ursa following her operation, and then marries her; because of his affair with Vivian, he and Ursa are divorced, in Gayl Jones's *Corregidora*.

Mrs. Margie (Marge) McCoy. Companion of Doremus Blodgett; finds George Brush's ideas ludicrous and is the first of many people to call him "nuts" in Thornton Wilder's *Heaven's My Destination*.

William McCoy. Dour Scottish seaman who is a leader of the rebellion aboard HMS *Bounty* in Charles Nordhoff and James Norman Hall's *Mutiny on the Bounty*; his love of alcohol precipitates the final violence between the Tahitians and the whites and leads to his suicide in *Pitcairn's Island*.

Joe McCoyne. President of the Abilene stockyards who buys the cattle driven there from Texas in Emerson Hough's *North of 36*.

Reverend Mister McCrae. Assistant to the Reverend Hodder in Winston Churchill's *The Inside of the Cup*.

Fenian "Fainy" McCreary (Mac). Itinerant radical who forsakes all, most notably his wife and family, to labor for the workingman in John Dos Passos's *U.S.A.* trilogy.

McCudden. British pilot in William Faulkner's *A Fable*.

Mary McCullogh. White prostitute, pawn of J. D. Carson and proponents of school segregation, whose allegation of rape by three blacks leads to racial violence in Julian Mayfield's *The Grand Parade*.

Skinny McCullough. Foreman of Drag Gibson's ranch in Ishmael Reed's *Yellow Back Radio Broke-Down*.

Elias McCutcheon. Fort Hill settler who becomes a wealthy landowner, common law husband of Jane Nail, and a leader of Confederate raiders in Jesse Hill Ford's *The Raider*.

Isaac McCutcheon. First-born son of Elias McCutcheon and Jane Nail; kills a man in a duel and is injured in the Civil War in Jesse Hill Ford's *The Raider*.

Jake McCutcheon. Slave given to Elias McCutcheon by Shokotee McNeilly; becomes McCutcheon's faithful friend and companion in Jesse Hill Ford's *The Raider*.

Patsy Jo McCutcheon. See Patricia Josephine McCutcheon Shafer.

Thomas Gideon (Tom) McCutcheon. Father of Patsy Jo McCutcheon and longtime member of the Sligo County community; murders Eleanor Fite at her wedding to Gratt Shafer before killing himself in Jesse Hill Ford's *Mountains of Gilead*; apparently descended from Elias McCutcheon in *The Raider*.

Willy McCutcheon. Second son of Elias McCutcheon and Jane Nail; marries Sallie Parham before being killed in the Civil War in Jesse Hill Ford's *The Raider*.

Gerald (Jerry) McDermott. Playwright who is the longtime friend and probable future husband of Olivia Lattimore in Mary Austin's *A Woman of Genius*.

Mrs. Simon McEachern. Wife of Simon McEachern; with her husband, adopts Joe Christmas, who eventually steals her money, in William Faulkner's *Light in August*.

Simon McEachern. Farmer who, with his wife, adopts Joe Christmas, who possibly murders McEachern, in William Faulkner's *Light in August*.

Angus Mcellhenny. Old miner and prospector who identifies Clay Turner as the Bad Man in E. L. Doctorow's *Welcome to Hard Times*.

Sheen McEvoy. Deformed and retarded man who tries to throw Mazie Holbrook down a mine shaft in Tillie Olsen's *Yonnondio*.

Annie McGairy. See Annie McGairy Brown.

Jim McGarrity. Kindly saloonkeeper and friend of the Nolans in Betty Smith's *A Tree Grows in Brooklyn*.

Marietta McGee-Chavéz. Wife of Thomas Harold MacDougal; yearns to restore a wholeness to herself through artifacts and fantasy of Spain in William Goyen's *In a Farther Country*.

Mary McGeeney. Biographer who teaches John Gilson and who is Balso Snell's childhood sweetheart in Nathanael West's *The Dream Life of Balso Snell*.

Agnes Bedford McGehee. Sister of Malcolm Bedford, wife of Hugh McGehee, and mother of Edward and Lucinda McGehee; travels from Natchez to Shiloh to find and bring home her dead son in Stark Young's *So Red the Rose*.

Edward McGehee. Son of Hugh and Agnes McGehee and admirer of Jefferson Davis; enlists in the Confederate army and dies at Shiloh in Stark Young's *So Red the Rose*.

Hugh McGehee. Husband of Agnes McGehee and father of Edward and Lucinda McGehee; opposes slavery and secession; owner of Montrose plantation, which is looted and burned by Union soldiers, in Stark Young's *So Red the Rose*.

Lucinda (Lucy) McGehee. Daughter of Hugh and Agnes McGehee; loves her cousin Charlie Taliaferro, who is killed at Shiloh, in Stark Young's *So Red the Rose*.

Leslie (Red) McGivers. Graduate student in history who moves to Detroit when her thesis adviser changes universities; studies karate, befriends Bernie Guizot, and tries to expose Honor Rogers to feminist ideas in Marge Piercy's *The High Cost of Living*.

Gowan McGland. Womanizing alcoholic Scotch-Welsh poet on a personal appearance tour in America; commits suicide in Peter De Vries's *Reuben, Reuben*.

Theresa McGoun. Swift and pretty stenographer for the Babbitt-Thompson Realty Company in Sinclair Lewis's *Babbitt*.

McGovern. One of Henry Miller's assistants at the telegraph company in Henry Miller's *Tropic of Capricorn*.

Gregory (Greg) McGovern. Movie actor and lover of Orpha Chase; marries Chase's daughter Wanda in Jessamyn West's *The Life I Really Lived*.

Sims McGrother. Greedy neighbor of Old Jack Beechum; abuses other people, his animals, and his land for profit in Wendell Berry's *The Memory of Old Jack*.

Terence McGuffy. Night-beat policeman in Albert Halper's *Union Square*.

Hugh McGuire. Altamont doctor and friend of the Gant family in Thomas Wolfe's *Look Homeward, Angel* and *Of Time and the River*.

Ross McGurk. Founder of the McGurk Institute of Biology in Sinclair Lewis's *Arrowsmith*.

James J. (Admiral Ass) McHabe. Administrative assistant at Calvin Coolidge High School; spends time writing circulars and keeping everyone innundated with paperwork, little of which makes any sense, in Bel Kaufman's *Up the Down Staircase*.

Lloyd McHarg. Well-known American novelist and close friend of George Webber in Thomas Wolfe's *You Can't Go Home Again*.

Arthur McHenry. Law partner and trusted friend of Joe Chapin I in John O'Hara's *Ten North Frederick*; Lockwood family lawyer in *The Lockwood Concern*.

Watts McHurdie. Civil War veteran; poet, philosopher, and harness maker in William Allen White's *A Certain Rich Man*.

Sergeant McIllhenny. Amorous sergeant who is three times reduced in rank to private; member of the 918th Bomb Group killed in battle in Beirne Lay, Jr., and Sy Bartlett's *Twelve O'Clock High!*

Bobby McIlvaine. Avant-garde theatrical designer in Edmund Wilson's *I Thought of Daisy*.

Clay McInnis. Country doctor of Port William, Kentucky, in Wendell Berry's *The Memory of Old Jack*.

David McInnis. Financial manager of Rebecca Carrington's estate and subsequently her husband in Robert Penn Warren's *A Place to Come To*.

Maria McInnis. See Maria McInnis Beaufort.

Rose McInnis. Wife and widow of Clay McInnis and lover of Jack Beechum; burns to death when her house catches fire in Wendell Berry's *The Memory of Old Jack*.

Reverend Kenneth McIntoch. Shady, unctuous minister aboard the *Castel Felice* in Calvin Hernton's *Scarecrow*.

Henry (Big Henry) McIntosh. Boyfriend of Dessie; boyhood playmate then houseboy of Tracy Deen; lynch mob victim when he is mistakenly identified as Deen's murderer in Lillian Smith's *Strange Fruit*.

Alice McIntyre. College friend and later New York roommate of Derrick Thornton in Helen Hooven Santmyer's *Herbs and Apples*.

Ben McKarkle. Son of Solomon McKarkle; avenges Sally Lacey's insult to his father by leading the group of young men who "crop" her hair in Mary Lee Settle's *O Beulah Land*.

Gideon McKarkle. Son of Peregrine Lacey Catlett's former overseer; hunting companion and trusted friend of Johnny Catlett; joins Johnny's Confederate army unit because his father told him to keep the Union troops out of Virginia in Mary Lee Settle's *Know Nothing*.

Jeb McKarkle. Inefficient brother of Gideon McKarkle in Mary Lee Settle's *Know Nothing*.

Mr. McKarkle. Overseer of Beulah and manager of the inn; moves to western Virginia to farm on his own; father of Gideon and Jeb McKarkle in Mary Lee Settle's *Know Nothing*.

Solomon McKarkle. Former hat maker driven out of business by British trade laws; settles at Beulah, defends Johnny Lacey, but is insulted when Sally Lacey does not really like the thimble bed he has made for Sara Lacey Catlett and so is indirectly responsible for the retaliatory "cropping" of Sally Lacey's hair in Mary Lee Settle's *O Beulah Land*.

Tad McKarkle. Son of Solomon McKarkle; marries the granddaughter of Mother Carver in Mary Lee Settle's *O Beulah Land*.

Bryan McKay. Brother of Cass McKay and drunken veteran of World War I in Nelson Algren's *Somebody in Boots*.

Cass McKay. Ignorant, dirt-poor Texas drifter who becomes a petty criminal in Chicago in Nelson Algren's *Somebody in Boots*.

Nancy McKay. Sister of Cass McKay; becomes a prostitute in Nelson Algren's *Somebody in Boots*.

Stuart (Stub, Stubby) McKay. Brutal father of Cass and Nancy McKay; his treatment of Cass causes Nancy to leave home in Nelson Algren's *Somebody in Boots*.

Mrs. McKeckeran (Mrs. McBales). Wife of a factory executive; as a gospel worker, visits the housing development where Gertie and Clovis Nevels live; later wants carved dolls for a Christmas bazaar in Harriette Arnow's *The Dollmaker*.

Calvin McKee. Grandson of Walter and Lois McKee; elopes with Etoile Momeyer; organizes the western ritual enacted on Tom Scanlon's ninetieth birthday in Wright Morris's *Ceremony in Lone Tree*.

Eileen McKee. Daughter-in-law of Walter and Lois McKee and mother of Calvin and Gordon McKee in Wright Morris's *Ceremony in Lone Tree*.

Emily Dodsworth McKee. Civic-minded daughter of Fran and Sam Dodsworth and wife of Harry McKee in Sinclair Lewis's *Dodsworth*.

Gordon Scanlon McKee. Five-year-old grandson of Walter and Lois McKee; falls under the influence of Gordon Boyd in Wright Morris's *The Field of Vision* and *Ceremony in Lone Tree*.

Harry McKee. Husband of Emily Dodsworth McKee and assistant general manager of the Vandering Bolt and Nut Company in Zenith in Sinclair Lewis's *Dodsworth*.

Lois Scanlon McKee. Wife of Walter McKee; still influenced by an adolescent kiss from Gordon Boyd in Wright Morris's *The Field of Vision*; frantically opposes male authority and fires a precipitating gunshot in *Ceremony in Lone Tree*.

Walter McKee. Proponent of typical middle class values; avatar of the average in Wright Morris's *The Field of Vision* and *Ceremony in Lone Tree*.

Becky Thurston McKelva. First wife of Judge Clinton McKelva and mother of Laurel McKelva Hand; West Virginia native who loses her vision and dies after an eye operation in Eudora Welty's *The Optimist's Daughter*.

Clinton (Clint, Judge Mac) McKelva. Seventy-one-year-old judge in Mt. Salus, Mississippi; father of Laurel McKelva Hand and widower of Becky McKelva; marries Fay Chisom McKelva one and a

half years before his eye operation and subsequent death in a New Orleans hospital in Eudora Welty's *The Optimist's Daughter*.

Wanda Fay Chisom McKelva. Second wife of Judge Clinton McKelva; inherits the McKelva family home in Eudora Welty's *The Optimist's Daughter*.

Albert McKisco. Novelist who fights a duel with Tommy Barban in F. Scott Fitzgerald's *Tender Is the Night*.

Sarah McKlennar. Motherly widow of a British officer; hires Gil Martin to farm for her during the Mohawk Valley campaign in Walter D. Edmonds's *Drums along the Mohawk*.

Andrew (Andy) McLane. Lover of Christina Goering until she leaves him for a gangster in Jane Bowles's *Two Serious Ladies*.

Red McLaughlin. Boyfriend of Marsan Vaiden, whom he impregnates, in T. S. Stribling's *Unfinished Cathedral*.

Patrick (Pat) McLear. Handsome San Francisco poet and friend of Jack Duluoz, who admires McLear's unpublished poem "Dark Brown," in Jack Kerouac's *Big Sur*; also appears in *Desolation Angels*.

McLeod (Mac). Experienced labor organizer and mentor of Jim Nolan; instigates the strike among the fruit pickers in John Steinbeck's *In Dubious Battle*.

Allan McLeod. Orphan reared by Mrs. John Durham; rises to political power during Reconstruction in Thomas Dixon's *The Leopard's Spots*.

Beverly Guinevere McLeod. Landlady of the boardinghouse, wife of William McLeod, mother of Monina, and lover of Leroy Hollingsworth in Norman Mailer's *Barbary Shore*.

William (Bill) McLeod. Former communist revolutionary who has stolen a mysterious "black box" from the U.S. government; pursued by Leroy Hollingsworth, befriended by Michael Lovett, and married to Beverly Guinevere McLeod in Norman Mailer's *Barbary Shore*.

Eloise (Eloise Hunter) McLindon. Struggling single parent of David Hunter; moves from Virginia to New Jersey following the death of her daughter, Clair Hunter, in Hal Bennett's *The Black Wine*.

Eva McLoch. See Christine Monahan.

Kevin McLoch. See Sean Monahan.

Casey McMahon. Handsome, superficial man who is Betsy Allbright's fourth husband in Ludwig Bemelmans's *Dirty Eddie.*

Mrs. Ella McManus. Fort Worth medium whom George Brush visits but refuses to pay because he learns that she is a fraud in Thornton Wilder's *Heaven's My Destination.*

Daniel (Dan) McMasters. Texas Ranger and sheriff who is responsible for the success of the cattle drive in Emerson Hough's *North of 36.*

Randle Patrick (Mack, McMurry, R. P.) McMurphy. Fast-talking and irrepressible inmate who challenges Big Nurse's dictatorial control of a mental hospital ward in Ken Kesey's *One Flew Over the Cuckoo's Nest.*

McNab. See Vadim Vadimovich.

William (Sandy) McNab. Employee of John Bonnyfeather and friend of Anthony Adverse in Hervey Allen's *Anthony Adverse.*

Cornelia McNabb. See Cornelia McNabb Tillinghast Brainard.

Gus McNiel. Milkman represented in a personal injury suit by the ambulance-chasing attorney George Baldwin in John Dos Passos's *Manhattan Transfer.*

Nellie McNiel. Wife of Gus McNeil seduced by George Baldwin while he is representing her husband in a personal injury suit in John Dos Passos's *Manhattan Transfer.*

Shokotee McNeilly. Chickasaw leader and father of Pettecasockee; gives Jane Nail to Elias McCutcheon for a wife in Jesse Hill Ford's *The Raider.*

Princess McNott. Yankton Indian wife of Sergeant Rob't McNott in Kenneth Roberts's *Northwest Passage.*

Sergeant Rob't (Mac) McNott. Soldier and trader who searches for a route to the Pacific Ocean; friend of Major Robert Rogers in Kenneth Roberts's *Northwest Passage.*

McPherson. Dispatcher for the South Eastern Railway whose office is broken into in Michael Crichton's *The Great Train Robbery.*

Jane McPherson. Wife of John (Windy) McPherson and mother of Sam McPherson in Sherwood Anderson's *Windy McPherson's Son.*

John (Windy) McPherson. Civil War veteran and house painter who is the drunken father of Sam and Kate McPherson in Sherwood Anderson's *Windy McPherson's Son.*

Kate McPherson. Daughter of John (Windy) McPherson and sister of Sam McPherson in Sherwood Anderson's *Windy McPherson's Son.*

Roger A. (Rog) McPherson. Head of the Neuropsychiatric Research Unit who authorizes the stage-three operation on Harold Benson in Michael Crichton's *The Terminal Man.*

Sam McPherson. Son of John (Windy) McPherson; newspaperboy who becomes a business giant and then wanders off in search of truth; loves Janet Eberly and marries Sue Rainey in Sherwood Anderson's *Windy McPherson's Son.*

Sue Rainey McPherson. See Sue Rainey.

Rev. Alex McPhule. White fundamentalist preacher, founder of True Faith Christ Lovers' Church, and leader of a lynch mob in George S. Schuyler's *Black No More.*

Laura McRaven. Nine-year-old only cousin of India Fairchild; leaves Jackson, Mississippi, after her mother's death to attend Dabney Fairchild's wedding at Shellmound plantation in Eudora Welty's *Delta Wedding.*

Malcolm M'Crea. Proprietor of the house in which Constantia and Stephen Dudley live after their financial ruin; sells a locket belonging to Constantia in Charles Brockden Brown's *Ormond.*

Sergeant Michael McShane. Brooklyn police officer and loving second husband of Katie Nolan in Betty Smith's *A Tree Grows in Brooklyn.*

Ev McTaggart. Smart but mediocre former catcher for the New York Mammoths; becomes manager of the team when Dutch Schnell dies in Mark Harris's *It Looked Like For Ever.*

Trina Sieppe McTeague. First wife of McTeague; develops pathological miserly traits, thus hastening McTeague's degeneration and precipitating his murdering her, in Frank Norris's *McTeague.*

McTeague (Mac). Dentist who degenerates to a brutish condition, murders his wife and steals her savings, and is last seen handcuffed to the corpse of his pursuer, Marcus Schouler, in Frank Norris's *McTeague.*

Anthony McVay. White lawyer who supports the civil rights efforts of the Reverend Phillip Martin in Ernest J. Gaines's *In My Father's House.*

Anne McVey. See Anne Sparrow.

Clara Butterworth McVey. See Clara Butterworth.

Hugh McVey. Young Missourian of poor white background who seeks to improve himself through education; becomes a railway station master and later a successful inventor of labor-saving machinery; marries Clara Butterworth in Sherwood Anderson's *Poor White*.

John Endicott (Johnny) McVey. First husband of Anne Sparrow; business failure who moves to California, where he dies of cholera, in Joseph Kirkland's *Zury*.

Margaret (Meg) McVey. Illegitimate daughter of Anne Sparrow and Zury Prouder in Joseph Kirkland's *Zury*.

Philip (Phil) McVey. Illegitimate son of Anne Sparrow and Zury Prouder in Joseph Kirkland's *Zury*.

McWatt. Air force pilot and show-off; commits suicide by crashing his plane into a mountainside after buzzing the squadron and accidentally killing Kid Sampson in Joseph Heller's *Catch-22*.

Mollie Catharine (Katy) McWhorter. Flutist, high school senior, and close friend of Susie Schnitzer; her father is accused of being a Communist during the McCarthy era in Harriette Simpson Arnow's *The Weedkiller's Daughter*.

Harvey McWilliams. Attorney who offers to defend Tyree Tucker and Dr. Bruce against possible charges of negligence resulting in the fire at the Grove; defends Fish Tucker against a charge of attempted rape in Richard Wright's *The Long Dream*.

McWillie. Jockey in William Faulkner's *The Reivers*.

M'Donald. Scottish gentleman who provides cynical commentary on the observations of Captain John Farrago in Hugh Henry Brackenridge's *Modern Chivalry*.

Ann Eliza Meacham. Pretty and apparently devout Methodist renowned for her prayers; seeks to marry Morton Goodwin in Edward Eggleston's *The Circuit Rider*.

George Gordon Meade. Union general who assumes command of the Army of the Potomac shortly before the Battle of Gettysburg in Michael Shaara's *The Killer Angels*.

Zebulun (Zeb) Meader. First and most important client of Austen Vane in Winston Churchill's *Mr. Crewe's Career*.

Essie Meadowfill. See Essie Meadowfill Smith.

Harry Meadows. Editor of the Amity *Leader* who agrees to conceal the facts about Christine Watkins's death from the public; discloses the truth after the Great White Shark kills two more people in Peter Benchley's *Jaws*.

O. B. Meadows. Obnoxious defensive lineman for the Dallas Cowboys who teams with Jo Bob Williams to make life miserable for Phil Elliott in Peter Gent's *North Dallas Forty*.

George Means. Refined young friend of Aunt Abby; falls in love with Jane Bellmont and with her defies Mrs. Bellmont's demands that Jane marry Henry Reed in Harriet E. Wilson's *Our Nig*.

Israel W. (Bud) Means. Twenty-year-old son of Jack Means and a leader among the schoolboys; won over by Ralph Hartsook in Edward Eggleston's *The Hoosier School-Master*.

Jack Means. Farmer and influential trustee of the Flat Creek school district in Edward Eggleston's *The Hoosier School-Master*.

Minerva (Minnie Mouse) Means. Owner of the Adirondacks cabin rented by Ambrose Clay; informs Violet Clay of Ambrose's suicide in Gail Godwin's *Violet Clay*.

Sophronie Meanwell. Neighbor of Gertie and Clovis Nevels, factory worker, and wife of Whit Meanwell in Harriette Arnow's *The Dollmaker*.

Whit Meanwell. Fellow worker of Clovis Nevels and husband of Sophronie Meanwell; joins Clovis in his union activities and aids him in taking revenge against an attacker in Harriette Arnow's *The Dollmaker*.

Benjaman (Ben) Mears. Unemployed writer who returns to Jerusalem's Lot to write a book based on the haunted Marsten House in Stephen King's *'Salem's Lot*.

Bessie Mears. Girlfriend of Bigger Thomas, who bashes in her skull and throws her body down an elevator shaft, in Richard Wright's *Native Son*.

Media. King of Odo and Taji's companion in Herman Melville's *Mardi*.

Principessa Margaret dei Medici. Woman James Boswell marries in a hopeless attempt to attain immortality through family life and in denial of his basically solitary nature in Stanley Elkin's *Boswell*.

Medina. Gypsy woman with seductive eyes in Gayl Jones's *Eva's Man*.

Lewis (Lew) Medlock. Physical fitness devotée who believes himself capable of withstanding the wilderness in its most primitive state; group leader during the canoe trip in James Dickey's *Deliverance*.

Medusa. Abductor of Perseus after his shipwreck in the *Perseid*, a novella in John Barth's *Chimera*.

Caroline (Carrie Madenda, Sister Carrie, Mrs. Wheeler) Meeber. Woman from Wisconsin who moves to Chicago to find work; runs away with George Hurstwood to New York, where she becomes a successful actress, in Theodore Dreiser's *Sister Carrie*.

Benjamin (Ben) Meecham. Elder son of Bull and Lillian Meecham; protagonist of Pat Conroy's *The Great Santini*.

Karen Meecham. Younger daughter of Bull and Lillian Meecham in Pat Conroy's *The Great Santini*.

Lillian Meecham. Wife of Bull Meecham and mother of Ben, Mary Anne, Karen, and Matt Meecham in Pat Conroy's *The Great Santini*.

Mary Anne Meecham. Elder daughter of Bull and Lillian Meecham in Pat Conroy's *The Great Santini*.

Matthew (Matt) Meecham. Younger son of Bull and Lillian Meecham in Pat Conroy's *The Great Santini*.

W. P. (Bull) Meecham. Marine lieutenant colonel; exacting husband of Lillian Meecham and father of Ben, Mary Anne, Karen, and Matt Meecham in Pat Conroy's *The Great Santini*.

Rev. Bartholomew Luther Meeks. Preacher who came to Somerton in 1842 to hold a protracted camp meeting and named the mounds outside town "the Mountains of Gilead"; predicted Christ's return in 1843 in Jesse Hill Ford's *Mountains of Gilead*.

Mr. Meeks. Rivermouth apothecary in Thomas Bailey Aldrich's *The Story of a Bad Boy*.

Mr. Meeks. Traveling copper flue salesman who gives Francis Marion Tarwater a ride to the city and hopes to hire him at minimal cost to help with his business in Flannery O'Connor's *The Violent Bear It Away*.

Arthur (Henry, Junior) Meesum. Sixty-two-year-old son of Joseph Meesum; mayor of Avalon, Connecticut, and part of the "new blood" at the Stilton Club in Peter De Vries's *The Mackerel Plaza*.

Joseph Meesum. Patriarch of the Stilton Club in Peter De Vries's *The Mackerel Plaza*.

Ludus Meggs. Murderer of Pammy Lee Sparkman in T. S. Stribling's *Unfinished Cathedral*.

Mehevi. Chief of the Typees in Herman Melville's *Typee*.

Daisy Meissner. See Daisy Meissner Coleman.

Kurt Meissner. Composer, former lover of Mabel Dingle, and Nazi supporter in Upton Sinclair's *Dragon's Teeth*.

Cherry Melainie. Nightclub singer and lover of Stephen Rojack in Norman Mailer's *An American Dream*.

Melba. Singer who falls in love with Malcolm immediately after meeting him; weds Malcolm but runs off with a Cuban valet in James Purdy's *Malcolm*.

Mr. Melbourne. Friend of Stephen Dudley; judge who supports the Dudleys in order to alleviate their poverty in Charles Brockden Brown's *Ormond*.

Paul Melia. Husband of Tante Melia; hangs himself in Henry Miller's *Black Spring*.

Tante Melia. Manager, with her husband Paul Melia, of a saloon; committed to an insane asylum in Henry Miller's *Black Spring*.

Augustus Mellon. Confederate soldier believed by Lee Mellon to be his great-grandfather and a general in Richard Brautigan's *A Confederate General from Big Sur*.

Lee Mellon. Dropout and smalltime criminal, who claims to be the great-grandson of a Confederate general; living hand-to-mouth, he eventually moves to Big Sur in Richard Brautigan's *A Confederate General from Big Sur*.

Dr. and Sarah Melmoth. Guardians of Ellen Langton; he is the president of Harley College in Nathaniel Hawthorne's *Fanshawe*.

Melody. Apricot-colored mulatto known as a "white man's woman"; Juba fears Melody's beauty will attract Gabriel Prosser in Arna Wendell Bontemps's *Black Thunder*.

Melody. See Melody Moss.

Henry Webster Melrose. Lawyer of Joseph Detweiler in Thomas Berger's *Killing Time*.

Dorothy and Robert Melville. Childless farm couple with whom Mary Fowler stays while Jerry Fowler works on the canal and in whose home Mary bears a child in Walter D. Edmonds's *Erie Water*.

Memoria. Pretty, nearly white woman who, when she was three, was saved from a burning house by George Birdsong; continues as Birdsong's lover following his marriage in Ellen Glasgow's *The Sheltered Life*.

Anita Mendelsohn. Headmistress of a Jewish school and lover of Charlie Sapistein after the death of her husband, Murray Mendelsohn, in Jay Neugeboren's *An Orphan's Tale*.

Ephraim Mendelsohn. Son of Murray and Anita Mendelsohn; Daniel Ginsberg sends him a short story in Jay Neugeboren's *An Orphan's Tale*.

Hannah Mendelsohn. Daughter of Murray and Anita Mendelsohn; kissing partner of Daniel Ginsberg in Jay Neugeboren's *An Orphan's Tale*.

Murray (Moses, Moshe) Mendelsohn. Husband of Anita Mendelsohn and friend of Charlie Sapistein; headmaster at a Jewish school who dies playing football in Jay Neugeboren's *An Orphan's Tale*.

Mendelssohn. Deceased superintendent of the Diamond County Home for the Aged; notorious alcoholic who often ignored the needs of the residents, who now glorify him, in John Updike's *The Poorhouse Fair*.

General Mendoza. Treacherous general and leader of the Opposition in the Olancho Senate who overthrows the government in Richard Harding Davis's *Soldiers of Fortune*.

Josephine (Fina) Mendoza. Young Puerto Rican woman who befriends Benny Profane; involved with street gangs in New York in the 1950s in Thomas Pynchon's *V*.

Louis Mendoza. Mexican criminal who informs the police about Roy Earle and Marie Garson in William Riley Burnett's *High Sierra*.

Valerie (Val) Mendoza. Lover of Leslie McGivers; chooses to stay behind in Grand Rapids, Michigan, when McGivers moves to Detroit in Marge Piercy's *The High Cost of Living*.

Menelaos. Brother of Agamemnon and husband of Helen; refuses to kill Helen; professes traditional views of love and morality but acts according to Helen's wishes in John Erskine's *The Private Life of Helen of Troy*.

Mendy Menendez. Racketeer friend of Terry Lennox in Raymond Chandler's *The Long Goodbye*.

Roberto Ortega Menéndez y Castillo. See Robert Webster.

Herbert Menti. Communist party member who murders Lionel Lane in Richard Wright's *The Outsider*.

Mentu. Old stableman at Pharoah's castle; companion, friend, and mentor of Moses; inventor of stories and bearer of legends in Zora Neale Hurston's *Moses, Man of the Mountain*.

Rachel Menzies. Jewish university student and aspiring social worker who marries Bunny Ross and helps him plan his labor college in Upton Sinclair's *Oil!*

Valencia Merble. See Valencia Merble Pilgrim.

Mercedes. Indian prostitute under the protection of Comandante Guzmán in Peter Matthiessen's *At Play in the Fields of the Lord*.

Roger Merchant. Degenerate Kentucky landowner and distant cousin of Mat Feltner in Wendell Berry's *A Place on Earth*.

Merchant of Sex. See A. J.

Chester Mercury. Teenaged son of Harry Mercury and Elsie Marvel; affects Elizabethan speech in Peter De Vries's *Through the Fields of Clover*.

Harry Mercury. Television comedian, "the latest Last of the Clowns"; former husband of Elsie Marvel and father of Lee and Chester Mercury in Peter De Vries's *Through the Fields of Clover*.

Lee Mercury. Nineteen-year-old daughter of Harry Mercury and Elsie Marvel; apprentice at Smuggler's Cove Theatre; courted by Malcolm Johnsprang, Bill Prufrock, and Neil Sligh in Peter De Vries's *Through the Fields of Clover*.

Meredith. Suspicious and ill-tempered oldest daughter of Hugh and Catherine and older sister of twins Dolores and Eveline in John Hawkes's *The Blood Oranges*.

Colin Meredith. Student and follower of Eleanor Norton; attempts suicide after being forcibly removed from the Brunists' influence and made an example by the Common Sense Committee in Robert Coover's *The Origin of the Brunists*.

Miss Mergan. Librarian and member of the school board who dies of lung cancer in August Derleth's *The Shield of the Valiant*.

James Merivale. Son of Jefferson Merivale who prospers in business with his father in John Dos Passos's *Manhattan Transfer*.

Jefferson Merivale. Successful banker, uncle of Jimmy Herf who offers his nephew a job and is turned down in John Dos Passos's *Manhattan Transfer*.

Francis (Frank) Meriwether. Cousin of Mark Littleton and husband of Lucretia Hazard Meriwether; Southern gentleman and master of Swallow Barn who graciously permits his neighbor Isaac Tracy to win an old lawsuit over a worthless piece of land in John Pendleton Kennedy's *Swallow Barn*.

Lucretia Hazard Meriwether. Sister of Ned Hazard and wife of Frank Meriwether; vigilant nurse to both white and black children in John Pendleton Kennedy's *Swallow Barn*.

Lucy Meriwether. Daughter of Frank and Lucretia Meriwether in John Pendleton Kennedy's *Swallow Barn*.

Philip (Rip) Meriwether. Son of Frank and Lucretia Meriwether in John Pendleton Kennedy's *Swallow Barn*.

Prudence (Pru) Meriwether. Spinster sister of Frank Meriwether; devoted to poetry, Virginia's past glories, elegant dress, and temperance in John Pendleton Kennedy's *Swallow Barn*.

Victorine Meriwether. Daughter of Frank and Lucretia Meriwether in John Pendleton Kennedy's *Swallow Barn*.

Dr. Merkle. Abortionist whom Charity Royall consults to confirm her pregnancy in Edith Wharton's *Summer*.

Madame Serena Merle. Mother, by her lover Gilbert Osmond, of Pansy Osmond; nemesis of Isabel Archer in Henry James's *The Portrait of a Lady*.

Merlin. Wizard who aspires to spiritual powers in Thomas Berger's *Arthur Rex*.

Merlin. Camelot wizard who is bested by Hank Morgan's nineteenth-century tricks in Samuel Langhorne Clemens's *A Connecticut Yankee in King Arthur's Court*.

Robert Merlin. Former lover of Margot Lamar; producer and codirector of the film being shot at Belle Isle in Walker Percy's *Lancelot*.

Vera Meroving. See V.

Jane Merrill. Sister of Susan Merrill; pampered but devoted friend of Cynthia Wetherell in Winston Churchill's *Coniston*.

Merissa Merrill. Twenty-seven-year-old British society columnist who has an eight-year-old son in boarding school, a rich father, a Spanish maid, and an American husband she is divorcing; inspires Henry Bech as a model for the heroine of his next novel, *Think Big*, in John Updike's *Bech: A Book*.

Stephen (Steve) Merrill. Father of Susan and Jane Merrill; mildly ethical railroad executive in Winston Churchill's *Coniston*.

Susan Merrill. Sister of Jane Merrill; pampered but devoted friend of Cynthia Wetherell in Winston Churchill's *Coniston*.

Sally Merrillee. Neighbor and girlhood sweetheart of Johnny Fraser in James Boyd's *Drums*.

Lankester Merrin. Elderly Jesuit priest, philosopher, and paleontologist who is called on to exorcise the demon possessing Regan MacNeil in William Peter Blatty's *The Exorcist*.

Fred Merrit. Embittered half-black and half-white lawyer who moves into a white neighborhood in Rudolph Fisher's *The Walls of Jericho*.

Arthur Mervyn. Bumpkin narrator who relates his coming-of-age in 1793 Philadelphia in Charles Brockden Brown's *Arthur Mervyn*.

Angeline Meserve. Second child of Arvay and Jim Meserve, wife of Hatton Howland, and socialite in Citrabelle, Florida, in Zora Neale Hurston's *Seraph on the Suwanee*.

Arvay Meserve. See Arvay Henson.

Earl David Meserve. Eldest child and handicapped son of Arvay and Jim Meserve; shot and killed by a posse of men that includes his father in Zora Neale Hurston's *Seraph on the Suwanee*.

James Kenneth (Kenny) Meserve. Third child of Arvay and Jim Meserve; blues musician first instructed by Joe Kelsey in Zora Neale Hurston's *Seraph on the Suwanee*.

Jim Meserve. Entrepreneurial hero, husband of Arvay Henson, and father of Earl, Angeline, and Kenny Meserve in Zora Neale Hurston's *Seraph on the Suwanee*.

Lt. Palmer Metcalfe. Staff officer from New Orleans; narrates part of Shelby Foote's *Shiloh*.

Metro (Met). Tenor saxophonist with a crude sound who idolizes Edgar Pool in John Clellon Holmes's *The Horn*.

Metzger (Baby Igor). Lawyer and co-executor with Oedipa Maas of the estate of Pierce Inverarity; former child actor in Thomas Pynchon's *The Crying of Lot 49*.

Roger Mexico. Young English statistician and lover of Jessica Swanlake; with Seaman Bodine, an active member of The Counterforce in Thomas Pynchon's *Gravity's Rainbow*.

Tadeusz Mey. Polish pianist; roomer at Rosa Reichl's boardinghouse in Katherine Anne Porter's *The Leaning Tower*.

Meyers. American gambler; gives tips about crooked horse races to Frederic Henry and Catherine Barkley in Milan in Ernest Hemingway's *A Farewell to Arms*.

Anya Meyers. See Anya Savikin.

Harry (Mad-Man) Meyers. Jewish teacher of Hebrew who captures Jackson and wins the respect of Ruben Fontanez; narrator of Jay Neugeboren's *Listen Ruben Fontanez*.

Lulu Meyers. Rising actress who has an affair with Sergius O'Shaugnessy and later with Charles Eitel in Norman Mailer's *The Deer Park*.

Mrs. Meyers. Effusive wife of Meyers; brings gifts to wounded soldiers in the American hospital in Milan in Ernest Hemingway's *A Farewell to Arms*.

Sarah Meyers. Dead wife of Harry Meyers, who often imagines that she is alive, in Jay Neugeboren's *Listen Ruben Fontanez*.

Big Mac M'Gann. Famous fixer and fence who buys Roy Earle's pardon; dies in his sleep before he can fence a half-million dollars in stolen jewelry in William Riley Burnett's *High Sierra*.

Miami. Former stripper and pornographic movie actress; member of Big Red Smalley's traveling gospel show in George Garrett's *Do, Lord, Remember Me*.

Michael. College student, lover of Donald, and failed lover of Djuna in Anaïs Nin's *Children of the Albatross*.

Michael. Journeyman in Rayal's House in Octavia E. Butler's *Patternmaster*.

Michael. Irish terrier pup; brother of Jerry in Jack London's *Jerry of the Islands*.

Roger Michael. Pen name of an Englishwoman author; Fabian socialist who enlightens young Hagar Ashendyne about a larger role in life for women in Mary Johnston's *Hagar*.

Sebastian Michaels. Middle-aged homosexual writer; lover of Tony Lewis and friend of Johnny Rio in John Rechy's *Numbers*.

Lou Michaelson. Rich fiancé of Marsha Zelenko in Herman Wouk's *Marjorie Morningstar*.

Michelle. Intelligent teenager with great potential; becomes belligerent after being hit by a teacher; lives at home with her mother, aunt, younger sisters, and brother, frustrated, bitter, and cynical, in Alexis Deveaux's *Spirits in the Street*.

Lawrence (Larry) Mickler. Advertising man and Dostoyevski aficionado in Edmund Wilson's *I Thought of Daisy*.

Middleton. American captain in William Faulkner's *A Fable*.

Carl Middleton. Pastor of Day Spring Baptist Church; husband of Larraine Henson but admirer of her sister, Arvay Henson, in Zora Neale Hurston's *Seraph on the Suwanee*.

Duncan Uncas Middleton. Grandson of Duncan Heyward and Alice Munro; military officer who pursues his kidnapped bride, Inez de Certavallos, onto the prairie and rescues her with the help of Natty Bumppo in James Fenimore Cooper's *The Prairie*.

Larraine (Raine) Henson Middleton. Sister of Arvay Henson and wife of Carl Middleton in Zora Neale Hurston's *Seraph on the Suwanee*.

Luigi Migliore. Italian policeman, Fascist, and student of humanistic philosophy; lectures Cass Kinsolving about Cass's self-destructive behavior in William Styron's *Set This House on Fire*.

Miguel. Mexican gamecock fighter in Nathanael West's *The Day of the Locust*.

Miguel. Employee of Feliu Viosca; assists in rescuing the baby Conchita in Lafcadio Hearn's *Chita*.

Miguel. Leader of a band of thieves who waylay Dobbs and his gold dust on the road to Durango in B. Traven's *The Treasure of the Sierra Madre*.

Miguelito. Young bullfighter who has been humiliated when a bull tore his pants during a bullfight in Anaïs Nin's *Seduction of the Minotaur*.

Jenny Wheelwright Milbury. Friend of Evalina Bowen; as a young woman, jilts Theodore Colville in William Dean Howells's *Indian Summer*.

Miles. Brother of Flora; apparently dies when confronted by the governess about the ghosts in Henry James's *The Turn of the Screw*.

Enoch Miles. Hired man of Jess and Eliza Birdwell in Jessamyn West's *The Friendly Persuasion* and *Except for Me and Thee*.

Mr. Miles. Episcopal minister who officiates at the burial of Mary Hyatt in Edith Wharton's *Summer*.

Shannon Fairchild (Great-Aunt Shannon) Miles. Widowed aunt of Battle Fairchild; lives with the Fairchild family at Shellmound plantation in Eudora Welty's *Delta Wedding*.

Carol Milford. See Carol Milford Kennicott.

Victor Milgrim. Motion-picture producer who affects an air of refinement and literary taste; employs Manley Halliday as a screenwriter in order to increase his own prestige in Budd Schulberg's *The Disenchanted*.

Warren Milholland. English professor turned manager of a commercially successful book club, the Readers' Circle, in Edmund Wilson's *Memoirs of Hecate County*.

Milkman. See Macon Dead III.

Phil Millard. White homosexual photographer and friend of Terry Bluvard in Ann Allen Shockley's *Loving Her*.

Rosa (Granny) Millard. Mother-in-law of John Sartoris and grandmother of Bayard Sartoris II; killed by Major Grumby; appears in William Faulkner's *The Unvanquished* and *The Hamlet*.

Jack Millay. One-armed man who dies in the fire at the Silver Sun in E. L. Doctorow's *Welcome to Hard Times*.

Anna Miller. Wife of Harry Miller; later divorces him; narrates part of Frederick Busch's *Domestic Particulars*.

Annie P. (Daisy) Miller. Innocent and audacious American traveling in Europe with her mother and brother; dies of malaria in Henry James's *Daisy Miller*.

Claire Miller. Jewish freelance editor; wife of Mac Miller and mother of Harry Miller; narrates part of Frederick Busch's *Domestic Particulars*.

Daisy Miller. See Annie P. Miller.

Duane (Duke) Miller. Prisoner and surprise witness for the prosecution in Robert Traver's *Anatomy of a Murder*.

Esmerelda Miller. Black American student at McCarthy College in Wisconsin; middle-class woman who adopts Marxism and exposes Hakim Ellelloû, her occasional lover, to it as well in John Updike's *The Coup*.

Eva Miller. Owner of the boardinghouse where Ben Mears stays; vampires seek refuge in her dark basement during the day in Stephen King's *'Salem's Lot*.

Gregory (Greg) Miller. Black problem student who eventually respects his teacher Richard Dadier in Evan Hunter's *The Blackboard Jungle*.

Harry Miller. Son of Mac and Claire Miller; lover of Katherine and later husband of Anna Miller, who divorces him; maintains minimal contact with his parents, returning to see his mother only after his father dies; narrates part of Frederick Busch's *Domestic Particulars*.

Henry Miller. Famous writer with whom a drunken Jack Duluoz breaks an appointment in Jack Kerouac's *Big Sur*.

Henry V. (Joe) Miller. Narrator who tells of his experiences in Paris in Henry Miller's *Tropic of Cancer*; narrator who describes the customers in his father's Brooklyn tailor shop in *Black Spring*; employee of the Cosmodemonic Telegraph Company and narrator of *Tropic of Capricorn* (where he also appears as Müller). See also, Gottlieb Leberecht Müller.

Howard Miller. Homosexual orderly suspected of an attempted rape of Maria Alvarez at Sacred Heart Hospital in Edward Lewis Wallant's *The Children at the Gate*.

Hugh Miller. Attorney general under Willie Stark; resigns because of a real estate scandal in Stark's administration in Robert Penn Warren's *All the King's Men*.

Jackie Miller. Dance-marathon partner of Mario Petrone; after Petrone's arrest, she is partnered with Kid Kamm in Horace McCoy's *They Shoot Horses, Don't They?*

Justin (Tiger) Miller. High school basketball wonder and editor of the *West Condon Chronicle*; makes fun of the Brunist cult while becoming sexually obsessed with the prophet's sister, Marcella Bruno, in Robert Coover's *The Origin of the Brunists*.

Lulu (L. L.) Miller. Married woman who befriends the adolescent Felix Fay and takes him to sophisticated parties in Floyd Dell's *Moon-Calf*.

Mac Miller. Professor of English, husband of Claire Miller, and father of Harry Miller; suffers and later dies from heart disease; narrates part of Frederick Busch's *Domestic Particulars*.

Mrs. Miller. Nervous woman traveling in Europe with her children Daisy and Randolph Miller in Henry James's *Daisy Miller*.

Randolph Miller. Brother of Daisy Miller; an uncontrollable brat who hates being in Europe in Henry

James's *Daisy Miller*.

Willard Miller. Boss Snake of the Mystic High School Rattlers in Harry Crews's *A Feast of Snakes*.

Dr. William Miller. Afro-American surgeon educated in Vienna; adversary of Major Philip Carteret in Charles W. Chesnutt's *The Marrow of Tradition*.

John Millet. English knight who hires and befriends Israel Potter in Herman Melville's *Israel Potter*.

Sergeant Millhouse. Devoted adherent of Captain Porgy and overseer of Glen-Eberley in William Gilmore Simms's *Woodcraft*.

Ernest (Putsi) Mills. Television director who directs Isolde Poole and Dick in P.T.A. entertainment in Peter De Vries's *The Tunnel of Love*.

Henry Mills. Chicago attorney and husband of Pauline Mills; offers Olivia Lattimore financial help, which she refuses, in return for her silence to his wife about his attentions to actresses in Mary Austin's *A Woman of Genius*.

Howard Mills. Deacon in the Reverend Phillip Martin's church; active in the civil rights struggle in Ernest J. Gaines's *In My Father's House*.

Martha Mills. Actress and singer who is the girlfriend of Harry Bogen in Jerome Weidman's *I Can Get It for You Wholesale*; becomes the mistress of Theodore Ast and runs off with Bogen's money in *What's in It for Me?*

Pauline Allingham Mills. Wife of Henry Mills and long-time friend of Olivia Lattimore; moralizes instead of helping Olivia financially in Mary Austin's *A Woman of Genius*.

Vera Mills. Diner waitress, Eliot-quoting feminist, and briefly love object of Billy Bumpers in Peter De Vries's *I Hear America Swinging*.

Lafayette (Lafe) Millspaugh. Neighbor of the Birdwells; has a long-standing aversion to bathing in Jessamyn West's *The Friendly Persuasion*.

Charles (Charlie) Millthorpe. Poor boyhood friend of Pierre Glendinning III; tries too late to help the imprisoned Glendinning in Herman Melville's *Pierre*.

Milly. Slave of Loo Nesbit; works as a housekeeper to help the ailing finances of Canema plantation but is shot by her employer; eventually flees to New York, where she rears orphan children, in Harriet Beecher Stowe's *Dred*.

Milly. Los Angeles social worker and Abel's girlfriend in N. Scott Momaday's *House Made of Dawn*.

Arnold Francis (Babe) Milnik. Inexperienced criminal who is killed in a car crash in William Riley Burnett's *High Sierra*.

Margaret Rose Peck (Meg, Meggie) Milsom. Daughter of Justine and Duncan Peck; married to a minister in Anne Tyler's *Searching for Caleb*.

George Milton. Wandering ranch hand who is the traveling companion, caretaker, and executioner of Lennie Small in John Steinbeck's *Of Mice and Men*.

Michael Milton. Graduate student who has an affair with his teacher, Helen Holm; dies when T. S. Garp crashes into Milton's car in John Irving's *The World According to Garp*.

Rytza Miltz. Sister of Herman; offers refuge to Zeftel and later manages Herman's prostitution operation in Isaac Bashevis Singer's *The Magician of Lublin*.

Mimi (Turtle Dove). Indian mother in James Kirke Paulding's *Koningsmarke*.

Min. Middle-aged woman who lives with William Jones in Ann Petry's *The Street*.

Fanny Minafer. Sister of Wilbur Minafer; middle-aged spinster secretly in love with Eugene Morgan, who loves Isabel Amberson Minafer, in Booth Tarkington's *The Magnificent Ambersons*.

George Amberson (Georgie) Minafer. Son of Isabel and Wilbur Minafer; proud and arrogant heir to Major Amberson's dwindling wealth in Booth Tarkington's *The Magnificent Ambersons*.

Isabel Amberson Minafer. Daughter of Major Amberson and widow of Wilbur Minafer; stopped by her son George Amberson Minafer from marrying Eugene Morgan in Booth Tarkington's *The Magnificent Ambersons*.

Wilbur Minafer. Quiet businessman and husband of Isabel Amberson Minafer; ignored by his son George Amberson Minafer in Booth Tarkington's *The Magnificent Ambersons*.

Minarii. Tahitian chieftain who joins Fletcher Christian in attempting to establish a democracy; killed by Matthew Quintal in Charles Nordhoff and James Norman Hall's *Pitcairn's Island*.

Milo Minderbinder. Squadron mess officer who creates the megalithic and multinational M & M Enterprises to put the war "on a businesslike basis" in

Joseph Heller's *Catch-22*.

Selig Mindish. Friend of the Isaacsons who testifies against them at their espionage trial in E. L. Doctorow's *The Book of Daniel*.

Steve Minetta. Italian-American soldier who fakes insanity but fails to get a discharge in Norman Mailer's *The Naked and the Dead*.

Minette. See Henrietta Anne Stuart.

Mingo. Boyfriend of Harriett Williams; his insistence on going to a dance leads Sandy Rodgers to his first encounter with the secular world in Langston Hughes's *Not Without Laughter*.

Mingo. Freedman and saddlemaker; friend to the rebelling slaves; often reads aloud to the slaves from the Bible and other books in Arna Wendell Bontemps's *Black Thunder*.

Catherine Spicer (Mrs. Manson Mingott) Mingott. Obese matriarch of the Mingott family; instrumental in preventing her granddaughter, Ellen Olenska, from having to return to a cruel husband in Edith Wharton's *The Age of Innocence*; mentioned in *The Old Maid*.

Mrs. Lovell Mingott. Member of the old New York Mingott family by marriage; sister-in-law of Augusta Welland and daughter-in-law of Catherine Mingott in Edith Wharton's *The Age of Innocence*.

John Minify. Vital editor in chief of a weekly magazine who hires Phil Green and becomes his friend and mentor in Laura Z. Hobson's *Gentleman's Agreement*.

Minister Q. Black Muslim leader in John A. Williams's *The Man Who Cried I Am*.

Minna. Catlett slave, wife of Jim, mother of Toey, mistress of Peregrine Lacey Catlett, and mammy to the Catlett children in Mary Lee Settle's *Know Nothing*.

Minnie. Part-time maid of Erskine Fowler in Richard Wright's *Savage Holiday*.

Minnie. Maid of Reba Rivers in William Faulkner's *Sanctuary*, *The Mansion*, and *The Reivers*.

Minnie. Pregnant heroin addict who convinces Terry Wilson to become a prostitute in order to support their drug addictions in Donald Goines's *Dopefiend*.

Ward Minogue. Crook who robs Morris Bober, blackmails Frank Alpine, attempts to assault Helen Bober, and dies setting a fire in Julius Karp's store in Bernard Malamud's *The Assistant*.

Marie Minotti. See May Wynn.

Harry Minowitz. Neighbor and first sexual partner of Mick Kelly in Carson McCullers's *The Heart Is a Lonely Hunter*.

Barbara (Babs) Mintner. Nurse at the Hauptman Clinic who is seduced by Ralph Edwards in Terry Southern's *Flash and Filigree*.

Claire Minton. Wife of Horlick Minton; together they form a "Duprass" in Kurt Vonnegut's *Cat's Cradle*.

Horlick Minton. Liberal diplomat who with his wife, Claire Minton, forms a "Duprass" in Kurt Vonnegut's *Cat's Cradle*.

Harold Mintouchian. Sybaritic Armenian lawyer who tries to teach Augie March by precept—but not by example—to accept himself and his fate in Saul Bellow's *The Adventures of Augie March*.

Fanny Mintz. Secretary of David Dehn; kills Hella Drachenfels, Dehn's wife, when Drachenfels reveals the source of Dehn's money; commits suicide in Jerome Weidman's *The Temple*.

Count Mippipopolous. Count who lavishly entertains Lady Brett Ashley and Jake Barnes in Ernest Hemingway's *The Sun Also Rises*.

Mira (née Ward). College professor who recounts her life as daughter, wife, mother, divorcée, graduate student, lover, and friend in Marilyn French's *The Women's Room*.

Mirabelle. Nubile daughter of Konrad Vost and Claire; Vost reports her to police for prostitution in John Hawkes's *The Passion Artist*.

Miranda. Asthmatic widow in whose house Skipper, Cassandra, and Pixie live for ten months on the gentle island in John Hawkes's *Second Skin*.

Miranda. Drama critic for the *Blue Mountain News* who, after nearly dying of influenza, awakens to what she perceives as an unsatisfactory world in Katherine Anne Porter's *Pale Horse, Pale Rider*; Catholic woman who elopes at age eighteen; rebels against Southern society, only to question her unromantic reality and alienation from her family in *Old Mortality*.

Miriam. Black friend and co-worker of Eliza Quarles in Alice Adams's *Listening to Billie*.

Miriam. One-handed first cousin and first lover of Zeke Gurevich in William Herrick's *The Itinerant*.

Miriam. See Miriam Schaefer.

Miriam. Sister of Aaron and perhaps of Moses; daughter of Amram and Jochebed; prophetess and first high priestess of the Hebrews in Zora Neale Hurston's *Moses, Man of the Mountain*.

Miss (Brigid Lawson, Lady Charlotte Simms) Miriam. Mistress and accomplice of Edward Pierce in Michael Crichton's *The Great Train Robbery*.

Mrs. Miriam. Eighty-one-year-old woman to whom Harry Miller turns for help in remembering his youth in Frederick Busch's *Domestic Particulars*.

Missouri. Long-time housekeeper for the McKelvas in Eudora Welty's *The Optimist's Daughter*.

Mister Man. See Scooter.

Mitch. Mafia hit man hired by Jackie Cogan to kill Frankie, Squirrel Amato, and Mark Trattman; turned in to police by Cogan for parole violation in George V. Higgins's *Cogan's Trade*.

Mitchell. Gentleman who sympathizes with Hugh Wolfe but prosecutes him for grand larceny in Rebecca Harding Davis's *Life in the Iron Mills*.

Anthony Mitchell. Father of Joan Mitchell and first husband of Aurelie Caillet; dies following his divorce from Aurelie in Shirley Ann Grau's *The House on Coliseum Street*.

Bernie (Itchy Mitch) Mitchell. Car thief and burglar; plagued by hives in Joseph Wambaugh's *The Black Marble*.

Eddie Mitchell. Friend of Jim Cowan; takes Helen from Cowan in Nathan Asch's *Pay Day*.

Frances Rankin Mitchell. Iowa native who is the daughter of Judd Rankin, the wife of Leonard Mitchell, and the mother of Judson and Madeleine Mitchell; searches for the meaning of life in Susan Glaspell's *Judd Rankin's Daughter*.

Harry Mitchell. First husband of Belle Mitchell Benbow and father of Titania Mitchell in William Faulkner's *Sartoris (Flags in the Dust)* and *Sanctuary*.

Joan Claire Mitchell. Daughter of Aurelie Caillet and Anthony Mitchell; protagonist who becomes pregnant after a brief love affair and has an abortion in Shirley Ann Grau's *The House on Coliseum Street*.

Judson Mitchell. Son of Frances and Leonard Mitchell and grandson of Judd Rankin; soldier who has a breakdown during World War II in Susan Glaspell's *Judd Rankin's Daughter*.

Leonard (Len) Mitchell. Husband of Frances Mitchell, father of Judson and Madeleine Mitchell, and son-in-law of Judd Rankin; literary critic who re-

views Rankin's book in Susan Glaspell's *Judd Rankin's Daughter*.

Madeleine (Maddie) Mitchell. Daughter of Frances and Leonard Mitchell and granddaughter of Judd Rankin in Susan Glaspell's *Judd Rankin's Daughter*.

Miss Mitchell. Violence coordinator for NESTER in Scott Spencer's *Last Night at the Brain Thieves Ball*.

Titania (Little Belle) Mitchell. Daughter of Harry and Belle Mitchell in William Faulkner's *Sartoris (Flags in the Dust)* and *Sanctuary*.

Mitchy Mitchett. Friend of Mrs. Brookenham and potential husband of Nanda Brookenham in Henry James's *The Awkward Age*.

Mitka (the Cuckoo, the Master). Crippled sharpshooter who reads poetry aloud to the narrator of Jerzy Kosinski's *The Painted Bird*.

Herr Mittelburger. German immigrant whose family accompanies the Laceys to Beulah in Mary Lee Settle's *O Beulah Land*.

Max Mittleman. Vulgar real estate agent at whose house Daniel Ginsberg stays; fond of crude Jewish jokes in Jay Neugeboren's *An Orphan's Tale*.

M'Kewn. Sinister, cunning, and unscrupulous mercenary in William Gilmore Simms's *Woodcraft*.

Moby Dick. White whale pursued by Captain Ahab in Herman Melville's *Moby-Dick*.

Woodenlips Mockett. Befuddled Los Angeles police lieutenant in Joseph Wambaugh's *The Black Marble*.

Moddle. Man-handled nurse of Maisie Farange's nursery days with Beale Farange in Henry James's *What Maisie Knew*.

Ilse Moeller. German immigrant who lives in a Second Avenue apartment managed by Norman Moonbloom in Edward Lewis Wallant's *The Tenants of Moonbloom*.

Elmer Moffatt. Swaggering Wall Street speculator; as a shiftless outcast in Apex City, he was Undine Spragg's first husband; later, a wealthy railroad magnate, he becomes her fourth husband in Edith Wharton's *The Custom of the Country*.

Tom Moffatt. True aristocrat, according to some, because he never questions prices at the tailor shop, because he never pays his bills, in Henry Miller's *Black Spring*.

Undine Moffatt. See Undine Spragg.

Alf Moffet. Fun-loving stagecoach driver who tells Blue about the destruction of Kingsville, Kansas, in E. L. Doctorow's *Welcome to Hard Times*.

Alberto (Albert [Bert, Bertie] Kalandyk) Mogadiscio. Italian owner of the Hippodrome; connected with the Syndicate in Cyrus Colter's *The Hippodrome*.

Mohi (Braid-Beard). Historian from Odo and Taji's companion in Herman Melville's *Mardi*.

Orang Mohole. Kingpin of "alternate physics" and twice winner of the Cheops Feeley Medal in Don DeLillo's *Ratner's Star*.

Moise. Eccentric female painter who announces her withdrawal from "the world of reason" because of her inability to function as an artist in society in Tennessee Williams's *Moise and the World of Reason*.

Moldorf. Friend of Henry Miller; has a wife and two children in the United States, but claims to be falling in love with Tania in Henry Miller's *Tropic of Cancer*.

Henry A. Mollenhauer. Philadelphia politician who helps ruin Frank Cowperwood in Theodore Dreiser's *The Financier*.

Molly. Bountiful waitress whom J. Henry Waugh tries to seduce for Lou Engel in Robert Coover's *The Universal Baseball Association, Inc., J. Henry Waugh, Prop.*

Bud Momeyer. Husband of Maxine Momeyer, father of Etoile Momeyer, and brother-in-law of Walter McKee; postman and archery enthusiast in Wright Morris's *Ceremony in Lone Tree*.

Etoile Momeyer. Audacious daughter of Bud and Maxine Momeyer; elopes with Calvin McKee; stars as the Girl of the Golden West in the ritual for Tom Scanlon's ninetieth birthday in Wright Morris's *Ceremony in Lone Tree*.

Lee Roy Momeyer. Nephew of Bud Momeyer; protests high school bullying by running over three of his tormenters with his car in Wright Morris's *Ceremony in Lone Tree*.

Maxine Momeyer. Wife of Bud Momeyer, sister of Lois McKee, and mother of Etoile Momeyer in Wright Morris's *Ceremony in Lone Tree*.

Momma. Owner of a bar in Naples frequented by homosexual soldiers in John Horne Burns's *The Gallery*.

Mon Cul. Baboon extraordinaire; dies with John Paul Ziller and The Corpse on the Icarus XC solar balloon in Tom Robbins's *Another Roadside Attraction*.

Mona. Empty-headed, occasional girlfriend of Waldo in Paul Theroux's *Waldo*.

Mona. New York girlfriend of Henry Miller; promises to come to Paris in Henry Miller's *Tropic of Cancer*.

Christine (Eva McLoch) Monahan. Placid and hospitable wife of Sean Monahan in Jack Kerouac's *The Dharma Bums*; also appears in *Desolation Angels*.

Mary Monahan. Boston Irish woman who is George Apley's first love; rejected by Apley's family as an unsuitable wife for Apley in John P. Marquand's *The Late George Apley*.

Sean (Kevin McLoch) Monahan. Carpenter and Buddhist; husband of Christine Monahan and host of Japhy Ryder and Ray Smith in Jack Kerouac's *The Dharma Bums*; also appears in *Desolation Angels*.

Kurt Mondaugen. German radio electronics engineer; employee of Yoyodyne, Inc.; tells Herbert Stencil about his adventures in Africa in 1922, where he met Lieutenant Weissmann at the "Siege Party" on Foppl's plantation, in Thomas Pynchon's *V.*; works for Weissmann on the V-2 rocket at Peenemünde and is the link between Weissmann and Franz Pökler in *Gravity's Rainbow*.

Gloria Monday. Kindhearted prostitute and comforter of Carl Reinhart in Thomas Berger's *Reinhart in Love* and *Vital Parts*.

Monee. Factotum of Deacon Ereemear Po-Po in Herman Melville's *Omoo*.

Shadrach Moneypenny. Emissary from William Penn in James Kirke Paulding's *Koningsmarke*.

Monica. Lover, briefly, of Henry Miller; her hands smell of grease from working in a restaurant in Henry Miller's *Tropic of Capricorn*.

Sister Monica. See Irene Shane.

Monina. Daughter whom Beverly Guinevere would like to make into a movie star in Norman Mailer's *Barbary Shore*.

Monique. Second mistress of Hippolyte in Susan Sontag's *The Benefactor*.

Monk. Gunman in the Palm Garden whose gunfire kills Mrs. Layden in Horace McCoy's *They Shoot Horses, Don't They?*

Monk. White drug pusher for whom Jake Adams works in St. Louis's black community in Herbert Simmons's *Corner Boy*.

Dr. Talbot Waller (Trick) Monk. Disturbed young physician and poet; acquaintance of Jesse Vogel in Joyce Carol Oates's *Wonderland*.

The Monkey. See Mary Jane Reed.

Jacques Monod. Nobel Prize-winning French biologist and philosopher; attended in his final days by George Levanter in Jerzy Kosinski's *Blind Date*.

Mononotto. Pequod chief and father of Magawisca and Oneco; perpetrator of the massacre at the Fletcher homestead in Catharine Maria Sedgwick's *Hope Leslie*.

Guillaume de Monparnasse. See Mlle Ida Larivière.

Max Monroe. Owner of the Spider club in Gayl Jones's *Corregidora*.

Ursula Monrose. See Martinette de Beauvais.

Lorenz (Lorry) Monsanto. San Francisco poet and bookstore owner whose remote cabin Jack Duluoz uses for periodic retreats in Jack Kerouac's *Big Sur*.

Guy Montag. Fireman whose job is to burn books; rebels against the antiliterate society in Ray Bradbury's *Fahrenheit 451*.

Mildred Montag. Suicidal housewife who reports her husband Guy Montag to authorities for owning books in Ray Bradbury's *Fahrenheit 451*.

Dr. Randolph Spenser Montag. Psychoanalyst of Myra/Myron Breckinridge in Gore Vidal's *Myra Breckinridge*.

Dr. John Montague. Anthropologist interested in supernatural phenomena who plans to investigate the spectral occurrences at Hill House; Eleanor Vance and Theodora come to Hill House at his invitation in Shirley Jackson's *The Haunting of Hill House*.

Mrs. Montague. Wife of Dr. John Montague; rabid but unscientific detective of paranormal phenomena; dominates her husband and takes over his investigation of Hill House in Shirley Jackson's *The Haunting of Hill House*.

Sarah Nevada (Flips) Montague. Actress and stunt performer who assists Merton Gill in Hollywood and introduces him to Jeff Baird, who makes Gill a star, in Harry Leon Wilson's *Merton of the Movies*.

Montana Slim. Sardonic hitchhiker and slaphappy drunk who befriends Sal Paradise in Jack Kerouac's *On the Road*.

Pete Montana. Chicago crime boss who tries to make peace with Rico Bandello in William Riley Burnett's *Little Caesar*.

Montcalm (Louis de Saint Véran, Marquis of Montcalm). French commander who captures Fort William Henry and unwittingly sends his prisoners into an Indian massacre in James Fenimore Cooper's *The Last of the Mohicans*.

Doña Clara de Montemayor. Daughter of Doña María de Montemayor; moves from Peru to Spain to escape her mother; Doña María's letters to Doña Clara become famous in Thornton Wilder's *The Bridge of San Luis Rey*.

Doña María (Marquesa de Montemayor) de Montemayor. Wealthy but ugly native of Lima, Peru, who clings desperately to her daughter, Doña Clara de Montemayor; her letters to her daughter become famous; dies in the fall of the bridge in Thornton Wilder's *The Bridge of San Luis Rey*.

Montezuma Montez. Gambler and macho police detective in Joseph Wambaugh's *The Black Marble*.

Anne Montgomery. Friend of Isabel Otis; forced by her family's attitude toward women to sacrifice a musical career and to become a caterer in Gertrude Atherton's *Ancestors*.

Ellen (Ellie) Montgomery. Young heroine who learns to make her way in the world when her parents leave her with her aunt, Fortune Emerson; becomes a devout Christian who submits to others in Susan Warner's *The Wide, Wide World*.

Jake Montgomery. Lumberman murdered by Crawford Gowrie in William Faulkner's *Intruder in the Dust*.

Mrs. Montgomery. Invalid mother of Ellen Montgomery; dies abroad where she had traveled with her husband in hope of curing her disease in Susan Warner's *The Wide, Wide World*.

Mrs. Montgomery. Widowed sister of Morris Townsend; warns Dr. Sloper not to let her brother marry Catherine Sloper in Henry James's *Washington Square*.

Charles Edward Montmorency. See Squire Raglan.

Captain Morgan Montgomery. Father of Ellen Montgomery; dies on his return passage to America in the ship *Duc d'Orleans* in Susan Warner's *The Wide, Wide World*.

Christopoher (Chris) de Monti (De Monti). Friend of Andrei Androfski and lover of Deborah Bronski; American journalist who publicizes the story of extermination centers in Poland and Germany; author of the final entry in Alexander Brandel's journal in Leon Uris's *Mila 18*.

Baltazar Montoya. Early eighteenth-century friar and missionary at Ácoma who kills an Indian serving boy and who is thrown off a cliff by the Indians in Willa Cather's *Death Comes for the Archbishop*.

Jack Montraville. Seducer of Charlotte Temple; convinced by Belcour that Charlotte has become sexually promiscuous, he abandons her, only to learn too late that he has been deceived; he then kills Belcour and, filled with remorse by his treatment of Charlotte, visits her grave regularly in Susanna Rowson's *Charlotte*.

Julia Franklin Montraville. See Julia Franklin.

Gilbertson Montrose. Scenario writer in whose movie on the sex life of Dolly Madison Lorelei Lee wishes to appear in Anita Loos's *"Gentlemen Prefer Blondes"*.

Miguel (Papa) Monzano. President of San Lorenzo and adoptive father of Mona Aamons Monzano in Kurt Vonnegut's *Cat's Cradle*.

Mona Aamons Monzano. Adopted daughter of Papa Monzano and fiancée of John in Kurt Vonnegut's *Cat's Cradle*.

Moodie (Old Moodie, Fauntleroy). Father of Zenobia and Priscilla, by different women, in Nathaniel Hawthorne's *The Blithedale Romance*.

Colonel Moodus. Despised son-in-law of General Dreedle in Joseph Heller's *Catch-22*.

Elvira Moody. Cellmate of Eva Medina Canada in a psychiatric prison; kills three men with bad whiskey in Gayl Jones's *Eva's Man*.

Fluvanna Moody. Granddaughter of Aunt Mehitable Green and companion of Dorinda Oakley in Ellen Glasgow's *Barren Ground*.

Maud Eva Moody. Wife of Judge Oscar Moody; her car accidentally ends up hanging on the edge of Banner Top in Eudora Welty's *Losing Battles*.

Oscar Moody. Judge in Boone County, Mississippi, who sentences Jack Renfro to Parchman State Penitentiary in Eudora Welty's *Losing Battles*.

Ralph Moody. Mortician in charge of the funeral of Caddy Hibbard in Wright Morris's *The World in the Attic*.

Mook. Half-wit who lives on the farm formerly owned by Ebenezer Cowley in Sherwood Anderson's *Winesburg, Ohio*.

Moon. See Walter Porter.

Alvin (Joe Redcloud) Moon. Father of Lewis Moon; becomes for his son a symbol of the lost power and dignity of his Indian ancestors in Peter Matthiessen's *At Play in the Fields of the Lord*.

Carolina Moon. Prostitute and police groupie in Joseph Wambaugh's *The Choirboys*.

Dolly Moon. Comic actress who becomes a close friend of Billy Orsini during the filming of Vito Orsini's *Mirrors*, for which she wins an Oscar, in Judith Krantz's *Scruples*.

Irma (Big Irma) Moon. Mother of Lewis Moon in Peter Matthiessen's *At Play in the Fields of the Lord*.

Meriwether Lewis (Kisu-Mu) Moon. American mercenary, part Cheyenne Indian, who parachutes into the jungle village of the Niaruna Indians and, posing as Kisu-Mu, Spirit of Rain, attempts to organize them against the encroachment of the white men in Peter Matthiessen's *At Play in the Fields of the Lord*.

Irwin Moonbloom. Owner of I. Moonbloom Realty Corp.; employs his brother Norman as agent for four tenements in Edward Lewis Wallant's *The Tenants of Moonbloom*.

Norman (Norm) Moonbloom. Agent and rent collector for four tenements owned by his brother Irwin in Edward Lewis Wallant's *The Tenants of Moonbloom*.

Kathleen Mooney. Younger friend and co-worker of Eliza Quarles in Alice Adams's *Listening to Billie*.

Adam Moorad. Beat poet; friend and host of Leo Percepied in Jack Kerouac's *The Subterraneans*.

Daniel Vivaldo (Viv) Moore. Bohemian novelist from Brooklyn who falls in love with Ida Scott; friend of Rufus Scott, Eric Jones, and Cass and Richard Silenski in James Baldwin's *Another Country*.

Denis Moore. Father, by Maria Bonnyfeather, of Anthony Adverse in Hervey Allen's *Anthony Adverse*.

Dennis Patrick (Denny) Moore. Cause of his mother's death in childbirth, younger brother reared by Maggie Moore, and husband of Tessie Vernacht in Betty Smith's *Maggie-Now*.

Duane Moore. Star athlete at Thalia High School who rooms with Sonny Crawford; joins the army in Larry McMurtry's *The Last Picture Show*.

Reverend Duncan Moore. Successor to Francis Prescott as rector of Justin Martyr School in Louis

Auchincloss's *The Rector of Justin*.

Isabel Moore. Guilt-ridden daughter of a possessive father; begins her life at age thirty when her paralyzed father dies; narrator of Mary Gordon's *Final Payments*.

John Moore. Gambler and pious thief; runs a rooming house where Sidney Wyeth stays in Oscar Micheaux's *The Forged Note*.

John Moore. Los Angeles deputy public defender; first to defend Gregory Powell in Joseph Wambaugh's *The Onion Field*.

Joseph Moore. Arch-conservative Catholic father of Isabel Moore and a professor who, though dead at the novel's beginning, dominates much of the action in Mary Gordon's *Final Payments*.

Julia Moore. Stepdaughter of Baron R. and friend of Armande Chamar Person; has a one-night affair with Hugh Person in Vladimir Nabokov's *Transparent Things*.

Kathleen Moore. Englishwoman who is the former mistress of a king; Monroe Stahr's lover in F. Scott Fitzgerald's *The Last Tycoon*.

Margaret Rose (Maggie, Maggie-Now) Moore. Only child of Mary Moriarity and Patrick Dennis Moore; "mother" to Brooklyn orphans and her little brother, Denny Moore; housekeeper for her widowed father; and loyal wife of Claude Bassett in Betty Smith's *Maggie-Now*.

Mrs. Moore. First employer of Frado after her indenture to the Bellmont family in Harriet E. Wilson's *Our Nig*.

Nat Moore. Rubber worker and companion of Larry Donovan and Jasper Collins in Jack Conroy's *The Disinherited*.

Patrick Dennis (Deef Pat, Patsy) Moore. Spoiled son of an Irish widow, immigrant to New York, stable boy for Mike Moriarity, husband of Mary Moriarity, and rascal father of Maggie Moore; later husband of Mary O'Crawley and the one who scatters Claude Bassett's ashes from the Statue of Liberty in Betty Smith's *Maggie-Now*.

Rosemary Moore. Mistress of Lyle Wynant; linked to a terrorist group planning to bomb the New York Stock Exchange in Don DeLillo's *Players*.

Thomas Moore. Farmer who buys Nat Turner from Alexander Eppes for $450 in William Styron's *The Confessions of Nat Turner*.

Ginnie Moorehead. Town whore and brassiere factory worker who marries Dave Hirsh after the annulment of her marriage to an ex-Marine in James Jones's *Some Came Running*.

Myron Moorhen. Accountant who keeps books in a bait shack in Thomas McGuane's *Ninety-Two in the Shade*.

Jabez Moorhouse. Hired hand and elderly confidant of Judith Blackford in Edith Summers Kelley's *Weeds*.

Patricia Moors. Wealthy, glittering society woman and owner of the New York Mammoths baseball team in Mark Harris's *The Southpaw, Bang the Drum Slowly, A Ticket for a Seamstitch*, and *It Looked Like For Ever*.

Dr. Mootry. See Lucius Kimbell.

Alvin Mopworth. English television actor; friend and aspiring posthumous biographer of Gowan McGland; widely suspected of homosexuality for his intense pursuit of women; marries Geneva Spofford in Peter De Vries's *Reuben, Reuben*.

Captain Mora. Leader of the fascist group that attacks El Sordo's men in Ernest Hemingway's *For Whom the Bell Tolls*.

Morache. French soldier in William Faulkner's *A Fable*.

José Morales. Mexican Communist, lover of Helen Jackson, and resident of Twenty-Door City in Albert Halper's *Union Square*.

Mordred. Illegitimate son of Arthur and Margawse; kills and is killed by his father in Thomas Berger's *Arthur Rex*.

Doris More. First wife of Tom More; leaves him to follow the English guru Alistair Fuchs-Forbes in Walker Percy's *Love in the Ruins*.

Samantha More. Dead daughter of Tom More; her faith and love inspire her father in Walker Percy's *Love in the Ruins*.

Thomas (Doc, Tom, Tommy) More, Jr. Psychiatrist who tries to save America from self-destruction; narrator of Walker Percy's *Love in the Ruins*.

John Moredock. Colonel who hates Indians yet has a loving heart in Herman Melville's *The Confidence-Man*.

Morehouse. Catholic bishop who sells his possessions and works for the poor; killed during the Chicago Commune labor riots in Jack London's *The Iron*

Heel.

J. Ward Morehouse. Ambitious journalist and advertising man who sees the need for public relations and forges a very successful career in that field in John Dos Passos's *U.S.A.* trilogy.

T. K. Morehouse. United States Deputy Marshall from Memphis who serves warrants on several prominent white citizens of Somerton for violating a black person's civil rights in denying access to a park; narrates part of Jesse Hill Ford's *The Liberation of Lord Byron Jones.*

Shep Morelli. Thuggish former boyfriend of Julia Wolf who feels he is a suspect in her murder and asks Nick Charles to help avoid charges in Dashiell Hammett's *The Thin Man.*

Katherine (Kit) Moresby. Wife of Porter Moresby; heroine of Paul Bowles's *The Sheltering Sky.*

Porter (Port) Moresby. Traveler and disillusioned writer; hero of Paul Bowles's *The Sheltering Sky.*

Ettore Moretti. Thrice-wounded Italian from San Francisco serving in the Italian army in Ernest Hemingway's *A Farewell to Arms.*

Francisco Morez. See Juan Martinez.

Mademoiselle Marie-Astrée-Luce de Morfontaine. Member of the Cabala; "Second Century Christian" who is obsessed with seeing the throne of France restored to the Bourbons and with restoring the divine right of kings to church dogma; her simple faith is destroyed by Cardinal Vaini's intellectual games in Thornton Wilder's *The Cabala.*

Constance Morgan. Childlike innocent and protégée of the narrator in Randall Jarrell's *Pictures from an Institution.*

Dr. Morgan. Kindly, retired Presbyterian minister who practices medicine and cares for Kike Lumsden in Edward Eggleston's *The Circuit Rider.*

Earl Morgan. Husband of Lillian Douglas Morgan and father of Virgil Morgan; music teacher and composer in Scott Spencer's *Preservation Hall.*

Ed Morgan. Bootlegger, muskrat trapper, and tenant on the farm Peter Leland inherits in Fred Chappell's *Dagon.*

Eugene Morgan. Widower who courts Isabel Amberson Minafer; pioneer in the automobile industry whose name replaces Amberson as the most significant family name in Booth Tarkington's *The Magnificent Ambersons.*

Frederick Morgan. Actor with whom Dorothy Shaw sleeps after resisting the advances of the deputy sheriff; she joins his acting company in Anita Loos's *"But Gentlemen Marry Brunettes."*

Genevieve Morgan. Middle-aged night waitress at Thalia's café who listens to Sonny Crawford in Larry McMurtry's *The Last Picture Show.*

Hank (The Boss) Morgan. Nineteenth-century man who, after being hit on the head, awakens in sixth-century England; introduces nineteenth-century ideas to Camelot; author of the manuscript "Tales of the Lost Land" in Samuel Langhorne Clemens's *A Connecticut Yankee in King Arthur's Court.*

Harry Morgan. Boat owner engaged in various illegal activities; a narrator of and central character in Ernest Hemingway's *To Have and Have Not.*

Harry Morgan. Millionaire from Long Island who is shunned by Boston society; fathers a child by Hopestill Mather in Jean Stafford's *Boston Adventure.*

Henrietta (Nettie) Morgan. Spirited daughter of Dr. Morgan; falls in love with Kike Lumsden while he is recuperating in the Morgan home in Edward Eggleston's *The Circuit Rider.*

Henry Morgan. British businessman and contact of Daniel Cable Wills; reveals Wills's career as a spy and the blood kinship of Andrew Collier and Daniel Compton Wills in George V. Higgins's *Dreamland.*

Jane Lightfoot Morgan. Mother of Emma Lou Morgan in Wallace Thurman's *The Blacker the Berry.*

Jim Morgan. Father of Emma Lou Morgan in Wallace Thurman's *The Blacker the Berry.*

Joe Morgan. Father of Mary Morgan; drunken pauper who becomes successful after giving up alcohol in T. S. Arthur's *Ten Nights in a Bar-Room.*

Uncle Joe Morgan. Uncle of Emma Lou Morgan; sends her to the University of Southern California and attempts to discourage her preoccupation with skin color in Wallace Thurman's *The Blacker the Berry.*

Joseph (Joe) Morgan. Colleague of Jacob Horner and husband of Rennie Morgan in John Barth's *The End of the Road.*

J. Pierpont Morgan. Multimillionaire whose library is besieged by Coalhouse Walker, Jr., and his insurrectionists in E. L. Doctorow's *Ragtime.*

Lillian Belsito Douglas (Lil) Morgan. Mother of Tommy Douglas and wife of Earl Morgan in Scott Spencer's *Preservation Hall*.

Lucy Morgan. Daughter of Eugene Morgan; loves the arrogant George Minafer in Booth Tarkington's *The Magnificent Ambersons*.

Marie Morgan. Wife of Harry Morgan in Ernest Hemingway's *To Have and Have Not*.

Mary Morgan. Brave daughter of Joe Morgan; her dying request is that her father give up alcohol in T. S. Arthur's *Ten Nights in a Bar-Room*.

Mina Morgan. Fishlike daughter of Ed Morgan, priestess of Dagon, object of Peter Leland's obsession, and agent of Leland's psychological and physical destruction in Fred Chappell's *Dagon*.

Mr. Morgan. Butler to the Hawkline family; sixty-eight-year-old, seven-foot, two-inch giant killed by the Hawkline Monster and revivified upon the monster's destruction in Richard Brautigan's *The Hawkline Monster*.

O'Reilly Morgan. Morning servant of Kermit Raphaelson; walks through the house either unclad or in a kimono in James Purdy's *Malcolm*.

Renée MacMahon (Rennie) Morgan. Wife of Joseph Morgan and lover of Jacob Horner; dies while undergoing an abortion in John Barth's *The End of the Road*.

Capt. Rex Morgan. Officer of the Royal Guard and devoted lover of Amber St. Clare; killed in a duel over her with Bruce Carlton in Kathleen Winsor's *Forever Amber*.

Cardinal Thaddeus Morgan. Church dignitary who visits the prison and helps Jody escape, an action which inspires Zeke Farragut, in John Cheever's *Falconer*.

Tracy Keating Morgan. Book designer married to Virgil Morgan in Scott Spencer's *Preservation Hall*.

Virgil (Fatboy, Vernon) Morgan. Businessman who accidentally kills his stepbrother Tommy Douglas; narrator of Scott Spencer's *Preservation Hall*.

William A. (Bumper) Morgan. Twenty-year veteran Los Angeles beat patrolman; protagonist and narrator of Joseph Wambaugh's *The Blue Knight*.

Morgan la Fey. Evil sister of Margawse and aunt of Mordred in Thomas Berger's *Arthur Rex*.

Morgan le Fay. Ruthless sister of Arthur in Samuel Langhorne Clemens's *A Connecticut Yankee in King Arthur's Court*.

Adolph Morgenroth. Farmer whose injured arm Will Kennicott amputates in Sinclair Lewis's *Main Street*.

Arnold Morgenstern. Father of Marjorie Morningstar and part owner of a feather importing business in Herman Wouk's *Marjorie Morningstar*.

Marjorie (Marjorie Morningstar) Morgenstern. Young Jewish woman who aspires to become an actress; lives with her parents in New York City in the 1930s in Herman Wouk's *Marjorie Morningstar*.

Rose Kupperberg Morgenstern. Mother of Seth Morgenstern and Marjorie Morningstar in Herman Wouk's *Marjorie Morningstar*.

Seth Morgenstern. Brother of Marjorie Morningstar in Herman Wouk's *Marjorie Morningstar*.

Dean Moriarty. Reform school veteran and free-spirited hipster philosopher; friend and cross-country traveling companion of Sal Paradise in Jack Kerouac's *On the Road*.

Mary Moriarity. Only child of Mike and Molly Moriarity, kindly but determined spinster school teacher, wife of immigrant Patrick Dennis Moore, and mother of Maggie and Denny Moore in Betty Smith's *Maggie-Now*.

Mike (The Boss) Moriarity. Tammany ward heeler indicted for graft and corruption but killed by a stroke before his trial; husband of Molly Moriarity and father of Mary Moriarity in Betty Smith's *Maggie-Now*.

Molly (The Missus) Moriarity. Wife of Mike Moriarity and mother of Mary Moriarity; beloved by her son-in-law, Patrick Dennis Moore, until she takes off for Boston with her dead husband's insurance money in Betty Smith's *Maggie-Now*.

Elizabeth Blaney (Bess) Morison. Wife of James Morison and mother of Robert and Peter Morison; dies of pneumonia, a complication of flu contracted during the 1918 epidemic, soon after giving birth to her third son in William Maxwell's *They Came Like Swallows*.

James B. Morison. Father of Robert and Peter Morison and an unnamed newborn son; seen primarily presiding at meals, playing solitaire, and reading the paper, until the death of his wife, Elizabeth Morison, in William Maxwell's *They Came Like Swallows*.

Peter (Bunny) Morison. Introverted eight-year-old who dislikes being outside, preferring to construct elaborate stories, have his mother read to him, and eavesdrop on conversations between his mother and her sister, in William Maxwell's *They Came Like Swallows*.

Robert Morison. Thirteen year old who as a young child lost one leg in an accident; enjoys rough games and alternately bullies and protects his younger brother, Peter Morison, in William Maxwell's *They Came Like Swallows*.

Morley (Molly). Timid assistant to Carl Belcher in Robert Cantwell's *The Land of Plenty*.

Henry (Morl) Morley. Librarian and skilled mountain climber; accompanies Japhy Ryder and Ray Smith in their ascent of Matterhorn mountain in Jack Kerouac's *The Dharma Bums*.

Morning Star. Son of Little Big Man and Sunshine in Thomas Berger's *Little Big Man*.

Marjorie Morningstar. See Marjorie Morgenstern.

Joey (Morph) Morphy. Friend of Ethan Allen Hawley and teller at the First National Bank in New Baytown who unknowingly gives Hawley the idea of robbing the bank in John Steinbeck's *The Winter of Our Discontent*.

James Morrell. Friend of Ellen and Ralph Putney; friend and admirer of Annie Kilburn in William Dean Howells's *Annie Kilburn*.

Morris (Q). Detective who discovers the location of the missing maid Hannah Chester in Anna Katharine Green's *The Leavenworth Case*.

Arthur Morris. Computer programmer who checks the computers at Project Wildfire and misses a simple mechanical problem that keeps the teleprinter from alerting the scientists to important information in Michael Crichton's *The Andromeda Strain*.

Corinne Morris. Mistress of Thomas Spellacy in John Gregory Dunne's *True Confessions*.

Julian Morris. See Louis Eugene Dupont.

Robert Morris. Surgeon and member of the Neuropsychiatric Research Unit in Michael Crichton's *The Terminal Man*.

Syra Morris. Book editor at the *Denver Call* who encourages Homer Zigler's literary ambitions in Clyde Brion Davis's *"The Great American Novel–."*

James Morrisey. Irish lawyer who falls in love with Theresa Dunn but is incapable of satisfying her sexually in Judith Rossner's *Looking for Mr. Goodbar*.

Hannah Morrison. Daughter of a drunkard; blames her troubles on Bartley Hubbard in William Dean Howells's *A Modern Instance*.

Mistress Morrison. Housekeeper at Dove Cote in John Pendleton Kennedy's *Horse-Shoe Robinson*.

Wendell Morrison. Former writing student of Henry Bech; appears on Martha's Vineyard and gets Bech, Norma Latchett, and Bea Cook high on marijuana in John Updike's *Bech: A Book*.

Jack Morrissey. Idealistic young lawyer who becomes romantically involved with Elena Howe in Joyce Carol Oates's *Do with Me What You Will*.

Mrs. Morrow. Mother of Holden Caulfield's schoolmate Ernest Morrow; charms Holden when he meets her on the train to New York City in J. D. Salinger's *The Catcher in the Rye*.

Ruth Morse. Society woman who inspires Martin Eden to become a writer, but who loves him only for the fame his writing brings in Jack London's *Martin Eden*.

Victor Morse. American ace aviator from Crystal Lake, Nebraska, who goes to Canada to enlist in the British army in Willa Cather's *One of Ours*.

Julia Mortimer. Unmarried retired teacher of Banner School who sends Gloria Short Renfro to the Normal school for training teachers and tries to discourage her from marrying Jack Renfro; cared for in retirement by Lexie Renfro in Eudora Welty's *Losing Battles*.

Edmund Mortimer (Radclyffe). Conniving nobleman and third husband of Amber St. Clare; unknown to her, the jilted fiancé of her mother; almost succeeds in poisoning Amber, but she abets his murder during the London Fire in Kathleen Winsor's *Forever Amber*.

Amelia (Amy) Mortis. Short, balding woman in her eighties with a goiter; resident of the Diamond County Home for the Aged; makes quilts to sell at the annual fair in John Updike's *The Poorhouse Fair*.

Captain Morton. Petty antagonist of Mr. Roberts and more of an enemy to his crew than are the Japanese in Thomas Heggen's *Mister Roberts*.

Jeannie Morton. Friend of Isadora Wing; housewife and poet awarded the Pulitzer Prize for her third book of poems, *Holy Fool's Day*; commits suicide in Erica Jong's *How to Save Your Own Life*.

Mr. Morton. Clergyman who is a friend of Evalina Bowen and suitor of Imogene Graham in William Dean Howells's *Indian Summer*.

Mrs. Morgan Morton. See Mrs. Herman Muller.

Angèle Mory. See Angela Murray.

Darlene Mosby. See Darlene Mosby Carlisle.

William (Sonny Boy) Mosby. Large black man returning from Kansas City to Somerton, where thirteen years before he was beaten by Stanley Bumpas; soon after arriving, he beats Jimmy Bivens to death and offers to become the bodyguard of Lord Byron Jones in Jesse Hill Ford's *The Liberation of Lord Byron Jones*.

Moses. "Son" of Princess Royal, "grandson" of Pharaoh, "nephew" of Ta-Phar, and commander in chief of the Egyptian armies; "adopted" son and later son-in-law of Jethro, husband of Zipporah, and emancipator of the Hebrews in Zora Neale Hurston's *Moses, Man of the Mountain*.

Moses (Moze). Shell-shocked veteran, who may or may not be a Jew; member of Big Red Smalley's traveling gospel show in George Garrett's *Do, Lord, Remember Me*.

Adam Moss. Nature-loving recluse who falls in love with Georgiana Cobb; narrator of James Lane Allen's *A Kentucky Cardinal*; marries Georgiana in *Aftermath*.

Chinatown (China) Moss. Innocently hedonistic half brother of Mat and Melody Moss; blinded in an industrial holocaust in William Attaway's *Blood on the Forge*.

Georgiana Cobb Moss. See Georgiana Cobb.

Hector Moss. Stupid commander in the Los Angeles Police Department; concerned with regulations and his IQ score of 107 in Joseph Wambaugh's *The Choirboys*.

Mat (Big Mat) Moss. Devoutly religious eldest of three half brothers who are collectively the protagonists of William Attaway's *Blood on the Forge*.

Melody Moss. Black sharecropper and musician whose move to the steel mills of Pennsylvania with his half brothers, and their subsequent destruction, are at the center of William Attaway's *Blood on the Forge*.

Serphin Moss. Sheepherder in H. L. Davis's *Honey in the Horn*.

Mostro. Prisoner of Il Gufo; all the fathers of Sasso Fetore desire his release so he can marry their daughters; after killing the village's four ganders, he escapes but is recaptured and hanged in John Hawkes's *The Owl*.

Hazel (Haze) Motes. Young man trying to evade redemption by sinning, owning a car, and preaching a Church Without Christ; blinds himself and adopts other severe penitential practices which lead to his death in Flannery O'Connor's *Wise Blood*.

Major Motes. Pompous censorship officer from Virginia who thinks reading letters is more important than fighting in John Horne Burns's *The Gallery*.

Mother. Wife of Father and mother of Little Boy; marries Tateh after the death of Father in E. L. Doctorow's *Ragtime*.

Mother Red-Cap. Leader of London criminals in the Whitefriars district; protects Amber St. Clare during Amber's first childbirth but expects to be repaid in Kathleen Winsor's *Forever Amber*.

Mother's Younger Brother (Younger Brother). Brother of Mother, lover of Evelyn Nesbit, and admirer of Emma Goldman and socialism; designs fireworks and bombs; joins the gang of Coalhouse Walker, Jr., but drives to Mexico to join Francisco Villa's revolutionaries; dies in a skirmish with government troops in E. L. Doctorow's *Ragtime*.

Rims Mott. Forty-five-year-old house painter and lover of Miss Margaret Treasure in Alice Walker's *Meridian*.

Wesley Mouch. Washington lobbyist for Henry Rearden; betrays him to become economic director of the nation in Ayn Rand's *Atlas Shrugged*.

Mowanna. King of Nukuheva in Herman Melville's *Typee*.

Colonel Mowbray. Befuddled executive officer for General Ira N. Beal; cannot handle administrative difficulties in James Gould Cozzens's *Guard of Honor*.

Lump Mowbray. Former slave assaulted by Polycarp Vaiden; attempts to persuade other former slaves to leave their plantations after the Civil War in T. S. Stribling's *The Forge* and *The Store*.

Mow-Mow. One-eyed Typean chief in Herman Melville's *Typee*.

Mowree. See Bembo.

M. T. Reader of Hank Morgan's manuscript in Samuel Langhorne Clemens's *A Connecticut Yankee in King Arthur's Court*.

Mtalba. Fat, pampered royal sister of Queen Willatale; offers herself in marriage to Eugene Henderson with presents and a ritual dance in Saul

Bellow's *Henderson the Rain King*.

Mtesa. Traitorous driver for Colonel Ellelloû; when Mtesa refuses to identify him to a mob, Ellelloû is deposed in John Updike's *The Coup*.

Lieutenant Mudd. Replacement pilot killed in combat before being checked in to Yossarian's squadron; because his death is unofficial, his belongings cannot be removed from Yossarian's tent in Joseph Heller's *Catch-22*.

Earl Mudger. Head of Radial Matrix, an intelligence organization, and one of many interested in a movie rumored to include footage of Hitler at an orgy in Don DeLillo's *Running Dog*.

Alexander Mueller. Son of Hans and Elizabeth Mueller and possible father of Robert Mueller; blinded in a suicide attempt in Nicholas Delbanco's *Fathering*.

Elizabeth Mueller. Wife of Hans Mueller and mother of Alexander Mueller; killed when hit by an automobile, a possible suicide, in Nicholas Delbanco's *Fathering*.

Hans Mueller. Husband of Elizabeth Mueller, father of Alexander Mueller, and possible father of Robert Mueller; killed in an automobile accident in Nicholas Delbanco's *Fathering*.

Marian Mueller. First wife of Alexander Mueller; dies of cancer at age twenty-one in Nicholas Delbanco's *Fathering*.

Robert Mueller. Actor of ambiguous paternity, the son of Chloe Duboise and either Hans or Alexander Mueller; adopted by Alexander and Susan Mueller in Nicholas Delbanco's *Fathering*.

Susan Mueller. Second wife of Alexander Mueller in Nicholas Delbanco's *Fathering*.

Thomas (Cooky, Tommy) Mugridge. Cook aboard the *Ghost* who abuses Hump Van Weyden; George Leach tries to kill him in Jack London's *The Sea-Wolf*.

David (Davy) Muir. Traitorous British quartermaster killed by Arrowhead in James Fenimore Cooper's *The Pathfinder*.

Diony Hall Jarvis Muir. See Diony Hall Jarvis.

Evan Muir. Provider for and second husband of Diony Hall Jarvis; loses Diony when Berk Jarvis, her first husband, returns from Indian captivity in Elizabeth Madox Roberts's *The Great Meadow*.

Sidi Mukhtar. Shrewd caravan leader who transports contraband goods through Kush; guides Colonel Ellelloû and Sheba through the Balak in search of King Edumu's severed head in John Updike's *The Coup*.

Arnold Mulcahy. Federal man who arranges for Fred Trumper to return to the United States and who wants to hire Dante Callicchio in John Irving's *The Water-Method Man*.

Father Mulcahy. Pastor, counselor, and friend of the Moores in Mary Gordon's *Final Payments*.

Norah Muldoon. Irish nursemaid to Patrick Dennis in Patrick Dennis's *Auntie Mame*.

Roberta (Captain Energy, Robert) Muldoon. Professional football player who becomes a transsexual; bodyguard for Jenny Fields and friend of the Garps; dies after doing wind sprints in John Irving's *The World According to Garp*.

Blanshard Muller. Widower who wants Myra Nelson to divorce her departed husband and marry him in Philip Roth's *When She Was Good*.

Gottlieb Leberecht Müller. Name used by Henry Miller when he is born anew and assumes a new identity in Henry Miller's *Tropic of Capricorn*.

Mrs. Herman (Miss Idell, Mrs. Morgan Morton, Mrs. Seth Parton) Muller. Lover of Aaron Starr and wife of Seth Parton; poses as a colonel's wife during the Civil War and befriends Amantha Starr in Robert Penn Warren's *Band of Angels*.

Margaret (Duchess of Müller, Mag, Maggie) Müller. Opportunistic and materialistic mother of Kenyon Adams; marries Henry Fenn, but divorces him to marry Thomas Van Dorn in William Allen White's *In the Heart of a Fool*.

Hannah Mullett. Faithful servant of the March family in Louisa May Alcott's *Little Women*.

Fern Mullins. Gopher Prairie teacher who is fired for having attended a party at which alcohol was served in Sinclair Lewis's *Main Street*.

Michael J. (Mike) Mulrooney. Kindly manager of the minor league team on which Henry Wiggen first played in Mark Harris's *The Southpaw*.

Bennie Mulry. Friend of Jimmie Vaiden; itinerant Methodist preacher and proslavery advocate who foretells the fall of Fort Sumter in T. S. Stribling's *The Forge*.

Gerda Miller Mulvaney. Longtime friend of Jane Clifford and publisher of the feminist newspaper *Feme Sole* in Gail Godwin's *The Odd Woman*.

Ludlow Mumm. Inept, politically liberal screenwriter for Olympia Studios in Ludwig Bemelmans's *Dirty Eddie.*

Carl Munchin. Wealthy California movie producer who wants to revise John Wilder's autobiographical movie *Bellevue* by having the central figure suffer a complete mental breakdown ("wipe him out") in Richard Yates's *Disturbing the Peace.*

Bobby (Will) Muncy. City-born son of Clyde Muncy in Wright Morris's *The Home Place* and *The World in the Attic.*

Clara Cropper Muncy. Rural Nebraska aunt of Clyde Muncy and wife of Harry Muncy; staunch believer in country virtues in Wright Morris's *The Home Place.*

Clyde Muncy. Returned Nebraska native forced to decide between country and city living; narrator of Wright Morris's *The Home Place*; ponders the nature of small-town nostalgia in *The World in the Attic.*

Harry (Uncle Harry) Muncy. Husband of Clara Muncy and uncle of Clyde Muncy in Wright Morris's *The Home Place.*

Peg Muncy. City-bred wife of Clyde Muncy in Wright Morris's *The Home Place* and *The World in the Attic.*

Peggy Muncy. Daughter of Clyde and Peg Muncy in Wright Morris's *The Home Place* and *The World in the Attic.*

Nella Liseth Mundine. Half-Scandinavian wife of Steve Mundine; appalled by the racial prejudice in Somerton; narrates part of Jesse Hill Ford's *The Liberation of Lord Byron Jones.*

Steve Mundine. Nephew and law partner of Oman Hedgepath; he and his wife, Nella Liseth Mundine, shock Somerton with their liberal racial views in Jesse Hill Ford's *The Liberation of Lord Byron Jones.*

Charlie Munger. Mass murderer in Wright Morris's *Ceremony in Lone Tree.*

Mrs. Munger. Socialite who instigates the Social Union scheme in William Dean Howells's *Annie Kilburn.*

Paul Muniment. Subversive deeply involved in revolutionary work; initiates Hyacinth Robinson into socialist activities in Henry James's *The Princess Casamassima.*

Mrs. Munkey. Loquacious cleaning woman for Joe and Naughty Sandwich in Peter De Vries's *The Vale of Laughter.*

Munn. Grizzled Civil War major who calls Molly Riordan "daughter"; dies of a stroke, whereupon his body is eaten by buzzards, in E. L. Doctorow's *Welcome to Hard Times.*

May Cox Munn. Wife of Percy Munn in Robert Penn Warren's *Night Rider.*

Percy (Barclay, Perse) Munn. Lawyer who becomes involved with the Association of Growers of Dark Fired Tobacco and with its violent arm, the Free Farmers' Brotherhood of Protection and Control, the night riders; lover of Sukie Christian in Robert Penn Warren's *Night Rider.*

Alice Munro. Daughter of Colonel Munro; loves Duncan Heyward in James Fenimore Cooper's *The Last of the Mohicans.*

Colonel Munro. Commander of Fort William Henry and father of Cora and Alice Munro in James Fenimore Cooper's *The Last of the Mohicans.*

Cora Munro. Daughter of Colonel Munro; loved by Uncas and desired as a wife by Magua; killed when she refuses to marry Magua in James Fenimore Cooper's *The Last of the Mohicans.*

Sally Munro. See Sally Munro Tallant.

Jefferson Davis Munroe. Midget and legendary karate master in Harry Crews's *Karate Is a Thing of the Spirit.*

Carlyle (Collie) Munshin. Movie producer known for pirating scripts in Norman Mailer's *The Deer Park.*

Dr. Barker Munsing. Father of Eunice Munsing in Thomas Berger's *Vital Parts.*

Eunice Munsing. Secretary of Robert Sweet in Thomas Berger's *Vital Parts.*

Buford Munson. Black neighbor of the Tarwaters in Powderhead; buries Mason Tarwater, marks his grave with a cross, and plows his field after Francis Marion Tarwater has gotten drunk, burned the house down, and run away to the city in Flannery O'Connor's *The Violent Bear It Away.*

Robert Durham (Bob) Munson. Senior senator from Michigan and Senate Majority Leader who eventually supports the Senate and House of Representatives even above his party's president in the controversial nomination of Robert Leffingwell for Secretary of State in Allen Drury's *Advise and Consent.*

Baroness Eugenia-Camilla-Dolores Münster. Complex baroness of the German province of Silberstadt-Schreckenstein who comes to the United States to seek her fortune; courted by Robert Acton, whom she rejects, in Henry James's *The Europeans*.

Munt. Police lieutenant who investigates the death of Tommy Douglas in Scott Spencer's *Preservation Hall*.

Anthony Joseph (Tony) Murascho. See Al Grecco.

Bogan Murdock. Unscrupulous developer and entrepreneur who manages to bilk the legislature on a land deal in Robert Penn Warren's *At Heaven's Gate*.

Sue Murdock. Daughter of Bogan Murdock and fiancée of Jerry Calhoun; breaks the engagement and enters relationships with Slim Sarrett and then Jason Sweetwater; killed by Sarrett in Robert Penn Warren's *At Heaven's Gate*.

Murf. Bat-faced cockney sidekick of Valentine Hood in Paul Theroux's *The Family Arsenal*.

Albert Murillio. Pimp and racketeer who controls the section of Harlem where Sol Nazerman has his pawnshop in Edward Lewis Wallant's *The Pawnbroker*.

Basil (Blackie) Murphy. Brother of Tasmania Orcino and Blix Hollister in Jessamyn West's *A Matter of Time*.

Father Murphy. Irish priest on Tahiti in Herman Melville's *Omoo*.

Ike (Mr. Ike) Murphy. Night desk clerk for the Somerton police department; aids Stanley Bumpas and Willie Joe Worth in their violation of civil rights, especially those of blacks, in Jesse Hill Ford's *The Liberation of Lord Byron Jones*.

Le Cid (Cid) Murphy. Brother of Tasmania Orcino and Blix Hollister in Jessamyn West's *A Matter of Time*.

Marmion Murphy. Brother of Tasmania Orcino and Blix Hollister in Jessamyn West's *A Matter of Time*.

Maude Hobhouse Murphy. Mother of Tasmania Orcino and Blix Hollister in Jessamyn West's *A Matter of Time*.

Orland Murphy. Father of Tasmania Orcino and Blix Hollister in Jessamyn West's *A Matter of Time*.

Angela Murray (Angèle Mory). Young painter from a modest Philadelphia home who "passes for white" in New York City until she sees the error of her ways in Jessie Redmon Fauset's *Plum Bun*.

Junius Murray. Dark-skinned black father of Angela Murray in Jessie Redmon Fauset's *Plum Bun*.

Mattie Murray. Light-skinned black mother of Angela Murray in Jessie Redmon Fauset's *Plum Bun*.

Virginia (Jinny) Murray. Teacher; kind-hearted, dark-skinned sister of Angela Murray in Jessie Redmon Fauset's *Plum Bun*.

Mrs. Murrett. Rich American woman of doubtful reputation to whom Sophy Viner is an assistant in Edith Wharton's *The Reef*.

Biff Musclewhite. Ruthless guardian of European values in America; former European serf, former police commissioner, and curator of the Center of Art Detention who boards the *Titantic* in Ishmael Reed's *Mumbo Jumbo*.

Allen Musgrove. Father of Mary Musgrove; Tory partisans burn his farm in John Pendleton Kennedy's *Horse-Shoe Robinson*.

Amalie Musgrove. Virginia-born first wife of Clement Musgrove; dies when she is forced to watch Indians boil her son in burning oil in Eudora Welty's *The Robber Bridegroom*.

Ann Chapin Musgrove. See Ann Chapin.

Clement Musgrove. Planter whose plantation is near Rodney's Landing on the Mississippi River; father of Rosamond Musgrove; unwittingly promises to reward Jamie Lockhart with Rosamond's hand in marriage if he kills the bandit who stole her clothes–Lockhart himself–in Eudora Welty's *The Robber Bridegroom*.

Mary Musgrove. Daughter of Allen Musgrove; warns Arthur Butler of Wat Adair's plot to betray him; accompanies the Lindsays on their trip to see Cornwallis in John Pendleton Kennedy's *Horse-Shoe Robinson*.

Rosamond Musgrove. See Rosamond Musgrove Lockhart.

Salome Thomas Musgrove. Second wife of Clement Musgrove; marries him after they are released by Indians who have killed their spouses in Eudora Welty's *The Robber Bridegroom*.

Norman Mushari. Avaricious lawyer who seeks to prove Eliot Rosewater insane in Kurt Vonnegut's *God Bless You, Mr. Rosewater*.

Musso. Army supply room clerk who eventually reclaims the pistol in the possession of Richard Mast in James Jones's *The Pistol*.

Mustache Sal. Mail-order wife of Drag Gibson; lover of the Loop Garoo Kid, who brands her with a Hell's bat; poisons Gibson, but he discovers her action and feeds her to his swine, in Ishmael Reed's *Yellow Back Radio Broke-Down*.

Baby Lou (Baby Sister) Mustian. Youngest of the Mustian children in Reynolds Price's *A Long and Happy Life* and *A Generous Man*.

Horatio (Rato) Mustian, Jr. Brother of Rosacoke Mustian in Reynolds Price's *A Long and Happy Life*; runs off to keep his "rabid" dog from being put to sleep in *A Generous Man*.

Jasper (Papa) Mustian. Grandfather of the Mustian children in Reynolds Price's *A Long and Happy Life* and *A Generous Man*.

Milo Mustian. Brother of Rosacoke and Rato Mustian in Reynolds Price's *A Long and Happy Life*; loses his virginity to Lois Provo and searches for his brother in *A Generous Man*.

Rosacoke Mustian. Female protagonist whose fierce love for Wesley Beavers forms the plot of Reynolds Price's *A Long and Happy Life*; appears as a child in *A Generous Man*.

Pauline Mustian. Dead wife of Papa Mustian, often quoted by him, in Reynolds Price's *A Long and Happy Life* and *A Generous Man*.

Sissie Abbott Mustian. Pregnant wife of Milo Mustian; gives birth to a dead child in Reynolds Price's *A Long and Happy Life*; mentioned in *A Generous Man*.

Mutchkin. Grocer whose daughter is courted by Teague Oregan in Hugh Henry Brackenridge's *Modern Chivalry*.

Vincente Pesola (Vince) Muzguiz. Relative who provides shelter, support, and help for Kat Alcazar in California; janitor and nursing student in M. F. Beal's *Angel Dance*.

M'Whorter. Young clergyman deranged because of Teague Oregan in Hugh Henry Brackenridge's *Modern Chivalry*.

Adolph Myers. See Wing Biddlebaum.

Marvin Myles. Self-made New York career woman and lover of Harry Pulham; marries a wealthy classmate of Pulham in John P. Marquand's *H. M. Pulham, Esquire*.

Myrna. See Vahine.

Myshkin. Soviet Writers' Union official in charge of Henry Bech's itinerary in Russia in John Updike's *Bech: A Book*.

Mysis. Servant of Chrysis and special companion of Glycerium in Thornton Wilder's *The Woman of Andros*.

N

Jim Nabours. Foreman of the Laguna del Sol ranch and advisor to Taisie Lockhart in Emerson Hough's *North of 36*.

Fabrizio Naccarelli. Handsome young Florentine who falls desperately in love with a retarded American girl, Clara Johnson, whose childlike innocence bewitches him in Elizabeth Spencer's *The Light in the Piazza*.

Signor Naccarelli. Father of the young Italian in love with an American girl whose mental retardation the Signor may or may not be aware of; his designs are on the girl's mother in Elizabeth Spencer's *The Light in the Piazza*.

President Harmon Nagel. College president afraid of the alumni and clever bargainer for Raymond Blent's right to play football in Howard Nemerov's *The Homecoming Game*.

George Nagle. Captain of the *Katopua*; treats Terangi as a son, does not help him escape, sees him pardoned, leaves the *Katopua* to him, and dies shortly after the hurricane in Charles Nordhoff and James Norman Hall's *The Hurricane*.

Matilda Nagy. Zagreb midwife assisting at the birth of Rudolf Stanka; charged with being a liaison between Stanka's mother and the Dug family in Louis Adamic's *Cradle of Life*.

Jane Nail. Common law wife of Elias McCutcheon, a gift to McCutcheon of Shokotee McNeilly, and mother of Isaac and Willy McCutcheon; her cheek is slashed open by a group of marauders, and she becomes reclusive as a result in Jesse Hill Ford's *The Raider*.

Eliot Nailles. Suburbanite and model citizen with an ideal family, though unable to function except under the effect of drugs; foil to the fanatic Paul Hammer in John Cheever's *Bullet Park*.

Nellie Nailles. Model but mindless suburban wife and mother in John Cheever's *Bullet Park*.

Tony Nailles. Son of Eliot and Nellie Nailles; psychosomatic youth who is saved from sacrificial death at the hands of Paul Hammer in John Cheever's *Bullet Park*.

Nameless. Adolescent girl raped by George Levanter at a Russian youth camp in Jerzy Kosinski's *Blind Date*.

Nana (Mrs. Greenfield, Ray). Beautiful, elegant, and influential aunt of the narrator of Aline Bernstein's *The Journey Down*.

Nana-dirat. Young woman who inhabits C. Card's fantasies of Babylon in Richard Brautigan's *Dreaming of Babylon*.

Nanantatee. Hindu representing himself as a wealthy merchant; lives in poverty and has not worked in five years in Henry Miller's *Tropic of Cancer*.

Aurore De Grapion Nancanou. Young Creole widow who marries Honoré Grandissime in George Washington Cable's *The Grandissimes*.

Clotilde De Grapion Nancanou. Daughter of Aurora Nancanou; marries Joseph Frowenfeld in George Washington Cable's *The Grandissimes*.

Nancy. Daughter of Till and an unknown white man; mulatto slave of Sapphira Dodderidge Colbert; runs away to Canada to avoid the sexual advances of Martin Colbert in Willa Cather's *Sapphira and the Slave Girl*.

Nancy. Cook for Clarissa and Edward Packard; fired for rudeness in Caroline Gilman's *Recollections of a Housekeeper*.

Nandy. Woman devoted to George Cain; helps him break his drug addiction in George Cain's *Blueschild Baby*.

Nanny. Grandmother who arranges Janie Crawford's marriage to Logan Killicks in Zora Neale Hurston's *Their Eyes Were Watching God*.

Nanny. Old nurse of Lillian's children and chief protector of familial harmony in Lillian's home in Anaïs Nin's *Ladders to Fire*.

Nanny Lisa. White woman who poses as a black nanny; works for the Louisiana Red Corporation and brings up Minnie Yellings to hate black men; murders Ed Yellings and is killed by Max Kasavubu in Ishmael Reed's *The Last Days of Louisiana Red*.

Miss Naomi. Former slave and keeper of Tangierneck's slave history in Sarah E. Wright's *This Child's Gonna Live*.

Napoleon. Slave of Sally and Brandon Lacey; carriage driver on their visit to Beulah in Mary Lee Settle's *Know Nothing*.

Narciss. Black housekeeper for Sam and Daniel Ponder in Eudora Welty's *The Ponder Heart*.

Gabriel Nash. Talkative friend of Nick Dormer in Henry James's *The Tragic Muse*.

Marcie Binnendale Nash. Owner, through inheritance, of a major department store; falls in love with Oliver Barrett IV, but drives him away with her shallowness and her unethical business practices in Erich Segal's *Oliver's Story*.

Phoebe Marvin Nason. See Phoebe Marvin.

Steven (Stevie) Nason. Maine woodsman who accompanies Benedict Arnold to Quebec to rescue Mary Mallinson; marries Phoebe Marvin in Kenneth Roberts's *Arundel*.

Mayor Nasta. Fascist collaborator given an opportunity to perform penitential service for Adano; circulates rumors about German advances and is banished from the town in John Hersey's *A Bell for Adano*.

Natahk. Leader of the Garkohn tribe in Octavia E. Butler's *Survivor*.

Natanis. Abenaki Indian friend of Steven Nason; helps Benedict Arnold's army in Kenneth Roberts's *Arundel*.

Lieutenant Nately. Patriotic companion of Yossarian; despises his wealthy father, falls in love with an Italian prostitute, and dies on a bombing mission in Joseph Heller's *Catch-22*.

Nathan. Young rabbi who creates a substitute home for Felix Fay before Fay becomes a reporter in Floyd Dell's *Moon-Calf*.

Dame (Aunt) Nauntje. Black servant to the Vancours in James Kirke Paulding's *The Dutchman's Fireside*.

Ralph Navarro. Lawyer for Joseph Chase and third husband of Orpha Chase in Jessamyn West's *The Life I Really Lived*.

Hester Nayburn. Blind girl seduced by Dalton Harron in Susan Sontag's *Death Kit*.

Jessie Nayburn. Aunt who rears Hester Nayburn after Hester is blinded by her mother in Susan Sontag's *Death Kit*.

Floyd Naylor. Farmer who, after marrying his cousin Lulu Bains, moves with his wife to Zenith in Sinclair Lewis's *Elmer Gantry*.

Ruth Nazerman. Deceased wife of Sol Nazerman in Edward Lewis Wallant's *The Pawnbroker*.

Sol (Pawnbroker, Solly) Nazerman. Polish survivor of the Holocaust and Harlem pawnbroker embittered by the deaths of his wife and children in a concentration camp in Edward Lewis Wallant's *The Pawnbroker*.

Henderson Neal. First husband of Maggie Ellersley; gambler and eventual suicide in Jessie Redmon Fauset's *There Is Confusion*.

Nearly Normal Jimmy. Ambitious businessman who tells Marx Marvelous about the zoo; shows *Tarzan's Triumph* in the holy city of Lhasa in Tom Robbins's *Another Roadside Attraction*.

Ned. Servant of the Glendinnings; seduces Delly Ulver in Herman Melville's *Pierre*.

Uncle Ned. Relative of Henry Miller; goes on a three-day drinking binge and dies from a head injury in Henry Miller's *Tropic of Capricorn*.

John Nefastis. Inventor of the Nefastis machine, which he claims contains a Demon that can violate the Second Law of Thermodynamics, in Thomas Pynchon's *The Crying of Lot 49*.

Drexa Neff. Viennese housekeeper and laundress for Captain Kudashvili; teaches Utch Thalhammer how to be a Russian in John Irving's *The 158-Pound Marriage*; also appears in *Setting Free the Bears*.

Stu Neihardt. High-school classmate of David Axelrod in Scott Spencer's *Endless Love*.

Annie Brandon Neill. See Annie Brandon O'Néill.

Dan Neill. Son of Big Dan O'Neill, husband of Lydia Catlett, owner of a livery stable, and politican advocating the separation of the wealthier western Virginia from the bankrupt eastern Virginia in Mary Lee Settle's *Know Nothing*.

James Peregrine Neill. Infant son of Dan and Lydia Catlett Neill in Mary Lee Settle's *Know Nothing*.

Lydia Catlett (Liddy, Liddy Boo) Neill. Daughter of Leah and Peregrine Lacey Catlett and sister of Lewis and Johnny Catlett; marries Dan Neill after her father's death and finances his ventures with her inheritance in Mary Lee Settle's *Know Nothing*.

Nelema. Aged Indian woman accused of witchcraft in Catharine Maria Sedgwick's *Hope Leslie*.

Nellie. Flirtatious former lover of Pete in Stephen Crane's *Maggie*.

Nelse. See Nelson Gaston.

Alice Nelson. Mistress of Robert Agar; turns Agar in to the police in Michael Crichton's *The Great Train Robbery*.

David Nelson. Dedicated Union man who considers moving West, but decides to remain in the South because such men as Comfort Servosse give him hope for a more tolerant Southern attitude, in Albion W. Tourgee's *A Fool's Errand*.

David Nelson. Botanist aboard HMS *Bounty* whose job is to collect Tahitian breadfruit in Charles Nordhoff and James Norman Hall's *Mutiny on the Bounty*; set adrift with Captain Bligh, whom Nelson assists with his scientific knowledge, in *Men against the Sea*.

Duane (Whitey) Nelson. Ne'er-do-well husband of Myra Carroll, who loves him, and father of Lucy Nelson, who detests him, in Philip Roth's *When She Was Good*.

George Nelson. Brother-in-law of Elsa Mason; Minneapolis attorney in Wallace Stegner's *The Big Rock Candy Mountain*.

Kristin Norgaard Nelson. Sister of Elsa Norgaard Mason; wife of George Nelson in Wallace Stegner's *The Big Rock Candy Mountain*.

Lucy Nelson. See Lucy Nelson Bassart.

Myra Carroll Nelson. Daughter of Willard Carroll, wife of Duane Nelson, and mother of Lucy Nelson Bassart in Philip Roth's *When She Was Good*.

Sterling Nelson. Urbane English businessman with whom Alice Prentice has an affair while her son is a child; Nelson's wealth, artistic tastes, and fidelity to Alice all prove fraudulent in Richard Yates's *A Special Providence*.

Professor Nemur. Research psychologist who, pushed by his wife for material success, designs an experiment for increasing intelligence and who, with Dr. Strauss, conducts the experiment on Charlie Gordon in Daniel Keyes's *Flowers for Algernon*.

Cornelius Nepos. Roman historian and biographer who keeps a commonplace book in Thornton Wilder's *The Ides of March*.

Bedelia Satterthwaite Nesbit. Wife of James Nesbit and mother of Laura Nesbit; helps care for young Kenyon Adams following Mary Adams's death in William Allen White's *In the Heart of a Fool*.

Evelyn Nesbit. Wife of Harry K. Thaw; seduced by Stanford White; becomes the lover of Mother's Younger Brother in E. L. Doctorow's *Ragtime*.

James Nesbit. Medical doctor and father of Laura Nesbit; his moral voice counterpoints Thomas Van Dorn's materialism in William Allen White's *In the Heart of a Fool*.

Louisa (Aunt Loo) Nesbit. Widowed aunt and companion of Nina Gordon; selfish devotee of com-

fortable Christianity in Harriet Beecher Stowe's *Dred*.

Milly Nesbit. See Milly.

Tomtit Nesbit. See Tomtit.

Elaine Nesbitt. Woman who has an affair with Bo Mason; Mason kills her before he commits suicide in Wallace Stegner's *The Big Rock Candy Mountain*.

Nessus. Young centaur who sets Jurgen on the road that will lead him to Koshchei the Deathless; gives Jurgen his multicolored shirt to wear on his journey in James Branch Cabell's *Jurgen*.

Eric Neuhoffer. Managing editor of the newspaper where Jerry Freeman works in Gail Godwin's *Glass People*.

Alpha Jones Neumiller. First wife of Martin Neumiller; a victim of uremia in Larry Woiwode's *Beyond the Bedroom Wall*.

Augustina Neumiller. Unmarried daughter of Otto Neumiller; nurse to her father in old age and at his death in Larry Woiwode's *Beyond the Bedroom Wall*.

Becky Neumiller. Daughter of Charles Neumiller (II) and Katherine Neumiller in Larry Woiwode's *Beyond the Bedroom Wall*.

Charles John Christopher Neumiller (I). Son of Otto Neumiller and inheritor of the Neumiller family farm; father of Martin Neumiller in Larry Woiwode's *Beyond the Bedroom Wall*.

Charles (Chuck, Chuckie) Neumiller (II). Middle son of Martin and Alpha Jones Neumiller; actor living in Greenwich Village and doing voiceovers for commercials in Larry Woiwode's *Beyond the Bedroom Wall*.

Cheri Neumiller. Wife of Tim Neumiller in Larry Woiwode's *Beyond the Bedroom Wall*.

Davey Neumiller. Son of Charles Neumiller (I) and Marie Krull in Larry Woiwode's *Beyond the Bedroom Wall*.

Elaine Neumiller. Oldest daughter of Charles Neumiller (I) and Marie Krull in Larry Woiwode's *Beyond the Bedroom Wall*.

Emil Neumiller. Son of Charles Neumiller (I) and Marie Krull in Larry Woiwode's *Beyond the Bedroom Wall*.

Fred Neumiller. Son of Charles Neumiller (I) and Marie Krull in Larry Woiwode's *Beyond the Bedroom Wall*.

Jay Neumiller. Son of Charles Neumiller (I) and Marie Krull in Larry Woiwode's *Beyond the Bedroom Wall*.

Jerome Neumiller. Oldest son of Martin and Alpha Jones Neumiller; physician in Illinois in Larry Woiwode's *Beyond the Bedroom Wall*.

Katherine Neumiller. Wife of Charles Neumiller (II) in Larry Woiwode's *Beyond the Bedroom Wall*.

Laura Neumiller. Second wife of Martin Neumiller; dies of breast cancer in Larry Woiwode's *Beyond the Bedroom Wall*.

Lucy Neumiller. Daughter of Otto Neumiller and wife of a cattle buyer in Larry Woiwode's *Beyond the Bedroom Wall*.

Marie Neumiller. Oldest daughter of Martin and Alpha Jones Neumiller in Larry Woiwode's *Beyond the Bedroom Wall*.

Martin Neumiller. Son of Charles Neumiller (I) and Marie Krull; husband of Alpha Jones Neumiller; teacher-principal, caretaker, and insurance salesman; twice a widower in Larry Woiwode's *Beyond the Bedroom Wall*.

Otto Neumiller. Patriarch of the Neumiller family; builder of the family farm in North Dakota; buried by his son, Charles Neumiller (I), in Larry Woiwode's *Beyond the Bedroom Wall*.

Rose Marie Neumiller. Daughter of Charles Neumiller (I) and Marie Krull in Larry Woiwode's *Beyond the Bedroom Wall*.

Susan Neumiller. Youngest daughter of Martin and Alpha Jones Neumiller in Larry Woiwode's *Beyond the Bedroom Wall*.

Timothy (Tim) Neumiller. Poet and youngest son of Martin and Alpha Jones Neumiller in Larry Woiwode's *Beyond the Bedroom Wall*.

Tom Neumiller Son of Charles Neumiller (I) and Marie Krull in Larry Woiwode's *Beyond the Bedroom Wall*.

Vince Neumiller. Son of Charles Neumiller (I) and Marie Krull in Larry Woiwode's *Beyond the Bedroom Wall*.

Amos Nevels. Youngest son of Gertie and Clovis Nevels; his mother urges an army officer and his driver to take him to a Kentucky village doctor when he is critically ill with diptheria in Harriette Arnow's *The Dollmaker*.

Cassie Marie Nevels. Youngest daughter of Gertie and Clovis Nevels; killed by a train when she is dis-tracted by playing with her imaginary playmate in Harriette Arnow's *The Dollmaker*.

Clovis Nevels. Husband of Gertie Nevels; mechanic who works as a repairman in a Detroit factory during World War II; driven to murder to revenge himself upon a young man hired to beat him up because of his union activities in Harriette Arnow's *The Dollmaker*.

Clytie Nevels. Oldest daughter of Gertie and Clovis Nevels in Harriette Arnow's *The Dollmaker*.

Enoch Nevels. Middle son of Gertie and Clovis Nevels in Harriette Arnow's *The Dollmaker*.

Gertie Kendrick Nevels. Dollmaker who leaves a Kentucky farm to join her husband, Clovis Nevels, who has gone to Detroit to work in a factory during World War II; destroys a statue of Christ she carved in order to use the wood to make dolls to help support her family in Harriette Arnow's *The Dollmaker*; also appears in *The Weed-Killer's Daughter*.

Reuben Nevels. Oldest son of Gertie and Clovis Nevels; returns to Kentucky because of his dislike for Detroit in Harriette Arnow's *The Dollmaker*.

Susan Newell. Eight-year-old daughter of Renie and Claud Newell; allegedly raped by Dr. Mark Channing in Lillian Smith's *One Hour*.

New Person. Probably the son of Lewis Moon and Pindi, though his paternity is attributed by the Niaruna Indians to the warrior Aeore in Peter Matthiessen's *At Play in the Fields of the Lord*.

Augusta (Gussie) Newcomb. Landlady and heir of Agee Ward; falls under Ward's mystical influence in Wright Morris's *The Man Who Was There*.

Victor (Prof) Newcool. Encouraging English professor; friend and mentor to Annie Brown in Betty Smith's *Joy in the Morning*.

Alyce (Ecstasy Pie) Newman. Astute Jewish lover and roommate of Jack Duluoz in New York in Jack Kerouac's *Desolation Angels*.

Christopher Newman. American millionaire who loses interest in business and visits Europe to increase his aesthetic sense; loves Claire de Cintré against her family's wishes in Henry James's *The American*.

Chadwick (Chad) Newsome. American expatriate living in Paris who remains in Europe against the wishes of his family; lover of Madame de Vionnet and friend of Lambert Strether in Henry James's *The Ambassadors*.

Mrs. Newsome. Rich, widowed mother of Chad Newsome; sends her fiancé, Lambert Strether, to Europe to disentangle her son from an involvement with Madame de Vionnet and bring him home to take over the family business in Woollett, Massachusetts, in Henry James's *The Ambassadors*.

Ralph Newsome. Washington spokesman whose favor Bruce Gold courts in Joseph Heller's *Good as Gold*.

Niceratus. Youthful guest at Chrysis's dinners; asks Chrysis to predict what life would be like in two thousand years in Thornton Wilder's *The Woman of Andros*.

Nichole. Italian-American white activist exploited by George Cain; gives birth to their child in George Cain's *Blueschild Baby*.

Brigadier General (J. J.,Jo-Jo) Nichols. Intuitive Chief of Air Staff whose almost preternatural intelligence manifests "an undeceived apprehension, a stern, wakeful grasp of the nature of things" in James Gould Cozzens's *Guard of Honor*.

James Nicholson. Eccentric printer who distributes cards and flyers containing gnomic messages in Albert Halper's *Union Square*.

Nick of the Woods. See Nathan Slaughter.

Brenda Nicol. Cousin who writes to Gary Gilmore in prison and helps him when he is released in Norman Mailer's *The Executioner's Song*.

John (Johnny) Nicol. Husband of Brenda Nicol in Norman Mailer's *The Executioner's Song*.

Fray Nicolás. Nineteenth-century priest living in Walatowa whose diary Father Olguin reads in N. Scott Momaday's *House Made of Dawn*.

Mario Nicolosi. Author who is the neighbor and friend of Virgil Morgan in Scott Spencer's *Preservation Hall*.

Fritz Jemand von Niemand. Nazi physician who forces Sophie Zawistowska to send one of her two children to the Birkenau crematoriums in William Styron's *Sophie's Choice*.

Lola Niessen. First piano teacher of Henry Miller; he seduces her because he is fascinated by her sallow complexion and abundance of body hair in Henry Miller's *Tropic of Capricorn*.

Nigel. Slave who befriends Dana Franklin and marries Carrie in Octavia E.Butler's *Kindred*.

Nigger. Lower East Side gang leader and later a gangster; Michael Gold's boyhood Jewish mentor in Michael Gold's *Jews without Money*.

Nigger Ed (Negro Ed). Town crier, drunkard, and buffoon who becomes the hero of Paul Laurence Dunbar's *The Fanatics*.

Night Shadow. Young Indian warrior in James Kirke Paulding's *Koningsmarke*.

Tug Nightingale. Painter and soldier in William Faulkner's *The Mansion*.

Arthur Nightwine. Thief turned Hollywood servant in Ludwig Bemelmans's *Dirty Eddie*.

Araba Nightwing. Trotskyite actress and underground leader of the Purple Group in Paul Theroux's *The Family Arsenal*.

Sam Niles. Divorced ex-Marine and claustrophobic who accidentally shoots Alexander Blaney; one of ten Los Angeles policemen-protagonists in Joseph Wambaugh's *The Choirboys*.

Woodsy Niles. Lover of Sally Buck; teaches Joe Buck to see himself as a cowboy in James Leo Herlihy's *Midnight Cowboy*.

Edgar Carl (Ed) Nillson. Oil speculator whose bribe causes the ruin of Senator Burden Day in Gore Vidal's *Washington, D.C.*

Peter Nilssen. Uncle of Helga Crane who pays for her education, disowns her after his marriage, but sends her $5,000 with the suggestion she go to Denmark in Nella Larsen's *Quicksand*.

Nimbus (George Nimbus, Nimbus Desmit, Nimbus Ware). Industrious black who flees his owner (Potem Desmit); enlists in the Union army (where he is given the name George Nimbus); returns to Horsford County and,as Nimbus Desmit, registers his marriage to Lugena; enrolls as a voter as Nimbus Ware; buys the Red Wing plantation, establishes a successful tobacco farm and freedmen's community, is forced to flee the Ku Klux Klan, returns to Horsford County, and eventually moves to Kansas to rejoin his family in Albion W. Tourgee's *Bricks without Straw*.

Edna Nimienski. Skinny peroxide blonde with whom Zeke Gurevich lives for three months in the Mojave desert in William Herrick's *The Itinerant*.

Nimni. Major Taparian on Pimminee and husband of Ohiro-Moldona-Fivona in Herman Melville's *Mardi*.

Nino. Wounded soldier who recovers in Castiglione and befriends Adeppi; friend of Edouard and Dolce in John Hawkes's *The Goose on the Grave*.

El Niño Muerto (The Dead Child). American boy in Mexico who transmigrates into other characters, finally becoming Xotoltl, his lover and comrade in the Mayan jungle, in William S. Burroughs's *The Wild Boys.*

Nioche. Father of Noémie Nioche; businessman who has experienced substantial losses and lives off Noémie, about whom he worries, in Henry James's *The American.*

Noémie Nioche. Heartless and calculating woman who wishes to become the mistress of a wealthy man; delighted when Valentin de Bellegarde and Stanislas Kapp fight a duel over her in Henry James's *The American.*

Leonard (Lenny) Nissem. Owner of a finance company that lends money to Harry Bogen on the basis of fraudulent dress orders in Jerome Weidman's *What's in It for Me?*

Richard Nixon. Vice-President of the United States, buffoon, scamp, and would-be lover of Ethel Rosenberg in Robert Coover's *The Public Burning.*

Mordecai Noah. Editor of the *Evening Star* and the only Jew ever to be appointed sheriff of New York City in Gore Vidal's *Burr.*

Charles Arnold (Charlie) Noble. Stranger who tells Frank Goodman about John Moredock; accused of being "a Mississippi operator" in Herman Melville's *The Confidence-Man.*

Maury Noble. Disloyal friend of Anthony Patch in F. Scott Fitzgerald's *The Beautiful and Damned.*

Mrs. Noble. Nursemaid for the Principino in Henry James's *The Golden Bowl.*

Jean-Marie Noblet. Drinking companion of Jean-Louis Lebris de Kérouac on a train trip to Brittany in Jack Kerouac's *Satori in Paris.*

Nobuko. Japanese actress who desires the spiritual freedom that Renate represents in Anaïs Nin's *Collages.*

Domina Nocturna. See Katje Borgesius.

N'Ogo. Relative and servant of N'Gana Frimbo in Rudolph Fisher's *The Conjure-Man Dies.*

Annie Laurie Nolan. Third child of Johnny and Katie Nolan; born after her father's death in Betty Smith's *A Tree Grows in Brooklyn.*

Cornelius John (Neeley) Nolan. Second child of Johnny and Katie Nolan; adored brother and friend of Francie Nolan in Betty Smith's *A Tree Grows in Brooklyn.*

Doctor Nolan. Woman psychiatrist who treats Esther Greenwood at Belsize, a private mental sanitarium, in Sylvia Plath's *The Bell Jar.*

Hezekiah (Uncle Hake) Nolan. Slovenly brother of Jenny Anderson and fifty-two-year-old husband of Lora Bowen Nolan; shot and killed by his nephew, Jan Anderson, in Fred Chappell's *The Inkling.*

Ida Nolan. Best friend of Louise Eborn; Louise suffers her fatal stroke at Ida's house; Ida's vision that the dead are always with the living closes Reynolds Price's *Love and Work.*

Jim Nolan. Young man who, as a result of his father's killing during a labor dispute, becomes a Communist organizer among migrant workers and is killed during the strike in John Steinbeck's *In Dubious Battle.*

John (Johnny) Nolan. Handsome, lovable son of Irish immigrants; poverty-ridden alcoholic dreamer and singing waiter; husband of Katie Nolan and father of Francie Nolan in Betty Smith's *A Tree Grows in Brooklyn.*

Katherine (Katie) Rommely Nolan. Child of Austrian immigrants, impoverished janitress, and loving wife of Johnny Nolan and mother of Francie Nolan; firm believer in education and role model for her daughter in Betty Smith's *A Tree Grows in Brooklyn.*

Lora Bowen Nolan. Nineteen-year-old housemaid who schemes first to marry Uncle Hake Nolan, then to usurp Jenny Anderson's position in the household, and finally to seduce Jan Anderson in Fred Chappell's *The Inkling.*

Mary Frances (Francie) Katherine Nolan. Brooklyn tenement child in the early 1900s, avid reader with a passion for beauty, first child of Johnny and Katie Nolan, and devoted big sister of Neeley and Annie Laurie Nolan; victim of near rape and determined heroine of Betty Smith's *A Tree Grows in Brooklyn.*

Sheriff Nolan. White authority with whom the Reverend Phillip Martin must negotiate in Ernest J. Gaines's *In My Father's House.*

William (Billy) Nolan. Boyfriend of Christine Hargensen; supplies the bucket of pig's blood that is emptied on Carrie White in Stephen King's *Carrie.*

Vincent (Vinc) Nolte. Successful banker and friend of Anthony Adverse; advises Adverse to invest in silver mines in Hervey Allen's *Anthony Adverse.*

Noomai. King of Hannamanoo in Herman Melville's *Omoo*.

Noonan. Chief of police and one of the four criminal bosses in Personville in Dashiell Hammett's *Red Harvest*.

Tim Noonan. Brother of the police chief; apparent suicide murdered by Bob MacSwain in Dashiell Hammett's *Red Harvest*.

Nord. Maintopman with a mysterious past aboard the *Neversink* in Herman Melville's *White-Jacket*.

Emil Nordquist. Free-verse poet known as the "Bard of the Prairie" in John Updike's *Bech: A Book*.

Karl Norgaard. Uncle of Elsa Norgaard Mason; store owner in North Dakota with whom Elsa goes to live as young woman; disapproves of her marriage to Bo Mason in Wallace Stegner's *The Big Rock Candy Mountain*.

Nels Norgaard. Father of Elsa Norgaard Mason; marries Elsa's girlhood friend, prompting Elsa to move away from home, in Wallace Stegner's *The Big Rock Candy Mountain*.

Sarah Norgaard. Wife of Nels Norgaard; girlhood friend of Elsa Norgaard Mason; her marriage to Elsa's father prompts Elsa to move away from home in Wallace Stegner's *The Big Rock Candy Mountain*.

Norm. Father by Mira of Normie and Clark; divorces Mira to marry another woman in Marilyn French's *The Women's Room*.

Norma. Shy young woman hired by Alice Chicoy to help at the diner; writes long, passionate letters to Clark Gable and fantasizes about getting a glamorous job in Hollywood; leaves on Juan Chicoy's bus in order to find a life away from the diner in John Steinbeck's *The Wayward Bus*.

Norman. Displaced caveman from Africa who worships peanuts in Stanley Elkin's *The Dick Gibson Show*.

Bernard B. (Bernie) Norman (Normanovitz). Owner of Norman Pictures later bought out by Jonas Cord, Jr.; develops the movie careers of Nevada Smith and Rina Marlowe in Harold Robbins's *The Carpetbaggers*.

Edward Norman. Christian journalist who excludes whiskey and tobacco advertising from the Raymond *Daily News* in Charles M. Sheldon's *In His Steps*.

Hose Norman. Son-in-law of Tom Camp; joins the Ku Klux Klan following his wife's murder in Thomas Dixon's *The Leopard's Spots*.

Mr. Norris. Man persuaded in a bar to try trout fishing; awakened his first night camping by the sound of men attempting to leave a dead body outside his tent in Richard Brautigan's *Trout Fishing in America*.

Abraham (Abe) North. Alcoholic composer and close friend of Dick and Nicole Diver in F. Scott Fitzgerald's *Tender Is the Night*.

Amy (Doctor) North. Unbalanced woman who marries Rick Martin in Dorothy Baker's *Young Man with a Horn*.

Frank North. Young black portrait painter who is a graduate of a New York art school and a member of the Charleston black artistic set; suitor of Lissa Atkinson in DuBose Heyward's *Mamba's Daughters*.

Mary North (Contessa di Minghetti). Wife, then widow, of Abe North; turns against Dick Diver after her marriage to a foreign potentate in F. Scott Fitzgerald's *Tender Is the Night*.

Resi North. German actress-wife of Howard Campbell, Jr., in Kurt Vonnegut's *Slaughterhouse-Five*. See Resi Noth.

Theodore Theophilus (Ted) North. Teacher who spends a summer in Newport, Rhode Island; while serving as a tutor, instructor, and reader, he is called upon to assist with several private problems; narrator of Thornton Wilder's *Theophilus North*.

Perry Northcutt. Brother of Roxie Biggers; bank cashier who is a hypocritical zealot and avowed fundamentalist; chief instigator of a revival by the Reverend Blackman to effect moral reform in T. S. Stribling's *Teeftallow*.

Norton. White trustee of a black college who is shocked by his experience with Jim Trueblood and the black veterans at the Golden Day bar in Ralph Ellison's *Invisible Man*.

Augustus Norton. Unnerved surgeon in Robert Herrick's *The Master of the Inn*.

Eleanor Norton. Schoolteacher whose obsessive spiritualism merges with others' superstition, religion, and grief following the mine disaster to create the Brunist sect; becomes Marcella Bruno's mother-figure in Robert Coover's *The Origin of the Brunists*.

John Norton. Quartermaster aboard the HMS *Bounty* who is set adrift with Captain Bligh in Charles Nordhoff and James Norman Hall's *Mutiny on the Bounty*; the only person to die on the difficult journey to Timor in *Men against the Sea*.

Susan (Susie, Suze) Norton. Lover of Ben Mears; helps Mears investigate the Marsten House and inadvertently becomes a vampire in Stephen King's *'Salem's Lot*.

Wylie Norton. Veterinarian and reverentially devoted husband of Eleanor Norton in Robert Coover's *The Origin of the Brunists*.

Helga Noth. German actress-wife of Howard Campbell and sister of Resi Noth in Kurt Vonnegut's *Mother Night*. See Resi North.

Resi Noth. Younger sister of Helga Noth and lover of Howard Campbell in Kurt Vonnegut's *Mother Night*. See Resi North.

Henry Novak. North Dakota farmer whose daughter dies from an allergic reaction to medicine administered by Martin Arrowsmith in Sinclair Lewis's *Arrowsmith*.

Molly (Molly N., Molly-O) Novotny. Lover of Frankie Machine in Nelson Algren's *The Man with the Golden Arm*.

Natalie Novotny. Lesbian stewardess in Thomas Berger's *Who Is Teddy Villanova?*

Antoinette Nowak. Private secretary to and mistress of Frank Cowperwood in Theodore Dreiser's *The Titan*.

Parker Nowell. Lawyer for the defense and narrator of Shelby Foote's *Follow Me Down* and *Jordan County*.

Catfoot Nowogrodski. Henchman of Bonifacy Konstantine; helps set up Bruno Lefty Bicek for arrest for murder in Nelson Algren's *Never Come Morning*.

Nung En (Elder, Wang the Eldest, Wang the Landlord). Pleasure-loving weakling married into a prosperous family in Pearl Buck's *The Good Earth*; moves with his wife to a big city because of their local unpopularity as grasping landlords in *Sons*; his sybaritic, parasitic ways continue in *A House Divided*.

Nung Wen (Wang the Second, Wang the Merchant). Grasping and tight-fisted mercantilist in Pearl Buck's *The Good Earth*; his successful business activities continue in Buck's *Sons* and *A House Divided*.

Arthur Nunheim (Albert Norman). Petty crook, stool pigeon, associate of Julia Wolfe's, and murder victim in Dashiell Hammett's *The Thin Man*.

Miriam Nunheim. Volatile wife of Arthur Nunheim in Dashiell Hammett's *The Thin Man*.

Cedric Nunnery. Youth whose disappearance leads to Eck Snopes's death in William Faulkner's *The Town*.

Daniel Nuñez. Consumptive peasant leader of a guerrilla band in the Spanish civil war; opposes both the military junta and the loyalists in William Herrick's *Hermanos!*

Nu-Nu. Member of the savage tribe that massacres the crew of the *Jane Guy*; captured by Arthur Gordon Pym and Dirk Peters in their escape from the island of Tsalal and subsequently dies of fright as the party nears the South Pole in Edgar Allan Poe's *The Narrative of Arthur Gordon Pym*.

Oliver (Ollie) Nuper. Hypocritical racist and voyeur always on the edge of violence; tenant of Walter Boyle in John Gardner's *The Sunlight Dialogues*.

Miss Abigail Nutter. Maiden sister of Grandfather Nutter and manager of the Nutter household in Thomas Bailey Aldrich's *The Story of a Bad Boy*.

Grandfather (Captain) Nutter. Soldier injured in the War of 1812; grandfather of Tom Bailey in Thomas Bailey Aldrich's *The Story of a Bad Boy*.

Nydia. Teenaged neighbor of Harry Meyers and wife of Carlos; wants Meyers to tutor her in Jay Neugeboren's *Listen Ruben Fontanez*.

Harold Nye. Special agent of the Kansas Bureau of Investigation; appointed to serve under Alvin Dewey in investigating the Clutter murders in Truman Capote's *In Cold Blood*.

Cora Nyhoff. Sanitarium roommate of Rena Baker in Peter De Vries's *The Blood of the Lamb*.

Nymwha. Shawnee Indian medicine man who serves as Salathiel Albine's mentor in Hervey Allen's *The Forest and the Fort*.

O

O. Daughter of Nimni and Ohiro-Moldona-Fivona in Herman Melville's *Mardi*.

Dr. Oakenburg (Oakenburger). Root doctor traveling with Lieutenant Porgy to join Francis Marion in William Gilmore Simms's *The Partisan*.

General Douglas D. Oakhart. President of the Patriot League in Philip Roth's *The Great American Novel*.

Dorinda (Dorindy, Dorrie) Oakley. Strong-willed woman seduced, impregnated, and abandoned by Jason Greylock; struggles for revenge by succeeding as a dairy farmer; marries Nathan Pedlar in Ellen Glasgow's *Barren Ground*.

Eudora Abernethy Oakley. Mother of Dorinda, Josiah, and Rufus Oakley; following the death of her missionary lover, marries into a life of hard, monotonous work and crazed African dreams in Ellen Glasgow's *Barren Ground*.

Francis (Frank) Oakley. Wastrel and half brother of Maurice Oakley; falsely accuses Berry Hamilton of stealing in Paul Laurence Dunbar's *The Sport of the Gods*.

Joshua Oakley. Father of Dorinda, Josiah, and Rufus Oakley; looks like John the Baptist; poor, humble, slow-witted man who lives as a slave of the land and is distant from his daughter in Ellen Glasgow's *Barren Ground*.

Josiah Oakley. Elder brother of Dorinda Oakley in Ellen Glasgow's *Barren Ground*.

Col. Maurice Oakley. Genteel southern landowner and employer of Berry Hamilton; believes the lie of his half brother that Hamilton stole money in Paul Laurence Dunbar's *The Sport of the Gods*.

Phoebe Thynne Oakley. Daughter of Mortimer Thynne; marries Tom Oakley in Australia; leaves her husband and their child and returns to England in Charles Nordhoff and James Norman Hall's *Botany Bay*.

Rufus Oakley. Handsome, spoiled younger brother of Dorinda Oakley; kills a man over a game of cards in Ellen Glasgow's *Barren Ground*.

Tom Oakley. English highwayman imprisoned in Australia; escapes from the penal colony and returns to England, but is caught and hanged when he resumes his old ways in Charles Nordhoff and James Norman Hall's *Botany Bay*.

Camille Oaks. Sexy, gorgeous blonde who works as a stripper in men's clubs and who, as a passenger on Juan Chicoy's bus, instantly becomes the center of attention of some men on the bus, to her dismay, in John Steinbeck's *The Wayward Bus*.

Owen Oarson. Former Texas football star and former tractor salesman who tries unsuccessfully to become a Hollywood film producer; lover of Jill Peel; narrates part of Larry McMurtry's *Somebody's Darling*.

Kayo Obermark. Slovenly but bright student who instructs Augie March about "the bitterness in the chosen thing" in Saul Bellow's *The Adventures of Augie March*.

Count Kurt von Obersdorf. Austrian count and banker; lover of Fran Dodsworth in Sinclair Lewis's *Dodsworth*.

Ford Obert. Painter and social observer in Henry James's *The Sacred Fount*.

O'Brien. One of the soldiers who tries to buy or steal the pistol in the possession of Richard Mast in James Jones's *The Pistol*.

Bernice (Mrs. W. B.) O'Brien. Favorite correspondent of Annabel Williams; mother of Echo O'Brien in James Leo Herlihy's *All Fall Down*.

Echo Malvina O'Brien. Daughter of Bernice O'Brien and lover of Berry-berry Williams; dies in an automobile accident in James Leo Herlihy's *All Fall Down*.

Harvey O'Brien. Rival of Homer Zigler on the staff of the *Denver Call* in Clyde Brion Davis's *"The Great American Novel—."*

J. J. O'Brien. World War I veteran, entrepreneur, and influential alumnus who pays for Jack Curran to play football at Boniface College in Mark Steadman's *A Lion's Share*.

Ingrid Ochester. Lover of Hugh Butterfield after he divorces his wife in Scott Spencer's *Endless Love*.

Mackate (Black Gown) Ockola. Indian conjurer in James Kirke Paulding's *Koningsmarke*.

O'Connor. Irishman who carries Mexican artifacts in his pockets and lives "the life of others" in Anaïs Nin's *Seduction of the Minotaur*.

Cecile (Ceci) O'Connor. Waitress, estranged wife of Walter Wong, and lover of Paul Cattleman in Alison Lurie's *The Nowhere City*.

Florinda (Splutter) O'Connor. Artist's model in love with Billie Hawker in Stephen Crane's *The Third*

Violet.

Guido O'Connor. Homosexual lover of Edward Henley in Shirley Ann Grau's *Evidence of Love.*

Dr. Matthew O'Connor. Transvestite Irishman from San Francisco who narrates much of Djuna Barnes's *Nightwood.*

Dr. Matthew O'Connor. Family physician to the Ryders and lover of Molly Dance in Djuna Barnes's *Ryder.*

Mary O'Crawley. Twice-widowed boardinghouse proprietor and second wife of Patrick Dennis Moore in Betty Smith's *Maggie-Now.*

Octavius. Nephew and later the adopted son of Caesar in Thornton Wilder's *The Ides of March.*

O'Daddy. See Rhino Gross.

Tommy Odds. Civil rights organizer who loses an arm to a sniper's bullets; rapes the white wife of his friend Truman Held in Alice Walker's *Meridian.*

Gaye Nell Odell. Daughter of Mavis Odell; beauty queen and brown belt karateka in Harry Crews's *Karate Is a Thing of the Spirit.*

Harry O'Dell. Owner of the Friendly Hearth Wood Yard and uncle of Lorena Hessenwinkle in Josephine Pinckney's *Three O'Clock Dinner.*

Mary Odell. See Mary Cheney Odell Curran.

Mavis Odell. Mother of Gaye Nell Odell in Harry Crews's *Karate Is a Thing of the Spirit.*

Brian O'Donnell. Art dealer who sells Jeremy Pauling's works; Mary Tell and her children find shelter in his boat house in Anne Tyler's *Celestial Navigation.*

Marcia Mae Hunt O'Donnell. Older widowed daughter of Nan and Jason Hunt and former fiancée of Duncan Harper, whom she jilted although she still loved him, in Elizabeth Spencer's *The Voice at the Back Door.*

James Michael (Big Boy) O'Doul. Powerful Chicago criminal in William Riley Burnett's *Little Caesar.*

Patsy O'Dowd. Bowery bartender famous for insulting wealthy patrons in Henry Miller's *Black Spring.*

Kermit (Boy) Oelsligle. Orphan who accompanies his great-uncle Floyd Warner from California to Nebraska; abandoned to the care of two hippies, Joy and Stanley, in Wright Morris's *Fire Sermon.*

Irene (Reenie) O'Farron. Best friend and co-worker of Margy Shannon; wife of Salvatore De Muccio in Betty Smith's *Tomorrow Will Be Better.*

Maizie O'Farron. Loving but difficult mother of Reenie O'Farron in Betty Smith's *Tomorrow Will Be Better.*

Dorothea O'Faye. Mother of Marion Faye; holds court at The Hangover in Norman Mailer's *The Deer Park.*

Peggy O'Flagherty. Housekeeper for the Dalton family in Richard Wright's *Native Son.*

Kevin O'Garvey. Member of Parliament who supports the Irish Party; lawyer who defends Irish farmers' rights in Leon Uris's *Trinity.*

Constance Ogden. Pretty, spoiled daughter of wealthy parents; infatuated with Frank Ellinger, whom she eventually marries, in Willa Cather's *A Lost Lady.*

George Ogden. Bank cashier who marries Abbie Brainard after the death of his first wife, Jessie Bradley, in Henry Blake Fuller's *The Cliff-Dwellers.*

Mary Ogden. See Countess Marie Zattiany.

Ellen (Ellie) Oglethorpe. Solicitous nurse and second wife of Tom More in Walker Percy's *Love in the Ruins.*

James (Jim) Oglethorpe. Son of Jane Oglethorpe and father of Janet Oglethorpe; advised by Lee Clavering to educate Janet about the real world in Gertrude Atherton's *Black Oxen.*

Jane Oglethorpe. Girlhood friend of Mary Ogden and self-sacrificing sexagenarian in Gertrude Atherton's *Black Oxen.*

Janet Oglethorpe. Self-assured but shallow flapper and granddaughter of Jane Oglethorpe; youthful rival of Mary Ogden for the love of Lee Clavering in Gertrude Atherton's *Black Oxen.*

Jem Oglethorpe. Wealthy rival of Billie Hawker for the affection of Grace Fanhall in Stephen Crane's *The Third Violet.*

Violet Ogure. Prostitute who refuses to move to Wahiawa with Robert E. Lee Prewitt after his transfer to G Company in James Jones's *From Here to Eternity.*

Aristides (Harry, Porky) O'Hara. Slightly crippled shoemaker and member of the Church of the Covenant community; best friend of Roger Ashley in Thornton Wilder's *The Eighth Day.*

Gerald O'Hara. Irish immigrant who acquires the Georgia plantation Tara in a poker game; father of

Scarlett O'Hara in Margaret Mitchell's *Gone with the Wind*.

Lance O'Hara. Homosexual Hollywood star; his legendary good looks begin to fade, leaving him increasingly lonely and dependent on alcohol, in John Rechy's *City of Night*.

Larry (Danny Richman) O'Hara. San Francisco bookstore owner and drinking buddy of Leo Percepied in Jack Kerouac's *The Subterraneans*; mentioned in *Book of Dreams*.

Samuel O'Hara. Grandfather of Porky O'Hara and deacon of the Covenant church; lets Roger Ashley know of John Ashley's interest in and assistance to the church in Thornton Wilder's *The Eighth Day*.

Scarlett O'Hara. Heroine married first to Charles Hamilton, then to Frank Kennedy, and finally to Rhett Butler; struggles to survive the horrors of Reconstruction in Margaret Mitchell's *Gone with the Wind*.

Tim O'Hara. Printer uncle of Mac who takes him to Chicago as a boy, teaches him the printing trade, and encourages his development as a radical in John Dos Passos's *U.S.A.* trilogy.

Tom O'Hara. Manager of one of Jake Hesse's shoe stores and lover of Orpha Chase in Jessamyn West's *The Life I Really Lived*.

Captain Bernard Eagle-1 (Daffodil-11) O'Hare. Pilot of President Wilbur Swain's helicopter in Kurt Vonnegut's *Slapstick*.

Bernard V. O'Hare. lieutenant who hunts down Howard Campbell in Kurt Vonnegut's *Mother Night*; friend and fellow prisoner of war who returns to Dresden with the author in *Slaughterhouse-Five*.

Mary O'Hare. Nurse, wife of Bernard V. O'Hare, and recipient of the dedication of Kurt Vonnegut's *Slaughterhouse-Five*.

Ohio. See Robes Smith.

Ohiro-Moldona-Fivona. Wife of Nimni in Herman Melville's *Mardi*.

Bernie Ohls. Sheriff's deputy in Raymond Chandler's *The Long Goodbye*.

Oh-Oh. Ugly antiquarian on Padulla in Herman Melville's *Mardi*.

Kenneth O'Keefe. Fellow American student and best friend of Sebastian Dangerfield; obsessed with his inability to lose his virginity, he returns to America broke and in despair in J. P. Donleavy's *The Ginger Man*.

Mary Martha O'Keefe. Common-law wife of Jarcey Pentacost; rescues Jarcey when the Kreggs try to burn him out, moves with him to Beulah, but later leaves with a land agent in Mary Lee Settle's *O Beulah Land*.

Olaf. Wireless officer on a cruise ship who competes with Allert Vanderveenan for Ariane's attention; relieved of duty and sedated when she disappears in John Hawkes's *Death, Sleep & the Traveler*.

O-lan. Wife of Wang Lung; achieves her greatest satisfaction from having borne children and from living to witness the marriage of her oldest son in Pearl Buck's *The Good Earth*.

Old Ben. Venerable bear in William Faulkner's *Go Down, Moses*.

Old Doctor. "Master" figure who absorbs newsreels and riot noises into himself and thereby stills them in William S. Burroughs's *The Ticket That Exploded*.

Old Hundred (John). Coachman at Canema plantation; first person to die in the cholera epidemic in Harriet Beecher Stowe's *Dred*.

Old Hurricane. See Major Ira Warfield.

Old Lodge Skins. Cheyenne adoptive grandfather of Little Big Man in Thomas Berger's *Little Big Man*.

Old Lord. See Lord Hwang.

Old Man. The Mississippi River in William Faulkner's *The Wild Palms*.

Old Running Water. Proprietor of the Lafayette Street warehouse who fires Hank Austin in Albert Halper's *Union Square*.

Master Oldale. Tavern keeper in James Kirke Paulding's *Koningsmarke*.

Sally Oldham. See Sally Oldham Collier.

Salvador Hassan (After Birth Tycoon, K. Y. Ahmed, Pepe El Culito, Hassan, Placenta Juan) O'Leary. Liquefactionist and possible secret Sender engaged in numerous international schemes; uses various aliases in William S. Burroughs's *Naked Lunch*.

Sergeant O'Leary. Soldier on the thirty-six-mile hike who annoys Lieutenant Culver by defending Colonel Templeton in William Styron's *The Long March*.

Countess Ellen Olenska. Granddaughter of Catherine Mingott and cousin of May Welland; leaves her abusive Polish husband and returns to her family in New York, where she falls in love with Newland Archer, her cousin's fiancé, in Edith Wharton's *The*

Age of Innocence.

Olga. Russian shoemaker; provides free meals for Henry Miller that always begin with soup in Henry Miller's *Tropic of Cancer.*

Olga the Wise One. Doctor and witch who buries the narrator to cure him of fever in Jerzy Kosinski's *The Painted Bird.*

Father Olguin. Walatowa priest who testifies at Abel's trial in N. Scott Momaday's *House Made of Dawn.*

Antonio Olivares. Wealthy don who contributes to Bishop Latour's cathedral fund in Willa Cather's *Death Comes for the Archbishop.*

Isabella Olivares. Wife of Antonio Olivares; forced to reveal her age in order to keep her husband's estate in Willa Cather's *Death Comes for the Archbishop.*

Earl Olive. Replacement manager of the Centennial Club; dynamites the dam and the main lodge when the members turn against him in Thomas McGuane's *The Sporting Club.*

Bump Oliver. Dapper card-shark who cheats during a card game in William Kennedy's *Billy Phelan's Greatest Game.*

Margaret Oliver. Younger daughter of Thomas Oliver; tries to be her father's son by participating in his business affairs in Shirley Ann Grau's *The Condor Passes.*

Stephanie Maria D'Alfonso Oliver. Wife of Thomas Oliver; descended from a Sicilian family prominent in the New Orleans business world; dies young after bearing two children in Shirley Ann Grau's *The Condor Passes.*

Thomas Henry (Old Man) Oliver. Millionaire protagonist who rises from a background of poverty to build a successful family and financial empire in Shirley Ann Grau's *The Condor Passes.*

Olivia. Hippie hitchhiker and lover of Jeremy Pauling; narrator of the eighth chapter of Anne Tyler's *Celestial Navigation.*

Olivia. Lover of Marius and rival to Hipparchia in H. D.'s *Palimpsest.*

Ollentangi. Aged warrior and sage in James Kirke Paulding's *Koningsmarke.*

Ollie (Ollie Miss). Farmhand employed by Uncle Alex, lover of Jule, and mother out of wedlock of Jule Jackson in George Wylie Henderson's *Ollie Miss* and *Jule.*

Mary Kathleen (Mrs. Jack Graham) O'Looney. Former lover of Walter F. Starbuck; bag lady who is in fact the powerful Mrs. Graham in Kurt Vonnegut's *Jailbird.*

Hans Olsa. Immigrant Norwegian farmer and friend of Per Hansa; his deathbed wish for a minister causes the death of his friend Per in O. E. Rölvaag's *Giants in the Earth.*

Sörine (Sörrina) Olsa. Wife and then widow of Hans Olsa in O. E. Rölvaag's *Giants in the Earth*; neighbor and confessor to the Norwegian community in *Peder Victorious*; appears in *Their Father's God.*

Axel Olsen. Copenhagen artist who paints a portrait of Helga Crane and proposes to her, but is rejected, in Nella Larsen's *Quicksand.*

Anita O'Malley. Tragic widow of a general and lover of a goatherd, both of whom died because of their love for her; forced by her father to go on the stage, she becomes famous for her coldness and self-isolation in Josefina Niggli's *Mexican Village.*

O'Mara. Friend and chief assistant of Henry Miller at the telegraph company; recently returned from the Philippines in Henry Miller's *Tropic of Capricorn.*

Dallas O'Mara. Artist and friend of Dirk DeJong in Edna Ferber's *So Big.*

Brackett Omensetter. "Unnaturally natural" newcomer to Gilean on the Ohio; his absolute intimacy with nature and lack of self-consciousness provide the narrative focus of William Gass's *Omensetter's Luck.*

Evan Ondyk. Psychotherapist and, briefly, lover of Kitty Dubin in Bernard Malamud's *Dubin's Lives.*

One-armed Pete. Western bank robber whose clothes Berkeley steals during a hotel fire in Samuel Langhorne Clemens's *The American Claimant.*

Oneco. Son of the Pequod chief Mononotto, brother of Magawisca, and husband of the Puritan Faith Leslie in Catharine Maria Sedgwick's *Hope Leslie.*

One Eye. Dog; mate of Kiche and father of White Fang in Jack London's *White Fang.*

Louis One Eye. Gangster, Tammany Hall employee, and pigeon fancier in Michael Gold's *Jews without Money.*

Adele O'Neill. Friend of Mira; beleaguered by multiple pregnancies and a philandering husband in Marilyn French's *The Women's Room.*

Annie Brandon O'Neill (Neill). Daughter of Stuart Brandon and niece of Mamie Brandon; comes to Beulah as an impoverished orphan with the hope of marrying Peregrine Lacey Catlett; remains there as a neurotic spinster, having an affair with Big Dan O'Neill (whom she ostensibly scorns); marries O'Neill after his wife has died and she has spent a year in Cincinnati "for her Brandon nerves" in Mary Lee Settle's *Know Nothing*.

Big Dan O'Neill (Neill). Irish "lifter" at Peregrine Lacey Catlett's salt furnace; marries Annie Brandon, becomes a "respectable" innkeeper, and changes his name to satisfy Annie and their son, Dan Neill, in Mary Lee Settle's *Know Nothing*.

Danny O'Neill. Boy who hangs around and admires Studs Lonigan in James T. Farrell's *Young Lonigan*; attends the University of Chicago and escapes the old neighborhood in *The Young Manhood of Studs Lonigan*.

Little Dan O'Neill. See Dan Neill.

Marie O'Neill. See Belinda.

Molly O'Neill. Younger sister of Dan Neill in Mary Lee Settle's *Know Nothing*.

Nubby O'Neill. Criminal who introduces Cass McKay to the criminal life and shares a cell with him in El Paso in Nelson Algren's *Somebody in Boots*.

Seamus O'Neill. Best friend of Conor Larkin; reporter for the Irish press, member of the Irish Republican Brotherhood, and revolutionary for the Irish Catholics in Leon Uris's *Trinity*.

Teeny O'Neill. Younger sister of Dan Neill and first sexual partner of Johnny Catlett in Mary Lee Settle's *Know Nothing*.

Valentine O'Neill. French-Irish fashion designer who leaves Paris for New York, only to be fired several times before moving to California to become chief buyer and designer for Scruples, Billy Ikehorn Orsini's boutique, in Judith Krantz's *Scruples*.

Bernadette Ong. Wife of John Ong and lover of Piet Hanema in John Updike's *Couples*.

John Ong. Korean nuclear physicist and husband of Bernadette Ong in John Updike's *Couples*.

Ono. Bandaged, sexless resident of the Golden Years Community in Jerzy Kosinski's *Cockpit*.

Fospe and Terese Ontstout. Impoverished citizens in James Kirke Paulding's *Koningsmarke*.

Opaku. Large, eventually traitorous bodyguard of Colonel Ellelloû in John Updike's *The Coup*.

Orchis (Doleful Dumps). Shoemaker who wins a lottery and forces China Aster to accept a loan in Herman Melville's *The Confidence-Man*.

Peter (Pete) Orcino. Second husband of Tasmania Orcino in Jessamyn West's *A Matter of Time*.

Tasmania (Tassie) Murphy Orcino. Older sister of Blix Hollister; helps Blix die when her cancer becomes unbearable in Jessamyn West's *A Matter of Time*.

Doctor (Doc) Orcutt. Physician whose effort to cure Henry Pimber's lockjaw cannot match the magical healing powers of Brackett Omensetter's special poultice in William Gass's *Omensetter's Luck*.

Matt Ord. Airplane builder in William Faulkner's *Pylon*.

Jack R. Ordway. Lighthearted, self-proclaimed office drunk; fabricates stories about drunken weekends with his rich wife's friends in Richard Yates's *Revolutionary Road*.

Teague Oregan (O'Regan). Ambitious and ignorant servant of Captain John Farrago; follows afoot behind Farrago's horse as he and his master tour the country; becomes involved in numerous careers, to his master's embarrassment, in Hugh Henry Brackenridge's *Modern Chivalry*.

O'Reilly. Irish lawyer and politician; relative of Mary Monahan; attempts to blackmail George Apley in John P. Marquand's *The Late George Apley*.

Orestes. Son of Agamemnon and Clytemnestra; in the name of duty, avenges his father's murder by killing Clytemnestra and her lover Aegisthus; violates the law of hospitality by killing Pyrrhus; runs off with Hermione in John Erskine's *The Private Life of Helen of Troy*.

Oribasius. Physician who befriends Julian as a youth and remains his lifelong companion in Gore Vidal's *Julian*.

Jose O'Riely. Married Spanish artist with whom Eveline Hutchins has an affair in John Dos Passos's *U.S.A.* trilogy.

Oriki. White-skinned daughter of Scarecrow in Calvin Hernton's *Scarecrow*.

Oris. Sun-colored Englishwoman who tries to bring poetry into Marietta McGee-Chávez's Spain in William Goyen's *In a Farther Country*.

Ork. Chief priest who believes he has been privileged to experience a visit from the divine presence in John Gardner's *Grendel*.

Edward (Ed) Orlin. Employee of Janoth Enterprises who is assigned by George Stroud to stake out Gil's Tavern in the search for the unidentified witness to Pauline Delos's murder; a narrator of Kenneth Fearing's *The Big Clock*.

Frankie Orloffski. Sailor and skindiver from South Jersey; Al Bonham's partner in a charter boat business; finally voted captain of the *Naiad* in James Jones's *Go to the Widow-Maker*.

Captain Robert Orme. Arrogant aide de camp to General Braddock; injured but survives the expedition to Fort Duquesne in Mary Lee Settle's *O Beulah Land*.

Ormond. Mysterious figure whose designs on Constantia Dudley lead him first to aid the Dudley family and then to instigate the murder of Stephen Dudley; killed by Constantia in Charles Brockden Brown's *Ormond*.

Marian Ormsby. See Marian Ormsby Forrester.

Violet Ames (Mother) Ormsby. Audacious representative of American Motherhood; asked by the navy to dedicate the USS *Ormsby* in Wright Morris's *Man and Boy*.

Virgil Ormsby. Son of Violet Ames and Warren K. Ormsby killed in World War II; the USS *Ormsby* is named after him in Wright Morris's *Man and Boy*.

Warren K. Ormsby. Husband of Violet Ames Ormsby and father of Virgil Ormsby in Wright Morris's *Man and Boy*.

Shad O'Rory. Politically powerful mobster who opposes Paul Madvig for control of the city in Dashiell Hammett's *The Glass Key*.

O'Rourke. Company detective at the Cosmodemonic Telegraph Company in Henry Miller's *Tropic of Capricorn*.

Orr. Air force pilot and inventive tentmate of Yossarian; intentionally ditches his plane and rows to Sweden and safety in an inflatable life raft in Joseph Heller's *Catch-22*.

Billy Ikehorn Orsini. See Wilhelmina Hunnenwell Winthrop Ikehorn Orsini.

Vito Orsini. Italian film producer who marries Billy Ikehorn Orsini and scores a major success with his film *Mirrors* in Judith Krantz's *Scruples*.

Wilhelmina Hunnenwell Winthrop Ikehorn (Billy, Honey) Orsini. Owner of Scruples, a Beverly Hills boutique; hires Valentine O'Neill and Spider Elliott, who make the store a great success; marries Vito Orsini after her first husband, Ellis Ikehorn, dies in Judith Krantz's *Scruples*.

Pedro Ortega. Dance partner of Lillian Bacon; assaults Bacon and Rocky Gravo when he learns that Rocky attempted to seduce Bacon in Horace McCoy's *They Shoot Horses, Don't They?*

Jesus Ortiz. Young Hispanic assistant to Sol Nazerman; killed by the bullet intended for Nazerman during the robbery in Edward Lewis Wallant's *The Pawnbroker*.

Hosea Ortman. Farm owner in Brand Whitlock's *J. Hardin & Son*.

Dudley (Uncle Dudley) Osborn. American picaro seeking a definition of bravery in Wright Morris's *My Uncle Dudley*.

Fremont Osborn. Uncle of Warren Howe and "the inventor of the dustbowl" in Wright Morris's *Cause for Wonder*.

Grace Osborn. Mother of the protagonists in Wright Morris's *The Man Who Was There*, *The Home Place*, *The World in the Attic*, and *Cause for Wonder*.

Hank Osborne. Failed novelist and onetime friend of Manley Halliday; teaches at Webster, an Ivy League college; Halliday resents Osborne's ability to pass gracefully from youth to middle age in Budd Schulberg's *The Disenchanted*.

Helen Osborne. Sister of Mildred Osborne in Paul Laurence Dunbar's *The Love of Landry*.

John Osborne. Father of Mildred and Helen Osborne in Paul Laurence Dunbar's *The Love of Landry*.

Mildred Osborne. Daughter of wealthy easterners; goes west to regain her health and falls in love with Landry Thayer, a cowboy who saves her life during a cattle stampede, in Paul Laurence Dunbar's *The Love of Landry*.

Oscar. Adolescent rapist falsely convicted of a rape committed by his friend George Levanter in Jerzy Kosinski's *Blind Date*.

Oscar. Lion that is the major attraction in Huguenine's circus; exhibited in five towns after he dies in Walter D. Edmonds's *Chad Hanna*.

Oscar X. Black American student at McCarthy College in Wisconsin; introduces Hakim Ellelloû to the Muslim faith and encourages him to overthrow the white-devil in John Updike's *The Coup*.

Iris Osgood. Plump, pretty student of George Caldwell in John Updike's *The Centaur*.

Brigid O'Shaughnessy (Miss Wonderly). Duplicitous temptress who hires Spade & Archer first, ostensibly, to help find a missing sister and who, after Archer's murder, hires Spade to help find the jewel-encrusted statuette in Dashiell Hammett's *The Maltese Falcon*.

Sergius (Gus, Mac, Slim, Spike) O'Shaugnessy. Air force veteran and narrator of Norman Mailer's *The Deer Park*.

Terry O'Shawn. Governor of Alabama and staunch advocate of white supremacy in T. S. Stribling's *The Store*.

Henry O'Shay. Itinerant showman who purports to display the mummified corpse of his faithless wife in Alice Walker's *Meridian*.

Robert O'Sheean. See Sugar-Boy.

Dr. Charles Osman. History professor who fails star football player Raymond Bent; loves Bent's girlfriend, Lily Sayre, in Howard Nemerov's *The Homecoming Game*.

Gilbert Osmond. Calculating dilettante and father, by his lover Madame Merle, of Pansy Osmond; marries Isabel Archer in Henry James's *The Portrait of a Lady*.

Pansy Osmond. Illegitimate daughter of Gilbert Osmond and Madame Merle; befriended by Isabel Archer in Henry James's *The Portrait of a Lady*.

Katrina Osterlaag. See Rina Marlowe.

Osterman. Wheat grower in the San Joaquin Valley who fails to influence the state commission regulating railroad shipping rates and who dies during a gunfight with the railroad's agents in Frank Norris's *The Octopus*.

Sean O'Sullivan. Military governor of Rombaden, special assistant to General Hansen, commander of an occupation team in post-World War II Germany, and lover of Ernestine Falkenstein in Leon Uris's *Armageddon*.

Ramón (The Greek) Otero. Mexican member of the Vettori gang dedicated to Rico Bandello; killed by the police in William Riley Burnett's *Little Caesar*.

Otis. Brother of Alfonso; regularly stops Alfonso from beating Jean in Gayl Jones's *Eva's Man*.

Otis. Troubled teenager in William Faulkner's *The Reivers*.

Isabel Otis. Californian who manages a chicken ranch and who is forced to choose between independence and marriage to John Gwynne in Gertrude Atherton's *Ancestors*.

Frances Melissa O'Toole. Irish immigrant lover of Salathiel Albine, by whom she has a child in Hervey Allen's *Toward the Morning*.

Philip Frederick Ottenburg. Son of a wealthy Chicago family; married to an heiress and later to Thea Kronborg in Willa Cather's *The Song of the Lark*.

Felix (N. J. Felix) Ottensteen. Magazine writer and friend of Leslie Braverman in Wallace Markfield's *To an Early Grave*.

Ottima. One of three sisters operating a wine shop; hired to be Samuele's maid in Thornton Wilder's *The Cabala*.

Señorita Vastie Oubaleta. Name assumed by Arista Prolo on a Spanish tour in Carlene Hatcher Polite's *Sister X and the Victims of Foul Play*.

Dr. Elvin R. Outerbridge. Kindly, wise elderly professor who tries to advise Lee Youngdahl in Mark Harris's *Wake Up, Stupid*.

Archy Outlaw. Son of a colonial North Carolina farmer; follows his fugitive brother Rion Outlaw to Tennessee, where Archy is captured by the Cherokee Indians and joins their tribe, in Caroline Gordon's *Green Centuries*.

Jocasta Dawson (Cassy) Outlaw. Sister of Francis Dawson and wife of Rion Outlaw; settles in Tennessee in Caroline Gordon's *Green Centuries*.

Orion (Rion) Outlaw. Son of a colonial North Carolina farmer; revolutionary who avoids hanging by settling in Tennessee in Caroline Gordon's *Green Centuries*.

Ouvrard. French banker and political manipulator in H. L. Davis's *Harp of a Thousand Strings*.

Blanche Overall. Girlfriend of Orlando Pratt; Maude Coffin Pratt accuses her of incest in Paul Theroux's *Picture Palace*.

Clay Overbury. Ambitious protégé of Burden Day and husband of Enid Sanford in Gore Vidal's *Washington, D.C.*

Enid Sanford Overbury. See Enid Sanford.

Miss Overmore. See Mrs. Beale Farange.

Merrill Overturf. Diabetic who befriends Fred Trumper in Austria; dies while trying to locate a German tank at the bottom of the Danube River in John Irving's *The Water-Method Man*.

Claire Ovington. Lover of David Kepesh; brings him Shakespeare records and provides him with what sexual pleasure he is capable of in his new form in Philip Roth's *The Breast*.

Doris Owen. Beautiful daughter of Israel and Martha Owen; temporarily attracted to the New York artist Dick Dale, but realizes that country ways suit her best and marries Dan Lester, her lifelong country suitor, in Sarah Orne Jewett's *A Marsh Island*.

Frederick Owen. New rector of St. John's Episcopal Church, eligible bachelor, and suitor of Sara Carroll in Constance Fenimore Woolson's *For the Major*.

Martha (Marthy) Owen. Wife of Israel Owen I and mother of Doris Owen and Israel Owen II; yearned for an exciting life, but learns to accept the life of the farm, in Sarah Orne Jewett's *A Marsh Island*.

Israel Owen (I). Elderly New England farmer who is the husband of Martha Owen and the father of Doris Owen and Israel Owen II; fights to maintain the farm and his own equanimity despite his grief over the death of his son in Sarah Orne Jewett's *A Marsh Island*.

Israel Owen (II). Son of Israel Owen I and Martha Owen; killed in the Civil War in Sarah Orne Jewett's *A Marsh Island*.

Barclay (Julius Caesar) Owens. American army captain fascinated with the ruins of Julius Caesar's camps, one of which he discovered, in Willa Cather's *One of Ours*.

Owl Eyes. Alcoholic guest at Jay Gatsby's parties in F. Scott Fitzgerald's *The Great Gatsby*.

Rachel Owlglass. Former lover of Benny Profane; helps pay for plastic surgery for her roommate, Esther Harvitz, in Thomas Pynchon's *V.*

Willy (Owlie) Owls. Manager of Curny Finnley in John Clellon Holmes's *The Horn*.

Gretchen Shurz Oxencroft. Mother of Paul Hammer; gives him his fanatical crucifixion mission in John Cheever's *Bullet Park*.

Oxie. See Ted Pape.

Oyp. Ancient Egyptian tomb robber in a dream had by Alexander Main in *The Bailbondsman*, a novella in Stanley Elkin's *Searches and Seizures*.

P

Widow Paarlenberg. Neighbor of Pervus and Selina DeJong; marries Klaas Pool in Edna Ferber's *So Big*.

Pablo. Leader of a partisan group that Robert Jordan leads in bridge blowing in Ernest Hemingway's *For Whom the Bell Tolls*.

Eddy Pace. Leader of a combo at Happy's Café in Gayl Jones's *Corregidora*.

Walter Pach. Translator of *History of Art* in Henry Miller's *Tropic of Cancer*.

Pacifica. Young Spanish prostitute from Panama who becomes the intimate friend and companion of Frieda Copperfield in Jane Bowles's *Two Serious Ladies*.

Clarissa Gray (Clara) Packard. Wife of Edward Packard; advocates women's relief from homemaking duties; narrator of Caroline Gilman's *Recollections of a Housekeeper*.

Edward Packard. Husband of Clarissa Packard; attorney who sympathizes with his wife's domestic problems in Caroline Gilman's *Recollections of a Housekeeper*.

Ralph Packer. Producer of underground films who moves to Greenwich Village in John Irving's *The Water-Method Man*.

Jack Packerton. Police captain and commander of West Valley Station in Los Angeles; unsatisfactory lover of Natalie Zimmerman in Joseph Wambaugh's *The Black Marble*.

Judith Paddock. Meddling wife of Zeno Paddock in James Kirke Paulding's *Westward Ho!*

Zeno Paddock. Busybody schoolmaster and editor in James Kirke Paulding's *Westward Ho!*

Paddy. Speakeasy proprietor in Nathan Asch's *Pay Day*.

Manny Padilla. Skinny Mexican who attends Crane College with Augie March; employs Augie as a textbook thief and helps him rescue Mimi Villars from near death after her visit to an abortionist in Saul Bellow's *The Adventures of Augie March*.

Paduk (Toad, Leader). Former schoolmate and adversary of Adam Krug; ruler of the totalitarian nightmare state and head of the Ekwilist party who tries to force Krug to accept the regime publicly, but fails in Vladimir Nabokov's *Bend Sinister*.

Luis Pagan. Spanish dancer who brings Ideal a daily cup of coffee; she seduces him in Carlene Hatcher Polite's *The Flagellants*.

Anson Page. Lawyer for a New York publishing company who must solve a complicated puzzle of missing royalties when he returns home to Pompey's Head, South Carolina, in Hamilton Basso's *The View from Pompey's Head*.

Ariah Page. Long-suffering wife of James Page and mother of Richard Page; understands how Richard accidentally caused the death of Horace Abbott, but cannot explain to her husband in John Gardner's *October Light*.

Clair (Miss Page) Page. Prostitute and former high school teacher whose juju frees and protects Bill Kelsey in Hal Bennett's *Seventh Heaven*.

Clara Page. Widowed cousin of Amory Blaine in F. Scott Fitzgerald's *This Side of Paradise*.

Evelyn Page. Widowed, overprotective mother of Norman Page, whom she dominates and stifles, in Grace Metalious's *Peyton Place*.

James L. Page. Seventy-three-year-old conservative Vermonter who threatens the life of his nonconformist sister, Sally Page Abbott, but eventually relents when he realizes how, by being too intimidating, he has caused the suicide of his son, Richard Page, in John Gardner's *October Light*.

Meg Page. Wife of Anson Page in Hamilton Basso's *The View from Pompey's Head*.

Norman Page. Shy and sheltered only son of Evelyn Page; childhood sweetheart of Allison MacKenzie in Grace Metalious's *Peyton Place*.

Richard Page. Son of James Page; commits suicide because his father's demands make him feel inadequate in John Gardner's *October Light*.

Rollin Page. Brother of Virginia Page and idle young clubman recently converted to Christianity in Charles M. Sheldon's *In His Steps*.

Virginia Page. Local heiress who finances a settlement house in Charles M. Sheldon's *In His Steps*.

Aristide Pailleron. Money-hungry white French professor who marries Teresa Cary in Jessie Redmon Fauset's *Comedy, American Style*.

Nerissa Paine. Night-nurse for John Laskell in Lionel Trilling's *The Middle of the Journey*.

Thomas Paine. English craftsman who migrates to America, where his passion for liberty and freedom for all men forces him to write such inflammatory works as *Common Sense*, *The Rights of Man*, and *The Age of Reason*, which aid the revolutionary cause, in Howard Fast's *Citizen Tom Paine*.

Adelaide Painter. American woman living in Paris for thirty years who remains avidly hostile to Gallic culture in Edith Wharton's *The Reef*.

Clara Morison Paisley. Aunt of Robert and Peter Morison; James Morison briefly considers allowing her to rear his sons upon the death of his wife in William Maxwell's *They Came Like Swallows*.

Palalakonuh. See Great World Snake.

Doctor Palas. Mexican physician stationed at Kulacan in Anaïs Nin's *Seduction of the Minotaur*.

Faith Paleologus. Housekeeper for John Bonnyfeather; seduces Anthony Adverse; lover of Marquis da Vincitata in Hervey Allen's *Anthony Adverse*.

Michael (Mike) Palgrave. See Morris Cohen.

Annie Palmer. Teacher who sells books for Sidney Wyeth and falls in love with him in Oscar Micheaux's *The Forged Note*.

Freddie Palmer. New York hoodlum and pimp and later a wealthy politician; takes Susan Lenox to Europe as his consort; out of jealousy he causes the death of his friend and Lenox's mentor, Robert Brent, in David Graham Phillips's *Susan Lenox*.

Mildred Palmer. Upper-class woman whom Alice Adams believes to be her closest friend; breaks the friendship because Alice is too affected in Booth Tarkington's *Alice Adams*.

Barbara Palmer, Lady Castlemaine. Cousin of the Duke of Buckingham and magnificently cunning mistress of Charles II; uses her influence and her beauty to attack her enemies and defend her position at Court in Kathleen Winsor's *Forever Amber*.

Carl Dean Palmers. Student and follower of Eleanor Norton; falls in love with Elaine Collins in Robert Coover's *The Origin of the Brunists*.

Mariana Paloma. Virginal Mexican waitress who becomes the fiancée of Serge Duran in Joseph Wambaugh's *The New Centurions*.

Pamphilus. Son of Simo and Sostrata; supposed to marry Philumena, but falls under the influence of Chrysis and in love with Glycerium; his introspective nature marks him as a Christian in a pre-Christian era in Thornton Wilder's *The Woman of Andros*.

Alexis Pan. Outrageous futurist poet with whom Sebastian Knight travels on a poetry-reading tour in

Vladimir Nabokov's *The Real Life of Sebastian Knight*.

William (Pinky) Panck. Soldier and follower of Johnny Church and Thankful Perkins; condemned to death for mutiny but spared in Cromwell's blanket pardon in Mary Lee Settle's *Prisons*.

Pancras. Homosexual superior at Remsen Park whose attempt to seduce Coverly Wapshot leads to Wapshot's doubts about his own sexual identity in John Cheever's *The Wapshot Chronicle*.

Pani. Blind guide on Maramma in Herman Melville's *Mardi*.

Reb Yidel Pankower. Rabbi who discovers David Schearl's intellect in Henry Roth's *Call It Sleep*.

Paoli (The Books Says Paoli). Sergeant who turns Richard Mast in for the pistol Mast possesses in James Jones's *The Pistol*.

Paolo. Italian servant of Theodore Colville in William Dean Howells's *Indian Summer*.

Paolo. Narcissistic gigolo who claims he loves Mrs. Karen Stone but runs off with an American film actress in Tennessee Williams's *The Roman Spring of Mrs. Stone*.

Papa. Father of Chantal and Pascal and husband of Honorine; plans to kill himself, Chantal, and his closest friend, Henri, by crashing the car he is driving into a stone barn; narrator of John Hawkes's *Travesty*.

Cora Smith Papadakis. Seductive wife of Nick Papadakis and lover of Frank Chambers, who helps Cora murder Nick; dies in an automobile accident in James M. Cain's *The Postman Always Rings Twice*.

Nick (the Greek) Papadakis. Restaurant owner murdered by his wife Cora and her lover Frank Chambers in James M. Cain's *The Postman Always Rings Twice*.

Nicholas (Nick, Pappy, the Greek) Papadoupalous. Restaurant owner whose scruples are questionable but who shows compassion for his ailing wife and for the Reverend MacCarland Sumpter in Robert Penn Warren's *The Cave*.

Ted (Oxie, Theodorik Paparikis) Pape. Gimlet Street pimp and hustler who has become a bail bondsman and attempts to become a political force in Fred Chappell's *The Gaudy Place*.

Alphonse (Al) Paquette. Bartender at the Thunder Bay Inn who sees Frederic Manion shoot Barney

Quill; although he testifies for the prosecution, his testimony helps Manion in Robert Traver's *Anatomy of a Murder*.

Sal Paradise. Disenchanted writer whose idealism and dreams of travel are rekindled by Dean Moriarty; narrator of Jack Kerouac's *On the Road*.

May Parcher. Daughter of Mr. Parcher; hosts Miss Lola Pratt for a summer; encourages her male acquaintances in their pursuit of Miss Pratt in Booth Tarkington's *Seventeen*.

Mr. Parcher. Father of May Parcher; his peaceful home life is shattered by the arrival of the simpering Miss Lola Pratt in Booth Tarkington's *Seventeen*.

William (Will) Parchment. Mate on the *Lillias Eden*, an old-timer and fairly good sailor, but a poor pilot; dies when the boat wrecks on Misteriosa Reef in Peter Matthiessen's *Far Tortuga*.

Doctor Parcival. Slovenly physician whose affected contempt for humanity leads him to disregard the young victim of a carriage accident in Sherwood Anderson's *Winesburg, Ohio*.

Pard. Friend of the narrator and of Trout Fishing in America; former machine-gunner and existentialist; lives with his girlfriend, the narrator, and the narrator's "woman" in the California bush in Richard Brautigan's *Trout Fishing in America*.

Theron Pardee. Former Union military captain who settles and establishes a law practice near Horsford County; belongs to the board that registers freedmen as voters, advises the Red Wing settlement, and serves as Hesden Le Moyne's agent in searching for the rightful owner of Mulberry Hill plantation in Albion W. Tourgee's *Bricks without Straw*.

Matthias Pardon. Journalist who proposes marriage to Verena Tarrant in Henry James's *The Bostonians*.

Cargile Parham. Physician and father of Sallie Parham in Jesse Hill Ford's *The Raider*.

Sallie Parham. Daughter of Cargile Parham and wife and widow of Willy McCutcheon in Jesse Hill Ford's *The Raider*.

Paris. Lover of Helen; his spirit appears to her in Egypt in H. D.'s *Helen in Egypt*.

Paris. Lover of Helen; killed in the Trojan War in John Erskine's *The Private Life of Helen of Troy*.

Memo Paris. Niece of Pop Fisher, lover of Bump Baily, and lover who sells out Roy Hobbs to Judge Banner in Bernard Malamud's *The Natural*.

Florence Udney Parish. Early love of Anthony Adverse; after being widowed, becomes Adverse's first wife; dies in a fire in Hervey Allen's *Anthony Adverse*.

Walter Parish. Retired New England sea captain; cousin and close friend of Miss Anna Prince in Sarah Orne Jewett's *A Country Doctor*.

Adeline (Addie) Parker. Teenaged granddaughter murdered by Clotilda Pilgrim; daughter of Ruby Parker and lover of Dunreith Smith in Cyrus Colter's *The Rivers of Eros*.

A. Hopkins Parker. Former student at Devon School who set a school swimming record that Finny later breaks unofficially in John Knowles's *A Separate Peace*.

Charles Parker. Cousin who commits Spiros Antonapoulos to an insane asylum in Carson McCullers's *The Heart Is a Lonely Hunter*.

Doc Parker. Operator of a health institute racket who helps his friend Roy Earle arrange for an operation on Velma Goodhue's clubfoot in William Riley Burnett's *High Sierra*.

Lester Parker. Grandson of Clotilda Pilgrim; watches the decline of his grandmother and his sister, Addie Parker, in Cyrus Colter's *The Rivers of Eros*.

Miss Laura Parker. High school teacher who persuades the family of Clay-Boy Spencer to allow him to try for a scholarship at the University of Richmond in Earl Hamner, Jr.'s *Spencer's Mountain*.

Mark Parker. American journalist friend of Kitty Fremont and David Ben Ami; breaks the story of children escaping to Israel on the *Exodus* in Leon Uris's *Exodus*.

Red Parker. Heavy-drinking salesman and widower whose apartment Bob Slocum uses for extramarital affairs; fired by Slocum in Joseph Heller's *Something Happened*.

Richard Parker. Mutineer who is spared when Arthur Gordon Pym, Augustus Barnard, and Dirk Peters retake the *Grampus*; when the group is adrift on the foundering vessel, he is cannibalized by his companions in Edgar Allan Poe's *The Narrative of Arthur Gordon Pym*.

Ruby Parker. Daughter of Clotilda Pilgrim and Chester Jackson, wife of Zack Parker, and mother of Addie and Lester Parker; murdered by Zack in Cyrus Colter's *The Rivers of Eros*.

Zack Parker. Auto mechanic, philanderer, and murderer of his wife, Ruby Parker, in Cyrus Colter's *The Rivers of Eros*.

Francois Parmentier. See Bebe Chicago.

Charles Stewart Parnell. Rich Protestant landowner; Irish anarchist and supporter of Irish Catholic causes in Leon Uris's *Trinity*.

Alison Parr. Estranged daughter of Eldon Parr and wife of John Hodder; independent and spirited architect in Winston Churchill's *The Inside of the Cup*.

Burt Parr. Filling station attendant and husband of Mollie Tyndale, until the marriage is annulled; tied to a tree and severely beaten in Mari Sandoz's *Capital City*.

Eldon Parr. Hypocritical church layman and viciously rapacious businessman; father of Alison and Preston Parr in Winston Churchill's *The Inside of the Cup*.

Preston Parr. Sensitive son of Eldon Parr; driven to alcoholism and death by his father in Winston Churchill's *The Inside of the Cup*.

Eva Parrington. Spinster cousin of Harry and Amy; Latin teacher devoted to women's suffrage in Katherine Anne Porter's *Old Mortality*.

Zed Parrum. Rustic hillman and close friend of Abner Teeftallow in T. S. Stribling's *Teeftallow*.

Al Parsons. See Alexander Portnoy.

Erleen Parsons. Wife of Henry Parsons; submits to sexual assault by Willie Joe Worth so she can win her husband's release from jail in Jesse Hill Ford's *The Liberation of Lord Byron Jones*.

Henry Parsons. Husband of Erleen Parsons falsely accused of public drunkenness and resisting arrest; later, in despair and humiliation, kills his son in Jesse Hill Ford's *The Liberation of Lord Byron Jones*.

Parthenia. Large yellow woman in a San Antonio red-light district and Augie's first date in Arna Wendell Bontemps's *God Sends Sunday*.

Parthenia (Partheny). Black nurse to the Fairchild children; invited to attend Dabney Fairchild's wedding in Eudora Welty's *Delta Wedding*.

Mrs. Seth Parton. See Mrs. Herman Muller.

Seth Parton. Union officer and friend of Tobias Sears; Amantha Starr falls in love with him before she marries Sears, but Parton rejects her in Robert Penn Warren's *Band of Angels*.

Pascal. Son of Papa and Honorine and younger brother of Chantal; dies from undisclosed causes in John Hawkes's *Travesty*.

Karl Pascal. Car mechanic and Communist; shares a concentration camp jail cell with Doremus Jessup in Sinclair Lewis's *It Can't Happen Here*.

Alexander Pascaleo. Italian Catholic friend and roommate of Marshall Pearl at Harvard University; rides the railroads with Pearl and works with him in a St. Louis meat packing plant in Mark Helprin's *Refiner's Fire*.

Eugénie Pasdemon. Aging Parisian actress snubbed by the Chatelaine in Henry Blake Fuller's *The Chatelaine of La Trinité*.

Paskingoe (One-eye). Mohawk chief in James Kirke Paulding's *The Dutchman's Fireside*.

Tony (Antonio Passalacqua) Passa. Youthful member of the Vettori mob who drives for holdups; killed by Rico Bandello in William Riley Burnett's *Little Caesar*.

Gene Pasternak. Writer who impregnates Christine and has an affair with Kathryn Hobbes in John Clellon Holmes's *Go*.

Father Pasziewski. Priest of Queenie Craven; prays on Fridays for George Brush; following Pasziewski's death, Brush receives a silver spoon from him in the mail in Thornton Wilder's *Heaven's My Destination*.

Pat. Black ex-college student in Copenhagen who wants money for an abortion in Cecil Brown's *The Life and Loves of Mr. Jiveass Nigger*.

Pat. Friend and heroin connection of William Lee in New Orleans in William S. Burroughs's *Junkie*.

Pat. Woman friend of Jimmy Low; discusses jazz and recipes in the taped conversations of Jack Kerouac's *Visions of Cody*.

Adam J. Patch. Multimillionaire reformist grandfather of Anthony Patch; disinherits Anthony in F. Scott Fitzgerald's *The Beautiful and Damned*.

Anthony Patch. Alcoholic dilettante who undergoes a process of deterioration while waiting for his inheritance in F. Scott Fitzgerald's *The Beautiful and Damned*.

Gloria Gilbert Patch. Pleasure-seeking wife of Anthony Patch in F. Scott Fitzgerald's *The Beautiful and Damned*.

Lillian Patch. Middle-class Harlem school teacher engaged to Max Reddick; frightened of the uncertainties of marriage to a writer in John A. Williams's *The Man Who Cried I Am.*

Mr. Patch-Withers. Substitute headmaster for the special summer session at Devon School in John Knowles's *A Separate Peace.*

Pathfinder. See Nathaniel Bumppo.

Ben Patimkin. Prosperous businessman and indulgent father of Brenda, Ron, and Julie Patimkin in Philip Roth's *Goodbye, Columbus.*

Brenda (Bren, Buck) Patimkin. Radcliffe student and lover of Neil Klugman; their affair ends when her parents discover her diaphragm in Philip Roth's *Goodbye, Columbus.*

Julie Patimkin. Spoiled younger sister of Brenda Patimkin in Philip Roth's *Goodbye, Columbus.*

Leo A. Patimkin. Lightbulb salesman and half brother of Ben Patimkin; confides in Neil Klugman in Philip Roth's *Goodbye, Columbus.*

Ronald (Ron) Patimkin. Athletic older brother of Brenda Patimkin; marries Harriet Ehrlich in Philip Roth's *Goodbye, Columbus.*

Henry (Pat) Patmore. Owner of a pool parlor and saloon who deals in illegal gambling and bootlegging in Rudolph Fisher's *The Walls of Jericho*; also appears in *The Conjure-Man Dies.*

Patricia (Pat). School teacher and lover of John; with John, downstairs neighbor of Constance Marlow and Bob and finder of the Logan brothers' bowling trophies in Richard Brautigan's *Willard and His Bowling Trophies.*

Michael Patrick. Lost, wandering soldier who attends a performance of *La Bohème* and searches for love in John Horne Burns's *The Gallery.*

Ferd Pattee. Salesman and frequent drinker in Henry Miller's *Black Spring.*

Bankey (Zack) Patterson. Old black man who meets Forrest Mayfield just after Forrest has been rejected by his wife, Eva Kendal, in Reynolds Price's *The Surface of Earth.*

Camack Patterson. Memphis lawyer, cousin who introduces Eleanor Fite to Gratt Shafer, and best man at their wedding in Jesse Hill Ford's *Mountains of Gilead.*

Jack Patterson. English professor and regular guest on the late-night radio show hosted by Dick Gibson; tells of his infatuation with a child singing star in Stanley Elkin's *The Dick Gibson Show.*

Louise Patterson. Artist who is admired and collected by George Stroud and who can identify Stroud as the missing witness; a narrator of Kenneth Fearing's *The Big Clock.*

Pattie Mae. Philo Skinner's assistant; a tyro dog handler in Joseph Wambaugh's *The Black Marble.*

Paul. Less-than-princely prince killed by a poisoned Vodka Gibson meant for Snow White in Donald Barthelme's *Snow White.*

Paul. Ranch owner who employs his neighbor Johnny Mack in Edwin Corle's *Fig Tree John.*

Paul. See Paul Melia.

Paul. See Typee.

Paul. Seventeen-year-old boy who is trapped by his parents; becomes the lover of Djuna in Anaïs Nin's *Children of the Albatross* and *The Four-Chambered Heart.*

Paul. Son of Lillian in Anaïs Nin's *Ladders to Fire.*

Father Paul. French Catholic missionary on Manukura who shelters Terangi; dies in his church during the hurricane before learning that he has been ordered back to France in Charles Nordhoff and James Norman Hall's *The Hurricane.*

Melissa Paul. Illegitimate cousin of Laurentine Strange; does not know she is the half sister of her boyfriend Malory Forten in Jessie Redmon Fauset's *The Chinaberry Tree.*

Lieutenant (jg) Ed Pauley. Special friend who shares Mr. Roberts's dislike of Captain Morton in Thomas Heggen's *Mister Roberts.*

Pauline. Concert pianist and lover of George Levanter in Jerzy Kosinski's *Blind Date.*

Amanda Pauling. Spinster sister of Jeremy Pauling; narrates part of Anne Tyler's *Celestial Navigation.*

Jeremy Pauling. Artist and agoraphobic; common-law husband of Mary Tell and father of five of her six children in Anne Tyler's *Celestial Navigation.*

Mary Pauling. See Mary Tell.

Wilma Pauling. Mother of Jeremy Pauling and owner of a boardinghouse in Anne Tyler's *Celestial Navigation.*

Pavel and Peter. Immigrants who left Russia in shame for having sacrificed a bride, bridegroom, and other friends to wolves in order to save themselves in Willa Cather's *My Ántonia.*

Katherine Lacey Pawling. See Katherine Lacey.

Clive (Old Man) Paxton. Father of Kathleen Paxton Hodge; so opposes her marriage to Taggert Hodge that he drives her into an institution; Taggert strangles him in revenge in John Gardner's *The Sunlight Dialogues.*

Joe Paxton. Black writer and resident of a Thirteenth Street building managed by Norman Moonbloom in Edward Lewis Wallant's *The Tenants of Moonbloom.*

Jerry (Boomaga) Payne. Introvert-turned-extrovert boyfriend of Pookie Adams; narrator of John Nichols's *The Sterile Cuckoo.*

Marcus (Marky) Payne. Intransigent young black man awaiting trial for murder; quietly defies racial taboos by having an affair with the wife of Sidney Bonbon; eventually killed by Bonbon in Ernest J. Gaines's *Of Love and Dust.*

Nicholas Payne. Young man who travels west on his motorcycle; falls in love with Ann Fitzgerald and helps C. J. Clovis build bat towers; operated on for hemorrhoids in Thomas McGuane's *The Bushwhacked Piano.*

Ensign Paynter. Assistant communications officer on the USS *Caine* in Herman Wouk's *The Caine Mutiny.*

Lucius Quintus Peabody. Physician in William Faulkner's *Sartoris (Flags in the Dust), The Sound and the Fury, As I Lay Dying, The Hamlet, The Town,* and *The Reivers.*

Eddie Peace. Small-time Hollywood actor with whom Marge Converse and Ray Hicks hide in Robert Stone's *Dog Soldiers.*

Eva (Pearl) Peace. Grandmother of Sula Peace and mother of Hannah and Plum Peace; owner of a boardinghouse in Toni Morrison's *Sula.*

Hannah Peace. Mother of Sula Peace and daughter of Eva Peace; dies from wounds suffered in a yard fire in Toni Morrison's *Sula.*

Ralph (Plum) Peace. Son of Eva Peace and brother of Hannah Peace; burned by his mother because of his excessive drug use in Toni Morrison's *Sula.*

Sula Peace. Daughter of Hannah Peace and granddaughter of Eva Peace; heroine engaged in the struggle for self-identity in Toni Morrison's *Sula.*

Calvin Peachtree. Black police detective in Thomas Berger's *Who Is Teddy Villanova?*

Luther Peacock. Deputy of Buddy Matlow; murdered by Joe Lon Mackey in Harry Crews's *A Feast of Snakes.*

Simeon Peake. Father of Selina Peake DeJong; gambler who is killed by a woman who intends to kill another man in Edna Ferber's *So Big.*

Maureen (Meringue Pie) Peal. Mulatto schoolgirl enviously nicknamed by Claudia and Frieda MacTeer in Toni Morrison's *The Bluest Eye.*

Pear Blossom. Young slave who becomes Wang Lung's mistress in Pearl Buck's *The Good Earth;* after Wang Lung's death, she cares for his and O-lan's retarded daughter; following the daughter's death, she enters a nunnery in *Sons.*

Pearl. Illegitimate daughter of Hester Prynne and Arthur Dimmesdale in Nathaniel Hawthorne's *The Scarlet Letter.*

Marshall Pearl. Son of Katrina Perlé and Lev, but orphaned and adopted by the Livingstons; inherits "visions" from his mother; mortally wounded while fighting the Syrians at Daughters of Jacob Bridge in Israel in Mark Helprin's *Refiner's Fire.*

Alf Pearson. White plantation owner and reputed real father of John Buddy Pearson in Zora Neale Hurston's *Jonah's Gourd Vine.*

Bruce William Pearson, Jr. Third-string catcher for the New York Mammoths and roommate of Henry Wiggen; learns he is dying of Hodgkin's disease in Mark Harris's *Bang the Drum Slowly.*

Captain Pearson. Captain of the *Serapis* who surrenders to John Paul Jones in order to stop the carnage in Herman Melville's *Israel Potter.*

Hattie Pearson. See Hattie Tyson.

James (Jamie) Pearson. Former lover of Hattie Sherbrooke in Nicholas Delbanco's *Possession.*

John Pearson. Elderly one-legged basketmaker and veteran of the War of 1812 who houses Shocky Thomson rather than see him bound over to a cruel master; falsely accused of aiding robbers in Edward Eggleston's *The Hoosier School-Master.*

John Buddy Pearson. Baptist preacher, carpenter, mayor of Eatonville, Florida, philandering husband of Lucy Potts, and hero of Zora Neale Hurston's *Jonah's Gourd Vine.*

Lucy Pearson. See Lucy Ann Potts.

Ray Pearson. Winesburg farmhand who is forced to evaluate the frustrated goals of his life when a younger worker asks him for advice in Sherwood Anderson's *Winesburg, Ohio.*

Thomas J. (Tub) Pearson. President of the Centaur State Bank and best friend of Sam Dodsworth in Sinclair Lewis's *Dodsworth.*

Curtis G. Peavey. Lawyer who plans to marry Roxy; accuses Chester Pomeroy of perversion in Thomas McGuane's *Panama.*

Caleb Peck. Musician and long-lost half brother of Daniel Peck; great-uncle of Duncan and Justine Peck and the object of the search in Anne Tyler's *Searching for Caleb.*

Caroline Peck. See Caroline Peck Mayhew.

Daniel (Judge Peck) Peck. Straight-backed and strait-laced grandfather of Justine and Duncan Peck and half brother of the missing Caleb Peck in Anne Tyler's *Searching for Caleb.*

Duncan Peck. Jack-of-all-trades given to wanderlust; grandson of Daniel Peck, husband of Justine Peck, and father of Meg Peck in Anne Tyler's *Searching for Caleb.*

Idella Peck. Infant daughter of Rev. Julius W. Peck; adopted by Annie Kilburn following her father's death in William Dean Howells's *Annie Kilburn.*

Jim Peck. Hippie who intrudes on Joe Allston's property and becomes Allston's intellectual foe in Wallace Stegner's *All the Little Live Things.*

Rev. Julius W. Peck. Liberal minister who stirs up the community and precipitates Annie Kilburn's social and moral awakening in William Dean Howells's *Annie Kilburn.*

Justine Peck. Fortuneteller; granddaughter and fellow-searcher of Daniel Peck, wife and cousin of Duncan Peck, and mother of Meg Peck in Anne Tyler's *Searching for Caleb.*

Meg Peck. See Margaret Rose Peck Milsom.

General P. P. Peckem. Rival of General Dreedle; scorned by ex-P.F.C. Wintergreen, who judges Peckem's prose pretentious and prolix, in Joseph Heller's *Catch-22.*

Peckover. Man who works for a newspaper and part time in a dentist's office to pay for his false teeth; saves cigarette butts to smoke in his pipe in Henry Miller's *Tropic of Cancer.*

Frederich Pedersen. Child musical prodigy; son of Karl and Mary Pedersen and brother of the adopted Jesse Harte in Joyce Carol Oates's *Wonderland.*

Hilda Pedersen. Child mathematics prodigy; daughter of Karl and Mary Pedersen and sister of the adopted Jesse Harte in Joyce Carol Oates's *Wonderland.*

Jesse Pedersen. See Jesse Harte.

Dr. Karl Pedersen. Demonic diagnostic physician who adopts the boy Jesse Harte and attempts to mold him in his own image in Joyce Carol Oates's *Wonderland.*

Marsha Pedersen. Graduate English student who shares a flight and a motel room with Jane Clifford in Gail Godwin's *The Odd Woman.*

Mary Pedersen. Subservient wife of Dr. Karl Pedersen and mother of Frederich and Hilda Pedersen; attempts, along with her adopted son, Jesse Harte, to escape her husband's control in Joyce Carol Oates's *Wonderland.*

Samanthetie Pedigo. Wild young girl whom other children view with suspicion; occasional student of Louisa Sheridan in Harriette Simpson Arnow's *Mountain Path.*

John Abner Pedlar. Clubfooted son of Nathan Pedlar in Ellen Glasgow's *Barren Ground.*

Lena Pedlar. Daughter of Nathan Pedlar; appears to be oversexed and weak-minded in Ellen Glasgow's *Barren Ground.*

Nathan Pedlar. Tall, homely man who reminds Dorinda Oakley of her father; becomes Dorinda's partner and husband in Ellen Glasgow's *Barren Ground.*

Rose Emily Milford Pedlar. First wife of Nathan Pedlar and teacher of Dorinda Oakley; faces death with illusions in Ellen Glasgow's *Barren Ground.*

Hester Pedlock. Sister-in-law and housekeeper for Andrew Mackerel; successful rival of Molly Calico for his hand in marriage in Peter De Vries's *The Mackerel Plaza.*

Jill Peel. Friend of Joe Percy and lover of Owen Oarson; former animation artist who becomes a Hollywood film director; narrates part of Larry McMurtry's *Somebody's Darling*; lover of Daniel Deck in *All My Friends Are Going to Be Strangers.*

John Peel. Tutor of Sophia Grieve Ryder whom he impregnates and marries; father of Wendell Ryder in Djuna Barnes's *Ryder.*

Beverly Peele. Lover and then husband of Patience Sparhawk; dies from an overdose of morphine in Gertrude Atherton's *Patience Sparhawk and Her Times.*

Harriet (Hal) Peele. Sister of Beverly Peele and friend and sister-in-law of Patience Sparhawk in Gertrude Atherton's *Patience Sparhawk and Her Times*.

Patience Sparhawk Peele. See Patience Sparhawk.

Peepi. Boy ruler of Valapee in Herman Melville's *Mardi*.

Francine Pefko. Secretary and mistress of Dwayne Hoover in Kurt Vonnegut's *Breakfast of Champions*.

Peg-leg. Morgue attendant who helps C. Card steal the corpse of a murdered prostitute in Richard Brautigan's *Dreaming of Babylon*.

Father Peitsch. Catholic priest who is critical of Preston Robinson's method of teaching in August Derleth's *The Shield of the Valiant*.

Peleg. An owner of the *Pequod* in Herman Melville's *Moby-Dick*.

Pelican. Assistant surgeon aboard the *Neversink* in Herman Melville's *White-Jacket*.

Dorothy (Doll) Pelky. Woman devoted to Dix Handley in William Riley Burnett's *The Asphalt Jungle*.

Master Sergeant Dominic (Danny) Pellerino. Crew chief for General Ira N. Beal; a seasoned enlisted veteran in James Gould Cozzens's *Guard of Honor*.

Dorothea O'Faye Pelley. See Dorothea O'Faye.

Miss Pemberton. White prostitute, sex show manager, and former civil rights worker in Hal Bennett's *The Black Wine* and *Wait Until the Evening*.

Sir Arthur (Pem) Pembroke. Rival of John Law for the love of Lady Catharine Knollys; killed by Indians in Emerson Hough's *The Mississippi Bubble*.

Harry Pena. Virile fisherman in Kurt Vonnegut's *God Bless You, Mr. Rosewater*.

Pender. Sergeant who allows Richard Mast to keep the pistol he possesses in James Jones's *The Pistol*.

Garrett Pendergass (Pendergrass). Owner of a frontier tavern and store who befriends Salathiel Albine; appears in Hervey Allen's *The Forest and the Fort* and *Bedford Village*.

Rose Pendergass. Wife of Garrett Pendergass in Hervey Allen's *The Forest and the Fort* and *Bedford Village*.

Leonora (The Lady) Penderton. Nominal wife of Captain Weldon Penderton and lover of Major Morris Langdon; bored with military life in Carson McCullers's *Reflections in a Golden Eye*.

Capt. Weldon (Captain Flap-Fanny) Penderton. Androgynous, self-tortured husband of Leonora Penderton; both attracted to and fearful of the handsome Private Ellgee Williams in Carson McCullers's *Reflections in a Golden Eye*.

Mr. Pendexter. Retired minister who questions the orthodoxy of Arthur Kavanagh in Henry Wadsworth Longfellow's *Kavanagh*.

Gabriel Pendleton. Former Confederate soldier and father of Virginia Pendleton; mild-mannered preacher who dies while trying to stop a lynching in Ellen Glasgow's *Virginia*.

Jig Pendleton. Superstitiously religious fisherman and drinking partner of Burley Coulter; his life on a shanty boat in the Kentucky River provides low comedy in Wendell Berry's *Nathan Coulter*.

Jill Pendleton. Eighteen-year-old runaway drug addict who comes to live with Rabbit Angstrom as his lover and dies in a fire in John Updike's *Rabbit Redux*.

Lucy Pendleton. Mother of Virginia Pendleton; naive idealist who lives in dignified poverty in Ellen Glasgow's *Virginia*.

Virginia (Jinny) Pendleton. Sentimental, loving, and provincial woman who marries Oliver Treadwell in Ellen Glasgow's *Virginia*.

Mrs. (Mrs. P.) Pendrake. Unfaithful wife of the Reverend Silas Pendrake and adoptive mother of Jack Crabb in Thomas Berger's *Little Big Man*.

Reverend Silas Pendrake. Missouri preacher and adoptive father of Jack Crabb in Thomas Berger's *Little Big Man*.

Julia Peniston. Wealthy widow and paternal aunt with whom Lily Bart lives in Edith Wharton's *The House of Mirth*.

Christine Penmark. Mother of Rhoda Penmark; after discovering that she herself was an adopted child and that her natural mother was a mass murderer, she feels responsible for implanting the "bad seed" in Rhoda; plans Rhoda's murder and commits suicide in William March's *The Bad Seed*.

Kenneth Penmark. Husband of Christine Penmark and father of Rhoda Penmark; devastated when he returns from South America to find that his wife committed suicide and tried to kill their daughter in William March's *The Bad Seed*.

Rhoda Penmark. Remorseless eight year old who murders people in order to gain possessions that she thinks are rightly hers in William March's *The Bad Seed.*

Connie Penn. Heterosexual high school classmate of Molly Bolt in Rita Mae Brown's *Rubyfruit Jungle.*

Elton Penn. Kentucky subsistence farmer and surrogate son of Jack Beechum; manages Beechum's land with the vision of responsible stewardship that Beechum's daughter, Clara Pettit, lacks in Wendell Berry's *The Memory of Old Jack.*

Mary Penn. Good-hearted wife of Elton Penn; her reliable country sensibility represents the values prized in Wendell Berry's *The Memory of Old Jack.*

Lavinia Sloper Penniman. Widowed sister of Austin Sloper and romantic, foolish aunt of Catherine Sloper; secretly encourages Morris Townsend's suit of Catherine in Henry James's *Washington Square.*

Lucretia Penniman. Author, teacher, and crusader for women's rights; friend of Cynthia Wetherell in Winston Churchill's *Coniston.*

Rose Timberlane Pennloss. Sister of Cass Timberlane in Sinclair Lewis's *Cass Timberlane.*

Pennoyer (Penny). Penniless artist; shares an apartment with Billie Hawker in Stephen Crane's *The Third Violet.*

John Penny. Gruff city editor of the *Morning Journal* who gives Homer Zigler his first newspaper job in Clyde Brion Davis's *"The Great American Novel–."*

Julius Penrose. Coldly rational lawyer crippled by polio; partner and friend of Arthur Winner in James Gould Cozzens's *By Love Possessed.*

Marjorie Penrose. Alcoholic, emotional woman of disturbing sexuality; wife of Julius Penrose; has had an affair with Arthur Winner and intends to convert to Catholicism in James Gould Cozzens's *By Love Possessed.*

Jarcey Pentacost. Quaker, printer, and friend of Johnny Lacey; transported to Virginia as a felon and there begins to publish a newspaper; moves to Beulah as settler, school teacher, and second in command after being burned out by the Kreggs for supporting the proclamation closing Indian lands to settlers in Mary Lee Settle's *O Beulah Land.*

Mary Martha O'Keefe Pentacost. See Mary Martha O'Keefe.

Will Pentacost. Friend of Johnny Church and Thankful Perkins; whipped and chased naked through the streets of Burford the night Cromwell's men round up dissenters in Mary Lee Settle's *Prisons.*

Lew Pentecost. Rival comedian engaged in a staged feud with Harry Mercury in Peter De Vries's *Through the Fields of Clover.*

Bascom Pentland. Scholar, retired preacher, and uncle of Eugene Gant in Thomas Wolfe's *Of Time and the River.*

Pepita. Orphan in the Convent of Santa María Rosa de las Rosas; sent by María del Pilar to live with Doña María de Montemayor; dies in the fall of the bridge in Thornton Wilder's *The Bridge of San Luis Rey.*

Dr. Pepper. Expert on drugs who adopts various disguises; visits Bucky Wunderlick in search of a mysterious drug in Don DeLillo's *Great Jones Street.*

Ned (Lucky Ned) Pepper. Leader of an outlaw gang that holds captive Mattie Ross, Rooster Cogburn, and LaBoeuf in Charles Portis's *True Grit.*

Alfred Peracca. Los Angeles judge in the second trial of Gregory Powell and Jimmy Smith; eventually relieved because of a heart condition in Joseph Wambaugh's *The Onion Field.*

Leo (Ti Leo) Percepied. Alcoholic writer and lover of Mardou Fox; narrator of Jack Kerouac's *The Subterraneans.*

Percival. See John.

Senator Lloyd Percival. U.S. Senator with a secret collection of erotic art; investigated by Moll Robbins and is himself investigating PAC/ORD, a government intelligence operation, in Don DeLillo's *Running Dog.*

Bainbridge (Pooh) Percy. Ellen Jamesian who blames T. S. Garp for Cushie Percy's death; after killing Garp and being institutionalized and discharged, she becomes a mother at age fifty-four and works with retarded children in John Irving's *The World According to Garp.*

Cushman (Cushie, Cushion) Percy. Sister of Stewart Percy, Jr., and Pooh, Randolph, and William Percy; T. S. Garp's first sexual partner; dies in childbirth in John Irving's *The World According to Garp.*

Joe Percy. Aging screenwriter and friend of Jill Peel; dies of a stroke; narrates part of Larry McMurtry's *Somebody's Darling.*

Randolph (Dopey) Percy. Brother of Stewart Percy, Jr., and Pooh, Cushman, and William Percy; dies of a heart attack in John Irving's *The World According to Garp.*

Stewart (Fat Stew, Paunch, Stewie) Percy. Father of Stewart Percy, Jr., and William, Randolph, Cushman, and Pooh Percy; history teacher at Steering School; dies of a heart attack in John Irving's *The World According to Garp.*

Stewart (Stewie Two) Percy, Jr. Brother of Cushman, Pooh, Randolph, and William Percy; married and divorced in John Irving's *The World According to Garp.*

William (Shrill Willy) Percy. Brother of Stewart Percy, Jr., and Cushman, Pooh, and Randolph Percy; Yale graduate killed during the war in John Irving's *The World According to Garp.*

Reeny (Reen) Jimson Perdew. Friend and accomplice of Podjo Harris and Rufus Hutton in Shelby Foote's *September September.*

R. G. Perdew. Writer who passes himself off as Ezra Pound in Paul Theroux's *Picture Palace.*

Doc Peret. Pragmatic army medic in Vietnam in Tim O'Brien's *Going after Cacciato.*

Camila (Micaela Villegas) Perichole. Great actress who becomes the mistress of Don Andres de Ribera, by whom she has three children; becomes a recluse after having smallpox in Thornton Wilder's *The Bridge of San Luis Rey.*

Miguel Perigua. Wild and impulsive leader of a group for the union of Pan-Africa and Pan-Asia; plots to wreck a train filled with Ku Klux Klansmen in W. E. B. Du Bois's *Dark Princess.*

Effie Perine. Secretary of Sam Spade in Dashiell Hammett's *The Maltese Falcon.*

Bernard (Bernie) Perk. Pharmacist and regular guest on the late-night radio show hosted by Dick Gibson; tells of his attraction to a female customer with very large genitals in Stanley Elkin's *The Dick Gibson Show.*

Adrien Perkheimer. Jewish tourist photographer; to overcome clichés, he photographs Greece with no film in his camera in Wright Morris's *What a Way to Go.*

Frederick Perkins. American tourist from Detroit who tries to use Samuele to secure entrance to private villas and sites; when he jumps over the wall at the Villa Colonna, he discovers the body of Marcantonio d'Aquilanera in Thornton Wilder's *The Cabala.*

Orville (Flash) Perkins. Uneducated friend of John Wickliff Shawnessy; dies in the Civil War in Ross Lockridge, Jr.'s *Raintree County.*

Peter Perkins. See Israel Potter.

Thankful Perkins. Closest friend of Johnny Church; executed for advocating greater democracy and opposing Cromwell's Irish campaign, but remains pious and trusting throughout, in Mary Lee Settle's *Prisons.*

Kathryn Perl. Attorney who represents Virgil Morgan in Scott Spencer's *Preservation Hall.*

Katrina Perlé. Russian Jew arrested at Riga during World War II; wife of Lev; because she is forgotten by the crew of the *Lindos Transit,* on which she is a passenger, she dies after giving birth to Marshall Pearl in Mark Helprin's *Refiner's Fire.*

Morton (Morty) Perlmutter. Cultural anthropologist and mentor of James Boswell in Stanley Elkin's *Boswell.*

Farrell Permalee. Brother of Harold Permalee and member of Ned Pepper's gang in Charles Portis's *True Grit.*

Harold Permalee. Brother of Farrell Permalee and member of Ned Pepper's gang in Charles Portis's *True Grit.*

Perrault. Elderly Frenchman who makes deceptive card boxes for faro dealers in H. L. Davis's *Beulah Land.*

Dr. Roderick Perrault. Renowned brain surgeon and mentor of Jesse Vogel in Joyce Carol Oates's *Wonderland.*

Mr. Perriam. Odious millionaire lover of Ida Farange during her marriage to Sir Claude in Henry James's *What Maisie Knew.*

Charity M. Perrin. Teacher of Barry Rudd who resists the "sale" of the boy to the United Lymphomilloid Company; harassed by the Committee on Education, Welfare, and Public Morality for her participation in a teachers' strike years before in John Hersey's *The Child Buyer.*

Yolande Perrotti. Schoolmate of Cress Delahanty and house party participant in Jessamyn West's *Cress Delahanty.*

Perry. Houston hustler who befriends then betrays Joe Buck in James Leo Herlihy's *Midnight Cowboy.*

Nathan Perry. Superintendent of an independent mine; supporter of Grant Adams's reforms in William Allen White's *In the Heart of a Fool.*

Dr. Sam Perry. Physician to Colored Town in Maxwell, Georgia; saves Ed Anderson from a lynch mob and is willing to marry Nonnie Anderson after the death of Tracy Deen in Lillian Smith's *Strange Fruit.*

Perseus. Performer of heroic deeds who is now twenty years older, bored, and overweight; narrator of the *Perseid*, a novella in John Barth's *Chimera.*

Mr. de Persia. Miraculous restorer and repairman who escapes his enemies in a balloon, descends by parachute, and discovers the body of Addis Adair in William Goyen's *Come, The Restorer.*

Armande Chamar Person. Daughter of Madame Charles Chamar and wife of Hugh Person, who puts up with her capricious behavior and peculiar sexual proclivities; murdered by her husband as he dreams he is saving her from a fire in Vladimir Nabokov's *Transparent Things.*

Dr. Henry Emery (Person Senior) Person. Father of Hugh Person; dies trying on a pair of trousers in a clothing store in Switzerland while on a trip with his son in Vladimir Nabokov's *Transparent Things.*

Hugh (Percy) Person. Editor for a New York-based publishing house; makes a pilgrimage to Switzerland to find traces of his dead wife, Armande Chamar Person; trip discloses the story of his life and loves and his gradual transformation into someone dwelling in a realm of transparent things in Vladimir Nabokov's *Transparent Things.*

Perta. Female canary who, in Birdy's fantasy, becomes Birdy's mate in William Wharton's *Birdy.*

Perth. Blacksmith aboard the *Pequod* in Herman Melville's *Moby-Dick.*

Pete. Bartender who seduces and deserts Maggie Johnson in Stephen Crane's *Maggie.*

Pete. Brother of Red and blackmailer/lover of Temple Drake in William Faulkner's *Requiem for a Nun.*

Pete. Operator of the gas station where Clyde Stout works; married to an ill-tempered woman in Jack Matthews's *Hanger Stout, Awake!*

M. A. (Medium Asshole) Pete. Assistant to the procurement manager of Pure Pores Filters Company; goes on the Alaskan hunting expedition with Rusty Jethroe in Norman Mailer's *Why Are We in Vietnam?*

Pete (Jake). Owner and bartender at Pete's, favorite bar of J. Henry Waugh, in Robert Coover's *The Universal Baseball Association, Inc., J. Henry Waugh, Prop.*

Pete the Finn. Bootlegger and one of the four criminal bosses in Personville in Dashiell Hammett's *Red Harvest.*

Peter. Handsome sailor aboard the *Neversink* who is flogged for fighting in Herman Melville's *White-Jacket.*

Peter. Lover of Ursula Vanderveenan and oldest friend of Allert Vanderveenan; psychiatrist who dies of a heart attack in his sauna in John Hawkes's *Death, Sleep & the Traveler.*

Peter. See Long Ghost.

Peter. See Pavel and Peter.

Peter. Aged black carriage driver and friend of Porgy; falsely accused of murdering Robbins, until the real murderer is revealed, in DuBose Heyward's *Porgy.*

Peter Sanford (Sandford). Dashing army major who wishes to avenge men's treatment by coquettes through his relationship with Eliza Wharton in Hannah Webster Foster's *The Coquette.*

Cleon (Oil King) Peters. Itinerant preacher in William Goyen's *Come, The Restorer.*

Dirk Peters. Half-breed sailor who befriends Augustus Barnard and Arthur Gordon Pym after the mutiny on the *Grampus*; accompanies Pym on the last half of his journey in Edgar Allan Poe's *The Narrative of Arthur Gordon Pym.*

Harold (Brother Harold) Peters. Member of the Order of St. Clement assigned to do cooking and menial labor at St. Clement's Hill Retreat House in J. F. Powers's *Morte D'Urban.*

Ivy (Poison Ivy) Peters. Cruel, arrogant, and unethical lawyer who uses his relationship with Marian Forrester to advance himself in Willa Cather's *A Lost Lady.*

Lymie Peters. Son of Lymon Peters and best friend of Spud Latham; attempts suicide in William Maxwell's *The Folded Leaf.*

Lymon Peters. Father of Lymie Peters; turns to drink and a transient way of life after the death of his wife and infant daughter in William Maxwell's *The Folded Leaf.*

Mabel Peters. See Mabel Peters Fry.

Rollo Peters. Floor judge for the dance marathon in Horace McCoy's *They Shoot Horses, Don't They?*

Alton Christian Peterson. See Alexander Portnoy.

Carl Peterson. Man whom Dr. Benway turns into a homosexual in William S. Burroughs's *Naked Lunch*; transformed into a woman in *The Soft Machine*; mentioned in *The Ticket That Exploded*.

Harold Peterson. Ambitious actor and playwright married to Kay Leiland Strong in Mary McCarthy's *The Group*.

Melody Oriole-2 von Peterswald. Granddaughter of Wilbur Swain in Kurt Vonnegut's *Slapstick*.

Jenny Petherbridge. Middle-aged American widow who takes Robin Vote from Nora Flood, becomes Robin's lover, and then loses her in Djuna Barnes's *Nightwood*.

Maximilian (Arthur Phillips) Petion. Husband of Christina Jansen; leader in the Brotherhood of Destruction who serves as Gabriel Weltstein's guide to America under the Oligarchy in Ignatius Donnelly's *Caesar's Column*.

Junior Petman. Son of Marvin Petman and adolescent clairvoyant in T. S. Stribling's *Unfinished Cathedral*.

Marvin Petman. Realtor and father of Junior Petman in T. S. Stribling's *Unfinished Cathedral*.

Athanase Petrescu. Rumanian translator of American literature and escort of Henry Bech in Rumania; wears sunglasses everywhere in John Updike's *Bech: A Book*.

Andrew D. Petrie. Charismatic politician and right-wing political theorist whose murder initiates the action of Joyce Carol Oates's *The Assassins*.

Hugh (Hughie) Petrie. Cartoonist brother of Andrew Petrie; his bungled suicide attempt renders him quadriplegic; narrates part of Joyce Carol Oates's *The Assassins*.

J. Adlee Petrie. Liberal high school science teacher and cynic; marries his student Marsan Vaiden and becomes a beneficiary of the Vaiden fortune in T. S. Stribling's *Unfinished Cathedral*.

Mark Petrie. Friend of Ralphie and Daniel Glick; escapes 'Salem's Lot with Ben Mears after Petrie's parents are murdered by the owners of Marsten House in Stephen King's *'Salem's Lot*.

Stephen Petrie. Religious mystic and brother of Andrew Petrie in Joyce Carol Oates's *The Assassins*.

Yvonne Radek Petrie. Wife of slain politician Andrew Petrie; editing and completing her husband's manuscripts, she retreats into a life of intellect and emotional non-involvement in Joyce Carol Oates's *The Assassins*.

Mario (Giuseppe Lodi) Petrone. Convicted murderer who participates in the dance marathon under an assumed name; apprehended by policemen who come to watch the contest in Horace McCoy's *They Shoot Horses, Don't They?*

Petrov. Bulgarian novelist turned playwright; friend of Vera Glavanakova in John Updike's *Bech: A Book*.

Pettecasockee. Chickasaw Indian who follows Elias McCutcheon into the Civil War; son of Shokotee McNeilly and husband of Denise Chatillion in Jesse Hill Ford's *The Raider*.

Petterman. Shopkeeper and deputy sheriff who trades with Agocho in Edwin Corle's *Fig Tree John*.

Pettibone. Virginia plantation owner who indirectly insults Thomas Sutpen in William Faulkner's *Absalom, Absalom!*

Regal Pettibone. Son of Pourty Bloodworth; brother of Amos-Otis Thigpen, Noah Grandberry, and LaDonna Scales (who is also his lover); half brother of Jonathan Bass; friend of Nathaniel Turner Witherspoon in Leon Forrest's *The Bloodworth Orphans*.

Stefanie Pettigrew. Vivacious finishing school graduate who becomes William's son's fiancée in Cynthia Ozick's *Trust*.

Pettingil. Owner of a bar and a confectionery store in Thomas Bailey Aldrich's *The Story of a Bad Boy*.

Adolphus (Dolly) Pettingill. Stutterer in Louisa May Alcott's *Little Men*.

Letitia (Litt) Pettingill. Mountaineer loved inordinately by Fee Guthrie in Mary Noailles Murfree's *In the "Stranger People's" Country*.

Clara Beechum Pettit. Daughter of Jack and Ruth Beechum; marries a Louisville banker to escape the tobacco farming life of her father in Wendell Berry's *The Memory of Old Jack*.

Gladston (Glad) Pettit. Husband of Clara Beechum Pettit; Louisville banker completely estranged from the farming and community values of Port William, Kentucky, in Wendell Berry's *The Memory of Old Jack*.

Red Pettus. Bigoted bully who murders Toomer Smalls and is then killed by Toomer's dogs in Pat

Conroy's *The Great Santini*.

Sherman (Sherman Jones) Pew. Mulatto son of Nigra Jones and Joy Little; rebels against his boss, Judge Fox Clane, by renting a house in a white neighborhood in Carson McCullers's *Clock Without Hands*.

Adélaïde-Hortense-Aimée Peyronnette. Daughter of Madame Léonie Peyronnette and mother of Mayotte; contracts pleurisy and dies two years after her marriage to Louis Desrivières in Lafcadio Hearn's *Youma*.

Léonie Peyronnette. Mother of Aimée Peyronnette and grandmother of Mayotte; discourages the romance between her slave Youma and Gabriel in Lafcadio Hearn's *Youma*.

Bena Peyton. Plump and valuable friend of Jenny Blair Archbald; brags about her wealth and is curious about sexual matters in Ellen Glasgow's *The Sheltered Life*.

Jeanette Peyton. Cousin of Peyton Dunwoodie and maiden aunt of Frances, Henry, and Sarah Wharton in James Fenimore Cooper's *The Spy*.

Tiff (Old Tiff) Peyton. Slave of Sue Peyton Cripps; protects Cripps's children from their depraved father after Cripps's death by securing a Christian education for them and by fleeing with them to Dred Vesey's camp and then to New England in Harriet Beecher Stowe's *Dred*.

Fatty Pfaff. Medical school classmate of Martin Arrowsmith; becomes an obstetrician in Sinclair Lewis's *Arrowsmith*.

Othman Pfegel. Councilman in James Kirke Paulding's *Koningsmarke*.

Phantom. Embodiment of Communism and archenemy of Sam Slick in Robert Coover's *The Public Burning*.

Pharaoh. Egyptian ruler, "grandfather" of Moses, and enslaver of the Hebrews in Zora Neale Hurston's *Moses, Man of the Mountain*.

Pharoah. Slave on the Prosser plantation in Arna Wendell Bontemps's *Black Thunder*.

William Francis (Billy) Phelan. Brassy bowler, pool player, and gambler in William Kennedy's *Billy Phelan's Greatest Game*.

Benny Phelps. Daughter of Silas and Sally Phelps; courted by Brace Dunlap against her parents' wishes in Samuel Langhorne Clemens's *Tom Sawyer, Detective*.

Phil. Charming, astute publisher of Baron R. and employer of Hugh Person; according to R., Phil would like him to write books less like his own but more like those of other authors in Vladimir Nabokov's *Transparent Things*.

Phil. First lover of Miriam Berg who shares her with Douglas MacArthur Jackson; drunkard and failed poet in Marge Piercy's *Small Changes*.

Philadelphy. Sartoris servant and wife of Loosh in William Faulkner's *The Unvanquished*.

Philemon. Female slave belonging to Sally Lacey; accompanies the Laceys to Beulah and finally back to the Tidewater in Mary Lee Settle's *O Beulah Land*.

Père Philéas. Hardworking priest of St. Médard parish; rears the young orphan Cribiche in Grace King's *The Pleasant Ways of St. Médard*.

Philip. Brother of Hipparchia; killed by Romans in H. D.'s *Palimpsest*.

Philip. German who sings "Tristan and Isolde" on the Provincetown beach; one of Sabina's lovers in Anaïs Nin's *A Spy in the House of Love*.

Uncle Philip. Witness to all family events in Anaïs Nin's *Children of the Albatross*.

Philippe of Orléans (Duke of Orléans, Grace Philippe). Regent of France whose greed destroys the banking system in Emerson Hough's *The Mississippi Bubble*.

Mrs. Philipson. Cook for Clarissa and Edward Packard; fired for dishonesty in Caroline Gilman's *Recollections of a Housekeeper*.

Arthur Phillip. Royal navy captain who becomes the first governor of the Australian penal colony; revered by the convicts for treating them as humanely as possible in Charles Nordhoff and James Norman Hall's *Botany Bay*.

Phillips. Princeton-educated official at the U.S. Embassy in Rumania; in charge of Henry Bech's schedule in John Updike's *Bech: A Book*.

Arthur Phillips. See Maximilian Petion.

Phil Phillips. Friend and colleague of George Caldwell in John Updike's *The Centaur*.

Undine Phillips. Landlady of Kennerly Kendal in Reynolds Price's *The Surface of Earth*.

Ursula Phillips. Grandmother who tells the narrator about his grandfather's career as a writer killed by a lecherous Hollywood producer in Tennessee Williams's *Moise and the World of Reason*.

Old Mammy Phillis. Black housekeeper in James Kirke Paulding's *Westward Ho!*

Philocles. Aged and insane sea captain and friend of Chrysis, who provides for his support, in Thornton Wilder's *The Woman of Andros.*

Palmyre (Madame Inconnue) la Philosophe. Quadroon freed slave and widow of Bras-Coupé; uses voodoo to seek revenge on Agricola Fusilier in George Washington Cable's *The Grandissimes.*

The Philosopher. Russian university student who seeks privacy in public lavatories and commits suicide in one of them in Jerzy Kosinski's *Steps.*

Philumena. Daughter of Chremes; supposed to marry Pamphilus in Thornton Wilder's *The Woman of Andros.*

Phineas (Finny). Outstanding natural athlete who breaks his leg in a fall from a tree; dies during surgery when his leg is being set after a second break in John Knowles's *A Separate Peace.*

Phoebe (Fibby). Wife of Roscius and mother of Thucydides in William Faulkner's *Go Down, Moses.*

Phyllis. Loquacious friend of Clyde Stout and his mother; urges Clyde to be a better friend to his mother and to stop letting people take advantage of him; works at the Dairy Freeze in Jack Matthews's *Hanger Stout, Awake!*

Luigi Piani. Italian ambulance driver who remains with Frederic Henry during the retreat from Caporetto in Ernest Hemingway's *A Farewell to Arms.*

Piano Girl. See Abeba Williams Lavoisier Torch.

Dr. Almus Pickerbaugh. Director of Public Health in Nautilus, Iowa, who employs Martin Arrowsmith and is later elected to Congress in Sinclair Lewis's *Arrowsmith.*

George Pickett. Confederate general famous for his charge against the enemy on Cemetery Ridge during the Battle of Gettysburg in Michael Shaara's *The Killer Angels.*

Luray Spivey Pickett. Café waitress and stepdaughter-in-law of Caleb Peck in Anne Tyler's *Searching for Caleb.*

Picklock. French soldier in William Faulkner's *A Fable.*

Edward (Robert Jeffers, Andrew Miller, John Simms, Arthur Wills) Pierce. Mastermind of the great train robbery of 1855 in Michael Crichton's *The Great Train Robbery.*

Herbert (Bert) Pierce. Formerly successful developer who loses his money in the Depression; first husband of Mildred Pierce; remarries Mildred following her divorce from Monty Beragon in James M. Cain's *Mildred Pierce.*

Loren Pierce. Wealthy businessman and tightfisted church trustee who conspires with Erastus Winch against Levi Gorringe in Harold Frederic's *The Damnation of Theron Ware.*

Mildred Pierce. Divorced woman who works her way to success, only to have her money drained away by the men in her life and by her demanding daughter Veda Pierce in James M. Cain's *Mildred Pierce.*

Moire (Ray) Pierce. Daughter of Herbert and Mildred Pierce; dies in James M. Cain's *Mildred Pierce.*

Veda Pierce. Snobbish, social-climbing daughter of Herbert and Mildred Pierce; ashamed of her mother's working-class background; becomes a famous singer and betrays her mother by sleeping with Mildred's husband, Monty Beragon, in James M. Cain's *Mildred Pierce.*

Mort Piercy. Overweight, mentally unbalanced political "radical" who involves Jules Wendall in the Detroit riots of the late 1960s in Joyce Carol Oates's *them.*

Pig Butcher. Devoted follower of Wang the Tiger in Pearl Buck's *Sons* and *A House Divided.*

Pigg-O. See Blind Pig.

Jack Wilson Pike. Animal lover who accompanies David Bell and friends on a trip west to make a film in Don DeLillo's *Americana.*

Lorinda (Linda, Lindy) Pike. Tavernkeeper, suffragist, pacifist, and mistress of Doremus Jessup in Sinclair Lewis's *It Can't Happen Here.*

Reverend Andrew (Andy) Pike. Deceased predecessor of Jethro Furber to whom Furber silently and perpetually confides in William Gass's *Omensetter's Luck.*

Piko. Joint king, with Hello, of Diranda; they control the population size by holding deadly games in Herman Melville's *Mardi.*

Mary Pilant. Former hostess at the Thunder Bay Inn, girlfriend of Barney Quill, and proprietor of the inn after Quill's death in Robert Traver's *Anatomy of a Murder.*

Pilar. Former mistress of matadors; gypsy woman and leader of partisan band in Ernest Hemingway's *For Whom the Bell Tolls.*

Madre María del Pilar. Abbess at the Convent of Santa María Rosa de las Rosas, where she has watched Pepita, Manuel, and Esteban grow up; becomes a comforter for Camila Perichole and Doña Clara de Montemayor after their losses in Thornton Wilder's *The Bridge of San Luis Rey.*

Billy Pilgrim. Soldier, prisoner of war, optometrist, and time traveler; husband of Valencia Pilgrim and mate of Montana Wildhack on Tralfamadore in Kurt Vonnegut's *Slaughterhouse-Five.*

Clotilda (Clo) Pilgrim. Guilt-ridden, widowed seamstress who owns and manages a rooming house; mother of Ruby Parker by her brother-in-law, Chester Jackson; suffocates her granddaughter, Addie Parker, in Cyrus Colter's *The Rivers of Eros.*

The Pilgrim. See Sarah Abbott Maulsby.

Valencia Merble Pilgrim. Overweight wife of Billy Pilgrim; dies of carbon monoxide poisoning driving to her wounded husband in Kurt Vonnegut's *Slaughterhouse-Five.*

Adam Pilitzky. Catholic lord after whom the town of Pilitz is named, employer of Jacob Eliezer, and adulterous husband of Theresa Pilitzky; eventually hangs himself in Isaac Bashevis Singer's *The Slave.*

Theresa Pilitzky. Promiscuous wife of Adam Pilitzky resisted by Jacob Eliezer in Isaac Bashevis Singer's *The Slave.*

Pills. Blacksmith who allows Greer, Cameron, and Magic Child to spend the night in his stables in Richard Brautigan's *The Hawkline Monster.*

Pills. Surgeon's steward aboard the *Neversink* in Herman Melville's *White-Jacket.*

Pilon. Penniless, opportunistic friend of Danny; rents one of Danny's houses without really paying rent; his chief interest in life is obtaining liquor in John Steinbeck's *Tortilla Flat.*

Charles Pilsudski. Black playwright and friend of Osgood Wallop in Peter De Vries's *Mrs. Wallop.*

Henry Pimber. Landlord of Brackett Omensetter; seduced by the mysterious ease of his tenant and finally driven to suicide by Omensetter's neglect of worship in William Gass's *Omensetter's Luck.*

Pindi. Niaruna Indian, wife of Tukanu, lover of Lewis Moon, and mother of New Person in Peter Matthiessen's *At Play in the Fields of the Lord.*

July Pinesett. Gambler who is the fun-loving twin of June Pinesett, husband of Mary Pinesett, father of

Unexpected Pinesett, and conjured lover of Cinder in Julia Peterkin's *Scarlet Sister Mary.*

June Pinesett. Hardworking twin of July Pinesett and father, by Mary Pinesett, of Seraphine Pinesett in Julia Peterkin's *Scarlet Sister Mary.*

Mary (Sister Mary) Pinesett. Ward of Maum Hannah, wife of July Pinesett, rival of Doll and Cinder, and lover of June Pinesett and others; excommunicated from Heaven's Gate Church for sexual indiscretions, but later re-baptized, in Julia Peterkin's *Scarlet Sister Mary.*

Seraphine Pinesett. Illegitimate daughter of Mary Pinesett and June Pinesett in Julia Peterkin's *Scarlet Sister Mary.*

Unexpected (Unex) Pinesett. Son of Mary and July Pinesett; dies in childhood in Julia Peterkin's *Scarlet Sister Mary.*

Pinhead. Idiot nephew of George Bennett; comes to Pickerel Beach in the care of Miss Whitaker and is murdered by Mickey McCane in Doris Betts's *The River to Pickle Beach.*

Mimi Pinseau (Pinson). Spinster who runs a small school in her home to support herself and her widowed father in Grace King's *The Pleasant Ways of St. Médard.*

Uncle Pio. Discoverer of Camila Perichole, whom he trained to become one of the world's great actresses; trains her son Don Jaime de Ribera; dies in the fall of the bridge in Thornton Wilder's *The Bridge of San Luis Rey.*

Piotr (Pierre Bouc, Zsettlani). Soldier in William Faulkner's *A Fable.*

Pip (Pippin). Alabama black who becomes insane and who is befriended by Ahab in Herman Melville's *Moby-Dick.*

Hans (I Drink, Minikoue) Pipe. Drunken, troublemaking Indian in James Kirke Paulding's *The Dutchman's Fireside.*

Christina Piper. Daughter of Heer Peter Piper and beloved of Koningsmarke in James Kirke Paulding's *Koningsmarke.*

Edith Piper. Shrewish sister of Heer Peter Piper in James Kirke Paulding's *Koningsmarke.*

Heer Peter (Pepper Pot Peter) Piper. Governor of Elsingburgh, New Sweden, in James Kirke Paulding's *Koningsmarke.*

Pipistrello. Blind husband of Arsella; killed by a falling boulder during a walk with Adeppi in John

Hawkes's *The Goose on the Grave*.

Annie and Bill Pippinger. Parents of Judith, Lizzie May, and Luella Pippinger in Edith Summers Kelley's *Weeds*.

Judith Pippinger. See Judith Pippinger Blackford.

Lizzie May and Luella Pippinger. Twin daughters of Annie and Bill Pippinger and sisters of Judith Pippinger in Edith Summers Kelley's *Weeds*.

Pirate. Huge, broad, bearded wood seller who lived in a deserted chicken house with his five dogs before Pilon persuaded him to live in Danny's house in an attempt by Pilon to acquire Pirate's stashed money in John Steinbeck's *Tortilla Flat*.

Jasper Pistareen. Seedy writer for and editor of a semi-pornographic tabloid newspaper in Paul Theroux's *Waldo*.

Pitch (Coonskins). Bachelor backwoodsman who buys a boy worker in Herman Melville's *The Confidence-Man*.

Lemuel Pitkin. Teenaged Vermonter who, in trying to make his fortune, is victimized by almost everyone in Nathanael West's *A Cool Million*.

Miss Jane (Jane Brown, Ticey) Pittman. Strong-willed black woman whose life from the Civil War to the civil rights movement is chronicled in Ernest J. Gaines's *The Autobiography of Miss Jane Pittman*.

Joe (Chief) Pittman. Husband of Miss Jane Pittman and horse breaker in Ernest J. Gaines's *The Autobiography of Miss Jane Pittman*.

James Elmo (Dummy) Pitts. Deaf-mute witness in the trial of Luther Eustis; narrates part of Shelby Foote's *Follow Me Down*.

Miz Pitts. Homesteader on an island in the Mississippi River; mother of Dummy Pitts in Shelby Foote's *Follow Me Down*.

Otto (Gordon) Pivner. Aspiring playwright who takes up with Esther Gwyon in William Gaddis's *The Recognitions*.

Pixie. Daughter of Cassandra and granddaughter of Skipper and Gertrude; born seven and one half months after Cassandra and Fernandez's wedding; sent to live with Gertrude's cousin after Cassandra's death in John Hawkes's *Second Skin*.

Placenta Juan. See Salvador Hassan O'Leary.

Mars Plasair. Tubercular old slave on the plantation at Bréda in Arna Wendell Bontemps's *Drums at Dusk*.

Stephanie Platow. Actress and lover of Forbes Gurney and Frank Cowperwood in Theodore Dreiser's *The Titan*.

Leo Platt. Dumur County locator and suitor of Libby Slogum in Mari Sandoz's *Slogum House*.

Augustus (Gus) Plebesly. Timorous Los Angeles policeman who learns to live with fear in Joseph Wambaugh's *The New Centurions*.

Catharine Pleyel. See Catharine Pleyel Wieland.

Henry Pleyel. Beloved of Clara Wieland; misled by Carwin to doubt Clara's purity, although he ultimately marries her in Charles Brockden Brown's *Wieland*.

Plotinus (Welsh) Plinlimmon. Author of *Ei*, a volume of lectures that includes "Chronometricals and Horologicals," in Herman Melville's *Pierre*.

Manny Plinski. Seventeen year old who puts turtles into Will Brady's pockets and assists Brady as Santa Claus's helper in Wright Morris's *The Works of Love*.

Angus Plow. Food-hating passenger on the *Here They Come* who plans to expose food as evil in Gregory Corso's *The American Express*.

Hope Plowman. Sincere and honest wife of Noah Ackerman; her positive influence furnishes his life with meaning and dedication to higher values in Irwin Shaw's *The Young Lions*.

Zeddy Plummer. Buddy of Jake Brown and lover of Gin-head Susy in Claude McKay's *Home to Harlem*.

Freddy Plympton. English landowner whose estate contains a private zoo where Brewster Ashenden encounters a female bear in heat in *The Making of Ashenden*, a novella in Stanley Elkin's *Searches and Seizures*.

Liza Pnin. See Dr. Elizaveta Innokentievna Bogolepov Pnin Wind.

Timofey (Timosha) Pavlovich Pnin. Émigré professor of Russian at Waindell College; his trials in adjusting to life in America form the basis of Vladimir Nabokov's *Pnin*.

Pocahontas. Indian princess deflowered by Captain John Smith in John Barth's *The Sot-Weed Factor*.

Jim Pocock. Husband of Sarah Newsome Pocock; controls the Newsome business in Woollett, Massachusetts, during Chad Newsome's absence in Europe; sent to Europe to retrieve Chad in Henry James's *The Ambassadors*.

Mamie Pocock. Sister of Jim Pocock; encouraged by Mrs. Newsome to marry Chad Newsome, whom she is sent to Paris to retrieve; becomes engaged to John Little Bilham in Henry James's *The Ambassadors*.

Sarah (Sally) Newsome Pocock. Sister of Chad Newsome and wife of Jim Pocock; sent to Paris to retrieve Chad in Henry James's *The Ambassadors*.

Arthur (Don Arturo) Poinsett. Handsome young man who tries to set wills and inheritances straight in Bret Harte's *Gabriel Conroy*.

Frank Pointer. Team doctor for the New York Mammoths in Mark Harris's *It Looked Like For Ever*.

Edward W. A. (Ned) Pointsman. English doctor involved in Pavlovian experiments at The White Visitation; engineers a scheme to study Tyrone Slothrop's responses to rocket technology in Thomas Pynchon's *Gravity's Rainbow*.

Franz Pökler. German engineer manipulated by Lieutenant Weissmann to cooperate in the building of rocket 00000 in Thomas Pynchon's *Gravity's Rainbow*.

Poky. Tahitian who befriends Typee in Herman Melville's *Omoo*.

Morris Polatkin. Manager of Olivia Lattimore in Mary Austin's *A Woman of Genius*.

Polchek. Soldier who betrays Stefan in William Faulkner's *A Fable*.

Tom Polhaus. Police detective who is investigating the murder of Miles Archer and Floyd Thursby in Dashiell Hammett's *The Maltese Falcon*.

Sam Polidor. Scheming landlord of Russel Wren in Thomas Berger's *Who Is Teddy Villanova?*

Tris Polk. Cattleman and suitor of Morissa Kirk in Mari Sandoz's *Miss Morissa*.

Asinius Pollio. Confidential agent of Caesar; risks his life to defend Caesar in an early assassination attempt in Thornton Wilder's *The Ides of March*.

Bart Pollock. General sales manager of Knox Business Machines; offers Frank Wheeler a promotion that undermines the Wheelers' plans to leave for Europe in Richard Yates's *Revolutionary Road*.

Guy Pollock. Gopher Prairie lawyer and intellectual in Sinclair Lewis's *Main Street*.

Polly. Scullery maid for Clarissa and Edward Packard; led into dishonesty by Mrs. Philipson in Caroline Gilman's *Recollections of a Housekeeper*.

Aunt Polly. Gullible guardian of Tom Sawyer in Samuel Langhorn Clemens's *The Adventures of Tom Sawyer*, *Adventures of Huckleberry Finn*, *Tom Sawyer Abroad*, and *Tom Sawyer, Detective*.

Sergeant Jefferson Polly. Confederate cavalry scout; narrates part of Shelby Foote's *Shiloh*.

Polyeidus. Tutor of Bellerophon; equipped with limited faculties in the *Bellerophoniad*, a novella in John Barth's *Chimera*.

Pomaree Vahinee I (Aimata). Queen of Tahiti in Herman Melville's *Omoo*.

Pomaree-Tanee. See Tanee.

Cody Pomeray. Charismatic ex-car thief turned railroad brakeman; husband of Evelyn Pomeray and idealized friend and traveling companion of Jack Duluoz in Jack Kerouac's *Visions of Cody*; also appears in *Dharma Bums*, *Book of Dreams*, *Big Sur*, and *Desolation Angels*.

Cody (The Barber) Pomeray, Sr. Improvident drifter; father of Cody Pomeray in Jack Kerouac's *Visions of Cody*.

Evelyn Pomeray. Second wife of Cody Pomeray and mother of their three children; participates in the taped conversations of Jack Kerouac's *Visions of Cody*; also appears in *Book of Dreams*, *Big Sur*, and *Desolation Angels*.

Chester (Chet) Hunnicutt Pomeroy. Formerly famous performer who tries to deal with life after fame; seeks to renew his relationship with Catherine Clay and invents the death of his living father in Thomas McGuane's *Panama*.

Cynthia Pomeroy. Seventeen year old who exemplifies "the wisdom of the body" and is attractive to a variety of male imaginations; marries Arnold Soby at the conclusion of Wright Morris's *What a Way to Go*.

Jim Pomeroy. Brother of Chet Pomeroy; dies on the day of the Boston subway fire in Thomas McGuane's *Panama*.

Kate Pomeroy. Wife of Rob Pomeroy; cannot forget her affair with Tommy Ryden; gives Milo Mustian his second sexual experience in Reynolds Price's *A Generous Man*.

Rob (Rooster) Pomeroy. Sheriff who heads the search for Rato Mustian in Reynolds Price's *A Generous Man*.

Alice Pomfret. Daughter of Fanny Pomfret; marries Humphrey Crewe in Winston Churchill's *Mr.*

Crewe's Career.

Fanny Pomfret. Rich, snobby mother of Alice Pomfret; wants American politics to emulate English politics in Winston Churchill's *Mr. Crewe's Career.*

Judge Pommeroy. Uncle of Niel Herbert and close friend of and counsel to Daniel Forrester in Willa Cather's *A Lost Lady.*

Pomoroy. Executive editor at a commercial book publishing house; commissions a book on the Jewish-American experience from Bruce Gold in Joseph Heller's *Good as Gold.*

Annie (Girl Fried Egg) Pompa. Front-office chief of the newspaper *West Condon Chronicle* in Robert Coover's *The Origin of the Brunists.*

Pompeia. Wife of Caesar; replaced as his wife by Calpurnia following the scandalous events at the Ceremonies of the Good Goddess in Thornton Wilder's *The Ides of March.*

Pompey Ducklegs. Slave of Cuthbert Dangerfield in James Kirke Paulding's *Westward Ho!*

Pompey the Little. Grandson of Pompey Ducklegs; jockey for Cuthbert Dangerfield in James Kirke Paulding's *Westward Ho!*

Bonnie Dee Peacock Ponder. Seventeen-year-old second wife of Daniel Ponder; leaves him after five years of marriage, then returns to oust him from his home; dies laughing when Daniel tickles her in Eudora Welty's *The Ponder Heart.*

Daniel Ponder. Youngest child of Sam Ponder; gives the Beulah Hotel to his niece and contemporary, Edna Earle Ponder; acquitted of the charge of murdering his second wife, Bonnie Dee Ponder, in Eudora Welty's *The Ponder Heart.*

Edna Earle Ponder. Unmarried manager of the Beulah Hotel in Clay, Mississippi; granddaughter of Sam Ponder and narrator of Eudora Welty's *The Ponder Heart.*

Sam Ponder. Original owner of the Beulah Hotel, his wife's inheritance; father of Daniel Ponder and grandfather of Edna Earle Ponder in Eudora Welty's *The Ponder Heart.*

Teacake (Miss Teacake) Sistrunk Magee Ponder. First wife of Daniel Ponder, whom she marries and divorces in 1944, in Eudora Welty's *The Ponder Heart.*

Phineas Delfase Ponniman. Eminent New York attorney and avowed agnostic who defends six blacks accused of raping a white woman in T. S. Stribling's *Unfinished Cathedral.*

John Ponta. Brutal boxer who kills Joe Fleming in a boxing match in Jack London's *The Game.*

Edna Pontellier. Wife of Léonce Pontellier and mother of Etienne and Raoul Pontellier; artist and outsider in Creole society, who, during an infatuation with Robert Lebrun, awakens to her individuality and sensuality; walks into the ocean to her death at the end of Kate Chopin's *The Awakening.*

Etienne Pontellier. Four-year-old son of Edna and Léonce Pontellier in Kate Chopin's *The Awakening.*

Léonce Pontellier. Possessive Creole husband of Edna Pontellier and father of Etienne and Raoul Pontellier; New Orleans cotton merchant in Kate Chopin's *The Awakening.*

Raoul Pontellier. Five-year-old son of Edna and Léonce Pontellier in Kate Chopin's *The Awakening.*

Edgar (Eddie, Horn) Pool. Superlative saxophonist fallen on hard times in John Clellon Holmes's *The Horn.*

Klaas Pool. Truck farmer who marries Widow Paarlenberg following the death of his first wife Maartje in Edna Ferber's *So Big.*

Maartje Pool. Wife of Klaas Pool and mother of Roelf Pool; dies during childbirth in Edna Ferber's *So Big.*

Roelf Pool. Famous sculptor in Edna Ferber's *So Big.*

Agatha Poole. Mother of Delia Poole; moves from Excelsior, Ohio, to live with her daughter after the suicide of James Poole in Janet Flanner's *The Cubical City.*

Augie Poole. Unsuccessful cartoonist "in whom a first-rate gagman was trying to claw his way out"; husband of Isolde Poole; philanderer who unwittingly adopts his own bastard in Peter De Vries's *The Tunnel of Love.*

Delia Poole. New York City costume designer employed by Goldstein; heroine of Janet Flanner's *The Cubical City.*

Isolde Poole. Former actress, wife of Augie Poole, and aspiring parent who becomes pregnant after successful adoption in Peter De Vries's *The Tunnel of Love.*

James Poole. Father of Delia Poole; loses much of the family fortune and then kills himself in Janet Flanner's *The Cubical City.*

Poo Poo. Nightmare figure that haunts Bradly in William S. Burroughs's *The Ticket That Exploded*.

Bub Poor. Younger son of Captain Red Poor; disguises himself as Jomo to delay Skipper from finding Cassandra in John Hawkes's *Second Skin*.

Jomo Poor. Elder son of Captain Red Poor; lost a hand in the fighting at Salerno and wears a hook in John Hawkes's *Second Skin*.

Red (Captain Red) Poor. Father of Bub and Jomo Poor; owner and captain of the *Peter Poor* in John Hawkes's *Second Skin*.

Pop. Alcoholic father of Lutie Johnson; his only source of income is selling bootlegged liquor in Ann Petry's *The Street*.

Pop. Father of Henry Wiggen in Mark Harris's *The Southpaw* and *Bang the Drum Slowly*.

Teddy (Mr. T) Pope. Homosexual actor who is forced to appear straight by movie industry executives in Norman Mailer's *The Deer Park*.

Popeye. See Popeye Vitelli.

Popkoff (Dr. P.). Pharmacologist employed by NESTER in Scott Spencer's *Last Night at the Brain Thieves Ball*.

Deacon Ereemear (Darer-of-Devils-in-the-Dark, Jeremiah, Jeremiah-in-the-Dark, Narmo-Nana) Po-Po. Native of Partoowye who hosts Typee and Long Ghost in Herman Melville's *Omoo*.

Clarence Popp. Hired hand and close friend of Otto Neumiller; helps Charles Neumiller (I) bury Otto in Larry Woiwode's *Beyond the Bedroom Wall*.

Coach Herman Popper. High-school coach who is cruel and abusive to boys and to his wife in Larry McMurtry's *The Last Picture Show*.

Ruth Popper. Ignored and lonely wife of Coach Herman Popper; lover of Sonny Crawford in Larry McMurtry's *The Last Picture Show*.

Claud Walsingham Popple. Society portrait painter who impresses Undine Spragg with his flattery and pomposity in Edith Wharton's *The Custom of the Country*.

The Popsicle Queen. See Mrs. Schnitzer.

Porcia. Wife of Brutus; suffers a miscarriage in Thornton Wilder's *The Ides of March*.

Peter Porcupine. Blackguard journalist in Pittsburgh whose pamphlet against the Jacobins brings to a head the issue of a free press in Hugh Henry Brackenridge's *Modern Chivalry*.

Porfirio. Woodcarver of Hidalgo known for his parsimony; tries to conduct a courtship on a budget in Josefina Niggli's *Mexican Village*.

Porgy. Crippled black beggar who takes Bess as a lover after Crown deserts her; kills Crown in self-defense in DuBose Heyward's *Porgy*.

Lieutenant Porgy. Officer under Francis Marion; fond of good food in William Gilmore Simms's *The Partisan*; as Captain Porgy, preoccupied with reclaiming his place and property as gentleman, cavalier, and master of Glen-Eberley plantation in Low Country South Carolina at the close of the American Revolution in *Woodcraft*.

Rev. Eclair Porkchop. Bishop of Soulville and head of the Church of the Holy Mouth in Ishmael Reed's *The Free-Lance Pallbearers*.

Porky. Fat heroin dealer who supplies drugs to Terry Wilson and Teddy and who enjoys degrading his addicts in Donald Goines's *Dopefiend*.

Private Milt Porsum. Bank president and war hero duped by Bogan Murdock; helps reveal Murdock's swindle in Robert Penn Warren's *At Heaven's Gate*.

Big Joe Portagee. Army veteran and friend of Danny and Pilon; fond of living in jail, but when released, and upon hearing of Danny's good fortune, quickly becomes friendlier with Pilon and Danny in order to stay in Danny's home in John Steinbeck's *Tortilla Flat*.

Alexander Thornton (Lex) Porter. Closest friend of Alfred Eaton at Princeton and later his partner in an airplane manufacturing business in John O'Hara's *From the Terrace*.

Henry Porter. Tenant of Macon Dead II, lover of First Corinthians Dead, and member of the racial revenge group called the Seven Days in Toni Morrison's *Song of Solomon*.

Mitch Porter. Unctuous steakhouse owner who pampers Lou Engel and J. Henry Waugh in Robert Coover's *The Universal Baseball Association, Inc., J. Henry Waugh, Prop.*

Walter (Moon) Porter. Pimp on the lam after killing a corrupt policeman; former member of a black high school athletic team and neighborhood gang gathering for a birthday testimonial honoring Chappie Davis in John A. Williams's *The Junior Bachelor Society*.

Portia. Compassionate and free-spirited daughter of Benedict Mady Copeland; like his other children, she rebels against Copeland's teachings in Carson

McCullers's *The Heart Is a Lonely Hunter*.

Alexander (Alex, Alex P, Breakie, Al Parsons, Alton Christian Peterson) Portnoy. Member of the American Civil Liberties Union, Assistant Commissioner of Human Opportunity for New York City, and special counsel to a United States Congressional subcommittee; describes his emotional and sexual trials to his psychiatrist; narrator of Philip Roth's *Portnoy's Complaint*.

Hannah Portnoy. See Hannah Portnoy Feibish.

Harold (Heshie) Portnoy. Handsome, muscular cousin of Alex Portnoy; prevented by his father from marrying Alice Dembosky and killed in World War II in Philip Roth's *Portnoy's Complaint*.

Jack (Jake) Portnoy. Devoted employee of the Boston and Northeastern Life Insurance Company, husband of Sophie Portnoy, and father of Alex Portnoy; perpetually constipated in Philip Roth's *Portnoy's Complaint*.

Sophie Ginsky (Red) Portnoy. Overprotective mother of Alex Portnoy and wife of Jack Portnoy in Philip Roth's *Portnoy's Complaint*.

George (Brother George) Posey. Husband of Susan Posey and brother of Jane Posey; provides arms for a Confederate battalion; loner who kills his wife's brother and the slave who attacked his sister; drives his wife mad; afraid of death in Allen Tate's *The Fathers*.

Jane Posey. Sister of George Posey; agrees to marry Semmes Buchan but is assaulted by Yellow Jim and enters a nunnery in Allen Tate's *The Fathers*.

Aunt Jane Anne Posey. Mother of George Posey; concerned only with her personal health, has little concept of reality in Allen Tate's *The Fathers*.

Susan Buchan (Susie) Posey. Daughter of Major Lewis Buchan and wife of George Posey; instigates an assault on Jane Posey to stop Jane's marriage to Semmes Buchan; her hair turns white after the death of her brother Semmes in Allen Tate's *The Fathers*.

Sergeant-Major Postalozzi. Expectant father who loses his legs in combat in Martha Gellhorn's *Wine of Astonishment*.

Thelma Postgate. See M Evans.

Edward Postoak. Son of John Postoak; slave and butler of Isaac Jameson in Shelby Foote's *Jordan County*.

John (Chisahahoma) Postoak. Choctaw convert to Christianity; reports the Choctaws' ritual killing of two trappers in Shelby Foote's *Jordan County*.

Anastasia Petrovna Potapov. See Madame Charles Chamar.

Charlie Potteiger. Former farmer who sold out to developers; owns Potteiger's Store, where George Caldwell shops for food nearly every day, in John Updike's *The Centaur*.

Ann Potter. Daughter of Natty Potter, whom she accompanies to Michilimackinac; marries Langdon Towne in Kenneth Roberts's *Northwest Passage*.

Benjamin Potter. Last surviving child of Israel Potter and his wife; accompanies his aged father to the United States from England in Herman Melville's *Israel Potter*.

Benny Potter. Wisecracking student at Steering School; works for a New York magazine in John Irving's *The World According to Garp*.

Senator Boyd Potter. United States senator who employs Hazel Stone; tries to take over the government by use of the atomic bomb in Mari Sandoz's *The Tom-Walker*.

Harlan Potter. Powerful newspaper publisher; father of Sylvia Lennox and Linda Loring in Raymond Chandler's *The Long Goodbye*.

Israel (Peter Perkins, Yellow-hair) Potter. Farmer from the Berkshires who fights at Bunker Hill, talks with King George III, serves as courier to and for Benjamin Franklin, fights with John Paul Jones aboard the *Bon Homme Richard* against the *Serapis*, and sees Ethan Allen before spending most of the remainder of his life in unfortunate circumstances in London in Herman Melville's *Israel Potter*.

Joseph (Red) Potter. Young gang member who is killed in an automobile crash in William Riley Burnett's *High Sierra*.

J. Pennington Potter. Upper-class black advocate of social mixing of the races in Rudolph Fisher's *The Walls of Jericho*.

Muff Potter. Accomplice of Injun Joe; framed by Injun Joe for the murder of Dr. Robinson in Samuel Langhorne Clemens's *The Adventures of Tom Sawyer*.

Nathaniel (Natty) Potter. Alcoholic father of Ann Potter and secretary to Major Robert Rogers; accompanies Rogers to Michilimackinac in Kenneth Roberts's *Northwest Passage*.

Nora Potter. Foster cousin of Austin King; her romantic attachment to him causes complications in William Maxwell's *Time Will Darken It.*

Randolph Potter. Preening bachelor and brother of Nora Potter in William Maxwell's *Time Will Darken It.*

Reuben S. Potter. Foster relative of Austin King; entices some of King's friends into a fraudulent land scheme in William Maxwell's *Time Will Darken It.*

Richard (Ricky) Potter. Young composer in Alison Lurie's *Real People.*

Calvin Potts. Black alcoholic; one of ten Los Angeles policemen-protagonists in Joseph Wambaugh's *The Choirboys.*

James (Alexis) Potts. College dropout, heroin addict, black separatist/nationalist, and friend of Dunreith Smith in Cyrus Colter's *The Rivers of Eros.*

Lucy Ann Potts. Wise and supportive wife of John Buddy Pearson and mother of their children in Zora Neale Hurston's *Jonah's Gourd Vine.*

Eustache Poupin. French exile, socialist, and bookbinder who befriends Hyacinth Robinson and takes him as an apprentice in Henry James's *The Princess Casamassima.*

Gregory Ulas (Greg) Powell. Habitual criminal convicted of and sentenced to die for the murder of Ian Campbell in Joseph Wambaugh's *The Onion Field.*

Harry (Preacher) Powell. Psychotic murderer in search of Ben Harper's stolen money; marries Harper's widow, murders her, and pursues her children down the river; ultimately convicted of Willa Harper's murder in Davis Grubb's *The Night of the Hunter.*

James Powell. Boat builder who constructs a skiff for Thomas Skelton in Thomas McGuane's *Ninety-Two in the Shade.*

Willa Harper Powell. See Willa Harper.

Alexander Powers. Superintendent of a railway maintenance shop who reports his discovery that the railway has been systematically violating regulations in Charles M. Sheldon's *In His Steps.*

Captain Powers. Former English professor serving as a Marine company commander in France during World War I and who is killed during an artillery barrage in Thomas Boyd's *Through the Wheat.*

Dorothy (Dot) Powers. Sixteen-year-old girlfriend of Cross Damon; becomes pregnant by Damon and tells his estranged wife of her intention to have him arrested for statutory rape in Richard Wright's *The Outsider.*

Mr. Powers. Hired man of Cress Delahanty's grandfather in Jessamyn West's *Cress Delahanty.*

Richard Powers. Husband of Margaret Powers; killed in World War I in William Faulkner's *Soldiers' Pay.*

Samuel (Sam) Powers. Suitor of Hattie Sherbrooke in Nicholas Delbanco's *Possession.*

Betty Prail. Girlfriend of Lemuel Pitkin; raped and sold into prostitution in Nathanael West's *A Cool Million.*

Doctor Mary J. Prance. Physician who attends Miss Birdseye in Henry James's *The Bostonians.*

Jonas W. Prather. First love and fiancé of Ellen Chesser, whom he abandons, in Elizabeth Madox Roberts's *The Time of Man.*

Anastasia (Annie, Chalkline Annie, Virgin Jekyll and Miss Hyde) Pratt. Schoolgirl who becomes Joe Buck's first lover behind the screen of the World movie theatre in James Leo Herlihy's *Midnight Cowboy.*

Chester (Chet) Pratt. Author of *Burn All Your Cities,* a successful novel made into a movie; becomes Pamela Hendricks's lover when he is hired as a speech writer for Robert Kennedy in Richard Yates's *Disturbing the Peace.*

Dean (Whaddayamean) Pratt. Wimpiest of the ten Los Angeles policemen-protagonists of Joseph Wambaugh's *The Choirboys.*

Helen Pratt. Good friend of Clare Bishop, acquaintance of Sebastian Knight, and typist for Mr. Goodman; helps V. in his quest for information about Knight in Vladimir Nabokov's *The Real Life of Sebastian Knight.*

Jeannine (Jen) Pratt. New classmate who befriends Conrad Jarrett in Judith Guest's *Ordinary People.*

Miss Lola Pratt. Lovely summer guest of the Parchers; drives the young men of the town into an adolescent frenzy, but her simpering ways disturb Mr. Parcher, in Booth Tarkington's *Seventeen.*

Mama and Papa Pratt. Wealthy Cape-Codders and benign despots; parents of Phoebe, Orlando, and Maude Coffin Pratt in Paul Theroux's *Picture Palace.*

Maude Coffin Pratt. Outspoken photographer, incestuous lover, and narrator of Paul Theroux's *Picture*

Palace.

Orlando (Ollie) Pratt. Brother of Maude Coffin Pratt and lover of his younger sister, Phoebe Pratt, in Paul Theroux's *Picture Palace.*

Phoebe Pratt. Younger sister of Maude Coffin Pratt and lover of their brother, Orlando Pratt, in Paul Theroux's *Picture Palace.*

Polly Pratt. Gushing proselytizer for Catholicism whose emotional fervor governs her life in James Gould Cozzens's *By Love Possessed.*

Preacher. See Harry Powell.

Preacher. See James D. Smathers, Jr.

Lon Preiser. Barrowville, Ohio, theater manager and boyfriend of Velma Goodhue in William Riley Burnett's *High Sierra.*

Bobby Prell. Orphaned West Virginian and corporal who returns from duty in the South Pacific nearly incapacitated by leg injuries; refuses to allow army doctors to amputate his leg and ends up selling war bonds in James Jones's *Whistle.*

Marshall Preminger. Professional lecturer, perpetual graduate student, and youngest owner in a Chicago condominium complex; commits suicide by leaping from a balcony in *The Condominium*, a novella in Stanley Elkin's *Searches and Seizures.*

Philip (Phil) Preminger. Father of Marshall Preminger; squanders his son's inheritance on a late-in-life romance in *The Condominium*, a novella in Stanley Elkin's *Searches and Seizures.*

Alice Grumbauer Prentice. Devoted but irresponsible mother of Robert Prentice; unflaggingly attempts to achieve artistic and social success through sculpturing fanciful garden statuary in Richard Yates's *A Special Providence.*

Captain Geoffrey (Pirate) Prentice. British officer in the Special Operations Executive; capable of having other people's fantasies and famous for his Banana Breakfasts in Thomas Pynchon's *Gravity's Rainbow.*

George Prentice. Former husband of Alice Prentice and father of Robert Prentice; stolid but kind man who is mystified by Alice's artistic and social aspirations in Richard Yates's *A Special Providence.*

Robert J. (Bob, Bobby) Prentice. Awkward, introspective, self-effacing son of Alice Prentice and George Prentice; attains some measure of independence from his mother through infantry service in World War II in Richard Yates's *A Special*

Providence.

Mr. Prentiss. Owner of a card and printing shop where Sandy Rodgers works; his daughter allows Sandy to read literary classics in Langston Hughes's *Not Without Laughter.*

Portia Prentiss. Young black woman from a deprived background; student of Jane Clifford in Gail Godwin's *The Odd Woman.*

Wayne Prentiss. Head of the Employment Department at Margy Shannon's firm; attractive bachelor and devoted son to a demanding mother in Betty Smith's *Tomorrow Will Be Better.*

Ephraim (Eph) Prescott. Patronage seeker sponsored by Jethro Bass in Winston Churchill's *Coniston.*

Francis (Frank, Rector of Justin) Prescott. Episcopal priest; founder and long-time headmaster of an exclusive boys' boarding school in Massachusetts; central character in Louis Auchincloss's *The Rector of Justin.*

Harriet Winslow Prescott. Wife of Francis Prescott; austere intellectual from an old Boston family in Louis Auchincloss's *The Rector of Justin.*

Selina Rosheen Prescott. Wife of Wylie Prescott; former rodeo star who, following her husband's death, becomes the richest woman in Texas in William Goyen's *Come, The Restorer.*

Wylie Prescott. Husband of Selina Rosheen Prescott; responsible for the destruction of the wilderness and for the growth of the polluted city of Rose, Texas, which he helped found, in William Goyen's *Come, The Restorer.*

The President. United States president and former governor of California; unscrupulous in using the powers of his office to secure his nomination of Robert Leffingwell for Secretary of State in Allen Drury's *Advise and Consent.*

Presley (Pres). Would-be poet who fails to create the epical "Song of the West" he has attempted and who resorts to a species of transcendental philosophy to cope with the suffering that he has observed in the San Joaquin Valley in Frank Norris's *The Octopus.*

Tom Preston. Brother-in-law of Johnny Lacey; settles at Winchester and inspires Johnny to move west in Mary Lee Settle's *O Beulah Land.*

Mrs. Prevost. Neighbor of Birdy; raises canaries in William Wharton's *Birdy.*

Robert E. Lee (Prew) Prewitt. Army private who transfers out of the Bugle Corps to G Company; wrongly imprisoned for assaulting Ike Galovitch; killed by sentries while trying to join the American defense against the Japanese at Pearl Harbor in James Jones's *From Here to Eternity*.

Count Percy de Prey. Stout, foppish neighbor of the Veens of Ardis; his supposed affair with Ada Veen drives Van Veen to fits of jealousy and torment in Vladimir Nabokov's *Ada*.

Countess Cordula (Cordula Tobak) de Prey. Cousin of Percy de Prey, friend of Ada Veen, and, at one time, mistress of Van Veen in Vladimir Nabokov's *Ada*.

Laura (Mrs. de Shamble) Pribble. Retired motion picture actress and, under an assumed name, brokerage client and briefly paramour of Joe Sandwich; finally marries Uncle Hamilton in Peter De Vries's *The Vale of Laughter*.

Ian (Pricey) Price. English mining associate of Oliver Ward; severely beaten in a mining dispute in Wallace Stegner's *Angle of Repose*.

Miss Lucy Pride. Aristocratic Bostonian; guardian of Hopestill Mather and benefactress of Sonia Marburg in Jean Stafford's *Boston Adventure*.

Priest. Old junky who sells Christmas seals in William S. Burroughs's *Nova Express* and *The Wild Boys*; gives his last fix to a cripple in pain in *Exterminator!*

Alexander Priest. Brother of Lucius Priest II in William Faulkner's *The Reivers*.

Alison Lessep Priest. Wife of Maury Priest I and mother of Lucius Priest II in William Faulkner's *The Reivers*.

Junius (June, Juny) Priest. Pianist influenced by Edgar Pool in John Clellon Holmes's *The Horn*.

Lessep Priest. Brother of Lucius Priest II in William Faulkner's *The Reivers*.

Lucius (Boss) Priest (I). Father of Maury Priest I and bank president in William Faulkner's *The Reivers*.

Lucius (Loosh) Priest (II). Grandson of Lucius Priest I in William Faulkner's *The Reivers*.

Lucius Priest (III). Grandson of Lucius Priest II and narrator of William Faulkner's *The Reivers*.

Maury Priest (I). Son of Lucius Priest I and father of Lucius Priest II in William Faulkner's *The Reivers*.

Maury Priest (II). Brother of Lucius Priest II in William Faulkner's *The Reivers*.

Sarah Edmonds Priest. Grandmother of Lucius Priest II in William Faulkner's *The Reivers*.

Charles de Marigny Prieur-Denis. Kinsman of Hamish Bond included in Bond's coterie in Robert Penn Warren's *Band of Angels*.

Nina Gitana de la Primavera. Captivating actress befriended by Renate and Bruce in Anaïs Nin's *Collages*.

Hester Prime. Strict Methodist spinster who adopts Frederick Brent after his father disappears and his mother dies of alcoholism; marries Eliphalet Hodges, who is less rigid religiously than she, in Paul Laurence Dunbar's *The Uncalled*.

Priming. Gunner's mate who blames White-Jacket for accidents and illnesses that have befallen members of their mess aboard the *Neversink* in Herman Melville's *White-Jacket*.

Primitivo. Member of Pablo's partisan band in Ernest Hemingway's *For Whom the Bell Tolls*.

Adeline Thacher (Addy) Prince. Daughter of old Mrs. Thacher; estranged from her family by her wildness and difficult temper; although dying of alcoholism and tuberculosis, she manages to get her child, Nan Prince, safely to Mrs. Thacher's New England farmhouse in Sarah Orne Jewett's *A Country Doctor*.

Anna (Nan) Prince. Orphaned ward of Dr. John Leslie; forgoes both marriage to George Gerry and inheritance from her rich aunt Nancy Prince to become a country doctor in Sarah Orne Jewett's *A Country Doctor*.

Anna (Nancy) Prince. Elderly, rich, spinster aunt of the orphaned Nan Prince; decides too late to bequeath her house and wealth to her niece in Sarah Orne Jewett's *A Country Doctor*.

John Prince. New York fashion designer who fires Valentine O'Neill when she begins producing her own designs in Judith Krantz's *Scruples*.

Mort Prince. Writer of clichéd existential novels about salvation through love in Walker Percy's *The Last Gentleman*.

Prince o'Light. Minister of Church Zealous who tries to save Savata in William Goyen's *The Fair Sister*.

Miss Princip. Efficient secretary of Ludlow Mumm in Ludwig Bemelmans's *Dirty Eddie*.

Principino. First-born child of Maggie Verver and Prince Amerigo in Henry James's *The Golden Bowl*.

Doctor Prine. Sadistic female psychiatrist in Thomas Berger's *Regiment of Women*.

Artie Pringle. Boyhood friend of Billy Bumpers; lecture agent and leader of the Baredevils orgy group in Peter De Vries's *I Hear America Swinging*.

Dash Pringle. Daughter of Lucius Pringle and love interest of Marshall Pearl and Farrell in Mark Helprin's *Refiner's Fire*.

Lucius Pringle. Friend of Marshall Pearl; British colonist in Jamaica who tries, because he lost his father and three brothers to raids by Rastas, to destroy the Rasta camp, although he has only limited success, in Mark Helprin's *Refiner's Fire*.

Mary-Ann Pringle. Girlfriend of Rusty Godowsky, object of Myra Breckinridge's desire, and eventual wife of Myron Breckinridge in Gore Vidal's *Myra Breckinridge*.

Priscilla (Veiled Lady). Daughter of Moodie and half sister of Zenobia; controlled by Professor Westervelt; loves Hollingsworth and is loved by Miles Coverdale in Nathaniel Hawthorne's *The Blithedale Romance*.

Priscus. Hellenist scholar and philosopher who becomes Julian's friend and mentor; narrates part of Gore Vidal's *Julian*.

Bernice Pritchard. Dainty, frigid, and headache-prone wife of Elliott Pritchard traveling to Mexico on Juan Chicoy's bus with her husband and their daughter Mildred Pritchard in John Steinbeck's *The Wayward Bus*.

Elliott Pritchard. Clannish, outwardly upright, and well-to-do businessman who, because he is taking his wife Bernice Pritchard and their daughter Mildred Pritchard on a vacation to Mexico, is a passenger on Juan Chicoy's bus in John Steinbeck's *The Wayward Bus*.

Mildred Pritchard. Daughter of Bernice and Elliott Pritchard; accompanies her parents on a vacation to Mexico; has a sexual encounter with Juan Chicoy after he leaves his stranded bus in John Steinbeck's *The Wayward Bus*.

Patrick (Pat) Pritchard. Major general at Pinetree in Beirne Lay, Jr., and Sy Bartlett's *Twelve O'Clock High!*

Gaston Probert. Frenchman who falls in love with Francie Dosson; must decide, after her interview appears in *The Reverberator*, whether to honor her or his family in Henry James's *The Reverberator*.

Andreas Procopirios. Eldest son of Apelis and Nicoletta Procopirios in Nicholas Delbanco's *The Martlet's Tale*.

Apelis Procopirios. Middle, and favorite, son of Orsetta Procopirios in Nicholas Delbanco's *The Martlet's Tale*.

Eleni Procopirios. Wife of Manos Procopirios in Nicholas Delbanco's *The Martlet's Tale*.

Manos Procopirios. Youngest son of Orsetta Procopirios in Nicholas Delbanco's *The Martlet's Tale*.

Nicoletta Procopirios. Deceased wife of Apelis Procopirios and mother of Andreas and Sotiris Procopirios in Nicholas Delbanco's *The Martlet's Tale*.

Orsetta Procopirios. Eighty-year-old matriarch of the Procopirios family and holder of a hidden family treasure; mother of Manos, Apelis, and Triphon Procopirios; dying of peritonitis in Nicholas Delbanco's *The Martlet's Tale*.

Sotiris (Sotis) Procopirios. Son of Apelis Procopirios and grandson of Orsetta Procopirios, who entrusts him with the supposed location of a hidden family treasure, in Nicholas Delbanco's *The Martlet's Tale*.

Triphon Procopirios. Eldest son of Orsetta Procopirios; now living in the United States in Nicholas Delbanco's *The Martlet's Tale*.

Jesse Lasky Proctor. Ineffectual political activist against fascism; under the influence of Charles Lawrence, shoots himself in the foot, defies Senator Joseph McCarthy, and nearly kills himself in Wright Morris's *The Huge Season*.

Major Proctor. Commander of the British garrison at Dorchester, South Carolina, in William Gilmore Simms's *The Partisan*.

Benny Profane. Former seaman called a "yo-yo" for riding back and forth on subway trains; involved with Josefina Mendoza, Rachel Owlglass, and the Whole Sick Crew; left on Malta by Herbert Stencil in Thomas Pynchon's *V.*

Professor. Teacher aboard the *Neversink* in Herman Melville's *White-Jacket*.

Professor Mephesto. Lecherous professor who seduces Candy Christian in Terry Southern and Mason Hoffenberg's *Candy*.

Arista (Sister X) Prolo. Exotic dancer who confronts sexism and racism in her pursuit of international artistic success as the "First Lady of American Jazz

Dance" in Carlene Hatcher Polite's *Sister X and the Victims of Foul Play*.

Elias Proops. Veteran of the Revolutionary War, Chad Hanna's confidant and advisor, and porch sitter at the Yellow Bud Hotel in Walter D. Edmonds's *Chad Hanna*.

Gabriel (Gen'l Gabriel) Prosser. Stately young slave on the Prosser plantation; leads other slaves in a nearly successful revolt; protagonist of Arna Wendell Bontemps's *Black Thunder*.

Thomas (Marse Prosser) Prosser. Wealthy Virginia plantation owner in Arna Wendell Bontemps's *Black Thunder*.

Anita Proteus. Wife of Paul Proteus; leaves him for Lawson Shepherd in Kurt Vonnegut's *Player Piano*.

Paul Proteus. Husband of Anita Proteus and manager-engineer at Ilium Works; becomes the messiah of the revolutionary Ghost Shirt Society in Kurt Vonnegut's *Player Piano*.

Mary (Pokey) Prothero. Heavy, cheerful daughter of a wealthy New York family; member of the Group in Mary McCarthy's *The Group*.

Anne Prouder. See Anne Sparrow.

Ephraim Prouder. Father of Zury Prouder; settles in frontier Illinois and, following the death of his wife and daughter, relinquishes his affairs to Zury in Joseph Kirkland's *Zury*.

Zury Prouder. Illinois dirt farmer whose hard character helps him become wealthy; learns humanity and compassion, finally finding happiness in marriage to Anne Sparrow, who had borne their illegitimate children, in Joseph Kirkland's *Zury*.

Caleb Proudhammer. Disgruntled Harlem youth who becomes a preacher after a series of misadventures which include being tortured on a southern prison farm; brother of Leo Proudhammer in James Baldwin's *Tell Me How Long the Train's Been Gone*.

Leo Proudhammer. Black actor from an impoverished Harlem family who struggles to establish himself in the "white" world of theaters and movies; the effort to prove himself leads to exhaustion and temporary heart failure; lover of Barbara King and Black Christopher; narrator of James Baldwin's *Tell Me How Long the Train's Been Gone*.

Willie (Man - with - hair - white - like - wind - on - water) Proudfit. Farmer who befriends and hides Barclay Munn after Munn is accused of killing a witness against Doctor MacDonald in Robert Penn Warren's *Night Rider*.

Lois Provo. Young woman who helps with the snake show at the fair and provides Milo Mustian with his first sexual experience in Reynolds Price's *A Generous Man*.

Selma Provo. "Aunt" of Lois Provo, later revealed as her unmarried mother, in Reynolds Price's *A Generous Man*.

Jane Provost. See Jean Dean.

Bill Prufrock. Half-breed Indian, collector of fools, satirist, writer for comedian Harry Mercury, and suitor and possible husband of Lee Mercury; his surname is translated from the Indian for "Rolling Stone" in Peter De Vries's *Through the Fields of Clover*.

John William Prutt. President of the Second National Bank of Grand Republic in Sinclair Lewis's *Kingsblood Royal* and *Cass Timberlane*.

Hester Prynne. Wife of Roger Chillingworth, lover of Arthur Dimmesdale, and mother of Pearl; forced to wear the letter A to symbolize her adulterous behavior in Nathaniel Hawthorne's *The Scarlet Letter*.

Ms. Prynne. Manageress of an omega-shaped desert resort for errant clergy; recipient of the Reverend Thomas Marshfield's amorous letters and sermons and ultimately Marshfield's lover in John Updike's *A Month of Sundays*.

Pucento. Ward of Il Gufo; leads the band of soldiers escorting the prisoner into the village in John Hawkes's *The Owl*.

Murray (The Goose) Pucinski. Killer for Legs Diamond; stalks Diamond and Speed Fogarty after being double-crossed in William Kennedy's *Legs*.

Brigadier Ernest Pudding. Senile figurehead at The White Visitation; dotes on his recollections of World War I trench warfare; involved in a sadomasochistic relationship with Katje Borgesius in Thomas Pynchon's *Gravity's Rainbow*.

Jonathan Pue. Custom-house surveyor who wrote a manuscript about Hester Prynne in Nathaniel Hawthorne's *The Scarlet Letter*.

Harold Herman Pugh. Murderer of Lois Fazenda in John Gregory Dunne's *True Confessions*.

Jack Pugh. Illiterate Mississippi gambler and World War I Marine private who befriends William Hicks in France in Thomas Boyd's *Through the Wheat*.

Clodia (Claudilla, Mousie) Pulcher. Intelligent socialite and gossip who attracts men, and especially Catullus; Caesar orders her out of Rome in Thornton Wilder's *The Ides of March.*

Publius Clodius Pulcher. Undisciplined troublemaker and brother of Clodia Pulcher; his sister introduces him as a votary at the all-female ceremony Mysteries of the Good Goddess, thus creating a city-wide disturbance, in Thornton Wilder's *The Ides of March.*

Cornelia Motford (Kay) Pulham. Boston aristocrat and wife of Harry Pulham; commits adultery with Bill King in John P. Marquand's *H. M. Pulham, Esquire.*

Henry Moulton (Harry, H. M.) Pulham. Boston aristocrat and investment counselor who adheres to the values of his social class; husband of Kay Motford Pulham and lover of Marvin Myles; narrator of John P. Marquand's *H. M. Pulham, Esquire.*

Ensign Frank Pulver. Hero-worshipping friend decidedly influenced by Mr. Roberts's friendship, transfer, and death in Thomas Heggen's *Mister Roberts.*

Maurice (Mr. P.) Pulvermacher. Co-owner of Pulvermacher, Betschmann & Kalisch, manufacturers of Pulbetkal women's garments; first person to contract with Harry Bogen for delivery of garments during the strike Bogen has started in Jerome Weidman's *I Can Get It for You Wholesale.*

The Pumpkin. See Kay Campbell.

Eunice Punck. Widowed mother of Mary Spofford; marries Dr. Emil Rappaport despite her daughter's efforts to match her with Frank Spofford in Peter De Vries's *Reuben, Reuben.*

William Purcell. Surly carpenter aboard the HMS *Bounty* who thinks that Captain Bligh is responsible for the rebellion, but whose sense of duty requires him to follow Bligh in being cast adrift, in Charles Nordhoff and James Norman Hall's *Mutiny on the Bounty*; backs down from a duel with Bligh in *Men against the Sea.*

L. Westminster (Brother Dallas, Plucky) Purcell III. Goofy-grinned, aristocratic ex-Duke halfback, drug dealer, abortion arranger, and fake priest; brings back The Corpse from the Vatican; shot to death while attempting to board the Icarus XC solar ballooon in Tom Robbins's *Another Roadside Attraction.*

Huldah Purdick. Teacher of Indian children at the Bois des Morts Mission; ends her engagement to Balthazar Harge in order to move to St. Paul in Sinclair Lewis's *The God-Seeker.*

Lemuel T. Purdy. Confidant of Clyde Muncy regarding the funeral of Caddy Hibbard in Wright Morris's *The World in the Attic.*

Paul Purdy. Wise and patient friend and colleague of Lee Youngdahl; wants to produce Youngdahl's play at the university in Mark Harris's *Wake Up, Stupid.*

Purple Better One. See Homer Mandrill.

Lord Frederick Purvis. Father of Hyacinth Robinson in Henry James's *The Princess Casamassima.*

Captain N. Purvis. American officer whose report results in Major Joppolo's reassignment to Algiers in John Hersey's *A Bell for Adano.*

Dorothy (Dot, Dottie) Pusey. Daughter of Pug Pusey; engaged to marry Tracy Deen when he is shot in Lillian Smith's *Strange Fruit.*

Pug Pusey. Father of Dorothy Pusey; owner of the Supply Store in Maxwell, Georgia, in Lillian Smith's *Strange Fruit.*

Nancy Putnam. College girlfriend of Pookie Adams in John Nichols's *The Sterile Cuckoo.*

Ellen Putney. Long-suffering but loving wife of Ralph Putney; close friend of Annie Kilburn in William Dean Howells's *Annie Kilburn.*

Ralph Putney. Lawyer whose career is thwarted by his alcoholism; defends Julius W. Peck in William Dean Howells's *Annie Kilburn.*

Winthrop (Win) Putney. Invalid child of Ellen and Ralph Putney in William Dean Howells's *Annie Kilburn.*

Harry Pyecraft. Motel owner whose Dew Drop Inn, scene of Gowan McGland's amours and suicide, becomes a literary tourist attraction in Peter De Vries's *Reuben, Reuben.*

Arthur Gordon Pym. Well-bred Nantucket youth; narrator of Edgar Allan Poe's *The Narrative of Arthur Gordon Pym.*

Alice Pyncheon. Daughter of Gervayse Pyncheon; plants posy seeds and plays the harpsichord in Nathaniel Hawthorne's *The House of the Seven Gables.*

Clifford Pyncheon. Brother of Hepzibah Pyncheon; unjustly imprisoned for the death of Jaffrey Pyncheon I in Nathaniel Hawthorne's *The House of the Seven Gables.*

Colonel Pyncheon. Patriarch of the Pyncheon family; claims the Maule land, after having Matthew Maule convicted of witchcraft; dies mysteriously in Nathaniel Hawthorne's *The House of the Seven Gables*.

Gervayse Pyncheon. Father of Alice Pyncheon in Nathaniel Hawthorne's *The House of the Seven Gables*.

Hepzibah Pyncheon. Cousin of Jaffrey Pyncheon II; runs a cent-shop in the Pyncheon house in Nathaniel Hawthorne's *The House of the Seven Gables*.

Phoebe Pyncheon. Cousin of Hepzibah and Clifford Pyncheon and of Jaffrey Pyncheon II; marries Holgrave in Nathaniel Hawthorne's *The House of the Seven Gables*.

Jaffrey Pyncheon (I). Uncle of Clifford Pyncheon and Jaffrey Pyncheon II; his death is mistakenly blamed on Clifford Pyncheon in Nathaniel Hawthorne's *The House of the Seven Gables*.

Judge Jaffrey Pyncheon (II). Nephew of Jaffrey Pyncheon I; arranges evidence so as to convict Clifford Pyncheon of murdering Jaffrey Pyncheon I; owner of the Pyncheon house; dies mysteriously in Nathaniel Hawthorne's *The House of the Seven Gables*.

Amanda (Pinnie) Pynsent. Poor dressmaker who is a friend of Florentine Vivier and the guardian of Hyacinth Robinson in Henry James's *The Princess Casamassima*.

Pyrrhus. Son of Achilles; killed by Orestes in John Erskine's *The Private Life of Helen of Troy*.

Q

Cliff Quackenbush. Crew manager at Devon School in John Knowles's *A Separate Peace.*

Catherine (Cat) Quarles. Affectionate daughter of Eliza Quarles and mother of an illegitimate son in Alice Adams's *Listening to Billie.*

Eliza Erskine Hamilton (Liza) Quarles. Passionate woman who struggles to find success and independence; protagonist of Alice Adams's *Listening to Billie.*

Evan Quarles. Overweight, heavy-drinking older husband of Eliza Quarles; dies from an overdose of sleeping pills in Alice Adams's *Listening to Billie.*

Dr. Willoughby Quarles. President of Terwillinger College, which Elmer Gantry attends, in Sinclair Lewis's *Elmer Gantry.*

Hazel Quarrier. American missionary, wife of Martin Quarrier, and mother of Billy Quarrier; driven mad by the hardships of the South American jungle in Peter Matthiessen's *At Play in the Fields of the Lord.*

Martin (Mart) Quarrier. American missionary, husband of Hazel Quarrier, and father of Billy Quarrier; murdered by one of the Indians he attempts to convert in Peter Matthiessen's *At Play in the Fields of the Lord.*

William (Billie) Martin Quarrier. Son of Martin and Hazel Quarrier; accidental victim of his parents' misguided efforts as missionaries; dies of blackwater fever in Peter Matthiessen's *At Play in the Fields of the Lord.*

Lieutenant Commander Philip Francis Queeg. Tyrannical captain of the USS *Caine* who loses his command in a mutiny in Herman Wouk's *The Caine Mutiny.*

Queen Mab (Old Deb). Old, wise, and respected Indian woman; remains behind when other Indians depart for a more remote wilderness in Charles Brockden Brown's *Edgar Huntly.*

Queenie. Sister of Herman and Verman; her huge goiter attracts the neighborhood children, until she drives them away, in Booth Tarkington's *Penrod.*

David (Davy) Queenslace. Anglican monk who believes that he is to write a new book of the Bible; drowns in a pond in Sinclair Lewis's *The God-Seeker.*

Queequeg (Quohog). Cannibal who is Starbuck's harpooner and who is Ishmael's good friend; his coffin saves Ishmael's life in Herman Melville's *Moby-Dick.*

Waldo Quigley. Pump organ salesman in Jessamyn West's *The Friendly Persuasion.*

Barney Quill. Owner of the Thunder Bay Inn who is killed by Frederic Manion for allegedly having raped Manion's wife Laura in Robert Traver's *Anatomy of a Murder.*

Flora Quill. Englishwoman and proprietor of the Panamanian Hotel de las Palmas, frequented mainly by prostitutes; friend of Frieda Copperfield and Pacifica in Jane Bowles's *Two Serious Ladies.*

Geoffrey Quill. Cousin of Marjorie Morningstar; an author in Herman Wouk's *Marjorie Morningstar.*

Clare (Cue) Quilty. Famous playwright with whom Dolores Haze deceives Humbert Humbert and whom Humbert murders in Vladimir Nabokov's *Lolita.*

Virginia Quilty. Beautiful pursuer of Randy Rivers, then Osgood Wallop, whom she marries, in Peter De Vries's *Mrs. Wallop.*

Emmett Quincy. Member of Ned Pepper's outlaw gang that holds captive Mattie Ross, Rooster Cogburn, and LaBoeuf in Charles Portis's *True Grit.*

Jacob Quincy. Commander of the Oligarchy's air forces who sells out to the Brotherhood of Destruction and bombs the Oligarchy's army in Ignatius Donnelly's *Caesar's Column.*

B. A. Quinlan. Unemotional head coach of the Dallas Cowboys who would rather deal with ideas than with people in Peter Gent's *North Dallas Forty.*

Harrison Quinn. Philandering neighbor of the Charleses who romances Dorothy Wynant in Dashiell Hammett's *The Thin Man.*

James (Jim) Quinn. Detroit businessman who owns a cabin on the grounds of the Centennial Club; long-time friend who always loses wax bullet duels with Vernor Stanton in Thomas McGuane's *The Sporting Club.*

Quint. Amity fisherman hired to hunt the Great White Shark; killed during the hunt in Peter Benchley's *Jaws.*

Bill Quint. I.W.W. instigator sent to organize the mineworkers in Personville in Dashiell Hammett's *Red Harvest.*

John Quint. Articulate, self-confident soldier with whom Robert Prentice longs to establish a close-buddy relationship; killed by a land mine while Prentice is hospitalized with pneumonia in Richard Yates's *A Special Providence*.

Peter Quint. Ghost who the governess believes influences Miles in Henry James's *The Turn of the Screw*.

Matthew Quintal. Largest and most obnoxious crewman aboard the HMS *Bounty* who, as a leader of the mutineers, nearly kills Captain Bligh before being persuaded to set him adrift in Charles Nordhoff and James Norman Hall's *Mutiny on the Bounty*; kills Minarii and is killed by Alexander Smith in *Pitcairn's Island*.

Quoin. Ill-natured quarter-gunner aboard the *Neversink* in Herman Melville's *White-Jacket*.

R

Mr. R. (Baron R.). Demanding German writer whose books Hugh Person edits; confesses before he dies that his stepdaughter, Julia Moore, is the only woman he ever loved in Vladimir Nabokov's *Transparent Things*.

Mrs. Rabbage. Maid who works for the Turners in Alison Lurie's *Love and Friendship*.

Rabbit. See Harry Angstrom.

Jascha Rabinowich. See Johannes Robin.

Lynne Rabinowitz. Civil rights activist, wife of Truman Held, and mother of Camara in Alice Walker's *Meridian*.

Rachel. Reliable maid of Austin and Martha King; leaves town to protect her daughter from sexual abuse but later returns to work for the Kings in William Maxwell's *Time Will Darken It*.

Rachel. See Maria.

Rachel. Slave who helps Leslie Collins care for a baby boy rejected by his mother in Harriette Simpson Arnow's *The Kentucky Trace*.

Aunt Rachel. Elderly black woman who constantly pleads with powerful whites to keep her sons off the chain gang and to allow her to have food and shelter in W. E. B. Du Bois's *The Quest of the Silver Fleece*.

Philip Rack. Young married musician who gives piano lessons to Lucette Veen while reputedly carrying on a love affair with Ada Veen; Van Veen wants to challenge him to a duel, but changes his mind when he sees that Rack is dying in Vladimir Nabokov's *Ada*.

Mrs. Rackover. Housekeeper for the Levs who constantly rebukes Asher Lev in Chaim Potok's *My Name Is Asher Lev*.

Radclyffe. See Edmund Mortimer.

Lady Radclyffe. See Amber St. Clare.

Nadine Rademacher. Nude storyteller who leaves New York and travels to Texas with Glen Selvy in Don DeLillo's *Running Dog*.

Male (Rad) Raditzer. Sinister and unsought companion of Charlie Stark; falls overboard to his death in Peter Matthiessen's *Raditzer*.

Arthur (Boo) Radley. Mysterious, reclusive neighbor and "mockingbird" who leaves gifts for Jem and Scout Finch; thwarts Bob Ewell's attempt to murder Scout and Jem in Harper Lee's *To Kill a Mockingbird*.

Radney. Mate aboard the *Town-Ho* who has an altercation with Steelkilt; killed by Moby Dick in Herman Melville's *Moby-Dick*.

Rafael. Gypsy member of Pablo's partisan band in Ernest Hemingway's *For Whom the Bell Tolls*.

Andalous (Andy) Raffine. American painter in Paris who imagines enounters with various types of women; narrator of Lawrence Ferlinghetti's *Her*.

Captain Rafton. British ex-army officer who befriends Helen Fairwood and gives her a tour of Karnak in H. D.'s *Palimpsest*.

Squire (Josiah Devotion, Charles Edward Montmorency) Raglan. Vicar's son turned London pickpocket; lover of Hannah Bridewell at Newgate Prison and father of the child she leaves with the Indians; transported to Virginia and bought by Peregrine Cockburn; steals Witcikti's English tomahawk as well as Peregrine's sash, horse, and silverhandled crop; becomes a frontier lawyer and is killed by Jeremiah Catlett in Mary Lee Settle's *O Beulah Land*; his grave is the basis for a local myth of tragic Indian lovers in *Know Nothing*.

Ragnell. Wife of Gawaine in Thomas Berger's *Arthur Rex*.

Count (Rags) Ragsdale. Itinerant gambler and rival of Augie for the love of Florence Dessau in Arna Wendell Bontemps's *God Sends Sunday*.

Rahim. "Soul at the seventh aspect" of Ralph Himebaugh in Robert Coover's *The Origin of the Brunists*.

Faye (Faysie) Raider. Roommate and lover of Molly Bolt at the University of Florida in Rita Mae Brown's *Rubyfruit Jungle*.

Raider (Big Raider). Jazz singer and boyfriend of Osella Barnes in Diane Johnson's *The Shadow Knows*.

Railroad Tommy. Co-owner of the local barbershop and member of the racial revenge group called the Seven Days in Toni Morrison's *Song of Solomon*.

Rain. Female follower of Coransee in Octavia E. Butler's *Patternmaster*.

Rainbow. Village resident who rapes a young Jewess and, finding himself trapped by a vaginal spasm, mutilates and kills her in Jerzy Kosinski's *The Painted Bird*.

Sue Rainey. Wealthy daughter of Colonel Tom Rainey; marries Sam McPherson, miscarries three times, and leaves her husband in Sherwood Anderson's *Windy McPherson's Son.*

Colonel Tom Rainey. President of the Rainey Arms Company who helps Sam McPherson succeed and then commits suicide in Sherwood Anderson's *Windy McPherson's Son.*

Colonel Rainsborough. Officer in Cromwell's army who speaks out for greater democracy; reassigned to the North and mysteriously murdered, possibly by Cromwell's agents, in Mary Lee Settle's *Prisons.*

Dudley Rainsford. Temporarily insane, melancholy frontier hero in James Kirke Paulding's *Westward Ho!*

Raisl. Wife who has deserted Yakov Bok in Bernard Malamud's *The Fixer.*

Gabriela (Gaby) Rak. Employee of the American Embassy in Warsaw who helps supply money and weapons to the Warsaw ghetto fighters; lover of Andrei Androfski in Leon Uris's *Mila 18.*

Carew Ralegh. Sir Walter Ralegh's son in George Garrett's *Death of the Fox.*

Elizabeth Throckmorton (Bess) Ralegh. Wife of Sir Walter Ralegh in George Garrett's *Death of the Fox.*

Sir Walter (Wat) Ralegh. Poet, scholar, soldier, and courtier awaiting execution in George Garrett's *Death of the Fox.*

Ralph. Friend of Wendy Gahaghan; agrees to accept her and her unborn baby in Alison Lurie's *The War Between the Tates.*

Clementina (Teeny, Tina) Lovell Ralston. Illegitimate daughter of Charlotte Lovell and Clement Spender; adopted by her aunt, Delia Ralston, when her mysterious origins prevent her from marrying a socially correct suitor in Edith Wharton's *The Old Maid.*

Delia Lovell Ralston. Wife of James Ralston and thus a member of one of the most conservative and wealthy families of old New York in Edith Wharton's *The Old Maid.*

James (Jim) Ralston. Wealthy and socially prominent husband of Delia Ralston in Edith Wharton's *The Old Maid.*

Joseph (Joe) Ralston. Cousin of Jim Ralston and fiancé of Charlotte Lovell until the engagement is broken in Edith Wharton's *The Old Maid.*

Clarence (Crimson Rambler) Rambo. Class bully who is rousted by Edwin Kibbler, Jr., in Jessamyn West's *Cress Delahanty.*

Mary Rambo. Harlem woman who owns a boardinghouse where the narrator lives in Ralph Ellison's *Invisible Man.*

White-Eye Ramford. Blind New Orleans blues guitarist and street-music partner of Caleb Peck in Anne Tyler's *Searching for Caleb.*

Arthur Ramírez. Police chief in Key Bonita, Florida, who looks after Clinton Williams in James Leo Herlihy's *All Fall Down.*

Ramírez-Suárez. Attentive hotel owner in Majorca in Gail Godwin's *The Perfectionists.*

Ramos. Psychiatrist for Janet Ross in Michael Crichton's *The Terminal Man.*

Madame Ramoz. Dictator's wife persuaded by George Levanter to influence the release of political prisoners in Jerzy Kosinski's *Blind Date.*

David Ramsay. Father of John Ramsay and neighbor of Allen Musgrove; Tory partisans burn his farm in John Pendleton Kennedy's *Horse-Shoe Robinson.*

Rob Ramsay. War veteran who commits suicide by walking off a pier in Henry Miller's *Black Spring.*

John Ramsay (Ramsey). Son of David Ramsay and beau of Mary Musgrove; helps Horse Shoe Robinson free Arthur Butler; dies while protecting Butler from Tory marauders in John Pendleton Kennedy's *Horse-Shoe Robinson.*

Mrs. Rance. American-born friend of Dotty and Kitty Lutch; travels in the Ververs' social circle in Henry James's *The Golden Bowl.*

Ben Rand. Circuit court clerk who narrates part of Shelby Foote's *Follow Me Down.*

Benjamin Turnbull Rand. Dying chairman of the board of First American Financial Corporation and adviser to the president of the United States; befriends Chance and launches his political career in Jerzy Kosinski's *Being There.*

Billie Rand. Aspiring starlet and companion of Al Manheim; becomes a prostitute in Budd Schulberg's *What Makes Sammy Run?*

Elizabeth Eve (EE) Rand. Sexually frustrated wife of billionaire power broker Benjamin Turnbull Rand; falls in love with Chance in Jerzy Kosinski's *Being There.*

Julie (Aunt Julie, Miss Julie) Rand. Elderly aunt of Marcus Payne; has knowledge of Marshall Hebert's earlier criminal acts in Ernest J. Gaines's *Of Love and Dust.*

Lewis Rand. Ambitious son of a tobacco roller; attorney and husband of Jacqueline Churchill; protégé of Thomas Jefferson and conspirator with Aaron Burr to rule Mexico; murders his magnanimous rival Ludwell Cary in Mary Johnston's *Lewis Rand.*

Sam Rand. Arkansas-born infantryman who becomes a companion of John Quint and Robert Prentice; having lost his index finger, he fires his rifle with his "social finger" in Richard Yates's *A Special Providence.*

Dr. (Ran) Randall. Contentious druggist; discusses social problems with Sidney Wyeth in Oscar Micheaux's *The Forged Note.*

Elizabeth Thornwell Alvin (Betty) Randall. See Elizabeth Thornwell Alvin.

Merrill Randall. Elegant poet; Jack Duluoz walks out on Randall's poetry reading in Jack Kerouac's *Desolation Angels.*

James Heyward (Jim) Randolph. College classmate idolized by George Webber in Thomas Wolfe's *The Web and the Rock.*

Jim Randolph. Married college instructor whom Maureen Wendall seduces and marries in Joyce Carol Oates's *them.*

John Randolph, Earl of Almsbury. Cavalier, best friend of Bruce Carlton, and frequent companion and guide of Amber St. Clare in Kathleen Winsor's *Forever Amber.*

Varnum Random. Poetry consultant for the Library of Congress and patient host of Raphael Urso and Jack Duluoz in Jack Kerouac's *Desolation Angels.*

Rango. Self-destructive Guatemalan guitar player and nightclub singer; husband of Zora and lover of Djuna in Anaïs Nin's *The Four-Chambered Heart.*

Frances Rankin. See Frances Rankin Mitchell.

Judd (Juddie) Rankin. Homespun Iowa newspaper editor and author; father of Frances Rankin Mitchell, grandfather of Judson and Madeleine Mitchell, and second cousin of Adah Logan in Susan Glaspell's *Judd Rankin's Daughter.*

Peggy Rankin. High school English teacher and occasional lover of Jacob Horner in John Barth's *The End of the Road.*

Basil Ransom. Cousin of Olive Chancellor; Mississippi gentleman who plans to marry Verena Tarrant in Henry James's *The Bostonians.*

Sammy Ransom. Young black man and putative father of Mildred Sutton's illegitimate child in Reynolds Price's *A Long and Happy Life.*

Fred (Freddie) Ransome. British poet and soldier; lover of Mavis Landour and former husband of Raymonde Ransome in H. D.'s *Palimpsest.*

Raymonde Ransome. American poet living in London and formerly the wife of Freddie Ransome in H. D.'s *Palimpsest.*

Henryk Rapaport. Socialist who, despite political differences with many of those also trapped within the Warsaw ghetto, joins in the united effort to survive destruction at the hands of the Nazis in John Hersey's *The Wall.*

Kermit Raphaelson. Midget artist married to Laureen Raphaelson; Malcolm is exposed to the couple's marital problems soon after meeting them in James Purdy's *Malcolm.*

Laurel Raphaelson. Woman with a sordid past married to Kermit Raphaelson; leaves Kermit and marries Girard Girard in James Purdy's *Malcolm.*

Emil Rappaport. Widowed physician who treats and later marries Eunice Punck in Peter De Vries's *Reuben, Reuben.*

Rare Spectacled Bears. Bears who escape the animal massacre in John Irving's *Setting Free the Bears.*

Rartoo. Chief of Tamai in Herman Melville's *Omoo.*

Ras the Exhorter (Ras the Destroyer). Violent black nationalist who starts a riot in Ralph Ellison's *Invisible Man.*

Raschid. See Keith Cain.

Shelly Rasmussen. Berkeley dropout and secretary to Lyman Ward in Wallace Stegner's *Angle of Repose.*

Sona Rasmussen. Half-Japanese, half-Norwegian professor at Benton College and maker of welded sculpture in Randall Jarrell's *Pictures from an Institution.*

Nurse (Big Nurse, Miss Rat-shed, Mother Ratched) Ratched. Domineering head nurse of a mental hospital ward; antagonist of Randle McMurphy in Ken Kesey's *One Flew Over the Cuckoo's Nest.*

Senator Silas P. Ratcliffe. Illinois senator, then Secretary of the Treasury; his proposal of marriage to

Madeleine Lee is rejected after she learns of his improper political dealings in Henry Adams's *Democracy*.

Henrietta Rathbone. Small-town dressmaker; loves Tommy Bettersworth, who turns to her when his wife, Olivia Lattimore, is away on acting engagements in Mary Austin's *A Woman of Genius*.

Adèle Ratignolle. Friend of Edna Pontellier and a "mother-woman" who bears a child every two years in Kate Chopin's *The Awakening*.

V. K. Ratliff. Sewing machine salesman in William Faulkner's *The Hamlet*, *The Town*, and *The Mansion*. See also Suratt.

Shazar Lazarus Ratner. Discoverer of Ratner's Star; kept alive in a biomembrane in Don DeLillo's *Ratner's Star*.

Rau-Ru (the k'la, Lieutenant Oliver Cromwell Jones). Trusted black employee who turns against Hamish Bond in Robert Penn Warren's *Band of Angels*.

Dr. Rausch. Physician who treats Henry Miller's father and also lectures Miller on the evils of "going against Nature" in Henry Miller's *Tropic of Capricorn*.

Angela Ravage. Movie starlet and prize in an essay contest won by Tom Waltz in Peter De Vries's *Let Me Count the Ways*.

Raven. Model for Renate; owns a raven in Anaïs Nin's *Collages*.

Blaine Raven. Father of Genevieve Raven Reinhart and father-in-law of Carl Reinhart in Thomas Berger's *Reinhart in Love* and *Vital Parts*.

Elijah Raven. Best man at Bukka Doopeyduk's wedding; heretic Nazarene apprentice whose greeting is "Flim Flam Alakazam!" in Ishmael Reed's *The Free-Lance Pallbearers*.

Genevieve Raven. See Genevieve Raven Reinhart.

Gaylord Ravenal. Actor on the *Cotton Blossom* who is also a gambler; marries Magnolia Hawks in Edna Ferber's *Show Boat*.

Magnolia Hawks Ravenal. Daughter of Andy and Parthenia Ann Hawks; actress on the *Cotton Blossom* who later appears on the New York stage; marries Gaylord Ravenal, by whom she has a daughter, in Edna Ferber's *Show Boat*.

Doctor Ravenel. Father of Lillie Ravenel; his loyalty to the Union cause during the Civil War begins the process of Lillie's conversion to that cause in John

William DeForest's *Miss Ravenel's Conversion from Secession to Loyalty*.

Lillie Ravenel. See Lillie Ravenel Carter.

Ravenspur. See Gerald Stanhope.

Lady Ravenspur. See Amber St. Clare.

Ravenstone. See Jakob Gradus.

Turner Ravis. Virtuous Victorian who breaks her engagement to Vandover when she discovers his seduction of Ida Wade and Wade's suicide in Frank Norris's *Vandover and the Brute*.

Ravus. See Jakob Gradus.

Joan Rawshanks. Movie star on location in San Francisco; appears in a reverie of Jack Duluoz in Jack Kerouac's *Visions of Cody*.

Harriet Ray. Conventional young woman who admires old New York society; seen by Mrs. Marvell as a marriage prospect for Ralph Marvell in Edith Wharton's *The Custom of the Country*.

John Ray, Jr. Editor of the manuscript Humbert Humbert writes while in prison; author of the foreword to that published manuscript, which is Vladimir Nabokov's *Lolita*.

Rayal. Patternmaster, husband of Jansee, and father of Teray and Coransee in Octavia E. Butler's *Patternmaster*.

Bishop Rayber. Idiot child of Bernice Bishop and Mr. Rayber; inadvertently baptized by Francis Marion Tarwater in the act of drowning him in Flannery O'Connor's *The Violent Bear It Away*.

Mr. Rayber. Schoolteacher, husband of Bernice Bishop, father of Bishop Rayber, and uncle of Francis Marion Tarwater; fails in his attempt to reclaim Tarwater from the religious influence of Mason Tarwater; young Tarwater seeks out Rayber after Mason Tarwater's death in Flannery O'Connor's *The Violent Bear It Away*.

George Rayburn. Owner of the house the Tussies rent in Jesse Stuart's *Taps for Private Tussie*.

Dorothy Raycroft. Mistress of Anthony Patch when he is a soldier in World War I in F. Scott Fitzgerald's *The Beautiful and Damned*.

Raymond. Student who serves on the Cinema Committee with Hill Gallagher during the student rebellion in James Jones's *The Merry Month of May*.

Raymond (Ray). Railroad dining car waiter and intellectual who shares his knowledge with Jake Brown in Claude McKay's *Home to Harlem*; black American writer who plans to write about the expatriates living in Marseilles in *Banjo*.

Charles Raymond. White manager of the Phosphate Mining Company; former lover of Kate Wentworth, whose son, Saint Wentworth, Raymond employs, in DuBose Heyward's *Mamba's Daughters*.

Everett Raymond. Junior partner in the law firm of Veeley, Carr, and Raymond who, because he does not think that Eleanore Leavenworth killed her uncle, starts his own investigation of the case; narrator of Anna Katharine Green's *The Leavenworth Case*.

Helen Raymond. Librarian who helps Felix Fay continue his education after he drops out of high school in Floyd Dell's *Moon-Calf*.

Mr. Raymonds. Retired university professor; lecherous employer of Meridian Hill in Alice Walker's *Meridian*.

Read. Womanizer and senior partner with Glymmer Read in Nathan Asch's *The Office*.

Billy Reagan. Hoodlum and brother of Tim Reagan; his quarrels with Legs Diamond result in the Hotsy Totsy Club shootout in William Kennedy's *Legs*.

Christian Reagan. Private in the United States Army; a double for Agee Ward in Wright Morris's *The Man Who Was There*.

Tim Reagan. Hoodlum and brother of Billy Reagan; killed by Legs Diamond in William Kennedy's *Legs*.

Henry (Hank) Rearden. Steel producer who invents a revolutionary new metal; joins with Dagny Taggart to build the John Galt Line in Ayn Rand's *Atlas Shrugged*.

Lillian Rearden. Wife of Henry Rearden, against whom she conspires to defeat, in Ayn Rand's *Atlas Shrugged*.

Reb. Black North Carolinian and boyhood chum of George Washington in Cecil Brown's *The Life and Loves of Mr. Jiveass Nigger*.

Reba. See Rebecca Dead.

The Rebbe. Leader of Hasidic Jews who uses Aryeh Lev as an emissary and who assists Asher Lev in Chaim Potok's *My Name Is Asher Lev*.

Nina (Madame Lecerf, Ninka) Toorovetz de Rechnoy. Russian woman whose letters V. finds in Sebastian Knight's apartment; V. tries to track her down after destroying the letters without reading them, according to Knight's instructions, in Vladimir Nabokov's *The Real Life of Sebastian Knight*.

Red. Bouncer murdered by Popeye; appears in William Faulkner's *Sanctuary* and *Requiem for a Nun*.

Red. Drug addict in Herbert Simmons's *Corner Boy*.

Red Bull. Magical bull who chases all but one unicorn into the sea below King Haggard's castle in Peter S. Beagle's *The Last Unicorn*.

Red Clay (Lufki-Humma). Natchez Indian who is an ancestor of Agricola Fusilier in George Washington Cable's *The Grandissimes*.

Red-Eye. Huge, atavistic enemy of Big-Tooth in Jack London's *Before Adam*.

Red John. Drinker and womanizer said to be "devil possessed" in Carlene Hatcher Polite's *The Flagellants*.

Red Man. Wrestling opponent of Laughing Boy; hopes to marry Slim Girl in Oliver La Farge's *Laughing Boy*.

Red Max. See Max.

Red Whiskers. Sailor aboard the *Indomitable* whom Billy Budd strikes in Herman Melville's *Billy Budd*.

Mr. Redbrook. Reforming grassroots political organizer in Winston Churchill's *Mr. Crewe's Career*.

Eddie Win(g)field (Wing) Redburn. Major alto saxophonist in John Clellon Holmes's *The Horn*.

Wellingborough (Boots, Buttons, Jack, Jimmy Dux, Lord Stormont, Pillgarlic) Redburn. Narrator who sails to Liverpool and back to New York in Herman Melville's *Redburn*.

Fenwick (Fen, Uncle Wick) Redcliff. Father-in-law of Judith Redcliff; Charleston patriarch and entrepreneur in Josephine Pinckney's *Three O'Clock Dinner*.

Judith (Judy) Redcliff. Widow of a prominent Charlestonian; has a genteel job at the Fuel and Welfare Society in Josephine Pinckney's *Three O'Clock Dinner*.

Lucian Quintillian Redcliff. Half brother of Fenwick Redcliff and real estate agent in Josephine Pinckney's *Three O'Clock Dinner*.

Tat Redcliff. Young brother-in-law of Judith Redcliff; part owner of several gas stations and a socialist; smitten by Lorena Hessenwinkle, whom he marries for a short time, not knowing she was his brother's lover, in Josephine Pinckney's *Three O'Clock Dinner*.

Margrit (Maggie) Westoever Reddick. Estranged spouse of Max Reddick to whom he returns in

John A. Williams's *The Man Who Cried I Am*.

Max (Mox) Reddick. Afro-American journalist and novelist dying of cancer; receives from his murdered mentor and rival, Harry Ames, the story of a CIA contingency plan for removing the minority population of the United States into concentration camps in John A. Williams's *The Man Who Cried I Am*.

Joab Ellery Reddington. Well-educated but corrupt high-school principal and clergyman who starts Gloria Wandrous sniffing ether and seduces her in John O'Hara's *Butterfield 8*.

Brian Redfield. Physician husband of Irene Redfield; charmed by Clare Kendry in Nella Larsen's *Passing*.

Irene ('Rene) Redfield. Chicago native, member of Harlem's social set, and wife of Brian Redfield; renews an acquaintance with Clare Kendry and keeps secret the knowledge that Clare is passing for white in Nella Larsen's *Passing*.

Martha Redford. Judge in the Timothy Landry case who lectures patrolman Bumper Morgan after he perjures himself in Joseph Wambaugh's *The Blue Knight*.

Redlaw. See Ben Redmond.

Stuart (Stu) Redman. East Texan chosen by Mother Abagail to lead The Stand against Randall Flagg's forces in Stephen King's *The Stand*.

Ben (Redlaw) Redmond. Lawyer who murders Colonel John Sartoris; appears in William Faulkner's *Sartoris (Flags in the Dust)*, *The Unvanquished*, and *Requiem for a Nun*.

Henry Reed. Neighbor and fiancé of Jane Bellmont, to whose money he is attracted; Jane rejects him in favor of George Means; later conspires with Mrs. Bellmont against Jenny Bellmont in Harriet E. Wilson's *Our Nig*.

Mary Jane (The Monkey) Reed. Semiliterate fashion model from West Virginia and lover of Alex Portnoy, who abandons her in an Athens hotel, in Philip Roth's *Portnoy's Complaint*.

Doctor Reefy. Winesburg physician who has a brief, platonic affair with Elizabeth Willard in Sherwood Anderson's *Winesburg, Ohio*.

Martha Goddard Reeves. School board member who speaks the Apache language and aids in spreading fear among whites concerning the ferocity of Agocho in Edwin Corle's *Fig Tree John*.

Vivian Sternwood Regan. Older daughter of General Sternwood; her husband Rusty Regan is murdered by her sister Carmen Sternwood, in Raymond Chandler's *The Big Sleep*.

Martha Reganhart. Former wife of an artist; single-handedly supports two children with her work as a waitress; lives with Gabe Wallach for a time before she gives in to Sid Jaffe's proposal of marriage in Philip Roth's *Letting Go*.

Reggie. Attractive, French-looking young woman; heroin addict who as a child was sexually abused by her mother in Calvin Hernton's *Scarecrow*.

Regina. Young male homosexual and transvestite who caters to the perverse sexual appetite of Harry Black until Black no longer has money to lavish on him in Hubert Selby, Jr.'s *Last Exit to Brooklyn*.

Paul Reichelderfer. Yale classmate of Sidney Tate; introduces Tate to Grace Brock Caldwell in John O'Hara's *A Rage to Live*.

Rosa Reichl. Landlady of Charles Upton in Berlin in Katherine Anne Porter's *The Leaning Tower*.

Roberta Reid. See Roberta Reid Fairchild.

Frank (Weary) Reilley. Violent young man whom Studs Lonigan beats up in a fight in James T. Farrell's *Young Lonigan*; starts a fight at a football game in *The Young Manhood of Studs Lonigan*; reported to have raped a young woman in *Judgment Day*.

Kathleen (Kate) Lynch Reilley. Mother of Jack Curran and Susy Reilley and ex-wife of Johnny Curran in Mark Steadman's *A Lion's Share*.

Susy Reilley. Daughter of Kathleen Reilley and younger half sister of Jack Curran in Mark Steadman's *A Lion's Share*.

Reilly. Police lieutenant working with Jack Rose in Paul Cain's *Fast One*.

Frank Reilly. Coworker of Charlie Gordon; pities Gordon after the intelligence experiment fails in Daniel Keyes's *Flowers for Algernon*.

Harry Reilly. Socially ambitious and wealthy Irish-American in John O'Hara's *Appointment in Samarra*.

Blaine Reinhart. Rebellious but later conformist son of Carl and Genevieve Reinhart in Thomas Berger's *Vital Parts*.

Carlo B. (Carl) Reinhart. American soldier in Europe in World War II who later marries Genevieve Raven and fathers Blaine and Winona Reinhart; recurrent protagonist of Thomas Berger's *Crazy in Berlin*, *Reinhart in Love*, and *Vital Parts*.

Dick Reinhart. Older university student who lives at the same boarding house as Lymie Peters and Spud Latham; confidant of Latham in William Maxwell's *The Folded Leaf.*

Genevieve Raven (Gen) Reinhart. Manipulative wife and later ex-wife of Carl Reinhart in Thomas Berger's *Reinhart in Love* and *Vital Parts.*

George Reinhart. Father of Carlo Reinhart in Thomas Berger's *Reinhart in Love.*

Maw Reinhart. Cantankerous mother of Carlo Reinhart in Thomas Berger's *Reinhart in Love.*

Mrs. Reinhart. White woman for whom Aunt Hager Williams washes clothes in Langston Hughes's *Not Without Laughter.*

Winona Reinhart. Daughter of Carl and Genevieve Reinhart in Thomas Berger's *Vital Parts.*

Peter Reinick. Lover of Rita Salus and anti-Nazi who once ran an underground newspaper; caught and tortured by the Gestapo in Martha Gellhorn's *A Stricken Field.*

Mademoiselle Reisz. Ill-tempered pianist whose music inspires Edna Pontellier in Kate Chopin's *The Awakening.*

Joanne Remington. Fiancée of Emmett Hunter; her affair with Phil Elliott helps get Elliott kicked out of football in Peter Gent's *North Dallas Forty.*

Phil (CO) Renaldi. Conscientious objector who works in an army hospital and befriends Alfonso Columbato in William Wharton's *Birdy.*

Renata (Contessa, Daughter). Italian lover of Richard Cantwell in Ernest Hemingway's *Across the River and into the Trees.*

Renate. Painter, part-time hostess at the Paradise Inn nightclub, and central character in Anaïs Nin's *Collages.*

Renato. Young barber who serves as a kind of confessor for his patrons, and friend who listens to Paolo's stories of female conquest in Tennessee Williams's *The Roman Spring of Mrs. Stone.*

Corinna Rendlesham. Spinster choir leader at St. John's Episcopal Church in Constance Fenimore Woolson's *For the Major.*

Dorothy (Dottie) Renfrew. Aspiring social worker and lover of Dick Brown in Mary McCarthy's *The Group.*

Beulah Beecham Renfro. Wife of Ralph Renfro, mother of Jack Jordan Renfro and four other chil-dren, granddaughter of Granny Vaughn, and hostess of Granny's birthday reunion in Eudora Welty's *Losing Battles.*

Ella Fay Renfro. Sixteen-year-old sister of Jack Renfro; removes an heirloom wedding ring from the family Bible only to have it taken from her by Curly Stovall, who is attacked by Jack Renfro and subsequently has him arrested, in Eudora Welty's *Losing Battles.*

Gloria Short Renfro. Orphan, wife of Jack Renfro, and former teacher at Banner School who attended the state Normal school for teachers in Eudora Welty's *Losing Battles.*

Jack Jordan Renfro. Oldest son of Beulah and Ralph Renfro and husband of Gloria Short Renfro; serves one and a half years in Parchman State Penitentiary for aggravated battery and robbery, escapes to attend Granny Vaughn's birthday celebration, and rescues Maud Eva Moody's car from the edge of Banner Top in Eudora Welty's *Losing Battles.*

Lady May Renfro. Baby daughter of Jack and Gloria Renfro; born while her father is in prison in Eudora Welty's *Losing Battles.*

Lexie Renfro. Unmarried sister of Ralph Renfro; cares for Julia Mortimer before her death in Eudora Welty's *Losing Battles.*

Ralph Renfro. Husband of Beulah Renfro and father of Jack Renfro and four other children; limps as the result of a dynamiting accident in Eudora Welty's *Losing Battles.*

Mr. Renling. Wealthy haberdasher for the carriage trade who, along with his wife, introduces Augie March to luxury and tries in vain to adopt him legally in Saul Bellow's *The Adventures of Augie March.*

Mrs. Renling. Wealthy haberdasher who, with her husband, wishes to adopt Augie Marsh legally and refine him in Saul Bellow's *The Adventures of Augie March.*

Amy (Baby) Rennsdale. Youngest member of the neighborhood dancing class; Penrod Schofield ruins her birthday party in Booth Tarkington's *Penrod and Sam*; her youth generally works to her disadvantage with other children in *Penrod* and *Penrod Jashber.*

Red (Monsignor Renton) Renton. Rector of the cathedral in the Roman Catholic diocese in J. F. Powers's *Morte D'Urban.*

Michael (Mike) S. Reusing (Rushing). Businessman who meets Francesca Bolt in an airport; his brief affair with her stimulates her short-lived effort at independence in Gail Godwin's *Glass People.*

Alfred Revere. Black sexton at Christ Church; patriarch of a family of respectable workers; failing in health and concerned about his approaching death in James Gould Cozzens's *By Love Possessed.*

Clara Walpole Revere. Daughter of migrant farm workers, wife of Curt Revere, and lover of Lowry, by whom she has a son, Swan Revere; protagonist of Joyce Carol Oates's *A Garden of Earthly Delights.*

Curt Revere. Wealthy businessman who marries Clara Walpole in Joyce Carol Oates's *A Garden of Earthly Delights.*

Steven (Swan) Revere. Son of Clara Walpole by her lover Lowry; kills his stepfather, Curt Revere, and himself in Joyce Carol Oates's *A Garden of Earthly Delights.*

Lucius (Lucky) Rexford. Fair, bright Chancellor of the University in John Barth's *Giles Goat-Boy.*

John Reyes. Doctor of Blix Hollister in Jessamyn West's *A Matter of Time.*

Douglass Reynolds. Alcoholic suitor of Adah Logan; commits suicide in Susan Glaspell's *Judd Rankin's Daughter.*

Elizabeth Reynolds. Daughter and older child of Margaret and Paul Reynolds in Anne Richardson Roiphe's *Up the Sandbox!*

Ellen Reynolds. Wife of Skip Reynolds in John Updike's *Bech: A Book.*

John Reynolds. Northern general who is offered command of the Union army but declines because he is not promised full control; dies at the beginning of the Battle of Gettysburg in Michael Shaara's *The Killer Angels.*

Margaret Ferguson Reynolds. Wife of Paul Reynolds and mother of Elizabeth and Peter Reynolds; housewife who fantasizes about what she could have been as she narrates Anne Richardson Roiphe's *Up the Sandbox!*

Paul Reynolds. Husband of Margaret Reynolds and father of Elizabeth and Peter Reynolds; history student who spends much time in the library researching revolutions in Anne Richardson Roiphe's *Up the Sandbox!*

Peter Reynolds. Son and younger child of Margaret and Paul Reynolds in Anne Richardson Roiphe's *Up the Sandbox!*

Skip Reynolds. Contact man for Henry Bech at the American embassy in Russia; former basketball player from Wisconsin; husband of Ellen Reynolds in John Updike's *Bech: A Book.*

Rhea Rhadin. Head receptionist at Silver Publishing Company in Rita Mae Brown's *Rubyfruit Jungle.*

Fahyi Rhallon. Captain in the Iranian secret police; interrogates the American soldiers who are chasing Cacciato in Tim O'Brien's *Going after Cacciato.*

Rheba. White librarian in the art library where Jimson is employed; he rejects her advances in Carlene Hatcher Polite's *The Flagellants.*

Colonel Nathan Rhenn. Impoverished Southern gentleman and Unionist, supporter of the Reconstruction Acts, and chairman of the meeting to elect delegates to the Constitutional Convention in Albion W. Tourgee's *A Fool's Errand.*

George Rhewold. Physician who temporarily takes over the practice of the injured Doctor Caldwell; successfully courts William Caldwell in Mary Austin's *Santa Lucia.*

Lola Rhoades. Cello-playing siren who invites Tom More to share her idyllic life of the Old South in Walker Percy's *Love in the Ruins.*

Leonard (Len) Rhodes. Rural politician severely beaten by Fee Guthrie in Mary Noailles Murfree's *In the "Stranger People's" Country.*

Leo (Lee) Rhynor. Dashing army corporal and romantic interest of Francie Nolan in Betty Smith's *A Tree Grows in Brooklyn.*

Giuseppe Ribaudo. Former illegal alien in the United States who becomes interpreter and assistant to Major Joppolo in John Hersey's *A Bell for Adano.*

Don Andrés de Ribera. Viceroy of Peru who fathers three children by Camila Perichole in Thornton Wilder's *The Bridge of San Luis Rey.*

Don Jaime de Ribera. Son of Camila Perichole and Don Andrés de Ribera; goes to Lima to be taught by his Uncle Pio; dies in the fall of the bridge in Thornton Wilder's *The Bridge of San Luis Rey.*

Ric (Armando) and Rac (Dolores). Spanish twins who exhibit demonic, uncontrollable behavior in Katherine Anne Porter's *Ship of Fools.*

Francesca Ricci. Daughter of Michele Ricci; employed as a maid in the home of Mason Flagg, who rapes and kills her, in William Styron's *Set This House on Fire.*

Michele Ricci. Tubercular Italian peasant for whom Cass Kinsolving steals medicine; father of Francesca Ricci in William Styron's *Set This House on Fire*.

Bessie (Sister Bessie) Rice. Noseless, self-appointed evangelist who plans an automobile crusade with her teenaged husband, Dude Lester, in Erskine Caldwell's *Tobacco Road*.

Graham Rice. Co-conspirator in Willie Hall's plan to lynch a white policeman; kills Thomas Wilkerson in John Edgar Wideman's *The Lynchers*.

Mrs. J. J. Rice. Perfectionistic white employer of Mrs. Annjee Rodgers in Langston Hughes's *Not Without Laughter*.

Richard. Common law husband of Elizabeth Grimes and father of John Grimes; moves with Elizabeth to New York and commits suicide after he is falsely accused of armed robbery in James Baldwin's *Go Tell It on the Mountain*.

Richards. Computer specialist who is an assistant to Gerhard at the Neuropsychiatric Research Unit in Michael Crichton's *The Terminal Man*.

James (Black Jim) Richards. Grandfather of Hester Le Moyne and cousin of Red Jim Richards, whose land grant Black Jim fraudulently assumes, thus depriving Red Jim's descendants of a large tract of North Carolina land in Albion W. Tourgee's *Bricks without Straw*.

James (Red Jim) Richards. New England shipowner/captain who holds the original land grant of which Mulberry Hill and Red Wing plantations are a part; dies in Philadelphia after executing a will leaving his property to his wife and daughter in Albion W. Tourgee's *Bricks without Straw*.

Richardson. Doctor who tends to the dying Charlotte Rittenmeyer in William Faulkner's *The Wild Palms*.

Seth Richmond. Friend of George Willard; has a brief encounter with Helen White before his intended departure from Winesburg in Sherwood Anderson's *Winesburg, Ohio*.

Virginia Richmond. Mother of Seth Richmond; admires her son to the point that she is unable to be a proper parent to him in Sherwood Anderson's *Winesburg, Ohio*.

Carl Richter. German-born supporter of freedom who dies for the Union cause in Winston Churchill's *The Crisis*.

Rico. See Frederick.

Beverly Ricord. College sweetheart and lover of Shepherd Lewis in Ernest J. Gaines's *In My Father's House*.

Albert Riddell. Boyfriend of the sixteen-year-old Louise Attwater; his date with her is responsible for her meeting her future husband, Todd Eborn, in Reynolds Price's *Love and Work*.

Mrs. Evans Riddle. Proprietor of the Victory Thought-power Headquarters in New York City, for which Elmer Gantry teaches prosperity classes, in Sinclair Lewis's *Elmer Gantry*.

Harry Riddle. Nice but feckless lover who absconds with Mrs. Sarah Temple in Winston Churchill's *The Crossing*.

Mary Ridgeley. Friend of Sophia Westwyn; her discovery of a locket, featuring Sophia's likeness, that once belonged to Constantia Dudley, prompts Sophia to investigate Constantia's dire circumstances in Charles Brockden Brown's *Ormond*.

Evalina (Lina) Ridgely. See Evalina Ridgely Bowen.

Siegfried Rieber. Anti-Semitic publisher of a women's trade journal who has a grotesque romance with Lizzi Spöckenkieker in Katherine Anne Porter's *Ship of Fools*.

Tillie Ried. Wife of Willie Ried and second cousin of Jacob Upshur; tongue lasher of Tangierneck in Sarah E. Wright's *This Child's Gonna Live*.

Willie Ried. Husband of Tillie Ried; migrant worker in Sarah E. Wright's *This Child's Gonna Live*.

Etta Rieff. Wife of Morroe Rieff in Wallace Markfield's *To an Early Grave*.

Morroe Rieff. Speechwriter for a Jewish organization; gathers some friends of Leslie Braverman to attend Braverman's memorial service in Wallace Markfield's *To an Early Grave*.

Erwin Riemenschneider. Former convict who masterminds a million dollar jewelry robbery and whose weakness for young women causes his capture in William Riley Burnett's *The Asphalt Jungle*.

Paul Riesling. Close friend and former college roommate of George Babbitt; accidentally shoots his wife in the shoulder during a domestic argument and is sentenced to prison in Sinclair Lewis's *Babbitt*.

Zilla Colbeck (Zil) Riesling. Wife of Paul Riesling; becomes religious after her husband shoots her in the shoulder during a domestic argument in Sinclair Lewis's *Babbitt*.

Riga. Russian-born captain of the *Highlander* in Herman Melville's *Redburn*.

Riggs. Servant of Frank Walker; kidnaps Halsey Innes in Mary Roberts Rinehart's *The Circular Staircase*.

Harvey Riggs. Go-between for Isaac Tracy and Frank Meriwether in the litigation over worthless land in John Pendleton Kennedy's *Swallow Barn*.

Rigolo. Fifty-year-old bald man who owns the junk yard that Clyde Stout frequents in Jack Matthews's *Hanger Stout, Awake!*

Gus J. (G. J., Gussie, Mouse, Mouso, Yanni, Yanny) Rigopoulos. Blustery Greek boyhood friend and hero of Jack Duluoz in Jack Kerouac's *Doctor Sax*, *Maggie Cassidy*, *Book of Dreams*, and *Desolation Angels*.

Rigs. Second mate aboard the *Highlander* in Herman Melville's *Redburn*.

Evelyn Riker. Woman friend of Philip Preminger in *The Condominium*, a novella in Stanley Elkin's *Searches and Seizures*.

Joanne Riley. Reformatory cellmate of Eva Medina Canada in Gayl Jones's *Eva's Man*.

Brian Rimsky. Boyhood friend of Jerome Neumiller and Charles Neumiller (II) in Larry Woiwode's *Beyond the Bedroom Wall*.

Leo Rimsky. Boyhood friend of Jerome Neumiller and Charles Neumiller (II) in Larry Woiwode's *Beyond the Bedroom Wall*.

Rinaldi. Lieutenant in the Italian army and a skilled surgeon; introduces Frederic Henry to Catherine Barkley in Ernest Hemingway's *A Farewell to Arms*.

B. P. (Rine, Rine the Runner) Rinehart. Well-dressed preacher and numbers man for whom the narrator is often mistaken in Ralph Ellison's *Invisible Man*.

John Ringman. Husband of Goneril; following his wife's death, he wears a widower's weed in his hat in Herman Melville's *The Confidence-Man*.

Ringo. See Marengo.

Jett Rink. Poor ruffian who becomes an oil baron; married and divorced several times in Edna Ferber's *Giant*.

Sergeant Rink. Police officer who solves the mystery of the murdered prostitute and the theft of her corpse in Richard Brautigan's *Dreaming of Babylon*.

Johnny Rio. Attractive Chicano homosexual from Texas who compulsively seeks impersonal sex with multiple partners in Los Angeles in John Rechy's *Numbers*.

Anne Riordan. Newspaper reporter and daughter of an honest police chief; she helps Philip Marlowe in Raymond Chandler's *Farewell, My Lovely*.

Maude Riordan. Talented young violinist loved by both Collin Fenwick and Riley Henderson; marries Riley after he becomes a successful businessman in Truman Capote's *The Grass Harp*.

Mike Riordan. One-legged, hard-drinking, Irish-Catholic coal miner; friend of Tom Donovan and boyhood hero of Larry Donovan in Jack Conroy's *The Disinherited*.

Molly Riordan. Wife of Blue; raped by Clay Turner and burned in a fire Turner sets; molds Jimmy Fee into another Bad Man; accidentally killed when the mortally wounded Turner grabs her and Jimmy fires a shotgun in E. L. Doctorow's *Welcome to Hard Times*.

Polly Ann Ripley. Loving and capable pioneer wife of Tom McChesney; friend of David Ritchie in Winston Churchill's *The Crossing*.

Risley. Sheriff of the Nevada territory whose absence from Bridger's Wells when Greene brings word of the alleged murder of Larry Kinkaid convinces the townspeople to take the law into their own hands in Walter Van Tilburg Clark's *The Ox-Bow Incident*.

Rita. Good sport and traveling companion of Humbert Humbert, who picks her up after Dolores Haze abandons him, in Vladimir Nabokov's *Lolita*.

David (David Trimble, Davy) Ritchie. Orphan whose wanderings take him, during the Revolutionary War, to Kentucky, St. Louis, and New Orleans; husband of Hélène de St. Gré; narrator of Winston Churchill's *Coniston*.

Charlotte Rittenmeyer. Wife of Rat Rittenmeyer; dies as her lover Harry Wilbourne attempts to perform an abortion on her in William Faulkner's *The Wild Palms*.

Francis (Rat) Rittenmeyer. Husband of Charlotte Rittenmeyer in William Faulkner's *The Wild Palms*.

Jamie Ritter. Baby who survives the Andromeda Strain attack in Michael Crichton's *The Andromeda Strain*.

Frau Rittersdorf. Notebook keeper who is returning to Germany from Mexico, where she had gone to find a rich husband, in Katherine Anne Porter's

Ship of Fools.

Dr. Morris Ritz. Charlatan brought from Chicago by Verena Talbo to market Dolly Talbo's dropsy medicine; flees after stealing Verena's money in Truman Capote's *The Grass Harp.*

Rivenoak. Wise Huron chief who captures and tortures Natty Bumppo for killing Le Loup Cervier in James Fenimore Cooper's *The Deerslayer.*

Buddy Rivers. Teenaged protagonist who is on his own after his father is hospitalized; remains suspended from school because there is no parent to sign for his return; rescues his fourteen-year-old girlfriend, Angela Figueroa, from a girls' shelter and hides out with her in his father's house in June Jordan's *His Own Where.*

Clementine (Tish) Rivers. Pregnant black teenager and lover of Fonny Hunt; narrator of James Baldwin's *If Beale Street Could Talk.*

Condé (Condy, Conny) Rivers. Journalist-fictionist who successfully initiates his career as a writer with the aid of Travis Bessemer, falling in love with her during the process, in Frank Norris's *Blix.*

Connie Rivers. Husband of Rose of Sharon Joad Rivers and brother-in-law of Tom Joad II; abandons his wife after they move west in John Steinbeck's *The Grapes of Wrath.*

Don Rivers. Road superintendent and lover of Inez Charlesbois in Jessamyn West's *Cress Delahanty.*

Earl of Rivers. Grandfather of Mary Conant; leaves her a legacy in Lydia Maria Child's *Hobomok.*

Ernestine (Sis) Rivers. Settlement house worker and sister of Tish Rivers in James Baldwin's *If Beale Street Could Talk.*

Joseph (Joe) Rivers. Father of Tish Rivers in James Baldwin's *If Beale Street Could Talk.*

Mrs. Lydia Ann Rivers. Nursery customer of Jess Birdwell; her fatal illness puts Birdwell's own worries into perspective in Jessamyn West's *The Friendly Persuasion.*

Randall (Randy) Rivers. Appleton, Indiana, novelist whose succès de scandale, *Don't Look Now, Medusa,* brings fame and distress in Peter De Vries's *Mrs. Wallop.*

Reba (Miss Reba) Rivers. Proprietor of a Memphis brothel in William Faulkner's *Sanctuary, The Mansion,* and *The Reivers.*

Rose of Sharon Joad (Rosasharn) Rivers. Sister of Tom Joad II; strives, in the face of her family's dif-

ficult trek west, to keep intact her marriage to Connie Rivers in John Steinbeck's *The Grapes of Wrath.*

Sharon Rivers. Mother of Tish Rivers in James Baldwin's *If Beale Street Could Talk.*

Stella Slobkin Rivers. Mother of Randy Rivers and victim of "literary matricide" in Peter De Vries's *Mrs. Wallop.*

Ruthie (Ruthalle) Rivkin. Girlfriend of Harry Bogen, who leaves her because he thinks she looks too Jewish in Jerome Weidman's *I Can Get It for You Wholesale;* engaged to Murray Heimowitz in *What's in It for Me?*

Carlo Rizzi. Abusive husband of Connie Corleone; killed in Michael Corleone's final purge in Mario Puzo's *The Godfather.*

Enrico Salvatore (Ratso, Rico) Rizzo. Swindler befriended by Joe Buck; dies on the bus to Florida with Joe in James Leo Herlihy's *Midnight Cowboy.*

Howard (Bricktop, Red) Roark. Creative architect and uncompromising hero in Ayn Rand's *The Fountainhead.*

Rob. Young black man who suffers at the hands of the Cresswells when he neglects his crop to care for his sick wife; lynched by Sheriff Colton's mob in W. E. B. Du Bois's *The Quest of the Silver Fleece.*

Robair. New Orleans Creole valet, butler, and friend first to Jonas Cord, then to Jonas Cord, Jr., in Harold Robbins's *The Carpetbaggers.*

Robbins. Black resident of Catfish Row; killed by Crown after being accused of cheating in a crap game in DuBose Heyward's *Porgy.*

Arabella (Bella) Robbins. Romantic desperate for marriage; former girlfriend of Horace Larkin in Hjalmar Hjorth Boyesen's *The Mammon of Unrighteousness.*

Dr. Robbins. Eccentric (or perhaps just "too well") psychiatrist of Sissy Hankshaw Gitche and self-acknowledged author of Tom Robbins's *Even Cowgirls Get the Blues.*

Dwight Robbins. Boyish, self-consciously unacademic president of Benton College in Randall Jarrell's *Pictures from an Institution.*

Le Roy Robbins. See Henry Ritchie Clavering.

Moll Robbins. Writer for *Running Dog* researching an article on sex as big business in Don DeLillo's *Running Dog.*

General Roberdeau. Leader of the Philadelphia militia who first denies and later supports Thomas Paine and the American Revolution in Howard Fast's *Citizen Tom Paine.*

Irene Roberdeau. Daughter of General Roberdeau; falls in love with Thomas Paine, only to marry another man when he rejects her, in Howard Fast's *Citizen Tom Paine.*

Robert. Economics professor with whom Tarden lives and studies English; during a psychotic episode, tries to kill Tarden with a knife in Jerzy Kosinski's *Cockpit.*

Roberto. Cuban revolutionary who kills Albert Tracy and shoots Harry Morgan in Ernest Hemingway's *To Have and Have Not.*

Roberts. Detective who interrogates Stephen Rojack on suspicion of murder in Norman Mailer's *An American Dream.*

Dave and Debbie Roberts. Siblings who perform sex scenes in Boris Adrian's pornographic movie in Terry Southern's *Blue Movie.*

Dick Roberts. Real estate agent at Camp Morgan who is so despondent over the Depression that his wife asks George Brush to watch him in order to keep him from committing suicide in Thornton Wilder's *Heaven's My Destination.*

Henry Roberts. Merchant from Wheeling, Virginia, in Herman Melville's *The Confidence-Man.*

Jeffrey Roberts. WASPish southern advertising man and poet; friend and lover of Isadora Wing in Erica Jong's *How to Save Your Own Life.*

Judson (Jud) Roberts. State secretary of the Y.M.C.A. who persuades Elmer Gantry to attend a prayer meeting, at which Gantry becomes religious, in Sinclair Lewis's *Elmer Gantry.*

Lieutenant (jg) Doug A. Roberts. Best-loved officer aboard the *Reluctant* and the only one with a desire to participate in World War II; battles the envious Captain Morton in Thomas Heggen's *Mister Roberts.*

Marion (Kiki) Roberts. Mistress of Legs Diamond; with Diamond when he kidnaps Clem Streeter and Dickie Bartlett in William Kennedy's *Legs.*

Robertson. Head of the President's Science Advisory Committee who is the contact person between Project Wildfire and the president in Michael Crichton's *The Andromeda Strain.*

Dutch Robertson. Ex-army private who turns unsuccessfully to crime when he is unable to make a living honestly in John Dos Passos's *Manhattan Transfer.*

Robey. Eccentric millionaire and stutterer who employs Augie March briefly to assist him in writing a history of human happiness from the perspective of the wealthy, a book he intends to entitle *The Needle's Eye,* in Saul Bellow's *The Adventures of Augie March.*

Jonathan Robillard. Assistant pastor to the Reverend Phillip Martin in Ernest J. Gaines's *In My Father's House.*

Freddi Robin. Son of Johannes Robin; freed from Dachau through the efforts of Lanny Budd in Upton Sinclair's *Dragon's Teeth.*

Johannes (Jascha Rabinowich) Robin. Jewish-German arms dealer naive to the Nazi threat to Jews; forced to give his fortune to the Nazis in Upton Sinclair's *Dragon's Teeth.*

Commodore Robinette. American naval officer imprisoned by Tripoli pirates; soldier of fortune, Indian trader, pioneer, and cofounder of a town in Oklahoma in H. L. Davis's *Harp of a Thousand Strings.*

Raine Robinette. Vacant actress who helps to corrupt the admiring Lucy Lamar in Walker Percy's *Lancelot.*

Professor Robinolte. Owner of The Tattoo Palace; gives Malcolm a tattoo to prepare him for marriage in James Purdy's *Malcolm.*

Robinson. Street criminal who accidentally kills Jesus Ortiz instead of Sol Nazerman during a robbery in Edward Lewis Wallant's *The Pawnbroker.*

Robinson (Robby). Movie technician in F. Scott Fitzgerald's *The Last Tycoon.*

Doctor (Sawbones) Robinson. Accomplice of Injun Joe and Muff Potter; murdered by Injun Joe in Samuel Langhorne Clemens's *The Adventures of Tom Sawyer.*

Doris Robinson. High-school student whom Birdy reluctantly takes to the junior prom in William Wharton's *Birdy.*

Enoch Robinson. Artist who leaves Winesburg for New York; returns home when he is unable to find the solitude he craves in Sherwood Anderson's *Winesburg, Ohio.*

Galbraith (Horse Shoe) Robinson. Patriot hero who is a guide for Arthur Butler; escapes captivity and guides the Lindsays to Cornwallis; rescues Butler in John Pendleton Kennedy's *Horse-Shoe Robinson.*

Helen Robinson. Wife of Tom Robinson; taunted by Bob Ewell in Harper Lee's *To Kill a Mockingbird.*

Henry Robinson. Husband and killer of Dolores Brittain in Hal Bennett's *Wait Until the Evening.*

Horse Shoe Robinson. See Galbraith Robinson.

Hyacinth (Hyacinthe Vivier) Robinson. Son of the impoverished French dressmaker Florentine Vivier and her lover Lord Frederick Purvis; becomes involved with a group of politically radical activists in Henry James's *The Princess Casamassima.*

Ira Robinson. Employee of NESTER in Scott Spencer's *Last Night at the Brain Thieves Ball.*

Joan Robinson. Ex-wife of Joey Robinson and mother of their three children; refined, elegant woman with a distant personality in John Updike's *Of the Farm.*

Joey Robinson. Thirty-five-year-old, Harvard-educated son of Mary Robinson; returns to the family farm to mow the fields and introduce his new wife and stepson; narrator of John Updike's *Of the Farm.*

Mary Robinson. Mother of Joey Robinson; aging, yet strong-willed and determined woman whose love for her only son and her family farm causes her interpersonal problems in John Updike's *Of the Farm.*

Peggy McCabe Robinson. Second wife of Joey Robinson and mother of Richard McCabe; perceiving her new mother-in-law, Mary Robinson, as an enemy and rival, she exhibits jealousy and impatience in John Updike's *Of the Farm.*

Preston (Pres) Robinson. Controversial Sac Prairie history teacher who is suspected of being a communist and anti-Catholic; withstands church criticism for years before accepting a job in Madison in August Derleth's *The Shield of the Valiant.*

Taft Robinson. Star running back and first black enrolled by Logos College in Don DeLillo's *End Zone.*

Thomas (Tom) Robinson. Black man falsely accused of raping and beating Mayella Ewell; killed by police while trying to escape in Harper Lee's *To Kill a Mockingbird.*

Patricia Robyn. Niece of Patricia Maurier and twin of Theodore Robyn; attends the yacht party in William Faulkner's *Mosquitoes.*

Theodore (Gus, Josh) Robyn. Nephew of Patricia Maurier and twin of Patricia Robyn; attends the yacht party in William Faulkner's *Mosquitoes.*

Maria Rocco. Italian who works at the American PX and falls in love with Moses Shulman in John Horne Burns's *The Gallery.*

Harvey (Father Urban) Roche. Priest whose attempt to remodel his fusty Order of St. Clement after the Jesuits ends in failure and humiliation; ultimately becomes the head of his province, but by then his "be-a-winner" spirit is dead in J. F. Powers's *Morte D'Urban.*

Rochus. Son of the Saltmaster; appears to take advantage of the love of Benedicta in Ambrose Bierce's adaptation of *The Monk and the Hangman's Daughter.*

Marah Rocke. Deserted wife of Major Ira Warfield; raises their son, Traverse Rocke, in desperate poverty and serves as foster mother to Herberty Greyson in E.D.E.N. Southworth's *The Hidden Hand.*

Traverse Rocke. Disowned son of Major Ira Warfield; struggles through poverty to succeed brilliantly as a physician in E.D.E.N. Southworth's *The Hidden Hand.*

Rocketman. See Lieutenant Tyrone Slothrop.

Gordon (Lord Stane) Roderick. Associate of Frank Cowperwood; in love with Berenice Fleming in Theodore Dreiser's *The Stoic.*

Mrs. Annjee (Annjelica Williams) Rodgers (Rogers). Daughter of Aunt Hager Williams and mother of Sandy Rodgers; devotion to her adventurous, irresponsible husband leads her to leave home in Langston Hughes's *Not Without Laughter.*

James (Sandy) Rodgers (Rogers). Son of Mrs. Annjee Rodgers; central character whose growth from childhood to adolescence is explored in Langston Hughes's *Not Without Laughter.*

Jimboy Rodgers (Rogers). Freespirited husband of Mrs. Annjee Rodgers and father of Sandy Rodgers; leaves home frequently to find work in Langston Hughes's *Not Without Laughter.*

Seth Rodgers. Boyhood foe of Tom Bailey; becomes a grocer with Bill Conway in Thomas Bailey Aldrich's *The Story of a Bad Boy.*

Willy Roebuck. Deputy sheriff in Shelby Foote's *Follow Me Down.*

Camille (Cam) Rogers. More liberal sister of Honor Rogers; leaves home to live with a man in Marge Piercy's *The High Cost of Living*.

Elizabeth Browne Rogers. Early love of Langdon Towne; marries Major Robert Rogers and accompanies him to Michilimackinac in Kenneth Roberts's *Northwest Passage*.

Honor (Honorée) Rogers. Over-protected seventeen year old whose main contacts with the outside world are Leslie McGivers and Bernie Guizot in Marge Piercy's *The High Cost of Living*.

Jimmie Rogers. Belligerent soldier who challenges Wilson and later is shot in battle in Stephen Crane's *The Red Badge of Courage*.

Joe Rogers. Agent who works as a CIA aide in the expedition against the wild boys in William S. Burroughs's *The Wild Boys*.

Milton K. Rogers. Former business partner of Silas Lapham; tries to involve Lapham in a shady investment deal in William Dean Howells's *The Rise of Silas Lapham*.

Mrs. (Mama) Rogers. Overprotective mother of Honor Rogers in Marge Piercy's *The High Cost of Living*.

Patricia (Pat) Rogers. New Zealand Salvation Army worker and lover of Andy Hookans in Leon Uris's *Battle Cry*.

Major Robert Rogers. American commander of Rogers' Rangers during the French and Indian War; appointed royal governor of Michilimackinac; dreams of finding a route to the Pacific Ocean in Kenneth Roberts's *Northwest Passage*.

Tom Rogers. Colleague of Homer Zigler on the staff of the *San Francisco Tribune* in Clyde Brion Davis's *"The Great American Novel—."*

Victoria (Victoria Maria San Felipe Sanchez) Rogers. Puerto Rican prostitute allegedly raped by Fonny Hunt in James Baldwin's *If Beale Street Could Talk*.

Deborah Kelly Rojack. Daughter of Barney Kelly; murdered by her husband, Stephen Rojack, in Norman Mailer's *An American Dream*.

Stephen Richards (Raw-Jock) Rojack. War hero, congressman, and college professor who murders his wife, Deborah Kelly Rojack; narrator of Norman Mailer's *An American Dream*.

Rojos (Pizarro). Leader of the revolutionary movement in South America who lacks imagination; sends Ramón Cordes and his band to their deaths at the silver mine in William Herrick's *The Last to Die*.

Dan Rolfe. Tubercular victim and companion to Dinah Brand in Dashiell Hammett's *Red Harvest*.

Loretta Lonigan Rolfe. See Loretta Lonigan.

Phillip (Phil) Rolfe. Jewish boyfriend of Loretta Lonigan; converts to Catholicism in James T. Farrell's *The Young Manhood of Studs Lonigan*; marries Loretta in *Judgment Day*.

Rolling Thunder. Indian chief and orator in James Kirke Paulding's *Koningsmarke*.

Indiana Frusk Rolliver. Rival of Undine Spragg when they are girls in Apex City and role model for Undine's habit of marrying to obtain social status in Edith Wharton's *The Custom of the Country*.

Bertrande (Madame Martin Guerre) de Rols. Wife of Martin Guerre; after being deserted by her husband, she lives with Arnaud du Tilh, who resembles Guerre and pretends to be him, in Janet Lewis's *The Wife of Martin Guerre*.

Dee Romano. Laconic chief of police for West Condon in Robert Coover's *The Origin of the Brunists*.

Natashya Romanov. See Natashya Romanov Everett.

Romarkin (Rom). Political refugee from Stalinist Russia; close friend of George Levanter in Jerzy Kosinski's *Blind Date*.

Pedro Romero. Young bullfighter from Pamplona; lover of Lady Brett Ashley in Ernest Hemingway's *The Sun Also Rises*.

Romilayu. Patient African guide who takes Eugene Henderson to his eventful encounters with the Arnewi and Wariri tribes in Saul Bellow's *Henderson the Rain King*.

Evy Rommely. See Evy Rommely Flittman.

Katie Rommely. See Katherine Rommely Nolan.

Mary (Granma) Rommely. Saintly wife of a brute and mother of four daughters; Austrian immigrant, storyteller, and believer in education; grandmother of Francie Nolan in Betty Smith's *A Tree Grows in Brooklyn*.

Sissy Rommely. Oldest child of Mary Rommely, energetic and zany wife of three husbands, and mother of eleven babies, ten of them born dead; Francie Nolan's favorite aunt and model of a stubborn spirit in Betty Smith's *A Tree Grows in Brooklyn*.

Dunstan Rondo. Methodist minister who officiates at the wedding of Dabney Fairchild and Troy Flavin in Eudora Welty's *Delta Wedding*.

Ronnie. Bartender at the Village Tavern; friend of Roe Billins, Jerry Payne, and Harry Schoonover in John Nichols's *The Sterile Cuckoo*.

Peter (Pete) Rood. Sullen, mysterious mountaineer who disgraces Mink Lorey in Mary Noailles Murfree's *In the Clouds*.

Miriam Rooth. Parisian actress loved by Peter Sherringham; marries Basil Dashwood in Henry James's *The Tragic Muse*.

Rope Yarn (Ropey). Landlubber aboard the *Julia* who dies at Papeetee in Herman Melville's *Omoo*.

John Roper. Brother of Simeon Roper, Puritan soldier, and follower of Johnny Church and Thankful Perkins; condemned to death for mutiny but spared in Cromwell's blanket pardon in Mary Lee Settle's *Prisons*.

Simeon Roper. Puritan soldier who, like his brother, John Roper, is condemned to death for mutiny but spared in Cromwell's blanket pardon in Mary Lee Settle's *Prisons*.

Ropey. See Rope Yarn.

Al Roquefort. Literary agent in Peter De Vries's *Comfort Me with Apples*.

Rosa (Roslin). Concubine of Sir Philip Gardiner; disguises herself as a boy called Roslin in Catharine Maria Sedgwick's *Hope Leslie*.

Wanda (Marie) Rosario. Lover of Beth Walker; sent to jail and loses custody of her children; with Walker, steals her children back and is forced to go underground in Marge Piercy's *Small Changes*.

Roscius (Roskus). Husband of Phoebe and father of Thucydides in William Faulkner's *Go Down, Moses*.

Vernon (A. H. Dory, Verne) Roscoe. Oil investor who gets J. Arnold Ross to buy influence in the Harding administration; cheats Bunny and Bertie Ross out of most of their inheritance in Upton Sinclair's *Oil!*

Rose. Entertainer at the Congo cabaret; loves Jake Brown and wants to support him financially, if only he would be her man forever, in Claude McKay's *Home to Harlem*.

Rose. Manager of the night club where Jake Jackson is robbed by a pickpocket in Richard Wright's *Lawd Today*.

Dr. Burton L. Rose. Third psychiatrist of John Wilder; solemn young doctor who compulsively eats mint candies in Richard Yates's *Disturbing the Peace*.

Jack (Jakie, Jake Rosencrancz) Rose. Gambler who plans to control Los Angeles in Paul Cain's *Fast One*.

Simon (Sim) Rosedale. Ambitious, social-climbing Jewish investor who falls in love with Lily Bart but refuses to marry her after her reputation becomes tarnished in Edith Wharton's *The House of Mirth*.

Rosella. South European peasant who poses nude for Hugh's photography and works as a maid for Cyril in John Hawkes's *The Blood Oranges*.

Rosemarie. See Rosemarie Buchanan.

Fernie Mae (Fern) Rosen. Southerner of black and Jewish heritage; the narrator is attracted to her but discovers she is emotionally beyond his understanding in Jean Toomer's *Cane*.

Gottfried Knosperl Rosenbaum. Jewish expatriate from Austria and husband of Irene Rosenbaum; teaches music at Benton College in Randall Jarrell's *Pictures from an Institution*.

Irene Rosenbaum. Retired singer of opera and lieder; wife and spiritual complement to Gottfried Rosenbaum in Randall Jarrell's *Pictures from an Institution*.

Ethel Greenglass Rosenberg. Convicted traitor, atom spy, and love object of Richard Nixon in Robert Coover's *The Public Burning*.

Joey Rosenberg. Long-haired young beatnik and former champion athlete who reminds Jack Duluoz of Jesus Christ in Jack Kerouac's *Big Sur*.

Julius Rosenberg. Convicted traitor, atom spy, and husband of Ethel Rosenberg in Robert Coover's *The Public Burning*.

Harold Rosenblatt. Wise and scholarly colleague who tries to give Lee Youngdahl good advice in Mark Harris's *Wake Up, Stupid*.

Harris Rosenblatt. Wealthy former college classmate of Bruce Gold and financial adviser to the White House in Joseph Heller's *Good as Gold*.

Roseveldt. Shopkeeper who sells to Martinette de Beauvais the lute that formerly belonged to Constantia Dudley in Charles Brockden Brown's *Ormond*.

Caroline Rosewater. Socially pretentious and alcoholic wife of Fred Rosewater in Kurt Vonnegut's

God Bless You, Mr. Rosewater.

Eliot Rosewater. Eccentric philanthropist, son of Lister Rosewater, husband of Sylvia Rosewater, and fan of Kilgore Trout; central character in Kurt Vonnegut's *God Bless You, Mr. Rosewater*; hospital patient with Billy Pilgrim in *Slaughterhouse-Five*, and patron of Trout in *Breakfast of Champions.*

Fred Rosewater. Suicidal insurance salesman descended from the poor Rhode Island branch of the Rosewater family in Kurt Vonnegut's *God Bless You, Mr. Rosewater.*

Lister Ames Rosewater. Conservative U.S. Senator and father of Eliot Rosewater in Kurt Vonnegut's *God Bless You, Mr. Rosewater.*

Sylvia DuVrais Zetterling Rosewater. Wife of Eliot Rosewater in Kurt Vonnegut's *God Bless You, Mr. Rosewater.*

Rosey. Best friend of Mariah Upshur; brings shame on Tangierneck and dies in childbirth in Sarah E. Wright's *This Child's Gonna Live.*

Rosie. Slovenly roommate of Sylvia and girlfriend of Frank in Jim Harrison's *A Good Day to Die.*

Edward (Ned) Rosier. Member of the American circle in Paris and suitor of Pansy Osmond in Henry James's *The Portrait of a Lady.*

Madame Rosita. Prostitute with whom Malcolm has his first sexual experience as preparation for his marriage to Melba in James Purdy's *Malcolm.*

Eino Roskinen. Dairy worker and rival of Cass Timberlane for the affections of Jinny Marshland; killed in World War II in Sinclair Lewis's *Cass Timberlane.*

Roskus. See Roskus Gibson and Roscius.

Roslin. See Rosa.

Alberta (Bertie, Birdie) Ross. Sister of Bunny Ross; disagrees with Bunny's political beliefs in Upton Sinclair's *Oil!*

Ardis (Bonita, Ardis Carter, Ardis Kármán, Marya Sharp, Mrs. Nigel Stock) Ross. Self-centered mother of Elena Ross Howe in Joyce Carol Oates's *Do with Me What You Will.*

Beulah (Sue) Ross. Prostitute murdered by her lover, Luther Eustis, in Shelby Foote's *Follow Me Down.*

Mrs. Cora Ross. Wife of Colonel Norman Ross; her intelligent observations and willingness to fulfill obligations bring her credit in James Gould Cozzens's *Guard of Honor.*

Elena Ross. See Elena Ross Howe.

Frank Ross. Father of Mattie Ross; killed by Tom Chaney in Charles Portis's *True Grit.*

Janet (Jan) Ross. Psychiatrist at the Neuropsychiatric Research Unit who counsels against giving Harold Benson the stage-three operation in Michael Crichton's *The Terminal Man.*

J. Arnold (Jim, Mr. Paradise) Ross. Millionaire father of J. Arnold Ross, Jr.; independent oil operator who becomes involved in a political scandal in Upton Sinclair's *Oil!*

J. Arnold (Bunny, Jim, Jr., Alex H. Jones) Ross, Jr. Son of J. Arnold Ross; becomes involved in the labor movement and plans to start a labor college; marries Rachel Menzies in Upton Sinclair's *Oil!*

Larry Ross. Young and upcoming studio executive seen by Sammy Glick as a future threat in Budd Schulberg's *What Makes Sammy Run?*

Leo Ross. Mentally disturbed father of Elena Howe in Joyce Carol Oates's *Do with Me What You Will.*

Mattie Ross. Narrator who hires Rooster Cogburn to capture Tom Chaney, her father's murderer, in Charles Portis's *True Grit.*

Colonel Norman (Judge) Ross. Air Inspector of Ocanara Army Air Base whose reasoned understanding of human nature solves General Ira N. Beal's personnel crisis; moral center in James Gould Cozzens's *Guard of Honor.*

Rachel Menzies Ross. See Rachel Menzies.

Sybil Ross. Sister of Madeleine Lee; she and John Carrington inform Madeleine of Senator Ratcliffe's improper political dealings to keep her from marrying him in Henry Adams's *Democracy.*

Thomas (Tommy) Ross. Boyfriend of Susan Snell; takes Carrie White to the prom as a favor to Snell in Stephen King's *Carrie.*

Michael (Mike) Rossi. See Tomas Makris.

Steffi Rostenkowski. Girlfriend of Bruno Lefty Bicek; remains faithful to Bicek after he betrays her into prostitution in Nelson Algren's *Never Come Morning.*

Lady Jane Rotherhall. Hostess for the Mensa meeting where Dane Tarrant meets her future husband, John Empson, in Gail Godwin's *The Perfectionists.*

Sam Rothmore. Head of Paramount's New York office; hires Noel Airman as an assistant story editor in Herman Wouk's *Marjorie Morningstar*.

Arnold Rothstein. Gangster who sponsors Legs Diamond's criminal beginnings in William Kennedy's *Legs*.

Chuck Rouncivale. Sportswriter for the *Blue Mountain News* in Katherine Anne Porter's *Pale Horse, Pale Rider*.

Gloria Rowan. Daughter of Thomas Rowan and lover of George Washington in Copenhagen in Cecil Brown's *The Life and Loves of Mr. Jiveass Nigger*.

Janet Rowan. Rich, spoiled blonde who humiliates Ada Fincastle and who, through her father's social power, traps Ralph McBride into marrying her rather than Ada in Ellen Glasgow's *Vein of Iron*.

Thomas Rowan. American political analyst in Copenhagen; has incestuous relations with his daughter, Gloria Rowan, in Cecil Brown's *The Life and Loves of Mr. Jiveass Nigger*.

Roxana (Roxy). Slave of Percy Driscoll; fearing that her baby Valet de Chambre will be sold, she switches him with the baby Thomas à Becket Driscoll and rears Driscoll as her son in Samuel Langhorne Clemens's *Pudd'nhead Wilson*.

Roxie. Black cook for the Battle Fairchild family in Eudora Welty's *Delta Wedding*.

Roxy. Stepmother of Chet Pomeroy; plans to marry Curtis Peavey in Thomas McGuane's *Panama*.

Roxy. See Roxana.

Roy. First morphine customer of William Lee and his partner in lush working in William S. Burroughs's *Junkie*.

Roy. See Hogo de Bergerac.

Mrs. Roy. American in Rome who is seeking a divorce under Pauline Privilege from the pope in Thornton Wilder's *The Cabala*.

Royal. Bastard child of Gabriel Grimes and Esther, unacknowledged by his father; killed in a Chicago saloon in James Baldwin's *Go Tell It on the Mountain*.

Princess Royal. Only daughter of Pharaoh, "mother" of Moses, and sister of Ta-Phar in Zora Neale Hurston's *Moses, Man of the Mountain*.

Charity Royall. Daughter of Mary Hyatt and lover of Lucius Harney; eventually marries her guardian, Lawyer Royall; heroine of Edith Wharton's *Summer*.

Lawyer Royall. Guardian and eventually husband of Charity Royall in Edith Wharton's *Summer*.

Enid Royce. Devout, prohibitionist, vegetarian Nebraskan who marries Claude Wheeler, only to depart for China to aid her ailing sister, in Willa Cather's *One of Ours*.

Rita Royce. Blonde starlet who accompanies Sammy Glick to high profile events in Budd Schulberg's *What Makes Sammy Run?*

Nellie Royster. Elderly domestic and friend of Mrs. Greco; slain and set afire by Bobby Bryant in Hal Bennett's *Seventh Heaven*.

Mama Rua. Widowed mother of Terangi; visited by her husband's ghost; dies shortly before the hurricane in Charles Nordhoff and James Norman Hall's *The Hurricane*.

The Rube. Junky friend deserted by William Lee in William S. Burroughs's *Naked Lunch*; undercover agent for the Nova Police and master of the reverse con in *Nova Express*.

Rubén. Poor candymaker who falls in love with a gypsy; raids a neighboring village with Pepe Gonzales in order to steal the bones of a local hero in Josefina Niggli's *Mexican Village*.

Tessie Rubin. Jewish widow and Holocaust survivor; mistress of Sol Nazerman in Edward Lewis Wallant's *The Pawnbroker*.

Ruby. Bootlegger's daughter and prostitute visited by Albert Riddell in Reynolds Price's *Love and Work*.

Ruby. Oldest of the orphaned girls under Rachel Cooper's care; reveals to Preacher that John and Pearl Harper are also in Cooper's care in Davis Grubb's *The Night of the Hunter*.

Sim Rudabaugh. Carpetbagging Texas politician and rustler; tries to keep Del Sol cattle from getting to Kansas in Emerson Hough's *North of 36*.

Barry Rudd. Ten-year-old genius and expert in biological classification and etymology; recruited as a "brain specimen" by Wissey Jones; subject of an investigation by the State Senate Standing Committee on Education, Welfare, and Public Morality in John Hersey's *The Child Buyer*.

Lambert Rudd. Landscape painter from Boston; husband of Maizie Jekyll and lover of Leda March in Nancy Hale's *The Prodigal Women*.

Maud Purcells (Mrs. Paul Rudd) Rudd. Mother of Barry Rudd; overcomes hardship to provide for

Barry, but when she is threatened, intimidated, and bribed by Wissey Jones, she succumbs and permits the sale of her son in John Hersey's *The Child Buyer*.

May Rudge. See May Rudge Harrington.

Jurgis (Michael O'Flaherty, Serge Reminitsky, Johann Schmidt) Rudkus. Lithuanian immigrant to America and husband of Ona Rudkus; finds work in the Chicago stockyards in Upton Sinclair's *The Jungle*.

Ona Lukoszaite Rudkus. Stepdaughter of Elzbieta and wife of Jurgis Rudkus; coerced into having sex with Phil Connor; dies during childbirth because of inadequate medical attention in Upton Sinclair's *The Jungle*.

Robert Rudleigh. Tourist fisherman who, with his wife, hires Thomas Skelton as a guide in Thomas McGuane's *Ninety-Two in the Shade*.

Dr. Jeffery Rudner. Psychoanalyst, lover of Isadora Wing, and tennis partner of Bennett Wing in Erica Jong's *How to Save Your Own Life*.

Matthew Rudolph. Servant to Prince Cabano; secret member of the Brotherhood of Destruction who arranges Estella Washington's escape from Cabano in Ignatius Donnelly's *Caesar's Column*.

Ruel. See Jethro.

Hamm (Rufer Hammond) Rufe. Son of Hallie Rufer Hammond and Michael Hammond; youthful runaway who assumes a new identity as an adult and returns to Franklin as a labor reporter; estranged husband of Stephani Kolhoff in Mari Sandoz's *Capital City*.

Marmaduke (Colonel Ruggles) Ruggles. British valet who is won in a poker game by Egbert Floud, with whom Ruggles goes to the United States; narrator of Harry Leon Wilson's *Ruggles of Red Gap*.

Henry (Roscoe) Rules. Meanest of the ten Los Angeles policemen-protagonists of Joseph Wambaugh's *The Choirboys*.

Ironwood (Landlord) Rumble. Foundling and blind musician in Leon Forrest's *The Bloodworth Orphans*.

Billy Rumbly. Part-Indian brother of Henry Burlingame; civilized savage who marries Anna Cooke in John Barth's *The Sot-Weed Factor*.

Beatrice (Bea) Rumfoord. Wife of Winston Niles Rumfoord and mate of Malachi Constant in Kurt Vonnegut's *The Sirens of Titan*.

Bertram Rumfoord. Harvard professor and military historian researching the Dresden raid in Kurt Vonnegut's *Slaughterhouse-Five*.

Winston Niles Rumfoord. Wealthy space and time traveler who enters a chrono-synclastic infundibulum in Kurt Vonnegut's *The Sirens of Titan*.

Jacob Rumpel. Stolid Pennsylvania farmer whose unaffected manner and good sense inspire Thomas Paine to revolutionary writing in Howard Fast's *Citizen Tom Paine*.

Sarah Rumpel. Daughter of Jacob Rumpel; exemplifies a uniquely American civilization to Thomas Paine, who rejects her in favor of his revolutionary writing, in Howard Fast's *Citizen Tom Paine*.

Jack Rumsen. Private detective hired by Ned Beaumont to help him find Bernie Despain in Dashiell Hammett's *The Glass Key*.

Bobby Rupp. Boyfriend of Nancy Clutter; briefly a suspect in the murder case because of her father's disapproval of the romance in Truman Capote's *In Cold Blood*.

Michael S. Rushing. See Michael S. Reusing.

Eliza Rushmore. Literary agent of Isadora Wing in Erica Jong's *How to Save Your Own Life*.

Professor Rolfe Alan Ruskin. Husband of the much younger Sarah Ruskin; card-carrying nuclear physicist, Nobel laureate, and scientific consultant to the Spanish Republic in William Herrick's *Hermanos!*

Sarah Ruskin. Fellow Communist party worker and lover of Jake Starr and wife of Rolfe Ruskin; aids British volunteers on their way to the Spanish civil war in William Herrick's *Hermanos!*

Frank Russel. Cynical friend of Edward Clayton; rejects Edward's radicalism in favor of caution and acceptance of the local mores in Harriet Beecher Stowe's *Dred*.

Russell. Small-time thief and drug addict; robs an illegal mafia card game with Frankie and is turned in to the authorities for drug peddling by Jackie Cogan in George V. Higgins's *Cogan's Trade*.

Arthur Russell. Summer-long boyfriend of Alice Adams; leaves her upon discovering her pretensions in Booth Tarkington's *Alice Adams*.

Buck Russell. Posse member who favors sexual experiences with black women; lover of Della Brame in Reynolds Price's *A Generous Man*.

James (Father Jim) Russell. Priest; as a child, lived in Old Halvorsen Place in Larry Woiwode's *Beyond the Bedroom Wall*.

Puss and Emily Russell. Society sisters in Winston Churchill's *The Crisis*.

Rusty. Thug employed by Shad O'Rory in Dashiell Hammett's *The Glass Key*.

Ruta. Maid to Deborah Kelly Rojack and spy for Barney Kelly; seduced by Stephen Rojack after he murders Deborah in Norman Mailer's *An American Dream*.

George Herman (Babe) Ruth. Star outfielder for the New York Yankees who is the lover of Mason Tidewater, according to Tidewater's memoirs, in Jay Neugeboren's *Sam's Legacy*.

Damon Rutherford. Imaginary wonderboy rookie pitcher for the Pioneers; killed by a bean ball in Robert Coover's *The Universal Baseball Association, Inc., J. Henry Waugh, Prop.*

Helen Rutherford. Alleged daughter of Leander Wapshot from a brief early marriage; believes that Wapshot abandoned her in infancy in John Cheever's *The Wapshot Chronicle*.

Miles Rutherford. Churlish bully beaten by Ned Hazard in John Pendleton Kennedy's *Swallow Barn*.

Willie Rutledge. Drownder preacher who bases his belief in brotherly love and a fervently spiritual life on a supernatural vision of heavenly glory in T. S. Stribling's *Unfinished Cathedral*.

Ada Rutter. Trashy denizen of the Peaks of Laurel and scheming mother of Ada Belle Rutter in Andrew Lytle's *The Velvet Horn*.

Ada Belle Rutter. Young mountain woman whom Lucius Cree marries when he learns she is pregnant with their child in Andrew Lytle's *The Velvet Horn*.

Willy Rutter. Thug and bully in Paul Theroux's *The Family Arsenal*.

Swami Rutuola. Indian faith healer who succeeds in curing Tony Nailles of the sadness that confines him to bed for a month in John Cheever's *Bullet Park*.

Elizabeth (Liz) O'Brien Ryan. Friend and confidante of Isabel Moore in Mary Gordon's *Final Payments*.

John Ryan. Husband of Liz Ryan and unscrupulous seducer of her friend, Isabel Moore, in Mary Gordon's *Final Payments*.

Pegeen Ryan. Fiery redhead who teaches French and marries Patrick Dennis; appears in Patrick Dennis's *Auntie Mame* and *Around the World with Auntie Mame*.

Hawkins Ryden. Uncle of the mysterious Tommy Ryden; rides with the posse on the chance of finding something belonging to Tommy that will repay him for having taken care of Tommy and his mother in Reynolds Price's *A Generous Man*.

Miss Jack Ryden. Mother of Tommy Ryden in Reynolds Price's *A Generous Man*.

Tommy Ryden. Father of Lois Provo and lover of Kate Pomeroy; supposedly killed in World War II in Reynolds Price's *A Generous Man*.

Cynthia Ryder. Mother of Sophia Grieve Ryder in Djuna Barnes's *Ryder*.

Japheth M. (Japh, Japhy) Ryder. Oregon-born poet, Oriental scholar, and Zen Buddhist; idealized friend of Ray Smith in Jack Kerouac's *The Dharma Bums*.

Jonathan Buxton Ryder. Father of Sophia Grieve Ryder in Djuna Barnes's *Ryder*

Sophia Grieve Ryder. Daughter of Jonathan Buxton Ryder and Cynthia Ryder, wife of John Peel and Alex Alexson, and mother of Wendell Ryder in Djuna Barnes's *Ryder*.

Wendell Ryder. Son of John Peel and Sophia Grieve Ryder; husband of Amelia de Grier; lover of Kate-Careless; father, by Amelia, of five children and father, by Kate, of three children; and lover of Molly Dance in Djuna Barnes's *Ryder*.

Ekaterina Alexandrovna (Kate) Ryleyeva. Russian translator and escort of Henry Bech; translates science fiction into Ukrainian; helps Bech spend the rubles given to him as Russian royalties in John Updike's *Bech: A Book*.

Coke Rymer. Blond youth who helps Mina Morgan destroy Peter Leland but is destined to be her victim in an even more hideous destruction in Fred Chappell's *Dagon*.

S

Cecile Sabat. Great aunt of Wiley Wright and grandmother of Helene Wright; her death causes Helene's emotionally wrenching visit to her Louisiana birthplace in Toni Morrison's *Sula*.

Rochelle Sabat. Daughter of Cecile Sabat and mother of Helene Wright; estranged from her daughter because of her life as a madam in a Louisiana bordello in Toni Morrison's *Sula*.

Sabatini. Bookie who allows Samuel Paul Berman to develop a large gambling debt in Jay Neugeboren's *Sam's Legacy*.

Nicholas (Nick) Sabb. London fence imprisoned in Australia; escapes from the penal colony and settles in Rotterdam in Charles Nordhoff and James Norman Hall's *Botany Bay*.

Timothy Sabb. Nephew of Nick Sabb; takes over Nick's illicit activities when Nick is taken to an Australian penal colony in Charles Nordhoff and James Norman Hall's *Botany Bay*.

Hassan i Sabbah. Prophet whose teachings represent a threat to control addicts in William S. Burroughs's *The Ticket That Exploded* and *Nova Express*.

Sabina. Woman who searches for herself in a series of affairs and has a failed lesbian relationship with Lillian in Anaïs Nin's *Ladders to Fire, Children of the Albatross, The Four-Chambered Heart*, and *A Spy in the House of Love*.

Sabino. Coroner who investigates Chalmers Egstrom's death and who enters into Marietta McGee-Chavéz's Spain in William Goyen's *In a Farther Country*.

Henri Guerlac de Sabrevois. British sympathizer and enemy of Steven Nason; abducts Mary Mallinson in Kenneth Roberts's *Arundel*.

Marie de Sabrevois. See Mary Mallinson.

Sabrina (Bu, Sabu). Daughter of George Cain and Nichole in George Cain's *Blueschild Baby*.

Nicola (Nick) Sacco. Anarchistic Italian shoe-factory worker and night watchman who, unjustly charged with robbery and murder, is executed with Bartolomeo Vanzetti, to the horror of many, in Upton Sinclair's *Boston*.

Sally Sachs. Painter and lover of Ricky Potter in Alison Lurie's *Real People*.

Sackett. District attorney who fails to convict Frank Chambers for the murder of Nick Papadakis, but convicts him of murdering Cora Papadakis, who dies accidentally, in James M. Cain's *The Postman Always Rings Twice*.

Lorna Sackville. See Susan Lenox.

Joe Sagessa. Police sergeant assigned to drive Alfonso Columbato and Birdy while they catch stray dogs in William Wharton's *Birdy*.

Count Armand De Sacy. Parisian visiting the Haitian estate of his cousin, the absent owner of Bréda, in Arna Wendell Bontemps's *Drums at Dusk*.

The Sailor. Heroin addict briefly mentioned in William S. Burroughs's *Junkie*; gatherer of reptile eggs and buyer of time in *Naked Lunch*; hangs himself in jail in *The Soft Machine*; mentioned in *Nova Express* and *Exterminator!*

Arthur St. Clair. Former British army officer; landowner in Hervey Allen's *The Forest and the Fort, Bedford Village*, and *Toward the Morning*.

Emilia St. Claire. Wealthy eccentric who buys a castle in Lowell, Massachusetts, and renames it Transcendenta in Jack Kerouac's *Doctor Sax*.

Amber St. Clare (Mrs. Luke Channell; Mrs. Samuel Dangerfield; Mrs. Edmund Mortimer, Countess of Radclyffe; Mrs. Gerald Stanhope, Countess of Danforth and Duchess of Ravenspur). Fifteen-year-old country maid who becomes the mistress of King Charles II; unbeatable heroine who survives, among other trials, debtors' prison, a bout of plague, a murderous husband, the gossip of Court, and the London Fire, but cannot win the enduring affection and attention of her first love, Bruce Carlton, in Kathleen Winsor's *Forever Amber*.

Augustine St. Clare. Husband of Marie St. Clare and father of Eva St. Clare; second owner of Uncle Tom; influenced by Tom and Eva to replace his cynicism with faith before being stabbed to death in Harriet Beecher Stowe's *Uncle Tom's Cabin*.

Evangeline (Little Eva) St. Clare. Daughter of Marie and Augustine St. Clare; befriends Uncle Tom and inspires and reforms those around her, such as her father and Topsy, before dying of consumption in Harriet Beecher Stowe's *Uncle Tom's Cabin*.

Henrique St. Clare. Young cousin of Eva St. Clare; his aristocratic cruelty is tempered by Eva's admonitions in Harriet Beecher Stowe's *Uncle Tom's Cabin*.

Mammy St. Clare. See Mammy.

Marie St. Clare. Wife of Augustine St. Clare and mother of Eva St. Clare; suffers from debilitating headaches; disapproves of her husband's benevolent management of their slaves and sells Uncle Tom when she disposes of Augustine's estate in Harriet Beecher Stowe's *Uncle Tom's Cabin.*

Ophelia St. Clare. Vermonter who manages the New Orleans household of her cousin Augustine St. Clare in Harriet Beecher Stowe's *Uncle Tom's Cabin.*

Waldo St. Cloud. Narrator and protagonist of Osgood Wallop's *The Duchess of Obloquy* in Peter De Vries's *Mrs. Wallop.*

Albert St. Dennis. Aging British poet and visiting Distinguished Professor of Poetry at Woodslee University in Joyce Carol Oates's *Unholy Loves.*

Antoinette de St. Gré. Woman who marries Nick Temple in Winston Churchill's *The Crossing.*

Auguste de St. Gré. Degenerate son of Philippe de St. Gré and brother of Antoinette de St. Gré in Winston Churchill's *The Crossing.*

Hélène Victoire Marie de (Hélène d'Ivry-le-Tour) St. Gré. Widow; friend and later the wife of David Ritchie in Winston Churchill's *The Crossing.*

Philippe de St. Gré. Generous friend of David Ritchie and father of Antoinette and Auguste de St. Gré in Winston Churchill's *The Crossing.*

Edgar St. Jermyn. Brother of Captain St. Jermyn; captured by Horse Shoe Robinson and Christopher Shaw in John Pendleton Kennedy's *Horse-Shoe Robinson.*

Captain St. Jermyn (Tyrrel). British spy who induces Philip Lindsay to join the British and Tory forces at King's Mountain; hanged after the British defeat in John Pendleton Kennedy's *Horse-Shoe Robinson.*

Angela Grace St. John. Wife of a Los Angeles doctor; has an affair with Abel in N. Scott Momaday's *House Made of Dawn.*

Mary St. John. See Mary St. John Eaton.

Sal. Friend and partner in crime of the youthful Vinni; later friend and drinking companion of Mike Kelly in Hubert Selby, Jr.'s *Last Exit to Brooklyn.*

Sakia (Love). Wife of Paskingoe in James Kirke Paulding's *The Dutchman's Fireside.*

Salem. American sailor who confronts the English consul aboard the *Julia* and who fights Bembo in Herman Melville's *Omoo.*

Art Salerno. Employee and best friend of Stan Waltz; husband of Lena Salerno in Peter De Vries's *Let Me Count the Ways.*

Lena Salerno. Wife of Art Salerno and quasi-mistress of Stan Waltz in Peter De Vries's *Let Me Count the Ways.*

Mac Sales. Airplane inspector in William Faulkner's *Pylon.*

John (Angel of Death, The Grim Reaper) Sallow. Professional wrestler who defeats James Boswell and precipitates a crisis of the will and a lengthy reappraisal of Boswell's personal values in Stanley Elkin's *Boswell.*

Sally. Commune-mate of Beth Walker; rears an illegitimate child with the help of the women's commune in Marge Piercy's *Small Changes.*

Salo (Old Salo). Tralfamadorian robot friend of Winston Niles Rumfoord and Malachi Constant in Kurt Vonnegut's *The Sirens of Titan.*

Saltmaster. Overseer of a salt mine; father of Rochus and, unknown to others, of Benedicta in Ambrose Bierce's adaptation of *The Monk and the Hangman's Daughter.*

Solly (Professor, Sparrow) Saltskin. Petty criminal forced to betray Frankie Machine, his best friend, in Nelson Algren's *The Man with the Golden Arm.*

Ben Saltz. Jewish scientist and husband of Irene Saltz; they are involved in partner swapping with Carol and Eddie Constantine in John Updike's *Couples.*

Irene Saltz. Community social activist and wife of Ben Saltz in John Updike's *Couples.*

Rita Salus. Lover of Peter Reinick and Communist refugee from the Nazis who is deported to Germany in Martha Gellhorn's *A Stricken Field.*

Doña Dolores (Grace Conroy) Salvatierra. Sister of Gabriel Conroy; poses as an Indian in Bret Harte's *Gabriel Conroy.*

Sam. First of two fetuses spontaneously aborted by Anne Sorenson; narrates part of Frederick Busch's *Manual Labor.*

Sam. Pedigreed fox hound named for a preacher and treated as a member of the family; Nunn Ballew buys him to chase King Devil in Harriette Arnow's *Hunter's Horn.*

Sam. Registrar who refuses to allow Will Harris to register to vote in Junius Edwards's *If We Must Die.*

Sam. White civil rights activist who researches the life of Tunis G. Campbell on the Georgia Sea Islands in Nicholas Delbanco's *News.*

Sam (Sammy-O). Friend of Fish Tucker; enlists in the army and is sent to France in Richard Wright's *The Long Dream.*

HARRY SAM. Polish dictator of HARRY SAM and former used-car salesman who disappears into the John for thirty years after catching a ravaging illness in Ishmael Reed's *The Free-Lance Pallbearers.*

Sam the Lion. Owner of the picture show, pool hall, and café in Thalia; one-time lover of Lois Farrow; dies of a stroke in Larry McMurtry's *The Last Picture Show.*

The Saminone. Black-talking inner voice–the voice of the Sam or Sambo in one–signifying in mysterious hallucinatory appearances to Max Reddick in John A. Williams's *The Man Who Cried I Am.*

Mr. Samm. Operator of the Go Hole in John Clellon Holmes's *The Horn.*

Artur (Slim-Jim, Uncle Sammler) Sammler. Elegant septuagenarian and Anglophile; survivor of a mass grave in Nazi-occupied Poland; concerned observer and critic of twentieth-century America's sexual emancipation, crime in the streets, technological mania, cultural leveling, and moral decline; protagonist and central intelligence of Saul Bellow's *Mr. Sammler's Planet.*

Shula (Shula-Slawa) Sammler. Daughter of Artur Sammler, ex-wife of Eisen, and a scavenger and collector who devotes herself to unconnected intellectual pursuits and to her father's nonexistent "project" on H. G. Wells in Saul Bellow's *Mr. Sammler's Planet.*

Cornelia (Corny) Samms. Schoolmate of Cress Delahanty and house party participant in Jessamyn West's *Cress Delahanty.*

Sammy The Butcher. Member of the Nova Mob in William S. Burroughs's *Nova Express* and *The Ticket That Exploded.*

Samoa. Upoluan aboard the *Parki*; married to Annatoo; killed by Aleema's sons in Herman Melville's *Mardi.*

Kid Sampson. Pilot sliced in two by a propeller in a freak accident, after which McWatt commits suicide, in Joseph Heller's *Catch-22.*

Robert Samson. White owner of the plantation on which Miss Jane Pittman lives during the civil rights movement; father of Tee Bob Samson and the mulatto Timmy in Ernest J. Gaines's *The Autobiography of Miss Jane Pittman.*

Robert (Tee Bob) Samson, Jr. Privileged white son of Robert Samson and half brother by the same father of the mulatto Timmy; commits suicide after being rejected by Mary Agnes LeFabre in Ernest J. Gaines's *The Autobiography of Miss Jane Pittman.*

Samuel. Abolitionist lecturer who falsely claims to be a fugitive slave; marries Frado, deserts her and their child, and dies of yellow fever in New Orleans in Harriet E. Wilson's *Our Nig.*

Reb Samuel. Chassidic immigrant owner of an umbrella store in Michael Gold's *Jews without Money.*

Samuele (Samuelino). Narrator named by Alix d'Espoli after Alix's dog in Thornton Wilder's *The Cabala.*

Brenda Samuels. Prostitute who gives Thomas Spellacy information that helps him solve the murder of Lois Fazenda in John Gregory Dunne's *True Confessions.*

Tony San Antonio. Saloonkeeper who makes a fortune during the Civil War by hoarding and selling cotton; becomes a wealthy financier in Grace King's *The Pleasant Ways of St. Médard.*

Dr. Sanborn. Physician, member of Chicago society, and proponent of the New Woman; marries Isabel Herrick in Hamlin Garland's *Rose of Dutcher's Coolly.*

Isabel Herrick Sanborn. See Isabel Herrick.

Sanchez. Faithful Mexican rider with the Del Sol herd in Emerson Hough's *North of 36.*

Manuel (Kid Sanchez) Sanchez. Ex-boxer who works for Everett Henshaw during apricot season; idolized by Tasmania Orcino in Jessamyn West's *A Matter of Time.*

Pablo Sanchez. Poor, gluttonous friend of Pilon; released from jail and convinced by Pilon to live in Pilon's house, if Sanchez agrees to pay the rent, in John Steinbeck's *Tortilla Flat.*

Raphael Nicholas (Nicky) Sanchez. Homosexual set designer for Boris Adrian's pornographic movie in Terry Southern's *Blue Movie.*

Max Sand. See Nevada Smith.

James Sandage. County trustee and overseer of the Lane County, Tennessee, poor farm; guardian of

Abner Teeftallow and murderer of Railroad Jones in T. S. Stribling's *Teeftallow*.

Sandbach. Intellectual and anarchist; rival of Jasper Ammen in Conrad Aiken's *King Coffin*.

Aleck Sander. Black friend of Chick Mallison in William Faulkner's *Intruder in the Dust* and *The Town*.

Billy Sanderlee. Pianist and friend who accompanies Harriett Williams in her singing act in Langston Hughes's *Not Without Laughter*.

Granny Sanders. Hag with a reputation for almost supernatural knowledge in Edward Eggleston's *The Hoosier School-Master*.

Tony Sanders. Screenwriter for Boris Adrian's pornographic movie in Terry Southern's *Blue Movie*.

George Sanderson. Professor of history and thesis adviser who takes a special interest in Leslie McGivers; having an "open marriage," he takes Honor Rogers as his lover in Marge Piercy's *The High Cost of Living*.

Luke Sanderson. Unambitious liar and thief; heir to Hill House in Shirley Jackson's *The Haunting of Hill House*.

Tommy Sanderson. Opportunist who is the supposed leader of the Union League but who is distrusted by the true Unionists in Albion W. Tourgee's *A Fool's Errand*.

Naomi (Mary Joy) Sandifer. Mother of Ralph Sandifer and wife of Buddy Sandifer; author of lurid, erotic adventures in Thomas Berger's *Sneaky People*.

Ralph Virgil (Ralphie) Sandifer. Fifteen-year-old midwestern hero of Thomas Berger's *Sneaky People*.

Virgil (Buddy) Sandifer. Unctuous used car salesman, unfaithful husband of Naomi Sandifer, and father of Ralph Sandifer in Thomas Berger's *Sneaky People*.

Sandra. See Mayo.

Gus Sands. King of the bookies in Bernard Malamud's *The Natural*.

Judith Sands. Reclusive novelist sought out by Doctor Mann; permits Renate to read her hidden manuscript; contributor to Renate's planned magazine in Anaïs Nin's *Collages*.

Felix (The Great Sandusky) Sandusky. Strongman and early teacher who advises James Boswell to deny his impulse for ego aggrandizement in Stan-

ley Elkin's *Boswell*.

George Sandusky. Customer at the tailor shop who works at a hotel loading taxis in Henry Miller's *Black Spring*.

James (Jaky) Sandusky. Self-serving attorney who defends Toussaint Vaiden; appears in T. S. Stribling's *The Store* and *Unfinished Cathedral*.

Betty Sandwich. See Betty MacNaughton.

Hamilton (Ham) Sandwich. Infant son of Joe and Naughty Sandwich; named for Uncle Hamilton in the hope of an inheritance in Peter De Vries's *The Vale of Laughter*.

Joe Sandwich. Inept stockbroker and perpetual "life of the party"; dies in a spectacular bicycle mishap; narrates part of Peter De Vries's *The Vale of Laughter*.

Sandy (Alisande de la Carteloise). Sixth-century wife of Hank Morgan; tells unending tales of knights' adventures in Samuel Langhorne Clemens's *A Connecticut Yankee in King Arthur's Court*.

Blaise Delacroix Sanford. Fierce, ambitious publisher of the prestigious *Washington Tribune*; uses his power and wealth to manipulate others in Gore Vidal's *Washington, D.C.*

Enid Sanford. Volatile wife of Clay Overbury; sent to an asylum by her father, Blaise Sanford; killed in a car crash in Gore Vidal's *Washington, D.C.*

Frederika Sanford. Harshly critical mother of Peter Sanford; wife of Blaise Sanford in Gore Vidal's *Washington, D.C.*

Peter Sanford. Sharp-tongued editor of *The American Idea*; son of Blaise and Frederika Sanford in Gore Vidal's *Washington, D.C.*

Peter Sanford (Sandford). Dashing army major who wishes to avenge men's treatment by coquettes through his relationship with Eliza Wharton in Hannah Webster Foster's *The Coquette*.

Lola San-Marquand. Artistic director of the Actors' Means Workshop and wife of Saul San-Marquand in James Baldwin's *Tell Me How Long the Train's Been Gone*.

Saul San-Marquand. Artistic director of the Actors' Means Workshop and husband of Lola San-Marquand in James Baldwin's *Tell Me How Long the Train's Been Gone*.

Miss Amy Skully Sansom. Wife of Edward Sansom, whom she marries after her cousin, Randolph Skully, shot and paralyzed him, in Truman Capote's *Other Voices, Other Rooms*.

Edward R. (Ed) Sansom. Bedridden father of Joel Harrison Knox; unable to communicate except with red tennis balls after his accidental shooting in Truman Capote's *Other Voices, Other Rooms*.

Joel Harrison Knox Sansom. See Joel Harrison Knox.

Sansori. Japanese ornithologist who relates the tale of how a dodo bird helped a medieval emperor defeat his enemies in Stanley Elkin's *The Dick Gibson Show*.

Santiago. Old Cuban fisherman who catches a huge marlin, only to have it eaten by sharks before he can bring it to land, in Ernest Hemingway's *The Old Man and the Sea*.

El (Sordo) Santiago. Leader of a partisan group in Ernest Hemingway's *For Whom the Bell Tolls*.

Danny Santini. Father of Gil Santini; stays with Harry Meyers to protect Meyers from possible attack by Jackson's brother in Jay Neugeboren's *Listen Ruben Fontanez*.

Gil Santini. Murdered five-year-old son of Danny Santini in Jay Neugeboren's *Listen Ruben Fontanez*.

Dr. Abe Sapirstein. Devil worshipper and physician to Rosemary Woodhouse during her pregnancy with Satan's son in Ira Levin's *Rosemary's Baby*.

Charlie (Chaim) Sapistein. Real estate agent, father figure to Daniel Ginsberg, and lover of Anita Mendelsohn after Murray Mendelsohn's death; dreams of becoming a rabbi despite being unable to read, because of dyslexia, in Jay Neugeboren's *An Orphan's Tale*.

Sarah. See Wanda Bzik.

Sarah. Betrothed of Coalhouse Walker, Jr.; killed while trying to talk with Vice President James Sherman in E. L. Doctorow's *Ragtime*.

Aunt Sarah. Slave mother of Nigel; befriends Dana Franklin in Octavia E. Butler's *Kindred*.

Alexis Saranditis. Father of Dania Saranditis and friend of Mehemet Effendi in Nicholas Delbanco's *The Martlet's Tale*.

Dania Saranditis. Daughter of Alexis Saranditis and lover of Mehemet Effendi and Sotiris Procopirios in Nicholas Delbanco's *The Martlet's Tale*.

Lee Sarason. Satanic secretary of state who deposes President Berzelius Windrip and succeeds him as president in Sinclair Lewis's *It Can't Happen Here*.

Frank Sargent. Mining associate of Oliver Ward; loves Susan Ward in Wallace Stegner's *Angle of Repose*.

Kit Sargent. Mannish and assertive novelist and screenwriter who is instrumental in the formation of a Hollywood writers' guild; sometime girlfriend of Sammy Glick and later wife of Al Manheim in Budd Schulberg's *What Makes Sammy Run?*

Aunt Saro Jane. Folk seer and former slave in Sarah E. Wright's *This Child's Gonna Live*.

Slim Sarrett. College boxer, poet, graduate student, and friend of Sue Murdock until she learns of his homosexuality; strangles her in Robert Penn Warren's *At Heaven's Gate*.

Father Sarria. Mission priest in the San Joaquin Valley who counsels Vanamee, whose fiancée has been raped and has died during childbirth, in Frank Norris's *The Octopus*.

Sarsefield. Lover of Euphemia Lorimer driven away by her brother, Arthur Wiatte, but eventually returns to marry her; friend and mentor of Edgar Huntly in Charles Brockden Brown's *Edgar Huntly*.

Bayard Sartoris (I). Brother of Col. John Sartoris; killed in the Civil War; appears in William Faulkner's *Sartoris (Flags in the Dust)* and *The Unvanquished*.

Bayard Sartoris (II). Son of Col. John Sartoris; mayor of Jefferson and president of a bank; kills Major Grumby, his grandmother's murderer; appears in William Faulkner's *Sartoris (Flags in the Dust)*; *The Unvanquished*; *The Hamlet*; *Go Down, Moses*; *Requiem for a Nun*; *The Town*; *The Mansion*; and *The Reivers*.

Bayard Sartoris (III). Grandson of Bayard Sartoris II; killed while testing an airplane; appears in William Faulkner's *Sartoris (Flags in the Dust)*, *Requiem for a Nun*, *The Town*, and *The Mansion*.

Benbow (Bory) Sartoris. Son of Narcissa Benbow and Bayard Sartoris III in William Faulkner's *Sartoris (Flags in the Dust)*, *Sanctuary*, *The Town*, and *The Mansion*.

Drusilla Hawk Sartoris. Fearless young woman who fights with the regiment of Col. John Sartoris and becomes his second wife in William Faulkner's *The Unvanquished*.

Col. John Sartoris. First Sartoris in Yoknapatawpha County; Confederate officer and father of Bayard Sartoris II; murdered by his partner Ben Redmond; appears in William Faulkner's *Sartoris (Flags in the Dust)*; *The Sound and the Fury*; *Light in August*;

Absalom, Absalom!; *The Unvanquished*; *The Hamlet*; *Go Down, Moses*; *Requiem for a Nun*; *The Town*; *The Mansion*; and *The Reivers*.

Narcissa Benbow Sartoris. Sister of Horace Benbow, second wife of Bayard Sartoris III, and mother of Benbow Sartoris; appears in William Faulkner's *Sartoris (Flags in the Dust)*, *Sanctuary*, *The Town*, and *The Mansion*.

Mr. de Sastago. Alleged marquis of Spain married to Honora Wapshot for eight months in her youth in John Cheever's *The Wapshot Chronicle*.

Cecily Saunders. See Cecily Saunders Farr.

Danny Saunders. Brilliant friend of Reuven Malter; leaves his Hasidic faith to become a psychologist in Chaim Potok's *The Chosen*; marries Rachel after treating her catatonic cousin Michael in *The Promise*.

Reb Isaac Saunders. Anti-Zionist Hasidic rabbi who passes on his deep faith to his son Danny by rearing him in silence in Chaim Potok's *The Chosen* and *The Promise*.

Leonard Saunders. Co-conspirator in Willie Hall's plan to lynch a white policeman in John Edgar Wideman's *The Lynchers*.

Levi Saunders. Sickly younger son of Reb Saunders; becomes Reb's designated successor as rabbi when Danny Saunders becomes a psychologist in Chaim Potok's *The Chosen*; gradually grows into the role of rabbi in *The Promise*.

Minnie Saunders. Wife of Robert Saunders I and mother of Cecily Saunders and Robert Saunders II in William Faulkner's *Soldiers' Pay*.

Robert Saunders (I). Husband of Minnie Saunders and father of Cecily Saunders and Robert Saunders II in William Faulkner's *Soldiers' Pay*.

Robert Saunders (II). Son of Robert and Minnie Saunders and brother of Cecily Saunders Farr in William Faulkner's *Soldiers' Pay*.

Savacol. Dissolute, egocentric gambler and first husband of Ruhama Warne in H. L. Davis's *Beulah Land*.

Eleanor Savage. Eccentric young woman with whom Amory Blaine is poetically involved in F. Scott Fitzgerald's *This Side of Paradise*.

Frank Savage. Demanding but successful commanding officer of the 918th Bomb Group in Beirne Lay, Jr., and Sy Bartlett's *Twelve O'Clock High!*

Richard Ellsworth Savage. Associate of J. Ward Morehouse's who has an affair with Anne Elizabeth Trent in Italy during World War I and refuses to marry her in John Dos Passos's *U.S.A.* trilogy.

Thomas (Tom) Savage. Lookout for men who try to ambush Comfort Servosse; after being injured and nursed back to health, he becomes a supporter of Servosse and warns the Regulators not to bother Servosse in Albion W. Tourgee's *A Fool's Errand*.

Tony Savanola. Catholic neighbor of the Luries; although he does not hate Jews, he bows to Eddie Kulanski's pressure and helps torment David Lurie in Chaim Potok's *In the Beginning*.

Savata. Sister of Ruby Drew; becomes a bishop in the Light of the World Holiness Church, but finally resists her sister's efforts to save her in William Goyen's *The Fair Sister*.

Miguel Saveda. Sailor whose corpse burns aboard the *Highlander* in Herman Melville's *Redburn*.

Maria Savor. Mother of a child that Annie Kilburn sends to the seaside for its health but which dies; with her husband, William, she forms the foundation of the Social Union in William Dean Howells's *Annie Kilburn*.

William Savor. Husband of Maria Savor and father of a deceased child in William Dean Howells's *Annie Kilburn*.

Pete Sawmill. Simple, free black who has rapport with animals and nature; serves first as Rose Wentworth's servant and then as Barton Cathcart's bodyguard during the Civil War; helps Cathcart escape from Gettysburg in Henry Ward Beecher's *Norwood*.

Nancy Sawyer. Kindly old maid who aids the ill Shocky Thomson in Edward Eggleston's *The Hoosier School-Master*.

Sidney (Sid) Sawyer. Do-gooder half brother of Tom Sawyer in Samuel Langhorne Clemens's *The Adventures of Tom Sawyer*.

Taylor Sawyer. Wastrel brother of Sally Lacey in Mary Lee Settle's *O Beulah Land*.

Thomas (Sid, Tom) Sawyer. Mischievous boy who witnesses the murder of Dr. Robinson and finds $12,000 in gold in Samuel Langhorne Clemens's *The Adventures of Tom Sawyer*; helps Huck Finn free Jim and is shot in the process in *Adventures of Huckleberry Finn*; pilots a balloon across North Africa in *Tom Sawyer Abroad*; solves the murder Silas Phelps is accused of in *Tom Sawyer, Detective*.

Doctor (Adolphus Asher Ghoulens, King of Anti Evil, Raymond) Sax. Lurking, green-faced phantom who vows to destroy the Great World Snake; imaginary boyhood companion of Jack Duluoz in Jack Kerouac's *Doctor Sax*; also appears in *Book of Dreams*.

Gramma Julie Saxinar. Maternal grandmother of Neil and Robert Kingsblood in Sinclair Lewis's *Kingsblood Royal*.

Madeleine Saxon. See Mary-Jane Saxon Kirkland.

Alethea Ann (Lethe) Sayles. Mountaineer loved by Mink Lorey and Ben Doaks in Mary Noailles Murfree's *In the Clouds*.

Herman Sayre. Wealthy alumnus of "the College" and father of Lily Sayre; overzealous supporter of Raymond Blent's eligibility to play football in Howard Nemerov's *The Homecoming Game*.

Lily Sayre. Daughter of Herman Sayre and girlfriend of Raymond Blent; loved by Dr. Charles Osman in Howard Nemerov's *The Homecoming Game*.

Giovanni Scabby. Underworld informer who seeks Rico Bandello in order to gain revenge on Bandello for having destroyed the Vettori mob in William Riley Burnett's *Little Caesar*.

Justina (Cousin Justina) Wapshot Molesworth Scaddon. Ancient cousin of Leander and Honora Wapshot; former dancer and piano player who lives in the ramshackle castle Clear Haven and attempts to control Moses Wapshot's marriage to her ward, Melissa, in John Cheever's *The Wapshot Chronicle*.

LaDonna Scales. Daughter of Pourty Bloodworth; sister of Amos-Otis Thigpen, Noah Grandberry, and Regal Pettibone (who is also her lover); half sister of Jonathan Bass in Leon Forrest's *The Bloodworth Orphans*.

Jimmy Scalisi. Bank robber and skilled craftsman with a pistol who works with Eddie Coyle in George V. Higgins's *The Friends of Eddie Coyle*.

Red Scalotta. Millionaire bookmaker and sexual pervert in Joseph Wambaugh's *The Blue Knight*.

Lucy Scanlan. Girlfriend of Studs Lonigan in James T. Farrell's *Young Lonigan*; although she has moved away, she remains the object of Lonigan's fantasies in *The Young Manhood of Studs Lonigan* and *Judgment Day*.

Scanlon. Last of the patients influenced by Randle McMurphy left at the mental hospital after McMurphy dies and Chief Bromden escapes in Ken Kesey's *One Flew Over the Cuckoo's Nest*.

Timothy Scanlon. Father of Tom Scanlon and the real subject of Tom's "autobiographical" musings in Wright Morris's *The Field of Vision*.

Tom Scanlon. Father of Lois McKee; myopic myth-making frontiersman in Wright Morris's *The Field of Vision*; his ninetieth birthday is the central occasion in *Ceremony in Lone Tree*; appears also in *The World in the Attic*.

Scar. Best friend of Jake Adams; addicted to heroin; later tries the cure in Herbert Simmons's *Corner Boy*.

Scarecrow. Successful black writer and expatriate; confusion over racial and sexual roles leads to his murdering four people and his own death; protagonist of Calvin Hernton's *Scarecrow*.

Peter Scatterpatter. Translator of the anonymous *A Manual for Sons* in Donald Barthelme's *The Dead Father*.

Miller (Mill) Schabb. Partner in the mob-run Regents Sportsmen's Club, Inc.; with Croce Torre, attempts to kill The Greek Almas in George V. Higgins's *The Digger's Game*.

Beatrice (Bea) Schachter. Experienced teacher who befriends Sylvia Barrett and helps her make it through her first year at Calvin Coolidge High School; respected and loved by students in Bel Kaufman's *Up the Down Staircase*.

Miriam Schaefer. American artist in Italy who loves Donatello and signals him to kill Brother Antonio in Nathaniel Hawthorne's *The Marble Faun*.

Anna Schaeffer. Agent for Asher Lev; bolsters Lev and sells Lev's paintings to the Manhattan Museum of Art in Chaim Potok's *My Name Is Asher Lev*.

Moira Schaffner. Secretary at the Love Clinic and naively romantic girlfriend of Tom More in Walker Percy's *Love in the Ruins*.

Schatzi (Ernst). German black marketeer in Thomas Berger's *Crazy in Berlin*.

Albert Schearl. Austrian immigrant ill-suited for life in New York; husband of Genya Schearl and father of David Schearl in Henry Roth's *Call It Sleep*.

David (Davy) Schearl. Son of Albert and Genya Schearl; absorbs the hectic conditions of Jewish immigrant life in New York in Henry Roth's *Call It*

Sleep.

Genya Schearl. Wife of Albert Schearl; perceptive and protective mother of David Schearl in Henry Roth's *Call It Sleep.*

Scheherazade (Sherry). Sister of Dunyazade; must invent a way to prevent the king from raping and killing a virgin every night in the *Dunyazadiad,* a novella in John Barth's *Chimera.*

Lieutenant Scheisskopf. Humorless and absurdly ambitious officer obsessed with uniformity and winning parades; eventually promoted to general in Joseph Heller's *Catch-22.*

Dr. Schiff. Woman psychiatrist who treats Hilary Wiggen; enamored of Henry Wiggen in Mark Harris's *It Looked Like For Ever.*

Nathan (Nate) Schild. Communist sympathizer and friend of Carlo Reinhart; murdered in Thomas Berger's *Crazy in Berlin.*

Lawrence (Larry) Schiller. Journalist who investigates Gary Gilmore's life in Norman Mailer's *The Executioner's Song.*

Richard (Dick) F. Schiller. Young man with job prospects in Alaska; husband of Dolores Haze and father of their stillborn child in Vladimir Nabokov's *Lolita.*

Father Schimmelpfennig. Catholic priest, spiritual adviser to the Neumiller family in Hyatt, North Dakota, and special friend of Martin Neumiller in Larry Woiwode's *Beyond the Bedroom Wall.*

Ed Schindel. Friend of Hart Kennedy in John Clellon Holmes's *Go.*

Nicholas Schliemann. Socialist-anarchist theorist whose ideas inspire Jurgis Rudkus to work for socialism in Upton Sinclair's *The Jungle.*

Schlossberg. Journalist and Jewish patriarch whose wise humanism leads Asa Leventhal to aspire to the "exactly human" and to "choose dignity" in Saul Bellow's *The Victim.*

Schmendrick. Magician who frees the unicorn from Mommy Fortuna's Midnight Carnival and helps her find other unicorns in Peter S. Beagle's *The Last Unicorn.*

Achilles Schmidt. Legless giant whose obsession with the prostitute Hallie Breedlove causes him to cripple Dove Linkhorn in Nelson Algren's *A Walk on the Wild Side.*

Alma (Lorene) Schmidt. Prostitute at Gert Kipfer's brothel; has an affair with Robert E. Lee Prewitt

and hides him after he kills Fatso Judson in James Jones's *From Here to Eternity.*

Nectar Schmidt. College roommate of Geneva Spofford; paramour then second wife of Jack Dumbrowski in Peter De Vries's *Reuben, Reuben.*

Frau Otto Schmitt. Woman who escorts her husband's body home to Germany in Katherine Anne Porter's *Ship of Fools.*

Schmuel. Father-in-law of Yakov Bok in Bernard Malamud's *The Fixer.*

Herman H. (Dutch) Schnell. Manager of the New York Mammoths baseball team in Mark Harris's *The Southpaw, Bang the Drum Slowly, A Ticket for a Seamstitch,* and *It Looked Like For Ever.*

Millie Schnell. Widow of Dutch Schnell in Mark Harris's *It Looked Like For Ever.*

Brandon Schnitzer. Younger brother of Susie Schnitzer; shares their father's values, not Susie's, in Harriette Simpson Arnow's *The Weedkiller's Daughter.*

Herman (Bismarck) Schnitzer. Radically right-wing father of Susie Schnitzer; racial bigot on a weedkilling campaign; fears having his Detroit suburb overrun by weeds and blacks in Harriette Simpson Arnow's *The Weedkiller's Daughter.*

Mrs. (The Popsicle Queen) Schnitzer. Mother of Susie Schnitzer; conforms to her husband's WASP-ish country club lifestyle in Harriette Simpson Arnow's *The Weedkiller's Daughter.*

Susan Marie (Susie) Schnitzer. Intelligent, self-aware fifteen-year-old heroine of Harriette Simpson Arnow's *The Weedkiller's Daughter.*

Sammy Schoelkopf. Son of the next-farm neighbors of Mary Robinson; occasionally mows the fields for her in John Updike's *Of the Farm.*

Marvin Schoenbrun. Tenant of the 70th Street building managed by Norman Moonbloom in Edward Lewis Wallant's *The Tenants of Moonbloom.*

Connie Schoffstal. Best friend and confidante of Grace Brock Caldwell in John O'Hara's *A Rage to Live.*

Henry Passloe Schofield. Father of Penrod Schofield; administers corporal punishment to his son, when necessary, in Booth Tarkington's *Penrod, Penrod and Sam,* and *Penrod Jashber.*

Margaret Passloe Schofield. Sister of Penrod Schofield; her suitors, with the exception of Robert Williams, are driven away when they become the target of Penrod's antics in Booth Tarkington's *Penrod, Penrod and Sam,* and *Penrod Jashber.*

Mrs. Schofield. Mother of Penrod Schofield; she generally deals well with her son's creativity and energy in Booth Tarkington's *Penrod, Penrod and Sam,* and *Penrod Jashber.*

Penrod (George B. Jashber) Schofield. Boy whose imagination, creativity, and energy lead him into numerous adventures, experiments, and escapades in Booth Tarkington's *Penrod, Penrod and Sam,* and *Penrod Jashber.*

Buddy Schonbeck. Boyhood friend of Jerome Neumiller and Charles Neumiller (II) in Larry Woiwode's *Beyond the Bedroom Wall.*

Harry (Schoons) Schoonover. College roommate and drinking buddy of Jerry Payne; owner of the Screaming Bitch, an automobile, in John Nichols's *The Sterile Cuckoo.*

Dr. Schott. President of Wicomico State Teachers College in John Barth's *The End of the Road.*

Marcus (Mark) Schouler. Friend of McTeague; upon believing that McTeague has cheated him, acts to have McTeague's license to practice dentistry revoked, thus triggering McTeague's economic and personal decline, in Frank Norris's *McTeague.*

Rudolph Schreiker. Kommisar of Warsaw after Nazi occupation in Leon Uris's *Mila 18.*

Kenneth (Kenny, Dr. Yankem) Schreuer. Dentist, tennis and radio soap-opera enthusiast, and former student of George Caldwell in John Updike's *The Centaur.*

Peter (Dutchman) Schroeder. German immigrant whose house is robbed in Edward Eggleston's *The Hoosier School-Master.*

O. Schrutt. Former Nazi Storm Trooper; dope-taking night watchman who beats the zoo animals; put in a cage with a ratel in John Irving's *Setting Free the Bears.*

Schuldig. Messenger hired by Henry Miller; spends twenty years in prison for a crime he didn't commit; eventually goes insane in Henry Miller's *Tropic of Capricorn.*

Marshall Schulman. Los Angeles deputy district attorney who prosecutes Gregory Powell and Jimmy Smith in Joseph Wambaugh's *The Onion Field.*

Schumann. Ship's doctor who falls in love with his drug-addicted patient La Condesa as he is returning, a dying man, to Germany in Katherine Anne Porter's *Ship of Fools.*

Frau Natalie Schuschnigg. Governess-housekeeper employed by Arbogast von Hohengraetz; becomes Rudolf Stanka's *mamitsa* when he is restored to a noble position; marries Herr Ottokar Bukuwky in Louis Adamic's *Cradle of Life.*

Kurt von Schuschnigg. Chancellor of Austria coerced by Hitler into agreeing to the German *Anschluss* in 1938 in John Irving's *Setting Free the Bears.*

Charles (Charlie, Old Patroon) Schuyler. Law clerk in Aaron Burr's office commissioned to write Burr's memoirs; narrator of Gore Vidal's *Burr.*

Nancy Schuyler. Servant of the Demooths who is impregnated by a British soldier, runs away, and becomes an Indian squaw in Walter D. Edmonds's *Drums along the Mohawk.*

Dr. Abigail Schwartz. Psychoanalyst of Isadora Wing in Erica Jong's *How to Save Your Own Life.*

Manny Schwartz. Ruined movie producer who commits suicide in F. Scott Fitzgerald's *The Last Tycoon.*

Milton (Milt) Schwartz. Law partner of Lou Michaelson; marries Marjorie Morningstar in Herman Wouk's *Marjorie Morningstar.*

Roger Schwartz. Boyfriend of Rose MacMahon, about whose pregnancy he is concerned, in Robert Cantwell's *The Land of Plenty.*

Mattie Schwengauer. Innocent girlfriend of Dirk DeJong in Edna Ferber's *So Big.*

Zero Schwiefka. Owner of a Polish gambling house in Chicago and Frankie Machine's employer in Nelson Algren's *The Man with the Golden Arm.*

Scipio. Freed slave who accompanies Mark Littleton on the final part of Littleton's journey to the plantation in John Pendleton Kennedy's *Swallow Barn.*

Scooter (Mister Man). Young black narrator of Albert Murray's *Train Whistle Guitar.*

Carlos Scotobal. Bank clerk and police informer in Merida, Mexico, in Nicholas Delbanco's *News.*

Scott. Professor and member of the Centennial Club in Thomas McGuane's *The Sporting Club.*

Scott. See Hud.

David (David Darling) Scott. American painter traveling with Jenny Brown, with whom he has a hopeless affair, in Katherine Anne Porter's *Ship of Fools.*

General Hector Scott. Retired military officer and lover of Aurora Greenway in Larry McMurtry's

Terms of Endearment.

Ida Scott. Promising black jazz singer from Harlem; sister of Rufus Scott and lover of Vivaldo Moore in James Baldwin's *Another Country.*

General John Scott. Nearly toothless old slave on the Prosser plantation; serves as treasurer of the slave revolt in Arna Wendell Bontemps's *Black Thunder.*

Rufus Scott. Down and out black jazz musician who commits suicide in a frenzy of despair; brother of Ida Scott, friend of Vivaldo Moore and Cass Silenski; one-time lover of Eric Jones; lover and abuser of Leona in James Baldwin's *Another Country.*

Samuel (Honorable Sammy, Sam, Sammy) Scott. Leading black politician of Chicago; in reality, a shrewd businessman in W. E. B. Du Bois's *Dark Princess.*

Lieutenant Colonel Walter Scott. Good-humored battalion commander in Willa Cather's *One of Ours.*

Weeden Scott. Mining engineer who rescues White Fang from the dogfights and tames him into a loyal dog in Jack London's *White Fang.*

Baby Lazar Scruggs. Exotic dancer Arista Prolo cannot outdance; overprotected by her mother in Carlene Hatcher Polite's *Sister X and the Victims of Foul Play.*

Ian Scuffling. See Lieutenant Tyrone Slothrop.

Louie Scurrah. Experienced woodsman who marries Genny Luckett; he deserts her and runs off with her sister Achsa Luckett to the western territories in Conrad Richter's *The Trees*; his death is mentioned in *The Fields.*

Dominic (Scuz) Scuzzi. Los Angeles police sergeant in charge of the vice squad in Joseph Wambaugh's *The Choirboys.*

Sarah Seabrooke. Spinster great-aunt of Jim Calder and Clothilde Wright; considered by Calder to embody the New England tradition in John P. Marquand's *Wickford Point.*

Fletcher Lynd (Fletch, Fletcher Gull) Seagull. Young seagull from Jonathan Livingston Seagull's flock who, after perfecting his flying, returns to the flock to teach the young gulls in Richard Bach's *Jonathan Livingston Seagull.*

Jonathan Livingston (Jon, Jonathan Gull) Seagull. Seagull who refuses to accept ordinary life and seeks a more meaningful existence by striving to perfect his flying skills, which he does after tran-scending life, in Richard Bach's *Jonathan Livingston Seagull.*

Vurl Seaman. College boyfriend of Blix Hollister in Jessamyn West's *A Matter of Time.*

Dr. Kennard Sear. Tiresias-figure who heads the college infirmary in John Barth's *Giles Goat-Boy.*

Lloyd Searight. Head of a nursing agency who falls in love with Ward Bennett but is alienated from him when he prevents her from doing her duty as a nurse in Frank Norris's *A Man's Woman.*

Harry Searle. Hack writer of soap operas who wants Lee Youngdahl to join his Dollar a Word Club in Mark Harris's *Wake Up, Stupid.*

Tobias Sears. Union officer who marries the mulatto Amantha Starr and makes her feel free in Robert Penn Warren's *Band of Angels.*

Ivor (Istvan Szegedyi) Sedge. Hungarian refugee, painter, and former lover of Violet Clay in Gail Godwin's *Violet Clay.*

Ethan Segal. Lover of Jack Laws and friend of Pammy Wynant; shares an office with her in Don DeLillo's *Players.*

Cruz Segovia. Los Angeles police sergeant and best friend of Bumper Morgan; killed by a robber in Joseph Wambaugh's *The Blue Knight.*

George Selby. Confederate colonel murdered by Laura Hawkins in Samuel Langhorne Clemens and Charles Dudley Warner's *The Gilded Age.*

T. Selby. Friend of J. Boyer; advises Boyer against further involvement with Eliza Wharton in Hannah Webster Foster's *The Coquette.*

Lawrence Selden. New York lawyer who loves and is loved by Lily Bart but whom she considers too poor to marry in Edith Wharton's *The House of Mirth.*

Father Seldon. Priest who introduces Cross Damon to Ely Houston in Richard Wright's *The Outsider.*

Bertha Selig. Sister with whom Sol Nazerman lives in Edward Lewis Wallant's *The Pawnbroker.*

Beatrice Fetner (Bebe) Sellars. Wife of Jack Sellars; amateur philosopher who is much in love with her husband after many years of marriage in Doris Betts's *The River to Pickle Beach.*

Jack S. Sellars. Husband of Bebe Sellars; nature lover who read and studied while a maintenance man at Duke University; has successfully lived down the childhood trauma of his father's murder in Doris

Betts's *The River to Pickle Beach.*

Colonel Beriah/Eschol/Mulberry (Berry, Earl of Rossmore) Sellers. Entrepreneur given to such wild schemes as the Salt Lick Pacific Extension and the Knobs Industrial University in Samuel Langhorne Clemens and Charles Dudley Warner's *The Gilded Age* (where he is known as Eschol, in the first edition, or as Beriah, in subsequent editions); plans to reincarnate spirits in Clemens's *The American Claimant* (where he is known as Mulberry and pretends to be the Earl of Rossmore).

Polly Sellers. Wife of Colonel Sellers in Samuel Langhorne Clemens's *The American Claimant* and Clemens and Charles Dudley Warner's *The Gilded Age.*

Sarah (Lady Gwendolen, Sally) Sellers. Daughter of Mulberry and Polly Sellers; falls in love with and marries Berkeley, whom she first knows as Howard Tracy, in Samuel Langhorne Clemens's *The American Claimant.*

Selvagee. Effeminate lieutenant aboard the *Neversink* in Herman Melville's *White-Jacket.*

Glen Selvy. Buyer of erotic art for Senator Lloyd Percival, undercover agent of Radial Matrix, and lover of Moll Robbins and Nadine Rademacher; murdered in Don DeLillo's *Running Dog.*

Irving (Krankeit) Semite. Psychiatrist with bizarre theories and therapies in Terry Southern and Mason Hoffenberg's *Candy.*

Alfred Semple. Husband of Lillian Semple and shoe-store owner; dies of pneumonia in Theodore Dreiser's *The Financier.*

Doña Maria Sepulvida. Fiery Latina and romantic interest of men, good and evil, in Bret Harte's *Gabriel Conroy.*

Mother Sereda. Mythical woman who bleaches the color from the cloth of life; flattered by Jurgen into granting him a year of youth, she sends her shadow along to observe his behavior; appears in various guises to Jurgen throughout his journeys in James Branch Cabell's *Jurgen.*

Serena. Mysterious prostitute and lover of George Levanter; murders a chauffeur with a metal rat-tail comb in Jerzy Kosinski's *Blind Date.*

Serge. Russian truck driver who hires Henry Miller as an English teacher in exchange for a room and one meal a day in Henry Miller's *Tropic of Cancer.*

Mrs. May Server. Promiscuous woman who is supposedly using Guy Brissenden as a front for an affair, although she actually loves him, in Henry James's *The Sacred Fount.*

Servilia. Mother of Brutus; she urges her son to become part of the conspiracy against Caesar and hints that Brutus might even be Caesar's son in Thornton Wilder's *The Ides of March.*

Comfort (Fool) Servosse. Captain of the Peru Invincibles who buys Warrington Place after the Civil War; after moving South, he antagonizes his neighbors by associating with teachers from the freedmen's school; becomes disillusioned with the North's failure to protect freedmen and Unionists in the South; dies of yellow fever after a trip to Central America in Albion W. Tourgee's *A Fool's Errand.*

Lily (Lil) Servosse. Daughter of Comfort Servosse; she warns her father and Thomas Denton of the Ku Klux Klan's plans to ambush them; refuses to marry Melville Gurney without his father's approval in Albion W. Tourgee's *A Fool's Errand.*

Metta Ward Servosse. Wife of Comfort Servosse in Albion W. Tourgee's *A Fool's Errand.*

William Severance. Professor of English who teaches Lymie Peters, Hope Davison, and Sally Forbes at a midwestern university in William Maxwell's *The Folded Leaf.*

Erect Severehead. Television news analyst who reports on the assassination of Trick E. Dixon in Philip Roth's *Our Gang.*

Birdie Sewall. Sister of Kivden Sewall and friend of Rena Janney in August Derleth's *The Shield of the Valiant.*

John Sewall. Banker who opposes the romance of his son Kivden Sewall and Rena Janney in August Derleth's *The Shield of the Valiant.*

Kivden (Kiv) Sewall. Boyfriend of Rena Janney; quits working in his father's bank and joins a Madison jazz band; enlists in the military at the beginning of World War II in August Derleth's *The Shield of the Valiant.*

William Seward. See William Lee.

Seymour. Murderous black cook and an instigator of the mutiny on the *Grampus*; killed when the ship is retaken by Arthur Gordon Pym, Augustus Barnard, and Dirk Peters in Edgar Allan Poe's *The Narrative of Arthur Gordon Pym.*

Frank Shabata. Jealous and spiteful husband of Marie Shabata; kills his wife and her lover Emil Bergson in Willa Cather's *O Pioneers!*

Marie Tovesky Shabata. Wife of Frank Shabata, who kills her and her lover Emil Bergson, in Willa Cather's *O Pioneers!*

Kalik Shabazz. Tailor who is a Muslim convert saving his money for a trip to Mecca; formerly the operator of an "all-nite" barbecue and shrimp shack in Carlene Hatcher Polite's *Sister X and the Victims of Foul Play.*

Booker Shad. Jazz musician encouraged by Jimson and Charlie Parker; disintegrates through the use of drugs in Carlene Hatcher Polite's *The Flagellants.*

Hazel Shade. Beloved daughter of John and Sybil Shade; commits suicide after a blind date, Pete Dean, walks out on her in the last of many frustrations in her short life in Vladimir Nabokov's *Pale Fire.*

John Francis (S) Shade. Author of the poem *Pale Fire,* professor of English, and expert on Alexander Pope; mistakenly murdered by an escaped lunatic who intended to shoot Judge Goldsworth, Shade's neighbor; Charles Kinbote interprets the murder in a more personal light in Vladimir Nabokov's *Pale Fire.*

Sybil (Mrs. S) Shade. Wife of John Shade portrayed lovingly in his poem *Pale Fire;* in contrast, Charles Kinbote's commentaries jealously depict her as a harpy in Vladimir Nabokov's *Pale Fire.*

Shadrack. Shell-shocked war veteran who befriends Sula and leads the annual Suicide Day Parade in Toni Morrison's *Sula.*

Adam Shafer. Head of the Department of Anthropology at Vanderbilt University, husband of Octavia Shafer, and father of Gratt Shafer; comes to Somerton to explore the forty mounds there in Jesse Hill Ford's *Mountains of Gilead.*

Adam Gideon Shafer. Infant son of Gratt and Patsy Jo Shafer; named for his grandfathers in Jesse Hill Ford's *Mountains of Gilead.*

Gratt Shafer. Graduate of Vanderbilt University in 1939, son of Adam and Octavia Shafer, and father of Adam Gideon Shafer; has a lengthy affair with Patsy Jo McCutcheon before marrying Eleanor Fite and marries Patsy Jo after Eleanor's death in Jesse Hill Ford's *Mountains of Gilead.*

Octavia Ashmore (Madam) Shafer. Wife of Adam Shafer and mother of Gratt Shafer in Jesse Hill Ford's *Mountains of Gilead.*

Patricia Josephine (Patsy Jo) McCutcheon Shafer. Daughter of Thomas McCutcheon, lover and later

wife of Gratt Shafer, and mother of Adam Gideon Shafer in Jesse Hill Ford's *Mountains of Gilead.*

Frank Shallard. Seminary student who, with his friend Elmer Gantry, works as an intern pastor at a country church; becomes a Baptist minister in Sinclair Lewis's *Elmer Gantry.*

Eileen Shallcross. Divorced stepdaughter of Sheridan Dale; falls in love and has an affair with Timothy Colt in Louis Auchincloss's *The Great World and Timothy Colt.*

Mrs. de Shamble. See Laura Pribble.

Irene (Sister Monica) Shane. Daughter of Julia Shane; teaches English to millworkers and becomes a nun, Sister Monica, to the disappointment of her mother, in Louis Bromfield's *The Green Bay Tree.*

Julia Shane. Wealthy Protestant with two daughters, in Louis Bromfield's *The Green Bay Tree.*

Lily Shane. Daughter of Julia Shane; after Lily becomes pregnant by the state governor, who will not marry her, her mother sends her to Europe, where she flourishes, in Louis Bromfield's *The Green Bay Tree.*

Sonny Shanks. Rodeo star and lover of Eleanor Guthrie; dies in an automobile accident in Larry McMurtry's *Moving On.*

Father Shannon. Priest who preaches sermons against Sinclair Lewis and H. L. Mencken in James T. Farrell's *The Young Manhood of Studs Lonigan.*

Flo Shannon. Possessive, nagging, yet devoted mother of Margy Shannon in Betty Smith's *Tomorrow Will Be Better.*

Henny Shannon. Brooklyn shop worker; angry and argumentative husband of Flo Shannon and gentle, philosophical father of Margy Shannon in Betty Smith's *Tomorrow Will Be Better.*

Margaret (Margy) Shannon. Seventeen-year-old mail reader at the Thomson-Johnson Mail Order House; conscientious worker with unfulfilled dreams; child of Henry and Flo Shannon and wife of Frankie Malone in Betty Smith's *Tomorrow Will Be Better.*

Shaper. Blind harpist who creates a history of noble causes to justify the aggression of the Scyldings in John Gardner's *Grendel.*

Dr. Ben Shapiro. Army friend and best man of Walter F. Starbuck in Kurt Vonnegut's *Jailbird.*

Max Shapiro. Heroic marine commander killed at Saipan in Leon Uris's *Battle Cry*.

Shar. See Sherton.

Sharon. Pregnant woman slain in her Beverly Hills home in a Charles Manson-style massacre in Jerzy Kosinski's *Blind Date*.

Norah Sharon. Lover of Jerry Fowler; rescued by Fowler and Issachar Bennet from a severe beating in Walter D. Edmonds's *Erie Water*.

Buckingham Sharp. Shrewd, manipulative lawyer and admirer of Adelaide Jones in T. S. Stribling's *Teeftallow*; confidant to Agatha Pomeroy and lawyer for Risdale Balus in *Bright Metal*.

Marya Sharp. See Ardis Ross.

Shattuck. Archaeologist friend of Leonard Rhodes; interested in the "stranger people's" graveyard in Mary Noailles Murfree's *In the "Stranger People's" Country*.

Christopher Shaw. Nephew of Allen Musgrove; helps Horse Shoe Robinson capture Edgar St. Jermyn in John Pendleton Kennedy's *Horse-Shoe Robinson*.

Dorothy Shaw. Wise-cracking brunette companion of Lorelei Lee in Anita Loos's *"Gentlemen Prefer Blondes"*; her impractical romances and marriages occupy most of the sequel, *"But Gentlemen Marry Brunettes"*

Jimmy Shaw. Retired pugilist who operates The Queen's Head, the pub where Edward Pierce meets Edgar Trent, in Michael Crichton's *The Great Train Robbery*.

Matt Shaw. Owner and editor of the Hickory, Massachusetts, *Blade*; pays Ben Marvel $15 for the "Edgewise" column, minus deductions "for quoted matter" in Peter De Vries's *Through the Fields of Clover*.

Reggie Shaw. Doctor whose insensitivity and drinking are a mask for his despair over the inevitability of his patients' folly and death in James Gould Cozzens's *By Love Possessed*.

David Shawcross. Friend and publisher of Abe Cady in Leon Uris's *QB VII*.

Shawn. Rock star who joins the Indians and becomes a brother to Corey in Marge Piercy's *Dance the Eagle to Sleep*.

Margaret (Maggie) Rose Shawn. Sweetheart of Patrick Dennis Moore and namesake of his daughter, Maggie Moore; cause of the beating and public humiliation of Moore by her brother, Timothy Shawn, in Betty Smith's *Maggie-Now*.

Roger Shawn. Army lieutenant looking for the downed Scoop VII satellite in Michael Crichton's *The Andromeda Strain*.

Timothy (Big Red, Tim, Timmy) Shawn. Bowery police officer who avenges the honor of his sister, Maggie Rose Shawn; godfather to Maggie Moore in Betty Smith's *Maggie-Now*.

Esther Root Shawnessy. Second wife of John Wickliff Shawnessy, though half his age, in Ross Lockridge, Jr.'s *Raintree County*.

John Wickliff (Jack, Johnny) Shawnessy. Idealistic Indiana native whose dreams and disappointments mirror those of nineteenth-century America in Ross Lockridge, Jr.'s *Raintree County*.

Susanna Drake Shawnessy. See Susanna Drake.

Sheba. Gentle, often stoned fourth wife of Colonel Ellelloû; accompanies him to the Balak only to be kidnapped by his enemies in John Updike's *The Coup*.

Bobby Sheen. Playboy from Wichita Falls who seduces Jacy Farrow in Larry McMurtry's *The Last Picture Show*.

Aunt Chloe Shelby. See Aunt Chloe.

George Shelby. Son of the owners of Uncle Tom, Aunt Chloe, and Eliza Harris; after having failed to save the venerated Uncle Tom from the hands of Simon Legree, George dedicates his life to the gradual emancipation of his remaining slaves in Harriet Beecher Stowe's *Uncle Tom's Cabin*.

Timothy (Tim) Shelby. Black politician who is lynched for having tried to kiss a white woman in Thomas Dixon's *The Leopard's Spots*.

Uncle Tom Shelby. See Uncle Tom.

Anne-Maria Sherbrooke Sheldon. Daughter of Daniel Sherbrooke and wife of Willard Sheldon; Mormon missionary in Guatemala whose letters are read by Maggie Sherbrooke in Nicholas Delbanco's *Sherbrookes*; mentioned in *Possession*.

P.G. Sheldon. Poet and good friend of Sebastian Knight and Clare Bishop; supplies V. with information about Knight in Vladimir Nabokov's *The Real Life of Sebastian Knight*.

Willard Sheldon. Husband of Anne-Maria Sherbrooke; Mormon missionary in Guatemala in Nicholas Delbanco's *Sherbrookes*.

Shenly. Foretopman aboard the *Neversink* who dies of pulmonary problems as White-Jacket tends to him in Herman Melville's *White-Jacket*.

Henry Shepard. Railroad station master in Mudcat Landing, Missouri; hires Hugh McVey as an assistant and helps change Hugh's life for the better in Sherwood Anderson's *Poor White*.

Sarah Shepard. Wife of Henry Shepard; sets out to improve the life of Hugh McVey through his education and hard work in Sherwood Anderson's *Poor White*.

Shepherd. Father of Ophelia Shepherd and Mrs. Martin; enraged with Ophelia for her actions with Mr. Martin, but charges Martin with her seduction and death, in William Hill Brown's *The Power of Sympathy*.

Goode Shepherd. Dutiful but ineffective preacher; father of Mateel Shepherd in E. W. Howe's *The Story of a Country Town*.

Lawson Shepherd. Subordinate to Paul Proteus who eventually takes Proteus's job and wife in Kurt Vonnegut's *Player Piano*.

Lenny Shepherd. New York cowboy-style disk jockey who picks up Doreen in Sylvia Plath's *The Bell Jar*.

Mateel Shepherd. Daughter of Goode Shepherd; divorced by her first husband, Jo Erring, who kills her second husband, Clinton Bragg, in E. W. Howe's *The Story of a Country Town*.

Ophelia Shepherd. Sister of Mrs. Martin; commits suicide after having a child by Mr. Martin in William Hill Brown's *The Power of Sympathy*.

Harney Shepherdson. Member of the family that is feuding with the Grangerfords; elopes with Sophia Grangerford, thus precipitating a deadly battle between the two families, in Samuel Langhorne Clemens's *Adventures of Huckleberry Finn*.

Fred (Signor Rossello) Shepley. High rider, as Signor Rossello, for Huguenine's circus; enamored of Albany Yates in Walter D. Edmonds's *Chad Hanna*.

Moseley Sheppard. Virginia planter and gentleman in Arna Wendell Bontemps's *Black Thunder*.

Robin (Marse Robin) Sheppard. Young son of Moseley Sheppard; student at the College of William and Mary in Arna Wendell Bontemps's *Black Thunder*.

Randy Shepperton. Childhood friend of George Webber in Thomas Wolfe's *You Can't Go Home Again* and *The Web and the Rock*.

Anne-Maria Sherbrooke. See Anne-Maria Sherbrooke Sheldon.

Daniel (Peacock) Sherbrooke. Grandfather of Judah Sherbrooke and builder of the Sherbrooke mansion in Nicholas Delbanco's *Sherbrookes*.

Harriet (Hattie) Sherbrooke. Spinster sister of Judah Sherbrooke in Nicholas Delbanco's *Possession* and *Sherbrookes*.

Ian Daniel Sherbrooke. Son of Judah and Maggie Sherbrooke and an actor in Nicholas Delbanco's *Sherbrookes*.

Judah (Jude) Porteous Sherbrooke. Owner of Sherbrooke estate, husband of Maggie Sherbrooke, and father of Ian and Seth Sherbrooke in Nicholas Delbanco's *Possession* and *Sherbrookes*.

Lisbeth McPherson Sherbrooke. First wife of Judah Sherbrooke; killed in an accident in Nicholas Delbanco's *Possession*.

Margaret (Maggie, Meg, Megan) Cutler Sherbrooke. Wife of Judah Sherbrooke and mother of Ian and Seth Sherbrooke in Nicholas Delbanco's *Possession* and *Sherbrookes*.

Seth Sherbrooke. Son of Judah and Maggie Sherbrooke who dies of crib death in Nicholas Delbanco's *Possession* and *Sherbrookes*.

Colonel Sherburn. Upper-class Arkansan who talks a mob out of lynching him in Samuel Langhorne Clemens's *Adventures of Huckleberry Finn*.

Louisa Sheridan. Young schoolteacher from Lexington, Kentucky; accepts her first job in the remote Cal Valley; central character in Harriette Simpson Arnow's *Mountain Path*.

Lila Sherman. See Lila Swallow.

Nickie Sherman. Best friend, Wildean dramatic collaborator, and brother-in-law of Chick Swallow; sometime policeman, later private detective in Peter De Vries's *Comfort Me with Apples*.

Peter Sherringham. Brother of Julia Sherringham Dallow; diplomat who loves Miriam Rooth and is loved by Biddy Dormer in Henry James's *The Tragic Muse*.

Sherton (Shar). Race car driver and rebellious lover of Karen Herz; commits suicide by racing his car into a retaining wall in Joyce Carol Oates's *With Shuddering Fall*.

Vida Sherwin. Gopher Prairie teacher and friend of Carol Kennicott in Sinclair Lewis's *Main Street*.

Barbara Sherwood. Court stenographer who lives briefly with Arthur Axelrod before her death in Scott Spencer's *Endless Love.*

Sam Shields. Father of Marie Shields Griswold; brings charges of manslaughter against Joseph Chase in Jessamyn West's *The Life I Really Lived.*

Shimerda. Bohemian weaver and musician; father of Ántonia Shimerda and an unsuccessful farmer who commits suicide in Willa Cather's *My Ántonia.*

Ambroz (Ambrosch) Shimerda. Sullen and surly brother of Ántonia Shimerda; a good farmer in Willa Cather's *My Ántonia.*

Ántonia Shimerda. Daughter of Shimerda and childhood friend of Jim Burden; plans to marry Larry Donovan, but he deserts her after impregnating her; happily married to Anton Cuzak in Willa Cather's *My Ántonia.*

Mr. Shipley. Georgia cotton farmer who employs Grange and Margaret Copeland; rumored to be the father of Margaret's illegitimate son Star in Alice Walker's *The Third Life of Grange Copeland.*

Seth Shipley. Partner in Jim's business; marries Mag Smith after Jim's death and convinces her to abandon Frado to the Bellmont family in Harriet E. Wilson's *Our Nig.*

Helen Shires. Girlfriend of Studs Lonigan in James T. Farrell's *Young Lonigan;* reported to be a lesbian in *The Young Manhood of Studs Lonigan.*

Shirley. Best friend of Michelle; disillusioned with school and teachers; smokes pot and hangs out on the streets in Alexis Deveaux's *Spirits in the Street.*

Shirley. Prostitute in Key Bonita, Florida, who befriends Clinton Williams in James Leo Herlihy's *All Fall Down.*

Shirley. Secretary to General Braddock and son of the Massachusetts governor; killed at Fort Duquesne in Mary Lee Settle's *O Beulah Land.*

Uncle Preston (Press) Shiveley. Proprietor of a toll station in Shoestring Valley, Oregon; father of Wade Shiveley and adoptive father of Clay Calvert in H. L. Davis's *Honey in the Horn.*

Wade Shiveley. Son of Uncle Preston Shiveley; ne'er-do-well accused of murdering four men; hanged by homesteaders in H. L. Davis's *Honey in the Horn.*

Bo Shmo. Dynamic and charismatic cowboy who gained fame by playing "Buttermilk Sky" backwards; believes, with his neosocial realist gang, that all art must be for the end of liberating the masses; tries to kill the Loop Garoo Kid for being too abstract in Ishmael Reed's *Yellow Back Radio Broke-Down.*

Hoover (Onnie Jay Holy) Shoats. Preacher in competition with Hazel Motes after Haze refuses to cooperate with him; hires false prophet Solace Layfield as a stand-in for Motes in Flannery O'Connor's *Wise Blood.*

Captain Godfrey Gerald Sholto. Revolutionary who is temporarily the favorite of Princess Casamassima in Henry James's *The Princess Casamassima.*

Jan Sholto. Active telepath and mother of two children by Doro in Octavia E. Butler's *Mind of My Mind.*

Earle Shoop. Arizona cowboy and model who is one of Faye Greener's lovers in Nathanael West's *The Day of the Locust.*

Gloria Short. See Gloria Short Renfro.

Gid Shorter. Younger son of Hattie Mayfield in Reynolds Price's *The Surface of Earth.*

Hatt Shorter. See Hattie Mayfield.

James Shorter. Dead husband of Hattie Mayfield in Reynolds Price's *The Surface of Earth.*

Whitby Shorter. Older son of Hattie Mayfield in Reynolds Price's *The Surface of Earth.*

Shorty. Employee at the Sunk Creek ranch; killed by Trampas in Owen Wister's *The Virginian.*

Shorty (Cockney). Cockney planter on Martair in Herman Melville's *Omoo.*

Yakima Shorty. Thug housebreaker shot by Elihu Willsson in Dashiell Hammett's *Red Harvest.*

Shosha (Shoshele). Oldest daughter of Bashele and Zelig; as a adult, she remains childlike both physically and intellectually, and her innocence captivates Aaron Greidinger, whom she loves and marries, in Isaac Bashevis Singer's *Shosha.*

Chief Showcase. Patarealist Crow Indian whose people were destroyed by coming out into the open instead of staying hidden; tries to get the white man by introducing him to smoking so he will die of lung cancer in Ishmael Reed's *Yellow Back Radio Broke-Down.*

Mary Shrike. Wife of Willie Shrike; permits Miss Lonelyhearts to take physical liberties with her, but will not let him sleep with her, in Nathanael West's *Miss Lonelyhearts.*

Willie Shrike. Newspaper feature editor and Miss Lonelyhearts's humiliating boss in Nathanael West's *Miss Lonelyhearts*.

Edwin Shuck. American Embassy operative who tries to include Jack Flowers in a blackmail scheme in Paul Theroux's *Saint Jack*.

Moses (Moe) Shulman. Second lieutenant in love with Maria Rocco; shot and killed by a German officer in John Horne Burns's *The Gallery*.

Jack Shumann. Son of Laverne Shumann and either Roger Shumann or Jack Holmes in William Faulkner's *Pylon*.

Laverne Shumann. Wife of Roger Shumann and mother of Jack Shumann in William Faulkner's *Pylon*.

Roger Shumann. Husband of Laverne Shumann; stunt pilot killed in an airplane crash in William Faulkner's *Pylon*.

Shumla. Seventeenth-century Turkish war hero who is the subject of the consul's wife's latest biography and with whom she falls in love in Anaïs Nin's *Collages*.

Reverend Dr. Alfred Shumway. Con man posing as a missionary; actually running contraband guns in Patrick Dennis's *Around the World with Auntie Mame*.

Rosemary Shumway. Con artist posing as Dr. Shumway's daughter in Patrick Dennis's *Around the World with Auntie Mame*.

James T. Shuster. Police homicide detective in Thomas Berger's *Killing Time*.

Lady Caroline Sibly-Biers. Corrupt Englishwoman in F. Scott Fitzgerald's *Tender Is the Night*.

Jer Sidone. Drummer who shares an apartment with Stanley Katz in Edward Lewis Wallant's *The Tenants of Moonbloom*.

August Sieppe. Brother of Trina Sieppe; wets his pants while at the Orpheum theater, embarrassing his mother and sister before McTeague, in Frank Norris's *McTeague*.

Trina Sieppe. See Trina Sieppe McTeague.

Mother (Ma) Sigafoos. Formulator and purveyor of "Mother Sigafoos's Bloody Mary Mix" and other Land's Sakes Brands products in Peter De Vries's *I Hear America Swinging*.

Monica Ehrmann Sigelman. Sister of Noel Airman in Herman Wouk's *Marjorie Morningstar*.

Silas. Servant at Plumfield in Louisa May Alcott's *Little Men*.

Silas Rents His Ox. Pimp and drug dealer and mentor to Berry-berry Williams in James Leo Herlihy's *All Fall Down*.

Fay Silberman. Widow who meets Gabe Wallach's father on a European tour and later becomes engaged to him in Philip Roth's *Letting Go*.

Mr. Silbermann. Traveling businessman and former detective; meets V. in a train and helps him determine the identity of Sebastian Knight's former Russian mistress in Vladimir Nabokov's *The Real Life of Sebastian Knight*.

Solomon Moses David Menelik Silberstein. Card-playing companion of William Demarest in Conrad Aiken's *Blue Voyage*.

Clarissa (Cass) Silenski. Friend and patron of Vivaldo Moore and Rufus Scott; wife of Richard Silenski and lover of Eric Jones in James Baldwin's *Another Country*.

Richard Silenski. New York school teacher and novelist; husband of Cass Silenski in James Baldwin's *Another Country*.

Silent One. Speechless inmate of the child center; befriends the narrator and together they derail a trainload of peasants coming home from market in Jerzy Kosinski's *The Painted Bird*.

Mrs. Tempy Williams Siles. Daughter of Aunt Hager Williams and wife of a postal clerk; ashamed of her background, she joins the Episcopal Church in Langston Hughes's *Not Without Laughter*.

Dean Silva. Medical school dean in Sinclair Lewis's *Arrowsmith*.

Maria Silva. Poor woman from the South Pacific with whom Martin Eden boards in Jack London's *Martin Eden*.

Eli Silver. Dedicated pediatrician whose son died in an automobile accident while Silver attended to his wife's minor injuries; arranges the adoption by Phil and Annie Sorenson of Elizabeth Bean's baby in Frederick Busch's *Rounds*.

Gwen Silver. Wife of Eli Silver; leaves him following their son's death in an automobile accident, but returns to try to salvage the marriage in Frederick Busch's *Rounds*.

Mattie (Matt) Silver. Cousin of Zenobia Frome and beloved of Ethan Frome, with whom she fails in a joint suicide attempt that leaves her an invalid, in Edith Wharton's *Ethan Frome.*

Sid Silver. University of Chicago student and part-time reporter for the *Daily Globe*; investigates the murder of Paulie Kessler and covers the trial of Artie Straus and Judd Steiner in Meyer Levin's *Compulsion.*

Mannie Silverhorn. Attorney for Elmer Gantry; ambulance chaser in Sinclair Lewis's *Elmer Gantry.*

Shirley Silverstein. See Maggie MacGregor.

Peter Sim. Childhood friend and schoolmate of Nicholas Delbanco in Nicholas Delbanco's *In the Middle Distance.*

Harvey Simkin. Wealthy and clever New York lawyer of Moses Herzog in Saul Bellow's *Herzog.*

Mr. (Bee-lips) Simmons. Lawyer who sets up a deal between Harry Morgan and the Cubans in Ernest Hemingway's *To Have and Have Not.*

Della Simmons. Young black woman, former playmate of Rachel Hutchins, and now servant to the Hutchins family; deeply in love with Rob Mayfield, she remains his mistress even during his engagement to Rachel in Reynolds Price's *The Surface of Earth.*

Flem Simmons. Eccentric early settler in the mountains of Oregon who befriends Clay Calvert in H. L. Davis's *Honey in the Horn.*

Henry Simmons. English valet who is engaged to Edweena Wills; becomes a close friend of and confidant to Theophilus North in Thornton Wilder's *Theophilus North.*

Jake Simmons. Harlem cabaret owner who befriends Jule Jackson in George Wylie Henderson's *Jule.*

Maisie (Maise) Simmons. Wife of Jake Simmons and friend of Jule Jackson in George Wylie Henderson's *Jule.*

Payette Simmons. Sheepherder in H. L. Davis's *Honey in the Horn.*

Ralph (Enrico Del Credo, Sim) Simmons. American opera singer studying in Italy; gives civilian clothes to Frederic Henry after Henry deserts the Italian army in Ernest Hemingway's *A Farewell to Arms.*

Simms. Sidewalk preacher who pursues Jake Blount in Carson McCullers's *The Heart Is a Lonely Hunter.*

Elvira K. Tewksbury Simms. Mother of Jed Tewksbury and remarried widow of Buck Tewksbury; encourages Jed to seek his fortune away from Dugton, Alabama, in Robert Penn Warren's *A Place to Come To.*

Jake Simms. Bumbling bank robber and kidnapper of Charlotte Emory; father of Mindy Callender's unborn child in Anne Tyler's *Earthly Possessions.*

Rosalie Simms-Peabody. World traveler and adventurer; guest lecturer for the Ithaca Parlor Lecture Club in William Saroyan's *The Human Comedy.*

Simo. Father of Pamphilus and prominent trader and owner of warehouses and ships in Thornton Wilder's *The Woman of Andros.*

Simon. Passenger on the *Here They Come* who exchanges fairy tales for Dad Deform's religious statues in Gregory Corso's *The American Express.*

Simon. See Simon Strother.

Erin (Chippo) Simon. Friend of both the Reverend Phillip Martin and Martin's former lover, Johanna Sims, in Ernest J. Gaines's *In My Father's House.*

Tom Simon. Employee of NESTER in Scott Spencer's *Last Night at the Brain Thieves Ball.*

Charity Prudence Eversole Simons. Married woman from Philadelphia who has given birth to the son of a man other than her husband and wishes to abandon the child, whom Leslie Collins finally adopts, in Harriette Simpson Arnow's *The Kentucky Trace.*

Carolyn Simpson. High school classmate and lover of Molly Bolt in Rita Mae Brown's *Rubyfruit Jungle.*

Elizabeth (Lizzie) Simpson. Daughter of Rev. Mr. Simpson; lover of Frederick Brent in Paul Laurence Dunbar's *The Uncalled.*

Homer Simpson. Iowa bookkeeper who shares a house with Faye Greener, who will not let him love her, in Nathanael West's *The Day of the Locust.*

Kermit Simpson. Rich, politically idealistic owner and editor of a liberal monthly newspaper and friend of John Laskell in Lionel Trilling's *The Middle of the Journey.*

Mark Simpson. Pennsylvania state senator and friend of Henry Mollenhauer in Theodore Dreiser's *The Financier.*

Rev. Mr. Simpson. Methodist preacher and father of Elizabeth Simpson in Paul Laurence Dunbar's *The Uncalled.*

Sam (Bub) Simpson. Discoverer of Roy Hobbs; takes Hobbs to Chicago to play baseball in Bernard Malamud's *The Natural.*

Samantha (Sam) Simpson. Friend of Mira; forced by an improvident husband to become financially independent in Marilyn French's *The Women's Room.*

Stephen (Steve) Simpson. College roommate of Oliver Barrett IV; helps Barrett following the death of Barrett's wife Jenny in Erich Segal's *Oliver's Story.*

Chris Sims. Black youth murdered by an angry white mob for associating with white women in Richard Wright's *The Long Dream.*

Etienne Sims. See Robert X.

Johanna Sims. Deserted mother of the Reverend Phillip Martin's unacknowledged, illegitimate children, including Robert X, in Ernest J. Gaines's *In My Father's House.*

Pearl Sims. Piano teacher of Renay Davis from sixth through twelfth grade in Ann Allen Shockley's *Loving Her.*

Mr. Sing. Man who hires Harry Morgan to transport twelve Chinese men; killed by Morgan in Ernest Hemingway's *To Have and Have Not.*

Fred Singer. Television commentator who attends many of the gatherings of expatriate Americans at the home of the Gallaghers during the student riots in Paris in James Jones's *The Merry Month of May.*

John Singer. Lonely deaf-mute mistakenly idealized by Mick Kelly and other townspeople; commits suicide in despair over the death of his friend Spiros Antonapoulos in Carson McCullers's *The Heart Is a Lonely Hunter.*

Sidney (Sid) Singer. Lawyer who is David Dehn's partner; helps Dehn build a temple and establish the Beechwood Jewish community in Jerome Weidman's *The Temple.*

Sergeant Singles. American prisoner of war in England who is married to Jenny, Israel Potter's boyhood sweetheart, in Herman Melville's *Israel Potter.*

Emily Singleton. Dying sister of Robert Singleton; takes refuge at the home of her uncle, Richard Walton, following the burning of her ancestral home in William Gilmore Simms's *The Partisan.*

Major Robert Singleton. Leader of a small band of partisans under Francis Marion in South Carolina in William Gilmore Simms's *The Partisan.*

Sam Singleton. American painter of small landscapes who travels in Europe looking for subject matter; finds Roderick Hudson dead at the bottom of a cliff in Henry James's *Roderick Hudson.*

Frank (J. Yák) Sinisterra. Counterfeiter who inadvertently kills Wyatt Gwyon's mother; his son is romantically involved with Gwyon's model Esme in William Gaddis's *The Recognitions.*

Valerie Sinnot. Screenwriter at Olympia Studios in Ludwig Bemelmans's *Dirty Eddie.*

Sinton. Black preacher and leader of the Princes and Potentates of Ethiopia, a benevolent association; works for equality, justice, and opportunity for blacks in T. S. Stribling's *Unfinished Cathedral.*

Henry De Soto (de Sota) Sippens. Real estate company owner and associate of Frank Cowperwood in Theodore Dreiser's *The Titan*; sent to London to investigate railway investments in *The Stoic.*

Sissie. Prostitute whose murder Willie Hall plans in John Edgar Wideman's *The Lynchers.*

Sister X. See Arista Prolo.

Dr. Archibald Sitgreaves. Comic military surgeon of the Virginia dragoons in James Fenimore Cooper's *The Spy.*

Sittina (Queen of Shendy). Artistic, prolific third wife of Colonel Ellelloû; only one of his wives to go with him into exile in John Updike's *The Coup.*

Miriam Skates. Artistic rival of Moise whose jealousy over Moise's recognition by a college art professor leads her to embarrass Moise publicly in Tennessee Williams's *Moise and the World of Reason.*

Arthur Gallup (Galloper) Skeel. Young man who aids Theophilus North in ridding his sister, Elspeth Skeel, of her terrible headaches in Thornton Wilder's *Theophilus North.*

Elspeth Skeel. Sister of Arthur Skeel; has excruciating headaches which seem incurable until Theophilus North uses his so-called "electric hands" in Thornton Wilder's *Theophilus North.*

Suggie (Miss Suggie) Skeete. Flamboyant tenant of Silla Boyce and confidante of Selina Boyce; after a week of trying to get ahead, rewards herself with rum and a new lover every weekend in Paule Marshall's *Brown Girl, Brownstones.*

Skeeter. See Hubert H. Farnsworth.

Skelton. Father of Thomas Skelton; pretends to be an invalid but is discovered to be out on the town late each night in Thomas McGuane's *Ninety-Two in the Shade.*

Goldsboro Skelton. Grandfather of Thomas Skelton; shady businessman who lends his grandson money for a boat in Thomas McGuane's *Ninety-Two in the Shade*.

Thomas Skelton. Key West fishing guide killed by his business competitor, Nichol Dance, in Thomas McGuane's *Ninety-Two in the Shade*.

Fred Skinner. Husband of Susy Skinner and colleague of Paul Cattleman in Alison Lurie's *The Nowhere City*.

Philo (Richard) Skinner. Chain-smoking dog handler and dognapper in Joseph Wambaugh's *The Black Marble*.

Susy Skinner. Wife of Fred Skinner and friend of Katherine Cattleman in Alison Lurie's *The Nowhere City*.

Skipper. Young black man, recently paroled, who is a hostile student of Eric Eisner in the New York literacy program in Phillip Lopate's *Confessions of Summer*.

Skipper (Edward, Papa Cue Ball, Skip). Father of Cassandra and the baby born to Catalina Kate, grandfather of Pixie, husband of Gertrude, and father-in-law of Fernandez; served four years on the USS *Starfish*; fifty-nine-year-old narrator of John Hawkes's *Second Skin*.

Fradrik Skotoma. Iconoclastic philosopher whose benevolent conception of mankind, "Ekwilism," first appeared as a pamphlet printed by Paduk's father and was later transformed by Paduk into a violent political doctrine in Vladimir Nabokov's *Bend Sinister*.

Vladimir Skrapinov. Soviet ambassador to the United States who believes Chance can speak Russian in Jerzy Kosinski's *Being There*.

Percival Skrogg. Journalist who helps Wilkie Barron print the handbill that prompts Jeremiah Beaumont to kill Colonel Cassius Fort in Robert Penn Warren's *World Enough and Time*.

Egbert Skully. Persistent Dublin landlord whom Sebastian Dangerfield manages to elude in J. P. Donleavy's *The Ginger Man*.

Randolph Lee Skully. Homosexual cousin of Amy Sansom; reclusive owner of Skully's Landing; person Joel Harrison Knox must finally turn to in Truman Capote's *Other Voices, Other Rooms*.

Ben Skutt. "Lease-hound" for J. Arnold Ross's oil company and spy for Petroleum Employers' Federation in Upton Sinclair's *Oil!*.

Skyeman. See Jarl.

Senator Skypack. Philistine member of the committee investigating the attempted "purchase" of Barry Rudd by Wissey Jones; eager to allow the sale for alleged reasons of national defense in John Hersey's *The Child Buyer*.

Slab. Artist who compulsively paints pictures of cheese Danishes; member of the Whole Sick Crew in Thomas Pynchon's *V*.

Frank Slade. Son of Simon Slade; becomes a drunk and murders his father in T. S. Arthur's *Ten Nights in a Bar-Room*.

Hugh Slade. Married veterinarian with whom Isabel Moore has an abortive affair in Mary Gordon's *Final Payments*.

Simon Slade. Owner of the Sickle and Sheaf tavern, which is the source of Cedarville's corruption; murdered by his son Frank Slade in T. S. Arthur's *Ten Nights in a Bar-Room*.

Willard Slade. Gifted artist; first love and inspiration of Alice Prentice in Richard Yates's *A Special Providence*.

The Great (Meester) Slashtubitch. Pornographic film star and director in William S. Burroughs's *Naked Lunch* and *The Wild Boys*.

Baxter Slate. Intellectual and suicide; one of ten Los Angeles policemen-protagonists of Joseph Wambaugh's *The Choirboys*.

Emmie Slattery. Mother, by Jonas Wilkerson, of illegitimate children in Margaret Mitchell's *Gone with the Wind*.

Mike Slattery. County political leader and mentor of Joe Chapin I in John O'Hara's *Ten North Frederick*.

Peg Slattery. Wife and confidante of Mike Slattery in John O'Hara's *Ten North Frederick*.

Slaughter. Farmhand and fellow employee of Ollie Miss on Uncle Alex's farm in George Wylie Henderson's *Ollie Miss*.

Nathan (Jibbenainosay, Nick of the Woods) Slaughter. Quaker pioneer who avenges his family's massacre by killing Indians and leaving the mark of The Jibbenainosay, or Nick of the Woods, who is believed to be an avenging spirit, in Robert Montgomery Bird's *Nick of the Woods*.

Ormand Slaughter. Retarded hired man who is the object of Orpha Chase's first infatuation in Jessamyn West's *The Life I Really Lived*.

Sledge (Doctor). Illegitimate and crippled infant son of Mildred Sutton; named after the doctor who delivered him because no one will admit to being his father in Reynolds Price's *A Long and Happy Life*.

Sam (Uncle Sam, The Yankee Peddler) Slick. Quintessential American spirit in Robert Coover's *The Public Burning*.

Neil Sligh. Potential blackmailer of Alma Marvel; suitor of Lee Mercury in Peter De Vries's *Through the Fields of Clover*.

Jane Sligo. Wife of Salathiel Albine in Hervey Allen's *The Forest and the Fort*.

Slim. Jerkline skinner whose country wisdom helps George Milton care for Lennie Small in John Steinbeck's *Of Mice and Men*.

Slim Girl (Came With War, Lillian, Lily). Beautiful Indian who struggles between leading Indian and white life-styles; married to Laughing Boy; dies of an arrow wound in Oliver La Farge's *Laughing Boy*.

Ed Slipper. Fourth-oldest prisoner in America and a trustee in the prison where Leo Feldman is incarcerated in Stanley Elkin's *A Bad Man*.

Linda Sliski. Roommate of Wendy Gahaghan in Alison Lurie's *The War Between the Tates*.

Mrs. Sliter. Cook for Clarissa and Edward Packard; fired for drunkenness in Caroline Gilman's *Recollections of a Housekeeper*.

Bijelo Slivinca. Father and leader of the Slivinca family, all of whom work for the Ustashi terrorists; plans Gottlob Wutt's death; killed by Wutt in John Irving's *Setting Free the Bears*.

Todor Slivinca. Son of Bijelo Slivinca; teaches Vratno Javotnik to ride a motorcycle; survives Gottlob Wutt's grenade attack and kills Javotnik after the war in John Irving's *Setting Free the Bears*.

Clere Sloane. Retired stage beauty married to Campbell Kitchen; Emma Lou Morgan is employed as her personal maid in Wallace Thurman's *The Blacker The Berry*.

Bob (Bobby) Slocum. New York market research executive whose ambitions consist of being awarded Andy Kagle's job as head of sales and the opportunity to give a speech at the company convention in Puerto Rico; narrator of Joseph Heller's *Something Happened*.

Derek Slocum. Brain-damaged third child and second son of Bob Slocum in Joseph Heller's *Something Happened*.

Jaffrey (Sloco) Slocum. Cunning lawyer in Robert Herrick's *The Memoirs of an American Citizen*.

Mrs. Slocum. Bored and lonely wife of Bob Slocum; drinks and flirts to excess in Joseph Heller's *Something Happened*.

Annette and Cellie Slogum. Twin daughters of Gulla and Ruedy Slogum; prostituted by their mother in order to gain power over the Dumur County sheriff and county judge in Mari Sandoz's *Slogum House*.

Cash Slogum. Second son of Gulla and Ruedy Slogum; forced by his mother to commit crimes in order to help build the Slogum House property in Mari Sandoz's *Slogum House*.

Fannie Slogum. Fourth daughter of Gulla and Ruedy Slogum and twin of Ward Slogum; returns home from an eastern boarding school, suffering from frequent abortions, venereal disease, and consumption in Mari Sandoz's *Slogum House*.

Haber (Hab) Slogum. Oldest son of Gulla and, possibly, Ruedy Slogum; forced by his mother to commit crimes in order to help build the Slogum House property in Mari Sandoz's *Slogum House*.

Libby Slogum. Oldest daughter of Gulla and Ruedy Slogum; responsible for the clean beds and good meals at Slogum House in Mari Sandoz's *Slogum House*.

Regula Haber (Gulla) Slogum. Wife of Ruedy Slogum and mother of seven children; proprietor of the roadhouse, Slogum House, in Mari Sandoz's *Slogum House*.

Ruedy Slogum. Husband of Gulla Haber and father, by her, of seven children in Mari Sandoz's *Slogum House*.

Ward Slogum. Third son of Gulla and Ruedy Slogum and twin of Fannie Slogum; beaten severely by the brothers of his Polish girlfriend after they are incited by his mother in Mari Sandoz's *Slogum House*.

Betty (Bettyle) Slonim. American actress who performs in Yiddish theaters, melancholy mistress of Sam Dreiman, and, briefly, lover of Aaron Greidinger; commits suicide in Isaac Bashevis Singer's *Shosha*.

Lazar Slonim. Jewish resistance fighter in Warsaw during the Nazi occupation; escapes through the ghetto wall, travels to the Treblinka death camp, and reveals the truth about the so-called Nazi resettlement of the Jews in John Hersey's *The Wall*.

Doctor Austin Sloper. Wealthy New York physician and widowed father of Catherine Sloper; determines to disinherit Catherine if she marries Morris Townsend, whom he despises, in Henry James's *Washington Square*.

Catherine Sloper. Daughter of Dr. Austin Sloper and niece of Lavinia Penniman; jilted by Morris Townsend in Henry James's *Washington Square*.

Jillsy Sloper. Charwoman at a publishing house; admires T. S. Garp's *The World According to Bensenhaver*, which Garp dedicates to her, in John Irving's *The World According to Garp*.

Harry Sloss. Associate of Paul Madvig's who, from a distance, witnesses the murder of Taylor Henry in Dashiell Hammett's *The Glass Key*.

Lieutenant Tyrone (Ian Scuffling, Rocketman) Slothrop. American officer assigned to the Political Warfare Executive, which studies him while he studies the V-2 rocket; lover of Katje Borgesius, Greta Erdmann, and Geli Tripping; subject of Pavlovian experiments as a child in Thomas Pynchon's *Gravity's Rainbow*.

Doctor Slovotkin. Sadistic prison physician; hanged by rioting women convicts in John Hawkes's *The Passion Artist*.

Saul Slowns. Yankee soldier who stays on in Tennessee after the Civil War; bachelor friend of Peter Legrand in Andrew Lytle's *The Velvet Horn*.

Slug. See Dagny Taggart.

Billy Small. Black alcoholic and robber; partner of Gregory Powell in Joseph Wambaugh's *The Onion Field*.

Dr. Henry Small. Young and apparently upright medical doctor who is actually the sinister leader of a band of robbers in Edward Eggleston's *The Hoosier School-Master*.

Lennie Small. Retarded companion of George Milton; helpless ranch worker whose misunderstood strength leads to his death in John Steinbeck's *Of Mice and Men*.

William Small. See Max Disher.

William Small. Small-minded principal of North Manual Trades High School in Evan Hunter's *The Blackboard Jungle*.

Big Red (L. J. Griggs) Smalley. Traveling evangelist and faith healer in George Garrett's *Do, Lord, Remember Me*.

Arrabelle Smalls. Black housekeeper for the Meecham family and mother of Toomer Smalls in Pat Conroy's *The Great Santini*.

Toomer Smalls. Black merchant of flowers, herbs, and honey; son of Arrabelle Smalls; killed by Red Pettus in Pat Conroy's *The Great Santini*.

James D. (Jimmy, Preach, Preacher) Smathers, Jr. Red-haired friend and alter ego of James Christopher; dies as the result of a severe beating by Jack Davis in Fred Chappell's *It Is Time, Lord*.

Smiley. Leader of a gang of black men hired by Miss Ann and Mr. Cleveland to steal the corpse of a murdered prostitute in Richard Brautigan's *Dreaming of Babylon*.

Smith. British lieutenant in William Faulkner's *A Fable*.

Smith. Sheet music salesman from New Orleans and fictitious father of William Demarest in Conrad Aiken's *Blue Voyage*.

Alexander (John Adams, Alex, Reckless Jack) Smith. Londoner, whose real name is John Adams, who signs aboard HMS *Bounty* as Alexander Smith; joins in the rebellion in Charles Nordhoff and James Norman Hall's *Mutiny on the Bounty*; treats the Tahitians humanely; as the sole survivor of Fletcher Christian's experiment with democracy, narrates the second half of *Pitcairn's Island*.

Anna Castagne Bolling Smith. Prosaic mother of Binx Bolling and of his six half brothers and sisters in Walker Percy's *The Moviegoer*.

Beauty (Pinhead) Smith. Yukon "Sour-dough" who buys White Fang to use in dogfights in Jack London's *White Fang*.

Benny Smith. Brother of Mama Lavorn and handyman for L. B. Jones; serves as a professional mourner at funerals in Jesse Hill Ford's *The Liberation of Lord Byron Jones*.

Boots Smith. Cold, hard young black musician who works for Mr. Junto and is beaten to death by Lutie Johnson in Ann Petry's *The Street*.

Clark (Clarkie) Smith. Insurance executive married to Janet Belle Smith in Alison Lurie's *Real People*.

Clinch Smith. Excommunicated Scientologist and rejected lover who goes berserk and kills Scientologists in William S. Burroughs's *Exterminator!*

Dunreith (Smitty) Smith. Troublemaker and married lover of Addie Parker in Cyrus Colter's *The Rivers* *of Eros.*

Essie Meadowfill Smith. Wife of McKinley Smith in William Faulkner's *The Mansion.*

George Smith. Closet pederast who annoys Sol Nazerman with long-winded monologues on literature and philosophy in Edward Lewis Wallant's *The Pawnbroker.*

Harold (little-Smith) Smith. Securities broker married to Marcia Smith in John Updike's *Couples.*

Herbert (Herb) Smith. Father of Johnny Smith; argues with his wife Vera over her newfound religious convictions in Stephen King's *The Dead Zone.*

Mrs. Horace Smith. Widow for whom Rabbit Angstrom works temporarily as a gardener in John Updike's *Rabbit, Run.*

Jack Tom Smith. World War I navy buddy of Alfred Eaton; becomes a wealthy Texas oil man and befriends Eaton during World War II in John O'Hara's *From the Terrace.*

Janet Belle Smith. Short story writer, mother of three children, wife of Clark Smith, and lover of Nick Donato in Alison Lurie's *Real People.*

Jimmy Lee (Jimmy Youngblood) Smith. Mulatto drug addict and partner of Gregory Powell; convicted of and sentenced to die for the murder of Ian Campbell in Joseph Wambaugh's *The Onion Field.*

John Smith. Soldier of fortune and founder of Virginia in John Pendleton Kennedy's *Swallow Barn.*

John (Johnny) Smith. Psychically acute man whose brain is permanently damaged--thus creating the dead zone--following an automobile accident in Stephen King's *The Dead Zone.*

Capt. John Smith. Colonial hero who saves himself from execution by Indians by successfully penetrating the impervious hymen of Pocahontas in John Barth's *The Sot-Weed Factor.*

Lafe Smith. Junior senator from Iowa; playboy in his private life but an honorable politician and close friend of Sen. Brigham Anderson in Allen Drury's *Advise and Consent.*

Lonnie Smith. Fatally ill and fervently Roman Catholic half brother of Binx Bolling in Walker Percy's *The Moviegoer.*

Mag Smith. White washerwoman who marries a black man, Jim, and gives birth to their daughter Frado; abandons Frado to the Bellmont family in Harriet E. Wilson's *Our Nig.*

Marcia Burnham (little-Smith) Smith. Wife of Harold Smith; they partner swap with Janet and Frank Appleby in John Updike's *Couples.*

McKinley Smith. Texan who marries Essie Meadowfill in William Faulkner's *The Mansion.*

Miguel Moreno (Brown, Brownie, Miguelito) Smith. Engineer aboard the *Lillias Eden* who leaves the boat to join the Jamaicans who threaten its safety in Peter Matthiessen's *Far Tortuga.*

Nevada (Max Sand) Smith. Half-blood Kiowa Indian who avenges the brutal deaths of his parents and becomes an outlaw; works for Jonas Cord, Sr.; teaches Jonas Cord, Jr., to ride horses and serves as a father figure for him; becomes a film star in movie Westerns and the husband of Rina Marlowe in Harold Robbins's *The Carpetbaggers.*

Perry Edward Smith. Psychotic criminal, man of ungovernable anger, and murderer of the Clutter family in Truman Capote's *In Cold Blood.*

Peter Smith. Self-made man who rises from overseer to plantation owner and justice of the peace; father of Potestatem Dedimus Smith in Albion W. Tourgee's *Bricks without Straw.*

Peter Charles Smith. Senator who pays a high price for his seat when he represents interests not to his liking; brother of Sarah Smith in W. E. B. Du Bois's *The Quest of the Silver Fleece.*

Potestatem Dedimus Smith. See Colonel Potem Desmit.

Ray Smith. Los Angeles defense attorney; first to defend Jimmy Smith in Joseph Wambaugh's *The Onion Field.*

Raymond (Ray, Tiger) Smith. Writer and cross-country traveler introduced to mountain climbing and asceticism by Japhy Ryder; narrator of Jack Kerouac's *The Dharma Bums.*

Rebel Smith. Okie cherry orchard boss and friend of Pretty Boy Floyd; the narrator works for her as a child in Richard Brautigan's *Trout Fishing in America.*

Father Rinaldo Smith. Addled but dedicated priest and Tom More's confessor in Walker Percy's *Love in the Ruins.*

Robert Smith. North Carolina Mutual Life Insurance salesman who commits suicide by jumping from the top of Mercy Hospital in Toni Morrison's *Song of Solomon.*

Robes (Ohio) Smith. Admirer of Abeba Torch; considered shiftless by Angela Lavoisier in Ellease Southerland's *Let the Lion Eat Straw*.

Roger Smith. California newspaper editor; anti-liberal sometime employer of Peter Gale in Louis Adamic's *Grandsons*.

Ruth Smith. American consul in Copenhagen and lover of George Washington; commits suicide in Cecil Brown's *The Life and Loves of Mr. Jiveass Nigger*.

Miss Sarah Smith. White school teacher from the North who comes to teach black children in Alabama and is instrumental in Zora's development; sister of Peter Charles Smith in W. E. B. Du Bois's *The Quest of the Silver Fleece*.

Smith Smith. Hero of C. Card's latest daydream; most famous private investigator of Babylon and beloved of Nana-dirat in Richard Brautigan's *Dreaming of Babylon*.

Tony Smith. Art professor from South Orange, New Jersey, whose patronage of the emotionally distraught Moise is Moise's salvation in Tennessee Williams's *Moise and the World of Reason*.

Vera Helen Smith. Religiously fanatical mother of Johnny Smith; believes that her son's psychic gifts should be used to further "God's Plan" in Stephen King's *The Dead Zone*.

Ware Smith. Health-food devotee who lives in the mountains with Kate and fathers their child in Gail Godwin's *Glass People*.

Word (Frederico, Smitty) Smith. Sportswriter and author of a history of the suppressed or imagined Patriot League in Philip Roth's *The Great American Novel*.

Lieutenant Colonel John Dawson (Johnny) Smithers. Anti-Semitic Georgian and U.S. infantry commander; becomes the lover of Dorothy Brock in Martha Gellhorn's *Wine of Astonishment*.

Smithson. Medical officer for the Arizona highway patrol in Michael Crichton's *The Andromeda Strain*.

Smoke. Black hotel porter lynched for allegedly assaulting a tough young man in Brand Whitlock's *J. Hardin & Son*.

Smokey. Drug addict wife of Porky; handles her husband's drug money in Donald Goines's *Dopefiend*.

Turk Smollet. Isolated Winesburg wood chopper in Sherwood Anderson's *Winesburg, Ohio*.

Freddy Smoot. Youth who explores the young Eva Medina Canada sexually with a dirty popsicle stick in Gayl Jones's *Eva's Man*.

Smoothbore. See Sylvania Berlew.

Smothers. Tiresias-figure whose prophetic voice cannot prevent industrial disaster or save the souls of the steel mill workers in William Attaway's *Blood on the Forge*.

Maudel Smothers. Best friend with whom Harriett Williams is arrested for prostitution in Langston Hughes's *Not Without Laughter*.

Wellington Smythe. Supposed English aristocrat who is actually the son of a charwoman; advises southern women on fashion, manners, and entertainments in Mary Lee Settle's *Know Nothing*.

Snake. See Kenneth Dumpson.

Snake. Drug addict and pimp who is killed during a robbery in Donald Goines's *Dopefiend*.

Snapper. Handsome homosexual who emasculates male patrons of porno theaters while performing fellatio on them in Jerzy Kosinski's *Cockpit*.

Corporal Snark. Snobbish mess officer who mashes soap into sweet potatoes to prove soldiers have no taste in Joseph Heller's *Catch-22*.

Aramintha Snead. Churchwoman who seeks advice from N'Gana Frimbo in Rudolph Fisher's *The Conjure-Man Dies*.

Balso Snell. Poet who crawls into a Trojan horse inhabited by unread writers in Nathanael West's *The Dream Life of Balso Snell*.

Ralph Fielding Snell. Prissy "Man of Letters" whose Foreword and Epilogue frame Jack Crabb's oral autobiography in Thomas Berger's *Little Big Man*.

Susan (Sue, Suze) Snell. Sympathetic classmate of Carrie White and author of *My Name is Susan Snell* in Stephen King's *Carrie*.

Clem (Private Ass Hole) Snide. Protean character who ruins a sex/death cinema party in William S. Burroughs's *The Soft Machine*; appears briefly in *Naked Lunch*.

Abner (Ab) Snopes. Father of Flem Snopes in William Faulkner's *The Unvanquished*, *The Hamlet*, *The Town*, and *The Mansion*.

Bilbo Snopes. Son of I. O. Snopes in William Faulkner's *The Town* and *The Mansion*.

Byron Snopes. Brother of Virgil Snopes and father of the little Indian Snopeses; bank bookkeeper in

William Faulkner's *Sartoris (Flags in the Dust)*, *The Town*, and *The Mansion*.

Clarence Eggleston Snopes. Son of I. O. Snopes; state senator in William Faulkner's *Sanctuary*, *The Town*, and *The Mansion*.

Admiral Dewey Snopes. Son of Eck Snopes in William Faulkner's *The Town* and *The Mansion*.

Doris Snopes. Son of I. O. Snopes in William Faulkner's *The Town* and *The Mansion*.

Eckrum (Eck) Snopes. Cousin of Flem Snopes and father of Wallstreet Panic and Admiral Dewey Snopes in William Faulkner's *The Hamlet*, *The Town*, and *The Mansion*.

Eula Varner Snopes. Daughter of Will Varner; has a child, Linda Snopes, by Hoake McCarron; marries Flem Snopes and has a long affair with Manfred de Spain; appears in William Faulkner's *The Hamlet*, *The Town*, and *The Mansion*.

Flem Snopes. Son of Ab Snopes and husband of Eula Varner; progresses from store clerk to bank president; appears in William Faulkner's *Sartoris (Flags in the Dust)*, *As I Lay Dying*, *The Hamlet*, *The Town*, *The Mansion*, and *The Reivers*.

I. O. Snopes. Cousin of Flem Snopes and father of Bilbo, Clarence, Doris, Montgomery Ward, Saint Elmo, and Vardaman Snopes; appears in William Faulkner's *The Sound and the Fury*, *The Hamlet*, *The Town*, and *The Mansion*.

Isaac (Ike) Snopes. Cousin of Flem Snopes; loves Jack Houston's cow in William Faulkner's *The Hamlet*.

Launcelot (Lump) Snopes. Clerk, succeeding his cousin Flem Snopes, at Jody Varner's store in William Faulkner's *The Hamlet* and *The Mansion*.

Linda Snopes. See Linda Snopes Kohl.

Mink Snopes. Cousin of Flem Snopes; murders Jack Houston; appears in William Faulkner's *The Hamlet*, *The Town*, and *The Mansion*.

Montgomery Ward Snopes. Son of I. O. Snopes in William Faulkner's *Sartoris (Flags in the Dust)*, *The Town*, and *The Mansion*.

Orestes (Res) Snopes. Farmer in William Faulkner's *The Mansion*.

Saint Elmo Snopes. Son of I. O. Snopes in William Faulkner's *The Hamlet*.

Vardaman Snopes. Son of I. O. Snopes in William Faulkner's *The Town* and *The Mansion*.

Virgil Snopes. Son of Wesley Snopes in William Faulkner's *Sanctuary*, *The Town*, and *The Mansion*.

Vynie Snopes. First wife of Ab Snopes in William Faulkner's *The Hamlet*.

Wallstreet Panic (Wall) Snopes. Son of Eck Snopes in William Faulkner's *The Hamlet*, *The Town*, and *The Mansion*.

Watkins Products Snopes. Carpenter in William Faulkner's *The Mansion*.

Wesley Snopes. Father of Virgil Snopes in William Faulkner's *The Mansion*.

Yettie Snopes. Wife of Mink Snopes in William Faulkner's *The Hamlet* and *The Mansion*.

Rev. Lazarus Snortgrace. Frontier preacher in James Kirke Paulding's *Westward Ho!*

Ernst (Ernie) Snow. Christ-driven husband of Stella Snow in John Hawkes's *The Cannibal*.

Stella Snow. Aristocratic personification of German nationalism; participates in the cannibalization of her nephew in John Hawkes's *The Cannibal*.

Uncle Snow. New Yorker who employs his nephew Tom Bailey in his counting house in Thomas Bailey Aldrich's *The Story of a Bad Boy*.

Snow White. Disillusioned "horsewife" and proponent of the women's movement; lives with seven "dwarfs" while waiting for Paul, her "prince," to arrive in Donald Barthelme's *Snow White*.

Snowden. Air force gunner wounded by flak on a bombing mission over Avignon; dies in Yossarian's arms after Yossarian treats him for the wrong wound in Joseph Heller's *Catch-22*.

Mott (Pinky) Snyth. Husband of Vashti Hake Snyth; ex-cowhand who helps manage the Hake cattle operation in Edna Ferber's *Giant*.

Vashti Hake (Vash) Snyth. Daughter of a wealthy cattle rancher, wife of Pinky Snyth, and friend of Leslie Benedict in Edna Ferber's *Giant*.

Henry Soames. Overweight owner of a diner and surrogate father to Callie Wells's son in John Gardner's *Nickel Mountain*.

Iggy Soames. Son of an artist; friend and confidant of Susie Schnitzer in Harriette Simpson Arnow's *The Weedkiller's Daughter*.

Sobaka. Head of the Soviet Writers' Union who becomes a non-person in John Updike's *Bech: A Book*.

Egon Sobotnik. Czechoslovakian prisoner at the Jadwiga concentration camp; provides a surgical record book that is used against Adam Kelno in a libel trial in Leon Uris's *QB VII*.

Arnold Soby. Middle-aged pursuer of Cynthia Pomeroy; college professor in search of "the wisdom of the body" in Wright Morris's *What a Way to Go*.

Robert Hopper Softly. Physically stunted director of Logicon Project, an attempt to develop a cosmic language based on mathematical principles, in Don DeLillo's *Ratner's Star*.

Rita Greenough Sohlberg. Mistress of Frank Cowperwood; injured by the jealous Aileen Cowperwood in Theodore Dreiser's *The Titan*.

Rachel Sojourner. Sister-in-law of Beulah Renfro and possibly the mother of Gloria Short Renfro in Eudora Welty's *Losing Battles*.

Alice (Mamaw) Sole. Mother of Lillian Meecham and grandmother of Ben, Mary Anne, Karen, and Matt Meecham in Pat Conroy's *The Great Santini*.

Roy Soleil. Dockmaster wounded with a fishing gaff by Nichol Dance in Thomas McGuane's *Ninety-Two in the Shade*.

Virgil (Turk) Sollozzo. Narcotics importer who is responsible for the shooting of Don Corleone in Mario Puzo's *The Godfather*.

Solomon. African slave who, according to myth, literally flies away from the Virginia plantation where he is enslaved, leaving his wife and twenty-one children behind; his descendants are the erroneously named Dead family in Toni Morrison's *Song of Solomon*.

Ermentrude (Ermy) Solomon. Friend about whom Raymonde Ransome composes a poem in H. D.'s *Palimpsest*.

Leon Solomon. Philosophy professor and one of two teachers on whom Raymond Blent's eligibility to play football depends in Howard Nemerov's *The Homecoming Game*.

Dr. Isidore Solow. Selfless, socially conscious Lower East Side physician in Michael Gold's *Jews without Money*.

Henry Solum. Norwegian-American farmer who becomes a teacher in O. E. Rölvaag's *Giants in the Earth*; appears in *Peder Victorious*.

Sam Solum. Norwegian-American farmer who sells a farm to Store-Hans Holm (Hansa) and then goes west in O. E. Rölvaag's *Giants in the Earth* and *Peder Victorious*.

Lottie Somers. Widow Henry Miller attempts to seduce because she is now weak and vulnerable in Henry Miller's *Tropic of Capricorn*.

Mr. Somerset. Aging resident of Wilma Pauling's boarding house in Anne Tyler's *Celestial Navigation*.

Julia Valette Somerville. Orphan adopted by Malcolm and Sarah Bedford; pretty coquette who marries Duncan Bedford in Stark Young's *So Red the Rose*.

Gustaf Sondelius. Famous "soldier of science" who travels the world promoting medical research and who later works with Martin Arrowsmith in Sinclair Lewis's *Arrowsmith*.

Sonny. Black petty officer on the USS *Starfish* and loyal friend and companion of Skipper in John Hawkes's *Second Skin*.

Sophie. German immigrant who is the cook for the Morison family in William Maxwell's *They Came Like Swallows*.

Sordino. See Edmond Behr-Bleibtreau.

George (Big George, Rub-a-dub) Sorensen. Mental patient obsessed with cleanliness who captains the fishing boat in Ken Kesey's *One Flew Over the Cuckoo's Nest*.

Sorenson. Longtime clipperman at the Past Bay Manufacturing Company factory; reluctant striker in Robert Cantwell's *The Land of Plenty*.

Anne (Annie) Sorenson. Artist who, with her husband, Phil Sorenson, renovates a house in Maine and comes to terms with the loss of two children by spontaneous abortions; narrates part of Frederick Busch's *Manual Labor*; she and Phil adopt Elizabeth Bean's baby in *Rounds*.

Bea Sorenson. Employee of Carol Kennicott; dies of typhoid fever in Sinclair Lewis's *Main Street*.

Michael (Mike) Sorenson. Baby born to Elizabeth Bean and adopted by Annie and Phil Sorenson; kidnapped by Horace L'Ordinet, his natural father, but later returned to the Sorensons; found to have sickle-cell anemia as passed on genetically from L'Ordinet in Frederick Busch's *Rounds*.

Philip (Phil) Sorenson. Poet, home handyman, husband of Anne Sorenson, and father of the dead fetus, Sam; narrates part of Frederick Busch's *Manual Labor*; with Anne, adopts a son in *Rounds*.

Sostrata. Wife of Simo and mother of Argo in Thornton Wilder's *The Woman of Andros*.

Brother Soulsby. Itinerant evangelist and husband of Candace Soulsby in Harold Frederic's *The Damnation of Theron Ware*.

Sister Candace Soulsby. Pragmatic evangelist and fund raiser; adviser and refuge of the disgraced Theron Ware in Harold Frederic's *The Damnation of Theron Ware*.

Allen Southby. Harvard professor and literary scholar who aspires to write the definitive novel about Wickford Point; second husband of Bella Brill in John P. Marquand's *Wickford Point*.

Eleanor (Ellie) Sowerby. Cousin of Roy Bassart and close friend of Lucy Nelson in Philip Roth's *When She Was Good*.

Julian Sowerby. Womanizing uncle of Roy Bassart; earns Lucy Nelson Bassart's unyielding animosity by his opposition to the continuation of her marriage to Roy in Philip Roth's *When She Was Good*.

Space Wanderer. See Malachi Constant.

Sam Spade. Private detective hired by Brigid O'Shaughnessy first, ostensibly, to help find her missing sister and then to help her locate the jewel-encrusted statuette in Dashiell Hammett's *The Maltese Falcon*.

Major de Spain. Landowner and sheriff of Yoknapatawpha County; appears in William Faulkner's *Absalom, Absalom!*; *The Hamlet*; *Go Down, Moses*; *Intruder in the Dust*; *The Town*; *The Mansion*; and *The Reivers*.

Manfred de Spain. Son of Major de Spain; banker and mayor; appears in William Faulkner's *The Town, The Mansion*, and *The Reivers*.

Thomas (Tom) Spangler. Manager of the telegraph office where Homer Macauley works in William Saroyan's *The Human Comedy*.

Wolvert Spangler. Ballad-singing cobbler in James Kirke Paulding's *Koningsmarke*.

John Spaniard. Companion of Doctor Reefy in Sherwood Anderson's *Winesburg, Ohio*.

Patience (Patitia) Sparhawk. Orphaned daughter of an alcoholic mother; falsely accused of murdering her husband Beverly Peele, but is saved from execution by Garan Bourke in Gertrude Atherton's *Patience Sparhawk and Her Times*.

Sparicio. Louisiana fisherman who transports Julien La Brierre to Viosca's Point in Lafcadio Hearn's *Chita*.

Pammy Lee Sparkman. Black cook of Drusilla Lacefield Crowninshield; seduced by Jerry Catlin the Second and murdered by Ludus Meggs; appears in T. S. Stribling's *The Store* and *Unfinished Cathedral*.

Kitty Sparks. Mother of Jane Clifford, wife of Ray Sparks, and mother of Emily, Jack, and Ronnie Sparks in Gail Godwin's *The Odd Woman*.

Ray Sparks. Contractor, husband of Kitty Sparks, and stepfather of Jane Clifford in Gail Godwin's *The Odd Woman*.

Sparling. Surgeon-general of Java who offers relief for the men of the HMS *Bounty*; provides a place for Thomas Ledward to recall and record his ordeal in Charles Nordhoff and James Norman Hall's *Men against the Sea*.

Anne Sparrow. Teacher in Wayback, Illinois, whose fear of darkness leads to a brief relationship with Zury Prouder; marries John McVey, bears children by Prouder, and later marries Prouder in Joseph Kirkland's *Zury*.

Col. Harold J. Sparrow. See Frank Wirtanen.

Willard Sparser. Wild friend of Clyde Griffiths; involves Griffiths in a fatal hit-and-run accident in Theodore Dreiser's *An American Tragedy*.

Peter Spavic. Close friend of Agee Ward; responsible for maintaining and continuing Ward's album in Wright Morris's *The Man Who Was There*.

Bill Spear. See Willie Spearmint.

Mrs. Spearman. Elderly, virtuous housekeeper for Judge Honeywell in Ellen Glasgow's *The Romantic Comedians*.

Willie (Bill Spear) Spearmint. Black writer trying to write his first book and lover of Irene Bell; destroys the manuscript of Harry Lesser's unfinished novel in Bernard Malamud's *The Tenants*.

Patty Speed. Ruthless black queen of the numbers game and secret lover of City Councilman Randolph Banks in Julian Mayfield's *The Grand Parade*.

Elsie Speers. Mother of Rosemary Hoyt in F. Scott Fitzgerald's *Tender Is the Night*.

Thomas Garrison (T. G.) Speidel. Cynical journalist who forms an early friendship with Roger Ashley in Chicago; becomes a significant part of Roger's education in Thornton Wilder's *The Eighth Day*.

Desmond (Des) Spellacy. Brother of Thomas Spellacy; monsignor in the Los Angeles diocese whose career is ruined because of his business dealings with corrupt businessmen, including Jack Amsterdam and Dan T. Campion, in John Gregory Dunne's *True Confessions*.

Mary Margaret Maher Spellacy. Wife of Thomas Spellacy; confined to a mental hospital in John Gregory Dunne's *True Confessions*.

Thomas (Tom) Spellacy. Brother of Desmond Spellacy; Los Angeles policeman who sets up the arrest of Jack Amsterdam for the murder of Lois Fazenda; narrates parts of John Gregory Dunne's *True Confessions*.

Miss Mary (Cornelia) Spence. Teacher of Penrod Schofield; he sorely tries her patience in Booth Tarkington's *Penrod, Penrod and Sam*, and *Penrod Jashber*.

Clay-Boy Spencer. Oldest son of Clay and Livia Spencer; becomes the first in his family and the first resident of New Dominion, Virginia, to go to college in Earl Hamner, Jr.'s *Spencer's Mountain*.

Clayton (Clay) Spencer. Virginia mill worker and father of eleven children; sacrifices his dream of building his own home atop Spencer's Mountain so his oldest son will have the opportunity to go to college in Earl Hamner, Jr.'s *Spencer's Mountain*.

Elizabeth (Eliza) Spencer. Mother of Clay Spencer and matriarch of the Spencer clan; forced to learn to cope with life without her husband, Zebulon Spencer, who is killed when a tree falls on him, in Earl Hamner, Jr.'s *Spencer's Mountain*.

Maisie Spencer. Mac's wife whom he abandons along with their two young children to work for social revolution in John Dos Passos's *U.S.A.* trilogy.

Mr. Spencer. History teacher whom Holden Caulfield visits before leaving Pencey Prep in J. D. Salinger's *The Catcher in the Rye*.

Olivia (Livia, Livy) Spencer. Mother of eleven children in depression-era Virginia and mainstay of the Spencer family in Earl Hamner, Jr.'s *Spencer's Mountain*.

Sharon Spencer. Tutor of Regan MacNeil; becomes horrified as she watches Regan become possessed by a demon in William Peter Blatty's *The Exorcist*.

Virgil Spencer. Brother of Clay Spencer and uncle of Clay-Boy Spencer, who lives with Virgil while going to college in Richmond, in Earl Hamner, Jr.'s *Spencer's Mountain*.

Zebulon Spencer. Father of Clay Spencer and patriarch of the Spencer clan; predicts his grandson Clay-Boy will follow a new, unknown path for killing a white deer in Earl Hamner, Jr.'s *Spencer's Mountain*.

Clement (Clem) Spender. Former suitor of Delia Ralston; jilted by Delia because he will not give up painting and become a lawyer; lover of Charlotte Lovell and father of their illegitimate child, Clementina Ralston, in Edith Wharton's *The Old Maid*.

Spengler. Centennial Club member who writes a history of the club for its anniversary in Thomas McGuane's *The Sporting Club*.

Roderick (Rod) Spenser. Cincinnati reporter and aspiring playwright who takes Susan Lenox to New York, abandons her, and is later rescued from alcoholism by her in David Graham Phillips's *Susan Lenox*.

McClintic Sphere. Black jazz musician and lover of Paola Maijstral; provides the advice, "keep cool, but care," in Thomas Pynchon's *V.*

Spider. Dice player, gambler, and friend of Jake Adams and Scar; victim left crippled by a street gang in Herbert Simmons's *Corner Boy*.

Sol Spiegel. Specialist in salvage and fallout survival equipment; accompanies Warren Howe to Schloss Riva in Wright Morris's *Cause for Wonder*.

Dr. Maximilian (Max) Spielman. Mathematical Psycho-Proctologist and first tutor of George Giles; wishes to protect Giles from the disappointments of human existence by concealing from him that he is a boy and not a goat in John Barth's *Giles Goat-Boy*.

Dr. O. (Doc) Spielvogel. Psychiatrist who treats Alex Portnoy and labels his condition "Portnoy's Complaint" in Philip Roth's *Portnoy's Complaint*.

Spirit of Alternatives (But on the Other Hand, Tu As Raison Aussi). Intellectual discussant whom Joseph generates imaginatively for private colloquies on the nature of reality and morality in Saul Bellow's *Dangling Man*.

Spitz. Member of Buck's dog team; killed by Buck in a fight over control of the team in Jack London's *The Call of the Wild*.

Dr. Henry J. Spivack. Sarcastic, garrulous Bellevue mental patient encountered by John Wilder in Richard Yates's *Disturbing the Peace*.

Doctor (Doc) Spivey. Psychiatrist pliably under the domination of Big Nurse in Ken Kesey's *One Flew Over the Cuckoo's Nest*.

Lizzi Spöckenkieker. Spinster who has a comical affair with Siegfried Rieber in Katherine Anne Porter's *Ship of Fools*.

Henry Spoffard. Wealthy and stingy censor of plays; Lorelei Lee marries him to finance a movie in which she will appear in Anita Loos's *"Gentlemen Prefer Blondes"*; he is further manipulated in *"But Gentlemen Marry Brunettes."*

Frank Spofford. Retired chicken farmer and aspiring author who reads assiduously hoping to qualify as a "derivative writer"; father of George Spofford and grandfather of Geneva Spofford; narrates part of Peter De Vries's *Reuben, Reuben*.

Geneva Spofford. Daughter of George and Mary Spofford and granddaughter of Frank Spofford; educated at Wycliffe College for Women, jilted by Tad Springer, impregnated by Gowan McGland; miscarries, then marries Alvin Mopworth in Peter De Vries's *Reuben, Reuben*.

George Spofford. Son of Frank Spofford, husband of Mary Spofford, and father of Geneva Spofford; runs the family poultry business in Peter De Vries's *Reuben, Reuben*.

Mary Punck (Mare) Spofford. Wife of George Spofford and mother of Geneva Spofford; fabricates an affair with Gowan McGland to preserve her daughter's reputation in Peter De Vries's *Reuben, Reuben*.

Icey Spoon. Wife of Walt Spoon; befriends Willa Harper after Ben Harper's execution in Davis Grubb's *The Night of the Hunter*.

Walt Spoon. Husband of Icey Spoon; store owner who employs Willa Harper out of charity in Davis Grubb's *The Night of the Hunter*.

Cherub Spooney. River barge deckhand in James Kirke Paulding's *Westward Ho!*

Sportin' Life. Carefree mulatto drug dealer who persuades Bess to take cocaine in DuBose Heyward's *Porgy*.

Whacker Spradlin. Town drunk of Port William, Kentucky, in Wendell Berry's *A Place on Earth*.

Abner E. Spragg. Father of Undine Spragg; his numerous business endeavors fund his daughter's zealous quest for social status in Edith Wharton's *The Custom of the Country*.

Leota B. Spragg. Ineffectual mother of Undine Spragg in Edith Wharton's *The Custom of the Country*.

Undine (Countess Raymond de Chelles, Undine Marvell, Undine Moffatt) Spragg. Relentlessly ambitious heroine who marries four times, twice to the same man, in her quest for wealth and acceptance in fashionable society in Edith Wharton's *The Custom of the Country*.

Jane Sprague. Pregnant and mildly retarded wife of Jim Sprague; lives in the Seventieth Street building managed by Norman Moonbloom in Edward Lewis Wallant's *The Tenants of Moonbloom*.

Jim Sprague. Slightly retarded husband of Jane Sprague; lives in a tenement managed by Norman Moonbloom in Edward Lewis Wallant's *The Tenants of Moonbloom*.

Marva Sprat. Wife of Jack Sprat; fantasizes love affairs with major-league baseball players in Mark Harris's *It Looked Like For Ever*.

Newton (Jack) Sprat. Husband of Marva Sprat and manager of the California baseball team in Mark Harris's *It Looked Like For Ever*.

Clive Springer. Lover of Selina Boyce; aimless and nonproductive because of guilt heaped on him by his mother, Clytie Springer, in Paule Marshall's *Brown Girl, Brownstones*.

Clytie Springer. Mother of Clive Springer; uses her "illnesses" to keep him close to her in Paule Marshall's *Brown Girl, Brownstones*.

Frederick (Fred) Springer. Car dealer, husband of Rebecca Springer, and father of Janice Angstrom in John Updike's *Rabbit, Run* and *Rabbit Redux*.

Mr. Springer. Traveling drug salesman who frequently stays at the Beulah Hotel in Eudora Welty's *The Ponder Heart*.

Rebecca Springer. Wife of Fred Springer and mother of Janice Angstrom in John Updike's *Rabbit, Run* and *Rabbit Redux*.

Roberta (Bobsy) Springer. Mother of Tad Springer and paramour of Gowan McGland in Peter De Vries's *Reuben, Reuben*.

Thaddeus (Tad) Springer. Son of Bobsy Springer; courts then jilts Geneva Spofford in Peter De Vries's *Reuben, Reuben*.

Sprog. Main character in Fred Trumper's translation of *Akthelt and Gunnel*; castrated and exiled for attempting to make love with Akthelt's wife in John

Irving's *The Water-Method Man.*

William Japheth Sproul III. Theology student who becomes an ardent follower of Nathan Vickery in Joyce Carol Oates's *Son of the Morning.*

Squeak. Sailor aboard the *Indomitable* who lies about Billy Budd in Herman Melville's *Billy Budd.*

Henrietta C. Stackpole. Brilliant and opinionated American journalist who is interested in Isabel Archer's life in Henry James's *The Portrait of a Lady.*

Ralph (Roaring Ralph) Stackpole. Loudmouth frontiersman and Indian fighter in Robert Montgomery Bird's *Nick of the Woods.*

Robert Stadler. Prominent scientist who surrenders his integrity to power-seeking government officials in Ayn Rand's *Atlas Shrugged.*

Lionel Stafford. Ill-fated "intellectual"-cum-coal miner in Jack Conroy's *The Disinherited.*

Maury Stafford. Rival of Richard Cleave for the affections of Judith Cary; sends a false order which disgraces Cleave and leads to the destruction of the Stonewall Brigade; confesses, and does penance in the trenches, in Mary Johnston's *The Long Roll* and *Cease Firing.*

Dr. Heinrich Stahlmann. Scholar at the University of Chicago under whom Jed Tewksbury studies classical literature in Robert Penn Warren's *A Place to Come To.*

Monroe Stahr. Brilliant movie producer who falls in love with Kathleen Moore in F. Scott Fitzgerald's *The Last Tycoon.*

Antrim Stairs. Biology professor who marries Julia Maybury in Mary Austin's *Santa Lucia.*

Julia Maybury Stairs. See Julia Maybury.

Jane (Janie) Staley. Cleaning woman and lover of Parkman's old men; grandmother of Edith Barclay in James Jones's *Some Came Running.*

Major Staley. Commander of Air Force ROTC at Logos College and expert on modern warfare in Don DeLillo's *End Zone.*

Dave Stallworth. Basketball player for the New York Knicks whose determination to come back after a heart attack is admired by Samuel Paul Berman in Jay Neugeboren's *Sam's Legacy.*

Henry (Old Henry) Stamper. Independent and stubborn patriarch of a family of non-union loggers; father of Hank and Lee Stamper in Ken Kesey's *Sometimes a Great Notion.*

Henry (Hank, Hankus) Stamper, Jr. Strong and self-reliant leader of a family of non-union Oregon loggers; son of Henry Stamper and in conflict with his half brother Lee Stamper in Ken Kesey's *Sometimes a Great Notion.*

Joe Benjamin (Joby, Joe Ben, Josephus) Stamper. Good-natured cousin of Hank and Lee Stamper; drowns when caught under a log in Ken Kesey's *Sometimes a Great Notion.*

Leland (Lee) Stamper. Younger half brother of Hank Stamper; returns to Oregon from Yale University seeking revenge on Hank in Ken Kesey's *Sometimes a Great Notion.*

Pat Stamper. Horse trader in William Faulkner's *The Hamlet* and *The Mansion.*

Vivian (Viv) Stamper. Wife of Hank Stamper caught in the middle of his conflict with his half brother Lee in Ken Kesey's *Sometimes a Great Notion.*

Baron Egon Bodo von Stams. Attaché at the Austrian embassy in Washington; he and Theophilus North become great friends, and he enlists North to help him win the attention of Persis Tennyson in Thornton Wilder's *Theophilus North.*

Constance Standish. See Constance MacKenzie.

Lord Stane. See Gordon Roderick.

Dr. Stanhope. White liberal physician who testifies at the trial of Ida Carlisle in Hal Bennett's *A Wilderness of Vines.*

George Stanhope. Literary agent who helps Jim Calder revise Calder's writing in order to attain commercial success in John P. Marquand's *Wickford Point.*

Gerald Stanhope, Earl of Danforth and Duke of Ravenspur. Foppish fourth husband of Amber St. Clare; selected by King Charles II to offer respectability to Amber's pregnancy with the king's child in Kathleen Winsor's *Forever Amber.*

James Staniford. Friend of Charley Dunham; marries Lydia Blood in William Dean Howells's *The Lady of the Aroostook.*

Lydia Blood Staniford. See Lydia Blood.

Rudolf Stanislaus (Rudek, Rudo) Stanka. Illegitimate son of Countess Zdenka von Studenitz and Crown Prince Rudolf von Hapsburg; reared by Dora Dugova, a Croatian peasant; uses his restored family position for the betterment of the peasants; narrator of Louis Adamic's *Cradle of Life.*

Zorka Dugova Stanka. See Zorka Dugova.

Walter F. Stankiewicz. See Walter F. Starbuck.

Stanley. Black chauffeur and attendant of Thomas Oliver; narrates part of Shirley Ann Grau's *The Condor Passes*.

Stanley. Catholic organist who writes a concerto for his dying mother; buried in a church's collapse at the end of William Gaddis's *The Recognitions*.

Stanley. Hippie; with Joy, his girlfriend, travels with Floyd Warner and Kermit Oelsligle and apparently causes the fire which destroys a house in Wright Morris's *Fire Sermon*.

Stanley. Retired janitor and leader of an underground movement for male liberation in Thomas Berger's *Regiment of Women*.

Joseph (Joe) Stanley. Caretaker at St. Jude's church in Sac Prairie in August Derleth's *The Shield of the Valiant*.

Glendinning (Glen) Stanly. Cousin of Pierre Glendinning III; tries to save Lucy Tartan from Pierre in Herman Melville's *Pierre*.

Dr. Stanpole. Physician at Devon School who performs the surgery during which Finny dies in John Knowles's *A Separate Peace*.

Joel Stansky. Editor at the *Village Voice* with whom Salley Gardens is sexually intimate on a periodic basis in Susan Cheever's *Looking for Work*.

Charlotte Stant. School friend of Maggie Verver; marries Adam Verver in Henry James's *The Golden Bowl*.

Adam Stanton. Brother of Anne Stanton, friend of Jack Burden's youth, and physician whom Willie Stark selects to head his new hospital; assassinates Stark after learning of Stark's affair with Anne in Robert Penn Warren's *All the King's Men*.

Anne Stanton. Sister of Adam Stanton, mistress of Willie Stark, and later wife of Jack Burden in Robert Penn Warren's *All the King's Men*.

Governor Stanton. Father of Anne and Adam Stanton and friend of Judge Irwin in Robert Penn Warren's *All the King's Men*.

Vernor Stanton. Insanely competitive member of the Centennial Club who has a dueling gallery in his basement; incites a battle between club members and friends of Earl Olive in Thomas McGuane's *The Sporting Club*.

Gertrude Staple. Second wife of J. Ward Morehouse in John Dos Passos's *U.S.A.* trilogy.

Neva Stapleton. See Neva Blanche Stapleton Manning.

Star. Illegitimate son of Margaret Copeland and, allegedly, her white employer, Mr. Shipley; poisoned by his mother in infancy in Alice Walker's *The Third Life of Grange Copeland*.

Starbuck. Chief mate aboard the *Pequod* who is unable to challenge Ahab successfully in Herman Melville's *Moby-Dick*.

Ruth Starbuck. Translator and former refugee; wife of Walter F. Starbuck in Kurt Vonnegut's *Jailbird*.

Walter F. (Walter F. Stankiewicz) Starbuck. Protégé of Alexander McCone; later diplomat, presidential adviser, convict, and corporate officer; protagonist and narrator of Kurt Vonnegut's *Jailbird*.

Charles P. (Char, Charlie) Stark. Navy enlisted man of good family and artistic ambitions; forced by his association with Raditzer to face his own frailty in Peter Matthiessen's *Raditzer*.

Charlotte Sylvester (Shar) Stark. Wife betrayed by Charlie Stark in Peter Matthiessen's *Raditzer*.

Lucy Stark. Wife of Willie Stark and mother of Tom Stark in Robert Penn Warren's *All the King's Men*.

Maylon Stark. Cook transferred to G Company; relates stories of Karen Holmes's sexual promiscuity at Fort Bliss to Milton Warden in James Jones's *From Here to Eternity*.

Tom Stark. Son of Willie and Lucy Stark; his sexual indiscretions cause political problems for Willie Stark; dies of a football injury in Robert Penn Warren's *All the King's Men*.

Willie (Cousin Willie, Boss, Governor) Stark. Lawyer, governor, father of Tom Stark, and employer of Jack Burden; rises from naive politico to ruthless demagogue in Robert Penn Warren's *All the King's Men*.

Oliver "Reno" Starkey. Mobster who is challenging Lew Yard for control of thievery in Personville in Dashiell Hammett's *Red Harvest*.

Joseph (Jody, Joe) Starks. Entrepreneur who becomes mayor of Eatonville, Florida, and Janie Crawford's second husband in Zora Neale Hurston's *Their Eyes Were Watching God*.

Berryben (Ben) Starnes (Ganchion). Son of Malley and Walter Warren Starnes; wanderer who leaves his family in Charity in William Goyen's *The House* *of Breath.*

Jessy Starnes. Sickly daughter of Malley and Walter Warren Starnes; dies at the age of nineteen in William Goyen's *The House of Breath.*

Jimbob Starnes. Husband of Lauralee Starnes; father of Maidie and Swimma Starnes in William Goyen's *The House of Breath.*

Lauralee (Aunty) Starnes. Daughter of Granny Ganchion; wife of Jimbob Starnes and mother of Maidie and Swimma Starnes; dies in Dallas in William Goyen's *The House of Breath.*

Maidie Starnes. See Maidie Starnes Suggs.

Malley Ganchion Starnes. Daughter of Granny Ganchion; wife of Walter Warren Starnes and mother of Jessy and Berryben Starnes; becomes blind in William Goyen's *The House of Breath.*

Sue Emma (Swimma) Starnes. Daughter of Lauralee and Jimbob Starnes; becomes a model and actress, marries, and has several deformed children; finally operates a boardinghouse in Texas in William Goyen's *The House of Breath.*

Walter Warren Starnes. Husband of Malley Ganchion Starnes; father of Jessy and Berryben Starnes in William Goyen's *The House of Breath.*

Doctor Alexander Alexandrovich Starov. Physician of V.'s mother; meets Sebastian Knight by chance and treats him in his final illness in Vladimir Nabokov's *The Real Life of Sebastian Knight.*

Aaron Pendleton Starr. Father of Amantha Starr; refuses to accept his daughter's black blood and sends her to school in Ohio; dies unexpectedly without "freeing" her in Robert Penn Warren's *Band of Angels.*

Amantha (Manty, Mrs. Tobias Sears) Starr. Daughter and slave of Aaron Starr, slave and mistress of Hamish Bond, and wife of Tobias Sears; repeatedly asks, "Who am I?"; narrator of Robert Penn Warren's *Band of Angels.*

Andrew Starr. Man whose wife and daughter were murdered by Joseph Detweiler in Thomas Berger's *Killing Time.*

Jacob (Jacobito, Jacques, Jake, Jakey, Capitán Jacobito Estrella, Comrade Comic Star) Starr. American revolutionary fighting for the loyalist cause in the Spanish civil war; union organizer, Latin-American expert, protégé of Carl Vlanoc, lover of Sarah Ruskin, and friend of Greg Ballard; tormented romantic who becomes a cold-blooded killer in William Herrick's *Hermanos!*

Walter Starr. Family friend who accompanies Andrew Lynch to the scene of the accident in which Jay Follet dies in James Agee's *A Death in the Family.*

Francis Starwick. Harvard schoolmate of Eugene Gant and secret homosexual in Thomas Wolfe's *Of Time and the River.*

Emil (Professor) Staubmeyer. Superintendent of schools in Fort Beulah and later a Minute Man officer in Sinclair Lewis's *It Can't Happen Here.*

Charlie Stavros. Lover of Janice Angstrom and salesman at her father's car dealership in John Updike's *Rabbit, Run* and *Rabbit Redux.*

Shep Stearns. Junior writer for a Hollywood film studio who, after submitting a screenplay for a college musical, is assigned to collaborate on the project with Manley Halliday, a writer whose work he greatly admires; not knowing that Halliday is an alcoholic, he presses him into sharing two bottles of champagne, inducing the drinking binge that will take Halliday's life in Budd Schulberg's *The Disenchanted.*

Johann (Hans) Steckfuss. Dubious Swiss doctor supervising cybernetic experiments in Thomas Berger's *Vital Parts.*

Margaret Gale (Maggie) Stedman. Granddaughter of Anton Galé in Louis Adamic's *Grandsons.*

Morgan Steele. Editor of the New York newspaper for which Patience Sparhawk works in Gertrude Atherton's *Patience Sparhawk and Her Times.*

Steelkilt. Lakeman aboard the *Town-Ho* who has an altercation with Radney in Herman Melville's *Moby-Dick.*

Steenie. See George Villiers.

Pepper Steep. Modern dance instructor and regular guest on the late-night talk show hosted by Dick Gibson in Stanley Elkin's *The Dick Gibson Show.*

Stefan (Corporal). Soldier killed by a firing squad for leading a mutiny in William Faulkner's *A Fable.*

Harper Steger. Attorney for Frank Cowperwood in Theodore Dreiser's *The Financier* and *The Titan.*

Carl Stein. Colleague of Paul Galambos in Scott Spencer's *Last Night at the Brain Thieves Ball.*

James I. (Bugger, Jim) Stein. Jewish attorney and National Guard captain who serves as commanding officer of C-for-Charlie Company until relieved of his post by Colonel Gordon Tall in James Jones's *The Thin Red Line.*

Genevieve (Jenny) Steinbauer. Blonde who attends the yacht party with Pete Ginotta in William Faulkner's *Mosquitoes*.

Judah (Judd) Steiner, Jr. Kidnapper and murderer (along with Artie Straus) of Paulie Kessler in Meyer Levin's *Compulsion*.

Judah Steiner, Sr. Father of Judd Steiner and Chicago garment industry millionaire in Meyer Levin's *Compulsion*.

Stella. Wheelchair-bound muscular dystrophy victim and lover of Samuel Paul Berman in Jay Neugeboren's *Sam's Legacy*.

Herbert Stencil. Son of Sidney Stencil; has been searching since 1945 for the mysterious V., who is mentioned in Stencil's father's diary; involved with the Whole Sick Crew; takes Benny Profane to Malta in Thomas Pynchon's *V.*

Sidney Stencil. Father of Herbert Stencil; works for the British Foreign Office; stationed in Florence in 1899, encounters Hugh and Evan Godolphin and Victoria Wren; stationed on Malta in 1919, encounters Father Fairing and Veronica Maganese in Thomas Pynchon's *V.*

George W. Stener. Philadelphia city treasurer and agent for powerful politicians; refuses a loan to Frank Cowperwood in Theodore Dreiser's *The Financier*.

Uncle Birdie Steptoe. Drunken fisherman who befriends John Harper; discovers Willa Harper's body submerged in the river in Davis Grubb's *The Night of the Hunter*.

Angela (Helen Brown) Sterling. World's highest paid movie actress who commits suicide after performing explicit sex acts in Boris Adrian's pornographic movie in Terry Southern's *Blue Movie*.

Felicia Sterling. Cousin of Rachel Winslow and resident of Chicago in Charles M. Sheldon's *In His Steps*.

Philip (Phil) Sterling. College friend of Henry Brierly and boyfriend of Ruth Bolton; unsuccessful at numerous jobs, but goes West with Brierly to make money from the railroads in Samuel Langhorne Clemens and Charles Dudley Warner's *The Gilded Age*.

Irving Stern. Middle-aged socialist critic in John Updike's *Bech: A Book*.

Moran Sternersen. Largely uncivilized, amorally predatory woman with whom Ross Wilbur falls in love; killed on the *Bertha Millner* in Frank Norris's *Moran of the Lady Letty*.

Artie Sternlicht. Columbia University student and political activist; friend of Susan Isaacson Lewin in E. L. Doctorow's *The Book of Daniel*.

Bertha Sternowitz. Enormous sister of Genya Schearl and possessor of a sharp Yiddish wit in Henry Roth's *Call It Sleep*.

Carmen Sternwood. Homicidal and nymphomaniacal younger daughter of General Sternwood in Raymond Chandler's *The Big Sleep*.

General Guy Sternwood. Dying father of Carmen and Vivian; Philip Marlowe's client in Raymond Chandler's *The Big Sleep*.

Dominie Stettinius. Clergyman and tutor of Sybrandt in James Kirke Paulding's *The Dutchman's Fireside*.

Steve. Friend of the Virginian in Owen Wister's *The Virginian*.

Coach (Steve) Stevens. Baseball coach at Lopin High School and friend of Carl Brown in Betty Smith's *Joy in the Morning*.

Colonel Stevens. Fatherly administrator of Kilrainey Army Hospital in James Jones's *Whistle*.

Don Stevens. Radical and abrasive newspaperman, an acquaintance of Eleanor Stoddard and Eveline Hutchins, he organizes a protest of the Sacco and Vanzetti execution with the help of Mary French in John Dos Passos's *U.S.A.* trilogy.

Dr. Stevens. Physician who nurses Arthur Mervyn to health following Mervyn's brush with yellow fever; becomes Mervyn's friend and adviser after listening to Mervyn tell about his adventures in Charles Brockden Brown's *Arthur Mervyn*.

Gavin Stevens. Attorney in William Faulkner's *Light in August*; *Go Down, Moses*; *Intruder in the Dust*; *Requiem for a Nun*; *The Town*; and *The Mansion*.

George Kingfish Stevens. Radio character jailed for robbing Amos's place; freed from jail by Minnie Yellings in Ishmael Reed's *The Last Days of Louisiana Red*.

Gladys Stevens. Woman whose voice is used in the voice-reminder system at Project Wildfire in Michael Crichton's *The Andromeda Strain*.

Gowan Stevens. Cousin of Gavin Stevens in William Faulkner's *The Town*; Temple Drake's husband in Faulkner's *Requiem for a Nun*; abandons his wife in Faulkner's *Sanctuary*.

Lemuel Stevens. Judge and father of Gavin and Margaret Stevens; appears in William Faulkner's *Intruder in the Dust*, *The Town*, *The Mansion*, and *The Reivers*.

Margaret Stevens. See Margaret Stevens Mallison.

Melisandre Backus Stevens. Wife of Gavin Stevens in William Faulkner's *The Mansion*.

Temple Drake Stevens. As Temple Drake, a flapper raped with a corncob by Popeye in William Faulkner's *Sanctuary*; wife of Gowan Stevens in *Requiem for a Nun*.

Stony Stevenson. Soldier friend of Malachi Constant in Kurt Vonnegut's *The Sirens of Titan*.

Agnes (Aggie, Jim) Stewart. Daughter of Jack Stewart and a woman of Ethiopian heritage; true love of Jean Baptiste in Oscar Micheaux's *The Homesteader*.

Col. Alexander Stewart. Copperhead, two-term Ohio legislator, and one of the oldest citizens of Dorbury, Ohio; father of Walter Stewart in Paul Laurence Dunbar's *The Fanatics*.

Cora Gordon Stewart. Sister of Harry Gordon and half sister of Nina and Tom Gordon; after having attempted to claim the Mississippi plantation left to her by her white husband, she is seized and thrown back into slavery; kills her children to prevent them from living enslaved, and is hanged as a murderess in Harriet Beecher Stowe's *Dred*.

Frances Stewart. Beautiful courtesan who supplants Barbara Palmer as the chief interest of King Charles II; smallpox destroys her beauty and she finally becomes a close friend of Queen Catherine in Kathleen Winsor's *Forever Amber*.

Jack Stewart. Scottish immigrant and farmer; father of Agnes Stewart in Oscar Micheaux's *The Homesteader*.

Walter Stewart. Only son of Alexander Stewart; supports the Union during the Civil War and is denounced by his father in Paul Laurence Dunbar's *The Fanatics*.

Jerusalem Webster (Perfessor) Stiles. Cynical, fraudulent professor and alter ego of John Wickliff Shawnessy in Ross Lockridge, Jr.'s *Raintree County*.

Edith Stilling. Widowed neighbor of Terry Bluvard; accepts the relationship between Bluvard and Renay Davis in Ann Allen Shockley's *Loving Her*.

Sam Stillings. Former butler at the Cresswell plantation who becomes Register of the Treasury in Washington, D.C., and marries Miss Caroline Wynn after he double-crosses Blessed Alwyn and Tom Teerswell in W. E. B. Du Bois's *The Quest of the Silver Fleece*.

Kevin Stillman. High school bully and friend of Conrad Jarrett in Judith Guest's *Ordinary People*.

Greg Stillson. Unscrupulous insurance and real estate agent, congressman, and presidential candidate whose plans for starting a nuclear war Johnny Smith discovers; assassinated by Smith in Stephen King's *The Dead Zone*.

Stilwell. Gunners mate second class who is at the helm of the USS *Caine* when the ship is seized by mutineers; obeys the mutineers in Herman Wouk's *The Caine Mutiny*.

Stinger. Bourne Island cane cutter who befriends Saul Amron in Paule Marshall's *The Chosen Place, the Timeless People*.

Stingo (Cracker, the Reverend Wilbur Entwistle, Stinky). Aspiring southern writer who chronicles his relationship with Sophie Zawistowska and Nathan Landau in Brooklyn in 1947; narrator of William Styron's *Sophie's Choice*.

Alec Stivvens. Friend of Thomas Paine; thief in London's Gin Row who is hanged for stealing in Howard Fast's *Citizen Tom Paine*.

Mrs. Nigel Stock. See Ardis Ross.

Stockton. Failed merchant and friend of Clarissa and Edward Packard in Caroline Gilman's *Recollections of a Housekeeper*.

Bernice Stockton. Domineering story-writer who ignores her husband Bruce Dudley, whom she knows as John Stockton, because of his lack of ambition in Sherwood Anderson's *Dark Laughter*.

John Stockton. See Bruce Dudley.

Stock Stockton. Police officer who investigates Frederick Eichner's automobile accident in Terry Southern's *Flash and Filigree*.

Freddy Stockwell. Father of Emily Turner in Alison Lurie's *Love and Friendship*.

Patricia Stockwell. Mother of Emily Turner in Alison Lurie's *Love and Friendship*.

Eleanor Stoddard. Designer and eventual companion of J. Ward Morehouse who through hard work and skillful management of her image becomes a successful businesswoman and socialite in John Dos Passos's *U.S.A.* trilogy.

Hopton Stoddard. Guilt-ridden philanthropist who commissions Howard Roark to build a temple in Ayn Rand's *The Fountainhead.*

David Stofsky. Jobless homosexual poet and former Columbia University student who has visions in John Clellon Holmes's *Go.*

Anastasia (Stacey) Stoker. Nurse in the New Tammany Psyche Clinic, wife of Maurice Stoker, daughter of Virginia R. Hector, and nymphomaniacal lover of George Giles; she and Giles couple in the belly of a computer in John Barth's *Giles Goat-Boy.*

Giles Stoker. See Stoker Giles.

Maurice Stoker. Brother of Lucky Rexford and ruler of the dark Power Plant in John Barth's *Giles Goat-Boy.*

Boney Stokes. Nosy and self-righteous store owner; opposes the Stampers in Ken Kesey's *Sometimes a Great Notion.*

Melba Stokes. Christian Scientist and employer of Tisha Dees in Arthenia J. Bates's *The Deity Nodded.*

Brian Stollerman. First husband of Isadora Wing; she divorces him when he becomes schizophrenic in Erica Jong's *Fear of Flying.*

Dora Stolnitz. First lover of Aaron Greidinger and Communist party member who becomes disenchanted by its policies under Stalin in Isaac Bashevis Singer's *Shosha.*

Andrew Stone. Self-made millionaire; father of Angel Stone and her half brother and husband, Michael Tarleton; spends years trying to gain control of Angel's company in M. F. Beal's *Angel Dance.*

Angel Stone. American feminist author and heiress to her grandmother's company of organized drug smugglers; estranged wife of Michael Tarleton and partner of Julia; hires Kat Alcazar as her companion, secretary, and bodyguard in M. F. Beal's *Angel Dance.*

Arabella Stone. See Milo Hamilton.

Bob Stone. Scion of a former slaveholding family whose sexual attraction to Louisa leads to his death and the lynching of her black lover in Jean Toomer's *Cane.*

Dr. Edgar Stone. Self-important English master whose refusal to take a salary cut is a partial cause of Dorset Academy's demise in Richard Yates's *A Good School.*

Edith Stone. Pretty, dreamy, teenaged daughter of Dr. Edgar Stone; a romantic image to the boys of Dorset Academy, she experiences sexual initiation with Student Council president Larry Gaines in Richard Yates's *A Good School.*

Hazel Stone. Wife of Milton Stone II; administrative assistant to Senator Boyd Potter, whom she tries to stop from using the atomic bomb against the president of the United States, in Mari Sandoz's *The Tom-Walker.*

Hiram Stone. Husband of Sarah Stone and father of Milton Stone; profit-raker during the Civil War in Mari Sandoz's *The Tom-Walker.*

Jeremy Stone. Stanford University bacteriology professor who developed the idea of Project Wildfire and who is the leader of a group of scientists in Michael Crichton's *The Andromeda Strain.*

Mrs. Karen (Miss Priss, The Pet) Stone. Retired fifty-year-old actress who reflects on her marriage and stage career; sensing she is losing her beauty, she depends on gigolos for emotional and sexual gratification in Tennessee Williams's *The Roman Spring of Mrs. Stone.*

Lucinda Martin (Lucie) Stone. Wife of Milton Stone I, whom she marries despite his loss of a leg; mother of Martin Stone in Mari Sandoz's *The Tom-Walker.*

Lyster Stone. Bohemian artist and friend of Isabel Otis and John Gwynne; introduces Gwynne to the underside of San Francisco life in Gertrude Atherton's *Ancestors.*

Martin (Marty) Stone. World War I veteran with gassed lungs; husband of Penny Turner Stone and father of three children; spends time in an insane asylum in Mari Sandoz's *The Tom-Walker.*

Milton (Milty) Stone (I). Civil War veteran with an iron peg leg who is the son of Sarah and Hiram Stone, the husband of Lucinda Martin Stone, and the father of Martin Stone in Mari Sandoz's *The Tom-Walker.*

Milton Stone (II). Son of Martin Stone and husband of Hazel Stone; World War II veteran with shrapnel located near his heart; knows the Portable Extradimensional Hole trick in Mari Sandoz's *The Tom-Walker.*

Miriam Berg Stone. Independent woman who trades a Ph.D. and a promising career in computers for a husband and children, but begins to regain self-confidence, self-esteem, and independence by the end of Marge Piercy's *Small Changes.*

Neil Stone. Husband of Miriam Berg in Marge Piercy's *Small Changes*.

Penny Turner Stone. Wife of Martin Stone and mother of three children; helps her husband homestead on a Wyoming ranch in Mari Sandoz's *The Tom-Walker*.

Rachel Stone. Millionaire mother of Andrew Stone and grandmother of Angel Stone; leaves her millions to Angel in M.F. Beal's *Angel Dance*.

Sarah Stone. Wife of Hiram Stone and mother of Milton Stone; plans her son's wedding to Lucinda Martin while unaware that he is returning from the Civil War as an amputee in Mari Sandoz's *The Tom-Walker*.

Thomas J. (Tom) Stone. Childlike, impotent husband of Mrs. Karen Stone; his death from heart trouble leaves her alone in Tennessee Williams's *The Roman Spring of Mrs. Stone*.

Hiram Stonebraker. United States major general who coordinates the Berlin airlift in Leon Uris's *Armageddon*.

Austin (Great Commoner) Stoneman. United States congressman, legislative force behind Reconstruction, and father of Phil and Elsie Stoneman in Thomas Dixon's *The Clansman*.

Elsie Stoneman. Daughter of Austin Stoneman; influences Abraham Lincoln to pardon Ben Cameron, whom she loves, in Thomas Dixon's *The Clansman*.

Phil Stoneman. Union army captain who becomes sympathetic to the southern white cause; trades places with Ben Cameron, who is awaiting execution, and is rescued by the Ku Klux Klan in Thomas Dixon's *The Clansman*.

Captain Bruno Storm. See Raymond Mainwaring.

Paula Arnold Storm. Friend of Dirk DeJong; marries a man more than twice her age in Edna Ferber's *So Big*.

Raymond (Ray) Stothard. Drunkard who organizes an aggressive movement of poor white ruffians and corrupt politicians to assault the black contrabands in Paul Laurence Dunbar's *The Fanatics*.

Brigit Stott. Novelist and academic who teaches at Woodslee University; involved in a turbulent love affair with music professor Alexis Kessler in Joyce Carol Oates's *Unholy Loves*.

Colonel Stotz. Early investigator of the murder of Breckenridge Lansing; as a private citizen he solves the mystery in Thornton Wilder's *The Eighth Day*.

Clyde (Hanger) Stout. Kind teenager who works as a mechanic at Pete's gas station, where he practices free-hanging; after being drafted into the army, he wins the free-hanging competition, but does not receive the prize money; narrator of Jack Matthews's *Hanger Stout, Awake!*

Harvey Stovall. Attorney from Columbus, Ohio; adjutant for the 918th Bomb Group in Beirne Lay, Jr., and Sy Bartlett's *Twelve O'Clock High!*

Marshal Excell Prentiss (Curly) Stovall. Storekeeper in Banner, Mississippi, who takes an heirloom wedding ring and Jack Renfro's horse and truck in payment for Renfro debts in Eudora Welty's *Losing Battles*.

Roma Stover. Yellow-haired girl from Roy Earle's boyhood in William Riley Burnett's *High Sierra*.

Joe Stowe. Friend and Harvard classmate of Jim Calder; first husband of Bella Brill; achieves critical and financial success as a writer of serious fiction in John P. Marquand's *Wickford Point*.

Marian Strademyer. Secretary for George Lockwood I at Lockwood & Co.; mistress of Penrose Lockwood in John O'Hara's *The Lockwood Concern*.

Ward Stradlater. Hotshot roommate of Holden Caulfield; Holden worries Stradlater might take advantage of Jane Gallagher in J. D. Salinger's *The Catcher in the Rye*.

Richard Throckett Straker. Partner of Barlow; buys the Marsten House as a home for the vampire Barlow in Stephen King's *'Salem's Lot*.

Annabelle Marie Strang. Society girl who becomes pregnant by young J. Ward Morehouse, marries him, and aborts the pregnancy; he divorces her for being unfaithful in John Dos Passos's *U.S.A.* trilogy.

Arline Strange. Actress who employs Emma Lou Morgan as her maid in Wallace Thurman's *The Blacker The Berry*.

John (Johnny Stranger, Mother Strange) Strange. Texan and mess sergeant; returns from duty in the South Pacific with metal fragments in his hand to discover that his wife loves another man and that his plans to start a new life as a restaurateur will never become reality in James Jones's *Whistle*.

Laurentine Strange. Illegitimate mulatto daughter of Sarah Strange; courted successfully by Stephen Denleigh in Jessie Redmon Fauset's *The Chinaberry Tree*.

Linda Sue Strange. Wife of Johnny Strange; while Johnny is stationed in the South Pacific, she becomes involved with a more adventurous married lover and abandons her plans to open a restaurant with her husband in James Jones's *Whistle*.

Sarah (Aunt Sal) Strange. Black servant and lover of the white Colonel Halloway; mother of Laurentine Strange in Jessie Redmon Fauset's *The Chinaberry Tree*.

Victor (Don Victor) Strasser. Father-in-law of Grace Strasser-Mendana and father of four warring sons; takes over Boca Grande from his wife's family and dies at age ninety-five in Joan Didion's *A Book of Common Prayer*.

Antonio Strasser-Mendana. Youngest son of Victor Strasser, husband of Isabel Strasser-Mendana, and brother of Edgar, Luis, and Little Victor Strasser-Mendana; succeeds Little Victor to power in Boca Grande in Joan Didion's *A Book of Common Prayer*.

Bianca Strasser-Mendana. Wife of Little Victor Strasser-Mendana in Joan Didion's *A Book of Common Prayer*.

Edgar Strasser-Mendana. Oldest son of Victor Strasser, husband of Grace Strasser-Mendana, and father of Gerardo Strasser-Mendana; upon his death, leaves Grace 59.8 percent of the arable land in Boca Grande in Joan Didion's *A Book of Common Prayer*.

Elena Strasser-Mendana. Widow of Luis Strasser-Mendana; attracted to her nephew, Gerardo Strasser-Mendana, in Joan Didion's *A Book of Common Prayer*.

Gerardo Strasser-Mendana. Son of Grace Strasser-Mendana and lover of Charlotte Douglas; makes a failed power grab in Boca Grande in Joan Didion's *A Book of Common Prayer*.

Grace Tabor Strasser-Mendana. Widow of Edgar Strasser-Mendana and daughter-in-law of Victor Strasser; narrator of Joan Didion's *A Book of Common Prayer*.

Isabel Strasser-Mendana. Wife of Antonio Strasser-Mendana in Joan Didion's *A Book of Common Prayer*.

Luis Strasser-Mendana. Second son of Victor Strasser; killed after being president of Boca Grande for fifteen months in Joan Didion's *A Book of Common Prayer*.

Victor (Little Victor) Strasser-Mendana. Third son of Victor Strasser and lover of Charlotte Douglas; succeeds to power in Boca Grande after the death

of his brother Luis in Joan Didion's *A Book of Common Prayer*.

Ray Stratton. College roommate of Oliver Barrett IV in Erich Segal's *Love Story*.

Artie (James Singer) Straus. Kidnapper and murderer (along with Judd Steiner) of Paulie Kessler in Meyer Levin's *Compulsion*.

Randolph Straus. Father of Artie Straus and millionaire director of the Straus Corporation in Meyer Levin's *Compulsion*.

Doctor Strauss. Neurosurgeon who teams with Nemur to perform the intelligence operation on Charlie Gordon in Daniel Keyes's *Flowers for Algernon*.

Streamline. Unemployed friend of Jake Jackson; named for his slick, straight black hair in Richard Wright's *Lawd Today*.

Scotty Streck. Bowler beaten in a match by Billy Phelan; dies of a heart attack in William Kennedy's *Billy Phelan's Greatest Game*.

Clem Streeter. Trucker tortured by Legs Diamond in William Kennedy's *Legs*.

Michael (Mike) Strelchuk. Miner whose heroism following a mine explosion is unavailing; he and his companions are among the dead in Robert Coover's *The Origin of the Brunists*.

Lewis Lambert Strether. Middle-aged editor from Woollett, Massachusetts, engaged to Mrs. Newsome, who sends him to Paris to persuade her son Chad Newsome to stop his affair with Madame de Vionnet and return to a respectable life in America, in Henry James's *The Ambassadors*.

Luke Strett. London physician who encourages the dying Mildred Theale to enjoy life fully in Henry James's *The Wings of the Dove*.

Susan Shepherd Stringham. Elderly widow and writer who is Mildred Theale's traveling companion; schoolgirl friend of Maud Lowder in Henry James's *The Wings of the Dove*.

Phillipos Stritsas. Lover of Chrysanthi and look-alike of Sotiris Procopirios in Nicholas Delbanco's *The Martlet's Tale*.

Aloysius James Strohe. Brewer; grandfather of Ellen Strohe in Larry Woiwode's *What I'm Going to Do, I Think*.

Ellen Sidone Anne Strohe. Newly married wife of Chris Van Eenanam and a central character in Larry Woiwode's *What I'm Going to Do, I Think*.

Grandma Strohe. Wife of A. J. Strohe and grandmother of Ellen Strohe in Larry Woiwode's *What I'm Going to Do, I Think.*

Charley Strong. Outstanding student of Francis Prescott; World War I hero wounded in action; lives in Paris with Prescott's daughter, Cordelia Turnbull, after the war; author of a manuscript collected by Brian Aspinwall in Louis Auchincloss's *The Rector of Justin.*

Kay Leiland Strong. Vassar graduate who works in merchandizing at Macy's, marries and is divorced from Harold Peterson, and falls to her death from the twentieth floor of a building; police rule her death an accident, but other members of the Group believe it to be suicide in Mary McCarthy's *The Group.*

Simon Strother. Coachman for Bayard Sartoris II in William Faulkner's *Sartoris (Flags in the Dust)*; Marengo's father in *The Unvanquished.*

George Stroud. Executive editor of *Crimeways* magazine and husband of Georgette Stroud; unidentified witness who can link Earl Janoth to the murder of Pauline Delos, Stroud's sometime lover; a narrator of Kenneth Fearing's *The Big Clock.*

Georgette Stroud. Wife of George Stroud in and a narrator of Kenneth Fearing's *The Big Clock.*

Daniel Strunk. Loner once married to a Cherokee Indian who was killed in an Indian massacre; helps Leslie Collins make saltpeter in Harriette Simpson Arnow's *The Kentucky Trace.*

Mrs. Lemuel Struthers. Wife of a millionaire shoe polish businessman whose soirées are initially deplored by old New York society but later accepted in Edith Wharton's *The Age of Innocence.*

Asa M. Stryker. Duck fancier turned commercial breeder of snapping turtles; murdered by Clarence Latouche in Edmund Wilson's *Memoirs of Hecate County.*

Captain Stuart. English captain, late of the Gordon Highlanders, serving as commander of the bodyguard of President Alvarez of Olancho; killed during the overthrow of the government in Richard Harding Davis's *Soldiers of Fortune.*

Charles Stuart (Charles II). King of Restoration England and lover of Amber St. Clare in Kathleen Winsor's *Forever Amber.*

Cornelius Stuart. Son-in-law of Montague Lacey; former Virginia congressman who opposes and fears secession in Mary Lee Settle's *Know Nothing.*

Henrietta Anne (Minette) Stuart. Physically delicate sister and closest friend of King Charles II in Kathleen Winsor's *Forever Amber.*

James (Jamie) Stuart, Duke of York. Controversy-fomenting brother of King Charles II in Kathleen Winsor's *Forever Amber.*

J. E. B. (Jeb) Stuart. Colorful and untrustworthy Southern general who fails to keep Robert E. Lee informed of the movements of the Union army preceding the Battle of Gettysburg in Michael Shaara's *The Killer Angels.*

Jack Stuart. Leader of Jack Stuart and His Collegians; hires Rick Martin, but makes Martin play in a restrained style so the band will not sound like a black band in Dorothy Baker's *Young Man with a Horn.*

Jamie Stuart. Provincial officer, friend of Johnny Lacey, and beau of Sally Lacey's sister; killed in the battle at Fort Duquesne in Mary Lee Settle's *O Beulah Land.*

Lancelot Stuart. Friend of Johnny Catlett; resigns a U.S. Army commission to join the Confederate army in Mary Lee Settle's *Know Nothing.*

Stubb. Carefree second mate aboard the *Pequod* in Herman Melville's *Moby-Dick.*

Count Yaromir (Friend) von Studenitz. Father of Countess Zdenka von Studenitz and maternal grandfather of Rudolf Stanka in Louis Adamic's *Cradle of Life.*

Countess Zdenka von Studenitz. Daughter of Count Yaromir von Studenitz, lover of Rudolf von Hapsburg, and mother of Rudolf Stanka in Louis Adamic's *Cradle of Life.*

Sir Lewis Stukely. Sir Walter Ralegh's kinsman and betrayer in George Garrett's *Death of the Fox.*

Stupid Ludmila. Half-crazed woman living in the forest with her dog; her father allowed her to be raped by "a herd of drunken peasants" because she refused to marry the son of the village psalmist; killed when village women, angry because Ludmila entices their husbands, break a glass bottle of feces inside her vagina in Jerzy Kosinski's *The Painted Bird.*

Ella Lowry Sturgis. Promiscuous wife of Hector Sturgis and daughter of an Irish laborer in Shelby Foote's *Jordan County.*

Esther (Little Esther) Wingate Sturgis. Wife of John Sturgis and domineering mother of Hector Sturgis in Shelby Foote's *Jordan County.*

Hector (Heck) Wingate Sturgis. Ineffectual husband of Ella Lowry Sturgis; city planner, artist, failed farmer, and father in Shelby Foote's *Jordan County.*

John Sturgis. Merchant, husband of Esther Wingate Sturgis, and father of Hector Sturgis in Shelby Foote's *Jordan County.*

Clyde Sturrock. Childhood friend of Paul Hardin; unscrupulous lawyer and congressman; a drinker who seizes the cause of prohibition in Brand Whitlock's *J. Hardin & Son.*

The Subliminal Kid. Technical sergeant specializing in putting out Rewrite Bulletins at the subliminal level in William S. Burroughs's *The Ticket That Exploded*; defector from the Nova Mob working in collaboration with the Nova Police in *The Soft Machine.*

Sue. Narrator of Helen Hooven Santmyer's *Herbs and Apples.*

Sue. See Beulah Ross.

Sugar-Boy (Roger/Robert O'Sheean). Irish driver and bodyguard for Willie Stark in Robert Penn Warren's *All the King's Men.*

Sugarman. Candy butcher on the Grand Central railroad; lives in the Thirteenth Street building managed by Norman Moonbloom in Edward Lewis Wallant's *The Tenants of Moonbloom.*

Maidie Starnes Suggs. Daughter of Lauralee and Jimbob Starnes; moves to Dallas, where she is unhappy, in William Goyen's *The House of Breath.*

Sula. See Sula Peace.

Suleau (I). Father of Suleau II; police spy in H. L. Davis's *Harp of a Thousand Strings.*

Suleau (II). Son of Suleau I; journalist killed by a mob in Paris in H. L. Davis's *Harp of a Thousand Strings.*

Suliana. Mute female who is abused by Patternists in Octavia E. Butler's *Patternmaster.*

Sullivan Female sculptor who accompanies David Bell and friends on a trip west to make a documentary film in Don DeLillo's *Americana.*

Sullivan (Sully). Seagull who is Jonathan Livingston Seagull's first flight instructor after Jonathan transcends earthly life in Richard Bach's *Jonathan Livingston Seagull.*

Betty Sullivan. Pianist married briefly to Stephen Lewis in Clyde Brion Davis's *"The Great American Novel–."*

Anna Summers. See Anna Leath.

Dick Summers. Veteran mountain man who teaches Boone Caudill the ways of the wilderness in A. B. Guthrie's *The Big Sky*; guide for a wagon train in *The Way West.*

Gina Summers. Prostitute specializing in sado-masochism; one of her clients is Los Angeles policeman Baxter Slate in Joseph Wambaugh's *The Choirboys.*

Lucy Freeman Sumner. Friend who counsels Eliza Wharton about the dangers of the adventurous life in Hannah Webster Foster's *The Coquette.*

Isaac (Ikey) Sumpter. Son of the Reverend MacCarland Sumpter; exploits Jasper Harrick's being trapped in a cave and is partly responsible for Harrick's death in Robert Penn Warren's *The Cave.*

Reverend MacCarland (Brother Sumpter, Ole Mac) Sumpter. Baptist preacher and father of Isaac Sumpter; goes into the cave and finds Jasper Harrick dead but lies to protect Isaac in Robert Penn Warren's *The Cave.*

Sun. Underworld drug dealer in George Cain's *Blueschild Baby.*

Sunshine. Indian second wife of Little Big Man and mother of their son, Morning Star, in Thomas Berger's *Little Big Man.*

Supercargo. Enormous attendant of shell-shocked black veterans who rebel against him at the Golden Day bar in Ralph Ellison's *Invisible Man.*

Suratt. Sewing machine salesman in William Faulkner's *Sartoris (Flags in the Dust)* and *As I Lay Dying.* See also V. K. Ratliff.

Buffy Surface. Former girlfriend of Brewster Ashenden in *The Making of Ashenden*, a novella in Stanley Elkin's *Searches and Seizures.*

Susan. Sixteen year old who becomes pregnant after sleeping with Lee Mellon; becomes a North Beach character in Richard Brautigan's *A Confederate General from Big Sur.*

Susie. Servant to Leonora and Captain Weldon Penderton in Carson McCullers's *Reflections in a Golden Eye.*

Susy. See Gin-head Susy.

Bruce Sutherland. British military commander of Cyprus who keeps secret his Jewish ancestry in Leon Uris's *Exodus.*

Clytemnestra (Clytie) Sutpen. Daughter of Thomas Sutpen and a black slave; burns down the Sutpen mansion, killing Henry Sutpen and herself, in William Faulkner's *Absalom, Absalom!*

Ellen Coldfield Sutpen. Second wife of Thomas Sutpen and mother of Henry and Judith Sutpen in William Faulkner's *Absalom, Absalom!*

Eulalia Bon Sutpen. Probable first wife of Thomas Sutpen and probable mother, by Sutpen, of Charles Bon; Sutpen divorces her when he learns that she has black blood in William Faulkner's *Absalom, Absalom!*

Henry Sutpen. Son of Thomas and Ellen Coldfield Sutpen and brother of Judith Sutpen; kills his half brother, Charles Bon, in William Faulkner's *Absalom, Absalom!*

Judith Sutpen. Daughter of Thomas and Ellen Coldfield Sutpen and sister of Henry Sutpen; engaged to her half brother, Charles Bon, in William Faulkner's *Absalom, Absalom!*

Thomas Sutpen. Probably the father, by Eulalia Bon Sutpen, of Charles Bon; father, by a black slave, of Clytemnestra Sutpen; by Ellen Coldfield Sutpen, of Henry and Judith Sutpen; by Milly Jones, of a daughter; killed by Milly's grandfather, Wash Jones; appears in William Faulkner's *Absalom, Absalom!*; *The Unvanquished*; *Go Down, Moses*; *Requiem for a Nun*; and *The Reivers.*

Tobe Sutterfield. Groom and minister in William Faulkner's *A Fable.*

Mary Sutton. Mother of Mildred Sutton in Reynolds Price's *A Long and Happy Life.*

Mildred Sutton. Young black woman and childhood friend of Rosacoke Mustian; dies in childbirth in Reynolds Price's *A Long and Happy Life.*

Nessie Sutton. Milliner's assistant, mother of an illegitimate daughter by her lover Abner Teeftallow, and wife of A. M. Belshue in T. S. Stribling's *Teeftallow.*

Colonel Sutton-Smith. Retired English colonel who invents the Do Easy method for doing things in William S. Burroughs's *Exterminator!*

Suzie. Indian prostitute under the protection of Comandante Guzmán in Peter Matthiessen's *At Play in the Fields of the Lord.*

Per Svenberg. Expert cinematographer who, though he fails to win an Oscar, becomes famous for his work on Vito Orsini's *Mirrors* in Judith Krantz's *Scruples.*

Emiscah Svenson. Girlfriend of Charley Anderson who gets pregnant by his best friend and convinces Charley to marry her; he arranges an abortion and breaks off their engagement in John Dos Passos's *U.S.A.* trilogy.

Eliza Mellon (Betty Brown) Swain. Giant Neanderthaloid twin sister of Wilbur Swain in Kurt Vonnegut's *Slapstick.*

Henry Swain. Father of Patty and Tom Swain; honest barrister and friend of Richard Carvel in Winston Churchill's *Richard Carvel.*

Letitia Vanderbilt Rockefeller Swain. Wife of Wilbur Swain in Kurt Vonnegut's *Slapstick.*

Patty Swain. Generous and hardworking woman who loves Richard Carvel in Winston Churchill's *Richard Carvel.*

Thomas (Tom) Swain. Wastrel son of Henry Swain and brother of Patty Swain in Winston Churchill's *Richard Carvel.*

Wilbur Rockefeller Daffodil-11 (Bobby Brown) Swain. Giant Neanderthaloid who becomes a doctor and president of the United States; twin brother of Eliza Mellon Swain; narrator of Kurt Vonnegut's *Slapstick.*

Charles (Chick) Swallow. Writer who succeeds his father-in-law as "The Lamplighter" advice columnist in the Decency, Connecticut, *Picayune Blade*; narrator of Peter De Vries's *Comfort Me with Apples.*

Lila Swallow. Younger sister of Chick Swallow and wife of Nickie Sherman in Peter De Vries's *Comfort Me with Apples.*

Effingham Swan. Military judge of the Minute Men who sentences Fowler Greenhill to death; dies when Mary Jessup Greenhill crashes her airplane into his in Sinclair Lewis's *It Can't Happen Here.*

Ella Swan. Servant of the Loftis family and a follower of Daddy Faith in William Styron's *Lie Down in Darkness.*

Jessica Swanlake. Lover of Roger Mexico in Thomas Pynchon's *Gravity's Rainbow.*

Singleton Oglethorpe Swansdown. Plantation owner whose poetry Ned Hazard mocks; arbitrator in Isaac Tracy's litigation with Frank Meriwether over worthless land in John Pendleton Kennedy's *Swallow Barn.*

Carol Severin Swanson. Narrator who, in his mid-life crisis, reminisces about his sexual conquests; retreats to the Huron Mountains of Michigan to renew his spirit and to see a wolf in the daylight in Jim Harrison's *Wolf*.

Mister Swanson. Member of the review board for the post office where Jake Jackson is employed in Richard Wright's *Lawd Today*.

Aurelia Swartout. Wife of Jerry Catlin the Second; murdered by a group of blacks who are irate because of mortgage foreclosures in T. S. Stribling's *Unfinished Cathedral*.

Sam Swartwout. Collector of the Port of New York and longtime friend of Aaron Burr in Gore Vidal's *Burr*.

Romana Swartz. Poet, nudist, and lover of Dave Wain; witnesses Jack Duluoz's alcoholic breakdown during a retreat at Big Sur in Jack Kerouac's *Big Sur*.

Dame Swaschbuckler. Wife of Gottlieb Swaschbuckler in James Kirke Paulding's *Koningsmarke*.

Master Gottlieb Swaschbuckler. Village jailer in James Kirke Paulding's *Koningsmarke*.

Sweeney. Head of the Provos, a terrorist group, in Paul Theroux's *The Family Arsenal*.

Dan Sweeney. Friend of Conor Larkin, gunrunner, and head of the Irish Republican Brotherhood in Leon Uris's *Trinity*.

Berenice Sweet. Older sister of Hard Candy Sweet, student at the University of Georgia, and Miss Rattlesnake of 1975; murdered by Joe Lon Mackey in Harry Crews's *A Feast of Snakes*.

Hard Candy Sweet. Cheerleader at Mystic High School and girlfriend of Willard Miller in Harry Crews's *A Feast of Snakes*.

Robert (Bob, Sweetie) Sweet. High school classmate and later employer of Carl Reinhart; owner of a rejuvenation clinic in Thomas Berger's *Vital Parts*.

Sweetman. See Orin Wilkerson.

Jason (Sweetie) Sweetwater. Son of an Episcopal bishop, union organizer opposing Bogan Murdock and father of Sue Murdock's aborted child in Robert Penn Warren's *At Heaven's Gate*.

Lila Swenson. Sioux woman who befriends Samantha De Vere after De Vere is raped by three men in Gail Godwin's *Violet Clay*.

George Swiebel. Former actor turned contractor in Chicago, best friend of Charlie Citrine, streetwise mingler with many types, and host of the poker party that leads to Citrine's troubles with Rinaldo

Cantabile in Saul Bellow's *Humboldt's Gift*.

Elizabeth Swift. Mother of Kate Swift in Sherwood Anderson's *Winesburg, Ohio*.

Kate Swift. Worldly Winesburg teacher; her attempt to counsel George Willard on his writing career becomes an aborted romantic encounter in Sherwood Anderson's *Winesburg, Ohio*.

Mark Swift. Model supported by his wife's dowry in Henry Miller's *Tropic of Cancer*.

Swift One. Mate of Big-Tooth; ancestor of the narrator in Jack London's *Before Adam*.

Pluto Swint. Obese and perspiring candidate for sheriff; suitor of Darling Jill Walden in Erskine Caldwell's *God's Little Acre*.

Swoop. See Swoop Ferguson.

Sybil. Married white woman who simulates a rape with the narrator in Ralph Ellison's *Invisible Man*.

Colonel Sydenham. Coxcomb British officer in James Kirke Paulding's *The Dutchman's Fireside*.

Sydney Ben. Australian sailor who fights Bembo aboard the *Julia* in Herman Melville's *Omoo*.

Isaac Syfe. Jewish farmer and partner of Augustus M. Barr in Oscar Micheaux's *The Homesteader*.

Granville Sykes. Plantation owner who evicts Berry Lawson for having attended a Republican political meeting, and then, a few months later, sues Lawson for having left the plantation in Albion W. Tourgee's *Bricks without Straw*.

Uncle Jim Sykes. Elderly black man who is accused of idleness by Harry Cresswell when he injures his leg and cannot work; eagerly attends Zora's meetings that promise freedom from such mistreatment in W. E. B. Du Bois's *The Quest of the Silver Fleece*.

Sylvain. Black leader of the attack on the home of de Kersaint I; killed by de Kersaint II in Lafcadio Hearn's *Youma*.

Pierre Sylvain. Owner of a printing establishment and friend of the young Diron Desautels in Arna Wendell Bontemps's *Drums at Dusk*.

Sylvester. Boyfriend of Tania in Henry Miller's *Tropic of Cancer*.

Sylvia. File clerk who leaves her job to go West with her lover Tim and the unnamed narrator; has an affair with the narrator and returns to Valdosta, Georgia, in Jim Harrison's *A Good Day to Die*.

Sylvie. Black servant whose service in the Kendal household spans three generations in Reynolds Price's *The Surface of Earth*.

Robert Syverten. Aspiring director who narrates his experiences as Gloria Beatty's partner in a dance marathon; sentenced to be put to death for killing Beatty in accordance with her wishes in Horace McCoy's *They Shoot Horses, Don't They?*

Istvan Szegedyi. See Ivor Sedge.

T

Tachechana (the Skipping Fawn). Sioux "Indian Princess"; daughter of Le Balafré and wife of Mahtoree; becomes the wife of the Pawnee chief Hard Heart, after he has defeated Mahtoree, in James Fenimore Cooper's *The Prairie*.

Tad. Nephew of 'Gustus Griff; presumably killed when Griff's mill is destroyed in Mary Noailles Murfree's *In the Clouds*.

Tadlock. Self-serving politician and captain of the wagon train in A. B. Guthrie's *The Way West*.

Tadziewski (Tad). Lover of Valerie in Marilyn French's *The Women's Room*.

Tommy Taft. One-legged retired sailor and town character who has a paternal interest in Barton Cathcart in Henry Ward Beecher's *Norwood*.

Dagny (Slug) Taggart. Operations vice-president of Taggart Transcontinental Railroad; heroine of Ayn Rand's *Atlas Shrugged*.

James (Jim) Taggart. President of Taggart Transcontinental Railroad; compromises its control and ownership for political favors in Ayn Rand's *Atlas Shrugged*.

Tahneh. Female Tehkohn tribal leader who befriends Alanna Verrick in Octavia E. Butler's *Survivor*.

Taji. Narrator who pursues Yillah in Herman Melville's *Mardi*.

Dolly Augusta Talbo. Unworldly maiden cousin who helps rear Collin Fenwick, becoming the boy's beloved friend and companion, in Truman Capote's *The Grass Harp*.

Verena Talbo. Efficient, rich sister of Dolly Talbo; unmarried, she supports the household and controls the lives of the people in it in Truman Capote's *The Grass Harp*.

Mariana Talbot. Wife of Mr. Talbot and mother of their four children in Grace King's *The Pleasant Ways of St. Médard*.

Mr. Talbot. Wealthy lawyer with a thriving practice in New Orleans before the Civil War; forced to endure wartime poverty and hardship and to adjust to the loss of his position after the war in Grace King's *The Pleasant Ways of St. Médard*.

Charles (Charlie) Taliaferro. Cousin of Lucinda McGehee, whom he loves; killed at Shiloh in Stark Young's *So Red the Rose*.

Gordon (Shorty) Tall. Lieutenant colonel and battalion commander who relieves James Stein of his command and replaces him with George Band, whom he also removes from that post, in James Jones's *The Thin Red Line*.

Bella Grantham Tallant. Wife of Jimmy Tallant, who married her largely because of his friendship with her father, Bud Grantham, so that her expected child, not Tallant's, would not be branded illegitimate, in Elizabeth Spencer's *The Voice at the Back Door*.

Hugh Tallant. American loyalist who seeks redress in England following the American Revolution; turns to crime and is imprisoned in Australia, but escapes from the penal colony and returns to England, where he is pardoned and marries Sally Munro, with whom he returns to Australia as a free settler; narrator of Charles Nordhoff and James Norman Hall's *Botany Bay*.

Jimmy Tallant. Partner of Bud Grantham and one-time bootlegger; largely through the example of his friend and antagonist Duncan Harper, he undergoes a significant transformation of character in Elizabeth Spencer's *The Voice at the Back Door*.

Sally Munro Tallant. Free Englishwoman who accompanies her father to Australia; falls in love with Hugh Tallant, whom she marries in England, whence they return to Australia as free settlers, in Charles Nordhoff and James Norman Hall's *Botany Bay*.

Ernest Talliaferro. Widower who attends the yacht party in William Faulkner's *Mosquitoes*.

Jean-Lambert Tallien. French revolutionary politician/statesman and opponent of Robespierre in H. L. Davis's *Harp of a Thousand Strings*.

Taloufa. Nigerian former servant to an Englishman; supports the Back-to-Africa movement in Claude McKay's *Banjo*.

Tambur-Ola. Civil War veteran who marries Sörine Olsa in O. E. Rölvaag's *Peder Victorious*; also appears in *Their Father's God*.

Dr. Tamkin. Charlatan psychologist who loses the savings of Tommy Wilhelm in the stock market but who teaches him the difference between the "true soul" and the "pretender soul" and urges him to "Seize the Day" in Saul Bellow's *The Victim*.

Mr. Tamworth. Black-bearded secretary of Baron R.; begins collecting material to write the definitive biography of his employer in Vladimir Nabokov's *Transparent Things*.

Francis Tanaguchi. Japanese-American practical joker; one of ten Los Angeles policemen-protagonists in Joseph Wambaugh's *The Choirboys.*

Tanee (Pomaree-Tanee). Henpecked husband of Queen Pomaree Vahinee in Herman Melville's *Omoo.*

Tanga. African servant of Louis Desrivières; tends to the slave children on Desrivières's plantation while their mothers work in the fields in Lafcadio Hearn's *Youma.*

Tangee. Black hoodlum and friend of Jesus Ortiz in Edward Lewis Wallant's *The Pawnbroker.*

Tania. Supposed girlfriend of Sylvester; tries to convince Henry Miller to live with her in Russia in Henry Miller's *Tropic of Cancer.*

Cornelia Tanner. Nurse who cares for Miranda in Katherine Anne Porter's *Pale Horse, Pale Rider.*

Flight Lieutenant Tanner. Fellow patient with Ben Flesh in a tropical disease ward in a North Dakota hospital; suffers from leukopenia in Stanley Elkin's *The Franchiser.*

Tanya. Teacher who is the girlfriend of Thomas Wilkerson in John Edgar Wideman's *The Lynchers.*

Psyche Tanzer. Young woman given a fatal dose of a drug by Victor Bruge in Theodore Dreiser's *The Bulwark.*

Ta-Phar. Son of Pharaoh, brother of Princess Royal, "uncle" of Moses, and second ruler of Egypt; frees the Hebrews and dies trying to reclaim them in Zora Neale Hurston's *Moses, Man of the Mountain.*

Oliver Tappan. Small-town boy who seeks his fortune in New York and Washington; becomes a congressman and marries a calculating society woman, Madeline Carter, in Hjalmar Hjorth Boyesen's *The Golden Calf.*

Albert Taylor (A. T.) Tappman. Mild-mannered air force chaplain and Anabaptist; befriends Yossarian in Joseph Heller's *Catch-22.*

Tar Baby. Mixed-race recluse who boards at the home of Eva Peace in Toni Morrison's *Sula.*

Tarden. Pseudonym by which the anonymous Ruthenian exile, ex-intelligence agent, and narrator is made known to the reader of Jerzy Kosinski's *Cockpit.*

Tarleton. British colonel who prevents his foraging troops from burning the home of a deceased Patriot colonel's widow; courteously receives Mildred and Henry Lindsay at Cornwallis's camp in John Pendleton Kennedy's *Horse-Shoe Robinson.*

Michael B. Tarleton. Illegitimate half-black son of Andrew Stone; married to Angel Stone, who he does not know is his half sister; murdered while investigating drug-smuggling activities in the company Angel has inherited in M.F. Beal's *Angel Dance.*

William D. Tarleton. Adoptive father of Michael Tarleton in M.F. Beal's *Angel Dance.*

Dane Tarrant. See Dane Tarrant Empson.

Mrs. Tarrant. Daughter of a Boston abolitionist; attempts to promote the speaking career of her daughter Verena Tarrant in Henry James's *The Bostonians.*

Doctor Selah Tarrant. Mesmeric healer who attempts to promote the speaking career of his daughter Verena Tarrant in Henry James's *The Bostonians.*

Verena Tarrant. Naive inspirational speaker who defies Olive Chancellor by going off to marry Basil Ransom in Henry James's *The Bostonians.*

Frederic Tartan. Older brother of Lucy Tartan, whom he tries to protect from Pierre Glendinning III, in Herman Melville's *Pierre.*

Lucy Tartan. Fiancée of Pierre Glendinning III; dies upon learning that Glendinning is married to his half sister Isabel Banford in Herman Melville's *Pierre.*

Taru. Head of the Rumanian Writers' Union in John Updike's *Bech: A Book.*

Francis Marion Tarwater. Fourteen-year-old country boy who goes to the city after the death of his great-uncle to learn whether what he has been taught is accurate; tries unsuccessfully to evade his calling as a prophet, but ends up baptizing his idiot cousin, Bishop Rayber, even as he drowns him in Flannery O'Connor's *The Violent Bear It Away.*

Mason Tarwater. Backwoods preacher and great-uncle of Francis Marion Tarwater, upon whom he lays the calling to be a prophet like himself and the instruction to baptize the idiot Bishop Rayber; his death motivates young Tarwater's visit to the city in Flannery O'Connor's *The Violent Bear It Away.*

Francis Tasbrough. Owner of a granite quarry; becomes the Minute Men District Commissioner in Sinclair Lewis's *It Can't Happen Here.*

Vasily Tashikov. Soviet ambassador to the United States; exhibits an open contempt for American leaders and the American political system in Allen

Drury's *Advise and Consent*.

Tashtego (Tash). American Indian who is Stubb's harpooner in Herman Melville's *Moby-Dick*.

Brian Tate. Professor of political science, husband of Erica Tate, father of Muffy and Jeffo Tate, and lover of Wendy Gahaghan in Alison Lurie's *The War Between the Tates*.

Erica Parker Tate. Wife of Brian Tate, mother of Muffy and Jeffo Tate, and the object of Sanford Finkelstein's devotion in Alison Lurie's *The War Between the Tates*.

Grace Brock Caldwell Tate. Beautiful, selfish daughter of the oldest, most respectable family in Fort Penn; lives on a Caldwell family farm with her husband Sidney Tate in John O'Hara's *A Rage to Live*.

Sheriff Heck Tate. Sheriff of Maycomb County, Alabama, who decides to proclaim that Bob Ewell "fell on his knife" rather than expose Boo Radley, Ewell's assailant, to the generosity of the townspeople in Harper Lee's *To Kill a Mockingbird*.

Jeffrey (Jeffo) Tate. Teenaged son of Erica and Brian Tate in Alison Lurie's *The War Between the Tates*.

Matilda (Muffy) Tate. Teenaged daughter of Erica and Brian Tate in Alison Lurie's *The War Between the Tates*.

Norah (Nory) Tate. Poor Farm inmate who marries James Conboy, the superintendent's son, in Jessamyn West's *The Witch Diggers*.

Rosa (Aunt Piggie, Rosy) Tate (Tait). Unmarried sister of Sarah Tate Bedford; lives at Portobello and helps instruct the Bedford children; dies of heart disease in Stark Young's *So Red the Rose*.

Sidney Tate. Yale-educated New Yorker who becomes a gentleman farmer after marrying the imperious Grace Brock Caldwell; establishes himself in the Fort Penn society in John O'Hara's *A Rage to Live*.

Tateh (Baron Ashkenazy). Husband of Mameh and father of The Little Girl; moviemaker who marries Mother in E. L. Doctorow's *Ragtime*.

Phillip Tattaglia. Sicilian gangster and head of the Tattaglia family, rivals of the Corleones, in Mario Puzo's *The Godfather*.

Tavi. Brother of Fakahau, husband of Marunga, and father of Mako and Hitia; storekeeper who survives the hurricane in Charles Nordhoff and James Norman Hall's *The Hurricane*.

Taweeda. Old Niaruna Indian woman in Kori's band and love object of Tukanu in Peter Matthiessen's *At Play in the Fields of the Lord*.

Tawney. Old black aboard the *Neversink* who tells White-Jacket tales of the War of 1812 in Herman Melville's *White-Jacket*.

Angela Taylor. Girlfriend of Willie Hall in John Edgar Wideman's *The Lynchers*.

Cletus (Old Man Taylor) Taylor. Abusive father of Molly Taylor, father-in-law of Eddie White, and grandfather of Jimmy and Joe White; dies from having drunk lye in Larry McMurtry's *Leaving Cheyenne*.

Danny Taylor. Childhood friend of Ethan Allen Hawley and town drunk who drinks himself to death after signing over the rights to his land to Hawley for $1,000, with which he was presumably to enter a rehabilitation center, in John Steinbeck's *The Winter of Our Discontent*.

Douglas Taylor. Idealistic reform mayor of Gainesboro; assassinated by white supremacist Hank Dean after leading a group of black children into a public school in Julian Mayfield's *The Grand Parade*.

Franklin Pierce Taylor. Wealthy natural father of Paul Hammer in John Cheever's *Bullet Park*.

George Taylor. Advertising agency boss of John Wilder; wealthy, handsome, married, and a compulsive womanizer in Richard Yates's *Disturbing the Peace*.

John Taylor. Brother of Mary Taylor and confidential clerk for Grey and Easterly, Brokers; his interest in the cotton-belt leads him to encourage his sister to teach in the South, where he meets and marries Helen Cresswell, in W. E. B. Du Bois's *The Quest of the Silver Fleece*.

Mary Taylor. Sister of John Taylor and wife of Harry Cresswell; teacher at Miss Sarah Smith's school, where she never feels comfortable with the dark-skinned children and indistinct personalities of her colleagues; because she desires glory, she marries the cold and selfish Cresswell, who almost destroys her, in W. E. B. Du Bois's *The Quest of the Silver Fleece*.

Molly Taylor. See Molly Taylor White.

Owen Taylor. Mountaineer and mine owner who offers Rose Dutcher a life in the West, which she refuses, in Hamlin Garland's *Rose of Dutcher's Coolly*.

Sonny Taylor. Sixteen-year-old neighbor of Francie Coffin and member of the Ebony Earls gang; provides the alibi which is instrumental in Junior Coffin's release from jail in Louise Meriwether's *Daddy Was a Number Runner.*

Weldon Taylor. Student working to save money for dental school; first lover of Emma Lou Morgan in Wallace Thurman's *The Blacker the Berry.*

Vaslav Tchitcherine. Soviet intelligence officer, lover of Geli Tripping, and half brother of Oberst Enzian, whom Vaslav is determined to find and kill, in Thomas Pynchon's *Gravity's Rainbow.*

Tea Cake. See Vergible Woods.

Teacher. See Bruce Thomas.

Zephi Teal. First officer on river barges in James Kirke Paulding's *Westward Ho!*

Teal Eye. Daughter of a Piegan chief and lover of Boone Caudill in A. B. Guthrie's *The Big Sky.*

The Technician. Dispeptic operator of sound and image control devices and consumer of bicarbonate of soda in William S. Burroughs's *Naked Lunch, Nova Express,* and *Exterminator!*

Clovis Techy. Older woman Waldo has an affair with and murders in Paul Theroux's *Waldo.*

Ted. Blond teenaged driver of the soft-drink truck; backs into and breaks down part of the stone wall in John Updike's *The Poorhouse Fair.*

Ted. Colleague of Thomas Eborn; writes a sensitive poem on the death of Eborn's mother in Reynolds Price's *Love and Work.*

Ted. Seventy-year-old Provincial soldier with Braddock's army; nurses his aching feet, warns Doggo Cutwright not to kill the visiting Catawbas, and is captured, tortured, and killed by the Shawnees in Mary Lee Settle's *O Beulah Land.*

Teddy. Drug addict and boyfriend of Terry Wilson in Donald Goines's *Dopefiend.*

Teddy (Teddybear). Owner and bartender of the Snag saloon in Ken Kesey's *Sometimes a Great Notion.*

Abner (Ab) Teeftallow. Ignorant and naive orphan; railroad construction worker, lover of Nessie Sutton and Adelaide Jones, and inheritor of large land claims from his grandfather in T. S. Stribling's *Teeftallow.*

Tom Teerswell. Longtime escort of Caroline Wynn, until she meets Blessed Alwyn; plots with Sam Stillings to win her back but loses her forever when she marries Stillings in W. E. B. Du Bois's *The Quest of the Silver Fleece.*

Teets. Black man who has slept with his sister in Paul Theroux's *Picture Palace.*

Teganisoris. Iroquois Indian chief whose tribe captures John Law and Sir Arthur Pembroke in Emerson Hough's *The Mississippi Bubble.*

Tehani. Tahitian of royal birth who marries Roger Byam, by whom she has a daughter; dies shortly after Byam leaves Tahiti in chains in Charles Nordhoff and James Norman Hall's *Mutiny on the Bounty.*

Tekla. Peasant chambermaid for Aaron Greidinger; her earthy sensuality not only lures him into bed but also proves to him, he says, the existence of God in Isaac Bashevis Singer's *Shosha.*

Telemachus. Elderly slave who tells Peregrine Lacey Catlett when Johnny Catlett breaks the rules by going to the salt furnace; son of Jonathan Lacey and Lyddy in Mary Lee Settle's *Know Nothing.*

Telemachus. Son of Odysseus; visits Menelaos to learn what happened to Odysseus, only to be besotted by Helen, in John Erskine's *The Private Life of Helen of Troy.*

John Telfer. Small town idler who befriends young Sam McPherson in Sherwood Anderson's *Windy McPherson's Son.*

Darcy Tell. Daughter of Mary Tell and common-law stepdaughter of Jeremy Pauling in Anne Tyler's *Celestial Navigation.*

Mary Tell. Common-law wife of Jeremy Pauling; mother of Darcy Tell and five children by Pauling; narrates part of Anne Tyler's *Celestial Navigation.*

Juan (Spanish Johnny) Tellamantez. Mexican laborer and musician; friend of Thea Kronborg in Willa Cather's *The Song of the Lark.*

Charlotte Temple. Young British woman seduced by Jack Montraville; taken from her family to the United States, where Montraville abandons her and she dies shortly after giving birth to their child in Susanna Rowson's *Charlotte.*

Elizabeth (Bess) Temple. Daughter of Judge Marmaduke Temple; twice rescued by Natty Bumppo; marries Oliver Effingham in James Fenimore Cooper's *The Pioneers.*

Henry Temple. Husband of Lucy Eldridge Temple and father of Charlotte Temple; travels from England to the United States in hopes of rescuing Charlotte, but instead witnesses her death hours after his arrival in Susanna Rowson's *Charlotte.*

Lucy Eldridge Temple. Doting mother of Charlotte Temple; despite the grief she suffers at Charlotte's death, she and her husband rear their motherless grandchild in Susanna Rowson's *Charlotte*.

Marmaduke Temple. Leading citizen of Templeton and father of Elizabeth Temple; grants to Oliver Effingham the land Effingham claims in James Fenimore Cooper's *The Pioneers*.

Nicholas (Nick) Temple. Adventurous and irresponsible friend of David Ritchie; marries Antoinette de St. Gré in Winston Churchill's *The Crossing*.

Rex Temple. Aging Pulitzer Prize-winning novelist who has not produced a novel in twenty years; heavy drinker and friend of Scarecrow in Calvin Hernton's *Scarecrow*.

Sarah (Mrs. Clive, Sally) Temple. Mother of Nicholas Temple; becomes repentant after taking a lover in Winston Churchill's *The Crossing*.

Colonel (Old Rocky) Templeton. Marine officer who orders an unnecessary thirty-six-mile march for a group of out-of-shape reserve soldiers in William Styron's *The Long March*.

Francie Templeton. Wife of Joe Templeton in Joan Didion's *Run River*.

Joe Templeton. Father of Lily Knight McClellan's aborted baby; schemes for land that was once in the McClellan family in Joan Didion's *Run River*.

Jake Tench. Heavy drinking handyman who marries Mistress Bartram, although he knows that she is pregnant by another man, in Conrad Richter's *The Fields*; also appears in *The Trees* and *The Town*.

Rosa Tench. Illegitimate daughter of Mistress Bartram and Portius Wheeler in Conrad Richter's *The Fields*; loves her half brother Chancey Wheeler, but when the community censures this relationship, she commits suicide in *The Town*.

One-Eye Tenczara. Unforgiving police captain who arrests Bruno Lefty Bicek for murder in Nelson Algren's *Never Come Morning*.

Eve Tennant. Aristocratic daughter of the British port collector; liked by Johnny Fraser in James Boyd's *Drums*.

Joyce Tennant. Girlfriend of Felix Fay and secretary to her uncle in Floyd Dell's *Moon-Calf*.

Tennie. See Tennie Beauchamp.

Tennie's Jim. See James Thucydides Beauchamp.

Archer Tennyson. Husband of Persis Tennyson; commits suicide under highly suspect circumstances in Thornton Wilder's *Theophilus North*.

Persis Tennyson. Granddaughter of Dr. James Bosworth and widow of Archer Tennyson; becomes friends with Theophilus North, who clears her husband's name, in Thornton Wilder's *Theophilus North*.

Herman (Mr. T.) Teppis. Producer at Supreme Pictures in Norman Mailer's *The Deer Park*.

Ter. Son of Susie Schnitzer's godfather; cousin whom Susie harbors in her room after he robs a bank and is wounded in Harriette Simpson Arnow's *The Weedkiller's Daughter*.

Terangi Matokia. Son of Mama Rua, husband of Marama, and father of Tita; leads people from Manukura to a nearby island to begin a new life; pardoned by the governor for an earlier altercation as a result of his valiant deeds during the hurricane in Charles Nordhoff and James Norman Hall's *The Hurricane*.

Teray. Brother of Coransee and son of Rayal and Jansee who challenges his brother for the Pattern in Octavia E. Butler's *Patternmaster*.

Ellen Terhune. Avant-garde composer and mistress of the Vallombrosa estate in Edmund Wilson's *Memoirs of Hecate County*.

Kermit Terkel. Agent who tries to find Martha Mills a job in Hollywood in Jerome Weidman's *What's in It for Me?*

Miss Terkle. Caseworker for "Rock-a-Bye" adoption agency in Peter De Vries's *The Tunnel of Love*.

Fats Terminal. Drug dealer who is a server of the Black Meat and knows the Algebra of Need in William S. Burroughs's *Naked Lunch*; mentioned in *Nova Express*.

Mamere Terrebonne. Oldest resident and spiritual mother of Isle aux Chiens, setting for Shirley Ann Grau's *The Hard Blue Sky*.

Terri. Student who serves on the Cinema Committee with Hill Gallagher during the student rebellion in James Jones's *The Merry Month of May*.

Alma Caldwell Terrio. Sister of George Caldwell and aunt of Peter Caldwell; lives in Troy, New York, in John Updike's *The Centaur*.

Terry. Grandson of Leah; idolizes Augie in Arna Wendell Bontemps's *God Sends Sunday*.

Terry. Young, married migrant woman with whom Sal Paradise becomes infatuated in Jack Kerouac's *On the Road.*

William Denis Terwilliger, Jr. See Billy Twillig. f lTessa. Adventurer who owns a gold mine in Ghost Town and uses the gold dust to gamble in Anaïs Nin's *Collages.*

Tessio. Gangster who betrays the Corleone family in Mario Puzo's *The Godfather.*

Mark Tesslar. Polish Jewish doctor who testifies against Adam Kelno in Leon Uris's *QB VII.*

Gerald (Gerry) Tetley. Sickly, vacillating son of Major Willard Tetley; forced by his father to participate in the hanging of Donald Martin; commits suicide by hanging himself in his father's barn in Walter Van Tilburg Clark's *The Ox-Bow Incident.*

Major Willard Tetley. Former Confederate cavalry officer who leads the lynch mob; throws himself on his sword after learning of the suicide of his son Gerald Tetley in Walter Van Tilburg Clark's *The Ox-Bow Incident.*

Agnes Andresen (Little Aggie) Tewksbury. First wife of Jed Tewksbury; dies, diseased, in a Chicago hospital in Robert Penn Warren's *A Place to Come To.*

Buck Tewksbury. Father of Jed Tewksbury and husband of Elvira K. Tewksbury; killed when his mule-drawn wagon runs over him in a freak accident in Robert Penn Warren's *A Place to Come To.*

Elvira K. Tewksbury. See Elvira K. Tewksbury Simms.

Jediah (Jed, Old Broke-Nose) Tewksbury. Native of Dugton, Claxford County, Alabama, who tries to escape his past only to return to it after receiving a Ph.D. from the University of Chicago, becoming an internationally known Dante scholar, and being absorbed into the society life in Nashville; narrator of Robert Penn Warren's *A Place to Come To.*

Mrs. Thacher. Kindly widowed mother of Adeline Thacher Prince and grandmother of Nan Prince; cares for Nan in Sarah Orne Jewett's *A Country Doctor.*

Max "Whisper" Thaler. The criminal boss in charge of gambling in Personville in Dashiell Hammett's *Red Harvest.*

Anna Agati (Utch, Utchka) Thalhammer. Wife of the unnamed narrator and mother of Bart and Jack; has an affair with Severin Winter when she and her husband and the Winters swap mates in John Irving's *The 158-Pound Marriage.*

Beata Thangbee. Spiritualist who interprets dreams and picks numbers for gamblers; pointed out to Ideal as an example of an "evil thing" in Carlene Hatcher Polite's *The Flagellants.*

Flora Thangue. Gentle Englishwoman prevented from marriage by familial duty in Gertrude Atherton's *Ancestors.*

Min (Minnie) Tharrington. Lover of Rob Mayfield before, during, and after his marriage to Rachel Hutchins in Reynolds Price's *The Surface of Earth.*

Ed Thatcher. Accountant, father of actress Ellen Thatcher in John Dos Passos's *Manhattan Transfer.*

Ellen Thatcher (Elaine, Elena). Successful actress and journalist who is frustrated in her quest for true art in John Dos Passos's *Manhattan Transfer.*

Dr. Joe Thatcher. Physician and first mentor of Rose Dutcher in Hamlin Garland's *Rose of Dutcher's Coolly.*

Judge Thatcher. Father of Becky Thatcher in Samuel Langhorne Clemens's *The Adventures of Tom Sawyer* and *Adventures of Huckleberry Finn.*

Rebecca (Becky, Bessie) Thatcher. Daughter of Judge Thatcher and girlfriend of Tom Sawyer in Samuel Langhorne Clemens's *The Adventures of Tom Sawyer* and *Adventures of Huckleberry Finn.*

Susie Thatcher. Wife of Ed Thatcher and mother of Ellen Thatcher, whose birth is the opening scene of John Dos Passos's *Manhattan Transfer.*

Harry K. Thaw. Profligate son of a millionaire and husband of Evelyn Nesbit; shoots Stanford White, his wife's lover; judged insane and sentenced to the State Hospital in E. L. Doctorow's *Ragtime.*

Pierre Thaxter. Friend of Charlie Citrine and fellow editor on *The Ark,* a proposed prestigious journal for intellectuals; mismanages funds and is kidnapped in Argentina in Saul Bellow's *Humboldt's Gift.*

Landry Thayer. Colorado ranch hand who falls in love with Mildred Osborne; saves her life during a cattle stampede and later proves himself a Victorian gentleman in Paul Laurence Dunbar's *The Love of Landry.*

Margaret Thayer. Helpful librarian at Waindell College and wife of Roy Thayer; suggests to Timofey Pnin that he board at the home of Laurence G. Clements in Vladimir Nabokov's *Pnin.*

Roy Thayer. Member of the English department at Waindell College, hypochondriac, expert in eighteenth-century poetry, and husband of Margaret Thayer, with whom he attends a party given by Timofey Pnin, in Vladimir Nabokov's *Pnin*.

Mildred (Milly) Theale. Wealthy American dying of an unnamed disease and in love with Merton Densher; discovering Densher's desire to marry her in order to inherit her wealth destroys her will to live in Henry James's *The Wings of the Dove*.

Theodora. Lebanese intelligence agent who gives Tarden the coded documents that lead to his enlistment with "the Service" in Jerzy Kosinski's *Cockpit*.

Theodora (Theo). Spoiled, carefree telepath who forms a bond with Eleanor Vance at Hill House which the house determines to break in Shirley Jackson's *The Haunting of Hill House*.

Theodore (Thedo). Bartender at Happy's Café in Gayl Jones's *Corregidora*.

Mrs. Therwald. Wife of a high Ku Klux Klansman; hints to her husband the importance of supporting Matthew Towns's release from prison in W. E. B. Du Bois's *Dark Princess*.

Theseus. Greek hero and foster father who protects and advises Helen in H. D.'s *Helen in Egypt*.

Thetis. Greek goddess and mother of Achilles; speaks to Helen in H. D.'s *Helen in Egypt*.

Théodore. Orphan reared by Lafitte in Joseph Holt Ingraham's *Lafitte*.

Anne-Joseph Théroigne. Daughter of a small landholder in the village of Jean-Labert Tallien; political agitator in the French Revolution in H. L. Davis's *Harp of a Thousand Strings*.

Clara Thicknesse. Quasi-mistress of Chick Swallow in Peter De Vries's *Comfort Me with Apples*.

Thiele. Arrogant, authoritarian captain of the German NM *Vera* in Katherine Anne Porter's *Ship of Fools*.

Amos-Otis Thigpen. Son of Pourty Bloodworth; brother of Regal Pettibone, LaDonna Scales, and Noah Grandberry; half brother of Jonathan Bass in Leon Forrest's *The Bloodworth Orphans*.

Thomas. Butler at Sunnyside; dies when he believes he sees Paul Armstrong's ghost in Mary Roberts Rinehart's *The Circular Staircase*.

Thomas. Cabin boy aboard the *Aroostook* and steward of Lydia Blood in William Dean Howells's *The Lady of the Aroostook*.

Thomas. Motherless son and possible murderer of The Dead Father in Donald Barthelme's *The Dead Father*.

Bigger Thomas. Twenty-year-old black man convicted and sentenced to death for the murder of Mary Dalton; murders his girlfriend, Bessie Mears, in Richard Wright's *Native Son*.

Bruce (Teacher) Thomas. Peer of Raymond Douglas noted for his wit and talent in providing information in Herbert Simmons's *Man Walking on Eggshells*.

Buddy Thomas. Younger brother of Bigger Thomas in Richard Wright's *Native Son*.

Ed Thomas. Friend who, on his deathbed, helps convince James Page that life is good if one submits to its seasons and cycles and that, in the end, nothing is irrelevant in John Gardner's *October Light*.

Esther Thomas. Alienated, low-level employee of Glymmer, Read who is unaffected by the firm's bankruptcy in Nathan Asch's *The Office*.

Jack (Jackie) Thomas. Son of Robin Thomas and halfbrother of Morissa Kirk, who sends him to the safety of his father, in Mari Sandoz's *Miss Morissa*.

Joe Thomas. Thirty-nine-year-old postal worker pushed from a sixth floor hotel window by Cross Damon in Richard Wright's *The Outsider*.

Mack Thomas. Former pimp, fighter, and gambler; performs in the Hippodrome and is a favorite "stud horse" of the customers in Cyrus Colter's *The Hippodrome*.

Marilla Thomas. Housekeeper to Dr. John Leslie; famous for her strange bonnets; crusty but kind to Nan Prince in Sarah Orne Jewett's *A Country Doctor*.

Mrs. Thomas. Mother of Bigger Thomas in Richard Wright's *Native Son*.

Mutt Philmore Thomas. Husband of Ursa Corregidora; throws the pregnant Ursa down a flight of stairs, causing her to undergo a hysterectomy, in Gayl Jones's *Corregidora*.

Robin Thomas. Father of Jack Thomas and stepfather of Morissa Kirk, whom he urges not to homestead, in Mari Sandoz's *Miss Morissa*.

Sister M. Thomas. See Jennie Denton.

Vera Thomas. Younger sister of Bigger Thomas in Richard Wright's *Native Son*.

William (Will) Thomas. Eccentric pianist and music instructor who becomes the lover of Emily Turner in Alison Lurie's *Love and Friendship*.

Florabel Thompkins. Ultrafeminine twin of Idabel Thompkins, her opposite in all things, in Truman Capote's *Other Voices, Other Rooms*.

Idabel Thompkins. Tomboy who longs to be male; alternately Joel Knox's friend and nemesis; twin sister of Florabel Thompkins in Truman Capote's *Other Voices, Other Rooms*.

Thompson (Doctor). Well-paid, religious, black cook aboard the *Highlander* in Herman Melville's *Redburn*.

Arthur and Herbert Thompson. Sons of Ellie and Royal Earle Thompson in Katherine Anne Porter's *Noon Wine*.

Bo Thompson. Obnoxious friend of Clyde Stout; works at Pete's gas station with Clyde in Jack Matthews's *Hanger Stout, Awake!*

Caesar Thompson (Wharton). Faithful black servant to the Whartons in James Fenimore Cooper's *The Spy*.

Ellen Bridges (Ellie) Thompson. Fragile, ailing wife of Royal Earle Thompson in Katherine Anne Porter's *Noon Wine*.

Ferris P. Thompson. Son of the richest farmer in Rock County, Indiana; marries Catherine Conboy in Jessamyn West's *The Witch Diggers*.

Henry T. Thompson. Father of Myra Thompson, father-in-law of George Babbitt, and partner in the Babbitt-Thompson Realty Company in Sinclair Lewis's *Babbitt*.

Colonel Marcus Thompson. Ku Klux Klansman who seeks the support of Negro voters in a race for sheriff of Rockford County; attacked in newspapers and handbills as the man responsible for murdering John Walters and for stealing two thousand dollars from Walters's body in Albion W. Tourgee's *A Fool's Errand*.

Miss Thompson. Neighborhood hairdresser and good friend of Selina Boyce in Paule Marshall's *Brown Girl, Brownstones*.

Rosamond Walden Thompson. Daughter of Ty Ty Walden and wife of Will Thompson in Erskine Caldwell's *God's Little Acre*.

Royal Earle Thompson. South Texas dairy farmer who kills Homer Hatch; although acquitted of the murder, he commits suicide in Katherine Anne Porter's *Noon Wine*.

Tommy Thompson. Chief of the American Embassy in Warsaw who helps direct American money and weapons to the Warsaw ghetto fighters; friend of Gabriela Rak in Leon Uris's *Mila 18*.

Will Thompson. Promiscuous weaver and strike leader who is killed by the company police in Erskine Caldwell's *God's Little Acre*.

Wilhelmina Thoms. Longtime and loyal secretary at the Coaltown mines who makes Breckenridge Lansing appear to be more effective at his job than he is by doing the work herself in Thornton Wilder's *The Eighth Day*.

Hannah Thomson. Eighteen year old bound into servitude upon her father's death; falls in love with Ralph Hartsook, whom she ultimately marries, in Edward Eggleston's *The Hoosier School-Master*.

Mrs. Thomson. Blind and widowed English-born mother of Hannah and Shocky Thomson; sent to the poorhouse upon the death of her husband in Edward Eggleston's *The Hoosier School-Master*.

W. J. (Shocky) Thomson. Orphan living with the family of John Pearson; "most faithful and affectionate child in the school" in Edward Eggleston's *The Hoosier School-Master*.

Margaretta Thorn. White author of a testament to the veracity of Harriet E. Wilson's *Our Nig*.

Billy Thorne. Firebrand leftist writer and husband of Diana Day in Gore Vidal's *Washington, D.C.*

Eleanor Thorne. Head nurse at the Hauptman Clinic in Terry Southern's *Flash and Filigree*.

Freddy Thorne. Dentist and husband of Georgene Thorne; arranges an abortion for Foxy Whitman in John Updike's *Couples*.

Georgene Thorne. Wife of Freddy Thorne and lover of Piet Hanema in John Updike's *Couples*.

Derrick Thornton. Midwesterner who goes to college in the East and works as a magazine editor in New York City in Helen Hooven Santmyer's *Herbs and Apples*.

Dr. Dick Thornton. Physician in a small midwestern town who influences his daughter, Derrick Thornton, by permitting her to read any book in the house in Helen Hooven Santmyer's *Herbs and Apples*.

Frederick (Fritz) Thornton. Wealthy New York uncle of Lex Porter and genial father-figure to Alfred Eaton in John O'Hara's *From the Terrace*.

John Thornton. Gold prospector whose life Buck twice saves, but who is eventually killed by Indians in Jack London's *The Call of the Wild*.

Reneltje (Nell) Thornton. Wife of Dick Thornton and mother of Derrick Thornton; rears a large family and then has no time for an artistic career in Helen Hooven Santmyer's *Herbs and Apples*.

Cornelia (Mrs. Nonna Cornell) Thornwell. Spirited sixty-year-old widow of the former governor of Massachusetts who, after her husband's death, abandons her blue-blooded life-style and becomes a laborer; through her friendship with Bartolomeo Vanzetti she becomes a supporter, for a brief time, of oppressed workers; attempts to save Vanzetti from execution in Upton Sinclair's *Boston*.

Thorpe. British pilot in William Faulkner's *A Fable*.

Mary Thorpe-Wharton. Wealthy American traveling with her mother and boyfriend in Egypt; friend of Helen Fairwood in H. D.'s *Palimpsest*.

Three Little Prigs. Harvard alumni hired onto the English faculty at Polycarp College; objects of harrassment by Tom Waltz in Peter De Vries's *Let Me Count the Ways*.

Sandor Thrilling. Director at Olympia Studios in Ludwig Bemelmans's *Dirty Eddie*.

Mary Throckmorton. Cousin of Bess Ralegh and a guest at Sir Walter Ralegh's last dinner in George Garrett's *Death of the Fox*.

Sir Thicknesse Throgmorton. Pompous British officer in James Kirke Paulding's *The Dutchman's Fireside*.

Winifred (Winnie) Throop. Aunt and chaperone of Cynthia Pomeroy; confidante of Arnold Soby in Wright Morris's *What a Way to Go*.

Thucydides. Son of Roscius and Phoebe; marries Eunice before she gives birth to Tomasina in William Faulkner's *Go Down, Moses*.

Floyd Thursby. Thug enticed by Brigid O'Shaughnessy to protect her during her search for the jewel-encrusted statuette; she initially hires Spade & Archer as part of a scheme to rid herself of him in Dashiell Hammett's *The Maltese Falcon*.

Mrs. Andrew Thwaites. Mean-spirited widow who donates to the Order of St. Clement the sanitarium that becomes the St. Clement's Hill Retreat House; mother of Sally Thwaites Hopwood in J. F. Powers's *Morte D'Urban*.

Mortimer Thynne. London society thief who is imprisoned in Australia; becomes a bureaucrat in the new government, which leads to his refusal to join his friends in their escape from the penal colony, in Charles Nordhoff and James Norman Hall's *Botany Bay*.

Ticey. See Miss Jane Pittman.

George Tichnor. Copyreader for the *Kansas City Times* and friend of Homer Zigler in Clyde Brion Davis's *"The Great American Novel—."*

Mason Tidewater. Light-skinned black who pitched for the Brooklyn Royal Dodgers and is a janitor in a charity rummage shop; author of his baseball memoir in Jay Neugeboren's *Sam's Legacy*.

Tien. Daughter of Alanna Verrick and Diut in Octavia E. Butler's *Survivor*.

Michael (Smiling Mike) Tiernan. Saloon owner and first ward boss in Theodore Dreiser's *The Titan*.

Tierney. Homicide detective and lover of Betty Bayson; capriciously murdered in Thomas Berger's *Killing Time*.

Tig. Personal slave of Johnny Catlett and husband of Toey; sold to Crawford Kregg, runs away, and is killed by a slave-hunter when Toey bears Johnny's child in Mary Lee Settle's *Know Nothing*.

Kathleen Tigler. See Kathleen Fleisher.

Gustave Nicholas (Nick) Tilbeck. Former lover of Allegra Vand and father of her only child in Cynthia Ozick's *Trust*.

Miss Tilbeck. Daughter of Nick Tilbeck and Allegra Vand; unravels the secrets of her origin and eventually meets her biological father; narrator of Cynthia Ozick's *Trust*.

Arnaud (Pansette) du Tilh. Lover of Bertrande de Rols and father, by her, of two children, while pretending to be her husband, Martin Guerre, in Janet Lewis's *The Wife of Martin Guerre*.

Till. Mother of Nancy and slave of Sapphira Dodderidge Colbert in Willa Cather's *Sapphira and the Slave Girl*.

Sue Annie Tiller. Old midwife and most opinionated, free-thinking adult in Little Smokey Creek, Kentucky; neighbor of Nunn Ballew in Harriette Arnow's *Hunter's Horn*; mentioned in *The Dollmaker*.

Elijah Tilley. Retired fisherman who takes the narrator to Elijah's house, which is a shrine to Tilley's dead wife, in Sarah Orne Jewett's *The Country of the*

Pointed Firs.

Aunt Tillie. Relative whom Henry Miller dislikes because she is ugly, smells of sweat, and has a dirty scalp in Henry Miller's *Tropic of Capricorn.*

Tim (Timmy). Vietnam War veteran who is killed when he, his lover Sylvia, and the unnamed narrator blow up an earthen dam in Jim Harrison's *A Good Day to Die.*

Blanche Lebanon Timberlane. See Blanche Lebanon Timberlane Boneyard.

Cass Timberlane. Judge of Grand Republic in Sinclair Lewis's *Kingsblood Royal*; becomes disillusioned with his wife Jinny Marshland Timberlane and loses her to Bradd Criley in *Cass Timberlane.*

Virginia Marshland (Jinny) Timberlane. Second wife of Cass Timberlane and lover of Bradd Criley in Sinclair Lewis's *Cass Timberlane*; also appears in *Kingsblood Royal.*

Jay Timlow. Secessionist who taunts Hesden Le Moyne about being a "Unioner," responds to Le Moyne's challenge by enlisting with him in the Confederate army, and becomes Le Moyne's friend and the cause of his losing his arm and horse in Albion W. Tourgee's *Bricks without Straw.*

Timmy. Mulatto half brother of Tee Bob Samson; banished by Robert Samson, his white father, in Ernest J. Gaines's *The Autobiography of Miss Jane Pittman.*

Tinch (Stench). Stuttering, foul-breathed English teacher at Steering School; freezes to death in John Irving's *The World According to Garp.*

Ora Lee Tingle. Prostitute and police groupie in Joseph Wambaugh's *The Choirboys.*

Solomon Tinkle. Owner of the *Nancy Harkins* and friend of Daniel Harrow in Walter D. Edmonds's *Rome Haul.*

Robert Tinkler. Midshipman aboard the HMS *Bounty* who saves Roger Byam from being hanged in Charles Nordhoff and James Norman Hall's *Mutiny on the Bounty*; provides comic relief among those cast adrift in *Men against the Sea.*

Tinor. Mother of Kory-Kory in Herman Melville's *Typee.*

Tiny. Chief guard in cellblock F and organizer of the great cat massacre in John Cheever's *Falconer.*

Benjamin (Ben) Tipton. Husband of Minna Tipton and father of Tom Tipton; helps expose Minna as the false Lady Fauntleroy in Frances Hodgson Burnett's *Little Lord Fauntleroy.*

Dick Tipton. New York bootblack who is the brother of Ben Tipton and a friend of Cedric Errol in Frances Hodgson Burnett's *Little Lord Fauntleroy.*

Minna (Lady Fauntleroy) Tipton. Wife of Ben Tipton; claims to be Lady Fauntleroy in Frances Hodgson Burnett's *Little Lord Fauntleroy.*

Colonel Tishnar. Former member of the British Intelligence Service whom Renate meets at Paradise Inn in Anaïs Nin's *Collages.*

Tita. Daughter of Terangi and Marama; survives the hurricane in Charles Nordhoff and James Norman Hall's *The Hurricane.*

James (Buck) Titus. Horse breeder and cynical friend of Doremus Jessup; prints anti-government leaflets for the New Underground and is sent to a concentration camp in Sinclair Lewis's *It Can't Happen Here.*

Tjerck. Old black servant of the Vancours in James Kirke Paulding's *The Dutchman's Fireside.*

Toad. See Paduk.

Joan Toast. London whore transformed by Ebenezer Cooke into a goddess of love in John Barth's *The Sot-Weed Factor.* See Susan Warren.

Cordula Tobak. See Countess Cordula de Prey.

Toby. Companion of Tommo in Herman Melville's *Typee.*

Toby. Friend of Pacifica; wants to help restore the Hotel de las Palmas and become rich; his plans collapse when he discovers that Flora Quill, its proprietor, has very little money in Jane Bowles's *Two Serious Ladies.*

Mike Todarescu. Director of the little theater at People's Liberal Church; marries Molly Calico in Peter De Vries's *The Mackerel Plaza.*

Almira Blackett (Almiry) Todd. Widowed landlady of the narrator; her engaging personality and skill with home remedies make her an ideal connection with people the narrator wishes to meet in Sarah Orne Jewett's *The Country of the Pointed Firs.*

Benton Todd. Son of Captain Todd; killed during the Bardsville raid on tobacco buyers' warehouses in Robert Penn Warren's *Night Rider.*

Captain Todd. Member of the board of directors of the Association of Growers of Dark Fired Tobacco, but a non-supporter of its violent secret branch, the Free Farmers' Brotherhood of Protection and

Control, in Robert Penn Warren's *Night Rider*.

Joanna Todd. Cousin of Almira Todd's late husband; lives and dies on the deserted Shell-Heap Island in Sarah Orne Jewett's *The Country of the Pointed Firs*.

Toey. Daughter of Peregrine Lacey Catlett and Minna, personal slave of Melinda Lacey Kregg, wife of Tig, and mother of Johnny Catlett's mulatto son in Mary Lee Settle's *Know Nothing*.

Bruce Tollifer. Hired diversion for the bored Aileen Cowperwood in Theodore Dreiser's *The Stoic*.

Abigail Howland Mason Tolliver. Granddaughter of William Howland; becomes the final keeper of the Howland land and fortune; principal narrator of Shirley Ann Grau's *The Keepers of the House*.

Senator Edmund Tolliver. Member of the board of directors of the Association of Growers of Dark Fired Tobacco; resigns when the organization becomes violent in Robert Penn Warren's *Night Rider*.

Ellen (Lilli Barr) Tolliver. Talented pianist whom Lily Shane helps leave a small town; becomes a star as Lilli Barr in Louis Bromfield's *The Green Bay Tree*.

John Tolliver. Husband of Abigail Mason Tolliver; lawyer and politician who loses his bid for governor when his wife's grandfather's marriage to a black woman is revealed in Shirley Ann Grau's *The Keepers of the House*.

Mr. Tolliver. Poor white farmer opposed to the aristocratic Cresswells; willing to sell his land to Sarah Smith in order to spite them in W. E. B. Du Bois's *The Quest of the Silver Fleece*.

Tom. Attacker who joins Jeff and Luke in attempting to castrate Will Harris in Junius Edwards's *If We Must Die*.

Tom. Native African who is a slave at Glen-Eberley; Captain Porgy's loyal cook in William Gilmore Simms's *Woodcraft*.

Tom. Paid companion of Harry in Jerzy Kosinski's *Cockpit*.

Uncle Tom. Longtime faithful slave to the Shelby family; sold to the St. Clares and then to Simon Legree, who tortures him to death for maintaining his Christian principles, in Harriet Beecher Stowe's *Uncle Tom's Cabin*.

Tom the Tinker. Chief of the Whiskey Rebels reduced to exhibiting his old kettles at the village fair, where Captain John Farrago encounters him, in Hugh Henry Brackenridge's *Modern Chivalry*.

Tomasina (Tomey). Daughter of Carothers McCaslin and Eunice and mother of Tomey's Turl Beauchamp in William Faulkner's *Go Down, Moses*.

Tomasino. Fisherman who leads the villagers of Adano to resume fishing; his support heightens the respect earned by Major Joppolo in John Hersey's *A Bell for Adano*.

Salvatore (Sally) Tomato. Convict in Sing Sing prison whom Holly Golightly visits every Thursday for a fee in Truman Capote's *Breakfast at Tiffany's*.

Geneva Tomblin. Dance-marathon contestant who is introduced, with the fiancé she met during the contest, to the audience after her elimination in Horace McCoy's *They Shoot Horses, Don't They?*

Tomek. Ruthenian child whom Tarden taunts during an airplane flight in Jerzy Kosinski's *Cockpit*.

Mama (Mama T.) Tomek. Aging, bitter prostitute and heroin addict who operates Bonifacy Konstantine's brothel in Nelson Algren's *Never Come Morning*.

Claas Tomeson. White captive tortured and killed by Indians in James Kirke Paulding's *Koningsmarke*.

Tomey. See Tomasina.

Tomey's Turl. See Tomey's Turl Beauchamp.

Tommo. Narrator who lives with the Typees and escapes from them in Herman Melville's *Typee*.

Tommy. Bootlegger murdered by Popeye in William Faulkner's *Sanctuary*.

Tomtit (Thomas). Comic grandson of Milly, whom he accompanies to freedom, in Harriet Beecher Stowe's *Dred*.

Tongue. Overseer of Swallow Barn in John Pendleton Kennedy's *Swallow Barn*.

Reverend Tonkle. Tabernacle evangelist who "converts" Greta Wanderhope in Peter De Vries's *The Blood of the Lamb*.

Tonoi. Chief of the fishermen on Martair in Herman Melville's *Omoo*.

Kjersti Tönseten. Wife of Syvert Tönseten in O. E. Rölvaag's *Giants in the Earth*, *Peder Victorious*, and *Their Father's God*.

Syvert Tönseten. Leader of the local and then the state Norwegian community in O. E. Rölvaag's *Giants in the Earth*, *Peder Victorious*, and *Their Father's God*.

Tony. Imaginary friend of Daniel Torrance; reveals to Torrance the dangers of the Overlook Hotel in

Stephen King's *The Shining*.

Too-wit. Chief of the savage tribe on the island of Tsalal who leads the massacre of the crew of the *Jane Guy* in Edgar Allan Poe's *The Narrative of Arthur Gordon Pym*.

Ellsworth Monkton (Elsie, Monk) Toohey. Pseudo-humanitarian journalist and villain in Ayn Rand's *The Fountainhead*.

Horne Tooke. One of three Englishmen, sympathetic to the American cause, who send Israel Potter as courier to Benjamin Franklin in Herman Melville's *Israel Potter*.

Rev. Wesley R. Toomis. Methodist bishop who persuades Elmer Gantry to become the minister of a small church in Sinclair Lewis's *Elmer Gantry*.

Hamilton (Ham) Tooting. Embittered party worker in Winston Churchill's *Mr. Crewe's Career*.

Dawn Melody Topp. See Dawn Melody Batelle.

Sheila Anne (Topper) Topp. Ex-convict and lesbian friend of Carole Batelle; raises Dawn Batelle as her own daughter until Carole takes the child away in M. F. Beal's *Amazon One*.

Julius Shaw Toppan. Anarchist friend of Jasper Ammen; suggests to Ammen the idea of following strangers in Conrad Aiken's *King Coffin*.

Topper. See Sheila Anne Topp.

Harriet Toppingham. Fashion editor of *Fashion and Interiors* who hires Spider Elliott as a fashion photographer, but fires him when he discovers that she is a lesbian, in Judith Krantz's *Scruples*.

Topsy (Tops). Young slave bought from the slave warehouse and given to Ophelia St. Clare to test her educational ideas in Harriet Beecher Stowe's *Uncle Tom's Cabin*.

Abeba Williams Lavoisier (African Flower, Piano Girl) Torch. Wife of Daniel Torch and mother of nine sons and six daughters; dies of cancer when the youngest are still small in Ellease Southerland's *Let the Lion Eat Straw*.

Askia-Touré Torch. Second oldest son of Abeba and Daniel Torch in Ellease Southerland's *Let the Lion Eat Straw*.

Daniel A. (Reverend Brother) Torch. Husband of Abeba Torch and father of their fifteen children; struggles with bouts of madness in Ellease Southerland's *Let the Lion Eat Straw*.

Daniel-Jr. Torch. Oldest son of Abeba and Daniel Torch in Ellease Southerland's *Let the Lion Eat Straw*.

Kora Torch. Oldest daughter of Abeba and Daniel Torch in Ellease Southerland's *Let the Lion Eat Straw*.

Daniel (Danny) Torrance. Five-year-old son of John and Winnifred Torrance; has the ability to shine (to be sensitive to supernatural phenomena), and communicates psychically with Dick Hallorann in Stephen King's *The Shining*.

John Daniel (Jack) Torrance. Husband of Winnifred Torrance and father of Daniel Torrance; former alcoholic who accepts a job as winter caretaker at the Overlook Hotel; under the influence of ghosts, he tries to murder his wife and son in Stephen King's *The Shining*.

Winnifred (Wendy) Torrance. Wife of John Torrance and mother of Daniel Torrance in Stephen King's *The Shining*.

Croce (Richey Torrey) Torre. Mafia member who runs Regents Sportsmen's Club, Inc., with The Greek Almas and Miller Schabb; plans gambling junkets to Mafia establishments; killed when he attempts to eliminate The Greek Almas in George V. Higgins's *The Digger's Game*.

Leon Tortshiner. Survivor of concentration camps in Poland and Russia and husband of Masha Bloch Tortshiner; refuses to divorce her until she becomes pregnant with Herman Broder's child in Isaac Bashevis Singer's *Enemies, A Love Story*.

Masha Bloch Tortshiner. Polish concentration camp survivor, wife of Leon Tortshiner, mistress and, after her divorce from Tortshiner, third wife of Herman Broder; commits suicide after the death of her mother and Broder's desertion in Isaac Bashevis Singer's *Enemies, A Love Story*.

John Big Bluff (Priest of the Sun) Tosamah. American Indian spiritual leader living in Los Angeles in N. Scott Momaday's *House Made of Dawn*.

Marty Tothero. Former high school basketball coach of Rabbit Angstrom; introduces Rabbit to Ruth Leonard; suffers a stroke in John Updike's *Rabbit, Run*.

Israbestis Tott. Senile historian and town ancient whose fragmented recollections of the main events of the novel open William Gass's *Omensetter's Luck*.

Daniel Tracy Touchett. American banker and long-time resident of England; Isabel Archer's uncle in

Henry James's *The Portrait of a Lady*.

Lydia Touchett. Deliberate, eccentric wife of Daniel Tracy Touchett and mother of Ralph Touchett; invites her cousin, Isabel Archer, to Europe in Henry James's *The Portrait of a Lady*.

Ralph Touchett. Clever, charming invalid who is emotionally supportive of his cousin Isabel Archer in Henry James's *The Portrait of a Lady*.

Toussaint. Dreamy-eyed middle-aged coachman at Bréda and one of the few literate slaves; joins the revolt in Arna Wendell Bontemps's *Drums at Dusk*.

Marie Tovesky. See Marie Tovesky Shabata.

Ann Potter Towne. See Ann Potter.

Langdon Towne. Member of Rogers' Rangers and admirer of Major Robert Rogers; successful painter of American Indians; narrator of Kenneth Roberts's *Northwest Passage*.

Matthew (George, Mat) Towns. Black American who becomes disillusioned with democracy when he experiences the horrors of racism as a porter and a prisoner; allows himself to be used politically by Sammy Scott and Sara Andrews, his first wife, in W. E. B. Du Bois's *Dark Princess*.

Sara Andrews Towns. Self-made and independent stenographer employed by Sammy Scott; first wife of Matthew Towns; organizes the Chicago Colored Woman's Council, a powerful political force, in W. E. B. Du Bois's *Dark Princess*.

Arthur Townsend. Stockbroker married to Marian Almond; cousin of Morris Townsend in Henry James's *Washington Square*.

Edith (Edy) Townsend. College roommate of and later resident of the same New York apartment with Derrick Thornton in Helen Hooven Santmyer's *Herbs and Apples*.

Marian Almond Townsend. See Marian Almond.

Mary (Towney) Townsend. Writer of "Ye Towne Gossyp," a society column; friend of Miranda in Katherine Anne Porter's *Pale Horse, Pale Rider*.

Morris Townsend. Handsome, mercenary suitor of Catherine Sloper, whom he jilts when her father resolves to disinherit her if she marries Morris, in Henry James's *Washington Square*.

Rosanna Townsend. Mistress of a brothel at 41 Thomas Street in New York City in Gore Vidal's *Burr*.

Albert R. (Bert) Tozer. Modern businessman and brother of Leora Tozer in Sinclair Lewis's *Arrowsmith*.

Mr. and Mrs. Andrew Jackson Tozer. Parents of Bert and Leora Tozer; they persuade Martin Arrowsmith to live with them while he is establishing his medical practice in Sinclair Lewis's *Arrowsmith*.

Leora Tozer. First wife of Martin Arrowsmith; supports her husband in his career and dies of the bubonic plague in Sinclair Lewis's *Arrowsmith*.

T. P. See T. P. Gibson.

Albert Tracy. Friend of Harry Morgan killed by Roberto; a narrator of Ernest Hemingway's *To Have and Have Not*.

Bel Tracy. Daughter of Isaac Tracy and fiancée of Ned Hazard; infatuated with medieval falconry in John Pendleton Kennedy's *Swallow Barn*.

Catharine Tracy. Educated daughter of Isaac Tracy in John Pendleton Kennedy's *Swallow Barn*.

Isaac Tracy. Revolutionary War veteran and widowered father of Bel, Catharine, and Ralph Tracy; obsessed with a lawsuit against Frank Meriwether for a worthless piece of swampland that separates their estates; distressed at the resolution of the litigation in his favor in John Pendleton Kennedy's *Swallow Barn*.

Ralph Tracy. Coarse son and heir of Isaac Tracy in John Pendleton Kennedy's *Swallow Barn*.

Viola (Vee) Tracy. Star of such movies as *The Virgin Vamp*; loves Bunny Ross, but does not accept his political activities, in Upton Sinclair's *Oil!*

Traddle. Illiterate weaver elected to the Pennsylvania assembly when Teague Oregan declines the honor in Hugh Henry Brackenridge's *Modern Chivalry*.

Tralala. Adolescent initiated without feeling into sexual activity at age fifteen; undergoes rapid moral disintegration and becomes a figure of scorn on the part of her associates—"johns," fellow thieves, and prostitutes—in Hubert Selby, Jr.'s *Last Exit to Brooklyn*.

Trampas. Foe and shootout victim of the Virginian in Owen Wister's *The Virginian*.

Kutunda Traoré. Last lover of Colonel Ellelloû; formerly an itinerant beggar, she uses her position as concubine to become Ellelloû's adviser, then betrays him to become the consort of his successor and a governmental minister in her own right in

John Updike's *The Coup*.

Berwyn Phillips (Red) Traphagen. Crusty intellectual catcher for the New York Mammoths; later becomes a professor at San Francisco State College in Mark Harris's *The Southpaw, Bang the Drum Slowly, A Ticket for a Seamstitch,* and *It Looked Like For Ever.*

Adam Trask. California settler whose wife, Cathy Ames Trask, shoots and deserts him, leaving him to rear the twins, Caleb and Aron; later devastated financially when his lettuce shipment is ruined by a failure in his experimental refrigeration system; dies in John Steinbeck's *East of Eden.*

Aron (Aaron) Trask. Quiet and earnest twin brother of Caleb Trask; plans to become a minister, but when Caleb reveals to him that their mother, supposed to be dead, is living in Salinas, where she operates a successful brothel, he is devastated and runs off to join the army in John Steinbeck's *East of Eden.*

Caleb (Cal) Trask. Twin brother of Aron Trask; discovers the existence of his mother, the madam Kate Ames Trask, believed by the boys to be long dead, and uses this knowledge to destroy his brother, whom he believes their father Adam prefers to Caleb, in John Steinbeck's *East of Eden.*

Cathy Ames (Catherine Amesbury, Kate) Trask. Beautiful but cruel and deceitful woman who marries Adam Trask and who is the mother of Caleb and Aron Trask, whom she abandons soon after their birth; becomes madam of a successful Salinas brothel in John Steinbeck's *East of Eden.*

Charles Trask. Half brother of Adam Trask; seduced by Cathy Ames on the night of her marriage to Adam and is the true father of one or both of her twins, Caleb and Aron, in John Steinbeck's *East of Eden.*

Father Trask. Priest who leads a wake for Chalmers Egstrom in William Goyen's *In a Farther Country.*

Mark (Markie) Trattman. Compulsive womanizer who runs an illegal card game for the mob; robs his own card game but is killed by Jackie Cogan for a robbery committed by Frankie and Russell in George V. Higgins's *Cogan's Trade.*

Emory Travis. Middle-aged homosexual friend of Sebastian Michael and Tony Lewis; unsuccessfully propositions Johnny Rio in John Rechy's *Numbers.*

Joseph Travis. Wheelwright, small farmer, and last owner of Nat Turner; killed in the slave insurrection of August 21, 1831, in William Styron's *The Confessions of Nat Turner.*

Rutherford (Rusty) Trawler. Much-married millionaire; Holly Golightly considers marrying him, but her rival, Mag Wildwood, captures him in Truman Capote's *Breakfast at Tiffany's.*

Belinda Bolingbroke Treadwell. Wife of Cyrus Treadwell, whose stinginess forces her to sell her family silver, in Ellen Glasgow's *Virginia.*

Cyrus Treadwell. Wealthy tobacco manufacturer, leader of the New South, and father of Susan Treadwell in Ellen Glasgow's *Virginia.*

Dewey Treadwell. Los Angeles police lieutenant and sycophantic underling of Hector Moss in Joseph Wambaugh's *The Choirboys.*

Henry (Harry) Treadwell. Spoiled, brilliant second child of Virginia Pendleton and Oliver Treadwell in Ellen Glasgow's *Virginia.*

Laura Treadwell. Aristocratic fiancée of Col. Henry French; rejects French because of his liberal racial attitudes in Charles W. Chesnutt's *The Colonel's Dream.*

Mary Treadwell. American divorcée who attempts to remain disengaged from the lives of the ship's passengers in Katherine Anne Porter's *Ship of Fools.*

Oliver Treadwell. Energetic, idealistic, and egocentric playwright; cousin of Susan Treadwell and unfaithful husband of Virginia Pendleton in Ellen Glasgow's *Virginia.*

Susan Treadwell. Independent, assertive, and sensible friend and foil of Virginia Pendleton in Ellen Glasgow's *Virginia.*

Virginia Pendleton Treadwell. See Virginia Pendleton.

Miss Lucille (Little Sister Lucille) Treasure. Old woman proud of her virginity and contemptuous of her fallen sister in Alice Walker's *Meridian.*

Miss Margaret Treasure. Septuagenarian spinster; convinced she is pregnant following her first sexual experience in Alice Walker's *Meridian.*

Clay Tredgold. President of Steel Windmill Company and friend of Martin Arrowsmith in Sinclair Lewis's *Arrowsmith.*

Felix (Mrs. Hugo Gross) Treevly. Patient who is killed by his dermatologist, Frederick Eichner, in Terry Southern's *Flash and Filigree.*

John (Ezekiel Hook) Treeworgy. British sympathizer who sabotages Benedict Arnold's army in Kenneth

Roberts's *Arundel*.

Silas Trefethen. Rivermouth grocer who buys old cannons in Thomas Bailey Aldrich's *The Story of a Bad Boy*.

Cass Trehune. Wealthy woman Joe Buck hopes will be his first New York client in James Leo Herlihy's *Midnight Cowboy*.

Tremlow. Wireless operator of the USS *Starfish*; leads a mutiny and physically assaults Skipper in John Hawkes's *Second Skin*.

Harriet Tremont. Aunt and surrogate mother of Patience Sparhawk in Gertrude Atherton's *Patience Sparhawk and Her Times*.

Charles Augustus (Gus) Trenor. Wealthy investor to whom Lily Bart becomes financially indebted in Edith Wharton's *The House of Mirth*.

Judy Trenor. Wealthy friend of Lily Bart; ends the friendship when she discovers that her husband, Gus Trenor, has given Bart a great deal of money in Edith Wharton's *The House of Mirth*.

Agnes Johnson Trent. College classmate of Jane Ward, successful writer and playwright, and wife of Jimmy Trent in Margaret Ayer Barnes's *Years of Grace*.

Anne Elizabeth Trent (Daughter). Kind-hearted volunteer for the Near East Relief who has an affair with Richard Ellsworth Savage and becomes pregnant; in a final act of despair, she takes up with a French flier and is killed in a plane crash after she encourages him to daring maneuvers in John Dos Passos's *U.S.A.* trilogy.

Edgar Trent. President of Huddleston & Bradford, a banking firm whose gold Edward Pierce steals in Michael Crichton's *The Great Train Robbery*.

Elizabeth Trent. Daughter of Edgar Trent; romanced by Edward Pierce, who wishes to gain information from her, in Michael Crichton's *The Great Train Robbery*.

James (Jimmy) Trent. Composer and music critic; husband of Agnes Johnson Trent, but in love with Jane Ward, who rejects him; dies in World War I in Margaret Ayer Barnes's *Years of Grace*.

Joe Trent. College student who makes sexual advances toward Ellen Chesser in Elizabeth Madox Roberts's *The Time of Man*.

Harris (Bunk) Trevelyan. Tobacco farmer who joins the Free Farmers' Brotherhood of Protection and Control and is subsequently killed by members of the brotherhood in Robert Penn Warren's *Night Rider*.

Andrés Treviño. Owner of goats and friend of Pepe Gonzales, Bob Webster, and Porfirio; his wedding provides a funny scene in Josefina Niggli's *Mexican Village*.

Carlo Treviso. Famous music teacher who encourages and defends Veda Pierce's snobbery and alienation from her mother in James M. Cain's *Mildred Pierce*.

Agnes Trevor. Friend of Mary Ogden; engages in social work rather than express her passion in Gertrude Atherton's *Black Oxen*.

Marquise de Trézac (Nettie Wincher). Young woman at a Virginia resort envied by Undine Spragg because of her higher social class; later provides Undine with advice about French society in Edith Wharton's *The Custom of the Country*.

Annabelle Puckett (Mrs. Duncan) Trice. Adulteress whose affair with Cass Mastern results in her husband's suicide in Robert Penn Warren's *All the King's Men*.

Caroline (Carolina) Trid. Wife of Chad Hanna and, as Carolina, lady high rider in Walter D. Edmonds's *Chad Hanna*.

Janet and Peter Trimble. Married friends of Arthur Ketcham in John Clellon Holmes's *Go*.

Moses Tripp. Man who is stabbed by Eva Medina Canada when he makes sexual advances toward her in Gayl Jones's *Eva's Man*.

Bobby Trippe. Popular but weak-willed suburbanite who is sodomized by vicious mountain men in James Dickey's *Deliverance*.

Geli Tripping. Young German witch; lover of Vaslav Tchitcherine and Tyrone Slothrop in Thomas Pynchon's *Gravity's Rainbow*.

Father Trissotin. Priest who counsels Hippolyte in Susan Sontag's *The Benefactor*.

Tristessa. Mexican-Indian morphine addict idealized by the narrator of Jack Kerouac's *Tristessa*; mentioned in *Desolation Angels*.

Tristram. Lover of La Belle Isold and husband of Isold of the White Hands in Thomas Berger's *Arthur Rex*.

Tom Tristram. American in Paris and friend of Christopher Newman in Henry James's *The American*.

Mrs. Tom Tristram. Wife of Tom Tristram; introduces Christopher Newman to Claire de Cintré in Henry James's *The American*.

Vaso Trivanovich. Olympic wrestler who becomes a Chetnik freedom fighter and flees Tito's Yugoslavia to live in Vienna; teaches Severin Winter to wrestle in John Irving's *The 158-Pound Marriage*.

Florrie Trotman. Friend who sympathizes with Silla Boyce's desire to own property in Paule Marshall's *Brown Girl, Brownstones*.

Carrie Trout. Mother, by her half brother William Body, of Abraham Dolphin in Leon Forrest's *The Bloodworth Orphans*.

Kilgore Trout. Prolific science fiction writer in Kurt Vonnegut's *God Bless You, Mr. Rosewater* and *Breakfast of Champions*; mentioned in *Slaughterhouse-Five* and the pseudonym of Dr. Robert Fender in *Jailbird*.

Leo Trout. Ornithologist on Bermuda and father of Kilgore Trout in Kurt Vonnegut's *Breakfast of Champions*.

Trout Fishing in America. Embodiment and voice of the American spirit; occasionally appears in human form and at other times as an activity, a hotel, a slogan, or a costume; writes letters to Pard and an "ardent admirer"; friend of the narrator of Richard Brautigan's *Trout Fishing in America*.

Trout Fishing in America Shorty. Legless, middle-aged wino and occasional resident of San Francisco; the narrator imagines shipping him to Nelson Algren in a large crate in Richard Brautigan's *Trout Fishing in America*.

Elux Troxl. Agent for a Honduran cartel attempting to hire Billy Twillig to help manipulate the money curve in Don DeLillo's *Ratner's Star*.

Christine Truax. Teenaged daughter of Valerie; her rape motivates Valerie's militant feminism in Marilyn French's *The Women's Room*.

Captain Truck. Captain of the *Typhoon*, which takes Tom Bailey from New Orleans to Boston in Thomas Bailey Aldrich's *The Story of a Bad Boy*.

Harriet Truckenmiller. Wife of Kenny Truckenmiller; owns and operates Nanette's Beauty Salon in John Irving's *The World According to Garp*.

Kenny Truckenmiller. Husband of Harriet Truckenmiller; wife- and child-beater who assassinates Jenny Fields in John Irving's *The World According to Garp*.

Trudchen. German teenager who sleeps with Carlo Reinhart in Thomas Berger's *Crazy in Berlin*.

Jim Trueblood. Black sharecropper who shocks Norton with the story of how Trueblood made his own daughter pregnant in Ralph Ellison's *Invisible Man*.

John Truman. President of and transfer agent for the Black Rapids Coal Company in Herman Melville's *The Confidence-Man*.

Colm Trumper. Son of Fred Trumper and Sue Kunft Trumper in John Irving's *The Water-Method Man*.

Fred (Boggle, Bogus, Thump-Thump) Trumper. Graduate student at the University of Iowa who translates *Akthelt and Gunnel*; husband of Sue Kunft Trumper and father of Colm Trumper; after being divorced, marries Tulpen; tries the water-method cure for his urinary tract infection; narrator of parts of John Irving's *The Water-Method Man*.

Sue Kunft Trumper. See Sue Kunft Trumper Bennett.

Louise Trunnion. Young woman with whom George Willard has his first sexual experience in Sherwood Anderson's *Winesburg, Ohio*.

Angela Whittling Trust. Aged owner of the Tri-City Tycoons; lover of many baseball greats, including Luke Gofannon, and tempter of Roland Agni in Philip Roth's *The Great American Novel*.

George Tryon. Best friend of John Walden; falls in love with Rowena Walden but rejects her when he learns she is black in Charles W. Chesnutt's *The House Behind the Cedars*.

Dr. A. DeWitt Tubbs. Director of the McGurk Institute of Biology in Sinclair Lewis's *Arrowsmith*.

Euphus Tubbs. Jailer in William Faulkner's *Intruder in the Dust*, *Requiem for a Nun*, and *The Mansion*.

Dan Tucker. Cincinnati lawyer and long-time friend of Alexander Main in *The Bailbondsman*, a novella in Stanley Elkin's *Searches and Seizures*.

Emma (Mama) Tucker. Wife of Tyree Tucker and mother of Fish Tucker; tries to keep Fish in school and away from his father's illegal business establishments in Richard Wright's *The Long Dream*.

Rex (Fish, Fishbelly, Fishy-O) Tucker. Young man growing up in Clintonville, Mississippi; drops out of school to work for his father, is accused of raping a white woman, and spends three years in jail without being convicted; leaves Mississippi for France after his release in Richard Wright's *The*

Long Dream.

Tyree (Papa) Tucker. Husband of Emma Tucker and father of Fish Tucker; owns a funeral home and illegal business establishments; murdered by Gerald Cantley, who believes Tucker to possess incriminating cancelled bribery checks, in Richard Wright's *The Long Dream.*

Edward (King Edward VI, Prince of Wales) Tudor. English prince who exchanges places with the impoverished Tom Canty and discovers the injustices of the English class system; vows to rule with compassion when he becomes king in Samuel Langhorne Clemens's *The Prince and the Pauper.*

Harry Tugman. Supervisor of newspaper carriers and first boss of Eugene Gant in Thomas Wolfe's *Look Homeward, Angel.*

Tukanu (Farter). Niaruna Indian warrior with a talent for exuberant farting in Peter Matthiessen's *At Play in the Fields of the Lord.*

Cora and Vernon Tull. Married couple in William Faulkner's *As I Lay Dying, The Hamlet, The Town,* and *The Mansion*; Vernon Tull is a farmer in Faulkner's *Sanctuary.*

Tulpen. English-born film editor who eventually marries Fred Trumper in John Irving's *The Water-Method Man.*

Margaret Mary Bernadette (Peggy) Tumulty. Faithful secretary and ultimately lover of Russel Wren in Thomas Berger's *Who Is Teddy Villanova?*

Tunner. Lover of Katherine Moresby and friend of Porter Moresby in Paul Bowles's *The Sheltering Sky.*

Second Lieutenant Amanda Turck. WAC officer at Ocanara Army Air Base; intelligent and introspective divorcée who has a sexual encounter with Captain Nathaniel Hicks in James Gould Cozzens's *Guard of Honor.*

Turfmould. Sexton and undertaker who buries Norwood's leading citizens in Henry Ward Beecher's *Norwood.*

Cordelia (Cordie) Turnbull. Embittered, twice-married daughter of Francis Prescott; carries on an affair with her father's former student, Charley Strong, in Louis Auchincloss's *The Rector of Justin.*

Frank Turnbull. Repentant womanizer, parishioner of Andrew Mackerel, and instigator of the Mackerel Plaza project in Peter De Vries's *The Mackerel Plaza.*

Steven (Steve, Stevie) Turnbull. Seventeen-year-old son of Frank Turnbull; author of *Some Notes Toward an Examination of Possible Elements of Homosexuality in Mutt and Jeff* in Peter De Vries's *The Mackerel Plaza.*

Turner. Black wide receiver on a college football team; takes boxing lessons from Phil Sorenson; roommate of I.R. Demby in Frederick Busch's *Rounds.*

Clay (Bad Man) Turner. Sadistic killer who devastates the first Hard Times by killing people, raping prostitutes, and burning the town; wounded by Blue and killed by Jimmy Fee in E. L. Doctorow's *Welcome to Hard Times.*

Ellen Turner. Younger sister of Marie Turner; worker at the Past Bay Manufacturing Company factory who falls in love with Johnny Hagen in Robert Cantwell's *The Land of Plenty.*

Emily Stockwell (Emmy) Turner. Wife of Holman Turner and lover of Will Thomas in Alison Lurie's *Love and Friendship.*

George Albert Turner. High school teacher of Vridar Hunter; makes Hunter realize that masturbation does not lead to insanity and helps Hunter attain intellectual growth and honesty in Vardis Fisher's *In Tragic Life*; also appears in *Orphans in Gethsemene.*

Holman Turner. English instructor at Convers College and husband of Emily Turner in Alison Lurie's *Love and Friendship.*

Hyacinth Turner. New Orleans spiritualist who attempts to get Clotilda Pilgrim to face the past in Cyrus Colter's *The Rivers of Eros.*

Lou-Ann Turner. House slave and mother of Nat Turner; dies when her son is fifteen in William Styron's *The Confessions of Nat Turner.*

Marie Turner. Elder sister of Ellen Turner; worker at the Past Bay Manufacturing Company factory who becomes ill following an abortion; briefly kidnapped by Walt Connor in Robert Cantwell's *The Land of Plenty.*

Nathaniel (Nat) Turner. Literate slave and preacher who leads an insurrection of other slaves against their Virginia owners on August 21, 1831; hanged in William Styron's *The Confessions of Nat Turner.*

Penny Turner. See Penny Turner Stone.

Samuel Turner. Owner of Turner's Mills who teaches Nat Turner carpentry and promises him his freedom, but then sells him to pay the mill's debts in

William Styron's *The Confessions of Nat Turner*.

Jacob Turnesa. Peddler who gives Daniel Harrow a ride into Rome in Walter D. Edmonds's *Rome Haul*; also appears in *The Big Barn*.

Lucius Mamilius Turrinus. Devoted friend and correspondent of Caesar; severely maimed in war; lives in self-imposed exile on Capri in Thornton Wilder's *The Ides of March*.

Arimithy (Grandma) Tussie. Wife of Press Tussie and mother of Kim and Mott Tussie in Jesse Stuart's *Taps for Private Tussie*.

Ben Tussie. Nephew of Press Tussie; moves in with the parvenu Tussies but reports them to the relief board in Jesse Stuart's *Taps for Private Tussie*.

George Tussie. Brother of Press Tussie; fiddle-playing wanderer who marries Vittie Tussie in Jesse Stuart's *Taps for Private Tussie*.

Kim Tussie. Son of Press and Arimithy Tussie; army private supposedly killed in the war who returns to reclaim his wife in Jesse Stuart's *Taps for Private Tussie*.

Mott Tussie. Son of Press and Arimithy Tussie and brother of Kim Tussie; falsely identifies a corpse as Kim's in order to court Kim's wife, Vittie Tussie, in Jesse Stuart's *Taps for Private Tussie*.

Press (Grandpa) Tussie. Father of Kim and Mott Tussie and patriarch of the shiftless Tussie clan; exploits the relief program through political power in Jesse Stuart's *Taps for Private Tussie*.

Sid Tussie. Orphan and observer of the Tussie clan who learns that he is not a Tussie but is rather the illegitimate son of a wealthy mine owner and Vittie Tussie; narrator of Jesse Stuart's *Taps for Private Tussie*.

Vittie Tussie. Wife of Kim Tussie and mother of Sid Tussie; inherits ten thousand dollars at Kim's supposed death and marries George Tussie before Kim returns in Jesse Stuart's *Taps for Private Tussie*.

L. Clark Tuttle. Pesky young American interviewer who writes an article for the London *Observer* titled "Bech's Best Not Good Enough" in John Updike's *Bech: A Book*.

Noah Tuttle. Senior law partner who has long juggled trust funds to conceal a $200,000 embezzlement he committed to save investors in a bankrupt trolley line in James Gould Cozzens's *By Love Possessed*.

Twelvemough. Writer of romantic fiction who defends America against Homos's criticisms in William Dean Howells's *A Traveler from Altruria*.

Billy (William Denis Terwilliger, Jr.) Twillig. Young mathematical genius and first winner of the Nobel Prize for mathematics; recruited for Field Experiment Number One, an attempt to decode mysterious signals from outer space, in Don DeLillo's *Ratner's Star*.

Kitty Twist. Vagabond who briefly spends time with Dove Linkhorn in Nelson Algren's *A Walk on the Wild Side*.

Tyke. Pet cat mourned by Jack Duluoz in Jack Kerouac's *Big Sur*.

Rick Tyler. Fugitive whose escape, after he has been apprehended, is thought to have been arranged by Hiram Kelsey in Mary Noailles Murfree's *The Prophet of the Great Smoky Mountains*.

Mollie Tyndale. Wife of Burt Parr, until the marriage is annulled, in Mari Sandoz's *Capital City*.

Typee (Paul). Narrator of Herman Melville's *Omoo*.

Tyrone. Saxophonist and lover of Marie Canada; has sex with the young Eva Medina Canada in Gayl Jones's *Eva's Man*.

Tyrrel. See Captain St. Jermyn.

Hattie Tyson. Mistress of John Buddy Pearson before she uses voodoo to become his second wife in Zora Neale Hurston's *Jonah's Gourd Vine*.

U

Madame Fanny Uccelli. American expatriate and friend of Evalina Bowen in William Dean Howells's *Indian Summer*.

Florence Udney. See Florence Udney Parish.

Ugly One. One of the wives of Boronai in Peter Matthiessen's *At Play in the Fields of the Lord*.

The Ugly Spirit. See Mr. Bradly Mr. Martin.

Uhia. King of Ohonoo who desires to be king of Mardi in Herman Melville's *Mardi*.

Stuart Ullman. Employee of the Overlook Hotel who interviews John Torrance for the position of winter caretaker in Stephen King's *The Shining*.

Delly Ulver. Servant of the Glendinnings who is seduced by Ned and who accompanies Pierre Glendinning and Isabel Banford to the city in Herman Melville's *Pierre*.

Walter Ulver. Father of Delly Ulver; Isabel Banford stays with his family in Herman Melville's *Pierre*.

Uncas (le Cerf Agile). Son of Chingachgook; killed trying to rescue his beloved Cora Munro, leaving his father as the last of their tribe, in James Fenimore Cooper's *The Last of the Mohicans*.

Larry Underwood. Rock star in love with Nadine Cross; second lead in Stephen King's *The Stand*.

Mary Underwood. Teacher who befriends young Sam McPherson in Sherwood Anderson's *Windy McPherson's Son*.

Unferth. Brother-killer and Scylding hero who seeks an honorable death from Grendel but is refused in John Gardner's *Grendel*.

Unk. See Malachi Constant.

Annabel Upchurch. Disillusioned daughter of Bella Upchurch; marries Gamaliel Bland Honeywell in order to get money for her mother in Ellen Glasgow's *The Romantic Comedians*.

Bella Upchurch. Widow whose pragmatism leads her to marry her daughter, Annabel, to Gamaliel Bland Honeywell in Ellen Glasgow's *The Romantic Comedians*.

Dr. Updike. Neighbor of the Fincastles who frequently intervenes to help them in Ellen Glasgow's *Vein of Iron*.

Bard Tom Upshur. Husband of Margaret Upshur and father of Percy Upshur; once owned Tangierneck in Sarah E. Wright's *This Child's Gonna Live*.

Bardetta Tometta Upshur. Daughter of Mariah Upshur and Dr. Albert Grene in Sarah E. Wright's *This Child's Gonna Live*.

Bertha Ann (Mamma Bertha) Upshur. Sister of Aunt Cora Lou, wife of Percy Upshur, and mother of Jacob, Levi, Thomas, and Emerson Upshur in Sarah E. Wright's *This Child's Gonna Live*.

Emerson Upshur. Son of Bertha Ann and Percy Upshur; singer in Sarah E. Wright's *This Child's Gonna Live*.

Gesus (Little Gee, Gezee) Upshur. Youngest son of Mariah and Jacob Upshur in Sarah E. Wright's *This Child's Gonna Live*.

Horace (Rabbit) Upshur. Middle son of Mariah and Jacob Upshur in Sarah E. Wright's *This Child's Gonna Live*.

Jacob (Sparrow) Upshur. Husband of Mariah Upshur and father of William, Horace, and Gesus Upshur; singer in Sarah E. Wright's *This Child's Gonna Live*.

Levi (Lark) Upshur. Son of Bertha Ann and Percy Upshur and brother of Jacob, Thomas, and Emerson Upshur; singer in Sarah E. Wright's *This Child's Gonna Live*.

Margaret (Mom Margaret) Upshur. Wife of Bard Tom Upshur and grandmother of Percy Upshur in Sarah E. Wright's *This Child's Gonna Live*.

Mariah Harmon (Rah) Upshur. Wife of Jacob Upshur and mother of Gesus, William, Horace, and Bardetta Tometta Upshur; twenty-three-year-old protagonist of Sarah E. Wright's *This Child's Gonna Live*.

Percy (Pop Percy) Upshur. Husband of Bertha Ann Upshur, father of Jacob, Levi, Thomas, and Emerson Upshur, and lover of Bannie Upshire Dudley; once owned Tangierneck in Sarah E. Wright's *This Child's Gonna Live*.

Thomas (Tom) Upshur. Son of Bertha Ann and Percy Upshur; singer in Sarah E. Wright's *This Child's Gonna Live*.

William (Skeeter) Upshur. Oldest son of Jacob and Mariah Upshur in Sarah E. Wright's *This Child's Gonna Live*.

Charles Upton. Young American painter who visits Berlin during the Depression in Katherine Anne Porter's *The Leaning Tower*.

Uranian Willy (The Heavy Metal Kid, Willy The Fink, Willy The Rat). Nova Police agent in William S. Burroughs's *Nova Express*; member of the Nova Mob who goes over to the other side, offering a plan of total exposure of the mob's operations, in *The Soft Machine*.

Father Urban. See Harvey Roche.

Raphael (Raff) Urso. Poet, former sexual rival of Jack Duluoz, and author of the tribute "To Jack Duluoz, Buddha-fish" in Jack Kerouac's *Desolation Angels*; also appears in *Book of Dreams*. See also Yuri Gligoric.

Uru (Brother Uru). Leader of the Bantu revolt in Walker Percy's *Love in the Ruins*.

John Ushant. Sexagenarian captain of the forecastle aboard the *Neversink* who refuses to have his beard shaved in Herman Melville's *White-Jacket*.

Pete Uspy. Agent for the Cracker Foundation who rescues Candy Christian from the police in Terry Southern and Mason Hoffenberg's *Candy*.

U2 Polyglot. College dean who writes "The Egyptian Dung Beetle in Kafka's 'Metamorphosis,' " pushes a light ball of excrement by the tip of his nose, and removes the hoodoo from Bukka Doopeyduk in Ishmael Reed's *The Free-Lance Pallbearers*.

Uyuyu (Yoyo). Tiro Indian who is converted first to Catholicism and then to Protestantism; ultimately murders Protestant missionary Martin Quarrier in Peter Matthiessen's *At Play in the Fields of the Lord*.

V

V. Half brother of Sebastian Knight, whose biography V. is trying to write as the narrator of Vladimir Nabokov's *The Real Life of Sebastian Knight*.

V. (The Bad Priest, The lady V., Veronica Manganese, Vera Meroving, Victoria Wren). Mysterious woman for whom Herbert Stencil searches; continuously replaces parts of her body with inanimate materials; as Victoria Wren, has an affair with a spy in Egypt and encounters Hugh and Evan Godolphin and Sidney Stencil in Florence in 1899; as "the lady V.," has an affair with Mélanie l'Heuremaudit in Paris in 1913; as Veronica Manganese, becomes involved with Italian politics on Malta with Sidney Stencil, Father Fairing, and Evan Godolphin in 1919; as Vera Meroving, attends Foppl's "Siege Party" in South-West Africa in 1922 with Lieutenant Weissmann and Kurt Mondaugen; as the Bad Priest, presumably dies on Malta in the 1940s in Thomas Pynchon's *V.*

Vadim (McNab) Vadimovich. Famous author of books in Russian and English; coy about revealing his name in the autobiography he narrates, which comprises Vladimir Nabokov's *Look at the Harlequins!*

Vahine (Heinie, Myrn, Myrna). Singer of Chinese and Hawaiian ancestry; sexual partner of Charlie Stark in Peter Matthiessen's *Raditzer*.

Alberta Sydna Crowninshield Vaiden. Daughter of Emory and Drusilla Lacefield Crowninshield, loved by Jerry Catlin the Second, second wife of Miltiades Vaiden, mother of Marsan Vaiden, and later the wife of Lucius Handback; appears T. S. Stribling's *The Store* and *Unfinished Cathedral*.

Augustus (Gus) Vaiden. Son of Jimmie and Laura Vaiden; wounded in his first battle of the Civil War; appears in T. S. Stribling's *The Forge* and *The Store*.

Cassandra Vaiden. Eldest daughter of Jimmie and Laura Vaiden; bluestocking spinster and a dominant influence in the Vaiden household; appears in T. S. Stribling's *The Forge* and *The Store*.

Gracie (Gracie Beekman, Gracie Dill, Gracie Light) Vaiden. Unacknowledged quadroon daughter of Jimmie Vaiden and a black slave; mother of Toussaint Vaiden by Miltiades Vaiden; mistress to several white men; appears in T. S. Stribling's *The Forge*, *The Store*, and *Unfinished Cathedral*.

Jimmie Vaiden. Patriarch of a large family of yeoman farmers in northern Alabama; father of the quadroon slave Gracie Vaiden in T. S. Stribling's *The Forge*.

Laura Vaiden. Wife of Jimmie Vaiden and mother of Cassandra, Marcia, Miltiades, Augustus, and Polycarp Vaiden in T. S. Stribling's *The Forge*.

Lucy Lacefield Vaiden. Educated black who marries Toussaint Vaiden and founds a school for black children at the former Lacefield Manor in T. S. Stribling's *The Store*.

Marcia (Marsh) Vaiden. Sentimental and romantic daughter of Jimmie and Laura Vaiden and wife of Jerry Catlin; appears in T. S. Stribling's *The Forge* and *The Store*.

Marsan Vaiden. Daughter of Miltiades and Sydna Crowninshield Vaiden and cousin of Jerry Catlin the Second; impregnated by Red McLaughlin; marries J. Adlee Petrie, her high school science teacher, in T. S. Stribling's *Unfinished Cathedral*.

Miltiades (Milt) Vaiden. Son of Jimmie and Laura Vaiden, husband first of Ponny BeShears Vaiden and then of Sydna Crowninshield Vaiden, and father of Marsan Vaiden and the octoroon Toussaint Vaiden; store clerk, overseer of Lacefield Manor, colonel in the Fourth Alabama Regiment, leader of the Ku Klux Klan, and eventual bank president; appears in T. S. Stribling's *The Forge*, *The Store*, and *Unfinished Cathedral*.

Polycarp (Carp) Vaiden. Son of Jimmie and Laura Vaiden and lover of Ponny BeShears; possibly killed by the Leatherwood gang in T. S. Stribling's *The Forge*.

Ponny BeShears Vaiden. See Ponny BeShears.

Toussaint Vaiden. Illegitimate son of Miltiades and Gracie Vaiden; victim of a lynch mob in T. S. Stribling's *The Store*.

Joseph (Blanchet) Vaillant. French missionary and long-time friend of Bishop Latour; works with Latour in New Mexico and later works in Colorado in Willa Cather's *Death Comes for the Archbishop*.

Cardinal Vaini. Eighty-year-old former missionary to China who has retired to Rome to read, meditate, and play with animals; his brilliant intellect holds him aloof from others; in an intellectual game, he undermines the faith of Marie-Astrée-Luce de Morfontaine, who later tries to shoot him, in Thornton Wilder's *The Cabala*.

Erik Valborg. Swedish tailor and lover of poetry who befriends Carol Kennicott in Sinclair Lewis's *Main Street.*

Magdalena Valdez. Mexican who is rescued from her murderous husband by Bishop Latour and who works for Latour until his death in Willa Cather's *Death Comes for the Archbishop.*

B. Valentine. Florist with whom J. Henry Waugh discusses funeral flowers in Robert Coover's *The Universal Baseball Association, Inc., J. Henry Waugh, Prop.*

Basil Valentine. Art critic in league with Recktall Brown in art fraud; stabbed (but not killed) by Wyatt Gwyon in William Gaddis's *The Recognitions.*

Lee Valentine. Bandleader who hires Rick Martin away from Jack Stuart; takes Martin to New York in Dorothy Baker's *Young Man with a Horn.*

Stephano Valentine. Lover of Junior Everett; helps Everett perpetuate a colossal scam that nets millions of dollars but also leads to their death in Peter Gent's *Texas Celebrity Turkey Trot.*

Dr. Valentini. Skilled Italian surgeon who removes shrapnel from Frederic Henry's knee in Ernest Hemingway's *A Farewell to Arms.*

Velma Valento (Mrs. Lewin Lockridge Grayle). Former showgirl who marries a wealthy older man; object of Moose Malloy's quest in Raymond Chandler's *Farewell, My Lovely.*

Valerie. Lobotomized fellow patient with Esther Greenwood at a private mental hospital in Sylvia Plath's *The Bell Jar.*

Valerie. Resident in orthopedics specializing in joint injuries and lover of Tarden until, in hiding while supposedly out of town, he watches and listens as she makes love with another man in Jerzy Kosinski's *Cockpit.*

Valerie (Val). Harvard graduate student and social activist slain by police during an act of militant feminism in Marilyn French's *The Women's Room.*

Valeska. Secretary hired by Henry Miller; he falls in love with her and brings her home to meet his wife; gives Miller's wife a hundred dollars for an abortion and later commits suicide in Henry Miller's *Tropic of Capricorn.*

Valet de Chambre (Tom Driscoll). Son of Roxy, who switches him at birth with Thomas à Becket Driscoll; reared as Tom Driscoll; murders York Leicester in Samuel Langhorne Clemens's *Pudd'nhead Wilson.*

Alex Valnikov. Brother of A. M. Valnikov; butcher, grocer, and caterer in Joseph Wambaugh's *The Black Marble.*

Andrei Mikhailovich (A. M., Andrushka, Val) Valnikov. Alcoholic Los Angeles burglary detective; protagonist of Joseph Wambaugh's *The Black Marble.*

Red Valsen. Soldier who unsuccessfully resists Sergeant Croft in Norman Mailer's *The Naked and the Dead.*

Marquesa Daisy de Valverde. Worldly Tangier socialite who tries to help Nelson Dyar in Paul Bowles's *Let It Come Down.*

Van. Finnish sailor aboard the *Julia* in Herman Melville's *Omoo.*

Harry Van. Composer and friend of Duff Conway in Shelby Foote's *Jordan County.*

Fred Van Ackerman. Junior senator from Wyoming and chief spokesman for a liberal group called COMFORT (Committee on Making Further Offers for a Russian Truce); eventually censured by the Senate for his unscrupulous and fanatical actions against Senator Brigham Anderson in Allen Drury's *Advise and Consent.*

Mr. Vanaker. Elderly garage employee, drunkard, and unhygienic inmate of the apartment house where Joseph lives; though he shares many of the same vices, Joseph vehemently denounces Vanaker's vulgarity, spying, and thievery in Saul Bellow's *Dangling Man.*

Letitia Van Allen. Masochistic talent agent and lover of Rusty Godowsky in Gore Vidal's *Myra Breckinridge.*

Vanamee. Wandering-shepherd figure who copes with the death of his fiancée by elaborating upon St. Paul's teachings concerning the resurrection in order to effect a denial of death itself in Frank Norris's *The Octopus.*

Abraham Van Brunt. Hired Dutchman who manages Fortune Emerson's farm; becomes Ellen Montgomery's loyal defender and later marries Fortune in Susan Warner's *The Wide, Wide World.*

Fortune Emerson Van Brunt. See Fortune Emerson.

Laura Van Brunt. See Laura Hawkins.

Mr. Van Brunt. Cantankerous old man who irritates Juan Chicoy by arguing with him about the danger of driving in a storm; has a stroke while waiting for the stranded bus to be rescued in John Steinbeck's

The Wayward Bus.

Martin (Matty Van) Van Buren. Lawyer and politician believed to be the illegitimate son of Aaron Burr in Gore Vidal's *Burr.*

Miss Van Campen. Supervising nurse at the American hospital in Milan; hastens Frederic Henry's return to the front by accusing him of self-inflicted alcoholic jaundice in Ernest Hemingway's *A Farewell to Arms.*

Eleanor (Nell) Vance. Thirty-two-year-old woman who, as a child, was the focus of poltergeist activity; invited to Hill House because of her susceptibility to spectral phenomena in Shirley Jackson's *The Haunting of Hill House.*

Margaret Vance. New Yorker who tries to introduce the Dryfoos sisters to high society; convinces Conrad Dryfoos to help the poor workers of New York in William Dean Howells's *A Hazard of New Fortunes.*

Mr. and Mrs. Vance. New York neighbors of Carrie Meeber and George Hurstwood, whom the Vances know as the Wheelers, in Theodore Dreiser's *Sister Carrie.*

Ariel (Auriel) Vancour. Youngest brother of the patroon family in James Kirke Paulding's *The Dutchman's Fireside.*

Catalina (Catty) Vancour. Daughter of Egbert and Madame Vancour; heroine of James Kirke Paulding's *The Dutchman's Fireside.*

Colonel Egbert Vancour. Oldest brother of the patroon family in James Kirke Paulding's *The Dutchman's Fireside.*

Dennis Vancour. Middle brother of the patroon family in James Kirke Paulding's *The Dutchman's Fireside.*

Madame Vancour. Wife of the patroon Egbert Vancour in James Kirke Paulding's *The Dutchman's Fireside.*

Allegra Vand. Pretentious heir of a family trust, money from which supports her flamboyant lifestyle and the activities of others in Cynthia Ozick's *Trust.*

Enoch Vand. Formerly radical husband of Allegra Vand in Cynthia Ozick's *Trust.*

Pieter Van Damm. Violinist, eunuch, and prisoner at the Jadwiga concentration camp; testifies against Adam Kelno in Leon Uris's *QB VII.*

William Robespierre Vandamm. Bachelor uncle of Gloria Wandrous; provides for Gloria's education and supports her mother, his younger sister, in John O'Hara's *Butterfield 8.*

Clare Van Degen. Elegant, restless cousin of Ralph Marvel and wife of Peter Van Degen in Edith Wharton's *The Custom of the Country.*

Peter Van Degen. Wealthy socialite and womanizer who leaves his wife, Clare Van Degen, to become Undine Spragg's companion for several months in Edith Wharton's *The Custom of the Country.*

Gustavus (Van) Vanderbank. Handsome man who loves but does not marry Nanda Brookenham in Henry James's *The Awkward Age.*

Horst Vanderhoof. Los Angeles park violinist; plays Russian music for A. M. Valnikov and Natalie Zimmerman in Joseph Wambaugh's *The Black Marble.*

Mrs. Walter J. Vander Meer. Wealthy widow who briefly acts as patroness to Alice Prentice in Richard Yates's *A Special Providence.*

Mrs. Vanderpool (née Wells). Wealthy northern matron who refines Zora and ruins Mary Taylor Cresswell in society in W. E. B. Du Bois's *The Quest of the Silver Fleece.*

Allert (Alan) Vanderveenan. Husband of Ursula and shipboard lover of Ariane; middle-aged Dutchman who may have once been a psychiatric patient; unwillingly takes a cruise at Ursula's insistence and is later tried and acquitted of responsibility for Ariane's disappearance; narrator of John Hawkes's *Death, Sleep & the Traveler.*

Ursula Vanderveenan. Sensual wife of Allert Vanderveenan and lover of Peter; leaves Allert after his trial in John Hawkes's *Death, Sleep & the Traveler.*

Caroline (Mrs. Erasmus Van de Weyer) Van de Weyer. Half sister of Peter Alden and socialite aunt of Oliver Alden in George Santayana's *The Last Puritan.*

Edith Van de Weyer. Cousin who rejects Oliver Alden's marriage proposal in George Santayana's *The Last Puritan.*

Mario (Marius, Vanny) Van de Weyer. Euopeanized cousin of Oliver Alden in George Santayana's *The Last Puritan.*

Robert (Black Rider, Bob) Van Doren. Confederate soldier who falls in love with Mary Waters, a Union sympathizer; son of Stephen Van Doren in Paul

Laurence Dunbar's *The Fanatics*.

Stephen Van Doren. Genteel white southerner and democrat who migrates to Dorbury, Ohio, and becomes a defender and protector of the northern black contrabands; father of Robert Van Doren in Paul Laurence Dunbar's *The Fanatics*.

Laura Nesbit Van Dorn. Daughter of James and Bedelia Nesbit; deserted by her husband Thomas Van Dorn; establishes a kindergarten for mine workers' families in William Allen White's *In the Heart of a Fool*.

Lila Van Dorn. Daughter of Thomas and Laura Van Dorn; marries Kenyon Adams in William Allen White's *In the Heart of a Fool*.

Thomas (Tom) Van Dorn. Materialistic judge who divorces Laura Nesbit Van Dorn to marry Margaret Müller Fenn; falls from power and social position in William Allen White's *In the Heart of a Fool*.

Vandover (Van). Weak-willed, unanalytical artist who comes to ruin, suffering multiple physical and mental disorders as he degenerates, in Frank Norris's *Vandover and the Brute*.

Vane (Vanio). Composer and lover of Julia Ashton in H. D.'s *Bid Me to Live*.

Austen (Aust) Vane. Reformist antirailroad lawyer and politician; marries Victoria Flint in Winston Churchill's *Mr. Crewe's Career*.

Hilary Vane. Father of Austen Vane; judge, railroad lawyer, and major political force in Winston Churchill's *Mr. Crewe's Career*.

Victoria Flint Vane. See Victoria Flint.

George Augustus Vane-Basingwell. Employer of the valet Marmaduke Ruggles; loses Ruggles to Egbert Floud in a poker game in Harry Leon Wilson's *Ruggles of Red Gap*.

Nevil (Earl of Brinstead) Vane-Basingwell. Brother of George Augustus Vane-Basingwell; tries to prevent his brother from marrying an unsuitable American woman, but marries her himself, in Harry Leon Wilson's *Ruggles of Red Gap*.

Christofer (Chris) Van Eenanam. Husband of Ellen Strohe; graduate student and a central character in Larry Woiwode's *What I'm Going to Do, I Think*.

Ellen Sidone Anne Strohe Van Eenanam. See Ellen Sidone Anne Strohe.

Edward Van Harrington. Unethical and rapacious youth who becomes a meatpacker and entrepreneur; husband of Sarah Gentles; narrator of Robert Herrick's *The Memoirs of an American Citizen*.

Van Horn (Skipper). Captain of the *Arangi*, a ship taking indentured servants to the British Solomons; killed by Bashti in Jack London's *Jerry of the Islands*.

Madeleine Van Leyden. College roommate of and later resident of the same New York apartment with Derrick Thornton; serves in World War I in Helen Hooven Santmyer's *Herbs and Apples*.

Spencer Van Moot. Complainer and scrounger; one of ten policemen-protagonists in Joseph Wambaugh's *The Choirboys*.

Van Norden (Joe). Jewish friend of Henry Miller; plans to write a book "someday" in Henry Miller's *Tropic of Cancer*.

JR Vansant. Eleven-year-old tycoon from Long Island whose short-lived financial career drives the action in William Gaddis's *JR*.

Kate Van Schaak. Aristocratic New Yorker who directs the career of her husband, Horace Larkin, and attempts to buy a diplomatic post for him in Hjalmar Hjorth Boyesen's *The Mammon of Unrighteousness*.

Baltus (Captain, Skipper) Van Slingerland. Hudson River sloop captain in James Kirke Paulding's *The Dutchman's Fireside*.

Felice Van Verdighan. See Avis Cunningham Everhard.

Helen Van Vleck. See Helen Van Vleck Barber.

Humphrey (Hump) Van Weyden. Narrator rescued at sea by the *Ghost*; saves the ship when the crewmen fight among themselves in Jack London's *The Sea-Wolf*.

Bartolomeo (Bart, Bartholomew) Vanzetti. Italian pastry cook and agnostic who immigrates to the United States to find a better life but sees such cruel exploitation of workers by the rich that he becomes an anarchist; unjustly charged with the murder of two men during a robbery; executed, despite the efforts of Cornelia Thornwell and others to save him, in Upton Sinclair's *Boston*.

Varda. Creator of collages who lives on a converted ferry boat in Sausalito in Anaïs Nin's *Collages*.

Ludwig Varlett. Shoemaker and councilman killed by Indians in James Kirke Paulding's *Koningsmarke*.

Eula Varner. See Eula Varner Snopes.

Jody Varner. Son of Will Varner and store manager; appears in William Faulkner's *As I Lay Dying, Light in August, The Hamlet, The Town,* and *The Mansion.*

Will (Uncle Billy) Varner. Father of, among others, Jody Varner and Eula Varner Snopes; appears in William Faulkner's *As I Lay Dying, Light in August, The Hamlet, Intruder in the Dust, The Town,* and *The Mansion.*

Joseph (Joe) Varney. Marine colonel and rival of Bull Meecham in Pat Conroy's *The Great Santini.*

Varvy. Deaf hermit who operates a still near Taloo in Herman Melville's *Omoo.*

Vanya (Danny Spellbinder) Vashvily. Hollywood producer who discovers Belinda in Ludwig Bemelmans's *Dirty Eddie.*

Whiskey Vassos. Thug employed by Shad O'Rory in Dashiell Hammett's *The Glass Key.*

Scratch Vatic. Perpetually hungry passenger on the *Here They Come* in Gregory Corso's *The American Express.*

Cecilia Vaughan. Friend of Alice Archer; in marrying Arthur Kavanagh, she causes Alice to die of a broken heart in Henry Wadsworth Longfellow's *Kavanagh.*

Colonel Ezekiel (Zeke) Vaughn. An original secessionist of Rockford County who never served in the Confederate army; surrenders to Comfort Servosse, takes financial advantage of him in the sale of Warrington plantation, but becomes his enemy when Servosse indignantly refuses to stop associating with the teachers at the freedmen's school; eventually accepts Servosse as harmless and tends to him during Servosse's final illness in Albion W. Tourgee's *A Fool's Errand.*

Lawrence P. Vaughan. Power- and money-hungry mayor of Amity; his refusal to close the beaches results in two deaths in Peter Benchley's *Jaws.*

Thurzah Elvira Jordan (Granny) Vaughn. Widowed grandmother of Beulah Beecham Renfro and her six Beecham brothers; rears them when their parents drown; celebrates her ninetieth birthday at a family reunion in Eudora Welty's *Losing Battles.*

Chandler Vaught. Genial automobile tycoon and patriarch of the family that befriends Will Barrett in Walker Percy's *The Last Gentleman.*

Jamison MacKenzie (Jamie, Jimmy) Vaught. Son of Chandler Vaught; scientific prodigy who is baptized before he dies in Walker Percy's *The Last Gentleman.*

Katherine Gibbs (Kitty) Vaught. Daughter of Chandler Vaught; Will Barrett's uncertain love in Walker Percy's *The Last Gentleman.*

Mrs. Vaught. Wife of Chandler Vaught; detects conspiracies to destroy the South and America in Walker Percy's *The Last Gentleman.*

Rita (Ree) Vaught. Meddlesome former wife of Sutter Vaught; her altruism conceals her own selfishness in Walker Percy's *The Last Gentleman.*

Sutter Vaught. Son of Chandler Vaught; libertine and suicidal coroner who refuses to be Will Barrett's mentor in Walker Percy's *The Last Gentleman.*

Valentine (Sister Johnette Mary Vianney, Val) Vaught. Daughter of Chandler Vaught; becomes a fierce but compassionate nun in Walker Percy's *The Last Gentleman.*

Zaza (Ali Zaza) Vauriselle. Mentally retarded adolescent given to masturbating in public; adopted by Jack Duluoz and his friends in Jack Kerouac's *Doctor Sax* and *Maggie Cassidy.*

Mrs. Vawse. Swiss native who lives on a remote mountain outside Thirlwall; befriends Ellen Montgomery and helps her learn French in Susan Warner's *The Wide, Wide World.*

Nancy Vawse. Mischievous young granddaughter of Mrs. Vawse; Ellen Montgomery overcomes her dislike of Nancy and befriends her in Susan Warner's *The Wide, Wide World.*

James Vayle. Fiancé of Helga Crane while both are teachers at a southern black school in Nella Larsen's *Quicksand.*

Agapito Vázquez de Anda. Wealthy banker and family tyrant who interferes with his son Domingo's desire to be a doctor and tries to force his son Cardito into being a banker in Josefina Niggli's *Step Down, Elder Brother.*

Brunhilda Vázquez de Anda. Extravagant daughter of the Vázquez de Anda family who is sent to New York to study piano; allies herself with her uncle Agapito and marries her brother Domingo's best friend in Josefina Niggli's *Step Down, Elder Brother.*

Domingo Vázquez de Anda. Oldest son torn between loyalty and duty to his family and his love for Márgara Bárcenas; finally rebels against his tyrannical uncle; protagonist of Josefina Niggli's *Step Down, Elder Brother.*

Lucio (Uncle Lucio) Vázquez de Anda. Gentle failure in an illustrious family; takes correspondence courses in Josefina Niggli's *Step Down, Elder Brother*.

Ricardo (Cardito) Vázquez de Anda. Younger brother of Domingo Vázquez de Anda; impregnates the housemaid and flees all responsibility in Josefina Niggli's *Step Down, Elder Brother*.

Sofía Vázquez de Anda. Daughter thwarted in her business ambitions by stultifying traditions; marries out of her class, suggesting the social and economic changes beginning to bring Monterrey, Mexico, into a new era, in Josefina Niggli's *Step Down, Elder Brother*.

William Veal. Slave and butler on the McGehee estate; accompanies Agnes McGehee to Shiloh to find and bring home the dead Edward McGehee in Stark Young's *So Red the Rose*.

Vee-Vee. Dwarf and page to Media in Herman Melville's *Mardi*.

Adelaida (Ada, Adochka) Veen. Daughter of Demon Veen and Marina Veen, half sister of Lucette Veen, sister and lover of Van Veen, and wife of Andrey Vinelander; the subject of Van's chronicle, Vladimir Nabokov's *Ada*.

Aqua Durmanov Veen. Twin of Marina Veen, wife of Demon Veen, and supposedly mother of Van Veen; commits suicide after a life of anguish and madness in Vladimir Nabokov's *Ada*.

Ivan (Van) Veen. Famous doctor, professor, and expert on Terra and theories of time; son of Demon Veen and Marina Veen, brother of Ada Veen, and half brother of Lucette Veen; celebrates his long love affair with Ada in his chronicle, Vladimir Nabokov's *Ada*.

Lucinda (Lucette) Veen. Daughter of Marina and Daniel Veen and half sister of Ada and Van Veen; commits suicide when Van, with whom she is hopelessly in love, rejects her once too often in Vladimir Nabokov's *Ada*.

Marina Durmanov Veen. Famous actress in her day; twin sister of Aqua Veen, wife of Daniel Veen, mistress of Demon Veen, and mother of Van, Ada, and Lucette Veen; substitutes Van for her sister's dead child in Vladimir Nabokov's *Ada*.

Walter D. (Dan, Daniel, Red, Durak Walter) Veen. Husband of Marina Veen and father of Lucette Veen; unaware that Ada is his cousin Demon Veen's daughter, he brings her up as his own in Vladimir Nabokov's *Ada*.

Walter D. (Dementiy, Demon, Raven, Dark Walter) Veen. Rich and notorious rake; husband of Aqua Veen, lover of Marina Veen, and father by Marina of Van and Ada in Vladimir Nabokov's *Ada*.

Veiled Lady. See Priscilla.

Constanza Velasquez. Betrothed of Count Alphonse D'Oyley; loved by Lafitte, who sacrifices much for her, in Joseph Holt Ingraham's *Lafitte*.

Mrs. Edward Venable. Newport socialite and hostess for Bodo Stams; has many elaborate social gatherings at her "cottage" in Thornton Wilder's *Theophilus North*.

Felice Venable. Wife of Lewis Venable and mother of Sabra Venable Cravat; moves her family from Mississippi to the Midwest before the Civil War in Edna Ferber's *Cimarron*.

Jean Sweet Venable. Journalist gathering information for an article on Robert Softly's Logicon Project in Don DeLillo's *Ratner's Star*.

Lewis Venable. Husband of Felice Venable and father of Sabra Venable Cravat; supports Sabra's trek west in Edna Ferber's *Cimarron*.

Arthur Vendler. Delicatessen owner who provides promotional dinners to radio talk show guests in Stanley Elkin's *The Dick Gibson Show*.

Uncle Venner. Workman friend of Hepzibah and Clifford Pyncheon in Nathaniel Hawthorne's *The House of the Seven Gables*.

Vera. Stripper at the Frolic Club, wife of Carl, and lover of E. L. Fletcher in Jerry Bumpus's *Anaconda*.

Edward Fairfax (Starry) Vere. Captain of the *Indomitable* who decides to have Billy Budd hanged in Herman Melville's *Billy Budd*.

Daniel (O. B. Haverton, Old Bitch Haverton, Virgin) Verger. Tubercular and masochistic former Harvard University student who lives in Spanish Harlem and has an affair with Georgia in John Clellon Holmes's *Go*.

Verily. Housekeeper of Judge Fox Clane; quits after fifteen years when the judge refuses to pay social security in Carson McCullers's *Clock Without Hands*.

Verman. Tongue-tied brother of Herman; his antics, both physical and verbal, provide comic relief for Penrod Schofield and his friends in Booth Tarkington's *Penrod*, *Penrod and Sam*, and *Penrod Jashber*.

T'ressa (Tessie) Vernacht. Daughter of German immigrants and wife of Denny Moore in Betty Smith's *Maggie-Now*.

Vernier. Colleague of Dr. Kersaint; patiently listens to Kersaint's story of the hurricane in Charles Nordhoff and James Norman Hall's *The Hurricane.*

Veronika. Belgian woman who marries a wealthy industrialist as part of a sexual pact with Tarden; when she becomes unruly, Tarden has her raped by derelicts and finally kills her by exposing her to the radiation from a fighter plane's radar system while he sits in its cockpit in Jerzy Kosinski's *Cockpit.*

Gulian C. Verplanck. Defeated anti-Tammany candidate in New York; a writer-lawyer in Gore Vidal's *Burr.*

Alanna (Lanna) Verrick. Afro-Asian orphan adopted by Jules and Neila Verrick; narrates part of Octavia E. Butler's *Survivor.*

Jules Verrick. Adoptive father of Alanna Verrick and leader of the Verrick Colony of Missionaries in Octavia E. Butler's *Survivor.*

Neila Verrick. Wife of Jules Verrick and adoptive mother of Alanna Verrick in Octavia E. Butler's *Survivor.*

Verrus. Roman esthete and lover of Hipparchia in H. D.'s *Palimpsest.*

Versh. See Versh Gibson.

Comtesse Lilianne de Vertdulac. Poor French countess who provides room and board for Billy Winthrop in Paris, teaches her French, and improves her fashion sense in Judith Krantz's *Scruples.*

Adam Verver. Wealthy American living in England; marries Charlotte Stant in Henry James's *The Golden Bowl.*

Charlotte Stant Verver. See Charlotte Stant.

Maggie (Mag, Princess) Verver. Wealthy woman whose attachment to her father Adam Verver threatens her marriage to Prince Amerigo in Henry James's *The Golden Bowl.*

Dred Vesey. Charismatic proselytizer of slave revolt based on Christian scriptures; inhabits the Dismal Swamp, where he hides and defends outlaw slaves until he is killed by Tom Gordon's gang, in Harriet Beecher Stowe's *Dred.*

Wilhelmina (Vesta Stover) Vesta. Illegitimate daughter of Jennie Gerhardt and George Brander; dies of typhoid fever in Theodore Dreiser's *Jennie Gerhardt.*

Anastasius Vetch. Violinist and friend of Amanda Pynsent and Hyacinth Robinson in Henry James's *The Princess Casamassima.*

Fleda Vetch. Heroine with great aesthetic appreciation; companion to Adela Gereth in Henry James's *The Spoils of Poynton.*

Maggie Vetch. Sister of Fleda Vetch in Henry James's *The Spoils of Poynton.*

Sam Vettori. Head of a Chicago gang and proprietor of the Club Palermo; pushed aside by Rico Bandello in William Riley Burnett's *Little Caesar.*

Sister Johnette Mary Vianney. See Valentine Vaught.

Paulette Viard. Beautiful but dangerous member of the aristocracy; suspected of masterminding the death of her late husband; rejected by Diron Desautels in Arna Wendell Bontemps's *Drums at Dusk.*

Ashton Vickery. Callous, unreflective uncle of Nathan Vickery in Joyce Carol Oates's *Son of the Morning.*

Elsa Vickery. Rural teenager who is brutally raped and gives birth to religious seeker Nathan Vickery in Joyce Carol Oates's *Son of the Morning.*

Nathanael William (Nathan) Vickery. Monomaniacal, tormented religious leader whose search for God brings him to the brink of madness in Joyce Carol Oates's *Son of the Morning.*

Opal Sayer Vickery. Protective grandmother of Nathan Vickery in Joyce Carol Oates's *Son of the Morning.*

Thaddeus Aaron Vickery. Physician and grandfather of Nathan Vickery; his pragmatic, atheistic outlook puts him at odds with his religious grandson in Joyce Carol Oates's *Son of the Morning.*

Norman Victman. Shopping-center idea man whose advancement is deliberately sabotaged by Leo Feldman in Stanley Elkin's *A Bad Man.*

Victoria Regina (Vickie). Madeline Whitfield's champion miniature schnauzer; stolen and mutilated by Philo Skinner in Joseph Wambaugh's *The Black Marble.*

Vidal. Brother of Abel; dies during Abel's childhood in N. Scott Momaday's *House Made of Dawn.*

Terasina Vidavarri. First love of Dove Linkhorn in Nelson Algren's *A Walk on the Wild Side.*

Lucky Videndi. See Lucia Angelina Elena Videndi Grant.

Jean Claude Vigneron. Urologist who prescribes the water-method technique for Fred Trumper's urinary tract problems in John Irving's *The Water-Method Man.*

Viking. See Jarl.

Marina Vilar. Terrorist plotting to bomb the New York Stock Exchange in Don DeLillo's *Players.*

Rafael Vilar. Terrorist arrested for killing a man on the floor of the New York Stock Exchange in Don DeLillo's *Players.*

Teddy Villanova. Non-existent character and red herring in Thomas Berger's *Who Is Teddy Villanova?*

Chela Villareal. Homely daughter of the village mayor; Joaquin Castillo falls in love with her but she chooses the village professor in Josefina Niggli's *Mexican Village.*

Mimi Villars. Pretty waitress and free-love advocate whom Augie March nurses through a botched abortion in Saul Bellow's *The Adventures of Augie March.*

George (Steenie) Villiers. Duke of Buckingham and favorite of King James I in George Garrett's *Death of the Fox.*

George Villiers, Duke of Buckingham. Cunning, powerful nobleman involved in many intrigues dangerous to himself and to King Charles II; cousin of Barbara Palmer in Kathleen Winsor's *Forever Amber.*

Jane Villiers de l'Isle-Adam. "Wicked witch" who attempts to poison Snow White but accidentally poisons Paul in Donald Barthelme's *Snow White.*

Vincent (Vincennti, Vinnie). Youngster arrested at age twelve for stealing a hearse; follows a career of theft and debauchery, largely because of his association with male transvestites and homosexuals; at age forty, marries and produces children but is no more fulfilled by this part of his life than by his earlier years in Hubert Selby, Jr.'s *Last Exit to Brooklyn.*

Marquis (Don Luis Guzman Sotomyer y O'Connell, conde de Azuaga) da Vincitata. Cuckolded husband of Maria Bonnyfeather; plots to kill Anthony Adverse, his wife's son, in Hervey Allen's *Anthony Adverse.*

Marquise da Vincitata. See Maria Bonnyfeather.

Andrey Andreevich Vinelander. Arizona rancher of Russian heritage and orthodox faith who marries Ada Veen in Vladimir Nabokov's *Ada.*

Viner. Trader on Tahiti who once sailed with John Jermin in Herman Melville's *Omoo.*

Sophy Viner. Vivacious, independent young woman who has a brief affair with George Darrow and later becomes governess for the daughter of Anna Leath, Darrow's fiancée, in Edith Wharton's *The Reef.*

Vineria (Vinie). Much-admired pup treated like a family member; white female of the pair of pedigreed fox hounds that Nunn Ballew buys to chase King Devil in Harriette Arnow's *Hunter's Horn.*

Vinogradus. See Jakob Gradus.

Carmen Viosca. Barcelonan wife of Feliu Viosca; rears their foster daughter, Conchita Viosca, to respect God and the sea in Lafcadio Hearn's *Chita.*

Mildred Vinton. Bookstore clerk and member of the Pauling household; narrates part of Anne Tyler's *Celestial Navigation.*

Jeanne de Vionnet. Pretty daughter of Madame de Vionnet in Henry James's *The Ambassadors.*

Mme. Marie de Vionnet. Estranged wife of a French count; friend of Maria Gostrey, mother of Jeanne de Vionnet, and mistress of Chad Newsome in Henry James's *The Ambassadors.*

Conchita (Chita, Concha, Eulalie, Lil, Zouzoune) Viosca. Daughter of Julien La Brierre; found at sea following a storm and adopted by Feliu and Carmen Viosca in Lafcadio Hearn's *Chita.*

Feliu Viosca. Husband of Carmen Viosca; Spanish fisherman who rescues the baby Conchita after the storm that destroys Last Island in Lafcadio Hearn's *Chita.*

Virginian. Gallant foreman at Sunk Creek ranch who upholds the laws of the West; has a shootout with Trampas in Owen Wister's *The Virginian.*

Maria Viskova. Polish Jewish doctor and Communist; colleague of Adam Kelno in the Jadwiga concentration camp in Leon Uris's *QB VII.*

Apollonia Vitelli. Young Sicilian woman and first wife of Michael Corleone; killed by a bomb meant for her husband in Mario Puzo's *The Godfather.*

Popeye Vitelli. As Popeye Vitelli, a gangster in William Faulkner's *Requiem for a Nun;* as Popeye, a bootlegger and murderer who is hanged for a murder he did not commit in *Sanctuary.*

Vivian (Vee). Mistress of Karl Larkin believed to be mute in Octavia E. Butler's *Mind of My Mind.*

Vivian (Vive). Singer at Happy's Café; Ursa Corregidora catches Vivian in bed with Ursa's husband, Tadpole McCormick, in Gayl Jones's

Corregidora.

Hyacinthe Vivier. See Hyacinth Robinson.

Florentine Vivier. Impoverished French dressmaker imprisoned for murdering her lover, Lord Frederick Purvis; mother, by Purvis, of Hyacinth Robinson in Henry James's *The Princess Casamassima.*

Vladek. Illegitimate child reared by Dora Dugova and Yuro Dug; permitted to die in Louis Adamic's *Cradle of Life.*

Carl (Comrade Truth, Untruth, General Carlos Verdad) Vlanoc. Representative of Joseph Stalin in the Western Hemisphere; supervisor of Jake Starr in William Herrick's *Hermanos!*

Helene Cady Vogel. Daughter of Benjamin Cady and wife of Jesse Vogel in Joyce Carol Oates's *Wonderland.*

Jesse Vogel. See Jesse Harte.

Serenus Vogel. See Kelcey.

Shelley Vogel. Runaway daughter of Jesse and Helene Vogel in Joyce Carol Oates's *Wonderland.*

Franz Vogelsang. Socialist political mentor of Felix Fay in Floyd Dell's *Moon-Calf.*

Ben Voler. Mira's fellow graduate student and lover in Marilyn French's *The Women's Room.*

Baron Felix Volkbein. Orphan who marries Robin Vote, loses her, and rears their son Guido Volkbein in Djuna Barnes's *Nightwood.*

Guido Volkbein. Son of Felix Volkbein and Robin Vote in Djuna Barnes's *Nightwood.*

Robin Vote Volkbein. See Robin Vote.

Kurt Vonnegut, Jr. Editor of the "Confessions of Howard Campbell Jr." in Kurt Vonnegut's *Mother Night;* appears briefly in *Slaughterhouse-Five* and *Breakfast of Champions.*

Hinckle Von Vampton. Grand Master of the Knights Templar who has acquired powers from the Arabians; starts a magazine, *The Benign Monster,* for which he creates a Negro Viewpoint and a Talking Android in Ishmael Reed's *Mumbo Jumbo.*

Hugo Von Vorst. Nonagenarian actor and possible villain in the legends of Jane Clifford's family in Gail Godwin's *The Odd Woman.*

Adolph Voss. Nazi colonel; physician who heads the medical experimental section at the Jadwiga concentration camp in Leon Uris's *QB VII.*

Konrad Vost. Widower of Claire, father of Mirabelle, and son of Eva Laubenstein and Konrad Vost the Father; taught to respect and love women as a prisoner of rioting women convicts, one of whom is his mother, in John Hawkes's *The Passion Artist.*

Konrad Vost the Father. Father of Konrad Vost; drenched in flammable liquid and set afire by his wife, Eva Laubenstein, in John Hawkes's *The Passion Artist.*

Robin Vote. Wife of Felix Volkbein, mother of Guido Volkbein, and lover of Nora Flood and Jenny Petherbridge; teeters between her human and bestial natures in Djuna Barnes's *Nightwood.*

Valerie de Voudrai. See Valerie Maret.

Captain de Vriess. Captain of the USS *Caine* prior to Captain Queeg in Herman Wouk's *The Caine Mutiny.*

Helen Vrobel. Wardrobe lady for Boris Adrian's pornographic movie in Terry Southern's *Blue Movie.*

Charles (Charles II) Xavier Vseslav, The Beloved. Last king of Zembla and son of Queen Blenda in Vladimir Nabokov's *Pale Fire.* See Dr. Charles Kinbote.

Vyella (Vy). Self-made preacher and friend to Mariah Upshur in Sarah E. Wright's *This Child's Gonna Live.*

W

Wadal. Ragged leader of itinerant beggars; former owner of Kutunda who denies knowing Colonel Ellelloû at the end of John Updike's *The Coup.*

Eileen Wade. Beautiful wife of Roger Wade, previously married to Terry Lennox; she murders Wade and Sylvia Lennox in Raymond Chandler's *The Long Goodbye.*

Ellen (Nelly) Wade. Eighteen-year-old dependent and relative by marriage of Esther and Ishmael Bush; helps free Inez de Certavallos; returns to the settlements with her beloved, Paul Hover, in James Fenimore Cooper's *The Prairie.*

Ida Wade. Woman who commits suicide after being seduced by Vandover and either being made pregnant or afflicted with a venereal disease by him in Frank Norris's *Vandover and the Brute.*

Johnston (Roy Earle) Wade. Crazed insurance magnate and acquaintance of Lee Mellon in Richard Brautigan's *A Confederate General from Big Sur.*

Roger Wade. Alcoholic writer murdered by his wife in Raymond Chandler's *The Long Goodbye.*

Walter Wade. Arbiter of style in Binx Bolling's fraternity; fiancé of Kate Cutrer in Walker Percy's *The Moviegoer.*

Elsa (Sarah) Wagner. Wife of Jacob Wagner; avoids arrest by the British by moving from North Carolina to Tennessee in Caroline Gordon's *Green Centuries.*

Jacob Wagner. North Carolina storekeeper and husband of Elsa Wagner; avoids arrest by the British by moving to Tennessee, where he establishes a grist mill, in Caroline Gordon's *Green Centuries.*

Jarry Wagner. Buddhist, poet, and friend who introduces Jack Duluoz to mountain climbing in Jack Kerouac's *Desolation Angels*; mentioned in *Big Sur.*

Peter Wagner. Philosophical and suicidal character in the comic-fantastic paperback *The Smugglers of Lost Souls' Rock,* the interior novel within John Gardner's *October Light.*

Wah-ta!-Wah (Hist-oh!-Hist). Kidnapped lover of Chingachgook in James Fenimore Cooper's *The Deerslayer.*

Dave Wain. Poet, friend and traveling companion of Jack Duluoz, and lover of Romana Swartz in Jack Kerouac's *Big Sur.*

Joseph Wainsworth. Harnessmaker in Bidwell, Ohio; because he is distressed at the coming industrialization, he goes crazy and kills Jim Gibson, his assistant, for having publicly humiliated him; shoots Steve Hunter for having opened the first factory in Bidwell; scratches and bites Hugh McVey for being the inventor who caused many of these changes in Sherwood Anderson's *Poor White.*

Edward Walcott. Harley College student who marries Ellen Langton in Nathaniel Hawthorne's *Fanshawe.*

Waldegrave. Brother of Mary Waldegrave; his murder initiates Edgar Huntly's derangement in Charles Brockden Brown's *Edgar Huntly.*

Mary Waldegrave. Sister of Waldegrave and sweetheart of Edgar Huntly in Charles Brockden Brown's *Edgar Huntly.*

Wald Waldemar. Horse player and only surviving blood relative of Von Humboldt Fleisher; Charlie Citrine gives Uncle Waldemar half his share of the money from the *Caldofredo* script in Saul Bellow's *Humboldt's Gift.*

Buck Walden. Son of Ty Ty Walden and husband of Griselda Walden; kills Jim Leslie Walden, who is courting Griselda, in Erskine Caldwell's *God's Little Acre.*

Darling Jill Walden. Voluptuous, sensual daughter of Ty Ty Walden in Erskine Caldwell's *God's Little Acre.*

Griselda Walden. Wife of Buck Walden; courted by Will Thompson and Jim Leslie Walden in Erskine Caldwell's *God's Little Acre.*

Jim Leslie Walden. Son of Ty Ty Walden; successful cotton broker who rejected his family; his passion for Griselda Walden causes Buck Walden to kill him in Erskine Caldwell's *God's Little Acre.*

John (John Warwick) Walden. Octoroon son of Molly Walden and elder brother of Rowena Walden; migrates to South Carolina, changes his name, and passes for white in Charles W. Chesnutt's *The House Behind the Cedars.*

Molly (Mis' Molly) Walden. Mulatto mother of John and Rowena Walden in Charles W. Chesnutt's *The House Behind the Cedars.*

Rosamond Walden. See Rosamond Walden Thompson.

Rowena (Rena) Walden. Octaroon daughter of Molly Walden and sister of John Walden; falls in love with George Tryon, who rejects her when he learns her true racial identity in Charles W. Chesnutt's *The House Behind the Cedars*.

Shaw Walden. Son of Ty Ty Walden in Erskine Caldwell's *God's Little Acre*.

Ty Ty Walden. Patriarch, prophet, and voyeur; Georgia farmer who digs for gold and does not plant the acre set aside for God in Erskine Caldwell's *God's Little Acre*.

Waldo. Juvenile delinquent and aspiring writer who goes to jail and college and shoots his older lover in Paul Theroux's *Waldo*.

Elaine (Estelle Walovsky) Wales. Young secretary of Phil Green; so ashamed of her heritage that she changed her name and cannot understand why anyone would admit to being Jewish in Laura Z. Hobson's *Gentleman's Agreement*.

Garvin Wales. Aging novelist who is the key to locating the missing money in Hamilton Basso's *The View from Pompey's Head*.

Lucy Devereaux Wales. Daughter of an old-line family who marries Garvin Wales for his fame and money in Hamilton Basso's *The View from Pompey's Head*.

Coalhouse Walker, Jr.. Educated black ragtime pianist whose Model T is trashed by Willie Conklin and others; organizes a gang to blow up the Emerald Isle fire station and occupies the Morgan Library; shot when he surrenders to the New York police in E. L. Doctorow's *Ragtime*.

Elizabeth Ann (Beth, Bethie, Cindy, Cynthia) Walker. Woman who leaves her traditional marriage and finds independence and her true identity as a lesbian in Marge Piercy's *Small Changes*.

Esther Walker. Society schemer who tries to swindle people into purchasing her husband's art; on a trip to Paris, tries to convince Aline Aldridge to have an affair with her in Sherwood Anderson's *Dark Laughter*.

Frank Walker. Physician who helps Paul Armstrong fake Armstrong's death; tries to force Louise Armstrong to marry him in Mary Roberts Rinehart's *The Circular Staircase*.

James (Jim) Hayes Walker. Husband of Beth Walker in Marge Piercy's *Small Changes*.

Mrs. Jamison Walker. Married American aristocrat who gives Paolo ruby cuff links and pays the Contessa for his services before her husband beats Paolo up in Tennessee Williams's *The Roman Spring of Mrs. Stone*.

Joe Walker. Painter who lets his wife Esther Walker set up schemes to sell his inferior art in Sherwood Anderson's *Dark Laughter*.

Mrs. Walker. American living in Rome; scandalized by Daisy Miller's disregard for her own reputation in Henry James's *Daisy Miller*.

Shurley (Shurl) Walker. Proprietor of a successful bar and former member of a black high school athletic team and neighborhood gang gathering for a birthday testimonial honoring Chappie Davis in John A. Williams's *The Junior Bachelor Society*.

Susan Walker. Boston woman who enrolls freed slaves in northern colleges in Thomas Dixon's *The Leopard's Spots*.

Tump Walker. Coach of the Mystic High School Rattlers in Harry Crews's *A Feast of Snakes*.

Mrs. Waldo Wallace Walker. Mother of Caroline English in John O'Hara's *Appointment in Samarra*.

Leesy Walkes. Elderly widow and great-aunt of Vere Walkes in Paule Marshall's *The Chosen Place, the Timeless People*.

Vere (Vereson) Walkes. Grand-nephew of Leesy Walkes; befriends Allen Fuso in Paule Marshall's *The Chosen Place, the Timeless People*.

Hugh Wall. Welsh former union organizer who lives on the income of his wife, an advertising copywriter; they rent a room to Eric Eisner in their Holland Park, London, home in Phillip Lopate's *Confessions of Summer*.

Aubrey Wallace. See Arnold Armstrong.

Binny Wallace. Boyhood friend of Tom Bailey; lost at sea in Thomas Bailey Aldrich's *The Story of a Bad Boy*.

Freddy Wallace. Bar owner who lends Harry Morgan a boat in Ernest Hemingway's *To Have and Have Not*.

Lucien Wallace. Son of Lucy Haswell and Arnold Armstrong (Aubrey Wallace) in Mary Roberts Rinehart's *The Circular Staircase*.

Gabriel (Gabe) Wallach. Live-in lover of Martha Reganhart and friend of Paul and Libby Herz, with whose separate and combined fortunes he is constantly involved, in Philip Roth's *Letting Go*.

Ina Inez Wallenius. Unpopular schoolmate befriended by Cress Delahanty in Jessamyn West's *Cress Delahanty*.

Mr. Wallenius. Father of Ina Wallenius; his disturbing behavior, including the torture of a gopher snake, forces Cress Delahanty to cut short her overnight stay with Ina in Jessamyn West's *Cress Delahanty*.

Emelyn Walley. Black radical and murderer in Nicholas Delbanco's *News*.

Evelyn Walling. Daughter of itinerant actors; adulterous lover of Paul Hardin in Brand Whitlock's *J. Hardin & Son*.

Wallner. Hot-rodding member of Gottlob Wut's German Motorcycle Unit Balkan 4; succeeds Wut as leader of the group, although he is later relieved of command, in John Irving's *Setting Free the Bears*.

Emma Wallop. Widow, retired nurse, erstwhile landlady of Randy Rivers, and putative model for his fictional "Mrs. Lusk"; actual model for Osgood Wallop's "Mrs. St. Cloud" in *The Duchess of Obloquy*, the film of which she finances; narrates part of Peter De Vries's *Mrs. Wallop*.

Osgood Wallop. Son of Emma Wallop; author of the novella *The Duchess of Obloquy* in Peter De Vries's *Mrs. Wallop*.

Ralph Wallop. Homosexual son of Cora Frawley; theatrical designer in Peter De Vries's *Mrs. Wallop*.

Estelle Walovsky. See Elaine Wales.

Carleton Walpole. Migrant farm worker and father of Clara Walpole in Joyce Carol Oates's *A Garden of Earthly Delights*.

Clara Walpole. See Clara Walpole Revere.

Walter. Mistreated German shepherd guard dog; nearly castrates dognapper Philo Skinner in Joseph Wambaugh's *The Black Marble*.

John Walters. Union League member who had refused to be conscripted into the Confederate army and who is murdered while attending the county nominating convention in Albion W. Tourgee's *A Fool's Errand*.

Mrs. Walters. Gossipy neighbor of Adam Moss in James Lane Allen's *A Kentucky Cardinal*; also appears in *Aftermath*.

Rover Walters. Black half brother of Forrest Mayfield from his mother's affair with Robinson Mayfield in Reynolds Price's *The Surface of Earth*.

Katharine (Kate) Walton. Daughter of Richard Walton and inamorata of both the British major Proctor and the partisan Robert Singleton in William Gilmore Simms's *The Partisan*.

Colonel Richard Walton. Important landholder who rejects offers of rank in the British service to join the American revolutionaries; captured at the Battle of Camden and sentenced to hang in William Gilmore Simms's *The Partisan*.

Elsie Wishnotski Waltz. Wife of Stan Waltz, mother of Tom Waltz, and "saved" evangelical Christian; successfully manages a furniture moving business when her husband is incapacitated in Peter De Vries's *Let Me Count the Ways*.

Stanley (Stan) Waltz. Agnostic owner of a moving and storage business, husband of Elsie Waltz, father of Tom Waltz, and victim of a twelve-year hangover; framing narrator and one of two protagonists of Peter De Vries's *Let Me Count the Ways*.

Thomas (Tom) Waltz. Son of Stan and Elsie Waltz and psychological product of his parents' antithetical religious views; member of the English faculty and eventually acting-president of Polycarp College; taken acutely ill at the shrine of Lourdes; central narrator and co-protagonist of Peter De Vries's *Let Me Count the Ways*.

Sarkin Aung Wan. Refugee from the Vietnam War and girlfriend of Paul Berlin, whom she urges to deny his obligations, in Tim O'Brien's *Going after Cacciato*.

Wanda. Flashy girlfriend of Jimmy Scalisi; has some scruples and a big mouth in George V. Higgins's *The Friends of Eddie Coyle*.

Wanda (Kickapoo). Adopted daughter of Orpha Chase; marries her mother's lover, Gregory McGovern, in Jessamyn West's *The Life I Really Lived*.

Ben Wanderhope. Dutch immigrant father of Don Wanderhope; delivers ice, then hauls garbage; fluctuates "between Faith and Reason" and is finally confined to an asylum in Peter De Vries's *The Blood of the Lamb*.

Carol Wanderhope. Daughter of Don and Greta Wanderhope; dies of leukemia at age twelve in Peter De Vries's *The Blood of the Lamb*.

Don Wanderhope. Son of Ben Wanderhope, husband of Greta Wanderhope, and father of Carol Wanderhope; reared in the Dutch Reformed faith; briefly confined to a tuberculosis sanitarium; succeeds his father in the garbage business and later becomes successful in advertising; narrator of Peter De Vries's *The Blood of the Lamb*.

Greta Wigbaldy Wanderhope. Youthful lover, then alcoholic wife of Don Wanderhope; a suicide in

Peter De Vries's *The Blood of the Lamb*.

Louie Wanderhope. Elder brother of Don Wanderhope; studies medicine at the University of Chicago and dies at age twenty in Peter De Vries's *The Blood of the Lamb*.

Gloria Wandrous. Beautiful brunette wanton leading a dissolute life in New York speakeasies in John O'Hara's *Butterfield 8*.

Mrs. (née Vandamm) Wandrous. Widowed mother of Gloria Wandrous; lives in Greenwich Village and is supported by her elder brother William Vandamm in John O'Hara's *Butterfield 8*.

Wang Lung. Peasant farmer who rises from poverty to wealth; ultimately leaves his mansion to retire to his land in Pearl Buck's *The Good Earth*; dies early in *Sons*.

Wang the Eldest, Wang the Landlord, Wang the Merchant, Wang the Second. See Nung En.

Wang the Third (Wang the Tiger). Serious student who falls in love with Pear Blossom; when he discovers that she is his father's mistress, he joins the army in Pearl Buck's *The Good Earth*; warlord and husband of three women in *Sons*; weakened warlord disappointed with his son and finally defeated by bandits in *A House Divided*.

Betsey MacCaffery Wapshot. Discontented wife of Coverly Wapshot in John Cheever's *The Wapshot Chronicle*; identified as Betsey Marcus Wapshot in *The Wapshot Scandal*.

Coverly Wapshot. Second son of Leander Wapshot; good-hearted but ineffectual dreamer in John Cheever's *The Wapshot Chronicle* and *The Wapshot Scandal*.

Ezekiel Wapshot. Emigrant from England aboard the *Arbella* in 1630; founds the Wapshot line in New England in John Cheever's *The Wapshot Chronicle*.

Honora Wapshot. Eccentric matriarch of the current Wapshot family and patroness of her cousins Moses and Coverly Wapshot; sometime foil to Leander Wapshot's schemes in John Cheever's *The Wapshot Chronicle*; fugitive from income tax authorities in *The Wapshot Scandal*.

Leander Wapshot. Father of Moses and Coverly Wapshot and current male head of the Wapshot clan; captain of the excursion boat *Topaze* and compulsive chronicler of his own life in John Cheever's *The Wapshot Chronicle* and *The Wapshot Scandal*.

Melissa Scaddon Wapshot. Beautiful ward of Justina Wapshot and subsequently wife of Moses Wapshot in John Cheever's *The Wapshot Chronicle*; has an affair with a grocery boy and settles in Rome in *The Wapshot Scandal*.

Moses Wapshot. Elder son of Leander Wapshot and a youth of considerable promise that remains unfulfilled as he passes into alcoholic failure in John Cheever's *The Wapshot Chronicle* and *The Wapshot Scandal*.

Sarah Coverly Wapshot. Wife of Leander Wapshot, village club organizer, and keeper of a floating gift shop converted from her husband's excursion boat in John Cheever's *The Wapshot Chronicle* and *The Wapshot Scandal*.

Warbler. See Yoomy.

Lord Warburton. Upper-class English radical, friend of Ralph Touchett, and admirer of Isabel Archer in Henry James's *The Portrait of a Lady*.

Ted Warburton. Television executive and colleague of David Bell; writes anonymous memos from fictional characters in Don DeLillo's *Americana*.

Agee Ward. Orphan seeking knowledge of his past; title character reported missing in Wright Morris's *The Man Who Was There*.

Billy Ward. Thirteen-year-old boy who has suffered a nervous breakdown in Louisa May Alcott's *Little Men*.

Jane Ward. See Jane Ward Carver.

John Ward. Chicago businessman and father of Jane and Isabel Ward in Margaret Ayer Barnes's *Years of Grace* and *Wisdom's Gate*.

Lizzie Ward. Conventional wife of John Ward and mother of Jane and Isabel Ward in Margaret Ayer Barnes's *Years of Grace* and *Wisdom's Gate*.

Lyman Ward. Retired history professor who researches and writes about his grandparents, Oliver and Susan Ward; narrator of Wallace Stegner's *Angle of Repose*.

Neal Dow Ward. Secretary to John Barclay and later editor of the Sycamore Ridge *Banner*; marries Jeanette Barclay when her father's wealth no longer threatens his moral integrity in William Allen White's *A Certain Rich Man*.

Oliver Ward. Mining engineer who is the husband of Susan Ward and the grandfather of Lyman Ward; pursues various jobs across the West and in Mexico, including a large irrigation project in Idaho, in

Wallace Stegner's *Angle of Repose.*

Oliver Burling (Ollie) Ward. Son of Susan and Oliver Ward in Wallace Stegner's *Angle of Repose.*

Susan Burling (Sue) Ward. Artist and writer who portrays the West while seeking to return to the more cultivated East; wife of Oliver Ward and grandmother of Lyman Ward in Wallace Stegner's *Angle of Repose.*

Ed Warden. Fellow railroad worker of Larry Donovan in Jack Conroy's *The Disinherited.*

Milton Anthony (Milt) Warden. First sergeant of G Company; has an affair with Karen Holmes, wife of his commanding officer, in James Jones's *From Here to Eternity.*

Alice Hastings Ware. Devoted wife of Theron Ware, who suspects her of infidelity with Levi Gorringe, in Harold Frederic's *The Damnation of Theron Ware.*

Cynthia Ware. See Cynthia Ware Wetherell.

Lugena Ware. See Lugena.

Nimbus Ware. See Nimbus.

Silas Ware. Overseer at Colonel Desmit's plantation and the person whose surname the freed slave Nimbus adopts in Albion W. Tourgee's *Bricks without Straw.*

Reverend Theron Ware. Naive and intellectually pretentious Methodist minister whose exposure to free-thinkers leads to a breakdown, after which he gives up religion for the real estate business; husband of Alice Hastings Ware in Harold Frederic's *The Damnation of Theron Ware.*

Major Ira (Old Hurricane) Warfield. Guardian of Capitola Le Noir and proprietor of Hurricane Hall in E.D.E.N. Southworth's *The Hidden Hand.*

Sarah McClellan Warfield. Twice-married sister of Everett and Martha McClellan; abandons the family farm and moves to Philadelphia in Joan Didion's *Run River.*

Ruth Warham. Cousin of Susan Lenox; wants to marry Lenox's boyfriend in David Graham Phillips's *Susan Lenox.*

Elison Warne. Half-white, half-Cherokee Indian younger daughter of Ewen Warne; wife of Savacol in H. L. Davis's *Beulah Land.*

Ewen Warne. Husband of Sedaya Gallet and father of Elison and Ruhama Warne in H. L. Davis's *Beulah Land.*

Ruhama Warne. Half-white, half-Cherokee Indian daughter of Ewen Warne; wife of Savacol and later of Askwani in H. L. Davis's *Beulah Land.*

Floyd Warner. Aged man on an archetypal journey involving conflict between young and old; abandons his great-nephew Kermit Oelsligle to the care of two hippies in Wright Morris's *Fire Sermon;* ritually killed by George Blackbird in *A Life.*

Albert Warren. President of Longevity Life Insurance Company; forces Erskine Fowler into early retirement in Richard Wright's *Savage Holiday.*

Beth Evan (Baby) Warren. Unprincipled sister of Nicole Warren in F. Scott Fitzgerald's *Tender Is the Night.*

Charles (Devereux) Warren. Millionaire father and seducer of Nicole Warren in F. Scott Fitzgerald's *Tender Is the Night.*

Nicole Warren. See Nicole Warren Diver.

Robert Warren. Son of Albert Warren; given Erskine Fowler's position as district manager for Manhattan as a wedding present from his father in Richard Wright's *Savage Holiday.*

Susan (Susie) Warren. Swinemaid almost raped by Ebenezer Cooke; actually Joan Toast in disguise in John Barth's *The Sot-Weed Factor.*

Philpot (Philly) Wart. Revolutionary War veteran; attorney in whom Frank Meriwether confides in John Pendleton Kennedy's *Swallow Barn.*

John Warwick. See John Walden.

Great Grief Warwickson. Impoverished artist who shares an apartment with Billie Hawker in Stephen Crane's *The Third Violet.*

Donald Washburn II. Character who appears in many guises and under many pseudonyms in Thomas Berger's *Who Is Teddy Villanova?*

Booker T. Washington. Educator and unsuccessful negotiator between the New York police and Coalhouse Walker, Jr., in E. L. Doctorow's *Ragtime.*

Estella Washington. Mistress, against her will, of Prince Cabano; rescued by Gabriel Weltstein, whom she marries, in Ignatius Donnelly's *Caesar's Column.*

George (Byron, Efan, Julius Makewell, Anthony Miller, Paul Winthrop) Washington. Young black American and part-time gigolo stranded in Copenhagen; protagonist of Cecil Brown's *The Life and Loves of Mr. Jiveass Nigger.*

George (Harper) Washington. Commander-in-chief of the Continental army during the American Revolution in James Fenimore Cooper's *The Spy*.

General George Washington. American Revolutionary War commander-in-chief who relies on Thomas Paine to keep the soldiers loyal, only to forget about him when Washington is president of the United States and Paine is jailed in France, in Howard Fast's *Citizen Tom Paine*.

Louisa Wasserman. See Louisa Calloway.

Michael Wasserman. Husband of Louisa Calloway; writer of an ongoing psychology dissertation and compulsive reader of detective novels in Alice Adams's *Families and Survivors*.

Eddie Watanabe. Parole officer of David Axelrod in Scott Spencer's *Endless Love*.

Charles Waterlow. American painter in Paris who encourages Gaston Probert in Henry James's *The Reverberator*.

Bradford Waters. Prominent republican pioneer of Dorbury, Ohio, who sympathizes with the Union; father of Mary Waters in Paul Laurence Dunbar's *The Fanatics*.

Harmonia H. (H. H.) Waters. Elderly female writer in Alison Lurie's *Real People*.

John (Jack) Waters. Resident of the Puerto Rican section of Harlem who commits himself to a sanitarium in John Clellon Holmes's *Go*.

Johnny Waters. Drug-taking movie actor who seduces Maria Wyeth in Joan Didion's *Play It As It Lays*.

Mary Waters. Union sympathizer who falls in love with Robert Van Doren, a Confederate soldier; daughter of Bradford Waters in Paul Laurence Dunbar's *The Fanatics*.

Mrs. Waters. Prostitute and mother of Toby Waters; Ironside outsider and challenger of the village's values who saves Ada Fincastle from the village mob in Ellen Glasgow's *Vein of Iron*.

Rev. Mr. Waters. Aged minister whose religious doubts lead him to abandon his church and native land; confidant of Theodore Colville and friend of Evalina Bowen in William Dean Howells's *Indian Summer*.

Toby Waters. Young Ironside idiot, social outcast, and victim of basic appetites in Ellen Glasgow's *Vein of Iron*.

C-J Watkins. Uncle of Abeba Torch who poses as her friend but sexually molests her over the period of a year in Ellease Southerland's *Let the Lion Eat Straw*.

Christine (Chrissie) Watkins. First victim of the Great White Shark in Peter Benchley's *Jaws*.

Eli (T. C. Brown) Watkins. Brother of Paul Watkins; radio preacher in Upton Sinclair's *Oil!*

Paul (Comrade Watkins) Watkins. Idealistic carpenter admired by Bunny Ross; member of the Communist party who is beaten and killed to suppress his political beliefs in Upton Sinclair's *Oil!*

Byrum (Big Byrom) Powery Watler. Experienced fisherman and turtler; dies when the *Lillias Eden* wrecks on Misteriosa Reef in Peter Matthiessen's *Far Tortuga*.

Belle Watling. Atlanta prostitute and mistress of Rhett Butler; lies to the Union soldiers in order to save the lives of Ashley Wilkes, Frank Kennedy, and other Confederate sympathizers in Margaret Mitchell's *Gone with the Wind*.

Watney. English rock musician who visits Bucky Wunderlick hoping to get from him a mysterious drug in Don DeLillo's *Great Jones Street*.

Bibleback Watrobinski. Witness to Bruno Lefty Bicek's murder of a nameless man; intimidated by Bonifacy Konstantine into turning Bicek in to the police in Nelson Algren's *Never Come Morning*.

Grover Watrous. Piano player with a club foot and a nose that "runs like a sewer"; believes it is a sin to bowl in Henry Miller's *Tropic of Capricorn*.

Anne Watson. Sister of Lucy Haswell and housekeeper at Sunnyside; confesses to murdering Arnold Armstrong in Mary Roberts Rinehart's *The Circular Staircase*.

Benjamin (Sailor Ben) Watson. Tattooed Nantucket sailor married to Kitty Collins; returns to her after a ten-year absence in Thomas Bailey Aldrich's *The Story of a Bad Boy*.

Johnnie Watson. Friend of William Baxter; one of Baxter's rivals for the affections of Miss Lola Pratt in Booth Tarkington's *Seventeen*.

Katherine Epps Watson. Wife of Thad Watson; dies giving birth to Eva Kendal's mother in Reynolds Price's *The Surface of Earth*.

Kenny Watson. Girlfriend of Scar; has difficulty finding employment after high school in Herbert Simmons's *Corner Boy*.

Kitty Watson. See Kitty Collins.

Matthew (Mat) Watson. Town blacksmith who employs Brackett Omensetter in William Gass's *Omensetter's Luck.*

Miss Watson. Owner of the slave Jim, whom she frees in her will, in Samuel Langhorne Clemens's *Adventures of Huckleberry Finn.*

Phoeby Watson. Best friend of Janie Crawford in Eatonville, Florida, and person to whom Janie's life story is addressed in Zora Neale Hurston's *Their Eyes Were Watching God.*

Thad Watson. Grandfather of Eva Kendal; killed himself when Eva's grandmother died giving birth to Eva's mother in Reynolds Price's *The Surface of Earth.*

Tom Watson. Denver pool shark who befriends young Cody Pomeray in Jack Kerouac's *Visions of Cody.*

Tom Watson. Lover of Nana; serenades her family in Aline Bernstein's *The Journey Down.*

Luther Watt. Friend of Mabry Jenkins; twice wins the all-around rodeo championship in Peter Gent's *Texas Celebrity Turkey Trot.*

Mr. Watterson. First officer aboard the *Aroostook* in William Dean Howells's *The Lady of the Aroostook.*

Mrs. Leora Watts. Prostitute who has the "friendliest bed in town"; Hazel Motes visits her on his arrival in Taulkinham to prove that sin is a meaningless concept in Flannery O'Connor's *Wise Blood.*

Ernst Watzek-Trummer. Austrian egg man; portrays the Austrian eagle by donning chicken feathers and parading through Vienna; moves to Kaprun with the Marters; keeper of the 1939 Grand Prix racing motorcycle in John Irving's *Setting Free the Bears.*

J. Henry Waugh. Actuarial, neurotic inventor of the dice-driven, imaginary Universal Baseball League in Robert Coover's *The Universal Baseball Association, Inc., J. Henry Waugh, Prop.*

Ike Wayfish. Liquor-loving clown in Huguenine's circus in Walter D. Edmonds's *Chad Hanna.*

Mr. Waymarsh. American lawyer and friend of Lambert Strether, whom he accompanies to Paris; reports to Mrs. Newsome on Strether's failure to encourage Chad Newsome to return to America in Henry James's *The Ambassadors.*

Mead Weaks. Short, slight, breathless chairman of a college English department; unable to relate to his son, Mead Weaks II; ineffective in relating to people in Frederick Busch's *Rounds.*

Mead Weaks II. Son of the chairman of a college English department; short, thin boy with gold-rimmed glasses; has a reputation for being mentally unstable and a drug user; leads authorities to rescue Mike Sorenson after Horace L'Ordinet kidnaps the baby in Frederick Busch's *Rounds.*

Wealtheow. Hostage queen to Hrothgar and comforter of warriors decimated by Grendel, who respects her as a source of grace in a problematic universe, in John Gardner's *Grendel.*

Roland Weary. Prisoner of war who dies of gangrene in Kurt Vonnegut's *Slaughterhouse-Five.*

Timothy (Varmounter) Weasel. Indian fighter in James Kirke Paulding's *The Dutchman's Fireside.*

Farmer Weatherbeat. Original owner of Dirty Eddie in Ludwig Bemelmans's *Dirty Eddie.*

Joseph Weatherby. Impoverished preacher who serves as minister to the wagon train in A. B. Guthrie's *The Way West.*

Twink Weatherby. Woman loved by Lem Forrester and Oliver Hutto; chooses Hutto over Forrester in Marjorie Kinnan Rawlings's *The Yearling.*

Harlan Weaver. Judge who presides over Frederic Manion's trial in Robert Traver's *Anatomy of a Murder.*

Robert Weaver. Childhood and college friend of Eugene Gant; his impulsiveness and love of alcohol lead Gant to suspect that rumors of insanity in the Weaver family might not be unfounded in Thomas Wolfe's *Of Time and the River.*

Samson Weaver. Owner of the *Sarsey Sal*, which Daniel Harrow owns upon Weaver's death, in Walter D. Edmonds's *Rome Haul.*

Charles Webb. White man who befriends Cecil Braithwaite in Europe in John Edgar Wideman's *Hurry Home.*

George Josiah (Monk, Monkus, Paul) Webber. Young writer who becomes a successful novelist in Thomas Wolfe's *You Can't Go Home Again* and *The Web and the Rock*; also appears in *The Hills Beyond.*

John Webber. Father of George Webber; causes a scandal in Libya Hills by abandoning his family to live openly with another man's wife in Thomas Wolfe's *The Hills Beyond* and *The Web and the Rock.*

Aaron Webster. Thoughtful and learned astronomer and pacifist; uncle and guardian of Holly Webster in Mark Harris's *The Southpaw.*

Cromwell (Ace) Webster. Incompetent commanding officer of an American battalion in the Spanish civil war in William Herrick's *Hermanos!*

Holly Webster. See Holly Webster Wiggen.

Robert (Bob, Roberto Ortega Menéndez y Castillo) Webster. Mexican-American protagonist who comes to the town of Hidalgo to work as quarry manager; discovers his kinship with the ruling house of Castillo and fully accepts his Mexican heritage in Josefina Niggli's *Mexican Village.*

Thayer (Web) Webster. Aged Massachusetts Superior Court judge who, in his intense hatred of anarchists, conspires with the prosecuting attorney to make Sacco and Vanzetti look like anti-social, murderous villains, despite evidence of their innocence, in Upton Sinclair's *Boston.*

Lorna Weech. Widow of Ron Weech and lover of his slayer, Valentine Hood, in Paul Theroux's *The Family Arsenal.*

Ron Weech. Cruel thug and thief murdered by Valentine Hood in Paul Theroux's *The Family Arsenal.*

Caroline Weed. See Caroline Weed Hubble.

Frederick Murdoch (Freddie) Weed. Shipyard owner and father of Caroline Weed in Leon Uris's *Trinity.*

Bunny Weeks. Homosexual restaurateur in Kurt Vonnegut's *God Bless You, Mr. Rosewater.*

Gabriel Weeks. Professor of Art History, husband of Ann Weeks, and lover of Jane Clifford in Gail Godwin's *The Odd Woman.*

Virgil Weeks. Watchman of the cabin used by Chris Van Eenanam and Ellen Strohe on their honeymoon in Larry Woiwode's *What I'm Going to Do, I Think.*

Robin and Ethel Weems. Researchers in sex physiology and friends of Joe and Naughty Sandwich in Peter De Vries's *The Vale of Laughter.*

Rollie Weems. Idealistic worker and union man; led by faith in his union's strike to an early death in Jack Conroy's *The Disinherited.*

Isaac Weeps-by-Night. Indian who teaches the Sioux language to Aaron Gadd in Sinclair Lewis's *The God-Seeker.*

Florence Wegenlied. Sister of Carrie Bolt and mother of Jennifer Denman in Rita Mae Brown's *Rubyfruit Jungle.*

Dr. Weidman. Physician to the Luries; his misdiagnosis of David Lurie's deviated septum leaves David vulnerable to a variety of childhood diseases in Chaim Potok's *In the Beginning.*

Nell Weil. Woman who identifies Joe Massara as a member of the gang that killed Jim Courtney in William Riley Burnett's *Little Caesar.*

Lieutenant Weincheck. Friend who shares Alison Langdon's appreciation of classical music; takes her and Anacleto to concerts in Carson McCullers's *Reflections in a Golden Eye.*

Barnet (Barn) Weiner. Poet and critic; friend of Leslie Braverman in Wallace Markfield's *To an Early Grave.*

Lester Weinstock. Public relations agent for Arvey Film Studio who is assigned to Dolly Moon following her success in Vito Orsini's *Mirrors*; falls in love with Moon, even though she is eight months pregnant by another man, in Judith Krantz's *Scruples.*

David (Dave) Weintraub. Expatriate American who introduces Samantha Everton to the Gallaghers in James Jones's *The Merry Month of May.*

Major S. O. Weiss. Army psychiatrist who tries to learn about Birdy from Alfonso Columbato in William Wharton's *Birdy.*

Maxie Weiss. Press agent for Glory Green in Alison Lurie's *The Nowhere City.*

Lieutenant (Captain Dominus Blicero, Major Weissmann) Weissmann. Debauched German officer encountered by Kurt Mondaugen at Foppl's Siege Party in Thomas Pynchon's *V.*; former lover of Oberst Enzian and, while engaged in building rocket 00000, the sexual manipulator of Katje Borgesius and Gottfried, finally firing the latter inside the completed rocket, in *Gravity's Rainbow.*

Thomas Welbeck. Forger and confidence man who attempts to use Arthur Mervyn in several schemes in Charles Brockden Brown's *Arthur Mervyn.*

John Welch. Orphaned cousin of Eva Birdsong; grows up to be a critical realist and to study medicine in Ellen Glasgow's *The Sheltered Life.*

Terrence (Genial) Weld. Thief considered by Inspector Lee to be responsible for the suicide of John Harrison in William S. Burroughs's *The Ticket That Exploded.*

Tom Weld. Neighbor of Joe Allston; develops a hillside into a subdivision in Wallace Stegner's *All the Little Live Things.*

Martin Welding. Mentally disturbed victim of social upheaval who seduces, impregnates, and abandons Milly Burden; marries Mary Victoria Littlepage in Ellen Glasgow's *They Stooped to Folly.*

Mary Victoria Littlepage Welding. Daughter of Victoria and Virginius Littlepage; nurse in the Balkans during World War I; virtuous idealist who, in trying to reunite Martin Welding and Milly Burden, eventually marries Welding in order to save him in Ellen Glasgow's *They Stooped to Folly.*

Arthur (Brother) Weldon. Meek, straw-hatted minister who travels the Nebraska countryside recruiting students for Temple College in Lincoln, where he teaches, in Willa Cather's *One of Ours.*

Augusta Welland. Daughter of Catherine Mingott, aunt of Ellen Olenska, and mother of May Welland in Edith Wharton's *The Age of Innocence.*

May Welland. Fiancée and then wife of Newland Archer; her conventionality contrasts with the independence of her cousin, Ellen Olenska, her rival for Archer's affections in Edith Wharton's *The Age of Innocence.*

Mr. Welland. Hypochondriacal father of May Welland and husband of Augusta Welland in Edith Wharton's *The Age of Innocence.*

Colmar (Cobby) Welles. Son of Susan Colmar Welles; president of the Franklin National Bank and Trust Company who commits suicide at the Kanewa Coronation in Mari Sandoz's *Capital City.*

Susan Colmar Welles. Widowed mother of Colmar Welles; owner of the Franklin National Bank and Trust Company in Mari Sandoz's *Capital City.*

Joe Welling. Standard Oil agent in Winesburg; courts Sarah King and befriends Tom and Edward King in Sherwood Anderson's *Winesburg, Ohio.*

Marion Wellington. Episcopalian "aristocrat," instructor of comparative religion at Polycarp College, and fiancée then wife of Tom Waltz in Peter De Vries's *Let Me Count the Ways.*

Mercy Wellington. Beautiful socialite who marries Compton Keith in Janet Flanner's *The Cubical City.*

Colonel Wellmere. Cowardly British officer who courts Sarah Wharton and is about to marry her when Harvey Birch reveals that Wellmere is already married in James Fenimore Cooper's *The Spy.*

Calliope (Callie) Wells. Abandoned sixteen year old who weds Henry Soames for the sake of her illegitimate son, Jimmy, in John Gardner's *Nickel Mountain.*

Floyd Wells. Cellmate of Richard Hickock in the Kansas State Penitentiary; tells Hickock about the Clutter family; informs police after the murders and becomes the most important witness in the murder trial in Truman Capote's *In Cold Blood.*

Will Wells. Black hired hand on Jack Beechum's farm; they work together until a destructive rage leads Wells into a fist fight with Beechum in Wendell Berry's *The Memory of Old Jack.*

Edward Welsh. Ill-tempered first sergeant who hates Private Witt and is instrumental in Witt's transfer out of C-for-Charlie Company in James Jones's *The Thin Red Line.*

Plotinus Plinlimmon Welsh. See Plotinus Plinlimmon.

Gabriel Weltstein. Ugandan sheep rancher, friend of Maximilian Petion, and husband of Estella Washington; exposes the Oligarchy's plot to destroy the Brotherhood of Destruction; founds a utopian community in Uganda after civilization falls; as a letter writer, he is the narrator of Ignatius Donnelly's *Caesar's Column.*

Heinrich Weltstein. Recipient of the letters of his brother Gabriel in Ignatius Donnelly's *Caesar's Column.*

Howard Wendall. Policeman who rapes and then marries the young Loretta Botsford; killed in a factory accident in Joyce Carol Oates's *them.*

Jules Wendall. Son of Loretta Wendall; young, idealistic pursuer of the American dream; becomes involved in the Detroit riots of the late 1960s in Joyce Carol Oates's *them.*

Loretta Botsford Wendall. Poor Detroit woman, mother of Jules and Maureen Wendall, wife of Howard Wendall and later of Pat Furlong; her life between 1936 and the late 1960s is chronicled in Joyce Carol Oates's *them.*

Mama Wendall. Domineering mother-in-law of Loretta Wendall in Joyce Carol Oates's *them.*

Maureen (Reeny) Wendall. Daughter of Loretta Wendall; becomes involved in prostitution and is badly beaten by her stepfather, Pat Furlong; seduces Jim Randolph away from his wife and marries him in Joyce Carol Oates's *them.*

Victor Wenk. Hack writer who tries to simplify Lee Youngdahl's play sufficiently for it to appear on Broadway in Mark Harris's *Wake Up, Stupid.*

Wenonga. Shawnee chief responsible for the massacre of Nathan Slaughter's family; killed by Slaughter in Robert Montgomery Bird's *Nick of the Woods*.

Charlotte Wentworth. Steadfast daughter of William Wentworth; marries Mr. Brand in Henry James's *The Europeans*.

Clifford Wentworth. Son of William Wentworth; marries Lizzie Acton in Henry James's *The Europeans*.

Dr. Kerstine Wentworth. Anthropologist sailing on the *Castel Felice*; becomes the companion of Dr. Norman Yas in Calvin Hernton's *Scarecrow*.

Elizabeth Wentworth. See Elizabeth Wentworth Acton.

Gertrude Wentworth. High-spirited daughter of William Wentworth; marries Felix Young in Henry James's *The Europeans*.

Hugh Wentworth. White novelist who attends integrated social and charitable functions in Nella Larsen's *Quicksand* and *Passing*.

Katherine (Kate) Wentworth. Widow whose family, once plantation aristocrats, have lost their wealth and prominence; mother of Saint and Polly Wentworth, whom she desires to be recognized by elite Charleston society, in DuBose Heyward's *Mamba's Daughters*.

Polly Wentworth. Daughter of Kate Wentworth in DuBose Heyward's *Mamba's Daughters*.

Reuben Wentworth. Town physician and leading citizen of Norwood who espouses a natural philosophy, teaches his daughter Rose to love nature, and practices a holistic form of medicine in Henry Ward Beecher's *Norwood*.

Rose Wentworth. Intelligent, loving, and sensitive daughter of Reuben Wentworth, who teaches her to love nature; becomes a nurse during the Civil War, rejects the advances of Frank Esel and Thomas Heywood, and marries Barton Cathcart in Henry Ward Beecher's *Norwood*.

St. Julien de Chatigny (Saint) Wentworth. Artistic and materialistic son of Kate Wentworth; manager of the commissary at the Phosphate Mining Company in DuBose Heyward's *Mamba's Daughters*.

Valerie Land lWentworth. See Valerie Land.

William Wentworth. Reserved American uncle of Eugenia Münster and Felix Young; acts as their host in Henry James's *The Europeans*.

William (Bill) Wentworth. Superintendent at the Casino who befriends Theophilus North by permitting him to give private tennis lessons to youngsters in Thornton Wilder's *Theophilus North*.

Arnold Wermy. Cliché-spouting president of Rugg College in Paul Theroux's *Waldo*.

Wolfgang Werner. Los Angeles policeman from Stuttgart and one object of Francis Tanaguchi's practical jokes in Joseph Wambaugh's *The Choirboys*.

Wes. Doctor of Richard Cantwell in Ernest Hemingway's *Across the River and into the Trees*.

WESCAC. West Campus Automatic Computer and true father of George Giles in John Barth's *Giles Goat-Boy*.

Wesley. Black man who helps Harry Morgan run a shipment of liquor to the Florida Keys in Ernest Hemingway's *To Have and Have Not*.

Emily (Aunt Wess) Wessels. Good-natured, simple aunt of Laura and Page Dearborn in Frank Norris's *The Pit*.

Arthur Francis (Artie) West. Student who threatens to knife Richard Dadier in Evan Hunter's *The Blackboard Jungle*.

Aurelia R. West. American from Rochester, New York, who travels through Europe with the Chatelaine in Henry Blake Fuller's *The Chatelaine of La Trinité*.

David West. Yacht steward in William Faulkner's *Mosquitoes*.

John Henry West. Bespectacled six-year-old cousin and playmate of Frankie Addams; dies of meningitis in Carson McCullers's *The Member of the Wedding*.

Josiah West. Internationally known painter in Brand Whitlock's *J. Hardin & Son*.

Julian West. Nineteenth-century Bostonian who, when he is hypnotized and awakens in the year 2000, learns how society has progressed; loves Edith Leete in Edward Bellamy's *Looking Backward*.

Tessie West. Friend of Ellen Chesser; Ellen runs away to find Tessie in Elizabeth Madox Roberts's *The Time of Man*.

Harold (Schultzy) Westbrook. Director of the *Cotton Blossom* company and husband of Elly Chipley in Edna Ferber's *Show Boat*.

Sybrandt Westbrook. Wilderness adventurer, fighter in the French and Indian War, and hero in James

Kirke Paulding's *The Dutchman's Fireside*.

Mary Westerman. Gossip who describes Mabel Blake as an unfit mother in Richard Wright's *Savage Holiday*.

Jasper Western. American inland sailor who leads a relief expedition to the Thousand Islands; loves and marries Mabel Dunham in James Fenimore Cooper's *The Pathfinder*.

Professor Westervelt. Mesmerist who uses Priscilla as the Veiled Lady in Nathaniel Hawthorne's *The Blithedale Romance*.

John Westlock. Father of Ned Westlock; religious fanatic who deserts his wife and their son in E. W. Howe's *The Story of a Country Town*.

Ned Westlock. Son of John Westlock and husband of Agnes Deming; narrator of E. W. Howe's *The Story of a Country Town*.

Clarence Weston, Sr. Corporation chairman aided and exploited by George Levanter in Jerzy Kosinski's *Blind Date*.

Sophia Westwyn (Courtland). Friend of Constantia Dudley; narrates the story of Constantia's battle with Ormond in Charles Brockden Brown's *Ormond*.

Caleb Wetherbee. Religious fanatic and cousin of Peter Alden; builds a Benedictine monastery in George Santayana's *The Last Puritan*.

Cynthia (Cynthy) Wetherell. Daughter of Cynthia Ware and William Wetherell; beloved ward of Jethro Bass following the death of her parents; marries Robert Worthington in Winston Churchill's *Coniston*.

Cynthia Ware (Cynthy) Wetherell. Beloved of Jethro Bass; marries William Wetherell; mother of Cynthia Wetherell in Winston Churchill's *Coniston*.

William (Will) Wetherell. Kind and loving, but ineffectual and sickly, husband of Cynthia Ware Wetherell; father of Cynthia Wetherell in Winston Churchill's *Coniston*.

Mrs. Wetwilliam. Mayflower Society luminary and regional chairman of the D.A.R.; social rival of Alma Marvel in Peter De Vries's *Through the Fields of Clover*.

Weucha. Treacherous Sioux warrior, a subordinate of Mahtoree; menaces Natty Bumppo and Bumppo's companions in James Fenimore Cooper's *The Prairie*.

Lottie Weyerhauser. Sister of Roberta Weyerhauser; convinces Roberta to marry George Brush and later convinces George to let Roberta divorce him in Thornton Wilder's *Heaven's My Destination*.

Roberta Weyerhauser. Young farm woman George Brush meets in Kansas; after they have sex, he searches for her, because, according to his beliefs, they are married; after finding her, he learns that she has been pregnant and apparently had an abortion; they marry and divorce in Thornton Wilder's *Heaven's My Destination*.

Alice Greenwood (Alice Jackson) Weylin. Freeborn black ancestor of Dana Franklin; enslaved by Rufus Weylin in Octavia E. Butler's *Kindred*.

Margaret Weylin. Mother of Rufus Weylin and wife of Tom Weylin in Octavia E. Butler's *Kindred*.

Rufus (Rufe) Weylin. White ancestor of Dana Franklin in Octavia E. Butler's *Kindred*.

Tom Weylin. Father of Rufus Weylin and husband of Margaret Weylin in Octavia E. Butler's *Kindred*.

Weymouth. Friend of Waldegrave; his inquiry about money he gave to Waldegrave which Edgar Huntly planned to keep leads to Huntly's further derangement in Charles Brockden Brown's *Edgar Huntly*.

Herbert (Spermwhale, Spermy) Whalen. Veteran Los Angeles policeman; one of ten protagonists in Joseph Wambaugh's *The Choirboys*.

Rev. Quintus Whaley. Oldtime black preacher who ministers to black workers at the Phosphate Mining Company in DuBose Heyward's *Mamba's Daughters*.

Walter (Whammer) Whambold. Famous homerun hitter who makes a bet with Sam Simpson over Roy Hobbs's pitching in Bernard Malamud's *The Natural*.

Richard Wharfinger. Seventeenth-century playwright and author of *The Courier's Tragedy*, which in one variant mentions the mysterious Tristero, in Thomas Pynchon's *The Crying of Lot 49*.

Eliza Wharton. Strong-willed society woman who dies because of her relationship with Peter Sanford in Hannah Webster Foster's *The Coquette*.

Frances Wharton. Younger daughter of Mr. Wharton; patriot sympathizer who marries Peyton Dunwoodie in James Fenimore Cooper's *The Spy*.

Henry Wharton. Son of Mr. Wharton; British army captain captured by the Virginia dragoons and condemned to death for espionage; escapes with the help of Harvey Birch in James Fenimore Cooper's *The Spy*.

M. Wharton. Affectionate and supportive mother of Eliza Wharton in Hannah Webster Foster's *The Coquette*.

Mr. Wharton. English father of Frances, Henry, and Sarah Wharton; secretly sympathizes with the royalists and lives on neutral ground hoping to escape the hostility of both sides in James Fenimore Cooper's *The Spy*.

Sarah Wharton. Elder daughter of Mr. Wharton flattered by the attention of British officers; suffers a breakdown when the existing marriage of her bridegroom, Colonel Wellmere, is revealed in James Fenimore Cooper's *The Spy*.

Mr. What's-his-name. Alliteration-prone United States vice-president who succeeds Trick E. Dixon in Philip Roth's *Our Gang*.

Gladys Wheatley. Detroit socialite, daughter of a wealthy banker, whom Charley Anderson marries and later abandons, prompting a financially crippling divorce in John Dos Passos's *U.S.A.* trilogy.

Mabel Wheatly. Young black prostitute who loves Jesus Ortiz and tries to discourage him from associating with hoodlums in Edward Lewis Wallant's *The Pawnbroker*.

April Wheeler. Failed actress and wife of Frank Wheeler; her dreams of moving to Paris with her family are thwarted, and she dies attempting to abort her third child in Richard Yates's *Revolutionary Road*.

Bayliss Wheeler. Eldest son of the Wheeler family who runs a farm-implement business and is a prohibitionist and pacifist in Willa Cather's *One of Ours*.

Chancey Wheeler. Youngest child of Sayward and Portius Wheeler; after being favored by his mother, he becomes a rebel, rejecting the pioneering values of struggle and hard work; edits a newspaper in Cincinnati, which his mother ultimately underwrites so he can continue his writing, in Conrad Richter's *The Town*.

Claude Wheeler. Restless Nebraskan seeking the meaning of life as a private college student, farmer, and lieutenant in World War I in Willa Cather's *One of Ours*.

Earl Wheeler. Father of Frank Wheeler; experiences lifelong disappointment because a promised promotion never occurs in Richard Yates's *Revolutionary Road*.

Evangeline Wheeler. Vermonter who goes to Nebraska to be a high school principal; she and her husband, Nat Wheeler, are the parents of Claude, Ralph, and Bayliss Wheeler in Willa Cather's *One of Ours*.

Franklin H. (Frank) Wheeler. Husband of April Wheeler; outwardly supports her plans to move to Paris, but inwardly is afraid to abandon his job at Knox Business Machines in Richard Yates's *Revolutionary Road*.

Guerdon Wheeler. Son of Sayward and Portius Wheeler; restless and hardworking man who marries a loose woman, kills one of her lovers, flees westward, and is never heard from again; appears in Conrad Richter's *The Fields* and *The Town*.

Colonel Isaiah Wheeler. Honest but combative Revolutionary War officer; Kike Lumsden turns to Wheeler for support against Enoch Lumsden in Edward Eggleston's *The Circuit Rider*.

Jason Wheeler. Former poet and former Communist, alcoholic pulp writer, friend of Leon Fisher, and resident of Twenty-Door City in Albert Halper's *Union Square*.

Luke Wheeler. Temporary farmhand at Pretty Pass and probable second husband of Ma Sigafoos in Peter De Vries's *I Hear America Swinging*.

Nat Wheeler. Wealthy Nebraska farmland owner who is neighborly, charitable, and likeable; he and his wife, Evangeline Wheeler, are the parents of Claude, Ralph, and Bayliss Wheeler in Willa Cather's *One of Ours*.

Portius Wheeler. Lawyer who flees his family in Massachusetts and lives a reclusive life in the Ohio territory until he marries Sayward Luckett in Conrad Richter's *The Trees*; resumes the practice of law and fathers an illegitimate child in *The Fields*; prospers in the activities of the community, builds a huge town mansion, becomes a judge, and dies in *The Town*.

Ralph Wheeler. Younger brother of Claude Wheeler; chief mechanic of the Wheelers' Nebraska farm and a Colorado rancher in Willa Cather's *One of Ours*.

Resolve Wheeler. First child of Sayward and Portius Wheeler; studies at the local academy and reads law with his father in Conrad Richter's *The Fields*; becomes a lawyer and eventually is elected governor of Ohio in *The Town*.

Jenny Wheelwright. See Jenny Wheelwright Milbury.

Judge Whimplewopper. Midget with a long, detachable nose that is the subject of a series of features in the *National Inquirer* in Ishmael Reed's *The Free-Lance Pallbearers*.

Mortimer (Mort) Whipple. Mayor of West Condon in Robert Coover's *The Origin of the Brunists*.

Nathan (Shagpoke) Whipple. Former president of the United States and founder of the National Revolutionary party; convinces Lemuel Pitkin to seek his fortune in New York in Nathanael West's *A Cool Million*.

Silas Whipple. Pro-Union lawyer and judge; friend of Stephen Brice in Winston Churchill's *The Crisis*.

Kenneth Whistler. Union organizer and spellbinding speaker in Kurt Vonnegut's *Jailbird*.

Laura Whitacre. Troubled wife of Michael Whitacre; moves with the fast set in Hollywood and New York and is finally divorced in Irwin Shaw's *The Young Lions*.

Michael Whitacre. Indecisive liberal and disillusioned stage director smothered by a sour marriage and stifled by the immoral life in Hollywood and New York; joins the army at the beginning of World War II and champions the ideals of patriotism and democracy in Irwin Shaw's *The Young Lions*.

Miss Whitaker. Nurse of the idiot Pinhead; murdered by Mickey McCane in Doris Betts's *The River to Pickle Beach*.

Corporal Whitcomb. Atheist and assistant to Chaplain Tappman; sends fill-in-the-blank form letters of condolence in Joseph Heller's *Catch-22*.

Donald (Don) Whitcomb. Reclusive Steering School teacher mistakenly thought to be Helen Holm's lover following T. S. Garp's death; writes Garp's biography in John Irving's *The World According to Garp*.

Elihue Micah (Soaphead Church) Whitcomb. Spiritualist and psychic reader consulted by Pecola Breedlove in her search for blue eyes in Toni Morrison's *The Bluest Eye*.

Pepper Whitcomb. Boyhood friend of Tom Bailey, who accidentally shoots Pepper in the mouth with an arrow; captured in the snowball fight; becomes a judge in Thomas Bailey Aldrich's *The Story of a Bad Boy*.

Abiram White. Brother of Esther Bush, brother-in-law of Ishmael Bush, principal kidnapper of Inez de Certavallos, and murderer of Asa Bush, his nephew, in James Fenimore Cooper's *The Prairie*.

Carietta (Carrie) White. High school student who uses her telekinetic powers for vengeance against classmates who tormented her in Stephen King's *Carrie*.

Eddie White. Husband of Molly Taylor White; dies after falling from an oil derrick in Larry McMurtry's *Leaving Cheyenne*.

Florence J. (Florrie) White. Business associate and rival of Eugene Witla; strives to have Witla fired in Theodore Dreiser's *The "Genius."*

Francis White. Officer in Cromwell's army and Cromwell's emissary to the dissenting soldiers; pleads with Cromwell to keep his word, but is considered cowardly by Johnny Church in Mary Lee Settle's *Prisons*.

Gary Cooper White. Drifter from Florida who, after being picked up by Theresa Dunn, kills her in Judith Rossner's *Looking for Mr. Goodbar*.

Helen White. Daughter of Winesburg's most prosperous citizen; has an occasional affair with George Willard in Sherwood Anderson's *Winesburg, Ohio*.

Joe White. See Joe.

Judith Stoloff (Jude) White. Mother of Isadora Wing; former artist who cannot tolerate anything ordinary in Erica Jong's *Fear of Flying*.

Margaret White. Religious fanatic who believes that the powers of her daughter, Carrie White, are evil in Stephen King's *Carrie*.

Miriam (Miri) White. Sister of Patsy White Carpenter and sister-in-law of Jim Carpenter; saved from drug addiction by her sister in Larry McMurtry's *Moving On*.

Molly Taylor White. Daughter of Cletus Taylor, wife of Eddie White, lover of Gideon Fry and Johnny McCloud, and mother of Jimmy and Joe; narrates part of Larry McMurtry's *Leaving Cheyenne*.

Stanford (Stanny) White. Famous architect who seduces Evelyn Nesbit; killed by Nesbit's husband Harry K. Thaw in E. L. Doctorow's *Ragtime*.

Wylie White. Screenwriter who hopes to marry Cecilia Brady in F. Scott Fitzgerald's *The Last Tycoon*.

White Fang. Part wolf, part dog; his vicious wolf nature is brought out by Lip-lip and Beauty Smith;

his loyal dog nature, by Weeden Scott, in Jack London's *White Fang*.

Chief White Halfoat. Half-blooded Creek Indian from Oklahoma, where his family moved from place to place, pursued as "human divining rods" by geologists in search of oil, in Joseph Heller's *Catch-22*.

White-Jacket. Narrator who, after many attempts, is finally able to rid himself of his jacket in Herman Melville's *White-Jacket*.

Margaret Whitehead. Young girl who befriends Nat Turner when he works for her mother; only white person Turner kills in the insurrection in William Styron's *The Confessions of Nat Turner*.

Sister Whiteside. Friend and neighbor of Aunt Hager Williams; gossips about "sinners" in the neighborhood and peddles vegetables in Langston Hughes's *Not Without Laughter*.

John Whitewood, Jr. Wealthy son of a famous college professor; becomes Edward Colburne's rival for Lillie Ravenel Carter's affections after the death of John Carter in John William DeForest's *Miss Ravenel's Conversion from Secession to Loyalty*.

Ben Whitey. Friend who joins the Home Guard with Joshua Birdwell when the Rebels threaten Vernon, Indiana, in Jessamyn West's *The Friendly Persuasion*.

Whitfield. Minister in William Faulkner's *The Hamlet*; father of Addie Bundren's son Jewel Bundren in *As I Lay Dying*.

Madeline Dills Whitfield. Pasadena divorcée; owner of the victim of a dognapping in Joseph Wambaugh's *The Black Marble*.

Elizabeth Fox (Foxy) Whitman. Pregnant wife of Ken Whitman; lover and later wife of Piet Hanema in John Updike's *Couples*.

Ken Whitman. Research biologist married to Foxy Whitman in John Updike's *Couples*.

Psyche Whitmore. Lover of Japhy Ryder who has to be thrown off the boat on which Ryder sails for Japan in Jack Kerouac's *The Dharma Bums*.

Florence (Flo) Whittaker. Tactless and disorganized but ingenuous wife of Jerrold Whittaker in Randall Jarrell's *Pictures from an Institution*.

Jerrold Whittaker. Teacher of sociology, professed liberal, and pretender to a familiarity with French literature in Randall Jarrell's *Pictures from an Institution*.

Big Foot Whitten. Mountain man who is Don Joaquin MacGillivray's assistant in H. L. Davis's *Harp of a Thousand Strings*.

Miss Whittle. Chief matron of the Alcanthia county home for light-skinned orphan girls in Burnside, Virginia, in Hal Bennett's *A Wilderness of Vines*.

Ishmael Whittman. Incompetent white officer promoted along a separate and unequal track intersecting the career of his black nemesis Abraham Blackman only during combat in World War II, Korea, and Vietnam in John A. Williams's *Captain Blackman*.

The Whole Sick Crew. Name given to a group that includes the artist Slab, record executive Gouverneur (Roony) Winsome, his wife Mafia, Fu, and Charisma in Thomas Pynchon's *V*.

Arthur Wiatte. Unsavory brother of Euphemia Lorimer; drives away Sarsefield; murdered by Clithero Edny; his death motivates the attempted murder of his sister in Charles Brockden Brown's *Edgar Huntly*.

Clarice Wiatte. See Clarice.

Ada Wickersham. Hotel operator in Manantiales; last person known to have befriended John Ashley; helps Ashley escape to Chile in Thornton Wilder's *The Eighth Day*.

Terry Wickett. Chemist at the McGurk Institute of Biology and friend of Martin Arrowsmith in Sinclair Lewis's *Arrowsmith*.

Harry Widener. Playboy and junior partner with Glymmer, Read in Nathan Asch's *The Office*.

Catharine Pleyel Wieland. Sister of Henry Pleyel and wife of Theodore Wieland; murdered by her husband in Charles Brockden Brown's *Wieland*.

Clara Wieland. Sister of Theodore Wieland; forces Carwin to confess his culpability in the murders committed by her brother; narrator of Charles Brockden Brown's *Wieland*.

Theodore Wieland. Brother of Clara Wieland and husband of Catharine Pleyel Wieland; led to kill his wife and their children by Carwin's biloquism in Charles Brockden Brown's *Wieland*.

Henry Whittier (Author, Hank) Wiggen. Brash left-handed pitcher for the New York Mammoths; hero and not entirely literate narrator of Mark Harris's *The Southpaw*, *Bang the Drum Slowly*, *A Ticket for a Seamstitch*, and *It Looked Like For Ever*.

Hilary Margaret Wiggen. Youngest daughter of Henry Wiggen; expresses her frustrations in screaming fits in Mark Harris's *It Looked Like For Ever*.

Holly Webster Wiggen. Girlfriend, then wife of Henry Wiggen in Mark Harris's *The Southpaw*, *Bang the Drum Slowly*, *A Ticket for a Seamstitch*, and *It Looked Like For Ever*.

Richard (Bubbles) Wiggins. Prosperous blue collar worker in a local factory and former member of a black high school athletic team and neighborhood gang gathering for a birthday testimonial honoring Chappie Davis in John A. Williams's *The Junior Bachelor Society*.

Theo G. (Tio) Wiggins. Wealthy black father of Martha Kinship and grandfather of Teddy and Lucinda Kinship in Shelby Foote's *September September*.

Harry Wilbourne. Medical intern imprisoned for killing his lover, Charlotte Rittenmeyer, during an attempted abortion in William Faulkner's *The Wild Palms*.

Ross Wilbur. Effeminate society-man who is shanghaied in San Francisco and who "becomes a man" under the influence of his lover, Moran Sternersen, in Frank Norris's *Moran of the Lady Letty*.

Jack Wilcox. American smuggler who lures Nelson Dyar to Tangier in Paul Bowles's *Let It Come Down*.

The Wild Child (Wile Chile). Feral adolescent girl whom Meridian Hill tries to befriend; struck and killed by a speeding car in Alice Walker's *Meridian*.

Janice Brady Wilder. Long-suffering wife of John Wilder; divorces him and marries their friend Paul Borg in Richard Yates's *Disturbing the Peace*.

John C. Wilder. Heavy-drinking advertising-space salesman whose plans to make a movie of his experiences in Bellevue Mental Hospital lead to further emotional collapses in Richard Yates's *Disturbing the Peace*.

Marjorie Wilder. Mother of John Wilder; wants John to assume control of her highly successful candy company, but he rejects the prospect in Richard Yates's *Disturbing the Peace*.

Tom (Tommy) Wilder. Lonely, withdrawn son of John and Janice Wilder; characteristically replies "I don't know, I don't care" to his father's inquiries in Richard Yates's *Disturbing the Peace*.

Jere Wilder-Halliday. Unstable, aging flapper; Manley Halliday's ex-wife and the object of his obsessions in Budd Schulberg's *The Disenchanted*.

Bert Wilderman. Free-hanging opponent of Clyde Stout in Jack Matthews's *Hanger Stout, Awake!*

Arty Wildgans. Head of the Wildgans Chase Agency in Ludwig Bemelmans's *Dirty Eddie*.

Montana Wildhack. B-movie starlet and Billy Pilgrim's mate on Tralfamadore in Kurt Vonnegut's *Slaughterhouse-Five*.

Margaret Thatcher Fitzhue (Mag) Wildwood. Tall, elegant fashion model; competes with Holly Golightly for eligible rich men in Truman Capote's *Breakfast at Tiffany's*.

Tommy (Wilhelm Adler, Velvel, Wilky) Wilhelm. Overweight, slovenly son of Dr. Adler, estranged husband, displaced father of two sons, unemployed former executive for the Rojax Corporation, and desperate struggler for a true identity and a better life; anti-hero badly advised and abandoned by quack psychologist Dr. Tamkin in Saul Bellow's *The Victim*.

Jonathan Wilk. Defense attorney for Artie Straus and Judd Steiner; argues that his clients are products of their environment and are not deviant criminals in Meyer Levin's *Compulsion*.

Jonas Wilkerson. Carpetbagger who raises the taxes on Tara in order to claim it as his own plantation; father of Emmie Slattery's illegitimate children in Margaret Mitchell's *Gone with the Wind*.

Orin (Sweetman) Wilkerson. Drunken, philandering father of Thomas Wilkerson; jailed for murder in John Edgar Wideman's *The Lynchers*.

Thomas Wilkerson. Teacher involved in Willie Hall's plan to lynch a white policeman; killed by fellow conspirator Graham Rice in John Edgar Wideman's *The Lynchers*.

Ashley Wilkes. Husband of Melanie Hamilton; pursued relentlessly as a love interest by Scarlett O'Hara in Margaret Mitchell's *Gone with the Wind*.

India Wilkes. Unmarried sister of Ashley Wilkes; accuses her brother and Scarlett O'Hara of being lovers, after witnessing them in a tender embrace, in Margaret Mitchell's *Gone with the Wind*.

John Wilkes. Phoenix gardener who assumes the role of a successful young millionaire businessman who agrees to back Renate's planned magazine in Anaïs Nin's *Collages*.

Melanie Hamilton (Miss Melly) Wilkes. Sister of Charles Hamilton, wife of Ashley Wilkes, and sister-in-law of Scarlett O'Hara; a devoted friend and defender of Scarlett in Margaret Mitchell's *Gone with the Wind*.

Joanna, Mary Jane, and Susan Wilks. Sisters and heirs of their father's wealth; saved by Huckleberry Finn from the Duke of Bridgewater and the Dauphin's scheme to steal their inheritance in Samuel Langhorne Clemens's *Adventures of Huckleberry Finn*.

Will. Slave cruelly treated by his owner; brutally kills many whites in the insurrection in William Styron's *The Confessions of Nat Turner*.

Willard. Three-foot-high papier-mâché bird placed by John and Patricia among the Logan brothers' stolen bowling trophies in Richard Brautigan's *Willard and His Bowling Trophies*.

Buddy Willard. Yale medical student and steady boyfriend of Esther Greenwood; their romance ends with his stay at a tuberculosis sanitorium and her suicide attempt in Sylvia Plath's *The Bell Jar*.

Elizabeth Willard. Mother of George Willard and owner of the New Willard House hotel; has a brief platonic affair with Doctor Reefy shortly before her death in Sherwood Anderson's *Winesburg, Ohio*.

George Willard. Aspiring writer and reporter for the *Winesburg Eagle*; his curiosity about human nature leads the townspeople to reveal their grotesqueries to him in Sherwood Anderson's *Winesburg, Ohio*.

Mr. Willard. Father of Buddy Willard; takes Esther Greenwood to visit his son at a sanitorium for tuberculosis patients in Sylvia Plath's *The Bell Jar*.

Mrs. (Nelly) Willard. Overbearing mother of Buddy Willard in Sylvia Plath's *The Bell Jar*.

Tom Willard. Father of George Willard and marginally successful proprietor of the New Willard House hotel in Sherwood Anderson's *Winesburg, Ohio*.

Willatale. Queen of the Arnewi tribe; bisexual and transcendental wise woman who sees in Eugene Henderson the spirit of vital life in Saul Bellow's *Henderson the Rain King*.

Eddie Willers. Personal secretary to Dagny Taggart in Ayn Rand's *Atlas Shrugged*.

Colin Willes. Thriller writer, socialite, and ladies' man with whom Salley Gardens has a protracted affair in Susan Cheever's *Looking for Work*.

Willett. Logging camp owner in William Dean Howells's *A Modern Instance*.

William. Attorney for his former wife Allegra Vand and guardian of her inheritance in Cynthia Ozick's *Trust*.

William. Watchman of the Bear Flag Restaurant; commits suicide with an ice pick following his rejection by the residents of the Palace Flophouse and Grill in John Steinbeck's *Cannery Row*.

Williams. Patriot colonel who helps free Arthur Butler from captivity in John Pendleton Kennedy's *Horse-Shoe Robinson*.

Williams. Black handyman and janitor at the Isaacson building in E. L. Doctorow's *The Book of Daniel*.

Williams. Witty maintopman aboard the *Neversink* in Herman Melville's *White-Jacket*.

Annabel Holznagel Williams. Wife of Ralph Williams and mother of Berry-berry and Clinton Williams in James Leo Herlihy's *All Fall Down*.

Annjelica Williams. See Mrs. Annjee Rodgers.

Berry-berry Williams. Wayward son of Ralph and Annabel Williams, older brother of Clinton Williams, and lover of Echo O'Brien; his treatment of Echo almost causes Clinton to murder him in James Leo Herlihy's *All Fall Down*.

Bessie Williams. Black singer at Mildred Sutton's funeral in Reynolds Price's *A Long and Happy Life*.

Clinton (Clint, Willy) Williams. Teenaged son of Ralph and Annabel Williams and younger brother of Berry-berry Williams; travels to Florida in search of Berry-berry and falls in love with his brother's girlfriend, Echo O'Brien, in James Leo Herlihy's *All Fall Down*.

Del Williams. Cowboy who falls in love with Taisie Lockhart; murdered by Cal Dalhart, his rival, in Emerson Hough's *North of 36*.

Edward (Eddie) Williams. Black student at Calvin Coolidge High School who sees every event as racially discriminatory in Bel Kaufman's *Up the Down Staircase*.

Father Williams. Priest to Susie Dahoney Holm; tries to befriend her husband Peder Holm in O. E. Rölvaag's *Their Father's God*.

Aunt Hager Williams. Overbearing yet jovial Christian grandmother of Sandy Rodgers; washes clothes and tends to the sick for a living in Langston Hughes's *Not Without Laughter*.

Harriett (Harrietta) Williams. Prodigal daughter of Aunt Hager Williams; resents her mother's piety and becomes both a prostitute and a blues singer in Langston Hughes's *Not Without Laughter*.

Jack Williams. Marshall of Billy, Oregon, and saloon owner; friend of Magic Child in Richard Brautigan's *The Hawkline Monster*.

Janey Williams. Ambitious stenographer and confidential secretary of J. Ward Morehouse in John Dos Passos's *U.S.A.* trilogy.

Jeffrey (Jeff) Williams. Black bandleader in Dorothy Baker's *Young Man with a Horn*.

Jennie Williams. Woman bludgeoned by the New York police when she accidentally appears in a crowd protesting the Sacco-Vanzetti executions in Nathan Asch's *Pay Day*.

Jo Bob Williams. Aggressive offensive lineman for the Dallas Cowboys who spends much of his time making life miserable for Phil Elliott and various rookies in Peter Gent's *North Dallas Forty*.

Joe Williams. Sailor brother of Janey Williams who goes AWOL from the U.S. Navy, is arrested as a spy in England, and marries unhappily, in John Dos Passos's *U.S.A.* trilogy.

John Williams. Blacksmith aboard the HMS *Bounty* who joins the rebellion in Charles Nordhoff and James Norman Hall's *Mutiny on the Bounty*; helps precipitate the violence between Tahitians and whites by seducing a Tahitian wife in *Pitcairn's Island*.

Marion Averley Williams. Abandoned, vengeful wife of Stuart Williams; divorces him after an eleven-year separation in Susan Glaspell's *Fidelity*.

Mrs. Williams. Mother of Jennie Williams; lives in the same building as the Cowans in Nathan Asch's *Pay Day*.

Nathan (Slim) Williams. Postal worker and friend of Jake Jackson; suffers from tuberculosis in Richard Wright's *Lawd Today*.

Private L. G. (Ellgee) Williams. Young soldier and stablekeeper so infatuated with Leonora Penderton he spies on her while she sleeps; followed and eventually killed by Captain Weldon Penderton in Carson McCullers's *Reflections in a Golden Eye*.

Ralph Williams. Husband of Annabel Williams and father of Berry-berry and Clinton Williams; works jigsaw puzzles in the basement in James Leo Herlihy's *All Fall Down*.

Robert (Bob) Williams. Older brother of Sam Williams; he alone, of all of Margaret Schofield's suitors, wins Penrod Schofield's approval, thus avoiding Penrod's antics; appears in Booth Tarkington's *Penrod*, *Penrod and Sam*, and *Penrod Jashber*.

Samuel (Sam) Williams. Best friend of Penrod Schofield; blithely follows Penrod into numerous adventures and troubles in Booth Tarkington's *Penrod*, *Penrod and Sam*, and *Penrod Jashber*.

Stuart Williams. Midwestern businessman who leaves his wife, Marion Averley Williams, and runs away with Ruth Holland in Susan Glaspell's *Fidelity*.

T. T. Williams. Restaurant owner and suitor of Berenice Sadie Brown in Carson McCullers's *The Member of the Wedding*.

Wash Williams. Winesburg telegraph operator; his misogyny results from his wife's indiscretions and his mother-in-law's subsequent perverse attempt to reconcile the couple in Sherwood Anderson's *Winesburg, Ohio*.

William (Clean Willy) Williams. Accomplice of Edward Pierce in Michael Crichton's *The Great Train Robbery*.

William Carlos Williams. Seventy-two-year-old physician and poet; Jack Duluoz visits Williams in New Jersey, accompanied by Irwin Garden, Simon Darlovsky, and Raphael Urso, in Jack Kerouac's *Desolation Angels*.

Willie. Crew member on Thomas Hudson's boat during submarine hunting in Ernest Hemingway's *Islands in the Stream*.

Willie (Little Willie). Twenty-year-old farmhand and, for a brief time, lover of Ollie in George Wylie Henderson's *Ollie Miss*.

Will Willing. Friend and biographer of George Apley; outdoes Apley in devotion to social convention in John P. Marquand's *The Late George Apley*.

Gerald (Gerry) Willis. Son of Kitty Willis Dubin by her first marriage; rejects his adoptive father's name after deserting the army and fleeing to Stockholm in Bernard Malamud's *Dubin's Lives*.

Martin Willis. Arizona highway patrol officer who kills five people and then commits suicide after being exposed to the Andromeda Strain in Michael Crichton's *The Andromeda Strain*.

Second Lieutenant Stanley M. Willis. Black officer struck by Benny Carricker for nearly causing the crash of General Ira N. Beal's plane; awarded a medal for an earlier exploit in James Gould

Cozzens's *Guard of Honor*.

Walter Willis. Customer in a hair salon in John Edgar Wideman's *Hurry Home*.

Stan Williston. Affluent gentile whose persistent apologies for Kirby Allbee are a constant source of chagrin to Asa Leventhal in Saul Bellow's *The Victim*.

John C. Willoughby. Millionaire playboy in William Riley Burnett's *Little Caesar*.

Daniel Cable Wills. Boston attorney and father of Daniel Compton Wills and Andrew Collier; serves as control to OSS agent General Aubrey Gammage in World War II; frees the formula for synthetic rubber from the Nazis for use by the Allies in George V. Higgins's *Dreamland*.

Daniel Compton (Comp) Wills. Boston attorney, son of Daniel Cable Wills, and half brother of Andrew Collier; denies blood kinship with Collier and seduces Collier's wife; narrator of George V. Higgins's *Dreamland*.

Edweena (Toinette) Wills. Fiancée of Henry Simmons in Thornton Wilder's *Theophilus North*.

Tom Wills. Friend of Bruce Dudley; newspaperman who shares with Dudley Wills his love of art and his desire to do more with his writing ability in Sherwood Anderson's *Dark Laughter*.

Donald Willsson. Newspaper publisher, son of Elihu Willsson, who initially engages the Continental Detective Agency to investigate corruption in Personville in Dashiell Hammett's *Red Harvest*.

Elihu Willsson. Wealthy, corrupt patriarch of Personville in Dashiell Hammett's *Red Harvest*.

Willy The Fink, Willy The Rat. See Uranian Willy.

Uncle Willy. See Uncle Willy Christian.

Billy Wilmerdings. Incorrigible son of a butcher; goes to sea in Henry Wadsworth Longfellow's *Kavanagh*.

George Wilmington. Husband of Lyra Wilmington and owner of the stocking mill in which his wife previously worked in William Dean Howells's *Annie Kilburn*.

Jack Wilmington. Nephew of Lyra Wilmington in William Dean Howells's *Annie Kilburn*.

Lyra Goodman Wilmington. Friend of Annie Kilburn; her marriage to an older, prosperous man causes scandal in William Dean Howells's *Annie Kilburn*.

Lee Wilshire. Girlfriend of Bernie Despain in Dashiell Hammett's *The Glass Key*.

Wilson. British consul on Tahiti in Herman Melville's *Omoo*.

Wilson. Loud soldier who comforts the wounded Henry Fleming and later fights alongside him in Stephen Crane's *The Red Badge of Courage*.

Anthony (Tony) Wilson. Abusive husband of Sarah Grimes Wilson in Richard Yates's *Easter Parade*.

Baby Wilson. Niece of Biff Brannon and daughter of Lucile and Leroy Wilson; survives a gunshot wound in Carson McCullers's *The Heart Is a Lonely Hunter*.

Clyde Wilson. Husband of Evalin McCabe Wilson in Diane Johnson's *The Shadow Knows*.

David (Pudd'nhead) Wilson. Eccentric and intelligent lawyer and surveyor whom the residents of Dawson's Landing consider a fool; his long-term hobby of fingerprinting helps him solve the murder of York Driscoll in Samuel Langhorne Clemens's *Pudd'nhead Wilson*.

Edward (Beau) Wilson. Londoner killed in a duel by John Law in Emerson Hough's *The Mississippi Bubble*.

Evalin McCabe (Ev) Wilson. Maid and babysitter for N. Hexam; Hexam believes that Wilson was murdered in Diane Johnson's *The Shadow Knows*.

Geoffrey Wilson. Father of Tony Wilson; falsely claims to be a London war refugee, inherits a dilapidated mansion, and becomes the object of Esther Grimes's flirting in Richard Yates's *Easter Parade*.

George B. Wilson. Husband of Myrtle Wilson; murders Jay Gatsby in F. Scott Fitzgerald's *The Great Gatsby*.

Leroy Wilson. Father of Baby Wilson; twice marries and twice deserts Lucile Wilson in Carson McCullers's *The Heart Is a Lonely Hunter*.

Lucile Wilson. Cosmetologist ambitious to develop the talents of her four-year-old daughter, Baby Wilson; wife of Leroy Wilson and sister-in-law of Biff Brannon in Carson McCullers's *The Heart Is a Lonely Hunter*.

Myrtle Wilson. Mistress of Tom Buchanan; killed in a hit-and-run accident by Daisy Buchanan in F. Scott Fitzgerald's *The Great Gatsby*.

Peter Wilson. Second son of Tony and Sarah Grimes Wilson; acts as guardian to his aunt, Emily Grimes, in her last days in Richard Yates's *Easter Parade*.

Samuel (Gunner) Wilson. Jet pilot who does night-time reconnaissance of Piedmont, Arizona, in Michael Crichton's *The Andromeda Strain*.

Sarah Grimes Wilson. Older sister of Emily Grimes and wife of Tony Wilson; becomes alcoholic in middle age, endures abuse by her husband, and dies after a fall in Richard Yates's *Easter Parade*.

Terry Wilson. Girlfriend of Teddy, who leads her into the world of drugs and prostitution; institutionalized after Minnie's suicide in Donald Goines's *Dopefiend*.

Woodrow Wilson. Hard-drinking southern soldier in Norman Mailer's *The Naked and the Dead*.

Benjamin (Ben) Wilton. Inadequately Charleston-educated brother of Cornelia Wilton in Caroline Gilman's *Recollections of a Southern Matron*.

Cornelia Wilton. Submissive wife of Arthur Marion; nurse of both white and black plantation children; narrator of Caroline Gilman's *Recollections of a Southern Matron*.

Henry Wilton. Dashing, witty, and generous father of Cornelia Wilton Marion in Caroline Gilman's *Recollections of a Southern Matron*.

Richard (Dick) Wilton. Brother of Cornelia Wilton; injured in a college duel in Caroline Gilman's *Recollections of a Southern Matron*.

Luke Wimble. Orchardist whose praise of Ellen Chesser Kent restores her spirits in Elizabeth Madox Roberts's *The Time of Man*.

Erastus Winch. Farm equipment salesman and trader in cheese; conspires with fellow church trustee Loren Pierce to cheat Levi Gorringe in Harold Frederic's *The Damnation of Theron Ware*.

Martin (Mart) Winch. Middle-aged first sergeant who returns from duty in the South Pacific with a heart ailment to find that his wife is promiscuous; becomes involved with Carol Firebaugh; continues to help three of his men—John Strange, Marion Landers, and Bobby Prell—after their return to the United States in James Jones's *Whistle*.

Nettie Wincher. See Marquise de Trézac.

Mrs. Winchester. Wealthy, cultured, kindly old aunt of Dick Dale in Sarah Orne Jewett's *A Marsh Island*.

Dr. Elizaveta (Lise, Liza) Innokentievna Bogolepov Pnin Wind. Former wife of Timofey Pnin; works as a psychologist with her second husband, Dr. Eric Wind, by whom she has the child Victor; goes on

to marry twice again in Vladimir Nabokov's *Pnin*.

Dr. Eric Wind. Psychotherapist for whom Liza Pnin leaves her husband and with whom she collaborates on psychology projects in Vladimir Nabokov's *Pnin*.

Victor Wind. Enormously talented child artist and son of Drs. Eric and Liza Wind; fantasizes about an imaginary father and seems genuinely fond of Timofey Pnin, whom he visits one Easter vacation, in Vladimir Nabokov's *Pnin*.

Berzelius Noel Weinacht (Buzz) Windrip. Democratic candidate for president who, when elected, turns the United States into a fascist state in Sinclair Lewis's *It Can't Happen Here*.

Cudge Windsor. Owner of a pool hall in Stanton, Kansas, where many local black men and boys hang out; Sandy Rodgers goes to the pool hall to escape his snobbish aunt, Mrs. Tempy Siles, in Langston Hughes's *Not Without Laughter*.

Bennett Wing. Chinese psychoanalyst and second husband of Isadora Wing in Erica Jong's *Fear of Flying* and *How to Save Your Own Life*.

Isadora Zelda White Stollerman Wing. Jewish poet who searches for herself through affairs and two marriages in Erica Jong's *Fear of Flying* and *How to Save Your Own Life*.

Esther Pollard Wingate. Mother of Esther Wingate Sturgis; successful farmer and land developer in Shelby Foote's *Jordan County*.

Ezra Wingate. Barn owner whose stagecoach Tom Bailey and others steal in Thomas Bailey Aldrich's *The Story of a Bad Boy*.

Hector Wingate. Husband of Esther Pollard Wingate and father of Esther Wingate Sturgis in Shelby Foote's *Jordan County*.

Jed Wingate. Son of Jesse and Molly Wingate and brother of Little Molly Wingate in Emerson Hough's *The Covered Wagon*.

Jesse Wingate. Leader of the Oregon-bound wagon train in Emerson Hough's *The Covered Wagon*.

Molly Wingate. Wife of Jesse Wingate and mother of Jed and Little Molly Wingate in Emerson Hough's *The Covered Wagon*.

Molly (Little Molly) Wingate. Daughter of Jesse and Molly Wingate; heroine of Emerson Hough's *The Covered Wagon*.

Stephen Wingate. Financial agent for the imprisoned Frank Cowperwood in Theodore Dreiser's *The*

Financier.

Brother Wingfare. Evangelical preacher whose religious activity contrasts with the nonreligious righteousness of Old Jack Beechum in Wendell Berry's *The Memory of Old Jack.*

Barbara Winkle. Governess and housekeeper at Swallow Barn in John Pendleton Kennedy's *Swallow Barn.*

Arthur Winner Junior. Prosperous and respected lawyer who regards the passions as subverting order and who believes that "youth's a kind of infirmity" in James Gould Cozzens's *By Love Possessed.*

Arthur Winner Senior. Dead father of Arthur Winner Junior; in his intellectual detachment and avoidance of emotional excess, epitomizes the Man of Reason in James Gould Cozzens's *By Love Possessed.*

Clarissa Henderson Winner. Sensible and devoted younger wife of Arthur Winner Junior in James Gould Cozzens's *By Love Possessed.*

Winnie. Tall Times Square night person; drug addict and thief in John Clellan Holmes's *Go.*

Suzanne Winograd. Professional tennis player who behaves childishly in Mark Harris's *It Looked Like For Ever.*

Rachel Winslow. Prominent parishioner of Henry Maxwell; gifted singer and friend of Virginia Page in Charles M. Sheldon's *In His Steps.*

Euston Peters Winslow-Davis. Horribly deformed dwarf who is wealthy enough to travel continuously; friend of Hellos and witness to Scarecrow's murder of her in Calvin Hernton's *Scarecrow.*

Mafia Winsome. Novelist who has developed a theory known as "Heroic Love"; a member of the Whole Sick Crew in Thomas Pynchon's *V.*

Mark Winsome. Mystic who warns Frank Goodman to beware of Charlie Noble in Herman Melville's *The Confidence-Man.*

Winstock. Army corporal who uses his authority to take the pistol from Richard Mast, who later steals it back, in James Jones's *The Pistol.*

Dorabella Winter. Younger daughter of Edith and Severin Winter, sister of Fiordiligi Winter, and friend and playmate of Jack and Bart; badly cut by shattering glass in John Irving's *The 158-Pound Marriage.*

Edith Fuller Winter. Wife of Severin Winter, mother of Dorabella and Fiordiligi Winter, and close friend of Utch Thalhammer and the unnamed narrator; has an affair with the narrator when the couples swap mates; attempts to seduce and humble George James Bender in John Irving's *The 158-Pound Marriage.*

Fiordiligi Winter. Older daughter of Edith and Severin Winter, sister of Dorabella Winter, and playmate and friend of Jack and Bart; badly cut by shattering glass in John Irving's *The 158-Pound Marriage.*

Kurt Winter. Husband of Katrina Marek and father of Severin Winter; famous painter who does nude, erotic paintings of Katrina in John Irving's *The 158-Pound Marriage.*

Miss Winter. Music teacher who befriends Meridian Hill in Alice Walker's *Meridian.*

Severin Winter. Son of Kurt and Katrina Marek and nephew of Vaso Trivanovich and Zivan Knezevich, who teach him to wrestle; husband of Edith Fuller Winter and father of Dorabella and Fiordiligi Winter; university German teacher and wrestling coach who has an affair with Audrey Cannon in John Irving's *The 158-Pound Marriage.*

Frederick Forsyth Winterbourne. American in Europe fascinated with Daisy Miller and jealous of her relationship with Giovanelli; unable to decide if Daisy is respectable in Henry James's *Daisy Miller.*

Ex-P.F.C. Wintergreen. Mail clerk whose control over communications gives him virtual command of the Twenty-seventh Air Force Headquarters; "a snide little punk who enjoyed working at cross purposes" in Joseph Heller's *Catch-22.*

Thor Wintergreen. Idealistic descendant of the European elite and member of Berbelang's Third World group; outsmarted and killed by Biff Musclewhite in Ishmael Reed's *Mumbo Jumbo.*

Ed Winters. Half-breed saw crewman at the Past Bay Manufacturing Company factory who proposes a walk-out to force Carl Belcher out as foreman; assaults Belcher during the power outage in Robert Cantwell's *The Land of Plenty.*

Hal Winters. Winesburg farmhand who asks Ray Pearson for advice in Sherwood Anderson's *Winesburg, Ohio.*

Amos (Amos Jordan) Winthrop. Father of Monica Winthrop and rival of Jonas Cord, Sr.; atones for his feud with the elder Cord by saving the life of Jonas Cord, Jr., after a plane crash in Harold Robbins's *The Carpetbaggers.*

Billy (Honey) Winthrop. See Wilhelmina Hunnenwell Winthrop Ikehorn Orsini.

Monica Winthrop. Daughter of Amos Winthrop, ex-wife of Jonas Cord, Jr., and mother of Jo-Ann in Harold Robbins's *The Carpetbaggers*.

Ralph Winwood. Painter who secretly paints a portrait of his cousin Pierre Glendinning II in Herman Melville's *Pierre*.

Frank (Blue Fairy Godmother, Col. Harold J. Sparrow) Wirtanen. United States Army major and spymaster of Howard Campbell in Kurt Vonnegut's *Mother Night*.

Eva Wiseman. Sister of Julius Kauffman and guest at the yacht party in William Faulkner's *Mosquitoes*.

Miss Wisteria. Midget in a traveling show; young Idabel Thompkins falls in love with her in Truman Capote's *Other Voices, Other Rooms*.

Mrs. William Wallace Witcher. Vice-president of the Mothers' League for Good Morals in Horace McCoy's *They Shoot Horses, Don't They?*

Witcikti (the Bald Eagle). Catawba warrior who accompanies the Shawnee raiding party that attacks Beulah; kills Jeremiah and Hannah Catlett and is killed by Ezekiel Catlett in Mary Lee Settle's *O Beulah Land*.

Witherby. Dishonest Boston newspaper publisher in William Dean Howells's *A Modern Instance*.

Nathaniel Turner (Spoons) Witherspoon. Custodian at Dolphin's Lounge and keen observer of the lives of his many friends; confidant and eulogizer of Regal Pettibone in Leon Forrest's *The Bloodworth Orphans*.

Angela Witla. Daughter of Angela Blue and Eugene Witla; her birth awakens her father's aesthetic sense in Theodore Dreiser's *The "Genius."*

Angela Blue Witla. Wife of Eugene Witla; dies giving birth to Angela Witla in Theodore Dreiser's *The "Genius."*

Eugene Tennyson (Genie, Henry Kingsland) Witla. Failed artist and businessman who becomes successful following the birth of his daughter Angela; lover of many women in Theodore Dreiser's *The "Genius."*

Private Witt. Boxer from Kentucky whose antagonistic behavior toward James Stein and Edward Welsh causes him to be transferred to the Cannon Company in James Jones's *The Thin Red Line*.

Pia Wittkin. Best friend of Isadora Wing in high school and college in Erica Jong's *Fear of Flying*.

Anthony (Antek the Owner) Witwicki. Alcoholic owner of the Tug & Maul Bar in Nelson Algren's *The Man with the Golden Arm*.

Mrs. Wix. Dowdy, much-loved governess of Maisie Farange; ignores textbooks to focus instead on her charge's sense of responsibility and moral development in Henry James's *What Maisie Knew*.

Dr. Woestijne. Superintendent of Health for whom Martin Arrowsmith works in Sinclair Lewis's *Arrowsmith*.

Charlotte Wolf. Noncirculating librarian at Calvin Coolidge High School who says students are not to be sent to the school library for any reason whatsoever and no books are to be removed from library shelves until the card catalog is brought up to date in Bel Kaufman's *Up the Down Staircase*.

Hat and Luke Wolf. Sharecropper neighbors of Jerry and Judith Blackford in Edith Summers Kelley's *Weeds*.

John Wolf. Honorable publisher who uses his cleaning woman, Jillsy Sloper, as a barometer of a book's probable success in John Irving's *The World According to Garp*.

Julia (Nancy Kane) Wolf. Clyde Wynant's consort and confidential secretary with a criminal past who is murdered in Dashiell Hammett's *The Thin Man*.

Wolf-Boy. Character from Dalton Harron's lost manuscript who appears in Harron's recurrent dreams in Susan Sontag's *Death Kit*.

Dr. Wolfe. Physician who first diagnoses Ben Flesh's multiple sclerosis in Stanley Elkin's *The Franchiser*.

Hugh Molly Wolfe. Oppressed laborer and artist who takes his life to avoid imprisonment in Rebecca Harding Davis's *Life in the Iron Mills*.

Old Wolfe. Welsh emigrant and laborer; father of Hugh Wolfe in Rebecca Harding Davis's *Life in the Iron Mills*.

John Wolff. Tory storekeeper who is imprisoned in a Connecticut mine, escapes, and searches vainly for his wife in Walter D. Edmonds's *Drums along the Mohawk*.

Rodger Wolfherald. Passenger who burns the *Here They Come* in Gregory Corso's *The American Express*.

Wolfie (Fat Morty). American mercenary, Jew, and confederate of Lewis Moon; bombs and strafes the Niaruna village on orders from Comandante Guzmán in Peter Matthiessen's *At Play in the Fields of the Lord*.

Fred Wolfpits. Homosexual collector of Orientalia and college classmate of Waldo in Paul Theroux's *Waldo*.

Meyer Wolfsheim. Racketeer who fixed the 1919 World Series; Jay Gatsby's partner in F. Scott Fitzgerald's *The Great Gatsby*.

Womwom. "Soul at the seventh aspect" of Wylie Norton in Robert Coover's *The Origin of the Brunists*.

Walter Wong. Fuller brush salesman and husband of Ceci O'Connor in Alison Lurie's *The Nowhere City*.

John Wood. Elderly farmer and participant in the Indian massacre who pleads guilty and is hanged in Jessamyn West's *The Massacre at Fall Creek*.

John (Johnny) Wood, Jr. Participant in the Indian massacre who is given a last-minute reprieve at the gallows in Jessamyn West's *The Massacre at Fall Creek*.

Mary Stark (Molly) Wood. Vermont aristocrat who goes to the West to teach; marries the Virginian in Owen Wister's *The Virginian*.

Reba Reese Wood. Second wife of John Wood and sister of George Benson in Jessamyn West's *The Massacre at Fall Creek*.

Susannah Wood. Starlet paramour of Carter Lang; beaten up by an actor in Joan Didion's *Play It As It Lays*.

Woodburn. Virginia colonel who is writing a book about the merits of slavery in William Dean Howells's *A Hazard of New Fortunes*.

Miss Woodburn. Daughter of Colonel Woodburn; marries Fulkerson in William Dean Howells's *A Hazard of New Fortunes*.

John Woodcock. One of three Englishmen sympathetic to the American cause who send Israel Potter as courier to Benjamin Franklin in Paris; dies of apoplexy while keeping Potter in a hidden chamber in Herman Melville's *Israel Potter*.

Luther (Woodie) Woodcock. Light-skinned black medic from Abraham Blackman's Charlie Company in Vietnam; infiltrated along with other such "white" soldiers by Blackman into strategic positions to thwart racist command decisions in the American military in John A. Williams's *Captain Blackman*.

Andrew John Woodhouse. Infant son of Satan and Rosemary Woodhouse; born with yellow eyes, orange hair, and budding horns, claws, and tail in Ira Levin's *Rosemary's Baby*.

Guy Woodhouse. Actor-husband of Rosemary Woodhouse; to further his career, conspires with devil worshippers in the seduction of his wife by Satan in Ira Levin's *Rosemary's Baby*.

Rosemary Woodhouse. Young New Yorker and wife of Guy Woodhouse; chosen without her knowledge to be the mother of Satan's first-born son in Ira Levin's *Rosemary's Baby*.

Samuel Payson (Sam) Woodhull. Wagon-train leader who contests with Will Banion for the love of Molly Wingate in Emerson Hough's *The Covered Wagon*.

Colonel (Woody) Woodman. Disgruntled alcoholic commander at Sellers Field who, passed over for advancement, commits suicide in James Gould Cozzens's *Guard of Honor*.

Bill Woodruff. Cuckold who gets revenge on his wife by beating her in Henry Miller's *Black Spring*.

Thurston Printise (Piney) Woods. Immature and unpredictable young catcher for the New York Mammoths in Mark Harris's *Bang the Drum Slowly* and *A Ticket for a Seamstitch*.

Vergible (Tea Cake) Woods. Hedonistic young man who becomes Janie Crawford's third husband; takes her from Eatonville, Florida, to the Everglades, where she shoots and kills him after he has been bitten by a rabid dog during a hurricane, in Zora Neale Hurston's *Their Eyes Were Watching God*.

Woody. Priest and golf player at the retreat in John Updike's *A Month of Sundays*.

Kerney Woolbright. Ambitious candidate for the state senate who for political gain betrays his friend Duncan Harper in Elizabeth Spencer's *The Voice at the Back Door*.

Dr. Emerson Woolcape. Black dentist in Sinclair Lewis's *Kingsblood Royal*.

David (Dave, Davidele, Davy) Woolf. Nephew of Bernie Norman; takes over management of Norman's movie studio after it is bought by Jonas Cord, Jr.; dies at Anzio in World War II in Harold Robbins's *The Carpetbaggers*.

Eliot Woolf. New York lawyer and Jewish convert to Episcopalianism who questions Noah Tuttle's irregular financial accounts in James Gould Cozzens's *By Love Possessed*.

Harrison Woolf. See Harrison Hawke.

Wooloo. Polynesian servant of Captain Claret aboard the *Neversink* in Herman Melville's *White-Jacket*.

Arnold (Little Arnie) Worch. Jewish gang chief run out of Chicago by Rico Bandello in William Riley Burnett's *Little Caesar*.

Belle Worsham. Spinster in William Faulkner's *Go Down, Moses*.

Doctor Worsham. Minister in William Faulkner's *The Unvanquished*.

Hamp Worsham. Brother of Molly Beauchamp and Belle Worsham's servant in William Faulkner's *Go Down, Moses*.

General Daniel Worth. Confederate general and plantation owner who disapproves of the romance of his daughter Sallie Worth with Charles Gaston in Thomas Dixon's *The Leopard's Spots*.

Sallie Worth. Daughter of General Daniel Worth; marries Charles Gaston against her father's wishes in Thomas Dixon's *The Leopard's Spots*.

Willie Joe Worth. Former alcoholic, police officer in Somerton, and lover of Emma Jones; to keep his name from being revealed in divorce proceedings against her, Worth murders L. B. Jones and mutilates his body in Jesse Hill Ford's *The Liberation of Lord Byron Jones*.

Worthington (Mr. W.). Supervisor of Paul Galambos; promises to let Galambos do sex experiments in Scott Spencer's *Last Night at the Brain Thieves Ball*.

Cynthia Wetherell Worthington. See Cynthia Wetherell.

Daria Erskine Paulus Worthington. Introspective wife of Smith Worthington and half sister of Eliza Quarles; treated in a sanitarium after her fourth miscarriage in Alice Adams's *Listening to Billie*.

Isaac Dudley Worthington. Father of Robert Worthington; rapacious and vicious businessman and opponent of Jethro Bass in Winston Churchill's *Coniston*.

Robert (Bob) Worthington. Principled son of Isaac Worthington; husband of the younger Cynthia Wetherell in Winston Churchill's *Coniston*.

Smith Worthington. Hardworking international businessman married to Daria Worthington in Alice Adams's *Listening to Billie*.

Jack Worthy. Friend and correspondent of Tommy Harrington in William Hill Brown's *The Power of Sympathy*.

Ben Wosznik. Brunist songwriter and spiritual whip in Robert Coover's *The Origin of the Brunists*.

Wounded Face. Uncle of Laughing Boy; opposes his nephew's association with Slim Girl in Oliver La Farge's *Laughing Boy*.

Woytek. Childhood friend George Levanter encourages to defect to the West; with his lover Gibby and others, slain in a Charles Manson-style massacre in Jerzy Kosinski's *Blind Date*.

Russel (Russ) Wren. Erudite detective whose imagination fuels his bizarre adventures; narrator of Thomas Berger's *Who Is Teddy Villanova?*

Clothilde Brill Wright. Twice-widowed mother of Harry and Bella Brill; cousin of Jim Calder; lives on small income with her unemployed adult children in the decaying ancestral home Wickford Point in John P. Marquand's *Wickford Point*.

Helene Sabat Wright. Mother of Nel Wright and daughter of Rochelle Sabat in Toni Morrison's *Sula*.

Heritage (Kam, Kamikazee) Wright. Activist with a penchant for spray-painting the sides of buildings; survives the explosion, goes on the run, and murders Bill Armiston for betraying the group in M. F. Beal's *Amazon One*.

Lucille Wright. Inquisitive friend of Helen Clarke; accompanies Helen to the Blackwood home for tea; relates the story of the Blackwood family poisonings in Shirley Jackson's *We Have Always Lived in the Castle*.

Nel Wright. Best friend of Sula Peace; daughter of Helene Wright and wife of Jude in Toni Morrison's *Sula*.

Robert Wright. Philadelphia publisher who agrees to publish Charles Schuyler's memoirs of Aaron Burr by a ghostwriter in Gore Vidal's *Burr*.

Tom Wright. Rival of Augie; a "bad nigger" who contends with Joe Baily for the affection of Florence Dessau in Arna Wendell Bontemps's *God Sends Sunday*.

Wiley Wright. Husband of Helene Wright in Toni Morrison's *Sula*.

Willie (Father) Wright. Religious fanatic; one of ten Los Angeles policemen-protagonists in Joseph Wambaugh's *The Choirboys*.

Wrinkles (Wrink). Starving artist; shares an apartment with Billie Hawker in Stephen Crane's *The Third Violet*.

Walter (Wally) Wronken. Assistant stage manager at South Wind camp for adults; pursues Marjorie Morningstar; becomes a successful playwright in Herman Wouk's *Marjorie Morningstar*.

Maurice Xavier Wu. Anthropologist with a special interest in caves; unearths evidence for a prehistoric temporary reversal of the evolutionary process ("reverse evolution") in Don DeLillo's *Ratner's Star*.

Bucky Wunderlick. Popular rock singer who suddenly quits his band, escapes to a small New York apartment, and gets involved in elaborate intrigue over a mysterious drug; narrator of Don DeLillo's *Great Jones Street*.

Jerry Wung. Chinese-American tenant in the Mott Street building managed by Norman Moonbloom in Edward Lewis Wallant's *The Tenants of Moonbloom*.

Professor A. Wunsch. Drunken German musician who gives the young Thea Kronborg piano lessons in Willa Cather's *The Song of the Lark*.

Gottlob Wut. Leader of the German Motorcycle Unit Balkan 4; killed by his men in an outhouse in John Irving's *Setting Free the Bears*.

Vida Sherwin Wutherspoon. See Vida Sherwin.

Ellis Wyatt. Ingenious oil producer who invents the means of extracting petroleum from shale; destroys his operation and disappears in protest against dictatorial government directives in Ayn Rand's *Atlas Shrugged*.

Sarah Wyatt. Friend of Walter F. Starbuck and wife of Leland Clewes in Kurt Vonnegut's *Jailbird*.

Tracy Wyatt. Multimillionaire who marries Donna Cravat in Edna Ferber's *Cimarron*.

Norine Wyckoff. Elderly woman who enlists the aid of Theophilus North in ridding her house of its ghosts in Thornton Wilder's *Theophilus North*.

Sarah Wydman. English lady and lover of Abe Cady; speaks for the English Jewish community in Leon Uris's *QB VII*.

Francine Wyeth. Mother of Maria Wyeth and wife of Harry Wyeth; runs her car off a highway in Nevada and is eaten by coyotes in Joan Didion's *Play It As It Lays*.

Harry Wyeth. Gambler father of Maria Wyeth in Joan Didion's *Play It As It Lays*.

Maria (Mrs. Lang) Wyeth. Depressed movie actress who is committed to a sanitarium after abetting the suicide of BZ; wife of Carter Lang and mother of Kate Lang in Joan Didion's *Play It As It Lays*.

Sidney (Books, Brown Skin) Wyeth. Author who sells his book throughout the South; eventually marries Mildred Latham in Oscar Micheaux's *The Forged Note*.

Wymontoo-Hee (Luff). Native of Hannamanoo who joins the crew of the *Julia* in Herman Melville's *Omoo*.

Gail Wynand. Tabloid publisher who builds an empire by serving mediocrity in Ayn Rand's *The Fountainhead*.

Clyde Wynant. Eccentric inventor who is the missing person and title character of Dashiell Hammett's *The Thin Man*.

Dorothy Wynant. Daughter of the eccentric inventor Clyde Wynant; she enlists the help of Nick Charles in locating her missing father in Dashiell Hammett's *The Thin Man*.

Gilbert Wynant. Bookish son of Clyde Wynant and brother of Dorothy Wynant in Dashiell Hammett's *The Thin Man*.

Lyle Wynant. Wall Street businessman who, as a government informer, becomes involved in a plot to bomb the Stock Exchange in Don DeLillo's *Players*.

Pammy Wynant. Employee of Grief Management Council in the World Trade Center; wife of Lyle Wynant and friend of Ethan Segal and Jack Laws in Don DeLillo's *Players*.

Ashby Porsum Wyndham. Cousin of Private Porsum and poor white who quits his job with the Massey Mountain Lumber Company and becomes a religious witness; writes the Statement of Ashby Wyndham while in jail in Robert Penn Warren's *At Heaven's Gate*.

Miss Caroline (Carrie) Wynn. School teacher who becomes involved in politics in an attempt to save her job; marries Sam Stillings because he has more money and position than her other suitors in W. E. B. Du Bois's *The Quest of the Silver Fleece*.

May (Marie Minotti) Wynn. Singer and girlfriend of Willie Keith in Herman Wouk's *The Caine Mutiny*.

XYZ

Robert X (Etienne Sims). Illegitimate son of Johanna Sims and the Reverend Phillip Martin; mysteriously and inopportunely appears to identify himself and to confront his father in Ernest J. Gaines's *In My Father's House.*

Father Xantes. Roman Catholic missionary who competes with his Protestant counterparts for the souls of the South American Indians in Peter Matthiessen's *At Play in the Fields of the Lord.*

Father Xavier. Childhood guardian of Anthony Adverse; tells Adverse that John Bonnyfeather is Adverse's grandfather in Hervey Allen's *Anthony Adverse.*

Xolotl. Mayan boy into whom the narrator is transformed in William S. Burroughs's *The Soft Machine*; lover and comrade of El Niño Muerto in the Mayan Jungle in *The Wild Boys.*

Samuel (Sad Sam) Yale. Aging star pitcher for the New York Mammoths replaced by Henry Wiggen in Mark Harris's *The Southpaw.*

Robert (Bob) Yamm. Midget pinch hitter for the Kakoola Reapers; commanded under threat of death not to swing his bat in Philip Roth's *The Great American Novel.*

Nick Yanov. Field sergeant of the Wilshire Police Station in Joseph Wambaugh's *The Choirboys.*

Lew Yard. The criminal boss in charge of thievery and fencing in Personville in Dashiell Hammett's *Red Harvest.*

Yardley. Cynical and senior drinking buddy of Jack Flowers in Singapore in Paul Theroux's *Saint Jack.*

Joab Yarkoni. Moroccan Jew and military trainer of refugee children in Leon Uris's *Exodus.*

Dr. Norman Yas. Sixty-one-year-old beatnik psychiatrist; self-proclaimed "existential psychotherapist" with a novel approach to schizophrenia; traveler aboard the *Castel Felice* in Calvin Hernton's *Scarecrow.*

Yates. Quiet drinking buddy of Jack Flowers in Singapore in Paul Theroux's *Saint Jack.*

Adelaide Yates. Wife of Stephen Yates; her comments about the "stranger people's" burial ground lead some to think her a murderess in Mary Noailles Murfree's *In the "Stranger People's" Country.*

Albany (Lady Lillian) Yates. Manipulator of men and school rider for Huguenine's circus; deserts the circus, but returns after being rescued from Burke and Walsh's circus by Chad Hanna, in Walter D. Edmonds's *Chad Hanna.*

Edward Hamilton Yates. Scottish lawyer who befriends Salathiel Albine and later becomes his partner; appears in Hervey Allen's *The Forest and the Fort, Bedford Village,* and *Toward the Morning.*

Stephen (Steve) Yates. Husband of Adelaide Yates; joins some outlaws while seeking a doctor for Leonard Rhodes, although people think he has disappeared mysteriously, in Mary Noailles Murfree's *In the "Stranger People's" Country.*

Hrant Yazdabian. Owner of a dress manufacturing firm; becomes a partner of Harry Bogen, but Bogen steals from their firm, in Jerome Weidman's *What's in It for Me?*

José Ybarra-Jaegar. Brazilian government official with whom Holly Golightly falls in love; deserts her when she is linked to a drug scandal in Truman Capote's *Breakfast at Tiffany's.*

Jackson (William [Bill, Willie] Carter) Yeager. Former writer and member of the editorial staff of Black Christian Publishing Company; killed his wife's lover, decapitated his wife, and joined the Hippodrome's cast in Cyrus Colter's *The Hippodrome.*

Ed Yellings. Black American itinerant who succeeds in the gumbo business and who is murdered by agents of the Louisiana Red Corporation because he is close to discovering a cure for heroin addiction in Ishmael Reed's *The Last Days of Louisiana Red.*

Minnie (Minnie the Moocher, Queen of the Moochers) Yellings. Youngest daughter of Ed Yellings; brought up by Nanny Lisa on Louisiana Red stories which depict black men as brutish louts; burns her father's gumbo business, frees Andy Brown and Kingfish Stevens from jail, and, as she is hijacking an airplane, is shot by Chorus, but not fatally because PaPa LaBas goes to the underworld to plead for her, in Ishmael Reed's *The Last Days of Louisiana Red.*

Street Yellings. Son of Ed Yellings; prisoner who has his consciousness raised while in jail; upon escaping, he is granted asylum in an "emerging" African nation, but Max Kasavubu returns him to the United States, where he and his brother, Wolf Yellings, kill each other in a quarrel over which of them will run their father's gumbo business in Ishmael Reed's *The Last Days of Louisiana Red*.

Wolf Yellings. Wise son of Ed Yellings; runs the gumbo business following his father's murder, but is killed in a shootout with his brother, Street Yellings, in Ishmael Reed's *The Last Days of Louisiana Red*.

Yellow Hand. Comanche Indian chief who punishes Sim Rudabaugh in Emerson Hough's *North of 36*.

Yellow Jim (Yaller Jim). Slave sold by George Posey to buy an expensive mare; returns and assaults Jane Posey; killed by George Posey in Allen Tate's *The Fathers*.

Sir Henry Yelverton. Attorney general of England in George Garrett's *Death of the Fox*.

Johnny Yen (Yenshe). Switch artist who performs by changing sexes in William S. Burroughs's *Nova Express*, *The Soft Machine*, and *The Ticket That Exploded*.

Sam Yerger. Hemingway-like writer and longtime friend of Emily Bolling in Walker Percy's *The Moviegoer*.

Yillah. White woman saved from death by Taji, captured by Queen Hautia, and pursued by Taji in Herman Melville's *Mardi*.

August (Gus) Yoder. German immigrant who farms land adjacent to the Wheelers for thirty years and is charged with disloyalty at the outbreak of World War I in Willa Cather's *One of Ours*.

Yoky. Deformed king of Hooloomooloo, the island of cripples, in Herman Melville's *Mardi*.

Yoomy (Warbler). Minstrel from Odo and Taji's companion in Herman Melville's *Mardi*.

York. See James Stuart, Duke of York.

Kakosan Yoshida. Exotic young Japanese woman taken up by Boston society; mistress of both Harry Morgan and Nathan Kadish in Jean Stafford's *Boston Adventure*.

Yossarian (Yo-Yo). Air force captain in World War II, bombardier, and malingerer traumatized by the death of Snowden and the absurdity and malignity of Catch-22 in Joseph Heller's *Catch-22*.

Youma. Loyal servant of Madame Léonie Peyronnette and lover of Gabriel; burned to death in a fire during a black riot in the West Indies in Lafcadio Hearn's *Youma*.

Edward (Ned) Young. Midshipman aboard the HMS *Bounty* who sleeps through the rebellion but later joins the mutineers in Charles Nordhoff and James Norman Hall's *Mutiny on the Bounty*; survives the violence between Tahitians and whites, but dies of asthmatic complications shortly after teaching Alexander Smith to read and write in *Pitcairn's Island*.

Felix Young. Bohemian artist and brother of Eugenia Münster; marries Gertrude Wentworth in Henry James's *The Europeans*.

Gertrude Wentworth Young. See Gertrude Wentworth.

Guy Young. Handsome actor and homosexual; has a brief sexual encounter with Johnny Rio in John Rechy's *Numbers*.

Linda (Lindy) Young. Maid to Agatha Cramp and Fred Merrit; falls in love with Joshua (Shine) Jones in Rudolph Fisher's *The Walls of Jericho*.

Pansetta Young. Classmate and first girlfriend of Sandy Rodgers; invites Sandy and other boys to her house while her mother works in Langston Hughes's *Not Without Laughter*.

Rosalie Young. Accident victim who stays with the Wapshots while recovering; her intimacy with Moses Wapshot, inadvertently witnessed by Honora Wapshot, leads to his being sent out into the world to make his way in John Cheever's *The Wapshot Chronicle*.

Margie Young-Hunt. Attractive tarot card reader; lover and confidante of several New Baytown men who tries unsuccessfully to compromise Ethan Allen Hawley's new-found status by seducing him in John Steinbeck's *The Winter of Our Discontent*.

Jimmy Youngblood. See Jimmy Lee Smith.

Beth Youngdahl. Pregnant wife of Lee Youngdahl in Mark Harris's *Wake Up, Stupid*.

Dee Youngdahl. Brother of Lee Youngdahl in Mark Harris's *Wake Up, Stupid*.

Lee W. Youngdahl. College teacher, playwright, former professional boxer, and dissatisfied protagonist of Mark Harris's *Wake Up, Stupid*.

Younger Bear. Cheyenne friend of Little Big Man; becomes a "Contrary" in Thomas Berger's *Little Big Man*.

Younger Brother. See Mother's Younger Brother.

Mark Youngerman. Basketball player at Olinger High School and student of George Caldwell in John Updike's *The Centaur*.

Perry Yturbide. Ex-convict and friend of Cody Pomeray and Billie Dabney; his excessive affection for young girls frightens Jack Duluoz in Jack Kerouac's *Big Sur*.

I. Y. Yunioshi. Neighbor of Holly Golightly in New York; photographer who discovers the carved wooden head of Holly in Africa years after she has fled New York in Truman Capote's *Breakfast at Tiffany's*.

Yves. French male prostitute with whom Eric Jones falls in love in James Baldwin's *Another Country*.

Yvette. French prostitute who is hired as a body double for Arabella in Boris Adrian's pornographic movie in Terry Southern's *Blue Movie*.

Zagayek. Adulterous husband of a paralytic wife who has an incestuous bond with his daughter; his lasciviousness, sadism, and greed oppress the village peasants; tavern owner and bailiff who arranges Jacob Eliezer's freedom in Isaac Bashevis Singer's *The Slave*.

Moishe (Reb Moishe) Zakolkower. Civic leader of Josefov, Poland, and one of three men who ransom Jacob Eliezer out of slavery in Isaac Bashevis Singer's *The Slave*.

Alan Zapalac. Exobiology instructor at Logos College in Don DeLillo's *End Zone*.

Vera Chipmunk-5 Zappa. Farmer, slave owner, and friend of Wilbur Swain in Kurt Vonnegut's *Slapstick*.

Zar. Russian immigrant who arrives with four prostitutes in Hard Times, where he builds a saloon; killed by one of Leo Jenks's wild shots in E. L. Doctorow's *Welcome to Hard Times*.

Countess Marie Ogden (Gräfin, Countess Josef, Mary) Zattiany. Fifty-eight-year-old woman faced with the choice between power and influence as the wife of an Austrian diplomat and rejuvenation as the wife of Lee Clavering in Gertrude Atherton's *Black Oxen*.

Pete Zavras. Cameraman helped by Monroe Stahr in F. Scott Fitzgerald's *The Last Tycoon*.

Eva Maria Zawistowska. Eight-year-old daughter of Sophie Zawistowska; dies in a Birkenau crematorium in William Styron's *Sophie's Choice*.

Jan Zawistowska. Ten-year-old son of Sophie Zawistowska confined in the children's camp at Auschwitz; his fate remains unknown in William Styron's *Sophie's Choice*.

Zofia Maria Biegańska (Irma Griese, Sophie, Zosia) Zawistowska. Polish Catholic survivor of Auschwitz, lover of Nathan Landau, and central character in Stingo's tale in William Styron's *Sophie's Choice*.

Bolek Zbarski. Son of Elzbieta Zbarski and brother of Magda Zbarski; loathes Yasha Mazur for bringing ignominy on Magda in Isaac Bashevis Singer's *The Magician of Lublin*.

Elzbieta Zbarski. Widowed mother of Magda and Bolek Zbarski; obese, loquacious, and sorrowful, she depends on Yasha Mazur for income and sympathy in Isaac Bashevis Singer's *The Magician of Lublin*.

Magda Zbarski. Mistress of Yasha Mazur, daughter of Elzbieta Zbarski, and sister of Bolek Zbarski; travels with Yasha and performs as an acrobat in his magic show; commits suicide when she believes Yasha will abandon her for another woman in Isaac Bashevis Singer's *The Magician of Lublin*.

Dr. Bruno Zechlin. Professor at Mizpah Seminary whose career Elmer Gantry ruins in Sinclair Lewis's *Elmer Gantry*.

Zed. See Sanford Finkelstein.

Zeftel. Deserted wife of a prison escapee; peasant lover of Yasha, whom she follows to Warsaw; leaves Warsaw with Herman to become madam of their brothel in Isaac Bashevis Singer's *The Magician of Lublin*.

Baron Zeitgeist. Amateur musician and scientist who admires the Chatelaine, whom he guides through the Tyrol, in Henry Blake Fuller's *The Chatelaine of La Trinité*.

Zeke (Keekee). American planter on Martair in Herman Melville's *Omoo*.

Marsha Zelenko. Friend of Marjorie Morningstar at Hunter College; encourages Marjorie to act in Herman Wouk's *Marjorie Morningstar*.

Zelig. Father of Shosha; leaves his wife, Bashele, for another woman in Isaac Bashevis Singer's *Shosha*.

Madam Zelma. Clairvoyant who in attempting to help recover a lost fur cap predicts stormy times and then triumph ahead for the narrator of Aline Bernstein's *The Journey Down*.

Zenobia. Daughter of Moodie and half sister of Priscilla; writer who lives at Blithedale and who apparently commits suicide by drowning in Nathaniel Hawthorne's *The Blithedale Romance*.

Zerkow. Junk man whose mania for gold eventually leads to the murder of his wife, Maria Macapa, in Frank Norris's *McTeague*.

Zeusentell. Participant in a drinking party; persuaded to recite "Patrick Clancy's Pig" in Stephen Crane's *George's Mother*.

Sabbatai Zevi. Supposed Messiah who, with his followers, divides seventeenth-century Jewish communities in Europe; eventually forsakes his messianic claim and converts to Islam; appears in Isaac Bashevis Singer's *Satan in Goray*, *The Slave*, and *Shosha*.

Horace Zifferblatt. "Militant clockwatcher" and J. Henry Waugh's manager in Robert Coover's *The Universal Baseball Association, Inc., J. Henry Waugh, Prop.*

Byron Zigler. Son of Homer and Pearl Zigler in Clyde Brion Davis's *"The Great American Novel–."*

Homer Zigler. Journalist who, through successive newspaper jobs in Buffalo, Cleveland, Kansas City, San Francisco, and Denver, continues to cherish the ambition of writing a supreme work of fiction; diarist/narrator of Clyde Brion Davis's *"The Great American Novel–."*

Pearl Hawkins Zigler. Wife of Homer Zigler; oblivious to her husband's most fundamental feelings and ambitions in Clyde Brion Davis's *"The Great American Novel–."*

Amanda Ziller. Vegetarian wife of John Paul Ziller, mother of Baby Thor, and lover of many men and women, including Plucky Purcell; admirer of butterflies, mysticism, and motorcycles; eye-opener of Marx Marvelous and heroine in Tom Robbins's *Another Roadside Attraction*.

John Paul Ziller. Husband of Amanda Ziller, co-owner of Captain Kendrick's Hot Dog Wildlife Preserve, drummer, artist, and magician; wears a loincloth on his body and a bone through his nose; dies with Mon Cul and The Corpse on the Icarus XC solar balloon in Tom Robbins's *Another Roadside Attraction*.

Heinz Zimmerman. Navigator in the 918th Bomb Group; commits suicide after having made an error in navigation in Beirne Lay, Jr., and Sy Bartlett's *Twelve O'Clock High!*

Louis M. Zimmerman. Lecherous principal of Olinger High School; disliked by George Caldwell

and others; rumored to have fathered Corinna Appleton's son, Skippy Appleton, in John Updike's *The Centaur*.

Natalie Kelso (Natasha) Zimmerman. Los Angeles burglary detective; A. M. Valnikov's partner and eventually his fiancée in Joseph Wambaugh's *The Black Marble*.

Danielle Zimmern. Instructor of French and divorced wife of Leonard Zimmern in Alison Lurie's *The War Between the Tates*.

Leonard (Lennie) Zimmern. Professor of English and former husband of Danielle Zimmern in Alison Lurie's *The War Between the Tates*.

Leonard D. Zimmern. Critic and teacher in Alison Lurie's *Real People*.

Ruth (Roo) Zimmern. Daughter of Danielle and Leonard Zimmern in Alison Lurie's *The War Between the Tates*.

Zing. Fox hound owned by Nunn Ballew and considered the best hunting dog in the county; dies in pursuit of the elusive King Devil in Harriette Arnow's *Hunter's Horn*.

Zipporah. Midianite, eldest daughter of Jethro, and wife of Moses in Zora Neale Hurston's *Moses, Man of the Mountain*.

Zizendorf (Editor). Insane neo-Nazi who plans to assassinate the American military overseer in Germany; narrator in John Hawkes's *The Cannibal*.

Madame Zoe. Palm reader who predicts for Sissy Hankshaw marriage, good sex, and children–but not all with the same man, or woman–in Tom Robbins's *Even Cowgirls Get the Blues*.

Zora. Invalid wife of Rango in Anaïs Nin's *The Four-Chambered Heart*.

Zora. Wild, elf-like girl who grows into a serious, productive young woman and challenges the entire sharecropping system when she fights to help her people in W. E. B. Du Bois's *The Quest of the Silver Fleece*.

Zsettlani. See Piotr.

Nathan Zuckerman. Young Jewish writer whose stories are resented by his family; a guest in the home of his literary hero, E. I. Lonoff, Zuckerman develops an elaborate fiction in which Amy Bellette is Anne Frank; narrator of Philip Roth's *The Ghost Writer*.

Zuckor. Father-in-law of Goodman; daily opens the office of Glymmer, Read and greets the other employees in Nathan Asch's *The Office*.

Constantine (Connie, Ski) Zvonski. Marine radio operator killed at Guadalcanal in Leon Uris's *Battle Cry*.

Harry Zwingli. Police detective in Thomas Berger's *Who Is Teddy Villanova?*

Madame Zyszynski. Spiritual medium consulted by the Budds in Upton Sinclair's *Dragon's Teeth*.

Index

Louis Adamic
Cradle of Life–H.A.C.
  Herr Ottokar Bukuwky
  Yuro Dug
  Dora Dugova
  Zorka Dugova
  Don Franyo
  Count Rudolf von Hapsburg
  Prince Arbogast von Hohengraetz
  Yozhé Kozak
  Matilda Nagy
  Frau Natalie Schuschnigg
  Rudolf Stanislaus Stanka
  Count Yaromir von Studenitz
  Countess Zdenka von Studenitz
  Vladek

Grandsons–H.A.C.
  Beverly Boyd
  Andrew Gale, Jr.
  Andrew Gale, Sr.
  Anthony Adams Gale
  Anton Galé
  Jack Gale
  Mildred Adams Gale
  Peter Gale
  Tony Gale
  Jesus Jiminez
  L
  Roger Smith
  Margaret Gale Stedman

Alice Adams
Families and Survivors–M.C.M.
  Caroline Calloway
  Jack Calloway
  Louisa Calloway
  Kate Flickinger
  John Jeffreys
  King
  Michael Wasserman

Listening to Billie–M.C.M.
  Harry Argent
  Reed Ashford
  Billie Holiday
  Miriam
  Kathleen Mooney
  Catherine Quarles
  Eliza Erskine Hamilton Quarles
  Evan Quarles
  Daria Erskine Paulus Worthington
  Smith Worthington

Henry Adams
Democracy–C.L.S.

Mrs. Samuel Baker
John Carrington
Schuyler Clinton
Victoria Dare
Lord Dunbeg
Baron Jacobi
Madeleine Ross Lee
Senator Silas P. Ratcliffe
Sybil Ross

James Agee
A Death in the Family–R.R.S.
  Catherine Follet
  Jay Follet
  Mary Follet
  Ralph Follet
  Rufus Follet
  Father Jackson
  Andrew Lynch
  Catherine Lynch
  Hannah Lynch
  Joel Lynch
  Walter Starr

Conrad Aiken
Blue Voyage–S.E.O.
  Cynthia Battiloro
  Seward Trewlove Clark
  Daisy Dacey
  Peggy Davis
  William Demarest
  Pauline Faubion
  Clarence Hay-Lawrence
  Major Kendall
  Solomon Moses David Menelik Silberstein
  Smith

Great Circle–S.E.O.
  Andrew Cather
  Bertha Cather
  David Cather
  Doris Cather
  John Cather
  Thomas Lowell Crapo

King Coffin–S.E.O.
  Jasper Ammen
  Gerta
  Karl N. Jones
  Sandbach
  Julius Shaw Toppan

Louisa May Alcott
Little Men–S.L.
  Thomas Buckminster Bangs
  Ned Barker

Friedrich Bhaer
Robin Bhaer
Nathaniel Blake
Daisy Brooke
John Brooke
John Brooke
Dick Brown
George Cole
Dan
Emil
Jack Ford
Franz
Annie Harding
Bess Laurence
Theodore Laurence
Amy Curtis March
Jo March
Margaret March
Adolphus Pettingill
Silas
Billy Ward

Little Women–S.L.
  Friedrich Bhaer
  Daisy Brooke
  John Brooke
  John Brooke
  James Laurence
  Theodore Laurence
  March
  Amy Curtis March
  Aunt March
  Elizabeth March
  Margaret March
  Mrs. March
  Jo March
  Hannah Mullett

Thomas Bailey Aldrich
The Story of a Bad Boy–B.F.
  Phil Adams
  Mat Ames
  Thomas Bailey
  Harry Blake
  Aunt Chloe
  Kitty Collins
  Bill Conway
  Widow Conway
  Miss Dorothy Gibbs
  Nelly Glentworth
  Mr. Grimshaw
  Gypsy
  Jack Harris
  Wibird Hawkins
  Dame Jocelyn
  Fred Langdon

Charley Marden
Mr. Meeks
Miss Abigail Nutter
Grandfather Nutter
Pettingil
Seth Rodgers
Uncle Snow
Silas Trefethen
Captain Truck
Binny Wallace
Benjamin Watson
Pepper Whitcomb
Ezra Wingate

Nelson Algren
The Man with the Golden Arm–D.I.
Record Head Bednar
Blind Pig
Louie Fomorowski
Violet Koskozka
Cousin Kvorka
Francis Majcinek
Sophie Majcinek
Molly Novotny
Solly Saltskin
Zero Schwiefka
Anthony Witwicki

Never Come Morning–D.I.
Casimir Benkowski
Bruno Bicek
Finger Idzikowski
Fireball Kodadek
Bonifacy Konstantine
Catfoot Nowogrodski
Steffi Rostenkowski
One-Eye Tenczara
Mama Tomek
Bibleback Watrobinski

Somebody in Boots–D.I.
Dill Doak
Norah Egan
Luther Gulliday
Herman Hauser
Olin Jones
Matches
Bryan McKay
Cass McKay
Nancy McKay
Stuart McKay
Nubby O'Neill

A Walk on the Wild Side–D.I.
Hallie Breedlove
Oliver Finnerty
Rhino Gross
Velma Gross
Byron Linkhorn
Dove Linkhorn
Fitz Linkhorn
Luther
Luther
Achilles Schmidt

Kitty Twist
Terasina Vidavarri

Hervey Allen
Action at Aquila–W.E. & G.G.
Judge Bristline
Elizabeth Crittendon
Margaret Crittendon
Nathaniel T. Franklin
Flossie Kiskadden

Anthony Adverse–W.E. & G.G.
Anthony Adverse
Napoleon Bonaparte
John Bonnyfeather
Maria Bonnyfeather
Dolores de la Fuente
Angela Guessippi
William McNab
Denis Moore
Vincent Nolte
Faith Paleologus
Florence Udney Parish
Marquis da Vincitata
Father Xavier

Bedford Village–W.E. & G.G.
Salathiel Albine
Phoebe Davison
Simeon Ecuyer
Captain Jack Fenwick
James Callowhill Gladwin
Samuel Japson
James McArdle
Garrett Pendergass
Rose Pendergass
Arthur St. Clair
Edward Hamilton Yates

The Forest and the Fort–W.E. & G.G.
Salathiel Albine
Big Turtle
Simeon Ecuyer
Samuel Japson
Kaysinata
Mawakis
James McArdle
Nymwha
Garrett Pendergass
Rose Pendergass
Arthur St. Clair
Jane Sligo
Edward Hamilton Yates

Toward the Morning–W.E. & G.G.
Salathiel Albine
Bridget McCandliss
Frances Melissa O'Toole
Arthur St. Clair
Edward Hamilton Yates

James Lane Allen
Aftermath–L.E.H.
Georgiana Cobb

Joseph Cobb
Margaret Cobb
Sylvia Cobb
Adam Moss
Mrs. Walters

A Kentucky Cardinal–L.E.H.
Georgiana Cobb
Joseph Cobb
Margaret Cobb
Sylvia Cobb
Adam Moss
Mrs. Walters

Sherwood Anderson
Dark Laughter–W.L.M.
Ted Copeland
Bruce Dudley
Rose Frank
Aline Aldridge Grey
Fred Grey
Sponge Martin
Bernice Stockton
Esther Walker
Joe Walker
Tom Wills

Poor White–C.L.S.
Clara Butterworth
Kate Chanceller
Ezra French
Jim Gibson
Judge Horace Hanby
Steve Hunter
Hugh McVey
Henry Shepard
Sarah Shepard
Joseph Wainsworth

Windy McPherson's Son–R.M.M.
Janet Eberly
Mike McCarthy
Jane McPherson
John McPherson
Kate McPherson
Sam McPherson
Sue Rainey
Colonel Tom Rainey
John Telfer
Mary Underwood

Winesburg, Ohio–C.D.B.
Jesse Bentley
Katherine Bentley
Wing Biddlebaum
Henry Bradford
Belle Carpenter
Ebenezer Cowley
Elmer Cowley
Ned Currie
Tom Foster
Ed Handby
Tandy Hard
Tom Hard

Albert Hardy
David Hardy
Harriet Hardy
John Hardy
Louise Bentley Hardy
Mary Hardy
Reverend Curtis Hartman
Will Henderson
Hop Higgins
Alice Hindman
Will Hurley
Edward King
Sarah King
Tom King
Mook
Doctor Parcival
Ray Pearson
Doctor Reefy
Seth Richmond
Virginia Richmond
Enoch Robinson
Turk Smollet
John Spaniard
Elizabeth Swift
Kate Swift
Louise Trunnion
Joe Welling
Helen White
Elizabeth Willard
George Willard
Tom Willard
Wash Williams
Hal Winters

Harriette Arnow
The Dollmaker—W.Mc.
Homer Anderson
Mrs. Anderson
John Ballew
Battle John Brand
Andy Hull
Henley Kendrick
Mrs. Kendrick
Mrs. McKeckeran
Sophronie Meanwell
Whit Meanwell
Amos Nevels
Cassie Marie Nevels
Clovis Nevels
Clytie Nevels
Enoch Nevels
Gertie Kendrick Nevels
Reuben Nevels
Sue Annie Tiller

Hunter's Horn—S.B.
Jaw Buster Anderson
John Ballew
Lee Roy Ballew
Lucy Ballew
Milly Ballew
Nunnely Danforth Ballew
Suse Ballew
William Danforth Ballew

Battle John Brand
Keg Head Cramer
Lureenie Cramer
Mark Cramer
Rans Cramer
J. D. Duffey
King Devil
Andrew Haynes
Andy Hull
Sam
Sue Annie Tiller
Vineria
Zing

The Kentucky Trace—S.B.
William David Collins
William David Leslie Collins II
Sadie Hawkins
Isaac Huffacre
Jethro
Little Brother Leaping Fish
Rachel
Charity Prudence Eversole Simons
Daniel Strunk

Mountain Path—S.B.
Chris Bledsoe
Corie Calhoun
Haze Calhoun
Lee Buck Calhoun
Mabel Calhoun
Rie Calhoun
Samanthetie Pedigo
Louisa Sheridan

The Weedkiller's Daughter—S.B.
Robert Thomas Hedrick IV
Helene Holman
Mollie Catharine McWhorter
Gertie Kendrick Nevels
Brandon Schnitzer
Herman Schnitzer
Mrs. Schnitzer
Susan Marie Schnitzer
Iggy Soames
Ter

T. S. Arthur
Ten Nights in a Bar-Room—G.G.
Harvey Green
Willy Hammond
Lyman
Joe Morgan
Mary Morgan
Frank Slade
Simon Slade

Nathan Asch
The Office—E.M.
Henry Clarke
Jim Denby
Gertrude Donovan
Edward Foley
John T. Glymmer

Goodman
Samuel Jacobs
Miss James
Marc Krantz
Read
Esther Thomas
Harry Widener
Zuckor

Pay Day—E.M.
Daisy Patricia Cowan
Eugene Cowan
James Cowan
Martha Cowan
Helen
Phillip Laurie
Eddie Mitchell
Paddy
Jennie Williams
Mrs. Williams

Gertrude Atherton
Ancestors—C.S.M.
Dolly Boutts
Anabel Colton
Thomas Colton
John Elton Cecil Gwynne
Lady Victoria Gwynne
Julia Kaye
Leslie
Anne Montgomery
Isabel Otis
Lyster Stone
Flora Thangue

Black Oxen—C.S.M.
Lee Clavering
Gora Dwight
Prince Moritz Franz Ernst Hohenauern
James Oglethorpe
Jane Oglethorpe
Janet Oglethorpe
Agnes Trevor
Countess Marie Ogden Zattiany

Patience Sparhawk and Her Times—C.S.M.
Miss Beale
Garan Bourke
Honora Tremont Mairs
Beverly Peele
Harriet Peele
Patience Sparhawk
Morgan Steele
Harriet Tremont

William Attaway
Blood on the Forge—J.C.S.
Chinatown Moss
Mat Moss
Melody Moss
Smothers

Louis Auchincloss
The Great World and Timothy Colt—C.C.D.

Ann Colt
Timothy Colt
Sheridan Dale
Larry Duane
George Emlen
David Fairchild
Henry Knox
Eileen Shallcross

The Rector of Justin–C.C.D.
Brian Aspinwall
Eliza Dean
David Griscam
Jules Griscam
Horace Havistock
Reverend Duncan Moore
Francis Prescott
Harriet Winslow Prescott
Charley Strong
Cordelia Turnbull

Mary Austin
Santa Lucia–R.G.B.
Luella Bixby
Dr. Edward Caldwell
William Caldwell
James J. Halford
Edward K. Jasper
Evan Lindley
Serena Haven Lindley
Julia Maybury
George Rhewold
Antrim Stairs

A Woman of Genius–R.G.B.
Thomas Bettersworth
Sarah Croyden
Mark Eversley
Helmeth Garrett
Ephemia Lattimore
Olivia May Lattimore
Sally Lattimore
Leon Lawrence
Gerald McDermott
Henry Mills
Pauline Allingham Mills
Morris Polatkin
Henrietta Rathbone

Richard Bach
Jonathan Livingston Seagull–V.W.
Chiang
Fletcher Lynd Seagull
Jonathan Livingston Seagull
Sullivan

Dorothy Baker
Young Man with a Horn–G.G.
Arthur Hazard
Daniel Jordan
Edward Richard Martin
Amy North
Jack Stuart
Lee Valentine

Jeffrey Williams

James Baldwin
Another Country–T.D.
Steve Ellis
Jane
Eric Jones
Leona
Daniel Vivaldo Moore
Ida Scott
Rufus Scott
Clarissa Silenski
Richard Silenski
Yves

Giovanni's Room–T.D.
David
Giovanni
Guillaume
Hella

Go Tell It on the Mountain–T.D.
Esther
Deborah Grimes
Elizabeth Grimes
Florence Grimes
Gabriel Grimes
John Grimes
Roy Grimes
Richard
Royal

If Beale Street Could Talk–T.D.
Daniel
Arnold Hayward
Adrienne Hunt
Alonzo Hunt
Frank Hunt
Mrs. Hunt
Sheila Hunt
Clementine Rivers
Ernestine Rivers
Joseph Rivers
Sharon Rivers
Victoria Rogers

Tell Me How Long the Train's Been Gone–T. D.
Christopher Hall
Jerry
Barbara King
Caleb Proudhammer
Leo Proudhammer
Lola San-Marquand
Saul San-Marquand

Djuna Barnes
Nightwood–J.W.H.
Nora Flood
Dr. Matthew O'Connor
Jenny Petherbridge
Baron Felix Volkbein
Guido Volkbein
Robin Vote

Ryder–J.W.H.
Alex Alexson
Molly Dance
Amelia de Grier
Kate-Careless
Dr. Matthew O'Connor
John Peel
Cynthia Ryder
Jonathan Buxton Ryder
Sophia Grieve Ryder
Wendell Ryder

Margaret Ayer Barnes
Wisdom's Gate–J.Re.
Alden Carver, Junior
Jane Ward Carver
Stephen Carver
Flora Furness
Cicily Carver Bridges Lancaster
Muriel Lester Lancaster
John Ward
Lizzie Ward

Years of Grace–J.Re.
Alden Carver, Junior
Cicily Carver
Jane Ward Carver
Stephen Carver
André Duroy
Flora Furness
Lily Furness
Albert Lancaster
Cicily Carver Bridges Lancaster
Muriel Lester Lancaster
Agnes Johnson Trent
James Trent
John Ward
Lizzie Ward

John Barth
Chimera–V.H.
Bellerophon
Calyxa
Dunyazade
Genie
Medusa
Perseus
Polyeidus
Scheherazade

The End of the Road–T.C.
Ethel Banning
Dr. Harry Carter
Mrs. Dockey
Doctor
Jacob Horner
Joseph Morgan
Renée MacMahon Morgan
Peggy Rankin
Dr. Schott

The Floating Opera–T.C.
Captain Jacob R. Adam
Thomas T. Andrews

Todd Andrews
Betty June Gunter
Mr. Haecker
Captain Osborn Jones
Julia Lake
Jane Paulsen Mack
Jeannine Paulsen Mack
Harrison A. Mack, Jr.

Giles Goat-Boy–V.H.
Leonid Andreich Alexandrov
Harold Bray
Croaker
Eblis Eierkopf
Enos Enoch
George Giles
Stoker Giles
Peter Greene
Virginia R. Hector
George Herrold
Lucius Rexford
Dr. Kennard Sear
Dr. Maximilian Spielman
Anastasia Stoker
Maurice Stoker
WESCAC

The Sot-Weed Factor–V.H.
Henry Burlingame III
Bertrand Burton
Charles Calvert, Lord Baltimore
John Coode
Anna Cooke
Ebenezer Cooke
Pocahontas
Billy Rumbly
Capt. John Smith
Joan Toast
Susan Warren

Donald Barthelme
The Dead Father–L.O.
The Dead Father
Edmund
Emma
Julie
Peter Scatterpatter
Thomas

Snow White–L.O.
Hogo de Bergerac
Bill
Clem
Dan
Edward
Henry
Hubert
Kevin
Paul
Snow White
Jane Villiers de l'Isle-Adam

Sy Bartlett
Twelve O'Clock High!–B.F.

Jesse Bishop
Joe R. Cobb
Keith Davenport
Ben Gately
Ed Henderson
Don Kaiser
Pamela Mallory
Sergeant McIllhenny
Patrick Pritchard
Frank Savage
Harvey Stovall
Heinz Zimmerman

Hamilton Basso
The View from Pompey's Head–J.R.M.
Wyeth Blackford
Phillip Greene
Dinah Blackford Higgins
Mico Higgins
Anna Jones
Anson Page
Meg Page
Garvin Wales
Lucy Devereaux Wales

Arthenia J. Bates
The Deity Nodded–V.W.S.
Flora Dees
Heflin Dees
Katie Mae Dees
Ludd Dees
Lyman Portland Dees
Squire Dees
Tisha Dees
Obidiah Funches
Kovel Henry
Detroit Kemp
Melba Stokes

Peter S. Beagle
The Last Unicorn–S.W.A.
Lady Amalthea
Captain Cully
Mommy Fortuna
Molly Grue
King Haggard
Prince Lír
Red Bull
Schmendrick

M. F. Beal
Amazon One–L.L.A.
William Armiston
Carole Batelle
Dawn Melody Batelle
Jersey Carmody
Marina Karsh
Atlas Androgyne Maartens
Sheila Anne Topp
Heritage Wright

Angel Dance–L.L.A.
Maria Katerina Lorca Guerrera Alcazar
Julia

Lenore
Vincente Pesola Muzguiz
Andrew Stone
Angel Stone
Rachel Stone
William D. Tarleton

Henry Ward Beecher
Norwood–E.J.H.
Hiram Beers
Agate Bissell
Uncle Buddy
Abiah Cathcart
Alice Cathcart
Barton Cathcart
Rachel Liscomb Cathcart
Frank Esel
Thomas J. Heywood
Jerry Marble
Pete Sawmill
Tommy Taft
Turfmould
Reuben Wentworth
Rose Wentworth

Edward Bellamy
Looking Backward–G.G.
Edith Bartlett
Barton
Leete
Edith Leete
Julian West

Saul Bellow
The Adventures of Augie March–M.G.P.
Hymie Bateshaw
Stella Chesney
William Einhorn
Thea Fenchel
Sophie Geratis
Grandma Lausch
Augie March
Georgie March
Mama March
Harold Mintouchian
Kayo Obermark
Manny Padilla
Mr. Renling
Mrs. Renling
Robey
Mimi Villars

Dangling Man–M.G.P.
Myron Adler
Amos
Kitty Daumler
Etta
Iva
Joseph
Spirit of Alternatives
Mr. Vanaker

Henderson the Rain King–M.G.P.
Atti

Dahfu
Eugene H. Henderson
Itelo
Mtalba
Romilayu
Willatale

Herzog–M.G.P.
Lucas Asphalter
Ramona Donsell
Valentine Gersbach
June Herzog
Madeleine Pontritter Herzog
Moses Elkanah Herzog
Sandor Himmelstein
Harvey Simkin

Humboldt's Gift–M.G.P.
Rinaldo Cantabile
Charles Citrine
Kathleen Fleisher
Von Humboldt Fleisher
Menasha Klinger
Renata Koffritz
Louie Lutz
Naomi Lutz
George Swiebel
Pierre Thaxter
Wald Waldemar

Mr. Sammler's Planet–M.G.P.
Margotte Arkin
Walter Bruch
Eisen
Lionel Feffer
Angela Gruner
Dr. Arnold Gruner
Dr. V. Govinda Lal
Artur Sammler
Shula Sammler

The Victim–M.G.P.
Dr. Adler
Kirby Allbee
Daniel Harkavy
Asa Leventhal
Schlossberg
Dr. Tamkin
Tommy Wilhelm
Stan Williston

Ludwig Bemelmans
Dirty Eddie–L.R.N.A.
Betsy Allbright
Belinda
Belladonna
Raoul de Bourggraff
Maurice Cassard
Beverly Copfee
Dirty Eddie
Envelove
Moses Fable
Grippenwald
Ma Gundel

Jerome Hack
Buddy van der Lynn
Casey McMahon
Ludlow Mumm
Arthur Nightwine
Miss Princip
Valerie Sinnot
Sandor Thrilling
Vanya Vashvily
Farmer Weatherbeat
Arty Wildgans

Peter Benchley
Jaws–C.W.
Ellen Brody
Martin Brody
Great White Shark
Matthew Hooper
Harry Meadows
Quint
Lawrence P. Vaughan
Christine Watkins

Hal Bennett
The Black Wine–R.W.
Dolly Anderson
Viola Anderson
Lizzie Bartley
Robert Bartley
Maybelline Cobb
Reverend Winston Cobb
Norman Eisenberg
Judith Finkel
Clair Hunter
David Hunter
Henry Hunter
Jerry Kaplan
Eloise McLindon
Miss Pemberton

Lord of Dark Places–R.W.
Miss Lavinia Barton
Tony Brenzo
Mary Cheap
Reverend Winston Cobb
Lamont Cranston Jones
Mavis Lee
Madame Eudora Market
Joe Market
Odessa Barton Market
Ramona Market
Roosevelt Market
Titus Market

Seventh Heaven–R.W.
Viola Anderson
Herman Baskerville
Maria Beñes
Bobby Bryant
Maybelline Cobb
Reverend Winston Cobb
Dicey
Mrs. Greco
Bill Kelsey

Serena Kelsey
Zachary Kelsey
Aunt Keziah
Clair Page
Nellie Royster

Wait Until the Evening–R.W.
Cora Brittain
Dolores Brittain
Kevin Brittain
Minnie Brittain
Paul Brittain
Percy Brittain
Shadrach Brittain
Maybelline Cobb
Reverend Winston Cobb
The Idiot
Eric Magee
Janet Magee
Miss Pemberton
Henry Robinson

A Wilderness of Vines–R.W.
Luann Asher
Birchie Bartley
Calvin LeRoy Bartley
Lizzie Bartley
Robert Bartley
Blessed Belshazzar
Darlene Mosby Carlisle
Ida Carlisle
Maybelline Cobb
Reverend Winston Cobb
Charlie Hooker
Janus Manning
Neva Blanche Stapleton Manning
Otha Manning
Dr. Stanhope
Miss Whittle

Thomas Berger
Arthur Rex–J.F.D.
Agravaine
Arthur
Gawaine
Guinevere
Isold of the White Hands
La Belle Isold
Lady of the Lake
Launcelot
Merlin
Margawse
Mordred
Morgan la Fey
Ragnell
Tristram

Crazy in Berlin–J.F.D.
Bach
Veronica Leary
James T. Marsala
Carlo B. Reinhart
Schatzi
Nathan Schild

Trudchen

Killing Time–J.F.D.
Arthur Bayson
Betty Starr Bayson
Harry C. Clegg
Joseph Detweiler
Henry Webster Melrose
James T. Shuster
Andrew Starr
Tierney

Little Big Man–J.F.D.
Buffalo Wallow Woman
Caroline Crabb
Jack Crabb
Olga Crabb
George Armstrong Custer
James Butler Hickok
Hump
Little Horse
Morning Star
Old Lodge Skins
Mrs. Pendrake
Reverend Silas Pendrake
Ralph Fielding Snell
Sunshine
Younger Bear

Regiment of Women–J.F.D.
Lieutenant Aster
Georgie Cornell
Harriet
Charlie Harrison
Doctor Prine
Stanley

Reinhart in Love–J.F.D.
Beatrice Fedder
Niles Fedder
Lorenz T. Goodykuntz
Claude Humbold
Gloria Monday
Blaine Raven
Carlo B. Reinhart
Genevieve Raven Reinhart
George Reinhart
Maw Reinhart

Sneaky People–J.F.D.
Horse Hauser
Clarence Honeywell
Leo Kirsch
Laverne Linda Hogan Lorraine
Naomi Sandifer
Ralph Virgil Sandifer
Virgil Sandifer

Vital Parts–J.F.D.
Raymond Mainwaring
Splendor Gallant Mainwaring
Gloria Monday
Dr. Barker Munsing
Eunice Munsing

Blaine Raven
Blaine Reinhart
Carlo B. Reinhart
Genevieve Raven Reinhart
Winona Reinhart
Johann Steckfuss
Robert Sweet

Who Is Teddy Villanova?–J.F.D.
Gus Bakewell
Alice Ellish
Carl Knox
Natalie Novotny
Calvin Peachtree
Sam Polidor
Margaret Mary Bernadette Tumulty
Teddy Villanova
Donald Washburn II
Russel Wren
Harry Zwingli

Aline Bernstein
The Journey Down–S.T.S.
Amelia
Carl
Daddy
Mr. Flick
Francie
Cousin Julia
Mrs. Lindow
Aunt Mamie
Nana
Tom Watson
Madam Zelma

Wendell Berry
The Memory of Old Jack–D.T.C.
Nettie Banion
Joe Banion
Jack Beechum
Lightening Berlew
Sylvania Berlew
Milton Burgess
Andy Catlett
Bess Feltner Catlett
Henry Catlett
Wheeler Catlett
Burley Coulter
David Coulter
Hannah Coulter
Jarrat Coulter
Mathew Burley Coulter
Nathan Coulter
Jonah Crow
Ben Feltner
Margaret Feltner
Margaret Finley Feltner
Mat Feltner
Nancy Beechum Feltner
Mrs. Hendrick
Frank Lathrop
Jasper Lathrop
Ruth Lightwood
Sims McGrother

Clay McInnis
Rose McInnis
Elton Penn
Mary Penn
Clara Beechum Pettit
Gladston Pettit
Will Wells
Brother Wingfare

Nathan Coulter–D.T.C.
Jack Beechum
Big Ellis
Kate Helen Branch
Burley Coulter
David Coulter
Jarrat Coulter
Nathan Coulter
Tom Coulter
Margaret Finley Feltner
Mat Feltner
Jig Pendleton

A Place on Earth–D.T.C.
Joe Banion
Nettie Banion
Jack Beechum
Big Ellis
Milton Burgess
Andy Catlett
Bess Feltner Catlett
Henry Catlett
Wheeler Catlett
Burley Coulter
Hannah Coulter
Jarrat Coulter
Nathan Coulter
Tom Coulter
Annie Crop
Gideon Crop
Ida Crop
Jonah Crow
Margaret Feltner
Margaret Finley Feltner
Mat Feltner
Virgil Feltner
Ernest Finley
Stanley Gibbs
Mrs. Hendrick
Frank Lathrop
Jasper Lathrop
Roger Merchant
Whacker Spradlin

Doris Betts
The River to Pickle Beach–S.L.K.
George Bennett
Pauline Buncombe
Willis Buncombe
Foley Dickinson
Earl Fetner
Grace Fetner
Randy Fetner
Treva Fetner
Troy Fetner

Mickey McCane
Pinhead
Jack S. Sellars
Miss Whitaker

Ambrose Bierce
The Monk and the Hangman's Daughter–H.H.
Ambrosius
Amula
Andreas
Benedicta
Rochus
Saltmaster

Robert Montgomery Bird
Nick of the Woods–G.G.
Richard Braxley
Colonel Bruce
Pardon Dodge
Abel Doe
Telie Doe
Edith Forrester
Captain Roland Forrester
Major Roland Forrester
Nathan Slaughter
Ralph Stackpole
Wenonga

William Peter Blatty
The Exorcist–S.A.A.
Burke Dennings
Captain Howdy
Damien Karras
William F. Kinderman
Chris MacNeil
Regan Teresa MacNeil
Lankester Merrin
Sharon Spencer

Arna Wendell Bontemps
Black Thunder–K.C.J.
Ben
Alexander Biddenhurst
Bundy
Creuzot
Ditcher
Drucilla
Juba
Laurent
Melody
Mingo
Pharoah
Gabriel Prosser
Thomas Prosser
General John Scott
Moseley Sheppard
Robin Sheppard

Drums at Dusk–K.C.J.
Angélique
Annette
Boukman
Choucoune
Claire

Diron Desautels
Philippe Desautels
Captain Frounier
Céleste Juvet
Hugo Juvet
Mme. Jacques Juvet
Bayou de Libertas
Mars Plasair
Count Armand De Sacy
Pierre Sylvain
Toussaint
Paulette Viard

God Sends Sunday–K.C.J.
Augie
Joe Baily
Biglow Brown
Horace Church-Woodbine
Mississippi Davis
Florence Dessau
Bad-foot Dixon
Della Green
Barney Jones
Leah
Lissus
Parthenia
Count Ragsdale
Terry
Tom Wright

Jane Bowles
Two Serious Ladies–R.E.L.
Arnold
Ben
Frieda Copperfield
J. C. Copperfield
Lucie Gamelon
Christina Goering
Andrew McLane
Pacifica
Flora Quill
Toby

Paul Bowles
Let It Come Down–S.E.O.
Thami Beidaoui
Nelson Dyar
Eunice Goode
Hadija
Marquesa Daisy de Valverde
Jack Wilcox

The Sheltering Sky–S.E.O.
Eric Lyle
Mrs. Lyle
Katherine Moresby
Porter Moresby
Tunner

James Boyd
Drums–R.W.
Hugh Clapton
Nathaniel Dukinfield
Captain Flood

John Fraser
John Fraser, Jr.
John Paul Jones
Sally Merrillee
Eve Tennant

Thomas Boyd
Through the Wheat–H.H.
John R. Adams
Lieutenant Bedford
King Cole
Kerfoot Harriman
William Hicks
Kitty Kahl
Captain Powers
Jack Pugh

Hjalmar Hjorth Boyesen
The Golden Calf–R.S.F.
Cyrus Carter
Madeline Carter
Dr. Habicht
Ferdinand Habicht
Minna Habicht
Oliver Tappan

The Mammon of Unrighteousness–R.S.F.
Dr. Archibald Hawk
Alexander Larkin
Gertrude Larkin
Horace Larkin
Obed Larkin
Arabella Robbins
Kate Van Schaak

Hugh Henry Brackenridge
Modern Chivalry–D.M.
Monsieur Douperie
Captain John Farrago
Duncan Ferguson
Marquis de Marnessie
Kate Maybone
M'Donald
Mutchkin
M'Whorter
Teague Oregan
Peter Porcupine
Tom the Tinker
Traddle

Ray Bradbury
Fahrenheit 451–G.G.
Beatty
Faber
Granger
Clarisse McClellan
Guy Montag
Mildred Montag

Richard Brautigan
The Abortion–B.H.
Mrs. Charles Fine Adams
Harlow Blade, Jr.
Foster

Vida Kramar
Mr. Librarian

A Confederate General from Big Sur–B.H.
Cynthia
Elaine
Elizabeth
Jesse
Augustus Mellon
Lee Mellon
Susan
Johnston Wade

Dreaming of Babylon–B.H.
Miss Ann
C. Card
Mr. Cleveland
Dr. Abdul Forsythe
Dr. Francis
Sam Herschberger
Nana-dirat
Peg-leg
Sergeant Rink
Smiley
Smith Smith

The Hawkline Monster–B.H.
Cameron
Greer
Jane Hawkline
Professor Hawkline
Susan Hawkline
Hawkline Monster
Marvin Cora Jones
Magic Child
Mr. Morgan
Pills
Jack Williams

Trout Fishing in America–B.H.
Art
Maria Callas
Alonso Hagan
Charles Hayman
The Mayor of the Twentieth Century
Mr. Norris
Pard
Rebel Smith
Trout Fishing in America
Trout Fishing in America Shorty

Willard and His Bowling Trophies–B.H.
Bob
John
Logan brothers
Patricia
Willard

Louis Bromfield
The Green Bay Tree–L.R.N.A.
René de Cyon
Governor
William Harrison
Stepan Krylenko

Irene Shane
Julia Shane
Lily Shane
Ellen Tolliver

Cecil Brown
The Life and Loves of Mr. Jiveass Nigger–J.M.B.
Ned Green
Bob Jacobs
Jero
Melvin Jerrell
Pat
Reb
Gloria Rowan
Thomas Rowan
Ruth Smith
George Washington

Charles Brockden Brown
Arthur Mervyn–J.C.
Achsa Fielding
Mr. Hadwin
Arthur Mervyn
Dr. Stevens
Thomas Welbeck

Edgar Huntly–W.Mc.
Clarice
Clithero Edny
Edgar Huntly
Euphemia Wiatte Lorimer
Queen Mab
Sarsefield
Waldegrave
Mary Waldegrave
Weymouth
Arthur Wiatte

Ormond–C.D.B.
Balfour
Sarah Baxter
Martinette de Beauvais
Helena Cleves
Thomas Craig
Constantia Dudley
Stephen Dudley
Malcolm M'Crea
Mr. Melbourne
Ormond
Mary Ridgeley
Roseveldt
Sophia Westwyn

Wieland–C.D.B.
Thomas Cambridge
Francis Carwin
Judith
Henry Pleyel
Catharine Pleyel Wieland
Clara Wieland
Theodore Wieland

Rita Mae Brown
Rubyfruit Jungle–R.B.

Alice Bellantoni
Polina Bellantoni
Leota B. Bisland
Carl Bolt
Carrie Bolt
Molly Bolt
Calvin
Ep Denman
Jennifer Denman
Leroy Denman
Ted Denman
Brockhurst Detwiler
Paul Digita
Holly
Connie Penn
Faye Raider
Rhea Rhadin
Carolyn Simpson
Florence Wegenlied

William Hill Brown
The Power of Sympathy–B.F.
Harriot Fawcet
Maria Fawcet
Fidelia
Mrs. Francis
Amelia Harrington
J. Harrington
Myra Harrington
Tommy Harrington
Henry
Mrs. Eliza Holmes
Mr. Martin
Mrs. Martin
Shepherd
Ophelia Shepherd
Jack Worthy

Pearl Buck
The Good Earth–P.A.D.
Ching
Cuckoo
Lord Hwang
Lotus
Nung En
Nung Wen
O-lan
Pear Blossom
Wang Lung
Wang the Third

A House Divided–P.A.D.
Nung En
Nung Wen
Pig Butcher
Wang the Third

Sons–P.A.D.
Hawk
Leopard
Nung En
Nung Wen
Pear Blossom
Pig Butcher

Wang Lung
Wang the Third

Ed Bullins
The Reluctant Rapist–L.S a.
Steven Benson
Aunt Bess
Jack Bowen
Marie Ann Bowen
Uncle Clyde
Ricardo S. Evans
Lenard
Lou Ellen

Jerry Bumpus
Anaconda–S.G.
Carl
Claire
Adaline Fletcher
E. L. Fletcher
Jimmy
Alonzo McCaferty
Vera

Frances Hodgson Burnett
Little Lord Fauntleroy–E.D.F.
Cedric Errol
Captain Cedric Errol
Mrs. Cedric Errol
John Arthur Molyneux Errol
T. Havisham
Silas Hobbs
Benjamin Tipton
Dick Tipton
Minna Tipton

William Riley Burnett
The Asphalt Jungle–D.A.N.
Louis Bellini
Bob Brannom
Charles Cobb
Joe Cool
Eddie Donato
Alonzo D. Emmerich
Lou Farbstein
Angela Finlay
Dolph Franc
Dix Handley
Theo J. Hardy
Dorothy Pelky
Erwin Riemenschneider

High Sierra–D.A.N.
John Dillinger
Roy Earle
Marie Garson
Jim Goodhue
Velma Goodhue
Vince Healy
Barmy Johnson
Kranmer
Louis Mendoza
Big Mac M'Gann
Arnold Francis Milnik

Doc Parker
Joseph Potter
Lon Preiser
Roma Stover

Little Caesar–D.A.N.
Cesare Bandello
Blondy Belle
Jim Courtney
DeVoss
Jim Flaherty
Magdalena
Joe Massara
Father McConagha
Pete Montana
James Michael O'Doul
Ramón Otero
Tony Passa
Giovanni Scabby
Sam Vettori
Nell Weil
John C. Willoughby
Arnold Worch

John Horne Burns
The Gallery–D.G.B.
Chaplain Bascom
Father Donovan
Ginny
Giulia
Hal
Sergeant Joe
Louella
Momma
Major Motes
Michael Patrick
Maria Rocco
Moses Shulman

William S. Burroughs
Exterminator!–A.J.
A. J.
Dr. Benway
B. J.
Audrey Carsons
Ali Juan Chapultepec
Clancy
Dib
Jerry
Johnny
William Lee
Homer Mandrill
Tío Mate
Priest
The Sailor
Clinch Smith
Colonel Sutton-Smith
The Technician

Junkie–A.J.
Gene Doolie
Bill Gains
Herman
Ike

Pat
The Sailor
William Lee
Roy
The Sailor

Naked Lunch–A.J.
A. J.
Dr. Benway
The Great Blashtubitch
The County Clerk
Clem Ergot
Jody Ergot
Bill Gains
Mr. Hyslop
Ike
Johnny
William Lee
Salvador Hassan O'Leary
Carl Peterson
The Rube
The Sailor
The Great Slashtubitch
Clem Snide
The Technician
Fats Terminal

Nova Express–A.J.
Dr. Benway
Ali Juan Chapultepec
Tony Green
The Intolerable Kid
Izzy the Push
Johnny
Kiki
K9
William Lee
Mr. Bradly Mr. Martin
Priest
The Rube
Hassan i Sabbah
The Sailor
Sammy The Butcher
The Technician
Fats Terminal
Uranian Willy
Johnny Yen

The Soft Machine–A.J.
A. J.
Dr. Benway
Joe Brundige
Ali Juan Chapultepec
The County Clerk
Bill Gains
Tony Green
Johnny
Kiki
K9
William Lee
Mr. Bradly Mr. Martin
Carl Peterson
The Sailor
Clem Snide

The Subliminal Kid
Uranian Willy
Xolotl
Johnny Yen

The Ticket That Exploded–A.J.
B. J.
Ali Juan Chapultepec
John Harrison
Izzy the Push
Johnny
Kiki
K9
William Lee
Lykin
Mr. Bradly Mr. Martin
Old Doctor
Carl Peterson
Poo Poo
Hassan i Sabbah
Sammy The Butcher
The Subliminal Kid
Terrence Weld
Johnny Yen

The Wild Boys–A.J.
A. J.
Colonel Bradly
Audrey Carsons
Ali Juan Chapultepec
Dib
Tony Green
General Lewis Greenfield
John Hamlin
Johnny
Kiki
Tío Mate
El Niño Muerto
Priest
Joe Rogers
The Great Slashtubitch
Xolotl

Frederick Busch
Domestic Particulars–N.L.T.
Samuel Dreff
Katherine
Anna Miller
Claire Miller
Harry Miller
Mac Miller
Mrs. Miriam

Manual Labor–J.G.H.
Abe
Baker
Sam
Anne Sorenson
Philip Sorenson

Rounds–J.M.
Elizabeth Bean
Alonzo I. R. Demby
Horace L'Ordinet

Eli Silver
Gwen Silver
Anne Sorenson
Michael Sorenson
Philip Sorenson
Turner
Mead Weaks
Mead Weaks II

Octavia E. Butler
Kindred–T.J.S.
Hagar Weylin Blake
Carrie
Edana Franklin
Kevin Franklin
Aunt Sarah
Alice Greenwood Weylin
Margaret Weylin
Rufus Weylin
Tom Weylin

Mind of My Mind–T.J.S.
Jesse Bernarr
Seth Dana
Rachel Davidson
Doro
Ada Dragan
Emma
Karl Larkin
Mary Larkin
Jan Sholto
Vivian

Patternmaster–T.J.S.
Amber
Coransee
Lady Darah
Iray
Jansee
Joachim
Michael
Rain
Rayal
Suliana
Teray

Survivor–T.J.S.
Choh
Diut
Gehl
Gehnahteh
Nathan James
Natahk
Tahneh
Tien
Alanna Verrick
Jules Verrick
Neila Verrick

James Branch Cabell
Jurgen
Dame Anaïtis
Chloris
Dorothy la Désirée

Florimel
Princess Guenevere
Jurgen
Koshchei the Deathless
Dame Lisa
Nessus
Mother Sereda

George Washington Cable
The Grandissimes–S.L.
Bras-Coupé
Clemence
Joseph Frowenfeld
Agricola Fusilier
Achille Grandissime
Honoré Grandissime
Honoré Grandissime f.m.c.
Sylvestre Grandissime
Raoul Innerarity
Doctor Charlie Keene
Charlie Mandarin
Aurore De Grapion Nancanou
Clotilde De Grapion Nancanou
Palmyre la Philosophe

George Cain
Blueschild Baby–E.B.
James Black
George Cain
Keith Cain
Mom Cain
Pop Cain
Ralph Cotton
Jose
Nandy
Nichole
Sabrina
Sun

James M. Cain
Mildred Pierce–G.G.
Montgomery Beragon
Wally Burgan
Lucy Gessler
Herbert Pierce
Mildred Pierce
Moire Pierce
Veda Pierce
Carlo Treviso

The Postman Always Rings Twice–G.G.
Madge Allen
Frank Chambers
Katz
Cora Smith Papadakis
Nick Papadakis
Sackett

Paul Cain
Fast One–G.G.
Shep Beery
John R. Bellmann
Crotti
Lee Fenner

S. Granquist
Gerry Kells
Reilly
Jack Rose

Erskine Caldwell
God's Little Acre–J.E.D.
Dave Dawson
Pluto Swint
Rosamond Walden Thompson
Will Thompson
Buck Walden
Darling Jill Walden
Griselda Walden
Jim Leslie Walden
Shaw Walden
Ty Ty Walden

Tobacco Road–J.E.D.
Lov Bensey
Pearl Lester Bensey
Ada Lester
Dude Lester
Ellie May Lester
Jeeter Lester
Mother Lester
Bessie Rice

Robert Cantwell
The Land of Plenty–R.M.R.
Gil Ahab
Carl Belcher
Walt Connor
Digby
Vin Garl
Hagen
John Hagen
Little Rock
Charles MacMahon
Rose MacMahon
Morley
Roger Schwartz
Sorenson
Ellen Turner
Marie Turner
Ed Winters

Truman Capote
Breakfast at Tiffany's–H.S.G.
Joe Bell
O. J. Berman
Fred
Doc Golightly
Holiday Golightly
Salvatore Tomato
Rutherford Trawler
Margaret Thatcher Fitzhue Wildwood
José Ybarra-Jaegar
I. Y. Yunioshi

The Grass Harp–H.S.G.
Judge Charlie Cool
Catherine Creek
Collin Talbo Fenwick

Riley Henderson
Little Homer Honey
Sister Ida Honey
Maude Riordan
Dr. Morris Ritz
Dolly Augusta Talbo
Verena Talbo

In Cold Blood–H.S.G.
Roy Church
Bonnie Fox Clutter
Herbert William Clutter
Kenyon Clutter
Nancy Clutter
Alvin Adams Dewey
Clarence Duntz
Richard Eugene Hickock
Susan Kidwell
Harold Nye
Bobby Rupp
Perry Edward Smith
Floyd Wells

Other Voices, Other Rooms–H.S.G.
Pepe Alvarez
Jesus Fever
Missouri Fever
Ellen Kendall
Joel Harrison Knox
Little Sunshine
Miss Amy Skully Sansom
Edward R. Sansom
Randolph Lee Skully
Florabel Thompkins
Idabel Thompkins
Miss Wisteria

Willa Cather
Death Comes for the Archbishop–G.G.
Jesus de Baca
Kit Carson
Bernard Ducrot
Eusabio
Gallegos
Jacinto
Jean Marie Latour
Marino Lucero
Antonio José Martínez
Baltazar Montoya
Antonio Olivares
Isabella Olivares
Joseph Vaillant
Magdalena Valdez

A Lost Lady–J.R.B.
Henry Collins
Francis Bosworth Ellinger
Ed Elliott
Captain Daniel Forrester
Marian Ormsby Forrester
Niel Herbert
Constance Ogden
Ivy Peters
Judge Pommeroy

My Ántonia–D.Sh.
Jim Burden
Gaston Cleric
Wycliffe Cutter
Anton Cuzak
Larry Donovan
Otto Fuchs
Peter Krajiek
Lena Lingard
Pavel and Peter
Shimerda
Ambroz Shimerda
Ántonia Shimerda

One of Ours–K.S.
Olive de Courcy
Augusta Erlich
Lieutenant Tod Fanning
Gladys Farmer
Lieutenant David Gerhardt
Ernest Havel
Mme. Joubert
Mahailey
Captain Harris Maxey
Victor Morse
Barclay Owens
Enid Royce
Lieutenant Colonel Walter Scott
Arthur Weldon
Bayliss Wheeler
Claude Wheeler
Evangeline Wheeler
Nat Wheeler
Ralph Wheeler
August Yoder

O Pioneers!–D.Sh. & J.R.
Alexandra Bergson
Emil Bergson
John Bergson
Lou Bergson
Mrs. Bergson
Oscar Bergson
Crazy Ivar
Carl Linstrum
Frank Shabata
Marie Tovesky Shabata

Sapphira and the Slave Girl–G.G.
Betty Blake
Mary Blake
Michael Blake
Rachel Colbert Blake
Mrs. Bywaters
Henry Colbert
Martin Colbert
Sapphira Dodderidge Colbert
Jefferson
Jezebel
Nancy
Till

The Song of the Lark–J.R.B.
Doctor Howard Archie

Madison Bowers
Andor Harsanyi
Ray H. Kennedy
Mr. and Mrs. Peter Kronborg
Thea Kronborg
Philip Frederick Ottenburg
Juan Tellamantez
Professor A. Wunsch

Raymond Chandler
The Big Sleep–R.L.
Lash Canino
Arthur Gwynn Geiger
Philip Marlowe
Eddie Mars
Mona Mars
Vivian Sternwood Regan
Carmen Sternwood
General Guy Sternwood

Farewell, My Lovely–R.L.
Jules Amthor
Lewin Lockridge Grayle
Moose Malloy
Philip Marlowe
Lindsay Marriott
Anne Riordan
Velma Valento

The Long Goodbye–R.L.
Sylvia Lennox
Terry Lennox
Linda Loring
Philip Marlowe
Mendy Menendez
Bernie Ohls
Harlan Potter
Eileen Wade
Roger Wade

Fred Chappell
Dagon–C.A.M.
Bella
Dagon
Enid
Annie Leland
Peter Leland
Sheila Leland
Ed Morgan
Mina Morgan
Coke Rymer

The Gaudy Place–C.A.M.
Clemmie
Andrew T. Harper
Katherine Harper
Linn Harper
Zebulon Johns Mackie
James Parker McClellan
Ted Pape

The Inkling–C.A.M.
Jan Anderson
Jenny Nolan Anderson

Timmie Anderson
Ronny Hughes
Hezekiah Nolan
Lora Bowen Nolan

It Is Time, Lord–C.A.M.
Virgil Campbell
Cory Christopher
David Christopher
James Christopher
Julia Christopher
Sylvia Christopher
Jack Davis
Judy Davis
Mavis
James D. Smathers, Jr.

John Cheever
Bullet Park–R.G.C.
Marietta Drum Hammer
Paul Hammer
Eliot Nailles
Nellie Nailles
Tony Nailles
Gretchen Shurz Oxencroft
Swami Rutuola
Franklin Pierce Taylor

Falconer–R.G.C.
Chicken Number Two
Deputy Warden Chisholm
Cuckold
Eben Farragut
Ezekiel Farragut
Marcia Farragut
Jody
Cardinal Thaddeus Morgan
Tiny

The Wapshot Chronicle–R.G.C.
Ray Badger
Uncle Peepee Marshmallow
Pancras
Helen Rutherford
Mr. de Sastago
Justina Wapshot Molesworth Scaddon
Betsey MacCaffery Wapshot
Coverly Wapshot
Ezekiel Wapshot
Honora Wapshot
Leander Wapshot
Melissa Scaddon Wapshot
Moses Wapshot
Sarah Coverly Wapshot
Rosalie Young

The Wapshot Scandal–R.G.C.
Mr. Applegate
Dr. Lemuel Cameron
Emile Cranmer
Griza
Norman Johnson
Gertrude Lockhart
Betsey Marcus Wapshot

Coverly Wapshot
Honora Wapshot
Leander Wapshot
Melissa Scaddon Wapshot
Moses Wapshot
Sarah Coverly Wapshot

Susan Cheever
Looking for Work–R.G.C.
Mike Abrams
Max Angelo
Jason Gardens
Salley Gardens
Joel Stansky
Colin Willes

Charles W. Chesnutt
The Colonel's Dream–J.G.H.
William Fetters
Col. Henry French
Laura Treadwell

The House Behind the Cedars–J.G.H.
George Tryon
John Walden
Molly Walden
Rowena Walden

The Marrow of Tradition–J.G.H.
Major Philip Carteret
Dr. William Miller

Lydia Maria Child
Hobomok–J.G.H.
Charles Brown
John Collier
Sally Oldham Collier
Charles Hobomok Conant
Mary Conant
Mrs. Mary Conant
Roger Conant
Corbitant
Governor Endicott
Hobomok
James Hopkins
Earl of Rivers

Kate Chopin
The Awakening–D.P.
Alcée Arobin
Madame Lebrun
Robert Lebrun
Dr. Mandelet
Edna Pontellier
Etienne Pontellier
Léonce Pontellier
Raoul Pontellier
Adèle Ratignolle
Mademoiselle Reisz

Winston Churchill
Coniston–W.H.
Jethro Bass
Sally Broke

Jane Merrill
Stephen Merrill
Susan Merrill
Lucretia Penniman
Ephraim Prescott
David Ritchie
Cynthia Wetherell
Cynthia Ware Wetherell
William Wetherell
Isaac Dudley Worthington
Robert Worthington

The Crisis–W.H.
Captain Elijah Brent
Stephen Atterbury Brice
Colonel Comyn Carvel
Virginia Carvel
George Catherwood
Tom Catherwood
Clarence Colfax
Ephum
Eliphalet Hopper
Carl Richter
Puss and Emily Russell
Silas Whipple

The Crossing–W.H.
Gignoux
Thomas McChesney
Harry Riddle
Polly Ann Ripley
Antoinette de St. Gré
Auguste de St. Gré
Hélène Victoire Marie de St. Gré
Philippe de St. Gré
Nicholas Temple
Sarah Temple

The Inside of the Cup–W.H.
Gordon Atterbury
Horace Bentley
Richard Garvin
Sally Grover
John Hodder
Kate Marcy
Reverend Mister McCrae
Alison Parr
Eldon Parr
Preston Parr

Mr. Crewe's Career–W.H.
Brush Bascom
Jacob Botcher
Euphrasia Cotton
Humphrey Crewe
Augustus P. Flint
Victoria Flint
Thomas Gaylord
Adam B. Hunt
Jabe Jenney
Zebulun Meader
Alice Pomfret
Fanny Pomfret
Mr. Redbrook

Hamilton Tooting
Austen Vane
Hilary Vane

Richard Carvel–W.H.
Reverend Allen
Grafton Carvel
Lionel Carvel
Philip Carvel
Richard Carvel
Duke of Chartersea
Captain Daniel Clapsaddle
Lord Comyn
Dorothy Manners
Margaret Manners
Marmaduke Manners
Henry Swain
Patty Swain
Thomas Swain

Walter Van Tilburg Clark
The Ox-Bow Incident–J.Cal.
Amigo
Bartlett
Canby
Gil Carter
Art Croft
Arthur Davies
Harley Drew
Jeff Farnley
Greene
Jenny Grier
Alva Hardwick
Laurence Liam Kinkaid
Donald Martin
Juan Martinez
Risley
Gerald Tetley
Major Willard Tetley

Samuel Langhorne Clemens
Adventures of Huckleberry Finn–G.G.
Dauphin
Widow Douglas
Duke of Bridgewater
Huckleberry Finn
Pap Finn
Emmeline Grangerford
Colonel Saul Grangerford
Sophia Grangerford
Jim
Aunt Polly
Thomas Sawyer
Harney Shepherdson
Colonel Sherburn
Judge Thatcher
Rebecca Thatcher
Miss Watson
Joanna, Mary Jane, and Susan Wilks

The Adventures of Tom Sawyer–G.G.
Widow Douglas
Huckleberry Finn
Pap Finn

Joseph Harper
Injun Joe
Amy Lawrence
Aunt Polly
Muff Potter
Doctor Robinson
Sidney Sawyer
Thomas Sawyer
Judge Thatcher
Rebecca Thatcher

The American Claimant–G.G.
Barrow
Kirkcudbright Llanover Marjoribanks Sellers
   Berkeley
Dan'l
Earl of Rossmore
Hattie Marsh
Rachael Marsh
One-armed Pete
Polly Sellers
Colonel Beriah/Eschol/Mulberry Sellers
Sarah Sellers

A Connecticut Yankee in King Arthur's Court–G.G.
Arthur
Clarence
Dinadan
Guenever
Merlin
Hank Morgan
Morgan le Fay
M. T.
Sandy

The Gilded Age–G.G.
Ruth Bolton
Henry Brierly
Dilsey
Henry Clay Hawkins
Laura Van Brunt Hawkins
Colonel Beriah/Eschol/Mulberry Sellers
Polly Sellers
Philip (Phil) Sterling

The Prince and the Pauper–G.G.
John Canty
Tom Canty
Miles Hendon
Earl of Hertford
Edward Tudor

Pudd'nhead Wilson–D.Sh.
Luigi and Angelo Capello
Percy Northumberland Driscoll
Thomas à Becket Driscoll
York Leicester Driscoll
Pembroke Howard
Roxana
Valet de Chambre
David Wilson

Tom Sawyer Abroad–G.G.
Huckleberry Finn

Jim
Aunt Polly
Thomas Sawyer

Tom Sawyer, Detective–G.G.
Brace Dunlap
Jake Dunlap
Jubiter Dunlap
Huckleberry Finn
Benny Phelps
Aunt Polly
Thomas Sawyer

Cyrus Colter
The Hippodrome–H.R.H.
Bea
Cleo
Darlene
Donald
Iris
Alberto Mogadiscio
Mack Thomas
Jackson Yeager

The Rivers of Eros–H.R.H.
Ambrose Hammer
Chester Jackson
Pearl Jackson
Adeline Parker
Lester Parker
Ruby Parker
Zack Parker
Clotilda Pilgrim
James Potts
Dunreith Smith
Hyacinth Turner

Evan Connell
Mr. Bridge–K.A.
Madge Arlen
Grace Barron
Virgil Barron
Carolyn Bridge
Douglas Bridge
India Bridge
Ruth Bridge
Walter Bridge
Harriett
Alice Jones
Julia

Mrs. Bridge–K.A.
Madge Arlen
Grace Barron
Virgil Barron
Carolyn Bridge
Douglas Bridge
India Bridge
Ruth Bridge
Walter Bridge
Dr. Foster
Harriett
Alice Jones
Julia

Jack Conroy
The Disinherited–J.C.S.
Helen Baker
Jasper Collins
Larry Donovan
Tom Donovan
Hans
Bonny Fern Haskin
Nat Moore
Mike Riordan
Lionel Stafford
Ed Warden
Rollie Weems

Pat Conroy
The Great Santini–L.M.M.
Virgil Hedgepath
Benjamin Meecham
Karen Meecham
Lillian Meecham
Mary Anne Meecham
Matthew Meecham
W. P. Meecham
Red Pettus
Arrabelle Smalls
Toomer Smalls
Alice Sole
Joseph Varney

James Fenimore Cooper
The Deerslayer–G.G.
Nathaniel Bumppo
Chingachgook
Hetty Hutter
Judith Hutter
Thomas Hutter
Le Loup Cervier
Henry March
Rivenoak
Wah-ta!-Wah

The Last of the Mohicans–G.G.
Nathaniel Bumppo
Chingachgook
David Gamut
Duncan Heyward
Magua
Montcalm
Alice Munro
Colonel Munro
Cora Munro
Uncas

The Pathfinder–G.G.
Arrowhead
Nathaniel Bumppo
Chingachgook
Charles Cap
Duncan of Lundie
Mabel Dunham
Serjeant Dunham
David Muir
Jasper Western

The Pioneers–G.G.
Nathaniel Bumppo
Chingach
Hiram Doolittlegook
Oliver Effingham
Louisa Grant
Hector
Richard Jones
Elizabeth Temple
Marmaduke Temple

The Prairie–J.G.H.
Obed Bat
Nathaniel Bumppo
Asa Bush
Esther Bush
Ishmael Bush
Inez de Certavallos
Hard Heart
Hector
Paul Hover
Le Balafré
Mahtoree
Duncan Uncas Middleton
Tachechana
Ellen Wade
Weucha
Abiram White

The Spy–G.G.
Harvey Birch
Peyton Dunwoodie
Elizabeth Flanagan
Captain John Lawton
Jeanette Peyton
Dr. Archibald Sitgreaves
Caesar Thompson
George Washington
Colonel Wellmere
Frances Wharton
Henry Wharton
Mr. Wharton
Sarah Wharton

Robert Coover
The Origin of the Brunists–M.D.
Father Battista Baglione
Abner Baxter
Frances Baxter
Nathan Baxter
Paul Baxter
Sarah Baxter
Angela Bonali
Charlie Bonali
Etta Bonali
Vince Bonali
Happy Bottom
Antonio Bruno
Emilia Bruno
Giovanni Bruno
Marcella Bruno
Joe Castiglione
Theodore Cavanaugh
Tommy Cavanaugh

Hiram Clegg
Clara Collins
Elaine Collins
Ely Collins
Wanda Cravens
Barney Davis
Domiron
Wesley Edwards
Elan
Jim Elliott
Wally Fisher
Ralph Himebaugh
Lou Jones
Karmin
Ko-li
Colin Meredith
Justin Miller
Eleanor Norton
Wylie Norton
Carl Dean Palmers
Annie Pompa
Rahim
Dee Romano
Michael Strelchuk
Mortimer Whipple
Womwom
Ben Wosznik

The Public Burning—M.D.
Dwight David Eisenhower
Richard Nixon
Phantom
Ethel Greenglass Rosenberg
Julius Rosenberg
Sam Slick

The Universal Baseball Association, Inc.—M.D.
Jock Casey
Benny Diskin
Lou Engel
Hettie Irden
Molly
Pete
Mitch Porter
Damon Rutherford
B. Valentine
J. Henry Waugh
Horace Zifferblatt

Edwin Corle
Fig Tree John—C.R.S.
Agocho
Joe
Jose
Kai-a
George Mack
Johnny Mack
Maria
Paul
Petterman
Martha Goddard Reeves

Gregory Corso
The American Express—D.L.

D.
Daphne
Dad Deform
Horatio Frump
Carrol Grilhiggen
Harry
Hinderov
Angus Plow
Simon
Scratch Vatic
Rodger Wolfherald

James Gould Cozzens
By Love Possessed—G.V.N.
J. Jerome Brophy
Fred Dealey
Helen Detweiler
Ralph Detweiler
Julius Penrose
Marjorie Penrose
Polly Pratt
Alfred Revere
Reggie Shaw
Noah Tuttle
Arthur Winner Junior
Arthur Winner Senior
Clarissa Henderson Winner
Eliot Woolf

Guard of Honor—G.V.N.
Captain Donald Andrews
Major General Ira N. Beal
Lieutenant Colonel Ben Carricker
Captain Clarence Ducheminny
Lieutenant James A. Edsell
Captain Nathaniel Hicks
Colonel Mowbray
Brigadier General Nichols
Master Sergeant Dominic Pellerino
Cora Ross
Colonel Norman Ross
Lieutenant Amanda Turck
Lieutenant Stanley M. Willis
Colonel Woodman

Stephen Crane
George's Mother—J.G.H.
Bleecker
Fidsey Corcoran
Maggie Johnson
Charley Jones
George Kelcey
Zeusentell

Maggie: A Girl of the Streets—D.Sh.
Blue Billie
Johnson
Jimmie Johnson
Maggie Johnson
Mary Johnson
Nellie
Pete

The Red Badge of Courage—J.G.H.

Jim Conklin
Henry Fleming
Tom Jamison
Jimmie Rogers
Wilson

The Third Violet—J.G.H.
Grace Fanhall
William Hawker
Florinda O'Connor
Jem Oglethorpe
Pennoyer
Great Grief Warwickson
Wrinkles

Harry Crews
A Feast of Snakes—J.L.R.
Duffy Deeter
Susan Gender
George
Lottie Mae
Lummy
Beatriz Dargan Mackey
Big Joe Mackey
Joe Lon Mackey
Shep Martin
Buddy Matlow
Willard Miller
Luther Peacock
Berenice Sweet
Hard Candy Sweet
Tump Walker

Car—J.L.R.
Homer Edge
Joe
Easton Mack
Herman Mack
Junell Mack
Mister Mack
Margaret

Karate Is a Thing of the Spirit—J.L.R.
Belt
George
John Kaimon
Lazarus
Marvin
Jefferson Davis Munroe
Gaye Nell Odell
Mavis Odell

Michael Crichton
The Andromeda Strain—D.L.Y.
Karen Anson
Alan Benedict
Charles Burton
Edgar Comroe
Lewis Crane
Mark William Hall
Peter Jackson
Jaggers
Christian Kirke
Peter Leavitt

Arthur Manchek
Arthur Morris
Jamie Ritter
Robertson
Roger Shawn
Smithson
Gladys Stevens
Jeremy Stone
Martin Willis
Samuel Wilson

The Great Train Robbery—D.L.Y.
Robert Agar
Sir John Alderston
Barlow
Richard Burgess
Teddy Burke
Bill Chokee
Laurence Chubb, Jr.
Henry Fowler
Edward Harranby
Jeremy Johnson, Sr.
Susan Lang
McPherson
Miss Miriam
Nelse
Edward Pierce
Jimmy Shaw
Edgar Trent
Elizabeth Trent
William Williams

The Terminal Man—D.L.Y.
John Anders
Craig Beckerman
Harold Franklin Benson
Angela Black
John Ellis
Farley
Gerhard
Manon
Roger A. McPherson
Robert Morris
Ramos
Richards
Janet Ross

Countee Cullen
One Way to Heaven—A.S.
Constancia Brown Brandon
Dr. George Brandon
Professor Seth Calhoun
Mary Johnson
Mattie Johnson
Sam Lucas
Aunt Mandy

H. D.
Bid Me to Live—J.Mi.
Julia Ashton
Rafe Ashton
Bella Carter
Frederick
Elsa Frederick

Vane

Hedylus—J.Mi.
Demetrius
Demion
Douris
Hedyle
Hedylus
Irene

Helen in Egypt—J.Mi.
Achilles
Helen
Paris
Theseus
Thetis

Palimpsest—J.Mi.
Julia Cornelia Augusta
Helen Fairwood
Hipparchia
Mavis Landour
Marius
Olivia
Philip
Captain Ratton
Fred Ransome
Raymonde Ransome
Ermentrude Solomon
Mary Thorpe-Wharton
Verrus

Clyde Brion Davis
"The Great American Novel—"—S.G.K.
Paul Clark
Frances Harbach
Syra Morris
Harvey O'Brien
John Penny
Tom Rogers
Betty Sullivan
George Tichnor
Byron Zigler
Homer Zigler
Pearl Hawkins Zigler

H. L. Davis
Beulah Land—S.G.K.
Askwani
Hube Dakens
Sedaya Gallet
Grandma Luttrell
Maruca
Perrault
Savacol
Elison Warne
Ewen Warne
Ruhama Warne

Harp of a Thousand Strings—S.G.K.
Apeyahola
Marquis René-Victor de Bercy
Jeanne-Marie Cabarrus de Fontenay
Fouché

Father Jarnatt
Luz
Don Joaquin MacGillivray
Ouvrard
Commodore Robinette
Suleau
Suleau II
Jean-Lambert Tallien
Anne-Joseph Théroigne
Big Foot Whitten

Honey in the Horn—S.G.K.
Clark Burdon
Clay Calvert
Orlando Geary
Pappy Howell
Foscoe Leonard
Isaac Lund
Serphin Moss
Uncle Preston Shiveley
Wade Shiveley
Payette Simmons

Rebecca Harding Davis
Life in the Iron Mills—J.G.H.
Clarke
Deborah
Janey
Kirby
John May
Mitchell
Hugh Wolfe
Old Wolfe

Richard Harding Davis
Soldiers of Fortune—H.R.H.
Madame Alvarez
President Alvarez
Robert Clay
Reginald King
Alice Langham
Andrew Langham
Hope Langham
Theodore Langham
MacWilliams
General Mendoza
Captain Stuart

Peter De Vries
The Blood of the Lamb—R.L.H.
Rena Baker
Mrs. Brodhag
Hank Hoos
Cora Nyhoff
Reverend Tonkle
Ben Wanderhope
Carol Wanderhope
Don Wanderhope
Greta Wigbaldy Wanderhope
Louie Wanderhope

Comfort Me with Apples—R.L.H.
Frank Carmichael
Pete Cheshire

Crystal Chickering
Harry Clammidge
Al Roquefort
Nickie Sherman
Charles Swallow
Lila Swallow
Clara Thicknesse

I Hear America Swinging—R.L.H.
Charlie Achorn
Hattie Brown
Herkimer Brown
William Bumpers
Clem Clammidge
Harry Clammidge
Ma Godolphin
Opal Kitchener
Claire de Lune
Vera Mills
Artie Pringle
Mother Sigafoos
Luke Wheeler

Let Me Count the Ways—R.L.H.
Dr. Bagley
Norman Littlefield
Angela Ravage
Art Salerno
Lena Salerno
Three Little Prigs
Elsie Wishnotski Waltz
Stanley Waltz
Thomas Waltz
Marion Wellington

The Mackerel Plaza—R.L.H.
Jack Analysis
Molly Calico
Pippa Calico
George Chance
Charlie Comstock
Reverend Andrew Mackerel
Ida May Mackerel
Arthur Meesum
Joseph Meesum
Hester Pedlock
Mike Todarescu
Frank Turnbull
Steven Turnbull

Mrs. Wallop—R.L.H.
Lena Bascombe
Edward R. Coffee
Cora Frawley
Will Gerstenslager
Charles Pilsudski
Virginia Quilty
Randall Rivers
Stella Slobkin Rivers
Waldo St. Cloud
Emma Wallop
Osgood Wallop
Ralph Wallop

Reuben, Reuben—R.L.H.
Pussy Beauseigneur
Edith Chipps
Jack Dumbrowski
Jack Haxby
Lucille Haxby
Gowan McGland
Alvin Mopworth
Eunice Punck
Harry Pyecraft
Emil Rappaport
Nectar Schmidt
Frank Spofford
Geneva Spofford
George Spofford
Mary Punck Spofford
Roberta Springer
Thaddeus Springer

Through the Fields of Clover—R.L.H.
Nat Bundle
Chaucer
Johnny Glimmergarden
Malcolm Johnsprang
Alma Marvel
Ben Marvel
Bushrod Marvel
Clara Marvel
Cotton Marvel
Elsie Marvel
Evelyn Shaw Glimmergarden Marvel
Chester Mercury
Harry Mercury
Lee Mercury
Lew Pentecost
Bill Prufrock
Matt Shaw
Neil Sligh
Mrs. Wetwilliam

The Tunnel of Love—R.L.H.
Audrey
Hugh Blair
Cornelia Bly
Dick
Mrs. Mash
Terry McBain
Ernest Mills
Augie Poole
Isolde Poole
Miss Terkle

The Vale of Laughter—R.L.H.
Benny Bonner
Gloria Bunshaft
Father Enright
Uncle Hamilton
Fido Harrison
Mother Hines
Wally Hines
MacNaughton
Betty MacNaughton
Mrs. Munkey
Laura Pribble

Hamilton Sandwich
Joe Sandwich
Robin and Ethel Weems

John William DeForest
Miss Ravenel's Conversion from Secession to Lo
John T. Carter
Lillie Ravenel Carter
Ravenel Carter
Edward Colburne
Major Gazaway
Mrs. Larue
Doctor Ravenel
John Whitewood, Jr.

Nicholas Delbanco
Fathering—G.L.M.
Chloe Duboise
Alain Hugues
Chantal Hugues
Alexander Mueller
Elizabeth Mueller
Hans Mueller
Marian Mueller
Robert Mueller
Susan Mueller

In the Middle Distance—G.L.M.
Jean Burling
Tunis G. Campbell
Andrea Delbanco
Barbara Delbanco
Evelyn Delbanco
Michael Delbanco
Nicholas Delbanco
Nat Kott
Peter Sim

The Martlet's Tale—G.L.M.
Anna-Maria Charaiambos
Chrysanthi
Mehmet Effendi
Andreas Procopirios
Apelis Procopirios
Eleni Procopirios
Manos Procopirios
Nicoletta Procopirios
Orsetta Procopirios
Sotiris Procopirios
Triphon Procopirios
Alexis Saranditis
Dania Saranditis
Phillipos Stritsas

News—G.L.M.
Adelina
Allan
Tunis G. Campbell
Elaine Dade
Gifford
Harrison
Karen
Sam
Carlos Scotobal

Emelyn Walley

Possession–G.L.M.
  Samson Finney
  James Pearson
  Samuel Powers
  Harriet Sherbrooke
  Judah Porteous Sherbrooke
  Lisbeth McPherson Sherbrooke
  Seth Sherbrooke
  Margaret Cutler Sherbrooke
  Seth Sherbrooke

Sherbrookes–G.L.M.
  Hal Boudreau
  Sarah Conover
  Samson Finney
  Andrew Kincannon
  Willard Sheldon
  Daniel Sherbrooke
  Harriet Sherbrooke
  Ian Daniel Sherbrooke
  Judah Porteous Sherbrooke
  Margaret Cutler Sherbrooke
  Seth Sherbrooke

Small Rain–G.L.M.
  Elise Crawford
  Reuben Crawford
  Harald von Einzeedle
  James von Einzeedle
  Maija von Einzeedle
  Thomas von Einzeedle
  Anthony Hope-Harding
  Janet Hope-Harding

Don DeLillo
Americana–K.A.
  Clinton Harkavy Bell
  David Bell
  Bobby Brand
  Clevenger
  Carol Deming
  Weede Denney
  Binky Lister
  Jack Wilson Pike
  Sullivan
  Ted Warburton

End Zone–K.A.
  Anatole Bloomberg
  Myna Corbett
  Emmett Creed
  Gary Harkness
  Taft Robinson
  Major Staley
  Alan Zapalac

Great Jones Street–K.A.
  Azarian
  Bohack
  Edward B. Fenig
  Globke
  Opel Hampson

  Hanes
  Dr. Pepper
  Watney
  Bucky Wunderlick

Players–K.A.
  J. Kinnear
  Jack Laws
  Rosemary Moore
  Ethan Segal
  Marina Vilar
  Rafael Vilar
  Lyle Wynant
  Pammy Wynant

Ratner's Star–K.A.
  Lester Bolin
  Henrik Endor
  Cheops Feeley
  LoQuadro
  Edna Lown
  Orang Mohole
  Shazar Lazarus Ratner
  Robert Hopper Softly
  Elux Troxl
  Billy Twillig
  Jean Sweet Venable
  Maurice Xavier Wu

Running Dog–K.A.
  Richie Armbriste
  Grace Delaney
  Lightborne
  Lomax
  Earl Mudger
  Senator Lloyd Percival
  Nadine Rademacher
  Moll Robbins
  Glen Selvy

Floyd Dell
Moon-Calf–W.R.
  Thomas Alden
  Miss Croly
  Felix Fay
  Stephen Frazer
  Rose Henderson
  Lulu Miller
  Nathan
  Helen Raymond
  Eve Tennant
  Joyce Tennant
  Franz Vogelsang

Patrick Dennis
Around the World with Auntie Mame–S.L.H.
  Elmore Jefferson Davis Burnside
  Vera Charles
  Mame Dennis
  Michael Dennis
  Patrick Dennis
  Captain Basil Fitz-Hugh
  Hermione Gravell-Pitt
  Baron von Hodenlohern

  Ito
  Pegeen Ryan
  Reverend Dr. Alfred Shumway
  Rosemary Shumway

Auntie Mame–S.L.H.
  Dwight Babcock
  Beauregard Jackson Pickett Burnside
  Vera Charles
  Mame Dennis
  Patrick Dennis
  Agnes Gooch
  Ito
  Norah Muldoon
  Pegeen Ryan

August Derleth
Evening in Spring–G.G.
  Granfather Adams
  August Derleth
  Constance Estabrook
  Margery Estabrook
  Stephen Grendon
  Will and Rose Grendon
  Simolean Jones
  May

The Shadow in the Glass–B.W.G.
  Helen Van Vleck Barber
  Joel Barber
  George Cox
  Garrett Denniston
  Charles Dewey
  Katherine Dunn Dewey
  Katie Dewey
  Nelson Dewey
  Henry Dodge
  Hercules Dousman
  Charles Dunn
  Stephen Grendon

The Shield of the Valiant–G.G.
  Granfather Adams
  Mrs. Janney
  Rena Janney
  Simolean Jones
  Miss Mergan
  Father Peitsch
  Preston Robinson
  Birdie Sewall
  John Sewall
  Kivden Sewall
  Joseph Stanley

Alexis Deveaux
Spirits in the Street–L.S.L.
  Roland Alexander
  Alexis
  Charles
  Lynda
  Michelle
  Shirley

James Dickey

Deliverance–G.V.N.
 Drew Ballinger
 Ed Gentry
 Lewis Medlock
 Bobby Trippe

Joan Didion
 A Book of Common Prayer–C.W.O.
  Carmen Arrellano
  Marin Bogart
  Warren Bogart
  Ardis Bradley
  Tuck Bradley
  Bebe Chicago
  Charlotte Amelia Douglas
  Leonard Douglas
  Victor Strasser
  Antonio Strasser-Mendana
  Bianca Strasser-Mendana
  Edgar Strasser-Mendana
  Elena Strasser-Mendana
  Gerardo Strasser-Mendana
  Grace Tabor Strasser-Mendana
  Isabel Strasser-Mendana
  Luis Strasser-Mendana
  Victor Strasser-Mendana

 Play It As It Lays–C.W.O.
  Benny Austin
  BZ
  Carlotta
  Freddy Chaikin
  Ivan Costello
  Felicia Goodwin
  Les Goodwin
  Helene
  Larry Kulik
  Carter Lang
  Kate Lang
  Mrs. Lang
  Johnny Waters
  Susannah Wood
  Francine Wyeth
  Harry Wyeth
  Maria Wyeth

 Run River–C.W.O.
  Rita Blanchard
  Henry Catlin
  Nancy Dupree Channing
  Ryder Channing
  China Mary
  Edith Knight
  Walter Knight
  Everett Currier McClellan
  Julia Knight McClellan
  Knight McClellan
  Lily Knight McClellan
  Martha Currier McClellan
  Francie Templeton
  Joe Templeton
  Sarah McClellan Warfield

Thomas Dixon

 The Clansman–G.G.
  Augustus Caesar
  Ben Cameron
  Margaret Cameron
  Richard Cameron
  Jake
  Alexander Lenoir
  Jeannie Campbell Lenoir
  Marion Lenoir
  Abraham Lincoln
  Silas Lynch
  Austin Stoneman
  Elsie Stoneman
  Phil Stoneman

 The Leopard's Spots–G.G.
  Flora Camp
  Tom Camp
  Stuart Dameron
  Dick
  Mrs. John Durham
  Rev. John Durham
  Charles Gaston
  Nelson Gaston
  George Harris
  Simon Legree
  Everett Lowell
  Allan McLeod
  Hose Norman
  Timothy Shelby
  Susan Walker
  General Daniel Worth
  Sallie Worth

E. L. Doctorow
 The Book of Daniel–E.C.R.
  Jacob Ascher
  Paul Isaacson
  Rochelle Isaacson
  Daniel Isaacson Lewin
  Lise Lewin
  Robert Lewin
  Susan Isaacson Lewin
  Selig Mindish
  Artie Sternlicht
  Williams

 Ragtime–E.C.R.
  Will Conklin
  Father
  Emma Goldman
  Harry Houdini
  Little Boy
  The Little Girl
  Mameh
  J. Pierpont Morgan
  Mother
  Mother's Younger Brother
  Evelyn Nesbit
  Sarah
  Tateh
  Harry K. Thaw
  Coalhouse Walker, Jr.
  Booker T. Washington

  Stanford White

 Welcome to Hard Times–E.C.R.
  Bert Albany
  Avery
  John Bear
  Helga Bergenstrohm
  Swede Bergenstrohm
  Blue
  Mrs. Clement
  Fee
  Jimmy Fee
  Hayden Gillis
  Hausenfield
  Leo Jenks
  Ezra Maple
  Isaac Maple
  Angus Mcellhenny
  Jack Millay
  Alf Moffet
  Munn
  Molly Riordan
  Clay Turner
  Zar

J. P. Donleavy
 The Ginger Man–S.Ba.
  Christine
  Percy Clocklan
  Marion Dangerfield
  Sebastian Dangerfield
  Lilly Frost
  MacDoon
  Tony Malarkey
  Mary
  Kenneth O'Keefe
  Egbert Skully

Ignatius Donnelly
 Caesar's Column–S.C.B.
  Frederika Bowers
  Nathan Brederhagan
  Prince Cabano
  Christina Jansen
  Caesar Lomellini
  Maximilian Petion
  Jacob Quincy
  Matthew Rudolph
  Estella Washington
  Gabriel Weltstein
  Heinrich Weltstein

John Dos Passos
 Manhattan Transfer–R.L.
  George Baldwin
  Anna Cohen
  Congo
  Stan Emery
  Joe Harland
  Jimmy Herf
  Jo-Jo
  Nevada Jones
  Bud Korpenning
  Gus McNiel

Nellie McNiel
James Merivale
Jefferson Merivale
Dutch Robertson
Ed Thatcher
Ellen Thatcher
Susie Thatcher

U.S.A. trilogy–R.L.
Charley Anderson
Joe Askew
G. H. Barrow
Nat Benton
Doc Bingham
Ben Compton
Gladys Compton
Margo Dowling
Mary French
Tony Garido
George Hall
Bill Haywood
Fred Hoff
Eveline Hutchins
Agnes Mandeville
Frank Mandeville
Fenian McCreary
Dirk McArthur
J. Ward Morehouse
Tim O'Hara
Jose O'Riely
Richard Ellsworth Savage
Maisie Spencer
Gertrude Staple
Don Stevens
Eleanor Stoddard
Annabelle Marie Strang
Emiscah Svenson
Anne Elizabeth Trent
Gladys Wheatley
Janey Williams
Joe Williams

Theodore Dreiser
An American Tragedy–C.L.S.
Roberta Alden
Hortense Briggs
Sondra Finchley
Asa Griffiths
Clyde Griffiths
Elvira Griffiths
Samuel Griffiths
Willard Sparser

The Bulwark–C.L.S.
Benecia Wallin Barnes
Etta Barnes
Hannah and Rufus Barnes
Solon Barnes
Stewart Barnes
Victor Bruge
Willard Kane
Volida La Porte
Psyche Tanzer

The Financier–C.L.S.
Edward Malia Butler
Aileen Butler Cowperwood
Frank Algernon Cowperwood
Henry Worthington Cowperwood
Lillian Semple Cowperwood
Seneca Davis
Henry A. Mollenhauer
Alfred Semple
Mark Simpson
Harper Steger
George W. Stener
Stephen Wingate

The "Genius."–C.L.S.
Stella Appleton
Christina Channing
Anatole Charles
Suzanne Dale
Margaret Duff
Miriam Finch
Ruby Kenny
Florence J. White
Angela Witla
Angela Blue Witla
Eugene Tennyson Witla

Jennie Gerhardt–C.L.S.
George Sylvester Brander
Letty Pace Gerald
Genevieve Gerhardt
William Gerhardt
Archibald Kane
Lester Kane
Robert Kane
Wilhelmina Vesta

Sister Carrie–C.L.S.
Bob Ames
Charles H. Drouet
Minnie Meeber Hanson
George W. Hurstwood
Julia Hurstwood
Caroline Meeber
Mr. and Mrs. Vance

The Stoic–C.L.S.
Marigold Shoemaker Brainerd
Hattie Carter
Aileen Butler Cowperwood
Frank Algernon Cowperwood
Lillian Semple Cowperwood
Berenice Fleming
Montague Greaves
Philip Henshaw
Jefferson James
Willard Jarkins
Lorna Maris
Gordon Roderick
Henry De Soto Sippens
Bruce Tollifer

The Titan–C.L.S.
Judah Addison

Claudia Carlstadt
Hattie Carter
Aileen Butler Cowperwood
Frank Algernon Cowperwood
Lillian Semple Cowperwood
Berenice Fleming
Forbes Gurney
Augustus M. Haguenin
Cecily Haguenin
Caroline Hand
Hosmer Hand
Edwin L. Kaffrath
Patrick Kerrigan
Peter Laughlin
Polk Lynde
General MacDonald
Truman Leslie MacDonald
Antoinette Nowak
Stephanie Platow
Henry De Soto Sippens
Rita Greenough Sohlberg
Harper Steger
Michael Tiernan

Allen Drury
Advise and Consent–M.Du.
Brigham M. Anderson
Celestine Barre
Raoul Barre
Seabright B. Cooley
Mrs. Phelps Harrison
Harley M. Hudson
Krishna Khaleel
Orrin Knox
Robert A. Leffingwell
Lord Claude Maudulayne
Lady Kitty Maudulayne
Robert Durham Munson
The President
Lafe Smith
Vasily Tashikov
Fred Van Ackerman

W. E. B. Du Bois
Dark Princess–A.G.M.
Mr. Amos
Mrs. Beech
Mr. Cadwalader
Corruthers
Congressman Doolittle
Jimmie Giles
Miss Gillespie
Mr. Graham
Mr. Green
Brother John Jones
Princess Kautilya
Miguel Perigua
Samuel Scott
Mrs. Therwald
Matthew Towns
Sara Andrews Towns

The Quest of the Silver Fleece–A.G.M.
Blessed Alwyn

Bertie
Colton
Harry Cresswell
Helen Cresswell
Colonel St. John Cresswell
Harry Cresswell
Edward Easterly
Elspeth
Emma
Mr. Job Grey
Mrs. Grey
Johnson
Jones
Aunt Rachel
Rob
Miss Sarah Smith
Peter Charles Smith
Sam Stillings
Uncle Jim Sykes
John Taylor
Tom Teerswell
Mr. Tolliver
Mrs. Vanderpool
Miss Caroline Wynn
Zora

Paul Laurence Dunbar
The Fanatics–D.L.L.
Nigger Ed
Col. Alexander Stewart
Walter Stewart
Raymond Stothard
Robert Van Doren
Stephen Van Doren
Bradford Waters
Mary Waters

The Love of Landry–D.L.L.
Anna Annesley
Arthur Heathcote
Helen Osborne
John Osborne
Mildred Osborne
Landry Thayer

The Sport of the Gods–D.L.L.
Berry Hamilton
Fannie Hamilton
Joe Hamilton
Kitty Hamilton
Francis Oakley
Col. Maurice Oakley

The Uncalled–D.L.L.
Frederick Brent
Margaret Brent
Tom Brent
Eliphalet Hodges
Hester Prime
Rev. Mr. Simpson
Elizabeth Simpson

John Gregory Dunne

True Confessions–G.G.
Jack Amsterdam
Dan T. Campion
Frank Crotty
Hugh Danaher
Lois Fazenda
Fuqua
Corinne Morris
Harold Herman Pugh
Brenda Samuels
Mary Margaret Maher Spellacy
Desmond Spellacy
Thomas Spellacy
Brenda Samuels

Walter D. Edmonds
Chad Hanna–W.We.
Bastock
B. D. Bisbee
Chad Hanna
Alonzo Dent Huguenine
Bettina Huguenine
Oscar
Elias Proops
Fred Shepley
Caroline Trid
Ike Wayfish
Albany Yates

Drums along the Mohawk–W.We.
Blue Back
Joe Boleo
Adam Helmer
Nicholas Herkimer
Gilbert Martin
Magdelana Borst Martin
Sarah McKlennar
Nancy Schuyler
John Wolff

Erie Water–W.We.
Issachar Bennet
Lester Charley
Harley Falk
Jeremiah Fowler
Mary Goodhill Fowler
Betsey Halleck
Caleb Hammil
Dorothy and Robert Melville
Norah Sharon

Rome Haul–W.We.
Joseph P. Calash
Fortune Friendly
Lucy Gurget
Daniel Harrow
Sam Henderson
Jotham Klore
Molly Larkins
Solomon Tinkle
Jacob Turnesa
Samson Weaver

Junius Edwards

If We Must Die–A.H.
Flip
Will Harris
Jeff
Luke
Sam
Tom

Edward Eggleston
The Circuit Rider–H.H.
Brady
Lewis Goodwin
Morton Goodwin
Captain Enoch Lumsden
Hezekiah Lumsden
Patty Lumsden
Mr. Magruder
Ann Eliza Meacham
Dr. Morgan
Henrietta Morgan
Colonel Isaiah Wheeler

The Hoosier School-Master–H.H.
Henry Banta
George H. Bronson
Ralph Hartsook
Martha Hawkins
Squire Hawkins
Walter Johnson
Peter Jones
Israel W. Means
Jack Means
John Pearson
Granny Sanders
Nancy Sawyer
Peter Schroeder
Dr. Henry Small
Hannah Thomson
Mrs. Thomson
W. J. Thomson

Stanley Elkin
A Bad Man–W.M.R.
Bisch
Leonard Dedman
Billy Feldman
Isidore Feldman
Leo Feldman
Lilly Feldman
Warden Fisher
Dr. Freedman
Silvia Lane
Ed Slipper
Norman Victman

Boswell–W.M.R.
James Boswell
Leon Herlitz
Nate Lace
Principessa Margaret dei Medici
Morton Perlmutter
John Sallow
Felix Sandusky

The Dick Gibson Show–W.M.R.
Edmond Behr-Bleibtreau
Lieutenant Collins
Louis Credenza
Dick Gibson
Henry Harper
Miriam Desebour Kranz
Norman
Jack Patterson
Bernard Perk
Sansori
Pepper Steep
Arthur Vendler

The Franchiser–W.M.R.
Julius Finsberg
Patty Finsberg
Finsberg children
Benjamin Flesh
Roger Foster
Dick Gibson
Flight Lieutenant Tanner
Dr. Wolfe

Searches and Seizures–W.M.R.
Brewster Ashenden
Joe Colper
Crainpool
Shirley Fanon
Glyp
Sid Harris
Lena Jacobson
Jane Löes Lipton
Alexander Main
Oyp
Freddy Plympton
Marshall Preminger
Philip Preminger
Evelyn Riker
Buffy Surface
Dan Tucker

Ralph Ellison
Invisible Man–G.G.
A. Hebert Bledsoe
Lucius Brockway
Brother Tod Clifton
Brother Hambro
Brother Jack
Norton
Mary Rambo
Ras the Exhorter
B. P. Rinehart
Supercargo
Sybil
Jim Trueblood

John Erskine
The Private Life of Helen of Troy–E.J.H.
Adraste
Aegisthus
Agamemnon
Charitas
Clytemnestra

Damastor
Eteoneus
Helen
Hermione
Idomeneus
Menelaos
Orestes
Paris
Pyrrhus
Telemachus

James T. Farrell
Judgment Day–G.G.
Catherine Banahan
Father Gilhooley
Dennis P. Gorman
Frances Lonigan
Loretta Lonigan
Mary Lonigan
Patrick J. Lonigan
William Lonigan
Frank Reilley
Phillip Rolfe
Lucy Scanlan

Young Lonigan–G.G.
Father Gilhooley
Dennis P. Gorman
Paul Haggerty
Frances Lonigan
Loretta Lonigan
Mary Lonigan
Patrick J. Lonigan
William Lonigan
Danny O'Neill
Frank Reilley
Lucy Scanlan
Helen Shires

The Young Manhood of Studs Lonigan–G.G.
Father Gilhooley
Dennis P. Gorman
Paul Haggerty
Frances Lonigan
Loretta Lonigan
Mary Lonigan
Patrick J. Lonigan
William Lonigan
Danny O'Neill
Frank Reilley
Phillip Rolfe
Lucy Scanlan
Father Shannon
Helen Shires

Howard Fast
Citizen Tom Paine–E.J.H.
Robert Aitken
Richard Bache
Joel Barlow
William Blake
Napoleon Bonaparte
Nicholas de Bonneville
Danton

Benjamin Franklin
General Nathanael Greene
Thomas Jefferson
Jordan
Doctor Kearsley
Lafayette
Mary Lambert
Thomas Paine
General Roberdeau
Irene Roberdeau
Jacob Rumpel
Sarah Rumpel
Alec Stivvens
General George Washington

William Faulkner
Absalom, Absalom!–B.F. & S.H.T.
Charles Bon
Charles Etienne Saint-Val Bon
Jim Bond
Goodhue Coldfield
Rosa Coldfield
Jason Lycurgus Compson II
Jason Lycurgus Compson III
Quentin Compson I
Alexander Holston
Ikkemotubbe
Milly Jones
Wash Jones
Luster
Shrevlin McCannon
Theophilus McCaslin
Pettibone
Col. John Sartoris
Major de Spain
Clytemnestra Sutpen
Ellen Coldfield Sutpen
Eulalia Bon Sutpen
Dulalia Bon Sutpen
Henry Sutpen
Judith Sutpen
Thomas Sutpen

As I Lay Dying–B.F. & S.H.T.
Henry Armstid
Martha Armstid
Addie Bundren
Anse Bundren
Cash Bundren
Darl Bundren
Dewey Dell Bundren
Jewel Bundren
Vardaman Bundren
Lafe
Lucius Quintus Peabody
Flem Snopes
Suratt
Cora and Vernon Tull
Jody Varner
Will Varner
Whitfield

A Fable–B.F. & S.H.T.
Philip Manigault Beauchamp

Bidet
Bridesman
Buchwald
Casse-tête
Collyer
Marthe Demont
Charles Gragnon
Harry
Jean
Lallemont
Lapin
Gerald David Levine
Luluque
Mannock
Marya
McCudden
Middleton
Morache
Picklock
Piotr
Polchek
Smith
Stefan
Tobe Sutterfield
Thorpe

Go Down, Moses–B.F. & S.H.T.
Henry Beauchamp
Hubert Beauchamp
James Thucydides Beauchamp
Lucas Quintus McCaslin Beauchamp
Molly Beauchamp
Samuel Worsham Beauchamp
Tennie Beauchamp
Tomey's Turl Beauchamp
Sophonsiba McCaslin Beauchamp
Jason Lycurgus Compson II
Carothers Edmonds
Carothers McCaslin Edmonds
Zachary Taylor Edmonds
Eunice
Walter Ewell
Sam Fathers
Boon Hogganbeck
Ikkemotubbe
Iseetibbeha
Will Legate
Lion
Amodeus McCaslin
Isaac McCaslin
Lucius Quintus Carothers McCaslin
Sophonsiba Beauchamp McCaslin
Theophilus McCaslin
Old Ben
Phoebe
Roscius
Bayard Sartoris II
Col. John Sartoris
Major de Spain
Gavin Stevens
Thucydides
Tomasina
Belle Worsham
Hamp Worsham

The Hamlet–B.F. & S.H.T.
Henry Armstid
Martha Armstid
Odum Bookwright
Major Grumby
Hope Hampton I
Buck Hipps
Jack Houston
Labove
Mrs. Littlejohn
Hoake McCarron
Theophilus McCaslin
Rosa Millard
Lucius Quintus Peabody
V. K. Ratliff
Bayard Sartoris II
Col. John Sartoris
Abner Snopes
Eckrum Snopes
Eula Varner Snopes
Flem Snopes
I. O. Snopes
Isaac Snopes
Launcelot Snopes
Mink Snopes
Saint Elmo Snopes
Vynie Snopes
Wallstreet Panic Snopes
Yettie Snopes
Major de Spain
Pat Stamper
Cora and Vernon Tull
Jody Varner
Will Varner
Whitfield

Intruder in the Dust–B.F. & S.H.T.
Lucas Quintus McCaslin Beauchamp
Molly Beauchamp
Jason Lycurgus Compson II
Carothers Edmonds
Sam Fathers
Bilbo Gowrie
Bryan Gowrie
Crawford Gowrie
N. B. Forrest Gowrie
Nub Gowrie
Vardaman Gowrie
Vinson Gowrie
Louis Grenier
Eunice Habersham
Doctor Samuel Habersham
Hope Hampton I
Boon Hogganbeck
Alexander Holston
Will Legate
Charles Mallison
Charles Mallison
Margaret Stevens Mallison
Buddy McCallum
Isaac McCaslin
Lucius Quintus Carothers McCaslin
Jake Montgomery
Aleck Sander

Major de Spain
Gavin Stevens
Lemuel Stevens
Euphus Tubbs
Will Varner

Light in August–B.F. & S.H.T.
Bobbie Allen
Henry Armstid
Martha Armstid
Miss Atkins
Byron Bunch
Lucas Burch
Joanna Burden
Juana Burden
Nathaniel Burden
Calvin Burden I
Calvin Burden II
Nathaniel Burrington
Joe Christmas
Mame and Max Confrey
Percy Grimm
Lena Grove
Gail Hightower
Mrs. Gail Hightower
Eupheus and Mrs. Hines
Milly Hines
Watt Kennedy
Mrs. Simon McEachern
Simon McEachern
Col. John Sartoris
Gavin Stevens
Jody Varner
Will Varner

The Mansion–B.F. & S.H.T.
Henry Armstid
Luther Biglin
Lucius Binford
Ephraim Bishop
Calvin Bookwright
Odum Bookwright
Joanna Burden
Uncle Willy Christian
Benjamin Compson
Candace Compson
Jason Lycurgus Compson IV
Quentin Compson I
Quentin Compson II
Colonel Devries
Virginia Du Pre
Walter Ewell
Brother Joe C. Goodyhay
Lonzo Hait
Hope Hampton I
Hope Hampton II
Lucius Priest Hogganbeck
Alexander Holston
Jack Houston
Barton Kohl
Linda Snopes Kohl
Charles Mallison
Charles Mallison
Margaret Stevens Mallison

Hoake McCarron
Isaac McCaslin
Tug Nightingale
V. K. Ratliff
Reba Rivers
Bayard Sartoris II
Bayard Sartoris III
Benbow Sartoris
Col. John Sartoris
Narcissa Benbow Sartoris
Essie Meadowfill Smith
McKinley Smith
Abner Snopes
Bilbo Snopes
Byron Snopes
Clarence Eggleston Snopes
Admiral Dewey Snopes
Doris Snopes
Eckrum Snopes
Eula Varner Snopes
Flem Snopes
I. O. Snopes
Launcelot Snopes
Mink Snopes
Montgomery Ward Snopes
Orestes Snopes
Vardaman Snopes
Virgil Snopes
Wallstreet Panic Snopes
Watkins Products Snopes
Wesley Snopes
Yettie Snopes
Major de Spain
Manfred de Spain
Pat Stamper
Gavin Stevens
Lemuel Stevens
Melisandre Backus Stevens
Euphus Tubbs
Cora and Vernon Tull
Jody Varner
Will Varner

Mosquitoes—B.F. & S.H.T.
Ayres
Dawson Fairchild
Mark Frost
Joe Ginotta
Pete Ginotta
Gordon
Dorothy Jameson
Julius Kauffman
Patricia Maurier
Patricia Robyn
Theodore Robyn
Genevieve Steinbauer
Ernest Talliaferro
David West
Eva Wiseman

Pylon—B.F. & S.H.T.
Frank Burnham
Vic Chance
Joe Ginotta

Pete Ginotta
Grady
Hagood
Hank
Jack Holmes
Art Jackson
Jiggs
Jug
Matt Ord
Mac Sales
Jack Shumann
Laverne Shumann
Roger Shumann

The Reivers—B.F. & S.H.T.
Bobo Beauchamp
James Thucydides Beauchamp
Lucas Quintus McCaslin Beauchamp
Tennie Beauchamp
Lucius Binford
Calvin Bookwright
Sam Caldwell
Uncle Willy Christian
Jason Lycurgus Compson II
Carothers Edmonds
Carothers McCaslin Edmonds
Zachary Taylor Edmonds
Walter Ewell
Sam Fathers
Louis Grenier
Hope Hampton I
Hope Hampton II
Boon Hogganbeck
Everbe Corinthia Hogganbeck
Lucius Priest Hogganbeck
Ikkemotubbe
Iseetibbeha
Colonel Linscomb
Butch Lovemaiden
Ludus
Luster
Isaac McCaslin
Lucius Quintus Carothers McCaslin
Ned McCaslin
Theophilus McCaslin
McWillie
Otis
Lucius Quintus Peabody
Alexander Priest
Alison Lessep Priest
Lessep Priest
Lucius Priest I
Lucius Priest II
Lucius Priest III
Maury Priest I
Maury Priest II
Sarah Edmonds Priest
Reba Rivers
Bayard Sartoris II
Col. John Sartoris
Flem Snopes
Major de Spain
Manfred de Spain
Lemuel Stevens

Requiem for a Nun—B.F. & S.H.T.
Jason Lycurgus Compson I
Jason Lycurgus Compson II
Virginia Du Pre
Louis Grenier
Alexander Holston
Ikkemotubbe
Iseetibbeha
Margaret Stevens Mallison
Nancy Mannigoe
Pete
Red
Ben Redmond
Bayard Sartoris II
Bayard Sartoris III
Col. John Sartoris
Gavin Stevens
Gowan Stevens
Temple Drake Stevens
Euphus Tubbs
Popeye Vitelli

Sanctuary—B.F. & S.H.T.
Belle Mitchell Benbow
Horace Benbow
Lucius Binford
Hubert Drake
Judge Drake
Virginia Du Pre
Lee Goodwin
Eustace Graham
Ruby Lamar
Minnie
Harry Mitchell
Titania Mitchell
Red
Reba Rivers
Benbow Sartoris
Narcissa Benbow Sartoris
Clarence Eggleston Snopes
Virgil Snopes
Gowan Stevens
Temple Drake Stevens
Tommy
Vernon Tull
Popeye Vitelli

Sartoris (Flags in the Dust)—B.F. & S.H.T.
Belle Mitchell Benbow
Horace Benbow
Virginia Du Pre
Eustace Graham
Joby
Louvinia
Harry Mitchell
Titania Mitchell
Lucius Quintus Peabody
Ben Redmond
Bayard Sartoris I
Bayard Sartoris II
Bayard Sartoris III
Benbow Sartoris
Col. John Sartoris
Narcissa Benbow Sartoris

Byron Snopes
Flem Snopes
Montgomery Ward Snopes
Simon Strother
Suratt

Soldiers' Pay–B.F. & S.H.T.
Emmy
Cecily Saunders Farr
George Farr
Joe Gilligan
Hank
Januarius Jones
Julian Lowe
Donald Mahon
Margaret Powers Mahon
The Reverend Mahon
Richard Powers
Minnie Saunders
Robert Saunders I
Robert Saunders II

The Sound and the Fury–B.F. & S.H.T.
Dalton Ames
Gerald Bland
Benjamin Compson
Candace Compson
Caroline Bascomb Compson
Jason Lycurgus Compson I
Jason Lycurgus Compson II
Jason Lycurgus Compson III
Jason Lycurgus Compson IV
Quentin Compson I
Quentin Compson II
Damuddy
Dilsey Gibson
Frony Gibson
Roskus Gibson
T. P. Gibson
Versh Gibson
Sidney Herbert Head
Luster
Shreve MacKenzie
Lucius Quintus Peabody
Col. John Sartoris
I. O. Snopes

The Town–B.F. & S.H.T.
Aleck Sander
Henry Armstid
Tomey's Turl Beauchamp
Calvin Bookwright
Uncle Willy Christian
Jason Lycurgus Compson II
Jason Lycurgus Compson IV
Virginia Du Pre
Carothers Edmonds
Carothers McCaslin Edmonds
Louis Grenier
Hope Hampton I
Eunice Habersham
Lonzo Hait
Mannie Hait
Boon Hogganbeck

Lucius Priest Hogganbeck
Alexander Holston
Jack Houston
Ikkemotubbe
Iseetibbeha
Linda Snopes Kohl
Matt Levitt
Lion
Mrs. Littlejohn
Charles Mallison
Charles Mallison
Margaret Stevens Mallison
Anse McCallum
Buddy McCallum
Hoake McCarron
Isaac McCaslin
Cedric Nunnery
Lucius Quintus Peabody
V. K. Ratliff
Bayard Sartoris II
Bayard Sartoris III
Benbow Sartoris
Col. John Sartoris
Narcissa Benbow Sartoris
Abner Snopes
Bilbo Snopes
Byron Snopes
Clarence Eggleston Snopes
Admiral Dewey Snopes
Doris Snopes
Eckrum Snopes
Eula Varner Snopes
Flem Snopes
I. O. Snopes
Mink Snopes
Montgomery Ward Snopes
Vardaman Snopes
Virgil Snopes
Wallstreet Panic Snopes
Major de Spain
Manfred de Spain
Gavin Stevens
Gowan Stevens
Lemuel Stevens
Cora and Vernon Tull
Jody Varner
Will Varner

The Unvanquished–B.F. & S.H.T.
Matt Bowden
Gavin Breckbridge
Jason Lycurgus Compson II
Nathaniel G. Dick
Virginia Du Pre
Brother Fortinbride
Major Grumby
Louisa Hawk
Joby
Louvinia
Lucius
Marengo
Amodeus McCaslin
Theophilus McCaslin
Rosa Millard

Philadelphy
Ben Redmond
Bayard Sartoris I
Bayard Sartoris II
Drusilla Hawk Sartoris
Col. John Sartoris
Abner Snopes
Simon Strother
Doctor Worsham

The Wild Palms–B.F. & S.H.T.
McCord
Old Man
Richardson
Charlotte Rittenmeyer
Francis Rittenmeyer
Harry Wilbourne

Jessie Redmon Fauset
The Chinaberry Tree–C.E.W.
Stephen Denleigh
Malory Forten
Philip Hackett
Colonel Halloway
Asshur Lane
Melissa Paul
Laurentine Strange
Sarah Strange

Comedy, American Style–C.E.W.
Henry Bates
Nicholas Campbell
Christopher Fidele Cary
Oliver Cary
Olivia Blanchard Cary
Teresa Cary
Phebe Grant
Aristide Pailleron

Plum Bun–C.E.W.
Martha Burden
Anthony Cross
Roger Fielding
Matthew Henson
Angela Murray
Junius Murray
Mattie Murray
Virginia Murray

There Is Confusion–C.E.W.
Peter Bye
Maggie Ellersley
Joanna Marshall
Joel Marshall
Philip Marshall
Sylvia Marshall
Henderson Neal

Kenneth Fearing
The Big Clock–R.M.R.
Pauline Delos
Gil
Steve Hagen
Earl Janoth

Don Klausmeyer
Emory Mafferson
Edward Orlin
Louise Patterson
George Stroud
Georgette Stroud

Edna Ferber
Cimarron–S.P.H.
Ruby Big Elk
Cimarron Cravat
Donna Cravat
Sabra Venable Cravat
Yancey Cravat
Isaiah
Dixie Lee
Sol Levy
Felice Venable
Lewis Venable
Tracy Wyatt

Giant–S.P.H.
Baldwin Benedict
Juana Benedict
Leslie Lynnton Benedict
Luz Benedict I
Luz Benedict II
Jordan Benedict the Third
Jordan Benedict the Fourth
Bob Dietz
Jett Rink
Mott Snyth
Vashti Hake Snyth

Show Boat–B.J.I.
Steve Baker
Kenneth Cameron
Kim Ravenal Cameron
Elly Chipley
Julie Dozier
Captain Andy Hawks
Parthenia Ann Hawks
Gaylord Ravenal
Magnolia Hawks Ravenal
Harold Westbrook

So Big–B.J.I.
Julie Hempel Arnold
Dirk DeJong
Pervus DeJong
Selina Peake DeJong
August Hempel
Dallas O'Mara
Widow Paarlenberg
Simeon Peake
Klaas Pool
Maartje Pool
Roelf Pool
Maartje Pool
Mattie Schwengauer
Paula Arnold Storm

Lawrence Ferlinghetti
Her–D.L.

Andalous Raffine

Rudolph Fisher
The Conjure-Man Dies–E.Q.T.
John Archer
Bubber Brown
Martha Crouch
Samuel Crouch
Perry Dart
N'Gana Frimbo
Jinx Jenkins
N'Ogo
Henry Patmore
Aramintha Snead

The Walls of Jericho–E.Q.T.
Bubber Brown
Agatha Cramp
Jinx Jenkins
Joshua Jones
Fred Merrit
Henry Patmore
J. Pennington Potter
Linda Young

Vardis Fisher
In Tragic Life–J.M.F.
Charley Bridwell
Jed Bridwell
Lela Bridwell
Neloa Doole
Diana Hunter
Dock Hunter
Joseph Charles Hunter
Mertyl Hunter
Prudence Branton Hunter
Vridar Baroledt Hunter
George Albert Turner

No Villain Need Be–J.M.F.
Robert Clark
Harrison Hawke
Mertyl Hunter
Prudence Branton Hunter
Vridar Baroledt Hunter
Athene Marvell

Orphans in Gethsemene–J.M.F.
Robert Clark
Neloa Doole
Harrison Hawke
Angele Lorelei Lee Hunter
Diana Hunter
Dock Hunter
Mertyl Hunter
Prudence Branton Hunter
Vridar Baroledt Hunter
Athene Marvell
George Albert Turner

Passions Spin the Plot–J.M.F.
Neloa Doole
Diana Hunter
Mertyl Hunter

Prudence Branton Hunter
Vridar Baroledt Hunter
A. M. McClintock

We Are Betrayed–J.M.F.
Neloa Doole
Diana Hunter
Mertyl Hunter
Prudence Branton Hunter
Vridar Baroledt Hunter
Athene Marvell

F. Scott Fitzgerald
The Beautiful and Damned–M.J.B.
Joseph Bloeckman
Richard Caramel
Maury Noble
Adam J. Patch
Anthony Patch
Gloria Gilbert Patch
Dorothy Raycroft

The Great Gatsby–M.J.B.
Jordan Baker
Daisy Fay Buchanan
Tom Buchanan
Nick Carraway
Dan Cody
Jay Gatsby
Henry C. Gatz
Ewing Klipspringer
Owl Eyes
George B. Wilson
Myrtle Wilson
Meyer Wolfsheim

The Last Tycoon–M.J.B.
Cecilia Brady
Pat Brady
Brimmer
Kathleen Moore
Robinson
Manny Schwartz
Monroe Stahr
Wylie White
Pete Zavras

Tender Is the Night–M.J.B.
Tommy Barban
Luis Campion
Collis Clay
Nicole Warren Diver
Richard Diver
Professor Dohmler
Royal Dumphry
Franz Gregorovious
Kaethe Gregorovious
Rosemary Hoyt
Albert McKisco
Abraham North
Mary North
Lady Caroline Sibly-Biers
Elsie Speers
Beth Evan Warren

Charles Warren

This Side of Paradise–M.J.B.
Amory Blaine
Beatrice O'Hara Blaine
Isabelle Borgé
Alec Connage
Rosalind Connage
Thomas Parke D'Invilliers
Monsignor Thayer Darcy
Burne Holiday
Clara Page
Eleanor Savage

Janet Flanner
The Cubical City–S.Bi.
Nancy Burke
Goldstein
Grafton
Paul Jarvis
Compton J. Keith
Agatha Poole
Delia Poole
James Poole
Mercy Wellington

Shelby Foote
Follow Me Down–R.L.P.
Kate Eustis
Luther Dade Eustis
Roscoe Jeffcoat
William Hezekiah Jimson
Parker Nowell
James Elmo Pitts
Miz Pitts
Ben Rand
Willy Roebuck
Beulah Ross

Jordan County–R.L.P.
Durfee Conway
Nora Conway
Colonel Nathan Frisbie
Pauly Green
Clive Jameson
Isaac Jameson
Julia Kinship
Captain Adam Lundy
Parker Nowell
Edward Postoak
John Postoak
Ella Lowry Sturgis
Esther Wingate Sturgis
Hector Wingate Sturgis
John Sturgis
Harry Van
Esther Pollard Wingate
Hector Wingate

Love in a Dry Season–R.L.P.
Amanda Barcroft
Florence Barcroft
Major Malcolm Barcroft
Amy Carruthers

Jeff Carruthers
Harley Drew

September September–R.L.P.
Podjo Harris
Rufus Hutton
Eben Kinship
Lucinda Kinship
Martha Wiggins Kinship
Theo Kinship
Reeny Jimson Perdew
Theo G. Wiggins

Shiloh–R.L.P.
Private Luther Dade
Private Otto Flickner
Captain Walter Fountain
Lt. Palmer Metcalfe
Sergeant Jefferson Polly

Jesse Hill Ford
The Liberation of Lord Byron Jones–D.Lo.
Jimmy Bivens
Stanley Bumpas
Toonker Burkette
Johnnie Price Burkhalter
Oman Hedgepath
Emma Lee Lessenbery Jones
George Gordon Lord Byron Jones
Mama Lavorn
T. K. Morehouse
William Mosby
Nella Liseth Mundine
Steve Mundine
Ike Murphy
Erleen Parsons
Henry Parsons
Benny Smith
Willie Joe Worth

Mountains of Gilead–D.Lo.
Toonker Burkette
Eleanor Fite
Gabe French, Sr.
Mattie French
George Gordon Lord Byron Jones
Bojack Markham
Thomas Gideon McCutcheon
Rev. Bartholomew Luther Meeks
Camack Patterson
Adam Shafer
Adam Gideon Shafer
Gratt Shafer
Octavia Ashmore Shafer
Patricia Josephine McCutcheon Shafer

The Raider–D.Lo.
Edward Ashe
Ellen Poe Ashe
Betsy
Dutt Callister
Fancy Callister
Denise Chatillion
Jasper Coon

Col. Ennis Dalton
Gabriel French
Sim Hornby
Timothy Laird
Leola
Elias McCutcheon
Isaac McCutcheon
Jake McCutcheon
Willy McCutcheon
Shokotee McNeilly
Jane Nail
Cargile Parham
Sallie Parham
Pettecasockee

Leon Forrest
The Bloodworth Orphans–J.L.G.
Jonathan Staunch Bass
Arlington Bloodworth, Sr.
Arlington Bloodworth III
Pourty Ford Worthy Bloodworth
William S. Body
Bella-Lenore Boltwood
Carl-Rae Bowman
Industrious Bowman
Abraham Ulysses Dolphin
Rachel Rebecca Carpenter Flowers
W. W. W. Ford
Noah Ridgerook Grandberry
Lavinia Masterson
Regal Pettibone
Ironwood Rumble
LaDonna Scales
Amos-Otis Thigpen
Carrie Trout
Nathaniel Turner Witherspoon

Hannah Webster Foster
The Coquette–M.K.G.
J. Boyer
Julia Granby
Peter Sanford
T. Selby
Lucy Freeman Sumner
Eliza Wharton
M. Wharton

Harold Frederic
The Damnation of Theron Ware–J.G.H.
Father Vincent Forbes
Levi Gorringe
Dr. Ledsmar
Celia Madden
Jeremiah Madden
Michael Madden
Terence Madden
Loren Pierce
Brother Soulsby
Sister Candace Soulsby
Alice Hastings Ware
Reverend Theron Ware
Erastus Winch

Marilyn French

The Women's Room–J.G.H.
Ava
Clarissa
Kyla Forrester
Isolde
Martha Jackson
Lily
Mira
Norm
Adele O'Neill
Samantha Simpson
Tadziewski
Christine Truax
Valerie
Ben Voler

Henry Blake Fuller
The Chatelaine of La Trinité–G.S.
Chatelaine of La Trinité
Fin-de-Siècle
Governor
Marquis of Tempo-Rubato
Eugénie Pasdemon
Aurelia R. West
Baron Zeitgeist

The Cliff-Dwellers–G.S.
Atwater
Sue Lathrop Bates
Jessie Bradley
Abbie Brainard
Abigail Brainard
Burton Tillinghast Brainard
Cornelia McNabb Tillinghast Brainard
Erastus M. Brainard
Marcus Brainard
Brower
Arthur J. Ingles
Cecilia Ingles
George Ogden

With the Procession–G.S.
Sue Lathrop Bates
Gilbert Belden
Thomas Bingham
Theodore Brower
David Marshall
Eliza Marshall
Jane Marshall
Richard Truesdale Marshall
Roger Marshall
Rosamund Marshall

William Gaddis
JR–S.M.
Stella Bast Angel
Edward Bast
Mr. Beaton
Governor John Cates
Dave Davidoff
Thomas Eigen
Jack Gibbs
Amy Moncrieff Joubert
JR Vansant

The Recognitions–S.M.
Anselm
Recktall Brown
Esme
Camilla Gwyon
Esther Gwyon
Reverend Gwyon
Wyatt Gwyon
Otto Pivner
Frank Sinisterra
Stanley
Basil Valentine

Ernest J. Gaines
The Autobiography of Miss Jane Pittman–T.R.H.
Jimmy Aaron
Big Laura
Corporal Brown
Albert Cluveau
Edward Stephen Douglass
Mary Agnes LeFabre
Miss Jane Pittman
Joe Pittman
Robert Samson
Robert Samson, Jr.
Timmy

In My Father's House–T.R.H.
Octave Bacheron
Billy
Angelina Bouie
Albert Chenal
Elijah Green
Shepherd Lewis
Alma Martin
Reverend Phillip J. Martin
Anthony McVay
Howard Mills
Sheriff Nolan
Beverly Ricord
Jonathan Robillard
Erin Simon
Johanna Sims
Robert X

Of Love and Dust–T.R.H.
Sidney Bonbon
Louise Bonbon
Pauline Guerin
Marshall Hebert
Frank James Kelly
Marcus Payne
Julie Rand

Zona Gale–K.A.A.
Miss Lulu Bett
Lulu Bett
Mrs. Bett
Neil Cornish
Diana Deacon
Dwight Herbert Deacon
Ina Bett Deacon
Ninian Deacon
Bobby Larkin

John Gardner
Grendel–L.C.
Dragon
Grendel
Hrothgar
Hrothulf
Hygmod
Ork
Shaper
Unferth
Wealtheow

Nickel Mountain–L.C.
Simon Bale
Doc Cathey
Norma Denitz
Willard Freund
Goat Lady
Jimmy
Fred Judkins
George Loomis
Henry Soames
Calliope Wells

October Light–L.C.
Horace Abbott
Sally Page Abbott
John F. Alkahest
Johann Fis
Dickey Hicks
Lewis Hicks
Virginia Page Hicks
Jane
Ariah Page
James L. Page
Richard Page
Ed Thomas
Peter Wagner

The Sunlight Dialogues–L.C.
Walter Boyle
Esther Clumly
Fred Clumly
Freeman
Arthur Taggert Hodge, Sr.
Benjamin Hodge, Sr.
Kathleen Paxton Hodge
Luke Hodge
Mildred Jewel Hodge
Taggert Faeley Hodge
William B. Hodge, Sr.
R. V. Kleppmann
Oliver Nuper
Clive Paxton

Hamlin Garland
Rose of Dutcher's Coolly–D.D.Q.
Carl
John Dutcher
Rose Dutcher
Caroline Harvey
Elbert Harvey
Willis Harvey
Warren Mason

Dr. Sanborn
Owen Taylor
Dr. Joe Thatcher

George Garrett
Death of the Fox–R.H.W.D.
Sir Francis Bacon
Gregory Brandon
Elizabeth I
James I
Carew Ralegh
Elizabeth Throckmorton Ralegh
Sir Walter Ralegh
Sir Lewis Stukely
Mary Throckmorton
George Villiers
Sir Henry Yelverton

Do, Lord, Remember Me–R.H.W.D.
Elijah J. Cartwright
Judith
Howie Loomis
Miami
Moses
Big Red Smalley

William Gass
Omensetter's Luck–A.M.S.
Reverend Jethro Furber
Clifford Huffley
Brackett Omensetter
Doctor Orcutt
Reverend Andrew Pike
Henry Pimber
Israbestis Tott
Kitty Watson

Willie Masters' Lonesome Wife–A.M.S.
Phil Gelvin
Babs Masters

Martha Gellhorn
A Stricken Field–J.E.O.
Lord Balham
Louis Berthold
General Labonne
Tom Lambert
Frau Markheim
Peter Reinick
Rita Salus

Wine of Astonishment–J.E.O.
Dorothy Brock
William Gaylord
Bert Hammer
Heinrich
Major Gordon Jarvis
Jacob Levy
Kathe Limpert
Royal Lommax
Sergeant-Major Postalozzi
Lieutenant Colonel John D. Smithers

Peter Gent

North Dallas Forty–E.J.H.
Bob Beaudreau
Charlotte Ann Caulder
Phillip J. Elliott
Clinton Foote
Conrad R. Hunter
Emmett John Hunter
Seth Maxwell
O. B. Meadows
B. A. Quinlan
Joanne Remington
Jo Bob Williams

Texas Celebrity Turkey Trot–E.J.H.
Titus Bean
Billy Bentson
George Billings
Stormy Claridge
Farah Everett
Jace Everett
Jace Everett, Jr.
Jason Everett III
LD Groover
Hondo Higgins
Mabry Jenkins
Ezra Lyttle
Stephano Valentine
Luther Watt

Caroline Gilman
Recollections of a Housekeeper–J.B.
Ma'am Bridge
Nancy
Clarissa Gray Packard
Edward Packard
Mrs. Philipson
Polly
Mrs. Sliter
Stockton

Recollections of a Southern Matron–J.B.
Anna Allston
Bill Barnwell
Lewis Barnwell
Joseph Bates
Charles Duncan
Arthur Marion
Benjamin Wilton
Cornelia Wilton
Henry Wilton
Richard Wilton

Ellen Glasgow
Barren Ground–J.R.R.
Doctor Burch
Bob Ellgood
Geneva Ellgood
James Ellgood
Doctor Faraday
Aunt Mehitable Green
Doctor Greylock
Jason Greylock
Mr. Kettledrum
Fluvanna Moody

Dorinda Oakley
Eudora Abernethy Oakley
Joshua Oakley
Josiah Oakley
Rufus Oakley
John Abner Pedlar
Lena Pedlar
Nathan Pedlar
Rose Emily Milford Pedlar

The Romantic Comedians–J.R.R.
Alberta
Dabney Birdsong
Colonel Bletheram
Angus Blount
Edmonia Honeywell Bredalbane
Ralph Bredalbane
Doctor Buchanan
Judge Gamaliel Bland Honeywell
Amanda Lightfoot
Mrs. Spearman
Annabel Upchurch
Bella Upchurch

The Sheltered Life–J.R.R.
Uncle Abednego
Cora Archbald
General David Archbald
Etta Archbald
Isabella Archbald
Jenny Blair Archbald
Delia Barron
Eva Howard Birdsong
George Birdsong
Joseph Crocker
Memoria
Bena Peyton
John Welch

They Stooped to Folly–J.R.R.
Colonel Bletheram
Milly Burden
Amy Paget Dalrymple
Louisa Goddard
Agatha Littlepage
Curle Littlepage
Duncan Littlepage
Marmaduke Littlepage
Victoria Brooke Littlepage
Virginius Curle Littlepage
Martin Welding
Mary Victoria Littlepage Welding

Vein of Iron–J.R.R.
Minna Bergen
Mr. Black
Ada Fincastle
Grandmother Fincastle
John Fincastle
Maggie Fincastle
Mary Evelyn Fincastle
Abigail Geddy
Mrs. McBride
Ralph McBride

Ranny McBride
Janet Rowan
Dr. Updike
Mrs. Waters
Toby Waters

Virginia–J.R.R.
Miss Priscilla Batte
Mandy
Gabriel Pendleton
Lucy Pendleton
Virginia Pendleton
Belinda Bolingbroke Treadwell
Cyrus Treadwell
Henry Treadwell
Oliver Treadwell
Susan Treadwell

Susan Glaspell
Fidelity–E.D.F.
Edith Lawrence Blair
Amy Forrester Franklin
Dr. Deane Franklin
Annie Morris Herman
Cyrus Holland
Ruth Holland
Ted Holland
Marion Averley Williams
Stuart Williams

Judd Rankin's Daughter–E.D.F.
Gerald Andrews
Stuart Jackson
Adah Elwood Logan
Joe Logan
Frances Rankin Mitchell
Judson Mitchell
Leonard Mitchell
Madeleine Mitchell
Judd Rankin
Douglass Reynolds

Gail Godwin
Glass People–J.C.M.
Cameron Bolt
Francesca Fox Bolt
Nina Brett
M Evans
Grace Fairfield
Jerry Freeman
Jonathan
Kate
Eric Neuhoffer
Michael S. Reusing
Ware Smith

The Odd Woman–J.C.M.
Edith Dewar Barnstorff
James Bruton
Jane Clifford
Cleva Dewar
Eleanor
Sonia Marks
Gerda Miller Mulvaney

Marsha Pedersen
Portia Prentiss
Kitty Sparks
Ray Sparks
Hugo Von Vorst
Gabriel Weeks

The Perfectionists–J.C.M.
Count Bartolomé
Dane Tarrant Empson
John Dominick Empson
Robin Empson
Henrietta Hart
Karl Heykoop
Polly Heykoop
Penelope MacMahon
Ramírez-Suárez
Lady Jane Rotherhall

Violet Clay–J.C.M.
Sheila Benton
Conrad Chakravorti
Ambrose Valentine Clay
Violet Isabel Clay
Samantha De Vere
Carol M. Gruber
Milo Hamilton
Stewart Landsborough
Lewis Lanier
Minerva Means
Ivor Sedge
Lila Swenson

Donald Goines
Dopefiend–G.G.
Billy Banks
Bessy Mae
Minnie
Porky
Smokey
Snake
Teddy
Terry Wilson

Michael Gold
Jews without Money–C.C.N.
Dr. Marcus J. Axelrod
Joey Cohen
Esther Gold
Herman Gold
Katie Gold
Michael Gold
Nigger
Louis One Eye
Reb Samuel
Dr. Isidore Solow

Caroline Gordon
Green Centuries–M.E.R.W.
Francis Dawson
Archy Outlaw
Jocasta Dawson Outlaw
Orion Outlaw
Elsa Wagner

Jacob Wagner

Mary Gordon
Final Payments–J.R.Ma.
Margaret Casey
Eleanor Lavery
David Lowe
Joseph Moore
Father Mulcahy
Elizabeth O'Brien Ryan
John Ryan

William Goyen
Come, The Restorer–T.E.D.
Ace Adair
Addis Adair
Jewel Adair
Mr. de Persia
Cleon Peters
Selina Rosheen Prescott
Wylie Prescott

The Fair Sister–T.E.D.
Ruby Drew
Cubsy Hall
Canaan Johnson
Orondo McCabe
Prince o'Light
Savata

The House of Breath–T.E.D.
Hattie Clegg
Boy Ganchion
Christy Ganchion
Folner Ganchion
Hannah Ganchion
Berryben Starnes
Jessy Starnes
Jimbob Starnes
Lauralee Starnes
Malley Ganchion Starnes
Sue Emma Starnes
Walter Warren Starnes
Maidie Starnes Suggs

In a Farther Country–T.E.D.
Sister Angelica
Thwaite Cumberly
Eddie
Chalmers Egstrom
Jack Flanders
Lois Fuchs
Louisa
Thomas Harold MacDougal
Marietta McGee-Chavéz
Oris
Sabino
Father Trask

Shirley Ann Grau
The Condor Passes–J.C.
Anna Oliver Caillet
Anthony Caillet
Aurelie Caillet

Robert Caillet
Maurice Lamotta
Mama
Margaret Oliver
Stephanie Maria D'Alfonso Oliver
Thomas Henry Oliver
Stanley

Evidence of Love—J.C.
Harold Evans
Abigail Morton Henley
Edward Milton Henley
Eleanor Halsey Henley
Lucy Roundtree Evans Henley
Stephen Henley
Thomas Henley
Guido O'Connor

The Hard Blue Sky—J.C.
Julius Arcenaux
Ignatius D'Alfonso
Adele Landry
Alistair Landry
Annie Landry
Henry Livaudais
Pete Livaudais
Mamere Terrebonne

The House on Coliseum Street—J.C.
Fred Aleman
Aurelie Caillet
Doris
Michael Kern
Anthony Mitchell
Joan Claire Mitchell

The Keepers of the House—J.C.
Oliver Brandon
Edward Delatte
Margaret Carmichael Howland
Robert Carmichael Howland
William Howland
Abigail Howland Mason
Gregory Edward Mason
Abigail Howland Mason Tolliver
John Tolliver

Anna Katharine Green
The Leavenworth Case—J.K.
Amy Belden
Hannah Chester
Henry Ritchie Clavering
Thomas Dougherty
Ebenezer Gryce
James Trueman Harwell
Eleanore Leavenworth
Horatio Leavenworth
Mary Leavenworth
Morris
Everett Raymond

Hannah Green
I Never Promised You a Rose Garden—B.J.P.
Anterrabae

Deborah Blau
Esther Blau
Jacob Blau
Susan Blau
Carla
Doctor Fried
Lactamaeon

Davis Grubb
The Night of the Hunter—C.D.B.
Bart
Macijah Blake
Clara
Rachel Cooper
Miz Cunningham
Ben Harper
John Harper
Pearl Harper
Willa Harper
Mary
Harry Powell
Ruby
Icey Spoon
Walt Spoon
Uncle Birdie Steptoe

Judith Guest
Ordinary People—C.S.R.
Karen Susan Aldrich
Tyrone C. Berger
Ray Hanley
Beth Jarrett
Calvin Jarrett
Conrad Keith Jarrett
Jordan Jarrett
Joe Lazenby
Jeannine Pratt
Kevin Stillman

A. B. Guthrie
The Big Sky—M.K.S.
Boone Caudill
Jim Deakins
Jourdonnais
Dick Summers
Teal Eye

The Way West—M.K.S.
Brownie Evans
Lije Evans
Rebecca Evans
Henry McBee
Mercy McBee
Dick Summers
Tadlock
Joseph Weatherby

Nancy Hale
The Prodigal Women—K.M.W.
Hector Connolly
Betsy Jekyll
Minnie May Jekyll
Thomas Jekyll
Adèle Macomb

James March
Leda March
Treat March
Lambert Rudd

James Norman Hall
Botany Bay—E.J.H.
Moll Cudlip
Robert Fleming
Nat Garth
Bella Goodwin
Dan Goodwin
Nellie Garth Goodwin
Ned Inching
Phoebe Thynne Oakley
Tom Oakley
Arthur Phillip
Nicholas Sabb
Timothy Sabb
Hugh Tallant
Sally Munro Tallant
Mortimer Thynne

The Hurricane—E.J.H.
Ah Fong
Arai
Fakahau
Farani
Hitia
Kauka
Kersaint
Eugene de Laage
Germaine Anne Marie de Laage
Mako
Marama
Marunga
Mata
George Nagle
Father Paul
Mama Rua
Tavi
Terangi Matokia
Tita
Vernier

Men Against the Sea—E.J.H.
William Bligh
William Cole
William Elphinstone
John Fryer
Thomas Hayward
Thomas Ledward
David Nelson
John Norton
William Purcell
Sparling
Robert Tinkler

Mutiny on the Bounty—E.J.H.
Joseph Banks
William Bligh
Roger Byam
Fletcher Christian
William Cole

Edward Edwards
William Elphinstone
John Fryer
Hamilton
Thomas Hayward
Hitihiti
Thomas Ledward
Maimiti
William McCoy
David Nelson
John Norton
William Purcell
Matthew Quintal
Alexander Smith
Tehani
Robert Tinkler
John Williams
Edward Young

Pitcairn's Island–E.J.H.
Fletcher Christian
Maimiti
William McCoy
Minarii
Matthew Quintal
Alexander Smith
John Williams
Edward Young

Albert Halper
Union Square–R.M.R.
Miss Allen
Henry Austin
Milly Boardman
Quincy Boardman
Celia Chapman
Natasha and Otto Drollinger
Leon Fisher
Andre Franconi
Pete Garolian
Helen Jackson
Margie
Terence McGuffy
José Morales
James Nicholson
Old Running Water
Jason Wheeler

Dashiell Hammett
The Glass Key–R.L.
Ned Beaumont
Bernie Despain
M. J. Farr
Jeff Gardner
Janet Henry
Senator Ralph Bancroft Henry
Taylor Henry
Walter Ivans
The Kid
Opal Madvig
Paul Madvig
Eloise Matthews
H. K. Matthews
Shad O'Rory

Jack Rumsen
Rusty
Harry Sloss
Whiskey Vassos
Lee Wilshire

The Maltese Falcon–R.L.
Iva Archer
Miles Archer
Joel Cairo
Wilmer Cook
Lieutenant Dundy
Mr. Freed
Casper Gutman
Rhea Gutman
Capt. Jacobi
Brigid O'Shaughnessy
Effie Perine
Tom Polhaus
Sam Spade
Floyd Thursby

Red Harvest–R.L.
Helen Albury
Robert Albury
Dinah Brand
Ike Bush
The Continental Op
Charles Proctor Dawn
Dick Foley
Myrtle Jennison
Stanley Lewis
Mickey Linehan
Bob MacSwain
Noonan
Tim Noonan
Pete the Finn
Bill Quint
Dan Rolfe
Yakima Shorty
Oliver Starkey
Max Thaler
Donald Willson
Elihu Willsson
Lew Yard

The Thin Man–R.L.
Asta
Studsy Burke
Nick Charles
Nora Charles
John Guild
Christian Jorgensen
Mimi Jorgensen
Georgia Kelterman
Herbert Macaulay
Shep Morelli
Arthur Nunheim
Miriam Nunheim
Julia Wolf
Clyde Wynant
Dorothy Wynant
Gilbert Wynant

Earl Hamner, Jr.
Spencer's Mountain–E.B.B.
Claris Coleman
Colonel Coleman
Clyde Goodson
Miss Laura Parker
Clay-Boy Spencer
Clayton Spencer
Elizabeth Spencer
Olivia Spencer
Virgil Spencer
Zebulon Spencer

Mark Harris
Bang the Drum Slowly–N.L.
Sidney Jerome Goldman
Katie
Patricia Moors
Bruce William Pearson, Jr.
Pop
Herman H. Schnell
Berwyn Phillips Traphagen
Henry Whittier Wiggen
Holly Webster Wiggen
Thurston Printise Woods

It Looked Like For Ever–N.L.
Suicide Alexander
Barbara
Bertilia
Beansy Binz
Ben Crowder
Jerry Divine
Sidney Jerome Goldman
Ev McTaggart
Patricia Moors
Frank Pointer
Dr. Schiff
Herman H. Schnell
Millie Schnell
Marva Sprat
Berwyn Phillips Traphagen
Henry Whittier Wiggen
Hilary Margaret Wiggen
Holly Webster Wiggen
Suzanne Winograd
Newton Sprat

The Southpaw–N.L.
Sidney Jerome Goldman
Bradley Lord
Patricia Moors
Michael J. Mulrooney
Pop
Herman H. Schnell
Berwyn Phillips Traphagen
Aaron Webster
Victor Wenk
Henry Whittier Wiggen
Holly Webster Wiggen
Samuel Yale

A Ticket for a Seamstitch–N.L.
Sidney Jerome Goldman

Patricia Moors
Herman H. Schnell
Berwyn Phillips Traphagen
Henry Whittier Wiggen
Holly Webster Wiggen
Thurston Printise Woods

Wake Up, Stupid–N.L.
Clinton W. Blalock
Gabriella Bodeen
Bartholomew Enright
Abner Klang
Bartholomew Enright
Louis Garafolo
Whizzer Harlow
Alexander Irwin
Abner Klang
Dr. Elvin R. Outerbridge
Paul Purdy
Harold Rosenblatt
Harry Searle
Beth Youngdahl
Dee Youngdahl
Lee W. Youngdahl

Jim Harrison
A Good Day to Die–E.C.R.
Frank
Chief Joseph
Rosie
Sylvia
Tim

Wolf–E.C.R.
Barbara
Laurie
Carol Severin Swanson

Bret Harte
Gabriel Conroy–P.D.M.
Olympia Conroy
Gabriel Conroy
Dr. Pete Duchesne
Peter Dumphy
Jack Hamlin
Arthur Poinsett
Doña Dolores Salvatierra
Doña Maria Sepulvida

John Hawkes
Death, Sleep & the Traveler–C.B.C.
Ariane
Olaf
Peter
Allert Vanderveenan
Ursula Vanderveenan

Second Skin–C.B.C.
Big Bertha
Uncle Billy
Cassandra
Fernandez
Gertrude
Harry

Sister Josie
Kate
Miranda
Pixie
Bub Poor
Jomo Poor
Red Poor
Skipper
Sonny
Tremlow

The Beetle Leg–C.B.C.
Harry Bohn
Camper
Hattie Lampson
Luke Lampson
Ma Lampson
Cap Leech
Maverick

The Blood Oranges–C.B.C.
Catherine
Cyril
Dolores
Eveline
Fiona
Hugh
Meredith
Rosella

The Cannibal–J.G.H.
The Duke
Jutta
Leevey
Ernst Snow
Stella Snow
Zizendorf

The Goose on the Grave–C.B.C.
Adeppi
Arsella
Brother Bolo
Dolce
Edouard
Gregario Fabbisogno
Caporale Guiglielmo
Jacopo
Nino
Pipistrello
Pixie

The Owl–C.B.C.
Antonina Barabo
Ginevra Barabo
Signor Barabo
Il Gufo
Mostro
Pucento

The Passion Artist–J.G.H.
Claire
Gagnon
Hania
Hermann Herzenbrecher

Anna Kossowski
Kristel
Eva Laubenstein
Mirabelle
Doctor Slovotkin
Konrad Vost
Konrad Vost the Father

Travesty–J.G.H.
Chantal
Henri
Honorine
Papa
Pascal

Nathaniel Hawthorne
The Blithedale Romance–G.G.
Miles Coverdale
Silas Foster
Hollingsworth
Moodie
Priscilla
Professor Westervelt
Zenobia

Fanshawe–G.G.
Butler
Widow Butler
Hugh and Sarah Hutchins Crombie
Fanshawe
Glover
Ellen Langton
John Langton
Dr. and Sarah Melmoth
Edward Walcott

The House of the Seven Gables–G.G.
Ned Higgins
Holgrave
Thomas Maule
Matthew Maule I
Matthew Maule II
Alice Pyncheon
Clifford Pyncheon
Colonel Pyncheon
Gervayse Pyncheon
Hepzibah Pyncheon
Phoebe Pyncheon
Jaffrey Pyncheon I
Judge Jaffrey Pyncheon II
Uncle Venner

The Marble Faun–G.G.
Brother Antonio
Donatello
Hilda
Kenyon
Miriam Schaefer

The Scarlet Letter–G.G.
Bellingham
Roger Chillingworth
Arthur Dimmesdale
Mistress Hibbins

Pearl
Hester Prynne
Jonathan Pue

Lafcadio Hearn
Chita–J.Dy.
Carmelo
Henry Edwards
Harris
Julien Raymond La Brierre
Laroussel
Mateo
Miguel
Sparicio
Carmen Viosca
Conchita Viosca
Feliu Viosca

Youma–J.Dy.
Raoul-Ernest-Louis Desrivières
Douceline
Gabriel
de Kersaint I
de Kersaint II
Mayotte
Adélaïde-Hortense-Aimé Peyronnette
Léonie Peyronnette
Sylvain
Tanga
Youma

Thomas Heggen
Mister Roberts–D.L.T.L.
Doc
Ensign James L. Keith
Captain Morton
Lieutenant Ed Pauley
Ensign Frank Pulver
Lieutenant Doug A. Roberts

Joseph Heller
Catch-22–J.G.H.
Captain Aardvaark
Appleby
Captain Black
Colonel Cargill
Colonel Cathcart
Clevinger
Major de Coverley
Nurse Cramer
Doc Daneeka
Dobbs
General Dreedle
Sue Ann Duckett
Dunbar
Dori Duz
Captain Flume
Captain Havermeyer
Hungry Joe
Huple
Washington Irving
Lieutenant Colonel Korn
Luciana
Major Major Major Major

McWatt
Milo Minderbinder
Colonel Moodus
Lieutenant Mudd
Lieutenant Nately
Orr
General P. P. Peckem
Kid Sampson
Lieutenant Scheisskopf
Corporal Snark
Snowden
Albert Taylor Tappman
Corporal Whitcomb
Chief White Halfoat
Ex-P.F.C. Wintergreen
Yossarian

Good as Gold–J.R.
Andrea Biddle Conover
Pugh Biddle Conover
Belle Gold
Bruce Gold
Gussie Gold
Julius Gold
Sid Gold
Lionel Greenspan
Maxwell Lieberman
Ralph Newsome
Pomoroy
Harris Rosenblatt

Something Happened–L.S.T.
Arthur Baron
Johnny Brown
Jack Green
Andy Kagle
Virginia Markowitz
Martha
Red Parker
Bob Slocum
Derek Slocum
Mrs. Slocum

Mark Helprin
Refiner's Fire–T.S.
Nancy May Baker
Big Tub
Farrell
Lev
Lydia Levy
Paul Levy
Livingston
Alexander Pascaleo
Marshall Pearl
Katrina Perlé
Dash Pringle
Lucius Pringle

Ernest Hemingway
Across the River and into the Trees–G.G.
Barone Alvarito
Richard Cantwell
Gran Maestro
T5 Ronald Jackson

Renata
Wes

A Farewell to Arms–J.G.H.
Bartolomeo Aymo
Catherine Barkley
Aldo Bonello
Helen Ferguson
Count Greffi
Frederic Henry
Meyers
Mrs. Meyers
Ettore Moretti
Luigi Piani
Rinaldi
Ralph Simmons
Dr. Valentini
Miss Van Campen

For Whom the Bell Tolls–D.L.Y.
Andrés
Anselmo
Augustín
Lieutenant Paco Berrendo
Eladio
Fernando
Comrade General Golz
Captain Rogelio Gomez
Joaquín
Robert Jordan
Karkov
Maria
André Marty
Captain Mora
Pablo
Pilar
Primitivo
Rafael
El Santiago

Islands in the Stream–G.G.
Boise
Roger Davis
Eddy
Henry
Honest Lil
Andrew Hudson
David Hudson
Thomas Hudson
Tom Hudson
Willie

The Old Man and the Sea–G.G.
Manolin
Santiago

The Sun Also Rises–G.G.
Lady Brett Ashley
Jacob Barnes
Michael Campbell
Frances Clyne
Robert Cohn
Bill Gorton
Count Mippipopolous

Pedro Romero

To Have and Have Not–D.L.Y.
Captain Willie Adams
Frankie
Helen Gordon
Richard Gordon
Frederick Harrison
Mr. Johnson
John MacWalsey
Eddie Marshall
Harry Morgan
Marie Morgan
Roberto
Mr. Simmons
Mr. Sing
Albert Tracy
Freddy Wallace
Wesley

George Wylie Henderson
Jule–E.S.N.
Alex
Bob Benson
Bertha Mae
Rollo Cage
Caroline
Louise Davis
Old Douglas
Jeff Gordon
Zell Ingram
Jule Jackson
Jule
Boykin Keye
Lucius Kimbell
Ollie
Jake Simmons
Maisie Simmons

Ollie Miss–E.S.N.
Alex
Caroline
Della Dole
Jule
Knute Kelly
Mack MacLeod
Ollie
Slaughter
Willie

James Leo Herlihy
All Fall Down–J.R.W.
Bernice O'Brien
Echo Malvina O'Brien
Arthur Ramírez
Shirley
Silas Rents His Ox
Annabel Holznagel Williams
Berry-berry Williams
Annabel Holznagel Williams
Clinton Williams
Ralph Williams

Midnight Cowboy–J.R.W.

Juanita Collins Harmeyer Barefoot
Tombaby Barefoot
Joe Buck
Sally Buck
Townsend Pederson Locke
Woodsy Niles
Perry
Anastasia Pratt
Enrico Salvatore Rizzo
Cass Trehune

Calvin Hernton
Scarecrow–D.M.T.
Joseppi Banascalco
Cederberge
Martin Handson
Orville Handson
Putsy Handson
Kaisa
Wantman Krane
Maria
Reverend Kenneth McIntoch
Oriki
Reggie
Scarecrow
Rex Temple
Dr. Kerstine Wentworth
Euston Peters Winslow-Davis
Dr. Norman Yas

Robert Herrick
The Memoirs of an American Citizen–W.H.
John Carmichael
Hillary Cox
Henry Iverson Dround
Jane Dround
Sarah Gentles
Reverend Hardman
May Rudge Harrington
Will Harrington
Jaffrey Slocum
Edward Van Harrington

William Herrick
Hermanos!–M.L.A.
Gregory Ballard
Mack Berg
Archie Cohen
Charles Evans Flagg
Joe Garms
Rolfe Keepsake
Daniel Nuñez
Professor Rolfe Alan Ruskin
Sarah Ruskin
Jacob Starr
Carl Vlanoc
Cromwell Webster

The Itinerant–M.L.A.
Dr. Abe Abramson
Matthew Cahn
Ida Delson
Rachel Mary Conyngham Farrell
Simon Xavier Farrell

Charles Evans Flagg
Pacifici Bartola Ahmed Gurevich
Samuel Ezekiel Gurevich
Miriam
Edna Nimienski

The Last to Die–M.L.A.
Buteo
Ramón Cordes
Delgado
Marguerite
Max
Rojos

John Hersey
A Bell for Adano–G.J.B.
Sergeant Leonard Borth
Matteo Cacopardo
Errante Gaetano
Zito Giovanni
Major Victor Joppolo
Lieutenant Crofts Livingston
General Marvin
Mayor Nasta
Captain N. Purvis
Giuseppe Ribaudo
Tomasino

The Child Buyer–R.C.T.
Donald R. Broadbent
Sean Cleary
Dr. Frederika Gozar
Wissey Jones
Senator Aaron Mansfield
General Marvin
Charity M. Perrin
Barry Rudd
Maud Purcells Rudd
Senator Skypack

The Wall–R.C.T.
Rachel Apt
Dolek Berson
Noach Levinson
Rutka Mazur
Henryk Rapaport
Lazar Slonim

DuBose Heyward
Mamba's Daughters–E.J.P.
George P. Atkinson
Lissa Atkinson
Proctor Baggart
Gilly Bluton
Thomas Broaden
Rev. Thomas Grayson
Hagar
Valerie Land
Mamba
Maum Netta
Frank North
Charles Raymond
Katherine Wentworth
Polly Wentworth

St. Julien de Chatigny Wentworth
Rev. Quintus Whaley

Porgy–E.J.P.
Alan Archdale
Bess
Crown
Simon Frasier
Jake
Maria
Peter
Porgy
Robbins
Sportin' Life

George V. Higgins
Cogan's Trade–E.H.F.
John Amato
Barry Caprio
Steve Caprio
Jack Cogan
Frankie
Kenny Gill
Mark Trattman

Dreamland–E.H.F.
Andrew Collier
General Aubrey T. Gammage
Ellen Shipp Hadley
Henry Morgan
Russell
Daniel Cable Wills
Daniel Compton Wills

The Digger's Game–E.H.F.
The Greek Almas
Jerry Doherty
Paul Doherty
Harrington
Mitch
Miller Schabb
Croce Torre

The Friends of Eddie Coyle–S.A.A.
Jackie Brown
Eddie Coyle
Dillon
Dave Foley
Jimmy Scalisi
Wanda

Laura Z. Hobson
Gentleman's Agreement–S.A.A.
Anne Dettrey
Dave Goldman
Philip Green
Tom Green
Belle King
Katherine Lacey
John Minify
Elaine Wales

John Clellon Holmes
Go–B.F.

Liza Adler
Bill Agatson
Albert Ancke
Ben
Bianca
Christine
Will Dennison
Dinah
Estelle
Georgia
Rocco Harmonia
Kathryn Hobbes
Paul Hobbes
Hart Kennedy
Arthur Ketcham
Margo
Max
May
Gene Pasternak
Ed Schindel
David Stofsky
Janet and Peter Trimble
Daniel Verger
John Waters
Winnie

The Horn–B.F.
Walden Blue
Cleo
Kelcey Crane
Geordie Dickson
Thomas Finnley
Billy James Henry
Metro
Willy Owls
Edgar Pool
Junius Priest
Eddie Winfield Redburn
Mr. Samm

Emerson Hough
The Covered Wagon–D.E.W.
William Hays Banion
Jim Bridger
Christopher Carson
Bill Jackson
Rob't Kelsey
Jed Wingate
Jesse Wingate
Molly Wingate
Molly Wingate
Samuel Payson Woodhull

The Mississippi Bubble–D.E.W.
Mary Connynge
Du Mesne
Lady Catharine Knollys
Catharine Law
John Law
Will Law
Sir Arthur Pembroke
Philippe of Orléans
Teganisoris
Edward Wilson

North of 36–D.E.W.
Alamo
Cinquo Centavos
Cal Dalhart
Colonel Sandy Griswold
Wild Bill Hickok
Anastasie Lockhart
Joe McCoyne
Daniel McMasters
Jim Nabours
Sim Rudabaugh
Sanchez
Del Williams
Yellow Hand

E. W. Howe
The Story of a Country Town–M.B.
Damon Barker
Lytle Biggs
Clinton Bragg
Agnes Deming
Jo Erring
Goode Shepherd
Mateel Shepherd
John Westlock
Ned Westlock

William Dean Howells
Annie Kilburn–K.F.C.M.
Oliver Bolton
Pauliny Bolton
Percy Brandreth
Emmeline Gerrish
William B. Gerrish
Annie Kilburn
Judge Rufus Kilburn
James Morrell
Mrs. Munger
Idella Peck
Rev. Julius W. Peck
Ellen Putney
Ralph Putney
Winthrop Putney
Maria Savor
William Savor
George Wilmington
Jack Wilmington
Lyra Goodman Wilmington

A Hazard of New Fortunes–D.S.
Angus Beaton
Christine and Mela Dryfoos
Conrad Dryfoos
Jacob Dryfoos
Christine and Mel Dryfoos
Fulkerson
Alma Leighton
Berthold Lindau
Basil March
Isabel March
Margaret Vance
Woodburn
Miss Woodburn

Indian Summer–K.F.C.M.
  Mrs. Amsden
  Effie Bowen
  Evalina Ridgely Bowen
  Theodore Colville
  Imogene Graham
  Mrs. Graham
  Maddalena
  Jenny Wheelwright Milbury
  Mr. Morton
  Paolo
  Madame Fanny Uccelli
  Rev. Mr. Waters

The Lady of the Aroostook–K.F.C.M.
  Lydia Blood
  Charley Dunham
  Henshaw Erwin
  Josephine Erwin
  Miss Hibbard
  Mr. Hicks
  Captain Jenness
  Deacon Latham
  Maria Latham
  Mr. Mason
  James Staniford
  Thomas
  Mr. Watterson

A Modern Instance–D.S.
  Atherton
  Henry Bird
  Squire Gaylord
  Ezra Ben Halleck
  Bartley Hubbard
  Marcia Gaylord Hubbard
  Kinney
  Mrs. Macallister
  Hannah Morrison
  Willett
  Witherby

The Rise of Silas Lapham–D.S.
  Anna Bellingham Corey
  Bromfield Corey
  Tom Corey
  Bartley Hubbard
  Marcia Gaylord Hubbard
  Irene Lapham
  Penelope Lapham
  Persis Lapham
  Silas Lapham

Their Wedding Journey–G.G.
  Kitty Ellison
  Richard and Fanny Ellison
  Basil March
  Isabel March

A Traveler from Altruria–G.G.
  Reuben Camp
  Homos
  Lumen
  Mrs. Makely

Twelvemough

Langston Hughes
Not Without Laughter–D.Sh.
  Buster
  Madam Fannie Rosalie de Carter
  Uncle Dan Givens
  Earl James
  Sister Sarah Johnson
  Willie-Mae Johnson
  Jimmy Lane
  Mingo
  Mr. Prentiss
  Mrs. Reinhart
  Mrs. J. J. Rice
  Mrs. Annjee Rodgers
  James Rodgers
  Jimboy Rodgers
  Billy Sanderlee
  Mrs. Tempy Williams Siles
  Maudel Smothers
  Sister Whiteside
  Aunt Hager Williams
  Harriett Williams
  Cudge Windsor
  Pansetta Young

Evan Hunter
The Blackboard Jungle–G.G.
  Anne Dadier
  Richard Dadier
  Josh Edwards
  Lois Hammond
  Solly Klein
  Gregory Miller
  William Small
  Arthur Francis West

Zora Neale Hurston
Jonah's Gourd Vine–L.P.H.
  Amy Crittenden
  Ned Crittenden
  Sally Lovelace
  Alf Pearson
  John Buddy Pearson
  Lucy Ann Potts
  Hattie Tyson

Moses, Man of the Mountain–L.P.H.
  Aaron
  Amram
  God
  Jethro
  Jochebed
  Joshua
  Mentu
  Miriam
  Moses
  Pharaoh
  Princess Royal
  Ta-Phar
  Zipporah

Seraph on the Suwanee–L.P.H.

  Alfredo Corregio
  Arvay Henson
  Hatton Howland
  Dessie Kelsey
  Joe Kelsey
  Angeline Meserve
  Earl David Meserve
  James Kenneth Meserve
  Jim Meserve
  Carl Middleton
  Larraine Henson Middleton

Their Eyes Were Watching God–L.P.H.
  Janie Mae Crawford
  Logan Killicks
  Nanny
  Joseph Starks
  Phoeby Watson
  Vergible Woods

Joseph Holt Ingraham
Lafitte–R.W.W.
  Cudjoe
  Count Alphonse D'Oyley
  Juana
  Lafitte
  Lafon
  Gertrude Langueville
  Théodore
  Constanza Velasquez

John Irving
The 158-Pound Marriage–E.C.R.
  Bart
  George James Bender
  Willard Buzzard
  Audrey Cannon
  Jack
  Jefferson Jones
  Zivan Knezevich
  Kudashvili
  Katrina Marek
  Drexa Neff
  Anna Agati Thalhammer
  Vaso Trivanovich
  Dorabella Winter
  Edith Fuller Winter
  Fiordiligi Winter
  Kurt Winter
  Severin Winter

Setting Free the Bears–E.C.R.
  Engelbert Dollfuss
  Borsfa Durd
  Gallen
  Zahn Glanz
  Heine Gortz
  Hannes Graff
  Ana Helein
  Siegfried Javotnik
  Vratno Javotnik
  Kudashvili
  Mara Madoff
  Marter

Muttie Marter
Hilke Marter-Javotnik
Rare Spectacled Bears
O. Schrutt
Kurt von Schuschnigg
Bijelo Slivinca
Todor Slivinca
Wallner
Ernst Watzek-Trummer
Gottlob Wut

The Water-Method Man–E.C.R.
Cuthbert Bennett
Sue Kunft Trumper Bennett
Dante Callicchio
Lydia Kindle
Elsbeth Malkas
Arnold Mulcahy
Merrill Overturf
Ralph Packer
Sprog
Colm Trumper
Fred Trumper
Tulpen
Jean Claude Vigneron

The World According to Garp–E.C.R.
Bodger
Bonkers
Florence Cochran Bowlsby
Charlotte
Jennifer Fields
Alice Fletcher
Harrison Fletcher
Duncan Garp
Jenny Garp
T. S. Garp
Technical Sergeant Garp
Walt Garp
Ernie Holm
Helen Holm
Ellen James
Michael Milton
Roberta Muldoon
Bainbridge Percy
Cushman Percy
Randolph Percy
Stewart Percy
Stewart Percy, Jr.
William Percy
Benny Potter
Jillsy Sloper
Tinch
Harriet Truckenmiller
Kenny Truckenmiller
Donald Whitcomb
John Wolf

Shirley Jackson
The Haunting of Hill House–M.J.
Arthur
Mrs. Dudley
Mrs. Dudley
Dr. John Montague

Mrs. Montague
Luke Sanderson
Theodora
Eleanor Vance

We Have Always Lived in the Castle–M.J.
Charles Blackwood
Constance Blackwood
Julian Blackwood
Mary Katherine Blackwood
Helen Clarke
Henry Clarke
Jim Donell
Lucille Wright

Henry James
The Ambassadors–G.A.H.
John Little Bilham
Maria Gostrey
Chadwick Newsome
Mrs. Newsome
Jim Pocock
Mamie Pocock
Sarah Newsome Pocock
Lewis Lambert Strether
Jeanne de Vionnet
Mme. Marie de Vionnet
Mr. Waymarsh

The American–D.S.
Emmeline de Bellegarde
Henri-Urban de Bellegarde
Madame Urbain de Bellegarde
Urbain de Bellegarde
Valentin de Bellegarde
Catherine Bread
Claire de Bellegarde de Cintré
Lord Deepmore
Stanislas Kapp
Christopher Newman
Nioche
Noémie Nioche
Tom Tristram
Mrs. Tom Tristram

The Awkward Age–B.F.
Mrs. Edward Brookenham
Fernanda Brookenham
Mrs. Harry Grendon
Duchess Jane
Lady Julia
Mr. Longdon
Mitchy Mitchett
Gustavus Vanderbank

The Bostonians–S.L.
Miss Birdseye
Henry Burrage
Mrs. Burrage
Olive Chancellor
Mrs. Farrinder
Mr. Filer
Mr. Gracie
Adeline Luna

Matthias Pardon
Doctor Mary J. Prance
Basil Ransom
Mrs. Tarrant
Doctor Selah Tarrant
Verena Tarrant

Daisy Miller–D.S.
Mrs. Costello
Eugenio
Giovanelli
Annie P. Miller
Mrs. Miller
Randolph Miller
Mrs. Walker
Frederick Forsyth Winterbourne

The Europeans–S.L.
Elizabeth Acton
Mrs. Acton
Robert Acton
Augustine
Azarina
Mr. Brand
Barones Eugenia-Camilla-Dolores Münster
Charlotte Wentworth
Clifford Wentworth
Gertrude Wentworth
William Wentworth
Felix Young

The Golden Bowl–S.L.
Prince Amerigo
Fanny Assingham
Col. Robert Assingham
Mr. Blint
Lady Castledean
Dotty and Kitty Lutch
Mrs. Noble
Principino
Mrs. Rance
Charlotte Stant
Adam Verver
Maggie Verver

The Portrait of a Lady–S.L.
Isabel Archer
Caspar Goodwood
Madame Serena Merle
Gilbert Osmond
Pansy Osmond
Edward Rosier
Henrietta C. Stackpole
Daniel Tracy Touchett
Lydia Touchett
Ralph Touchett
Lord Warburton

The Princess Casamassima–L.I.
Prince Casamassima
Millicent Henning
Lady Aurora Langrish
Christina Light
Paul Muniment

Eustache Poupin
Lord Frederick Purvis
Amanda Pynsent
Hyacinth Robinson
Captain Godfrey Gerald Sholto
Anastasius Vetch
Florentine Vivier

The Reverberator–B.F.
Fidelia Dosson
Francina Dosson
Whitney Dosson
George P. Flack
Gaston Probert
Charles Waterlow

Roderick Hudson–G.A.H.
Augusta Blanchard
Prince Casamassima
Mary Garland
Cavaliere Giuseppino Giacosa
Gloriani
Madame Grandoni
Roderick Hudson
Sarah Hudson
Mr. Leavenworth
Christina Light
Mrs. Light
Rowland Mallet
Sam Singleton

The Sacred Fount–L.I.
Grace Brissenden
Guy Brissenden
Lady John
Gilbert Long
Ford Obert
Mrs. May Server

The Spoils of Poynton–S.L.
Mona Brigstock
Mrs. Brigstock
Adela Gareth
Owen Gareth
Madame de Jaume
Fleda Vetch
Maggie Vetch

The Tragic Muse–B.F.
Charles Carteret
Julia Sherringham Dallow
Basil Dashwood
Lady Agnes Dormer
Bridget Dormer
Grace Dormer
Nicholas Dormer
Percival Dormer
Gabriel Nash
Miriam Rooth
Peter Sherringham

The Turn of the Screw–D.S.
Douglas
Flora

Mrs. Grose
Miss Jessel
Miles
Peter Quint

Washington Square–G.A.H.
Elizabeth Almond
Marian Almond
Mrs. Montgomery
Lavinia Sloper Penniman
Doctor Austin Sloper
Catherine Sloper
Arthur Townsend
Morris Townsend

What Maisie Knew–D.B.R.
Susan Ash
Captain
Sir Claude
Countess
Lord Eric
Beale Farange
Mrs. Beale Farange
Ida Farange
Maisie Farange
Moddle
Mr. Perriam
Mrs. Wix

The Wings of the Dove–D.S.
Kate Croy
Merton Densher
Maud Lowder
Lord Mark
Luke Strett
Susan Shepherd Stringham
Mildred Theale

Randall Jarrell
Pictures from an Institution–J.A.B.
Camille Turner Batterson
Gertrude Johnson
Constance Morgan
Sona Rasmussen
Dwight Robbins
Gottfried Knosperl Rosenbaum
Irene Rosenbaum
Florence Whittaker
Jerrold Whittaker

Sarah Orne Jewett
A Country Doctor–J.M.F.
Eunice Fraley
George Gerry
Mrs. Graham
Dr. John Leslie
Walter Parish
Adeline Thacher Prince
Anna Prince
Anna Prince
Mrs. Thacher
Marilla Thomas

The Country of the Pointed Firs–J.M.F.

Mrs. Blackett
William Blackett
Susan Fosdick
Gaffett
Esther Hight
Captain Littlepage
Abby Martin
Elijah Tilley
Almira Blackett Todd
Joanna Todd

A Marsh Island–J.M.F.
Bradish
Richard Dale
Temperance Kipp
Dan Lester
Doris Owen
Martha Owen
Israel Owen I
Israel Owen II
Mrs. Winchester

Diane Johnson
The Shadow Knows–G.G.
Osella Barnes
Inspector Dyce
A. J. Harper
Bess Harvill
Gavin Hexam
N. Hexam
Mr. and Mrs. Hoaglund
Andrew Mason
Raider
Clyde Wilson
Evalin McCabe Wilson

Josephine Johnson
Now in November–M.H.M.
Arnold Haldmarne
Kerrin Haldmarne
Marget Haldmarne
Merle Haldmarne
Willa Haldmarne
Grant Koven

Mary Johnston
Cease Firing–R.C.
Edward Cary
Fauquier Cary
Judith Jacqueline Cary
Richard Cleave
Steven Dagg
Désirée Gaillard
Allan Gold
Joseph Eggleston Johnston
Maury Stafford

Hagar–R.C.
Colonel Argall Ashendyne
Hagar Ashendyne
Medway Ashendyne
Rachel Bolt
Ralph Coltsworth
John Fay

Denny Gayde
Edgar Laydon
Roger Michael

Lewis Rand–R.C.
Aaron Burr
Fairfax Cary
Ludwell Cary
Edward Churchill
Jacqueline Churchill
Unity Dandridge
Adam Gaudylock
Thomas Jefferson
Lewis Rand

The Long Roll–R.C.
Edward Cary
Fauquier Cary
Judith Jacqueline Cary
Lucy Cary
Richard Cleave
Steven Dagg
Allan Gold
General Thomas Jonathan Jackson
Joseph Eggleston Johnston
Maury Stafford

Gayl Jones
Corregidora–B.F.
Austin Bradley
Corregidora
Correy Corregidora
Dorita Corregidora
Gram Corregidora
Ursa Corregidora
Mr. Deak
Mr. Floyd
Mose Grundy
Harold
Jimmy
Catherine Lawson
Lurene
Martin
May Alice
Tadpole McCormick
Max Monroe
Eddy Pace
Theodore
Mutt Philmore Thomas
Vivian

Eva's Man–B.F.
Alfonso
Miss Billie
Eva Medina Canada
John Canada
Marie Canada
Davis Carter
Charlotte
James Hunn
Jean
Jeffy
Jimmy
Mr. Valentino Logan

Medina
Elvira Moody
Otis
Joanne Riley
Freddy Smoot
Moses Tripp
Tyrone

James Jones
From Here to Eternity–C.D.B.
Andy Anderson
Blues Berry
Isaac Nathan Bloom
Chief Choate
Salvatore Clark
Lieutenant Culpepper
Ike Galovitch
Captain Dana E. Holmes
Karen Holmes
James Judson
Mrs. Gert Kipfer
Angelo Maggio
John J. Malloy
Violet Ogure
Robert E. Lee Prewitt
Alma Schmidt
Maylon Stark
Milton Anthony Warden

Go to the Widow-Maker–S.E.G.
Hunt Abernathy
Al Bonham
Letta Bonham
Cathie Chandler Finer
Sam Finer
Lucia Angelina Elena Videndi Grant
Ron Grant
Jim Grointon
Lisa Halder
René Halder
Doug Ismaileh
Frankie Orloffski

The Merry Month of May–M.M.
Anne-Marie
Bernard
Edith de Chambrolet
Daniel
Samantha-Marie Everton
Florence
Harry Gallagher
Hill Gallagher
Louisa Dunn Hill Gallagher
McKenna Hartley Gallagher
Eleanor Hartley
Jonathan James Hartley III
Ferenc Hofmann-Beck
Martine
Raymond
Fred Singer
Terri
David Weintraub

The Pistol–M.M.

Thomas Burton
Fondriere
Grace
Richard Mast
Musso
O'Brien
Paoli
Pender
Winstock

Some Came Running–S.E.G.
Edith Barclay
Raymond Cole
Wallace French Dennis
Gracie Dill
William Howard Taft Dillert
Doris Frederic
Guinevere French
Robert Ball French
Vic Herschmidt
Clark Hibbard
Agnes Marie Towns Hirsh
David L. Hirsh
Dawn Hirsh
Frank Hirsh
Mrs. Elvira Hirsh
Walter Hirsh
Geneve Lowe
Ginnie Moorehead
Jane Staley

The Thin Red Line–L.I.
George R. Band
John Bell
Don Doll
Corporal Fife
James I. Stein
Gordon Tall
Edward Welsh
Private Witt

Whistle–L.I.
Colonel Baker
Carol Ann Firebaugh
Frances Highsmith
Major Hogan
Marion Landers
Bobby Prell
Colonel Stevens
John Strange
Linda Sue Strange
Martin Winch

Erica Jong
Fear of Flying–D.L.T.L.
Charles Fielding
Adrian Goodlove
Brian Stollerman
Judith Stoloff White
Bennett Wing
Isadora Zelda White Stollerman Wing
Pia Wittkin

How to Save Your Own Life–D.L.T.L.

Josh Ace
Michael Cosman
Britt Goldstein
Rosanna Howard
Gretchen Kendall
Hope Lowell
Jeannie Morton
Jeffrey Roberts
Dr. Jeffery Rudner
Eliza Rushmore
Dr. Abigail Schwartz

June Jordan
His Own Where–L.S.L.
Angela Figueroa
Buddy Rivers

Bel Kaufman
Up the Down Staircase–S.H.W.
Sylvia Barrett
Paul Barringer
Samuel Bester
Alice Blake
Maxwell E. Clarke
Frances Egan
Joseph Ferone
Sadie Finch
Ella Friedenberg
Harry Kagan
James J. McHabe
Beatrice Schachter
Edward Williams
Charlotte Wolf

Edith Summers Kelley
Weeds–B.L.
Jerry Blackford
Judith Pippinger Blackford
Jabez Moorhouse
Annie and Bill Pippinger
Lizzie May and Luella Pippinger
Hat and Luke Wolf

John Pendleton Kennedy
Horse-Shoe Robinson–J.B.
Walter Adair
Arthur Butler
Cornwallis
James Curry
Nancy Dimock
Endymion
Ferguson
Stephen Foster
Hugh Habershaw
Innis
Isaac
Henry Lindsay
Mildred Lindsay
Philip Lindsay
Mistress Morrison
Allen Musgrove
Mary Musgrove
David Ramsay
John Ramsay

Galbraith Robinson
Edgar St. Jermyn
Captain St. Jermyn
Christopher Shaw
Tarleton
Williams

Swallow Barn–J.B.
Abe
Ben
Hafen Blok
Mike Brown
Absalom Bulrush
Carey
Chub
Crab
Mammy Diana
Edward Hazard
Ned Hazard
Walter Hazard
Zachary Huddlestone
Mark Littleton
Lucy
Francis Meriwether
Lucretia Hazard Meriwether
Lucy Meriwether
Philip Meriwether
Prudence Meriwether
Victorine Meriwether
Harvey Riggs
Miles Rutherford
Scipio
John Smith
Singleton Oglethorpe Swansdown
Tongue
Bel Tracy
Catharine Tracy
Isaac Tracy
Ralph Tracy
Philpot Wart
Barbara Winkle

William Kennedy
Billy Phelan's Greatest Game–E.C.R.
Angie
Morrie Berman
Honey Curry
Daddy Big
Edward Daugherty
Katrina Daugherty
Martin Daugherty
Mary Daugherty
Peter Daugherty
Georgie Fox
Marcus Gorman
Harvey Hess
Hubert Maloy
Bindy McCall
Charlie Boy McCall
Matt McCall
Patsy McCall
Bump Oliver
William Francis Phelan
Scotty Streck

Legs–E.C.R.
Dickie Bartlett
Jimmy Biondo
Billy Blue
Patrick Delaney
Alice Diamond
Eddie Diamond
John Thomas Diamond
Mendel Feinstein
Charlie Filetti
Flossie
Joe Fogarty
Marcus Gorman
Hubert Maloy
Murray Pucinski
Billy Reagan
Tim Reagan
Marion Roberts
Arnold Rothstein
Clem Streeter

Jack Kerouac
Big Sur–J.G.H.
George Baso
Ron Blake
Rosemarie Buchanan
Elliott Dabney
Willamine Dabney
Ange Duluoz
Emil Alcide Duluoz
Gerard Duluoz
Ben Fagan
Irwin Garden
Julien Love
Arthur Ma
Patrick McLear
Henry Miller
Lorenz Monsanto
Cody Pomeray
Evelyn Pomeray
Joey Rosenberg
Romana Swartz
Tyke
Jarry Wagner
Dave Wain
Perry Yturbide

Book of Dreams–J.G.H.
Old Bull Balloon
Vinny Bergerac
Deni Bleu
Paul Boldieu
Austin Bromberg
Rosemarie Buchanan
Slim Buckle
Maggie Cassidy
Pauline Cole
Ange Duluoz
Catherine Duluoz
Emil Alcide Duluoz
Gerard Duluoz
Mardou Fox
Irwin Garden
Bull Hubbard

DALC

Huck
June
John Kerouac
Albert Lauzon
Julien Love
Balliol MacJones
Larry O'Hara
Cody Pomeray
Evelyn Pomeray
Gus J. Rigopoulos
Doctor Sax
Raphael Urso

Desolation Angels–J.G.H.
Blacky Blake
Deni Bleu
Maggie Cassidy
Pauline Cole
Emil Lazarus Darlovsky
Simon Darlovsky
Geoffrey Donald
Ange Duluoz
Catherine Duluoz
Emil Alcide Duluoz
Gerard Duluoz
Jean Louis Duluoz
Bull Gaines
Irwin Garden
Ruth Heaper
Bull Hubbard
Huck
June
Rose Wise Lazuli
Julien Love
Harvey Marker
Patrick McLear
Christine Monahan
Sean Monahan
Alyce Newman
Cody Pomeray
Evelyn Pomeray
Merrill Randall
Varnum Random
Gus J. Rigopoulos
Tristessa
Raphael Urso
Jarry Wagner
William Carlos Williams

The Dharma Bums–J.G.H.
Rosemarie Buchanan
Rheinhold Cacoethes
Bud Diefendorf
Alvah Goldbook
Christine Monahan
Sean Monahan
Henry Morley
Cody Pomeray
Japheth M. Ryder
Raymond Smith
Psyche Whitmore

Doctor Sax–J.G.H.
Old Bull Balloon

Amadeus Baroque
Vinny Bergerac
Joe Bissonnette
Paul Boldieu
Count Condu
Ange Duluoz
Catherine Duluoz
Emil Alcide Duluoz
Gerard Duluoz
Jean Louis Duluoz
Great World Snake
Richard Hampshire
Bull Hubbard
Albert Lauzon
Gus J. Rigopoulos
Emilia St. Claire
Doctor Sax
Zaza Vauriselle

Maggie Cassidy–J.G.H.
Vinny Bergerac
Joe Bissonnette
Paul Boldieu
Maggie Cassidy
Pauline Cole
Ange Duluoz
Catherine Duluoz
Emil Alcide Duluoz
Gerard Duluoz
Jean Louis Duluoz
Joe Garrity
Johnny Kazarakis
Albert Lauzon
Lu Libble
Gus J. Rigopoulos
Zaza Vauriselle

On the Road–G.V.N.
Remi Boncoeur
Camille
Ed Dunkel
Inez
Chad King
Carlo Marx
Marylou
Montana Slim
Dean Moriarty
Sal Paradise
Terry

Satori in Paris–J.G.H.
Raymond Baillet
Jean-Louis Lebris de Kérouac
Ulysse Lebris
Jean-Marie Noblet

The Subterraneans–J.G.H.
Austin Bromberg
Frank Carmody
Mardou Fox
Yuri Gligoric
John Golz
Arial Lavalina
Balliol MacJones

Adam Moorad
Larry O'Hara
Leo Percepied

Tristessa–J.G.H.
Cruz
Bull Gaines
El Indio
Jack
Tristessa

Visions of Cody–J.G.H.
Old Bull Balloon
Deni Bleu
Helen Buckle
Slim Buckle
Joanna Dawson
Diane
Catherine Duluoz
Gerard Duluoz
Jean Louis Duluoz
Irwin Garden
Val Hayes
Bull Hubbard
Huck
Earl Johnson
Helen Johnson
June
Lu Libble
Julien Love
Jimmy Low
Justin G. Mannerly
Pat
Cody Pomeray
Cody Pomeray, Sr.
Evelyn Pomeray
Joan Rawshanks
Tom Watson

Visions of Gerard–J.G.H.
Old Bull Balloon
Ange Duluoz
Catherine Duluoz
Emil Alcide Duluoz
Gerard Duluoz
Jean Louis Duluoz
Manuel

Ken Kesey
One Flew Over the Cuckoo's Nest–S.L.T.
William Bibbit
Chief Broom Bromden
Charles Cheswick
Dale Harding
Randle Patrick McMurphy
Nurse Ratched
Scanlon
George Sorensen
Doctor Spivey

Sometimes a Great Notion–S.L.T.
Jonathan Bailey Draeger
Floyd Evenwrite
Lester Gibbons

503

Indian Jenny
Henry Stamper
Henry Stamper, Jr.
Joe Benjamin Stamper
Leland Stamper
Vivian Stamper
Boney Stokes
Teddy

Daniel Keyes
Flowers for Algernon–E.J.H.
Algernon
Joe Carp
Charles Gordon
Alice Kinnian
Professor Nemur
Frank Reilly
Doctor Strauss

Grace King
The Pleasant Ways of St. Médard–M.W.H.
Aglone
Doctor Botot
Coralie Chépé
Thomas Cook
Cribiche
Jerry
Madame Joachim
Père Philéas
Mimi Pinseau
Tony San Antonio
Mariana Talbot
Mr. Talbot

Stephen King
Carrie–C.W.
Miss Desjardin
Christine Hargensen
William Nolan
Thomas Ross
Susan Snell
Carietta White
Margaret White

The Dead Zone–C.W.
Frank Dodd
Sarah Bracknell Hazlett
Herbert Smith
John Smith
Vera Helen Smith
Greg Stillson

'Salem's Lot–C.W.
Barlow
Matthew Burke
Donald Callahan
James M. Cody
Daniel Francis Glick
Ralphie Glick
Benjamin Mears
Eva Miller
Susan Norton
Mark Petrie
Richard Throckett Straker

The Shining–C.W.
Delbert Grady
Dick Hallorann
Tony
Daniel Torrance
John Daniel Torrance
Winnifred Torrance
Stuart Ullman

The Stand–C.W.
Nick Andros
Glen Bateman
Nadine Cross
Tom Cullen
Donald Merwin Elbert
Farris
Randall Flagg
Abagail Freemantle
Frances Goldsmith
Lloyd Henreid
Kojak
Harold Emery Lauder
Stuart Redman
Larry Underwood

Joseph Kirkland
Zury–T.C.F.
John Endicott McVey
Margaret McVey
Philip McVey
Ephraim Prouder
Zury Prouder
Anne Sparrow

John Knowles
A Separate Peace–D.S.F.
Chet Douglass
Gene Forrester
Brinker Hadley
Mr. Hadley
Phil Latham
Elwin Lepellier
A. Hopkins Parker
Mr. Patch-Withers
Phineas
Cliff Quackenbush
Dr. Stanpole

Jerzy Kosinski
Being There–M.D.
Chance
Tom Courtney
Thomas Franklin
Benjamin Turnbull Rand
Elizabeth Eve Rand
Vladimir Skrapinov

Blind Date–J.G.H.
Svetlana Alliluyeva
Captain Barbatov
Chairman Mao's Robot
Foxy Lady
Gibby
Jolene

JP
Mary-Jane Saxon Kirkland
George Levanter
Jacques Monod
Nameless
Oscar
Pauline
Madame Ramoz
Romarkin
Serena
Clarence Weston, Sr.
Woytek

Cockpit–M.D.
Anthony Duncan
Fiammetta
Harry
Richard Lasker
Madame Leuwen
Ono
Robert
Snapper
Tarden
Theodora
Tom
Tomek
Valerie
Veronika

The Painted Bird–M.D.
Anton
Anulka
Black One
Ewka
Garbos
Gavrila
Jealous
Labina
Lekh
Makar
Marta
Mitka
Olga the Wise One
Rainbow
Silent One
Stupid Ludmila

Steps–J.G.H.
The Philosopher

Judith Krantz
Scruples–E.J.H.
Curt Arvey
Aunt Cornelia
Peter Elliott
Comte Edouard de la Cote Grace
Fiorio Hill
Joshua Isaiah Hillman
Ellis Ikehorn
Maggie MacGregor
Dolly Moon
Valentine O'Neill
Vito Orsini
Wilhelmina Hunnenwell Ikehorn Orsini

John Prince
Per Svenberg
Harriet Toppingham
Comtesse Lilianne de Vertdulac
Lester Weinstock

Oliver La Farge
Laughing Boy—A.F.
George Hartshorn
Jesting Squaw's Son
Laughing Boy
Red Man
Slim Girl
Wounded Face

Nella Larsen
Passing—M.W.B.
John Bellew
Margery Bellew
Dave Freeland
Felise Freeland
Bob Kendry
Clare Kendry
Gertrude Martin
Brian Redfield
Irene Redfield
Hugh Wentworth

Quicksand—M.W.B.
Dr. Robert Anderson
Helga Crane
Katrina Nilssen Dahl
Poul Dahl
Reverend Mr. Pleasant Green
Anne Grey
Miss Hartley
Jeanette Hayes-Rore
Peter Nilssen
Axel Olsen
James Vayle
Hugh Wentworth

Beirne Lay, Jr.
Twelve O'Clock High!—B.F.
Jesse Bishop
Joe R. Cobb
Keith Davenport
Ben Gately
Ed Henderson
Don Kaiser
Pamela Mallory
Sergeant McIllhenny
Patrick Pritchard
Frank Savage
Harvey Stovall
Heinz Zimmerman

Harper Lee
To Kill a Mockingbird—D.Sh.
Aunt Alexandra
Miss Maudie Atkinson
Calpurnia
Miss Stephanie Crawford
Mayella Violet Ewell

Robert E. Lee Ewell
Atticus Finch
Jean Louise Finch
Jeremy Atticus Finch
Charles Baker Harris
Miss Rachel Haverford
Arthur Radley
Helen Robinson
Thomas Robinson
Sheriff Heck Tate

Ira Levin
Rosemary's Baby—C.F.L.
Minnie Castevet
Roman Castevet
Terry Gionoffrio
Dr. Hill
Edward Hutchins
Steven Marcato
Dr. Abe Sapirstein
Andrew John Woodhouse
Guy Woodhouse
Rosemary Woodhouse

Meyer Levin
Compulsion—S.J.R.
Charles Kessler
Jonas Kessler
Martha Kessler
Paulie Kessler
Sid Silver
Judah Steiner, Jr.
Judah Steiner, Sr.
Artie Straus
Randolph Straus
Jonathan Wilk

Janet Lewis
The Wife of Martin Guerre—B.F.
Carbon Bareau
Jean Espagnol
Martin Guerre
Monsieur Guerre
Pierre Guerre
Sanxi Guerre
Bertrande Rols
Arnaud du Tilh

Sinclair Lewis
Arrowsmith—C.L.S.
Martin Arrowsmith
Clif Clawson
Angus Duer
Madeline Fox
Professor Max Gottlieb
Dr. Rippleton Holabird
Latham Ireland
Joyce Lanyon
Dr. Oliver Marchand
Ross McGurk
Henry Novak
Fatty Pfaff
Dr. Almus Pickerbaugh
Dean Silva

Gustaf Sondelius
Albert R. Tozer
Mr. and Mrs. Andrew Jackson Tozer
Leora Tozer
Clay Tredgold
Dr. A. DeWitt Tubbs
Terry Wickett
Dr. Woestijne

Babbitt—C.L.S.
George F. Babbitt
Katherine Babbitt
Myra Thompson Babbitt
Theodore Roosevelt Babbitt
Verona Babbitt
Rev. John Jennison Drew
William Washington Eathorne
Kenneth Escott
Stanley Graff
Vergil Gunch
Tanis Judique
Eunice Littlefield
Howard Littlefield
Theresa McGoun
Paul Riesling
Zilla Colbeck Riesling
Henry T. Thompson

Cass Timberlane—C.L.S.
Blanche Lebanon Timberlane Boncyard
Rev. Evan Brewster
Bradd Criley
Dr. Roy Drover
Avis Criley Elderman
Sweeney Fishberg
Lucius Fliegend
Christabel Grau
Tilda Hatter
Mrs. Higbee
Jay Laverick
Rose Timberlane Pennloss
John William Prutt
Eino Roskinen
Cass Timberlane
Virginia Marshland Timberlane

Dodsworth—C.L.S.
Fernande Azeredo
Edith Cortright
Brent Dodsworth
Frances Voelker Dodsworth
Samuel Dodsworth
Major Clyde Lockert
Emily Dodsworth McKee
Harry McKee
Count Kurt von Obersdorf
Thomas J. Pearson

Elmer Gantry—C.L.S.
George F. Babbitt
Lulu Bains
Cleo Benham
Hettie Dowler
Oscar Dowler

Sharon Falconer
Eddie Fislinger
Elmer Gantry
Mrs. Logan Gantry
Jim Lefferts
Floyd Naylor
Dr. Willoughby Quarles
Mrs. Evans Riddle
Judson Roberts
Frank Shallard
Mannie Silverhorn
Rev. Wesley R. Toomis
Dr. Bruno Zechlin

The God-Seeker–C.L.S.
Black Wolf
Aaron Gadd
Elijah Gadd
Uriel Gadd
Rev. Balthazar Harge
Mercie Harge
Caesar Lanark
Selene Lanark
Huldah Purdick
David Queenslace
Isaac Weeps-by-Night

It Can't Happen Here–C.L.S.
Mrs. Candy
Mr. Dimick
Julian Falck
Reverend Falck
Dr. Fowler Greenhill
Mary Jessup Greenhill
Cecilia Jessup
Doremus Jessup
Emma Jessup
Philip Jessup
Oscar Ledue
Hector Macgoblin
Karl Pascal
Lorinda Pike
Lee Sarason
Emil Staubmeyer
Effingham Swan
Francis Tasbrough
James Titus
Berzelius Noel Weinacht Windrip

Kingsblood Royal–C.L.S.
Rodney Aldwick
Rev. Evan Brewster
Sophie Concord
Dr. Roy Drover
Belfreda Gray
Drexel Greenshaw
Elizabeth Kingsblood
Faith Kingsblood
Dr. Kenneth M. Kingsblood
Neil Kingsblood
Robert Kingsblood
Vestal Kingsblood
John William Prutt
Gramma Julie Saxinar

Cass Timberlane
Virginia Marshland Timberlane
Dr. Emerson Woolcape

Main Street–C.L.S.
Mrs. Bogart
Sam Clark
Mr. and Mrs. Luke Dawson
Dave Dyer
Harry and Juanita Haydock
Carol Milford Kennicott
Dr. Will Kennicott
Adolph Morgenroth
Fern Mullins
Guy Pollock
Vida Sherwin
Bea Sorenson
Erik Valborg

Ross Lockridge, Jr.
Raintree County–D.J.G.
Cassius P. Carney
Susanna Drake
Neil Gaither
Laura Golden
Garwood B. Jones
Orville Perkins
Esther Root Shawnessy
John Wickliff Shawnessy
Jerusalem Webster Stiles

Jack London
Before Adam–L.R.N.A.
Big-Tooth
Lop-Ear
Red-Eye
Swift One

The Call of the Wild–L.R.N.A.
Buck
Spitz
John Thornton

The Game–L.R.N.A.
Joe Fleming
Genevieve
John Ponta

The Iron Heel–G.G.
John Cunningham
Avis Cunningham Everhard
Ernest Everhard
Jackson
Morehouse

Jerry of the Islands–L.R.N.A.
Bashti
Mister Haggin
Jerry
Harley Kennan
Lamai
Michael
Van Horn

Martin Eden–L.R.N.A.
Russ Brissenden
Professor Caldwell
Lizzie Connolly
Joe Dawson
Martin Eden
Bernard Higginbotham
Ruth Morse
Maria Silva

The Sea-Wolf–L.R.N.A.
Maud Brewster
Johansen
Johnson
Death Larsen
Wolf Larsen
George Leach
Louis
Thomas Mugridge
Humphrey Van Weyden

White Fang–L.R.N.A.
Gray Beaver
Kiche
Lip-lip
Matt
One Eye
Weeden Scott
Beauty Smith
White Fang

Henry Wadsworth Longfellow
Kavanagh–E.J.H.
Alice Archer
Alfred Churchill
Mary Churchill
Mr. Churchill
Hiram Adolphus Hawkins
Martha Amelia Hawkins
Arthur Kavanagh
Lucy
Sally Manchester
Mr. Pendexter
Cecilia Vaughan
Billy Wilmerdings

Anita Loos
"But Gentlemen Marry Brunettes"–R.J.S.
Charlie Breene
Lorelei Lee
Lester
Frederick Morgan
Dorothy Shaw
Henry Spoffard

"Gentlemen Prefer Blondes"–R.J.S.
Sir Francis Beekman
Gus Eisman
Gerald Lamson
Lorelei Lee
Gilbertson Montrose
Dorothy Shaw
Henry Spoffard

Phillip Lopate
Confessions of Summer–T.S.
Jack Bogardes
Cora
Marie Curtin
Eric Eisner
Bruno Fisher
Teddy Forster
Horace Hinton
Charles Kroegel
Skipper
Hugh Wall

Alison Lurie
Love and Friendship–L.M.
Julian Fenn
Miranda Fenn
Allen Ingram
William Wigglesworth Lumkin
Mrs. Rabbage
Freddy Stockwell
Patricia Stockwell
William Thomas
Emily Stockwell Turner
Holman Turner

The Nowhere City–L.M.
Katherine Cattleman
Paul Cattleman
Dr. Isidore Einsam
Glory Green
Cecile O'Connor
Fred Skinner
Susy Skinner
Maxie Weiss
Walter Wong

Real People–L.M.
Charlie Ryan Baxter
Theodore Berg
Nick Donato
Kenneth Foster
Gerald Grass
Caroline Kent
Richard Potter
Sally Sachs
Clark Smith
Janet Belle Smith
Harmonia H. Waters

The War Between the Tates–L.M.
Sanford Finkelstein
Wendy Gahaghan
Dr. Bernard M. Kotelchuk
Ralph
Linda Sliski
Brian Tate
Erica Parker Tate
Jeffrey Tate
Matilda Tate
Danielle Zimmern
Leonard Zimmern
Leonard D. Zimmern
Ruth Zimmern

Andrew Lytle
A Name for Evil–M.T.L.
Ellen Brent
Henry Brent
Major Brent

The Velvet Horn–M.T.L.
Captain Joe Cree
Julia Cropleigh Cree
Lucius Cree
Beverly Cropleigh
Dickie Cropleigh
Duncan Cropleigh
Jack Cropleigh
Peter Legrand
Ada Rutter
Ada Belle Rutter
Saul Slowns

Norman Mailer
An American Dream–J.W.B.
Eddie Ganucci
Barney Oswald Kelly
Lieutenant Leznicki
Cherry Melanie
Roberts
Deborah Kelly Rojack
Stephen Richards Rojack
Ruta

Barbary Shore–J.W.B.
Willie Dinsmore
Ed Leroy Hollingsworth
Michael Lovett
Lannie Madison
Shago Martin
Beverly Guinevere McLeod
William McLeod
Monina

The Deer Park–J.W.B.
Charles Francis Eitel
Elena Esposito
Marion Faye
Lulu Meyers
Carlyle Munshin
Dorothea O'Faye
Sergius O'Shaugnessy
Teddy Pope
Herman Teppis

The Executioner's Song–J.W.B.
April Baker
Nicole Kathryne Baker Barrett
Mont Court
Vern Damico
Bessie Gilmore
Gary Mark Gilmore
Mikal Gilmore
Brenda Nicol
John Nicol
Lawrence Schiller

The Naked and the Dead–J.W.B.
Sergeant William Brown
Staff Sergeant Samuel Croft
Major General Edward Cummings
Casimir Czienwicz
Major Dalleson
Roy Gallagher
Joey Goldstein
Lieutenant Robert Hearn
Sergeant Julio Martinez
Steve Minetta
Red Valsen
Woodrow Wilson

Why Are We in Vietnam?–J.W.B.
Ollie Totem Head Water Beaver
M. A. Bill
D. J.
Luke Fellinka
Gottfried Hyde, Jr.
Gottfried Hyde, Sr.
Alice Hallie Lee Jethro
Rusty Jethroe
M. A. Pete

Bernard Malamud
The Assistant–D.C.
Frank Alpine
Helen Bober
Ida Bober
Morris Bober
Nick Fuso
Julius Karp
Louis Karp
Ward Minogue

Dubin's Lives–J.C.M.
Fanny Bick
Kitty Willis Dubin
Maud Dubin
William B. Dubin
Roger Foster
Evan Ondyk
Gerald Willis

The Fixer–D.C.
B. A. Bibokov
Yakov Shepsovitch Bok
Marfa Vladimirovna Golov
Zhenia Golov
Gregor Gronfein
Vladislav Grigorievitch Grubeshov
Nikolai Maximovitch Lebedev
Zinaida Nikolaevna Lebedev
Raisl
Schmuel

The Natural–D.C.
Bump Baily
Judge Goodwill Banner
Harriet Bird
Pop Fisher
Roy Hobbs
Iris Lemon
Memo Paris

Gus Sands
Sam Simpson
Walter Whambold

A New Life—N.L.T.
Leo Duffy
Dr. Gerald Gilley
Pauline Gilley
Seymour Levin

The Tenants—R.B.M.
Irene Bell
Sam Clemence
Harry Lesser
Irving Levenspiel
Willie Spearmint

William March
The Bad Seed—C.W.
Monica Breedlove
Claude Daigle
Burgess, Claudia, and Oct Fern
Leroy Jessup
Christine Penmark
Kenneth Penmark
Rhoda Penmark

Wallace Markfield
To an Early Grave—G.G.
Inez Braverman
Leslie Braverman
Holly Levine
Felix Ottensteen
Etta Rieff
Morroe Rieff
Barnet Weiner

John P. Marquand
H. M. Pulham, Esquire—K.C.S.
Bo-jo Brown
Bill King
Marvin Myles
Cornelia Motford Pulham
Henry Moulton Pulham

The Late George Apley—K.C.S.
Catharine Bosworth Apley
Eleanor Apley
George William Apley
John Apley
Thomas Apley
William Apley
Mary Monahan
O'Reilly
Will Willing

Point of No Return—K.C.S.
Roger Blakesley
Malcolm Bryant
Anthony Burton
Charles Gray
John Gray
Nancy Gray
Jessica Lovell

Laurence Lovell
Jack Mason

Wickford Point—K.C.S.
Bella Brill
Harry Brill
Jim Calder
Patricia Leighton
Sarah Seabrooke
Allen Southby
George Stanhope
Joe Stowe
Clothilde Brill Wright

Paule Marshall
Brown Girl, Brownstones—W.L.M.
Deighton Boyce
Ina Boyce
Selina Boyce
Silla Boyce
Beryl Challenor
Percy Challenor
Virgie Farnum
Iris Hurley
Maritze
Miss Mary
Suggie Skeete
Clive Springer
Clytie Springer
Miss Thompson
Florrie Trotman

The Chosen Place, the Timeless People—E.B.B.
Harriet Shippen Amron
Saul Amron
Cuffee Ned
Delbert
Ferguson
Allen Fuso
Lyle Hutson
Merle Kinbona
Stinger
Leesy Walkes
Vere Walkes

Jack Matthews
Hanger Stout, Awake!—R.J.F.
Penny Barker
Jim Boynton
Dan Comisky
Pete
Phyllis
Rigolo
Clyde Stout
Bo Thompson
Bert Wilderman

Peter Matthiessen
At Play in the Fields of the Lord—W.W.
Aeore
Azusa
Boronai
Dick
Padre Fuentes

El Comandante Rufino Guzmán
Fausto Guzmán
Señora Dolores Estella Cruz y Peralta Guzmán
Andy Huben
Leslie Huben
Kori
Mercedes
Alvin Moon
Irma Moon
Meriwether Lewis Moon
New Person
Pindi
Hazel Quarrier
Martin Quarrier
William Martin Quarrier
Suzie
Taweeda
Tukanu
Ugly One
Uyuyu
Wolfie
Father Xantes

Far Tortuga—H.W.
Captain Andrew Avers
Jim Eden Avers
Captain Raib Avers
Junior Bodden
Athens Ebanks
Captain Desmond Eden
Vemon Dilbert Evers
Wodie Greaves
William Parchment
Miguel Moreno Smith
Byrum Powery Watler

Raditzer—J.G.H.
Carter Adams
Robert Ariyoshi
Carl
Jack Gioncarlo
Hoak
Male Raditzer
Charles P. Stark
Charlotte Sylvester Stark
Vahine

William Maxwell
The Folded Leaf—M.H.M.
Hope Davison
Alfred Dehner
Sally Forbes
Charles Latham
Evans Latham
Helen Latham
Mrs. Latham
Lymie Peters
Lymon Peters
Dick Reinhart
William Severance

They Came Like Swallows—G.J.B.
Ethel Blaney

Boyd Hiller
Irene Blaney Hiller
Elizabeth Blaney Morison
James B. Morison
Peter Morison
Robert Morison
Clara Morison Paisley
Sophie

Time Will Darken It—G.J.B.
Alice Beach
Lucy Beach
Miss Ewing
Abbey King
Austin King
Martha Hastings King
Nora Potter
Randolph Potter
Reuben S. Potter
Rachel

Julian Mayfield
The Grand Parade—E.W.T.
Alonzo Banks
Randolph Banks
Chick Bolton
Clarke Bryant
Jonah Dean Carson
Angus Cleveland
Hank Dean
Mary McCullogh
Patty Speed
Douglas Taylor

The Hit—E.W.T.
Sister Clarisse
Gertrude Cooley
Hubert Cooley
James Lee Cooley
John Lewis

The Long Night—E.W.T.
Frederick Brown
Mae Brown
Paul Brown

Mary McCarthy
The Group—M.C.M.
Elizabeth Andrews
Dick Brown
Hartshorn Priss Crockett
Helena Davidson
Elinor Eastlake
Elizabeth MacAusland
Harold Peterson
Mary Prothero
Dorothy Renfrew
Kay Leiland Strong

Horace McCoy
They Shoot Horses, Don't They?—C.D.B.
Mack Aston
Lillian Bacon
Mattie Barnes

James Bates
Ruby Bates
Gloria Beatty
Vincent Donald
Jere Flint
Freddy
Rocky Gravo
Mary Hawley
Mrs. J. Franklin Higby
Kid Kamm
Mrs. Layden
Rosemary Loftus
Vee Lovell
John Maxwell
Jackie Miller
Monk
Pedro Ortega
Rollo Peters
Mario Petrone
Robert Syverten
Geneva Tomblin

Carson McCullers
Clock without Hands—D.Sh.
Judge Fox Clane
John Jester Clane
Johnny Clane
Judge Fox Clane
Grown Boy
Dr. Kenneth Hale Hayden
Nigra Jones
Joy Little
Ossie Little
J. T. Malone
Martha Malone
Sherman Pew
Verily

The Heart Is a Lonely Hunter—J.G.H.
Spiros Antonapoulos
Jake Blount
Alice Brannon
Bartholomew Brannon
Benedict Mady Copeland
Grandpapa Copeland
William Copeland
Lancy Davis
Highboy
Love Jones
Junebug
Bill Kelly
Etta Kelly
George Kelly
Hazel Kelly
Mick Kelly
Ralph Kelly
Wilbur Kelly
Harry Minowitz
Charles Parker
Portia
Simms
John Singer
Baby Wilson
Leroy Wilson

Lucile Wilson

The Member of the Wedding—J.G.H.
Frances Addams
Jarvis Addams
Royal Quincy Addams
Berenice Sadie Brown
Honey Camden Brown
Janice Evans
Ludie Freeman
Mary Littlejohn
Barney MacKean
John Henry West
T. T. Williams

Reflections in a Golden Eye—D.Sh.
Anacleto
Firebird
Alison Langdon
Major Morris Langdon
Leonora Penderton
Capt. Weldon Penderton
Susie
Lieutenant Weincheck
Private L. G. Williams

Thomas McGuane
The Bushwhacked Piano—G.G.
Cletus James Clovis
Wayne Codd
Ann Fitzgerald
Duke and Edna Fitzgerald
Nicholas Payne

Ninety-Two in the Shade—K.A.
Faron Carter
Miranda Cole
Nichol Dance
Myron Moorhen
James Powell
Robert Rudleigh
Skelton
Goldsboro Skelton
Thomas Skelton
Roy Soleil

Panama—G.G.
Catherine Clay
Jesse James
Curtis G. Peavey
Chester Hunnicutt Pomeroy
Jim Pomeroy
Roxy

The Sporting Club—K.A.
Mary Beth Duncan
Fortescue
Janey
Earl Olive
James Quinn
Scott
Spengler
Vernor Stanton

Claude McKay
Banjo—G.G.
  Buchanan Malt Avis
  Jake Brown
  Lincoln Agrippa Daily
  Sister Geter
  Goosey
  Latnah
  Lonesome Blue
  Raymond
  Taloufa

Home to Harlem—W.L.M.
  Agatha
  Billy Biasse
  Jake Brown
  Miss Lavinia Curdy
  Uncle Doc
  Felice
  Gin-head Susy
  Zeddy Plummer
  Raymond
  Rose

Larry McMurtry
All My Friends Are Going to Be Strangers—S.R.D.
  Daniel Deck
  Lorena Deck
  Sally Bynum Deck
  Emma Greenway Horton
  Tommy Horton
  Thomas Horton
  Jill Peel

Horseman, Pass By—S.R.D.
  Homer Lisle Bannon
  Jewel Bannon
  Lonnie Bannon
  Halmea
  Hud
  Jesse Logan

The Last Picture Show—D.D.Q.
  Abilene
  Billy
  Frank Crawford
  Sonny Crawford
  Charlene Duggs
  Gene Farrow
  Jacy Farrow
  Lois Farrow
  Lester Marlow
  Duane Moore
  Genevieve Morgan
  Coach Herman Popper
  Ruth Popper
  Sam the Lion
  Bobby Sheen

Leaving Cheyenne—S.R.D.
  Adam Fry
  Gideon Fry
  Mabel Peters Fry
  Jimmy

  Joe
  Jonathan McCloud
  Cletus Taylor
  Eddie White
  Molly Taylor White

Moving On—S.R.D.
  David Carpenter
  James Carpenter
  Patsy White Carpenter
  Clara Clark
  Eleanor Guthrie
  Emma Greenway Horton
  Teddy and Tommy Horton
  Thomas Horton
  Hank Malory
  Sonny Shanks
  Miriam White

Somebody's Darling—S.R.D.
  Owen Oarson
  Jill Peel
  Joe Percy

Terms of Endearment—S.R.D.
  Daniel Deck
  Rosie Dunlup
  Royce Dunlup
  Aurora Starrett Greenway
  Emma Greenway Horton
  Melanie, Teddy, and Tommy Horton
  Thomas Horton
  General Hector Scott

Herman Melville
Billy Budd—B.F.
  William Budd
  John Claggart
  The Dankster
  Red Whiskers
  Squeak
  Edward Fairfax Vere

The Confidence-Man—B.F.
  China Aster
  Black Guinea
  Charlemont
  William Cream
  Egbert
  Thomas Fry
  Goneril
  Francis Goodman
  James Hall
  John Moredock
  Charles Arnold Noble
  Orchis
  Pitch
  John Ringman
  Henry Roberts
  John Truman
  Mark Winsome

Israel Potter—B.F.
  Ethan Allen

  James Bridges
  Benjamin Franklin
  George III
  Jenny
  John Paul Jones
  John Millet
  Captain Pearson
  Benjamin Potter
  Israel Potter
  Sergeant Singles
  Horne Tooke
  John Woodcock

Mardi—B.F.
  A
  Abrazza
  Alanno
  Aleema
  Almanni
  Annatoo
  Babbalanja
  Bardianni
  Bello
  Borabolla
  Donjalolo
  Hautia
  Hello
  Hevaneva
  Hivohitee
  I
  Jarl
  Lombardo
  Media
  Mohi
  Nimni
  O
  Ohiro-Moldona-Fivona
  Oh-Oh
  Pani
  Peepi
  Piko
  Samoa
  Taji
  Uhia
  Vee-Vee
  Yillah
  Yoky
  Yoomy

Moby-Dick—B.F.
  Ahab
  Bildad
  Bulkington
  Daggoo
  Elijah
  Fedallah
  Flask
  Ishmael
  Father Mapple
  Moby Dick
  Peleg
  Perth
  Pip
  Queequeg

Radney
Starbuck
Steelkilt
Stubb
Tashtego

Omoo–B.F.
Arfretee
Arheetoo
Baltimore
Beauty
Bell
Bembo
Captain Bob
Bungs
Crash
Guy
Lem Hardy
John Jermin
Jim
Johnson
Kooloo
Long Ghost
Loo
Marbonna
Monee
Father Murphy
Noomai
Poky
Pomaree Vahinee I
Deacon Ereemear Po-Po
Rartoo
Rope Yarn
Salem
Shorty
Sydney Ben
Tanee
Tonoi
Typee
Van
Varvy
Viner
Wilson
Wymontoo-Hee
Zeke

Pierre–B.F.
Isabel Banford
Dates
Falsgrave
Dorothea Glendinning
Mary Glendinning
Pierre Glendinning I
Pierre Glendinning II
Pierre Glendinning III
Aunt Llanyllyn
Charles Millthorpe
Ned
Plotinus Plinlimmon
Glendinning Stanly
Frederic Tartan
Lucy Tartan
Delly Ulver
Walter Ulver

Ralph Winwood

Redburn–B.P.
Jack Blunt
Harry Bolton
Carlo
Danby
Goodwell
Gun-Deck
Handsome Mary
Jackson
Betsey Jennings
Jones
Larry
Lavender
Lord Lovely
Max
Wellingborough Redburn
Riga
Rigs
Miguel Saveda
Thompson

Typee–B.F.
Fayaway
Jimmy
Karakoee
Karky
Kolory
Kory-Kory
Marheyo
Marnoo
Mehevi
Mowanna
Mow-Mow
Tinor
Toby
Tommo

White-Jacket–B.F.
Antone
Baldy
Bland
Bridewell
Jack Chase
Claret
Colbrook
Cadwallader Cuticle
John
Lemsford
Mad Jack
Mark
Nord
Pelican
Peter
Pills
Priming
Professor
Quoin
Selvagee
Shenly
Tawney
John Ushant
White-Jacket

Williams
Harrison Woolf

Louise Meriwether
Daddy Was a Number Runner–M.W.B.
Maude Caldwell
Rebecca Caldwell
Vallejo Caldwell
China Doll Coffin
Francie Coffin
Henrietta Coffin
James Adam Coffin
James Adam Coffin, Jr.
Sterling Coffin
Sukie Maceo
Mabel Mackey
Sonny Taylor

Grace Metalious
Peyton Place–L. I.H.
Betty Anderson
Seth Buswell
Ted Carter
Lucas Cross
Nellie Cross
Selena Cross
Leslie Harrington
Rodney Harrington
Bradley Holmes
Allison MacKenzie
Constance MacKenzie
Tomas Makris
Evelyn Page
Norman Page

Oscar Micheaux
The Forged Note–J.R.W.
Jefferson Bernard
Vance R. Coleman
Constance Jacobs
Wilson Jacobs
Ernestine Jacques
Mildred Latham
Legs
John Moore
Annie Palmer
Dr. Randall
Sidney Wyeth

The Homesteader–J.R.W.
Jean Baptiste
Augustus M. Barr
Eugene Crook
E. M. Glavis
Ethel McCarthy Glavis
Peter Kaden
Newton Justine McCarthy
Orlean E. McCarthy
Agnes Stewart
Jack Stewart
Isaac Syfe

Henry Miller
Black Spring–J.D.P.

Albert F. Bendix
H. W. Bendix
R. N. Bendix
Jabberwhorl Cronstadt
Katya Cronstadt
George Denton
Paul Dexter
Brother Eaton
Baron Carola von Eschenbach
Julian Legree
Paul Melia
Tante Melia
Tom Moffatt
Patsy O'Dowd
Ferd Pattee
Rob Ramsay
George Sandusky
Bill Woodruff

Tropic of Cancer–J.D.P.
Bessie
Boris
Borowski
Carl
Mlle. Claude
Collins
Jabberwhorl Cronstadt
Elsa
Father
Fillmore
Germaine
Ginette
Kepi
Kruger
Macha
Marlowe
Henry Miller
Moldorf
Mona
Nanantatee
Olga
Walter Pach
Peckover
Serge
Mark Swift
Sylvester
Tania
Van Norden

Tropic of Capricorn–J.D.P.
Mr. Burns
Carnashan
Aunt Caroline
Mr. Clancy
Clausen
Curley
Father
Francie
Georgiana
Joe Gerhardt
Griswold
Roy Hamilton
Pauline Janowski
Hymie Laubscher

Jack Lawson
MacGregor
McGovern
Henry V. Miller
Monica
Gottlieb Leberecht Müller
Uncle Ned
Lola Niessen
O'Mara
O'Rourke
Dr. Rausch
Schuldig
Lottie Somers
Aunt Tillie
Valeska
Grover Watrous

Margaret Mitchell
Gone with the Wind–C.W.
Eugenie Victoria Butler
Rhett K. Butler
Charles Hamilton
Sarah Jane Hamilton
Frank Kennedy
Mammy
Gerald O'Hara
Scarlett O'Hara
Emmie Slattery
Belle Watling
Jonas Wilkerson
Ashley Wilkes
India Wilkes
Melanie Hamilton Wilkes

N. Scott Momaday
House Made of Dawn–C.A.E.
Abel
Ben Benally
Juan Reyes Fragua
Francisco
Martinez
Milly
Fray Nicolás
Father Olguin
Angela Grace St. John
John Big Bluff Tosamah
Vidal

Wright Morris
Cause for Wonder–J.J.W.
Katherine Morley Brownell
Brian Caffrey
Etienne Dulac
Seymour Gatz
Charles Ames Horney
Warren P. Howe
Fremont Osborn
Grace Osborn
Sol Spiegel

Ceremony in Lone Tree–J.J.W.
Gordon Boyd
Daughter
W. B. Jennings

Calvin McKee
Eileen McKee
Gordon Scanlon McKee
Lois Scanlon McKee
Walter McKee
Bud Momeyer
Etoile Momeyer
Lee Roy Momeyer
Maxine Momeyer
Charlie Munger
Tom Scanlon

The Field of Vision–J.J.W.
Gordon Boyd
Paul Kahler
Dr. Leopold Lehmann
Gordon Scanlon McKee
Lois Scanlon McKee
Walter McKee
Timothy Scanlon
Tom Scanlon

Fire Sermon–J.J.W.
Joy
Kermit Oelsligle
Stanley
Floyd Warner

The Fork River Space Project–J.J.W.
P. O. Bergdahl
O. P. Dahlberg
Kelcey
Alice Kelcey
Harry Lorbeer

The Home Place–J.J.W.
Eddie Cahow
Bobby Muncy
Clara Cropper Muncy
Clyde Muncy
Harry Muncy
Peg Muncy
Peggy Muncy
Grace Osborn

The Huge Season–J.J.W.
Lou Garbo Baker
Peter Nielson Foley
Charles Gans Lawrence
Richard Olney Livingston III
Jesse Lasky Proctor

Love among the Cannibals–J.J.W.
Eva Baum
Billie Harcum
Earl Horter
Dr. Leggett
Irwin K. Macgregor

Man and Boy–J.J.W.
Myrtle Dinardo
Private Lipido
Violet Ames Ormsby
Virgil Ormsby

Warren K. Ormsby

The Man Who Was There–J.J.W.
Eddie Cahow
Grandmother Herkimer
Roger Burns Lakeside
Augusta Newcomb
Grace Osborn
Christian Reagan
Peter Spavic
Agee Ward

My Uncle Dudley–J.J.W.
Cupid
Furman
Kid
Dudley Osborn

What a Way to Go–J.J.W.
Signor Condotti-Pignata
Dr. Luther Hodler
Konrad Holzapfel
Mathilde Kollwitz
Adrien Perkheimer
Cynthia Pomeroy
Arnold Soby
Winifred Throop

The Works of Love–J.J.W.
Mickey Ahearn
Ethel Bassett
Jr. Brady
Will Jennings Brady
Gertrude Long
T. P. Luckett
Opal Mason
Manny Plinski

The World in the Attic–J.J.W.
Angeline Hibbard
Bud Hibbard
Caddy Hibbard
Clinton Hibbard
Nellie Hibbard
Ralph Moody
Bobby Muncy
Clyde Muncy
Peg Muncy
Peggy Muncy
Grace Osborn
Lemuel T. Purdy
Tom Scanlon

Toni Morrison
The Bluest Eye–J.G.H.
Cholly Breedlove
Pauline Williams Breedlove
Pecola Breedlove
Sammy Breedlove
Claudia MacTeer
Frieda MacTeer
Miss Marie
Maureen Peal
Elihue Micah Whitcomb

Song of Solomon–C.C.D.
Guitar Bains
Crowell Byrd
Heddy Byrd
Sing Byrd
Susan Byrd
Circe
Reverend Cooper
First Corinthians Dead
Hagar Dead
Macon Dead I
Macon Dead II
Macon Dead III
Mary Magdalene Dead
Pilate Dead
Rebecca Dead
Ruth Foster Dead
Empire State
Freddie
Hospital Tommy
Henry Porter
Railroad Tommy
Robert Smith
Solomon

Sula–C.C.D.
Chicken Little
Dewey
Albert Jacks
Jude
Eva Peace
Hannah Peace
Ralph Peace
Sula Peace
Cecile Sabat
Rochelle Sabat
Shadrack
Tar Baby
Helene Sabat Wright
Nel Wright
Wiley Wright

Mary Noailles Murfree
In the Clouds–B.F.F.
Ben Doaks
'Gustus Thomas Griff
James Gwinnan
Bob Harshaw
Reuben Lorey
Peter Rood
Alethea Ann Sayles
Tad

In the "Stranger People's" Country–B.F.F.
Ephraim Guthrie
Felix Guthrie
Letitia Pettingill
Leonard Rhodes
Shattuck
Adelaide Yates
Stephen Yates

The Prophet of the Great Smoky Mountains–B.F.F.
Dorinda Cayce

John Cayce
Gid Fletcher
Micajah Green
Hiram Kelsey
Rick Tyler

Albert Murray
Train Whistle Guitar–E.S.
Miss Tee Boykin
Luzana Cholly
Luzana Cholly
Little Buddy Marshall
Scooter

Vladimir Nabokov
Ada–C.A.R.
Mlle Ida Larivière
Count Percy de Prey
Countess Cordula de Prey
Philip Rack
Adelaida Veen
Aqua Durmanov Veen
Ivan Veen
Lucinda Veen
Marina Durmanov Veen
Walter D. Veen
Andrey Andreevich Vinelander

Bend Sinister–C.A.R.
Dr. Alexander
President Azureus
Linda Bachofen
Mariette Bachofen
Mr. Ember
Professor Hedron
Professor Adam Krug
David Krug
Olga Krug
Maximov
Anna Petrovna Maximov
Paduk
Fradrik Skotoma

Lolita–C.A.R.
Mona Dahl
Jean Farlow
John Farlow
Gaston Godin
Dolores Haze
Charlotte Becker Haze Humbert
Humbert Humbert
Annabel Leigh
Clare Quilty
John Ray, Jr.
Rita
Richard F. Schiller

Look at the Harlequins!–C.A.R.
Gerard Adamson
Louise Adamson
Iris Black
Ivor Black
Anna Ivanovna Blagovo
Dolly von Borg

Baroness Bredow
Isabel
Ninel Ilinishna Langley
Vadim Vadimovich

Pale Fire–C.A.R.
Queen Blenda
Conmal
Jean Dean
Disa, Duchess of Payn
Judge Hugh Warren Goldsworth
Jakob Gradus
Dr. Charles Kinbote
Hazel Shade
John Francis Shade
Sybil Shade
Charles Xavi Vseslav

Pnin–C.A.R.
Betty Bliss
Laurence G. Clements
Jack Cockerell
Herman Hagen
Alexandr Petrovich Kukolnikov
Susan Marshall Kukolnikov
Timofey Pavlovi Pnin
Margaret Thayer
Roy Thayer
Dr. Elizaveta Bogolepov Pnin Wind
Dr. Eric Wind
Victor Wind

The Real Life of Sebastian Knight–C.A.R.
Clare Bishop
Mr. Goodman
Sebastian Knight
Virginia Knight
Alexis Pan
Helen Pratt
Nina Toorovetz de Rechnoy
P. G. Sheldon
Mr. Silbermann
Doctor Alexander Alexandr Starov
V.

Transparent Things–C.A.R.
Madame Charles Chamar
Julia Moore
Armande Chamar Person
Dr. Henry Emery Person
Hugh Person
Phil
Mr. R.
Mr. Tamworth

Howard Nemerov
The Homecoming Game–W.L.M.
Arthur Barber
Raymond Blent
Lou Da Silva
Mr. Giardineri
Coach Hardy
President Harmon Nagel
Dr. Charles Osman

Herman Sayre
Lily Sayre
Leon Solomon

Jay Neugeboren
An Orphan's Tale–G.G.
Eliezer Fogel
Daniel Ginsberg
Sol Kantor
Anita Mendelsohn
Ephraim Mendelsohn
Hannah Mendelsohn
Murray Mendelsohn
Max Mittleman
Charlie Sapistein

Listen Ruben Fontanez–G.G.
Manuel Alvarez
Carlos
Ruben Fontanez
Jackson
Marty
Harry Meyers
Sarah Meyers
Nydia
Danny Santini
Gil Santini

Sam's Legacy–G.G.
Benjamin Samson Berman
Samuel Paul Berman
Gabriel Cohen
Flo
Amos Johnson
George Herman Ruth
Sabatini
Dave Stallworth
Stella
Mason Tidewater

John Nichols
The Sterile Cuckoo–W.L.M.
Grandfather Adams
Marian and Bob Adams
Pookie Adams
Roe Billins
Joe Grubner
Jerry Payne
Nancy Putnam
Ronnie
Harry Schoonover

Josefina Niggli
Mexican Village–P.W.S.
Alejandro Castillo
Joaquín Castillo
María de las Garzas
Pepe Gonzales
Tía Magdalena
Anita O'Malley
Porfirio
Rubén
Andrés Treviño
Chela Villareal

Robert Webster

Step Down, Elder Brother–P.W.S.
Márgara Bárcenas
Mateo Chapa
Agapito Vázquez de Anda
Brunhilda Vázquez de Anda
Domingo Vázquez de Anda
Lucio Vázquez de Anda
Ricardo Vázquez de Anda
Sofía Vázquez de Anda

Anaïs Nin
Children of the Albatross–L.B.D.
Lillian Beye
Djuna
Donald
Faustin the Zombie
Jay
Lawrence
Matilda
Michael
Paul
Uncle Philip
Sabina

Collages–L.B.D.
Betty
Bill
Bruce
Emile
Harry
Henri
John
Ken
Count Laundromat
Leontine
Lisa
Doctor Mann
Max
Nobuko
Nina Gitana de la Primavera
Raven
Renate
Judith Sands
Shumla
Tessa
Colonel Tishnar
Varda
John Wilkes

The Four-Chambered Heart–L.B.D.
Djuna
Jay
Paul
Rango
Sabina
Zora

Ladders to Fire–L.B.D.
Adele
Lillian Beye
Djuna
Gerard

Jay
Larry
Nanny
Paul
Sabina

Seduction of the Minotaur–L.B.D.
Adele
Lillian Beye
Diana
Djuna
Edward
Fred
Mr. Hansen
Hatcher
Doctor Hernandez
Jay
Larry
The Lie Detector
Lietta
Michael Lomax
Maria
Miguelito
O'Connor
Doctor Palas

A Spy in the House of Love–L.B.D.
Alan
Cold Cuts
Djuna
Donald
Jay
John
The Lie Detector
Mambo
Philip
Sabina

Charles Nordhoff
Botany Bay–E.J.H.
Moll Cudlip
Robert Fleming
Nat Garth
Bella Goodwin
Dan Goodwin
Nellie Garth Goodwin
Ned Inching
Phoebe Thynne Oakley
Tom Oakley
Arthur Phillip
Nicholas Sabb
Timothy Sabb
Hugh Tallant
Sally Munro Tallant
Mortimer Thynne

The Hurricane–E.J.H.
Ah Fong
Arai
Fakahau
Farani
Hitia
Kauka
Kersaint

Eugene de Laage
Germaine Anne Marie de Laage
Mako
Marama
Marunga
Mata
George Nagle
Father Paul
Mama Rua
Tavi
Terangi Matokia
Tita
Vernier

Men Against the Sea–E.J.H.
William Bligh
William Cole
William Elphinstone
John Fryer
Thomas Hayward
Thomas Ledward
David Nelson
John Norton
William Purcell
Sparling
Robert Tinkler

Mutiny on the Bounty–E.J.H.
Joseph Banks
William Bligh
Roger Byam
Fletcher Christian
William Cole
Edward Edwards
William Elphinstone
John Fryer
Hamilton
Thomas Hayward
Hitihiti
Thomas Ledward
Maimiti
William McCoy
David Nelson
John Norton
William Purcell
Matthew Quintal
Alexander Smith
Tehani
Robert Tinkler
John Williams
Edward Young

Pitcairn's Island–E.J.H.
Fletcher Christian
Maimiti
William McCoy
Minarii
Matthew Quintal
Alexander Smith
John Williams
Edward Young

Frank Norris
Blix–J.R.M.

Travis Bessemer
Captain Jack
Condé Rivers

A Man's Woman–J.R.M.
Adler
Dr. Adler
Ward Bennett
Richard Ferriss
Lloyd Searight

McTeague–J.R.M.
Miss Baker
Cribbens
Old Grannis
Maria Miranda Macapa
Trina Sieppe McTeague
McTeague
Marcus Schouler
August Sieppe
Zerkow

Moran of the Lady Letty–J.R.M.
Josie Herrick
Captain Hodgson
Captain Alvinza Kitchell
Moran Sternersen
Ross Wilbur

The Octopus–J.R.M.
Annixter
S. Behrman
Caraher
Mr. Cedarquist
Mrs. Cedarquist
Delaney
Annie Derrick
Harran Derrick
Lyman Derrick
Magnus Derrick
Dyke
Genslinger
Minna Hooven
Mrs. Hooven
Osterman
Presley
Father Sarria
Vanamee

The Pit–J.R.M.
Sheldon Corthell
Landry Court
Carrie Cressler
Charles Cressler
Page Dearborn
Samuel Gretry
Curtis Jadwin
Laura Dearborn Jadwin
Emily Wessels

Vandover and the Brute–J.R.M.
Flossie
Charlie Geary
Dolliver Haight

Turner Ravis
Vandover
Ida Wade

Tim O'Brien
Going after Cacciato–M.W.R.
Paul Berlin
Cacciato
Corson
Stink Harris
Li Van Hgoc
Oscar Johnson
Sidney Martin
Doc Peret
Fahyi Rhallon
Sarkin Aung Wan

Flannery O'Connor
The Violent Bear It Away–L.S.
Bernice Bishop
Lucette Carmody
Mr. Meeks
Buford Munson
Bishop Rayber
Mr. Rayber
Francis Marion Tarwater
Mason Tarwater

Wise Blood–L.S.
Enoch Emery
Mrs. Flood
Asa Hawks
Sabbath Lily Hawks
Mrs. Wally Bee Hitchcock
Solace Layfield
Hazel Motes
Hoover Shoats
Mrs. Leora Watts

John O'Hara
A Rage to Live–T.R.S.
Roger Bannon
Brock Caldwell
Julian McHenry English
Catherine Grenville
John Hollister
Charlie Jay
Betty Martindale
Paul Reichelderfer
Connie Schoffstal
Grace Brock Caldwell Tate
Sidney Tate

Appointment in Samarra–T.R.S.
Ed Charney
Caroline Walker English
Julian McHenry English
William Dilworth English
Luther Leroy Fliegler
Al Grecco
Helene Holman
Harry Reilly
Mrs. Waldo Wallace Walker

Butterfield 8–A.I.B.
Major Boam
Eddie Brunner
Norma Day
Emily Liggett
Weston Liggett
Jimmy Malloy
Joab Ellery Reddington
William Robespierre Vandamm
Gloria Wandrous
Mrs. Wandrous

From the Terrace–T.R.S.
Martha Johnson Eaton
Mary St. John Eaton
Natalie Benziger Eaton
Raymond Alfred Eaton
Roland Eaton
Samuel Eaton
James Duncan MacHardie
Alexander Thornton Porter
Jack Tom Smith
Frederick Thornton

The Lockwood Concern–T.R.S.
Preston Hibbard
Morris Homestead
Abraham Lockwood
Adelaide Hoffner Lockwood
Agnes Wynne Lockwood
Ernestine Lockwood
George Bingham Lockwood I
George Bingham Lockwood, Jr.
Geraldine Lockwood
Moses Lockwood
Penrose Lockwood
Wilma Lockwood
George Bingham Lockwood
Arthur McHenry
Marian Strademyer

Ten North Frederick–T.R.S.
Charley Bongiorno
Ann Chapin
Benjamin Chapin
Charlotte Hofman Chapin
Edith Stokes Chapin
Joseph Benjamin Chapin I
Joseph Benjamin Chapin, Jr.
Kate Drummond
William Dilworth English
Harry Jackson
Arthur McHenry
Mike Slattery
Peg Slattery

Joyce Carol Oates
The Assassins–G.J.
Andrew D. Petrie
Hugh Petrie
Stephen Petrie
Yvonne Radek Petrie

Childwold–G.J.

Arlene Bartlett
Evangeline Ann Bartlett
Vale Bartlett
Fitz John Kasch

Cybele–G.J.
Risa Allen
Cathleen Diehl
Lobo
Cynthia Locke
Edwin Locke

Do with Me What You Will–G.J.
Meredith Dawe
Elena Ross Howe
Marvin Howe
Jack Morrissey
Ardis Ross
Leo Ross

Expensive People–G.J.
Elwood Everett
Natashya Romanov Everett
Richard Everett

A Garden of Earthly Delights–G.J.
Lowry
Clara Walpole Revere
Clurt Revere
Steven Revere
Carleton Walpole

Son of the Morning–G.J.
Esther Leonie Beloff
Reverend Marian Miles Beloff
William Japheth Sproul III
Ashton Vickery
Elsa Vickery
Nathanael William Vickery
Opal Sayer Vickery
Thaddeus Aaron Vickery

them–G.J.
Patrick Furlong
Bernard Geffen
Nadine Greene
Mort Piercy
Jim Randolph
Howard Wendall
Jules Wendall
Loretta Botsford Wendall
Mama Wendall
Maureen Wendall

Unholy Loves–G.J.
Alexis Kessler
Albert St. Dennis
Brigit Stott

With Shuddering Fall–G.J.
Karen Herz
Mr. Herz
Max
Sherton

Wonderland–G.J.
Dr. Benjamin Cady
Reva Denk
Jesse Harte
Dr. Talbot Waller Monk
Friedrich Pedersen
Hilda Pedersen
Dr. Karl Pedersen
Mary Pedersen
Dr. Roderick Perrault
Helene Cady Vogel
Shelley Vogel

Tillie Olsen
Yonnondio–M.K.G.
Elias Caldwell
Anna Holbrook
Jim Holbrook
Mazie Holbrook

Cynthia Ozick
Trust–M.K.G.
Stefanie Pettigrew
Gustave Nicholas Tilbeck
Miss Tilbeck
Allegra Vand
Enoch Vand
William

James Kirke Paulding
The Dutchman's Fireside–G.M.C.
Mr. Aubineau
Mrs. Aubineau
Colonel Barry Fitzgerald Macartney Gilfillan
Sir William Johnson
Dame Nauntje
Paskingoe
Hans Pipe
Sakia
Dominie Stettinius
Colonel Sydenham
Sir Thicknesse Throgmorton
Tjerck
Ariel Vancour
Catalina Vancour
Colonel Egbert Vancour
Dennis Vancour
Madame Vancour
Baltus Van Slingerland
Timothy Weasel
Sybrandt Westbrook

Koningsmarke–G.M.C.
Aonetti
Master Lazarus Birchem
Bombie of the Frizzled Head
Sir Robert Carre
Dan Cupid
Lob Dotterel
Restore Gosling
Dominie Kanttwell
Koningsmarke
Wolfgang Langfanger
Colonel Richard Lovelace

Mimi
Shadrach Moneypenny
Night Shadow
Mackate Ockola
Master Oldale
Ollentangi
Fospe and Terese Ontstout
Othman Pfegel
Christina Piper
Edith Piper
Heer Peter Piper
Rolling Thunder
Wolvert Spangler
Dame Swaschbuckler
Master Gottlieb Swaschbuckler
Claas Tomeson
Ludwig Varlett

Westward Ho!–G.M.C.
Mr. Barham
Black Warrior
Ambrose Bushfield
Cornelia Dangerfield
Colonel Cuthbert Dangerfield
Leonard Dangerfield
Virginia Dangerfield
Samuel Hugg
Father Jacques
Ulysses Littlejohn
Mr. Mactabb
Judith Paddock
Zeno Paddock
Old Mammy Phillis
Pompey Ducklegs
Pompey the Little
Dudley Rainsford
Rev. Lazarus Snortgrace
Cherub Spooney
Zephi Teal

Walker Percy
Lancelot–G.M.C.
Anna
Elgin Buell
Troy Dana
Janos Jacoby
John Northumberland
Lancelot Andrewes Lamar
Lily Lamar
Lucy Lamar
Lucy Cobb Lamar
Mary Margaret Reilly Lamar
Maury Lamar
Robert Merlin
Raine Robinette

The Last Gentleman–G.M.C.
Forney Aiken
Ed Barrett
Wilston Bibb Barrett
Father Boomer
Gamow
Mort Prince
Chandler Vaught

Jamison MacKenzie Vaught
Katherine Gibbs Vaught
Mrs. Vaught
Rita Vaught
Sutter Vaught
Valentine Vaught

Love in the Ruins–G.M.C.
Buddy Brown
Alistair Fuchs-Forbes
Max Gottlieb
Hester
Art Immelmann
Ives
Doris More
Samantha More
Thomas More, Jr.
Ellen Oglethorpe
Lola Rhoades
Moira Schaffner
Father Rinaldo Smith
Uru

The Moviegoer–G.M.C.
Dr. Bolling
John Bickerson Bolling
Emily Bolling Cutrer
Jules Cutrer
Kate Cutrer
Harold Graebner
Sharon Kincaid
Eddie Lovell
Nell Lovell
Anna Castagne Bolling Smith
Lonnie Smith
Walter Wade
Sam Yerger

Julia Peterkin
Scarlet Sister Mary–H.M.B.
Andrew
Budda Ben
Cinder
Daddy Cudjoe
Doll
Maum Hannah
July Pinesett
June Pinesett
Mary Pinesett
Seraphine Pinesett
Unexpected Pinesett

Ann Petry
The Street–E.B.B.
Granny
Mrs. Hedges
Bub Johnson
Jim Johnson
Lutie Johnson
William Jones
Mr. Junto
Min
Pop
Boots Smith

David Graham Phillips
Susan Lenox–J.R.B.
 Etta Brashear
 Robert Brent
 Robert Burlingham
 Jeb Ferguson
 Susan Lenox
 Freddie Palmer
 Roderick Spenser
 Ruth Warham

Marge Piercy
Dance the Eagle to Sleep–K.B.A.
 Billy Batson
 Corey
 Ginny
 Joanna
 Marcus
 Shawn

Small Changes–K.B.A.
 Dorine
 Douglas MacArthur Jackson
 Phil
 Wanda Rosario
 Sally
 Miriam Berg Stone
 Neil Stone
 Elizabeth Ann Walker
 James Hayes Walker

The High Cost of Living–K.B.A.
 Bernard Guizot
 Leslie McGivers
 Valerie Mendoza
 Camille Rogers
 Honor Rogers
 Mrs. Rogers
 George Sanderson

Josephine Pinckney
Three O'Clock Dinner–S.Ba.
 Lorena Hessenwinkle
 Harry O'Dell
 Fenwick Redcliff
 Judith Redcliff
 Lucian Quintillian Redcliff
 Tat Redcliff

David Plante
The Family–J.R.B.
 Albert B. Francoeur
 André J. Francoeur
 Aricie Melanie Atalie Lajoie Francoeur
 Arsace Louis Pylade Francoeur
 Daniel R. Francoeur
 Edmond R. Francoeur
 Julien E. Francoeur
 Philip P. Francoeur
 Richard A. Francoeur

Sylvia Plath
The Bell Jar–L.K.B.
 Betsy

 Constantin
 Dodo Conway
 Doreen
 Joan Gilling
 Doctor Gordon
 Esther Greenwood
 Mrs. Greenwood
 Philomena Guinea
 Hilda
 Irwin
 Jay Cee
 Marco
 Doctor Nolan
 Lenny Shepherd
 Valerie
 Buddy Willard
 Mr. Willard
 Mrs. Willard

Edgar Allan Poe
The Narrative of Arthur Gordon Pym–J.M.B.
 Augustus Barnard
 Mr. Barnard
 Captain Guy
 Nu-Nu
 Richard Parker
 Dirk Peters
 Arthur Gordon Pym
 Seymour
 Too-wit

Carlene Hatcher Polite
The Flagellants–H.W.S.
 Black Cat
 Mr. Coffee
 Mrs. Fitzpatrick
 Frog
 Ideal
 Inez
 Jimson
 Johnny Lowell
 Luis Pagan
 Red John
 Rheba
 Booker Shad
 Beata Thangbee

Sister X and the Victims of Foul Play–H.W.S.
 Abyssinia
 Belfast X
 Lila Chand Bibi
 Black Will
 Glynda, Girl of the Glen
 Hubby
 Señorita Vastie Oubaleta
 Arista Prolo
 Baby Lazar Scruggs
 Kalik Shabazz

Katherine Anne Porter
The Leaning Tower–D.J.C.
 Otto Bussen
 Hans von Gehring
 Hillentafel

 Kuno Hillentafel
 Lutte
 Tadeusz Mey
 Rosa Reichl
 Charles Upton

Noon Wine–P.A.Z.
 Burleigh
 Homer T. Hatch
 Olaf Eric Helton
 Arthur and Herbert Thompson
 Ellen Bridgés Thompson
 Royal Earle Thompson

Old Mortality–P.A.Z.
 Amy
 Gabriel Breaux
 Harry
 Miss Honey
 Keziah
 Maria
 Eva Parrington

Pale Horse, Pale Rider–P.A.Z.
 Adam
 Bill
 Danny Dickerson
 Hildesheim
 Miss Hobbe
 Miranda
 Chuck Rouncivale
 Cornelia Tanner
 Mary Townsend

Ship of Fools–P.A.Z.
 Karl Baumgartner
 Jenny Brown
 La Condesa
 William Denny
 Echegaray
 Wilhelm Freytag
 Karl Glocken
 Wilibald Graf
 Arne Hansen
 Hutten
 Käthe Hutten
 Johann
 Julius Lowenthal
 Heinrich Lutz
 Ric
 Siegfried Rieber
 Frau Rittersdorf
 Frau Otto Schmitt
 Schumann
 David Scott
 Lizzi Spöckenkieker
 Thiele
 Mary Treadwell

Charles Portis
True Grit–G.G.
 Tom Chaney
 Reuben Cogburn
 Daggett

Mrs. Floyd
Moon Garrett
LaBoeuf
Ned Pepper
Farrell Permalee
Harold Permalee
Emmett Quincy
Frank Ross
Mattie Ross

Chaim Potok
The Chosen–E.J.H.
  Davey Cantor
  Rav Gershenson
  David Malter
  Reuven Malter
  Manya
  Danny Saunders
  Reb Isaac Saunders
  Levi Saunders

In the Beginning–E.J.H.
  Miriam Bader
  Shmuel Bader
  Mrs. Horowitz
  Eddie Kulanski
  Alex Lurie
  David Lurie
  Max Lurie
  Meyer Lurie
  Ruth Lurie
  Sarah Lurie
  Tony Savanola
  Dr. Weidman

My Name Is Asher Lev–E.J.H.
  Rav Yosef Cutler
  Jacob Kahn
  Tanya Kahn
  Reb Yudel Krinsky
  Aryeh Lev
  Asher Lev
  Rivkeh Lev
  Yitzchok Lev
  Mrs. Rackover
  The Rebbe
  Anna Schaeffer

The Promise–E.J.H.
  Rav Gershenson
  Abraham Gordon
  Joseph Gordon
  Michael Gordon
  Rachel Gordon
  Sarah Gordon
  Rav Jacob Kalman
  David Malter
  Reuven Malter
  Manya
  Danny Saunders
  Reb Isaac Saunders
  Levi Saunders

J. F. Powers
Morte D'Urban–J.Ca.
  Wilfrid Bestudik
  Billy Cosgrove
  Sally Thwaites Hopwood
  John Kelleher
  Harold Peters
  Red Renton
  Harvey Roche
  Mrs. Andrew Thwaites

Reynolds Price
A Generous Man–E.B.L.
  Della Brame
  Yancey Breedlove
  Puss Ellis
  Dr. Joel Fuller
  Macey Gupton
  Marise Gupton
  Jake Hasty
  Baby Lou Mustian
  Horatio Mustian, Jr.
  Jasper Mustian
  Milo Mustian
  Pauline Mustian
  Rosacoke Mustian
  Sissie Abbott Mustian
  Kate Pomeroy
  Rob Pomeroy
  Lois Provo
  Selma Provo
  Buck Russell
  Hawkins Ryden
  Miss Jack Ryden
  Tommy Ryden

A Long and Happy Life–E.B.L.
  Landon Allgood
  Isaac Alston
  Marina Alston
  Willie Duke Aycock
  Wesley Beavers
  Estel
  Arnold Guptonle
  Frederick Gupton
  Macey Gupton
  Marise Gupton
  Manson Hargrove
  Mae
  Baby Lou Mustian
  Horatio Mustian, Jr.
  Jasper Mustian
  Milo Mustian
  Pauline Mustian
  Rosacoke Mustian
  Sissy Abbott Mustian
  Miss Pauline
  Sammy Ransom
  Sledge
  Mary Sutton
  Mildred Sutton
  Bessie Williams

Love and Work–E.B.L.
  Alix

Bo Browder
Cal
Jane Eborn
Jim Eborn
Louise Attwater Eborn
Thomas Eborn
Todd Eborn
Norman Gaul
Sybil Hedden
Ida Nolan
Albert Riddell
Ruby
Ted

The Surface of Earth–E.B.L.
  Thorne Bradley
  Margaret Jane Drewry
  Elvira Jane
  Veenie Goodwin
  Walter S. Grainger
  Rachel Hutchins
  Raven Hutchins
  Bedford Kendal
  Charlotte Watson Kendal
  Eva Kendal
  Kennerly Kendal
  Rena Kendal
  Mag
  Alice Matthews
  Anna Goodwin Mayfield
  Forrest Mayfield
  Hattie Mayfield
  Aunt Mannie Mayfield
  Raven Hutchins Mayfield
  Robinson Mayfield
  Bankey Patterson
  Undine Phillips
  Gid Shorter
  Hatt Shorter
  Whitby Shorter
  Della Simmons
  Sylvie
  Min Tharrington
  Rover Walters
  Katherine Epps Watson
  Thad Watson

James Purdy
Malcolm–D.Sh.
  Estel Blanc
  Eloisa Brace
  Jerome Brace
  Mr. Cox
  Girard Girard
  Madame Girard
  Gus
  George Leeds
  Malcolm
  Melba
  O'Reilly Morgan
  Kermit Raphaelson
  Laurel Raphaelson
  Professor Robinolte
  Madame Rosita

Mario Puzo
The Godfather—L.I.
Kay Adams
Luca Brasi
Peter Clemenza
Constanzia Corleone
Michael Corleone
Santino Corleone
Vito Corleone
Johnny Fontane
Thomas Hagen
Mark McCluskey
Carlo Rizzi
Virgil Sollozzo
Phillip Tattaglia
Tessio
Apollonia Vitelli

Thomas Pynchon
The Crying of Lot 49—E.B.S. & D.M.B.
Emory Bortz
Clayton Chiclitz
Genghis Cohen
Randolph Driblette
Mike Fallopian
Dr. Hilarius
Pierce Inverarity
Stanley Koteks
Oedipa Maas
Wendell Maas
Metzger
John Nefastis
Richard Wharfinger

Gravity's Rainbow—E.B.S & D.M.B.
Pig Bodine
Seaman Bodine
Katje Borgesius
Emil Bummer
Clayton Chiclitz
Oberst Enzian
Margherita Erdmann
Gerhardt von Göll
Gottfried
Professor Doctor Laszlo Jamf
Major Duane Marvy
Roger Mexico
Kurt Mondaugen
Edward W. A. Pointsman
Franz Pökler
Captain Geoffrey Prentice
Brigadier Ernest Pudding
Lieutenant Tyrone Slothrop
Jessica Swanlake
Vaslav Tchitcherine
Geli Tripping
Lieutenant Weissmann

V—E.B.S. & D.M.B.
Pig Bodine
Seaman Bodine
Clayton Chiclitz
Dudley Eigenvalue, D.D.S.
Father Fairing

Foppl
Evan Godolphin
Hugh Godolphin
Esther Harvitz
Mélanie L'Heuremaudit
Fausto Maijstral
Paola Maijstral
Signor Rafael Mantissa
Josephine Mendoza
Kurt Mondaugen
Rachel Owlglass
Benny Profane
Slab
McClintic Sphere
Herbert Stencil
Sidney Stencil
V
Lieutenant Weissmann
The Whole Sick Crew
Mafia Winsome

Ayn Rand
Atlas Shrugged—G.B.M.
Francisco Domingo Carlos Anconia
Orren Boyle
Ragnar Danneskjold
Floyd Ferris
John Galt
Wesley Mouch
Henry Rearden
Lillian Rearden
Robert Stadler
Dagny Taggart
James Taggart
Eddie Willers
Ellis Wyatt

The Fountainhead—G.B.M.
Henry Cameron
Lois Cook
Sean Xavier Donnigan
Dominique Francon
Catherine Halsey
Peter Keating
Steven Mallory
Howard Roark
Hopton Stoddard
Ellsworth Monkton Toohey
Gail Wynand

Marjorie Kinnan Rawlings
The Yearling—M.K.G.
Ezra Ezekial Baxter
Jody Baxter
Ory Baxter
Flag
Buck Forrester
Fodder-wing Forrester
Lem Forrester
Grandma Hutto
Oliver Hutto
Twink Weatherby

John Rechy

City of Night—E.S.N.
Miss Ange
Miss Destiny
Ed King
Lance O'Hara

Numbers—E.S.N.
Tony Lewis
Sebastian Michaels
Johnny Rio
Emory Travis
Guy Young

Ishmael Reed
The Free-Lance Pallbearers—P.N.
Cipher X
Bukka Doopeyduk
Fannie Mae
M/Neighbor
Rev. Eclair Porkchop
Elijah Raven
HARRY SAM
U2 Polyglot
Judge Whimplewopper

The Last Days of Louisianna Red—P.N.
Amos
Big Sally
Andy Brown
Chorus
Max Kasavubu
Nanny Lisa
George Kingfish Stevens
Ed Yellings
Minnie Yellings
Street Yellings
Wolf Yellings

Mumbo Jumbo—P.N.
Berbelang
Black Herman
Charlotte
Abdul Hamid
Woodrow Wilson Jefferson
PaPa LaBas
Biff Musclewhite
Hinckle Von Vampton
Thor Wintergreen

Yellow Back Radio Broke-Down—P.N.
Drag Gibson
John Wesley Hardin
Innocent
Zozo Labrique
Loop Garoo Kid
Skinny McCullough
Mustache Sal
Bo Shmo
Chief Showcase

Anne Rice
Interview with the Vampire—G.G.
Armand
Claudia

Babette Freniere
Lestat
Louis
Madeleine

Conrad Richter
The Fields–P.A.D.
Mistress Bartram
Achsa Luckett
Genny Luckett
Sayward Luckett
Wyitt Luckett
Louie Scurrah
Jake Tench
Rosa Tench
Guerdon Wheeler
Portius Wheeler
Resolve Wheeler

The Sea of Grass–P.A.D.
Black Hetty
Brock Brewton
Harry Brewton
Colonel James B. Brewton
Lutie Cameron Brewton
Brice Chamberlain

The Town–P.A.D.
Mistress Bartram
Genny Luckett
Sayward Luckett
Sulie Luckett
Worth Luckett
Wyitt Luckett
Jake Tench
Rosa Tench
Chancey Wheeler
Guerdon Wheeler
Portius Wheeler
Resolve Wheeler

The Trees–P.A.D.
Achsa Luckett
Genny Luckett
Jary Luckett
Sayward Luckett
Sulie Luckett
Worth Luckett
Wyitt Luckett
Louie Scurrah
Jake Tench
Portius Wheeler

Mary Roberts Rinehart
The Circular Staircase–J.K.
Liddy Allen
Arnold Armstrong
Fanny B. Armstrong
Louise Armstrong
Paul Armstrong
John Bailey
Nina Carrington
Lucy Haswell
Gertrude Innes

Halsey B. Innes
Rachel Innes
Jamieson
Riggs
Thomas
Frank Walker
Lucien Wallace
Anne Watson

Harold Robbins
The Carpetbaggers–D.L.T.L.
Jonas Cord, Sr.
Jennie Denton
Jo-Ann
Geraldine Marlowe
Harrison Marlowe
Rina Marlowe
Ronald Marlowe
Robair
Bernard B. Norman
Nevada Smith
Amos Winthrop
Monica Winthrop
David Woolf

Tom Robbins
Another Roadside Attraction–F.W.B.
Baby Thor
The Corpse
Father Gutstadt
Marx Marvelous
Mon Cul
Nearly Normal Jimmy
L. Westminster Purcell III
Amanda Ziller
John Paul Ziller

Even Cowgirls Get the Blues–F.W.B.
Chink
Countess
Delores del Ruby
Dr. Felix Dreyfus
Julian Gitche
Sissy Hankshaw Gitche
Bonanza Jellybean Dr. Robbins
Madame Zoe

Elizabeth Madox Roberts
The Great Meadow–
Daniel Boone
Betty Hall
Polly Brook Hall
Thomas Hall
Berk Jarvis
Diony Hall Jarvis
Elvira Jarvis
Evan Muir

The Time of Man–
Amanda Cain
Ellen Chesser
Henry Chesser
Nellie Chesser
Judge James Bartholomew Gowan

Chick Kent
Jasper Kent
Cassie Beal MacMurtrie
Scott MacMurtrie
Jonas W. Prather
Joe Trent
Tessie West
Luke Wimble

Kenneth Roberts
Arundel–E.D.F.
Benedict Arnold
Saved from Captivity Huff
Jacataqua
Mary Mallinson
Phoebe Marvin
Steven Nason
Natanis
Henri Guerlac de Sabrevois
John Treeworgy

Northwest Passage–E.D.F.
Captain Jonathan Carver
Sir William Johnson
Princess McNott
Sergeant Rob't McNott
Ann Potter
Nathaniel Potter
Elizabeth Browne Rogers
Major Robert Rogers
Langdon Towne

Anne Richardson Roiphe
Up the Sandbox!–J.S.
Dr. Beineke
Fidel Castro
Dora Grossbart
John
Dr. Maria Lopez
Elizabeth Reynolds
Margaret Ferguson Reynolds
Paul Reynolds
Peter Reynolds

Judith Rossner
Looking for Mr. Goodbar–C.S.R.
Ali
Katherine Dunn
Theresa Dunn
Thomas Dunn
Martin Engle
Brooks Hendell
Brigid Dunn Kelly
Tony Lopanto
James Morrisey
Gary Cooper White

Henry Roth
Call It Sleep–D.J.C.
Leo Dugovka
Luter
Reb Yidel Pankower
Albert Schearl
David Schearl

Genya Schearl
Bertha Sternowitz

Philip Roth
The Breast–G.G.
David Alan Kepesh
Dr. Klinger
Claire Ovington

The Ghost Writer–G.G.
Amy Bellette
Emanuel Isidore Lonoff
Hope Lonoff
Nathan Zuckerman

Goodbye, Columbus–J.G.H.
Harriet Ehrlich
Luther Ferrari
Aunt Gladys
Neil Klugman
Ben Patimkin
Brenda Patimkin
Julie Patimkin
Leo A. Patimkin
Ronald Patimkin

The Great American Novel–G.G.
Roland Agni
Ulysses S. Fairsmith
Gilbert Gamesh
Luke Gofannon
Michael Masterson
General Douglas D. Oakhart
Word Smith
Angela Whittling Trust
Robert Yamm

Letting Go–J.C.M.
Theresa Bigoness
Asher Buckner
Elizabeth DeWitt Herz
Paul Herz
Sid Jaffe
Martha Reganhart
Fay Silberman
Gabriel Wallach

Our Gang–J.G.H.
John F. Charisma
Billy Cupcake
Trick E. Dixon
Charles Curtis Flood
Lyin' B. Johnson
Erect Severehead
Mr. What's-his-name

Portnoy's Complaint–J.S.L.
Kay Campbell
Alice Dembosky
Hannah Portnoy Feibish
Sarah Abbott Maulsby
Alexander Portnoy
Harold Portnoy
Jack Portnoy

Sophie Ginsky Portnoy
Mary Jane Reed
Dr. O. Spielvogel

When She Was Good–J.C.M.
Lucy Nelson Bassart
Roy Bassart
Willard Carroll
Blanshard Muller
Duane Nelson
Myra Carroll Nelson
Eleanor Sowerby
Julian Sowerby

Susanna Rowson
Charlotte–W.H.C.
Emily Crayton Beauchamp
Belcour
Colonel Crayton
Mr. Eldridge
Julia Franklin
Mademoiselle La Rue
Jack Montraville
Charlotte Temple
Henry Temple
Lucy Eldridge Temple

O. E. Rölvaag
Giants in the Earth–D.D.Q.
Beret Holm Hansa
Per Hansa
Anna Marie Holm
Ole Haldor Holm
Peder Victorious Holm
Store-Hans Holm
Hans Olsa
Sörine Olsa
Henry Solum
Sam Solum
Kjersti Tönseten
Syvert Tönseten

Peder Victorious–D.D.Q.
Gjermund Dahl
Charles Doheny
Susie Doheny
Reverend Gabrielsen
Ted Gilbert
Beret Holm Hansa
Anna Marie Holm
Henry Percival Holm
Ole Haldor Holm
Peder Victorious Holm
Store-Hans Holm
Andrew Holte
Clarabelle Mahon
Sörine Olsa
Henry Solum
Sam Solum
Tambur-Ola
Kjersti Tönseten
Syvert Tönseten

Their Father's God–D.D.Q.

Gjermund Dahl
Charles Doheny
Susie Doheny
Beret Holm Hansa
Anna Marie Holm
Peder Victorious Holm
Store-Hans Holm
Andrew Holte
Nikoline Johansen
Sörine Olsa
Tambur-Ola
Kjersti Tönseten
Syvert Tönseten
Father Williams

J. D. Salinger
The Catcher in the Rye–J.R.S.
Robert Ackley
Mr. Antolini
James Castle
Allie Caulfield
D. B. Caulfield
Holden Caulfield
Phoebe Josephine Caulfield
Jane Gallagher
Sally Hayes
Carl Luce
Mrs. Morrow
Mr. Spencer
Ward Stradlater

Mari Sandoz
Capital City–B.R.
Abigail Allerton
Josina Kugler Black
Carl Halzer
Hallie Rufer Hammond
Asa Bruce Harcoot
Stephani Kolhoff
Burt Parr
Hamm Rufe
Mollie Tyndale
Colmar Welles
Susan Colmar Welles

Miss Morissa–B.R.
Calamity Jane
Edward Elton Ellis
Morissa Kirk
Tris Polk
Jack Thomas
Robin Thomas

Slogum House–B.R.
René Dumur
Butch Haber
Leo Platt
Annette and Cellie Slogum
Cash Slogum
Fannie Slogum
Haber Slogum
Libby Slogum
Regula Haber Slogum
Ruedy Slogum

Ward Slogum

The Tom-Walker–B.R.
Senator Boyd Potter
Hazel Stone
Hiram Stone
Lucinda Martin Stone
Martin Stone
Milton Stone I
Milton Stone II
Penny Turner Stone
Sarah Stone

George Santayana
The Last Puritan–S.E.O.
Harriet Bumstead Alden
Nathaniel Alden
Oliver Alden
Peter Alden
Dr. Bumstead
Austin Darnley
James Darnley
Rose Darnley
Letitia Lamb
Caroline Van de Weyer
Edith Van de Weyer
Mario Van de Weyer
Caleb Wetherbee

Helen Hooven Santmyer
Herbs and Apples–J.M.O.
Jack Devlin
Frances Higginson
Alice McIntyre
Sue
Derrick Thornton
Dr. Dick Thornton
Reneltje Thornton
Edith Townsend
Madeleine Van Leyden

William Saroyan
The Human Comedy–E.H.F.
Mr. Byfield
Lionel Cabot
Tobey Goerge
August Gottlieb
William Grogan
Miss Hicks
Homer Macauley
Marcus Macauley
Ulysses Macauley
Rosalie Simms-Peabody
Thomas Spangler

Budd Schulberg
The Disenchanted–J.M.B.
Professor Connolly
Professor Crofts
Douglas Halliday
Manley Halliday
Al Harper
Ann Loeb
Victor Milgrim

Hank Osborne
Shep Stearns
Jere Wilder-Halliday

What Makes Sammy Run?–J.M.B.
Julian Blumberg
Sheik Dugan
Sidney Fineman
Sammy Glick
Israel Glickstein
Rosalie Goldbaum
Harrington
Laurette Harrington
Al Manheim
Billie Rand
Larry Ross
Rita Royce
Kit Sargent

George S. Schuyler
Black No More–N.R.J.
Dr. Shakespeare Agamemnon Beard
Madame Sisseretta Blandish
Bunny Brown
Dr. Samuel Buggerie
Dr. Junius Crookman
Max Disher
Helen Givens Fisher
Reverend Henry Givens
Rev. Alex McPhule

Catharine Maria Sedgwick
Hope Leslie–E.H.F.
Everell Fletcher
William Fletcher
Sir Philip Gardiner
Faith Leslie
Hope Leslie
Magawisca
Mononotto
Nelema
Oneco
Rosa

Hubert Selby, Jr.
Last Exit to Brooklyn–W.H.C.
Harry Black
George Hanson
Mike Kelly
Regina
Sal
Trahlala
Vincent

Mary Lee Settle
Know Nothing–C.A.M.
Stuart Brandon
Lawyer Carver
Maury Carver
Preston Carver
Johnny Catlett
Leah Cutwright Catlett
Lewis Catlett
Mamie Brandon Catlett

Peregrine Lacey Catlett
Rebecca Catlett
Sara Lacey Catlett
Cuffee
Jim
Brandon Kregg
Crawford Kregg
Dr. Noah Kregg
Lacey Kregg
Melinda Lacey Kregg
Brandon Lacey
Peregrine Lacey
Sally Crawford Lacey
Loady
Maria
Reverend Charles McAndrews
Gideon McKarkle
Jeb McKarkle
Mr. McKarkle
Minna
Napoleon
Dan Neill
James Peregrine Neill
Lydia Catlett Neill
Annie Brandon O'Neill
Big Dan O'Neill
Molly O'Neill
Teeny O'Neill
Wellington Smythe
Cornelius Stuart
Lancelot Stuart
Telemachus
Tig
Toey

O Beulah Land–C.A.M.
Baucis
Backwater Brandon
Ralph Burton
Mother Carver
Ezekiel Catlett
Hannah Bridewell Catlett
Jeremiah Catlett
Rebecca Catlett
Ensign Peregrine Cockburn
Mister Corey
Brandon Crawford
Doggo Cutwright
Jacob Cutwright
Maggie Cutwright
Christopher Gist
Colonel Halkett
Azariah Keel
Moses Kregg
Sanhedron Kregg
Jonathan Lacey
Montague Crawford Bacchus Lacey
Peregrine Lacey
Sally Sawyer Lacey
Spotteswood Lewis
Joe Little Fox
Lydia
Mrs. Stacy McAndrews Mason
Ben McKarkle

Solomon McKarkle
Tad McKarkle
Herr Mittelburger
Mary Martha O'Keefe
Captain Robert Orme
Jarcey Pentacost
Philemon
Tom Preston
Squire Raglan
Taylor Sawyer
Shirley
Jamie Stuart
Ted
Witcikti

Prisons–C.A.M.
  Baxter
  John Cantloe
  Charity
  Corporal Jonathan Church
  Oliver Cromwell
  Cornet Henry Denne
  William Dogood
  Sir Thomas Fairfax
  Nell Lacy
  Peregrine Lacy
  Sir Valentine Lacy
  Lazarus
  Robbie Lokyar
  Gideon MacKarkle
  Laodocious Martin
  William Panck
  Will Pentacost
  Thankful Perkins
  Colonel Rainsborough
  John Roper
  Simeon Roper
  Francis White

Michael Shaara
  The Killer Angels–W.W.R.
  Lewis Armistead
  John Buford
  Joshua Lawrence Chamberlain
  Richard Ewell
  Arthur Lyon Fremantle
  Richard Brooke Garnett
  Winfield Scott Hancock
  Ambrose Powell Hill
  Robert Edward Lee
  James Longstreet
  George Gordon Meade
  George Pickett
  John Reynolds
  J. E. B. Stuart

Irwin Shaw
  The Young Lions–W.W.R.
  Noah Ackerman
  Johnny Burnecker
  Christian Diestl
  Gretchen Hardenburg
  Lieutenant Hardenburg
  Hope Plowman

Laura Whitacre
Michael Whitacre

Charles M. Sheldon
  In His Steps–C.L.
  Rev. Calvin Bruce
  Jasper Chase
  President Donald Marsh
  Henry Maxwell
  Edward Norman
  Rollin Page
  Virginia Page
  Alexander Powers
  Felicia Sterling
  Rachel Winslow

Ann Allen Shockley
  Loving Her–H.R.H.
  Terrence Bluvard
  Fran Brown
  Denise Davis
  Jerome Lee Davis
  Renay Davis
  Jean Gail
  Mr. Herald
  Vance Kenton
  Phil Millard
  Pearl Sims
  Edith Stilling

Herbert Simmons
  Corner Boy–A.H.
  Jake Adams
  Old Man Adams
  Armenta Arnez
  Edna Arnez
  Henry Arnez
  Booker
  Georgia Garveli
  Pop Garveli
  Maxine Goldstein
  Evelyn Keyes
  Lobo
  Monk
  Red
  Scar
  Spider
  Kenny Watson

  Man Walking on Eggshells–A.H.
  Argustus Anderson
  Wilbur Anderson
  Banny Douglas
  Helen Douglas
  Hosea Douglas
  Mae Douglas
  Raymond Charles Douglas
  Carl Logan
  Codene McClusky
  Bruce Thomas

William Gilmore Simms
  The Partisan–H.H.
  Moll Blonay

Ned Blonay
John Davis
Frampton
Lancelot Frampton
Captain Amos Gaskens
General Horatio Gates
Walter Griffin
Sergeant Hastings
Bella Humphries
Richard Humphries
William Humphries
General Johann De Kalb
Francis Marion
Dr. Oakenburg
Liuetenant Porgy
Major Proctor
Emily Singleton
Major Robert Singleton
Katharine Walton
Colonel Richard Walton

Woodcraft–T.L.J.
  Mrs. Eveleigh
  Lancelot Frampton
  Mrs. Griffin
  Sergeant Millhouse
  M'Kewn
  Lieutenant Porgy
  Tom

Upton Sinclair
  Boston–M.H.L.
  Elizabeth Thornwell Alvin
  Governor Alvin Tufts Fuller
  Nicola Sacco
  Cornelia Thornwell
  Bartolomeo Vanzetti
  Thayer Webster

  Dragon's Teeth–G.G.
  Irma Barnes Budd
  Lanning Prescott Budd
  Mabel Budd Detaze Dingle
  Parsifal Dingle
  Hermann Wilhelm Göring
  Adolph Hitler
  Heinrich Jung
  Kurt Meissner
  Freddi Robin
  Johannes Robin
  Madame Zyszynski

  The Jungle–G.G.
  Marija Berczynskas
  Phil Connor
  Jack Duane
  Elzbieta
  Jurgis Rudkus
  Ona Lukoszaite Rudkus
  Nicholas Schliemann

  Oil!–G.G.
  Daniel Webster Irving
  Rachel Menzies

Vernon Roscoe
Alberta Ross
J. Arnold Ross
J. Arnold Ross, Jr.
Ben Skutt
Viola Tracy
Eli Watkins
Paul Watkins

Isaac Bashevis Singer
Enemies, A Love Story–J.S.L.
Shifrah Puah Bloch
Herman Broder
Tamara Luria Broder
Yadwiga Pracz Broder
Rabbi Milton Lampert
Leon Tortshiner
Masha Bloch Tortshiner

The Magician of Lublin–S.M.
Emilia Chrabotzky
Halina Chrabotzky
Herman
Esther Mazur
Yasha Mazur
Rytza Miltz
Bolek Zbarski
Elzbieta Zbarski
Magda Zbarski
Zeftel

Satan in Goray–S.M.
Benish Ashkenazi
Levi Ashkenazi
Eleazar Babad
Rechele Babad
Zeydel Ber
Reb Gedaliya
Granny
Moredecai Joseph
Itche Mates
Sabbatai Zevi

Shosha–S.M.
Bashele
Celia Chentshiner
Haiml Chentshiner
Sam Dreiman
Morris Feitelzohn
Aaron Greidinger
Shosha
Betty Slonim
Dora Stolnitz
Tekla
Zelig
Sabbatai Zevi

The Slave–S.M.
Jan Bzik
Wanda Bzik
Benjamin Eliezer
Jacob Eliezer
Gershon
Zelda Leah

Adam Pilitzky
Theresa Pilitzky
Zagayek
Moishe Zakolkower
Sabbatai Zevi

Betty Smith
Joy in the Morning–H.L.K.
Annie McGairy Brown
Carl Brown
Anthony Byrd
James W. Darwent
Margo Hansmon
Henry
Aggie Lopin
Goldie Lopin
Victor Newcool
Coach Stevens

Maggie-Now–H.L.K.
Claude Bassett
Dennis Patrick Moore
Margaret Rose Moore
Patrick Dennis Moore
Mary Moriarity
Mike Moriarity
Molly Moriarity
Mary O'Crawley
Margaret Rose Shawn
Timothy Shawn
T'ressa Vernacht

Tomorrow Will Be Better–H.L.K.
Salvatore De Muccio
Frances Xavier Malone
Nora Malone
Patrick Malone
Salvatore De Muccio
Irene O'Farron
Maizie O'Farron
Wayne Prentiss
Flo Shannon
Henry Shannon
Margaret Shannon

A Tree Grows in Brooklyn–H.L.K.
Ben Blake
Evy Rommely Flittman
Jim McGarrity
Sergeant Micheal McShane
Annie Laurie Nolan
Cornelius John Nolan
John Nolan
Katherine Rommely Nolan
Mary Frances Katherine Nolan
Leo Rhynor
Mary Rommely
Sissy Rommely

Lee Smith
Something in the Wind–D.C.H.
Bentley T. Hooks
Charles Windham Hughes
Brooke Kincaid

Carolyn Kincaid
Carter Kincaid
T. Royce Kincaid

Lillian Smith
Strange Fruit–R.V.C.
Bess Anderson
Ed Anderson
Ern Anderson
Nonnie Anderson
Tillie Anderson
Crazy Carl
Alma Mathews Deen
Laura Deen
Tracy Deen
Dr. Tutwiler Deen
Dessie
Brother Dunwoodie
Tom Harris
Henry McIntosh
Dr. Sam Perry
Dorothy Pusey
Pug Pusey

Susan Sontag
The Benefactor T.J.S.
Frau Anders
Professor Bulgaraux
Hippolyte
Jean-Jacques
Lucrezia
Maestro
Monique
Father Trissotin

Death Kit–T.J.S.
Jim Allen
Harron Dalton
Paul Harron
Joan Harron
Angelo Incardona
Myra Incardona
Mary
Hester Nayburn
Jessie Nayburn
Wolf-Boy

Ellease Southerland
Let the Lion Eat Straw–M.H.B.
Jackson Gold
Mamma Habblesham
Angela Williams Lavoisier
Arthur Lavoisier
Robes Smith
Abeba Williams Lavoisier Torch
Askia-Touré Torch
Daniel A. Torch
Daniel-Jr. Torch
Kora Torch
C-J Watkins

Terry Southern
Blue Movie–G.G.
Boris Adrian

Arabella
Pamela Dickensen
Feral
C. D. Harrison
Les Harrison
Tina Marie Holt
Morton L. Kanovitz
Cardinal von Kopf
Sidney H. Krassman
Abe Letterman
Nathan Malone
Dave and Debbie Roberts
Raphael Nicholas Sanchez
Tony Sanders
Angela Sterling
Helen Vrobel
Yvette

Candy–G.G.
Candy Christian
Jack Christian
Livia Christian
Sidney Christian
Doctor J. Dunlap
Emmanuel
Grindle
Howard Johns
Professor Mephesto
Irving Semite
Pete Uspy

Flash and Filigree–G.G.
Ralph Edwards
Frederick Eichner
Eddy Fiske
Martin Frost
Beth Jackson
Jean-baby
Howard Lester
Barbara Mintner
Stock Stockton
Eleanor Thorne
Felix Treevly

The Magic Christian–G.G.
Agnes and Esther Edwards
Guy Grand
Ginger Horton

E.D.E.N. Southworth
The Hidden Hand–J.D.
Black Donald
Clara Day
Nancy Grewell
Herbert Greyson
Capitola Le Noir
Craven Le Noir
Gabriel Le Noir
Marah Rocke
Traverse Rocke
Major Ira Warfield

Elizabeth Spencer
The Light in the Piazza–S.Ba.

Clara Johnson
Margaret Johnson
Noel Johnson
Fabrizio Naccarelli
Signor Naccarelli

The Voice at the Back Door–W.H.C.
Beckwith Dozer
Willard Follansbee
Bud Grantham
Duncan Harper
Louise Taylor Harper
Jason Hunt
Marjorie Angeline Hunt
Nan Hunt
Marcia Mae Hunt O'Donnell
Bella Grantham Tallant
Jimmy Tallant
Kerney Woolbright

Scott Spenser
Endless Love–M.M.
Arthur Axelrod
David Axelrod
Rose Axelrod
Ann Butterfield
Hugh Butterfield
Jade Butterfield
Keith Butterfield
Sam Butterfield
Ecrest
Susan Henry
Stu Neihardt
Ingrid Ochester
Barbara Sherwood
Eddie Watanabe

Last Night at the Brain Thieves Ball–M.M.
Acoraci
Leon Anderson
Paul Lloyd Galambos
Miss Mitchell
Popkoff
Ira Robinson
Tom Simon
Carl Stein
Worthington

Preservation Hall–M.M.
Melissa Cavanaugh
Thomas Douglas
Gary Fish
Bob Halpin
Gerald Healey
Earl Morgan
Lillian Belsito Douglas Morgan
Tracy Keating Morgan
Virgil Morgan
Munt
Mario Nicolosi
Kathryn Perl

Jean Stafford
Boston Adventure–M.E.W.W.

Countess Berthe von Happel
Nathan Kadish
Hermann Marburg
Ivan Marburg
Shura Korf Marburg
Sonia Marburg
Hopestill Mather
Harry Morgan
Dr. Philip McAllister
Miss Lucy Pride
Kakosan Yoshida

Mark Steadman
A Lion's Share–J.B.Mob.
George Bogger
Mackey Brood
Jack Curran
Johnny Curran
Mary Cheney Odell Curran
Critchwood Laverne Garfield
J. J. O'Brien
Kathleen Lynch Reilley
Susy Reilley

Wallace Stegner
All the Little Live Things–M.J.F.
Joseph Allston
Ruth Allston
Debby Catlin
John Catlin
Marian Catlin
Fran LoPresti
Julie LoPresti
Jim Peck
Tom Weld

Angle of Repose–M.J.F.
Augusta Drake
Thomas Hudson
Ian Price
Shelley Rasmussen
Frank Sargen
Lyman Ward
Oliver Ward
Oliver Burling Ward
Susan Burling Ward

The Big Rock Candy Mountain–W.M.
Jud Chain
Miss Hammond
Heimie Hellman
Bruce Mason
Chester Mason
Elsa Norgaard Mason
Harry G. Mason
Laura Mason
George Nelson
Kristin Norgaard Nelson
Elaine Nesbitt
Karl Norgaard
Nels Norgaard
Sarah Norgaard

John Steinbeck

Cannery Row–J.Cal.
  Horace Abbeville
  Alfred
  Lee Chong
  Doc
  Eddie
  Dora Flood
  Frankie
  Mack
  William

East of Eden–L.I.
  Abra Bacon
  Samuel Hamilton
  Will Hamilton
  Lee
  Adam Trask
  Aron Trask
  Caleb Trask
  Cathy Ames Trask
  Charles Trask

The Grapes of Wrath–K.H.O.
  Jim Casey
  Muley Graves
  Al Joad
  John Joad
  Ma Joad
  Noah Joad
  Tom Joad I
  Tom Joad II
  Connie Rivers
  Rose of Sharon Joad Rivers

In Dubious Battle–L.I.
  Alfred Anderson
  Doc Burton
  Dick
  Joy
  London
  McLeod
  Jim Noland

Of Mice and Men–K.H.O.
  Candy
  Crooks
  Curley
  George Milton
  Slim
  Lennie Small

The Pearl–M.H.L.
  Coyotito
  Juan Tomás
  Juana
  Kino

Tortilla Flat–M.H.L.
  Jesus Maria Corcoran
  Danny
  Pilon
  Pirate
  Big Joe Portagee
  Pablo Sanchez

The Wayward Bus–M.H.L.
  Edward Carson
  Alice Chicoy
  Juan Chicoy
  Ernest Horton
  Louie
  Norma
  Camille Oaks
  Bernice Pritchard
  Elliott Pritchard
  Mildred Pritchard
  Mr. Van Brunt

The Winter of Our Discontent–V.W.
  Mr. Baker
  Ethan Allen Hawley
  Mary Hawley
  Alfio Marullo
  Joey Morphy
  Danny Taylor
  Margie Young-Hunt

Donald Ogden Stewart
Mr and Mrs Haddock Abroad–J.K.
  Harriet N. Q. Haddock
  Mildred Haddock
  William P. Haddock

Robert Stone
Dog Soldiers–G.G.
  Antheil
  John Converse
  Marge Bender Converse
  Dieter
  Raymond Hicks
  Eddie Peace

Harriet Beecher Stowe
Dred–M.L.K.
  Frederic Augustus Carson
  Anne Clayton
  Edward Clayton
  Judge Clayton
  John Cripps
  Sue Seymour Cripps
  Emmeline
  Harry Gordon
  John Gordon
  Lisette Gordon
  Nina Gordon
  Thomas Gordon
  Aunt Katy
  Milly
  Louisa Nesbit
  Old Hundred
  Tiff Peyton
  Frank Russel
  Cora Gordon Stewart
  Tomtit
  Dred Vesey

Uncle Tom's Cabin–M.L.K.
  Senator and Mrs. Bird
  Cassy

  Aunt Chloe
  Emmeline
  Dan Haley
  Rachel Halliday
  Eliza Harris
  George Harris
  Harry Harris
  Simon Legree
  Tom Loker
  Mammy
  Augustine St. Clare
  Evangeline St. Clare
  Henrique St. Clare
  Marie St. Clare
  Ophelia St. Clare
  George Shelby
  Uncle Tom
  Topsy

T. S. Stribling
The Forge–E.J.P.
  Cyrus U. Beekman
  Alexander BeShears
  Ponny BeShears
  Drusilla Lacefield Crowninshield
  Emory Crowninshield
  John Handback
  A. Gray Lacefield
  Caruthers Lacefield
  Bill Leatherwood
  Lump Mowbray
  Bennie Mulry
  Augustus Vaiden
  Cassandra Vaiden
  Gracie Vaiden
  Jimmie Vaiden
  Laura Vaiden
  Marcia Vaiden
  Miltiades Vaiden
  Polycarp Vaiden

The Store–E.J.P.
  Cyrus U. Beekman
  Alexander BeShears
  Ponny BeShears
  Alex Cady
  Eph Cady
  Jeremiah Ezekiel Madison Catlin
  Jerry Catlin the Second
  Drusilla Lacefield Crowninshield
  John Handback
  Lucius Handback
  A. Gray Lacefield
  Landers
  Mayhew
  Lump Mowbray
  Terry O'Shawn
  James Sandusky
  Pammy Lee Sparkman
  Alberta Sydna Crowninshield Vaiden
  Augustus Vaiden
  Cassandra Vaiden
  Gracie Vaiden
  Lucy Lacefield Vaiden

Marcia Vaiden
Miltiades Vaiden
Toussaint Vaiden

Teeftallow–E.J.P.
Tug Beavers
A. M. Belshue
Roxie Biggers
Blackman
Peck Bradley
Ditmas
Adelaide Jones
David Jones
Perry Northcutt
Zed Parrum
James Sandage
Buckingham Sharp
Nessie Sutton
Abner Teeftallow

Unfinished Cathedral–E.J.P.
Jefferson Ashton
Jim Blankenship
William Yancey Bodine
Jerry Catlin the Second
Drusilla Lacefield Crowninshield
Lucius Handback
James Vaiden Hodige
Red McLaughlin
Ludus Meggs
Junior Petman
Marvin Petman
J. Adlee Petrie
Phineas Delfase Ponniman
Willie Rutledge
James Sandusky
Sinton
Pammy Lee Sparkman
Aurelia Swartout
Alberta Sydna Crowninshield Vadien
Gracie Vaiden
Marsan Vaiden
Miltiades Vaiden

Jesse Stuart
Taps for Private Tussie–F.H.L.
George Rayburn
Arimithy Tussie
Ben Tussie
George Tussie
Kim Tussie
Mott Tussie
Press Tussie
Sid Tussie
Vittie Tussie

William Styron
The Confessions of Nat Turner–S.E.G.
Jeremiah Cobb
Reverend Alexander Eppes
Thomas R. Gray
Hark
Thomas Moore
Joseph Travis

Lou-Ann Turner
Nathaniel Turner
Samuel Turner
Margaret Whitehead
Will

Lie Down in Darkness–L.M.S.
Dolly Bonner
Carey Carr
Daddy Faith
Helen Peyton Loftis
Maudie Loftis
Milton Loftis
Peyton Loftis
Ella Swan

The Long March–L.I.
Lieutenant Jack Culver
Corporal Hobbs
Major Billy Lawrence
Captain Al Mannix
Sergeant O'Leary
Colonel Templeton

Sophie's Choice–J.S.L.
Dr. Zbigniew Bieganska
Dr. Walter Dürrfeld
Morris Fink
Rudolph Franz Höss
Jozef Muck-Horch von Kretschmann
Wanda Muck-Horch von Kretschmann
Nathan Landau
Fritz Jemand von Niemand
Stingo
Eva Maria Zawistowska
Jan Zawistowska
Zofia Maria Bieganska Zawistowska

Set This House on Fire–L.I.
Flag
Celia Flagg
Mason Flagg
Cass Kinsolving
Poppy Kinsolving
Rosemarie de Laframboise
Peter Charles Leverett
Luigi Migliore
Francesca Ricci
Michele Ricci

Booth Tarkington
Alice Adams–D.S.
Alice Adams
Mrs. Adams
Virgil Adams
Walter Adams
J. A. Lamb
Mildred Palmer
Arthur Russell

The Magnificent Ambersons–D.S.
George Amberson
Major Amberson
Fanny Minafer

George Amberson Minafer
Isabel Amberson Minafer
Wilbur Minafer
Eugene Morgan
Lucy Morgan

Penrod–E.J.H.
Georgie Bassett
Roderick Magsworth Bitts, Junior
Rupe Collins
Della
Duke
Herman
Marjorie Jones
Mitchell Jones
Kinosling
Maurice Levy
Queenie
Amy Rennsdale
Henry Passloe Schofield
Margaret Passloe Schofield
Mrs. Schofield
Penrod Schofield
Mrs. Mary Spence
Verman
Robert Williams
Samuel Williams

Penrod Jashber–E.J.H.
Georgie Bassett
Roderick Magsworth Bitts, Junior
Herbert Hamilton Dade
Della
Duke
Herman
Marjorie Jones
Maurice Levy
Amy Rennsdale
Henry Passloe Schofield
Margaret Passloe Schofield
Mrs. Schofield
Penrod Schofield
Miss Mary Spence
Verman
Robert Williams
Samuel Williams

Penrod and Sam–E.J.H.
Georgie Bassett
Della
Duke
Herman
Marjorie Jones
Maurice Levy
Amy Rennsdale
Henry Passloe Schofield
Margaret Passloe Schofield
Mrs. Schofield
Penrod Schofield
Miss Mary Spence
Verman
Robert Williams
Samuel Williams

Seventeen–E.J.H.
  Freddie Banks
  Wallace Banks
  Jane Baxter
  Mrs. Baxter
  William Sylvanus Baxter
  Miss Boke
  Joe Bullitt
  Clematis
  George Crooper
  Flopit
  Genesis
  Mr. Genesis
  Mary Randolph Kirsted
  May Parcher
  Mr. Parcher
  Miss Lola Pratt
  Johnnie Watson

Allen Tate
The Fathers–B.P.
  Lacy Gore Buchan
  Major Lewis Buchan
  Semmes Buchan
  John Langton
  George Posey
  Jane Posey
  Aunt Jane Anne Posey
  Susan Buchan Posey
  Yellow Jim

Paul Theroux
The Family Arsenal–S.C.
  Lady Susannah Arrow
  Brodie
  Ralph C. Gawber
  Valentine Hood
  Mayo
  Murf
  Araba Nightwing
  Willy Rutter
  Sweeney
  Lorna Weech
  Ron Weech

Picture Palace–S.C.
  Frank Fusco
  Woodrow Leathers
  Blanche Overall
  R. G. Perdew
  Mama and Papa Pratt
  Maude Coffin Pratt
  Orlando Pratt
  Phoebe Pratt
  Teets

Saint Jack–S.C.
  Jack Flowers
  Desmond Frogget
  Gladys
  Gopi
  Gunstone
  Chop Hing Kheng Fatt
  William Leigh

  Edwin Shuck
  Yardley
  Yates

Waldo–S.C.
  Sybil Czap
  Edwin
  Emma
  Grammy
  Mona
  Jasper Pistareen
  Clovis Techy
  Waldo
  Arnold Wermy
  Fred Wolfpits

Wallace Thurman
The Blacker the Berry–J.D.P.
  Alva
  Mrs. Blake
  Bobbie
  Braxton
  Benson Brown
  Jasper Crane
  Tony Crews
  Geraldine
  Grace Giles
  Anise Hamilton
  John
  Gwendolyn Johnson
  Campbell Kitchen
  Maria Lightfoot
  Samuel Lightfoot
  Alma Martin
  Hazel Mason
  Jane Lightfoot Morgan
  Jim Morgan
  Uncle Joe Morgan
  Clere Sloane
  Arline Strange
  Weldon Taylor

Jean Toomer
Cane–N.Y.M.
  Avey
  King Barlo
  Becky
  Tom Burwell
  Carma
  Esther Crane
  Dorris
  Bona Hale
  Fred Halsey
  Samuel Hanby
  Paul Johnson
  Ralph Kabnis
  Karintha
  Louisa
  Fernie Mae Rosen
  Bob Stone

Albion W. Tourgee
Bricks without Straw–C.A.M.
  Mollie Ainslie

  Oscar Ainslie
  Colonel Potem Desmit
  Lucy Ellison
  Wasington Goodspeed
  Colonel Walter Greer
  Eliab Hill
  Jordan Jackson
  Berry Lawson
  Sally Ann Lawson
  Casaubon Le Moyne
  Hesden Le Moyne
  Hester Richards Le Moyne
  Hildreth Le Moyne
  Julia Lomax Le Moyne
  Hetty Lomax
  Lorency
  Lugena
  Nimbus
  Theron Pardee
  James Richards
  Peter Smith
  Granville Sykes
  Jay Timlow
  Silas Ware

A Fool's Errand–C.A.M.
  Andy
  Jayhu Brown
  John Burleson
  Alice E. Coleman
  Exum Davis
  Thomas Denton
  Mr. Eyebright
  George D. Garnett

B. Traven
The Treasure of the Sierra Madre–S.W.A.
  Curtin
  Dobbs
  Joaquin Escalona
  Howard
  Robert W. Lacaud
  Pat McCormick
  Miguel

Robert Traver
Anatomy of a Murder–G.G.
  Max Battisfore
  Paul Biegler
  Blaude Dancer
  Julian Durgo
  Gregory W. Harcourt
  Sulo Kangas
  Mr. Lemon
  Mitch Lodwick
  Sonny Loftus
  Maida
  Frederic Manion
  Laura Manion
  Parnell Emmett Joseph McCarthy
  Duane Miller
  Alphonse Paquette
  Mary Pilant
  Barney Quill

Harlan Weaver

Lionel Trilling
The Middle of the Journey–G.V.N.
Duck Caldwell
Emily Caldwell
Susan Caldwell
Arthur Croom
Nancy Croom
Miss Debry
Alwin Folger
Eunice Folger
Mrs. Folger
Elizabeth Fuess
Dr. Graf
Mr. Gurney
John Laskell
Gifford Maxim
Nerissa Paine
Kermit Simpson

Dalton Trumbo
Johnny Got His Gun–E.J.R.
Kareen Birkman
Mike Birman
Joe Bonham

Anne Tyler
Celestial Navigation–A.R.Z.
Brian O'Donnell
Olivia Amanda Pauling
Jeremy Pauling
Wilma Pauling
Mr. Somerset
Darcy Tell
Mary Tell
Mildred Vinton

The Clock Winder–A.R.Z.
Elizabeth Abbott
John Abbott
Julia Abbott
Mr. Cunningham
Andrew Emerson
Margaret Emerson
Matthew Emerson
Pamela Emerson
Peter Emerson
Timothy Emerson

John Updike
Bech: A Book–D.B.R.
Hannah Bech
Henry Bech
Mildred Belloussovsky-Dommergues
Bobochka
Eustace Chubb
Hannah Ann Collins
Mrs. Beatrice Latchett Cook
Char Ecktin
Ruth Eisenbraun
John Kingsgrant Forbes
Vera Glavanakova
Josh Glazer

Jòsh Josiah Goldschmidt
Eva Hassel
Miss Haynsworth
Jason Honeygale
Anatole Husač
Tory Ingersoll
Torquemada Langguth

The Centaur–D.B.R.
Corinna Appleton
Harry Appleton
Hester Appleton
Skippy Appleton
Catherine Kramer Caldwell
George W. Caldwell
Peter·Caldwell
Becky Davis
Johnny Dedman
Ray Deifendorf
Penny Fogleman
Heller
Mim Herzog
Al Hummel
Vera Hummel
Kegerise
Pop Krame
Minor Kretz
Judith Lengel
Reverend March
Iris Osgood
Phil Phillips
Charlie Potteiger
Kenneth Schreuer
Alma Caldwell Terrio
Mark Youngerman
Louis M. Zimmerman

The Coup–J.C.N.
Candace Cunningham
Dorfû
King Edumu IV, Lord of Wanjiji
Colonel Hakim Félix Ellel
Michaelis Ezana
Angelica Gibbs
Donald "X." Gibbs
Kadongolimi
Mr. Klipspringer
Barry Little
Esmerelda Miller
Mtesa
Sidi Mukhtar
Opaku
Oscar X
Sheba
Sittina
Kutunda Traorē
Wadal

Couples–L.M.
Frank Appleby
Janet Appleby
Carol Constantine
Eddie Constantine
Matt Gallagher

Terry Gallagher
Bea Guerin
Roger Guerin
Angela Hanema
Nancy Hanema
Piet Hanema
Ruth Hanema
Leon Jazinski
Bernadette Ong
John Ong
Ben Saltz
Irene Saltz
Harold Smith
Marcia Burnham Smith
Freddy Thorne
Georgene Thorne
Elizabeth Fox Whitman
Ken Whitman

Marry Me–L.M.
Jerry Conant
Ruth Conant
Richard Mathias
Sally Mathias

A Month of Sundays–D.B.R.
Amos
Thaddeus Bork
Doctor Reverend Wesley Chillingworth
Alicia Crick
Fred
Frances Harlow
Gerald Harlow
Jamie Ray
Jane Chillingworth Marshfield
Martin Marshfield
Reverend Thomas Marshfield
Stephen Marshfield
Ms. Prynne
Woody

Of the Farm–D.B.R.
Doc Graaf
Dean McCabe
Richard McCabe
Joan Robinson
Joey Robinson
Mary Robinson
Peggy McCabe Robinson
Sammy Schoelkopf
Frederick Springer
Rebecca Springer
Charlie Stavros
Marty Tothero

The Poorhouse Fair–D.B.R.
Walter Andrews
Dr. Angelo
Stephen Conner
Tommy Franklin
Grace
Billy Gregg
August Hay
Elizabeth Heinemann

John F. Hook
Mary Jamiesson
Mrs. Johnson
Buddy Lee
George R. Lucas
Martha Lucas
Mendelssohn
Amelia Mortis
Ted

Rabbit Redux–L.M.
Earl Angstrom
Harry Angstrom
Janice Springer Angstrom
Mary Angstrom
Miriam Angstrom
Nelson Frederick Angstrom
Rebecca June Angstrom
Hubert H. Farnsworth
Billy Fosnacht
Peggy Fosnacht
Beatrice Greene
Jill Pendleton
Frederick Springer
Rebecca Springer
Charlie Stavros

Rabbit, Run–J.G.H.
Earl Angstrom
Harry Angstrom
Janice Springer Angstrom
Mary Angstrom
Miriam Angstrom
Nelson Frederick Angstrom
Rebecca June Angstrom
Jack Eccles
Lucy Eccles
Fritz Kruppenbach
Ruth Leonard
Mrs. Horace Smith
Frederick Springer
Rebecca Springer
Charlie Stavros
Marty Tothero

Leon Uris
Armageddon–R.A.K. & S.D.D.
Shenandoah Blessing
Lotte Böhm
Nelson Goodfellow Bradbury
Scott Davidson
Ernestine Falkenstein
Hildegaard Falkenstein
Ulrich Falkenstein
Andrew Jackson Hansen
Neal Hazzard
Heinrich Hirsch
Marion Hodgkiss
Igor Karlovy
Sean O'Sullivan
Hiram Stonebraker

Battle Cry–R.A.K. & S.D.D.
Cyril Brown

Daniel Forrester
Joseph Gomez
Mortimer Gray
Andrew Hookans
Samuel Huxley
Lamont Quincy Jones
Jake Levin
Shining Lighttower
Mac
Patricia Rogers
Max Shapiro

Exodus–R.A.K. & S.D.D.
David Ben Ami
Akiva Ben Canaan
Ari Ben Canaan
Barak Ben Canaan
Jordana Ben Canaan
Karen Hansen Clement
Katherine Fremont
Dov Landau
Ernest Lieberman
Mark Parker
Bruce Sutherland
Joab Yarkoni

Mila 18–R.A.K. & S.D.D.
Andrei Androfski
Alexander Brandel
Wolf Brandel
Deborah Androfski Bronski
Paul Bronski
Rachael Bronski
Horst von Epp
Franz Koenig
Christopher de Monti
Gabriela Rak
Rudolph Schreiker
Tommy Thompson

QB VII–R.A.K. & S.D.D.
Thomas Bannister
Abraham Cady
Ben Cady
Terrence Campbell
Anthony Gilray
Robert Highsmith
Adam Kelno
Angela Brown Kelno
Stephan Kelno
David Shawcross
Egon Sobotnik
Mark Tesslar
Pieter Van Damm
Maria Viskova
Adolph Voss
Sarah Wydman

Trinity–R.A.K. & S.D.D.
Atty Fitzpatrick
Caroline Weed Hubble
Jeremy Hubble
Roger Hubble
Andrew Ingram

Brigid Larkin
Conor Larkin
Dary Larkin
Liam Larkin
Oliver Cromwell MacIvor
Shelley MacLeod
Kevin O'Garvey
Seamus O'Neill
Charles Stewart Parnell
Dan Sweeney
Frederick Murdoch Weed

Gore Vidal
Burr–B.J.E.
Dr. Dominie Bogart
William Cullen Bryant
Col. Aaron Burr
Theodosia Burr
Mary Eliza Chase
Nelson Chase
William de la Touche Clancey
Mr. Craft
Matthew L. Davis
Professor George Orson Fuller
Reginald Gower
Alexander Hamilton
Thomas Jefferson
Helen Jewett
Eliza Bowen Jumel
William Leggett
Mordecai Noah
Charles Schuyler
Sam Swartwout
Rosanna Townsend
Martin Van Buren
Guilian C. Verplanck
Robert Wright

Julian–C.C.
Julian Augustus
Callistus
Constantius Augustus
Eusebia
Gallus
Helena
Libanius
Maximus
Oribasius
Priscus

Myra Breckinridge–G.G.
Myra Breckinridge
Rusty Godowsky
Buck Loner
Dr. Randolph Spenser Montag
Mary-Ann Pringle
Letitia Van Allen

Washington, D.C.–E.L.R.
Diana Day
James Burden Day
Kitty Day
Harold Griffiths
Edgar Carl Nillson

Clay Overbury
Blaise Delacroix Sanford
Enid Sanford
Frederika Sanford
Peter Sanford
Billy Thorne

Kurt Vonnegut
Breakfast of Champions–P.J.R.
Fred. T. Barry
Col. Looseleaf Harper
Wayne Hoobler
Celia Hoover
Dwayne Hoover
George Hoover
Rabo Karabekian
Kazak
Harry LeSabre
Bonnie MacMahon
Francine Pefko
Eliot Rosewater
Kilgore Trout
Leo Trout
Kurt Vonnegut, Jr.

Cat's Cradle–P.J.R.
Julian Castle
Philip Castle
H. Lowe Crosby
Hazel Crosby
Angela Hoenikker
Dr. Felix Hoenikker
Franklin Hoenikker
Newton Hoenikker
John
Lionel Boyd Johnson
Dr. Schlichter von Koenigswald
Earl McCabe
Claire Minton
Horlick Minton
Miguel Monzano
Mona Aamons Monzano

God Bless You, Mr. Rosewater–P.J.R.
Amanita Buntline
Diana Moon Glampers
Norman Mushari
Harry Pena
Caroline Rosewater
Eliot Rosewater
Fred Rosewater
Lister Ames Rosewater
Sylvia DuVrais Zetterling Rosewater
Kilgore Trout
Bunny Weeks

Jailbird–P.J.R.
Leland Clewes
Dr. Robert Fender
Alexander Hamilton McCone
Daniel McCone
Mary Kathleen O'Looney
Dr. Ben Shapiro
Ruth Starbuck

Walter F. Starbuck
Kilgore Trout
Kenneth Whistler
Sarah Wyatt

Mother Night–P.J.R.
Howard W. Campbell, Jr.
George Kraft
Helga Noth
Resi Noth
Bernard V. O'Hare
Kurt Vonnegut, Jr.
Frank Wirtanen

Player Piano–P.J.R.
Shah of Bratpuhr
Bud Calhoun
Katharine Finch
Edward Francis Finnerty
Elmo C. Hacketts, Jr.
Edgar Rice Burroughs Hagstrohm
Doctor Ewing J. Halyard
Reverend James J. Lasher
Anita Proteus
Paul Proteus
Lawson Shepherd

The Sirens of Titan–P.J.R.
Boaz
Chrono
Malachi Constant
Bobby Denton
Kazak
Beatrice Rumfoord
Winston Niles Rumfoord
Salo
Stony Stevenson

Slapstick–P.J.R.
Cordelia Swain Cordiner
Captain Bernard Eagle-1 O'Hare
Melody Oriole-w von Peterswald
Eliza Mellon Swain
Lettita Vanderbilt Rockefeller Swain
Wilbur Rockefeller Daffod Swain
Vera Chipmunk-5 Zappa

Slaughterhouse-Five–P.J.R.
Howard W. Campbell, Jr.
Edgar Derby
Paul Lazzaro
Resi North
Bernard V. O'Hare
Mary O'Hare
Billy Pilgrim
Valencia Merble Pilgrim
Eliot Rosewater
Bertram Rumfoord
Kilgore Trout
Kurt Vonnegut, Jr.
Roland Weary
Montana Wildhack

Alice Walker

Meridian–J.G.H.
Camara
Anne-Marion Coles
George Daxter
Eddie
Eddie Jr.
Feather Mae
Truman Held
Gertrude Hill
Meridian Hill
Walter Longknife
Louvinie
Rims Mott
Tommy Odds
Henry O'Shay
Lynne Rabinowitz
Mr. Raymonds
Miss Lucille Treasure
Miss Margaret Treasure
The Wild Child
Miss Winter

The Third Life of Grange Copeland–J.G.H.
Brownfield Copeland
Daphne Copeland
Grange Copeland
Josie Copeland
Margaret Copeland
Mem R. Copeland
Ornette Copeland
Ruth Copeland
Judge Harry
Mr. Shipley
Star

Edward Lewis Wallant
The Children at the Gate–M.H.M.
Maria Alvarez
Angelo DeMarco
Esther DeMarco
Frank DeMarco
Theresa DeMarco
Samuel Abel Kahan
Dimitri Lebedov
Sister Louise
Howard Miller

The Pawnbroker–L.I.
Marilyn Birchfield
Albert Murillio
Ruth Nazerman
Sol Nazerman
Jesus Ortiz
Robinson
Tessie Rubin
Bertha Selig
George Smith
Tangee
Mabel Wheatly

The Tenants of Moonbloom–M.H.M.
Eva Baily
Minna Baily
Basellecci

Old Man Beeler
Sheryl Beeler
Bodien
Leni Cass
Del Rio
Bobby Hauser
Carol Hauser
Sherman Hauser
Mr. Hirsch
Arnold Jacoby
Betty Jacoby
Wade Johnson
Karloff
Stanley Katz
Gaylord Knight
Kram
J. T. Leopold
Milly Leopold
Aaron Lublin
Sarah Lublin
Ilse Moeller
Irwin Moonbloom
Norman Moonbloom
Joe Paxton
Marvin Schoenbrun
Jer Sidone
Jane Sprague
Jim Sprague
Sugarman
Jerry Wung

Joseph Wambaugh
The Black Marble–D.K.J.
Rocco Bambarella
Digby Bates
Chester Biggs
Clarence Cromwell
Nate Farmer
Frick and Frack
Millie Muldoon Gharoujian
Skipper Hooker
Charlie Lightfoot
Earl Scheib Lopez
Bernie Mitchell
Woodenlips Mockett
Montezuma Montez
Jack Packerton
Pattie Mae
Philo Skinner
Alex Valnikov
Andrei Mikhailovich Valnikov
Horst Vanderhoof
Victoria Regina
Walter
Madeline Dills Whitfield
Natalie Kelso Zimmerman

The Blue Knight–D.K.J.
Knobby Booker
Charlie Bronski
Herman Brown
Cassie
Glenda
Laila Hammad

Marvin Heywood
Zoot Lafferty
Timothy G. Landry
Reba McClain
William A. Morgan
Martha Redford
Red Scalotta
Cruz Segovia

The Choirboys–D.K.J.
Alexander Blaney
Harold Bloomguard
Stanley Drobeck
Filthy Herman
Alvin Finque
Theda Gunther
Reba Hadley
Adrian Lynch
Carolina Moon
Hector Moss
Sam Niles
Calvin Potts
Dean Pratt
Henry Rules
Dominic Scuzzi
Baxter Slate
Gina Summers
Francis Tanaguchi
Ora Lee Tingle
Dewey Treadwell
Spencer Van Moot
Wolfgang Werner
Herbert Whalen
Willie Wright
Nick Yanov

The New Centurians–D.K.J.
Whitney Duncan
Sergio Duran
Roy Fehler
Laura Hunt
Andy Kilvinsky
Mariana Paloma
Augustus Plebesly

The Onion Field–D.K.J.
Arthur Alarcon
Mark Brandler
Pierce R. Brooks
Sheldon Brown
Raymond Byrne
Adah Campbell
Chrissie Campbell
Ian James Campbell
Dino Fulgoni
Julius Griffin
Phil Halpin
Helen Hettinger
Karl Hettinger
Charles Hollopeter
Irving Kanarek
Thomas Le Sage
Charles Maple
John Moore

Alfred Peracca
Gregory Ulas Powell
Marshall Schulman
Billy Small
Jimmy Lee Smith
Ray Smith

Charles Dudley Warner
The Gilded Age–G.G.
Ruth Bolton
Henry Brierly
Abner Dilworthy
George Washington Hawkins
Henry Clay Hawkins
Laura Van Brunt Hawkins
George Selby
Polly Sellers
Philip Sterling

Susan Warner
The Wide, Wide World–S.E.G.
Ellen Chauncey
Fortune Emerson
Alice Humphreys
John Humphreys
Mr. Humphreys
Mr. Lindsay
Mrs. Lindsay
George Marshman
Mr. Marshman
Ellen Montgomery
Mrs. Montgomery
Captain Morgan Montgomery
Abraham Van Brunt
Mrs. Vawse
Nancy Vawse

Robert Penn Warren
All the King's Men–J.A.G.
Ellis Burden
Jack Burden
Sadie Burke
Tiny Duffy
Judge Montague M. Irwin
Gummy Larson
Mortimer Lonzo Littlepaugh
Cass Mastern
Hugh Miller
Adam Stanton
Anne Stanton
Governor Stanton
Lucy Stark
Tom Stark
Willie Stark
Sugar-Boy
Annabelle Puckett Trice

At Heaven's Gate–J.A.G.
Gerald Calhoun
Bogan Murdock
Sue Murdock
Private Milt Porsum
Slim Sarrett
Jason Sweetwater

Colonel Beriah/Eschol/Mulberry Sellers
Ashby Prosum Wyndham

Band of Angels–J.A.G.
  Hamish Bond
  Mrs. Herman Muller
  Seth Parton
  Charles de Marigny Prieur-Denis
  Rau-Ru
  Tobias Sears
  Aaron Pendleton Starr
  Amantha Starr

The Cave–J.A.G.
  Jo-Lea Bingham
  Timothy Bingham
  Celia Hornby Harrick
  Jasper Harrick
  John T. Harrick
  Jebb Holloway
  Nicholas Papadoupalous
  Isaac Sumpter
  Reverend MacCarland Sumpter

Night Rider–J.A.G.
  Professor Ball
  Bill Christian
  Lucille Christian
  Doctor MacDonald
  May Cox Munn
  Percy Munn
  Willie Proudfit
  Benton Todd
  Captain Todd
  Senator Edmund Tolliver
  Harris Trevelyan

A Place to Come to–J.A.G.
  Maria McInnis Beaufort
  Michael X. Butler
  James Lawford Carrington
  Rozelle Hardcastle Butler Carrington
  Dauphine Finkel
  Rebecca Carrington Jones-Talbot
  David McInnis
  Elvira K. Tweksbury Simms
  Dr. Heinrich Stahlmann
  Agnes Andresen Tewksbury
  Buck Tewksbury
  Jediah Tweksbury

World Enough and Time–J.A.G.
  Wilkie Barron
  Jeremiah Beaumont
  Rachel Jordan Beaumont
  Colonel Cassius Fort
  Gran Boz
  Morton Marcher
  Percival Skrogg

Jerome Weidman
  I Can Get It for You Wholesale–R.T.
    Theodore Ast
    Meyer Babushkin

Harry Bogen
Mrs. Bogen
Mrs. Heimowitz
Tootsie Maltz
Martha Mills
Maurice Pulvermacher
Ruthie Rivkin

The Temple–R.T.
  Monroe Blumenfeld
  Morris Cohen
  Rachel Cohen
  Anthony X. D'Allessandro
  Bella Biaggi Dehn
  David Dehn
  Hella Drachenfels
  Don Fortgang
  Rabbi Goldfarb
  Fanny Mintz
  Sidney Singer

What's in It for Me?–R.T.
  Theodore Ast
  Harry Bogen
  Mrs. Bogen
  Mrs. Heimowitz
  Murray Heimowitz
  Martha Mills
  Leonard Nissem
  Ruthie Rivkin
  Kermit Terkel
  Hrant Yazdabian

Eudora Welty
  Delta Wedding–L.G.
    Battle Fairchild
    Denis Fairchild
    Ellen Dabney Fairchild
    George Fairchild
    India Primrose Fairchild
    Jim Allen Fairchild
    Maureen Fairchild
    Primrose Fairchild
    Roberta Reid Fairchild
    Roy Fairchild
    Shelley Fairchild
    Troy Flavin
    Maureen Fairchild Laws
    Mary Lamar Mackey
    Laura McRaven
    Shannon Fairchild Miles
    Parthenia
    Dunstan Rondo
    Roxie

Losing Battles–L.G.
  Brother Bethune
  Aycock Comfort
  Maud Eva Moody
  Oscar Moody
  Julia Mortimer
  Beulah Beecham Renfro
  Ella Fay Renfro
  Gloria Short Renfro

Jack Jordan Renfro
Lady May Renfro
Lexie Renfro
Ralph Renfro
Rachel Sojourner
Marshal Excell Prentiss Stovall
Thurzah Elvira Jordan Vaughn

The Optimist's Daughter–L.G.
  Major Rupert Bullock
  Tennyson Bullock
  Tish Bullock
  Adele Courtland
  Mr. Dalzell
  Laurel McKelva Hand
  Philip Hand
  Mrs. Martello
  Becky Thurston McKelva
  Clinton McKelva
  Wanda Fay Chisom McKelva
  Missouri

The Ponder Heart–L.G.
  DeYancey Clanahan
  Tip Clanahan
  Narciss
  Bonnie Dee Peacock Ponder
  Daniel Ponder
  Edna Earle Ponder
  Sam Ponder
  Teacake Sistrunk Magee Ponder
  Mr. Springer

The Robber Bridegroom–L.G.
  Mike Fink
  Goat
  Little Harp
  Jamie Lockhart
  Rosamond Musgrove Lockhart
  Amalie Musgrove
  Clement Musgrove
  Salome Thomas Musgrove

Jessamyn West
  Cress Delahanty–A.D.F.
    Miss Iris Bird
    Inez Dresden Charlesbois
    Luther Charlesbois
    Frank Cornelius
    Joyce Cornelius
    Avis Davis
    Mavis Davis
    Bernadine Deevers
    Crescent Delahanty
    Gertrude Delahanty
    John Delahanty
    John Delahanty
    Maribeth Dufour
    Honor Gallagher
    Hubert
    Mrs. Edwin Kibbler
    Edwin Kibbler, Jr.
    Yolande Perrotti
    Mr. Powers

Clarence Rambo
Don Rivers
Cornelia Samms
Ina Inex Wallenius
Mr. Wallenius

Except for Me and Thee—A.D.F.
Elspeth Bent
Gardiner Bent
Eliza Cope Birdwell
Jane Birdwell
Little Jess Birdwell
Jesse Griffith Birdwell
Joshua Birdwell
Laban Birdwell
Martha Truth Birdwell
Sarah Birdwell
Enoch Miles

The Friendly Persuasion—A.D.F.
Alf Applegate
Elspeth Bent
Gardiner Bent
Eliza Cope Birdwell
Jane Birdwell
Little Jess Birdwell
Jesse Griffith Birdwell
Joshua Birdwell
Laban Birdwell
Martha Truth Birdwell
Laban Birdwell
Sarah Birdwell
Stephen Birdwell
Lidy Cinnamond
Homer Denham
Reverend Marcus Augustus Godley
Mrs. Hudspeth
Enoch Miles
Lafayette Millspaugh
Waldo Quigley
Mrs. Lydia Ann Rivers
Ben Whitey

The Life I Really Lived—A.D.F.
Joseph Raymond Chase
Orpha Chase
Alonzo T. Dudley
Burt Griswold
Marie Shields Griswold
Jacob Hesse
Crit Matthews
Ebon Matthews
Gregory McGovern
Ralph Navarro
Tom O'Hara
Sam Shields
Ormand Slaughter
Wanda

The Massacre at Fall Creek—A.D.F.
Luther Bemis
Ora Bemis
George Benson
Black Antler

Benjamin Cape
Caleb Cape
Hannah Cape
Lizzie Cape
Jud Clasby
Norah Culligan
Oscar Achilles Dilk
Folded Leaf
Charles Fort
John Wood
John Wood, Jr.
Reba Reese Wood

The Witch Diggers—A.D.F.
James Abel
Mary Abel
Catherine M. Conboy
Elizabeth Conboy
Emma Jane Conboy
James Conboy
Lincoln Conboy
Carmen Sylva Cope
Christian J. Fraser
Odis Korby
Norah Tate
Ferris P. Thompson

Nathanael West
A Cool Million—G.G.
Lemuel Pitkin
Betty Prail
Nathan Whipple

The Day of the Locust—G.G.
Faye Greener
Harry Greener
Tod Hackett
Abe Kusich
Miguel
Earle Shoop
Homer Simpson

The Dream Life of Balso Snell—G.G.
Beagle Hamlet Darwin
Janey Davenport
John Gilson
Maloney the Areopagite
Mary McGeeney
Balso Snell

Miss Lonelyhearts—G.G.
Betty
Fay Doyle
Peter Doyle
Miss Lonelyhearts
Mary Shrike
Willie Shrike

Edith Wharton
The Age of Innocence—K.A.F.
Adeline Archer
Dallas Archer
Newland Archer
Julius Beaufort

Regina Dallas Beaufort
Sillerton Jackson
Lawrence Lefferts
Henry van der Luyden
Louisa Dagonet van der Luyden
Marchioness Medora Manson
Catherine Spicer Mingott
Mrs. Lovell Mingott
Countess Ellen Olenska
Mrs. Lemuel Struthers
Augusta Welland
May Welland
Mr. Welland

The Custom of the Country—K.A.F.
Charles Bowen
Comte Raymond de Chelles
Urban Dagonet
Princess Lili Estradina
Laura Fairford
Mrs. Heeney
Mabel Blitch Lipscomb
Mrs. Marvell
Paul Marvell
Ralph Marvell
Elmer Moffatt
Claud Walsingham Popple
Harriet Ray
Indiana Frusk Rolliver
Abner E. Spragg
Leota B. Spragg
Undine Spragg
Marquise de Trézac
Clare Van Degen
Peter Van Degen

Ethan Frome—E.B.B.
Ethan Frome
Zenobia Pierce Frome
Harmon Gow
Ruth Varnum Hale
Miss Hatchard
Ally Hawes
Mary Hyatt
Verena Marsh
Mr. Miles
Mattie Silver

The House of Mirth—E.B.B.
Lily Bart
Bertha Dorset
George Dorset
Gertrude Farish
Carry Fisher
Percy Gryce
Julia Peniston
Simon Rosedale
Lawrence Selden
Charles Augustus Trenor
Judy Trenor

The Old Maid—K.A.F.
Lanning Halsey

Sillerton Jackson
Henry van der Luyden
Louisa Dagonet van der
    Luyden
Charlotte Lovell
Catherine Spicer Mingott
Clementina Lovell Ralston
Delia Lovell Ralston
James Ralston
Joseph Ralston
Clement Spender

The Reef–K.A.F.
Madame de Chantelle
George Darrow
Anna Leath
Effie Leath
Fraser Leath
Owen Leath
Mrs. Murrett
Adelaide Painter
Sophy Viner

Summer–K.A.F.
Annabel Balch
Lucius Harney
Miss Hatchard
Ally Hawes
Julia Hawes
Liff Hyatt
Mary Hyatt
Verena Marsh
Dr. Merkle
Mr. Miles
Charity Royall
Lawyer Royall

William Wharton
Birdy–G.G.
Alfonso
Birdie
Birdy
Alfonso Columbato
Mr. Lincoln
Corporal Lumbowski
Perta
Mrs. Prevost
Phil Renaldi
Doris Robinson
Joe Sagessa
Major S. O. Weiss

William Allen White
A Certain Rich Man–D.D.Q.
Jane Manson Barclay
Jeanette Barclay
John Barclay
Elijah Westlake Bemis
Adrian Pericles Brownwell
Molly Culpepper Brownwell
Martin Culpepper
Robert Hendricks
Watts McHurdie
Neal Dow Ward

In the Heart of a Fool–D.D.Q.
Amos Adams
Grant Adams
Kenyon Adams
Mary Sands Adams
Henry Fenn
Violet Mauling Hogan
Margaret Müller
Bedelia Satterthwaite Nesbit
James Nesbit
Nathan Perry
Laura Nesbit Van Dorn
Lila Van Dorn
Thomas Van Dorn

Brand Whitlock
J. Hardin & Son–P.W.M.
Billie Dyer
Malcolm Dyer
Winona Dyer
J. Hardin
Paul Hardin
Matilda
Hosea Ortman
Smoke
Clyde Sturrock
Evelyn Walling
Josiah West

John Edgar Wideman
Hurry Home–G.G.
Albert
Cecil Otis Braithwaite
Esther Brown Braithwaite
Simon Braithwaite
Carlos
Charles Webb
Walter Willis

The Lynchers–G.G.
Anthony
Willie Hall
Graham Rice
Leonard Saunders
Sissie
Tanya
Angela Taylor
Orin Wilkerson
Thomas Wilkerson

Thornton Wilder
The Bridge of San Luis Rey–D.Lo.
Captain Alvarado
Esteban
Brother Juniper
ManXuel
DonXa Clara de Montemayor
DonXa Mára de Montemayor
Pepita
Camila Perichole
Madre Mára del Pilar
Uncle Pio
Don Andrés de Ribera
Don Jaime de Ribera

The Cabala–D.Lo.
Mme. Agoropoulos
Julia d'Aquilanera
Leda Matilda Colonna,
    La Duchessa d'Aquilanera
Marcantonio d'Aquilanera
Bernice
Madame Anna Bernstein
James Blair
Léry Bogard
Princess Alix d'Espoli
Elizabeth Grier
Madamoiselle Marie-Astrée-Luce
    de Morfontaine
Ottima
Frederick Perkins
Mrs. Roy
Samuele
Cardinal Vaini

The Eighth Day–D.Lo.
Archbishop of Chicago
Constance Ashley
John Barrington Ashley
Lily Scolastica Ashley
Marie-Louise Scolastique
    Dubois Ashley
Roger Berwyn Ashley
Sophia Ashley
Peter Bogardus
Wellington Bristow
Olga Sergeievna Doubkov
Dr. Gillies
Beata Kellerman-Ashley
Anne Lansing
Breckenridge Lansing
Eustacia Sims Lansing
Félicité Marjolaine Dup
    Lansing
Fisher Lansing
George Sims Lansing
Aristides O'Hara
Samuel O'Hara
Thomas Garrison Speidel
Colonel Stotz
Wilhelmina Thoms
Ada Wickersham

Heaven's My Destination–D.Lo.
Bat
Reverend Doctor James
    Bigelow
Doremus Blodgett
George Marvin Brush
George Burkin
Judge Darwin Carberry
Judge Leonidas Corey
Mississippi Corey
Marcella L. Craven
Mrs. Crofut
Mrs. Efrim
Louie
Elizabeth Martin
Herbert Martin

Jessie Mayhew
Mrs. Margie McCoy
Mrs. Ella McManus
Father Pasziewski
Dick Roberts
Lottie Weyerhauser
Roberta Weyehauser

The Ides of March–D.Lo.
Marc Anthony
Marcus Junius Brutus
Caius Julius Caesar
Calpurnia
Gaius Valerius Catullus
Cicero
Cleopatra
Cytheris
Julia Marcia
Cornelius Nepos
Octavius
Asinius Pollio
Pompeia
Porcia
Clodia Pulcher
Publius Clodius Pulcher
Servilia
Lucius Mamilius Turrinus

Theophilus North–D.Lo.
Alice
Diana Bell
Dr. Bosco
Dr. James McHenry Bosworth
Sarah Bosworth
Mrs. Amelia Cranston
Flora Deland
Josiah Dexter
Mr. Diefendorf
Charles Fenwick
Eloise Fenwick
George Francis Granberry
Myra Granberry
Elbert Hughes
Hilary Jones
Mrs. Doris Keefe
Benjamino Matera
Theodore Theophilus North
Henry Simmons
Arthur Gallup Skeel
Elspeth Skeel
Baron Egon Bodo von Stams
Archer Tennyson
Persis Tennyson
Mrs. Edward Venable
William Wentworth
Edweena Wills
Norine Wyckoff

The Woman of Andros–D.Lo.
Apraxine
Argo
Chremes
Chrysis
Glycerium

Mysis
Niceratus
Pamphilus
Philocles
Philumena
Simo
Sostrata

John A. Williams
Captain Blackman–J.L.D.J.
Captain Abraham Blackman
Ishmael Whittman
Luther Woodcock

The Junior Bachelor Society–J.LD J.
Charles Davis
Kenneth Dumpson
Cudjo Evers
Swoop Ferguson
D'Artagnan Foxx
Clarence Henderson
Ezzard Jackson
Walter Porter
Shurley Walker
Richard Wiggins

The Man Who Cried I Am–J.L.D.J.
Charlotte Ames
Harry Ames
Moses Lincoln Boatwright
Michelle Bouilloux
Reverend Paul Durrell
Alfonse Edwards
Jaja Enzkwu
Minister Q
Lillian Patch
Margrit Westoever Reddick
Max Reddick
The Saminone

Tennessee Williams
Moise and the World of Reason–D.Sh.
Big Lot
Charlie
Invicta
Lance
Moise
Ursula Phillips
Miriam Skates
Tony Smith

The Roman Spring of Mrs. Stone–D.Sh.
Meg Bishop
Contessa
Signora Coogan
Fabio
Paolo
Renato
Mrs. Karen Stone
Thomas J. Stone
Mrs. Jamison Walker

Edmund Wilson
I Thought of Daisy–C.C.N.

Hugo Bamman
Pete Bird
Rita Cavanagh
Daisy Meissner Coleman
Ray Coleman
H. M. Grosbeake
Bobby McIlvaine
Lawrence Mickler

Memoirs of Hecate County–C.C.N.
Si Banks
Wilbur Flick
Jo Gates
Flagler Haynes
Clarence Latouche
Anna Lenihan
Imogen Loomis
Warren Milholland
Asa M. Stryker

Harriet Wilson
Our Nig–K.L.R.
Aunt Abby
Alfrado
James Bellmont
Jane Bellmont
Jenny Bellmont
John Bellmont
Lewis Bellmont
Mary Bellmont
Mrs. Bellmont
Susan Bellmont
Mrs. Capon
Pete Greene
Mrs. Hale
Mrs. Hoggs
Jim
Miss March
George Means
Mrs. Moore
Henry Reed
Samuel
Seth Shipley
Mag Smith
Magaretta Thorn

Harry Leon Wilson
Merton of the Movies–J.K.
Jeff Baird
Amos G. Gashwiler
Merton Gill
Sarah Nevada Montague

Ruggles of Red Gap–J.K.
Effie Floud
Egbert G. Floud
Mrs. Judson
Kate Kenner
Marmaduke Ruggles
George Augustus Vane-
Basingwell
Nevil Vane-Basingwell

Kathleen Winsor

Forever Amber–M.Du.
Lady Emily Almsbury
Nan Britton
Lady Carlton
Lord Carlton
Queen Catherine
Luke Channell
Bess Columbine
Samuel Dangerfield
Michael Godfrey
Nell Gwynne
Anne Hyde
Edward Hyde. Earl
of Clarendon
Black Jack Mallard
Capt. Rex Morgan
Edmund Mortimer
Mother Red-Cap
Barbara Palmer,
Lady Castlemaine
John Randolph,
Earl of Almsbury
Amber St. Clare
Gerald Stanhope, Earl of
Stanhope and Duke
of Ravenspur
Frances Stewart
Charles Stuart
Henrietta Anne Stuart
James Stuart, Duke of York
George Villiers, Duke
of Buckingham

Owen Wister
The Virginian–L.R.N.A.
Judge Henry
Shorty
Steve
Trampas
Virginian
Mary Stark Wood

Larry Woiwode
Beyond the Bedroom Wall–G.L.M.
Donny Ennis
Conrad Jones
Edward Jones
Electra Jones
Elling Jones
Jerome Jones
Lionell Jones
Marie Krull
Selmer Krull
Alpha Jones Neumiller
Augustina Neumiller
Becky Neumiller
Charles John Christopher
Neumiller I
Charles Neumiller II
Cheri Neumiller
Davey Neumiller
Elaine Neumiller
Emil Neumiller
Fred Neumiller

Jay Neumiller
Jerome Neumiller
Katherine Neumiller
Laura Neumiller
Lucy Neumiller
Marie Neumiller
Martin Neumiller
Otto Neumiller
Rose Marie Neumiller
Susan Neumiller
Timothy Neumiller
Tom Neumiller
Vince Neumiller
Clarence Popp
Brian Rimsky
Leo Rimsky
James Russell
Father Schimmelpfenning
Buddy Schonbeck

What I'm Going to Do, I Think–G.L.M.
Anna Clausen
Orin Clausen
Nelson Hartis
Aloyisius James Strohe
Ellen Sidone Anne Strohe
Grandma Strohe
Christofer Van Eenanam
Virgil Weeks

Thomas Wolfe
The Hills Beyond–L.I.
Hugh Fortescue
Edward Joyner
Emily Drumgoole Joyner
Gustavus Adolphus Joyner
Robert Joyner
Theodore Joyner
William Joyner
Zachariah Joyner
George Josiah Webber
John Webber

Look Homeward, Angel–L.I.
Benjamin Harrison Gant
Eliza E. Pentland Gant
Eugene Gant
Oliver Gant
George Graves
Laura James
Margaret Leonard
Hugh McGuire
Harry Tugman

Of Time and the River–L.I.
Ann
Elinor
Benjamin Harrison Gant
Eliza E. Pentland Gant
Eugene Gant
James Graves Hatcher
Hugh McGuire
Bascom Pentland
Francis Starwick

Robert Weaver

The Web and the Rock–L.I.
Gerald Alsop
Nebraska Crane
Esther Jack
Frederick Jack
Mag Joyner
Mark Joyner
Maw Joyner
James Heyward Randolph
Randy Shepperton
George Josiah Webber
John Webber

You Can't Go Home Again–L.I.
Nebraska Crane
Foxhall Edwards
Esther Jack
Frederick Jack
Mag Joyner
Mark Joyner
Maw Joyner
Else von Kohler
Lloyd McHarg
Randy Shepperton
George Josiah Webber

Constance Fenimore Woolson
For the Major–R.S.M.
Senator Godfrey Ashley
Madam Marion More Morris
Carroll
Sara Carroll
Scar Carroll
Major Scarborough Carroll
Louis Eugene Dupont
Mrs. Greer
Frederick Owen
Corinna Rendlesham

Herman Wouk
The Caine Mutiny–C.F.
Captain Blakely
Lieutenant Commander Jack
Challee
Ensign Farrington
Walter Feather
Lieutenant Barney Greenwald
Roland Keefer
Thomas Keefer
Edwin Keggs
Mrs. Keith
Willis Seward Keith
Lieutenant Stephen Maryk
Ensign Paynter
Lieutenant Commander Philip
Francis Queeg
Stilwell
Captain de Vriess
May Wynn

Marjorie Morningstar–C.F.
Noel Airman

George Drobes
Michael Eden
Billy Ehrmann
Samson-Aaron Fader
Guy Flamm
Sandy Goldstone
Maxwell Greech
Lou Michaelson
Arnold Morgenstern
Marjorie Morgenstern
Rose Kupperberg Morgenstern
Seth Morgenstern
Geoffrey Quill
Sam Rothmore
Milton Schwartz
Monica Ehrmann Sigelman
Walter Wronken
Marsha Zelenko

Richard Wright
Lawd Today–J.D.P.
Blanche
Blue Juice
Doc Higgins
Howard
Jake Jackson
Lil Jackson
Albert Johnson
Robert Madison
Rose
Streamline
Mister Swanson
Nathan Williams

The Long Dream–J.D.P.
James Bowers
Fats Brown
Dr. Bruce
Gerald Cantley
Gladys
Zeke Jordan
Gloria Mason
Harvey McWilliams
Sam
Chris Sims
Emma Tucker
Rex Tucker
Tyree Tucker

Native Son–J.D.P.
Mr. Bitten
David A. Buckley
Henry G. Dalton
Mary Dalton
Mrs. Dalton
Jan Erlone
Gus
Reverend Hammond
Max
Bessie Mears
Peggy O'Flagherty
Bigger Thomas
Buddy Thomas
Mrs. Thomas

Vera Thomas

The Outsider–J.D.P.
Mr. Blimin
Eva Blount
Gilbert Blount
Cross Damon
Gladys
Langley Herndon
John Hilton
Ely Houston
Robert Hunter
Sarah Hunter
Jenny
Rose Lampkin
Herbert Menti
Dorothy Powers
Father Seldon
Joe Thomas

Savage Holiday–J.D.P.
Mabel Blake
Tony Blake
Erskine Fowler
Minnie
Albert Warren
Robert Warren
Mary Westerman

Sarah E. Wright
This Child's Gonna Live–V.B.G.
Lettie Cartwright
Aunt Cora Lou
Haim Crawford
Bannie Upshire Dudley
Dr. Albert Grene
Effie Harmon
Pop Harmon
Frannie Jefferson
Ol Jefferson
Lil Bits
Mamie
Miss Naomi
Tillie Reid
Willie Reid
Rosey
Aunt Saro Jane
Bard Tom Upshur
Bardette Tometta Upshur
Bertha Ann Upshur
Emerson Upshur
Gesus Upshur
Horace Upshur
Jacob Upshur
Levi Upshur
Margaret Upshur
Mariah Harmon Upshur
Percy Upshur
Thomas Upshur
William Upshur
Vyella

Richard Yates
Disturbing the Peace–R.Ba.

Dr. Jules Blomburg
Paul R. Borg
Dr. Myron T. Brink
Dr. Chadwick
Charlie
Bill Costello
Nathan Epstein
Pamela Hendricks
Carl Munchin
Chester Pratt
Dr. Burton L. Rose
Dr. Henry J. Spivack
George Taylor
Janice Brady Wilder
John C. Wilder
Marjorie Wilder
Tom Wilder

Easter Parade–R.Ba.
Donald Clellon
Andrew Crawford
Howard Dunninger
Lars Ericson
John Flanders
Emily Grimes
Esther Grimes
Walter Grimes
Anthony Wilson
Geoffrey Wilson
Peter Wilson
Sarah Grimes Wilson

A Good School–J.S.Ba.
Alice Draper
Jack Draper
Robert Driscoll
Terry Flynn
Lawrence Mason Gaines
William Grove
W. Alcott Knoedler
Jean-Paul La Prade
Dr. Edgar Stone
Edith Stone

Revolutionary Road–R.Ba.
Milly Campbell
Sheppard Sears Campbell
Mrs. Helen Givings
Howard Givings
John Givings
Maureen Grube
Jack R. Ordway
Bart Pollock
April Wheeler
Earl Wheeler
Franklin H. Wheeler

A Special Providence–J.S.Ba.
Eva Grumbauer Forbes
Owen Forbes
Maude Larkin
Sterling Nelson
Alice Grumbauer Prentice
George Prentice

Robert J. Prentice
John Quint
Sam Rand
Willard Slade
Mrs. Walter J. Vander Meer

Stark Young

So Red the Rose–J.R.B.
   Duncan Bedford
   Malcolm
   Sarah Tate Bedford
   Mary Cherry
   Agnes Bedford McGehee
   Edward McGehee

Hugh McGehee
Lucinda McGehee
Julia Valette Somerville
Charles Taliaferro
Rose Tate
William Veal

Contributors

K.A. Ken Autrey
K.A.A. Katherine Anne Ackley
K.B.A. Kristin Berkey-Abbott
L.L.A. Lisa L. Antley
L.R.N.A. Leonard R. N. Ashley
M.L.A. Max L. Autrey
S.A.A. Suzanne A. Allen
S.W.A. Scott W. Allen

A.I.B. Anne I. Barton
C.D.B. Charles D. Brower
D.G.B. David G. Byrd
D.M.B. Donald M. Brown
E.B. Edith Blicksilver
E.B.B. Elizabeth B. Baker
E.B.Bo. Edward B. Borden
F.W.B. F. Wylie Brown
G.J.B. Gloria J. Bell
H.M.B. Harry McBrayer Bayne
J.A.B. J. A. Bryant, Jr.
J.B. Jan Bakker
J.M.B. Jean M. Bright
J.M.Br. J. M. Brook
J.R.B. James R. Bailey
J.S.Ba. Judith S. Baughman
J.W.B. John Whalen-Bridge
L.K.B. Linda K. Bundtzen
M.B. Martin Bucco
M.H.B. Mary Hughes Brookhart
M.J.B. Matthew Joseph Bruccoli
M.W.B. Muriel Wright Brailey
P.T.B. Paul T. Bryant
R.B. Ronald Baughman
R.Bu. Ron Buchanan
R.G.B. Rae Galbraith Ballard
S.B. Sandra Ballard
S.Ba. Sarah Barnhill
S.Bi. Suzann Bick
S.C.B. Stephen C. Brennan
W.K.B. William K. Bottorff

C.B.C. Carol Bebee Collins
C.C. Carol Cumming
D.C. Diane Carr
D.J.C. David J. Carroll
D.T.C. Daniel T. Cornell
G.M.C. Gary M. Ciuba
H.A.C. Henry A. Christian
J.C. John Canfield
J.Ca. John Calabro
J.Cal. Joseph Caldwell
L.C. Leonard Casper
R.C. Ronald Cella
R.G.C. R. G. Collins
R.V.C. Roseanne V. Camacho
S.C. Samuel Coale
T.C. Thomas Carmichael
W.H.C. William H. Castles, Jr.

C.C.D. Carolyn C. Denard
C.C.Da. Christopher C. Dahl
J.D. Joanne Dobson
J.Dy. Joyce Dyer
J.E.D. James E. Devlin
J.F.D. Joan F. Dean
L.B.D. Laurie Bernhardt Demarest
M.D. Marc Demarest
M.Du. Margaret Dunn
P.A.D. Paul A. Doyle
R.H.W.D. R. H. W. Dillard
S.D.D. Sharon D. Downey
S.R.D. S. Renee Dechert
T.D. Tom Dabbs
T.E.D. Thomas E. Dasher

B.J.E. Barbara J. Everson
C.A.E. Catherine A. Eckman
W.E. Wilton Eckley

A.D.F. Ann Dahlstrom Farmer
A.F. Abigail Franklin
B.F. Benjamin Franklin V
B.F.F. Benjamin Franklin Fisher
C.F. Carol Farrington
D.S.F. Dianne S. Fergusson
E.D.F. Elaine Dunphy Foster
E.H.F. Erwin H. Ford II
E.H.Fo. Edward Halsey Foster
J.M.F. Joseph M. Flora
J.M.Fr. June M. Frazer
K.A.F. Kathy A. Fedorko
M.J.F. Michael J. Freeman
R.J.F. Rebecca Jane Franklin
R.S.F. Robert S. Frederickson
T.C.F. Timothy C. Frazer

B.W.G. Boyd W. Geer
D.J.G. Donald J. Greiner
G.G. Gary Geer
H.S.G. Helen S. Garson
J.A.G. James A. Grimshaw, Jr.
J.L.G. Johanna L. Grimes
L.G. Linda Garner
M.K.G. Marcia Kinder Geer
S.E.G. Susan Elizabeth Gunter
S.G. Sinda Gregory
V.B.G. Virginia B. Guilford

A.H. Australia Henderson
B.H. Brooke Horvath
D.C.H. Dorothy Combs Hill
E.J.H. E. Jens Holley
G.A.H. Glenda A. Hudson
H.H. Herbert Hartsook
H.R.H. Helen R. Houston
J.G.H. Judith Giblin Haig
J.W.H. James W. Hipp

L.E.H. Lee Emling Harding
L.P.H. Lillie P. Howard
M.W.H. Melissa Walker Heidari
R.L.H. Robert L. Haig
S.L.H. Susan Luck Hooks
S.P.H. Steven P. Horowitz
T.R.H. Theodore R. Hudson
V.H. Vernon Hyles
W.H. William Higgins

B.J.I. Betty J. Irwin
D.I. Dennis Isbell
L.I. Laura Ingram

A.J. Allan Johnston
D.K.J. David K. Jeffrey
G.J. Greg Johnson
J.L.D.J. James L. de Jongh
K.C.J. Kirkland C. Jones
M.J. Michael Jasper
N.R.J. Norma R. Jones
T.L.J. Thomas L. Johnson

H.L.K. Harriet L. King
J.K. Jackie Kinder
M.L.K. Mary Lou Kete
R.A.K. Richard A. Kallan
S.G.K. Steven G. Kellman
S.L.K. Sue Laslie Kimball

B.L. Barbara Lootens
C.F.L. Charles F. Loveless
D.L. Dan Lee
D.L.L. Doris Lucas Laryea
D.Lo. Dennis Loyd
D.L.T.L. Dawn Lee Terry Leonard
E.B.L. Ellen B. Lane
F.H.L. Frank H. Leavell
J.S.L. Janet Sanders Land
L.S.L. Leota S. Lawrence
M.H.L. May Harn Liu
M.T.L. Mark T. Lucas
N.L. Norman Lavers
R.E.L. Robert E. Lougy
R.L. Richard Layman
S.L. Suzanne Leahy

A.G.M. Amanda Gwyn Mason
C.A.M. Charmaine A. Mosby
C.S.M. Charlotte S. McClure
D.M. Daniel Marder
E.M. Eva Mills
G.B.M. Gary B. Meyer
G.L.M. Gregory L. Morris
J.B.Mob. Judith B. Mobley
J.C.M. Jane Compton Mallison
J.M. Jo Mayer
J.Mi. Joseph Milicia

J.R.M. Joseph R. Millichap
J.R.Ma. John R. May
J.R.Mc. Joseph R. McElrath, Jr.
K.F.C.M. Karen F. Costello-McFeat
L.M. Len McCall
L.M.M. Lynn M. Morton
M.C.M. Mary Cease Megra
M.M. Michael Mullen
M.H.M. Mary H. McNulty
N.Y.M. Nellie Y. McKay
P.D.M. Patrick D. Morrow
P.W.M. Paul W. Miller
R.B.M. Robert M. Myers
R.S.M. Rayburn S. Moore
S.M. Steven Moore
S.Mo. Stephanie Morris
W.L.M. Wanda L. Mattress
W.Mc. Warren McInnis

C.C.N. Charles C. Nash
C.N. Christine Nelson
D.A.N. Douglas A. Noverr
E.S.N. Emmanuel S. Nelson
G.V.N. Gordon Van Ness III
J.C.N. Jennifer Castillo Norman
P.N. Peter Nazareth

C.W.O. Clark W. Owens
J.E.O. Jacqueline E. Orsagh
J.M.O. Julie M. Overton
K.H.O. Kevin Hunter Orr
L.O. Lance Olsen
S.E.O. Steven E. Olson

B.J.P. Barbara J. Price
D.P. Donna Padgett
E.J.P. Edward J. Piacentino
J.D.P. Jeffrey D. Parker
M.G.P. M. Gilbert Porter
R.L.P. Robert L. Phillips, Jr.

D.D.Q. Diane Dufva Quantic

B.R. Barbara Rippey
C.A.R. Christine A. Rydel
C.S.R. Carmen S. Rivera
D.B.R. Donna Brumback Romein
E.C.R. Edward C. Reilly
E.J.R. Edward J. Ruggero
E.L.R. Elizabeth Lee Rametta
J.L.R. Jennifer L. Randisi
J.R. Judith Ruderman
J.Re. Josephine Rentz
J.R.R. J. R. Raper
K.L.R. Katheryn L. Rios
M.W.R. Michael W. Raymond
P.J.R. Peter J. Reed
R.M.R. Robert M. Ryley
S.J.R. Stephen J. Rubin
W.M.R. William M. Robins
W.R. William Roba
W.W.R. Walter W. Ross

A.M.S. Arthur M. Saltzman
A.S. Alan Shucard
A.Sh. Allan Shepherd
C.L.S. Cynthia L. Storm
C.R.S. Carl R. Shirley
D.S. David Shetler
D.Sh. Dean Shackelford
E.B.S. Elaine B. Safer
E.S. Elizabeth Schultz
G.S. Guy Szuberla
H.W.S. Hammett Worthington-Smith
J.C.S. Jon Christian Suggs
J.R.Su. Jack R. Sublette
J.S. Jean Sims
K.C.S. Katherine C. Schwartz
K.S. Kathryn Snell
L.M.S. Lucille M. Schultz
L.S. Linda Schlafer
L.Sa. Leslie Sanders
M.K.S. Michael K. Simmons
P.W.S. Paula W. Shirley

R.J.S. Richard J. Schrader
R.R.S. Richard R. Schramm
S.T.S. Suzanne T. Stutman
T.J.S. Thelma J. Shinn
T.R.S. Thomas R. Smith
T.S. Teresa Steppe
V.W.S. Virginia Whatley Smith

D.M.T. David M. Taylor
E.Q.T. Eleanor Q. Tignor
E.W.T. Estelle W. Taylor
L.S.T. Lindsey S. Tucker
N.L.T. Nancy Lewis Tuten
R.C.T. Richard C. Taylor
R.T. Richard Tuerk
S.H.T. Susan Hayes Tully
S.L.T. Stephen L. Tanner

C.E.W. Carolyn E. Wedin
C.W. Crystal Williamson
D.E.W. Delbert E. Wylder
H.W. Holly Westcott
J.J.W. Joseph J. Wydeven
J.R.W. J. Randal Woodland
K.M.W. Kathleen Murat Williams
M.E.R.W. Mary Ellen R. Westmoreland
M.E.W.W. Mary Ellen Williams Walsh
R.W. Ronald Walcott
R.Wa. Richard Walser
R.W.W. Robert W. Weathersby II
S.H.W. Sylvia H. Weinberg
V.W. Virginia Weathers
W.W. Warren Westcott
W.We. William Wehmeyer

D.L.Y. Deborah L. Yerkes

A.R.Z. Anne R. Zahlan
P.A.Z. Pamela A. Zager